THE UNIVERSAL HOME LAWYER

IMPARTIAL JUSTICE
The symbolic figure that watches over the Old Bailey, London.

The
UNIVERSAL
HOME
LAWYER
ILLUSTRATED

ODHAMS PRESS LTD.
Long Acre, London, W.C.2.

Printed and Bound in Great Britain by
Greycaine Limited, Watford, Herts.

INTRODUCTION

ONE of the most valuable material assets a man may have is a knowledge of the law; and indeed the old maxim "Ignorance of the law is no excuse" is a cogent reason for one to acquire that knowledge. For the law prescribes our moral code, it regulates our behaviour in relation to our neighbours, and it safeguards our rights as citizens. In fact the law, on which the whole structure of our society is founded, impinges on nearly every one of our daily actions.

To acquire this knowledge is not always an easy task. The man in the street who has not had any legal training is often at a loss to lay his hands on the information he requires, or much less understand the legal issues involved even in ordinary business dealings. Matters are sometimes still further complicated by certain difficulties experienced in interpreting the language of the law.

This volume has been planned so as to provide a comprehensive and useful legal encyclopædia which will serve all the practical requirements of the "average man." It has been compiled by a large body of experts, including many distinguished practising barristers and solicitors, and is entirely new in every respect. The arrangement is strictly alphabetical for easy and rapid reference. There is an elaborate system of cross-references whereby the reader is enabled rapidly to consult kindred subjects in any way related to the matter on which he wishes to be informed.

One of the features of modern government is its continuous creation of new legislation; and the rapidity with which conditions change and with which new laws are brought into being to meet these new conditions, makes it absolutely essential for us to be conversant with the law as it is to-day. The very latest changes in legislation have been incorporated in THE UNIVERSAL HOME LAWYER.

As has already been mentioned, legal phraseology may often be difficult to follow. For this reason a definite attempt has been made in this volume to explain the various and intricate workings of our laws in a simple and straightforward way. Everyday examples have frequently been added to the text to bring out in an interesting way the real significance of the legal points involved. Moreover, to familiarise readers with the ordinary documents which they may be called upon to sign in the usual course of events, such as cheques, agreements for leases, hire-purchase agreements, etc., etc., the more common of these have been specially reproduced here for their guidance, and practical advice has been given on all the important points connected with such transactions.

The reader will also find a full description under the various headings of Constitutional Law and the workings of Parliament, Ecclesiastical Law, the Powers of Local Authorities, Trade Unions and Friendly Societies, Banking and Insurance, and the hundred and one legal points that affect the professional or the business man in the course of his employment. Scots law has besides been included and particular mention is made of the many differences between it and the law in England.

Attention has also been paid to what might be called the "human side" of the law. There has been included a large number of biographical notes of famous Judges and lawyers, past and present, who have made lasting contributions to the framing and establishment of our laws, or who have done much to clarify, interpret or maintain them. Again, the more celebrated trials have been described, as it was felt that their inclusion was justified both from their legal importance and from their general and dramatic interest.

At the end of the book has been placed a series of Special Supplements which deal with subjects of outstanding interest and practical utility. Each has been contributed by an acknowledged authority. Thus the Rt. Hon. Herbert Morrison, a former Minister of Transport, writes on "Road Traffic," and Major-General Sir Wyndham Childs, who was for many years in charge of the Criminal Investigation Department of Scotland Yard, on "The Police."

British justice, from the impartiality of our Judges and Courts and the fairness of our laws, is admired throughout the civilized world; and by reading this book the reader will be able to appreciate why this is so, and at the same time will be able to take full advantage, for his own personal benefit, of the great legal system which this country is fortunate enough to possess.

THE EDITORS.

The Temple,
London,
E.C.4.

CONTENTS

SPECIAL SUPPLEMENTS

The
UNIVERSAL
HOME LAWYER
Illustrated

A LICENCE.—This is one of the licences required by everyone whose business involves the carriage of goods by motor vehicles. (*See* CARRIER'S LICENCE.)

"A" LIST.—When a Company is wound up, the liquidator prepares two lists of the contributories (persons who are liable to pay money on shares held in the Company). On one of these lists, called the "A" List, he puts all those who were shareholders of the Company at the time of the winding up. On the other list called the "B" List he puts the names of those persons who have ceased to be shareholders of the Company within the last 12 months. Where the shares of a Company are fully paid there will of course be no necessity to prepare these lists. (*See* CONTRIBUTORIES.)

ABANDONMENT (Marine).—*See* MARINE INSURANCE.

ABATEMENT.—1. **Of actions.** When the Plaintiff or Defendant in an action dies before the verdict is given and nobody is entitled to take his place, the action abates or comes to an end. Where the dispute is a purely personal one, it must abate because nobody can inherit a personal right or liability. But where it affects a man's property, as in an action for debt, it does not abate on his death because his property still remains and passes to someone else together with all the rights and liabilities which affect it. (*See* ACTION.)

2. **Of legacies.** When a man dies and his estate turns out to be too small to provide all the legacies which his will directs, the general legacies must be reduced in amount proportionately. They are then said to abate. General legacies abate equally unless it is proved that the testator meant any of them to be paid in full before the others. Demonstrative legacies only abate if the fund provided for paying them is insufficient and specific legacies only if the general estate is too small to pay off all the testator's debts. (*See* LEGACIES.)

3. **Of nuisances.** Abatement of a nuisance is the removal or remedying of something which interferes with one's private rights. If my neighbour's trees overhang my garden so as to amount to a nuisance in a legal sense, I can abate the nuisance by lopping the offending branches. But if I do this I cannot also sue him for damages in respect of the nuisance. The abatement must be done with as little damage as possible and in most cases notice must be given beforehand. A public nuisance can only be abated by a private person so far as it does special injury to himself. Abatement is a dangerous remedy and the law does not encourage it. (*See* ACTION; LEGACY; NUISANCE.)

ABETTING.—A person abets a crime if he is present and aids its commission but does not actually perpetrate it by his own hand. To abet it is not necessary to be actually on the scene of the crime, it is enough to be sufficiently close at hand to lend assistance if needed. Watching a short distance away in order to give warning of interruption is abetting, and so is remaining close at hand merely to give courage to the person committing the crime. Abetting is punishable in the same way as is the crime which is abetted. (*See* ACCESSORY.)

ABORTION.—Any operation or administration of a drug to produce a miscarriage in a woman is termed procuring an abortion. Unless the miscarriage is essential for preserving the life of the woman and produced with that honest intention, the operation or administration of such a drug is a serious criminal offence punishable with penal servitude for life. Not only the woman herself may be convicted but also anyone who operates on her or assists her. Should the woman die as a result of an illegal operation or the taking of such a noxious drug, anyone who was a party to the crime may be indicted for manslaughter or even murder. It is further an offence to supply any instrument or other article with the knowledge that it is to be unlawfully used for procuring a miscarriage. This is punishable with a maximum sentence of five years' penal servitude.

ABSTRACT OF TITLE.—This is an epitome or list of the documents and facts constituting the "Vendor's" or seller's title to land and certain interests in land prepared when land is sold. It is a history setting out matters relating to, dealings with, and circumstances which have affected, the land over a number of years. In an Open Contract (q.v.) for the sale of land, that is to say, when the parties have made no special agreement as to the period which this history has to cover, the period covered by the abstract of title is thirty years. The earliest document set out is called the "Root of Title" (q.v.) and should be of such a nature that the Purchaser may fairly assume that when it came into existence the earlier title was thoroughly investigated. The best roots of title are "Conveyances on Sale" which are deeds whereby land is sold, or Mortgages of land, which are documents whereby an owner gives his land to another as security for a loan. The Abstract of Title is prepared by the Vendor's Solicitor and sent by him to the Purchaser's Solicitor, who must then verify all the documents mentioned by examining them, and confirm all facts, by making searches (q.v.), or inquiries in registries where the same are registered. (*See* LANDLORD AND TENANT; MORTGAGES; SALE OF LAND.)

ACCEPTANCE (BILL OF EXCHANGE).—The bill of exchange being an order on a person known as the Drawee to pay a sum of money, it is necessary in many cases that the Drawee should indicate on the bill that he is willing to carry out the order given to him. The method in which he does this is by accepting the bill. Until a Bill is accepted the Drawee is not liable upon it.

A bill may be accepted before it has been signed by the Drawer. Thus, if a firm in London owes money to a firm in Germany, they may meet their obligations by accepting a bill for the amount due and sending it to the firm in Germany which then adds its name as Drawer. Only the person to whom the bill is addressed as drawee can accept it, so if a bill is addressed to AB and accepted by CD it would be invalid.

The method of acceptance is usually by the Drawee writing across the bill the word "Accepted" with his signature. In some cases the Drawee may not be prepared to accept the bill exactly in the terms of the Order. Thus if a bill is drawn on a man for £100 he may be prepared only to accept it for £50, or he may be prepared to accept for the full amount subject to some condition, as that he must first receive the bills of lading relating to the goods for the price of which the bill of exchange is drawn.

Again a bill drawn payable one month after sight may be accepted only payable three months after. These acceptances are known as qualified acceptances and any holder who presents a bill for acceptance and is offered a qualified acceptance, may refuse it and treat the bill as dishonoured by non-acceptance. In this case he will not of course have any rights against the person refusing to accept, i.e. the Drawee, because his liability to a holder does not arise until he accepts, but the holder may have rights against the Drawer and all previous parties to the bill if it has been negotiated. The Drawer may have some rights against the Drawee if there has been any arrangement or contract between them under which the Drawee was bound to accept the bill, but any such liability will be quite independent of the bill itself. Although a holder, as has been seen, may refuse to take a qualified acceptance he is not bound to refuse, but if he takes a qualified acceptance he must obtain the consent of all previous endorsers and of the Drawer. If they do not consent they are released from liability on the bill. This does not apply to a partial acceptance, e.g. a bill drawn for £100 accepted for £50, for in that case the Drawer and previous endorsers will be liable if notice of the qualified acceptance is given to them, whether they expressly assent or not.

A bill may be transferred from one person to another before it has been accepted, and it may never be presented at all to the Drawee until the time for payment arrives. It is however always possible to present a bill for acceptance and whether it is desirable to do so or not will depend on the financial position of the persons who have drawn it and endorsed it. They will be liable on the bill whether the Drawee accepts it or not.

If they are not known to be of good financial credit then it would probably be impossible in practice for any holder of the bill to get anybody else to take it until it has been accepted. But if, for example, a bill were drawn by Rockefeller upon a comparatively unknown Drawee there is no doubt that presentment for acceptance would be quite unnecessary for the purpose of negotiating the bill. If the situation were reversed and the bill were drawn on Rockefeller by an unknown Drawer then for practical purposes the bill would have to be presented for acceptance before anyone would take it, since Rockefeller would not be liable until he had accepted.

When acceptance is necessary.—In some cases apart from these practical considerations it is legally necessary to present the bill for acceptance, e.g. when it is payable so many days after sight, i.e. after it has been presented to the Drawee. Presentment will be necessary in order to determine the date when the bill will fall due. Where presentment is necessary it will be excused and the bill may be treated as dishonoured by non-acceptance where the drawee is dead or bankrupt, or is a fictitious person, or has no capacity to contract by a bill, e.g. is an infant, or where it is impossible to effect presentment after the exercise of reasonable endeavours to do so. The mere fact that the holder has reason to believe that the bill will be dishonoured if he does present does not excuse him from presentment.

If the Drawee does not accept the bill within a reasonable time after it has been presented, usually 24 hours, the person presenting it must treat it as dishonoured. If he does not but gives the Drawee a longer

time he will not be able to sue the Drawer or previous endorsers. Where a bill is not accepted the Drawer and previous endorsers become immediately liable on it even though under the terms of the bill it is not yet due—e.g. is payable 30 days after sight.

Where a bill is dishonoured by non-acceptance it is possible, if the holder consents, for some person not a party to the bill to volunteer and accept it. He is called an acceptor for honour supra protest. He will be liable on the bill when the time for payment comes but it should first be presented again to the Drawee for payment. (*See* BILL OF EXCHANGE.)

ACCEPTANCE (BILLS OF EXCHANGE, SCOTS LAW).—There is one important difference between the effect of presenting a bill for acceptance in England and in Scotland. In Scotland presentment for acceptance operates as an assignation of any money belonging to the Drawer which the Drawee may have, even if the Drawee refuses to accept. Suppose A draws a bill for £100 on B in favour of C. C presents the bill to B who refuses to accept it. A of course is liable, but assume that he becomes bankrupt and that in fact B had £100 belonging to A in his hands at the time of the acceptance; A's trustee in bankruptcy cannot claim the £100 but C may take this instead of claiming against A's estate and receiving only a dividend. The presentment of a cheque for payment has the same effect. (*See* BILL OF EXCHANGE; CHEQUES.)

ACCESS. Access to Land.—If a piece of land is wholly surrounded by land owned by other persons, there may well be no means of approach to the property except by trespassing upon the lands of the adjoining owners. In most cases, however, property so entirely surrounded by other land is held by a separate owner, only as the result of a sale to him by an owner who *has* access to a highway through land which he retains, and who, before he sold the isolated plot, had access from the plot to the highway through other parts of his own land. When a man sells a plot out of the middle of his own lands in this way, the law implies that he intends at the same time to grant a right of way to the purchaser over his lands to the plot sold. Only by an express agreement that such a right of way does not exist will the vendor avoid having to allow the purchaser to pass over his lands; and no sane purchaser would buy land when he knew from the conveyance that he would be unable to reach it without trespassing. There is, therefore, little danger that the purchaser of land will find himself unable to obtain access to his property. A right of way which the law in this way implies to have been granted is called a "way of necessity."

Access of Husband to Wife.—A child born of a married woman is presumed to be the legitimate child of the marriage, and, if there was a real possibility that the husband was its father, any proof that its mother had adulterous intercourse with another man will be unavailing to prove the child illegitimate. If, however, it be proved that the husband had no access to his wife at all at the time when the child was conceived, the child will be declared illegitimate. Such proof of non-access may not be given by the husband or the wife personally: it must be supplied by other witnesses, e.g. persons who could swear that the husband lived in Paris at the time when the child was conceived in London.

The law considers it is contrary to public policy that a husband or wife should give evidence of the intimacies of married life in order to prove that their supposed child is illegitimate. This rule does not apply in cases where a child was conceived before marriage but born afterwards, the husband then being entitled to give evidence personally that he had had no connection with the mother before the marriage through which the child could have been begotten. Nor does the rule apply where there is no child alive who could be injured by such evidence given, e.g. if the child was still-born: in such a case, either spouse may give evidence that the child was illegitimate, and such evidence may be given for any purpose, e.g. to prove adultery on the part of the wife. (*See* ILLEGITIMATE CHILDREN.)

Access of Parent to Child.—When a decree of divorce is obtained, the custody of the children is usually given to the innocent party; if the father is the guilty party, he is usually allowed access to his children at times and places fixed by the Court or by agreement between the parties; but in the case of a mother who has been

guilty of adultery, the Court is sometimes less inclined to allow her to see the children. Apart from divorce, a Magistrate's Court may give the custody of a child to its mother or to its father exclusively if they consider it necessary, and may provide that, in such a case, the other parent is to have certain rights of access. (*See* CHILDREN; FATHER; MOTHER; AND ALSO SPECIAL SUPPLEMENT "DIVORCE.")

Access to Highways and Rivers.— Every person who has land adjoining a public road or public river has a right of access to the road or river, and, if that right is materially interfered with, such person may sue either for damages or for an injunction for the removal of the obstruction.

ACCESSORY.—Accessory is a term used to describe a person who is a party to the commission of a felony, or who conceals it or protects the felon. In the first case he is termed an accessory before the fact and in the latter case an accessory after the fact. It is important to note that there can only be accessories to felonies. A person who is a party to the commission of a misdemeanour is treated as a principal.

Accessory Before the Fact.—The essential point about an accessory before the fact is that he is not present at the commission of the felony. If he be present, of course, he becomes a principal. He is one therefore who, though absent from the scene of the crime incites or abets some other person to commit it. An accessory before the fact can be punished in the same way as the person who actually carries out the felony.

Accessory After the Fact.—If anyone knows that a felony has been committed by another yet receives or conceals him, or assists him to escape from justice, the person doing so becomes an accessory after the fact to that felony. The maximum punishments for accessories after the fact vary in some cases according to the particular felony. An accessory after the fact to murder may be sentenced to penal servitude for life. Where no special provision exists, two years' imprisonment with or without hard labour is the maximum punishment.

ACCIDENT.—An accident has been described as a "mishap or untoward event that is not expected or intended." If a person has been injured in an accident he can under certain circumstances bring an action against the person who caused the injury, but he cannot bring it unless he has suffered some damage as a result of the accident. If he has suffered such damage, his right to sue will depend on whether the person injuring him owed him some duty not to harm him which has been broken.

In law there are two kinds of duties which a person can be owed. The first is a duty arising out of a contract. For example A arranges with B that while B is travelling in his (A's) carriage, if he pays a shilling a mile, A will indemnify him for any injury that may befall him. If then B is injured he takes his action on the arrangement made between him and A. This is the simplest form of contractual duty. Sometimes however the duty is not expressed in actual terms in the contract but is to be implied or understood from it because of its nature. Such is the case where you arrange with a workman to come to your house to do some work for you there. If while he is there doing it he falls through a rotten floor, about which you knew but had not warned him, and is injured, you will be liable, because it is an implied term of the contract that you will protect him against such dangers, and you have neglected your duty towards him. (*See* DANGEROUS ARTICLES; DANGEROUS PREMISES.) The other kind of duty is owed by each person to his fellow men. It is a general duty to use care towards others. In other words to act as a reasonable man would act. If while acting unreasonably you harm another you will be liable. Thus the motorist owes a duty to every lawful user of the road to be careful in his driving and not wilfully or carelessly to drive into them. (*See* COLLISION; NEGLIGENCE.)

Right to Recover Damages.—These are the cases where the victim of an accident can recover damages. There are cases however where, though an accident has occurred and a person has been injured, there is no right to recover damages. Thus where an earthquake causes a wall or tree to fall on a passer-by no one is liable. Again, where a great storm caused ornamental waters to overflow and do damage, the owner was not liable. But if a person brings something dangerous on his land which is not naturally there, such as lions or tigers, or even if the dangerous thing is one that only becomes dangerous because it is collected in large quantities such as water in a reservoir, then he keeps it there at his peril, and if the lions escape, or the water breaks down the reservoir and they do damage, he will be liable.

If the person injured is himself the cause of the accident, as where a pedestrian dashes under a motor-car without giving the driver an opportunity to avoid him, the driver will not be liable. Even if the driver has not used care there are cases where he will not be liable, as where the victim was also careless and his carelessness was the decisive cause of the accident. (*See* CONTRIBUTORY NEGLIGENCE.) Thus it will be seen that when an accident occurs the injured person if he wants to recover damages must prove:—

1. That his injuries were caused by the accident;
2. That the accident was caused by the fault of the person against whom he is proceeding.

Death from Accident.—Where a person is killed in an accident and it can be proved that it is the fault of a third person, it used to be the law that no damages could be recovered.

This was so decreed because it was a principle of the Common Law that a personal action, e.g. an action dealing with a wrong to the person of the plaintiff, not to his property, died with the person. Now by statute the relatives of a dead man who were dependent upon his earnings can recover, but they must prove that they were dependent. A man can recover for the loss of the services of his wife if she is killed in an accident, but nothing can be recovered for the death of a child upon whom no one is dependent.

Liability for Accidents caused by others.—If a servant causes an accident, by his negligence, his master will be liable if it is committed in the course of his legitimate employment. (*See* MASTER AND SERVANT.) Thus if a person is knocked down by an omnibus that person can sustain an action against the company who own the omnibus. (*See* COLLISION; COMPENSATION; CONTRIBUTORY NEGLIGENCE; DAMAGES; MASTER AND SERVANT; NEGLIGENCE.)

ACCIDENT INSURANCE.— Most insurance companies now issue a policy insuring the holder against death or injury by accident, and some newspapers provide this policy free to registered readers. The principles governing this form of insurance are precisely the same as in the case of ordinary life insurance (q.v.), but the policy holders must prove that the cause of the death or injuries was in fact an accident, and the policy will not cover death or injury which, though apparently caused by an accident, is really the result of disease or inherent weakness. There is often a clause in such policies providing that the insured person shall not expose himself wilfully or negligently to unnecessary danger and this, as well as the other conditions on the policy, must be complied with in order to recover under the policy. Policies may also be obtained against illness as well as accident.

In the case of accident insurance which is provided free by newspapers, no premium is payable but the reader must remain registered with the newspaper in the prescribed manner if he wishes to be entitled to recover under the policy.

Many employers nowadays also insure themselves against any liability which they may incur under the Workmen's Compensation Acts (q.v.) for injury to their employees. Such a policy of insurance is very similar to the insurance of motor owners against third party risks and is governed by the same rules including the rule that, if the employer becomes bankrupt or compounds with his creditors, or being a company is wound up, the insured employee has a right to recover directly against the insurance company, and the policy does not pass to the trustee in bankruptcy for the benefit of the employer's creditors generally. (*See* INSURANCE; LIFE INSURANCE; THIRD PARTY INSURANCE.)

ACCOMMODATION BILL.— Although normally when A draws a bill of exchange upon B directing him to pay a certain sum of money, and B accepts that bill, he does so because he holds that sum of money belonging to A in his hands, or owes A that amount. In some cases however this is not so, and B will accept the bill through an arrangement with A although no money is due. Such a bill is said to be accepted for the accommodation of A and is called an accommodation bill. As between A and B, B is not liable for the money, but if A negotiates the bill to somebody who gives him some value for it, B will be liable to that person, whether the person taking the bill knew it was an accommodation bill or not. The accommodation party may sign the bill as the Drawer or endorser instead of as the acceptor.

Bills of this kind are frequently used for obtaining loans. Thus supposing A wishes to raise £1,000 from his Bank, the Bank may be unwilling to advance him so much, but they might be prepared to do so if they could have some other person or persons who would be liable for the money as well as A. The most convenient method by which this could be arranged would be for A to draw a bill on B in his (A's) own favour for £1,000 payable, say, in 6 months' time, arranging with B to accept the bill. A may then take this bill to the Bank who might be prepared to advance the £1,000 by discounting the bill, that is, by paying the £1,000 less the appropriate interest for the period before it falls due. They know that they can require either A or B or both to pay the money. If the Bank are still dissatisfied then a further person could be made liable by A drawing a bill on B in favour of C, and getting B to accept and C to sign his name as endorser. There are then 3 persons liable on the bill and the process may be extended by getting other persons to sign as endorsers also. When the bill becomes due A will give B the money to meet it. B will of course be liable to a holder who has given value even if A does not provide him with the money, but will not be liable to A or C. (*See* BILL OF EXCHANGE.)

ACCOMPLICE.—One who has assisted another to commit a crime. On the trial of a prisoner, the evidence of a person who was his accomplice in the crime may be received against the prisoner, but a Judge should warn juries that they should not accept the evidence of accomplices unless it is corroborated by other evidence. (*See* APPROVER; KING'S EVIDENCE.)

ACCORD AND SATISFACTION.—One of the methods in which the rights under a Contract may be discharged without the Contract itself having been performed is when the parties agree by a fresh contract to substitute new rights for those which they have under the old contract. This is known as accord and satisfaction. It also applies to cases in which one person has acquired rights against another arising not out of contracts but out of a tort, i.e. some wrong committed by the second person against the first

Amount due indefinite: A cheque taken in Settlement.—An example of the application of this rule in the case of contracts will arise where A has agreed to supply B with a 100 tons of coal and has admittedly failed to do so, so that B had a right of action against A for damages for breach of contract. The exact amount which A would be entitled to recover for breach of contract is at the moment uncertain and would have to be determined by a Court. A and B may make an agreement that A should pay B £100 as damages, and A may give him a cheque for that amount. This is said to be accord between the parties, that is, a new agreement has been made giving rise to new rights. Now assume that A's cheque is dishonoured. Can B then sue A for damages for the original breach of contract, or can he sue him only for £100 due on the cheque? This will depend on whether at the time the cheque was given the parties intended that the right of action for breach of contract should be exchanged for the right of action on the cheque, or whether they intended that it should be exchanged only for the £100 *payable on the cheque,* so that if the cheque were not met and the £100 therefore not paid, the rights of action for breach of contract should be preserved. Was it understood that the case of action for breach of contract should be given up only if the cheque were met?

If it was so understood, then the giving of the cheque will not prevent B suing for the breach of contract if the cheque is not met, for there is accord but no satisfaction. If, however, the parties intended that the right of action on the cheque should be substituted for the right of action for breach of contract in any event, then there is both accord and satisfaction, for in this case it is the giving of the cheque and not its being met which the parties have agreed should be satisfaction. There must be both accord and satisfaction, but what is satisfaction will depend on the agreement made by the parties.

Where the parties are in dispute as to whether a contract has been broken or not or as to whether one has committed a civil wrong against the other, the situation is somewhat different because they may then compromise their dispute, and if they do so they will not be allowed to rely on their breach of contract or right of action for a civil wrong but will be compelled to keep to the agreement of compromise. There must be a genuine dispute, each honestly believing that he is right.

It will be presumed in this case that they intended that their previous rights of action should be exchanged for the right of action under their new contract of compromise whether that is carried out or not. The discharge is thus presumed not to be conditional on the immediate fulfilment of the rights under the compromise.

The same situation arises where one person has wronged another. Thus if X has run into Y in his motor car and injured him, Y would have a claim against X. At the time of the accident or soon afterwards X may offer Y £5 in settlement of any claim for injuries he may have. If X pays the £5 the matter will certainly be concluded and Y will have no further claim against X; but if X does not pay the £5 and Y sues him for damages the question will have to be considered whether by the contract settling the claim X and Y intended that Y should give up his claim for damages in exchange for X's *promise* to pay £5, or whether it was intended that he should only give up his claim if X promised to pay *and did pay* £5. It is obvious therefore that if a claim of this kind is settled the money should be paid as soon as possible.

Amount due definite: Payment of a smaller sum.—The cases which have been dealt with above are those in which the parties have either been in dispute as to what are their rights against one another, or, if they have been agreed that one has committed a breach of contract or been guilty of a tort towards the other, the amount due by one to the other is uncertain—i.e. unliquidated. The position is very different where a contract is broken and there is no dispute as to the fact that it has been broken, and the amount due under it is certain and liquidated. Thus if A owes B a £100 and fails to pay it, A will not be released from his obligation to pay £100 merely by an agreement between himself and B that B should take £75 in settlement of the claim, even if A pays and B accepts £75.

The reason for this is to be found in the doctrine in English Law of Consideration. There would be no consideration moving from A, that is, no new promise given by A to act as consideration for B's promise to take £75 instead of £100. A is already liable to pay the £75 (and is indeed liable to pay £25 more) and the promise to do an act which one is already bound in law to do cannot be good consideration for a promise given by another person. Thus even after this agreement is made, and even if A pays the £75, B can still continue and sue him for the remaining £25. It would be different however if any consideration were given by A at all for B's promise to accept £75 instead of £100. Firstly, if there were any dispute between the parties as to A's obligation, as if A were contending that the money was not yet due, and B was contending that it was due; or if, although the parties were agreed that the money was due in a week's time, A agreed to pay the £75 in six days' time. In this last case B would be getting a new right, namely, a right to get £75 in six days' time in exchange for his giving up his right to claim £100 in seven days' time and A's promise to pay the £75 in six days' time is something which he was not already bound to do. He was not bound to pay anything before seven days.

Again there would certainly be consideration if A in addition to promising to pay the £75 said that he would give B something else as well. The value of the other thing to be given would not matter and it would be enough if A said he would give B his walking stick, and B agreed to take it, or if A and B agreed that A should give £75 and take B for a ride in his motor car in exchange for the release from the debt of £100. As the cause of action on a cheque is different from a cause of action on the debt alone it would be good consideration if B agreed to accept a cheque for £75 instead of the promise to pay £100.

Since the difficulties in discharging a debt by a smaller payment depend entirely on the Doctrine of Consideration, it is always possible to discharge the debt by entering into a deed, i.e. a contract under seal which is binding even though there is no consideration. (*See* CONSIDERATION; CONTRACT; DEED.)

ACCOUNT, Action for.—There are many cases where a debtor owes money to a creditor but the creditor does not know how much is due to him. For instance, A may have received several payments of money on account of B, and B may not know the exact amounts A has so received. Again, A may have agreed to pay commission to B out of sums received from business introduced by B. In such circumstances B can insist on A accounting to him by shewing the amounts received and paying over the balances found to be due. The method of enforcing this right is an action for an account. In such an action it is necessary first to prove that the relationship between plaintiff and defendant was such that it was the duty of the defendant to disclose his dealings to the plaintiff. If this requirement is satisfied the Court will order the defendant to make the necessary disclosure. The accounts are then examined before an official of the Court and the plaintiff secures judgment for the amount found to be due. (*See* AGENT.)

ACCOUNTANT OF COURT (SCOTS LAW).—The Accountant of Court is an official in Scotland who exercises a wide supervision over the Accounts of certain trustees such as trustees in bankruptcy and also over judicial factors. He corresponds to some extent to the Official Receiver in England.

ACCOUNTS (COMPANY).—A company is bound by law to keep certain Accounts of its transactions. It must keep books recording all receipts and expenses, all sales and purchases, and a list of its assets and liabilities. The books must be at the registered office and must be open to the inspection of the Directors. The directors are responsible for keeping these books and are liable to fine or imprisonment if they neglect their duty.

Each year the directors must lay before a General Meeting of the Company—i.e. of the shareholders—a profit and loss account and Balance Sheet for the year together with a report by them as to the state of the company's affairs. The Balance Sheet must show separately certain items specified in the Company's Act, the most important of which are the amounts which have been lent to Directors or paid to them as remuneration.

A copy of the Balance Sheets with the report must in the case of Public Companies be sent to all shareholders and debenture holders together with the auditors' report (*See* AUDITOR). Private companies do not require to send out these documents but shareholders are entitled to copies of them on request, and payment of a small sum.

The accounts of every Company must be audited every year by an auditor who is a disinterested person acting in the interests of the shareholders. (*See* AUDITOR.)

ACCUMULATION.—If the interest produced by a fund or sum of money, instead of being paid to some person or persons, each year is re-invested for the purpose of being paid to some person or persons in the future, it is said to accumulate. English law forbids unlimited accumulation, though before the year 1800 accumulation of income was allowed to any extent. In that year, however, one Peter Thellusson by his will left over £600,000 to accumulate for a remote descendant, and when it was realised what an enormous sum would result from such accumulation, the law was altered. Under the so-called Thellusson Act, 1800, and the Accumulations Act, 1892, money is allowed to accumulate only for twenty-one years after the death of the person making the will or during the minority of any person living at the date of his death. It follows that money cannot be left for the benefit only of a person who is not yet born at the time when the person who leaves the money dies. (*See* TRUST.)

ACQUITTAL.—When a person is tried on indictment and found Not Guilty by a jury he is said to have been acquitted. There is no appeal from an acquittal. Strictly speaking the term is applicable only to trials on indictment, since courts of summary jurisdiction do not "Acquit" but dismiss summonses or informations. A person acquitted on indictment cannot be tried again in respect of the same acts, but this rule does not in all cases apply to dismissals in court of summary jurisdiction. (*See* AUTREFOIS ACQUIT; DISMISSAL; AND NOT GUILTY.)

ACT OF BANKRUPTCY.—A person cannot be made bankrupt merely because he is insolvent—i.e. cannot pay his debts.

A petition to make him bankrupt cannot be presented against him until some act of a public nature has taken place in consequence of the financial difficulties of the debtor. These acts are called "acts of bankruptcy" and when one of them has taken place any creditor with a liquidated debt (i.e. fixed in amount) over £50 may ask the Court to make the debtor bankrupt. The effect of an act of bankruptcy for this purpose lasts for three months and after that time no petition to make the debtor bankrupt can rely on that act of bankruptcy.

By far the most usual of these acts is failure to comply with a bankruptcy notice, that is, to pay to a creditor who has obtained a judgment of the Court the amount due on that judgment when demanded by a written document called a bankruptcy notice. (*See* BANKRUPTCY NOTICE.) Other acts of bankruptcy are:

1. Where the debtor hands over his property to a Trustee for the benefit of his creditors generally. This may be done quite honestly, and therefore where a debtor makes a Deed of Arrangement (q.v.), which consists in handing over his property for this purpose to a trustee so that it may be divided among his creditors in order to avoid bankruptcy and as an alternative to it, an act of bankruptcy is committed. No creditor, however, who has agreed to accept the deed can rely on it as an act of bankruptcy for the purposes of presenting a petition, and even where a creditor has not assented to the deed the trustee of the deed may send him a notice of the deed, and the creditor, if he wishes to rely on it as an act of bankruptcy, must do so within one month of that notice instead of the three months from the deed otherwise allowed.

2. Where the debtor makes a fraudulent conveyance—i.e. transfer—or gift of any part of his property with the intention of preventing his creditors from getting hold of the property. This is quite a different transaction to the one considered above and the objection to it is that it indicates that the debtor is trying to give away property and put it out of the reach of his creditors at a time when he is really insolvent and when, therefore, the property belongs not truly to him but to his creditors. Usually a fraudulent conveyance is made to some relation or close friend of the debtor, or to a limited

company formed by him at a time when the debtor knows he is going bankrupt, with the secret understanding that it should be handed back to the debtor or used for his benefit after the bankruptcy is over; and so his creditors will be defrauded.

The conveyance may be a gift—e.g. of jewellery—or a sale under which the debtor gets something in return for his property. Further, it may be of all or practically all his property or of only a part of it; it may be a transfer of the property itself or the creation of some charge over it. Where the whole of the debtor's property is conveyed in this way and nothing is received for it in return, it is presumed to have been fraudulent and done with the intention of defrauding his creditors; but if only part of the property is transferred it will be necessary to prove that the debtor intended to defraud his creditors.

Where the property is not given away but sold or exchanged for something else of equivalent value, no harm will usually have been done because the creditors will have the money in place of the property; but where property is disposed of for less than its real value the evidence may be enough to satisfy the Court that it was not done in good faith. Even where a fair money value is received for the property the transaction may be fraudulent for it may be the debtor's object to turn his property into cash so that he may abscond with it.

In addition to being an act of bankruptcy a conveyance may be declared void, i.e. the person receiving the property may be compelled to hand it back—if it is made after the debtor has committed an act of bankruptcy and within three months before the date of the presentation of the petition, unless the person to whom the property was transferred had no knowledge of the act of bankruptcy. Where the conveyance is made more than three months before this date the property may also be claimed back, unless it is proved that the transfer was made in good faith and for good or valuable consideration, and the person taking it did not know of the debtor's intention to defraud creditors by making it. (*See* FRAUDULENT CONVEYANCE; VOLUNTARY SETTLEMENT.)

3. Where a debtor grants a fraudulent preference to one of his creditors, that is, at a time when he is insolvent in the sense that his liabilities exceeds his assets, he voluntarily and with the object of putting one creditor in a better position than others pays the debt of that creditor or gives him a security over part of his property for a debt which has been already incurred. (*See* FRAUDULENT PREFERENCE.)

4. Where a debtor with the intention of defeating his creditors leaves England or tries to keep out of the way of his creditors by leaving his home or by shutting himself up in his house—"Keeping house." (q.v.)

5. Where execution has been levied against the debtor's goods, i.e. where his goods have been seized by the sheriff to pay a debt due, and where they have either been sold to pay the debt or have remained in the Sheriff's hands for 21 days without the debt being paid.

6. Where the debtor formally draws up and files in court a document stating that he cannot pay his debts or presents a bankruptcy petition against himself, or where he notifies any of his creditors formally or informally that he has suspended payment of his debts or is about to do so.

Importance of "earliest Act of Bankruptcy."—It is very rarely that a bankruptcy petition is founded on a fraudulent conveyance or fraudulent preference as an act of bankruptcy, because the circumstances of these transactions are not usually found out or known to anyone except the debtor himself until bankruptcy proceedings have been taken on some other act of bankruptcy. The importance of them, however, is that by a rule known as the Doctrine of Relation Back the trustee's title to the property of the bankrupt dates back to the "earliest act of bankruptcy" committed by the debtor within three months before the petition was presented. The effect of this is that the trustee gets not only the property which the debtor has when the petition is presented but also all property and money which he had at the time of this earlier act of bankruptcy, even though he has got rid of it before he became bankrupt. Certain exceptions are, however, made in the case of persons receiving money or property from a debtor during this period without knowing that an act of bankruptcy has been committed, or paying him money, or delivering property to him even with knowledge of an act of bankruptcy but without notice that a petition has been presented against the debtor. (*See* BANKRUPTCY.)

The importance of this rule will be observed from the following illustration. On the 1st of June a debtor sells some of his property at a very low figure to a friend of his. This is a fraudulent conveyance, but at the time, of course, no one but the debtor and his friend know anything about it. On the 1st of August a petition is presented against the debtor to make him bankrupt,

ACT OF GOD.—Acts of God are occurrences which have their origin in the agency of natural forces. Sometimes they are events disastrous in their results to human life and property; as for instance a great and violent storm. It is only when this occurs that Act of God takes on any importance in the eyes of the law. Then like inevitable accident it constitutes a defence to an action for negligence. Thus where there was an extraordinary rainfall swelling the volume

Interior of the House of Commons, Westminster:

the act of bankruptcy alleged being the failure to comply with a bankruptcy notice served in July. During the public examination of the debtor and the investigation of his affairs by the trustee the fraudulent conveyance in June will probably be discovered, and then the trustee can not only claim back the property which was fraudulently sold but can also claim all property which the debtor had on the 1st of June and has since got rid of, unless the persons to whom he got rid of it gave money or some value for it and were not aware that an act of bankruptcy had already taken place previously. (*See* BANKRUPTCY; BANKRUPTCY NOTICE; RECEIVING ORDER; TRUSTEE IN BANKRUPTCY; *also* VOLUNTARY SETTLEMENT.)

of water in an artificial lake so that it burst its banks and did great damage, it was held that the damage was due to an Act of God and the owner of this lake was not liable. (*See* ACCIDENT; INEVITABLE ACCIDENT; AND NEGLIGENCE.)

ACT OF PARLIAMENT.—An Act of Parliament is a legislative enactment passed by the House of Commons, the House of Lords and assented to by the Crown. It has no force until the Royal Assent has been given, but, in practice, the Royal Assent is never withheld. By the Parliament Act, 1911, however, the power of the House of Lords was seriously curtailed, the Act providing that, with the exception of money bills and bills to extend the possible duration of Parliament beyond five years, any Bill which has been passed by the House of Commons in three successive sessions and which has been sent up to the House of Lords at least one month before the end of each such session, may be presented to the King for the Royal Assent in spite of the fact that the House of Lords has refused to pass it. The House of Lords is, in effect, able to hold up a bill for at least two years. The Irish Home Rule Act was passed in this way in 1914. Money Bills certified as such by the Speaker, may be presented for the Royal Assent after having been passed by the Commons, provided they are sent up to the House of Lords at least one month before the end of a session; the House of Lords is allowed one month to consider the Bill before the Royal Assent may be given. In cases of money Bills, therefore, the House of Lords is also practically powerless.

An Act of Parliament, it has been said, can do anything save change a man to a woman; in other words, there is no limit to the powers of Parliament, no check such as, in many other countries, is provided by the terms of a written constitution. In the United States of America, for example, the powers of Congress are limited in many respects, and any Act which violates the written constitution may be declared void by the Supreme Court; it has been held, for example, that an Act to abolish or control child-labour by Congress is outside its powers and void, since the constitution leaves such matters under the control of the individual States. But in England, there is no such control. The interpretation of Statutes falls upon the Judges, and a great deal may be done by them in mitigating the severity or injustice of Acts passed when manners and passions were far different from those of to-day. It has even been said by some Judges, that if an Act were clearly an outrageous infringement of natural justice, they would be entitled to ignore it, but it is unlikely that any such circumstances would arise. Since Parliament has supreme and sovereign powers, it may at any time alter any of its previous enactments, and it is, therefore, unable to fetter its future actions by passing a Statute with a provision that it shall be incapable of repeal.

A Statute applies to the Colonies and Dominions (including now the Irish Free State) only if it is expressed to be so applied. The Copyright Act, 1911, for example, was extended to the whole of His Majesty's Dominions, but, even in that Act it was provided that it should not extend to a self-governing Dominion unless declared by the Legislature of that Dominion to be in force therein. Since the Statute of Westminster in 1931, no Act of Parliament can bind a Dominion unless it is stated in the Act that the Dominion has requested that it should be included. (*See also* ATTAINDER; BILL (PARLIAMENTARY); PARLIAMENT.)

ACT OF SEDERUNT (SCOTS LAW).—These are rules made in Scotland corresponding to Statutory Rules and Orders made in England. They relate to such matters as the procedure of the Court and are made under the authority of the Lord President of the Court of Session.

ACTION.—An action is the most usual of the processes by which a person may enforce his legal rights against another person, or restrain the infliction of injury upon him by another person, through the medium of a Court of Justice. Strictly speaking the word covers also criminal proceedings, but as generally employed it is restricted to the processes by which a person can recover damages or injunctions in the civil courts.

A large portion of this volume is devoted to setting out the legal rights of the citizens of this country, and it is a general rule that wherever the law bestows upon a person a legal right, that person has also the power to assert that right in a Court of Justice and to recover compensation from any person who interferes with his enjoyment of that legal right.

In certain cases where rights have been bestowed by Act of Parliament, the Act provides a special and particular way of enforcing it, otherwise than by action, and in such cases the right can only be enforced in the manner provided. An example of this is the right which a workman has to recover in the police court any benefit which he may have lost by the failure of his employer to stamp his National Health Insurance cards. But even where the right is bestowed by a Statute the person whose right is infringed may bring an ordinary action in the Courts for it, provided either that the right existed before the Statute and the Statute did not take away the Common Law action, or where the Statute which bestows the right does not provide a special and exclusive method of enforcing it. (For the distinction between Common Law and Statute *see* these headings.)

The first test as to whether a person may bring an action in a Court of Justice is provided by the answer to the question: Has a right been infringed? If it has been, then generally an action will lie, but care must be taken to ascertain whether the right is what is called an absolute one, i.e. a right any breach of which may give a right of action even though no financial loss is caused—such as a right not to be libelled, or a right to prevent another person trespassing on one's land; or whether it is in the nature of a qualified right, where an action is only available if actual financial loss has been caused to the person complaining, such as a right to walk in safety along a public highway. Examples of these two different kinds of rights are given throughout this volume and should be referred to under their particular headings.

If the answer to the initial question "Has a right been infringed?" is in the negative, then no action will lie, despite the fact that a person has suffered the greatest damage by reason of the act complained of. Thus a slanderous statement made about another unless it falls within certain classes (*see* SLANDER) is not actionable, though the utmost grief and distress may have been occasioned to the sufferer, while the perpetrator may have been guilty of the worst motives. So also the bringing of an action against another person for which there is no justification and which does not succeed does not give any right to the other person to damages against the bringer of the action although the successful defendant may have been ruined by the proceedings.

Finally there is a rule of law which lays down that the Courts will not take notice of infinitesimal infringements of rights, but this maxim only applies where the infringement complained of is so small that it would be absurd or vexatious to take account of it.

Besides these limitations on the right of bringing an action there are certain cases where the right is suspended until certain formalities have been complied with. For example, if a person persistently commences actions without reasonable cause it is open to the Court to declare him to be a "vexatious litigant." The effect of this is that no action can be commenced by the litigant without the leave of the Court.

Arbitration.—One of the commonest ways in which a right of bringing an action is suspended is by entering into an agreement to arbitrate upon differences that may arise. Although it is not lawful for any person to enter into an agreement to arbitrate in such terms as to oust completely the right of the ordinary courts of law to adjudicate upon disputes, yet where a person has agreed to arbitration, the Court will not permit him to bring an action upon the subject of the dispute until the arbitration has been decided.

Criminal Acts.—Where the infringement of the right for which a person wishes to bring an action also amounts to a crime of either treason or felony, he is not entitled to bring his action until he has instituted criminal proceedings, but this rule does not apply, if either he has not sufficient evidence to institute criminal proceedings, or if the action arises not out of the crime itself, but out of the indirect consequences of the crime. The reason for this rule is that every citizen has a public duty to bring to justice an offender against the criminal law. (*See* ARBITRATION; COUNTY COURT PROCEDURE; HIGH COURT PROCEDURE; PARTIES; PLEADINGS.)

AD FACTUM PRAESTANDUM (SCOTS LAW).—An obligation is said to be "ad factum praestandum" when the person bound under the contract has agreed to do some specific act, e.g. to deliver some goods—and not merely to pay money. In some cases he may be compelled to carry out what he has undertaken by a decree ad factum praestandum instead of merely paying damages. Such a decree is equivalent to an order for a specific performance in England and is governed by the same considerations. (*See* SPECIFIC PERFORMANCE.)

ADJOINING OWNERS.—Adjoining owners of land owe a number of legal duties to each other and have a number of legal rights. Some of these rights and duties are the result of the general law of the land, viz:

Air and View.—The owner of a house or land has no legal right to have the free flow of air to his property or the view from it unobstructed. The owner of adjacent property may at any time build or alter it in such a way as to shut out his neighbour from either, and the latter will have no legal ground for complaint. (*See* ANCIENT LIGHTS.)

Dangerous Things.—Any person who brings upon his land anything which, if it escapes, is liable to cause damage will be responsible for such damage unless he can shew that this was the result of something entirely beyond his control. This principle was originally laid down in a case in which water was collected in a reservoir out of which it burst. It does not apply if it was natural and ordinary to act in such a way: thus a wall which collapses unexpectedly is outside the rule and it has also been decided that to leave land uncultivated and to permit thistle down and other seeds to escape falls within the exception.

Ditches, Fences and Walls.—There is no legal presumption that a boundary wall or fence belongs to either of the two adjoining owners and it is a question of fact in each case to which of them it belongs. There is, however, a strong presumption that a ditch which adjoins a fence belongs to the same person as the fence, as the practice used to be for a man to dig a ditch on the boundary, throwing back the earth on to his *own* land and planting a hedge on top of it. In the absence of any agreement to the contrary the owner of land is under no obligation to keep the fences, etc., in repair, or indeed to fence at all. If his neighbour's cattle stray on to his land he can sue him for trespass to which it would be no answer to say that the cattle would not have got in if the fences had been in order; a man's duty is to keep his own cattle in, not to keep his neighbour's cattle out. It has now been provided by statute to simplify the position with regard to party walls that they shall be considered to be cut perpendicularly down the centre and that each of the adjoining owners shall own half: they are each bound therefore to keep their own half in repair.

Easements.—These are rights which one owner of property may have over the property of another, such as rights of way, rights to draw water, rights to light, etc. They are subject to a number of technical rules and are the result either of express agreement or of long uninterrupted ownership. (*See* ANCIENT LIGHTS; EASEMENTS.)

Nuisance.—This is the technical name for any kind of disturbance which makes the enjoyment of land appreciably less in the eye of the law. It is however confined to the occupiers of land, for no person can sue or be sued "in nuisance" except as the occupier of a particular piece of land which is either affected by, or is the place of origin of, the nuisance. In determining whether any particular thing is a nuisance, one must take into account the general character of the neighbourhood and the pursuits which are usually carried on there (for the special rules relating to obstruction of the right to light *see* ANCIENT LIGHTS); if the result of the act complained of is to make the neighbouring property appreciably less comfortable than the normal property in the same district, then it is an actionable nuisance. Examples of acts which have been held to be nuisances on the particular facts of each case are excessive vibrations, noise (including piano playing, dancing, machinery, etc.), smell, smoke, chemical deposit on fruit trees and similar inconveniences.

It is no defence to an allegation that a particular act or trade is a nuisance to say that it cannot be carried on in any other way, or that it is situated at the only possible place; the attitude of the law is that if it cannot be carried on without creating a nuisance it must not be carried on at all. It is no defence to shew that in fact the nuisance was already there when the person who now complains of it first came to the land or first built in such a way as to notice it; nor apparently can long use give rise to a right to commit a nuisance.

The remedy for a nuisance is by way of an action for damages and for an injunction to restrain the further commission of the nuisance; the Court is not bound to give such an injunction when asked for and may give only damages instead. There is also a practical remedy known as abatement (q.v.), which remedy however should only be used in very urgent cases as it is not very favourably regarded by the Courts. Strictly speaking, any occupier of land who is aggrieved by a nuisance upon neighbouring land may take whatever steps are necessary to abate it—i.e. to stop it; but if this would involve going upon his neighbour's land he should first give the latter notice and a warning that if he does not abate it himself an entry will be made to do so.

Overhanging Trees.—If the roots or branches of a tree grow into the property of an adjoining owner this is a nuisance which he can abate by cutting them off at the point where they enter his land. If he can do this from his own land he may do so immediately, but, if it is necessary to go upon his neighbour's land he must first give him notice asking him to cut them himself. No action can be brought simply because the tree has grown over the boundary, but if its encroachments cause any material damage (as by injuring crops) an action to recover compensation for these will lie. If the tree is poisonous such as a yew, and it is eaten by neighbour's cattle, liability depends on whether or not it had grown over the boundary; if it had, its owner is liable for all consequential damage, whereas if the animals had to reach over a fence or hedge to get at it, their owner will have no right of action if they die. That part of a tree which overhangs a neighbour's land nevertheless remains the property of the owner of the land on which it grows; the same rule applies to fruit growing upon the tree.

If either the fruit, or the tree itself, or any part of it falls or is blown into a neighbour's land, its owner has a legal right to enter such land to reclaim it provided always that it came there by accident; if it fell as the result of any act of the owner though it would still remain his property and therefore might not be used by his neighbour, he would himself have no right to enter on his neighbour's property to get it back. The same principle applies to other things such as balls, etc., so it follows that legally speaking one never has a right to retrieve them, though of course this does not mean that they may be used by the owner of the land where they came to rest. Any such user would probably be the tort of conversion. Damage caused by the accidental fall of a tree cannot be recovered from its owner; the position would however be different if the owner knew or ought to have known as a reasonable man that it was dangerous.

Support.—The right to be supported by adjoining property is enjoyed by all land, and any subsidence which follows the withdrawal of such support is an actionable wrong. A house or other building, however, does not acquire a right to support until it has been in position for twenty years, but since in almost every case it is impossible to withdraw support from the house without also withdrawing it from the land, and since damages for the injury to the house may be recovered in any action for the withdrawal of support from the land (although the house has not been built for twenty years and therefore has not acquired a right for itself) the distinction is not important.

Water.—The rights of riparian owners (owners of land on a river bank) are rather complicated but broadly speaking each owner is entitled to take what water he needs for his riparian property provided he does not materially affect the flow of water to the riparian owners lower down the river.

As regards water flowing underground it has long been decided that unless this flows in a defined channel no person has any more right to it than any one else. It follows that there is no remedy at law if the percolating water to a well is dried up by boring or pumping operations on neighbouring land, unless it can be shown that at the place where it was abstracted it flowed in a defined channel. Owners of adjoining properties may also have rights and duties which are the result of agreements expressed or implied; the commonest of these are easements (q.v.). There are also rights known as restrictive covenants (q.v.) which entitle the owner of one property to forbid the owner of another to do certain things (e.g. building) upon it.

Animals.—The owner of an animal such as a dog or cat is not liable if it goes on to someone else's land and does damage to the garden. (*See* ANIMALS; EASEMENTS; NUISANCE; RESTRICTIVE COVENANTS.)

ADJUDICATION (SCOTS LAW). —Adjudication is the method by which the land of a debtor may be seized by his creditor. It can only be obtained by bringing an action in the Court of Session. Any land may be taken including leases, but not land belonging to a railway company or any other public utility company which is used for the purposes of their legitimate business.

The effect of a decree of adjudication is to vest the property in the land in the creditor. At any time within a period of ten years—known as the "legal"—the debtor may redeem the land by paying the amount due. If the debtor does not do this within ten years the creditor may bring another action which will prevent the debtor exercising the right of redemption, but if he does not do so the debtor may redeem at any time. When a summons of adjudication is served, a notice of it should be registered in the General Register of Inhibitions and Adjudications and after the ten years no proceedings by the debtor can affect the right of the creditor. (*See* DILIGENCE.)

ADJUDICATION ORDER.—This is the order of the Court following upon the petition and receiving order in bankruptcy which makes a debtor bankrupt, and for the first time takes his property away from him and gives it to a trustee to be divided among his creditors. When a receiving order has been made an adjudication will follow in most cases, for a debtor must be adjudicated bankrupt by the Court:

1. If the creditors pass a resolution to that effect at the first meeting of creditors, or pass no resolution at all or fail to meet; and

2. If they do not approve a composition (q.v.) or scheme (i.e. a proposal for the payment of his debts made by the debtor to his creditors as an alternative to adjudicating him bankrupt) within 14 days after the conclusion of the public examination (q.v.).

Where a debtor has presented a petition for his own bankruptcy the adjudication order will be made at the same time as the receiving order.

The Court may annul—i.e. cancel—the adjudication order

1. If the debtor ought not to have been made bankrupt, i.e. there is something wrong in the proceedings; or

2. Where the debts have been paid in full; or

3. Where a composition or scheme is put forward after the order is made and is approved by the Court.

Persons dealing with the bankrupt after the adjudication order in buying goods from him and paying him the price, or selling goods to him, will not be affected by the bankruptcy if the transactions are completed before the trustee intervenes, are not gifts, and are made in good faith. In such a case it does not matter whether or not the person receiving the money knew of the adjudication order, for although the trustee is entitled to all property and money which the bankrupt gets after the adjudication order and before he is discharged and can claim it from the bankrupt, yet if, before he does so, the bankrupt sells or deals with the property or spends the money, the trustee cannot claim it back from the person to whom the bankrupt has disposed of it. It makes no difference if the person taking the property knew of the bankruptcy.

This protection does not extend to cases where the bankrupt has given away any property as a gift but only where he has received something in return and where the transaction is genuine—i.e. is not a gift disguised as a sale.

This provision is of great value to bankers who receive money which is paid into a bankrupt's banking account, or who receive shares or other securities from a bankrupt to cover an overdraft given to him. But for the protection given, the banker would be compelled to hand over money or securities to the Trustee, even though the bankrupt had already drawn out money equal to what had been paid in or up to the amount of the overdraft.

Where a banker knows that one of his customers is a bankrupt he is still entitled to the protection, but unless he is satisfied that the customer's account is really on behalf of some one else—i.e. is a trust account—he must inform the customer's Trustee in bankruptcy or the Board of Trade. He must make no payments out of the account until he receives permission from the Trustee or the Court, but if he receives no instructions for a month after he has given the notice, he may make payments out of the account as before. (*See* BANKRUPTCY; TRUSTEE IN BANKRUPTCY.)

ADMINISTRATION ACTION.— Any personal representative, i.e. executor or administrator, or beneficiary under a will or intestacy, or any creditor of a deceased person, is entitled to seek the aid of the Court in deciding any question of doubt such as a right to receive a legacy or payment of a debt, etc. This power to go to the Court is most useful for executors and should be resorted to whenever questions of real doubt arise. If the total amount of the estate is less than £500 this can be done cheaply and expeditiously in the County Court of the district in which the deceased resided or one of the personal representatives resides. It may also be done in the County Court where a legatee seeks to recover a legacy not greater than £100, however large the total estate.

The executor or any other interested person desiring a decision upon the point in question should take out a summons at the office of the Registrar of the County Court. All persons whom he wishes to be bound by the decision of the Court may be made parties, but if it is only a question that concerns one legatee, that legatee alone need be defendant and served with the summons. Similarly a legatee or residuary legatee may take out a plaint and summons against the executors alone. With the plaint should be delivered full particulars of the point upon which a decision is desired, and in due course the case will be heard before the County Court Judge who will give his decision and make an order. If the estate is greater than £500 the action must take place in the High Court and should be started either by writ or by applying for an originating summons (q.v.), but in all such cases a solicitor should be employed.

A somewhat similar right is that of the personal representative to pay into Court any money or securities of which he has a doubt as to the person properly entitled, or of which the beneficiary is an infant or abroad. If the fund so desired to be paid into Court is less than £500 it can be paid into the County Court, and this can be done by a simple request addressed to the Registrar and signed by the personal representative. It must be accompanied by a certificate from the Inland Revenue showing that all death duties have been paid, and unless the beneficiary is an infant or abroad, the executor must file an affidavit explaining the circumstances and the reasons why he has paid it in. He must also send a notice that the money is lodged in Court to any person who is entitled to the money, who can then take the procedure mentioned above in order to settle the disputed question of ownership, etc. The executors however must not use this procedure merely to avoid their own duties under their executorship,

or where the matter could be decided as mentioned above without paying the money into Court.

Administration Proceedings. — A more drastic procedure, and one used generally when an estate is insolvent, is to start administration proceedings. If the estate is worth less than £500 these can be started in the ordinary way by plaint and summons in the County Court, or if the estate is greater than £500 by issuing a writ in the Chancery Division of the High Court. Any person who is interested in the estate, i.e. the personal representatives (executors or administrators), the beneficiaries or any creditor may start administration proceedings in this manner. Generally it is a creditor who starts such proceedings and he must name the executors or administrators as defendants in his writ or summons, nor can he name any other person as defendant without special leave of the Court. He may sue for administration of the estate either on behalf of himself alone, or on behalf of all other creditors, but when he gets a judgment for administration it will be for the benefit of all other creditors and from the moment of the judgment the personal representative loses his right of preferring creditors. This is generally the chief reason of such proceedings being started.

The judgment for administration may take many forms but the commonest is in the form of an order upon the executor to render a full and sufficient account of all his dealings as executor, and after such a judgment though he has still a right to retain his own debt in preference to the debts of other creditors, he is not entitled to do anything which gives one creditor an advantage over any other. The administration order may also order him to pay money into court or appoint a receiver of the estate, after which the executor will not be able to deal with the estate at all himself and will so lose his right to retainer as well.

When the estate of the deceased is insolvent, the order for administration of his estate obtained in this manner is treated as if it were an order for the administration of the estate of a bankrupt, and the same rules and procedure apply as in ordinary bankruptcy proceedings. (*See* BANKRUPTCY EXECUTORS AND ADMINISTRATORS; LETTERS OF ADMINISTRATION; PROBATE OF WILLS.)

ADMINISTRATION, LETTERS OF.—(*See* LETTERS OF ADMINISTRATION.)

ADMINISTRATION ORDER.—The easiest and cheapest method by which a small trader may be made bankrupt in cases where he is unable to pay his debts is by an administration order. This may be made by a County Court where a judgment for any amount has been obtained against a debtor who says he cannot pay it at once and further says that the whole of his debts do not exceed £50, or where the Court is asked to make a committal order, i.e. to send to prison a debtor against whom a judgment has been obtained on the ground that he is able to pay the debt but does not do so. In both of these cases it is necessary that the total liabilities of the debtor should not exceed £50.

The administration order provides for the debts being paid usually by instalments and either in full or to as great an extent as the County Court Judge thinks it possible. The debtor may be ordered to pay something towards his debts out of his future earnings.

Where the debtor has property which can be taken in execution and which appears to be over £10 in value, the registrar of the County Court must at the request of the creditor and without charge issue execution against the goods of the debtor, but household goods, wearing apparel, bedding of the debtor or his family and tools and implements of his trade to a total value of £20 are exempt.

Order may be cancelled.—If the debtor refuses or fails to pay any instalment he may be committed to prison, and if he fails to pay two or more of these instalments the Court may cancel the administration order. It may also do this in cases where a receiving order (q.v.) is made against the debtor or where the order was obtained by fraud, or the debtor has given wrong particulars as to his creditors, or subsequently to the order has obtained credit from someone to the extent of £5 or more without disclosing the fact that an administration order had been made.

When an order has been made the Registrar of the Court prepares a list of creditors and any creditor who proves his debt may have his name inserted on this list. Creditors whose debts were not due at the time of the order may also have their names put on the list, but will not be entitled to receive any money until all the creditors whose debts were due at the time of the order have been paid, not necessarily in full, but to the extent provided for in the order. When the debtor has paid his debts to this extent he is automatically discharged from all liabilities to creditors who have had their names entered in the list, but not to any other creditors.

ADMINISTRATOR'S BOND.—Before anyone is granted letters of administration (q.v.) of the estate of a person who has died without a will, he is required to enter into a bond known as an Administrator's Bond by which he binds himself to:

(1) Make an inventory, i.e. list, of the whole estate as fully and truly as possible and to exhibit this inventory at Somerset House, London.

(2) Well and truly to administer the estate.

(3) To make and render a true account of his administration whenever he is required to do so by law.

(4) To deliver up the letters of administration if a will is subsequently brought into the registry.

If he is a creditor of the deceased he must also swear not only not to pay his own debt before those of other creditors but to pay all in proportion if there is not enough for all.

The penalty for not complying with the bond is twice the value of the property that comes into the hands of the administrator, and if the administrator breaks his bond the registrar may transfer the bond to any person he likes who may sue the administrator for the penalty as trustee, i.e. for the benefit of all persons interested, and recover the full amount of the penalty.

In addition to the bond, which must always be given except when the administrator is the Public Trustee (q.v.) or some other public official or the estate is in Court, the registrar may demand two sureties, i.e. guarantors at his discretion, but he will not generally do this if more than one of the next of kin is appointed as administrator. (*See* LETTERS OF ADMINISTRATION.)

ADMIRALTY JURISDICTION. Historical.—The authority of the Crown to hear and determine matters connected with the sea and ships is of very ancient origin. As far back as the reign of Henry I we find references to the Court or Courts of the Admiral. Originally the coast of England was divided up into districts, each with its own Court presided over by an Admiral or Vice-Admiral and Deputies, whose business it was to administer justice in respect of piracy and other offences committed on the sea. The limited jurisdiction which these courts exercised did not satisfy the Admirals, however, who gradually acquired a jurisdiction over offences committed in inland

By "jurisdiction" is meant the authority which a Court has to decide matters that are the subject of litigation before it, or to take notice of matters submitted before it in a formal way for decision; this authority is usually derived from and governed by the Statute (i.e. Act of Parliament) or other instrument under, or by virtue of, which the Court is constituted. This jurisdiction may be limited in two ways, firstly as to the nature of the actions and matters over which

Interior of the Admiralty Court, London.

tidal waters and other places inland, which brought them into conflict with the Courts of Common Law, whose Judges resented this intrusion into their preserves, with the result that two Statutes were passed in the reign of Richard II, which defined the authority of the Admirals' Courts, and confined the Admirals and their Deputies to "things done upon the sea, and in the main streams of great rivers."

The Courts of the Admiral were later merged into one High Court of Admiralty, which in turn became, in common with the other Superior Courts, a component part of the Supreme Court, by the Supreme Court of Judicature Act passed in 1873.

the Court shall exercise its authority, and secondly as to the area over which this jurisdiction shall extend.

Extent of Jurisdiction (Criminal).— The jurisdiction of the Court of Admiralty, in so far as the matters over which it exercises authority, was limited at first to the arrest of the person, mostly in connection with piracy and other offences at sea. This criminal jurisdiction was by the Offences at Sea Act of 1536 transferred to Commissioners appointed by the King, but the present practice with regard to crimes committed within the Admiralty jurisdiction is that they may be tried by the Ordinary Superior Criminal Courts, and in this connection it may be noted that the Central Criminal Court (The Old Bailey) has power to try offences committed on the High Seas and other places within the jurisdiction of the Admiralty, but the various Courts of Assizes have also power to try any person for criminal acts done within the Admiralty jurisdiction, provided such person is committed to, or in prison in any gaol, in any County or other district within the jurisdiction of the particular Court of Assize. For instance, if A has been committed to prison in Winchester for an offence committed on a ship or other place within the Admiralty jurisdiction, he may be tried at the next Assize to be held in Winchester.

Extent of Jurisdiction (Civil Matters).

With regard to the Civil jurisdiction of the Admiralty Court (i.e. the jurisdiction which it exercises over matters in dispute between subject and subject as distinct from crimes), this also in the beginning appears to have been exercised by the arrest of the person of the defendant. This method known as an action *in personam*, i.e. against the person, was largely discontinued, however, and the Admiralty Court now exercises its civil jurisdiction for the most part by means of the arrest, i.e. seizure of the property the subject matter in dispute, usually a ship, and by the enforcement of its judgments against the property so arrested, by means of an action known as an *action in rem*, i.e. against the property, the ship. This right to arrest the property the subject matter in dispute, and to enforce the judgment of the Court upon such property, is based upon the theory of what is called a maritime lien; a lien being a right in one man to retain the property of another in his possession, until certain demands of the person in possession are satisfied. This right or lien, attaches to the property to the extent of the claim, and still remains even though the property in question should be bought by some person who knows nothing of the lien.

An action *in rem* cannot be brought against King's Ships, or foreign national ships; and certain mail ships in postal service and subsidized for the execution of that service are also exempt from arrest.

Sometimes, as where for example a ship had been lost, a plaintiff could take proceedings *in personam* against the owners of the ship, which would have been arrested if the proceedings had been *in rem*; but since the Judicature Act of 1873, the defendant in an Admiralty action *in personam* is liable as in other divisions of the High Court for the full amount of the plaintiff's proved claim. It should be noted also that a defendant who appears and puts in bail in an action *in rem* is now liable for the full amount of the plaintiff's claim and costs, even though such claim and costs exceed the value of the subject matter in dispute and the bail provided.

Jurisdiction—locality.

The authority of the Admiralty Court is limited to all matters arising upon the High Seas and not within the body of any County. Usually, the Admiralty Court has jurisdiction from the lowest bridges on a river, down to the sea, but this jurisdiction may not always hold sway, and it may be excluded by some local Court, and in this connection it may be of interest to note that a ship anchored at Limehouse is not within the Admiralty jurisdiction, but is subject to a Court called the Court of Conservancy.

In relation to matters happening below low water mark, the Court of Admiralty has sole and absolute jurisdiction; between high-water mark and low-water mark (i.e. between the tides) the Common Law and the Court of Admiralty have a divided and alternate jurisdiction; the Court of Admiralty, when the sea is at flood and the Common Law when the sea is ebbed. If part of the matter be done upon the sea and part in a county the Common Law has all the jurisdiction. In cases of damage by collision occurring within the body of a county the Court of Admiralty has jurisdiction provided the vessel involved is a seagoing vessel. The Admiralty jurisdiction of England extends over British vessels not only when they are sailing on the high seas, but also when they are in the rivers of a foreign country at a place below bridges, where the tide ebbs and flows and where great ships go.

Note that "roads" are not within the body of the land, and where a British ship is anchored in foreign roads she is within the jurisdiction of the Admiralty Court.

Similarly a strait, e.g. the Solent, between lands of the same county is deemed to be the high seas and so within that jurisdiction.

All causes and matters arising under the Admiralty jurisdiction of the High Court are dealt with in the Probate Divorce and Admiralty Division of the High Court in London, but all Divisions of the High Court are entitled to exercise Admiralty jurisdiction.

Appeals lie from the Admiralty Division of the Probate Divorce and Admiralty Division, to the Court of Appeal, and thence to the House of Lords, except where such Admiralty Court is exercising its jurisdiction as a Prize Court, when appeal lies to the Judicial Committee of the Privy Council.

In addition to the Admiralty jurisdiction exercised by the High Court, the following County Courts, including the City of London Court, exercise limited Admiralty Jurisdiction conferred by Statute:—

Newcastle-on-Tyne, Sunderland, West Hartlepool, Stockton-on-Tees, Middlesbrough, Kingston - upon - Hull, Great Grimsby, Boston, King's Lynn, Great Yarmouth, Lowestoft, Ipswich, Colchester, City of London, Rochester, Ramsgate, Dover, Brighton, Portsmouth, Southampton, Poole, Weymouth, Exeter, Torquay, Plymouth and East Stonehouse, Truro, Barnstaple, Bridgwater, Bristol, Gloucester, Newport (Mon.), Cardiff, Swansea, Carmarthen, Haverfordwest, Aberystwyth, Bangor, Chester, Liverpool, Manchester, Preston, Blackpool and Fleetwood, Barrow-in-Furness and Ulverston and Whitehaven.

These County Courts have jurisdiction over all cases of salvage of life or property, where the value of the property salved does not exceed £1,000, or where the amount claimed does not exceed £300, and they may also determine claims, not exceeding £150 for towage and necessaries; and claims not exceeding £300 for damage to cargo, or damage to a ship by collision or otherwise.

Such County Courts exercising Admiralty jurisdiction may also determine claims for wages by sailors not exceeding £150, but claims for wages below £50 must be brought in a Court of Summary jurisdiction, e.g. Petty Sessional Court or Police Court.

The following Courts also exercise a limited Admiralty jurisdiction, viz.:—the Court of Admiralty of the Cinque Ports, The Cinque Ports Salvage Commissioners and the Liverpool Court of Passage.

ADOPTION.—The Adoption of Children Act, 1926, came into force on 1st January, 1927. Until that date, legal adoption of children had not been recognized in England. The most that could previously be done was for a person to put himself by his conduct into the position of a parent to a child, and so take upon himself a number of the rights and duties of a natural parent. This may still be done to-day, but the results are, for several reasons, not nearly as satisfactory as a legal adoption, e.g. unless the adoption is a legal one the child's natural parents can claim the child back (*see* LOCO PARENTIS). As a result of the Act of 1926, legal adoption can now be effected in England, and has the result of putting the adopted child in practically the same position in relation to his adopter as if he were his legitimate child.

The right to obtain an adoption order is limited by the following seven restrictions: (i) the adopter must be over twenty-five; (ii) the child must be under twenty-one; (iii) the adopter must be not less than twenty-one years older than the child, unless within the prohibited degrees of consanguinity when the Court may make the order at its discretion, e.g. the Court will usually allow an aunt of twenty-six to adopt a niece of ten years of age; (iv) a male adopter may not adopt a female unless there are special circumstances to make it desirable; this does not apply when a man and his wife are adopting a child jointly; (v) the adopter must be resident and domiciled in England or Wales; (vi) the child must be a British subject and resident in England or Wales; and (vii) the child must never have been married.

In order to obtain an adoption order, the consent must be obtained of each of the following persons: the child's parents or guardians, or the person who has the actual custody of the child or who is liable to contribute to its support. The Court may, however, dispense with such consents if it is satisfied that the person whose consent is required has abandoned or deserted the child; or cannot be found; or is incapable of giving consent (e.g. is insane); or, in the case of a person who is liable to contribute to the support of the child, if he has persistently neglected so to do, or is, in the opinion of the Court, a person whose consent should be dispensed with, having regard to all the circumstances of the case. The only case in which more than one person can jointly adopt a child is that of a man and his wife. A married man or woman may also adopt a child without his or her spouse becoming a joint adopter, provided the consent of such spouse is obtained; this consent may be dispensed with if the man and his wife are permanently separated and living apart, or if the spouse whose consent is required cannot be found or is incapable of giving consent.

Before the Court will grant an adoption order, it must be satisfied (i) that every person whose consent is necessary has consented, fully understanding the effect of such consent, (ii) that the order will be for the welfare of the infant, and for this purpose the wishes of the child must, to a proper extent, be considered, (iii) that no payment or other reward has been made or is to be made to the adopter in consideration of the adoption without the sanction of the Court. The Court may make the order subject to any terms or conditions it sees fit.

Adoption orders are made either by the High Court in London, or, at the option of the applicant, by a County Court or Magistrate's Court in the area within its jurisdiction. The application is made in the County Court by means of a petition which must be filed in the Court and copies of which must be served on the persons whose consents are required.

Effect of Adoption Order.—When the order is made, all the rights and duties of the child's original parents or guardians are extinguished, and vested in the adopter as if the child had been born to the adopter in lawful wedlock. There is this one exception: the adopted child is not to be treated as the lawful child of the adopter(s) in respect of interests accruing on death, e.g. it will not be entitled to succeed to the property of the adopter on his death intestate; and, if the adopter leaves property to his "children," an adopted child will not share with natural children unless the will shews an intention that it should. Conversely, the adopted child is not deprived of its rights under any intestacy or disposition of property to which it would have been entitled if the adoption order had never been made. In other words, an adoption order has no effect on successions resulting from death either by intestacy or by legacy.

The Court may refuse to make an out-and-out adoption order, and may instead make an "interim" or probationary order on proper terms and conditions for a period not exceeding two years. Such an order has none of the effects of an adoption order except that it transfers the custody of the child to the proposed adopter, and will contain provisions as to the maintenance and education of the child. An adopted child may subsequently be adopted for a second time by another person, and in that case its first adoptive parents are the persons whose consent is required for the subsequent adoption.

A Register of Adopted Children is kept at Somerset House, London, W.C. 2, and every adoption order is automatically recorded in the register. An index to the Register may be inspected on payment of a small fee.

Where any single person (or any man jointly with his wife) has in effect adopted and maintained a child for two years or more before 1st January, 1927, the Court may make an adoption order without requiring any consents and even though the child is female and the adopter is a male. But the Court must be satisfied that such an order will be for the benefit of the child. (*See* FATHER; LEGITIMATION OF CHILDREN; LOCO PARENTIS; MOTHER.)

ADULTERATION.—The mixing in articles of food or drink of other ingredients in such a way as to alter the nature or composition of the article is adulteration. It is an offence to mix, stain, or powder any article of food in such a way as to make the article injurious to health. The penalty for this offence is a fine of £50. Similarly to adulterate any article of drink such as milk or spirit is an offence, except that in the case of spirit it can be mixed with water if the resulting mixture is not more than thirty-five degrees under proof. An article of food may be mixed with an ingredient which is not injurious to health provided that notice of the mixture is given to a purchaser by means of a label attached to the article.

To protect the public from injury to their health from adulterated food or drink, it is provided by the Food and Drugs Acts that local authorities shall appoint inspectors of weights and measures for their district.

These inspectors have power to take samples of any article of food which they suspect is being sold contrary to the provisions of the Acts of Parliament, and they can submit any sample thus taken to the public analyst for the district for his report.   If the public analyst certifies that the article analysed is adulterated then the seller may be prosecuted. (See DRUGS; FOOD; PUBLIC HEALTH.)

ADULTERY.—(See SPECIAL SUPPLEMENT "DIVORCE.")

ADVERTISEMENT.—A contract for the publication of an advertisement is generally bound by the same legal principles as any other contract. (See CONTRACT.)

Where damages are recoverable for the failure to publish an advertisement, such damages are not limited to the amount paid for the insertion of an advertisement, but may include the loss of the business which the publication of the advertisement might have brought.   An agreement or a contract for the publication of an advertisement if over £5 should bear a 6d. stamp.

Illegal advertisements.—Certain advertisements are illegal and their publication may render the printer and publisher of them liable to a penalty.   Thus any person who publishes, or causes to be published, any kind of advertisement which advertises a house where illegal betting is carried on may be liable to a penalty not exceeding £30.   The printer or publisher of any newspaper may be liable to forfeit the sum of £50 to any person who sues for it, if he prints or publishes any advertisement offering a reward for the recovery of stolen property and stating that no questions will be asked, or promising to repay any money that a pawnbroker may have advanced on the goods stolen if the pawnbroker returns them.

Such an action against the printer or publisher of a newspaper must be brought within six months of the publication of the advertisement, and the consent of the Solicitor-General or the Attorney-General must be obtained before any action can be brought.

When statements are made in an advertisement of goods for sale, the law allows to the advertiser a certain licence in praising his goods so long as he does so in general terms.   If, however, he makes specific statements, e.g. that his hair tonic is guaranteed to cure baldness in three weeks, or that he will pay £50 to any person who contracts influenza after using his medicine—the law will hold him to his word and compel him to pay if his advertisement is not borne out. For indecent advertisements see INDECENT PUBLICATIONS.

ADVOCATE (SCOTS LAW).—The advocate in Scotland corresponds to the Barrister in England.   His functions are to appear for his client in Court and he alone is entitled to represent his client in the Court of Session.   A person becomes an advocate by being admitted as a member of the Faculty of Advocates.   An advocate must be instructed by a solicitor and cannot act for his client direct.

The profession in Scotland is divided as in England into K.C.'s (called Senior Counsel) and Juniors, who perform the same work as in England.   Advocates wear a wig and gown as do barristers in England, but in the Scottish dress a white bow tie is substituted for the bands worn in England, while K.C.'s wear a type of white cravat. The head of the profession is known as the Dean of Faculty and there are in addition a Lord Advocate and Solicitor-General appointed as Law Officers by the Government.

Advocates do not have separate offices of their own corresponding to the chambers in the Inns of Court but conduct most of their business in the hall of the Parliament House in Edinburgh where the Law Courts are situated.   Consultations with clients take place at the advocates' homes which are situated in one district in Edinburgh within easy reach of Parliament House.   There is no system of chambers as in England under which a group of barristers occupy one set of buildings, and when occasion demands assist one another in their work.

No action can be brought against an advocate for any statement made by him in a Court on the ground that the statement is defamatory.   He is said to enjoy absolute privilege.   (See PRIVILEGE.)   Advocates cannot sue for their fees and have the corresponding benefit that they are not liable to any action for negligence in the carrying out of their work.

The term advocate is also applied to a member of a society of solicitors in Aberdeen. Such persons are really solicitors and are not advocates in the sense above considered.

ADVOWSON.—An Advowson is the right to instal (or "present") one's nominee to a church living, and the person who holds the right is called the patron. The Bishop may refuse to accept the nominee on the ground of immorality, want of learning or unorthodoxy, but otherwise he is bound to institute him. This right arose during the Middle Ages when the Barons began to build and endow churches on their land, whereupon the Church, to encourage this pious practice, gave the barons the privilege of presentation which remains to-day. This privilege was abused however, and, in an endeavour to check the scandal, the peculiar crime of simony was defined, consisting of the corrupt presentation of a clergyman to an ecclesiastical benefice in return for money, gift or reward. The punishment is forfeiture of the advowson to the Crown (*see* SIMONY).

Advowsons were, however, capable of being sold, provided the crime of simony was not committed, but such transactions have been long looked on with disfavour, and now, by a Measure passed in 1923, it is provided that almost every advowson will be unsaleable after two vacancies have occurred in the benefice since 14th July, 1924. The owner of an advowson is also entitled, even before that date, to make a declaration that the advowson is no longer saleable, and such declaration will be effective. Although advowsons thus will soon become unsaleable, they may, nevertheless, still be able to be transferred as gifts, but it is probable that the majority of owners of advowsons will now transfer them either gratis or for some small consideration to the Diocesan Boards of Patronage, which are bodies created in 1932 for the acquiring, holding and transferring of advowsons. (*See* BENEFICE.)

AERODROME.—An aerodrome is any definite and limited ground or water area intended to be used either wholly or in part for the landing or departure of aircraft. In this country aerodromes are of four main kinds.

(i) Private aerodromes. These are not used for the transport of passengers and consequently no licence is required.

(ii) Licensed aerodromes. No place may be used as a regular place of landing or departure by aircraft carrying passengers for hire or reward without a licence to that effect from the Minister for Air. There are two classes of licensed aerodromes (*a*) those licensed for public use and (*b*) those to be used only by the licensee and persons authorised by him.

(iii) Aerodromes controlled by the State for the purpose of civil aviation, such as Croydon, Lympne, and Penshurst. The Air Minister has powers of compulsory purchase of lands for this purpose.

(iv) Royal Air Force Aerodromes. The power of compulsory purchase may also be exercised in this case.

Customs aerodromes.—These are Croydon, Lympne, Heston and Barton (Manchester) for aeroplanes, and Cardington for airships. Dover, Southampton and Liverpool have customs aerodromes for seaplanes.

Aerodromes must be defined by red lights at night and the landing direction must be shown by a luminous T. The direction of the wind must be shown to all landing aeroplanes by one of the recognised methods. Trespass on an aerodrome is no more a crime than trespass on any other land, but malicious damage to an aerodrome is of course a criminal offence. (*See* AVIATION.)

AEROPLANE.—An aeroplane is one of that species of aircraft known as flying machines. This species includes also seaplanes, flying boats and other aircraft heavier than air which have means of propulsion. As to the steps to be taken on purchase, and how to obtain a licence, etc. *see* AVIATION.

AFFIDAVIT.—There are two methods by which facts may be proved in a Court of law. One is by calling somebody as a witness who knows the facts and can inform the Court as to them by verbal evidence on oath. The other is by a sworn statement in writing made on oath before some person authorised to take statements on oath. Usually an affidavit is sworn before a Solicitor who is a Commissioner for Oaths. Making an untrue statement in an Affidavit is perjury and a criminal offence just as if the statement were made verbally in Court.

English law does not allow all evidence to be given by Affidavit. In fact it is only in exceptional cases that facts may be proved in this way instead of by the production of a person who may speak to them in Court.

The reason for this is that it is considered essential to the discovery of the truth that a person should be cross-examined, and this of course is impossible in the case of an Affidavit, although where evidence by Affidavit is allowed an order may be made for the person who has sworn the Affidavit to attend for the purpose of being cross-examined.

Evidence may be in the form of Affidavits either if the parties to the case agree or if the Court makes a special order dispensing with verbal witnesses. The Court may order that certain facts in a case may be proved by Affidavit, as for example where the only witness who could prove it is at a distance, and the facts are not at this stage really disputed by the other party to the proceedings.

AFFILIATION ORDER.—An affiliation order is an order made by the Justices' Court or by a Magistrate's Court, which, having adjudged a man to be the father of a bastard child, orders him to pay not more than 20/- a week towards its maintenance. As to who is a bastard, *see* ILLEGITIMATE CHILDREN. The order can be made only if the child was born *alive* in England or in a British ship or, if born abroad, of English parents who are normally resident and domiciled in England. The father must, at the time of the proceedings, be present in England, for otherwise it would be impossible to serve the summons on him (*see* below as to soldiers, sailors, etc.). It is the mother who takes the proceedings, and she must be a "single woman"; this does not mean that she must be unmarried, for she will be considered single if she is living separately from her husband. It must be remembered that the evidence required to prove that the child of a married woman is a bastard is very difficult to obtain (*see* ILLEGITIMATE CHILDREN), and an affiliation order will not be made until it be proved; the separation must also be proved to be *bona fide* and not, e.g. purely temporary for the purposes of obtaining the affiliation order. If an unmarried woman has a bastard and then, before taking proceedings, marries some other person, she cannot obtain an affiliation order or continue with proceedings already instituted, even though she subsequently separates from her husband: the reason is that a man, who marries

a woman who already has a bastard, becomes liable to maintain the bastard in all circumstances, and there is therefore no need to take proceedings against a third person because the child is already provided for. No proceedings can be taken after the death of either the alleged father or the mother.

How to obtain an order.—Before the order can be made, two distinct steps must be taken: (i) the applicant must make an application for a summons; and (ii) the Justice to whom the application was made must issue the summons. The application must be made by the mother, and may be made at any time between the date when the child was conceived and twelve months after the birth of the child. It is to be made to any Justice of the Peace of the petty sessional division in which the mother resides. It is not sufficient to apply to the Justices' Clerk. When the application is made before the birth of the child, the mother must make a deposition on oath stating who is the father of the expected child. The purpose of the deposition is to preserve a record of the application in view of the fact that the proceedings cannot be heard until after the birth of the child.

There are exceptional cases in which an application may be made after the expiration of twelve months from the birth: (i) If the father has ceased to reside in England before the expiration of the twelve months, the application may be made within twelve months after his return, and in some cases may therefore be made many years later; (ii) If the father has paid money for the maintenance of the child within twelve months after the birth, the application may be made at any time; and (iii) Where the mother proves that she went through a ceremony of marriage with the alleged father, but that such marriage was void under the Age of Marriage Act, 1929 (i.e. because either party was under the age of sixteen), she may make application for a summons against the father at any time, provided that she can shew that the alleged father had access to her within twelve months before the birth. The making of an application does not prevent the making of a subsequent application, provided that every such application is made within the time limit mentioned above. If the first application resulted in a decision that the

2

alleged father was not the father of the child, the Court will, when dealing with the subsequent application, attach great weight to that decision, and will be disposed to grant the summons only if the mother can shew that her first proceedings failed for some technical reason or that new evidence has been obtained. Once an appeal at Quarter Sessions has been heard, no new application may be made. If the Justice grants the application, he then issues the summons on the alleged father. The summons ought to be issued by the same Justice as the one that heard the application, but if such Justice has ceased to hold office or is unable to act, any one of his brother Justices may issue the summons. The summons need not be issued immediately, and, indeed, the Justice will always hold the issue over if the mother says that the alleged father cannot be found. More than one summons may be issued on the same application even though more than twelve months have elapsed from the birth, but when once one of those summonses has been heard and the case decided, no new summons will issue except on a new application. The summons may issue before or after the birth of the child, but if before, the hearing is always fixed for a date after the time when the birth of the child is expected.

Service of Summons.—The next step to be taken is to serve the summons on the defendant, in order to give him notice of the proceedings. It must be served a reasonable time before the case is to come on, and, if the defendant cannot be found, the summons may be served by leaving it at his last place of abode. This does not mean his last *known* place of abode. In a case where a man had gone to America shortly before the summons was issued, and the summons was then served at his home, which was his last place of abode in England, it was decided that such service was void, because the defendant had taken up a new abode in a town in America by the time the summons was served. If, however, he had gone to America merely for a tour, the Court would have held that he had not acquired a new abode there, but that his abode was still at his home in England, and that the service was good. The Justices are always entitled to enquire, when the defendant does not appear at the trial,

whether sufficient service has been effected, and if the summons was served upon the defendant personally. The server must be called as a witness at the trial unless the defendant resided outside the petty sessional district when the server need only make an affidavit of service. If the case comes on without the summons having been properly served, or if there is any other informality, and the defendant appears at the hearing and raises no objection to such informality, he cannot raise the point later.

There are special rules relating to members of the Army, Navy or Air Force, e.g. a summons on a soldier or airman living outside the petty sessional division where the mother resides is served on the commanding officer together with a sum sufficient to pay the defendant's travelling expenses. In other cases, either the commanding officer or the defendant himself may be served, but in the latter case, a copy must be sent to the commanding officer by registered post. Naval ratings and Royal Marines are served by serving the commanding officer, or, where that is impossible, through the Admiralty. No member of the forces under orders for foreign service may be served with a summons.

The Hearing of the Case.—The hearing of any case must take place within forty days after service of the summons, except when the summons was served before the birth of the child, when the period is two months from the date of birth. But the hearing may, in certain circumstances, be adjourned beyond those periods. When the case comes on for hearing, either party may appear in person or be represented by counsel or a solicitor. If the defendant does not appear, the mother must still prove her case before the order will be made, and it is vital that she should be there in person to give her evidence. When she is cross-examined, she may be asked as to her connections with other men, but if she denies having had such connection, witnesses may not be called to prove that she was lying, unless it is contended on behalf of the defendant that the child was the result of such connection. The evidence of the mother must be *corroborated* by some independent testimony in some material particular, or the case will fail. Such corroborative evidence must shew not merely the possibility but the probability of the defendant's being the father of the child. That there was merely an *opportunity* for sexual intercourse between the parties is not usually enough, but in these cases the mother's evidence was held to have been sufficiently corroborated: (i) Where the mother's brother gave evidence that the defendant had confessed to him that he was the child's father; (ii) Where the mother's sister had overheard a conversation between the defendant and the mother in which the defendant admitted he was the child's father; (iii) Where a witness gives evidence of acts of familiarity between the parties, even before the time when the child was conceived; (iv) Where the mother was a servant-girl and was seen out with a person much above her social position in country lanes in the evening. No corroboration is required if the case rests upon the fact that the father has paid money for the maintenance of the child within twelve months after its birth.

The defendant himself may be summoned to give evidence for the mother, and must answer any relevant questions put to him. All witnesses who are not willing to attend at the Court may be summoned to appear, and money to pay for their travelling expenses must be offered to them when the summons is served.

The Order.—At the conclusion of the case, the Justices may adjudge the defendant to be the father of the child, and, on considering the circumstances of the case, may order the payment of a weekly sum not exceeding 20/– to the mother, or (where the mother dies, or becomes insane, or is imprisoned) to the person having custody of the child; they may also order the defendant to pay the costs of the summons, the expenses of the birth, and, if the child died before the hearing, the funeral expenses. The weekly maintenance will be payable until the child attains thirteen years of age, unless the justices fix a shorter period or extend it till sixteen. When application was made before the expiration of two months after the birth, the arrears are payable as from the date of birth. Money payable under the order is usually to be paid to the collecting officer, who, in turn, pays it over to the mother. The collecting officer may, on the authority of the mother, take proceedings for arrears.

When the mother dies, or while she is insane, or is imprisoned, the maintenance is to be paid to the person having the custody of the child, or, if the child comes on the parish, to the local authority. Although no order can be made when a mother marries after the birth of the bastard, still, once the order has been made, her subsequent marriage does not affect its validity. On the death of the father, the order becomes void. Orders may be revoked or varied on fresh evidence (e.g. if the father acquires a larger income he may be ordered to pay more, but not exceeding 20/– per week); the question of paternity can never be re-opened. If the father falls into arrears with his payments, execution may be levied on his goods, and if that does not suffice, he may be imprisoned for a period up to three months, but must be released on payment of all arrears and costs. The first step to obtain arrears is to apply to any one Justice for a warrant to bring him up before two Justices. The constable must produce the warrant when he effects the arrest, and the father is usually entitled to avoid arrest by paying arrears and costs to the constable. If the father thereafter neglects to pay, the distress warrant will be issued.

Appeals.—Appeals against affiliation orders, or refusals to make them, or variations of such orders lie to the Quarter Sessions, or, in some cases, to the High Court. When the appeal is made to Quarter Sessions the whole case is re-heard, and the original order of the Justices may be discharged, confirmed or varied.

Every person against whom an affiliation order has been made must give notice of any change of address to the collecting officer under penalty of not more than £2. (*See* BASTARDY; ILLEGITIMATE CHILDREN; POOR LAW.)

AFFIRMATION.—This is a substitute for the oath used in cases where the person giving evidence, whether verbally or by Affidavit, objects to take the oath because the taking of an oath is contrary to his religious belief or because he has no religious belief. In such a case he is said to "affirm." Instead of saying the words of the oath "I swear by Almighty God that . . ." he says "I AB do solemnly, sincerely and truly declare and affirm." If statements made after an affirmation are untrue the person making them will be liable to proceedings for perjury. Persons may claim to affirm either because the taking of an oath is contrary to their religious belief, e.g. where they are Quakers, or because they have no religious belief, i.e. are atheists.

AGENT.—In a great many matters it is necessary, or at least practically convenient, that one person should authorise another to do legal acts on his behalf, e.g. to enter into contracts. The person doing the acts is called the agent and the person on whose behalf they are done is called the principal.

Certain legal persons can only act through agents because they are artificial legal persons. Thus a limited company (q.v.) or corporation (q.v.) has no physical existence although it is a legal person, and so must act through its proper officers, which in the case of a company are its Directors, for some purposes, and employees who are not directors for other purposes.

Although the law allows a man to do through an agent most of the acts which he could do in person, there are certain acts which must be done by the man himself. Thus a contract of marriage cannot be entered into through an agent nor can many of the acts which a man is entitled or required to do as a citizen, e.g. voting at elections or serving on a Jury. There is a further rule that if a man has had delegated to him the performance of some duty so that he is himself in the position of an agent, he cannot usually employ another as his agent to do that work for him. This rule is expressed in the maxim "Delegatus non potest delegare" ("An agent cannot delegate"). Thus the Director of a Company would not have authority to appoint an agent to represent him at the Board Meetings of the Company although he is entitled to appoint an agent to carry out minor duties relating to the Company, but such a person is an agent of the Company and not an agent of the Director. Again a Trustee cannot, except in very rare cases, appoint another person to carry out his duties for him.

For most purposes the law allows an agent to be appointed without any particular formalities, so that his appointment may be by word of mouth or in a letter, but for certain purposes, e.g. to enable an agent to execute a deed (q.v.) or document under seal on behalf of his principal, the appointment itself must be under seal. Such an appointment is called a Power of Attorney (q.v.).

The exact duties of principals and agents and their relation to one another and to third parties will depend to a large extent on the purposes for which the agency is created and are dealt with under specific headings. (*See* AUCTIONEERS; COMMISSION; DEL CREDERE AGENT; FACTOR; HOUSE AGENT; POWER OF ATTORNEY; PRINCIPAL AND AGENT.)

AGISTMENT.—This is a form of contract by one man to take the cattle, horses or other animals of another to graze on his land for some payment or consideration until the owner demands their redelivery. The man who takes the beasts to graze (called the agister) is liable to the owner for injury caused to them by neglect of reasonable and proper care for them, as it is his duty under the contract not to be negligent and to take reasonable and proper care of the beasts. The agister cannot hold the beasts against the owner for the money due under the contract. His remedy is to sue the owner for the price of the grazing but he must deliver up the beasts to the owner on demand.

AGREEMENT.—The word Agreement is used in many senses, but in law it usually has the same meaning as contract, that is, an agreement which has legal consequences. An agreement may be made either orally, that is by word of mouth, between the persons making it, or in some written document, or by a document under seal called a Deed (q.v.). This last is the most formal way. It is always advisable that the parties to an agreement should put their agreement into writing for if they do not, but merely rely on their recollection of what was said by the one to the other, disputes may later arise and it may be difficult to prove the exact terms of the agreement, or indeed that there was ever an agreement at all. Even when both parties are perfectly honest their recollection of what was said may differ very widely.

Although agreements may frequently be quite valid when made orally, in some cases the law requires that they should be made in writing, or that some written document setting out their terms should be in existence, or that they should be made by deed. If an agreement is not made in the way required by the law the effect may be either that the law will not enforce it for the parties or else the agreement may be absolutely void and of no effect. (*See* WRITTEN CONTRACTS.)

Agreements should be distinguished from actual transfers of property. Thus if A agrees to sell to B 100 shares in a Company, that is an agreement to sell and not a transfer of the property in the shares, which still belong to A. The property in the shares will be transferred when A signs a document called a transfer, and B has this registered with the Company. If A refuses to transfer the shares after he has agreed to do so, B may compel him. The same distinction can be seen in the case of a Sale of Land where the parties first agree to sell it and later transfer it from one to the other by a Conveyance.

Stamps.—It is very important that all agreements should be properly stamped. The amount of stamp will depend on the purpose for which the agreement is entered into and the amount of money concerned in it. In most cases where no special duty is required the agreement must have a 6d. stamp if it is in writing. An oral agreement does not require any stamp. A deed requires at least a 10/- stamp. The following agreements do not need to be stamped.

1. An agreement relating to some matter under £5 in value;

2. An agreement relating to the hire of any labourer, artificer, manufacturer or menial servant;

3. An agreement for the sale of goods;

4. An agreement between the Master of a ship and the sailors for wages when the ship's voyage is from port to port in the United Kingdom;

5. A document acknowledging a debt to prevent it from becoming irrecoverable by reason of the Statute of Limitations.

Where an agreement requires only a 6d. stamp, an ordinary 6d. adhesive stamp may be put on before the agreement is signed and the signatures written across it; or, if this is not done, the agreement may be taken within 14 days to an Inland Revenue Office where on payment of 6d. a special stamp will be impressed on it. After that time the Inland Revenue Authorities are entitled to demand a penalty before putting on a stamp. The maximum penalty is £10

but usually a smaller sum only will be demanded varying with the amount of delay which there has been in putting on the stamp.

The special form which an agreement must take, if any is required, and the terms it should contain are set out under particular headings herein. Any person signing an agreement or signing a printed document put in front of him should be quite sure that he has read it and understands what it means; for if it turns out that it contains terms of which he was not aware, this will be no defence when he is sued upon the agreement, and he has only himself to blame. This note of warning refers particularly to agreements which a householder or shopkeeper is asked by a canvasser to sign at his house or shop relating to such matters as hire purchase of goods or advertising. The person asked to sign may be busy and may have little time to examine the document, but if he signs it without doing so he cannot afterwards complain. (*See* CLUBS; CONTRACT; HIRE PURCHASE; LANDLORD AND TENANT; MASTER AND SERVANT; SEPARATION; SOLICITOR; STAMP DUTIES; WRITTEN CONTRACTS.)

AGRICULTURAL HOLDINGS.—

The Common Law in general made no provision for the payment of compensation to an agricultural tenant when he had carried out improvements during his period of occupation which had increased the value of the land. The Agricultural Holdings Act, 1923, now provides compensation for improvements and for disturbance, and gives other valuable rights to the tenant. Any contract entered into by the tenant which seeks to limit or to deprive the tenant of these rights to compensation cannot be enforced by the landlord. The Act applies to tenancies of land which is agricultural and pastural, and it covers market gardens but not allotments.

The Contract of Tenancy.—The tenancy of an Agricultural Holding may commence either upon the date agreed in the tenancy agreement, or in default of agreement upon the date or dates usual according to the custom of the country. To end the tenancy 12 months' notice to quit expiring on the anniversary of the day on which the tenancy began is necessary except where the land may be required by the army, navy or air force, or the tenant has become bankrupt. Where the term is granted for two years or more, the tenancy will not end at the expiration of that period unless at least one year's notice is given by either party, otherwise the tenancy continues as a yearly tenancy.

Where a notice to quit has been given and then the person giving the notice agrees to sell the land, whether to the tenant or another person, the notice to quit ceases to have effect and the tenant can continue to stay on after the date fixed by the notice. He cannot stay on, however, if he has agreed in writing with the landlord that the notice to quit shall be valid.

The landlord has a right at all reasonable times to enter on the holding to view the state thereof, but he cannot recover any sum for breach of the terms of the tenancy beyond the actual damage suffered except, e.g. cases of breaking up permanent pasture, cutting trees, etc.

When a tenant is entitled to be paid for improving the farm.—The tenant becomes entitled to compensation from the landlord in three cases:

Improvements.—At the termination of his tenancy or quitting the holding, the tenant will be entitled to compensation for three classes of improvements:

(1) Improvements of a permanent nature, e.g. buildings, roads and bridges, planting of orchards, reclamation of land, provided the landlord has given written consent to the improvement being made;

(2) Drainage, provided the tenant has given to the landlord not more than three months' and not less than two months' notice of his intention;

(3) Improvements tending to benefit the soil, e.g. chalking, liming, marling, manuring of land, etc., and in the case of a market garden, the planting of fruit trees, strawberry plants, rhubarb, asparagus, etc. In this case, the landlord's consent is not necessary.

The compensation payable if not agreed must be fixed by arbitration and is, in general, the value of the improvements to the incoming tenant. Except in the case of manuring, however, the tenant is not entitled to claim compensation for any improvement begun by him within the last year of his tenancy, unless he has given notice of his intention and the landlord has agreed or has failed to object to the work.

Further, the tenant is entitled to compensation where by a continuous adoption of a system of farming he has increased the value of the holding, and the landlord is entitled to compensation from the tenant, if he shews that the holding has deteriorated in value by the failure of the tenant to cultivate the holding according to the rules of good husbandry.

Foxes and Pheasants. *Damage by Game.*—Where the tenant's crops have been damaged by game which the tenant has not written permission to kill, he is entitled to compensation from the landlord if the damage exceeds one shilling per acre, but only if :

(1) Notice in writing has been given to the landlord as soon as the damage is observed;

(2) The landlord has been given a reasonable opportunity for inspection;

(3) Notice in writing of the claim with particulars has been given within one month after the expiration of the current calendar year.

Disturbance.—Compensation is payable where the tenancy has been terminated by a notice to quit given by the landlord, and in consequence of that notice the tenant has quitted the holding; except where the notice states that it was given because the tenant had failed to cultivate the holding according to the rules of good husbandry, or has failed to pay rent, or has refused to arbitrate as to rent, or has become bankrupt, or has broken a material condition of the tenancy. If, however, the landlord offers to withdraw the notice to quit and the tenant unreasonably refuses to accept the offer, compensation is not payable. Where the landlord refuses to agree to a written demand by the tenant to arbitrate as to rent and the tenant in consequence gives notice to quit, the tenant will be entitled to compensation as though the notice had been given by the landlord.

The compensation payable is such as will cover any loss suffered by the tenant, e.g. by sale of stock, implements, etc., which is directly due to his quitting the holding. To avoid disputes the sum is fixed at one year's rent unless the tenant can prove it is greater. In any case the tenant cannot recover more than 2 years' rent.

How the amount due is fixed.—In default of agreement by the parties, compensation is to be fixed by a single arbitrator appointed by the parties, or if they cannot agree, elected by the Minister of Agriculture and Fisheries. The award must be made within 28 days of the appointment of the arbitrator and is binding on the parties and in the absence of misconduct cannot be set aside. The arbitrator may at any stage of the proceedings, and shall if so directed by the County Court, state a special case for the opinion of the County Court on any matter of law. Appeal is from the County Court to the Court of Appeal whose decision is final. (*See* ARBITRATION; DISTRESS FOR RENT; FIXTURES; NOTICE TO QUIT.)

AGRICULTURAL PRODUCE.— During the last few years important statutory provisions have been made for the grading, and compulsory organization by the State of the marketing of certain agricultural products, and for the regulation of the imports of such products. The Agricultural Produce (Grading and Marketing Act) of 1928, and the Agricultural Marketing Acts of 1931 and 1933, have provided the Minister of Agriculture with the necessary machinery and powers to introduce various regulations controlling production.

The Agricultural Produce (Grading and Marketing) Act was passed in order to enable the Minister of Agriculture to establish specified standards of quality of agricultural products and thereby facilitate their increased sale. The Act provides that the Minister of Agriculture may make provisions and regulations for the grading and branding by means of "Grade designations" of any agricultural produce, and it provides that if any agricultural produce is sold under such a grade designation, that is, sold under an official label, that label constitutes a guarantee that the produce is of the standard and quality provided for under the regulations applied to that product. In consequence if A purchases a tin of preserved plums, labelled as National Mark plums, he knows the exact quality of the plums he is buying, and that the plums are guaranteed to be of that quality.

If any produce which is governed by such regulations is sold with an official label on it, and the producer of the product is not a registered producer, the person who sells the product so marked may be liable to a fine or imprisonment. Regulations providing for the grading and marking of very many agricultural products have already been put into force. Among the many products so regulated are Apples, Pears, Broccoli, Canned Vegetables, Canned Fruits, Cider and Beef.

The aim of the Agricultural Marketing Acts of 1931 and 1933 was to provide for the organization and development of the marketing of agricultural products. They have provided for the application through The Minister of Agriculture, of regulations for compulsory organization of production of such products and their sale, and also provide, that when steps have been taken to reorganize the industry, then regulations may be made to regulate the imports of that product. Every scheme for the regulation of production, and every order for the regulation of the imports, is put into force after being submitted to both Houses of Parliament by means of a Statutory Rule and Order. Every scheme or order is drawn up in accordance with the provisions of the Agricultural Marketing Acts of 1931 and 1933.

Under the Acts every scheme must provide for the registration of producers, and may provide that any producer of a product may not sell the product unless he registers under the scheme. The Acts also provide that both the consumers and the producers of the products must be represented as consultative bodies, and they are called upon to consider and criticise every scheme. The committee of producers may submit schemes to the Minister of Agriculture. The Act also provides that after a given period, every scheme must provide for a poll of all producers in order to ascertain whether they desire the scheme to remain in force, and if the result of the poll is against the scheme remaining in force, then the scheme is to be revoked. Thus if the producers do not ultimately consider that the scheme is to their advantage, they may revoke it.

AGRICULTURAL RATES.—Since 1929 agricultural land and buildings have been exempt from liability as regards rates. Agricultural land includes the following: (1) Any land used as arable, meadow or pasture only; (2) a plantation or wood; (3) land used for the purpose of poultry farming, market gardens, orchards. or allotments.

The expression does not cover lands that are occupied together with a house as a park or garden, nor land that is kept for use as a sports ground or racecourse. It is a question of fact whether land is being used as meadow or pasture land only; a reasonable and normal interpretation must be given to the words "meadow or pasture" and if the words may fairly be applied to the land in question then it will be covered by the exemption from rates. Land used for a plantation or a wood is still exempt when underwood is grown on it to be sold; but not when it is occupied with a house as a park or preserved for the purposes of sport or recreation.

Cottage gardens when they exceed one quarter of an acre in size are included in the exemption given generally under the head of "allotments." It has been decided that a cottage garden is one that is attached to a dwelling of a person of the labouring classes.

Agricultural buildings mean buildings other than dwelling houses that are occupied in connection with agricultural land or form part of a market garden. The buildings must be used solely to further the agricultural operations carried on; this means that the building must be what is commonly known as a "farm building." Glass houses and frames form part of a market garden and are exempted. No building that is used as a dwelling house is covered by any of these exemptions; it will be liable to be rated although it is occupied by the occupier of the adjoining agricultural land.

Since 1929, however, a partial exemption is introduced in favour of such dwelling houses. It applies when the house is occupied in connection with agricultural land and the occupier is engaged in carrying on the operations on that land, or is the servant of the person so engaged. If these conditions are present then the gross value is to be estimated by reference to the rent that one could expect to obtain for the house, if these two uses were the only possible uses to which the house could be put.

AIR GUNS.—The provisions of the Fire Arms Act requiring police licences for the possession of fire arms do not apply to air guns. On the other hand the term "gun" under the Gun Licence Act, 1870, includes an air gun or any other kind of gun from which any missile can be dis-charged. A licence is therefore required under this Act by any person using a gun or who carries a gun, e.g. a gamekeeper, outside his residence. (*See* GUN LICENCE.)

AIR NAVIGATION ACT, 1920.—The principal statute regulating aircraft in this country. (*See* AVIATION.)

ALDERMEN.—Aldermen are the senior members of county councils or borough councils, and are chosen by the councillors. They hold office for six years, except in the case of the Aldermen of the City of London of whom there are twenty-five, and who, since 1394, have always been elected for life. Their duties do not differ from those of the ordinary councillors. (*See* LOCAL GOVERNMENT.)

ALIENS.—Every person who is not a British subject (*see* BRITISH SUBJECT) is an alien. Aliens are divided into two classes: alien friends and alien enemies. An alien enemy is an alien whose state is at war with the King of England. But a British subject becomes an alien enemy if he lives in the enemy state or trades with the enemy. Companies are alien enemies in certain cases. As to how a British subject may become an alien *see* BRITISH SUBJECT, and as to how an alien may become British *see* NATURALIZATION.

Legal Proceedings.—An alien friend is subject to the criminal law to the same extent as any British subject. While he is on British territory he owes temporary allegiance to the King, and may, therefore, be convicted of treason, which is the breach of allegiance. In one matter (apart from questions such as registration) aliens are subject to special criminal liabilities: if an alien attempts anything likely to cause disaffection among His Majesty's forces or among the civil population, he is liable to penal servitude for not more than ten years or, on summary conviction, to imprisonment for not more than three months. If he attempts to promote industrial unrest in any industry in which he was not bona fide engaged for at least two years immediately preceding such attempt, he is liable on summary conviction to imprisonment for not more than three months. Generally speaking, an alien may not be tried for offences committed abroad except in a few serious cases, e.g. murder, manslaughter, piracy. In the civil courts his rights are the same as those of a British subject. Even though he resides abroad, he may sue or be sued in the English courts for any wrong committed in England, or for any contract broken in England. Even though not resident in England, he may also bring an action in England against a British subject or against an alien wherever the wrong was committed, or wherever the contract was broken, provided the defendant is present in England; but in the case of wrongs, the injury must (i) have been of such a kind that, if it had been committed in England, an action would have lain for it by English law, and (ii) have been actionable in the country where it was committed.

For instance, when a man libelled another in Brazil and action was brought against him for the libel in England, had he proved that the Brazilian law allowed no action for such words, then the case would have been dismissed. The real fetter on actions by and against aliens in England has been imposed by the courts upon themselves by the Rules of Court, which provide that only in certain limited circumstances can a writ be served outside the jurisdiction, i.e. outside England or Wales. If the writ cannot be served, then the action cannot commence.

Writs can be served outside the jurisdiction only in the following cases and in a few other minor cases: (i) When the whole of the action relates to land within the jurisdiction; (ii) When the defendant is domiciled or ordinarily resident within the jurisdiction; (iii) Where the action is for the administration of the personal estate of a person who died domiciled within the jurisdiction, or is for the enforcement of English trusts of property within the jurisdiction; (iv) Where the defendant is not ordinarily resident in Scotland and the action relates to a contract made within the jurisdiction, or was made by an agent trading or residing within the jurisdiction, or made expressly or by implication to be governed by English law; or, except where the defendant ordinarily is resident in Ireland or Scotland, in respect of a breach of contract committed within the jurisdiction; (v) Where the action is for tort committed within the jurisdiction; (vi) Where the plaintiff claims an injunction relating to anything done within the jurisdiction.

Civil Rights.—An alien may do most things that a British subject is entitled to do.

He may own or deal in any kind of property with the one exception of British ships, but although he cannot own a British ship or any share in one (*see* MERCHANT SHIPPING), he may hold shares in any shipping company; he may be a trustee or take the benefit of a trust; he may have rights in patents or copyrights; he has the same parental rights and duties as regards his children as a British subject (*see* FATHER). He may be made bankrupt if, when the act of bankruptcy was committed, he had a place of residence in England or carried on business in England personally or by agent, or was a member of an English partnership, or if he was ordinarily resident in England, or was actually present in England. But in the following cases an alien is subject to disqualifications: He has no right to vote at parliamentary or local government elections. He may not become a Member of Parliament or a member of the civil service, nor may he hold civil or military positions of trust under the government. Shipping is particularly protected from alien influence; it has been noticed above that an alien may not own a British ship (or even a share therein), but further, an alien may not act as master, chief officer, or chief engineer, or skipper, or second hand of any merchant ship or fishing boat registered in the United Kingdom unless (i) in certain cases he held such a position during the Great War or (ii) such ship is habitually employed outside the United Kingdom. No alien may hold a pilot's certificate in the United Kingdom. Aliens may join the navy, army or air force with the consent of the appropriate ministry, but may not rise above the rank of warrant or non-commissioned officer. No military force may contain more than one alien to every fifty British subjects. An alien may not serve on a jury, but after being domiciled in England or Wales for ten years he may be called upon to serve at an inquest. There are certain restrictions on the rights of aliens to use any other than the name they were known by on 4th August, 1914. (*See* NAME, CHANGE OF.)

Immigration of Aliens.—The rights of aliens to enter the United Kingdom (including the Irish Free State) are regulated by the Aliens Restriction Amendment Act, 1919, and the regulations made thereunder and known as the Aliens Order, 1920. The Act is a temporary measure, and is continued in force only for a year at a time, but there appears to be no probability of its failing to be so continued in the future. An alien will be admitted only with the leave of an immigration officer, and such leave will not be granted in the following circumstances: (i) if he is not in a position to support himself and his dependants; (ii) in the case of an alien desiring to take employment, if he fails to produce a permit for his engagement issued to the employer by the Ministry of Labour; (iii) if he is a lunatic or mentally deficient; (iv) if a certificate has been given to the immigration officer by a medical inspector certifying that for medical reasons it is undesirable that he should be admitted; (v) if he has been sentenced by a foreign court for an extradition crime; (vi) if he is the subject of a deportation or expulsion order; (vii) if he has been prohibited from landing by the Home Secretary; (viii) if he fails to fulfil any other requirements that the Home Secretary may prescribe, whether of general application or framed to meet only his particular case. The requirements as to means are, since 1920, enforced even though the alien has fled from his own country to escape political or religious persecution. There is no limit to the number of aliens that may be admitted nor is there any literacy test such as is enforced in the colonies and in the United States, nor are political views grounds for exclusion, but in important cases the Home Secretary may exclude particular individuals by the exercise of his powers under (viii) above.

The immigration officer may, in accordance with the directions of the Home Secretary, attach conditions on admitting an alien or may subsequently add such conditions, especially with relation to the length of time during which the alien may remain. Aliens other than seamen may land only at certain approved sea- or air-ports (about twenty in number). But an alien to whom leave to land has been refused may be placed temporarily on land in custody. When leave is refused, it is the duty of the master of the ship to remove the alien to the country of which he is a national or from which he embarked. (For offences against these provisions, *see* below.)

Registration.—An alien, on entering the United Kingdom, must, as soon as may be, furnish to the chief officer of police in the police district in which he resides particulars of his name; sex; present and previous nationality; date and country of birth; profession or occupation; date, place and mode of arrival in the United Kingdom; address of residence in the United Kingdom and of last residence abroad; photograph; government services, country where such services were performed and nature and duration thereof, and rank or appointments held; passport or other document establishing nationality and identity; signature and fingerprints if required; and other matters at the discretion of the chief officer of police.

A passport produced for identification must be not more than five years old and must contain a photograph. Any occurrence altering the accuracy of such information must be notified within seven days, e.g. change of occupation.

If the alien intends to change his address, he must give information as to the date thereof and as to his intended place of residence, and, after making such change, must, if it takes him to another police district, give notice of his arrival within forty-eight hours to the chief officer of the new district. On being absent for more than two months continuously, he must give notice to the chief officer of the district where he was registered of his current address and every subsequent change of address, including his return to his residence. On effecting registration, a registration certificate is issued, which must be produced on demand to police officers, immigration officers, etc. Aliens having no residence in the United Kingdom may register with the chief officer of any police district and must thereafter report to the officer of any other district in which they stay for more than twenty-four hours, giving notice of intended changes of address to the police officer to whom they had last reported.

The burden of this repeated reporting may be alleviated by giving as an address that of a banker, solicitor, hotel-keeper or manager, tourist or theatrical agent or other person of good credit whom he must keep supplied with such information. It is the duty of any person with whom an alien lives or lodges to take steps to secure compliance with these regulations. These provisions as to registration do not apply to persons under sixteen or to persons who have been in the United Kingdom for less than two months since their last arrival.

Keepers of any premises, furnished or unfurnished, where lodging or sleeping accommodation is provided for reward must keep a register of aliens over the age of sixteen, containing certain particulars, e.g. date of arrival and departure. Registers for aliens are twofold, one being kept in the police district by the chief officer of police, the other (called the Central Register) being kept under the supervision of the Home Secretary in London.

The Home Secretary may impose on any alien or class of aliens any restrictions as he may deem necessary in the public interest, e.g. as to residence or use of firearms.

Deportation.—Deportation orders may be made in the following cases: (i) Where any court certifies that an alien has been convicted of certain offences (including any offence for which the court may impose imprisonment without the option of a fine, and offences relating to prostitution), and that the court recommends deportation; (ii) Where, in the case of an alien having entered the United Kingdom within twelve months previously, a Magistrate's court certifies that he· has been in receipt of parochial relief within the previous three months, or has been found wandering without ostensible means of subsistence within the previous three months, or has been sentenced abroad for an extradition crime; or (iii) Where the Home Secretary deems it conducive to the public good to make such order. The order is made by the Home Secretary under any condition he thinks proper. The alien may then be placed in any ship about to sail abroad, and may not return until the order has expired. Aliens are usually deported to the country of which they are nationals, as it is probable that any other country would refuse to receive them. Any property of the alien may be seized and used to pay the expenses of the voyage.

A recommendation for deportation will usually not be made if the alien has a family domiciled in England, or would be put to death on returning to his own country, or if he has lived for a very long period in England, or if, being a married woman, her deportation would amount to a divorce.

Penalties.—If any person fails to comply with any of the regulations, or any conditions imposed thereunder, or aids or abets any offences against them or knowingly harbours a person whom he has reasonable grounds to believe has committed such offences, or if he refuses to answer any questions reasonably put to him, or answers them falsely, or refuses to produce any docu ment in his possession, or makes false returns, or acts in contravention of the regulations, he is liable to a fine not exceeding £100 or to imprisonment with or without hard labour for not more than six months. Constables or immigration officers may take into custody without warrant any person whom they reasonably suspect of having broken any of the regulations.

Alien Enemies.—Alien enemies have practically no rights so long as they remain such. Their property may be seized by the Crown, but during the Great War the Crown resigned this power and all enemy property was transferred into the hands of an authority called the Custodian. The Peace Treaties declared that the Crown was entitled to retain all property so held, and the original alien owners were given rights of compensation against their own governments. Practically all their rights to bring actions in the courts are suspended during the continuance of a war. Alien enemies continuing to reside in England by special licence are allowed to retain their rights. Persons who were alien enemies during the Great War were subject to numerous disabilities, but these disabilities were removed in 1927, except that a former alien enemy may not serve in any British ship registered in the United Kingdom. (*See also,* ALLEGIANCE; BRITISH SUBJECT; DENIZEN; NAME, CHANGE OF; NATIONALITY; NATURALIZATION; PASSPORT.)

ALIMENTARY DEBT (SCOTS LAW).—A sum of money is said to be an alimentary debt when it is given to a person for the purpose of supplying him with the necessaries of life. The effect of making a debt alimentary is that it cannot be seized or taken by any of the creditors of the person to whom it is payable, except in so far as the amount payable is in excess of what is required for the maintenance and support of the person entitled. Thus an alimentary debt cannot be arrested (*see* ARRESTMENT), nor can it be claimed by the Trustee in Bankruptcy of the person to whom it is payable.

A debt may be alimentary because it is so described in some document creating it as where a liferent or annuity granted by one person to another is stated to be an alimentary provision, or it may be alimentary because of the general law. Debts alimentary by general law are salaries due to persons in an official position, e.g. government servants.

ALIMONY.—The allowance made by a husband to his wife by an order of the High Court of Justice. There are two kinds of alimony: pending suit and permanent. Alimony pending suit is ordered, as the name suggests, pending the disposal of some matrimonial suit. When a wife has filed a petition for a divorce, judicial separation or other matrimonial suit, she may file a further petition for alimony pending suit. The incomes of husband and wife are enquired into by an officer of the Court and an order for periodical payments by the husband to the wife can then be made. The practice is to name a figure which will have the result of bringing the income, if any, of the wife up to about one fifth of the joint incomes of husband and wife. When a decree of judicial separation has been made against a husband an order for permanent alimony can be obtained by the wife. The amount of this is usually calculated so as to bring her total income up to about a third of the joint incomes. In the case of a divorce a similar order can be obtained but in that case it is described as one for "permanent maintenance."

Where the financial circumstances of husband and wife change after the making of an an order for alimony, either party can petition for a variation of the order. It should be noted that the word "alimony" is applicable only to orders of the High Court of Justice. Similar orders in the police courts are called "Maintenance orders." (*See* MAINTENANCE; AND SPECIAL SUPPLEMENT "DIVORCE.")

ALLEGIANCE.—Allegiance is the tie which binds the subject to the King in return for that protection which the King affords the subject. Every person (with a few exceptions, such as ambassador's children) born within the King's dominions owe allegiance to the King: he is said to be born within the King's allegiance, i.e. within the territories that owe allegiance to the King. But every British subject owes allegiance, wherever he was born. Aliens, on the other hand, owe only "temporary" allegiance, during the time that they remain in the Empire, availing themselves of the King's protection. An alien who has been granted a certificate of naturalisation must take the oath of allegiance within one month thereafter. The oath is in the following form:

"I, John Robinson, swear by Almighty
"God that I will be faithful and bear
"true allegiance to His Majesty King
"George the Fifth, his heirs and suc-
"cessors, according to law."

(Signed) JOHN ROBINSON.

"Sworn as inscribed this first day of
"January, 193—, before me."

(Signed) THOMAS SMITH, Justice of the
Peace or Commissioner for Oaths.

(The fee payable to the Clerk to the Justice or to the Commissioner for Oaths, as the case may be, is 2/6.)

The oath must also be taken by Members of Parliament and by certain officials, e.g. most Cabinet Ministers, the Judges of the High Court and certain Justices of the Peace. It must also be made by persons taking clerical orders or preferment, and by all recruits to the Royal Forces. But whether the oath be taken or not, still every subject is under the same duties as if he had taken it.

Any offence against the duty of allegiance is treason, and therefore, as alien visitors owe temporary allegiance while in the Empire, they may be guilty of treason. But no acts done in their own country can amount to treason here, because, while they are abroad, they owe no allegiance to the King of England. (*See* ALIENS; BRITISH SUBJECT; DENIZEN; NATURALIZATION.)

ALLOTMENT.—Allotment is the method by which shares are issued by a Company to those who intend to invest money in it. When shares are bought from some other holder this is not known as allotment but as a transfer of the shares. It is only when the shares are for the first time issued by the Company that the transaction is called an allotment. An intending shareholder obtains shares by signing an application form. This constitutes his offer which the Company may accept and turn into a contract by sending him an allotment letter. The application form is usually so framed as a request to the Company to allot a certain number of shares "or any smaller number that may be allotted," and this enables the Company to accept the offer by allotting a less number than has in fact been applied for in the offer. Were this phrase not inserted the acceptance would not be in the same terms as the offer, and no contract would result. (*See* CONTRACT.) The allotment letter can be transferred from one holder to another. (*See* SHARES.)

ALVERSTONE, Baron (1842-1915). —After practising in the Commercial

Lord Alverstone.

Courts Richard Webster was made Attorney-General immediately on his entering the House of Commons, in the exceptional circumstances of never having held the office of Solicitor-General. He acted as counsel for *The Times* in the Parnell inquiry, and after being appointed Lord Chief Justice and raised to the peerage as Lord Alverstone he presided over the Alaska Boundary Commission in 1903.

AMBASSADOR.—Ambassadors and other diplomatic agents who are sent to this Country as representing foreign Countries are entitled to what is known as Diplomatic privilege. This means that they cannot be made liable for any criminal offences by the Courts of the State to which they are appointed and cannot be arrested. Further they cannot be sued nor can their goods or other property be seized to pay debts. They may of course not claim this privilege and if they waive it they may be tried or sued in the ordinary way. They cannot be compelled to attend as witnesses, and if their evidence is required application should be made not by the Court but by the Foreign Office to the Diplomatic agent.

The privilege extends to the family and servants of an Ambassador living with him in his house and also to the house itself, but in England they lose this right if they engage in trade. In practice an Ambassador who did not waive the immunity would probably be recalled by his own Country on complaints being made by the Foreign Office.

ANÆSTHETICS.—It is illegal and a criminal offence to perform certain operations on any horse, dog, cat or any cattle unless an anæsthetic is first administered to prevent the pain being felt. These operations include dishorning cattle over one month old, docking horses' tails, or the tail-docking and ear-clipping of dogs and cats over 6 months in age. (*See* ANIMAL.)

ANCIENT LIGHTS.—In the ordinary case the fact that a house has got a window through which light passes does not mean that the owner of the house can prevent other persons, such as the owners of adjoining land, from putting up buildings which interfere with the light of the window or which entirely prevent any light from reaching it. This is so even though the room in which the window is has no other source of light and is made entirely useless by the erection of the building on the adjoining land.

It is possible, however, for the owner of land to have a right to receive a certain amount of light through some of his windows, and to prevent any other person from interfering with this light by building or otherwise, and the windows which are so protected are called "Ancient Lights."

This means that the window to which it is applied has enjoyed the inflow of light under such circumstances and for such a length of time that its owner or occupier for the time being has acquired the right to this flow of light, and may take legal proceedings to prevent the erection of buildings which would obstruct it. Notice that it is only one or more particular windows which can acquire this right, not a house as a whole. The technical name for this right is the easement of light. Like all other easements (q.v.) its peculiar characteristic is that it is appurtenant to land, that is, it belongs to a particular piece of land or to a house, and passes with that land or house to the person who owns or occupies it for the time being. Moreover it is exercisable not against any particular person as such but only as the owner or occupier of the land which is subject to it. A right which is not so annexed to two neighbouring plots of land cannot be an easement but at the most can only be a contractual right against a particular person.

How much light?—The amount of light to which the dominant tenement (the house to which the right to have light belongs) is entitled as against the servient tenement (the neighbouring land over which the right is claimed) is judged by the ordinary standards of human comfort which the courts have held are the same for all classes and all districts, without any regard being paid to the wealth of the occupiers or the amount of light which they themselves would consider reasonable. Provided a reasonable amount of light is received it is no ground for complaint that there used formerly to be more; obstruction of view or air, or unsightliness, are also no ground for complaint though they may be offences against the local building regulations.

What is room used for?—In determining what is a reasonable amount of light one is entitled to take into consideration the purpose for which the house or room in question has been used, provided that the result of so doing is to *increase* the amount of light to which it is entitled.

Thus a room which has been used as a studio or for other purposes requiring a lot of light may (subject to what is said below) obtain a more extensive right to light than an ordinary sitting- or bed-room; but on the other hand the mere fact that such a room, which could be used as a bed- or sitting-room, has in fact been used as a box-room or even as a photographic dark room (provided that the windows have not been blocked up in such a way as to amount to an abandonment of the right) cannot deprive it of the right to receive an amount of light reasonably sufficient for its use as a bed- or sitting-room.

It is the common practice to gauge the reasonableness of the supply of light to any particular window by drawing an imaginary line at an angle of 45° from the sill; if this line would not cut into the building opposite but goes over the top of it, then prima facie

The Notice Affixed to a Wall.

that building does not infringe the right to light; if on the other hand the line would cut into the building, the presumption is that there is an infringement. But it cannot be too strongly stressed that, though this may be a convenient working rule, it is not the test which the law applies and the House of Lords has on more than one occasion declared that the question of infringement or no infringement must be decided on a consideration of all the facts of the individual case.

Amongst the facts that might be taken into consideration are the number and situation of other windows in the same room; for it is to the total amount of the light in the room that one must look in determining whether it has been diminished to an unreasonable extent.

But this statement is subject to an important qualification, for if the other windows in the same room have not acquired a right to light for themselves and are also liable to be obstructed, then any light which comes through them may be disregarded in calculating the amount of light which the room receives. This means that the light from windows which look out into the garden of the house must be taken into consideration, but the light from windows which look into a neighbour's property (whether across a narrow strip of passage or not) should not be considered, unless such windows have themselves acquired the right to "Ancient Lights."

How right is acquired.—It must be remembered that the right to light is not acquired simply by constructing a window through which light flows over neighbouring property. Apart from any express agreement between the owners of the respective properties it can only be acquired by use for a period of time in accordance either with Statute or the common law. By far the most important of these two methods is Statute Law and the material Statute is the Prescription Act of 1832. It is there provided that the enjoyment of the flow of light throughout the twenty years next, before any legal action is brought about the light, creates an easement of light unless this enjoyment was exercised under permission given by some written agreement.

Interference to prevent right being acquired.—Several important results follow from the wording of this statute. In the first place the bare fact of enjoyment for twenty years is enough in itself to create the right. Protests from the occupier of the servient tenement are of no avail; he has only two courses open to him, either to get the occupier of the dominant tenement to agree in writing or under seal (i.e. by deed [q.v.]) that he receives the light with the "licence," i.e. permission and consent of his neighbour, or to erect a building or hoarding which will exclude the light. Provided that he does so build within twenty years of the date on which the light was first received, he will be within his rights and cannot be interfered with for the dominant tenement will not yet have acquired any right to receive it. On the other hand the occupier of the dominant tenement who brings an action to assert an easement of light *must* shew that he has enjoyed the light throughout the twenty years *immediately preceding* his action. If therefore he can shew twenty years' enjoyment

(or more) but there has been a gap of a year or more between the end of that period and the date on which the action is brought during which the light has been obstructed, he cannot bring himself within the provisions of the Prescription Act and will acquire no right under it. Thus if he enjoyed the light from 1900 to 1930 but in 1930 the light was obstructed by a building, if he brings an action in 1934, he cannot shew the necessary 20 years' enjoyment *before* action brought.

Length of interference.—The Prescription Act also contains a proviso to the effect that no obstruction of the right shall be effective unless it is persisted in for a year. Two important results follow from this: Firstly, if the occupier of the servient tenement wishes to prevent the right accruing and cannot induce his neighbour to take a written licence, he must, if he erects a building or hoarding keep it in position for at least a year; and secondly if he neglects to do so until after the *commencement* of the twentieth year of enjoyment, the occupier of the dominant tenement—the house with the window—can assert his right as soon as the year is complete and there will be no defence to it; for he can prove enjoyment for twenty years and his neighbour cannot shew that he has obstructed the light *for at least one year.* Thus enjoyment for nineteen years and one day will in practice be enough for it is then too late to obstruct the light. For example, A builds a house which is erected on January 1st 1914, and which enjoys light for its windows until January 2nd, 1933. The light comes over ground owned by B which is unbuilt on from 1914 until 1933. On 2nd January 1933 B erects a building on the ground which deprives A's building of most of its light. A *at the moment* can do nothing to prevent him for he has not enjoyed the light for twenty years, but as soon as January 1st, 1934 arrives, A must take legal proceedings against B for interference with his right to light which he acquires *on that date.* B cannot rely on the obstruction from January 2nd, 1933 to January 1st, 1934 because it is for less than a year and must therefore be ignored. The position would be the same if B's land instead of being unbuilt on from 1914 to 1933 had had a building on it which allowed a certain amount of light to enter A's window, and if B had erected a higher building on January 2nd, 1933. A would not then be entitled to more light than the window had received between 1914 and 1933, but he would be entitled to that amount of light and could prevent B from increasing the height of his building.

Lost Deed.—Apart altogether from statute it is sometimes possible to persuade the Court to assure that there must at some time in the past have been a Deed which has been lost, granting the right to light; but there are technical difficulties in the way, and in any case it is necessary to shew that the light has been enjoyed for a considerably longer period than twenty years. Lastly the Courts will often infer a grant of the right to light, under the principle that a man must not derogate from his own grant, i.e. must not take away from what he has given, where one of two adjoining properties are sold by the person who owns them both as frequently happens in building and development schemes (*See* EASEMENT). Each of the properties will then be presumed to have a right to light over the other.

Effect of rebuilding.—Alteration or rebuilding of the premises for which ancient lights are claimed does not necessarily extinguish them. In every case it is a question of fact whether the new windows are in the same place and occupy such a substantial part of the space occupied by the old that they receive much the same flow of light. Are they in substance the same windows? If they are, then the right to light is not lost but is transferred to the new windows. Any substantial variation, however, will cause the right to be lost, the reason being that it is regarded as an abandonment of it just as much as would the *permanent* walling up of the windows.

If the windows are altered and the rights are lost, then in order to acquire ancient lights for such new windows twenty years' further enjoyment after the alteration would have to be proved. The same principle applies to internal alterations in structure or use, for the occupier of the dominant cannot increase the burden on the servient tenement simply by enlarging the size of his rooms, blocking up other windows or putting the room to new uses requiring an exceptional amount of light. In order to acquire the right to receive the new amount of light he must first prove that he has enjoyed it for twenty years before action brought. The fact that such alterations have been made, however, though it does not confer an increased right to light, does not nevertheless affect the right to receive that amount of light which would have been reasonable for the *ordinary* uses of the room before the alterations were made.

How to prevent interference.—There are two remedies open to the person who asserts that his ancient lights have been or will be infringed. He can obtain either an injunction—i.e. an order of the Court forbidding the erection of the building which is an infringement—or damages—i.e. a money payment for the loss of value to his property. An injunction will not be granted in every case. If the building work has not yet been commenced or does not yet obstruct the light, the proper procedure is to apply to the Chancery Division of the High Court of Justice for a "prohibitory" injunction (order) to forbid the erection of the building. If the building has already been put up and the rights are already obstructed a "mandatory" injunction is the proper remedy. This will order the other party to pull down so much of the building as infringes the right. To order a building which has been erected to be pulled down is a serious step and the Court has the right to give damages instead, and to allow the building to remain, and if the defendant has not acted improperly or unreasonably it very often does so. The effect of this is that the occupier of the dominant tenement loses his right to the light and must accept in its place the pecuniary compensation ordered by the Court. If a man knows, however, that some adjoining landowner is complaining that a building proposed to be erected infringes his right to light, he should not continue building regardless of the complaints, for if he does and the Court later holds that the building does infringe the right to light, he will be compelled to pull it down and will not be allowed to keep the building where it is merely by paying damages or compensation. It is not reasonable to go on building in such circumstances. Alternatively application may be made for damages alone.

The right to light is not a personal right of the owner of the house but pertains to the house itself whoever may own it or occupy it. Thus, if A owns a house which has rights of light over land belonging to B, and A sells the house to X and B sells his land to Y, then X can still claim for the house the same right to light over the land which it had when A owned it and B owned the land. The position would be the same if the house or land were sold before the elapse of the twenty years of use which are necessary to establish the light. X could add the period of use enjoyed in A's time to the period which was enjoyed by the house in his own time to make up the twenty years. (*See* EASEMENT.)

ANCIENT LIGHTS (SCOTS LAW).—While Scots law recognises that the owner from time to time of a house may be entitled to a certain proportion of light received by the windows of that house and may be able to prevent any interference with these lights, it does not allow such a right to be acquired except by the agreement between the owner of the house and the person over whose land the right to receive the light is created. The right therefore cannot be acquired by use without an agreement as in English Law. (*See* SERVITUDE.)

"AND REDUCED."—When a Company has been compelled to reduce its capital owing to losses which it has suffered, it is occasionally required to add to its name the words "and reduced" for some period of time. This is to inform all persons dealing with the Company that a reduction of capital has taken place. (*See* COMPANIES.)

ANIMAL.—In law animals (which word in this article includes birds, fish and insects) are divided into two classes, according as to whether they are wild animals or tame animals. Tame or domestic animals are such animals as cats, dogs, cattle, sheep, poultry and the general livestock of the farmyard, while wild animals includes all other animals from lions and tigers to rats, mice and insects.

Wild Animals.—A wild animal in its natural state cannot be the property of anyone as long as it is able to run wild. Thus a man cannot rightly speak of a rabbit or a pheasant as being his rabbit or his pheasant merely because its home is on his land, and if the rabbit or pheasant leaves his land and passes on to the land of somebody else, the owner of the land on which it originally lived has no right to claim it. This does not mean that any person may take or kill wild animals upon another person's land, since the owner of land has, as a general rule, an exclusive right to take and kill wild animals found upon his land, and this right he can dispose of to other persons, generally known as shooting tenants, and in most cases any person interfering with his right by poaching (q.v.) can be dealt with under the Game Laws.

When, however, a wild animal is captured or tamed it becomes the property of its captor and can be bought and sold, etc., and if stolen the thief can be prosecuted for larceny (q.v.). Thus a tame fox kept as a pet is the property of its possessor, as is a canary in a cage, or bees in a hive; but once the wild animal escapes from the control of its owner and returns to its natural state, the original owner loses all his rights in the animal. Thus, if the tame fox were to escape entirely from its owner and to return to the woodlands, the owner could not bring an action against anyone shooting it, whereas he would have been able to do so if the fox had been still within his control. Other examples of wild animals which have become the property of the person who has tamed or captured them, are deer in an enclosed park, fish in a fishpond or stew, and all performing or caged animals.

Bees which swarm may be followed and retaken by the owner of the hive, even if they settle on land belonging to some other person. The owner of the hive must, however, keep the swarm in sight all the time, as if he once loses sight of it, so that he can no longer identify it as his, the owner of the land on which the swarm settles may hive it.

In the same way the young of wild animals while they are too small to wander are the property of the owner of the land where they live. Thus rabbits too young to run away, or partridges or pheasants too small to fly away, belong to the owner of the land or of the sporting rights over the land where they are born, and this right of property continues until the animals or birds are big enough to be capable of escaping. This does not apply to birds' eggs, which are not the property of the owner of the land.

Although wild animals while alive cannot, except by being brought into captivity, become the property of any one, when they are dead they become immediately the property of the owner of the land or the sporting rights over the land where they are killed. There is, however, an exception to this in the case of an animal which has been started on the land of one owner and killed upon the land of another, and in this case the killer is the owner of the dead animal.

It is not larceny, though it may be an offence against the game laws to kill and take away an animal in its wild state from the land of another person. But if once a wild animal has been killed, the killer allows it to remain upon the land while he goes away, intending to abandon it, and returns for it later, it becomes larceny and is punishable as such, while the taking of a wild animal which is in confinement or tamed is of course larceny.

Any person who keeps a wild animal which is naturally dangerous is liable for any damage which it may do whether the damage is due to the negligence of the owner or not. Common sense is the best test as to whether an animal is naturally dangerous, but such animals as lions or tigers, monkeys or bears, however tame the individuals may be, come under this rule and the keeper of them is liable for the damage they cause even though he may not have been negligent at all.

Domestic Animals.—Domestic animals can be property in just the same manner as any other goods and can be bought, sold or stolen in the same way as a bag of flour or a packet of cigarettes. The young of domestic animals as a general rule belong to the owner of the mother animal, although there may be an individual agreement between the owners of the parent animals that the young shall belong to one or other of them in certain proportions. In the exceptional case of swans the cygnets are divided equally between the owners of the male and female birds, except on the Thames where they are divided in the proportion of three to the owner of the cock and two to the owner of the hen.

Liabilities of Owners.—The general rule as to the liability of owners of domestic animals for damage which they may do to the property or persons of other people is that no owner of a domestic animal is liable for damage which it is not in its

nature to do, unless the owner knows that the particular animal is likely to do such damage. Thus, it is not in the nature of any domestic animal to harm human beings and accordingly if a horse, a bull, a dog or a cat bites or injures a human being, the owner is not liable unless he knows that the animal in question was dangerous to human beings. In order therefore to recover damages for a bite from a dog or a kick from a horse, the person injured must be able to shew that the owner of the offending animal, knew or ought to have known that it was liable to attack human beings, and this he can generally prove by shewing that the owner knew that the animal had attacked human beings before. The knowledge of the dangerous propensity of a domestic animal is known as "scienter," and once the owner of the animal has scienter of its dangerous propensity, he is in the same position as the owner of a dangerous wild animal, and he keeps it at his peril and is liable to any person subsequently injured by it, even if the owner has not been negligent.

How scienter is proved.—In order to prove scienter, it is of course not necessary to prove that the animal has in fact bitten or kicked human beings before, it is sufficient if it has to the knowledge of the owner attempted to attack human beings. It is not sufficient in order to prove scienter of a propensity to attack human beings to shew that the animal has previously attacked other animals.

This does not mean that if a man keeps a dangerous dog or a dangerous bull in a field to which other persons have no right of access, he is liable if the dog or bull attacks someone trespassing in the place where it is confined; but if it attacks someone who passes through the place upon lawful business, such as canvassing or tradesmen delivering orders, or members of the public using a right of way or even a path, which although not a right of way has been frequently used by the public with the owner's consent, the owner will be liable for any damage that it may do.

An exception to the necessity of proving scienter exists in the case of dogs attacking sheep, cattle or poultry, in which case the dog's owner is liable for the damage although he had no reason to think that the dog was likely to be savage in this respect.

It is a defence open to anyone sued for damages for injury caused by a domestic animal, that the injury was due to the contributory negligence of the person injured, i.e. if a person deliberately teases an animal and is then bitten or kicked, he is not entitled to recover damages for his injury: but it must be remembered that merely to pat a dog does not amount to teasing it, and a person bitten by a dog that he has patted can recover damages against the owner, if he can prove scienter.

Apart from liability for injuries the owners of domestic animals are liable for any damage which they may do, which it is within their nature to do. The sort of injuries which animals are likely to do are best dealt with under their separate headings, but it will serve as an indication of the principle involved to point out that cattle, sheep, horses, etc., are likely to do damage to the herbage, if they trespass, and hence the owner is liable for that damage, but that dogs and cats are not likely to damage herbage or to kill and injure game, and accordingly the owner is not liable for damage that they may do, unless he has actually encouraged them to do it.

Duties of Owners.—The owner of a domestic animal has duties towards the animal which he owns, not to treat it with active cruelty or to underfeed or under water it, or to overwork it, or to work it when it is not in a fit state. (*See* Dog; Cat; Cattle; Cruelty to Animals; Game; Poaching; Sheep.)

ANNUAL MEETING.—Every Company is required to hold an annual general meeting at least once every calendar year and each meeting must be not more than 15 months after the previous meeting. At the meeting the balance sheets and profit and loss accounts together with the reports of the Directors and Auditors must be submitted to the Company. (*See* Companies; Director.)

ANNUAL RETURN.—Every year a Company must send to the registrar of Companies a return containing a list of its members with their addresses and occupations and the number of shares held by them. The Annual Return must also contain a summary called the Annual Summary which is designed to disclose the Company's position as shewn by its Balance Sheet, and also gives particulars of any shares issued by it during the last year. (*See* Companies.)

ANNUITY.—An annuity is a sum payable each year. The right to an annuity may be given by a person to take effect during his lifetime—when it is said to be "inter vivos," "between living persons"— or by will, when of course it begins to be paid only after the death of the person who has granted it. When an annuity is granted by one person to another inter vivos it should be by a deed (q.v.) i.e. by a document not only signed but also sealed by the person granting the annuity. If it is granted merely by word of mouth it cannot be enforced, for it is a contract which cannot be performed within one year, and must therefore be evidenced in writing by reason of the Statute of Frauds (q.v.).

Where it is granted by a written document but not under seal, the person granting it may be compelled to pay it by the Court by an order for specific performance of the written agreement. (*See* Specific Performance.)

An annuity inter vivos may be either a personal liability undertaken by the grantor (i.e. the person promising to pay it), or a charge on real property (i.e. land), or personal property (i.e. goods, or shares). When charged on land it is more usually called a Rentcharge (q.v.). When land on which an annuity is charged is sold, the purchaser takes the land without any liability for the annuity unless the annuity is registered.

When created by will annuities are included in the term legacies and are subject generally to the rules of law governing legacies (q.v.). Annuities created by will may be in the form of a simple bequest of an annuity, or of instructions to trustees to set apart a fund to pay the annuity, or to purchase an annuity or to set aside a given sum. When created in the form of a simple bequest the annuitant can claim to have sufficient property kept on one side as a security to make it practically certain that the annuity will be paid. Where trustees are instructed to set aside a sum of money or property sufficient to produce the money needed to pay the annuity, or to buy an annuity, or to invest a specific capital sum, the annuitant may claim to have the money or property which has been set aside paid over to him at once, unless the will has provided that after the death of the first annuitant the annuity or the capital sum shall be paid to some one else. This is called a gift over. Thus, if a will directs Trustees to set aside property to pay an annuity of £100 a year to A for his life, A can claim to have all the property handed to him right away instead of taking it in the form of an annuity. If however the annuity is to be paid to A for his life and after his death to B, this is a gift over and A cannot claim the capital sum but only the annuity each year.

Unless otherwise expressed an annuity created by deed commences from the date of the execution of the deed, and an annuity created by will commences from the death of the testator.

Annuities may be (i) perpetual, as in the case of an annuity to a man and his heirs; (ii) for the life of the annuitant or (iii) for some period other than the life of the annuitant, as in the case of an annuity to A for the life of B. In such a case the annuity continues even if A predeceases B, and A's next of kin, or the persons named by him in his will can receive the money. An annuity to several persons jointly, unless otherwise expressed, is payable in full to the survivor or survivors of them.

Unless the instrument is otherwise expressed, annuities, being legacies, are reduced proportionately where there is not enough money to pay them all. But an annuity charged upon real estate has priority over other annuities.

An annuitant must bear the Income Tax upon the annuity unless the deed or will is expressed in such a way as to shew a clear intention on the part of the donor or testator to make an additional gift out of his estate equal to the amount of the Tax.

The Apportionment Act applies to annuities, which are deemed therefore to accrue *de die in diem*—i.e. from day to day. Thus if an annuity is payable on the 1st January in each year and the annuitant dies on the 1st December, before the date for the payment of the annuity has arrived, his personal representatives are entitled to the proper proportion of the annuity for the period from the previous 1st January to the 1st December.

APARTMENTS. — An occupier of apartments may be either a tenant or a lodger. In the absence of an express tenancy agreement, the test is whether he has merely a right to enjoy the use of the apartments, in which case he is a lodger, or whether he has complete control over them, in which case he is a tenant. The occupier is thus a tenant unless the landlord resides on the premises and reserves to himself the general control over the whole; in fact remains master of the house; but the mere fact that the landlord lives on the premises will not necessarily make the occupier a lodger. If the occupier is a lodger, the law applying to boarding-houses will, in the absence of express agreement, govern the relationship between the landlord and himself, even if he is the only lodger. (*See* BOARDING-HOUSES.) If the occupier is a tenant, the ordinary law of landlord and tenant (q.v.) applies.

The main distinctions between furnished and unfurnished apartments are:—

(1) The Rent Restriction Acts do not apply to furnished apartments, but unfurnished apartments let to a tenant may, under certain circumstances, come within the Act, if neither board nor attendance is provided. (*See* SPECIAL SUPPLEMENT "RENT RESTRICTION.")

(2) In the case of furnished apartments there is an implied covenant by the landlord that they are reasonably fit for the purpose of human habitation; this does not apply to unfurnished apartments.

The landlord of premises where apartments are let is under a duty to the tenants to take reasonable care to see that the staircase and other conveniences of the house are in a fit condition, and is liable for any injury caused to a tenant or a visitor to a tenant as a result of his failure to do so.

A tenant of premises whose lease forbids the premises to be used either (i) for the purpose of any business or (ii) otherwise than as a private dwelling-house, is guilty of a breach of covenant if he lets apartments.

APOLOGY.—As a general rule an apology made in respect of and after some legal wrong has been done, is not recognised in law as a factor reducing the damages caused and recoverable in respect of the wrong. In certain cases, however, the behaviour of the wrongdoer after the wrong has been done may be taken into consideration in assessing the damages to be recovered, especially where the damages are "at large," that is to say, in the discretion of the Court, e.g. in an action for breach of promise or in an action for libel or slander. A statutory exception to this rule has been made in the case of any libel published in a newspaper. In such cases it has been provided, that, in certain circumstances, it is a complete defence to any action for a libel published in a newspaper for the newspaper to prove that an apology was made and a sum of money has been paid to the plaintiff by way of amends. In such a case, however, the newspaper must be able to prove that the publication was not made maliciously, that is to say, that there was no intention on the part of the newspaper to injure the plaintiff and that the statement was not made negligently, and at the earliest opportunity the newspaper published or offered to publish in any newspaper the plaintiff might select a full and wholehearted apology. (*See* DEFAMATION.)

APPEAL FROM COUNTY COURT.—Generally speaking any party to an action has a right of appeal against the judgment of the County Court Judge upon points of law, or upon the admission or rejection of evidence wherever the amount of the claim exceeds £20. The question of law must be raised at the trial and the Judge should be asked to take a note of the point at the time. Where there is no general right to appeal, the Judge should be asked, at the time that he delivers judgment, to grant leave to appeal. In any case the Judge should be asked to grant a stay of execution until the appeal has been heard.

The appeal goes from the County Court to the Divisional Court of the King's Bench Division, unless the appeal is on a Chancery or Probate matter when it will go to those divisions, and the person wishing to appeal must give notice of his intention to appeal at the Crown Office Department of the Central Office at the Royal Courts of Justice, Strand. The notice of appeal must also be served upon the other parties to the action and the Registrar of the County Court where the original action was heard. All this must be done within twenty-one days of the judgment, or the right to appeal will be lost, unless the person wishing to appeal applies to the High Court which is entitled to grant leave to appeal even after the 21 days has elapsed.

The mere fact that a notice of appeal has

been served does not prevent the successful litigant in the County Court from proceeding to enforce his judgment by execution (q.v.), unless the County Court Judge has so ordered, or unless the person wishing to appeal against the decision of the County Court has deposited with the Registrar of the County Court a sum of money sufficient to satisfy the judgment and costs, or some lesser sum, if the Registrar so decides. For this reason, it is very important to remember to ask the County Court Judge for a stay of execution pending appeal, if it is intended to appeal against his decision, and the County Court Judge can grant this stay upon what terms, as to payment of a sum of money into court or otherwise, he pleases.

Although it is possible to appeal against the decision of the County Court Judge upon a question of fact where the claim is for more than £20, it is very difficult to be successful on such an appeal, for in order to succeed it must be shown that the decision on the facts was one at which no reasonable man could have arrived, upon the evidence before the Court. (*See* COUNTY COURT PROCEDURE; NEW TRIAL; STAY OF EXECUTION.)

APPEAL IN CRIMINAL CASES. The rights of appeal in criminal cases are very extensive in this country. There are really two kinds of appeal—(1) from the decision of magistrates on summary conviction (the Police Court), and (2) from decisions of the higher criminal Courts, namely Quarter Sessions, Assizes and the Central Criminal Court.

Appeals from Courts of Summary Jurisdiction.—Every person has the right of appeal from the decision of magistrates to the Quarter Sessions for the area in which is situated the Court at which he was tried. An appeal against conviction to Quarter Sessions is really a fresh hearing, and both sides may call any proper witnesses whether or not they were called at the Court of first instance. The appeals are heard by such of the magistrates of the county who attend or, in the case of a Borough, by the Recorder. Another form of appeal is on a point of law to the King's Bench Division of the High Court of Justice. This is called an appeal by way of "case stated."

Appeals from Superior Courts.—Where any person has been convicted by a jury the only court to which he can appeal against either conviction or sentence, or both is the Court of Criminal Appeal. Although the Court of Criminal Appeal has power to hear fresh evidence it is only in the most exceptional circumstances that it will do so. Appeals to this court are conducted by means of argument addressed by counsel on questions of law, or mixed law and fact. The only appeal from the Court of Criminal Appeal is to the House of Lords and such appeals can only be heard if the Attorney-General certifies that they involve matters of great importance. In consequence they are extremely rare. The Attorney-General only gives his authority, called his "fiat," in the most exceptional cases. Indeed the late Lord Birkenhead when Attorney-General refused to give it in the case of Sir Roger Casement, whose appeal on most intricate historical questions of law had been rejected by the Court of Criminal Appeal. (*See* CASE STATED; COURT OF CRIMINAL APPEAL; LORDS, HOUSE OF; QUARTER SESSIONS.)

APPEAL IN HIGH COURT.—As a general rule when an action has been decided in the High Court, or where some preliminary order has been made (called an interlocutory order), there is an absolute right of appeal to a higher court. The chief exception to this is where under New Procedure (q.v.) the parties to an action have agreed to dispense with their right of appeal. In certain other cases, a right of appeal does not lie except when leave has been obtained either from the Court from which the appeal is being made, or from the Court of Appeal itself. From the judgment of the Court of first instance in any Division of the High Court of Justice, an appeal may be made to the decision of the Court of Appeal (q.v.). From the decision of a Master in Chambers upon interlocutory matters—i.e. matters arising in an action prior to the trial—an appeal lies first to the Judge in Chambers and thence to the Court of Appeal. From the decision of a Divisional Court upon an appeal from a County Court an appeal lies to the Court of Appeal but only by leave of the Divisional Court or of the Court of Appeal.

When a litigant wishes to appeal from the decision of the High Court he must do so within six weeks of the judgment in the Court below, and must give 14 days' notice of his intention to do so, serving the notice

which he can obtain from the Central Office, Royal Courts of Justice, Strand, upon the other party—i.e. the respondent.

If the appeal is against an interlocutory order the notice of appeal must be served within 14 days of the order appealed against.

The hearing of an Appeal.—The hearing of an appeal by the Court of Appeal amounts to a rehearing of the case, and all the documents which were produced before the Court of first instance may be produced to the Court of Appeal. The evidence which was taken on oath at the original trial of the action is produced in the form of the Judge's notes to the Court of Appeal, or if shorthand notes of the evidence have been taken these are used. The witnesses do not as a rule appear to give evidence in person in the Court of Appeal, though the Court is entitled to hear additional witnesses if they wish to do so.

After rehearing, the Court of Appeal gives its judgment upon the appeal, and makes what orders as to the costs of the appeal and of the original action it thinks fit. It may dismiss the appeal, or alter or reverse the judgment of the Judge in the original action, or it may send back the case for retrial.

A further right of appeal lies in most cases from the Court of Appeal to the House of Lords. (*See* COURT OF APPEAL; HIGH COURT PROCEDURE; NEW TRIAL; STAY OF EXECUTION; SUPREME COURT OF JUDICATURE.)

APPENDANT.—A right is said to be appendant when it is annexed to a particular piece of land by operation of law; it is opposed to appurtenant (q.v.). It is used in connection with rights of common and of profits a prendre (q.v.) and implies in each case that the nature of the holding is such that the law attaches the right to it. (*See* APPURTENANT; COMMONS; PROFITS À PRENDRE.)

APPRAISER.—An appraiser is one who is licensed to value land or personal property. He is often an auctioneer or estate agent and is usually known as a valuer. Anyone who does this work professionally or makes a valuation on which stamp duty is payable, must take out an appraiser's licence unless he is already licensed as an auctioneer or estate agent. The licence, which expires on the 5th of July following the date when it was granted, costs £2 per annum and is obtained from the local taxation officer. Failure to take out a licence makes the appraiser liable to a penalty of £50 and without one he cannot recover his fees.

Certain valuations are not chargeable with stamp duty but those which are must be written out by the appraiser and stamped within 14 days. Anyone who receives or pays for a valuation not in this form is liable to a fine.

An appraiser has a duty towards his employer and may have to pay him damages if his valuation is careless and inaccurate. Where he is employed in order to fix the purchase price of some property his employer is bound by his valuation.

APPRENTICESHIP.—With the advance of education, and especially with the advance of technical and vocational education at training colleges or institutions, the former importance of apprenticeship is considerably diminished, but it is by no means dead, particularly in respect of trades or occupations where practical experience is an essential.

The system of apprenticeship appears to have made its first appearance in about the twelfth century, and, until 1814, it was, in law and in practice, almost impossible for a man to exercise a trade without having served as an apprentice. A great many of the rules still in force in relation to apprenticeship date back to very early times.

An apprentice stands in many respects in the same legal relation towards his master as an ordinary servant, and it is therefore necessary to consider only the respects in which they differ.

Creation of the Contract.—The first step in binding a boy apprentice is the completion of the written contract under which he is to be bound. If the contract is to extend for more than a year, it must be written, and for that reason contracts of apprenticeship are almost invariably in writing. It need not be by deed of indenture (q.v.), although a deed is often used. No other formality is required except that "every writing relating to the service or tuition of any apprentice, clerk or servant placed with any master to learn any profession, trade or employment (except articles of clerkship to a solicitor or law agent or writer to the signet), is to be deemed to be an instrument of apprenticeship," and must therefore be stamped with

a half-crown stamp; no stamp is required in Ireland where the premium does not exceed £10, nor is a stamp required where the child is a poor child in charge of a parish or township or public charity.

The master would always be well advised to make it clear in the instrument that it is a contract of apprenticeship and not a mere contract of service, although it will always be recognized as apprenticeship if the child is entitled under the instrument to receive instruction in the trade. It is usual for a premium to be paid to the master on the commencement of the apprenticeship as remuneration to him for the education of the child, and this also is strong evidence of the fact that the contract is of apprenticeship.

It is important that the contract should be clearly a contract of apprenticeship since the child cannot then claim to rescind it on the grounds that he is an infant, for infants are always bound by contracts they enter into which are for their own benefit. It is common for the child's father, mother or other friend to be made a party to the contract (which is then made by deed), in order that the father or friend may bind himself for the good behaviour of the child; if the child then breaks the contract, his father or friend will be answerable, while the child is free from all liability for his breach of contract unless local custom imposes a liability upon him (as in London, *see* below).

The terms of the contract vary in each particular case, but if they are unfair or detrimental to the child's welfare, the child will be entitled to treat the whole contract as void: the contract must be regarded as a whole for the purposes of judging whether it is unfair or not, but it will be so considered if it provides for penalties to be imposed upon the child or if it omits any provision as to the child's wages or maintenance. The contract will also fix the time for which it is to continue, and, if it fixes a time of more than seven years, the contract will, nevertheless, end at the termination of seven years. At one time, seven years was the minimum period, and it still survives (in another sphere) in the period of seven years which is required to elapse between matriculation at a university and the taking of the degree of Master of Arts.

Transfer of the Contract.—A master cannot transfer his rights and duties under the contract to a new master without the consent of all the parties to the original instrument. Such assignment, if consented to, should be in writing and should bear a half-crown stamp and should state that the former contract is to be terminated.

Termination of the Contract.—The contract will normally come to an end at the date fixed in the instrument. If the apprentice was under twenty-one at the time of making the contract, he will be entitled to declare the contract void when he attains twenty-one or within a reasonable time thereafter; such a declaration, however, will not relieve from liability any adult person who covenanted in the original deed for the continuation of the service beyond the age of twenty-one. The contract will also cease if either the master or the apprentice dies, or if the apprentice becomes permanently ill.

On the bankruptcy of the master, the apprentice is free to terminate the contract by notice to the trustee in bankruptcy, who may refund a proportionate part of the premium (if any) paid by the apprentice at the commencement of the apprenticeship. The contract may, of course, be cancelled with the consent of all the parties, and this would probably be validly effected by writing the word "cancelled" across the instrument. The contract also terminates when the master changes his business in such a way as to be unable to continue the teaching of the apprentice, or, if the master was a partnership, when the partnership is dissolved by the death or retirement of a partner.

The master cannot dissolve the contract for misconduct on the part of the apprentice, unless there is a term in the contract that he may do so, or unless the misconduct was of a most gross or dangerous nature, and occurred in connection with the business to be taught, e.g. stealing from the till by a pawnbroker's apprentice.

The master or the apprentice may, however, if questions arise, apply under the Employers and Workmen Act, 1875, to a Magistrates' Court to settle disputes between them in all cases where the premium paid was £25 or less and in cases of apprenticeship to the sea service. The Court may, on such an application, rescind the contract, and may order the master to repay the whole or part of the premium, or again it may order the apprentice to perform his duties.

Rights and Duties of the Apprentice.—The apprentice binds himself to perform the lawful commands of his master and to serve his master faithfully. In return, he is entitled to receive instruction from the master. The fact that the master's business falls off will not dissolve the contract, but the apprentice would be entitled to sue the master for breach of contract if it fell off to such an extent that the master could no longer teach him the trade; even though the master ceases to own his business and becomes merely a journeyman, still the contract subsists, and the apprentice is bound still to serve his master. The master is entitled to the service of the apprentice at all reasonable times for all proper purposes, but he will not be entitled to services unconnected with the business that is to be taught, e.g. a tailor's apprentice could not be ordered to black shoes, nor could a bootmaker's apprentice be required to repair clothes.

The apprentice is entitled to such wages as have been agreed in the contract and to no more; but he is entitled to these even while he is away through illness; but usually the master is liable to pay wages only when the work is done, and therefore is not liable to pay them if the apprentice runs away or is imprisoned. The apprentice has no right to be absent from his work without leave, and, if he is so absent for an unreasonable time, the master will be entitled to refuse to receive him back. The apprentice may, however, always absent himself on Sundays, since it would be illegal for the master to require his services then. As regards the instruction that the apprentice is to receive, the contract usually contains a careful definition of the extent of the apprentice's rights, but, if it does not, the apprentice is entitled to learn the whole of his master's trade, and not merely one branch of it. He has no right to be taught by the master personally, but, if the master does not provide adequate teachers, the apprentice will be entitled to sue on the master's breach of covenant to teach.

Food and Clothing.—An apprentice may be either an "outdoor" or an "indoor" apprentice. Outdoor apprentices are those who come for instruction every day; indoor apprentices are those who live with, or under the care of, the master, and to whom the master agrees to supply "board, lodging and all other necessaries," or words to the same effect. The term "necessaries" will include all washing, mending and clothing, but the master is bound to supply only such things as are necessary to apprentices in the particular trade, and in the particular branch of that trade in which the master is engaged: an hotelier's apprentice, for example, would require greater expenditure on clothes than a chimney sweeper's apprentice. If the master undertakes to provide medicines and medical attendance, and he fails to do so, he is liable to be convicted of a misdemeanour. Failure to provide necessary food, clothing or lodging renders the master liable to the same conviction.

Punishment of Apprentices.—An apprentice is liable to reasonable chastisement by his master much in the same way as a child is liable to chastisement by its parent. Such punishment will not justify the child in leaving his master, but he would be justified in leaving if he had reasonable cause to fear that real bodily harm would be caused to him. The master may not authorize persons other than himself to inflict chastisement. In old cases, a master has been held to be entitled to chastise even his apprentices who were above the age of twenty-one, but it is almost certain that nowadays an action for assault and battery would be available in such cases, for, under modern conditions, such punishment would be deemed unreasonable.

There are also extensive powers vested in Magistrates' Courts to punish apprentices. In the first place, the Court may order the apprentice to perform his duties (*see* above TERMINATION OF CONTRACT), and, if he fails so to do within a month, he may be ordered to imprisonment (without hard labour) for fourteen days. After release, he is still bound to continue his service, and, on failure to do so a second time, may a second time be committed to prison. The mode of procedure is for the injured party to make a complaint before a justice, who will then issue the summons.

London.—The rules relating to apprentices bound in the City of London differ considerably from those applicable to apprentices elsewhere, the rules of the City of London being derived from ancient customary law, which has not survived in other cities to any material extent. As examples of the important differences between rules relating to London apprentices and other apprentices it may be noted that a deed of indenture is always required and must be enrolled; that the term of service may not be for less than four years; that the apprentice must be over fourteen and under twenty-one; that the apprentice himself, even though a minor, is liable to be sued for breach of the covenants of the indenture; and that the Chamberlain's Court takes the place of Magistrates' Court in relation to dispute between apprentices and their masters, the Chamberlain being able to commit the apprentice to prison for offences for not more than three months.

Apprentices to the Sea Service, Pawnbrokers, etc.—Many special rules also apply to apprentices for service at sea, the most notable being that no boy may be bound apprentice to this service under the age of thirteen or for more than seven years. If any pawnbroker employs any apprentice under the age of sixteen years to take pledges in pawn, he shall be liable to a penalty not exceeding £10. If a child under the age of sixteen is apprenticed to a chimney-sweeper, the indenture of apprenticeship shall be null and void. (*See also* CHIMNEY SWEEP.)

Insurance and Workmen's Compensation.—The National Health Insurance Acts and the Unemployment Insurance Acts apply to paid apprentices, whether the contract be written or oral, but they do not apply to unpaid apprentices. In deciding whether an apprentice is entitled to compensation under the Workmen's Compensation Acts, he is to be regarded as an ordinary servant in the service of his master; in other words, where an ordinary employee would have been entitled to compensation, an apprentice also will be entitled to compensation.

APPROVED SCHOOL.—An approved school is a school to which children and young persons who have committed an offence, or who are in need of care or protection, may be sent by the order of a Juvenile Court. Approved schools were formerly called Industrial Schools or Reformatory Schools but the name has been changed by the Children's and Young Persons' Act, 1933—the Act which has been fitly described as the "Children's Charter."

The managers of any school which is intended for the training and education of children who may have committed an offence may apply to the Secretary of State to have the school approved, and if the Secretary of State thinks fit he may approve the school and issue a certificate of approval to the managers. The certificate may be withdrawn by the Secretary of State if he gives six months' notice to the managers, and the managers may surrender their certificate after giving the Secretary of State six months' notice of their intention to do so.

The existing Reformatory and Industrial Schools have been converted into approved schools wherever application has been made for approval.

The managers of an approved school are bound to accept any child who is sent to the school, unless their school is for persons of a different religious belief than that of the child proposed to be sent, or unless the school is already full.

Who may be sent to an Approved School.—If a child or a young person is found guilty of an offence, which if committed by an adult would have been punishable with imprisonment, the Court may order him to be sent to an approved school. A child is defined as a person under fourteen years of age, and a young person is a person who is under seventeen years of age but over fourteen. If a Juvenile Court is satisfied that a child or young person brought before it by a local authority, police constable or other authorized person is in need of care or protection, it may order the child to be sent to an approved school. A child is held to be in need of care or protection if it is without a parent or guardian, or if its parent or guardian is an unfit person and the child is beyond control or exposed to moral danger; if it is a member of a household in which resides a person who has been convicted of the murder of a child, or a sexual offence against a child, or of cruelty to a child; if it is being prevented from receiving education or is found destitute and without the means of subsistence.

If a parent or guardian of a child or young person proves to a Juvenile Court that he is unable to control that child or young person, the Court may order him to be sent to an approved school if they are satisfied that the parent or guardian understands the results

which will follow from the making of the order and consents to it.

A local poor law authority may apply to a Juvenile Court to have a child or young person, who is boarded out in one of their institutions, sent to an approved school because he is refractory.

When a child is ordered to be sent to an approved school, the order is an authority for keeping him there for three years, and if at the time of the expiry of the three years he is under fifteen he may be detained until he reaches that age. If a young person is sent to an approved school he may be detained for three years if he was not sixteen when the order was made, or until he is nineteen years of age if he was over sixteen when the order was made. Upon discharge from an approved school, a child or young person remains under the supervision of the managers for the next three years and may be recalled by them to the school, if the Secretary of State so directs.

If a person who has been sent to an approved school escapes from the school, or while absent on temporary leave runs away or fails to return upon the expiry of his leave, he may be arrested without a warrant and brought before a Court of Summary Jurisdiction. That Court may order him to be brought back to the school and have his period of detention increased by six months, or if he is over sixteen years of age he may be sent to a Borstal Institution for two years.

Who Pays for the Maintenance of a Child?—When a child or young person is sent to an approved school, his father or stepfather, mother or stepmother may be ordered to make contributions towards his maintenance in the school. The Court which sends the child to the approved school makes a contribution order on any person who is liable to make contributions, for the payment of a weekly sum in accordance with his means. If the child is illegitimate and an affiliation order is in force with regard to it, the Court of Summary Jurisdiction for the area in which the father resides may direct that the money payable under the affiliation order is to be paid over to the person authorized to receive contributions on behalf of the approved school. A contribution order remains in force for as long as the child or young person is under the care of the managers of the school. (*See* COURT; EDUCATION; INDUSTRIAL SCHOOL; JUVENILE COURT; RELIGIOUS INSTRUCTION.)

APPROVED SOCIETY.—Under the scheme of National Health Insurance the right to benefit is generally administered through Friendly Societies which have been approved by the Minister of Health for the purposes of the scheme. These societies must not be run for profit and must be controlled and administered by their members.

Any person entitled to be insured is entitled to apply for membership of an approved society and if the application for membership is granted, he is bound by the rules of the society.

Although all approved Societies must give to their members the full benefits for medical treatment, sickness, disablement, maternity, etc., provided under the National Health Insurance Scheme, many of them also offer additional benefits to their members, such as a payment to widows and orphans upon the death of the member, a form of insurance against funeral expenses, etc., etc. (*See* DISABLEMENT BENEFIT; FRIENDLY SOCIETY; MATERNITY BENEFIT; MEDICAL BENEFIT; NATIONAL HEALTH INSURANCE; SICKNESS BENEFIT.)

APPROVER.—An old-fashioned term meaning a person who, when charged with felony himself, agrees to give evidence against other persons also charged, in other words to turn "King's Evidence." (*See* ACCOMPLICE; KING'S EVIDENCE.)

APPURTENANT.—A right is said to be appurtenant when it has been annexed to a particular holding or piece of land for the benefit of whoever may be its owner for the time being by some agreement between such owner, or his predecessors, and the owner of the land over which the right is exercisable. Both rights appurtenant and appendant, since they must be annexed to some particular holding of land, are contrasted with rights in gross which attach not to land but to a particular person and his heirs. (*See* APPENDANT; COMMONS; EASEMENT; PROFITS À PRENDRE.)

ARBITRATION.—The law confers on persons rights which may arise under contract or otherwise. For the enforcement of these rights the law has set up Courts to which any person, who is being refused what is his legal due, may complain. The law,

however, does not compel persons to rely solely on the Courts for the enforcement of their legal rights or for the settling of their disputes. It is frequently open to them, if they wish, to agree with one another that some dispute between them shall be settled not by the Court but by taking the decision of some private person on the matter, by whose decision each of them agrees to abide. Such a method of settling disputes is known as Arbitration. It has various advantages over the method of settling a dispute in Court; the chief of these is that the proceedings in an arbitration usually take place in private, and therefore no one except the parties to the actual dispute know anything about it. This aspect of arbitration makes it attractive to Insurance Companies who would hesitate to repudiate claims, even though they thought they might be entitled to do so, if the fact of the repudiation would be made public through the proceedings in Court, for this might injure their business reputation. Arbitration is also considered by some persons to be less expensive than litigation but this is by no means always the case.

Stay of Proceedings.—The law in England does not allow the parties to oust the jurisdiction of the Courts by an arbitration agreement in every case, but in practice this result can be obtained if the arbitration claim is properly framed. For if proceedings are begun in Court about a matter which the parties have agreed to arbitrate, the Court will order the proceedings in Court to be stayed until the arbitration has taken place. In certain cases, however, where it is in the public interest that the matter should be considered publicly by a Court, e.g. where one of the parties is charged with fraud, the Court will not stay the proceedings but will allow them to proceed, so that the party charged with fraud may have the opportunity of meeting in public the allegations made against him. For the same reasons no matter involving a crime can be referred to arbitration.

Before there can be an arbitration the parties must have entered into a contract agreeing that their dispute shall be settled in this way. They may do this either before a dispute arises or after it has arisen. Thus, if parties are entering into a contract for some matter during the course of which a great many questions are likely to arise, they may provide beforehand in their contract that any question so arising shall be decided by some named person. This happens frequently in building contracts where disputes arising during the carrying out of the work are usually settled by an Architect. Where there is no such provision in the contract the parties, if they wish to arbitrate, must make an agreement when the dispute arises agreeing to refer that dispute to arbitration.

The Submission.—The agreement by which parties refer their dispute to arbitration is known as a Submission. This may be made either by word of mouth or in writing, but special advantages are attached to submissions made in writing because it is to those only that the Arbitration Act, 1889, applies. Verbal submissions, however, may frequently be made in cases of an informal nature. Thus, if A has sold B some wheat and B says that the wheat is not of the quality promised, they may each agree to ask Y who is an expert in wheat and on whose judgment they are content to rely. If Y gives his decision as to the quality of the wheat, then A and B must abide by it, and if B tried to sue A in the Court he would not be allowed to allege that the wheat was not of the quality agreed to be sold.

When a submission is in writing it may of course contain such provisions as the parties please. But in the absence of any contrary intention the following provisions apply:—

1. If no other method of reference is provided the reference is to a single arbitrator;

2. If the reference is to two arbitrators they may appoint an Umpire to decide between them if they disagree;

3. The decision of the Arbitrator (i.e. the Award) must be given within 3 months after the beginning of the reference but the Arbitrator has power to extend the time;

4. If the time has expired without an award being made or if the arbitrators have indicated that they cannot agree the Umpire enters on the reference;

5. He must make his award within a month but again may extend the time;

6. The parties to the arbitration must answer questions on oath before the arbitrator and produce all books and documents relating to the dispute;

7. Witnesses may be examined on oath;

8. The award is final and binding on the parties;

9. The arbitrators or the Umpire can order one of the parties to pay the costs of the proceedings;

Appointment of Umpire.—The umpire may be named in the submission, or it may be provided in the submission that the parties shall choose an arbitrator at a later date. Where the parties cannot agree on their arbitrator the Court will appoint an arbitrator. If, where each party is to appoint an arbitrator, one of them fails or refuses to do so, the other party may serve a notice on him requiring him to make an appointment within 7 days, and if he still fails to do so the arbitration may proceed before the single arbitrator.

Duty of Arbitrator.—The arbitrator cannot delegate his powers to any person and must hear the dispute and give his decision himself. He may, however, if the parties do not object, have a legal assessor, that is, some person trained in law, to sit with him and assist him as to the legal points involved, and in all cases he may employ legal assistance in drawing up his award. The arbitrator should fix a time and place for the arbitration and inform the parties. If one does not attend the arbitration may proceed in his absence. He must hear any evidence tendered in the presence of both parties and must observe the legal rules of evidence. He cannot call a witness himself without the consent of the parties.

The arbitrator may decide any point of law arising in the case, but if he does not wish to do so, he may state his award in the form of a special case. This means that the arbitrator comes to a decision on the facts and then asks the Court certain specific questions of law based on these facts. When a question of law arises in a case the arbitrator may be compelled on application to the Court to state a special case to the Court on that question of law.

The Award.—Where the submission is in writing the award must also be in writing. The arbitrator must be careful to decide only the questions submitted to him for if he goes outside the submission the whole award may be void. On the other hand, he must be careful to consider all matters that have been referred. The award must be final. When an award has been made the arbitrator informs the parties who can take it up on paying his costs. An award may be enforced in the same way as a judgment of the Court if leave of the Court is first obtained. The award may be set aside in certain cases as where the arbitration has been improperly conducted, or where the arbitrator has been biased or secretly interested in the dispute or the subject matter of it.

Reference to Arbitration under the Order of the Court.—In any legal proceedings other than criminal proceedings the Court, if the parties consent, may order any part of the dispute to be tried by an Arbitrator or Official Referee (*see* OFFICIAL REFEREE) and in certain exceptional cases, where the matter is one which requires prolonged investigation, or the examination of scientific documents, or is purely a matter of figures, the Court can compel the parties to refer the matter to the Official Referee.

References to Arbitration under Statutory Powers.—Certain statutes provide that questions arising under them shall be referred to arbitration. Thus the Acquisition of Land (Assessment of Compensation) Act, 1919, provides that, where under any statute land is authorized to be compulsorily acquired, any question of disputed compensation shall be referred to arbitration before one of a panel of official arbitrators appointed under the Act. Questions under the Workmen's Compensation Act must also be determined by arbitration. On questions submitted to arbitration under the Acquisition of Land Act and under the Workmen's Compensation Act, the decisions of the Official Arbitrator on questions of fact are final and no right of appeal lies, but questions of law decided may be reviewed by the High Court. (*See* OFFICIAL REFEREE; WORKMAN'S COMPENSATION.)

ARBITRATION (SCOTS LAW).—The Scots Law of Arbitration differs in some respects from that of England. The Courts in Scotland are much more ready to exclude persons who have agreed to arbitrate from commencing any legal proceedings about the matter instead of arbitrating.

The person to whose decision the matter has been referred is called an Arbiter and any umpire appointed to decide, in the event of there being two arbiters who dis-

agree, is called the Oversman. Whereas in England it is always possible for parties to appeal from the decision of an Arbitrator by asking him to state a case on a point of law which has arisen, this is not possible in Scotland and the decision of an Arbiter is binding on the parties and conclusive in law as well as in fact. The attitude of the Courts is that, if the arbiter who has been chosen makes a decision which is wrong in law, the parties cannot complain for it is they who have chosen him.

Arbitration under special statutes in Scotland such as The Workmen's Compensation Acts follows the same rules as in England and in these cases an appeal may be made to the Court.

ARCHBISHOP.—There are two Archbishoprics in England, the province of Canterbury and the province of York. An Archbishop (or "Metropolitan") is appointed by the King (in effect, by the Prime Minister in office at the time of a vacancy), and exercises supreme power in his province in all ecclesiastical matters. Particularly, he has power over the Bishops within his see, and is entitled to try them and to deprive them of their dioceses, i.e. he is the Bishop's "Ordinary." It is also his duty to visit and inspect all the clergy within his province. He is president of Convocation, which is summoned by him. An Archbishop is chairman of the National Assembly, the Archbishop of Canterbury having precedence. His other duties are innumerable, e.g. to consecrate Bishops, and to hear appeals from the Bishop's Court.

The Archbishop of Canterbury has certain exclusive rights, including the right to grant special marriage licences; he is known officially as the "Primate and Metropolitan of all England" and signs himself by his christian name followed by the abbreviation "Cantuar:" (Cantuariensis = of Canterbury).

The Archbishop of York is known as "Primate and Metropolitan of England," and signs himself with his christian name followed by the abbreviation "Ebor:" (Eboracensis = of York). But, although he is second in precedence, the Archbishop of York is in no way controlled by the Archbishop of Canterbury. Both Archbishops are members of the House of Lords, but this right does not pass to their children.

ARCHDEACON.—Every diocese is divided into archdeaconries, each of which, in its turn, is divided into rural deaneries. The Archdeacon is governor in ecclesiastical matters of the area of his archdeaconry. He is usually appointed by the Bishop, and his duties include the examination of candidates for ordination; the admission of church-wardens and sidesmen; and the inspection of all clergy within his archdeaconry. His immediate superior is his diocesan Bishop.

ARCHES, COURT OF.—The Court of Arches is the Ecclesiastical Provincial Court of the Province of Canterbury (*see* PROVINCIAL COURT). It is so called because it used to be held in Bow Church, which had acquired its name from the stone arches (or bows) upon which its steeple was supported. The Judge is known as the Dean of Arches.

ARCHITECTS.—An architect need not in law have a special qualification. There is, however, the Register of Registered Architects in which he may register and then use the title of "Registered Architect." A person may be removed from this list if he is convicted of a criminal offence or his conduct is unprofessional.

The Duties of an Architect towards his Building Owner.—When an architect enters into a contract he always impliedly undertakes to exercise a reasonable amount of care and skill in carrying out the work to be done. If he does not do so the building owner can end the contract and recover damages from him for any loss he has caused by his want of care or skill. He must examine the site of a proposed building; for example, he must ascertain for himself by experiment the nature of the soil. He is liable if his plans and specifications are faulty from a technical point of view, or because he has not carried out the instructions of the building owner. His supervision need not be so thorough as to cover every small detail but it must be sufficiently minute to enable him to give a final certificate in good faith. Where bye-laws or general housing regulations apply to his locality, it is his duty to acquaint himself with them and see that his plans comply with them; where necessary he must submit his plans to the local authority for approval. If the building owner incurs loss through any failure to comply with any of these regulations the architect will have to make good the loss. The architect does not,

however, guarantee the contractor in any way and does not render himself liable in any way by recommending the acceptance of any tender from a particular contractor.

Liability of the Architect towards the Contractor.—Here again the architect gives no guarantee and he is not liable to the contractor for the actions of the building owner. He will only be personally liable if he exceeds his authority as agent of the building owner so that the contractor incurs loss.

Payment of Architects.—This will usually be a matter of express agreement between the architect and the building owner, but if no rate is fixed the general rule is that the architect is entitled to ask for a reasonable rate in the circumstances. He cannot ask for this if he only submits plans; they must have been accepted and used. There is a professional scale of charges worked out on a percentage of the cost of the proposed building, but which will not govern the contract unless it is actually a part of it; it may of course be an understood term. Payment will not become due until the entire work is done unless there is an agreement to pay by instalments. Where the architect has not completed the work to be done and the termination of the contract is due to some fault of the building owner, he may sue for damages. If, on the other hand, he has not exercised the skill and care that he should have, he cannot recover any payment and must refund any amount that he has been paid. (*See* BUILDING CONTRACT.)

ARMS, COAT OF. Assumption of Arms.—The grant of coats of arms is controlled nominally by the King, but virtually by the College of Arms and, to some extent, by the Home Secretary. Arms can be granted only by virtue of the King's prerogative and no person is entitled to bear arms if he cannot derive his title from a Royal grant. Application for arms is made in the same way as application for change of arms (*see* below). An excise licence must be taken out by every person who uses arms. The licence is obtainable at most Post Offices, and must be renewed every year. If the arms are used on a carriage the duty is £2 2s. 0d. per year; if not so used, £1 1s. 0d. Every licence expires on 31st December of each year, and must be renewed within twenty-one days thereafter.

The licence need not be taken out by the owner of a hackney carriage for the use of arms on his carriage, nor by the servants of a corporation for wearing the arms on a uniform, nor in cases where they are worn by virtue of some office—e.g. by a mayor. About 34,000 licences for armorial bearings are taken out annually.

Change of Arms.—If a person desires to change his armorial bearings, he must make application as if he were applying for the first time, i.e. he must make application to the College of Arms, where a petition will be drawn up for transmission through the Home Secretary to the King. The stamp duty in such a case is £10, unless the change is required in order to comply with a condition in a will requiring the beneficiary to assume the testator's arms, when the duty is £50. In ordinary cases, a change of arms will, in all, cost about £100.

Royal Arms.—The Royal Standard can only be flown with the King's permission, and such permission is given only when the King or Queen is present at the place where the Standard is to be flown. Under penalty of £20, the Royal Arms may not be used without a licence from the Crown in connection with any business, trade or profession so as to lead persons to believe that their use is authorized. Such licence must bear a £30 stamp. The Royal arms of foreign countries and the arms of a city or body corporate may be used as a trade mark, but, in order to secure registration of such trade marks, the applicant may be required to shew that he is authorized to use them. (*See also* RED CROSS; ROYAL WARRANT HOLDER.)

ARMSTRONG POISONING CASE, THE.—The little solicitor from Brecon was tried before Mr. Justice Darling at the Hereford Assizes in April, 1922, for the murder of his wife by poison. Sir Ernest Pollock, the Attorney-General (now Lord Hanworth), led for the Crown, and Sir Henry Curtis Bennett for the defence.

Armstrong, a small man weighing only 7 stone, was completely under the domination of his wife. Towards the end of 1920 Mrs. Armstrong was certified insane and remained in an asylum for four months. On her return she became very ill, and died on February 22, 1921. His subsequent conduct leading to suspicion, her body was exhumed nearly a year later and found to contain as much as $3\frac{1}{2}$ grains of arsenic.

Case for the Crown.—The prosecution alleged that a fatal dose had been administered by Armstrong within twenty-four hours of death. The motive they imputed to him was the pecuniary benefit he would derive from his wife's death; they also suggested that he desired his freedom on account of another woman, who was called as a witness but not named. This suggestion was strengthened by the fact that Armstrong had persuaded his wife to sign a new will, written out by him, which left everything to him who had not been left anything in the previous will, and which he as a solicitor knew did not comply with the requirements of law as to witnesses.

The defence never denied that Armstrong had bought quantities of weedkiller and packets of arsenic prior to his wife's death. His explanation was that he used to inject it with a syringe into the roots of dandelions on his lawn.

The defence was that Mrs. Armstrong was of suicidal tendencies and unsound mind and had herself taken the arsenic; that there was no evidence that he had actually administered the poison, and that he had no motive for doing so.

Armstrong was originally arrested on another charge of administering arsenic with attempt to murder a Mr. Martin. A dramatic moment came in the trial when the Attorney-General intimated that he wished to call evidence as to this and its admission was objected to by Sir Henry Curtis Bennett. It was allowed by the Judge to rebut the defence of suicide and to show that the prisoner's possession of arsenic at the time of his wife's death was not innocent.

The extraordinary story was then told which did much to convict Armstrong. It was proved that he had administered arsenic to Martin, a fellow-solicitor in the town, while his guest at tea, and his motive for doing so was that he was in financial difficulties and Martin was pressing for the repayment to a client of a deposit on a property deal which failed to go through. The Jury were undoubtedly largely influenced by the evidence as to Mr. Martin, and returned the verdict of guilty which sent this eccentric little poisoner to his death.

ARRAIGNMENT.—The arraignment

of a prisoner is the formal charging of him in open Court when he is about to be tried on indictment. It consists of three steps. First the prisoner is called upon by name. In former times he was, on being called upon, required to hold up his hand, but this now is no longer normally required. The next step is to read to him the indictment. The arraignment is then concluded by the question "How say you, are you Guilty or Not Guilty?" (*See* INDICTMENT.)

ARRAIGNS, CLERK OF.—An official at Assize Courts whose duty it is to arraign prisoners.

ARREST.—The term arrest in the sense of legal seizure is used in two connections: it may be applied either to persons or to ships.

Arrest of the person may be quite lawfully effected for a variety of causes, but in all cases, since the abolition of imprisonment for debt in 1869, arrest is for a criminal offence or for matters very similar to a criminal offence, whether actually committed or only suspected. There is an important distinction between the powers of a police constable and the powers of a private individual to effect arrests—the private individual may arrest only when he *knows* that a felony has been committed, and has reasonable grounds to suspect that the person arrested is the criminal. A constable, on the other hand, may effect an arrest when he has grounds merely to *suspect* that the felony has been committed and that the person arrested is the criminal. Either a constable or a private person may arrest a person who is about to commit a felony or breach of the peace. In the majority of other cases, a warrant will be required. If a person is unlawfully arrested, he may have an action for assault and battery and for false imprisonment; and a writ of habeas corpus will issue for his release. (*See* HABEAS CORPUS AND SPECIAL SUPPLEMENT "POLICE.")

If a ship causes damage, it may be detained until compensation has been paid in order to prevent evasion of liability by its sailing abroad. This is known as arrest of a ship.

ARREST OF JUDGMENT.—A prisoner who is being tried on indictment may, after he has been convicted by the Jury and before receiving sentence, move the Court in Arrest of Judgment. This a motion to set aside the proceedings on the ground of some fatal flaw in the indictment.

ARRESTMENT (SCOTS LAW).—Arrestment is the seizure of movable property, i.e. goods or debts which are owed to a person. It is used in Scots Law for three purposes:

Arrestment to found jurisdiction.—By a very convenient process it is possible in Scotland to sue any person, wherever the matter may have arisen about which the action is brought, and even though the person is a foreigner not living in Scotland, by arresting, that is, seizing, any property in Scotland belonging to him. This is most frequently used in the case of ships belonging to foreigners. This process cannot be used in actions affecting status (e.g. divorce), but is usually confined to matters relating to commerce. The fact that property has been arrested for this purpose does not give the person arresting any security over the property, or any right to have any debts, which may be due to him by the person to whom the property belongs, paid out of that property.

Arrestment in security or on the dependence.—In Scots Law a creditor is not compelled to wait until he has got an order of the Court against his debtor for the payment of money before he is entitled to seize the debtor's property. Even where there is no action, if the debtor is in financial difficulties or is thought to be about to leave the country, letters of arrestment may be obtained by the creditor authorizing him to seize the property. In the same way where an action has been begun in which some sum of money is claimed, the property may be seized before the decree, i.e. judgment in the action, has been given. This procedure has the advantage not only that the debtor is prevented from getting rid of his property during the delay which must follow before judgment can be obtained against him, but also the person arresting obtains a preference as against the other creditors, which will be of great value to him if the debtor becomes sequestrated, i.e. bankrupt. The absence of any equivalent form of procedure in England sometimes works great hardship.

Arrestment in execution.—This is the procedure which is equivalent to the execution in English law by which a creditor seizes the property of the debtor in payment of his debt. In Scotland the whole subject of execution is called diligence, and arrestment is one of the methods of doing diligence.

Arrestment is the method by which the creditor gets hold of property belonging to the debtor which is not in the debtor's possession. (As to property in the debtor's possession, *see* Poinding.) In this sense it corresponds to garnishee proceedings (q.v.) in English Law. It applies to goods belonging to the debtor which are in the hands of some other person and also to any sum of money which is owed to the debtor by any person, or to any right of action which the debtor has, e.g. shares in a Company. Future debts, that is, debts which are not yet payable—e.g. rent which will be due in a month's time—cannot be arrested. Debts which are alimentary cannot be arrested. An alimentary debt is one which is given to a person for the purpose of supplying him with the necessaries of life, and a debt may become alimentary either because it is given under some document which states it is alimentary, e.g. a life-rent or annuity, or under some rule of law.

Thus, salaries, enjoyed by persons in some public office, such as all persons employed by the Crown, or a Parish Minister, are alimentary except in so far as the amount of the salary is in excess of what is required for the reasonable support of the debtor. The wages of labourers, farm servants, and workmen cannot be arrested except for any excess over 35/– a week.

An arrestment by itself is not a complete diligence and, in order to entitle the creditor to claim the money or property from the person by whom it is owed to the debtor, it must be followed by decree in an action in the Court called an action of forthcoming. The arrestment itself only prevents the person who owes the money from paying it to the debtor. (*See* Diligence.)

ARSON.—Arson is the crime of maliciously setting fire to buildings. It is a felony punishable according to the kind of building set fire to. Thus setting fire to any place of divine worship, or to any public building, or to any dwelling-house in which any human being is at the time, is punishable with penal servitude for life. Setting fire to other buildings is in general punishable with penal servitude for fourteen years. Accidental causing of fire, of course, is not arson, since the essence of the crime is the intent; but it is not necessary that there should be present any malice against the owner or occupier. The crime is committed if it is intentional, whatever the motive.

ARTICLES OF ASSOCIATION.— The Articles of Association of a Company are the documents which control the relationship of the shareholders to one another and to their directors. They deal with such matters as the shareholders' rights of voting, the powers of directors, and the dividend rights of the various classes of shares. When a Company is formed Articles of Association are deposited with the Registrar of Companies together with the Memorandum of Association. It is not necessary for a Company to deposit Articles of its own, for if it does not do so a set of model Articles called Table "A" will automatically apply to it. Many of the provisions in that Table, however, are not considered suitably by some Companies, and these frequently adopt certain clauses of Table A and file in addition some special Articles of their own dealing with the points on which they wish to differ from Table A. While a Public Company thus need not have special Articles, it is necessary for a Private Company in all cases to file special Articles forbidding it to make any issue of its shares to members of the public; for, unless this provision is contained in its Articles, it is not entitled to the privileges of a Private Company, and there is no such provision in Table A. (*See* Companies.)

Every member of a Company is bound by the Articles as fully as if he had signed a contract setting out their terms.

The Articles may be altered by the Company by a special resolution, i.e. a resolution passed by a three-quarters majority at a meeting of which 21 days' notice was given. Neither the articles as altered nor as originally prepared must infringe the Memorandum by giving power to the Company to do anything not included in that document. An alteration may be objected to if it constitutes which is called a "Fraud on the Minority." Thus if certain shareholders use their votes to carry a resolution which injures the interests of the minority of the shareholders and is not in the interests of the Company as a whole, the resolution will be set aside by the Court. This provision is of importance to-day since so many Companies have been desirous of taking advantage of the low rates of interest for money by passing resolutions reducing the rates of dividend payable on their preference shares. It frequently happens that a majority of the preference shareholders also hold almost all the ordinary shares, and in such a case they are prepared to reduce the preference dividend knowing that the money so saved will ultimately find its way into their pockets as dividend on the ordinary shares. Shareholders who think they are being unfairly treated in this way may apply to the Court.

ARTICLES (SHIP'S).—The name Ship's Articles is given to the agreement under which the crew of any ship must be engaged.

No seaman can be engaged to serve on a ship, except on ships of less than 80 tons registered tonnage engaged in coastal trade, unless upon an agreement in a form which has been specified by the Board of Trade. The agreement must state the nature, or, as far as practicable, the duration of the voyage, or its maximum period, and any places to which the voyage is not to extend, the number and description of the crew, the time when each seaman is to be on board to begin work, the capacity in which he is to serve, his wages, the scale of provisions to which he is entitled, and any regulations as to conduct on board, or as to fines or short allowance of provisions which may be imposed as a punishment. The Agreement must be signed by the Master of the ship before it is signed by the seaman.

Foreign-going Ships.—Where the ship is a foreign-going ship, that is, where it is bound to some place outside the United Kingdom and the Continent of Europe between the river Elbe and Brest, the agreement must be signed in the presence of the Superintendent of the Port where the seamen are engaged. He must have the agreement read over and explained to each seaman, before he signs it, and must witness his signature. The agreement may be for one voyage, or if the voyages of the ship average less than 6 months in length may be for two or more voyages. Such agreements are known as running agreements. A running agreement must not extend beyond the next following 30th day of June or 31st day of December after the signature, or the first arrival of the ship at her port of destination in the United Kingdom after that date, or the discharge of the cargo on arrival there.

Home Trade Ships.—In the case of agreements with the crew of home trade ships the crew may, if the Master wishes, be engaged before the Superintendent as in the case of foreign going ships, but if this is not done the Master himself, either before the ship puts to sea or as soon afterwards as possible, must read the agreement and explain it to each seaman, who must sign it in the presence of a witness.

At the commencement of every voyage a copy of the agreement must be posted up in some part of the ship where the crew can see it.

When seamen are engaged in a British possession abroad the agreement must either be made before the Superintendent of the Port or a Customs Officer, or it must be sanctioned by the Consular Officer. (*See* MERCHANT SHIPPING.)

ASSAULT.—An assault strictly speaking is an attempt to commit a forcible crime against the person. If it results in an actual striking or violent or insulting touching, it becomes a battery. For an act to amount to an assault it must be more than a mere threat. It has been held that if a person presents an unloaded firearm at another in a threatening way, such an act, if the person at whom it is presented does not know that it is unloaded, is an assault.

An assault is both a crime and a civil wrong. The person assaulted may, at his option, prosecute for the crime in a Criminal Court or sue in a Civil Court for the damage he has suffered.

Assault, as a crime, may be of various kinds. An assault unaccompanied by serious circumstances is called a common assault. If accompanied by circumstances of indecency it is called an indecent assault. There are also assaults with intent to murder, to do grievous bodily harm, or to commit a felony or other crime. In the case of a common assault a Police Court can inflict a punishment of two months' imprisonment or a fine not exceeding £5, and require the offender to enter into a recognizance to keep the peace for twelve months.

It is a good defence to a prosecution or action for assault to shew that the acts complained of were done in lawful protection of persons or property, and were necessary for that purpose, and did not in the circumstances involves force that was out of proportion to the violence offered. (*See* BATTERY.)

ASSESSMENT COMMITTEE.—

(For the subject of rating generally see "RATING" and the references given thereunder).

An assessment committee exists in every assessment area; the members being appointed by the rating authority of the area and the county council. The members are appointed for a term that must not exceed five years and they must not receive any remuneration in respect of their services. A member cannot take any part when the matter to be determined concerns property of which he is the owner or occupier; and a person who is a member of any committee dealing with the preparation of the valuation list is not qualified to be a member of the assessment committee. With the exception of a provision requiring a quorum of three, the committee has power to decide how their proceedings shall be conducted. The minutes of the committee have to be open to the public for inspection without payment of any fee. The committee may sue or be sued in the name of the clerk.

The assessment committee has to revise and amend the draft valuation list. The rating authority prepares the draft list and deposits it for public inspection at the offices of the authority. Notice is given that the list has been so deposited; the notice will state how, and by what date, objections must be made. Persons who wish to object to the draft list must then lodge their objections with the assessment committee within twenty-five days from the date of deposit. The assessment committee then holds meetings for considering these objections. Fourteen days notice must be given to the objector, the occupier, if he did not lodge the objection, and the rating authority. They are all entitled to be heard and call witnesses.

When the committee have come to a decision on an objection, notice of the decision must be sent to the same persons. If necessary the draft list will be altered. The committee may also make alterations although there is no objection lodged with them; if this is done any person aggrieved by such alteration must be given fourteen days within which to lodge an objection. Lastly the committee have to approve the draft list by a signed certificate. The list is then returned to the rating authority who deposit the list at their office where it is open for inspection.

The above provisions are those applying to committees outside the Metropolitan area; those within the area are governed by very similar provisions. Notices must be in writing and sent by post; they must specify the grounds of objection and the correction in the list that is desired. They must be lodged within twenty-five days of deposit. When an assessment committee in the area has made any alteration in the list, the list must be redeposited after approval. Then after public notice has been given, objections to the alteration may be lodged within seven days.

ASSESSOR (INSURANCE).—

When an event has happened giving rise to a claim against an Insurance Company under an Insurance policy—e.g. a fire—the exact extent of the claim and the amount which the Insurance Company should pay are usually arrived at by persons called Assessors. One of these will represent the Insured person and the other the insurance company. After examining the premises or goods which have been damaged by the fire these assessors will agree the amount of the claim.

ASSIGNATION (SCOTS LAW).—

When rights under a contract are transferred from one person to another the transaction is called an assignation and is equivalent to the assignment (q.v.) in English law. The assignation should be by a deed and must be intimated to the debtor. There is no distinction in Scots Law between legal and equitable assignments.

ASSIGNMENT.—

When A and B have made a contract under which A is bound to do something for B—e.g. to pay him £100— it is in some cases possible for B to arrange with C, a third person, that A shall do the act or pay the money to C instead of to B. This is known as an assignment to C of B's rights under the contract—i.e. of a chose in action (q.v.). B is called the assignor and C the assignee.

The arrangement may be made in either of two ways. Firstly A, B, and C may meet and may agree that B's rights shall be transferred to C. This is not really an assignment for, since A's consent has been obtained, it is a new contract under which A has agreed to do for C what he had previously agreed to do for B. This is known as

Novation. Secondly, without C's consent B may transfer to C the rights which he previously had against A. This is known as an assignment. It is not every right which can be assigned in this way but only rights in which it may be said that it makes no difference to A whether he does the acts to B or to C. This will usually be the case where B has done all that he has agreed to do under his contract with A. Thus, if B agrees to sell to A 100 bags of flour for £100, B cannot without C's consent transfer the contract to C so that C may be entitled to deliver the 100 bags of flour to A and then to claim £100. A is entitled to get his flour from B and it may be quite a different matter for him if he gets it from C, who may not supply such good flour. If, however, B has delivered the flour to A so that all remains of the contract is A's duty to pay £100, B may then transfer the right to receive the £100 to C.

Legal Assignment.—The most satisfactory method of assigning an obligation of this kind is by what is called a legal assignment. In this the person to whom the debt is due signs a written document transferring it to the assignee. It is also necessary that written notice of the assignment should be given to the debtor, although his consent, as has been seen above, is not required. If a debt is assigned to more than one person, the one entitled to the money is not the one whose assignment was first made but the person who first gives notice to the debtor. In a legal assignment the assignment must be absolute. This means that it must not be subject to any condition for, if B assigned the debt of £100 to C "provided that certain goods which C had agreed to sell to B were found to be satisfactory," A would not know whether he ought to pay his money to B or to C until he had satisfied himself that the goods were satifactory; and, if he paid to C and the goods turned out not to be satisfactory, he would have to pay again to B. This is considered to be an unfair burden to put upon the debtor for he is entitled to know beyond all doubt to whom he must pay the money.

A legal assignment must not be by way of charge. This does not mean that a debt cannot be assigned in security for money due by the assignor, but that it must be a complete legal assignment and that it must not merely have effect if the debt is not paid when due.

When an assignment complies with the above rules—i.e. is a legal assignment—the assignee (C in the illustration taken) may sue A for the money in his own name if A does not pay. In cases, however, where the assignment has not been made as above, it may still be effective, and although C may not be able to sue A in his own name he can compel B to allow him to sue in his (B's) name. An assignment of this kind is called an equitable assignment and it may be good although the assignment is subject to some condition and is not absolute.

The Assignee's rights.—In all cases of assignment the assignee takes "subject to equities." This means that he cannot be in a better position towards the debtor than was the person from whom he got the debt. Thus, if A in the illustration above had some answer to B's claim for £100, either, for example, because the flour which had been supplied was not up to contract quality, or because he had been induced to enter into the contract by fraud, or because B owed him some money on another transaction, A could claim to take advantage of these defences as against C and could only be required to pay to him the same amount as he really owed to B.

The effect of notice in a legal assignment is somewhat different from its effect in the case of an equitable assignment. In both cases once the debtor has received notice of the assignment he must pay his debt to the assignee and not to his original creditor, but if *before he receives notice* he has already paid it to the creditor he cannot be compelled to pay it over again to the assignee.

In the case of a legal assignment, however, notice is necessary in order to complete the assignment as between the assignor and assignee—but in the case of equitable assignment the assignment is complete as between assignor and assignee as soon as the agreement has been entered into regardless of whether notice has, or has not, been given to the debtor.

What cannot be assigned.—There are certain rights which cannot be assigned at all. Thus a mere right of action for damages either for breach of contract or for tort cannot be assigned. There are also certain rights which require to be assigned in certain formal ways. Thus Policies of Insurance or Marine Insurance must be assigned in forms specified by law, and shares in Companies are assigned by transfer in accordance with the Articles of Association (q.v.) of the Company followed by registration of the transfer in the books of the Company.

There is a type of assignment to which entirely different rules apply and that is the assignment of rights under what is known as a negotiable instrument (q.v.) such as a bill of exchange, cheque, or promissory note. The important distinction here is that the assignee for value of rights under a negotiable instrument (e.g. an endorsee) is not affected by any rights which the debtor may have against the assignor i.e. does not take subject to equities as mentioned above. (*See* HOLDER IN DUE COURSE.)

Assignment of liabilities.—It should be noticed that all that has been said above applies to the assignment of rights only and not to the assignment of liabilities. Thus, if A owes B £100 he cannot without B's consent transfer his obligation to pay to C in such a way that B can no longer claim the money from A but must claim it from C. The reason for this is obvious for, though in the case of assignment of rights it may not matter very much to A whether he pays his £100 to B or to some assignee, it obviously may be a very different matter to B in the case of an assignment of liabilities, if instead of being able to sue A (who may be a wealthy man) he can only sue C (who may be penniless.) Of course, if B consented to the transfer of the obligation to C there would be a new contract, but this is a Novation and not an assignment proper.

In some cases there may seem to be an apparent exception to this rule, as where A undertakes to do work for B, as to repair his motor car, and then sends the job out to be done by another person. A may be entitled to do this if he has not been chosen to do the work because of any special skill which he has; but this is not true assignment, for A still remains liable to B if the person to whom he has sent the work does not do it well.

Assignment by Law.—In the cases we have considered the assignment of the rights have all been brought about by the voluntary act of the creditor. Assignment may also be effected by the operation of law without any act of the creditor. Assignments of this kind take place in two cases:

1. Where a person acquired property and thereby comes under an obligation to do certain acts relating to the property, not because he has agreed to do them but because the person who originally acquired the property and from whom he has received it agreed to do these acts. Assignments of this kind occur when a lease is transferred by the Lessee to some third person. That third person will then be liable to the Landlord for the obligations in the Lease. (*See* ASSIGNMENT OF LEASE.) The same rule may also hold where a person purchases the freehold, that is, the ownership of land, and where a previous owner has undertaken certain obligations with some other person relating to the land e.g. has agreed not to build above a certain height on it, or not to use premises on the land for carrying on a business. Such obligations are known as covenants running with the land.

2. When a person dies or becomes bankrupt all his rights and liabilities will in the first case pass to his executor or administrator, and in the second case to his Trustee in Bankruptcy. These rights and liabilities will include rights of action to which the deceased or bankrupt was entitled and also obligations by which he was bound, that is, both rights and liabilities. Even in these cases, however, contracts which require some special skill or personal service from the deceased or bankrupt cannot be enforced against the executors or the trustee, nor can they claim to perform the contract and earn the money. Thus they could not insist on painting a picture which the deceased or the bankrupt had agreed to paint.

General assignment of book-debts.—When a person carrying on a business makes an assignment of the book-debts owed to him and is later adjudicated bankrupt, the trustee in bankruptcy is not bound by the assignment as to any debts not paid at the commencement of the bankruptcy, unless the assignment has been registered as if it were a bill of sale. (q.v.)

This will not apply to assignments of debts which are due at the date of the assignment from debtors who are specified in the assignment, or which are growing due under contracts specified in the assignment, or to debts which are assigned on the transfer of a business in good faith and for value or assigned for the benefit of creditors generally.

Garnishee.—The process by which a creditor who has obtained a judgment for his debt takes in payment any money due to his debtor by other persons is also an assignment. (*See* ATTACHMENT OF DEBTS; CONTRACT; GARNISHEE.)

ASSIGNMENT OF LEASE.—The parties to a Lease are the Landlord who has granted it and the Tenant to whom it has been granted. Either of these may assign to some other person the interest which he has. When the Landlord assigns he is said to assign his reversion.

An assignment should be distinguished from a sub-lease. There is an assignment when a tenant transfers to some other person either the whole or part of the property which has been let to him for the *whole period remaining* of the lease; there is a sub-lease when the Tenant, himself acting as a Landlord, lets to another person the whole or part of the premises for *some period shorter then the remaining period* of the lease. Thus, if A has a lease of premises of which 5 years are unexpired and he transfers the remaining 5 years of the lease to B, that is an assignment; but if he grants to B a lease of the premises for some period less than 5 years, even though it be 5 years all but a day, this is a sub-lease.

Can a tenant assign?—Every tenant who is not a tenant merely at will or at sufferance is entitled to assign or sub-let, unless he is expressly forbidden to do so by the terms of his letting, or unless there are some restrictions imposed upon him by law, as is the case where premises are held under the Rent Restrictions Act. It is usual to provide in leases that a Tenant must not assign, but almost invariably there is a further provision enabling him to do so if he obtains the consent in writing of his Landlord. Where there is this further provision the Landlord will be bound to give the consent so long as the proposed new tenant to whom the assignment is to take place is a suitable tenant and a responsible person financially. Until 1927 the Landlord could refuse to give his consent unless the above words were expressly inserted in the Lease, but now they are always implied and the Landlord cannot refuse.

Tenant not released by assignment. —The assignment must be made by a Deed, that is, a document not only signed by the tenant who is assigning but also bearing his seal. Tenants should remember that by making an assignment they do not relieve themselves from liability under the lease.

It is always implied in the assignment, even if not expressly stated, that the assignee should be liable to the Landlord for the payment of rent and for all covenants contained in the Lease.

But if the assignee is unable to pay the rent, or if he breaks the covenants, e.g. to repair of the premises, and is liable to damages which he cannot pay, the tenant himself will be liable to the Landlord, although he may have had nothing to do with the premises since he assigned them. Thus, where a tenant wishes to get rid of premises before the end of his lease, it is always more satisfactory if he can induce the Landlord to accept a surrender of the Tenant's lease and to grant a new lease to the person who is to take over the premises. If this is done the Tenant's liability ceases.

Liability of Assignee.—The assignee of a lease is liable to the Landlord for the rent in the lease and for all covenants relating to the land contained in the lease, such as a covenant to repair, for these covenants are said to run with the land, that is, to be binding on any person who may hold the land even though he has not expressly contracted with the Landlord to carry them out. In the case of covenants which do not run with the land, that is, covenants to do some positive act, such as to erect some new building on the land, the assignee will also be bound if the covenant in the lease was made after the 1st of January 1926. Covenants of a purely personal nature not relating to the land at all will not be binding upon the assignee.

When Assignee himself assigns.— The assignee will be liable only during the time while he holds the land, unless he enters into any contract with the Landlord to carry out the covenants of the lease. If he does, there will be what is called "privity of contract" between himself and the original Landlord. So long as he does not enter into any contract of this kind there is said to be "privity of estate" only between himself and the Landlord so long as he occupies the land; but once he ceases to do this the "privity of estate" is gone. Thus, if an assignee himself assigns the remainder of the lease to some other person, he will be in a position very different from that of the original tenant, for he will not be liable for any of the covenants in the lease after the time of the assignment. Thus, if A is a Tenant and assigns a lease to B and B after some time assigns the lease to C, B will be liable for the rent and other covenants after the date of A's assignment to him and before the date of his assignment to C; but he will not be liable for anything after that time, even if C fails to perform them. A

name for a lunatic asylum is mental hospital or institution.

There are now several different types of institution in which it is lawful to detain a person of unsound mind.

(1) Licenced houses. These are houses maintained by private persons for profit; and as no new licences for this type of institution could be granted after 1930 they are not common. All types of persons of unsound mind may be detained in them.

A Judge of Assize attends Church Service before opening the Assizes.

on the other hand, as has been seen, as being the original Tenant to whom the lease was granted, and as having therein agreed to pay the rent and perform the covenants of the lease, will remain liable both while B has the premises and while C has them, if they do not perform the covenants themselves. (*See* LANDLORD AND TENANT.)

ASSIZE.—A Judge of Assize derives his jurisdiction to try cases by virtue of various ancient writs. The old Writ of Assize was one of these, and it provides the name still given to the Court in which a circuit Judge tries cases.

ASYLUMS.—Since 1930 the proper

(2) State institutes. These are institutes maintained by the Board of Control in Lunacy, chiefly for violent patients.

(3) Registered hospitals. A hospital is defined by Act of Parliament as a place where mental patients are cared for without charge. Application for registration must be made to the Board of Control to whom notice of all structural alterations must be given.

(4) Institutes or hospitals maintained by a Local Authority.

(5) Certified houses. Application for certification is made to the Board of Control; and is appropriate when it is desired to run the house for private profit. It should be

noted that only mental defectives (q.v.) may be detained in such certified houses.

(6). Approved nursing homes, houses, etc. Approval must be obtained from the Board of Control and will only be granted where the object is charitable and treatment is provided wholly or partly out of voluntary contributions or donations. Such approved houses, etc., are only permitted to receive mental defectives and voluntary and temporary patients. (*See* CERTIFICATION OF LUNATICS; DETENTION OF LUNATICS.)

(7) Approved persons. If it is desired to receive a voluntary or temporary patient or a mental defective as a single patient, the guardian must be a person approved by the Board of Control. In the case of temporary patients the approval of the Board must also be obtained to the reception of each individual patient.

It is illegal to detain a person of unsound mind (unless he is a criminal lunatic) in any other place. All the places and persons described are subject to the supervision of the Board of Control. The Commissioners of the Board and its Inspectors make regular visits, require reports, and prescribe conditions of diet, accommodation, etc. in addition to being the " licensing " and " approving " Authority. (*See* LUNATIC.)

ATTACHMENT OF DEBTS.—When a debtor owes money to his creditor and the creditor has sued the debtor and established the debt by obtaining a judgment, the creditor is given by the law various rights to enable him to make his Judgment effective by seizing the debtor's property. These rights are known as Execution and enable the creditor to seize inter alia the debtor's goods or land. If however the debtor has certain sums of money which are owed to him, the creditor may obtain an order from the court directing the persons who owe money to the debtor to pay it to the creditor instead, in satisfaction of his debt. This process is known as attachment of debts. It would, for example, enable a creditor to obtain payment of money which was in the hands of the banker of his debtor in the debtor's bank account. The order made by the Court is called a Garnishee Order (q.v.).

It is not all debts which may be attached. The wages of a servant, labourer or workman cannot be taken (but other wages or salaries may be once they are due) nor can old age pensions, or police pensions, or money which a husband is bound to pay to his wife as alimony or maintenance. Half-pay of officers in the Army and Navy cannot be taken nor can deposits in the Post Office Savings Bank. A debt cannot be attached before it is due. Where the debt owed to the debtor exceeds the amount of the Judgment debt of the creditor, so much of it as is necessary to pay off the Judgment debt may be taken. (*See* GARNISHEE.)

ATTACHMENT (PERSONAL).—Attachment of the person is a process for summarily punishing those who commit criminal contempt of court or refuse to obey an order of the court. Another process is committal. By means of these two the Court is able to imprison anyone who refuses to obey it or attempts to interfere with the administration of justice.

The two processes are now equally applicable to most cases of contempt, but as a general rule a man should be attached for not doing what he is ordered to do, and committed for doing what he ought not to do. In each case he is sent to prison but the procedure is different. Of the two, attachment probably involves the less expense. The order for attachment is made by a judge and sent to the sheriff who has to arrest the offender and imprison him. If the sheriff cannot find him the order may be carried out by the sergeant-at-arms. Where the order is for committal it is carried out by an officer of the court called the tipstaff.

The person attached remains in prison until the court authorises him to be discharged. If he has "purged his contempt," for example, by obeying the order which he had previously disobeyed, he can himself apply to be discharged, or, if the Court thinks he has been punished sufficiently, it may discharge him without this. If his contempt consisted in refusing to obey an order to pay money, he cannot be kept in prison longer than a year. (*See* CONTEMPT OF COURT.)

Men and women who are imprisoned in London under these processes by the High Court are usually sent to Brixton and Holloway respectively. They receive special privileges and are not treated as criminals. The official solicitor is responsible to the Lord Chancellor for seeing that they are not being detained unreasonably.

ATTAINDER.—An Act of Attainder

was, in former times, a means of securing condemnation for some crime by Act of Parliament. During the reigns of the Tudor and Stuart Sovereigns it was not infrequently used for the purpose of obtaining the execution of political offenders. Attainder has not been resorted to since the eighteenth century.

ATTAINT.—When a person was sentenced to death or outlawry he was said to be "attaint," namely, stained or blackened. The effect in law was twofold. It involved forfeiture of property and "corruption of the blood." This last prevented him from inheriting property or any other person claiming property through him. The consequences of attaint, however, were gradually removed from English law and are now of merely historical interest.

ATTESTATION.—When any person executes a deed by signing his name and impressing his seal or, in modern practice, touching a wafer which is already placed on the deed, the execution is witnessed by the signature of a person, called the attesting witness, who was present at the time these acts were done. His signature is called the Attestation of the Deed. He signs his name at the side of the name of the person who is executing the deed, which is said to be "signed sealed and delivered by the above named AB in the presence of XY."

When a Deed is executed by a Company the company's seal is impressed on the deed in the presence of some officials of the company. The exact procedure to be followed and the officials who must sign as witnesses are usually laid down in the company's Articles of Association, but although these usually provide that the seal must be witnessed by two Directors and the Secretary, it is now always sufficient in England if the names of one director and the secretary appear whatever may be the provision in the articles.

In the case of Wills it is necessary that the signature of the Testator should either be made or acknowledged by the testator to be his own before two witnesses. Both these witnesses must sign their names as witnesses and each must be present when the other signs. The testator must also be present. A person who witnesses a will cannot take any property in the will and any bequest in the will to that person or to his wife (or her husband if the witness is a woman) will be void.

It is never necessary that the person signing the document should actually do so in the presence of the witnesses, and it will be enough if after he has signed it he states in the presence of the witnesses that the signature is his.

There is a widespread belief that a wife cannot witness her husband's signature. This is not the case, but if the document is a will, she will be unable to take any benefit under it, although the validity of the will is not otherwise affected. There is no reason however why she should not witness her husband's signature to other documents. (*See* DEED.)

ATTESTATION (SCOTS LAW).— The formalities required in the execution of probative writings in Scots Law are more strict than in English Law. When a document is attested the party to it must sign each page and also at the end of the document. In almost all cases the signature must be witnessed by two witnesses who sign on the last page. They do not require to sign every page. They must be over 14 years of age and must either see the Deed that is signed or must hear the person executing it acknowledge that the signature is his.

At the end of the deed an attesting clause is inserted describing the witnesses. It is the practice for witnesses in Scotland always to write the word "Witness" after their names.

It is no longer necessary to name in a deed the person who wrote it or typed it, or to specify the number of pages, and, if the deed is signed by the granter at the end and by two witnesses, it may be proved to be valid although some other formality has been omitted, e.g. although the granter has not signed on each page. A will in Scotland is attested in the same way as any other deed.

Where the person making the deed is blind or cannot write he may execute it in front of some law agent, notary, justice of the peace or a parish minister who will sign on his behalf after having read the deed over to him. The witnesses sign the deed in the ordinary way. (*See* HOLOGRAPH; WRITTEN CONTRACTS [SCOTS LAW].)

ATTORNEY-GENERAL.—The law officers of the Crown are two in number— the Attorney-General and the Solicitor-General. As such the Attorney-General has to advise the Government on legal questions of importance and to represent the Crown in Court. He also represents the public at large where their interests are at stake. Again, his sanction is necessary before certain prosecutions can be commenced or a criminal appeal to the House of Lords heard. He is head of the Bar of England and takes precedence over all other Barristers. The Attorney-General is not a permanent official. His appointment is a political one and he is, of course, a Member of Paraliament. He is frequently required to take part in debates in the House of Commons and to assist the Government with his legal knowledge. He has also to account to the House of Commons, if required, as to the performance of his duties.

ATTORNMENT.—An attornment is the act by which the tenant of land acknowledges a new landlord when a change takes place. He "puts one person in the place of another as his landlord." It may take the form of a written document but this is not necessary, and any act done by the tenant which unequivocally recognises the change —as by paying rent to the new landlord— will be sufficient. When the landlord of a property assigns his reversion—i.e. transfers to some other person the rights which he has to receive rent and after the lease has terminated the right to possession of the land—the attornment of the tenant is necessary to enable the new landlord to claim rent and to enforce the other provisions of the lease. (*See* Assignment of Lease; Landlord and Tenant.)

AUDITOR.—Every Company whether private or public is required by law to have an auditor. This auditor does not need to be an accountant although he usually is. No Director or Officer of the Company, nor any partner of, or any person employed by, an officer of the company can be an auditor, except in the case of a private company where a partner or employee of an officer may hold the office. When it is proposed to change the auditor notice of this intention must be given 14 days before the Annual General Meeting. This is to prevent the directors getting rid of auditors who may be unpopular with the directors, because they are taking too firm a line in the interests of the shareholders without giving the shareholders full notice that the auditors are being changed. Each year the auditors prepare a report relating to the financial position of the company and for this purpose they are entitled to access to all the books and papers of the company and to all information and explanations from its officers—i.e. the directors and the secretary.

Duties.—The general duties of an auditor are to safeguard the interests of the shareholders and to see that there is no irregularity in the dealings of the directors with the property of the company. It is very difficult to state exactly how far an auditor is bound to carry his investigations and the position has been summed up by saying it is his duty to be a "watch dog" and not a "blood hound," meaning that he is bound to be on the alert to detect anything suspicious but not bound to investigate every transaction until his suspicion are aroused. If an auditor wilfully makes any false statement in any report he is guilty of a criminal offence.

The Kylsant Case and "Secret Reserves."—The auditor usually states in his certificate that the accounts disclose the true position of the company and that he has been given all the information he has required. Questions have arisen recently in cases where a company has created in prosperous years what are called Secret Reserves by entering its assets in its Balance Sheets at less than their true value. The effect of this is to make it appear that the company has made less profits than is in fact the case. When it is desired later in a time of bad trade, the assets can once more be shown at their true value and a sum of money will thus be released for the payment of dividends, even though there may not have been a trading profit.

It has been suggested that an auditor should state in his report that such secret reserves are being created, but most auditors consider that this is not desirable and that it is in the interests of the shareholders that the true position of the company should be withheld from them. This would not, of course, apply in cases where the balance sheets shewed the company's position as being more prosperous than in fact was, and no auditor would then grant a certificate. These questions came into prominence in the prosecution of Lord Kylsant arising out of his management of the affairs of the Royal Mail Steam Packet Company.

AUCTIONEERS.—Auctioneers are persons who conduct auctions. No special qualifications are required and their duties are laid down by the Auctioneers' Act, 1845, which enacts that during an auction the auctioneer's full name and address must be displayed conspicuously in the auction rooms under penalty of £50.

Important provisions of this Act relate to the Auctioneer's licence which can be obtained by written application at Somerset House or at the applicant's local Inland Revenue Office. £10 duty is payable. The licence is annual from July 5th and should be renewed at least ten days before that date each year. With the exception of persons auctioning fish at its first landing place, persons auctioning under a distress warrant for non-payment of rent or tithes under £2 and officers of the Court, every person who acts as an auctioneer must take out an auctioneer's licence for himself. For conducting a sale without a licence the fine is £100. Other licences (e.g.) Excise, Hawker's must be taken out in addition whenever necessary. At the time of the sale the licence must be produced on demand to any officer of excise or of stamps and taxes or £10 deposited with the officer. In default the auctioneer may be arrested and imprisoned by a justice for a period of one month. The £10 may be imposed in addition as a penalty, but if it is deposited, it can be recovered by the auctioneer on production of his licence in good order.

The Auctioneer and the Vendor.—A man may auction his own property or some other person's. In the latter event he is the agent of the Vendor (i.e. the seller) and the ordinary rules of principal and agent (q.v.) apply. Unless there is an express agreement to the contrary the auctioneer has authority to sell according to the custom of auctioneers and to settle the conditions of the sale, which should be made known to bidders by exhibition in the auction rooms. In so doing he must act with the skill and knowledge of a competent auctioneer otherwise he may be liable to the vendor for negligence. The agency may be ended at any time before the property is finally knocked down, and the auctioneer cannot continue the auction even if he has incurred expense, nor can he at any time pass over his authority as an auctioneer to someone else.

An auctioneer is a Bailee (q.v.) for reward of the vendor's goods and, as such, must take reasonable care of them and give them back on demand—except where his charges and remuneration are unpaid for he has then, by custom, a lien or charge on the goods, or on the purchase money for the amount due to him. In addition, he must not give the goods to the purchaser until the purchase money, of which he is a trustee, is paid. If he does so and the purchaser defaults, he himself will have to pay the vendor.

An auctioneer may buy the goods but only with the vendor's consent.

Where the law requires a memorandum in writing of the contract (see WRITTEN CONTRACT) the auctioneer must see that this is signed so as to bind the purchaser as well as the vendor. For this purpose he is the agent of both parties except when selling on his own behalf. He must not get his clerk to sign on behalf of the purchaser but must do so himself at the time of the sale.

Remuneration is paid to the auctioneer in accordance with any arrangement made between him and the vendor. If there is no such agreement he is entitled to make a fair and reasonable charge. In most cases he receives an agreed percentage of the proceeds of sale. The auctioneer is entitled to his remuneration when he introduces a customer and the vendor sells privately. He has a further right to be indemnified for expenses or damages which he incurs by reason of the auction but all these rights are lost by his negligence or misconduct.

Auctioneer and Purchaser.—If the auctioneer does not disclose the vendor as his principal he will, according to the ordinary law of agency, be liable personally to the purchaser, first as if he were himself the vendor, and in all cases he may be liable to the purchaser for breach of warranty of authority if he sells without authority, and for fraud. So long as the auctioneer's charges are unpaid he may, by reason of his lien, sue the purchaser for the price of the goods.

The price is usually paid to the auctioneer though he has no implied authority to receive the price of land. Payment should be in cash where possible as the auctioneer cannot take cheques without permission from the vendor, and where he lacks this authority, payment by cheque will not discharge the purchaser. Any deposit can be paid by cheque to the auctioneer if he will take it. He is then a stakeholder of the deposit.

Statements by Auctioneers.—These may be mere puff or may be relied on by the purchaser. The dividing line is difficult to draw, but if the statements are actually misleading the purchaser can sue the auctioneer for fraud or misrepresentation, or the vendor for breach of warranty, if they are such as to be part of the contract. (*See* CONTRACT.)

An auctioneer may sue for trespass (q.v.) to, or conversion (q.v.) of, the goods. He, himself, is liable for conversion if he sells without the consent of the true owner. An auction room is not necessarily a market overt. (*See* MARKET OVERT.)

AUTREFOIS ACQUIT.—Once a person has been acquitted by a jury of a crime he cannot be tried again on the same charge. Should he be brought to trial again, when asked to plead to the charge he should say "Autrefois Acquit." If he establishes this plea he cannot be tried.

AUTREFOIS CONVICT.—This is a plea which can be raised in bar of trial by anyone who has already been convicted of a crime. Its effect is similar to that of "Autrefois Acquit.

AVERAGE.—Average may either be particular average or general average. In the case of particular average, when loss is sustained by any property or goods, the loss must fall on the owner of the property or goods; but in general average the loss must be shared by the owners of other property or goods which were not damaged in any way but were saved from damage by the destruction or loss of the first goods. This usually arises in insurance, as when in putting out a fire in a warehouse some goods may be damaged by water, but the rest of the goods in the warehouse are saved by this means at the price of the damage which the first goods have suffered.

The term is most frequently met with in the case of goods being carried at sea and the principle is of very great antiquity, being found among the ancient Greeks. It has always been recognised that, if a ship, for example, is in danger of sinking and in order to lighten the ship some part of the cargo is thrown overboard and the ship is thereby

saved, it is only fair that the owners of the other goods in the cargo, whose property has been saved by the sacrifice of the goods thrown overboard, should bear part of the loss suffered by the owners of those goods. Further, the ship herself has been saved by the sacrifice and her owners therefore should also bear part of the loss.

The Ship, the Cargo, the Freight.—In practice there are usually considered to be three interests affected—the owners of the ship, the owners of the cargo, and the persons who will receive freight if the ship completes her voyage and the cargo saved is delivered. These last may be the owners of the ship, who would thus have a double interest, or may be charterers who have chartered the ship and have then contracted to carry goods for others. Take a case where a fire has broken out on board a ship worth £10,000 and belonging to A. In order to extinguish the fire one of the holds is flooded and cargo in that hold belonging to B to the value of £3,000 is totally destroyed by the flooding. On board the ship in other holds is cargo belonging to C and D to the value of £5,000 each. The ship is under charter to E who will receive £1,000 in freight on the cargo saved but has lost £200 in freight on the cargo destroyed. After the fire the ship is able to proceed to her destination and deliver the cargo belonging to C and D. Had this cargo been lost E would have received no freight.

The total value of the interests affected will therefore be:

A (the ship)	£10,000
B's cargo (lost)	3,000
C's cargo (saved)	5,000
D's cargo do.	5,000
E (the freight)	1,000
E (freight lost)	200
	£24,200

All must contribute to the loss of £3,000 to B and of £200 to E in proportion to their interests. Thus B himself must bear 30/242 parts, C and D each 50/242 parts, A (the ship) 100/242 parts, and E 10/242 parts in respect of the freight saved and 2/242 parts in respect of the freight lost.

Before this principle of a general average loss can apply, it is necessary that the loss should have been incurred to avoid a danger which threatened interests other than that of the person who has suffered the loss. Thus, if there was a fire which never endangered more than a small part of the cargo, damage to that part caused by water used to put out the fire would not be a general average loss.

Loss must be intentional.—Again, the loss must have been caused by some voluntary act. Thus, if the ship were about to founder but were saved by some of the cargo being accidentally washed overboard, not deliberately thrown overboard, there is no general average loss. If, in the illustration first taken, some of B's cargo had been damaged by the fire before any water was let into the hold, then the damage so caused would have to be met by B alone.

The thing thrown overboard or sacrificed must have some value and not be already valueless, so that if goods which have already been ruined by sea water are jettisoned there is no general average loss. Of course if the loss does not result in the saving of the ship or cargo and all are destroyed, no question of general average will arise.

Cases of particular average arise where, for example, the mast of a ship is carried away, or where cargo is washed overboard. In such cases the persons who have suffered loss cannot require the others to share the loss. (*See* Carriage by Sea.)

AVERAGE CLAUSE.—It is frequently provided in an insurance policy against such risks as fire or burglary that the insurance company shall not be liable to pay the full amount of the loss, where part only of the goods insured have been stolen or damaged, but shall only pay the proportion of the loss which the amount of insurance bears to the value of the property. This is known as an average clause. Thus if goods worth £5,000 are insured under an average policy for £3,000 and are damaged by fire to the extent of £2,000, the insurance company will only be liable to pay £1,200. The total goods are only insured for three-fifths of their value and are therefore regarded as being insured as to three-fifths and uninsured as to two-fifths. Thus the damaged goods were also insured as to three-fifths and uninsured as to two-fifths. Therefore the insurance company should only pay for three-fifths of the loss, namely, £1,200.

AVIATION.—M. Bleriot crossed the Channel in the year 1909 and it was at once obvious to lawyers that it would be idle for individual countries to make laws as to the regulation of aviation, unless there was some firm international basis on which to raise a legal superstructual. In 1919, therefore, a convention was signed between the principal nations of the world, acknowledging that every nation has the exclusive right to regulate aviation within and in the air space over its territory. Every State, however, grants freedom of passage over its territory to aircraft of foreign nations under certain conditions. Aircraft wishing to fly over the territory of a foreign State must comply with the ordinances of that country as to carriage of goods, route, and prohibited areas and must bear the name and address of its owner, nationality and registration marks, licences, and so forth in the same manner as a motorcar being taken abroad.

Furthermore, no visiting aircraft is allowed passage without a special dispensation from the visited country if it is (i) carrying explosives or other warlike munitions; (ii) a military, customs or police aircraft; or (iii) flying in competition with the aircraft of the visited country in commercial transport. To give effect to this convention is of course impossible without the goodwill of all the nations, but in practice it has been found that satisfaction has always been obtained by forwarding complaints through the usual diplomatic channels whenever an aircraft of a particular nationality has offended against the international code.

The Air Navigation Act, 1920.—The statute which regulates aviation in this country is the Air Navigation Act, 1920, which was passed to give effect in English law to the international convention referred to above. By this Act it is provided that no one shall be liable for trespass or nuisance merely for flying over someone else's land, provided they fly at a reasonable height, so that it will be seen that although a country owns the air space above its territory, the rights of a private landowner cease when a "reasonable height" above his estate is attained. The Act further provides—and this is important—that whenever any accident occurs or any damage is done and an aircraft is involved, the aircraft is liable, and is presumed to be alone at fault unless it is shown by evidence that the other party was to blame. This enactment places a heavy burden upon aircraft, but its fairness will not be questioned. The interesting question was recently raised as to what would happen if two aircraft collided. In one case, where the collision took place between two aeroplanes one of which was stationary on the ground, the principle was held to apply instead of the ordinary rules of negligence.

Dangerous Flying.—The other section of the Act which most nearly affects the general public is that which provides that, where an aircraft is flown in such a manner as to be the cause of unnecessary danger to any person or property on land or water, the pilot or person in charge of the aircraft, and also the owner, unless he proves that the aircraft was so flown without his knowledge or consent, shall be liable to a fine not exceeding £200 or 6 months with or without hard labour or both. Prosecutions under this section are not infrequent and are chiefly brought in respect of an aeroplane which has been flying too low.

Carriage by Air Act, 1932.—There is one more statute which must be briefly noticed. This is the Carriage by Air Act, 1932, which was passed as the result of an international convention in Warsaw, and which as yet applies only to international traffic and not to internal transport, although provision is made to extend the ambit of the Act by Orders in Council when necessary.

The principal points to be kept in mind are as follows:

The carrier must deliver to each passenger a luggage and a passenger ticket, and if he does not do so he may not exclude or limit his ordinary common law liability.

Every consignor of goods must make out an "air consignment note" containing all relevant particulars, but its absence, etc., does not affect the validity of the contract of carriage. The consignor may stop the goods in the course of transit at any time before the consignee becomes entitled to delivery.

The carrier must give the consignee notice as soon as the goods arrive; but if he admits to having lost them, or they have not arrived seven days after the due date, the consignee may sue the carrier.

The carrier is liable for the death or personal injury of each of his passengers, up to a limit of 125,000 francs per head, unless it has been otherwise specially agreed.

He is liable for the loss of the goods while in his charge to a limit of 250 francs per kilogram, unless a special declaration of value has been made. He is also liable for the loss or damage of objects of which the passenger himself takes charge up to a limit of 5,000 francs per passenger. He is also liable to pay damages for delay.

Under certain circumstances he is, however, exempted from liability. These are: (i) If he has taken all necessary measures to avoid the damage, or if it was impossible to avoid the damage. (ii) In the case of goods, etc., if the damage was caused by negligent pilotage, or negligent navigation, and all other necessary steps have been taken. (iii) If the damage has been caused or contributed to by the negligence of the person injured, the carrier may be in whole or in part exonerated. But damage caused by the wilful misconduct of the carrier, or of his agent acting within the scope of his authority, renders the carrier liable, and he cannot escape by relying on any favourable provision of the Convention. Again, any provision in the contract tending to relieve the carrier of liability or fixing a lower rate of liability is null and void. This is important. If luggage or goods are damaged in transit, a complaint must be made in writing to the carrier within three days at latest in the case of luggage and seven days in the case of goods. In the case of delay 14 days are allowed for complaint.

If the consignor fails to make this complaint in time, he cannot sue, unless the carrier has been guilty of fraud. The right to sue lapses if no action is commenced within two years from the date on which the aircraft arrived, or ought to have arrived, or from the date on which carriage stopped.

Actions for damages must be brought at the option of the plaintiff in the territory of one of the signatories to the convention at one of the following four places:

(i) Where the carrier is ordinarily resident; or

(ii) has his principal place of business; or

(iii) has an establishment at which the contract was made; or

(iv) at the place of destination.

The provisions of this Act should be carefully noted, as they hold good all the world over, save internally in Great Britain.

A British Air Liner shewing the Nationality Mark, " G," and the group of four Registration Letters assigned by the Air Ministry.

Aircraft.—Having dealt with "Aircraft," the next point is to define that mysterious word. It appears to include craft of every kind which is capable of remaining in the air for a reasonable time without falling to the ground, irrespective of whether it has a means of propulsion or no. Thus balloons, kites, gliders, parachutes, are as much aircraft as aeroplanes, seaplanes and airships. The obvious and principal classification of aircraft is into two types, state and private, aircraft used for official and military purposes on the one hand, and aircraft used for private and civil aviation on the other.

Registration.—As there are certain preliminaries which have to be adjusted before a new-bought car may be put upon the road, so with an aeroplane. The first point is to comply with the requirements of nationality and registration. Suppose an aeroplane is purchased in England and subsequently registered here, it becomes *ipso facto* British aircraft. So much for nationality. An application for registration should be made out on the correct form and sent to the Secretary (D.C.A.), Air Ministry, London, W.C.2. A certificate of registration and a registration mark is then granted, the fee for which is £1. 1s. 0d. unless it is bought from a dealer who has already himself registered

it, in which case there is only 5/- to pay. On change of ownership, destruction of the aircraft, and so forth, the registration lapses and the Air Ministry should be notified.

Markings.—The nationality mark of British aircraft is a large G, and the registration marks are a group of four capital letters assigned by the Air Ministry. Other compulsory markings are the name and address of the owner, and the empty and maximum total authorized weight of the machine.

Airworthiness.—No aircraft may fly unless it is certified as airworthy. Certificates are granted by the Air Minister, and applications should be made as in the case of registration, stating the purpose of employment of the aircraft, and stating the required details. The certificate is only valid for the stated period, but is renewable on payment of £5 5s. 0d. Flying trials by an official pilot have to be made, and other stringent conditions complied with before the certificate will be granted. It is more readily obtained in the case of a "subsequent" machine, that is, a machine conforming to the design of another already certificated, than in that of a "type" machine, an individual model, the first of its kind. All aircraft of a public transport nature must be inspected and certified fit for flight within twenty-four hours of each and every trip, thus ensuring that an aircraft which has once been certificated as airworthy shall not subsequently lose that airworthiness.

Documents.—Every aircraft engaged in international aviation has to carry certain documents. These are: certificate of registration, certificate of airworthiness, certificates of competency, licences of the crew, and a log book, in which entries of the times and occurrences of each journey must be made in ink. A wireless licence must be carried, a list of names of the passengers, their passports and so forth, and in the case of British aircraft, a notice about smoking and the items making up the weight of the machine.

Instruments and Lights.—On all flights the following instruments are necessary: an altimeter, an air speed indicator, and a revolution indicator. Every person carried in an open cock-pit must be provided with a safety belt. On flights of more than three miles by radius from the departure point, signalling lights must be carried. On all flights at night, navigation lights of the prescribed kind, which must not be dazzling, and no others, must be carried. If these lights fail, the aircraft is in duty bound to land at once or as soon as possible without danger. The lights prescribed for a flying machine in the air are green on the right, red on the left, visible for at least five miles, and white aft, visible at least three miles from the rear. Various other lights are prescribed in the case of machines anchored or moored, or not under control.

Pilot's Licence.—An applicant for a pilot's licence must be not under 17 years of age and must undergo a medical examination with particular reference to nervous stability. This examination is very thorough and must be carried out in accordance with C. A. Form 61, which is forwarded on completion to the Secretary (D.C.A.) Air Ministry, W.C.2. The would-be pilot may be examined by his own doctor. To obtain an A licence, without which no one may fly, except, of course, a candidate undergoing a test for this purpose, the would-be pilot has to satisfy three conditions. First, he has to pass a practical test in flying: next, a technical examination on the rules for air traffic, the regulations as to lights and signals and kindred subjects, and finally he must show that he has done at least three hours solo flying in the year

preceding his application for a licence. After the candidate has successfully passed these tests, he pays £1 1s. 0d. for his flying test, 5/– for his technical examination and a further 5/– for his licence, and a private pilot's licence is granted to him for the period of twelve months. If an official medical examination has been required, he must pay £1 1s. 0d.

The licence is renewable, and the same fees are then payable save that the medical examination costs 10/6. He is liable on renewal to be called upon to pass once more the tests to which he submitted on applying for the licence.

B Licence.—To obtain a B licence is a much more difficult proposition. The private pilot has in all probability only his own life at stake, while the possessor of a B licence authorizing him to fly public transport aircraft and carry passengers or goods for hire, has a far greater responsibility. The successful candidate must be between the ages of 19 and 45, and must pass a preliminary and a special medical examination, the latter carried out by official doctors, and of extreme thoroughness. He must then pass the usual A licence tests, and in addition accomplish cross country or oversea flights of at least 200 miles, do a left and right hand spin, make forced landings under the eye of an examiner, fly by night at a height of at least 1,500 feet, and give such further practical demonstrations as may be required. He then undergoes a severe technical examination, and must, before his B licence is awarded, prove that he has flown at least 100 hours and made 30 landings within two years.

Other Aircraft Licences.—What has been set out before applies to aeroplanes; the candidates for A and B licences in respect of balloons have to pass similar examinations of varying severity. There are three classes of airship pilots' licences, and the candidate with the aid of experience and more detailed technical knowledge passes in similar fashion from the one to the others. The fee for the B licence flying test for aeroplanes is £10 and £1 1s. 0d. for the medical examination. The technical examination and the licence itself cost 5/–. The B licence is granted for a period of six months to men, and of three months to women, and it is renewable in a manner similar to that of an A licence.

A navigator's licence is difficult to obtain, and requires a knowledge of compasses, navigation by radio-goniometry, flight by dead reckoning, signalling, meteorology, and international air legislation. These licences are of two classes, a first-class licence requiring greater experience as a member of a crew of an aircraft.

A further licence is granted to persons who pass the requisite tests as an engineer, and possession of a ground engineer's licence entitles the possessor to inspect aircraft flying for public service and certify its fitness to start.

Master Pilot's Certificate.— Finally, the expert aviator may obtain a master pilot's certificate. The qualifications for this are difficult to obtain. The candidate must be the holder of a current B licence and in addition a current navigator's licence. Further he must have held his B licence for at least five years, during which he must have flown 1,000 hours as pilot, and must have accomplished 20 cross-country or oversea night flights of not less than one hour each. The Air Ministry may, however, grant a master pilot's certificate at its discretion to a pilot who is possessed of qualifications substantially equal to those set out above. It will thus be seen that a master pilot is an expert at his job.

Rules of the Air.—The most important rules regulating traffic in the air are as follows:

(i) **Taking Off.—**Always take off up-wind. If no wind, in the direction indicated by the landing T. Leave machines on the ground on your left. Do not turn until you are 500 yards from the aerodrome. When turning, bear left.

(ii) When flying by compass along an air traffic route, keep the line 500 yards on your left. When following a line of land

Mr. Justice Avory.

marks, keep it 300 yards on your left. When crossing such a line, do so as fast and as high as possible, and at right angles.

(iii) Proceed with caution in fog. Endeavour to make yourself visible.

(iv) If you are taxi-ing on water you are considered a steam vessel, and must observe the ordinary maritime rules.

(v) Flying machines must always give way to airships and balloons, and airships to balloons, the more mobile giving way to the less mobile.

(vi) Never cross ahead of aircraft to which you are required to give way.

(vii) **Overtake on the Right.** Do not pass by diving.

(viii) If you are crossing the course of another aircraft, give way if he is on your right, otherwise keep on.

(ix) If you are meeting end on, **Keep to the Right.**

(x) Give way to anyone about to land.

(xi) When landing, land upwind.

Customs. — The usual customs formalities must be observed as in any other form of transit and no pilot may leave Great Britain without authority in the shape of a clearance form duly signed by the Customs Officer.

Damage by an R.A.F. Pilot.—If an R.A.F. pilot does damage he may be sued as an individual, but the position of the owner of the damaged property is unattractive. The pilot himself may not be worth suing from a financial point of view, and his superiors will not be liable. If the damage is done during a flight not undertaken in the course of his duty, it is outside the scope of his employment, and he is alone liable. If the damage occurred during an authorized flight, the superiors of the pilot are still not liable as they are all fellow-servants of the Crown, which can do no wrong.

AVORY, Mr. Justice (1851—).— Besides being the Senior Judge of the King's

Bench Division he is perhaps the best-known figure in the Law to-day. As Senior Treasury Counsel at the Central Criminal Court he prosecuted for the Crown in many celebrated trials, among them that of Adolf Beck. When on the Bench, to which he was raised in 1910, he tried the English Blue-beard, Vacquier, Browne and Kennedy, and the Hatry case of 1930.

AWARD.—An Award in an arbitration is the decision or judgment of an arbitrator or arbitrators upon the matters submitted to them. An award is final and conclusive, that is to say, there is no right of appeal from an award and the parties are debarred from litigating upon the same subject matter. The principle upon which this rule is based has been expressed in this way: "You have con-stituted your own tribunal and you are bound by its decisions." The arbitrator must deliver his award within three months of entering upon the reference—i.e. of hear-ing the dispute. Although an award is unappealable, nevertheless the Court has the power in certain cases to remit the award to the arbitrator for reconsideration and in other cases the award may be set aside by the Court or Judge, e.g. on the ground of the misconduct of the arbitrator, or on the ground that the award was bad in that it was made on matters not included in the submission and, therefore, the arbitrator was acting *ultra vires*—i.e. beyond his powers. An application to set aside or remit an award must be made within six weeks of the award by motion to the Divisional Court or Judge. An award may be enforced by leave of the Court or Judge as though it were a judgment or order to the same effect. The leave of the Court or Judge is obtained by means of an origina-ting summons. (*See* ARBITRATION.)

B.B.C.—The British Broadcasting Corporation is a Body incorporated by Royal Charter in 1926, and it con-sists of a Chairman and Governors appointed by the Government. It was formed for the purpose of "carrying on a Broadcasting Service within the United Kingdom . . ." and it is expressly prohibited from opening negotiations of any kind with the Dominions or foreign governments except with the consent of the Postmaster-General. This Government official, and through him Parliament, is really the controlling authority on all questions except day to day adminis-tration; for the Postmaster-General has a complete monopoly of all wireless com-munications, broadcasting and receiving stations within the United Kingdom, and it is only under a licence from him that the B.B.C. can operate at all. He has power to revoke this licence if a state of emergency arises, or if he decided that the B.B.C are not properly carrying out their functions; he can forbid the broadcasting of any particular item, or alternatively could prob-ably compel it, and he can specify the hours between which broadcasting is to take place. The B.B.C. are bound to work their stations in such a way as not to interfere with naval or military signalling and they are expressly prohibited from permitting advertising over the wireless save in a few exceptional cases. (*See* POST OFFICE; WIRELESS LICENCE.)

B LICENCE.—This is one of the licences required by persons who use motor vehicles in their business for the carriage of goods. (*See* CARRIER'S LICENCE.)

"B" LIST.—When a company is being wound up and its shares are not all fully paid the liquidator prepares two lists of the shareholders who still owe money in respect of their shares. The "A" list contains the names of those who are shareholders at the time of the winding-up, the "B" list consists of those who have ceased to be shareholders within the last year. (*See* WINDING-UP.)

BABY-FARMING.—By the Children Act, 1908, and the Children and Young Persons Act, 1933, it is provided that, where a person undertakes for reward the nursing and maintenance of a child under the age of nine apart from its parents, or where it has no parents, he shall give notice in writing to the local authority (usually at the Town Hall) as follows:—(i) where it is the first child he proposes to receive in the dwelling occupied for the purpose, not less than seven days before he receives the child, or (ii) in any other case not less than forty-eight hours before he receives it.

If a person already looks after a child, but without remuneration, and then subsequently agrees to accept remuneration, he must give notice of such agreement within forty-eight hours after making it. A child may be received in an emergency without notice being given beforehand, provided it is given within twelve hours thereafter. The notice is to contain the

Sir Francis Bacon.

name, sex, and date and place of birth of the child, the name and address of the person receiving it, and the name of the person from whom it is received. Notice must be given of change of address within forty-eight hours. If the infant dies or is removed from the care of the foster-parent, notice must be given within forty-eight hours both to the local authority and to the person from whom the child was received. The local authority must appoint inspectors to discover whether children are being nursed and maintained without the proper notices having been given, and to visit the cases notified.

It is an offence to refuse to allow a visitor to visit the premises where a child is kept in respect of whom notice has been given. The justices may grant warrants to search premises. On the complaint of the local authority, a Magistrate's Court may order

the infant to be removed to a place of safety if it appears that the child was kept or was about to be received (i) in overcrowded, dangerous or insanitary premises, or (ii) by a person who, by reason of old age, infirmity, ill-health, ignorance, negligence, inebriety, immorality, or criminal conduct, or for any other reason is unfit to have care of it, or (iii) in an environment which is detrimental to it.

Notice of the death of a child must be given to the coroner within twenty-four hours. It is an offence for the foster-parent to insure the life of the child or for any insurer to attempt to procure the issue of such a policy. Any advertisements regarding nursing and maintenance of children under the age of nine must contain the name and address of the advertiser truly stated. Certain institutions, convalescent homes and hospitals are exempted from any of the above requirements. Any offence against the above provisions or failure to give any of the above notices is punishable with imprisonment for not more than six months and/or a fine of not more than £20. Notices may be sent by registered post, or delivered at the office of the local authority, or at the office or residence of the coroner as the case may require. (*See* CHILDREN.)

BACON, Sir Francis (1561-1626). —Known generally to the public as a philosopher and statesman, Bacon was no less great as an exponent of the law and his Maxims of the Law are quoted in the Courts to-day. While a law officer of the Crown he played an important part in the trial of Lord Essex and was later Lord Chancellor with the title of Lord St. Albans. His sensational fall from office, his trial and the heavy fines imposed upon him were the culmination of his public life; thereafter he lived in retirement occupied with his philosophical works.

BAILEE.—When goods which belong to one person are not in his possession but with his consent in the possession of another, the transaction is said to be a Bailment, the person to whom the goods belong being called the Bailor and the person in whose possession they are being called the Bailee. A bailment will arise in a great many of the contracts entered into in ordinary business—e.g. hire purchase (q.v.) and the duty of the bailor and bailee as to the goods will depend on the nature and purposes of of the particular bailment.

Six kinds of Bailment are recognized: 1. **Deposit:** when goods are given to the bailee for safe custody. The bailee may in some cases receive some money for looking after the goods and in other cases he may keep them gratuitously—i.e. for nothing. Examples of a bailment for reward are where goods are left in a railway or restaurant cloakroom, or a warehouse, or where a car is left in a garage; and of a gratuitous bailment where a visitor to a house hands his hat or coat to a maid, or puts his car in his friend's garage. The exact extent of the duties of the bailee will depend on whether the bailment is for some money or other reward, or is gratuitous. When the bailment is gratuitous the object of this bailment is to benefit the bailor, and therefore the bailee will only be liable for any damage to, or loss of, the goods if he is grossly negligent or wilfully injures the goods.

If the bailment is for reward the bailee must look after the goods with reasonable care, but will not be liable if they are damaged or stolen without any fault of his. Thus, if a car is stolen from a public garage, the garage proprietor will not be liable unless he has omitted to take reasonable care to see that his premises are secure. The distinction between ordinary lack of care or negligence and gross negligence is very difficult to define. Where a person is liable only for gross negligence, it is usually understood that he is only required to exercise the same degree of care over the goods bailed as he does over his own property.

The bailee cannot use any goods which have been deposited with him, and if he does so will be liable for any loss or damage that may ensue even without any negligence on his part. He must be prepared to hand back the goods when demanded by the bailor.

Special Contracts.—It should be pointed out that in almost all cases where the bailment is for reward there will be some special contract entered into with terms which lay down the liability of the parties, and, of course, in such a case the parties may, for example, provide that the bailee may be liable for any loss, or on the other hand that he shall not be liable for loss however caused. These special terms may be either written or printed on the contract itself or on some document handed to the bailor at the time of the contract, e.g. a railway cloakroom ticket; or they may be contained in some notice or other document to which the bailor's attention is directed, or which is brought to his notice at the time of the bailment.

Thus it is very frequent to see in a restaurant a notice to the effect that "the Management do not accept responsibility for coats or hats of customers hung on pegs near their table." If such a notice is displayed in a reasonably conspicuous place in the room a customer cannot complain or claim from the restaurant if his coat is lost, even though the restaurant has been negligent and even though he did not see or read the notice. In the case of railway cloakroom tickets it is usually provided that the company shall not be liable for any articles over £5 in value unless some extra charge is paid, and it is for the passenger to offer to pay the extra charge, not for the railway company to demand it.

Where foods are sent by a carrier—such as a railway company—the liability of the company will be that of a common carrier (q.v.) during the carriage and for a reasonable time afterwards to enable the consignee to collect the goods; but if the goods are not collected within a reasonable time the company will cease to be liable as a carrier and will only be liable as a bailee under a contract of deposit.

Even when the bailment is gratuitous, as has been seen, the bailee must use some care; and in a famous case a bailee who undertook for a friend to keep some hogsheads of brandy and did so negligently so that the casks broke, was held liable in damages.

2. **Commodatum.** This arises where goods are left with a friend gratuitously in order that he may use them, and is distinguished from deposit by the fact that it is for the benefit of the friend the bailee, and not of the bailor. Accordingly the bailee is here liable for even the smallest degree of negligence. He is not responsible for reasonable wear and tear: so if I lent a car to my friend to oblige him and a tyre is punctured through the car running over a nail on the road, which could not have been avoided, or through the ordinary wear of

the tyre, my friend is not liable to me for the tyre nor is he bound to repair the puncture. If, however, he does not put sufficient oil into the car so that the engine is damaged he will be liable. A gratuitous bailee even of this kind is not liable if the goods are stolen, so long as he has not by his carelessness in any way contributed to the theft, e.g. as by leaving open the door of the garage.

A Defective Car.—The lender is himself under some duty to the person who is borrowing and must tell him of any defects of which he actually knows in the article which has been lent. Thus, if A lends a car to B to oblige B, and to the knowledge of A the foot brake is defective and will not bring the car to a standstill within a reasonably short distance, A must tell B of this and if he does not and in consequence B has an accident injuring both himself and the car, A will not be able to claim from B for the damage to the car but will have to compensate B for the injuries that he has sustained.

3. **Hire.**—This is the same contract as the last with this difference, that the bailee is here paying something for the use of the goods whereas in the last case he was using them for nothing. (*See* HIRE.)

4. **Pledge.**—This is when goods are delivered to someone in security for a debt. The lender is entitled if the money is not paid to sell the goods and pay himself what is due to him out of the proceeds of sale. Very special rules apply to this contract when it is entered into with a pawnbroker (*see* PAWNBROKER). In other cases the person to whom the goods are pledged must hand back the goods when the debtor offers the money due in respect of the debt, provided that he does so within the time stipulated in the contract or, if no time is mentioned, within a reasonable time after the money has been demanded. If payment is not made the pledgee (i.e. the person with whom the goods have been pledged) may sell the goods, and after he has paid the expenses of sale and his own debts must return the balance to the pledger.

The pledgee must take reasonable care of the goods and cannot use them except possibly in cases where they will not depreciate through use, e.g. jewellery which may be worn; but if the goods are lost while being used in this way even without the fault of the pledgee, e.g. are stolen, he will be liable although he would not be liable if they were stolen while not in use.

This contract of pawn or pledge must be distinguished from a mortgage, in which the goods which are used as security for the debt remain in the possession of the debtor. Such a transaction must be entered into under a bill of sale. (q.v.) If the transaction is not to be carried out by a bill of sale, the possession of the goods *must* be given to the pledgee, otherwise the security will be of no effect.

5. When goods are delivered to some person who is to do something to them for which he is to receive money, the duty of the bailee will depend on the exact nature of what he has to do. Thus, if the goods are to be carried, the bailee may be a common carrier and will be under the most severe obligations (*see* COMMON CARRIER). If, however, the bailee has to do something to the goods other than carry them, e.g. to wash them as when goods are sent to the laundry, he is bound to use only ordinary reasonable care.

6. **Mandatum.**—This is the same contract as the last except that the bailee is not paid anything for doing what he has got to do to the goods. Here he will not be liable unless he is grossly negligent, as the bailment is for the benefit of the bailor. In all cases the bailor must warn the bailee of any defect in the goods known to him which renders them dangerous. If dangerous goods are sent by a carrier, or if clothes which are known to be infected are sent to a laundry, the bailor (i.e. the sender) will be liable for all damage.

If the bailee in any of these cases refuses to hand back the goods when the bailor asks him to do so, the bailor may sue him for detaining them by an action called Detinue. This of course could only be brought if the bailor is entitled to have the goods back again, and would not apply, for example, where he had agreed for reward to allow the bailee to use the goods for a period which had not elapsed at the time when the demand for return was made. The bailee cannot refuse to hand back the goods to the bailor on the ground that they really belong to some third party, unless that third party is making a claim for the goods. In that case the bailee may "interplead" by taking the proper steps in the Courts (*see* Interpleader). The effect of this is that he declares that he himself has no interest in the goods but that other persons are making conflicting claims against him for them.

If a bailee fraudulently does anything to the goods which is contrary to the terms of the bailment in such a way as to show that he intends to deprive the bailor of the goods permanently, e.g. if he himself sells them or pledges them, he will be guilty of theft. (*See* Bill of Sale; Common Carrier; Hire; Hire-purchase; Interpleader; Pawnbroker; Railway Cloakroom).

BAILIFF.—The most common use of this term is to note a person who distrains for rent on behalf of a landlord. Every bailiff must hold a certificate from a County Court Judge, and if he levies a distress without this certificate he is liable to a fine and also to pay damages to the person whose goods have been taken.

The word is also applied to the officers of the County Court whose duty it is to serve all summonses and orders, and execute all warrants, precepts and writs issued out of the County Court. They act under the high bailiff who is in most cases the registrar of the Court. They are appointed by the Lord Chancellor.

The term is also applied to persons who act as agents for a land owner in looking after his estate. They are usually known as farm bailiffs. (*See* Distress.)

BAILLIE - STEWART. — Norman Baillie-Stewart was the central figure of perhaps the most famous case ever tried before a British Court Martial. A subaltern in the Seaforth Highlanders serving with the Royal Army Service Corps, he was arrested by the military authorities and confined to the Tower of London. On the 20th March, 1933, he was arraigned before a General Court Martial on several charges under the Official Secrets Acts based upon his alleged dealings with a German secret service agent named Obst. He was defended by Mr. Norman Parkes and Mr. Conolly Gage.

The prosecution proved that the accused had received some £90 in bank-notes from a person in Germany who signed letters to him "Marie Louise." They also established

that he had paid several visits to Holland without the knowledge of the military authorities. They suggested that these visits were for the purpose of conveying military information to Obst and that the name "Marie Louise" was a mere pseudonym.

Baillie-Stewart admitted that he had made these visits and had received the money, but said that he did so in the course of a love affair with a beautiful German girl whom he knew under the name of "Marie Louise." He strenuously denied that he had ever been guilty of any treacherous conduct. After a trial lasting some ten days Baillie-Stewart was convicted on certain of the charges and was cashiered and sentenced to five years' penal servitude.

BAKING.—There are a number of legal provisions which govern the business of baking and the majority of them are concerned with the preservation of the health of the public. Only certain materials and preservatives may be used in baking, and if any prohibited ingredient is used the offender is liable to a penalty of £10. There are also regulations about premises used for baking. The most important of these are: no room which is so situated that the surface of the floor is more than three feet below the surface of the adjoining footway may be used as a bakehouse, unless it was being so used on the 17th of August, 1901, and has been certified by the local council as suitable for a bakehouse; no ashpit or W.C. may be placed in a building used as a bakehouse in such a way that it is in direct communication with the bakehouse.

No baking may be done on Sunday, but the dough can be prepared for the following day's baking. (*See* Bread, Factory, Food, Public Health.)

BANK.—The largest Banks in this country, now known as the "big five," are:

Barclays Bank,
Lloyds Bank,
National Provincial Bank,
Midland Bank,
Westminster Bank.

All these are limited Companies registered under the Companies Acts. There are, however, still in existence certain banks consisting of partners without any limited liability, but it is not now possible for more than ten persons to carry on the business of banking unless they are registered as a Company under the Companies Act.

The Bank must honour cheques.— One of the most important duties of Banks is to pay out money on cheques signed by persons who are customers of the Bank. The Bank must be careful to honour any cheque so long as there is any money in the customer's account to meet it, and if a cheque is dishonoured while there is money in the account, or while the Bank has agreed to allow the customer to overdraw to a certain amount which is in excess of the amount drawn by the cheque, the Bank will have to pay heavy damages to the customer for the injury which he has suffered in his commercial reputation. In the same way a Bank must not pay a cheque which has been stopped by the customer or after they have had notice of the customer's death. A cheque may be stopped by letter or telegram, but the cheque should be clearly described with the name of the payee and if possible with the number of the cheque. The banker's authority to pay cheques on behalf of his customer will also cease if he has received notice of a petition being presented to make the customer bankrupt, or if a receiving order in bankruptcy has been made whether the Bank has notice of it or not.

Forged Cheques.—A Bank is supposed to know the signature of the customer, and if it pays out a cheque on a signature which is forged it cannot charge the amount to the customer. The same applies to cases where it is not the signature that is forged, but where some other alteration has been made in the cheque, e.g. the amount has been altered. Here, however, the Bank is only required to exercise reasonable care, and if the customer has made the forgery easy by his carelessness—as by omitting to fill in the amount in words on the cheque— the Bank will not be responsible. It is not carelessness on the part of a customer to keep his cheque book in an unlocked drawer in his desk. Banks are also protected when they either pay or receive money on behalf of a customer on a cheque which has been crossed, if they act without negligence. (*See* CROSSED CHEQUES.)

Bank References.—Enquiries are frequently made of Banks as to the credit of customers. The Bank is bound to keep secret the state of its customer's account and so must not disclose any information about it unless it first obtains the customer's consent. Thus, where a person gives a Bank reference—for example, on becoming tenant of a house—he should also request his Bank to give the information to the person enquiring. There is a recognized exception to this in cases where the Bank is required to disclose information under legal compulsion, e.g. in evidence in a Court of law, or where there is a duty to the public to disclose, or where the interests of the Bank require disclosure, e.g. where the Bank are suing a customer for money owed to them on an overdraft.

When Banks give any reference or make any inquiries, they are usually extremely careful to state that they are doing so without accepting any liability for accuracy. Banks, however, are further protected by a statutory provision that no action can be brought in respect of any statement as to the "conduct, credit, ability, trade or dealings" of any person made with a view to the enquirer giving credit to the person about whom the enquiries are made, unless the statement is made in writing and is signed by the person giving it. Thus a statement by a Bank manager made verbally as to the credit of some other person would not give any cause of action to the person to whom it was made against the Bank, if it turned out that the statement was untrue, even though the banker knew that it was untrue at the time when he made it. In order to make the Bank liable it would be necessary to have a written statement signed not by the Bank manager, who is merely an agent for the Bank, but by the Bank itself, i.e. the limited company or the partnership.

It is now fortunately a rare event for a Bank in this country to become bankrupt or to be wound up as insolvent. When this does happen, however, it may have important effects on persons who have accounts with the Bank. Thus, if A gives B a cheque for £100 on the XY Bank and at the time had £100 to his credit there, and if B delays for more than a reasonable time in presenting the cheque and before it is presented the Bank becomes insolvent, B cannot call on A to pay him the £100. He must present the cheque to the Bank and claim in the insolvency for the £100 which belongs to A and which B would have received if he had presented the cheque in good time. Thus, if the Bank only pays 1/- in the £ it is B who suffers the loss and not A. This of course will not apply if the Bank becomes insolvent before a reasonable time for the presenting of the cheque has elapsed.

If it comes to the knowledge of a Bank that a customer is an undischarged bankrupt, the Bank must inform the trustee in bankruptcy or the Board of Trade and must not make any payments out of the account without an order of the Court or the trustee, unless he receives no instructions from the trustee within a month after he has sent the notice. (*See* BANKER; LIEU CHEQUES.)

BANKRUPTCY.—Bankruptcy is the method by which a debtor may be released from all his debts on condition that he surrenders all his property to be divided fairly among his creditors. There are thus two principles involved. The first is that a person should not be compelled to continue burdened by debts which he is unable to pay, but by becoming bankrupt should be able to be relieved of them for all time. Viewed from this aspect bankruptcy is a privilege given to a debtor, and formerly was only allowed to certain debtors who were considered likely to incur the risk of bankruptcy, namely, traders. To-day, however, any person (with certain exceptions) is entitled to this privilege and however wealthy he may become in the future cannot be made liable for debts which were incurred before he became bankrupt.

The second principle is that in return for this privilege a debtor is required to give up all his property and to do nothing to prevent it from being fairly divided according to law among his various creditors. This does not mean that the property will be shared equally among all creditors for some are entitled by law to be paid before others (*see* PREFERRED CREDITORS), but it does mean that the debtor must not do anything to interfere with the order of payment laid down by the law by giving to one creditor a preference to which the law does not entitle him over the others.

Bankruptcy as a Debtor's Privilege. —All the provisions of the acts relating to

bankruptcy are founded on one or other of these principles. Thus the debtor is required to undergo a very searching examination on oath as to his property and his dealings with it in order to make sure that he is fulfilling his side of the bargain by giving up all he has. Any dealings by the debtor with his property before his bankruptcy, which indicate that he is giving it away to other persons in expectation of going bankrupt so that these persons may, after his bankruptcy return the property to him, or use it for his benefit, will not be permitted under the law relating to fraudulent conveyances (q.v.). Further, if it is discovered that the debtor, knowing that he is likely to become bankrupt, has put one creditor in a better position than the others, either by paying him a debt due or giving him some security for a debt which is already due with the intention of preferring him, the transaction will also have no effect and will be regarded as a fraudulent preference (q.v.), and the creditor will be required to return the money or give up the security.

Who may be Bankrupt.—Although almost any person may be made bankrupt, yet there are one or two persons to whom this privilege is not extended. A married woman cannot be made bankrupt unless she carries on some trade, business or profession, or is judicially separated from her husband. This is a survival of the days when married women had not full power to make contracts. A Company registered under the Companies Acts may not be made bankrupt, but must be wound up under the provisions of the Companies Acts. (*See* WINDING-UP.) Lunatics and infants also cannot be made bankrupt by reason of the fact that they cannot enter into contracts binding upon them and so cannot incur debts on which bankruptcy proceedings could follow.

How a Debtor is made Bankrupt— Acts of Bankruptcy.—A man may be made bankrupt either by the acts of one of his creditors or by reason of steps taken by himself. Bankruptcy is brought about only by an order of the Court, called an Adjudication Order (q.v.), under which the Court "adjudges" the debtor bankrupt, and this order is obtained on a petition being presented either by the creditors or by the debtor himself. A debtor may at any time petition to have himself made bankrupt, but where a creditor wishes to make a debtor bankrupt he must prove certain facts. Firstly it is necessary that the debtor should have committed some act which amounts to a public manifestation of his financial difficulties. Such acts are called acts of bankruptcy (q.v.). Mere insolvency, that is, the inability to pay one's debts as they fall due, is not of itself an act of bankruptcy, although it is present in most acts of bankruptcy. The most common act of bankruptcy is the failure to comply with a bankruptcy notice (q.v.), that is, a notice requiring the debtor within 7 days to pay some money which is due by him to a creditor on a judgment of the Court which the creditor has obtained. (For other acts of bankruptcy, see ACT OF BANKRUPTCY.)

A Creditor's Petition.—The petition may be presented by the creditor who has served the actual bankruptcy notice or by any other creditor within 3 months of the failure to comply with the bankruptcy notice or of the commission of any act of bankruptcy. The Court in which the petition must be presented will depend on the residence or place of business of the debtor within the previous six months. If he has resided or carried on business throughout that period in one place the petition must be to the High Court, if that place is within a certain area round London called the London Bankruptcy District, and to the Local County Court if the place of residence or business is outside that area. In cases where the debtor has not resided or carried on business in one place for the six months, the petition is presented in the district in which he has resided or carried on business for the longest time during these six months. If he does not reside in England, or his residence cannot be ascertained, the petition must be presented in the High Court. Although a bankruptcy notice may be served for any amount however small, no creditor can present a petition unless the debtor owes to him at least £50, but if his debt is less than that amount he may find other creditors willing to join with him in order to bring the total amounts of debts up to £50. The debt, unlike that on which a bankruptcy notice is served, need not be a judgment debt—i.e. there need not have been any decision by a Court that the debtor

owes the money to the creditor, but it must be for a liquidated sum, that is to say, must not be merely a claim for damages the exact amount of which cannot be mathematically calculated, and which depends on evidence being called, and the amount fixed by a Judge and jury. A debt will be liquidated even though some calculation is necessary before the exact amount of it can be determined. Thus in a contract to pay £5 a ton for a stack of hay the amount due may be calculated by weighing the hay and the debt is therefore liquidated. When the petition is presented the creditor must in addition prove some act of bankruptcy by the debtor within 3 months before the presentation of the petition.

When a County Court may reverse House of Lords.—If the debt is disputed by the debtor the Court may adjourn the hearing of the petition until an action to establish the debt has been tried, and even where the debt is a judgment debt—i.e. where some Court has already decided in an action that the money is owing by the debtor to the creditor—the Court is not bound to accept it as final, but may go behind the judgment and see whether the money is really due. This provision is necessary because it sometimes suits the purpose of a debtor to arrange with a creditor that a false judgment shall be taken against him with a view to the creditor making the debtor bankrupt. If the Court therefore discovers that the judgment is not genuine, the petition will be dismissed.

Receiving Order.—If the petition is not dismissed, a receiving order will be made. This is an intermediate order in the process in making a man bankrupt, and does not deprive a debtor of the ownership of his property or enable the creditors to have it divided or sold for their benefit. That is done later by the adjudication order. The receiving order is merely of a protective nature and takes the property out of the control of the debtor, placing it under the charge of the Official Receiver and so preserving it, by preventing the debtor from dealing with it or any creditors from seizing any part of it by legal process, e.g. execution. When the debtor is finally adjudicated bankrupt, the property is taken by his trustee in bankruptcy and sold and divided among his creditors. (*See* TRUSTEE IN BANKRUPTCY.) If the receiving order is rescinded—i.e. cancelled—before an adjudication order has been made, the debtor is once more allowed to control his property and bankruptcy proceedings against him are at an end.

Petition by Debtor.—A debtor who wishes to file a petition in order to make himself bankrupt must fill up a form (which he will obtain at the offices in Carey Street, London, W.C.) in which he must state his name and description and address. The petition must be attested before a Solicitor or Justice of the Peace, or Official Receiver or Registrar of the Court. The debtor must deposit with the Official Receiver the sum of £5. When the petition is filed by a partnership in the firm name the debtors must in addition file a statement of the names and addresses of the partners as they appear in the register under the registration of Business Names Act 1916.

Statement of Affairs.—So soon as the receiving order has been made the debtor must make out and send to the Official Receiver a statement of affairs (q.v.). This shows the debtor's property and debts, and the names, residences and occupations of his creditors and any securities which they hold for their debts—e.g. mortgages or pledges—and is intended as a first step in ascertaining the exact financial position of the debtor. In practice, the values put by the debtor on his assets in his statement are much higher than the amounts those assets ultimately produce when sold.

Meeting of Creditors—Composition.—Next it is necessary for the creditors, for whose benefit all these proceedings are being taken, to hold their first meeting. This is a very important meeting for at it the debtor may bring forward some proposal for the payment of his debts, either by paying so much in the £, or by paying a lump sum to be divided among the creditors —i.e. a composition or scheme of arrangement. The creditors may be prepared to accept this proposal instead of making the debtor bankrupt. The meeting is held within a fortnight of the receiving order, and in the meantime the official receiver has considered the statement of affairs filed by the debtor and makes a report as to what he considers to have been the causes of

the debtor's failure. At the meeting the creditors will consider any composition or scheme of arrangement proposed by the debtor, and, if a majority in number of them and three-fourths in value (calculated on their debts) approve of the proposal and it is later sanctioned by the Court, the non-consenting creditors will also be bound, and the bankruptcy proceedings will be put an end to and the receiving order rescinded.

Appointment of Trustee.—If the bankruptcy proceedings continue, the creditors at their meeting will appoint a trustee (*see* TRUSTEE IN BANKRUPTCY) whose duty it will be to collect, and divide the debtor's property, and they may, if they please, also appoint a committee of inspection consisting of members of their own number to assist the trustee.

Public Examination.—In order to enable the creditors to make sure that they have got all the debtor's property, the debtor must submit to a public examination. He must there answer on oath all questions he may be asked by the Trustee, Official Receiver or any creditor even although his answers may tend to show that he has been guilty of some crime. The object of this examination is to discover whether the debtor has been giving his property away to some friends of his with a view to preventing his creditors getting at it (fraudulent conveyance [q.v.]), or has been treating one creditor in a way that amounts to giving him a preference over others, e.g. by giving him a security for an old debt (fraudulent preference [q.v.]). The examination may be adjourned from time to time. The debtor, for example, may be asked to explain payments of money which appear in his bank pass book in favour of some friend or relation, or gifts of property, and when these explanations have been given the examination will be adjourned to enable the official receiver or the trustee to discover whether they are correct or not. When the examination is at an end the Court formally declares the examination concluded, but it cannot make this order until the creditors have held their first meeting.

Adjudication Order.—If a proposal for a composition is not accepted at the first meeting as indicated above, the almost inevitable consequence is that the debtor will be adjudicated bankrupt by an adjudication order being made, for the law does not like persons to have receiving orders made against them without full bankruptcy proceedings being taken, or else the receiving order being rescinded. Therefore, unless the creditors positively accept a composition or scheme within 14 days after the conclusion of the public examination, the adjudication order will be made. The adjudication order for the first time takes away from the debtor the ownership of all his property and vests it in the trustee in bankruptcy.

Annulment of Adjudication Order.
—It is still possible,however,for the creditors to accept a composition or scheme and if this is done the adjudication order will be annulled, i.e. cancelled. As in the case of a composition or scheme before the adjudication order, the scheme must be approved by a majority in number and three - fourths in value of all creditors who have proved their debts and sanctioned by the Court. The adjudication order may also be annulled if it is proved that the debts have been paid in full, but for this purpose it is not enough to show that the creditors have released the debtor from his debt, e.g. have granted a full receipt although only a part of the debt has been paid. There must be actual payment of the full debt. The Court will not sanction a scheme until after the end of the public examination, because it is thought undesirable that the proceedings in bankruptcy should be put an end to without the debtor being required to answer questions which may show that he has other property in addition to what he has disclosed to the creditors, or has been guilty of some criminal offence.

The Court will not in every case approve of the scheme and in fact in some cases has not power to do so, e.g. where the scheme does not provide reasonable security for the payment of the composition.

Disqualifications of a Bankrupt.—
As soon as a man is adjudicated bankrupt certain disqualifications attach to him. These are not now of great importance but an undischarged bankrupt is usually unable to hold public office as a Justice of the Peace or Councillor. The most important provision is that which imposes a penalty on an undischarged bankrupt who acts as a Director or takes any part in the management of a Company registered under the Companies Act except with leave of the Court. It is an offence for an undischarged bankrupt to obtain credit for over £10 without disclosing the fact that he is a bankrupt.

Bankrupt must assist trustee.—It is the duty of the debtor to do everything in his power to assist the trustee in collecting his property and realising it for the purpose of distribution among the creditors, and if he does not do this he may find when he later applies for his discharge that his application will be refused. In particular, the debtor must attend the first meeting of creditors. Even after the debtor has been discharged he is bound to assist the trustee in getting in any property not yet realised. The Court may grant a warrant for the arrest of the debtor and for the seizure of his business books, money, or goods if he is thought to be absconding or removing his goods.

Discharge.—The debtor is entitled to apply for his discharge as soon as the public examination has been concluded. His discharge is quite unconnected with the realisation of his property by the trustee and may well take place before that is all distributed, or for that matter may not take place until long afterwards, if at all. The effect of the discharge is that the debtor is free from all debts which could have been proved in the bankruptcy and of course is deprived of all property which belonged to him before the bankruptcy, except in cases where his property is more than enough to pay all the debts, when any surplus is of course paid over to him. The discharge is granted by an Order of the Court, and the Court, before granting it, will consider a report on the debtor and his affairs which the Official Receiver makes, and may either grant a discharge, or refuse it, or suspend it for the specified time, or make it a condition of the discharge that the debtor shall pay some money to the trustee out of his future earnings. The most usual order is for the Court to suspend the discharge for a period of a few months.

In some cases the Court has not got power to grant immediate discharge. The most important of these are:

1. Where the debtor's assets are not 10/- in the £ of his debts;

2. Where he has not kept proper account books for 3 years before the bankruptcy;

3. Where he has traded when he knew he was insolvent, or contracted a debt without a reasonable expectation of being able to pay it;

4. Where he has not accounted satisfactorily for loss of his assets;

5. Where he has been speculating, or gambling, or living extravagantly or has neglected his business;

6. Where he has indulged in frivolous litigation;

7. Where he has preferred a creditor within 3 months before the receiving order;

8. Where he has previously been bankrupt or made a composition with his creditors;

9. Where he has been guilty of fraud or of fraudulent breach of trust.

Other grounds on which the discharge may be refused or suspended are where a debtor has before his marriage made a marriage settlement, at a time when he could not have paid his debts without the property which he has disposed of in the settlement.

The discharge may in certain cases be granted with a certificate to the effect that the bankruptcy was caused by misfortune without any misconduct on the part of the debtor. The only advantage of this certificate is that the disqualifications (which in some cases continue for five years after the discharge) are removed. The certificate might be granted, for example, where a man had been made bankrupt through being made liable for the acts of a partner who had criminally or fraudulently incurred debts or removed trust property.

Effect of Discharge.—It is by his discharge that the debtor is finally released from his debts. Until the discharge is given he is still liable for debts which could be proved in his bankruptcy, and therefore, if he acquires any property before he is discharged, his trustee may seize it and use it for the benefit of the creditors. Thus, if before his discharge the debtor receives a legacy of £5,000, the trustee may claim it. The same principle applies to all profits made by the debtor in any business but not to earnings which are in the nature of wages, for these cannot be taken by the trustee unless he obtains a special order from the Court. If a debtor remains undischarged for a long time and carries on business, as he may do, he may have incurred fresh debts since his bank-

ruptcy (although it is an offence for him to obtain credit for over £10 without disclosing that he is an undischarged bankrupt). If, however, he has obtained credit, his new creditors will want to have their debts paid and will not unnaturally object to the trustee in bankruptcy taking all the debtor's property for the purpose of paying additional sums to the persons who were creditors in the bankruptcy. They may prevent this by making the debtor bankrupt a second time, and then the trustee in the first bankruptcy will be entitled to claim in the second bankruptcy as a creditor in respect of the debts, provable in the first bankruptcy, which have not been discharged. The persons who have become creditors since the first bankruptcy will also claim, and the property which the debtor has obtained since his first bankruptcy will be divided.

Once, however, the debtor has got his discharge the trustee in his prior bankruptcy has no claim upon him. The debts from which he will be released by his discharge will be all those which could have been proved in his bankruptcy with certain exceptions. He will not be released from debts which could not have been proved in the bankruptcy, namely, from:

1. Claims for unliquidated damages arising otherwise than by reason of a contract, promise, or breach of trust. This will usually prevent any proof being made in respect of claims against the bankrupt for negligence (e.g. arising out of a motor car collision); but this provision will not be of great importance to-day because in most cases the bankrupt will be insured and the claim will be against the insurance company direct. (*See* THIRD PARTY INSURANCE.) Where the amount of damages has been liquidated before the Receiving Order by a Judgment or by agreement, the amount may be claimed.

2. Debts which the debtor has contracted with someone who knew at the time of contracting the debt that the debtor had committed an act of bankruptcy, which would have been available to support the petition on which he was made bankrupt, i.e. was within 3 months before it. Thus, if any person knows that a debtor has committed an act of bankruptcy, e.g. has made a fraudulent preference and nevertheless gives him credit, he will not be able to recover the debt

in the bankruptcy if a petition is presented against the debtor within 3 months.

3. Alimony awarded to a wife.

In addition to those debts which are not provable in the bankruptcy there are certain debts which are provable but from which the debtor is nevertheless not released by his discharge. Thus he is still liable on debts due to the Crown for offences against revenue statutes (e.g. in respect of Income Tax) and for any liability which has been incurred by fraud or a fraudulent breach of trust. Again, he remains liable under an affiliation order and his obligation to support his wife is not discharged even though he has made a separation deed, and although the wife has proved in the bankruptcy for the capital value of the sums due under the deed.

Persons dealing with Debtor.—The position of persons who deal with a debtor either shortly before or after he is adjudicated bankrupt requires some consideration. The trustee takes the property of the debtor not as at the date of the adjudication order but as at the date of the commencement of the bankruptcy, which may be very much earlier (*see* TRUSTEE IN BANKRUPTCY), for it is the time when the debtor committed the first act of bankruptcy within the 3 months before the petition was presented. Since that time the debtor may have traded with many persons and may have transferred his property either in a gift or by a sale, and those persons may have been entirely ignorant of the fact that he has committed an act of bankruptcy. It is accordingly provided that any person who receives money from the debtor which is due to him or any property from the debtor for value (i.e. not as a gift), will be protected so long as the transaction took place before the receiving order, and so long as the person dealing with the bankrupt did not know of the act of bankruptcy.

A somewhat wider protection is given to persons who pay money *to* the debtor or deliver property *to* him. They are protected and cannot be compelled to pay again to the Trustee, so long as the transaction took place before the receiving order and before the person paying knew that a bankruptcy petition had been presented, provided always that the transaction is in good faith. The effect of this is that a person may go on *paying* his debts *to* a

debtor even though he knows of an act of bankruptcy, so long as he does not know that a petition has been presented; but he cannot safely *receive* money *from* the bankrupt after he knows of an act of bankruptcy.

Transaction between Receiving Order and Adjudication.—Persons who deal with the debtor in this period are afforded very little protection, and if a banker makes payments out of the debtor's account after the date of the receiving order, he may be required to pay the money again to the trustee. Any person who paid any debt to the debtor or transferred to him any property after the receiving order would also be liable to the trustee. Where, however, a transaction has taken place after the receiving order but before it has been advertised in the *London Gazette*, the trustee cannot claim again from the person who has parted with property of the debtor, unless the Court is satisfied that it is not reasonably practicable for the trustee to recover the money or property from the person to whom it was paid or transferred. Thus, if a banker honours a debtor's cheque after the receiving order but before advertisement, the trustee could not claim from him again if it were possible to recover the money from the payee of the cheque.

Transactions after Adjudication.—Although anything that may be acquired by a debtor before his discharge may be taken by the trustee, it is recognized that the debtor will no doubt incur obligations and receive property, and a very wide protection is given to persons dealing with him. All transactions will be protected and valid so long as they are completed before the trustee intervenes to claim the property and are made in good faith and for value. It does not matter whether or not the person dealing with the bankrupt knows of the adjudication order. Thus, if the bankrupt receives a legacy for £5,000, the trustee may intervene and claim the money. If before he does so, however, the bankrupt buys a house with the £5,000 the trustee cannot claim the money from the person from whom the house was bought. He can of course claim the house, but if before he does so the bankrupt sells the house again the trustee cannot claim the house from the purchaser— although again he may claim the purchase money from the debtor. If, however, the debtor *gave away* the £5,000 or *gave away* the house, the trustee could claim the money or house from the person to whom it was given because the transaction was a gift and not "for value." For the protection of bankers it is specially provided that any money or security received by a banker from a customer, or paid or delivered by a banker to a customer, or by his direction, are to be considered transactions for value. Thus a banker who advances money to a bankrupt on the security of shares of the bankrupt deposited with him cannot be compelled to give the shares up to the trustee, even though he knew of the bankruptcy of his customer.

Bankruptcy Offences.—There are a very great many acts, which if done by a debtor who becomes bankrupt, are regarded as crimes making him liable to fine or imprisonment. The most important of them is probably that which makes it an offence for a person not to keep proper books of his trade or business during the period of 2 years prior to the presentation of a petition against him. The books must show and explain his transactions and financial position, and must contain entries from day to day of his cash sales and purchases and stock-taking. It is also an offence for an undischarged bankrupt to obtain credit for more than £10 without disclosing the fact that he is a bankrupt. Generally any failure of the bankrupt to do everything in his power to assist the trustee in recovering all the property to which he was entitled, whether the failure consists in removing the property or altering or destroying books, will be a bankruptcy offence. A debtor who within two years before the presentation of a petition has contributed to his insolvency by gambling or by rash speculation unconnected with his business, or who has lost any part of his property by gambling or speculation between the date of the presentation of the petition and the receiving order, is also guilty of a crime.

In addition to those acts which are criminal offences there are many acts, which, although they may not make a debtor liable to fine or imprisonment, may yet be regarded as offences in that they will be taken into account when he applies for his discharge, and may prevent his discharge being granted.

Small Bankruptcy.—In cases when the debtor's property is not likely to exceed £300 the estate may be administered as a "small bankruptcy." In such a case the proceedings are generally simplified with a view to saving expense. There is thus no committee of inspection and the Official Receiver acts as trustee.

The effects of bankruptcy may also be produced by means of an administration order (q.v.) in a County Court but this is limited to cases where the total debts do not exceed £50. Further, where an application is made on a judgment Summons for a committal order—i.e. to send a debtor to prison because he will not pay his debts—the Court has power with the consent of the creditor instead of making the committal order to make a receiving order against the debtor. The bankruptcy proceedings will follow their ordinary course. (*See* ADMINISTRATION ORDER; TRUSTEE IN BANKRUPTCY.)

BANKRUPTCY (SCOTS LAW).— The Scots Law Bankruptcy is founded on the same principles as English Law although the rules governing the various stages of the proceedings differ in many respects.

Bankruptcy itself is a term unknown to Scots Law, although the word bankrupt is used loosely to denote a person whose estate has been sequestrated, the order of sequestration being equivalent to the English adjudication order.

There are certain acts which must be done or suffered by the debtor before his property can be taken and given to his creditors. In England these acts are known as acts of bankruptcy; in Scotland a debtor in such a situation is said to be notour bankrupt.

Notour Bankruptcy.—Notour bankruptcy commences when a debtor is insolvent and when his insolvency has been made notour, i.e. notorious—by some part of his property being seized, or made liable to be taken in payment for debts which he owes to a creditor. This will happen where decree has been obtained against him, i.e. the Court has ordered him to pay money—and where although he has been directed to pay by a charge, i.e. notice—he does not do so within the period allowed, so that he may either have his goods poinded or be imprisoned. Poinding (q.v.) is the process by which a debtor's goods are taken from him and sold to pay a debt. The same effect of notour bankruptcy is created if his land is taken by an adjudication (q.v.) against his heritable property, or if his goods are sequestrated by the landlord. (*See* SEQUESTRATION.)

Effect of Notour Bankruptcy.—The main effect of notour bankruptcy is that a creditor with a debt of £50 may present a petition to have a debtor sequestrated at any time within 4 months, just as in England he may present a petition to have a receiving order made after an act of bankruptcy. Notour bankruptcy also makes of no effect any transfers of property which the debtor has given away within 60 days before the notour bankruptcy. In order to recover this property from the person to whom it was given, it must be shewn that it was a gift, that the debtor could not pay his debts when he made it, and has never since been solvent. In cases where the property has been given to what is known as a "conjunct or confident person," that is, someone either nearly related to the debtor—"conjunct"— or else someone closely connected with him in his business—"confident"—the transaction is presumed to have been done with the intention of defrauding the creditors, unless the debtor or the person who has got the property can shew that this was not the case or that he was solvent at the time.

Notour bankruptcy has also a considerable effect on creditors who have seized some of the debtors' property within the last 4 months and obtained payment of their debts out of it. In this respect Scots Law is more severe on creditors than English Law, for all property seized by creditors within 60 days before the notour bankruptcy and 4 months after it must be shared equally by all who have seized any property during that time. As it usually happens that a debtor will be sequestrated, i.e. made bankrupt before the 4 months have elapsed, and as sequestration puts the trustee in bankruptcy who is appointed in the position of a creditor who has seized property, the effect will usually be that creditors who have seized property at any time after 60 days before notour bankruptcy will have to share with all the creditors and get no benefit out of the property they have seized.

Fraudulent Preferences.—Notour bankruptcy has also an effect on payments made, or additional security given, to a creditor by the debtor at any time after 60 days before a notour bankruptcy. Where the transaction is voluntary, the money paid or property given as security may be claimed back unless it can be shewn that the debtor was solvent when he gave the preference. A transaction will not be voluntary for the purpose of this rule if it is made in the ordinary way of business in payment of a debt or in incurring a new obligation. Fraudulent preferences can also be made of no effect for the benefit of all the creditors however long before notour bankruptcy they may have taken place. But then the trustee or person wishing to have the preference reduced, i.e. set aside, must prove positively that the debtor was insolvent and knew he was insolvent when he made the preference, and has remained insolvent ever since; whereas, where preference is within 60 days of the notour bankruptcy, it is not for the trustee to prove these facts but for the person claiming the property under the preference to prove the contrary. The practical advantage of this is great as it is very difficult to prove that a man has been insolvent at a particular time and more difficult still to prove that he was aware of his insolvency.

Sequestration.—It does not follow because a person is a notour bankrupt that he will ultimately have his property taken away from him and distributed among his creditors, i.e. that an award of sequestration will be made—any more than it happens in all cases in England that a debtor who has committed an act of bankruptcy is adjudicated bankrupt. If, however, at any time within 4 months of the date on which a debtor has been notour bankrupt as described above, a petition is presented to the Court to have that debtor sequestrated, the award of sequestration will be made and the property of the debtor will thereafter belong to the trustee for the benefit of his creditors.

The Petition.—The petition may be presented either by the debtor or by one or more of his creditors. In England a debtor is always able to present a petition to have himself made bankrupt without requiring any of his creditors to join with him in the petition, but in Scotland a debtor cannot present a petition unless he has the concurrence of creditors who would be qualified to present a petition themselves without his assistance, that is, of creditors to whom the debtor owes in all at least £50.

When the petition is presented by a creditor the amount of his debt must, as has been stated above, be £50, but the debt may be either liquid, that is ascertained or capable of calculation mathematically, or illiquid. Here the position is different from that in England. The debt may be presently due, or not due until a future time, but it must not be contingent, i.e. it must be certain that the debt will be due at some future time, and its becoming due must not depend on the happening of any event, such, for example, as the failure of a person who has accepted a bill of exchange to pay the amount due. In such a case the drawer of the bill of exchange will be liable to pay only if the acceptor makes default and his liability is contingent, that is, will only arise if the acceptor fails to pay.

The creditor who presents the petition must make an oath or affirmation stating any security he holds for the debt, or any other persons who are liable as well as the debtor, that is, any other parties there may be to the contract such as the debtor's partners. He must also produce an account and voucher in support of the debt and evidence that the debtor is a notour bankrupt.

The date when the petition for sequestration is first presented is taken as the commencement of the sequestration for most purposes; whereas, in England the commencement of the bankruptcy dates back to the first act of bankruptcy within 3 months before the date of the petition, and is not the date of the receiving order or of the adjudication order.

The petition will be presented either to the Sheriff Court of the district in which the debtor lives or carries on business, or to the Court of Session. On the hearing of the petition, objections to it may be raised, but if an award of sequestration is made the lord ordinary or sheriff will fix a time for the creditors to meet. At the meeting, which is usually within a fortnight of the award of sequestration and is called the First Statutory Meeting, the creditors attend and produce and prove their debts. The bankrupt also attends and produces his state of affairs, disclosing all his property and debts. The creditors then elect a trustee

and also commissioners, usually three creditors who correspond to the Committee of Inspection in England.

The trustee is appointed by an Order of the Court, known as the Act and Warrant, and before this is made he must have entered into a bond of caution, that is, have given security for all the property which may come into his hands.

Examination of Bankrupt.—The first duty of the trustee is to apply to the Sheriff to fix a date for the examination of the bankrupt and to collect the estate belonging to the bankrupt. The bankrupt must attend the examination which is in much the same form as a public examination in an English bankruptcy. After the examination has been concluded the creditors hold their Second Statutory Meeting, and there the trustee presents a report as to the estate and gives an estimate of the dividend which he expects will be paid.

The debtor may either at the First Statutory Meeting, or at the Second, or at any later meeting put forward suggestions for the payment of his debts as an alternative to the continuation of the sequestration. These suggestions may either be in the form of a deed of arrangement under which all the debtor's property is transferred to a trustee, or in the form of a composition contract under which the proposal is not that the debtor should give up his property but that each of the creditors should agree to be content with a fixed proportion per £ of the debts due. Before these proposals can be accepted there must be a majority in number and a three-fourths majority in value of the creditors present in favour of them.

Effect of Sequestration.—Sequestration has a considerable effect on any attempts by creditors to seize the debtor's property in satisfaction of their debts. Thus all arrestments (q.v.) and poindings (q.v.) which any creditor has made on or after the sixtieth day before the sequestration are of no effect, except that the arrester or poinder will be entitled to a preference for the costs. An arrestment is the process by which a creditor gets hold of property belonging to the debtor which is in the hands of someone else and not in the debtor's hands, or of debts owed to the debtor. Poinding is the process by which a creditor seizes goods belonging to the debtor in his own hands.

Thus a creditor may arrest goods of the debtor which are in the possession of some third person and also any sums of money owed to the debtor by the third person.

Claims.—The creditors will have to make claim against the estate on two occasions, firstly, when they do so for the purposes of voting and, secondly, for the purposes of claiming dividends, and slightly different principles apply to each of the cases. When a creditor claims for voting purposes he has got to deduct from the amount of his claim, when he has any other person liable as well as the debtor on the same debt, the amount which the debtor would be able to claim from that other person if he the debtor paid the whole debt. Thus A who is bankrupt has guaranteed a loan of £1 made to C by B. C is called the principal debtor and B is called the cautioner—i.e. guarantor. B when voting on A's estate must deduct the value of the claim which A would have against C if he, A, were required to pay the full amount. A would be entitled to recover the full £1 from C, for A is only guaranteeing the debt, and therefore B would not have any vote against A's estate at all. Suppose, however, that C is also bankrupt and that his estate is paying 15/– in the £. If A had paid the full amount and claimed against C for £1 he would receive only 15/–, so that the value of A's claim against C is only 15/–, and B must therefore deduct 15/– from his claim against A and claim for 5/– only. In all cases when B is voting on C's estate he will vote for his full amount, namely, £1, because C has no right to any relief from A, since C is the principal debtor and A is merely the person guaranteeing the debt, and a principal debtor has no right of relief from the cautioner. It should be pointed out again that these rules apply only in cases where the claim is being made for the voting and not where the claim is being made for the purpose of sharing in the dividends. Then the creditor claims for the full amount against both principal debtor and cautioner although he will not be entitled to draw in dividends more than 20/– in £ from the combined estates.

Trustee.—The trustee's accounts must be made up immediately after 4 months from the deliverance, that is, order of the Court, actually awarding sequestration. These accounts are examined by the Commis-

sioners at a meeting and the dividend which can be paid from them is declared. The first dividend is payable 6 months after the award of sequestration, the second dividend 4 months later, and any subsequent dividends at intervals of 3 months. The commissioners may postpone these payments.

Discharge.—The bankrupt in Scotland does not obtain his discharge as easily as in England. He cannot be discharged unless he has paid 5/– in the £, or unless he proves that it is not his fault but his misfortune that he is not able to do so. The discharge is obtained on a petition to the Court after the consent of the creditors has been obtained and a report made by the trustee as to the conduct of the bankrupt. The majority of creditors, which is required in order to give the consent, will vary with the length of time which has elapsed since the sequestration. Thus, before 6 months from the sequestration every creditor must consent. Between 6 and 12 months a majority in number and four-fifths in value; between 12 and 18 months a majority in number and two-thirds in value; between 18 months and 2 years a majority in number and value; and after that time the consent of the creditors is dispensed with, although the Court may still refuse to grant the discharge.

Property of Trustee.—The trustee takes much the same property in Scotland as he does in England.

The creditors are divided into preferred, ordinary and deferred, and for the most part their rights will be same as in English law.

After the estate has been collected and distributed the trustee will be entitled to be discharged. Special provisions are also made in Scotland, by what is known as Summary Sequestration, for a debtor to be made bankrupt as inexpensively as possible. It is necessary that the assets should not exceed £300 and any creditors to whom £10 is owed may present a petition.

BANKRUPTCY NOTICE.—A bankruptcy notice is a formal document issued by the Court at a request of a creditor who has sued his debtor for some money and has obtained a judgment against him. The creditor serves the bankruptcy notice upon the debtor and in it the debtor is required to pay the amount specified in the notice within 7 days. If the debtor fails to do this he has committed an act of bankruptcy (q.v.), and not only the creditor who has served the notice but any creditor to whom the debtor owes £50 (see BANKRUPTCY) may, within 3 months of the date of the failure to comply with the notice, present a petition to the Court asking the Court to make the debtor a bankrupt.

The notice must be in the form prescribed by the Act and must state the amount of the debt which the debtor owes, and must require the debtor to pay the sum of money due in accordance exactly with the terms of the judgment which the creditor has obtained, or to give to the creditor security for the debt to his satisfaction or to the satisfaction of the Court. The notice must also state that if the debtor fails to comply with it a petition may be presented against him. The law requires that the form of the notice prescribed should be very strictly complied with. If, for example, the creditor has obtained a judgment which orders the debtor to pay a sum of money not to the creditor but to the Registrar of a County Court, and the creditor serves a bankruptcy notice requiring the debtor to pay the money to him, the notice will be invalid, although the only purpose of the money being paid to the Registrar was so that he might hand it over to the creditor.

The bankruptcy notice may be for any amount however small, and in this respect it should be noted that a creditor may be able to serve a bankruptcy notice in respect of a debt, although he may not be able to present a petition to have the debtor made bankrupt should the notice not be obeyed, for before any creditor can present a petition he must have due to him a debt of at least £50. In such a case the creditor might be able to get other creditors to join with him in presenting a petition if the total amount of their debts amounted to £50 or more. (See ACT OF BANKRUPTCY; BANKRUPTCY.)

BANNS.—(*See* MARRIAGE.)

BAR.—The Bar of England is an ancient institution going back to the Middle Ages. It is the term applied to the body of barristers. The right of audience in all the higher Courts is exclusively confined to members of the Bar. (*See* BARRISTERS.)

BARRATOR.—This is an archaic term meaning a person who stirs up trouble, and brings, or causes to be brought, un-

necessary actions in the Courts. A person who does this is said to be guilty of "barratry." This is a crime punishable with imprisonment. In order to secure a conviction for this offence, it is necessary to prove that the accused person "habitually moves, excites, or maintains suits and quarrels." In these days, however, prosecutions for this are extremely rare. (*See* CHAMPERTY; MAINTENANCE.)

BARRATRY.—This is an old word used in charter parties and in policies of Marine Insurance and means some wilful act of the master or crew of a ship which causes loss to the owner or the charterer. Instances of barratrous acts would be attempts to scuttle the ship, or a mutiny. "Barratry of the master and mariners of a ship" is usually one of the perils from which the charterer exempts himself from liability by his charter party. (*See* BILL OF LADING; CARRIAGE BY SEA; CHARTER PARTY.)

BARRISTER.—A barrister is a person who has been called to the Bar. In England no person may plead the cause of another in the High Court except a barrister. This restriction applies also at most Quarter Sessions and certain other Courts.

A barrister becomes qualified by being called to the Bar by an Inn of Court; he is required for three years to keep terms at his Inn of Court and his attendance is regulated by his being required to attend for dinner in the hall of his Inn on certain specified occasions. This is called "eating his dinners." He has also to pass in certain examinations and to pay certain fees. On being called to the Bar he becomes an "utter" or "outer" barrister, that is to say, a barrister who is allowed to plead from the outer Bar. If he becomes sufficiently distinguished he can, if he wishes, apply to the Lord Chancellor to be called within the Bar, that is to say, to sit in the front row of Counsels' seats in Court. When called within the Bar he becomes a King's Counsellor. A King's Counsellor may not in general appear in Court unless a junior or "outer" barrister is briefed with him.

A barrister cannot in cases which are likely to end in Court receive instructions from any person save through a solicitor; a solicitor is said to instruct counsel and to act as an intermediary between the client and the barrister. A barrister is paid for his services by means of a fee paid him by the solicitor, and the solicitor of course charges the client for the fee so paid.

In the Middle Ages barristers used to be exclusively ecclesiastical persons who appeared for poor and uneducated persons to plead their causes. They used of course to do so without charge. The practice eventually grew up of giving to barristers a gratuity in recognition of the services so rendered. Indeed barristers of those days used to have hung over their shoulders a small bag in which these tips were placed. So strong has been the effect of this curious origin of the barrister's profession, that even to-day his remuneration is, in theory, a gratuity and his services rendered gratuitously. No barrister therefore can sue for his fees and to compensate him for this no barrister can be sued by a dissatisfied client for negligence. An interesting relic of the mediæval practice is the small piece of black cloth still hanging from a barrister's gown which is a survival of the old bag in which those tips were placed.

BASEMENT.—The basement of a house is the storey below the ground floor. The term basement usually means the whole storey, whereas a cellar signifies a single room in the basement. Every house built in London since 1895 which has a habitable basement must be provided with an open space measuring at least one hundred square feet at the rear of the building to give light and air to the basement. A basement is habitable if it is adapted to be lived in, that is to say, if it fulfils the conditions attached to the using of a cellar for a living room. (*See* CELLAR; HOUSING; PUBLIC HEALTH.)

BASTARDY.—A bastard is the child of persons not joined in lawful wedlock, or the child begotten in adultery (*see* ILLEGITIMATE CHILDREN). But a person born a bastard may subsequently become legitimate (*see* LEGITIMATION). A bastard is regarded in law as having no natural relationship with any person except his mother, and, as a result, is incapable of succeeding to the property of any of his natural relations unless such property is left to him specifically. Thus, if his father or aunt dies intestate, he has no rights at all to the property they leave, and even if the father had bequeathed £50 to each of his " children," the word "children" means, primarily, legitimate children. Only

for the purpose of incest is a bastard regarded in law as having natural relationship with his relatives.

When the bastard himself dies intestate, only his mother, wife and descendants are entitled to succeed to his estate, and if they are all dead, his property will go to the Crown. The rights of succession as between the bastard and his mother were created in 1926, and apply only in cases of deaths occurring since 1st January, 1927; and, in any case, the bastard can succeed to his mother's property on her intestacy only if she dies leaving no legitimate issue. When there are no children the wife of a bastard has only a life interest in his intestate estate, and when she dies the property will pass either to the bastard's mother, or, if she be dead, to the Crown. If there were children, the property is divided between them and their mother as on an ordinary intestacy. The same rules apply when it was the mother and not the father that was the bastard. If a bastard was a member of a friendly, industrial and provident society, or of a trade union or of a savings bank, and died without nominating any person to receive moneys payable after his death, such moneys shall be paid as if the bastard had been legitimate. A bastard is often entitled to receive compensation for the death of his parent or grandparent under the Workmen's Compensation Act, 1925.

A bastard has no surname until he has acquired one by reputation: he usually takes his mother's, but there is nothing to prevent his taking his father's. He may, of course, be christened like any other child. When his birth is registered, the father's name is not to be entered in the register except at the joint request of the mother and father who then sign the register together.

The obligation to maintain a bastard falls on the mother, and continues until the child attains sixteen or, in the case of a girl, marries before attaining that age. The father is under no legal obligation towards the child until an affiliation order is made or in certain other circumstances (*see* below). He is, however, entitled to the custody of the child after the mother's death, but he is not bound to undertake its custody even then. The mother, then, is the person entitled to the custody of the child; her consent is required to the marriage of the child so long as it is under twenty-one (but the marriage is not void if her consent is not obtained); she must see to the education of the child; she has the right to choose its religion, even against the wishes of the father; she may appoint guardians by deed or will to act after her death, and if the father undertakes the guardianship of the child when she dies, the guardians she has appointed will act jointly with the father; and if the child desires to marry when under twenty-one the consent not of the father but of the guardians appointed by the mother is required. The mother's duties terminate when she dies: her executors have no duties towards her illegitimate child. Otherwise, the mother cannot escape her obligations to the child unless some other person adopts it. (*See* ADOPTION.)

The father himself, on the other hand, has no duties to the child unless they are subsequently imposed upon him; such duties may arise (i) by an affiliation order being made against him (*see* AFFILIATION ORDER); or (ii) by his entering into a contract with the mother to contribute towards the child's maintenance; or (iii) by an order being made for the father to contribute to the expenses of maintenance at an institution of a child under twenty-one who is mentally defective; or (iv) by an order being made for the father to contribute to the expenses of maintenance of a youthful offender; or (v) by the father obtaining an adoption order (*see* ADOPTION). The contract mentioned in (ii) above is binding even though not in writing; it forms no bar to affiliation proceedings; it terminates on the mother's death, but not on the bankruptcy of the father.

The only other persons who may be liable to maintain an illegitimate child are as follows: (i) the husband of a woman is always bound to maintain her illegitimate children if they were born before he married her, until they attain sixteen or until the mother dies, whichever be the earlier. Bastards born after the marriage he need not maintain, but before refusing to maintain them he should make sure that he has sufficient evidence to prove that they are bastards (as to the difficulties of proving that a child of a married woman is a bastard, *see* ILLEGITIMATE CHILDREN); (ii) a person cohabiting with the mother of a mentally defective

bastard under twenty-one may be ordered to contribute to its maintenance in an institution, and a person cohabiting with the mother of an illegitimate youthful offender may be ordered to contribute to its maintenance; (iii) persons in whose favour the Court has made an affiliation order on the grounds that he has the custody of the child must maintain the child. (*See also* AFFILIATION ORDERS; ILLEGITIMATE CHILDREN.)

BATTERY.—A battery is the unlawful beating of a person. The expression "beating" in law means any striking or even hostile touching of another or his clothes. The term "assault" is often used to include a battery, though strictly, assault is the offering of the violence and the battery is the actual violence. A battery is both a crime and a civil wrong. The injured party can seek redress for a battery in the same way as in an assault. Self defence is a good defence to a charge of battery. (*See* ASSAULT.)

BECK, ADOLF. — Happily almost unique in the modern administration of English Criminal Law, the trial of Beck was undoubtedly a genuine miscarriage of justice. To be twice convicted and sentenced for crimes he did not commit, and to serve five years' penal servitude for frauds of which he was innocent, was the tragic experience of this Norwegian adventurer.

The facts necessary for an understanding of this remarkable case began in 1877, when a certain John Smith was sentenced to five years' penal servitude for a series of frauds committed on women in London. He would accost them pretending he was a nobleman, and after acquaintance rob them by a trick of some of their jewellery. He was released from prison in 1881.

The next stage was in 1895, when a series of complaints were made by women declaring they had been swindled in an exactly similar manner. Adolf Beck, walking down Victoria Street, was recognized by one of them as the man who had defrauded her and given in charge to a constable.

He was tried at the Old Bailey before the Recorder, and prosecuted by Mr. Avory (later Mr. Justice Avory) on charge of defrauding ten different women by false pretences.

The evidence against him was his identification by these women and police officers who had known John Smith, and the evidence of Mr. Gurrin, the handwriting expert, that certain incriminating documents were in his handwriting.

Beck was convicted and sentenced to seven years' penal servitude.

He served his sentence and regained his freedom in 1901. In 1904 more frauds exactly similar were being perpetrated. Beck was recognized and identified by one of the

It is often remarked that a beer barrel is inscribed with three X's as shown here. Formerly, by law, a barrel of beer was marked with an X when the duty on it had been paid. Consequently beer thus marked was of a good and standard quality. To-day many brewers still use the one, two or three X's, to mark the different strengths of their beer.

women and charged with three separate frauds before Mr. Justice Grantham at the Old Bailey. He was convicted on June 27, but the Judge had doubts and postponed passing sentence.

On July 7, happily for Beck, John Smith was arrested for fraud and identified, and letters found upon him which were obviously in the same writing as the incriminating documents produced in the trial of Adolf Beck. Here was the man who was guilty of the frauds for which the wretched Beck had suffered. On July 27 a free pardon was given to Adolf Beck.

BEER.—The word beer includes ale, porter, spruce beer, black beer and any other description of beer containing alcohol.

All beers are intoxicating liquors and so an excise licence is required before any of them can be sold by retail. A justices' licence will also be required where it is desired to sell beer for consumption on the premises, and occasionally even when it is desired to sell it for consumption off the premises. (*See* INTOXICATING LIQUOR.) If beer only is to be sold the best course is to procure a beerhouse licence. This permits the holder to sell both beer and cider for consumption on or off the premises. Under a full licence beer can of course be sold by retail, as well as wine and spirits, for consumption on or off the premises.

If your house is under £8 in annual value you may brew beer for your own domestic use without taking out any kind of licence. If, however, your house is between £10 and £15 in annual value your licence to brew for domestic use will cost you 9/–; in any other case 4/–. If, however, you brew beer for sale you must pay duty according to the number of barrels brewed during the preceding year. It is £1 for the first hundred barrels and 12/– for every further fifty barrels. (*See* INTOXICATING LIQUOR.)

BEER HOUSES.—This is the name given to a house licensed only for the sale by retail of beer and cider for consumption on or off the premises. (*See* INTOXICATING LIQUOR AND PUBLIC HOUSES.)

BEGGING.—Begging in any public place is an offence and a person found guilty of begging may be convicted as an "idle and disorderly person." It is also an offence punishable in the same way to encourage any child to beg. The soliciting of contributions for a charitable object is not punishable as begging, although of course a person may well commit the offence of obstructing the public highway in the course of collecting.

Anyone convicted as an idle and disorderly person may be sentenced to one month's imprisonment or fined £5. A second conviction as an idle and disorderly person renders the offender punishable as "a rogue and vagabond," and as such may be sentenced to 3 months' imprisonment or a fine not exceeding £25. A second conviction as a rogue and vagabond renders the offender punishable as "an incorrigible rogue," as he is called, for which imprisonment up to one year may be inflicted by a magistrate.

BENEFICE.—The term benefice has many different meanings in different Acts of Parliament; in its broadest sense, it means any ecclesiastical promotion or living, but usually it is defined to include rectories, vicarages, perpetual curacies and chapelries, as distinct from "preferment" which includes such higher offices as archdeaconries and bishoprics. No person may be admitted to any benefice until he has been ordained a priest. (See PRIEST.) The right to present a priest to a benefice is often privately owned, and is known as an advowson. (See ADVOWSON.) The priest is admitted to his office by the Bishop by "institution," or, where the right to present belongs to the Bishop himself, by "collation;" and he then becomes the incumbent or minister of the benefice.

Exchange of Benefices.—Before a clergyman can exchange his benefice or living for another it is necessary to procure a licence from the Ordinary (see ORDINARY) to exchange; on the licence being granted, the exchange is effected by an instrument in writing. The fact that two clergymen have exchanged livings does not mean that they lose their right to claim each against the other in respect of dilapidations.

Union of Benefices.—One of the most difficult questions with which the Church has to deal is that of the Union of Benefices. A commission is appointed by the Bishop at the request of the Ecclesiastical Commissioners to report on the advisability of union. If, as is usually the case, the report favours the union the matter rarely ends there, for the residents in the parish which is to disappear would naturally almost always object if only on sentimental grounds. The Bishop transmits the report to the Ecclesiastical Commissioners who are to propose the scheme. They draw up the scheme for union and certify it, with the consent of the Bishop or Bishops affected, to the King in Council. The disaffected parishioners or patron, as the case may be, may appeal to the Privy Council against the union if they so desire. Provision is made for the pulling-down of the churches, parsonages and other buildings made superfluous by the union.

Loss of Benefices.—The incumbent loses his benefice in one of five ways: (i) by death; (ii) by resignation; (iii) by cession, i.e. by preferment or the taking of a new benefice of such a kind that he is not legally entitled to retain his original benefice (see PLURALITY); (iv) by exchange (see above); and (v) by deprivation. Deprivation may occur by reason of the incumbent's having committed an ecclesiastical offence, as a punishment for which he is deprived (see CHURCH OF ENGLAND: Ecclesiastical Courts); or because he or some other person has been guilty of simony in connection with the benefice (see SIMONY); or because he was disqualified from holding the benefice (e.g. had not been ordained a priest), or had been deprived by an Ecclesiastical Court of the right ever again to hold a benefice.

The Bishop is entitled to deprive a clergyman who has been found guilty of certain offences against morality by a lay Court. (See CLERGYMAN.)

The Bishop has power to appoint a commission to enquire into the conduct of an incumbent in respect of his official duties, and if his duties have been inadequately performed by reason of his negligence (i.e. not by reason of matters beyond his control) he may be deprived of his benefice; he may appeal from such deprivation to a Court consisting of the Archbishop and a Judge of the High Court. (See ADVOWSON, CHURCH OF ENGLAND; PLURALITY, AND SIMONY.)

BENEFIT OF CLERGY.—During the middle ages, a clergyman, which included any person who could read Latin verses chosen by the Judge from any book (known colloquially as his "neck verses"), was entitled to be tried by the Ecclesiastical and not by the ordinary Civil Courts for any felony he might have committed. This meant that, in the majority of cases, he escaped without punishment of any kind. The right to claim benefit of clergy was gradually restricted, and was finally abolished in 1827 for commoners and in 1841 for Peers.

BESTIALITY.—Bestiality is the commission of an unnatural carnal offence by a man or woman with an animal. It is punishable with penal servitude for life or for not less than three years, or with imprisonment with or without hard labour for not more than two years.

BICYCLES.—It is an offence punishable with a fine of 40/– wilfully to lead or ride any bicycle upon any public footpath. Bicycles are required during hours of darkness to carry one white light in the front. They need not carry a red rear light provided an efficient red reflector can be seen from the rear. If a bicycle is being wheeled by a person on foot on the near side of the carriage-way it is not required to carry any lamp at all. If a bicycle has a side-car attachment, two front lights are required.

BIGAMY.—The offence of bigamy is marrying a second person whilst an existing spouse is still alive. It is a felony punishable with seven years' penal servitude.

It is a good defence to a charge of bigamy to shew that at the time of the second marriage the first husband, or wife, had been absent for seven years, unless the person contracting the second marriage knew that, though absent, the first husband or wife was still alive. Even though the absence does not amount to seven years a person charged with bigamy should still be acquitted if he shews that he, on reasonable grounds, really believed that his first spouse was dead and had made proper enquiries as to this.

If the first marriage has been lawfully dissolved or declared null and void there is, of course, no offence committed by a second marriage But a divorce or nullity decree must, of course, be pronounced by a competent Court, a Court, that is to say, whose jurisdiction in matrimonial matters over the parties is recognized by the English Courts.

Bigamy is punishable by penal servitude for not more than seven years or by imprisonment for a period not exceeding two years. (*See* MARRIAGE.)

BILL OF EXCHANGE.—A Bill of Exchange is an unconditional order in writing given by a person called the drawer and signed by him, requiring another person called the drawee to pay a fixed sum of money to, or to the order of, a person named called the payee, or to the bearer, either on demand or at a future date which is fixed or determined. If these conditions are not strictly complied with—e.g. if something other than the payment of money is ordered —the instrument is not a bill.

Although not legally necessary, it is usual to specify the date, the place where drawn, and the fact that value has been given. The following is a common form of such a bill:—

"London 1st January 193–".
"£100. Three months after date pay Richard Roe or order the sum of one hundred pounds for value received. To William Styles (Signed) John Doe."

The person who is ordered to pay the £100 is William Styles, the "drawee." When he signs his name across the face of the bill, thereby agreeing to pay, he is called the "acceptor," for he thereby "accepts" the bill. When the bill comes into the payee's hands, he will indorse it. (*See* INDORSEMENT.) The commonest form of bills are cheques, which are dealt with elsewhere. The drawer, John Doe, can make a bill payable to himself or to his own order. Where drawer and drawee are the same, or the latter is fictitious or lacks capacity to contract, the holder may treat the instrument as a bill or a promissory note. There may be two drawees but there must not be alternative or successive drawees, instead there is a person called Referee in Case of Need, whose name is inserted by the drawer in the bill, and to whom the holder may go if the bill is not accepted or is not paid.

There may be several payees, the bill being payable to all or some of them. When the payee does not exist, the bill is payable to bearer like a cheque in the form "pay cash." Bills are rarely drawn payable to bearer, for this makes them negotiable by transfer alone. Other bills require indorsement but they may contain words prohibiting transfer such as "payee only," in which event they are not negotiable.

Interest.—A bill may direct that a sum be paid with interest or by stated instalments; 5 per cent. per annum is the rate of interest if none is named. Interest on the sum can always be claimed from the time of presentment or maturity of a bill.

When Bills are Payable.—A bill is payable on demand when it is drawn payable "on demand," or "at sight," or "on presentation," or when no time for payment is expressed. A bill is often made payable at a fixed period (three months) after its date, or after sight, or after the happening of some event which is bound to happen. "After sight" here means "after acceptance," not merely after a private exhibition to the drawee. On a promissory note "after sight" means after the note has been again shewn to the maker. Any holder can insert the true date of issue or acceptance in an undated bill.

Days of Grace.—These are three days added as of right to the time of payment fixed by any bill not payable on demand. The bill, which can always expressly exclude days of grace, is due on the last of the days except when that falls on a Sunday. It is then due on the preceding day.

Acceptance.—Only the drawee can accept. If anyone else purports to do so his action does not make him liable as acceptor on the instrument. The drawee is under no liability until his acceptance which may be general or qualified, that is to say, conditional, or as to part only of the amount of the bill, or with terms as to time or place. It must not say that the drawee will do anything other than the payment of money in fulfilment of his promise. A holder may always refuse to take a qualified acceptance and treat the bill as dishonoured by non-acceptance. A bill addressed to a partnership should be accepted in the firm name, for if a partner accepts it in his own name he alone is liable. The acceptance may be written by some person other than the payee if done with his authority, but the name written must be the payee's name, otherwise it is inoperative. A signature induced by fraud is generally invalid. Acceptance may be before the drawer has signed the bill, or after dishonour, or when the bill is overdue.

Alterations and Omissions.—The holder may fill up any omissions in any way he thinks fit. If the amount is left blank the holder has the right to fill in any sum the stamp will cover. Material alteration avoids the bill except as against the person altering.

Delivery.—Delivery of the bill is always necessary to make a person liable on it. Thus the payee has no rights if the drawer dies before delivery. Posting is delivery, for by the rules of the Post Office, a letter posted cannot be reclaimed. Delivery must be with the authority of the person who is to be made liable. It may be conditional or for some purpose other than transferring the property, but a valid delivery is presumed till the contrary is shewn. Where the possessor is a holder in due course (q.v.) the presumption cannot be upset. The payee, however, is not regarded as such a holder.

Liability on Bills.—Drawers, acceptors and indorsers are liable on a bill if they sign it as such, and any person who can make a contract can sign a bill. That one of the parties to a bill suffers from incapacity in no way negatives the liability of the others, for example, the drawer's infancy is no defence to the acceptor. An infant is not liable on a bill payable after he attains his majority, or on a cheque similarly post-dated.

The drawer's liability may be limited by the drawer or expressly negatived, so that the holder has no remedy against him. The usual method of thus limiting liability is by the addition of the words "sans recours." Conversely to save expense the drawer may waive the holder's duties. Indorsers have similar powers.

Signatures.—A trade or assumed name is treated as the name of the person signing. A firm's name is equivalent to the signature of all the partners. A forged signature puts no liability upon the person whose name it purports to be.

Agents' Signatures.—These do not exempt the agent from personal liability unless it is clear that he signs for, or on behalf of, his principal. To do this an agent may add the words "sans recours" and name his principal as well. If the agent signs the principal's name the principal is bound only if the agent acted within the scope of his apparent authority. When the agent signs "per pro" his principal this is notice to all concerned that the agent has only a limited authority to sign. If that authority is exceeded the principal is not liable.

Consideration or value must be given for a bill, other than an accommodation bill, at some time or other. It is presumed to have been given till the contrary is proved. Any consideration which will support a simple contract or, contrary to the usual rule, an existing debt or liability, is sufficient.

Presentment for Acceptance is necessary to fix the date of maturity when a bill is payable after sight, where presentment is stated by the bill itself to be necessary, or where it is payable elsewhere than at the place of business or residence of the drawee. Presentment must be within a reasonable time, otherwise the drawer and all indorsees prior to the holder are discharged. Where a bill is duly presented but is not accepted within the customary time (24 hours) it is treated as dishonoured by non-acceptance. Death, bankruptcy and the fact that the drawee cannot be found excuses presentment. The holder can then pursue his rights against the drawer and indorsers just as if the bill had been dishonoured by non-acceptance.

Presentment for Payment is necessary unless excused, or when the bill is already dishonoured by non-acceptance or when, after a reasonable effort, presentment is found to be impossible. Failure discharges the drawer and indorsers. The holder or his agent must present on the day the bill falls due, or, if payable on demand, within a reasonable time of its issue. What is a reasonable time depends on the circumstances of each case. Delay is excused when caused by matters beyond the control of the holder (e.g. his sudden death), otherwise they are discharged from liability. Agents may give and receive notice. A valid notice must be in writing or by personal communication, or both. It must identify the bill and state the dishonour. It may be given as soon as the bill is dishonoured and must be given within a reasonable time, which, in the absence of special circumstances, is one that reaches its destination on the day after dishonour where both parties live in the same place. Where they live in different places, a notice sent off on the day after dishonour is sufficient. In estimating time, an agent, a bank and a branch bank are each looked upon as independent holders.

A person receiving notice has the same time in which to pass it on to the other parties, e.g. to other indorsers. Return of the dishonoured bill is sufficient notice. Delay caused by circumstances beyond control is excused, as also is delay in the post. Notice is dispensed with altogether where the place of presentment must be the place of payment named in the bill. If none is specified then the bill should be presented at the address, place of business, or residence of the drawee or acceptor if named in the bill. If not, then presentment may be at the last known address or wherever the party can be found.

When a bill is duly presented and payment is refused, or is unobtainable, or when presentment is excused and the bill is over-

due and unpaid, it is said to be dishonoured by non-payment. The holder can then pursue his rights against the drawer and indorsers. Unless required by an express term of a qualified acceptance there need be no presentment for payment to the acceptor. When paid the holder should deliver the bill to the party paying it.

Notice of Dishonour must be given by the holder or by an indorser who is, at the time of giving it, himself liable on the bill, to the drawer and to each indorser. When the drawer or indorser cannot be found, or when the bill was made or accepted for the accommodation of the indorser, it is excused.

Noting and Protest.—Noting, or noting for protest, means the marking of a bill by a notary public at the time and place of its dishonour. When presented by post and returned dishonoured, it may be protested at the place to which it is returned. Protest is the formal certificate which shows that the bill has been dishonoured and in practice it is taken to show due presentment. It is based on the noting and contains a copy of the bill. Stamp duty is payable. Where no notary public is available, a resident of substance may give a protest attested by two witnesses. Protest is necessary before acceptance or payment for honour, and for a foreign bill, that is, a bill which is not either drawn and payable in Britain or drawn in Britain upon some person resident therein.

Discharges.—A bill is discharged when all rights of action thereon are extinguished. Payment in due course, that is, payment in good faith without notice of any defect, renunciation in writing and the intentional cancellation of the bill by the holder are the principal methods of discharge. Where the drawer pays the bill to a third party he may enforce payment from the acceptor, but may not re-issue the bill. If a banker pays a bill in the ordinary course of business he is deemed to have paid in due course even if the indorsement is forged.

Any party liable on a bill may be discharged by the intentional cancellation of his signature by the holder. Any indorser who would have a right to recover against a person thus discharged is also discharged.

Intervention for Honour.—Where a bill has been protested for dishonour by non-acceptance or for better security and is

4*

not overdue, any person not already liable may, with the consent of the holder, intervene and accept the bill supra protest for the honour of any party liable thereon, or of any person for whose account it is drawn.

Acceptance for honour is in the same form as an ordinary acceptance. It must indicate that it is for honour. It may be for part only of the bill.

Similarly anyone may pay a bill supra protest for the honour of any person liable where it is protested for non-payment.

Lost Bills.—Where a bill is lost before it is overdue the last holder may ask the drawer for a similar bill. If the drawer is given indemnity against all persons in case the lost bill is found again he can be compelled to give a duplicate bill.

The Bills of Exchange Act, 1882, governs the whole subject. (*See also* ACCOMMODATION BILL; CHEQUES; HOLDER FOR VALUE; HOLDER IN DUE COURSE; INDORSEMENT; PROMISSORY NOTE.)

BILL OF LADING.—When goods are sent to be carried at sea the sender may either arrange with the owner of a ship to take the whole of the ship's capacity or some definite part of it, in which case he will enter into a charter party; or he may arrange merely that the carrier shall take the specific goods which are required to be carried, in which case the transaction will be carried out by a bill of lading.

The bill of lading has three important functions:—

(1) It is a receipt for the goods and shews that they have been shipped and usually the condition in which they were shipped.

(2) It contains the terms of the contract made between the shipper of the goods and the carrier.

(3) It is a document of title to the goods, and the ownership of the goods may be transferred from one person to another by handing over of the bill of lading.

In the case of any goods which are sent from any port in Great Britain or Northern Ireland (except in coasting trade) under a bill of lading, the bill of lading must be in the terms prescribed by the Carriage of Goods by Sea Act, 1924. (*See* CARRIAGE BY SEA.)

BILL, PARLIAMENTARY.—A Bill is a proposed legislative enactment which,

after approval by the House of Commons, the House of Lords, and the King, becomes an Act of Parliament. (*See* ACT OF PARLIAMENT.)

Bills are either public bills or private bills, public bills relating to matters of general importance, and private bills relating to matters of purely personal or local interests. Once it has been passed, a private bill is no less binding than a public bill, but the distinction is of very great importance as regards the procedure by which such a bill passes through Parliament. A public bill may be introduced in the House of Lords by any member of the House without notice. A member of the House of Commons may introduce a public bill to the House of Commons after giving notice. The bill is then read for the first time without debate and is ordered to be printed. At the second reading, the principle of the bill is considered, and, if approved, the bill is passed for the second time, and is then examined by a Committee. It is then said to have reached the Committee Stage. The next stage is the Report Stage, which is followed by the third reading. This procedure, broadly speaking, is followed in both Houses, and the bill is then presented to the King for the Royal Assent.

A private bill cannot be introduced without the consent of the House, such consent being obtained by means of a petition by the promoters. A private bill passes through the same stages and readings as a public bill, but with different regulations as to time, mode and other matters of procedure. The regulations differ, also, according to the purpose of the bill, e.g. a railway bill, a bill for promoting companies and a bill to acquire working-class houses each has a different set of rules applicable to it. (*See also* ACT OF PARLIAMENT; PARLIAMENT.)

BILL OF SALE. Secret Transactions.—The law considers that where any person is in possession of goods, persons dealing with him in trade are likely to think that the goods belong to him and therefore may give credit to him.

It is most undesirable therefore that any third person should be able to claim the goods under a document by which they have been secretly transferred to the third person by their apparent owner to the exclusion of the person who has given credit. The law therefore says that all transfers of the ownership of goods, under which the goods remain in the possession of the person by whom they have been transferred, should be made public by being registered. All documents having this effect are known as Absolute Bills of Sale.

Impecunious Borrowers.—The law also considers it undesirable that persons in need of money should be induced to sign complicated documents which they do not understand, giving to a person from whom they have borrowed money a charge over goods which remain in their possession. All documents of this kind are known as Conditional Bills of Sale, or bills of sale in security, and the law here requires that they should be made in compliance with some form, which the law has prescribed, which sets out quite clearly the nature of the transaction and thus prevents the borrower from being misled. As these documents, if they were made secretly, would also have the effect of enabling the borrower to obtain false credit on the strength of the goods which he retains in his possession, it is further necessary that they should not be made secretly, and should be registered in the same way as Absolute Bills of Sale.

It should be noticed that it is only where these transactions are made by some written document that the law requires the observance of a particular form or registration. The transaction may be made orally and will be quite valid without registration. Further, if the possession of the goods is handed over, in the case of a conditional bill of sale, to the person who has a charge over them (in which case the transaction is really a pledge), or, in the case of an absolute bill of sale, to the person to whom they are being transferred, the law does not require either registration or the observance of the statutory form even if the transaction is set down in writing.

What is a Bill of Sale?—A document may be a Bill of Sale even though it is not described in the document by that name, and the law has defined a bill of sale as including:—

1. Bills of Sale strictly so called;
2. Assignments;
3. Transfers;
4. Declarations of Trust without transfer;
5. Inventories of goods with receipt

thereto attached, or receipts for purchase moneys of goods, and other assurances of personal chattels;

6. Licences to take possession of chattels as security for any debt, and also any agreement, whether intended or not to be followed by the execution of any other instrument, by which a right in equity to any personal chattels, or to any charge or security thereon, shall be conferred. A licence to seize goods which are already the property of the person who is entitled to seize them is not a bill of sale. Thus a hire-purchase agreement which allows the owner to seize if default is made in paying instalments, etc., is not a bill of sale. (*See* HIRE PURCHASE.)

In addition certain documents are " deemed to be" bills of sale, namely:

"Every attornment, instrument or agreement not being a mining lease whereby a power of distress is given, or agreed to be given by any person to any other person by way of security for any present, future or contingent debt or advance, and by which any rent is reserved or made payable as a mode of providing for the payment of interest on such debts or advance, or otherwise for the purpose of such security only."

Notice that such an agreement is a bill of sale only if the money described as rent is not really rent at all, but interest for money lent. This will be the case only where the power of distress is not the usual power which a landlord has, but is exceptional. Thus an agreement between brewers and a publican for the lease of a public house, under which the brewers took a right to distrain for *any* money that might be owing to them by the publican, their tenant, e.g. for beer supplied and not merely for rent, was held to be a bill of sale.

Where land has been mortgaged and the mortgagor has attorned, i.e. become a tenant of the mortgagee, so that the mortgagee can claim to distrain for rent, the transaction is not, however, to be considered as a bill of sale.

What is Not a Bill of Sale.—The law also states that certain transactions are not to be considered Bills of Sale. These are:

1. Assignments for the benefit of creditors. These must be registered as Deeds of Arrangement (q.v.).
2. Marriage Settlements, provided that they are made before the marriage takes

place. If, however, a man even after marriage, settles furniture or other goods on his wife the transaction need not be registered as a bill of sale if the furniture is at the house where they both live.

3. Transfers of ships or share therein. (*See* BILL OF SALE (SHIP); SHARES; SHIPPING.)

4. Transfers of goods in the ordinary course of trade. Thus, if A sells goods to B and in the ordinary course of business relationship is allowed by B to retain possession of the goods after they have passed into B's ownership, the transaction need not be registered. It should be noted, however, that if A sells the goods again to someone else or pledges them, that person will be entitled to claim the goods as against B. (*See* SALE OF GOODS.)

5. Debentures issued by a Company. These have to be registered under the Companies Act. (*See* DEBENTURES.)

6. Bills of Lading which transfer goods. (*See* BILLS OF LADING.)

7. Assignments of fixtures unless they are separately assigned. (*See* FIXTURES.)

"Personal Chattels."—It is, subject to one exception noted below, only assignments or transfers of "personal chattels" which require to be registered as Bills of Sale. Personal chattels include goods, furniture and articles capable of complete transfer by delivery, and fixtures and growing crops when separately assigned or charged, i.e. apart from the land on which they are situated. Trade machinery is also included in the term.

The following assignments, however, are not governed by the laws relating to bills of sale, namely, assignments of stocks or shares, contracts, or choses in action, e.g. book-debts. Although assignments of book debts are not bills of sale, yet certain assignments of book-debts must be registered "as if they were bills of sale," or else they will be void against the trustee in bankruptcy if the maker of the assignment becomes bankrupt. The assignments which require to be registered are those which are made by a person engaged in any trade or business and which affect existing or future book-debts. Even then registration is only necessary when the assignment is of book-debts *generally*, i.e. is not of some debt or debts actually specified in the document of assignment or of debts arising under contracts specified

therein. An assignment for the benefit of creditors generally does not require registration as a bill of sale for it is a deed of arrangement (q.v.) and must be registered as such. When a business is sold and the book-debts due are assigned even generally no registration is necessary. A special register for assignments of book-debts is kept.

Absolute Bills of Sale—Registration.—In the case of Absolute Bills of Sale the law is concerned, as has been seen, with the protection of persons who may trade with the person who has granted the bill, and not with the protection of that person himself from the wiles of money lenders, as in the case of Conditional Bills of Sale. The objects of the law are therefore here secured by requiring publicity by means of registration without prescribing in detail any particular form in which the transaction must be carried out. The bill must be registered within 7 clear days after it has been signed, and it must be attested by a solicitor of the Supreme Court, and the attestation clause must state that the effect of the bill has been duly explained by the solicitor to the grantor. The registration is effected by taking to the Bills of Sale Department in the Royal Courts of Justice the original bill with every schedule or inventory attached to it, and also a copy of the bill and schedule, and an affidavit verifying the execution and attestation and setting out the time when the bill was executed, the name, address and occupation of the grantor, and of the witness who has attested the bill. The original bill is shewn to the registrar or his officer but the copy is filed.

Where the affidavit describes the residence of the person making the bill as outside the London Bankruptcy District (*see* BANKRUPTCY) or where the chattels are stated to be outside that district, a copy of the bill is sent to the local County Court of the district where the debtor resides or the chattels are situated. Any person is entitled to examine the register on payment of a small fee. No reasons for making the search need be given.

Registration lasts for five years and may be renewed by filing with the registrar an affidavit stating the last registration of the bill. If the registration is not renewed at the proper time, then the bill becomes void just as though it had never been registered.

This Indenture

made the fourth
day of June One
thousand nine

hundred and thirty   B E T W E E N   JOHN WHITE of 6 Triglees Wells
Road Clapham Draper of the one part and SILAS GREEN of 664 Ash Lane
Clapham Butcher of the other part   W I T N E S S E T H   that in
consideration of the sum of SIXTY POUNDS now paid to John White by
Silas Green, the receipt of which the said John White hereby acknowledges
he the said John White DOTH HEREBY ASSIGN unto Silas Green his
executors administrators and assigns all and singular the several
chattels and things specifically described in the schedule hereto
annexed by way of security for the payment of the sum of Sixty pounds
and interest thereon at the rate of five per cent per annum   And the
said John White doth further agree and declare   that he will duly pay
to the said Silas Green the principal sum aforesaid together with
interest then due by six equal monthly payment of Ten pounds on the
fourth day of July One thousand nine hundred and thirty   and
on the fourth day of each and every succeeding month   And the said
John White doth also agree with the said Silas Green that he will at
all times during the continuance of this security insure and keep the
said chattels insured against loss and damage by fire in the sum of
Sixty pounds at least ───

   PROVIDED ALWAYS that the chattels hereby assigned shall not be
liable to seizure or to be taken possession of by the said Silas
Green for any cause other than those specified in section seven of the
Bills of Sale (1878) Amendment Act, 1882. ──────────────────────

   I N   W I T N E S S   whereof the parties to these presents have
hereunto set their hands and seals the day and year first above written

THE SCHEDULE above referred to
Furniture   at   6 Triglees Wells Road Clapham

DRAWING ROOM   DINING ROOM

Mahogany cabinet   Large Mahogany Table
Mahogany card table   6 Mahogany chairs
Arm chair   Carpet
Carpet
Small Mahogany table

SIGNED and SEALED by the above   )
named   John White   in the   )   John White.
presence of:-   )

     Frank. H. Connett

        1000 Redford Road. Clapham. S W
             Secretary

A Specimen Bill of Sale.

Duplicate Bills.—Attempts were at one time made to avoid the provisions requiring registration by drawing up a fresh bill just before the elapse of the seven days allowed for registration of the first bill. The fresh bill could then be allowed to be current for (say) six days and a third bill be drawn up before the time for registration had expired. This is now declared to be illegal and such duplicate bills, if given in security for the same debt or any part of it, and so far as respects the same chattels or any part of them as were comprised in the first bill, are absolutely void; unless it is proved that the subsequent bill was given in good faith for the purpose of correcting some material error in the prior bill, and not for the purpose of evading the provisions requiring registration. That these rules do not apply to a second bill given more than seven days after an earlier unregistered bill.

The bill must state the consideration for which it is granted, i.e. the money payment and this statement must be true. Thus, if part of the money is not paid until some time after the bill is signed it should not be stated that the money is "now paid." The consideration for an absolute bill of sale may be of any amount. The goods covered by the bill need not be set out in a schedule to it, but if they are then the schedule must be registered along with the bill. If there is any term in the bill which will enable it to be made void (called a defeasance), such as a term which would enable the grantor of the bill to recover back his property on certain conditions, or if there is any declaration of trust, this must be set forth on the paper which contains the bill.

Bills of Sale in Security.—Here the law, as has been seen, desires not only to make the transaction public, but to protect impecunious borrowers. The rules as to registration are the same as in the case of an absolute bill of sale. A very detailed form has been prescribed which must be exactly complied with. The form sets out the date of the bill, the names and addresses of the Grantor and Grantee, the consideration for which the bill is granted, the transfer of the property in security for the payment of the money lent and interest, an obligation by the borrower to pay the principal sum and interest, and also to do any acts necessary for the preservation of the goods taken in security, e.g. the taking out of an insurance policy over them. The bill need not be attested by a solicitor. Any credible witness will do.

The goods which are to be affected by the bill of sale must be set out in an inventory which is scheduled to the bill. The bill will be void, except as against the grantor, in respect of any chattels not specifically described in this schedule. Thus, if the schedule states that the goods covered by the bill of sale are "the Chippendale table and chair and other furniture" in a certain room, the grantee will not be able to claim the "other furniture" against any person, such as a trustee in bankruptcy or execution creditor of the debtor. He can, however, claim all the furniture if it is only a question between himself and the debtor, i.e. if no third party is making a claim.

The goods in the schedule must belong to the person granting the bill at the time when he granted it. Thus a bill of sale cannot be granted over stock which a trader has not yet acquired, and no transaction can be carried out having the same effect on the property of an individual as a debenture creating a floating charge has upon the property of a company. (*See* DEBENTURE.)

The bill must state a definite sum which is due for principal. There must be a definite time or times fixed for payment of principal and interest. No bill of sale in security can be granted for a less amount than £30.

When Goods may be Seized.—The object of the bill, of course, is to enable the person who has lent money to seize the goods if he thinks that the debtor will not be able to repay him the money, but, again, for the protection of borrowers, the law has stated that it is only in certain events that the lender of the money, i.e. the grantee of the bill, may seize the goods. These are:—

1. If the grantor makes default in paying any money secured by the bill at the time when he should do so, or fails to perform any of the obligations he has undertaken, e.g. to insure. The grantee does not need to remind the debtor of his obligations by demanding payment from him formally a short time before the date for payment arrives.

2. If the grantor becomes bankrupt or if

he allows the goods or any of them to be distrained upon by his landlord for rent or by the proper authorities for rates or taxes.

3. If the grantor either fraudulently removes the goods from his premises or allows them to be removed. Notice that the removal must be fraudulent, that is, it must be done with the intention of preventing the grantee seizing the goods.

4. If the grantor fails without a reasonable excuse to produce to the grantee his last receipts for rents, rates and taxes after he has been required to do so by a written demand from the grantee.

5. If execution has been levied against the goods of the grantor. Notice that this does not necessarily mean that the execution must be levied against the goods that are included in the bill of sale. If the bill of sale had been granted over the furniture in one room and execution were levied on the furniture in another room, this would be sufficient.

Even after the grantee has become entitled as above to seize the goods and has seized them, he must leave them on the place where they have been seized for 5 days and during that time the grantor of the bill may apply to a Judge of the High Court and ask him to prevent the goods being removed or sold; and an order to this effect will be made if the Judge is satisfied that the cause under which the goods were seized no longer exists, e.g. if the money has now been paid.

When Absolute Bill is Void.—If an Absolute Bill of Sale becomes void because it has not been registered, the effect is that it is void only with regard to any creditors of the person who granted it. This is what one would expect when one remembers the objects the law has in view in the case of Absolute Bills. When it is void, all goods which are in the "apparent possession" of the grantor may be taken by his trustee in bankruptcy, if he becomes bankrupt; by any person to whom they have been assigned for the benefit of his creditors; by any persons seizing them in execution, or on whose behalf they have been seized. Goods are said to be in the "apparent possession" of a person so long as they remain on any premises, private or business, occupied by him, or even if they are not on any premises of his but are used and enjoyed

by him on premises belonging to another person. Thus if the bill is made void it will not affect goods which before that time have been taken into the possession of the grantee. If the bill is duly registered the goods comprised in it are not within the "order and disposition" of the grantor for the purposes of bankruptcy. (*See* TRUSTEE IN BANK-RUPTCY.)

It should be noticed that if an Absolute Bill of Sale becomes void it will nevertheless remain valid as between the grantor and the grantee, so that the grantee can claim the goods from the grantor. It is only when the persons mentioned above are also claiming the goods from the grantor, i.e. trustee in bankruptcy, execution creditor, etc., that the effect of the bill is lost.

When Conditional Bill is Void.—Where a Conditional Bill of Sale becomes void, the effect will depend on the ground on which it is void. If it is not in the proper form or if the consideration for it is less than £30, it will be void as between the grantor and grantee as well as against all other parties. The grantee will lose his security and also will be unable to claim the interest at the rate specified in the bill. His only right will be to claim the actual principal paid and 5% interest per annum.

If the bill is void because it has not been properly registered or attested, or if the consideration is not clearly stated, it will again be void as between the parties and also as against third parties so far as any security is concerned, but the grantee may claim principal and interest at the rate specified in the bill

If the ground upon which the bill is defective is that the schedule which is attached to it does not specifically describe the chattels included in the bill, or that the grantor of the bill was not the true owner of the chattels at the time the bill is granted, the bill will be void against third parties mentioned above so far as these chattels are concerned, but may be enforced against the grantor in respect of all the chattels.

Even though a bill of sale complies with all the requirements above set out it may yet be made void if the debtor becomes bankrupt. Thus, if it was a transfer of practically the whole of the debtor's property in consideration for a sum of money which was already owing, it would be a fraudulent conveyance (q.v.) or assignment and an act of bankruptcy (q.v.). If the bill of sale is given partly as security for a debt already existing, but also in security for further advances of money which the grantee of the bill undertakes to make, it will not be void nor an act of bankruptcy if the fresh advance was made with the intention of enabling the borrower to carry on his business, and if the lender reasonably believed that the advance would enable him to do so. Again a bill of sale may be a fraudulent preference (q.v.), that is, given with the intention of preferring the grantee and enabling him to get his debt paid before other creditors. Before it can be a fraudulent preference the debtor must, however, be insolvent and must have as his main motive the object of preferring the creditor. Thus, if the bill of sale is only granted under genuine pressure by the creditor, the bill will be good. A bill may be attacked as a fraudulent preference only if it is given within 3 months before the debtor has a receiving order made against him. If it is a fraudulent preference, the creditor will not have any rights against the goods covered by the bill. (*See* BANKRUPTCY; FRAUDULENT CONVEYANCE; FRAUDULENT PREFERENCE.)

BILL OF SALE (SHIP).—The document by which the ownership of a ship is transferred from one person to another is known as a bill of sale. A bill of sale of this kind is governed by rules entirely different from those relating to bills of sale under the Bills of Sale Acts. (*See* SHIPPING.)

BILLIARDS.—A licence is required for any place where a billiard table, bagatelle board, or any like instrument is kept for the use of the public. But if the place happens to be a fully-licensed public house no other licence will be required.

Billiard licences are obtained at the general annual licensing meeting of the justices (*see* BREWSTER SESSIONS) and the same notices are required as in the case of justices' licences. Billiard licences may also be transferred in just the same way that justices' licences for the sale of drink are transferred, and again similar notices are necessary (*see* TRANSFER OF JUSTICES' LICENCES AND INTOXICATING LIQUOR), but no notices need be given for a renewal. Licensing Justices have full discretion as to granting or refusing new

Earl of Birkenhead.

licences, renewals and transfers, and no appeal lies against their refusal.

A place licensed for billiards must have a notice setting forth that fact in a conspicuous position and it is an offence not to do so. Billiards must not be played between 1 a.m. and 8 a.m. or on Sundays, Christmas Days, or any other day of public fasting or thanksgiving. Even a resident on the premises cannot play during such times. The police can enter on such premises when they think fit. A billiard licence costs six shillings, but if a place is kept for public billiard playing and no licence is obtained, a fine of £10 for every day on which it was so kept can be exacted, or the person keeping it may be sent to prison for six months. Playing in the prohibited hours is punishable by a fine of £10. (*See* BREWSTER SESSIONS; INTOXICATING LIQUOR; TRANSFER OF JUSTICES' LICENCE.)

BILLPOSTING.—Local authorities have very wide powers to make bye-laws for the regulation of advertising within their areas; they may, for example, regulate or prevent the exhibition of advertisements which disfigure or injuriously affect (i) views of rural scenery from public places or from public waters or from railways; or (ii) villages; or (iii) historic or public buildings to which the public resort chiefly on account of their beauty or historic interest. When these bye-laws are made, the existing advertisements are protected for a period of five years. The posting of bills upon property of another person without authority is a trespass and the billposter may be sued for damages for so doing, and, in certain cases may be prosecuted.

BINDING OVER.—A useful provision for dealing with persons who are convicted of minor offences, or, in the case of first offenders, who are convicted of more serious offences, is the power to bind over to be of good behaviour. A person so dealt with is required to give an undertaking to be of good behaviour, and, in some cases, to find other people who will go surety with him for this purpose. The effect is, that if the person so dealt with in effect remains of good behaviour during the time for which he is bound over, usually six or twelve months, he will hear no further of his conviction.

BIRDS.—By the Wild Birds Protection Acts, 1880–1906, no wild bird may be shot, snared, or trapped, or otherwise taken, or killed, or exposed or offered for sale between 1st March and 1st August in each year. The penalty for an offence in respect of "scheduled" birds is £1, and in respect of other birds a reprimand or, on second offence, 10/–. The schedule includes most rare birds and larks, kingfishers, plovers, snipe and wild duck. The occupier of land is not, however, liable if he kills or takes unscheduled birds on his own land, or if he authorizes other persons to do so. County Councils have wide powers, through the Home Secretary, to extend or restrict the operation of the Acts, and to protect wild birds' eggs. Any person may demand an offender's name and address. It is illegal to take alive for sale or to offer for sale alive any of the common wild birds of this country (*See also* PLUMAGE.)

BIRKENHEAD, Earl of (1872-1930.) F. E. Smith was one of the greatest advocates of his time. After a brilliant career in scholarship and sport at Oxford he was called to the Bar and practised on the Northern Circuit. He first won fame in London at the Central Criminal Court by the brilliant eloquence of his plea in mitigation of sentence for Goudie, who had pleaded guilty to gigantic frauds on the Bank of Liverpool. He was later in many famous cases among them the Lever Case and the Marconi share scandal. "F.E." was a well-known and popular figure with all sections of the people. In the House of Commons he was considered the ablest speaker on the Conservative side. He was made Attorney-General and later Lord Chancellor, being raised to the peerage with the title of Lord Birkenhead.

BIRKETT, Norman (1883-   ).— One of the leading advocates of the day and particularly noted for his oratory. His most famous case, perhaps, was his prosecution of Rouse, in the "Blazing Car Mystery." But his great triumphs have been in civil cases in the High Court.

BIRON, Sir Chartres (1863-   ).— Formerly Treasury Counsel at the London Sessions, he retired in 1933 from the post of Senior Magistrate at Bow Street where he was a well-known figure for many years.

BIRTH. Registration.—It is the duty of the father or mother of every child (since 1926, even if stillborn) to register the birth within 42 days thereafter, supplying all necessary particulars and signing the register personally. The father of a bastard, however, is under no such duty, but may sign the register with the mother's consent. Failing the father or mother, the duty rests on the occupier of the premises where the child was born, or a person present at the

Norman Birkett.

birth or a person having charge of the child. The particulars required are (i) date and place of birth; (ii) name (if any) and sex of the child (if no name is entered, such entry may be made on the application of a parent within twelve months); (iii) name and profession of the father; (iv) maiden name of the mother; (v) signature and address and description of the informant. In the case of a stillborn child, a doctor's or midwife's certificate that the child was stillborn, or a declaration that a doctor or midwife was not present at the birth are also required. Births at sea on British ships are registered with the Master who notifies the Registrar-General of Shipping.

The giving of false particulars is punishable on summary conviction by a penalty of not more than £50, or on indictment by penal servitude for not more than ten years. If registration is not effected within the 42 days, the registrar may by notice require the person responsible to attend his office within twelve months. After the expiration of twelve months, no registration can be effected save by leave of the Registrar-General (fee 10/-). There is, in every case, an additional duty on the father, if he resides in the house where the birth took place, and on any other person present at the birth to notify the birth within 36 hours to the District Medical Officer of Health by prepaid post; doctors and midwives may be supplied free of charge with stamped postcards for this purpose. (Penalty for failure, 40/-.)

BIRTH CERTIFICATE.—A complete record of all births registered in England and Wales since July 1st, 1837, is kept at Somerset House, Strand, London.

Anyone wishing to obtain a copy of a birth certificate can do so by visiting Somerset House between 9.30 and 4.0 on week-days (Saturdays 9.30 to 1.0). On payment of £1 the applicant can search the index for any time up to six consecutive hours. The charge is only 1/- if the object of the search is specified, and the records to be examined do not exceed a period of 5 years. A copy of certificate obtained at Somerset House (on payment of 2/7) is conclusive evidence of date of birth for all purposes.

If the applicant does not wish to attend in person, an official will make the search over a period of 5 years on a payment of 2/6.

District offices also exist where a register of local births is kept. The search fees here are 5/- and 1/- respectively. Copies obtained here are not conclusive legal evidence.

The following are also registered at Somerset House:—
  (i) British citizens born abroad and registered with the local Consul.
 (ii) Births in British ships.
(iii) Births in the Ionian Islands and certain British Protectorates in Asia and Africa.
 (iv) Births in the Army.

Certificates in respect of those born in Scotland, Ireland and the Dominions cannot be obtained at Somerset House as they are only registered locally.

BISHOP.—The Bishop is elected by the chapter of his cathedral church by virtue of a licence from the Crown. But in point of fact the nomination really lies with the Crown, or rather, with the Prime Minister in power when the vacancy occurs. When elected by the chapter, the new Bishop is confirmed in his office by the Archbishop on command of the King under penalty of præmunire (see PRÆMUNIRE).

Thereafter the Bishop may exercise his spiritual jurisdiction, but he is not completely Bishop until consecration. As soon as he is consecrated, all the benefices of which he was formerly possessed become void.

A Bishop removing from one see to another is said to be translated; the same formalities are observed on translation, except that no second consecration is required.

The duties of a Bishop are innumerable, including ordination of priests; granting of marriage licences; confirmation; licensing of curates; appointing certain diocesan and cathedral officials, e.g. Chancellors; and generally supervising ecclesiastical matters within his diocese. He is a member of the Upper House of Convocation, and president of his Diocesan Conference. The Bishops of London, Durham and Winchester are members of the House of Lords, together with the twenty-one other most senior Bishops. A Suffragan Bishop is an assistant to a Diocesan Bishop (see SUFFRAGAN).

BLACK LIST.—Large trading concerns and associations of traders in order to protect their trade have devised a scheme for dealing with persons who sell their goods at "cut" prices. If they find out that a trader has been selling their goods at less, or more than, the fixed price, they put his name on a "stop" or "black" list, and cut off supplies from him. This procedure is known as putting a person on the "Black List," and although some traders have attempted to obtain damages from an association or trade combine which had put them on the Black List for cutting prices or for some other infringement of their trading rules, they have been unsuccessful in their claim.

The Courts have held that such a procedure is a perfectly lawful one to protect the trade interests of the association or combine. In an important case in which the Motor Trade Association was concerned it was decided that it was lawful to form an association to secure that new goods should be sold only at a fixed price, and the steps taken to achieve this object were also held to be perfectly lawful. The Association agreed together to refuse to supply goods to a person who sold their goods at less or more than the fixed price. If any trader sold goods at prices other than the fixed price, then the association circulated his name on a stop list to members of the association, and took other steps to see that he was not supplied with goods either directly or indirectly. These drastic actions may have the effect of ruining the business of a person against whom they are taken, but unless he can prove that the association combined together to ruin him and not to further or protect their own trade interests, he will not succeed in an action for damages.

When a trader is put on a Black List he is usually informed by the association or combine that his name will be removed from the list if he pays a sum of money to a charity or to the funds of the association. This sum is paid by way of a penalty for the infringement of the price rules. Unfortunately the Court of Appeal dealing with Civil Cases and the Court of Appeal dealing with Criminal Cases are at variance upon this custom of demanding a sum of money as a penalty. The Court of Criminal Appeal refused to upset the conviction of the secretary of an association, who was

convicted of demanding money by menaces. The secretary acted upon the instructions of his association and wrote a letter to a trader who had sold goods at cut prices, saying that if he did not make a payment of a certain sum within a specified time his supplies would be cut off. The Court of Criminal Appeal held that this was in fact demanding money with menaces, but the Civil Court of Appeal is of the opinion that such a threat was only the logical consequence of putting a trader on the Black List, and as there was nothing unlawful in putting him upon that list, there could be nothing unlawful in this method of allowing him to obtain his removal from it.

The principle of putting a person on the Black List is really a form of boycott, that is to say, a complete obstruction of a person in the way of his livelihood, such as was practised at one time by the British Medical Association against a doctor of whose conduct they disapproved.

To put a person on a Black List in order to protect one's own interests is perfectly lawful, but to subject him to a boycott which ruins him or causes him substantial damage, with the motive only of putting him out of business and not to further one's own interests, is an actionable wrong for which the person damaged can claim compensation. (*See* CONSPIRACY ; PICKETING.)

BLACKBURN, Lord (1813-96).— Starting as a law reporter Colin Blackburn never achieved a large practice at the Bar, but during his period of nearly 30 years upon the Bench he came to be regarded as one of the highest exponents of the principles of the Common Law. He published eight volumes of law reports which are referred to by practising lawyers to-day.

BLACK-LEG LABOUR.—This is the name given to persons who take the place of, and work instead of, workmen who are out on strike. (*See* PICKETING; STRIKE; TRADE UNION.)

BLACKMAIL.—Blackmail is not a technical legal expression. It is used popularly to cover all kinds of extortion or attempts at extortion by means of threats to expose improper conduct, criminal or otherwise, on the part of the person blackmailed. It is a most serious crime and has been, not inaptly, described as "murder of the soul." Of recent years the Judges have allowed the names of prosecutors in blackmail cases to be kept secret, thus depriving the blackmailer of his chief weapon—his victim's fear of publicity. In a blackmail case it is, of course, no defence to shew that the matter as to which exposure was threatened was true. If a person is blackmailed his proper course is to inform the police at once. To pay anything to a blackmailer is merely to invite further threats. The appetite of the blackmailer is always whetted by success and he, almost invariably, returns to his victim with ever increasing demands.

The penalties for blackmail are very heavy. Any person who sends any letter demanding money or other property with menaces, or who by any other means attempts to extort by threatening to accuse of certain crimes may be sentenced to penal servitude for life. Any person who by menaces or force demands any money or other property with intent to steal it may be sentenced to penal servitude for a period not exceeding five years.

BLACKSTONE, Sir William (1723-1780).—The English Justinian, he was the first great authority to codify the law of England. By publishing his famous Commentaries, which were originally delivered as lectures at Oxford where he was Vinerian Professor of Law, he gave to lawyers and to the general public a clear exposition of the law, which up to that time could only be found with difficulty in Year Books and obscure reports. He was Solicitor-General to Queen Charlotte and later was raised to the Bench as a Judge in the Common Pleas.

BLASPHEMY.—Blasphemy is a criminal offence and consists of writing or speaking words tending to vilify the Christian religion. In practice the laws as to blasphemy are only invoked in the case of malicious publications or of behaviour intended to wound the feelings of others. Thus serious works of an anti-Christian nature however controversial, if couched with some regard to the decencies of controversy, are not made the subject of prosecutions and indeed could not be. The real test is whether the language used is of a kind reasonably likely to shock the feelings of normal people.

It is to be noted that the Christian religion is the only religion so protected. Thus attacks however violent upon non-Christian religions could not constitute the offence of blasphemy although of course they might be so phrased as to be punishable on other grounds.

Blasphemy is normally punished as blasphemous libel for which both imprisonment, with or without hard labour, and a fine may be imposed.

BLINDNESS.—A blind person has, generally speaking, no special standing in English law, but special provision is made for them in the following cases:—

Signing of Documents.—Documents to be signed by a blind person should, for safety, always be read out to him in full or accurately explained before he signs, and a blind man is entitled to have read out to him any document he is required to sign. If he chooses to dispense with the reading, and signs the document without having heard it read, he will be bound by it as if he had read it. But if a really material part of the document is omitted when the rest of it is read to him, or if he is satisfied with an explanation, and such explanation is inaccurate in any really material respect, he will not be bound by it, for he cannot be taken to have consented to something of which he could have known nothing. For the same reason, he is entitled to have the document read over in a language which he understands. The same rules apply to the signing of documents by illiterate persons. When a blind person makes an affidavit, the commissioner for oaths or other person who takes the affidavit must certify that in his presence the document was read over to the blind person and that he appeared to understand it.

Wills and Gifts.—In order to secure the validity of his will, a blind person should always have his will read out to him before signing it in the presence of persons, who will afterwards be able to give evidence of the reading; for, when probate for the will of a blind person is sought, the Registrar will refuse probate until he has been satisfied that the testator had the will read over to him and that he understood it, or that, by some other means, the testator was aware of the contents of the will.

It has been decided that a person born deaf, dumb and blind cannot validly make any gift; but it is probable that, with the advance of the education of such persons, such a gift would be valid nowadays if it were proved that he intended to make a gift and had sufficient understanding to realize the effect of his actions.

Education.—Parents are bound to see that their children receive suitable elementary instruction, even though the children be deaf or blind. It is, however, the duty of the local education authority to enable blind children to obtain education, and, if efficient and suitable provision is not otherwise made, the authority may either establish a special

A blind man with a specially-trained dog for which no licence is required.

school or contribute towards the establishment of such a school, or may make arrangements for boarding out blind children in homes conveniently near to a certified school. This does not apply to blind children who are idiots, imbeciles or resident in workhouses; the expression "blind" means too blind to be able to read the ordinary school books used by children. When a special school is within reach of the

child's residence, it is the duty of the parents to cause the child to attend the school, and the fact that a guide is necessary is no excuse for failure. When it appears that a blind child is not receiving adequate instruction, application may be made to the Justices for a suitable order, but an order may not, as a general rule, be made for the boarding out of a child unless the consent of the parent is obtained in writing The local authority must always, so far as possible, consider and give effect to the wishes of a child's parents.

Pensions.—A blind person who is so blind as to be unable to perform any work for which eyesight is essential, is entitled to an old age pension at the age of fifty under the same conditions as any normal person is entitled to such pension at the age of seventy. Blind persons, to whom work is given out by any charitable or philanthropic institution and who are not wholly or mainly dependent for their livelihood on their earnings in respect of that work, are not compulsorily insurable under the National Health Insurance Acts. Contributions to Unemployment Insurance are not payable in respect of a person in receipt of such pension.

Homes.—County and Borough Councils are bound to make arrangements to the satisfaction of the Minister of Health for promoting the welfare of blind persons ordinarily resident within their areas, and may for this purpose maintain or contribute towards the provision of workshops, hostels or homes for the reception of the blind. Special Council committees are often established for these purposes, and one-third of the committee may consist of persons who are not members of the council, but who are specially qualified by training or experience in matters relating to the blind. Local authorities also have powers under the Public Health Act, 1925, to make whatever arrangements they may think desirable for assisting in the prevention of blindness, and in particular for the treatment of persons ordinarily resident within the area suffering from any disease of or injury to the eyes.

Voting.—A blind person desiring to record his vote at a parliamentary election may make a declaration of his inability to read, and may require the presiding officer to record his vote on the ballot paper in the presence of the candidates' agents, and to place the ballot paper in the ballot-box. The name of every such voter is then entered in a list called "the list of votes marked by the presiding officer."

Wireless Licences.—By the Wireless Telegraphy (Blind Persons Facilities) Act, 1926, it is provided that where a person satisfies the Postmaster-General that he is a blind person, a licence to establish and maintain and work a wireless telegraph station for the purpose only of receiving messages may be granted to him by the Postmaster-General, subject to such terms, conditions and restrictions as the Postmaster-General may think fit, but without payment of any fee. A blind person is defined as any person (not being resident in a public or charitable institution or in a school) who produces a certificate issued by the Council of the County or Borough in which he is ordinarily resident, that he is registered as a blind person within the County or Borough area. The certificate should be taken to any money order office in order to obtain the licence.

Dog Licences.—No dog licence is required for a dog which is kept and used solely by a blind person for his or her guidance, and, unlike the case of dogs used for tending sheep or cattle, no certificate of exemption need be obtained by the blind person.

Registration.—The method and requirements for registration are prescribed by the Local Authority and differ according to the area in which the blind person is ordinarily resident, but a medical examination by a competent ophthalmic surgeon appointed by the local authority is always necessary before registration can be effected. Applications for registration should be made to the County or Borough Council or to the Committee of such Council appointed for the care of blind persons. Upon registration, the blind person, if a young person, is entitled to receive occupational training as provided by the Council, and, if of advanced years, and without other income, the Council may grant him a weekly sum for his maintenance. The amount of such weekly sum varies according to the area in which the blind person is resident; in the County of London the allowance is 25/- per week; and in the County of Middlesex 27/6 per week. But the allowance is considerably smaller in rural areas where the income from rates available for such purposes is smaller. Other advantages also arise from registration, e.g. the provision of free wireless licences (*see* above).

Postage Rates.—By a Post Office Warrant passed in 1926, it is provided that there shall be charged and paid on postal packets consisting of books and papers impressed with characters in relief, e.g. in Braille, for the use of the blind, the following rates of postage: on every packet not exceeding two pounds in weight, one halfpenny; on every packet exceeding two pounds and not exceeding five pounds, one penny; and, on every packet exceeding five pounds and not exceeding six and a half pounds, three halfpence. For postage abroad, the charges are: up to 2 lbs., $\frac{1}{2}$d.; 2–4 lbs., 1d.; 4–6 lbs., 1$\frac{1}{2}$d.; 6–8lbs., 2d.; 8–11 lbs., 2$\frac{1}{2}$d. Inland postage on all such packages must be prepaid, and, if it is insufficiently prepaid, double the deficiency will be charged. The packet may contain no ordinary printing or writing or other matter, except the title, date of publication, serial number, name and address of the printer and publisher, price and table of contents of the book or periodical, and any key to, or instructions for, the use of the special type. Nor may the package contain any enclosure except the label for the return of the package. Outside, the packet must bear the words "Literature for the Blind," and the name and address of the sender. It must be sent either without a cover or in a cover open at both ends so that it may easily be removed for inspection. It may not exceed 6$\frac{1}{2}$ lbs. in weight or 2×1×1 feet in dimensions, unless it be a roll, when it may not exceed 30 inches in length and 4 inches in diameter. Failure to observe any of these conditions will render the packet liable to be charged as if it had been sent by parcel postage or printed paper rate. For imperial and foreign postage, the same regulations apply as for printed paper, except that the upper left-hand corner must contain the words "Literature for the Blind."

BOARD MEETINGS.—The Directors of a Company are bound to meet and consider its affairs. A board meeting is valid although all directors do not attend so long as all have had notice. The quorum

—i.e. minimum number who must be present—is usually fixed by the Articles, but if not, then it will be the number of directors who usually act. Minutes of these meetings should be kept, but they are private documents and no shareholder has a right to inspect them. In this respect they differ from the Minutes of the meetings of the company itself.

A director is not bound to attend all board meetings but he cannot escape liability for the acts of his co-directors merely by neglecting to attend and giving his consent without consideration to all acts which they advise. (*See* DIRECTORS.)

BOARD OF CONTROL IN LUNACY.—This body, which consists of a chairman and senior Commissioners of whom some have legal and some medical experience, has been invested by Parliament with general supervisory authority over all persons of unsound mind and the hospitals, asylums, etc., in which they are treated. The only province which is still completely outside the powers of the Board is the administration of property, which is still performed by the Management and Administration Department of the High Court of Justice through an official called a Master in Lunacy.

In addition to maintaining their own institutions for violent patients the Commissioners of the Board must themselves make regular visits to all asylums and persons detained as being of unsound mind; there are also inspectors appointed by the board who make even more frequent visits and deal in addition with the details of administration, accommodation, etc.

The board cannot themselves declare a man to be of unsound mind but they can take proceedings to have him certified and a reception order (q.v.) made against him if they consider it desirable. On the other hand they can declare him sane and order his immediate release: any two commissioners being able at any time to order the release of any person detained as of unsound mind.

If it is thought that anyone is unjustly detained it is to the board that application should first be made; friends or relatives who desire to visit a patient or to have him medically examined should apply to the board who have a discretion to grant their request. If it is not known where a patient is kept application should be made to them to search the record to see where he is.

A person of unsound mind may not lawfully be detained in any place which has not been recognised by the Board of Control, and no doctor, keeper or other person may receive him as a patient without first obtaining the board's approval (*see* ASYLUMS). In some cases where a medical certificate is necessary the law requires that it be given by a doctor previously approved for this purpose by the board.

Stringent regulations have been laid down by the board for the conduct of hospitals and all other mental institutions. The buildings themselves must be approved and so must the diet provided. Detailed reports of all persons received, dying, escaping or discharged have to be submitted as well as reports on the treatment given and its effect. (*See* CERTIFICATION OF LUNATICS; LUNATICS.)

BOARDING-HOUSES.—A boarding-house means, in law, premises where board and lodging are provided for approved visitors, and for them only. A boarding-house thus differs from a hotel in that any visitor who is in a fit condition and can pay a reasonable sum must be admitted into the latter if there is room.

In each case it is a question of fact into which category any given premises fall. The mere name or description of the premises is not conclusive evidence; it would, however, in practice be dangerous for a person desirous of opening a boarding-house to call it a " hotel " without the qualification " residential " or " private." The main factors are the advertisements issued and the policy adopted regarding the reception of visitors. Precautions which would go at least a long way towards assuring the position are (i) a system of references; (ii) a system of personal interviews. If the management could show that, in fact, applicants have been refused from time to time as being unsatisfactory, that would be strong evidence of the premises being a boarding-house.

Liabilities of Proprietor.—A boarding-house keeper is not bound to receive any visitor: a prospective boarder thus differs from a traveller visiting a hotel in that the former has no right to be accepted on payment of a reasonable sum.

The proprietor and his boarder can arrange any terms as to the contract by which their relationship is to be governed, which terms need not be in writing unless the contract is for more than a year certain, but in the absence of express terms the following are the rights of the boarding-house proprietor and the boarder. The proprietor is bound to provide the boarder with the use of a bedroom and the public rooms until reasonable notice has been given by either party and has expired. As to what is reasonable notice depends chiefly on the arrangements made as to payment. When payment is weekly or monthly, the reasonable notice will usually be held to be a week or a month respectively.

The proprietor is not regarded as an insurer of the boarder's property. There is, however, a duty on the proprietor to carry on the business with reasonable care for the safety of the property of his boarders, and if such property is lost or damaged through his wilful default or through the negligence of himself or of his servants while acting within the scope of their employment, he will be liable for such loss or damage. What amounts to reasonable care depends on the normal conduct of a boarding-house of that nature, and so varies in each particular case, all the circumstances of which must be considered.

If the boarder's property is stolen by a servant of the proprietor, the proprietor is not liable unless he was negligent either in engaging the servant without taking up references with due care, or in failing to dismiss the servant after due cause for suspicion had been given.

If the boarder's property is stolen by a fellow boarder, the proprietor is not liable unless he has been negligent in admitting that fellow boarder. The degree of care that must be taken in regard to the admission of boarders varies according to the type of the boarding-house.

If the boarder hands over to the proprietor any of his property for safe custody, the latter's duty is to preserve the property with the same degree of care as a prudent man would take in respect of his own, and he will be liable for loss or damage suffered unless he can shew that neither his own wilful act nor his want of care was the cause.

In all the circumstances referred to above there is this modification to the proprietor's responsibility for the results of his negli-

gence: he will escape liability if he can shew that the loss or damage would not have happened if the boarder himself had used the ordinary care that a prudent man could be expected to have taken. The proprietor's liability for personal injury suffered by a boarder is identical with that of the management of a hotel, so also is the proprietor's duty in regard to the registration of aliens and to notification of cases of infectious diseases. (*See* HOTELS.)

Remedies of Proprietor.—In contrast to the case of hotel proprietors, the only remedy open to the proprietor of a boarding-house in respect of unpaid bills is to sue the boarder. He has no right to detain or to sell the boarder's property, nor any right of distress.

Rights of Boarders.—A boarder has an exclusive licence for the use of his room, but has no legal right of property in it and therefore cannot transfer to anyone else the right to use it. He also has the right to use the public rooms and accommodation. These rights continue until the expiration of a reasonable notice or, in the event of there being a special contract, until such contract is ended. (*See* APARTMENTS; HOTELS.)

BODY.—As in law there can be no ownership of a dead body it cannot be stolen, but it is a punishable offence to disinter a body without lawful authority. It is no defence to show that the disinterment was with pious or laudable object, or done in a decent and proper manner.

In the last century two men named Burke and Hare carried on a trade of what was popularly called Body Snatching, and sold the bodies for the purpose of anatomical examination by schools of anatomy. Burke was eventually executed for committing a murder with the object of obtaining a body for dissection. To prevent the commission of crime and ensure a sufficient supply of subjects for anatomical schools the Anatomy Act was passed soon after to regulate schools of anatomy. (*See* BURIAL.)

BONA FIDE.—This is a Latin expression meaning "in good faith." It is in constant legal use and occurs frequently in numerous contracts and other documents of legal importance.

BONA VACANTIA.—This is a Latin expression meaning goods which have no owner. Such goods must be distinguished from things which are incapable of having an owner. ⸰ They are articles of property which happen not to be owned at a particular time.

BOND.—A bond is a document under seal, i.e. a deed (q.v.) in which one person, called the Obligor, binds himself to pay a sum of money to another person, called the Obligee, either at once or at some fixed future time. A bond is very rarely found in this simple form and almost always has attached to it a condition, the provision usually being that if the person making the bond does a certain act then the bond shall be void, and the money payable under it shall not be due. In this way a bond is used to impose a penalty on a person who does not do what he has promised to do, although in practice the law will not allow the amount of the penalty to be recovered, but will instead award to the person suing the actual damages he has suffered through the failure of the other party to do what he promised to do.

⸰A usual form of bond, known as a common money bond, provides that the obligor shall pay the obligee a sum of money, say, £100, on a certain date with the condition that if a smaller sum of money, say, £50, is paid on an earlier date the bond shall be void. As has been stated above the law will treat this bond as a penalty which will not be enforced and will only allow the actual amount of money due with interest to be paid. Where the bond provides for the payment of a sum of money, if an agreement is not carried out, the person suing upon the bond can only recover the actual damage sustained by him and not the full amount of the bond.

Post obit bond.—This is a bond which is stated to become void if a sum of money is paid after the death of a specified person, and is usually given in respect of a loan.

Lloyds Bond.—These are bonds issued by a Company for money borrowed or in discharge of a liability already existing. They may be used in cases where a Company has already borrowed up to the amount authorized by its Memorandum and Articles, and the lender may recover from the Company even though the transaction is beyond the powers of the Company, if the money has to be used to pay off some of the Company's debts.

The condition in a bond must not be the doing of something which is illegal, and so a bond would be void which was made for the purpose of procuring a marriage between two persons, for a contract to procure a marriage is illegal.

BOND (SCOTS LAW).—A bond in Scots Law is merely a document containing an obligation to pay money. The personal obligation to pay money may be coupled with the transfer of some property which is to be held in security for the payment. Where the property is movable the transaction is called a bond and assignation in security, and where the property is heritable, i.e. land, the transaction is known as a bond and disposition in security. Thus, if a person wished to raise money on an insurance policy over his life, he would grant to the lender of the money a bond for the sum lent and an assignation of the policy.

A special kind of bond used for the purpose of obtaining an overdraft from the bank is known as a cash credit bond. Under this the person borrowing the money obtains certain other persons to join with him as cautioners, i.e. sureties, and each of them binds himself to repay the money which may be advanced by the Bank.

A bond usually contains a clause consenting to the registration of the document for "preservation and execution." This is of great importance. It allows the creditor to record the bond either in the register called the Books of Council and Session in Edinburgh or in the Books of a Sheriff Court. If the debtor fails to pay the money due under the bond the creditor is able to seize his goods and other property without first obtaining an order of the Court by bringing an action. He obtains an extract from the register which is equivalent to Judgment. This is known as Summary Diligence (q.v.). (*See* SECURITY.)

BONUS SHARES.—In certain cases when a Company has accumulated a large sum of money out of its profits, instead of paying it over to its shareholders in the form of dividends, it may issue to them bonus shares, keeping the money in payment for the shares, in this way increasing its capital. Any shareholder can of course sell the shares and so turn the bonus shares into cash as soon as he gets them. If he does not do so the shares will of course entitle him to a dividend on future profits like any other shares. There are two advantages of bonus shares. One is that the Company can use its profits more easily in the expansion of its business by capitalizing them, and the second is that profits distributed as bonus shares are not liable to surtax in the hands of the shareholder. Before a Company can issue bonus shares it must have a clause in its Articles authorizing it to increase its capital, and the amount of profits in its hands must be enough to pay the sums that would have been paid for the shares, had they been issued for cash instead of as bonus shares.

The issue of bonus shares is very different from the grant of a cash bonus which is in reality nothing but an additional dividend and is liable to surtax. The grant of a cash bonus does not increase the Company's capital. (*See* CAPITAL; DIVIDEND; SHARES.)

BOOK DEBTS.—When a person is carrying on business he will in the ordinary course be owed money by the persons with whom he is trading, and these debts are known as book debts. They may be transferred from one person to another by an assignment, but in certain cases this assignment will not be valid if the person to whom the debts are owed becomes bankrupt unless it is registered as a Bill of Sale. (*See* ASSIGNMENT; BILLS OF SALE.)

BOOKMAKER.—By the Finance Act, 1926, excise duties (known as "betting duties") were imposed upon bookmakers' certificates and entry certificates, but such duties were abolished in 1930. A duty which had been imposed upon bets made with bookmakers was abolished in 1929. By the Betting Act, 1853, it is provided that no house, office, room or other place may, under penalty not exceeding £100 or six months imprisonment, be kept for betting with persons resorting thereto; it has been held that an enclosure on a racecourse is not a "place" within the Act, but that it may become so if a bookmaker sets up a stool, umbrella or stand in such a way as to fix his position and to indicate the place where a man will be found who will accept bets. If, however, his apparatus serves to indicate merely his identity and his willingness to accept bets from anyone who will come to bet, it will not be a "place" within the Act. (*See* SPECIAL SUPPLEMENT "GAMBLING.")

BOROUGH.—A town acquires the title of "borough" either by Act of Parliament or by Royal grant. There are two kinds of boroughs: municipal boroughs and county boroughs. A county borough conducts its administration as if it were a separate and distinct county, but a municipal borough is, to some extent, controlled by the county council of the county in which it is situated. All boroughs are governed by a mayor, aldermen and councillors. The councillors are elected by the ratepayers, and after they have been elected they choose from their own number the mayor and the aldermen. For the powers and duties of borough councils, *see also* LOCAL GOVERNMENT.

BOROUGH COUNCIL.—A borough council is composed of the mayor, aldermen and councillors, all of whom are elected. The councillors are elected by the burgesses or citizens (i.e. the local government electors) to hold office for three years; the aldermen are elected by the councillors to hold office for six years; and the mayor is elected by the whole council to hold office for one year. For the powers and duties of a borough council, *see* LOCAL GOVERNMENT.

BORSTAL.—A Borstal Institution is a place where young persons of sixteen and no more than twenty-one years of age may be detained and subjected to discipline and industrial and other training. The objects of the Institution are to endeavour to prevent crime and to reform such young persons as are convicted of offences for which, on indictment, they would be liable to be sentenced to imprisonment or penal servitude. Both males and females may be sent to a Borstal Institution.

In the case of a person, within the limit of age already referred to, who has been summarily convicted of an offence for which a term of imprisonment for one month or upwards may be imposed without option of a fine, the Court may, instead of passing sentence, commit him to prison until the next Assizes or Quarter Sessions for consideration as to whether he should be detained in a Borstal Institution. This can only be done, however, if it is proved at the Court of Summary Jurisdiction where he is convicted that he has previously been convicted of an offence or, having been previously put on probation, he has failed to obey any condition of such probation and that because of his associations with bad characters and his own criminal tendencies and habits he should be detained in his own interests in an endeavour to reform him. A term of penal discipline in the Institution must not be for more than three years.

Any person, within the age limits already mentioned, who is undergoing sentence by way of imprisonment or penal servitude may be transferred to a Borstal Institution on the Authority of the Secretary of State addressed to the Prison Commissioners. This may be done if the Secretary of State considers it to the advantage of the prisoner. On such transfer the prisoner can be detained for a period representing the whole or any part of the unexpired term of his original sentence.

At any time after the expiration of six months from the commencement of detention, in the case of males, they may be released on licence. The licence is in a form containing conditions laid down by regulations made by the Secretary of State. In the case of females, a release on licence may be made at the expiration of three months. The licence can be revoked and the person again detained for a period not exceeding one year. During this period they can, however, be again released on licence.

BOTTOMRY.—Formerly when a ship was in a foreign port and in need of money the master would borrow the money and give in security for the loan a Bottomry Bond. The effect of this was that, if the debt was not paid within a certain time of the ship's arrival at her home port, the lender could take the ship and the money due for freight, and in some cases also the cargo on board in payment of the debt. If the ship never arrived home safely but was lost, no part of the debt was repayable. The person who lent money upon a bottomry bond took therefore a considerable risk and the rate of interest payable on money was usually high. Since methods of communication have so much improved in modern times it is almost always possible for a master to obtain funds by communicating with his owners, and bottomry bonds are now rarely found. (*See* SHIPPING.)

BOXING.—Boxing is regarded as a lawful sport. Prize fighting on the other hand is illegal. The two are distinguished by this test—is there any intention on the part of the contestant to injure his opponent? Where proper gloves are used it may be assumed that the contest is a boxing match, and not a prize fight. If a person is injured in the course of a lawful match, in the absence of any definite unfairness on the other side, the person inflicting the injury is not liable either civilly or criminally. The same applies if one of the boxers is accidentally killed.

BRAMPTON, Lord (1817-1907).— As Henry Hawkins he took part in many of the famous trials of his time, including the two Tichborne trials. On the Bench he had the reputation of "a hanging Judge" and his judicial conduct aroused great controversy. On his retirement he was made a peer.

BREACH OF CONTRACT.— Wherever a person enters into a contract (q.v.) it is his duty to do all those things which he has promised by the terms of his contract to do. As long as both parties to a contract fulfil their promises to each other's satisfaction the doctrines of law are not deeply concerned with their acts; but the moment one of the parties fails to fulfil the terms of the contract into which he has entered, it is open to the other party to invoke the assistance of the law courts either to compel performance of the contract or to award him damages for the other party's failure to perform it.

Any departure from the terms of a contract, or any failure to observe it, even in the minutest particular, is known as a breach of contract, and gives a right to the party who has been wronged to call the processes of the law into motion, by the issue of a writ in the High Court or of a Plaint and Summons in the County Court.

There are three chief methods by which a person may enforce in a Court of Law the observance of a contract, when its terms are being broken by the other party. The Court may: (1) Order the other party to carry out the contract, (2) Prevent the other party from breaking the contract or (3) Order that the party in the wrong shall pay pecuniary compensation to the party wronged; and at the same time it may or may not release the party wronged from his liability to perform his part of the contract. The first remedy is called specific performance, the second an injunction, while the third is known as damages for breach of contract. (*See* CONTRACT; DAMAGES; INJUNCTION; SPECIFIC PERFORMANCE.)

BREAD.—A baker can make or sell bread made with flour, meal of wheat, barley, rye, oats, buckwheat, Indian corn, peas, beans, rice or potatoes, and he may mix with these substances in any proportion he thinks fit the following ingredients: common salt, pure water, eggs, milk, barm, leaven, potato and other yeast. An ingredient to make flour self-raising may be used, and self-raising flour containing an ingredient to make cakes or puddings may be sold. Apart from these, no other ingredient may be used, and if such other ingredient is knowingly used, the offender is liable to a penalty of £10. The justices may order the name of an offender and his place of abode and offence to be advertised in a local newspaper. Similarly it is an offence to put any ingredient other than those set out above into flour which is intended for sale. The penalty for this offence is a fine of £20 maximum.

Apart from these statutory prohibitions it is a common law misdemeanour to sell bread containing any noxious or unwholesome material, and the addition of the noxious material need not be done by the baker personally, for he is responsible for the failings of any servant who is employed to use a material which might be dangerous.

Bread made of peas, or beans, or of any sort of grain other than wheat must be marked with a large letter M. Omission so to mark bread involves a penalty of 10/- for every pound weight of unmarked bread made for sale or sold.

Bread must be sold by net weight, but fancy bread and loaves not exceeding twelve ounces in weight are exempt from this provision. Ordinary bread sold by net weight must be at least 1 lb. in weight, and loaves must be made which weigh an integral number of pounds. That is to say you cannot sell a loaf weighing 1¾ lbs. Every person who sells bread must keep in a conspicuous part of his shop a correct weighing machine, and if requested to do so by either a purchaser or an inspector of weights and measures, must weigh bread in the presence of the person so requesting him. Every person who carries bread for sale or delivery to a purchaser must carry a correct weighing machine on his cart, and, if required to do so by an inspector of weights and measures, must permit the inspector to weigh the bread upon the said machine.

Bread, rolls and cakes may not be made on Sunday, and they may not be sold after 1.30 p.m. on Sunday. A baker must not do any work in the way of his trade as a baker on Sunday, except so far as may be necessary to prepare the bread or dough for the following day's bakery. He may, however deliver bakings to his customers up to 1.30 p.m. (*See* FOOD.)

BREWSTER SESSIONS.—This is the name given to the general annual licensing meeting of justices held in the first fourteen days of February of each year, at which a great part of the licensing business is conducted. One such meeting is held in each licensing district, which is a petty sessional division of the county. At these meetings and at their adjournments, applications for new licences, removals and renewals are heard in public. Twenty-one days before the annual meeting is held the justices must meet and appoint the day, hour and place of the meeting. When these are decided the clerk must, within five days, send notices to the police, who must place notices upon the door of the parish churches in all parishes of the district and also serve copies upon the licensing justices, holders of justices' licences and applicants for justices' licences. The same procedure must be followed in the case of adjournments of the licensing meeting.

BRIBERY.—To offer or receive a bribe is a serious criminal offence. To offer a bribe to any agent in order to influence him the way in which he discharges his principal's business is a misdemeanour punishable with two years' imprisonment with hard labour and a fine not exceeding £500. If an agent corruptly accepts or agrees to accept any bribe he becomes liable to the same penalties. Similar punishments may be inflicted in cases of bribery or attempted bribery of judicial officers or public servants. It is important to note that the offence of bribery can take place even though the bribe is not actually money, it may be any gift or consideration.

Bribery is of importance in respect not only to the criminal law but also to the ordinary law of contract. Acceptance of a bribe is sufficient ground to justify the immediate dismissal without notice of any servant or agent. Moreover, the employer or principal may require the person bribed to hand over the money he has received in respect of the bribe. (*See* CORRUPTION.)

BRIDES IN THE BATH CASE, THE.—The trial of George Joseph Smith, one of the most atrocious monsters in the history of crime, was not possessed of that dramatic interest generally associated with famous murder cases. There was no sympathy for Smith in Court, and it was clear from the first that he was a guilty man.

Mr. Justice Scrutton presided at his trial at the Old Bailey for the murder of Bessie Mundy. Smith was defended by Marshall Hall, K.C., while three famous Treasury Counsel, Archibald Bodkin, Travers Humphreys and Cecil Whitely, represented the Crown.

Evidence of System.—After legal argument as to its admissibility, evidence was given for the prosecution of the circumstances in which two other women had met their deaths. This was not to prove that Smith had murdered Bessie Mundy, but to negative the defence of accident and to show that the prisoner had a system of murdering these women, after going through a form of marriage, to obtain their money. Undoubtedly were it not for these other cases Smith would have escaped justice.

As the case for the prosecution proceeded a ghastly tale was unfolded. In each case the circumstances were the same: Smith would meet these lonely women, make love to them, go through a form of marriage, and by exercising his extraordinary powers of fascination persuade them to make all their money over to him. In each case the bride met her death shortly after the wedding in identical circumstances, being found dead from shock in a bath.

Smith did not go into the box nor did he call any witnesses. This gave his defender, Marshall Hall, the last word with the jury. At the end of 8 days the inevitable verdict of guilty was given. 112 witnesses were called for the prosecution, and over 260 exhibits shown in Court.

It was later shown that Smith had a bad criminal record, had served sentences for larceny, and had made eight bigamous marriages.

BRIEF.—When a solicitor instructs counsel—i.e. a barrister—to appear in Court, he places before him the papers in the case in the form of a Brief. The brief consists of the comments on the case made by the solicitor together with all other papers which have a bearing on it. The papers are usually tied together with red tape. The name of the barrister to whom they are delivered is marked on the outside together with the fee that is to be paid to him. After a case has been tried the barrister endorses his brief with the result of the case. Sometimes when a case is settled out of Court the barrister on each side endorses the settlement on the brief.

BRITISH SUBJECT.—A person may be a British subject either by birth, or by naturalization (*see* NATURALIZATION), or by the annexation to the British Empire of territory in which he lived, or, in the case of a woman, by marriage with a British subject.

Persons born in the British Empire.—Every child born within His Majesty's dominions is a British subject unless he was the child of a foreign ambassador or other personal representative of a foreign country. It makes no difference that his parents were aliens or, possibly, even that they were alien enemies, unless they were present within the dominions only as a result of foreign hostile invasion; but it is possible that the child of an enemy prisoner or person interned may be an alien. The term "His Majesty's dominions" is nowhere defined, but it does not, it seems, include protectorates.

Persons born at Sea.—Any person born on board a British ship is a British subject, whether or not the ship was, at the time, in foreign waters or even in a foreign port. A person born in a foreign ship is not a British subject merely by reason of the ship's having been in British territorial waters, or even in a British port at the time of the birth.

Persons born outside the British Empire.—A person born outside His Majesty's dominions is a British subject only: (i) if his father was, at the time of the birth, a British subject by reason of having been born within the King's dominions; or (ii) if he was born after 1st January, 1915, and his father was, at the time of the birth, a British subject by reason of having been naturalized or by reason of the annexation of territory to the British Crown; or (iii) if his father was a British subject and, at the time of the birth, was in the service of the Crown; or (iv) in the case of a person born after 1st January, 1915, if his father was a British subject and the birth was registered at the British Consulate within one year or, in special circumstances, two years; or (v) in the case of a person born before 1st January, 1915, if his father was a British subject and his paternal grandfather had been born on British soil, and the birth had been registered at the British consulate before 1st August, 1923; or (vi) if his father or mother was a British subject and he himself was born in any place where the King exercises jurisdiction over British subjects, e.g. in a protectorate. The broad rule, therefore, is that a person born after 1914 is a British subject if his father was born on British soil or was naturalized. The rule before 1915 was different, and still applies to persons born before that date; the rule then was, broadly, that a person born abroad was a British subject (i) if his father was born on British soil, or (ii) if his father was a British subject (though not born on British soil) *and* his paternal grandfather was born on British soil.

Loss of British Nationality.—When the birth has to be registered in order to obtain the status of British subject, such person will lose his British nationality unless, within one year of his attaining twenty-one, he makes a declaration of retention of his British nationality and divests himself, if possible, of any other nationality. The purpose of this provision is to meet cases where a person has acquired dual nationality, as in many cases he may, by having been born in a foreign country, whereby he became a subject of that country, and by having at the same time had his birth registered at the British consulate, whereby he became also a British subject. Conversely, any person who is a natural-born British subject by reason of having been born in British territory, and at the same time is a subject of a foreign state (e.g. born in England of French parents), may make what is known as a declaration of alienage, provided he is of full age and under no disability (e.g. is not insane). And any British subject born outside British territory may make such declaration, whether or not he is also a national of another state. In a few cases, naturalized persons may make a

similar declaration, and they thereupon revert to their former nationality. If a person residing in a foreign state becomes a naturalized subject of that state he automatically loses his British nationality; but he still remains liable for acts done while a British subject. Any person whose name was included in his parents' certificate of naturalization may, within a year after attaining twenty-one, make a declaration of alienage. A naturalized person will also cease to be a naturalized subject on revocation of his certificate of naturalization. Marriage will often deprive a woman of British nationality: if she marries an alien, she loses British nationality, but if she marries a British subject who subsequently loses his British nationality, she may make a declaration of retention of British nationality and thereby remain British. An alien woman becomes British by marrying a British subject and she remains British even after her husband's death. On revocation of a certificate of naturalization of a husband, the wife and children under twenty-one remain British unless (i) the revocation specifically mentions them or (ii) the wife, within six months, makes a declaration of alienage. In all other cases the children under twenty-one of a person losing British nationality also cease to be British, provided that, on ceasing to be British, they will become the subjects of a foreign country by the law of such country. This does not apply to the children of a widow who, by marrying an alien, herself becomes an alien.

No person who has lost British nationality may recover it unless he obtains a certificate of naturalization in the ordinary way. There is this exception: a person who has lost British nationality by his parent having become an alien may, within a year of attaining twenty-one, make a declaration that he desires to be readmitted to British nationality. As to the disadvantages under which aliens find themselves, *see* ALIENS. As to persons without nationality, *see* NATIONALITY. (*See also* ALLEGIANCE; DENIZENS; NATURALIZATION; PASSPORT.)

BROKER.—Any agent who negotiates transactions in connection with the sale of goods, stocks and shares, or insurance policies, is a broker. A broker is entitled to the customary reward for his services, and if he negotiates as agent only, he is not liable for his principal's duties. (*See* PRINCIPAL AND AGENT; STOCK EXCHANGE.)

BROTHEL.—Any house to which women and men are permitted to resort for immoral purposes is a brothel. A house used by one woman only is not a brothel. It is an offence to manage or take any part in the management of a brothel, or knowingly let a house or permit it to be used as a brothel. A person convicted of any such offence is liable to a fine of not more than £100 or to imprisonment with or without hard labour for not more than three months. A second offence is punishable more severely. A conviction of a tenant of a house for an offence of this nature entitles the landlord to obtain a fresh tenant. (*See* DISORDERLY HOUSE.)

BROUGHAM, Lord (1778-1868).—An able lawyer but chiefly famous on

Lord Brougham.

account of his political career. He was a powerful orator and possessed a peculiar and biting wit, this together with his tall bony appearance made him a favourite subject for caricaturists of the time. His greatest legal achievement was his spirited defence of Queen Caroline as her Attorney-General. He was made Lord Chancellor by the Whig Government.

BUCKMASTER, Lord (1861-   ).—A former Lord Chancellor and one of the most distinguished of the present Law Lords. He is a keen social reformer, both for the Divorce Laws of this country, and those relating to motorists. He was a Liberal member in the House of Commons and held the office of Solicitor-General in 1913. During the first two years of the Great War he was Director of the Press Bureau.

BUILDING CONTRACTS.—A building contract is entered into between the owner or person in possession of land, who is known as the building owner or employer, and the contractor who is to put up the building. When the owner has decided to build he will take the following steps. After a site has been chosen he will approach an architect and give him all possible particulars, such as the use to which the proposed building is to be put and the number of persons it is to house. Most important, of course, is the amount of money that the owner is willing to spend.

The architect will then work out a rough scheme and get out preliminary sketch plans. These will be submitted to the owner for his approval. If the preliminary sketch plans are approved, the owner will instruct the architect to prepare contract drawings and specifications. In these he will, in fact, have described the whole of the proposed building in detail. The specifications deal with the whole of the materials to be used and all the details of every trade concerned, such as electric lighting and water supply, etc. The contract drawings and specifications are sufficient to enable the architect to get in tenders. If the proposed building is to be a large one, bills of quantities are prepared by quantity surveyors, as the contract drawings and specifications alone do not give sufficient detail for tenders to be worked out when the work is very large. These bills give in greater detail the amount of materials needed; for example, there will be an estimate of the exact number of bricks required. The preparation of the contract drawings represents a definite stage in the relationship between the architect and the employer: the former is now entitled to a definite proportion of his fees.

The next step is for the architect to get in tenders from contractors. This may be by advertisement but in practice the architect will choose a few contractors known to him. He will send them the contract drawings and specifications from which the contractors will prepare their tenders, stating the amount for which they are prepared to execute the building as drawn and specified. There is a meeting at the architect's office at which the tenders that have been sent to the architect in sealed envelopes are opened. It is customary to accept the lowest figure sent in though there is no obligation to do so, unless it has been expressly stated that the lowest tender will be accepted.

The owner and the contractor, whose tender has been accepted, then enter into the building contract. This is drawn up by the architect. He will probably use the printed form that is issued by the Royal Institute of British Architects as being the most suitable form that can be used. This is then signed by the owner and the contractor with witnesses to the signatures. The architect is not a party to the building contract. The main clauses are those giving the amount to be paid by the owner and the conditions and methods of payment. The specifications rather than the contract itself describe exactly and in full the materials to be used and the standard of workmanship. They and the contract drawings, however, form part of the contract and are also signed.

Work under the contract will now start. It is the duty of the architect to see that the employer is getting both good and the agreed value for his money in the materials and the workmanship of the contractor. The architect cannot, however, supervise every detail and, where the work is large, a clerk of the works is employed. He is independent of the contractor, being paid by the owner. He is a trained man and remains permanently on the works on behalf of the architect to see that the work is being carried out properly. As the work continues the building contractor will become entitled to an instalment payment. This falls due when work to a certain value has been completed; the exact times being laid down in the conditions of payment in the contract. Before, however, the building contractor is entitled to payment he must get a progress certificate from the architect. This is a signed form from the architect that the work has been to the value mentioned. Actually the giving of a certificate

does not necessarily mean that the work has been done according to specification or that it will eventually be approved. Also it is the usual practice for the architect to retain a percentage of the money that he pays over under a progress certificate for maintenance for a given period after completion. While the work is in progress the architect can insist on reasonable variations from the specifications and drawings and it will not affect the continuance of the contract; but such variation must be within reasonable limits and not go so far as to alter the whole scheme of the work. When the work is finished the architect will give the contractor a certificate of completion if he is satisfied.

There then follows a period known as the maintenance period. During this period all defects that appear in the building have to be made good at the expense of the contractor. When this period is over the contractor will get a final certificate from the architect, who will pay him the balance of the money to be paid but which the architect retained in his own hands when giving progress certificates.

Arbitration.—In the event of the architect and the building contractor not being able to agree on a particular matter arising during the work, the dispute will be submitted to an arbitrator. The contract usually names two or three persons who may be called on to act when such a dispute arises.

Provisional Sums.—A building contract will often contain a clause setting aside a sum of money from the money to be paid and allotting it to work that must be carried out by a specialist; for example, the heating arrangements. The contract may specify a particular firm that is to do this work, or the architect may get tenders for it and so get it done for less than the sum named in the contract. The building contractor must always allow that sum to be set aside and has no control over it. It is under the complete control of the architect who may effect a saving on the total cost if he gets in tenders that are for less than the provisional sum. (*See* ARCHITECTS; QUANTITY SURVEYORS.)

BUILDINGS.—It is part of the duty of the local authority in each district to make bye-laws regulating the erection of new buildings and the alteration of existing ones in their district. Such bye-laws when made must be submitted to the Minister of Health for confirmation, and the Minister, if he is satisfied that the existing bye-laws in any district are handicapping the erection of any building, may require the local authority to revoke them or substitute new ones.

The great majority of the regulations apply to the erection of new buildings, but the following operations are considered to be equivalent to the erection of a new building:—

(a) The re-erection of any building pulled down to, or below, the ground floor.

(b) The re-erection wholly or partially of any building of which an outer wall is pulled down or burnt down to, or within, ten feet of the surface of the ground adjoining the lowest storey of the building.

(c) The conversion into a dwelling house of any building not originally constructed for human habitation, or the conversion into more than one dwelling house of a building originally constructed as one dwelling house only.

(d) The reconversion into a dwelling house of any building which has been discontinued as, or used for, any purpose other than that of a dwelling house.

(e) The making of any addition to an existing building by raising any part of the roof, by altering a wall, or making any projection from the building, but so far as regards the addition only.

(f) The roofing over of an open space between walls or buildings.

Plans are necessary before building can be started.— Before a new building, even a wooden shed like a small garage, can be erected plans must be prepared and deposited with the local authority. A local authority must either approve or disapprove the plans within one month after they are delivered to them. Until such approval is obtained no building may be commenced, and any building which is erected or commenced before the plans have been approved may in fact be pulled down by the direction of the local authority.

5

If plans are to obtain the approval of the local authority they must conform to the building regulations in force in the district. These regulations cover a very wide range of matters connected with building, and they may differ appreciably in different districts. In practically every district, however, regulations are in force with respect to the following matters:—

(1) The structure of the walls, foundations, roofs and chimneys of new buildings; these are to secure the stability of the building and to prevent fires.

(2) The adequacy of the space about the buildings, to secure the circulation of air and the ventilation of the buildings.

(3) The drainage of the buildings, water closets, etc.

(4) The structure of the floors, hearths and staircases and the height of rooms which are intended for human habitation.

(5) The height of the buildings themselves.

Every builder and architect must acquaint himself with the local restrictions upon buildings, and must make his plans or erect his building, as the case may be, in accordance with them.

What is the Building Line?—The building line is the general line of the buildings in any street, and no building may be erected beyond the line except with the consent of the local authority if the building line is within fifty feet of the highway. If the building line is more than fifty feet from the highway, then a building may not be erected within fifty feet of the highway. To build beyond the building line without the consent of the local authority is a criminal offence and any offending building may be ordered to be demolished.

Buildings in London.—The erection and alteration of buildings in London is governed by a local Act of Parliament, The London Building Act, 1930. This Act contains all the regulations with regard to structure, height, materials, etc., and the following are only a few of its most interesting and important provisions:—

(a) No building, except a church or a chapel, may be erected of, or increased to, a greater height than eighty feet. This limit does not include the height of an ornamental tower or turret. If a building is to be erected or altered on a site on the side of a street which was laid out after the 7th August, 1862, and the width of the street is less than fifty feet, then the height of that building must not exceed the distance from the front of it to the other side of the street.

(b) Every building in London must be enclosed with walls constructed of brick, stone or other hard and incombustible material.

(c) To be considered habitable the height of a room must be at least eight feet six inches from floor to ceiling over the whole area of the room; if, however, the room is in the attic, then the regulation is complied with if it is eight feet six inches in height over an area which is half the area of the whole room.

Places of Public Resort.—Public Buildings are governed by special regulations which are made with a view to ensuring the safety of persons using them. For example, there are very strict regulations about the means of escape from fire, the number of exits which must be provided, and the width of the passages leading into or out of the building. The District Surveyor's approval is necessary before a building may be used as a place of public resort. (*See* BUILDING CONTRACTS; HOUSING, LOCAL GOVERNMENT.)

BUILDING SCHEME.— Local authorities are given the power of submitting a scheme for Town or Country Planning to the Minister of Health, and, if such scheme is approved by him and not disallowed by Parliament, they may proceed in accordance with its provisions. Such a planning scheme necessarily involves the planning of new buildings to be comprised in the area, and a building scheme therefore has to be prepared within the framework of the general planning scheme. A Building Scheme usually includes provisions prescribing the space about the buildings, limiting the number, regulating the design and construction, and restricting the uses to which such buildings may be put. The provisions may be made to apply to existing buildings within the area comprised in the scheme, if such provisions will tend to produce uniformity throughout the planned area. The provisions of the scheme do not apply to any building or the erection of any building which is, or is to be, used mainly for agricultural purposes.

The term Building Scheme is loosely used to describe the houses or buildings when they are completed, but it really means the plan in accordance with which an area has been built over. (*See* HOUSING; LOCAL GOVERNMENT; TOWN PLANNING.)

BUILDING SOCIETIES.—The objects and rules of building societies differ one from another, but the general object is as follows: a number of persons agree together to contribute a fixed sum (say, £100) each to a common fund. Each contributor is issued with a £100 share and is bound to contribute, not in a lump sum, but by periodical (usually monthly) instalments, until he has made up the whole £100. Every member is entitled, before the full number of periodical payments has been made, to draw upon the common fund to the extent of his £100 share, on the understanding that he will continue to pay the monthly instalments as they fall due, and as security for such payments he mortgages his freehold or leasehold property to the society. In effect, the society advances him money in order that he may buy a house, which he then mortgages as security for the money so advanced. In most cases, the member is not entitled to obtain advances to the full extent of the £100 because such advance will usually be made only on the deduction of a discount, varying according to the number of monthly instalments still owing.

Formation and Constitution of a Society.—Practically all building societies are now controlled by Acts of Parliament, and are known as incorporated societies, though about thirty still exist in an older form, being known as unincorporated societies. Any new society must comply with the statutory requirements unless its members number less than twenty. But even a smaller number, provided it exceeds two, may (and, for safety, should) proceed under the Acts. In view of the rarity of unincorporated societies, it is not intended here to discuss the law relating to them, and the following remarks must be taken not to apply to such societies. The first step in the creation of an incorporated society is to effect the incorporation (fee, £10).

For this purpose, the promoters must agree upon the rules by which the society is to be governed. Two copies of these rules, together with the proper application form, must be sent to the Chief Registrar of Friendly Societies, 17 North Audley Street, London, W.1. If the proposed rules comply with the statutory requirements, they are approved by the Registrar, who grants a certificate of incorporation, whereby the society becomes a body corporate, so that it is entitled to perform its functions in its own name; but anything that the society does outside the powers specifically conferred upon it by statute or by the rules it has adopted is void. A penalty of £5 a day may be inflicted on a person who falsely represents that a business he is carrying on is incorporated as a building society. The officers of the society must include a board of directors or managing committee, two auditors and a manager or secretary.

Special provisions have been made to ensure the honesty of all such officers, e.g. they may not accept any gift in connection with any loan made by the society, and they may not purchase even in open auction any of the lands sold by the society as a result of foreclosure. The directors of a building society have very much the same powers and duties as the directors of ordinary limited companies. They will be liable to the society and, probably, to third persons, if they do anything outside the powers conferred upon them by the rules of the society, even though they have acted in the name of the society; and the society itself is not responsible for such acts. It is therefore always desirable to make sure that any unusual course adopted by a building society is authorized by its rules.

Rules.—The rules of a building society are, in the first place, made by the promoters and approved by the Registrar, who will reject any proposed rules which he considers would be unlawful. Every officer of the society and every member is bound by the rules, and it is not open to him to say that he has not read them. Copies of the current rules may always be obtained by any member of the public on application

to the secretary of the society, and on payment of a fee that may never exceed one shilling. Certain matters must be included in the rules, e.g. the manner in which advances are to be made, the purpose to which funds are to be applied, the investment of funds, the mode in which meetings are to be called, borrowing powers of the society, the mode in which members may withdraw from the society, etc. Any other additional matters may be included, provided they do not convert the society into something other than a building society, e.g. a trading company, or a bank, or a fire insurance company. Certain other rules are also forbidden, e.g. no rule may provide that shares cannot be withdrawn from the funds, and the terms upon which mortgages may be redeemed by a member must be bona fide and definite. The rules of societies formed after 25th August, 1894, may not provide for the granting of advances to members by ballot. Subject to certain limitations, rules may be altered or rescinded.

Members.—The members of a building society are of two classes, known as "advanced" (or "borrowing") members and "unadvanced" (or "investing") members. A member who has taken, say, a £100 share in the society may, as mentioned above, borrow up to about £100 *before* he has paid up the full £100. Until he avails himself of this right, he is an unadvanced member, but as soon as he draws on his share he immediately becomes an advanced member.

Both classes are bound to continue their periodical payments until such time as the full £100 has been paid up, and an advanced member will, in the end, pay considerably more than that sum, since he will also have covenanted in the mortgage deed to pay interest on the amount advanced.

Infants may join societies as unadvanced members, but until they attain their majority their powers are very limited; they cannot transfer their shares nor vote at meetings, and as they cannot hold any interest in land, they are unable to purchase and mortgage land so as to become advanced members. A married woman may hold shares, but if she purchased them with her husband's money without his consent, the Court may order the shares to be transferred to him. Shares may be held jointly by two or more persons. Unadvanced members are usually entitled, under the rules of the society, to interest on the amount paid up, and, when the share is fully paid up (or, sometimes, before that date), to a share in profits. When the share is fully paid up, the member may continue to hold it. If the society goes into liquidation, an unadvanced member is liable to pay each instalment on his share as it falls due as if the society had continued solvent. If he is in arrears with his payments, the liquidator will, of course, be found to insist upon immediate payment of all such arrears. Advanced members will, on liquidation, be liable to claims under the mortgage deed or other security they have given, but to nothing else unless the rules of the society specifically impose upon them some additional liability. Apart from liquidation, advanced members may be entitled under the rules to a share of the profits.

Death of a Member.—When a member or depositor dies intestate having a sum not exceeding £50 in the funds of a society, such sum may be paid to the person who shall appear to the directors to be entitled to it on the intestacy, without letters of administration having been taken out. Before the directors may make such payment, they must receive satisfactory evidence of the death and a statutory declaration that the member died intestate, and that the person claiming payment is entitled on intestacy.

When a payment has been made in this way, and it subsequently turns out that the person so paid was not the next of kin, the person who is in fact the next of kin cannot recover from the society, but is free to proceed against the person to whom the society made the payment. When an advanced member dies intestate, leaving an infant heir, the society, after selling the premises mortgaged to them by the deceased, may pay any money remaining in their hands to the administrator of the deceased's estate, provided the total sum so remaining in their hands does not exceed £150. In other cases, investments or other interests in building societies pass on the death of the member to his executor or administrator in practically the same way as do the shares in a limited company, and if the shares are

not fully paid up, then the estate of the deceased person will be liable for all deficiencies; but, as death operates as an automatic withdrawal from the society, such liability will only arise if the society goes into liquidation before the death occurred. But even in the case of a liquidation, the deceased person's estate is in an advantageous position, since moneys owing to the deceased member must be paid out before any payments may be made to other members.

Meetings.—A building society, like an ordinary limited company, is controlled and owned by the members, and the conduct of the business is entrusted by the members to the directors and other officers. The powers of the members are exercised at the meetings of members. Various kinds of meetings are held, and are known as "general meetings," "annual general meetings" and "special meetings." The mode of calling any of these meetings is prescribed in the rules of each society.

General meetings are usually held every month, and the business that a general meeting is empowered to deal with includes the fixing of the amount of security to be given by officers who have charge of the funds of the society; the taking of proceedings against persons wrongfully obtaining or misapplying the property of the society; the purchasing, leasing or furnishing of the society's premises; the payment to the administrators of deceased members of £150 as mentioned above ("Death of Member"). The duty of the annual general meeting is to receive the report of the retiring directors; to pass the accounts of the last year; and to appoint new directors and other officers.

A special meeting, or "general meeting specially called," is summoned by the delivery to each member of a notice specifying the purpose for which it is called. Such a meeting has power to change the society's name; to agree to the union of the society with another society; and to alter the rules —for these purposes, a three-fourths majority is required. A special meeting is often called at the same time as a general meeting, and, in these circumstances, it proceeds first to dispatch the business of a general meeting, and afterwards exercises the powers of a special meeting. On the application of one-tenth of the members or of 100 members, the Registrar may, if he sees fit, call a special meeting of the society to decide any questions that he deems desirable. The Registrar also has the same power on receiving a statutory declaration as to the facts from not less than three members. Subject to special provision in the rules, votes at all meetings are taken by a shew of hands, but if a poll or ballot is taken, then each member has one vote in respect of each share he holds; any member may demand a poll to be taken immediately after the shew of hands, and the chairman ought to comply with such a demand unless the rules otherwise provide. A resolution will be carried by the votes of a bare majority except in the cases mentioned above, or unless the rules of the society otherwise provide.

Shares.—The number of shares that may be issued by a building society is unlimited, depending solely upon the number of persons that apply for them. There is no limit to the nominal value of a share when issued, nor to the amount of the periodical subscriptions. Preferential shares may be, and often are, issued, entitling the owner to a guaranteed rate of interest in preference to the ordinary members, but such shares do not give a right to share in profits.

The person entitled to shares is the person whose name is registered in the books of the society as owner. Usually shares may be transferred without any difficulty, and no stamp duty is payable on such transfer. The rules of each society usually lay down the method by which transfer is to be effected. Once a transfer has been completed the transferor ceases to be a member or to have any connection with the society, and, in the event of the society becoming insolvent, he will not be liable for any amounts still owing to the society in respect of the share.

Shares may be withdrawn and no rule may be made prohibiting such withdrawal, though rules can lay down the method by which withdrawal is to be effected, and may provide for discounts to be deducted on withdrawal. Any member may withdraw the amount he has already paid by his periodical instalments, even though he has not completed the payments. The effect of withdrawal is to terminate all connection between the member and the society, so that he is no longer entitled to interest or to a share in the profits, and is no longer liable to continue his periodical payments. If a member desires to withdraw, he should notify the society in accordance with the provisions of the society's rules, every society being bound to declare in their rules the terms upon which withdrawal may be effected. Usually some period of notice is required, and a special form of application for withdrawal is often required by the rules.

If the society goes into liquidation, any member who has delivered a notice to withdraw is entitled to the amount owing to him as the result of such notice as if he were one of the creditors of the society, e.g. if there are not sufficient funds to pay both the withdrawing member and the continuing members, the withdrawing member will be entitled to be paid in full before the continuing members receive a penny. But he will not be entitled to this privilege unless his withdrawal has been completed, i.e. if he has not given the proper notice of withdrawal, or if the period of notice required has not expired before the date of the liquidation, he will come in on an equal footing with those members who have not given notice of withdrawal. It is therefore advisable to give notice of withdrawal as soon as possible if there is any probability of the society coming into financial difficulties. The rules of a society often provide that on failure to pay the due contributions, the share shall be forfeit, and that the amounts already paid to the society shall remain the property of the society. Any rule as to forfeiture must be reasonable, and would probably be invalid if it provided for forfeiture on failure to pay only one instalment.

The Mortgage.—Advances are made to members only when they are able to mortgage freehold or leasehold properties as security for the loan. But further security is often required in the form of a guarantee by some third person that any sums owing will be duly paid; local authorities (e.g. county councils and borough councils) are authorized to enter into such guarantees for the purpose of encouraging housing. A member is at any time entitled to redeem his mortgage, e.g. to pay off the society in a lump sum, and the amount payable on redemption is governed by the society's rules. The rules very often provide that when an instalment is not paid punctually on the due date, the whole amount of future instalments will become immediately payable, and great care should therefore be taken to ensure that instalments reach the society at the proper time. In other respects, a mortgage to a building society is similar to any ordinary mortgage, and is subject to foreclosure in the same way.

Disputes.—If any question arises between the society and one of its members, such dispute will be decided in the first instance by an arbitrator, or by the Registrar, or by the County Court, according as the rules of the society provide. Arbitrators are appointed or elected according to the society's rules. The award or decision of any of these bodies in any case is final and conclusive, and is enforceable by the County Court on proper application. But, if it seems desirable, the arbitrator, County Court or Registrar, as the case may be, may ' state a case ' for the opinion of the Supreme Court; this course is often adopted when any difficult question of law principle arises. This peculiar mode of settling disputes has been specifically authorized in the case of building societies in order to cheapen the expenses of litigation, in view of the fact that the members of building societies are usually persons of moderate means.

Permanent and Terminating Societies.—The most important building societies are of the class known as ' permanent ' societies, and the law as stated above refers to such permanent societies. Terminating societies are on almost precisely the same footing, and it has not been considered necessary in this article to indicate the minor differences between them. The main distinction is that a terminating society is intended to continue in existence only until a fixed date or until some result, as specified in its rules, has been attained, e.g. when the funds, as the result of the periodical contributions and the investment of sums so received, amount to a figure sufficient to pay off all the shares. During the time the society is operative, advances will be made in the

usual way as far as the funds will allow. When the date or desired result has been arrived at, the society distributes all its assets among its members. A permanent building society, on the other hand, contemplates no end to its activities. There is a tendency, therefore, that a permanent society, which desires to acquire a good name and to retain its members, will act with more consideration than a terminating society whose sole object is to swell its funds with a view to the final distribution. (*See also* FRIENDLY SOCIETIES; MORTGAGES.)

BURGLARY.—The word burglary is popularly used to describe any entering of a house for the purpose of stealing. In law, however, it has a strict meaning and is confined to the breaking and entering of a dwelling house at night with intent to commit a felony therein. A person " breaks" a house who gets in or out by a trick or by forcing some aperture through which to enter or leave. There need not, of course, be any fracturing or splitting. Thus opening a door by means of a key or by lifting a latch constitutes a breaking in law. A person "enters" who inserts any portion of his body however small, or any object held in his hand, inside the house. Where there is a breaking and entering at any time save at night the offence is called Housebreaking. Night means the interval between nine o'clock in the evening and six o'clock in the morning of the next succeeding day.

A person convicted of burglary may be sentenced to penal servitude for life or to imprisonment for not more than two years.

BURGLARY INSURANCE.—Insurance against theft or burglary is governed by precisely the same principles as fire insurance, but the greatest care must be taken to read the description of the risk insured against, e.g. an insurance against burglary alone will not cover loss by theft during the daytime. (*See* BURGLARY; FIRE INSURANCE; INSURANCE; THEFT.)

BURIAL.—It is the duty of the surviving near relations living with a deceased person at the time of his death to dispose of the body. Failing such survivors the duty falls upon the executors and, failing them, even upon the householder on whose premises the body lies. Neglect to do so may be an offence. It is not necessary to bury although this is the ordinary way of disposal. The body can be disposed of, for example, by cremation. Before the Cremation Act in 1902, it was not necessarily unlawful to cremate, but the Act regulated cremation and recognized it.

It is not necessary that a body should be buried in consecrated ground, or, indeed, in any particular place. It can even be buried in private ground if desired, provided that burial there does not constitute a nuisance, and also provided it does not offend against any law applying to any particular locality.

It is necessary to dispose of a body with decency. Failure to do so is a nuisance, and probably an offence punishable by fine or imprisonment, if it be done in such a way as to shock public decency. There are various prohibitions against burial without formality as, for example, in the case where a Coroner has reasonable grounds for holding an inquest. It is an offence to dispose of a body so as to prevent an inquest in such circumstances.

A body cannot be stolen as there is no property in a corpse, but it is an offence to disinter a body without lawful authority even for a pious and laudable purpose. Any person removing the remains of a deceased person without the licence of a Secretary of State, or without carrying out the conditions laid down by him as a condition of the licence, is liable on summary conviction to a fine. But a Coroner may order a disinterment within a reasonable time after death for the purpose of an inquest. It has not yet been decided whether the licence of a Secretary of State should be obtained to make the disinterment under such order legal.

The directions of a person as to the disposal of his body after death are not legally binding on his representatives, but they can be bound to carry out his written directions against his body being disposed of in any particular way, such as by cremation. Further, they can be bound by his directions as to any examination of his body anatomically he may desire.

Every inhabitant and parishioner of the parish has a right to burial in the parish churchyard or burial ground, and every person dying within the parish has a like right. The right to burial does not, however, give the right to the erection of a monument. A criminal executed by process of law must be buried within the walls of the prison in which he has been executed, unless there is no convenient space, in which case a Secretary of State appoints some other place. A person committing suicide while of years of discretion and sound mind must, on the direction of a Coroner, be buried in a churchyard or burial ground of the parish in which the body would normally by custom be interred. Formerly the Coroner directed such bodies to be buried in a public highway and a stake driven through them, but an Act of Parliament has now directed they should be buried privately in a churchyard or burial ground.

Generally, if the burial takes place in consecrated ground, it is necessary for the burial service of the Church of England to be performed by a duly authorized Minister of the Church. But, any person having the legal charge, or being responsible for the disposal of the body may give notice of intention that it is proposed to inter the body in the churchyard or cemetery without the performance of that service. In the case of a churchyard the notice should be left at the place of abode of the rector, or other incumbent, forty-eight hours before the proposed interment. In the case of a cemetery or burial ground other than a churchyard the notice should go to the Chaplain.

A burial may take place without any religious service at all, but it must be in a decent and orderly manner. A burial may also take place in unconsecrated ground with a full burial service according to the rites of the Church of England or of any other Christian creed.

Apart from Act of Parliament no fee is due for burial in a parish churchyard or a person entitled to be buried there, but by long custom fees may and, in fact, often are demanded. To be enforceable by law in the case of fees payable by long custom, it must be established that the custom has existed at that particular place before the commencement of the reign of Richard I, unless it can be shewn that the custom is uniform in modern times, when a presumption will arise that it is long established. This latter will be rebutted, however, if it can be shewn that the custom could not have existed prior to the reign of Richard I as, for example, that the churchyard did not exist at that time. Fees are payable on the burial of a person who is not entitled to be buried in that burial ground, as for example in the case of a non-parishioner. (*See* CREMATION; CEMETERIES.)

BUSINESS NAMES.—Until 1916, persons could carry on business under any name that they pleased. Now, however, the Registration of Business Names Act, 1916, restricts in many respects this practice.

Every person or firm having a place of business in the United Kingdom, and carrying on business under a name which does not consist only of the true surnames of all the partners, with or without the Christian names, is now required to be registered.

Registration is done by sending to the Registrar of the district in which the principal place of business of the firm or person is situated a written statement setting out certain particulars. These particulars must shew the business name in question, the general nature of the business, the principal place of the business, together with particulars as to the nationality and previous names, if any, of the persons involved in the said business. These particulars must be furnished within fourteen days after the firm or person commences business, and, further, should any change in connection with any of the particulars furnished occur, written notice of such change must be given within fourteen days of the change.

Non-compliance with these provisions renders the offender liable to a fine not exceeding £5 for every day on which business is carried on contrary to the provisions of the Act. Further, any person or firm which has failed to provide the proper particulars required is under certain disabilities in legal proceedings. Thus, a person or firm in default is not allowed to enforce in the Courts any contract entered into whilst he or it was in default, unless the judge, before whom the case is brought, grants special exemption from this provision.

A further important requirement is that where a person or firm is registered under the Business Names Registration Act, a certificate of registration, which is provided by the Registrar, shall be exhibited in a conspicuous position at the principal place of business of the person or firm. Failure to exhibit this renders the offender liable to a fine not exceeding £20.

Where any person or firm registered under the Business Names Registration Act ceases to carry on business, the partners in the firm or, in the case of a person who is dead, his executors or administrators, must, within three months after the business has ceased to be carried on, send a written notice to the Registrar stating that the person or firm has ceased to carry on business. Failure to comply with this renders any person whose duty it was to give the notice liable to a fine not exceeding £20.

There is an important provision which is intended to protect British firms from unfair competition. Where any business name contains the word " British," or any other word which, in the opinion of the Registrar, tends to cause people to believe that the business is under British ownership or control, when in fact the persons who wholly or mainly control it are not British, the Registrar may refuse to register it, or, if it is already registered, may remove it from the register. If any person is dissatisfied with the decision of the Registrar in this connection, he may appeal to the Board of Trade, but he has no other form of appeal.

There are also provisions requiring persons or firms carrying on business under a business name to publish their true names for the information of persons with whom they deal. Thus, is the case of an individual person, he must set out on all trade catalogues, trade circulars, show cards, and business letters, his Christian name or initials, his surname, any former names he may have borne, and, if he is not British, his nationality. Similar rules apply in the case of a firm, all partners being required to give this information. Non-compliance with these provisions renders any offender liable to a fine not exceeding £5.

BUTTER.—Is defined by the law as being the substance usually known as butter made exclusively from milk or cream or both, with or without salt or other preservative, and with or without the addition of colouring matter. Butter must not be sold which contains a preservative forbidden by regulations of the Minister of Health, and any colouring matter used in the manufacture must not be injurious to health. Butter containing more than sixteen per cent. of water must not be kept in, nor sent out from, any factory, and the occupier of the factory or person despatching such butter is guilty of an offence, unless he can prove that the butter was not made, blended, re-worked or treated in that factory. Butter containing more than sixteen per cent. of water must not be imported into this country nor sold or exposed for sale. Butter factories, that is, places where butter is blended, re-worked or subjected to any treatment, must be registered with the Food and Drugs Authority of the district, and they must not communicate except by a public road with any factory where margarine or milk-blended butter is manufactured. Failure to observe any of these provisions constitutes an offence which is punishable by fines of £20, £50, and £100 for first, second and third offences respectively.

Milk-blended Butter is a mixture produced by mixing and blending butter with milk and cream but not condensed milk or condensed cream.

Milk-blended butter is to be sold under a name approved by the Minister of Agriculture and Fisheries and packages containing it must be marked with such approved name in printed capital letters, and also the percentage of moisture or water which is contained in it. Milk-blended butter containing more than twenty-four per cent. of water must not be imported or sold. A factory where milk-blended butter is manufactured must be registered in the same way as a butter factory and the occupier must keep a register shewing the quantity of consignments sent out from the factory and their destination. (*See* Food.)

BYE-LAW.—A bye-law is a regulation made by some body such as a corporation, local authority, or railway company, which governs the conduct of either the members of the body itself or of the general public in some particular sphere of their activities. It is usually supported by a penalty for its non-observance.

Bye-laws are made by an authority under powers granted to it by Act of Parliament, and they have to be submitted for confirmation to a central authority, usually a Government department, before they come into force.

Bye-laws must be reasonable and must not be contrary to the general law of the land otherwise they will be disallowed. It should be noted, however, that if a bye-law is properly made and confirmed then it has the force of law as made by Act of Parliament (*See* Borough Council; Corporation; Local Government; also Railways.)

C **LICENCE.**—One of the licences required by persons who use motor vehicles in their business for the carriage of goods. (*See* Carrier's Licence.)

CAIRNS, Lord (1819-1885).—After practising on the Chancery side and earning a high reputation in the House of Commons, he was chosen by Disraeli as his Lord Chancellor. When on the Bench he was noted for his excellent work in framing the law in relation to Companies, a branch of the law which was then in its infancy.

CALLS.—When shares are issued by a company it is not usual to require the shareholders to pay over the full value of the share at once. In most cases some proportion, say, 5/- in the £, is payable when the shares are applied for, another 5/- on allotment, and the balance when "called." As the Directors find they require more money they may decide to make a call on the shareholders for the whole or part of the amount outstanding on the shares. Once a shareholder has paid the full amount due on the shares, he is not responsible for any of the debts of the company.

It is usual for a company to provide in its Articles that it shall have a lien on the shares of any shareholder—i.e. a right to refuse to allow the shareholder to transfer the shares, until all calls due have been paid, and to provide further that it may sell or forfeit the shares in order to pay itself the amount of the call. Unless there is such a provision in the articles, a company registered in England has no lien, but a company registered in Scotland has a lien by the Scots Common Law without any special provision.

When shares are sold the transferor is

liable for all calls on them that may have been made before the transfer, even though the date of payment fixed by the call is after the transfer. When a shareholder is owed money by the company either for dividends or in respect of some other matter he cannot, if the company is insolvent, claim to deduct the liability of the company to him from the amount of his liability on calls, and pay only the balance. He must pay the full amount of the call and claim against the company separately for what is due to him, even though he may, in fact, receive only a few shillings in the £1 owing to the insolvency of the company. There is an exception to this rule in cases where the shareholder who owes the money is himself bankrupt, and in such a case his trustee in bankruptcy is allowed to set off. (*See* CAPITAL [COMPANY]; SHARES; WINDING-UP.)

CAMERA.—In general, all Courts in this country sit in public. In certain cases, however, there is power to exclude the public, and all persons who are not connected with the actual case being dealt with at the time. This is called "Sitting in Camera."

The power to sit in camera is conferred by statute, but there is also an inherent right in every court to exclude the public, where, owing to the nature of the case, this is desirable. A Court, however, may only do so where it is satisfied that this course is essential in the interest of the State, or of public decency.

CAMPBELL, Lord (1779-1861).— Had an unrivalled judicial record, being successively Lord Chancellor of Ireland, Chief Justice of England, and Lord High Chancellor. He was a keen reformer of the Law and, besides the Fatal Accidents Act, which bears his name, he introduced the Statute of Limitations, the Newspaper Libel Act, and many other important statutes.

While in the House of Lords he published his well-known "Lives of the Chancellors" and "Lives of the Chief Justices."

CANTEENS.—Naval or military canteens—that is to say, canteens carried on under the authority of a Secretary of State or the Admiralty—do not require a justices' licence; though they are not, of course, exempted by this enactment from requiring an excise licence. It is not an offence to sell

intoxicating liquor to a civilian at such a canteen. The ordinary restrictions as to permitted hours do not apply to such canteens or to naval or military messes; in other words, apart from naval or military regulations, intoxicants may be sold at any hour in such places.

CANON LAW.—The papal ecclesiastical law is known as the Canon Law, and, although, since the Reformation, it has had no validity in England, a great deal of it survived in the form of customary observances, and was subsequently adopted by Parliament or was incorporated into the common law of England in relation to ecclesiastical matters.

The term "canon" is also used to describe certain rules framed by Convocation on ecclesiastical matter; such rules are binding on the clergy but not on the laity.

CAPITAL (COMPANY).—The word Capital is used in several senses:

1. Nominal Capital. This is the total amount of shares which the company has power to issue under its Memorandum. All these shares may not be issued by the company at once, or indeed at all.
2. Issued Capital. This is the nominal value of the shares which the company has issued.
3. Paid-up Capital. This is the total amount which has been paid by shareholders on the issued capital.

It will thus be seen that a company may have power to issue 10,000 shares of £1 each, making its nominal capital £10,000; it may in fact have issued £5,000 worth of these (its issued capital) and on each of these 5,000 shares ten shillings only of the £1 due may have been paid, making its paid-up capital £2,500.

A company occasionally creates what is known as Reserved Capital by passing a Special Resolution (q.v.). This means that the capital so declared to be reserved cannot be called up (*see* CALLS) or used by the company until the company is wound up. This gives to the creditors of the company an additional fund to which they may look for the payment of their debts.

Another use of the word "capital" is to be found in the expressions "fixed capital" and "circulating capital." Fixed capital is the property of a company which it owns and uses for the purpose of carrying on its business, and not with a view to re-selling, e.g. its factory premises.   Circulating capital is property which the company buys for the purpose of re-sale, e.g. stock-in-trade. This distinction is important in the calculation of the money available from the profits of a company to pay dividends. (*See* DIVIDENDS.)

The capital of the company may be divided into various classes of shares, or it may consist wholly or in part of stock (q.v.). This division of the capital may be made either in the memorandum or in the articles. If the division is made in the memorandum, it is much more difficult for the company to alter the rights of the different classes of shareholders, for if the shareholders' rights are fixed in the articles they may be altered by a special resolution (q.v.) at any time.   A minority of objecting shareholders is bound by any alteration of their rights carried out as provided in the articles or memorandum, but if they consider they are being unfairly treated they may protect their interests by applying to the Court.

Increase and Reduction.—A company may find either that its business is expanding and it requires more money than it has available to carry it on successfully, or else it may have been very unsuccessful and have lost a large part of its original capital.   In the first of these cases it will wish to increase its capital, and in the second to reduce it. As an increase of capital cannot possibly injure persons who are creditors of the company but will usually be in their interests (as it will give them more money to look to for the payment of their debts), whereas a reduction of capital may seriously prejudice their interests, it is much more easy to increase capital than to reduce it.   Capital may be increased by a resolution of the company in general meeting as provided by the articles. This power cannot be delegated to the directors.   When capital is to be reduced, however, a special resolution is necessary and the resolution must also be confirmed by the Court. (*See* DIVIDENDS; PREFERENCE SHARES; SHARES; WINDING-UP.)

CAPITAL   PUNISHMENT.—The punishment of a crime by death.   In English law, sentence of death can now only be passed in cases of High Treason, Murder, Piracy and setting fire to royal ships or dockyards

and of certain offences under the Army Act. It cannot be inflicted upon any person under the age of eighteen or upon any expectant mother.   Sentence of death is carried out by hanging, but in cases of High Treason the King may direct that it may be carried out by decapitation.   In foreign countries such sentences are carried out in a variety of ways.   Thus in most of the States of the United States of America, execution is effected by means of electrocution, in France and parts of Germany by guillotining, and in Spain by a form of garotting.

CARD PLAYING.   Card Debts.— Money won at cards cannot be recovered in a court of law unless there has been a subsequent legal contract between the loser and the winner on which the latter can sue. Thus, if the winner agrees not to report the loser to the committee of the club for defaulting, on condition that the debt is paid within a month, the winner can bring an action when the time has expired.   An I.O.U. for a card debt does not give the holder the right to sue.

Money lent with the knowledge that it is to be used for gambling at cards is also not recoverable, but is if lent to pay a gambling debt already incurred.   Again, a security given in respect of a gambling debt is void.

Gambling Offences.—It is a question of fact whether any game is one of chance or skill.   Baccarat, Chemin-de-Fer and Progressive Whist, where "partners are shuffled as well as the cards" have been held to be games of chance, but Bridge and ordinary Whist would probably be held to be games of skill.

Playing card games of chance for money may be unlawful for three reasons:

(i) Because the games played are absolutely illegal.

Ace of Hearts, Faro and Bassett are the only absolutely illegal card games.   Anyone playing them anywhere may be fined.

(ii) Because the game is played in a road or other public place.

A public place is any place to which the public have, or are permitted to have, access. It includes, in addition to any road, a railway carriage, omnibus, tram, hotel, park, beach, etc.   It is a separate offence to play cards for money in a public library.

(iii) Because the game is played in a place to which a large number of persons are habitually invited for the purpose of playing card games of chance for money. A place so used is called a common gaming house.

It is not necessary that the place should be open to the public, so that a members' club may be a common gaming house, and the committee may be convicted of assisting in its management.

The following offences may be committed in connection with gambling in a common gaming house:—

(a) Keeping the premises for such purpose.
(b) Owning the premises and permitting gambling to take place there.
(c) Managing or assisting in the management of such premises.
(d) Lending the players money with which to gamble.
(e) Playing in such premises.
(f) Obstructing the entrance of the police.
(g) Refusing to give names and addresses to the police.

Search warrants may be obtained and cards, etc., may be seized.

The premises must be habitually used for gambling and so the law is often evaded by holding gambling parties at different private houses each time.

The proprietor of licensed premises is guilty of a special offence if he permits gambling on card games of chance to take place there.

Cheating at Cards.—Cheating at cards, when the game is played for money, is a criminal offence, i.e. obtaining money by false pretences if successful, or attempting to obtain it if unsuccessful.

An accusation of cheating at cards can, therefore, be the subject of a slander action without special damage being proved, and such a serious charge should not be made unless it can be proved to be true. The publication of the slander may, however, be defended as privileged if honestly made to fellow players or by a fellow member to the committee of a Club.

The "Baccarat Case."—The most famous case arising out of an accusation of cheating at cards bears the legal title of "Cumming v. Green and Others," but is more commonly known as the "Tranby Croft" case, or by the title it was given at the time, the "Baccarat Case."

This was a slander action brought by Sir Edward Gordon Cumming, a well-known society figure and friend of long standing of the then Prince of Wales (afterwards Edward VII), against some fellow guests at a Doncaster Races house-party at Tranby Croft. The slander complained of consisted of a charge of cheating when playing baccarat at Tranby Croft. The alleged cheating consisted of increasing and diminishing the stakes after the result of the hands was known. The case achieved enormous publicity owing to the social position of the parties and all the witnesses. The fact that the then Prince of Wales was banker at the game and gave evidence for Gordon Cumming (he did not notice any cheating), and that the game was being played with the Prince's private set of cards and counters with his feathers on the back, enhanced public interest in the case.

The house-party took place in September, 1890, baccarat being played regularly in the evenings. Several members of the party watched Cumming's play as a result of an accusation made by the son of the house. They then charged him with cheating, which charge he denied, but signed an undertaking never to play cards again, those in the secret promising to keep silent. Despite this agreement, the secret leaked out next day and soon spread all over England. This agreement was entered into in the hope of avoiding publicity for the fact that the Prince of Wales played baccarat regularly for high stakes (the bank was £100). It was also suggested during the trial that the Prince, as Cumming's superior officer, had been under a duty to report the charge to the proper military authority if he thought him guilty.

The trial of the action which took place in June, 1891, lasted 7 days, and the Court was packed. The Prince of Wales sat on the bench beside the Judge. Despite a great closing speech by Sir Edward Clarke, for Cumming, which earned a burst of applause very rarely heard in a Court of Law, the jury only retired for 10 minutes before finding that the words were true. Seldom, if ever, in so long and hotly contested a trial, have the jury taken so short a time to agree on their verdict. Nevertheless, Sir Edward Clarke, among others, always maintained that Gordon Cumming was innocent although no further light has since been thrown on this extraordinary question.

Taxation.—There is an import duty of 3/9 per dozen packs of playing cards. When the customs duty is paid, the packs are enclosed in excise wrappers, and these must not be removed until the cards are sold. The wrapper may, however, be removed before a pack is sold to a member of a club, as this is not counted as a sale. Toy cards measuring less than $1\frac{3}{4}$ inches by $1\frac{1}{4}$ inches do not require wrappers.

There is also a duty of 3d. a pack on cards made in the United Kingdom and they, similarly, must be enclosed in excise wrappers before being sent out by the makers, unless they are for exportation, when no duty is chargeable. The maker requires a licence, which costs £1 and has to be renewed annually on September 1st. (*See* SPECIAL SUPPLEMENT "GAMBLING.")

CARRIAGE BY LAND.—The law which applies to the carriage of persons is different in several respects from that which applies to the carriage of goods; and in each case it is necessary to draw a further distinction between carriage by rail and carriage by road. The legal relationship between a passenger and the railway company, over whose line he travels, is defined partly by Act of Parliament, and partly by the Common Law, as also is that between the owner of goods and the railway company which contracts to carry them; but the result in each case is different, for whereas a railway company is only liable for an accident to a passenger if it was the result of some negligence on the part of the company's servants, it is, broadly speaking, liable for every loss of, or damage to, goods or luggage, no matter how caused (this general statement of the law must be read subject to several qualifications). (*See* RAILWAY GOODS TRAFFIC; RAILWAY PASSENGERS.)

The extent of the liability of any carrier by road depends on whether or not he is a "common carrier."

Common Carriers. — A common carrier is one who holds himself out as prepared to carry *all* goods which may be consigned to him between certain places; every railway company is a common carrier.

The common law of England attaches several important incidents to the legal status of the common carrier. In the first

place he may not refuse to carry any goods of the sort which he holds himself out as prepared to carry, unless he is unable to do so for some good reason such as lack of accommodation. If he should refuse, an action lies against him for damages.

In the second place he is an insurer of the goods; that is to say that if they are lost or damaged he must pay compensation, unless he can prove that the loss or damage was the result of an unusually violent storm, or other natural phenomenon, or to the inherent vice of the thing itself. Inherent vice means some quality which itself was responsible for the damage—the tendency of some animals to struggle violently, of liquid to evaporate, or of some solids to melt.

Valuables must be declared.—It has also been provided by Act of Parliament, the Carriers Act of 1830, that a carrier is not to be liable at all for the loss of, or damage to, money, valuables, furs, glass, books and pictures if there is more than £10 (railway companies £25) worth in any one package, unless at the time when they were delivered to him he was informed of their value.

There is nothing to prevent a common carrier from entering into a special contract with his customer either increasing or limiting his liability. The law set out above only applies if there is no such special contract. Carriers who are not common carriers (and a great many carriers by road now take care not to hold themselves out as carriers in such a way as to become "common" carriers) are not bound to accept all goods which are brought to them, but may pick and choose. In addition, they are only liable for loss or damage if it can be proved against them that this was caused by their negligence (q.v.), and, of course, there is nothing to prevent them contracting out of even this liability.

Ticket Conditions.—It is important in this connection to realize that the law assumes that all the terms of a contract, and any conditions printed upon it, or upon receipts, tickets, etc., have been read and agreed to by both parties. This assumption cannot be disproved in the case of conditions printed upon the contract itself; but where the conditions are contained not on the contract document itself but elsewhere, as in advertisements on the backs of tickets, in time-tables, etc., the carrier who relies upon them must shew that reasonable notice of their existence was given to the other party. This is why railway tickets always have across their face some statement that the ticket is issued subject to conditions. The tendency of the law at the moment seems to be that almost any notice will suffice to raise the assumption that the conditions were read and accepted. This principle applies equally to the carriage of goods and of passengers.

In other respects, however, the legal position of a carrier of persons is different. There may be common carriers of passengers. Most omnibus companies hold themselves out as prepared to carry any person who may present himself. A chara-banc proprietor does not; he reserves to himself the right to refuse to carry anybody, and he cannot be forced to carry them. A common carrier of passengers is not entitled so to refuse, unless there is some good reason such as drunkenness, or filth— or the absence of any accommodation to justify him. He is not, however, an insurer of the safety of his passengers; he is not liable if they are injured, unless they can prove that the injury was caused by the carrier's negligence, and that they have not entered into a contract which absolves him from liability in such a case.

When trains are late.—In general the publication of a time-table is a guarantee that it will be adhered to, but in practice no time-table is ever published without a statement that the carrier reserves the right to depart from it, and does not guarantee to make connections or to run to time. In such a case he is not liable if the vehicles do not keep to the time-table.

As a result of legislation in recent years it is now no longer permissible for anybody to set up as a carrier by road, whether of passengers or of goods, without first obtaining a special licence to do so from the Traffic Commissioners for his particular area. The only exception is that of the carrier who uses nothing but horse traction.

Vehicles used for the carriage of passengers may be divided into three classes: hackney carriages (which must seat less than eight persons—*see* "HACKNEY CARRIAGES") which are licensed under the Hackney Carriage Acts; and public service vehicles (to seat more than eight); and contract carriages which must both be licensed under the Road Traffic Act of 1930. (*See* SPECIAL SUPPLEMENT "ROAD TRAFFIC.") The distinction between the last two classes is that a public service vehicle plies for hire (for instance, an ordinary omnibus), whereas a contract carriage may only be employed as the result of a special contract (i.e. a char-a-banc hired for a private party).

Goods Vehicles.—Motor (which includes steam) vehicles used for the carriage of goods by road may also be divided into three classes: vehicles, which like public service vehicles, ply for hire as public carriers of goods; vehicles which are sometimes used for the public carriage of goods, and sometimes for the carriage of goods in connection with the trade or business of their owner; and vehicles which are used only for the latter purpose, such as a tradesman's van or a commercial traveller's adapted car.

The characteristics of these three classes are important as under the Road and Rail Act of 1933 a different kind of carriers' licence must be obtained for each. For the first, an A or public carriers' licence is necessary; for the second, a B or limited carriers' licence; and for the third, a C or private carriers' licence.

No licence is necessary for the carriage of goods in a motor vehicle which is not "constructed or adapted for the carriage of goods," or in a trailer which is drawn by a private motor vehicle with a seating capacity of not more than seven excluding the driver. A tradesman may therefore deliver goods in a private motor car without having to get a C licence, provided that he stacks them on the seats, but not if he removes the seats altogether and adapts the car for the carriage of goods. (*See* further CARRIERS' LICENCES.)

The same acts which imposed the necessity for a licence upon all carriers also laid upon them certain obligations. The fares which may be charged, and the time-tables which must be adhered to, by a passenger carrier are fixed for him at a public hearing by the Traffic Commissioners who may also impose further conditions upon him.

With regard to the carriage of goods the Commissioner's powers are more restricted; they cannot even in the case of a B licence (where their powers are greatest) specify the rates to be charged, nor in an A licence can they specify the kinds of goods which may be carried or the places which may be served. Practically no conditions may be attached to a C licence.

Condition of Vehicles.—Further, all carriers, whether of passengers or of goods, must maintain their vehicles in fit and proper condition to the satisfaction of examiners and certifiers appointed by the Minister of Transport.

These officials, and in addition, any police constable, have power to stop any goods vehicle on the road in order to inspect its licence and mechanical fitness. They have also power to enter garages and other private places for the same purposes. In each case they must first, if asked to do so, produce their authority. If they are not satisfied with the condition of the vehicle they may immediately prohibit its use, but if the defect is one which does not cause danger to the public and which could be remedied within ten days, they must make a conditional order which will prohibit the use of the vehicle after ten days, unless *any* examiner certifies that the repairs are being carried out.

Notice of any prohibition must be given by the examiner to the driver and owner of the vehicle and to the Traffic Commissioners who granted it a licence. From any decision of an examiner an appeal lies to the certifier and from the latter to the Minister of Transport.

In order to protect the public, carriers must not work drivers for more than a certain number of hours out of the twenty-four and must allow them adequate rest periods. To ensure that this is done they must keep records of the times worked by all their employees. They must also keep a record of the weights carried by any goods vehicle; this must, if required, be produced to any constable or examiner. (*See* CARRIERS' LICENCES; HACKNEY CARRIAGES; LONDON PASSENGER TRANSPORT BOARD; AND RAILWAYS.)

CARRIAGE BY AIR ACT, 1932.— This Act binds aircraft engaged in International Air Navigation, and was passed to give effect to a convention signed in Warsaw in 1929. The rules of the Convention may be applied by Order in Council to internal transport but no such order in Council has yet been made. For the substance of this Act *see* AVIATION.

CARRIAGE BY SEA.—When goods are carried by sea the contract may be either in the form of a charter party or a bill of lading, or a special contract under the Carriage of Goods by Sea Act, 1924. Sometimes both bills of lading and a charter party will be entered into for the carriage of the same goods, and in other cases the charterer, that is, the person who has taken out the charter party, will carry goods for other persons for whom he will issue bills of lading.

If no special provision is made in the contract of carriage, i.e. in the charter party, bill of lading or special contract, a carrier by sea will be a common carrier (q.v.) and liable to all obligations as such, but in almost all cases it is the practice for the carrier to alter the liabilities which would thus fall upon him by the insertion of special provisions in the charter party or bill of lading.

What is a Charter Party?—A charter party is an agreement under which the owner of the ship places it, or a specified part of it, at the disposal of a person desiring to ship goods for the purpose of carrying a cargo. The charter party may operate as a lease of the ship so that the person chartering it becomes for the time the owner of the ship and the master and crew become his servants, but as a general rule the charter party only gives the right to the charter to have his cargo carried by the ship. In return for this right the charterer agrees to pay a certain sum of money to the owner of the ship and this money is called freight.

A bill of lading is an agreement under which a carrier undertakes to carry certain goods described in the bill of lading to a named destination. A bill of lading may be issued either by the shipowner or by a charterer of the ship.

The charter party may be either a voyage charter or a time charter. In a voyage charter the charterer takes the ship for the purpose of carrying out a certain voyage or series of voyages, e.g. from London to New York. In a time charter the ship is taken for a fixed period of time commencing either from a particular date or from the date on which the ship arrives at a named port. If the ship is not ready to be handed over to the charterer by the date named or, in the case where the charter commences from its arrival at a named port, if it does not arrive at that port within a reasonable time from the date of the charter party, the charterer is entitled to refuse to take the ship.

Usual Terms in a Charter Party.—The form of a charter party varies very much in different cases depending on the purpose for which the charter is required. The following clauses will usually be found:

(1) A statement of the position of the ship at the date of the charter party. This is to enable the charterer to know when he may expect the ship to reach a port at which it is to be handed over to him. If in fact the ship is not at the place stated in the charter party the charterer will be entitled to repudiate the contract.

(2) An undertaking that the ship is seaworthy. If the charter party is in these terms, it is not enough for the shipowner to provide a ship seaworthy "so far as he can make it so." The obligation on him is an absolute one, and if the ship should turn out to be unseaworthy even without any fault of the shipowner, he will be liable for any loss. Even without any express provision in the charter party the shipowner will be bound to make the ship seaworthy. It should be noticed that his obligation only applies to seaworthiness at the time of sailing and of loading a cargo. He will not necessarily be responsible if the ship later becomes unseaworthy. Seaworthiness is a relative term and the exact meaning of it in any case will depend on the nature of the voyage and of the cargo which has to be carried. In one case it is held that a ship which had been to a plague-infected port and was therefore required by law to be fumigated, was unfit for the carriage of fruit which was damaged by the fumigation.

(3) In cases where the freight is to be calculated at so much per ton of the cargo carried the shipowner is usually anxious that no part of the ship shall be empty during the voyage, as this will mean a loss of freight to him, and for that purpose he usually provides that a full and complete cargo must be loaded. In such a case the charterer must load the ship to the full capacity even though this is above the capacity as stated in the charter party. The charterer, however, is not bound to load a deck cargo, i.e. on the deck of the ship, unless this is provided for either by the charter party or by some trade custom relating to the goods to be carried. If the charter party fixes the amount of cargo to be carried, the whole ship need not be filled if its capacity is in excess of the amount fixed.

(4) The charter party provides that the ship having gone to her loading port and loaded the cargo shall proceed to the port at which the charterer wishes the goods to be delivered. As the charterer is not bound to take delivery anywhere else than at the port named, e.g. not by lighters outside the port, unless this is so stated, it is usual to provide by the charter party that the ship shall go to the named port, or "so near thereunto as she may safely get." This will protect the shipowner if he is unable by reason of some obstacle to enter the named port itself.

When the selection of the port is left to the charterer, it is usual to provide for the protection of the shipowner that the ship shall not be sent to any port unless she can lie there "always afloat" with her full cargo, i.e. at all stages of the tide without touching the ground.

(5) As the shipowner in calculating what is a remunerative freight to him will have to take into account not only the time occupied during the voyage but also the time taken up in loading and unloading the cargo, the charter party usually provides that further sums shall be payable for every day which the ship is detained beyond the lay-days, i.e. the normal loading or unloading period. This payment is called demurrage (q.v.).

(6) What is called a "cesser clause" is frequently inserted, which provides that the charterer's liability under the charter is to cease when the cargo is loaded, and goes on to give to the master of the ship and the owners a lien on the cargo for the amount due in respect of freight and demurrage.

The effect of this is that the shipowner is content to look to the consignee, i.e. the person to whom the cargo is to be delivered, for the money due for the carriage. By virtue of his lien, the shipowner can refuse to deliver the cargo until the money due (i.e. the freight) is paid. (*See* LIEN; [SHIPOWNER].)

(7) Since, if no provision were made to the contrary in the charter party, the liability of the shipowner for the goods entrusted to him would be that of a common carrier,

i.e. he would be responsible for any loss however caused, whether by his negligence or not, it is the invariable practice to reduce his liability by inserting in the charter party a clause to the effect that the shipowner shall not be liable for any loss caused through certain "expected perils" set out. These usually are "restraints of princes and rulers, Act of God, the King's enemies, fire, and all and every other dangers and accidents of the seas, rivers and navigation of whatever nature and kind whatsoever," and frequently the following are also excepted: negligence on the part of the master and his crew, barratry (q.v.), pirates (q.v.), robbers or thieves.

"Perils of the sea" includes all losses caused to the goods by the action of the sea of an unusual character, e.g. a storm, so long as the shipowner or his servants have not by their negligence brought about the loss. Where the negligence of master and crew is also excepted, the shipowner will not be liable even where the loss is caused by negligence. Unless negligence is expressly excepted, the shipowner will only be protected from liability where the loss is caused by one of the excepted perils *and* without any fault of his or his servants. Thus he will be liable for a fire caused by the negligence of a stoker.

Deviation.—These clauses in the charter party apply only when the ship is on the voyage for which she was chartered, and, if the shipowner departs from the voyage which he has undertaken to carry out, without reasonable cause, i.e. deviates by going off the normal route or calling at other ports, he will cease to be protected by the clauses in the charter party.

Once the deviation has taken place the shipowner is no longer upon that voyage but upon another. The shipowner's liabilities then become those of a common carrier (q.v.). It should be noticed that once deviation has taken place and the shipowner has gone off the route indicated he will cease to be protected, even though after the deviation he returns to the route indicated and a loss takes place, after he has returned, which would have been excluded under the charter party. Again his liability is not confined to losses caused through the deviation, but once the deviation has taken place he is liable for all losses however caused.

Thus, in one case, where the shipowner was protected against the negligence of persons unloading the cargo, and during the voyage he deviated, he was not entitled to rely on the protection clause when at the end of the voyage the cargo was damaged on being unloaded at the port of destination. Deviation is allowed when necessary to save life or to avoid pirates or dangers of navigation, but not to save property. Thus a ship is entitled to go off her course for the purpose of giving assistance to another ship which is in difficulties, but not for the purpose of salving a ship which has been abandoned by her crew. Deviation to save property is, however, now allowed in all bills of lading which are covered by the Carriage of Goods by Sea Act, 1924, that is, bills of lading issued in respect of goods being carried on ships from any port in Great Britain or Northern Ireland.

Protection to Shipowners.—A protection is given to the owners of British ships by the Merchant Shipping Act, 1894, which provides that they shall not be liable for damage unless caused with their actual fault or privity in cases where goods are lost or damaged by fire on board ship, or where small articles of large value, such as gold, silver, diamonds, watches, jewels or precious stones, are lost or damaged by robbery, embezzlement, making away with, or secreting, unless their true nature and value have been declared in writing when they are shipped, so that a special care may be taken of them.

Whenever there is loss of life or personal injury to any person on the ship, or damage to goods, or where the ship is improperly navigated and loss of life, or personal injury, or damage to goods is caused to some person or goods on board another ship, or to another ship itself in collision or otherwise, the shipowner is again protected. If this loss is without his actual fault or privity he cannot be made liable for an amount exceeding £15 a ton of the ship's tonnage where there is loss of life or personal injury, or £8 per ton if goods are lost or damaged.

Dangerous Goods.—A shipowner or the master can refuse to take on board goods of a dangerous character, and if he finds them on board may throw them overboard without incurring liability, and it is an offence to send dangerous goods unless their nature is marked on the outside of the baggage, and the master or owner is further informed by writing.

What is a Bill of Lading ?—Whereas a charter party is taken out when the whole or a specific portion of a ship's capacity is required for the carriage of the cargo, persons desiring to send smaller quantities of goods will enter into a contract known as a bill of lading, under which the carrier agrees to carry these specific goods and not, as in the case of a charter party, to put any definite part of the ship's capacity at the disposal of the skipper. This document serves three purposes.

1. It is a receipt for the goods, showing that they have been put on board ship.

2. It contains the terms of the contract on which the goods are being carried.

3. It is a document of title to the goods.

The bill of lading must bear a 6d. stamp except when the goods are shipped abroad. The bill of lading is signed by the master, and once a master has granted a bill of lading he cannot deny that the goods have been shipped, although in fact they may never have been put on board; except in cases where the person who holds the bill of lading knows the goods have not been shipped, or where the master was induced to give a bill of lading by some fraud on the part of the person shipping the goods or the holder of the bill of lading, or some person from whom the holder has obtained the bill of lading. Notice that this only applies to the master. The shipowner may always shew that the goods were not in fact shipped, although once a bill has been signed by the master, it is for the shipowner to prove that the goods were not shipped, and not for the person claiming the goods to prove that they were. A bill of lading may state in terms that the goods have been shipped in good order and condition, and when it does so, it is called a clean bill of lading. This statement, however, only refers to the external condition of the goods, and the shipper, before he recovers damages from the shipowner, must shew that the goods shipped were in good condition internally when they were shipped, or that they had been damaged from some cause within the control of the shipowner.

What Carrier must Undertake.— The terms of contract as set out in a bill of lading will now be controlled in all cases in which goods are shipped from Great Britain or Northern Ireland by the terms of the Carriage of Goods by Sea Act, 1924, which makes considerable alterations in the liabilities of shipowners. Notice that this does not apply to charter parties.

When this Act applies the normal undertaking by the shipowner, that the ship is seaworthy, is modified, and in the event of the ship proving unseaworthy he will not be liable, unless he has failed to use proper care to make it seaworthy. He is under a similar duty to take reasonable care that the ship is properly manned, equipped and supplied, and that the holds, refrigerating and cold chambers and all other parts of the ship in which goods are carried are made fit and safe for the reception, carriage and preservation of the goods. The shipowner is further bound properly and carefully to load, handle, stow, carry, keep, care for and discharge the goods carried.

When goods are delivered the shipper can demand a bill of lading setting out:

1. The leading marks shewn upon the goods and identifying them.

2. The number of packages or pieces or quantity or weight as furnished in writing by the shipper.

3. The apparent order and condition of the goods. The bill must state in terms that it is issued subject to the rules set out in the act.

When Goods are Damaged.—These rules include a considerable protection for the carrier. If the goods are damaged notice must be given to him in writing before they are removed, except in cases where the state of the goods has been the subject of joint survey or inspection by representatives of the shipowner and the consignee. If the loss or damage is not apparent, notice must be given within 3 days. Unless this is done, it will be presumed that the goods have been delivered in accordance with the description on the bill of lading. Even when notice has been given as required, any action against the carrier for damages for the loss of, or damage to, the goods must be commenced within a year from the time when they were, or should have been, delivered. In all cases a carrier's liability is further limited to £100 per package unless the nature and value of the goods have been declared by the shipper and inserted in the bill of lading. If the shipper has knowingly misstated the value he cannot recover anything in respect of the goods either for loss or damage. When goods of an inflammable, explosive or dangerous character are shipped without disclosure of their nature, the carrier may destroy them without paying any compensation.

Even in cases when their dangerous nature has been disclosed, they may be destroyed if during the voyage they cause danger to the ship or cargo.

Deviation.—The carrier is now entitled to deviate when deviation is necessary for the purpose of saving life or property at sea or is otherwise reasonable.

"Excepted Perils."—The carrier is not responsible for loss or damage caused in certain ways known as excepted perils:

(i) The act, neglect or default of the master mariner, pilot or servants of the carrier in the navigation or the management of the ship.

Notice that this has the effect of exempting the shipowner from any loss or damage caused by the negligence of the master or crew *relating to the management of the ship*, but that the carrier is still liable if the goods are improperly *loaded, carried or discharged* in any respect not relating to the management of the ship;

(ii) Fire, unless caused by the actual fault or privity of the carrier;

(iii) Perils, dangers and accidents of the seas or other navigable waters (*see* above);

(iv) Act of God (q.v.);

(v) Act of war;

(vi) Act of public enemies;

(vii) Arrest or restraint of princes, (q.v.) rulers or people, or seizure under legal process;

(viii) Quarantine restrictions;

(ix) Act or omission of the shipper or owner of the goods, his agent or representative;

(x) Strikes, or lock-outs, or stoppage or restraint of labour from whatever cause, whether partial or general;

(xi) Riots and civil commotions;

(xii) Saving or attempting to save life or property at sea;

(xiii) Wastage in bulk or weight, or any other loss or damage arising from inherent defect, quality, or vice of the goods;

(xiv) Insufficiency of packing of goods;

(xv) Insufficiency or inadequacy of marks;

(xvi) Latent defects not discoverable by due diligence;

(xvii) Any other cause arising without the actual fault or privity of the carrier, or without the faulty neglect of the agents or servants of the carrier.

The carrier in this last case must, however, show that the loss has happened without the actual fault or privity of himself or his servants, and it is not for the shipper to prove how the loss in fact took place.

Carrier cannot " contract out."—The carrier cannot issue a bill of lading under which he exempts himself from liability as set out in the above rules in respect of making the ship seaworthy, or its equipment proper, or fitting it out in a way suitable to take the cargo, or in respect of the loading, stowing, carriage, or discharge of the cargo; but he may increase his liability in any respect, or abandon any of the protection or exemption given to him, provided that this is set out in the bill of lading in clear terms. These rules do not apply to charter parties, but where a ship is also under a charter party, the bills of lading must comply with the rules.

Except in certain cases.—When the goods carried are particular goods, that is, not ordinary shipments made in the usual course of trade, and, in coastal trade, for all goods, the carrier is entitled to make any special provisions that he pleases and can exclude himself from any liability or exemption imposed by these rules. No bill of lading, however, must be issued in such a case, but the terms must be set out in a receipt.

Goods Transferred by Bill of Lading.—It has been stated above that a bill of lading also fulfils the purpose of a document of title to the goods specified in it. This means that the ownership of the goods may be transferred from one person to another while the goods are at sea by the handing over of the bill of lading. The bill is handed over in much the same way as a bill of exchange. Thus, if it is drawn to order the holder must endorse it before handing it to the assignee, i.e. the person to whom he wishes to transfer the goods. He may endorse it in blank, and it will then become a document drawn to bearer. The person who has obtained a bill of lading by a transfer from some other holder, not only gets the ownership of the goods but can sue on the contract entered into by the shipper with the carrier for their carriage, just as if the contract contained in the bill of lading had been made with himself. The master is required to deliver the goods to the person who produces to him the bill of lading. Bills of lading are frequently made out in three copies, one for the shipper, one for the master and one to be sent to the consignee. In such a case they will contain a clause "one of these bills of lading accomplished, the others shall stand void."

If, where there are several bills of lading the goods have been transferred to more than one person, the person entitled to them is the one to whom the transfer was first made; but if the master of the ship in good faith and, without any knowledge that the person presenting the bill of lading is not entitled to the goods, delivers them to him, he will not be liable if that person is not entitled to them.

It has been stated above that a bill of lading in some respects resembles a bill of exchange, but a bill of lading is not a negotiable instrument (q.v.), that is, the person who receives a bill of lading for value and in good faith does not in every case receive a good title to the goods contained in it, if the bill has in fact been stolen by the person from whom he got it or by some prior holder.

If the bill of lading were made negotiable in the same way as a bill of exchange, any person taking it in good faith and for value would get a good title to the goods, even if the person who gave him the bill of lading had stolen it; but no holder of a bill of lading can get a better title to the goods than the person from whom he received it. Thus the only extent to which a bill of lading can be said to be negotiable is that the ownership of the goods may be transferred by mere delivery of the bill of lading while the goods themselves are on a ship at sea. Probably this only applies to bills of lading which are drawn to the order or assigns of the holder. The importance in law of this is that the consignor's right of stoppage in transitu (q.v.) is defeated by a transfer of the bill of lading. Thus, if A

sells goods to B in Antwerp and the goods are put on board ship, A will be entitled to notify the shipowner and require him not to deliver the goods to B if before the end of the voyage A has heard that B has become insolvent; but if B has obtained the bill of lading and transferred it to some other person, this right of stoppage in transitu is lost. (*See* SHIPPING.)

CARRIAGES AND CARTS.—Tax. —The annual excise duties payable upon a cart or carriage are (i) if it has less than four wheels, 15/–; (ii) if it has four wheels or more and is drawn by one horse or mule, £1 1s. 0d.; (iii) if it has four wheels or more and is drawn by two or more horses or mules, £2 2s. 0d. As to the tax upon armorial bearings used on carriages, *see* ARMS, COAT OF.

Offences.—The penalty for using a dog to draw, or to help to draw, a cart or barrow on a public highway is 40/– for the first offence and £5 thereafter. When the driver of a cart or carriage is arrested, the police may take charge of his cart or carriage and the magistrate may order it to be sold to satisfy a fine. Within the Metropolitan Police District, it is an offence (fine, 40/–) for any person having the control of a cart or carriage to ride on it, or on the horse, or on the shafts, without holding the reins; or to be at such a distance from the carriage or cart as not to have complete control over every animal drawing it. It is a similar offence to draw or drive in any public place any cart, carriage or barrow upon a footway, or to fasten any horse or animal so that it can stand across a footway; or, to the annoyance of the inhabitants or passengers, to feed or shoe horses, or to expose them for sale, or to clean or repair any part of a carriage or cart, except in cases of accident when repair on the spot is necessary.

It is an offence (fine, 5/–) for any person to ride upon carriages within the Metropolitan Police District without the owner's or driver's consent; if the offender is a child apparently under twelve years of age, a magistrate may cause him to be detained until the parent or guardian can attend to receive him; but when the Police Court closes for the day, the child may be discharged. In all urban districts and in many rural districts, there are similar offences to all the above and also the following: it is an offence to drive more than two carts or waggons at the same time; when driving two carts or waggons, it is an offence not to have the halter of the last cart's horse securely fastened to the back of the first cart, or to have such halter of a greater length than four feet. The owner of every waggon or cart must have his full name and address painted thereon in black and white, the letters to be at least one inch high (penalty for failure, 40/–); this does not apply to gigs, gentlemen's carriages, etc.

CARRIERS' LICENCES.—No person may now carry goods by road in a motor vehicle without first obtaining a carrier's licence for each vehicle under the Road and Rail Traffic Act of 1933, which came into effect on January 1st, 1934.

There are, however, a few exceptions where no licence is necessary. In the first place if no hire or other reward, i.e. money, is received in return for the carriage, it is not necessary to have a carrier's licence, unless the carriage is in connection with the carrier's own trade or business. A commercial traveller or tradesman carrying or delivering goods in the course of his business or trade, or a manufacturer taking goods from one factory to another, needs a licence; but if the goods were not connected with his trade or business, then no licence would be required unless some charge were made. A tradesman therefore, or a professional man who delivered goods for another *gratuitously*, would not need a licence.

In the second place the act only applies to vehicles or trailers constructed or adapted for the carriage of goods, and not even to trailers so constructed or adapted if they are drawn by a private vehicle built to seat not more than seven persons and a driver, and no hire or reward is received in return for the carriage. A commercial traveller therefore may not use a car specially adapted for the carriage of samples without first obtaining a C licence, but he may use a trailer drawn by an ordinary private car. A tradesman will be in the same position with regard to the delivery of his wares.

No carrier's licence is necessary for most agricultural vehicles, nor for ambulances and fire and police machines, nor for vehicles used solely for funerals (for the carriage of coffins, etc., and not of passengers). Breakdown lorries and machines used for towing or for removing goods from a disabled vehicle to a place of safety are also exempted.

Carriers' licences are personal to the carrier to whom they are issued and cannot be assigned or sold; on death, sale, etc., application should be made to the Traffic Commissioners for a transfer.

Different Kinds of Licences.—There are three kinds of licence; the public carrier's, called A, for short, the limited carrier's or B licence, and the private carrier's or C licence. An A licence entitles the licencee to use the licensed vehicle for the carriage of goods by road for hire or reward, but such vehicles may not be used in connection with any other trade or business of the licensee. The Traffic Commissioners have a discretion as to whether or not they will grant an A licence (except in a few cases, *see* below), but if they do grant it they cannot insert any conditions in it as to services, charges, etc. The normal duration of an A licence is two years from the date on which it was given.

If, in addition to using the vehicle for the carriage of goods for hire or reward, the licensee wishes to use it for the carriage of goods in connection with his own trade or business, he must obtain a B licence (a limited carrier's licence) which will entitle him to use the vehicle for both purposes.

In issuing these licences Traffic Commissioners have a much greater discretion than in the case of A licences for in addition to deciding whether or not they will grant a B licence at all they have also power to grant it subject to conditions affecting the right to use the licensed vehicle for the carriage of goods for hire or reward; as regards its use for the carriage of goods in connection with the licensee's trade or business, however, no conditions may be imposed. Of the conditions that may be attached the most important are those limiting the places between which the persons for whom and the nature or class of goods which may be carried. No conditions as to rates or charges may be imposed. A B licence lasts for one year and expires on the same dates as an A licence.

Both A and B licences entitle the licensee to act as a public carrier of goods for hire or reward, and a B licence entitles him also to use the same vehicles in his trade or business. In granting both A and B licences the authorities have a discretion and they may also attach certain conditions to a B licence. If therefore an applicant for a licence does not intend to use the vehicles for carriage for hire or reward but only in connection with his own trade or business, he should apply for a C licence; for no conditions can be attached to this and the licensing authority have no power to refuse to grant it, unless the applicant has at some time held a carrier's licence which was suspended or revoked.

A C licence entitles the licensee to use the licensed vehicles in connection with his own trade or business and, in the case of a farmer, to carry goods for another farmer in the same district for hire or reward. It lasts for three years and expires on the same dates as the A and B licences.

Short term A, B and C licences of three months' duration may be granted for work which only lasts for a short season.

How Application is Made.—Application for a carrier's licence should be made to the Traffic Commissioners (the licensing authority) for the area in which is situated the base, or centre, from which the business will be worked, or in the case of a C licence, in which is situated the head office of the applicant. Special forms should be obtained and all the particulars required filled in. An A or B licence can only be obtained for vehicles already owned or hired by the licensee, or which he intends to acquire immediately his licence is granted; but a C licence may be obtained for vehicles which the licensee does not yet own. When a C licensee does become owner or hirer under a hire-purchase agreement of such a vehicle, he must give notice to the licensing authority within one month. If the licensing authority cannot deal with applications at once, they have power to grant temporary licences of not more than twelve months for an A, six for a B, or three for a C, which will end automatically when the application for a full licence is granted or refused.

Carriers Already in Business.—In certain cases a licensing authority is bound to grant a licence. The position of an applicant for a C licence has already been discussed; they are usually entitled as of right to a licence. So also is any applicant for an A or B licence who applies before 1st April, 1934, and can prove that during the year 1st April, 1932, to 1st April, 1933, he acted as a carrier for hire or reward; but his *right* is confined to the grant of a licence for vehicles of the same unladen weight as he employed during that year; as regards any extra weight the licensing authority may exercise their usual discretion.

An applicant for an A licence who proves that the vehicles in question will only be used to carry the goods of a particular person or firm under a contract for at least one year, cannot be refused a licence, though when granted it will come to an end on the same date as his contract; nor may applications to vary a licence by reducing the maximum weight or number of vehicles licensed, or by replacing one vehicle with another of similar capacity, be refused. In all cases, except those in which they are bound to grant a licence, the Traffic Commissioners must publish particulars of every application they receive in order that any objectors may come forward. Apparently any person may object, but the Traffic Commissioners are only bound by law to listen to, and consider, the objections raised by persons already themselves engaged as carriers of goods (whether by rail, road or water), and in the case of applications for an A licence they cannot even be compelled to allow the holder of a B licence to object, though they must listen to the objections of another A licensee.

Conditions.—In addition to their powers of granting, refusing and varying licences and inserting conditions therein, licensing authorities have power to revoke or suspend a licence for breach of those conditions; but they may only do so if satisfied that the breach was frequent, or wilful, or entailed danger to the public, and they may be required to state in writing the grounds on which they acted. From any decision of a licensing authority the applicant or an objector (provided that he belongs to the class which they were bound to hear) may appeal to an Appeal Tribunal whose decision is in nearly every case final; in a few exceptional cases it may still be possible to resort further to the Ordinary Courts.

Using an unlicensed vehicle or one, the use of which has been prohibited by an examiner, or breaking any condition of the licence, is, in addition to being a ground for revocation or suspension of the licence, also a criminal offence and is punishable with a heavy fine.

CARRIER'S LIEN.—A common carrier (q.v.) has a right to withhold goods carried by him until the carriage charges have been paid. This is called a lien. (*See* CARRIAGE CHARGES; COMMON CARRIER.)

CASE STATED.—The method of appeal from a Police Court on a point of law is by means of "Case Stated" to a Divisional Court of the High Court of Justice. The party who is dissatisfied with the Police Court's decision can ask the magistrates to state a case; in other words, to set out their decisions on questions of fact, and to put for the decision of the High Court of Justice the questions of law arising from those decisions of fact. The case so stated is then considered by the Judges of a Divisional Court of the High Court of Justice, and they declare what is the legal effect of the findings of fact in the court below.

It is important to note that an appeal of this sort can be on a question of law only, since the High Court Judges must accept as right the decisions on questions of fact of the lower Court. This procedure is used, not only in appeals from Police Courts, but in connection with decisions of arbitrators also.

CASHIERING.—This is the most ignominious form of dismissal of an officer from the combatant services. It is only inflicted in cases of offences involving most discreditable conduct. An officer who has been cashiered can never again be employed under the Crown in any capacity.

CASUAL WARD.—Every County Council must provide within its area a casual ward for the use of the casual poor, who may require relief therein. Every casual poor person is to be admitted to the ward, fed, set to work and discharged, but he must not be discharged until 9 o'clock in the forenoon of the day following his admittance, nor until he has performed the work which he has been set to do.

Any person who applies for relief representing himself to be a casual poor person may be searched by the relieving officer or the Master of the Workhouse, and any money found in his possession may be used to pay for the expense of relieving him. (*See* POOR LAW; WORKHOUSE.)

CAT.—Cats are domestic animals and are the property of their owner, but since they are not dangerous, the owner of a cat cannot be held liable for the damage that it does unless it can be shewn that he knew that it was liable to cause that damage. As a general rule the owner of a cat is not liable if it kills the pet birds of neighbours, but once he knows that the cat is likely to do this he will be liable for keeping it. (*See* ANIMALS; CRUELTY TO ANIMALS.)

CATTLE.—Cattle, like other domestic animals, are the property of their owner, and he can maintain an action for damages against anyone who injures them, e.g. the negligent driver of a motor-car. If the injury is done by a dog, the owner of the cattle is entitled to shoot the dog if he catches it in the act of worrying, or he can take out a summons at the Petty Sessional Court for an order that the dog be kept under proper control or destroyed as a dangerous dog. If the damage which the dog has done is less than £5, he can recover the damages in a Court of Summary Jurisdiction. (*See* DOG.)

Cattle, including bulls, are not in law dangerous animals to human beings, and accordingly the owner of cattle is not liable for damages if they attack human beings unless he already knows that they are dangerous. Even then a farmer is perfectly entitled to keep a dangerous bull provided that he keeps it properly shut in, and he will not be liable if a trespasser is injured, though if he keeps it in a field through which a public footpath passes, or even in a field which he knows the public are accustomed to use, he will be liable.

If cattle trespass on to the land of another person the owner of the cattle is liable for any damage that they may do, unless he can shew that the trespass was caused by the failure of that other person to keep in order the fence through which the cattle trespassed. This applies only to trespass from one field into a neighbour's field, and if cattle are being driven along a highway and trespass into fields or premises bounding the highway the owner of the cattle is not liable, unless it can be shewn that the cattle were being negligently driven. Thus, if a bull, taking fright, goes into a china shop, the owner of the bull is not liable for the damage it may do, unless it was due to his negligence. Further, since no one is bound in law to keep his fences abutting on to a highway in proper repair, the owner of cattle is not liable if they escape from his field and wander on the highway where they may do damage, or cause accidents to traffic.

Distress Damage Feasant.—Where cattle trespass on to another person's land, the owner of the land is entitled to seize them and hold them until he has received compensation for the damage that they have done. This is known as distress damage feasant, and it applies not only to cattle, but to any chattels which are improperly upon another person's land.

The cattle must be distrained, i.e. seized at the time of the trespass; they cannot be followed after they have left the land; and after they have been seized they should at once be impounded. In some places there are still common pounds, and where these still exist, the distrainor should take the cattle there at once and hand them over to the pound keeper. Generally speaking, however, common pounds have gone out of use, and the distrainor will impound the cattle himself, i.e. put them in a field or barn on his own premises. While they are impounded the person distraining must provide the impounded animals with adequate food and water, under a penalty of £5 for failing to do so. If he fails to provide them with food and water for 6 consecutive hours, any person is entitled to enter the place where they are impounded in order to do so. The cost of the food and water the distrainor can recover from the owner of the animals by proceedings in a Court of Summary Jurisdiction.

The distrainor of animals impounded in this way is entitled to retain them only until the owner has offered him sufficient compensation for the damage that they have done. When a reasonable sum for damage has been tendered by the owner, the impounder must hand them back to the owner, and if he fails to do so, he will be liable in damages for retaining them.

For this reason the method of obtaining redress for trespass by cattle by distraining damage feasant is a dangerous one, and it must be remembered that each animal can be distrained only for the damage that it has done itself and not for damage done by animals which have not been distrained. Further, the distrainor is not entitled to use the animals himself, or to sell them, or indeed to do anything to them except to retain them until tender for the damage which they have done has been made. He cannot recover the cost of feeding them as part of the damage done, but must, if necessary, proceed through his proper remedy in the Court of Summary Jurisdiction.

Agistment.—Agistment is the contract whereby a farmer pays for his cattle to graze upon another man's land. The agister, upon whose land the cattle graze, must take reasonable care of them, e.g. he must not put them in a field with poisonous yews, or allow a dangerous animal of his own to go in the field with them, or leave gates open, etc. They are exempt from distraint for rent or tithe by the agister's landlord. Contracts of agistment are often made upon terms that the agister shall permit the cows to graze in return for their milk.

Diseases of Cattle.—Owners of cattle which they have reason to believe are affected with cattle plague, foot and mouth disease and other infectious diseases, must forthwith give notice to a local police constable, and take every possible step to isolate the animals. The local inspectors of the Ministry of Agriculture will then decide upon what further steps should be taken, which may include the prohibition of movement of all animals within the neighbourhood or orders for the destruction of cattle suspected of being infected. Compensation is payable for animals which have been slaughtered for the common good. There are penalties for failure to comply with these provisions. (*See* ANIMALS; CRUELTY TO ANIMALS.)

CAVEAT.—A Caveat is a document which may be obtained at the Principal Probate Registry by any person who wishes to object to a grant of Probate being made. It has the effect of preventing any grant of probate being made in respect of an estate until the person who has obtained the caveat, and who is known as the Caveator, has had an opportunity of voicing his objections to the grant of probate. If a caveat is obtained and applied for without sufficient reason, the caveator is liable to pay the costs occasioned by his acts. (*See* ADMINISTRATION ACTION; EXECUTORS AND ADMINISTRATORS; PROBATE OF WILLS.)

CAVEAT EMPTOR.—This is a Latin expression meaning "Let the purchaser beware." There is a general rule in the Law of contract that a purchaser makes his bargain at his peril, and if what he gets is not what he wanted, he has no redress. There are, of course, certain exceptions to this rule, such as where a seller misrepresents the quality or quantity of goods that he is selling, or where the buyer indicates to the seller that he is relying upon his skill or judgment in selecting him the goods. (*See* SALE OF GOODS.)

CELLARS.—A cellar, vault or underground room must not be used as a dwelling house unless it was let or occupied as a dwelling house upon the 11th of August, 1875. If it has been built or rebuilt since that date, then under no circumstances may it be used as a dwelling house. A cellar which was let or occupied before the 11th of August, 1875, may still be let if it is more than seven feet high all over, and if every part of the ceiling is more than three feet above the level of the ground. In order that it may comply with the legal regulations, the cellar must have an open area in front of it, proper drains, a water closet, window and fire-place. Any person who lets, or allows to be occupied, any cellar which does not comply with all these provisions is liable to a fine of twenty shillings for every day that the cellar remains occupied after a notice has been given by the local authority.

Cellars in London.—In London, cellars or underground dwellings may be let or occupied even although they were constructed after 1875, but certain strict conditions as to lighting, ventilation and drainage, similar to those already mentioned must be complied with. (*See* BASEMENT; HOUSING; PUBLIC HEALTH.)

CEMETERIES.—Generally speaking anyone may provide and keep a cemetery for burial of the dead, but in some localities, for example the Metropolis, or within two miles of any part of it, the sanction of the Ministry of Health must be obtained and further, no nuisance must be caused thereby. A registration book must, by law, be kept and all burials registered. There is a prohibition in law against a cemetery being constructed nearer to a dwelling house than 200 yards without the consent in writing of the owner, lessee or occupier of the dwelling. In some cases, however, the distance may be 100 yards. This, of course, does not apply to cemeteries already constructed before the

Act came into force in the last century. Any land which has been consecrated and used for burial may not be sold or disposed of for any other purpose, such as building, except in a few special instances. This does not, of course, prevent the building of chapels for the carrying out of burial services, or buildings for the purpose of embellishment of the cemetery, nor does it prevent the building of roads and proper fences.

A chapel for the performance of the burial service according to the rites of the Established Church may be erected on the consecrated portion. No body may be buried under any chapel in the cemetery or within fifteen feet of its outer wall.

The owners of the cemetery must provide proper drainage. If any streams to which others have a right of use be fouled by anything from the cemetery they are called upon to pay, and must pay, damages to any such person. The owners of the cemetery may have any part of it consecrated by the Bishop of the Diocese in which it is situated for burial in accordance with the rites of the Established Church, providing the Bishop is satisfied as to the title of the owners and he thinks fit to consecrate. This portion must be used for burials according to the rites of the Established Church subject, however, to the right of the person having charge of, or being responsible for, the burial giving notice in the prescribed form to the usual officiating minister of intention to bury without such rites. The consecrated and unconsecrated portion must be distinguished by suitable marks.

No body may be removed from its place of burial without both an ecclesiastical faculty, in the case of consecrated ground, and the license of a Secretary of State, and in the case of unconsecrated ground, the license of a Secretary of State alone.

The owners of the cemetery must appoint a clerk in Holy Orders to officiate as Chaplain and he must, unless, prevented by reasonable cause, perform when required the burial service of the Established Church over all bodies which are entitled to burial in consecrated ground, and are brought for burial in such ground; but he is under no obligation to perform any service in the case of a body being cremated. He may do so, however, by permission of the Bishop. The chaplain must be approved by the

Bishop who thereupon must license him, but such license can be withdrawn by the Bishop for reasonable cause. The owners are responsible for the stipend of the chaplain. (*See* BURIAL.)

CENTRAL CRIMINAL COURT.—

The Central Criminal Court is situated on the site of the ancient Criminal Court of the City of London, known as the Old Bailey. In fact, it is still popularly called by that name. It is under the control of the corporation of the City, but it exercises jurisdiction as the Assize Court of Middlesex as well as that of the City. By means of the Writ of Certiorari, important cases, which for various reasons are removed from other counties for trial, may be tried there.

The Central Criminal Court is not in constant session, but sits from time to time at frequent intervals, in order to deal with batches of prisoners. A Judge of the King's Bench Division sits at each session, and he is assisted by the Recorder of the City of London, the Common Sergeant, and an additional Judge, who is called the Commissioner. The Lord Mayor and Sheriffs of the City are frequently to be seen upon the Bench, but they take no actual part in the trial of prisoners.

CERTIFICATION OF LUNATICS.

—Before a person can be detained as a lunatic under a reception order (q.v. and *see* DETENTION OF LUNATICS) it is necessary in ordinary cases to obtain two medical certificates that he is of unsound mind.

Very strict rules have been laid down as to the circumstances under which these certificates can be given and the persons who can sign them, for there is frequently a danger that persons who are not insane may be shut up as lunatics by relations and others from spiteful motives.

Each certificate must, of course, be made out by a doctor and must state that in his opinion the person is of unsound mind. In addition, the facts must be set out on which the opinion is formed, facts observed by the doctor himself being distinguished from those of which he has been informed by others. The doctor must have examined the patient within seven clear days before the date on which the petition for a reception order is made, and if more than one certificate is required, it is necessary that the doctors should have examined the patient separately.

A doctor who is closely related by marriage or otherwise to the person who is applying for the detention of the lunatic cannot give a certificate, nor can a doctor who is the manager of, or the regular attendant in, the institution to which the lunatic is to be taken, or is interested in any payments to be made on account of the lunatic for his treatment, or who is related to, or an assistant or partner of, any of the above persons.

Where two certificates are required, the one cannot be given by an assistant, partner or relative of the person giving the other.

When it is intended to obtain an urgency order (*see* DETENTION OF LUNATICS), the doctor granting the certificate must have examined the patient not more than two clear days before the lunatic is received into the institution. (*See* DETENTION OF LUNATICS; LUNATICS.)

CERTIFIED SCHEMES.—Contract-

ing-out of the provisions of the Workmen's Compensation Act 1925 is not permitted except in one way, and that is by means of what is called a certified scheme. A certified scheme is a scheme for providing compensation for injured workmen which is approved by the Chief Registrar of Friendly Societies. If a scheme is put forward by the employer and approved by a majority of the workmen affected by it, then if the scheme is certified by the Registrar, the employer may contract with his workmen that the provisions of the scheme shall take the place of the provisions of the Workmen's Compensation Act, and the employer then becomes liable to his workmen in accordance with the scheme.

There are certain conditions which must be satisfied before the Registrar can certify a scheme and these are:—

(1) That the scale of payments by way of compensation under the proposed scheme must not be less favourable to both the workmen and their dependents than the scale laid down by the Compensation Act.

(2) That if a workman is required to make contributions under the scheme he must get benefits at least equal to his contributions in addition to the statutory benefits he would receive if there were no scheme.

(3) That a ballot of the workmen to be affected is taken and such ballot results in a majority in favour of the scheme.

(4) That a workman is not compelled to join in the scheme as a condition of his being employed.

(5) That there is a provision in the scheme enabling a workman to withdraw from it.

(6) That the scheme provides security against all liabilities which arise either during the existence of the scheme or after it has expired.

The Registrar may grant a certificate for a limited period of five years and he may renew the certificate when it expires. If it appears to him that the rules of the scheme relating to benefits have been altered so that the amounts payable are less favourable to the workman than those payable under the Act, then he may revoke the certificate. If the certified scheme provides that the payments by way of compensation should be made by a Friendly Society, then the provisions of the Friendly Societies Act 1896 which forbid a Friendly Society from paying an annuity of more than £50, or a gross sum of more than £300 do not apply. (*See* FRIENDLY SOCIETY; WORKMEN'S COMPENSATION.)

CERTIORARI.—Certiorari is a writ directed by a superior Court (usually the King's Bench Division of the High Court) to an inferior court (e.g. to a County Court), and ordering a case to be removed from such inferior Court to the superior Court in order that justice may be done. The writ is issued by the High Court in the exercise of the power that has always been vested in that court to supervise the Conduct and proceedings of all inferior Courts, the judges of the High Court being regarded as the direct representatives of the King who is the fountain of all justice. The writ is therefore known as a prerogative writ, being issued by virtue of the Royal prerogative. (*See* PREROGATIVE WRITS.)

The writ is issued for the following purposes:—

(i) To remove a civil case from an inferior Court to the High Court because it is desirable it should be tried in the High Court (e.g. if it involves a difficult question of law, or if it is possible that, due to local feeling or other causes, the inferior Court will not be fair tribunal).

(ii) To remove indictments (including coroners' inquests) to the King's Bench Division of the High Court or to the Central Criminal Court, either for the hearing of the trial or merely for the judgment;

(iii) In certain cases, to bring the case up to the King's Bench in order to "quash" (i.e. upset) the decision of an inferior criminal Court;

(iv) In certain civil or criminal cases, to remove the case into the High Court after the inferior Court has given judgment, for the purpose of enforcing such judgment.

The writ of certiorari will be issued in respect of almost every inferior Court in England, Wales and Berwick-upon-Tweed, but it cannot be issued against any Court that is itself a part of the High Court. The most important use of the writ is, however, of comparatively modern growth; a very considerable number of government departments and other administrative bodies have recently been invested with sweeping powers in respect of innumerable activities (e.g. town-planning), and in the course of their duties it often happens that they are empowered to act like a judicial body (e.g. in the assessing of compensation to be paid to members of the public or in the deciding upon plans or schemes to be adopted).

In the majority of such cases, no appeal lies to a public Court at the suit of a party aggrieved by their decision, even though the most flagrant injustice has been done. But in these cases, a writ of certiorari will often be issued by the High Court, which acts upon the grounds that it is entitled to supervise any public body which is entrusted with quasi-judicial functions. It was on this principle that, in 1933, a writ of certiorari was issued when it appeared that, at a meeting of a rural district council, a member of the council had voted, when not entitled so to vote, on whether permission should be given to erect buildings in an area scheduled as a town-planning area.

On similar grounds, the writ has been granted in order that the High Court might enquire whether a surgeon's certificate of disablement under the Workmen's Compensation Act, 1925, has been properly made, for the giving of such certificate is regarded as, to some extent, a judicial act. Similarly, when an official examiner of the quality of gas gave an adverse report as to the quality of a company's gas without taking the evidence of one party in the presence of the other, a writ of certiorari was issued in order to enable the Court, if it saw fit, to annul such report. But the writ will issue only against a person or body who acts in a judicial capacity, not against one acting in a purely administrative capacity, e.g. the grant of a certificate for the admission of an insane person into an asylum cannot be brought before the Court by certiorari, however improperly it may have been made, but the writ of habeas corpus may be available in such cases. (*See* HABEAS CORPUS.)

In a few cases, the Judge is bound to grant the writ on application being properly made, e.g. at the request of the Attorney-General in his official capacity; but in all other cases the Judge may exercise his discretion as to whether or not he will grant the writ, and, in a criminal case, he will never issue it unless either it appears that a fair and impartial trial could not be obtained in the local Court, or that some difficult question of law is involved, or that a special jury would be advisable. In all other cases the Judge must exercise his discretion, as in all cases of prerogative writs, according to established principles of law, and not in a purely arbitrary manner, e.g. it has now become a rule that the Judge will never issue the writ if he sees that no substantial benefit would accrue to the party asking for it, even if it were granted.

The cases in which a writ of certiorari is most used and most useful are where the Court, against whom the writ is issued, has acted beyond its powers (or "jurisdiction"), or where a member of a Court was biased in his decision. For example, justices are not entitled to convict for non-payment of a rate when the defendant disputes the validity of the rate in good faith, and, if they proceed to decide the case in spite of such a contention having been raised, they act outside their jurisdiction. Bias in a Judge or justice or other member of a judicial body must generally be pecuniary, e.g. when justices convicted a man for riding in a second class compartment with a third class ticket, a writ of certiorari was issued on its being shewn that some members of the bench were shareholders

in the prosecuting company, and the conviction was thereupon annulled.

The writ, when issued, must be served on the Court or person against whom it was issued, and it is then his duty to send all the original official documents (known as the "records") to the High Court. The case is then heard afresh either in the High Court in London or by a High Court Judge on assize. (*See also* PROCEDENDO.)

The writ is so called because it commands the case to be removed in order that the High Court may "be certified" as to the facts or conduct of the case in the Court below, i.e. may make itself certain that justice has been done. (*See* PREROGATIVE WRITS; PROCEDENDO.)

CESTUI QUE TRUST.—This is the person for whose benefit a trust is created. A cestui que trust is the owner of an equitable estate as opposed to the trustee, who is usually the owner of the legal estate. The cestui que trust is the beneficiary under the trust, i.e. the person who gets the money produced by the trust. (*See* TRUST.)

CESTUI QUE VIE.—It used to be a common practice when granting a lease to provide that it should last until the death of a particular person or persons named therein; since the length of the lease would depend on his life this person was called the cestui-que-vie, which is old law French for "he on whose life. . ." A similar position might be reached if a man who was entitled to land for his own life granted his interest to some one else; the grantee got an interest "pur autre vie" ("during the life of another") and the grantor, since it was on his life that this interest depended was called the cestui que vie. The Cestui-Que-Vie Act of 1706 provided a means by which other persons, who will be entitled to the land when the cestui que vie dies, can challenge the person in possession of the land to prove that he is still alive.

CHAMPERTY.—When a man, knowing that some dispute has arisen which is likely to lead to an action in the Courts, purchases an interest in the case, or renders assistance to one of the parties under an agreement to receive a share of the damages, he is said to be guilty of champerty. An agreement of this kind is called champertous. Champerty is a civil wrong, and is also a crime. Prosecutions for champerty, however, are extremely rare. (*See* MAINTAINANCE.)

CHANCEL.—The portion of a church where the altar is situated. It is under the direct legal control of the incumbent, and is reparable by the rector, who in some cases may be a layman.

CHANCELLOR.—This is a title frequently given to the principal official in a particular sphere or department: even, in Scotland, to the foreman of a jury. Various officers holding this title are dealt with below.

CHANCELLOR, LORD HIGH.— The Lord Chancellor, as he is generally called, is the chief judicial officer in England, and he has various duties. He is Speaker of the House of Lords (where he sits on the Woolsack), a Privy Councillor, President of the House of Lords sitting as the Supreme Court of Appeal, of the Court of Appeal, and of the Chancery Division of the High Court. He nominates the Judges of the High Court, except the Lord Chief Justice, and appoints County Court Judges and Justices of the Peace. He is also the guardian of infants and lunatics, is a member of the Cabinet, and goes out of office with the Government. He is appointed by the delivery of the Great Seal into his keeping.

He may not be a Roman Catholic, and among his titles is Keeper of the King's Conscience, a reminder of the times when he was a churchman and not a lawyer. Cardinal Wolsey was the last ecclesiastic to be Lord Chancellor.

His salary is £10,000 per annum, and his pension, £5,000 per annum.

CHANCELLOR OF THE EXCHEQUER.—The Chancellor of the Exchequer is the member of the Cabinet responsible for finance. Although the Prime Minister is nominally First Lord of the Treasury, the Chancellor of the Exchequer is the effective controller of the financial affairs of the government, and it is he who introduces the Budget every year, setting out the state of the nation's accounts, and arranging such new or modified taxation as he thinks necessary to " balance the budget." His salary is £5,000 per annum.

Among his duties is to compile a list— together with the Judges of the King's Bench Division—of three names for each post of Sheriff. These lists are submitted to the King, who chooses the first name on each list by the old custom of pricking it with a bodkin, that is, a small dagger.

CHANCELLOR OF THE DUCHY. —This officer of the Crown is nominally in charge of the Courts, lands and property in the royal Duchy of Lancaster: but as this work is all done by subordinate officials, the Chancellor in fact has virtually no duties. The office is therefore usually given to a minister whose assistance is of value to the government, but who cannot, for any reason, supervise one of the great departments. He receives £2,000 per annum.

CHANCELLOR OF A DIOCESE. —The official who presides over a Bishop's Court in his diocese, and hears cases in the Bishop's name, is called the Chancellor of the Diocese. He is usually a barrister.

CHANCELLOR OF A UNIVERSITY.—A University Chancellor is usually a nobleman or distinguished statesman. He is the head of the University, but his duties within it are very largely performed by a Vice-Chancellor. The principal concern of the Chancellor is to look after the interests of the University, especially in its relations with the government.

CHANCERY DIVISION.—The Chancery Division of the High Court of Justice has six judges assigned to it, and in this Division should be started all actions dealing with the administration of estates, actions affecting partnership agreements, or patent rights, redemption and foreclosure of mortgages, contracts for the sale or leasing of land or other real property, all trust matters and questions dealing with infants and the distribution of the proceeds of property subject to liens and charges. In addition to this, any action where the chief remedy sought is an injunction preventing another party from infringing rights, or for specific performance to force another party to carry out an agreement, or to rectify or to discover the true meaning and effect of a deed or written document should be commenced in this division.

The administration of the estates of bankrupts is dealt with by a special Court known as the Court of Bankruptcy, which sits in a building in Carey Street in London, and of which, district Courts sit in most of the large cities of the country. Although these are special Courts they are all part of the Chancery Division of the High Court of Justice.

Another special Court which is part of the

Chancery Division sits for the purpose of dealing with the management and winding up of companies. This sits in the same building as the Bankruptcy Court. (*See* COURTS; HIGH COURT OF JUSTICE; HIGH COURT PROCEDURE.)

CHARACTER (EVIDENCE OF).

—Questions of great difficulty often arise in criminal cases on points in connection with the character of the prisoner.

In general, the character of a prisoner cannot be made known to the tribunal until after he or she has been convicted. This is the attempt of the law to avoid the consequences of the old motto " give a dog a bad name, and hang him." There are, however, certain important exceptions to this rule. Although when a prisoner gives evidence on his own behalf he cannot usually be asked any question in cross-examination tending to show that he is of bad character, yet he or his advocate may so conduct his case, that such questions become perfectly proper. Questions of this kind are allowed in the following cases:—

Where the prisoner has given evidence of his own good character.

Where he or his advocate has attacked the character of the witnesses for the prosecution.

Where he has given evidence against any other prisoner charged with the same offence.

There are certain special offences which give the prosecution the right to call evidence tending to shew that the prisoner is a bad character. An example is the case of receiving stolen property. In such cases, the prosecutor may prove that the prisoner has, within five years before his trial, been convicted of other offences involving dishonesty.

A prisoner may, of course, if he wishes, give evidence as to his own good record, and may call witnesses to shew that he is of good character. This right is very frequently exercised, and such evidence sometimes turns the scale in favour of an accused person.

CHARACTER OF SERVANTS.—

In the absence of any special agreement there is no legal obligation binding a master to give a character to a servant who has left his employ, or whom he has dismissed, and he cannot be sued if he refuses to give him one.

If a master gives a character concerning the honesty of a servant who has been in his employ, which he knows to be false, and some person employs the servant on the strength of that character, and the servant then robs his new master, he, the new master, may be able to recover his loss, in the form of damages, from the former employer. It is a criminal offence for an employer to make a false statement as to the period during which a servant has been in his employ, or for any person falsely to represent himself as having employed a person of whom he purports to give a character.

If a master gives a character he must do so honestly and truthfully. If he does not, the character may be defamatory of the servant of whom it was given, and the servant may be entitled to bring an action for libel or slander. A character given by a master of a servant who has been in his employ to a prospective employer, or answers to questions put to him by the prospective employer are "privileged communications," (*see* PRIVILEGE); and before an action for libel or slander can be brought, the servant complain-of the statements must be able to prove that the statements or character were not only untrue but were given maliciously, that is to say, that they were not made honestly, but were statements made which the master knew to be false, or which he made out of spite. (*See* DEFAMATION.)

CHARGING ORDER.

—When a person against whom a judgment has been obtained owns Government stock, or shares in any company, or where there is a fund in Court to which he is entitled, an order may be made by the Court charging the stock, shares, or fund with the payment of the amount of the judgment. This is known as a Charging Order. The Order is made in two stages. First an Order nisi is made, calling upon the debtor to shew cause why the final charging order should not be made, and if the debtor does not shew good cause the order is made absolute. No proceedings can be taken to enforce the order until six months from the date of the order nisi, but then the judgment creditor may take proceedings to have the property sold. He will require for this purpose to take out an originating summons (q.v.).

CHARITY.

—In law the word charity has a much wider meaning than it has in ordinary speech. It includes not only the relief of poverty but also:—

1. the advancement of religion;
2. the advancement of education;
3. other objects of a like nature which are for the benefit of the community.

The last heading is very vague but it is clear that it is not every object which benefits the public which is a charity. Thus the advancement of sport is not a charity, but money left for the prevention of cruelty to animals is a charity for it is for the benefit of the community.

The importance of determining whether an object is charitable or not lies in the fact that, if money is left for charitable purposes under a charitable trust, the trust is in many respects in a more favoured position than ordinary trusts.

A trust may be charitable although it does not benefit the public at large. So a trust for the benefit of certain poor relatives of the person leaving the money is a charitable trust, although it can benefit only the particular persons mentioned, for it is for the public benefit that all classes of the poor should be provided for.

Gifts for the benefit of particular individuals not in poverty or a fluctuating body of particular individuals, for instance, gifts to persons residing in a particular street, or to a city company whose property is charged with no charitable trust, are never charitable, though they may be good as gifts to individuals.

Gifts for superstitious purposes, that is to say, gifts which have for their object the propagation or the rites of a religion not tolerated by the law, are void, and generally the Court will not allow the encouragement of imposture in the guise of a charitable trust. Thus a trust for the benefit of spiritualistic mediums is void. In the same way gifts which though charitable, are against public policy, are also void.

The Charity Commissioners have power to inquire into all charities.

How Created.—Like other trusts a charitable trust may be created by any clearly expressed intention on the part of the donor to devote certain property to charity, but again like other trusts it must be proved by some writing signed by some person who is able to declare such trust, or by his will. The writing need not have been in existence at the date of the creation of the trust, it is sufficient if it is in existence at the date of the action brought to enforce the trust.

Cy-Pres.—A charitable trust has two advantages. The first is that a charitable trust may be good although the objects of the trust are not clearly and certainly named in the document creating the trust, or although the objects are clearly named but have become impossible. In either of these cases an ordinary trust would fail, but in the case of a charitable trust the Court will always endeavour to find in the trust document a general charitable intention, i.e. will enquire whether the person leaving the money did not intend that, if the special object (if any) mentioned became impossible, the money should be used for some similar purpose of a charitable kind.

Thus, if A leaves money to maintain a certain school and before his death the school ceases to exist, the Court would have to consider whether A's object was to benefit that *particular school* or whether it was to benefit *education generally*. If it held that the first was his object the trust would fail, but if it came to the conclusion that A wanted generally to benefit education and merely selected the particular school as being the most convenient and desirable method of carrying out his general intention, then the trust would not fail but the Court would order the money to be applied "cy-pres"—that is, in a manner "near thereto"—and to be used for the benefit of some similar school or for similar educational purposes. Notice that once a trust has become devoted to charitable purposes it will not come to an end because the purposes later fail, but will always be applied cy-pres. Thus, if in the example above, the school had been in existence at A's death but had later been closed, the money would be applied to some other charitable purpose, whether the Court thought A had a general charitable purpose or merely a charitable intention to benefit that particular school.

Rule against perpetuities.—The Rule against Perpetuities, which says that a gift under a trust is bad if it may not become effective within a life in being and twenty-one years, (*see* PERPETUITIES) does not apply to charitable trust when there is a gift for charitable purposes and then another gift for charitable purposes on the failure of the first, even though the gift over may not vest within the required period.. Both the gift and the gift over must be for charitable purposes. Thus, if money is left to build a school subject to the condition that, if the Government should set up at any time a system of national education, the money should go to the sisters of the testator instead of the school, and if after the death of the testator a system of national education was set up, his sisters could not take, for the gift to them is against the rule against perpetuities and is not protected, for it is not for a charitable purpose.

Gifts of Land.—Land given by deed to a charity must be made at least twelve months before the death of the person giving it, and must take effect in possession and be without a power of revocation. Where land is left by will it must be sold within a year of the testator's death unless the charity to whom it is left is authorized to retain the land by the Court or the Charity Commissioners. (*See* Perpetuities; Trusts.)

CHARITY COMMISSIONERS.— These are a body of commissioners for England and Wales, appointed by the Crown under the Charitable Trusts Acts. **There** are four commissioners, of whom two must be barristers of twelve years standing. They have power to examine into all charities, and to prosecute all necessary inquiries by officers called assistant commissioners; to require trustees of charities and other persons to render written accounts and statements, or to attend and be examined on oath, in relation to any charity or its property; to authorise suits concerning any charity or its property.

CHARLES I.—Charles I was tried at Westminster Hall on the 20th January, 1648 before Commissioners appointed by Act of Parliament under the Lord President, John Bradshawe. Cromwell and Ireton were members. He was prosecuted by John Cook, the Solicitor-General for the Commonwealth, for High Treason and other high crimes and on the fourth day sentenced to death with the words: "This court doth adjudge the said Charles as a tyrant, traytor, murtherer and publique enimy to the good people of this nation shall be put to death by the severing of his heade from his body."

CHARTER (BOROUGH).—A borough is a town which has been given the title of "Borough" by Royal Charter or Act of Parliament. ;The charter lays down the internal constitution of the borough and incorporates it as a legal personality or corporation. The charter may provide that the borough is to be either a municipal or a county borough. There is little or no legal difference between a borough and a city except in name, and the distinction arises solely from the words used in the charter, but the title "City" is conferred only upon important towns and generally only upon towns which possess a cathedral. For the legal differences between municipal boroughs and county boroughs, *see* Local Government.

CHARTER PARTY.—When goods are sent by sea the person sending them may arrange to take the whole ship or some specific part of it for the purpose of carrying the goods, and the document by which this arrangement is set out is known as a Charter Party, the person sending the goods being known as the charterer. The amount payable is called the freight. A transaction of this kind must be distinguished from one in which the person sending the goods does not take the whole ship or any named part of it, but merely arranges with the owner of the ship that certain named goods shall be carried. In such a case the document setting out the transaction is known as a Bill of Lading (q.v.). (*See* Carriage by Sea; Freight.)

CHARTERED COMPANIES.— Although most Companies are limited Companies registered under the Companies Act a Company may also be incorporated, that is, given a legal personality by royal charter or under the Chartered Companies Acts. There are not now many Companies of this nature in existence. The powers of the company will depend on its charter. (*See* Companies.)

CHATTELS.—Personal as distinguished from real property. Real property includes all freehold interests in land and buildings. Chattels on the other hand include all movable articles of property of a tangible nature. Leasehold interests in land are called chattels real. (*See* Property.)

CHEATING AT CARDS.—This is a form of obtaining or of attempting to obtain money by false pretences. It is, of course, punishable criminally only where the game at which it takes place is for stakes. (*See* CARD PLAYING.)

CHEMISTS.—Every person who sells goods by retail as a chemist or who describes himself as a chemist and druggist, or druggist, or pharmaceutical chemist, must be registered with the Pharmaceutical Society. He should register in each year and his name may be removed from the register by the Statutory Committee of the Society if he is guilty of misconduct. If he sells poisons he must also exhibit his certificate of registration in his premises and have his premises registered.

CHEQUES.—A cheque is an unconditional order in writing to a banker to pay a definite sum of money on demand to, or to the order of, the person named on the cheque or to the bearer. The person who gives the order is called the drawer. The banker to whom it is given is in a position somewhat similar to the drawee of a bill of exchange; and the person who is to receive the money is called the payee. In short, a cheque is simply a bill of exchange payable on demand, and all the provisions of the Bills of Exchange Act, 1882, relating to such Bills apply. It is not necessary that the order should be written on a form supplied by the bank to which it is directed, though this is the usual practice. Legally it may be written on an ordinary piece of paper, or on a table napkin, or on whatever is most convenient, provided a twopenny stamp is affixed and cancelled.

A cheque should be dated, and the sum payable expressed both in words and figures, the former prevailing in the event of discrepancy between the two. The signature of the drawer or of some person who, to the knowledge of the banker, has the drawer's authority either to sign cheques "per pro" the drawer, that is, on behalf of the drawer, or by a power of attorney to operate upon the drawer's banking account, must appear on the cheque, otherwise it is not the drawer's order. For this reason if the drawer's signature is forged there is no order to the banker and he, not the customer, has to bear the loss. Other fraudulent alterations have a similar effect, but it is now settled law that the customer owes a duty to his banker to draw cheques with reasonable care to prevent forgery, and if the customer neglects this duty he must

compensate the bank for any loss. Each case is decided on its own facts. Thus it has been held that it was not negligent to fail to draw a line after the payee's name, but in another case it was negligent to fill up the cheque so that "two" was easily changed to "a hundred and twenty." The duty applies only to the "drawing," so it is not negligent to leave your cheque book in an unlocked drawer, however unwise such a practice may be.

Where a cheque is expressed as payable to bearer, or directs the banker to "pay cash," the person presenting the cheque will be paid, for the holder, like the possessor of a treasury note, has a prima facie right to payment. In other words, the title to such a cheque passes by delivery alone. A cheque payable to a named person or his order requires indorsement to make it negotiable (*see* INDORSEMENT). A cheque payable to "self" requires indorsement and all payees should be made to indorse to show that the cheque has passed through their hands, thus enabling the drawer to show a payment.

Cheques which are payable to a fictitious person, e.g. "pay Father Christmas," are treated as payable to the bearer. Cheques may be drawn for any sum, but postal orders are generally used for amounts under 21/-. These are not transferable but, like cheques, they can be crossed.

Banker and Customer.—The drawer of a cheque is usually the customer of the bank on which it is drawn with an account there. In theory he has lent money to the bank, so the relationship between the two parties is that of debtor and creditor, with this additional duty upon the banker, that he must pay his customer's cheques if there are funds in the account. If a banker dishonours a cheque for no good reason he can be sued by the drawer for damages for breach of contract, and often for defamation as well; for incalculable damage may be done to a man's financial credit by such an act. The payee has no remedy against the bank but he can sue the drawer. The banker's duty to pay is ended by notice of the customer's death, insanity, or bankruptcy, or by an order to stop payment, and if the drawer's signature or any other part of the cheque is suspicious the banker has a reasonable time in which to make enquiries for his own

6

Form of "Open" cheque.

A cheque is drawn in this form when it is intended that the payee may present it for cash at the counter of the Bank upon which it is drawn.

General form of "crossing."

The legal requirement of a "general" crossing is that two parallel transverse lines shall be drawn across the face of the cheque. The words "& Co." are frequently added but do not alter the effect of the crossing. It will be appreciated that the principle of crossing a cheque is to give added protection; i.e. the crossing indicates a requirement that the cheque shall be passed through a Bank account. It is usual for cheques sent by post to be "crossed."

Form of "general crossing" with the addition of the words "Not Negotiable."

Where a person other than the payee takes a crossed cheque bearing the words "not negotiable" he does not obtain, and is not able to give a better title to the cheque than that which was possessed by the person from whom he took it. The words do not imply that the cheque is not transferable.

Form of cheque crossed to a specified account at a stated Bank or Branch.
The object of the crossing is to ensure:
(a) that it shall go to the account of the person named in the crossing, and
(b) to that person's account at the Bank and Branch indicated.

PRACTICAL ADVICE IN REGARD TO CHEQUES.

Do not leave your cheque book unprotected.

Do not use any form but the protective cheque form supplied by your Bank.

Do not fill in your cheques with the aid of the typewriter; write clearly in ink.

Do not leave spaces which permit of subsequent insertions on either side. Many frauds have been occasioned by neglect of this kind.

Do not "cross" a cheque if cash is required. A "crossing" is a direct instruction to your Bank to pay only to a Bank.

If it is your general practice to "cross" your cheques, use cheques with printed crossings.

Do not anticipate that your initials will prove sufficient authority for your Bank to pay cash against your "crossed" cheque. Your full signature is requisite if you wish to "open" the "crossing."

Do not vary your signature.

Do not omit to fill in the counterfoil of each cheque as drawn.

Do not place your signature on a cheque form which is not in other respects completed.

Form of cheque with printed crossing.
Shewing the procedure to be followed by the drawer if he wishes to "open" the cheque, i.e. indicate his desire that the payee may receive cash on presentation of the cheque at the Bank's counter.
The necessity for adding the words "Pay cash" and the full signature of the drawer will be noted.

protection before payment. Where the cause of dishonour is lack of funds the drawer need not be notified; the usual course adopted by the bank is to mark the cheque "Refer to Drawer" or "R D" and return it to the person who presented it for payment.

The banker must not give any information about his customer's account except by the customer's order or by Order of the Court.

Pass Books, in which the customer's transactions are recorded are kept by the bank. An entry therein is a statement on which the customer is entitled to act and is, prima facie, an admission by the bank in his favour, but the law is uncertain and every case depends on its own facts.

Presentment.—A holder's failure to present a cheque for payment within a reasonable time does not relieve the drawer unless he suffers actual damage by reason of the failure of the bank. Presentment must be made within a reasonable time to make an indorser liable.

Crossing and its uses.—Cheques are often crossed because in practice a crossed cheque is paid only through a banker, and the risk of fraud is thus minimised. When a cheque has across its face two parallel straight lines with or without the words "and Company," or any abbreviation of these two words, the cheque is said to be crossed generally. The words "not negotiable" may be put between the lines in all cases, as a further safeguard. Where the name of a banker is added the cheque is said to be crossed specially and payment can be made to that banker alone. Thus, if bank A is directed by a crossed cheque to pay X £1, it does not pay X the money over the counter, but pays it to whatever bank X may have given the cheque to be collected on his behalf. If bank A is directed by a special crossing to pay through bank B then the money can be paid to bank B only. The bank receiving payment is known as a collecting bank, and the money collected is credited to X's account in each case. Where the recipient of a crossed cheque has no banking account he should indorse, (see INDORSEMENT), it to a friend who has, or to a local tradesman from whom in due course he can receive the money.

Holders as well as drawers may cross cheques generally or specially, and a holder may add "Not negotiable" to a crossed cheque, but he must not add to, or alter, or obliterate the crossing in any other way, for to do so may be forgery. The only way to open a cheque is to get the person who crossed it to obliterate the crossing by writing the words "pay cash" with his signature.

As crossing is merely a direction to the bank it does not restrain the negotiability of a cheque. If a banker disobeys the direction and pays otherwise than to a banker, he must make good any loss suffered by the true owner of the cheque. When he obeys the order or when he pays an uncrossed cheque, the drawer or payee must shoulder the loss. The money can always be recovered from the person who cashed the cheque, i.e. by forging the indorsement, if he can be found.

Not Negotiable.—The addition of the words "Not negotiable" leaves the cheque freely transferable, but anyone who takes it does so at his own risk, for no person can give a better title to such cheque than he has himself. For example, a cheque is payable to order and indorsed by the payee. It is then stolen and cashed by a tradesman. If the cheque was marked "not negotiable" the tradesman has no more right to it than the thief, and must bear the loss; but if it was not so marked he is probably a holder in due course and the loss falls on the payee.

Account Payee Only, or "account payee" is now a common form of crossing. It is a direction to the receiving banker to put the money received to the credit of the payee's account, and if disregarded he is, in the absence of a reasonable explanation, held to be guilty of negligence. If a receiving banker paid such a cheque to the person presenting it, or used it to open an account, this would, on the face of it, be negligence. In most other cases the careful banker receiving payment of a crossed cheque is fully protected by the Bills of Exchange Act. (*See* BILL OF EXCHANGE; HOLDER FOR VALUE; HOLDER IN DUE COURSE; INDORSEMENT.)

CHIEF JUSTICE.—The head of the Judges of the King's Bench Division is Lord Chief Justice of England. He takes precedence over all the other Judges of the King's Bench Division and also presides in the Court of Criminal Appeal. He is appointed from amongst eminent members of the Bar, though sometimes a Judge is promoted to that position. On appointment he is always raised to the peerage.

CHILDREN.—This article deals only with criminal offences in relation to children, and with the trial and treatment of children who are themselves guilty of criminal offences, and, to some extent, with the custody of children. The law governing children is contained in what is popularly known as the "Children's Charter," i.e. the Children and Young Persons Act, 1933, and in the few surviving parts of previous Acts.

Prevention of cruelty and exposure to moral and physical dangers.— If any person over sixteen, having custody of a child under that age, wilfully ill-treats, neglects, abandons or exposes him or causes him so to be ill-treated, etc., in a manner likely to cause *unnecessary* suffering or injury to health, he shall be liable to a fine of not more than £100 and/or imprisonment for not more than two years, or, on conviction before a Magistrate's Court, to a fine not exceeding £25 and/or imprisonment for not more than six months. A parent will be guilty under this section merely by wilfully failing to provide adequate food, clothing or medical aid, or, if too poor to do so, by failing to take the necessary steps under the Poor Law. The penalties may be increased if the person convicted was aware that he might receive any sum of money on the death of the child, e.g. a legacy or insurance money.

A person having the custody or care of a girl under sixteen is liable to imprisonment for not more than two years if he causes or encourages her seduction or prostitution or an indecent assault upon her; or if those results follow from his allowing her to consort with persons of known immoral character. Penalties are also provided for allowing children between the ages of four and sixteen to reside in or frequent brothels.

Begging, Intoxicants, Smoking and Pawning.—If any person causes or procures a child under sixteen to be in any street, premises or other place for the purpose of begging or receiving alms (even though accompanied by singing, performing or offering articles for sale), he is liable to be fined £25 and/or imprisoned for not more than three months. The same penalties apply if the person having the custody of the child *allows* him to act as mentioned, and the fact that he allowed the child to be in the street, premises or other place is evidence that he knew the purpose for which he was there, i.e. when a child has actually been found begging, the person in whose custody the child was, will be convicted unless he can prove that, although he allowed the child to be there, he did not know that he was there for the purpose of begging. The hiring out or lending of children to accompany beggars is prohibited.

Except by order of a doctor or for an urgent purpose, no intoxicants may be given to a child under five years of age (penalty: fine of not more than £3). The holders of licences to sell intoxicants may not allow children under fourteen to be in the bar during the permitted hours (penalty: first offence—40/–; subsequent offences— £5). Any person who attempts to cause or procure a child to be in the bar of such premises is liable to the same penalties. The licence-holder will escape if he can shew that he used due diligence to prevent the child from being there, or that the child was apparently fourteen years old, or that it was his own child, or that it was resident on the premises, or that the child was using the bar merely for the purpose of passing to some other part to which there was no other convenient means of access, or that the premises were primarily intended for some other purpose and that the licence was purely auxiliary, e.g. railway refreshment rooms.

Tobacco or cigarette-papers may not be sold to a child apparently under sixteen even though they are for some other person's use (penalty: not exceeding for first offence, £2; second offence, £5; subsequent offences, £10). But tobacco other than cigarettes may be sold to children if the seller had no reason to believe that the child was going to use it himself. Tobacco or cigarettes may be sold to the employees of tobacco-dealers or to messenger-boys employed by messenger companies. Uniformed park-keepers and constables may seize tobacco or cigarette-papers in the possession of persons apparently under sixteen who are found smoking in public places; tobacco so seized must be disposed of according to regulation. Automatic machines for the sale of tobacco may be ordered to be removed or to be made inaccessible to children, if it be proved to a Magistrate's Court that they are being extensively used by persons apparently under the age of sixteen. Pawnbrokers may not accept articles as pawns from children under fourteen, and marine store dealers or dealers in old metal may not buy articles from children under sixteen.

Safety from Burning and at Entertainments.—If any person over sixteen having the care of a child under seven allows the child to be in any room containing an open and insufficiently guarded fire-grate without taking reasonable precautions against risk of burning, and the child as a result is killed or suffers serious injury, such person shall be liable to a fine not exceeding £10. Where the audience of an entertainment consists mostly of children and the number of children exceeds one hundred, it is the duty of the person providing the entertainment (except where held in a private dwelling-house) to provide a sufficient number of adult attendants to control the children and to see to their safety, and the owner of a building hired out for entertaining children must take all reasonable precautions to see that these requirements are complied with (penalty: not exceeding, for first offence, £50; subsequent offence, £100).

Employment.—Generally, no child may be employed when under twelve years old; nor before six o'clock in the morning or after eight o'clock at night; nor for more than two hours on days when he is required to attend school; nor for more than two hours on Sundays; nor to lift or carry things so heavy as to be likely to cause injury. Local authorities may make bye-laws authorizing employment of children under twelve in light agricultural work and authorizing the employment of children before school for not more than one hour. They may also prohibit the employment of children in any specified occupation, and they may raise the age below which children may never be employed and may prescribe length of hours, holidays, etc., for children. But no regulations shall apply to children of fourteen or older, except that, to a limited extent, regulations may be made as to the hours and holidays, etc., of children up to eighteen.

Unless permitted by bye-laws, no person under sixteen shall be employed in street-trading, e.g. hawking newspapers, matches, etc., or playing, singing or performing, or shoe-blacking. Bye-laws may also prohibit street-trading of persons under eighteen. Offences against any of the above provisions or any of the above bye-laws are punishable by a fine of not more than £5 for a first offence, and for subsequent offences £20. But the child himself is never liable to a fine of more than 20/– for a first offence or 40/– for a subsequent offence.

Children under fourteen may not take part in any entertainment in connection with which any charge is made to the audience unless (i) a licence is obtained for the child to perform; or (ii) the child has not taken part in any such performance more than six times in the previous six months, and the net proceeds are devoted to purposes other than the private profit of the promoters, e.g. to charity.

Nevertheless, if the performance is to take place in premises licensed for the sale of intoxicants, even those exemptions do not apply, unless the premises are also licensed for the performance of stage plays, etc., or special permission has been obtained from two justices of the peace. The licence is obtainable from the local authority of the area in which the child lives, and can be granted only in respect of a child of, or over, twelve years of age. No child under sixteen may take part in any public performance in which his life or limbs are endangered. No child under twelve may be *trained* to take part in a performance of a dangerous nature, nor, without a licence from petty sessions, any child between twelve and sixteen. Fines for offences against these provisions as to performances may be inflicted on any person causing or procuring the performance or training of the child, or on a parent or guardian allowing such performance or training.

Employment Abroad.—No person may procure a child under the age of eighteen, nor may a parent or guardian allow such a child to go abroad for the purpose of singing, playing, performing or being exhibited for profit unless such child is over the age of fourteen and a police magistrate's licence has been granted for the purpose. Such licences are granted only after careful enquiry, and must be renewed every three months after further enquiry.

The licence may be varied or revoked at any time. Penalties for offences against these provisions do not exceed £100 fine and/or three months imprisonment. Police constables may, on the authority of a justice of the peace, take to a place of safety any person under the age of seventeen who, there is reason to believe, is about to go abroad in contravention of these provisions.

Criminal Proceedings.—The Act of 1933 contains various provisions as to the care until trial of persons under seventeen who are arrested. If some time must elapse before his trial can take place, such a person must always be released on bail unless he is arrested for murder or other grave crimes, or unless it is in his interests to keep him from the company of reputed criminals or prostitutes, or to prevent his escape.

If not bailed, the child usually is detained in a remand home. When any child is brought before a Court, his parent or guardian shall be, if he lives within a reasonable distance (and in any case may be), required to attend at the Court unless excused; and when a child is arrested his parent or guardian is to be warned by the police to attend. When children are charged with offences, the local authority or, in some cases, the probation officer must make investigations as to the home-surroundings, school record, etc., of the child and report the result to the Court. When a child gives evidence in cases of offences against morality the Court may be cleared while he is in the box, and the Court may prohibit the publication in newspapers of the name or any other means of identification of the child. In certain cases (e.g. incest with a child or ill-treatment) the Court may dispense altogether with the presence of the child. In all proceedings, it is the duty of the Court primarily to consider the welfare of the child.

Juvenile Courts.—The Magistrate's Court has special powers conferred upon it by the 1933 Act in respect of children under seventeen, and is then called a Juvenile Court. All charges against children must be brought in the Juvenile Court except in a few cases, e.g. where a charge is brought against a child and an adult jointly. Juvenile Courts sit as often as may be necessary, and in a different building

from that in which the ordinary proceedings are held, or on different days. No person may be present except the officers of the Court, parties and their lawyers, and other persons directly interested, and bona fide reporters. All other persons must obtain the consent of the Court to be present. No newspaper may publish reports or photographs that would identify a child involved either as accused or as witness in a case before the Juvenile Court without the consent of the Court, or under rules to be made by the Home Secretary.

No child under eight years of age can be guilty of any offence. No child under seventeen may be sent to penal servitude nor, except in exceptional cases of children over fourteen, be committed to prison on failure to pay fines or costs. No person under eighteen may be sentenced to death. Where an adult would be liable to imprisonment or penal servitude, the Court may order a child to be committed to custody in a remand home, but never for more than one month.

Where fine, damages or costs are the proper punishment for an offence, the Court may in the case of a child under seventeen, and must in the case of a child under fourteen, order the parent or guardian to pay such fine, etc., unless the parent or guardian cannot be found or can shew that he has not conduced to the commission of the offence by neglecting to exercise due care of the child. The parent or guardian may appeal. Where a child is found guilty before any Court other than a Juvenile Court, the case may be sent to a Juvenile Court for the purpose of dealing with the child, whether by punishment or otherwise. Any child found guilty of an offence which, in the case of an adult, would be punishable with imprisonment, may be sent to an "approved school" or committed to the care of a "fit person."

Children in need of Care or Protection.—The duties of a Juvenile Court are not solely directed to child-offenders; the Court also has power to deal with children "in need of care or protection," i.e. children under seventeen who, having no parent or guardian, or whose parent or guardian neglects his duties, is falling into bad associations, or is beyond control, or is exposed to moral danger. The term also includes children in respect of whom certain criminal offences have been committed, e.g. offences under the second paragraph of this article; and it includes children who are members of the same household as a person who has committed certain offences. Children found destitute or begging are assumed to be exposed to moral danger. All such children may be sent to approved schools, or committed to the care of fit persons, or placed under the supervision of a probation officer.

Refractory Children.—The Juvenile Court also has power, when a parent or guardian proves that he is unable to control his child, to send the child to an approved school or to place him under the supervision of the probation officer.

Approved Schools, Probation Officers, etc.—Children are sent to approved schools or remand homes, or put under the care of probation officers or "fit persons" in the circumstances mentioned above. A child sent to an approved school must be sent, where practicable, to one intended for persons of the same religious persuasion as himself. No child may be detained in an approved school beyond the age of nineteen. It is the duty of a probation officer to visit, advise and befriend a child put under his care, and, when necessary, to endeavour to find him employment. Remand homes are provided by County Councils or County Borough Councils.

If a child escapes from either an approved school or a remand home, he may be arrested and taken back without a warrant, and any person who assists or induces such an escape, or knowingly harbours, or conceals or prevents the return of such child, shall be liable to imprisonment for not more than two months and/or to a fine of not more than £20. When a child is committed to the care of a fit person, such person shall have the same powers as if he were the child's parent and shall be subject to the same duties to maintain the child, notwithstanding any claims of the child's actual parents (see FATHER). Local Authorities may be chosen as fit persons, and, when so appointed, they may board out the child on such terms as to payment, etc., as they think fit. Escapes from fit persons are treated in the same way as escapes from approved schools (see above). Contributions to the expenses of children committed to the care of fit persons or to approved schools may be obtained from (i) his father or stepfather; (ii) his mother or stepmother; (iii) any person who at the date of the order is cohabiting with the child's mother. The weekly amount payable is assessed by the Court having regard to the means of the person liable.

Voluntary Homes.—Homes for the care of poor children supported entirely by voluntary contributions are subject to careful inspection and control by the Home Office, and if the orders of the Home Office are not complied with so as to endanger the welfare of any of the children, they may be removed.

Infant Life Protection, Baby Farming.—By the Children and Young Persons Act, 1932, and the Children Act, 1908, various provisions were made to prevent the abuses that existed in respect of what is popularly known as baby-farming. For details, *see* BABY-FARMING. (*See also* ADOPTION; AFFILIATION ORDERS; CRUELTY TO CHILDREN; FATHER; LOCO PARENTIS; MOTHER.)

CHILDREN (EDUCATION OF).—The law makes provision for the compulsory education of children between the ages of five (in some districts six) and fourteen. (*See* EDUCATION; SCHOOL.)

CHILTERN HUNDREDS. — A member of Parliament, once elected, technically cannot relinquish his seat. In order to evade this restriction, a member wishing to resign applies for the office of Steward of the Chiltern Hundreds.

This is, in theory, an office of profit under the Crown, the holding of which unseats a member. It is now a purely nominal position and no duties or pay attach to it.

CHIMNEYS. Fires.—If any chimney accidentally catches fire, the occupier of the premises is liable to a penalty not exceeding ten shillings, unless he can prove that such fire was in no way due to his or his servants' omission, neglect or carelessness. If any person wilfully sets a chimney on fire or causes it to be so set on fire, he will be liable to a penalty of not more than £5; he may, of course, also be guilty of other more serious criminal offences if the fire should spread.

Smoke.—Any chimney (not being the chimney of a private dwelling house) sending forth black smoke in such quantity as to be a nuisance is a nuisance within the Public Health Act, 1875, and a person aggrieved, or any two householders, or a policeman or a relieving officer, or an officer of the Council may inform the Local Authority of the nuisance. The Local Authority will then (after enquiry) serve a notice on the person causing the nuisance requiring him to "abate" (or prevent) it.

If the notice is not complied with, the Local Authority may make a complaint before a justice, who will issue a summons, and, on the hearing of the summons, if the Court is satisfied that a nuisance has been caused, it will order it to be abated and may, at the same time, impose a penalty of not more than £50. By an Act of 1926 it is provided that the smoke need not be black, and the word smoke is to include soot, ash and grit. It is a good defence to shew that the best practicable means have been used for preventing the nuisance, having regard to the cost and to the local conditions and circumstances.

Local Authorities may make bye-laws regulating the emission of smoke of such colour and density of content as may be prescribed in the bye-law. Bye-laws may also be made in respect of the construction of new · buildings for use other than as private dwelling-houses to prevent smoke. Railway locomotives using coal or other similar fuel emitting smoke must be constructed on the principle of consuming, and must so consume their own smoke, under penalty of £5 per day. Smoke from ships may constitute a nuisance and may be dealt with by the Local Authority. (*See also* NUISANCE.)

CHIMNEY-SWEEPS.—Every chimney-sweep who employs a journeyman, assistant or apprentice must take out a certificate issued by the chief officer of police of the district. Application for such certificate is to be made to the police station nearest the applicant's dwelling-house. The certificate costs two shillings and is available for one year. Certificates may be indorsed (without fee) by the police officers of neighbouring districts. Penalties for failure to take out the certificate are ten shillings for the first offence and twenty shillings for every subsequent offence. The certificate must be produced on demand to the customer or to a constable. It is unlawful to compel or knowingly allow any child under the age of twenty-one to ascend or descend a chimney, or enter a flue for the purpose of cleaning or extinguishing fire therein (penalty: fine of not more than £10 or imprisonment for not more than six months). No chimney-sweep may, on entering a building for the purpose of cleaning a chimney or extinguishing a fire therein, cause or knowingly allow a person under sixteen years of age who is under his control to enter any part of such building while the chimney-sweep is present (penalty: fine not exceeding £10). Chimney-sweeps may not, for the purpose of soliciting employment, knock at houses from door to door, or ring a bell, or use any noisy instrument, or, to the annoyance of an inhabitant, ring a door-bell of any house (penalty: fine not exceeding, for first offence, 10/–; for subsequent offences, 20/–). As to the employment of children in general, *see* CHILDREN.

CHOSE IN ACTION.—This expression is one of great legal antiquity which comes to us from the old Norman-French and means literally "things in action," and in its present meaning is probably best conveyed by the description, "things recoverable by action" (as opposed to things in actual physical possession and ownership), and "personal rights enforceable by action." It is difficult to define the limits of its meaning at the present day because it has been used to describe a multitude of things from ancient times. It has been used to describe the right to a claim for a particular article and also the article itself. It has also been used to describe things of which no physical possession is possible, such as shares in a company, and even the proportion of a share of the dividend. An ordinary debt has been held to be a chose in action.

Choses in action can, generally speaking, be given or sold to another with certain exceptions. Thus, if A owes B a debt, B can, if he wishes, sell the right to C to recover the debt. He can also give C the right to recover the debt. But certain formalities have to be observed, and these vary in accordance with the type of chose in action. In the case of a simple debt for an ascertained amount, for example, the assignment from B to C must be in writing under the hand of B, and it must be an absolute out and out assignment and not a charge only. Notice in writing must be given to A or the person from whom the debt is due. The assignment must be of the whole amount outstanding and cannot be for a part only. Many points of difficulty may arise on the assignment of a chose in action. For instance, in the case of the example of the assignment of a simple debt just given, any rights which the debtor might have had against B the creditor will affect C who has bought the right to recover the debt. If the debtor A at the time of the assignment had a counterclaim against B the creditor, he can set it up against C who has bought the right to the debt.

Certain choses in action are incapable of being assigned because it would be against public policy to allow them to be so dealt with, e.g. pensions and salaries of public officers such as Judges, etc. Likewise alimony granted to a wife is not assignable. A right to recover damages for personal injury cannot be assigned, nor can a fire insurance policy ordinarily, in the latter case on the ground that it is a purely personal contract. It can, however, be assigned with the consent of the insurer. (*See* ASSIGNMENT.)

CHURCH OF ENGLAND.—The Church of England is considered, in law, to have had a continued existence from Anglo-Saxon times until the present day. By a series of statutes passed between 1532 and 1571 the Church was dissociated from Rome, and the King of England was declared to be its spiritual and temporal head. At the time of the Union with Ireland, the Irish and English Churches were also united as one established Church, but the Irish Church was disestablished in 1869. The Church in Wales was disestablished in 1914.

All matters of Church administration, management and ceremonial are laid down in Acts of Parliament or have by custom become a part of the law of England, and, until 1919, any changes in such matters had to be effected in the same way as any other changes in the law, namely, by Act of Parliament. In 1919, however, the Church of England Assembly (Powers) Act (popularly known as the "Enabling Act") was passed, whereby the National Assembly was created,

with power to consider Church Measures and to present such Measures to Parliament for approval. Parliament must then either adopt or reject the Measures, but may not amend them; in the dispute regarding proposed amendments to the Prayer Book in 1927, it was therefore not open to Parliament to adopt some of the proposals and to reject others. Once it has been passed, the Measure has the force of an ordinary Act of Parliament. It is still open to Parliament to pass ordinary enactments binding upon the Church, but Church legislation is now generally effected through the National Assembly. (*See* NATIONAL ASSEMBLY.)

Territorial Divisions.—For the purpose of administration, the whole of England is divided into two Provinces, the Province of Canterbury and the Province of York, each being controlled by its Archbishop. Each Province is divided into Dioceses, thirty for Canterbury and thirteen for York, every Diocese being under the government of its Bishop (*see* DIOCESE). Each Archbishop also has his Diocese in addition to his province (*see* ARCHBISHOP). The Diocese, in turn, is divided into Archdeaconries, the Archdeaconries into Rural Deaneries, and the Rural Deaneries into Parishes (*see* ARCHDEACON; DEAN; PARISH, ECCLESIASTICAL). Each of these divisions, except the Archdeaconry, has a representative body which, to some extent, controls the management and finances of the division: the Province is represented by Convocation; the Diocese by the Diocesan Conference, the Rural Deanery by the Ruri-decanal Conference (*see* DEAN); and the Parish by the Vestry and by the Parochial Church Council and Meeting.

Ecclesiastical Courts.—By reason of the Church of England being established by law, the control of the clergy and of the church ceremonies and property is maintained by legally constituted Courts with very considerable powers in such matters, but with no power to inflict corporal punishment or to inflict fines in the usual sense. The inferior Ecclesiastical Courts are the Consistory Courts (*see* CONSISTORY COURT); next come the two Provincial Courts (*see* PROVINCIAL COURT); and finally the Privy Council. There is also another Court composed of an Archbishop and a Judge of the High Court sitting together, for the trial of cases where the Bishop has refused to institute a clergyman in his benefice (e.g. on the grounds of immorality), and to hear appeals under the Benefices (Ecclesiastical Duties) Measure, 1926, by an incumbent who has been reported by the Bishop's Commission to have performed his duties inadequately by reason of his own negligence (see BENEFICE).

The punishments that may be inflicted by the Courts previously mentioned are mainly four in number: (1) *Monition*, which, as its name implies, is merely a warning to refrain from committing an ecclesiastical offence; (ii) *Suspension* of the right to perform clerical duties for a limited time, and, in some cases, temporary deprivation of the profits of the benefice; (iii) *Deprivation* of a benefice or other preferment for certain serious offences (e.g. on a third conviction for trading while in holy orders); (iv) *Incapability to hold preferment* in the future, this disability being imposed on all persons sentenced under number (iii) above, or who would have been so sentenced if they had been possessed of any benefice of which they could have been deprived. Deposition from holy orders (or "unfrocking") can be effected by the Bishop in respect of any person sentenced under (iii) or (iv) above, subject to appeal to the Archbishop (see also CLERGYMEN, PROCEEDINGS AGAINST). The Ecclesiastical Courts also have non-criminal powers in relation to matters of church property.

Ecclesiastical Law.—The law relating to ecclesiastical matters in England is as much a part of the law of the realm as the law relating to crimes or the law relating to contracts, and, like all branches of English law, is partly contained in Acts of Parliament and partly derived from usage or custom to be found largely in the reports of former cases and known as Common Law. But, unlike other branches of the law, ecclesiastical law was originally derived, to a very large extent, from the Canons of the Roman Church and from the Civil Law of ancient Rome (see CANON).

The main distinction between ecclesiastical law and other branches of the law is that it is administered by Ecclesiastical Courts, as distinct from the Ordinary Courts (see above), and that it usually relates solely to the clergy and not to the laity, e.g. the law relating to the exchange of benefices or the ordination of priests, or the constitution of Convocation can only have a very remote effect upon the laity. There are, however, some matters connected with the Church that are dealt with in the ordinary courts; usually they are offences committed by laymen, e.g. blasphemy or offences against the Lord's Day Observance Act.

CHURCH OF SCOTLAND.— The Church of Scotland is Presbyterian, that is, it is controlled and governed not solely by Clerics but to a large extent by lay-elders, and has no system of hierarchy in the Church such as Archbishops or Bishops. The constitution of the Church in this form is guaranteed by the Act of Union between England and Scotland in 1707, which declared that the continuance of a Presbyterian Church as then established should be "held and observed in all time coming as a fundamental and essential condition of any treaty or union to be concluded between the two Kingdoms."

The Church Courts.—The most important bodies in the Church are its Courts, namely, the Kirk-Session, the Presbytery, the Synod, and the General Assembly. These Courts have wide powers, which were frequently exercised until comparative recent times, of punishing persons who have been guilty of offences against morality and church discipline, and within those limits carried out a part of the work which is done in other countries by the Civil Courts. To enforce its decisions in these matters the Courts had power of imposing fines or imprisonment.

The lowest of the Courts is the Kirk Session which consists of the minister and elders of the Parish. It supervises generally all ecclesiastical matters which are not entirely in the hands of the Minister, and admits persons to membership of the Church. It keeps the Communion Roll, the Register of Baptisms and of the Proclamation of Banns.

The Presbytery consists of the Ministers of all Parishes in the District, the Professors of Divinity of any University who are also Ministers, and an Elder from each Kirk Session. The duties of the Presbytery are to examine students of Divinity and to grant licences to them to preach. It also controls and supervises the parishes within its district and the conduct of their ministers.

The Synod is a Court between the Presbytery and the General Assembly, and consists of the members of the Presbyteries within its district. It acts as a Court of Appeal upon the decisions of the Presbytery.

The General Assembly is the supreme Court of the Church. Its members are Ministers and Elders who are elected. In its judicial capacity it hears appeals from the other Courts. It has in addition wide powers of legislation in all matters relating to the Church, but every act proposed by it must be accepted by a majority of the Presbyteries before it becomes effective. The General Assembly meets once a year and is presided over by a Moderator who is appointed annually. While he is acting he takes rank in Scotland next after the Lord Chancellor, and in England after the Bishops who are in the House of Lords, but before all barons.

The Ministry.—The Church of Scotland does not recognise any hierarchy of priests and therefore with some few exceptions all ministers are of the same rank, namely, Parish Minister. There is now no patronage in the Church, that is, no private person is entitled to appoint a Minister, but all Ministers are elected by the congregation of the parish to which they are to be appointed, or, if the congregation fails to act, by the Presbytery. The Minister elect must sign the Confession of Faith and is then inducted, i.e. installed in his benefice. If he is guilty of immoral conduct or of neglect of his duties he will be deposed from office. He must reside in his Parish and has imposed on him certain disabilities, e.g. he cannot be a Member of Parliament.

The property in the Church and Manse was formerly in the hands of the heritors, i.e. landowners, of the Parish and they were responsible for the upkeep and repair. Since 1925, however, all church property has been transferred to a body known as The Church of Scotland General Trustees who are liable for repairs.

CHURCHWARDENS.—This ancient office existed before the thirteenth century. In most parishes one warden is chosen by the incumbent and another elected by the Vestry. (*See* VESTRY.) The latter is usually chosen by show of hands, but a poll may be demanded. Before undertaking their duties the churchwardens undergo the ceremony of "admission" at the visitation either of the bishop or the archdeacon. Minors, aliens, Jews, and persons who have been convicted of felony, perjury, or fraud may not be elected as churchwardens. Most parishioners are bound to act as churchwardens if elected, but exemption extends to almost all the professional classes; they may, however, if elected, waive that exemption and take office.

Duties.—Their duties are, briefly, the allocation of seats to the parishioners, provision of requisites for Divine Service, disposal of the proceeds of the collection where it has been for "church expenses," and the maintenance of order in the church. They may arrest anyone brawling in or about the church. When a vacancy occurs in a benefice, the churchwardens are usually appointed "sequestrators," and the income is taken by them and applied as circumstances require. (*See* SEQUESTRATION.)

Churchwardens may sue and be sued in their official capacity, but in almost every case it will be found that the parochial church council is the proper body. (*See* PARISH, ECCLESIASTICAL.)

CHURCHYARDS.—*See* BURIAL AND CEMETERIES.

CICERO, Marcus Tullius (106-43 B.C.).—Is sometimes called "the Father of Advocacy," and is famous both for his forensic skill and as a publicist. His two best known forensic speeches were those in defence of Sextus Roscius, made when he was 26, and when defending Milo for the murder of Clodius. His chief legal publication was "de Officiis" which Lord Mansfield advised all law students to master, calling them "Tully's Offices." His political fame was chiefly based on his tireless campaign of exposure of the Cataline conspiracy, for which he was banished on the ground that he had executed the conspirators without trial.

CIDER.—To sell cider by retail a justices' licence is required as well as an excise licence. A licence to retail beer for consumption on or off the premises permits the holder to retail cider as well, and so of course would a full licence. If it is only desired to retail cider off the premises then a cider off-licence must be applied for, unless a beer off-licence is already held. The latter is the only off-licence which includes a cider off-licence. (*See* INTOXICATING LIQUOR; ON- AND OFF-LICENCES.)

CIGARETTES.—It is a crime to sell to anybody apparently under the age of 16 any tobacco or cigarettes whether they are intended for the use of that person or not. Any police officer or park keeper must seize any tobacco or cigarettes in the possession of any person apparently under 16 who is seen smoking in the street or any public place.

It is not an offence, however, to sell to boy messengers in uniform in the course of their employment, or to persons employed by tobacconists buying in the course of their duties. If it is proved that an automatic cigarette machine is being used extensively by persons under 16, a Court may order the owner of the machine, or the occupier of the place where it is kept, to take steps to prevent this.

CINEMATOGRAPH. Licence.—A licence is required for the public exhibition of inflammable films by the Cinematograph Act, 1909. This Act applies only to places of public entertainment and so a licence is not required for the shewing of films in a private house or before prospective customers by a dealer in films, though probably it is needed for a club. Further the Act deals only with inflammable films, so no licence is required to shew non-inflammable pictures.

The licensing authority is the County or Borough Council of the area in which the cinema is situated. The Council is under the supervision of the Home Secretary, and may delegate its powers to justices sitting in petty sessions. An applicant for a licence, or for a transfer of a licence, must give not less than seven days' notice in writing to the Council and to the chief officer of police of the district in which the premises are, of his intention to apply for a licence. He then appears before the appropriate authority and makes his application.

Conditions.—The Council may attach conditions to the issue of the licence. It is by the use of this discretionary power that supervision is exercised over the type of film to be shewn and the manner of conducting a cinema. For instance, a Council may impose the condition that the licensed cinema shall not be open on Sundays, Good Friday or Christmas Day, or that no film shall be shewn which is of an objectionable or indecent nature, or which is likely to have a bad effect on the young, or to produce a riot or a breach of the peace. But these conditions must satisfy three requirements—they must be (i) reasonable, (ii) for the public benefit, and (iii) they must relate to the user of the premises. A condition which relates solely to the welfare of children—by prohibiting them to enter a cinema after certain hours—is invalid, because the licence is for the user of premises as a cinema, and the grounds for imposing the condition are not connected with that.

But a condition requiring undertakings by the licensee of the cinema to cease giving presents of sweets to the children, or, on receiving notice from a department of public health that a certain school had an infectious disease, to keep out children from that school, is reasonable.

Censor.—There is no censorship of films set up by law in this country. The character of films can be supervised by the imposition of conditions in the grant of the licence as shewn above. The British Board of Film Censors is a body appointed by the film industry to safeguard the film trade interests by the censorship of films to be shewn in England. It is unofficial and has no legal authority, statutory or otherwise.

It appears that a licensing authority can insist upon a condition in a licence that no film be shewn which has not been certified for public exhibition by the British Board of Film Censors, provided they reserve to themselves the right to review the decisions of the Board, but not otherwise.

Safety.—Besides the general provisions of the Public Health Acts as to structural and building requirements, the Cinematograph Act prohibits the public exhibition of films unless the regulations of the Home Secretary with regard to ensuring safety are complied with. By these regulations the exits must be clearly marked—with doors that open outwards on being pressed from within; the gangways, stairs and passages must be kept clear during the presence of the public, and no one allowed to stand or sit in gangways; the seating must give free access to the exits. There must be sufficient staff for securing safety, and suitable fire appliances on the premises. Premises must be adequately illuminated while the public is present, and form a separate source to that of the general lighting of the premises.

The regulations also deal with the technical apparatus, the projector, and rewinding room, etc.

Children.—By Section 121 of the Children's Act, 1908, special precautions must be taken to ensure safety for children at public entertainments. There must be a sufficient number of adults to control properly the children present.

Sunday Opening.—The Sunday Entertainments Act, 1932, which was prompted by proceedings taken under the old Sunday Observance Acts of 1625–1780, to recover penalties under them, gives the licensing authorities power to grant licences for the opening of cinemas in their areas. But they must impose the following conditions: that no employee who has worked for 6 days in the week shall work on the 7th; that a share of the profits shall go to the authority to be paid into the Cinematograph Fund, and the remainder to anyone specified by the authority, for the purpose of being applied to charitable objects. The Cinematograph Fund is a fund constituted by the Act, under the control and direction of the Privy Council, for the purpose of encouraging the use and development of the cinema as a means of entertainment and instruction. The Act does not extend to Scotland or Northern Ireland.

Quota.—The Cinematograph Films Act was passed in 1927 to secure that a certain proportion of British films should be exhibited each year from 1929 to 1938.

A British film is defined as follows: (1) It must have been made by a British subject or a British company, (2) The studio scenes must have been photographed in a studio in the British Empire, (3) the author of the scenario must have been British, (4) not less than 75% of the salaries and wages paid in the making of the film, exclusive of payment to one foreign actor, actress or producer, must be paid to British subjects.

The Board of Trade keeps a register of films on which it is stated whether each picture is British or foreign. No unregistered film may be exhibited. No film can be registered until it has been trade shewn, and since no one can exhibit new films unless they have been registered, the Act prevents blind booking, i.e., the hiring of pictures to an exhibitor who has never seen them. Further, Section 2 of the Act restricts advance booking by fixing maximum periods between the date of the agreement for exhibit and the actual date of the shewing. The period for agreements made since the 1st October, 1930, is six months.

Every exhibitor is to show British films in a gradually increasing proportion, starting, for renters, at 7½% for the year ending 31st March 1929 and up to 20% in 1938. The exhibitors have a slightly lower quota starting at 5%. Both renters and exhibitors must hold a licence from the Board of Trade, and must keep a record of films and theatres which must be open for Board of Trade inspection.

CIRCUIT.—England is divided into circuits. These are divisions of the country toured by the Assize Judges. In each circuit there is a certain number of towns in which Assizes are held. The present circuits are—the South Eastern, Midland, the Northern, the North Eastern, the Oxford, the Western and the North and South Wales circuit.

Barristers practise on a particular circuit which they join in the early days of their professional careers. If a client wishes to obtain the services of a barrister to appear in a case on a circuit other than that of which he is a member, he has to pay the barrister a special fee. A barrister who goes to a circuit other than his own to conduct a case, is said to "go special."

CIRCUMSTANTIAL EVIDENCE.—So frequently are crimes committed in the absence of witnesses that it is necessary to decide many cases either wholly or partly upon circumstantial evidence. This evidence is evidence of facts from which an inference may be drawn. Thus, in a poisoning case, though no one saw the poisoner prepare the deadly draught, and though none save his victim saw him present the cup, yet other witnesses may testify to facts from which an irresistible inference may be drawn as to both those acts. If a witness prove the purchase by the prisoner of a poison, if another the presence of that poison in the corpse of the deceased, if yet another testify as to the presence of the prisoner alone with the deceased at the probable time of the consumption of the draught, and yet another as to his cleaning of the dregs of the cup, it may well be that the only reasonable conclusion will be the guilt of the person charged.

Circumstantial evidence is not necessarily inferior to direct evidence, indeed it is sometimes said to be more trustworthy. "Facts cannot lie," while witnesses may. On the other hand, facts may deceive as often as witnesses may lie. Circumstantial evidence is therefore properly scrutinised with the utmost vigilance. It is only when the facts

Sir Edward Clarke.

lead to one inference and one alone that that inference can be said to be established.

CITATION.—This is a form of summons in use in the Probate, Divorce, and Admiralty Division of the High Court of Justice.

CIVIL LAW.—The term civil law is used in three connections. It is used, first, as a name for Roman Law as distinguished from English Law. The majority of continental codes are derived directly or indirectly from the old Roman Law, which was known to the Romans as *Jus Civile,* or State Law as opposed to Local Customary Law. English Law, on the other hand, owes very little to Roman Law: some of it is, in origin, Anglo-Saxon, but principally it has been evolved by the English legislature and judiciary, and, though naturally it has much in common with any other system of justice, there are

very wide differences between the Anglo-American system and the Roman system, especially in relation to such matters as succession on death and the ownership and tenure of land. The branch of English Law that owes to Roman Law is that relating to ecclesiastical matters.

The term civil law, is, secondly, used to distinguish non-criminal from criminal matters, and, as the procedure and effect of proceedings differ, according as the proceedings are civil or criminal in nature, the distinction is of importance. There are some matters which, though civil in form, are in substance criminal, e.g. for some offences the punishment is not fine or imprisonment as in the majority of other criminal offences, but it is left to private members of the public to enforce by an action in the Civil Courts for a specified sum of money, known as a penalty, the person suing being known as a common informer. This method of enforcing the criminal law now survives only in a few cases, and it is contrary to the policy of Parliament to extend it. The chief Civil Courts in England are the County Courts and the High Court, including the Court of Appeal, and the House of Lords. The chief Criminal Courts are the Police Magistrates' Courts (known as "Courts of Summary Jurisdiction"), and the High Court Judges sitting on assize for the hearing of criminal cases, or sitting as a Court of Criminal Appeal. A few criminal cases are taken to the House of Lords when they are of exceptional public importance.

Thirdly, the term civil law is used to distinguish the law applicable to laymen from the canon law, which is the law applicable to the Roman clergy. This distinction is little used in England, where ecclesiastical law is regarded as an integral part of the ordinary common law, but, in countries where the Roman Church is the national church, the distinction is of considerable importance. In such countries, the civil law is, in the majority of cases, derived from the Roman Law, while the canon law is generally the result of enactments of ecclesiastical councils. (*See also,* Canon Law.)

CLARKE, Sir Edward (1841-1931). —The last and perhaps the greatest of the Victorian orators. Starting with no other advantages than his natural ability Edward Clarke came to be one of the most noted figures of his day. During his 50 years at the Bar, among his most famous cases were the Penge Mystery, his defence of Adelaide Bartlett, and the Baccarat Case in which he appeared for Gordon Cumming.

CLAUSE.—A sub-division or paragraph of a legal document.

CLEAR DAYS.—When the law requires some act to be done so many "clear days" before a particular date, the days must be reckoned without counting either that date or the day on which the prescribed act is done. Thus, if a trial is fixed for the 10th of the month and one party is required to give the other five clear days' notice of it, the notice must be received on the 4th of the month because there will then be five whole days before the trial, exclusive of the 4th and the 10th.

CLERGYMAN. Ordination.—Since before ordination a candidate for ordination to the Church of England must take the oath of allegiance (*see* ALLEGIANCE), it is impossible for foreign subjects to be ordained. For the purpose, however, of ministering to persons residing outside the King's dominions, the Bishop of London may, by letters of ordination, ordain an alien without requiring him to take the oath of allegiance. A bastard desiring to be ordained usually obtains a dispensation from the Archbishop of Canterbury, but, though previously essential, this dispensation is not, in most cases, strictly required by law. As to the mode and effect of ordination, *see* ORDINATION.

Pensions.—The pensions of the clergy below the rank of Diocesan Bishops have been systematized by the Clergy Pensions Measures of 1926, 1927, and 1928 in the case of all clergymen who were engaged in rendering whole-time service to the Church, who had not attained the age of fifty-five on 1st January, 1927, and whose salary or benefice exceeded £100 a year in value. In some cases, a clergyman may be exempted from the scheme on his own application when he can shew that he will be entitled to a pension from elsewhere. Persons who have been compulsory contributors of the scheme for fifteen years, or who would have been compulsory contributors for that period if the Measures

had been in force at a previous date, are entitled to pensions when they have attained the age of seventy years or have retired by reason of permanent disability, provided they remain in retirement and continue to be members of the Church of England capable of holding preferment.

Proceedings against a Clergyman.—If a clergyman is convicted of treason or felony, or is convicted on indictment of a misdemeanour, or on any such conviction is sentenced to imprisonment with hard labour or any greater punishment; or if a bastardy order is made against him; or if he is found in a divorce case to have committed adultery; or if a separation order is made against him; he is automatically removed from his position by the Bishop of the diocese, unless the Crown grants the offender a free pardon. For immoral conduct, neglect of duty, and other offences, every ecclesiastical person may be called to account by his ecclesiastical superior, known as his ordinary (q.v.)

Immorality.—If a clergyman is alleged to have committed certain immoral acts or an offence against the ecclesiastical laws which is an offence against morality and not a question of doctrine or ritual, he may be prosecuted by any parishioner, by the Bishop or by a person approved by the Bishop. There is, however, a salutary provision in that the bishop may always disallow a prosecution which he considers too frivolous or vague. This is just as well, as the Ecclesiastical Canons which were drafted in 1603 still provide the standard of morality for the clergy, including, amongst other crimes against morality, that of wearing an embroidered nightcap in bed. The offender is tried by the consistory court (q.v.), or, on the request of the Bishop, by the Provincial Court (q.v.). A clergyman who is found guilty of immoral conduct is either deprived of his living or suspended for a term as the Bishop sees fit. In a particularly serious case, the Bishop may also pronounce the sentence of deposition from holy orders and unfrock the offender, who may appeal to the Archbishop whose decision is final. (*See* CHURCH OF ENGLAND; ECCLESIASTICAL COURTS.)

Neglect of Duty.—Anyone who wishes may prosecute a clergyman who neglects his duties, but the more usual procedure is for the Bishop, on complaint being made or information coming to his ears, to appoint a commission to inquire into the habits of the clergyman in question, and report their finding. If they report that there is no evidence of neglect, well and good; but if they report that the duties of the parish are being inadequately performed, then it all depends whether or no the commission reports that the inadequate performance of the duties is due to the negligence of the incumbent. If the vicar is not blamed, the Bishop may compel him to employ curates, on the grounds that the work is beyond the scope of one man; but if the incumbent has been personally neglectful, then the Bishop may inhibit him, that is, may forbid him to act as vicar and strip him of his office. The inhibited clergyman may appeal to a Court composed of the Archbishop of Canterbury and a High Court Judge sitting together, and the judgment of such Court is final.

The bitterest feelings are often provoked when parishioners do not like the method adopted by their vicar of carrying on the service. If they consider his conduct to be unlawful they, if members of the Church of England residing in the parish and having so resided for one year, may make complaint to the bishop. The complaint must be made by a parishioner, but it is of course impossible to prevent persons coming and settling in a parish for the required period simply for the purpose. Proceedings are taken, and, if the incumbent is found guilty, the Bishop either by inhibition debars him from his office or by monition commands him to abstain from the act complained of.

The most notable offences peculiar to the clergy have been mentioned above, but there are innumerable other rules of law that they are bound to obey; for example, as a general rule, no minister may hold two benefices at the same time (*see* PLURALITY); nor may the right to present a minister to benefices be unlawfully bought or sold (*see* SIMONY).

Relinquishment of Orders.—A clergyman cannot divest himself of the privileges and duties of a clerk in holy orders except by virtue of the Clerical Disabilities Act, 1870, by which special procedure for the purpose is prescribed. The chief formality is the execution of a deed of relinquishment

and the enrolment of the deed in the Central Office of the Supreme Court, London. A clergyman may also be deposed from orders by his Bishop for certain ecclesiastical offences (*see* above).

Bankruptcy.—When a Bankrupt is a Beneficed Clergyman the profits of the Benefice may be taken by the trustee by a sequestration, and this sequestration will have priority over any other issued in respect of a debt provable in the bankruptcy, except a sequestration issued before the date of a receiving order by a person who has had no notice of an available act of bankruptcy, i.e. of an act of bankruptcy which was committed within 3 months before the petition was presented. (*See* BANKRUPTCY.)

The trustee, if he sequestrates, must pay to the bankrupt such stipend as the Bishop thinks proper, and must also pay out of the profits of the benefice the salary due to any curate in respect of duties performed by him during the 4 months before the receiving order not exceeding £50. (*See* BANKRUPTCY AND SEQUESTRATION; BISHOP; CHURCH OF ENGLAND; CHURCH OF SCOTLAND; PRIEST.)

CLERK OF THE CROWN AND PEACE.—The Clerk of the Crown and Peace is an official of a county whose duty it is to ensure that indictments and other matters are brought before Quarter Sessions. He also acts as advisor on legal matters to the magistrates in Quarter Sessions.

CLERK TO THE JUSTICES.— Each Petty Sessional Division of a County and each Borough having a commission of the peace has a Clerk appointed to the Justices. His duties in general consist in keeping minutes of all convictions and orders made by the Court, and of the names of the parties, and of the justices trying the case and the nature of the complaint or offence; he is also required to keep accounts of the fines and penalties and of fees received and other matters relating to the business of the Court, and to pay the fees and fines to the proper authority.

His appointment is made by the Justices of the Peace and his salary is payable by the County Council in the case of petty sessional divisions of the County, or the Borough funds in the case of Boroughs holding a Court of Quarter Sessions. He holds office at the pleasure of the Justices and can be dismissed at any time. His qualification is that he must either be a barrister of not less than fourteen years' standing, a solicitor, or having service of not less than seven years as clerk to a stipendiary or Metropolitan magistrate. But there are certain discretionary exceptions to these qualifications. (*See* PETTY SESSIONS.)

CLOAK ROOMS.—The liability of railway companies and other carriers for luggage which has been deposited in their cloak rooms is very much less than their liability for the same luggage at other times, for they are not in the position of carriers at such a time and therefore are not insurers of its safety. They can only be held liable for loss or damage which can be shewn to be the result of their negligence. In addition, most persons who afford cloak room facilities almost invariably print on the back of the cloak room ticket conditions limiting even their liability, and such conditions if legibly printed (and conditions printed elsewhere than on the ticket if clearly referred to on the ticket) are binding on the depositor of the luggage, because he is presumed by the law to have read and assented to them, whether he did so in fact or not.

If cloak room charges are allowed to mount up, the owner of the cloak room acquires a lien over the article deposited—i.e. a right to detain it—and may refuse to hand it over until the charges are paid in full; but unless there is a special condition allowing them to do so they may not sell it. (*See* BAILEE; LOST PROPERTY; RAILWAYS.)

CLUBS.—A club has been defined as a society of persons associated together for any purpose except the acquisition of gain. Broadly speaking there are two kinds of club, the proprietary club and the members' club. The first, as the name denotes, is a club in which the club house, furniture, food and drinks, belong to a proprietor, to whom the members pay a subscription in return for the use of the club property. In law the position of such a club is a simple one; the proprietor may be sued for goods supplied to the club and can sue on behalf of the club. As owner he is virtually the club for the purpose of legal proceedings. The members in their turn, if wrongfully

excluded from the privileges for which they have paid, can bring an action against the proprietor for damages for breach of contract. They can also be sued by the proprietor for articles consumed, as well as for goods delivered.

Rather more complex, however, is the position of the members' club. In such cases there is no proprietor. The club house, furniture and property belong to all the members. The management of the club is in their hands and its business is conducted by them jointly in general meeting or, more usually, delegated by them to a committee. Thus a members' club is not a legal entity, which means that it is not recognized as having any legal existence apart from its members.

Dealings with Strangers.—The chief effect of a club not being a legal entity is made manifest in its dealings with strangers. It cannot sue or be sued as a club. Thus, if a person is injured, say, on club premises, or through the negligence of a club servant, and wishes to bring an action in tort against it, he must sue all the members of the committee or of the club. This of course is cumbersome and expensive, so the person suing can apply to the Court and have a representative or representatives appointed to defend on behalf of all the members. In the same way if a members' club wishes to take action against a stranger, the members can apply to have one of their number authorised to sue on their behalf.

In the case of goods ordered for the club one member cannot pledge the credit of another. In this of course clubs are unlike partnerships, where one partner can pledge the credit of the others. Thus, if goods are supplied to a club only those members who gave the order, or made the contract, can be liable. If the order was given by a servant of the club the ordinary laws of principal and agent would apply to determine who were the contracting parties. It has been held that in such cases credit was given to the persons composing the committee and they have been made liable. The mere fact that the defendants in an action are members of a managing committee is not sufficient to make them liable, but it may be evidence that the plaintiff looked to them for payment, and that they pledged their own credit and authorized the orders; but in cases of contract as in cases of tort a members' club cannot be sued as such.

Dealings between the Members.— Of course, if one member orders goods on behalf of the remainder, and the remainder have approved his doing so either by the rules or by resolution, the member who has ordered the goods, if he has been made to pay for them, can make the other members indemnify him.

Again, where money is borrowed under rules or a resolution of the club, or debentures are issued in pursuance of the rules or resolutions, or for any legitimate club purpose, there will be a lien on the club property. Club members will be liable to their committee for their proportionate share of money borrowed by the committee during their membership under the rules and with their knowledge and consent. If the obligation to repay is a continuing one, resignation will not save a member from his liability for such a debt, though of course he would not be liable for debts incurred by the club after his resignation.

What to do, if wrongfully expelled. —No one person need associate with another unless he wishes to do so, and no Court will compel him to do so. Thus a member expelled from a club cannot complain that his fellow-members refuse to associate with him. On the other hand by membership he is entitled to certain privileges and has a right of property in the club. If, then, he is deprived of these privileges and rights by wrongful expulsion, he can complain to the Courts, and if he makes out his case, they will restore them to him. The members of the club will succeed, however, if they can prove the following points:—

1. The rules providing for expulsion have been strictly observed.
2. The member expelled has had a full opportunity of answering the charges made against him and putting forward any explanation.
3. There has been no malice in exercising the power of expulsion.

If the Court is satisfied that all these matters have been observed they will not go behind the members' decision, even though they do not themselves agree with it.

The rules of a members' club form the contract between its members. Thus they will only be liable to pay the subscriptions and sums of money they have agreed to. Hence a "whip," i.e. a request that each member pay a sum of money to meet some financial emergency, is unenforceable.

A club may be incorporated under the Companies Act 1924. In such cases it can still be either a members' club or a proprietary club. If a proprietary club, it merely means that the company takes the place of the proprietor. If a members' club, the best method is to register it as a company, limited by guarantee, the members of the club for the time being constituting the company. The advantage of this is that the club while remaining a members' club can sue and be sued as a legal entity.

The Sale of Intoxicants in a Club. —When the question of selling intoxicants in clubs arises, the position of proprietary and members' clubs is again very different.

The proprietor of the former type of club, if intoxicating drink is supplied to members, must have a licence. In a members' club, however, where all the property belongs to the members jointly no licence is required. The reason for this is that the proprietor of the former type of club owns the liquor, and consequently when a member purchases a drink there is a sale to him from the proprietor, for which a licence is required. There is a means, however, of getting over the need of a licence in a proprietary club. It is as follows:—

The sale of drink is entrusted to a wine committee composed of members. This committee buys intoxicants on behalf of all the members and takes the sale of drinks out of the hands of the proprietor. Thus when a drink is sold in a club where such an arrangement is in force, there is a sale from the proprietor to a member, but the position is similar to that appertaining in a members' club. There the liquor belongs to the members, and, when one of them orders and pays for a drink, there is not a sale but merely a release to him of the proprietary rights of his co-owners, and, as there is no sale, a licence is not required.

A club, whether proprietary or otherwise, must be registered if intoxicating liquor is to be obtained on the premises. That is to say the secretary must furnish the clerk of the justices with a return containing the name and objects of the club, its address name of its secretary, number of its members, and the rules, together with a fee of 5/-. The clerk of the justices then enters these particulars on his register of clubs and the club is said to be registered, and intoxicants can be supplied off the premises. These, however, cannot be supplied except during the permitted hours nor can they be supplied on the premises. The long pull (*See* LONG PULL) is also prohibited. With these exceptions, however, the Licensing Acts do not apply to members' clubs and intoxicants can be sold to members for consumption on or off the premises. Though a licence is not required for such clubs duty must be paid on the intoxicants consumed there. This is done in the following way:—

The secretary of every registered club must deliver annually a statement of the purchases of intoxicating liquor during the previous year and a duty of 3d. in the £ is payable thereon.

Hours during which drinking is permitted in Clubs.—The regulations relating to permitted hours are slightly different for clubs situated in the metropolis and for clubs outside.

In the Metropolis.—The hours during which intoxicating liquor may be supplied or consumed must not exceed nine on week-days and five on Sundays, Christmas Day and Good Friday. The members may fix these hours, on week-days, between 11 a.m. and 11 p.m. with a two hour break after twelve noon; and on the other days two hours between noon and 3 p.m. and three between 6 and 10 p.m. During these hours intoxicating liquor can be supplied and consumed on the club premises, but for half an hour after them intoxicating liquor can be consumed with a meal, provided it was supplied and served with the meal before the permitted hours ended. Clubs may also add one hour to the permitted hours, so long as the justices are satisfied that drinking is not the principal business of the club, but only ancillary to the provision of substantial refreshment. But during that extra hour drink can only be supplied and consumed with a meal in the club dining room, and any other bar on the premises must be closed. In accordance with the rule already mentioned, however, consumption of intoxicants will be allowed for half an hour after the conclusion of the

extra hour. Hence, in the metropolis in clubs where the extra hour is in force, intoxicants can be supplied or consumed in any part of the premises up to 11 p.m., and after that, may be supplied and consumed in the dining room with a meal up to 12 p.m., and after 12 midnight they may not be supplied but may be consumed with a meal up to 12.30 a.m.

Outside the Metropolis.—The only difference is that the total number of hours on week-days during which intoxicating liquors may be supplied and consumed must not exceed eight as compared to nine in the metropolis, and the latest hour which may be fixed is 10 p.m. instead of 11 p.m. in the metropolis. Otherwise the law as to the permitted hours and extensions thereof are the same for clubs inside and outside the metropolis.

Of course intoxicants can be supplied at any time to a member who is residing upon the club premises, and a member may order intoxicants outside the permitted hours to be consumed off the club premises, and intoxicants so ordered may be despatched outside the permitted hours. A club may on conviction by the justices be struck off the register on all or one of the following grounds:—

1. That the club has ceased to exist or that the number of members is less than twenty-five.

2. That is is not conducted in good faith as a club or that it is habitually used for some unlawful purpose.

3. That there is frequent drunkenness on the club premises.

4. That illegal sales of intoxicating liquor have taken place on the premises.

5. That persons who are not members are habitually admitted to the club merely for the purpose of obtaining intoxicating liquor.

6. That the club occupies premises which within twelve months next preceding its formation have had a licence which has been forfeited. (This is to prevent a publican who has lost his licence carrying on under the guise of a club.)

7. That persons are habitually admitted as members without an interval of at least forty-eight hours between their nomination and admission.

8. That the supply of intoxicating liquor

to the club is not under the control of the members on a committee appointed by them.

Once struck off the register a club cannot be re-registered. (*See* INTOXICATING LIQUORS; LONG PULL; PERMITTED HOURS; WORKING MEN'S CLUBS.)

COAL MINES.—The coal industry is regulated by a considerable body of statute law. The Acts of Parliament dealing with the industry may, for convenience, be divided into two main classes. Of these, the first class was consolidated by an Act of 1911 and deals with what may be called the internal regulation and organization of a coal mine.

This includes such matters as hours, payment and safety measures. The statutes in the second group have all been passed since 1919, and represent the steps taken to reorganize the coal industry as a whole in the years after the Great War. Although summarized here, this legislation is of political and economic rather than of great legal importance.

Hours of Work.—The main Act dealing with hours of work is the Coal Mines Act 1908. This was the first act to introduce a limitation of hours of work that applied to the whole industry. The limit imposed was that no workman should remain below ground for more than eight hours in any consecutive twenty-four hours. The provision has gone through several amendments and the present position is as follows:— (1) The time limit is seven hours; (2) On sixty days in the year the time may be extended by not more than one hour a day. It is provided that, of the two periods required for lowering and raising workmen, one of them must be included in the seven hours while the other is not included. These limitations may be suspended by Order in Council during any national emergency, or in the event of any grave economic disturbance caused by the demand for coal exceeding the supply at any time. Also they do not apply during any local emergency; a workman may be below ground for a longer period for the purpose of rendering assistance when an accident occurs or there is some danger to the mine.

Wages.—Statutory provisions fixing a minimum wage for the industry were introduced by the Coal Mines (Minimum Wage)

Act 1912, which set up the machinery of joint district boards for settling the minimum wage for each district. Questions as to wages are, however, usually regulated by agreement between the owners and workmen of the particular district. If wages are paid by reference to the amount of coal worked by a workman, a check weigher may be appointed by the workmen. To protect the workmen's interests he must be given all facilities for examining and testing the weighing machines, and he will check the weighing of coal while it is being done.

General safety regulations are set out in the Coal Mines Act 1911. As regards ventilation, a place is not considered to be in a state for working if the air in it contains less than 19% of oxygen when tested. Locked safety lamps of the approved type must be used. An inspection of the part of the mine to be worked must be carried out before commencing work, and machinery must be examined at specified intervals. If it is found that a part of the mine is dangerous by reason of inflammable gases or from any other cause, every workman must be withdrawn. Every seam that is being worked must be in communication with at least two shafts or outlets. Persons who have had less than two years' experience must not work alone but must be under the supervision of some skilled workman.

Provisions as to accidents.—When an accident occurs that causes loss of life or serious personal injury, notice in writing must be sent to the inspector of the district. The place where the accident occurred must be left as it was at the time of the accident until an inspection has been carried out. If it appears expedient, a formal inquiry may be held.

Management.—Every mine must be under the control of one manager who is responsible for the control and direction of the mine, and who shall himself exercise daily personal supervision. A person is only qualified to act as manager if he holds a first class certificate of competency. The owner of a mine cannot take any part in the technical management of a mine unless he is so qualified. Competent persons must be appointed to make such inspections as to ventilation etc., as are required by the Act. Inspectors can enter and examine any mine at any reasonable time to ascertain whether the statutory provisions are being complied with, and to inspect generally to see that everything possible is being done to safeguard the persons employed in or about the mine.

Welfare Fund.—In 1920 the Mining Industry Act imposed a levy of 1d. per ton on the annual output of every coal mine, and in 1926 a Royalties Welfare Levy of a shilling in the pound was added. The

represent the attempts made by Parliament to reorganize the industry in recent years. The Mining Industry Act of 1920 established a Mines Department of the Board of Trade with power to make regulations for the industry and to hold inquiries into working methods, etc. The Department also collects and prepares information and statistics relating to the industry. The Mining Industry Act of 1926 deals with amalgamation and absorption as a possible

Numerous safety devices, enforced by law, are in use in all coal mining districts. Volunteer Rescue Brigades are maintained by colliery owners

money so raised is paid to the Welfare Fund. This is administered by the Welfare Committee for any purpose connected with social well-being and conditions of living of those employed in the mining industry. There is a statutory provision that the first object to which the Royalties Welfare Levy is to be applied is the provision of baths and of various facilities for drying clothes in all mines.

Reorganization of the Coal Industry.—The following statutes deal with the coal mining industry as a whole and

means of securing more efficient and economical working and disposal of coal. Two or more owners of coal mines may submit to the Board of Trade a scheme for complete or partial amalgamation. The Board of Trade is then to consider the proposed scheme, and if it is satisfied that the proposals submitted reveal a prima facie case for amalgamation—inasmuch as the scheme would promote more economical and efficient working—then it will refer the scheme to the Railway and Canal Commission. This Court will then confirm the scheme if it is satisfied that it is in the national interest to do so, and that the scheme is fair and equitable to all persons affected by it... It must be noted that by an absorption scheme an undertaking may be compelled to join in one of these schemes, though the owners of it are, in fact, unwilling to join in. The Coal Mines Act 1930 amends the last Act. A Coal Mines Reorganization Commission has been set up. The schemes dealt with by the Act of 1926 are to be certified by the Commission when they are proposed by mine owners. The Reorganization Committee can also introduce schemes itself although none of the owners of the undertakings concerned accept it. After certification by the Commission, the scheme still goes through the stages described above. The principles upon which the Railway and Canal Commission are to act when considering a scheme are differently expressed in the later Act. A scheme is not to be confirmed unless it would be in the national interest to do so. Secondly, the scheme must result in lowering the cost of production or disposal of coal, and must not be financially injurious to any of the undertakings concerned unless such undertaking is to be bought out at a price agreed on by arbitration. Thirdly, the terms must be fair and equitable.

COAL, SALE OF.—The Weights and Measures Act 1889 deals with the sale of coal. It provides that coal must always be sold by weight, except where it is being sold by boat load or in tubs delivered direct to the works of the purchaser from the colliery. The act imposes fines for the breach of any of the following requirements:—

(1) Where any quantity of coal exceeding two hundredweight is delivered in any vehicle to the purchaser the seller must send a ticket drawn up in the form set out in the statute which runs:—To Mr. A.B. Take notice that you are to receive herewith x cwt. of coal in sacks each containing y cwt. C.D. (being the name of the seller) E.F. (being the name of the person in charge of the vehicle). If the coal is sold in bulk there should be added the weight of coal and vehicle, tare weight of vehicle and the net weight of coal delivered to the purchaser.

(2) A second requirement is that when any quantity of coal exceeding two hundred-

weight is conveyed for delivery on sale in a vehicle in bulk, the tare weight of the vehicle shall be marked on the vehicle.

(3) The seller of coal by retail shall keep a weighing instrument stamped by an inspector of weights and measures, and shall, if required by the purchaser, weigh any coal before sale.

COCK FIGHTING.—The sport of Cock Fighting is illegal. The police may disperse any meeting assembled for the purpose of setting cocks to fight each other and prosecute the organisers, and in some cases even those present only as spectators.

COCKBURN, Sir Alexander (1802–80), first became known by his defence of McNaughten, when the law as to insanity

Sir Alexander Cockburn.

in criminal cases was settled. A small man, it was said of him "He rose up a pigmy and sat down a giant," so great was the power of his advocacy. His prosecution of Palmer the poisoner was masterly; and on his conviction Palmer handed down a note consisting of the words "It's the riding that has done it." Cockburn became Chief Justice, his best known case as Judge being his Award on the Alabama claims.

CODICIL.—A codicil is a document in which a testator varies the provisions contained in a will which he has previously made. It must be signed by the testator in the presence of two attesting witnesses with all the formalities of a will itself. A codicil may have the effect of adding new clauses to a will, or deleting clauses contained in the original will, or it may cancel the whole effect of a previous will. It is generally attached to the will which it is intended to vary. (*See* PROBATE OF WILLS: WILLS.)

CODIFICATION.—Codification means the enactment of the whole law of a country, or a part of the law, as a code. This has been done in many foreign countries, and has been the object of many famous lawmakers in history. Perhaps the greatest example of codification in the history of the world was that of the Emperor Justinian in the sixth century. He caused to be collected from various sources all the then existing principles of Roman law and issued them in the form of a code. Napoleon I carried out a similar scheme of codification for use in the French empire; his code still exists under the name of the Code Napoleon. The Code Napoleon has been the basis of many codes enacted in various European countries during the nineteenth and twentieth centuries.

The English speaking countries have never to any great extent adopted codification. They have always looked to the unwritten principles of English law, called the Common Law, as the basis of their legal systems. In England there have been isolated attempts to codify certain portions of the law; in 1882 the law relating to Bills of Exchange was codified in the Bills of Exchange Act. In India there is in existence a complete code of criminal law.

English lawyers have always been much divided on the question of whether or not codification is desirable. At first sight it may well be thought that to have in one large document the whole law of a country, laid down once for all, would be highly desirable, but a little thought shows that this might well create greater difficulties than it avoids. It is, obviously, humanly impossible to set out in one document, however long. the solution of every possible legal point that can arise. It is therefore at least arguable that the English system of having general principles of law in an unwritten form, which can be interpreted and extended by the Judges as practical points arise, is the

better method. It certainly has this great advantage: a written code sets out the views of the lawgivers at the time that the code was made, it remains thereafter in an unchangeable form. A living body of law on the other hand is a flexible one, and can be interpreted by the Judges in the light of present day ideas and modern public opinion.

There is at the present time in England no great demand for codification, indeed, to codify the enormous mass of English law would be an undertaking that could not be concluded in one, or even ten years. To commence a work of this nature, moreover, would be to raise all sorts of points for decision, and it is perhaps, in view of this, desirable to let sleeping dogs lie. However the question of codification or non-codification is an interesting one and a frequent source of subjects for debate in which it will be found, usually, that lawyers are against codification while laymen are in favour of it.

COINING.—There are many different offences in respect of counterfeit coins. Some of these are: falsely making or counterfeiting coins to pass for current coin, gilding, silvering, lightening or defacing coins, importing or tendering counterfeit coin. Unlawful possession of tools for making counterfeit coin is also a crime. Any person also commits a crime if he has in his custody or possession three or more pieces of counterfeit gold or silver coin knowing them to be counterfeit and intending to issue them. Coinage offences are very seriously regarded by the law. Most of them are felonies punishable with penal servitude.

Foreign Coin.—Any person who, with intent to defraud, uses any foreign coin resembling current coin of the realm and of less value, commits a misdemeanour.

COKE, Sir Edward (1552-1634).—Famous as the champion of the Common Law against the rival claims of Church, Equity, and the Royal Prerogative. His knowledge of the Common Law was not equalled even by his great rival Bacon, and his legal writings have been the material on which generations of lawyers have been trained.

COLERIDGE, Lord (1820-1894).—Starting practice on the Western Circuit, he reached fame by his masterly cross-examination of the Tichborne Claimant. As Lord

Chief Justice, he led a party of English lawyers on a visit to the United States at the invitation of the Bar Association of New York. He tried the case of Rex v. Dudley which aroused a great deal of interest at the time. In it he decided that ship-wrecked sailors were not justified in killing one of their number, a boy, in order to preserve their own lives from starvation.

COLLATERAL AGREEMENT.—

It is one of the rules of the English Law of

Lord Coleridge.

Evidence that where two persons have drawn up a written document setting out the terms of an agreement made between them, they are bound by these terms, and cannot introduce into the agreement any other matters which were discussed by them in their preliminary negotiations but which have not been set out in their written document. There are, however, exceptions to this rule. The first occurs where the document does not contain the real terms which the parties agreed upon. The parties may then ask the Court to rectify the document.

The second exception to this rule is to be found where one party alleges some collateral agreement, that is, a preliminary agreement, by which one of the parties made promises to the other in consideration of that other signing the written document which contains the final terms. This collateral agreement is distinct and separate from the later written document.

Suppose A is contemplating taking a lease of a house from B. In the negotiations the parties may discuss the repairs which have to be done to the house, and B may say that he will paper and paint a certain room. When the agreement for the lease is prepared, no reference may be made to B's obligation to paint and paper. If B later refuses to paint or paper the room, A could not compel him to do so by relying on the terms under which the premises were let. If he says that B is bound to paint and paper under the terms of the letting, B can point to the written document which contains *all* the terms of the letting and shews that no such term is included in it, and A is not allowed to bring into the written document terms discussed before the written document, but not included in it. The law, however, allows A, by what is really a legal fiction, to say that before the lease was signed he made a separate agreement with B that if B would promise to paint and paper the premises he, A, would sign the lease. This agreement is collateral to the agreement of letting, and A could enforce it against B either by saying that it was only on the basis of B's papering and painting that A signed the lease (i.e. making it a condition precedent), and that as this has not been done, A is not bound to take the premises, or by treating it as a warranty and suing B for damages, which will be the cost of papering and painting. A collateral agreement cannot be relied on if it contradicts some term of the written contract between the parties. (*See* CONTRACT.)

COLLATERAL RELATIVE.—

Collateral Relatives, frequently called collaterals, are persons who are neither ancestors nor descendants, thus not only brothers and sisters will be included in the term but also uncles and aunts or nieces and nephews.

COLLATERAL SECURITY.—

When, after a transaction has been entered into, one person gives to the other some money or property in security for the fulfilment of his obligations, that security is said to be Collateral. Thus if A has sold goods to B for £100 and after the transaction is over he gives B a Bill of Exchange for the amount, the bill is collateral security. Security of this kind is usually perfectly valid, but where the person giving the security becomes bankrupt the transaction may amount to a fraudulent preference.

COLLECTING SOCIETY is a friendly society which receives contributions collected from members who live at a distance of more than ten miles from its registered office. The subscriptions are collected by the society's collectors. A collecting society, whether registered or unregistered, is subject to the provisions of the Industrial Assurance Act, 1923, and the law requires that certain provisions must be contained in the rules of a collecting society.

The rules must contain provisions for giving members notice of forfeiture of their benefits, for the holding of general meetings, for the inspection and delivery of balance sheets and annual returns, and for the settlement of disputes. All notices of the society must have the name of the society printed upon it. Collecting societies have in recent years come to be associated almost entirely with the business of Industrial Assurance, which is the insurance of human life, the premiums for which are collected by the collectors of the society.

If a collecting society insures the lives of its members then it must be registered with the Chief Registrar of Friendly Societies, who is also known as the Industrial Assurance Commissioner when he is dealing with societies engaged in the business of industrial assurance.

The society must also deposit a sum of £20,000 with the Commissioner and such deposit must be maintained as long as the society continues to do life insurance.

A collecting society which does industrial assurance must keep a separate fund for the money received as premiums for life insurance, and the rules must provide that such a fund is the absolute security of the holders of life insurance policies. Separate valuations of the life insurance business must be made. (*See* FRIENDLY SOCIETY, INSURANCE.)

COLLISIONS ON LAND.—When two objects collide, it sometimes, but not always, gives rise to an action. Whether it does so or not depends on whether:

(a) The collision injured some person or thing;

(b) The collision has been caused by the

fault or negligence of some person or other.

The person who is injured will be the plaintiff, and the person who caused the accident is the person liable. When these two are united in one person there will, of course, be no cause of action. Very often it may happen that the person injured is not actually in the collision. He may be a bystander who is hurt by a flying fragment. This makes his case none the less actionable. Again the person who caused the collision may not himself be in the collision. For instance, a car coming suddenly from a side turning may cause another car to swerve and collide with a third. This would not debar both the second and third car from proceeding against the first. The three different classes of collision best known to the public are road collision, railway collision, and collision at sea.

As to the first, the principles governing liability in such cases will be found under the heading of Negligence.

Railway collisions differ but slightly in the principles governing liability from road collision. Usually the persons injured are passengers, and a passenger is owed two different kinds of duty. Firstly he is owed the duty that everyone is owed by their fellow men, namely, that the railway servants will behave as reasonable men towards him, and will not wilfully or negligently injure him. Secondly there is a contractual duty. The passenger has impliedly contracted with the company for safe carriage from one place to another, and is entitled to safe conveyance. The railway company, by allowing him to be injured in a collision, have committed a breach of this duty.

All drivers of trains are bound to drive as a reasonable man should drive a train. Thus a person run over on a railway can in many cases sue the company for its servants failing to exercise reasonable care.

Of course, in deciding the standard of care regard must be had to all the circumstances. A train takes a considerable time to pull up. The railway company fence their tracks and a train driver may expect to find the track free of pedestrians. So the injury or death of a person on a railway line must be connected with the negligence of the railway company's servants. If a man was found dead on a railway line, even if it were assumed that the railway company were negligent, the relatives would not succeed unless they connected the death with that negligence, e.g. it would not be enough to prove the man was killed by a train, and to prove that trains habitually did not whistle at the spot where the dead man was found, though it was the rule of the company that they should do so.

It would have to be proved that the train which killed the man did not whistle, and that it was the absence of the whistle which caused his death. (*See* ACCIDENT; CONTRIBUTORY NEGLIGENCE; NEGLIGENCE.)

COLLISIONS AT SEA.—When two ships collide at sea the law governing the liability for the collision is in many respects different from the law relating to collisions on land. The rule in the case of collisions on land is that blame must either be attributed to one vehicle or to the other vehicle or pedestrian, with the result that the one found to be in fault is solely to blame, or that if both are found to blame, neither is responsible for the damage caused to the other but each must bear his own loss. In the case of collisions at sea the Court endeavours, when each of the vessels has been negligent, to divide the responsibility between them, and to hold each liable for the damages in proportion to their responsibility. Thus one vessel may be held to be two-thirds to blame and the other one-third to blame, and in such a case the damage caused would be divided between the two ships in that proportion. (*See* SHIPPING.)

COLLUSION.—Where persons who are outwardly opponents in an action or suit have some secret agreement by means of which they intend to deceive the Court, they are said to be in collusion. Collusion chiefly arises in connection with divorce, as it not infrequently happens that a husband and wife, in order to end an unhappy marriage tie, will plot together to deceive the Court, into thinking that one or the other is bringing a perfectly proper suit. Consequently a petitioner must swear that no collusion exists between the parties. Further if collusion is discovered in any divorce suit it forms an absolute bar to the divorce being obtained. (*See* SPECIAL SUPPLEMENT " DIVORCE.")

COMBINATION ACTS.—From very early times combinations of workmen to regulate their wages or their conditions of labour, were frowned upon by the State, partly because the State itself regulated the conditions of labour, and partly because it did not like any combination of persons within itself which might be hostile to it. Throughout the centuries from the Thirteenth century onwards, Acts of Parliament have been passed making combinations among workmen illegal conspiracies, this series culminated in The Combination Act of 1800. That Act declared that any combination to obtain an advance in wages, to alter hours of work, to prevent any person employing whomsoever he thought fit to employ, or to attempt to induce workmen to leave their work was an illegal combination. In 1824, however, it was realised that such a law was unnecessarily harsh and oppressive, and the Combination Acts were repealed by an Act of that year. This Act was followed by an amending Act of 1825 which made it an offence to molest, intimidate or threaten a person to prevent him accepting or giving employment. (*See* CONSPIRACY; TRADE DISPUTE; TRADE UNION.)

COMMERCIAL COURT.—Special provision has been made by the Judges in the King's Bench division for the trial of what are called Commercial cases, that is, cases relating to business transactions, usually of considerable magnitude, which will take a long time to try and which do not require a jury but are suitable for trial by a Judge alone. Special Judges with considerable experience in commercial work are appointed to take these cases. The main characteristics of the Commercial Court are that matters, particularly in the preliminary stages, are much less formal than in other courts, and that the date for trial of the cases is fixed.

COMMERCIAL LAW.—This name is usually applied to those parts of the law which deal with business relations as distinct from law dealing with family relationship, e.g. marriage and divorce or other matters of a personal character or with Wills, or Land. Commercial law is concerned with such matters as the Sale of Goods, Bills of Exchange, Charter Parties, Bills of Lading and all the multiplicity of affairs which are found in modern business life.

COMMISSION.—Commission is the sum, generally a percentage, payable to an agent or employee by his principal or employer for introducing a purchaser, vendor, lender, tenant, partner etc., or for carrying through a transaction himself.

Where agents are concerned, commission is the most common form of remuneration, but it is not so common where the relations of master and servant exist; in the latter case it is usually additional to a salary. The law as to commission, except where stated, is the same for an agent as for an employee.

The three main questions regarding commission for introducing third parties are:

1. Was the agent the means of introducing the third party to the principal?

The transaction must have directly, but not necessarily immediately, resulted from the agent's introduction. It does not matter that other agents also introduced the third party, and so more than one agent may be entitled to commission in respect of the same transaction. The service rendered must be within the scope of the agent's employment, e.g. if an estate agent who is employed to let a house introduces someone who buys it, he is not entitled to commission.

2. Was the third party willing, or could he be compelled to carry through the transaction on substantially the same terms which the agent was instructed to obtain?

If an agent is employed to find a lender who requires 5%, he has not performed his task if he finds one who requires 10%, even if no one could be found to lend at the former figure.

In the absence of a trade custom or of an express term of the agreement to the contrary, e.g. commission to be paid on sale taking place, the agent is entitled to his commission when he has produced the willing or compellable third party. Even if the transaction afterwards falls through, whether owing to the inability or refusal of the principal to complete it—he may be unable to show a good title on the sale of the land —or for any other reason except one caused by the agent himself, the latter's commission is not affected. This is so, even if the principal obtains no benefit out of the transaction.

3. What amount of commission is due to the agent?

If the amount is not fixed by agreement,

it is fixed either by custom or by implication —in the latter case a reasonable sum in view of the service rendered and the sum involved. Thus, by the special scale drawn up by the Auctioneers and Estate Agents Institute, the following are typical rates of commission fixed:

(i) On sale of Freehold property—5% if price over £100.

(ii) On letting Unfurnished property— 5% of one year's rental if letting for £100 or less and for one year or less, or for over £100 and for under three years. 7½% if under £100 and over one year, or over £100 and under three years.

(iii) On letting Furnished property—5% of first year's rental and 2½% of subsequent rent paid. This last rate includes collecting of rent.

Commission for auctioneer's sales of goods under distraint, or seized by a sheriff, or belonging to a bankrupt are fixed by Statute. A "del credere" agent who guarantees the solvency of the third party is entitled to a higher rate of commission.

Not only has the rate of commission to be paid often to be implied, but a promise to pay commission at all is often only inferred, e.g. there is seldom an express promise to pay commission to an auctioneer or estate agent. The vendor or lessor is always responsible for the commission.

This claim for payment of a reasonable sum as commission is analogous to a quantum meruit, which is a contract implied by law to pay for services rendered and accepted. If an agent does not carry out his instructions and thereby disentitles himself to the commission, he can sue the principal on a "quantum meruit" for the beneficial work he did which was accepted. (See QUANTUM MERUIT.)

The agent is not entitled to his commission if:

(i) The transaction was unauthorised by the principal and not ratified by him.

(ii) The transaction was an unlawful or wagering one. (The term "turf commission agents" owes its origin to the time when their job was to place bets for a principal. A commission for placing a bet is not recoverable.)

(iii) The agent was an unlicensed appraiser (valuer). An unlicensed auctioneer or estate agent is, however, entitled to his commission.

(iv) The agent was guilty of wilful breach of duty or misconduct. An agent who accepts a secret commission, i.e. a bribe, from the third party, given to influence him to be disloyal to his principal, even though he is not so influenced, cannot claim his commission and is liable to pay the secret commission over to the principal. He is also guilty of a criminal offence.

(v) The agent's negligence has prevented the principal from obtaining any benefit out of the transaction. If the principal derives any benefit, the agent can claim his commission but is liable to a counter-claim for negligence.

If the principal prevents an agent earning his commission by a breach of an express or implied term of the agreement between them, the agent can sue him in an ordinary action for breach of contract. If he can shew that, but for the breach, he would have earned the commission, he is entitled to the whole amount of the commission as damages.

If an employee is wrongfully dismissed, he is entitled to the commission he would have earned. A principal can usually revoke an agent's authority without notice if the agency is not for a fixed period. An agent is usually not entitled to commission on business arising wholly as a result of an introduction previously effected by him after his agency has been rightfully revoked. To obtain such commission he must, in the absence of an express term to that effect, shew that such a term is to be implied from the nature of his employment.

An agent or employee paid by commission only (but probably not an employee paid salary and commission) is entitled to reasonable facilities to earn such commission. Further, it is an implied term that the employer or principal will do nothing to put an end to the circumstances under which alone the arrangement can be operative.

Thus a commercial traveller, paid by commission only, is entitled to be given a reasonable supply of goods to sell, and is able to claim damages if he is not so supplied, and this is so even though the employer has given up business or, in the case of a company, it has been voluntarily wound up.

A person appointed sole agent is entitled to claim as damages the commission he has lost by reason of the principal appointing other agents.

The most common form of agents on commission are estate agents and auctioneers, and of employees on commission, commercial travellers. Estate agents are not entitled to anything unless they are successful or have been specially authorized to incur expenditure, e.g. they are not entitled to charge for putting up a board outside a house unless instructed to do so. An auctioneer is, however, allowed to charge for necessary expenditure, the distinction being due to the fact that his expenditure is inevitable and therefore presumed to be authorized. An auctioneer has a right to retain out of the purchase money or deposit the amount due to him for commission, or if property of the principal has been left in his possession he has a lien on it, i.e. a right to retain it until his commission is paid. An auctioneer who is instructed to sell property by auction is entitled to commission if he sells it by private treaty. (*See* AUCTIONEERS; ESTATE AGENTS; MASTER AND SERVANT; PRINCIPAL AND AGENT; QUANTUM MERUIT.)

COMMISSIONER FOR OATHS. —Any practising solicitor and any fit and proper person may be appointed by the Lord Chancellor to be a Commissioner for Oaths. The function of a Commissioner is to administer oaths, affirmations and declarations, but he may not do so if he is a solicitor in any proceeding or action in any matter in which he is acting, or interested in his professional capacity.

Certain officers of the courts are empowered to administer oaths, and British ambassadors and diplomatic representatives, including consular officers in the course of exercising their functions in any foreign country may also do so.

The appointment of a solicitor as a Commissioner is not usually made unless he has been in continuous practice for six years, but it is a matter for the discretion of the Lord Chancellor, who is guided by the need of the locality, upon application to him of a solicitor of less than six years' standing in continuous practice. (*See* AFFIDAVITS.)

COMMON CARRIER.—A common carrier is one who holds himself out as ready to carry all goods brought to him for carriage between certain places.

Carriers who carry certain classes of goods only are not common carriers. Common carriers cannot refuse to carry goods if they have room, and are under a greater liability for the safety of the goods than ordinary carriers. (*See* CARRIAGE BY LAND.)

COMMON COUNCIL.—The Common Council of the City of London is equivalent to the Borough Council of any ordinary borough, although, since the City of London is still governed by its ancient charters, the powers of the Common Council are considerably wider than those of other borough councils. The Common Council consists of the Lord Mayor, 25 aldermen and 206 councilmen. The common councilmen are elected by the local government electors, and themselves choose the Lord Mayor and aldermen. (*See* ALDERMEN; LOCAL GOVERNMENT.)

COMMON LAW.—English law is not codified; that is to say, there s no basic written law to which reference may be made to decide unsettled points of law. In theory there has always been in England a fixed unwritten law dating back to remote antiquity. This is, of course, not really so, but it is a convenient fiction by means of which the law has developed as time goes on. Actually, as undecided points of law crop up the Judges decide them by reference to previous decisions on similar points involving similar principles. They try always to stretch back into the past in order to find out what the law always has been though not actually declared. This body of unwritten law as interpreted and extended by the decisions of the Judges is called "common law." The expression is used in contradistinction to equity, although since 1873 both law and equity have been administered in the same courts. (*See* EQUITY.)

COMMONS.—A common is the waste land of one of the manors into which the greater part of England used to be divided. In 1925 Parliament enacted that all the members of the public should have the right to use commons for purposes of air and exercise, but at the same time prohibited the unauthorized driving of cars or carts over them and the parking of cars except within 15 feet of the road. The prohibition also extends to camping and the lighting of fires.

Before 1925 the law, though it was seldom observed or enforced, was that only those persons who had rights of common over the land in question might use it. There were several different kinds of rights of common and they varied from manor to manor; the most usual was common of pasturage or the right to turn out on to the common as many cattle and horses as the commoner's land could support during the winter months. Other rights of common are estovers—the right to cut wood for fencing or burning, and turbary the right to cut turf.

Rights of common are either appendant or appurtenant (q.v.). Though there is an important difference in meaning between these two words they have one thing in common; they both imply that the right of common is annexed not to a particular person but to a particular piece of land, be it farm, house or field. As a result of this identification of the right with the land, it will pass to whomsoever is the owner or occupier of the land for the time being, but it can only be claimed by him so long as he is owner or occupier, and then only to satisfy the needs of the particular piece of land to which it is annexed. Thus a common of pasturage is confined to cattle levant et couchant on the land, that is, cattle which can be supported throughout the winter on the commoner's land. Common of turbary and common of estovers are also limited to the amount of wood or turf necessary for the commoner's house or fields, and he has no legal right to cut either for sale or even to cut them for use in another house of his own to which the right of common does not attach.

Appendant.—A common appendant is one which is annexed by operation of law to the commoner's holding; it is seldom met with nowadays as it can only be claimed for land which was anciently arable and which was granted by the lord of the manor before 1290 to the present tenant's predecessors in title. If it can be shewn that the right has been enjoyed for a long time and that it *might* have been granted before 1290, the law will presume that there must have been such a grant and that it has been lost. This is an example of the maxim that the law regards enjoyment of a right as being lawful unless it is shown to be unlawful.

Appurtenant.—A common appurtenant is one which is annexed to the commoner's holding not by operation of law but by some express agreement between the commoner or his predecessors and the lord of the manor. Such a right may have been created at any time in the past and may be created at the present day. Like common appendant, it is confined to the needs of the commoner's holding, but unlike it, it is not confined to pasturing cattle and may expand to pigs and other animals.

COMMONS, HOUSE OF.—The House of Commons is the supreme legislative power, subject only to the right of the House of Lords, to suspend the passing of any non-money bill for two years. Money bills when passed by the House of Commons go straight to the King for royal assent—this is since 1911, after a deadlock had been created by the House of Lords throwing out Mr. Lloyd George's Budget.

The House of Commons consists of 615 members and, subject to adjournments and recesses (intervals between the sessions), sits for 5 years, unless or until it is dissolved before the lapse of that period by the King on the advice of the Prime Minister. Each session is opened and closed by the King, who makes a speech respectively forecasting or reviewing the Government's activities.

The House has complete jurisdiction over anything that goes on within its walls, and governs its own procedure by its Standing Orders. The sittings are presided over by the Speaker or, in his absence, by the Chairman of Ways and Means who, in his turn, has a deputy. These officers are elected on the assembling of each new Parliament, the Speaker being nearly always re-elected. Government and Opposition members sit on the right and left of the Speaker respectively. Members are not allotted particular seats except that the Front Bench immediately on the Speaker's right (called the Treasury Bench) is reserved for Ministers, with the Opposition Leaders directly facing them.

The House sits at 2.45 p.m. from Monday to Friday; it usually rises at 11 p.m. but occasionally sits all night. Prayers are first read, followed by questions asked of Ministers by private members. Any member can ask a Minister material questions if he gives notice of the question. If he wants an oral reply he must say so: many questions are answered in writing. After question time the House proceeds to the business of the day which is settled by the leader of the House who is often, but by no means always, the Prime Minister.

Government bills are introduced by the Minister in charge, whose department is responsible for their drafting. A bill is first formally read. A discussion of its principles takes place on the second reading. It then goes to committee, either of the whole House or a small committee, where it is amended. It then comes up for a final reading. No bill may be introduced twice during a session. The Budget is introduced by the Chancellor of the Exchequer each April and is always considered by a committee of the whole House. In addition to Government bills, private members acquire by ballot the right to introduce bills. These are considered on Fridays and, unless they obtain Government support, are very seldom passed.

The voting is done by members walking into the "Aye" and "No" lobbies, two tellers being appointed by each side. They report the result to the Speaker. Members who are not actually sitting in the House are allowed to vote, and a bell is rung to warn them of a division.

Members speak when called upon; those desiring to do so giving their names to their Party Whips who are responsible for the management of each Party in the House, e.g. they see that members vote, etc. No member may speak twice in a debate, except that the opener has a right of reply.

Speeches of members are controlled by the following rules of procedure:

(i) Reading of speeches is forbidden.
(ii) The King's name must not be used disrespectfully or in an attempt to influence a debate.
(iii) No reference to debates in the House of Lords are allowed. When referred to, that House is spoken of as "another place."
(iv) Referring to members by name is forbidden.

Ministers are addressed by the office they hold and private members as the Honourable member for so-and-so. If of military rank, as the Honourable and Gallant member.

Members refusing to obey the rulings of the Speaker or otherwise behaving improperly may be "named" by him. It is then put to the vote of the House whether they be suspended; if it is carried, such suspension may last for any time up to the end of the session. Members are not allowed to read while sitting in the House.

The Speaker can always adjourn the House if, owing to chaos, business cannot be carried on, and must do so at the request of a member, if less than 40 members are present. If less than 40 are found to be present after 4 o'clock and not between 8.15 and 9.15 p.m. (dinner time) the House is adjourned for the day. The House is then said to be "counted out." This frequently occurs on Fridays (when the House can be "counted out" after 1 p.m.) when there are no questions and normally private members' bills instead of Government bills are discussed.

Complete freedom of speech is allowed in the House of Commons; no slander action can be brought in respect of words uttered in a speech there. A member is, of course, often called on to substantiate or withdraw an attack on any of his fellow-members.

Technically, the public is not allowed to be present in the House nor are debates allowed to be reported without authority. In point of fact, the latter is never enforced, although Hansard is the only official report, and the former only if a member says "I spy strangers," when it is put to the vote of the House whether the strangers be excluded. During the War the House sometimes used to sit in camera.

Admission is only by introduction from a member, and any visitor misbehaving during the sittings may be ejected. (*See* CHILTERN HUNDREDS; MEMBERS OF PARLIAMENT.)

COMPANIES.—To the average laymen a company almost always means a limited company incorporated under the Companies Acts, that is, a body having directors and shareholders whose liability is limited— i.e. is to pay for their shares, and who cannot be made liable for any debts incurred by the company. In law, however, a limited company is only one of the kinds of company which may be created. A company may be "unlimited," in which case its shareholders will be liable without limit for all its debts; or it may be "limited by guarantee" in which case its members are not shareholders (for there are usually no

shares) but undertake each to find so much money to pay the liabilities of the company when it is wound up (q.v.). Unlimited and guarantee companies are not often found, and attention may be confined to the company limited by shares, referred to as a limited company.

Company an Artificial Legal Person.—A company is in law a corporate body, that is, an artificial person created by the law. A legal person may be either a natural person, such as a human being, or an artificial person, such as a company.

"Legal person" means simply a being which is capable of having rights and liabilities. Thus an animal has no rights or liabilities because it is not a legal person, and if any one wished to leave a sum of money by will for the benefit of an animal, e.g. for the maintenance of a pet dog, it would not be possible to leave the money directly to the animal because the law would not recognize its right to take it, but it would be necessary to leave it to some legal person, e.g. a human being, and direct that person to spend it in looking after the animal.

A Company's Powers Limited.—Although both artificial legal persons, such as companies, and human beings are legal persons, yet their position is very different. The law allows a human being, so long as he is not an infant, i.e. under 21, or a lunatic, to enter into any contracts and acquire any rights or liabilities that he wishes. He may, for example, carry on at the same time two businesses, one for manufacturing boots and the other for manufacturing hats. The law has expressed this by saying he has a "full legal capacity." When the law allowed artificial legal persons to be created it could, if it had wished, have allowed them to have equally unlimited capacities to do any acts, but it has not chosen to do so and has required that whenever an artificial legal person, e.g. a company, is brought into existence those who are forming it must state clearly beforehand the things which they wish the company to have power to do. The law allows them to state as many things as they like, but once they have done so will not allow the company to do any acts for which they have not taken power. Thus a company which has been formed for the purpose of selling boots could not also sell hats, unless those forming it had provided that it should have power to do both these things. If it tried to sell hats without having power to do so the act would be ultra vires (q.v.)—that is beyond its powers and of no legal effect.

The persons who are forming a company are required to state beforehand in writing what its objects are in a document called the Memorandum of Association, and this document is filed in a public register with the Registrar of Companies, where anybody interested in the company may see it and so find out what the powers of the company are.

Company and Shareholders different legal persons.—It may now perhaps be appreciated that the company is a completely different legal person from any of its shareholders. When the company enters into contracts, the shareholders do not acquire any rights under them, nor are they liable for any debt which it has incurred. Their only duty is to pay to the company the amount of money which is due on the shares which they hold, i.e. £100 if they hold 100 £1 shares.

Advantages of a Company.—There are both advantages and disadvantages to be derived from turning a business which has been carried on by a partnership or a private individual into a limited company. The first advantage of a company, namely, that the liability of the shareholders is limited, has already been noticed. Again, a company makes it more easy for one of the proprietors who wishes to retire from active management to do so while yet retaining an interest, and without being liable for its debts. A company also enables new money to be put into the business by shareholders who will allow the directors to carry on the business without demanding a share in its administration, and employees may also be enabled to acquire a financial interest without their having any control of the management.

Saving of Surtax.—A final advantage is to be derived from the law relating to surtax (i.e. super-tax). When a private trader or a partnership makes profits, income tax and surtax must be paid even though the money is not taken out of the business but is used to extend it. In the case of a company, income tax, it is true, is paid by the company on its profits whether they are distributed or not, but the company

is not liable for surtax. This liability is borne by the shareholders who only pay it in respect of moneys which they receive as dividends. Thus, if the company wishes, its profits may be used to extend the business or to build up a reserve instead of being paid out as dividends, and later may be distributed in the form of bonus shares without ever having paid surtax. It is true that in some cases where a company is not paying out a reasonable proportion of its profits, the Inland Revenue Authorities are entitled to treat a part of these profits as if they had been paid to shareholders and claim surtax on them, but this claim does not often succeed.

Disadvantages of Companies.—The disadvantages of a company are that certain expenses are involved in its flotation, i.e. in bringing it into existence. Further the income received by a shareholder as dividends is not earned income for the purposes of income tax, and therefore the shareholder will not be entitled to claim the earned income allowance on it. In the case of some private companies where the directors hold all the shares, this difficulty may be overcome by paying out the profits in the form of directors' fees instead of as dividends, and they will then be regarded as earned income. Another disadvantage of a company is that the law requires that it should make public a large amount of information relating to its accounts and the carrying on of its business, and this may be considered undesirable as giving an advantage to trade competitors.

Private and Public Companies.—There are two kinds of companies, private and public. A private company is one:

1. Whose members, excluding employees on profit sharing schemes, are not more than 50 in number;

2. Which does not offer its shares or debentures for subscription to the public, but confines its shareholders usually to members of one family or their friends; and

3. Whose regulations prevent its shareholders from transferring their shares to any person they please.

Any other company is a public company even though it does not in fact make an offer of its shares to the public, but in practice a public company nearly always makes a public issue of shares with the result that the money invested in it belongs to a large number of persons, the vast majority of whom have no knowledge of the Directors who control the company and handle their money.

A Private company is frequently nothing more or less than a kind of family concern, usually the result of the conversion into a company of some private business, and provision is often made to prevent anyone but a member of the family holding the shares. Private companies are also widely used in order to reduce death duties. Public companies have to make their affairs much more public than private companies for the protection of the shareholders.

How to form a Company.—The first step in the formation of a company is to decide whether a public or private company is best suited to the purposes in view. The preliminary steps will be carried out by persons called promoters, who fulfil a very necessary function. Until a company has actually been brought into existence as a legal person, it can do no acts for itself nor can it have agents to act for it; for a thing which does not exist cannot give authority to agents, and so the promoters' business is to take all the preliminary steps necessary to bring the company into existence. These steps will vary in different cases, but will usually include securing expert reports, or the valuation of any business which it is proposed the company should purchase and carry on; negotiating the purchase price with the persons who at present own the business; and ascertaining the amount of money which will be required to buy and carry on the business, including the purchase price, working capital, preliminary expenses of forming the company (government duty printing professional accounts and lawyers' fees etc.) and reserves.

On the amount necessary for these purposes will depend how much money the company will need to have in shares, i.e. its capital. It may be proposed to raise some of the money not by shares but by borrowing on the security of debentures and in such a case the amount of capital will be reduced.

These preliminary steps are really very important because it is impossible for a company to carry on if in its early stages it is short of ready money, and many companies have failed for this very reason.

The Company comes into existence.—When all these matters have been arranged the promoters are ready to take the final steps of bringing the company into existence by registering certain documents at the office of the Registrar of Companies in London or Edinburgh, when on the payment of certain fees a certificate of incorporation will be given, and the new legal person will be brought into existence.

Memorandum and Articles.—The documents which have to be registered are the Memorandum of Association (q.v.) and Articles of Association (q.v.). The Memorandum is by far the most important document relating to the company because in it are set out the things which the company is to have power to do, and, as has been seen above, the company will not have power to do anything unless it is contained in the Memorandum. (See ULTRA VIRES.) The Articles control the internal management of the company and deal with such matters as voting rights, powers of directors, etc.

The Memorandum is signed by the persons forming the company who must be at least seven in number in the case of a public company and two in the case of a private company. The persons who sign it are the first shareholders and are called the subscribers.

Certain other documents must also be lodged with the registrar of companies at the time of incorporation, and these include a prospectus, a list of directors and contracts by them agreeing to take up the shares necessary to qualify them to act as directors (see QUALIFICATION SHARES) in the case of public companies, and, in the case of both public and private companies, a statement of the capital, the address of the registered office (which is the place where the company legally resides) and a statutory declaration (i.e. solemn statement) by a solicitor or director or the secretary that all the requirements of the Act relating to companies have been complied with.

Commencement of Business.—A Company is not entitled to start carrying on its business as soon as it is brought into existence unless it is a private company. Every public company must first obtain from the Registrar of Companies a certificate entitling it to do so. This will not be granted until shares payable in cash up to the amount of the minimum subscription (q.v.) (i.e. the lowest amount which it is necessary to receive from the public before the company can hope to carry on its business successfully) have been applied for, and every director has paid on every share which he holds, and for which he is liable to pay in cash the same amount as members of the public are required to pay at the time the shares are applied for, and also at the time when they are allotted. A statutory declaration must be made to this effect. If the company has issued a prospectus this must have been filed with the Registrar of Companies and if there has been no prospectus because no issue of shares has been made to the public, a statement in lieu of prospectus must be filed giving much the same information as the prospectus. Until this certificate to commence business has been obtained no shares may be allotted to shareholders who may have applied for them.

While any seven persons (or two in the case of a private company) may form a company, there are certain limits to the numbers of persons who can carry on business without forming themselves into a company as a separate legal person. Not more than 20 persons can carry on business as partners and the limit is 10 in the case of companies engaged in banking. (See DEBENTURES; DIRECTORS; DIVIDENDS; MEETINGS; MEMORANDUM OF ASSOCIATION; NAME [COMPANY]; PROSPECTUS; SHARES; WINDING-UP.)

COMPANIES (SCOTS LAW).—

The law of Companies in Scotland is in most respects the same as in England. Registration of all documents required to be lodged with the Registrar of Companies is made in Edinburgh at the office of the Registrar there and not in London. (See DEBENTURES; LIEN [COMPANIES].)

COMPANY PROMOTER.—Until a

company has been registered it has got no legal personality—i.e. cannot enter into any contracts, or acquire any rights or liabilities. (See COMPANIES.) Thus it cannot do any acts for itself as it is not yet in existence. It is therefore necessary that there should be some persons who will carry out the many preliminary acts, such as the preparation of the Memorandum (q.v.) and Articles of Association (q.v.) and the arrangements necessary for making any public issue of the shares—e.g. the preparation of the prospectus (q.v.). Such persons are known as the Promoters of the company and they fulfil a very useful function. The law allows them to make what profit they please out of the transactions they enter into in forming the company, but requires that their profit should not be secret, but should be disclosed to the company, either to a board of Directors who are independent of the Promoters—i.e. not their nominees, or to the shareholders themselves. Thus there is no objection to a promoter buying property at a low price and selling it again to the company at a high price, but the fact that he has done so must be disclosed in the prospectus, so that all persons who may take shares in the company may be aware of it. In this respect the promoters are in the position of trustees in much the same way as are directors. In many cases in practice the promoters later become the first directors of the company. (See COMPANIES; PROSPECTUS.)

COMPENSATION.—When a person

has been injured, and the court holds that he has been injured through the fault of some other person, it will either order that person to put the injured one back in the position he originally occupied, or if that is not possible, to pay him some sum by way of compensation. It is on this basis that damages are awarded to the successful litigant. Injuries do not necessarily mean injuries to the person; thus in libel or slander the injuries are to the reputation, and there are many cases where a man's property may be injured. For all such injuries, if wrongfully occasioned, he is entitled to compensation.

Position when Person entitled to Compensation dies.—In such a case, unless the wrongful injury is to the dead man's property, no compensation can be recovered. If a man is injured in his person or reputation and then dies, his representatives cannot recover anything, because it is the law that his right of action dies with him. The only exception is when a man is killed through the wrongful act of another. In this case if he has any relatives who were dependent for their livelihood upon him, they are entitled to compensation.

There are other cases in which the law allows compensation to be awarded. If a workman is killed or injured in the course of his employment he, or his dependents in a fatal case, are entitled to compensation. A tenant is entitled to compensation from his landlord for any improvements he may effect upon the premises let to him.

Where land is compulsorily taken over by some body or person by reason of an act of parliament, the original owner is, of course, entitled to compensation, and where a public house is closed on the grounds of redundancy all those interested in the house will be similarly entitled to compensation. (See DAMAGES; LANDLORD AND TENANT; WORKMEN'S COMPENSATION ACT.)

COMPENSATION AUTHORITY. —When the licensing justices of a district decide that a licensed house is no longer required they cannot themselves take away its licence but must refer the matter to the Compensation Authority. But in the case of an on-licence existing on August 15th 1904 in which (i) the premises have been ill-conducted; (ii) are structurally unsuitable; (iii) the licence holder is unfitted to hold a licence; (iv) a renewal of the licence would be void; and in the case of a beerhouse licence existing before 1st May 1869 (i) where the holder of the licence cannot, on renewal, produce satisfactory evidence of good character; (ii) the house or an adjacent house owned by the licence holder is of a disorderly character; (iii) the holder has forfeited a previous licence for misconduct; or (iv) is not qualified in law to hold one, the justices can themselves take away the licence.

Justices also need not refer to the Authority new on-licences, i.e. those granted after August 15th 1904, or beerhouse licences granted after 1st May 1869 and need not refer an off-licence, or an on-licence for the sale of wine and sweets alone, but can themselves deal with such licences. When the justices refer a licence, notice of objection must have been given to the licence holder at renewal and he must have an opportunity of giving sworn evidence before them. The Compensation Authority is the Quarter Sessions. They hold three meetings—the Preliminary Meeting held before the last day of May when reports on referred houses from the licensing justices are considered, (the chairman of the referring justices usually attends such a meeting to consult with the authority); next comes the Principal Meeting, where all persons interested in the referred licence are heard and evidence that the licence is not required is taken; it is then decided whether the licence is to be extinguished, finally there is the Supplemental Meeting where the persons entitled to compensation are ascertained, the amount of the compensation is approved when agreed, and the shares are settled.

The Amount of Compensation payable when a Licence is taken away.—This is a sum equal to the difference in value of the premises licensed and unlicensed and including the amount of depreciation of trade fixtures arising by reason of the refusal to renew the licence. If the premises are owned by a brewer and let to the tenant as a tied house at less than a full rent, the rent payable and the profits derived from the sale of liquor on the premises forms the basis of valuation of the premises licensed. (See INTOXICATING LIQUOR; MONOPOLY VALUE; REDUNDANCY LIST; RENEWAL AND TRANSFER OF JUSTICES' LICENCES.)

COMPETITIONS.—The winner of a competition is entitled to recover the prize unless the competition amounted to a wagering contract or a lottery. When, therefore, the competition involves the exercise of skill and does not depend upon chance, and when the competitors themselves contribute nothing towards the prize, there will be no doubt that the winner can recover his prize; but when chance plays a part or the competitors contribute, there may be a possibility that the competition is a wagering contract and unenforceable. If the prize is a monetary prize, it will be recoverable in the same way as an ordinary debt; if it is not monetary, an action for damages for breach of contract will lie, or an action for specific performance. A condition that the editor's decision shall be final is binding, and his decision can be attacked only on the grounds that it was given fraudulently or was not given at all (e.g. if it could be proved that he never opened the envelope in which the competitor's solution was contained). (See SPECIAL SUPPLEMENT "GAMBLING.")

COMPOSITION.—A composition is an arrangement under which the creditors of a debtor agree to accept so much in the £

of their debts, usually as an alternative to making the debtor bankrupt. A composition is frequently proposed by the debtor at the first meeting of the creditors held after the making of the receiving order or at a later meeting after the adjudication order has been made. (*See* BANKRUPTCY; DEED OF ARRANGEMENT; TRUSTEE IN BANKRUPTCY.)

COMPOUNDING A FELONY.— When a felony has been committed anyone who was injured by it but who nevertheless agrees with the felon that he will not prosecute him, is said to compound a felony. A familiar example of this is an agreement by a person from whom goods have been stolen to take them back from the thief or receiver without asking any questions. Compounding a felony is a criminal offence and renders the offender liable to imprisonment. If he receives money from the felon in consideration of not prosecuting, the offence, of course, becomes more serious.

CONCEALMENT OF BIRTH.— The birth of every child must be registered whether it is born alive or dead. When a child is born dead, or dies immediately, it is a serious crime to attempt to conceal the birth by failing to register it. If this were not so there would be nothing to prevent people from secretly disposing of unwanted babies. It is not necessary to register a miscarriage, but where a dead child is born so far developed that it would have had a reasonable chance of surviving if it had been born alive, it must be registered as still-born.

A woman who tries to dispose secretly of a living child and so causes its death is guilty of murder or infanticide; but if the child died before she got rid of it she can be sent to prison with hard labour for concealment of birth. Where a child survives, failure to register its birth is not so serious and only involves a fine. Registration must be made at the local registry of births and deaths. No fee is required. Where a still-birth is registered, there must be a certificate by a doctor or midwife or else a declaration that none was present.

CONDITION.— A condition is a promise made by one party to a contract, either set out in the contract or implied by law, which is considered to be so vital to the contract that, if it is not fulfilled, the other party is entitled to treat the contract as never having been made and to refuse to carry out his part of the bargain. It is distinguished from a warranty (q.v.) which is a term in a contract not of so great importance to the parties. If a warranty is broken by one of the parties, the other cannot refuse to carry out his side of the bargain but he may sue the other party for the damages which have been caused to him through the warranty being broken. Where a condition has been broken, the person who is entitled to treat the contract at an end need not do so unless he wishes but instead may fulfill his part of the bargain and claim damages. If he does this he is said to be treating the condition as a warranty. Whether a term is a condition or a warranty will depend entirely on the importance which the parties attach to it in their contract. It does not matter how they describe the term in the contract itself. They may set it out in the contract and describe it as a warranty and yet the Court may come to the conclusion that it is in reality a condition.

Precedent.— A condition may either be precedent or subsequent. A condition precedent occurs where the parties agree that one of them is to be liable to do something only if the other has first performed *his* obligations. If that other has failed to perform what he should have done then the first party never becomes liable under the contract. Instances of conditions precedent are to be found in Insurance Policies where the statements made on the proposal form by the person insured are stated by the Policy to be conditions precedent and the basis of the liability of the Insurance Company. If these statements turn out to be untrue, then a condition precedent has not been fulfilled and the Insurance Company's liability does not arise.

Subsequent.— A condition subsequent is found where parties agree that they shall be liable *until* a certain event happens. When this event happens the parties ceased to be liable to one another but they are liable for everything that may have taken place until the happening of the event. An illustration of this is to be found in the cesser clause in a Charter party, i.e. one under which the Charterer and shipowner agree that the Charterer's liability for the freight shall cease as soon as a cargo is loaded. Once this has happened the shipowner cannot claim against the charterer for the freight, because the condition has taken place on which as the parties agreed the liability of the charterer should cease. (*See* CONTRACT; SALE OF GOODS.)

CONDITIONAL FEE.—In the early part of the 13th century landowners who desired to settle their land tried to do so by means of a conveyance expressed to be to X and his descendants (technically to the heirs of his body) with the intention that the first recipient (X) and his heirs should all have interests in the land and enjoy the use of it, but should never be able to sell it. The Judges, however, placed a different construction upon such a conveyance; they decided that the use of such words gave the first recipient the absolute ownership of the land subject only to the condition that he should have a child, and that as soon as a child was born the condition was complied with. The interest which the first recipient had in the land until a child was born was called a conditional fee because he had the fee simple (absolute ownership) upon condition. This construction entirely defeated the intention of the landowners for it meant that the children never acquired any interest or ownership over the land and that as soon as one was born its father (the first recipient) could sell the land, so they procured the passing of the Statute of Westminster II "De Donis Conditionalibus" which enacted that the use of such words should create an estate tail. (*See* ESTATE TAIL; FEE SIMPLE.)

CONDITIONS OF SALE.—On a sale of land by auction the seller, or "Vendor" must set out in detail the terms subject to which the land is offered for sale. In particular he must be careful to disclose any matters in relation to the " title," that is to say, the history, of the property, which might affect an intending Purchaser in deciding whether or not to bid for the same. The Conditions of Sale are printed in one document with the "Particulars of Sale," which describe the property, and this document forms the Contract of Sale. After having bought, the Purchaser signs a copy, which he hands to the Auctioneer and pays a deposit on the purchase price. In return he receives another copy signed and receipted by the Auctioneer as agent for the Vendor. If it subsequently transpires that the Condi-

tions of Sale were incomplete, or inaccurate in any material respect, the Purchaser may have a right to rescind the Contract, that is, refuse to go on with the sale, or to claim damages or both. (*See also* SALE OF LAND.)

CONDONATION. — This means the forgiveness of an offence and the reinstatement of the offender. In practice it is confined to matrimonial offences and is constantly referred to in divorce cases. Condonation is a good answer to proceedings for divorce or judicial separation; but for it to be of value the injured party must have had full knowledge of all the circumstances at the time when he or she condoned the matrimonial offence. Obviously a person cannot condone what he does not know. On the other hand condonement is regarded as being dependent upon the offending party not repeating the offence, and the repetition of a matrimonial offence will revive any previous offence although condoned. (*See* SPECIAL SUPPLEMENT " DIVORCE.")

CONDUCT MONEY.—When a Subpœna is served upon a witness, the witness should be given by the person who serves it a sum of money sufficient to pay for his travelling and other expenses necessary to reach the Court at which he is to give evidence. This is called conduct money. A subpœna is not properly served unless conduct money is tendered with it. (*See* SUBPŒNA.)

CONFERENCE.—A Conference is a meeting at which a solicitor, either with or without his client, attends to confer with a barrister. Conferences usually take place at the barrister's chambers, but in an emergency are held elsewhere; indeed, sometimes they take place in the precincts of the Court itself. (*See* CONSULTATION.)

CONFESSION AND AVOIDANCE. —This expression is used in connection with legal pleadings, that is to say, the statements made by the parties to an action setting out their respective cases. When the one charged admits what is alleged against him, but sets up some new matter in order to deprive it of its legal effect, he is said to "confess and avoid." (*See* PLEADINGS.)

CONFESSIONAL.—No statement made in the confessional, whether it be of the Established or of the Roman Catholic Church, is privileged from disclosure in a

Court of Law. A priest can be compelled by the Judge to state what he has been told, though in practice the right to force him to do so probably would not be exercised.

CONFESSIONS.—English law examines very closely evidence of a confession by a prisoner. Before a confession can be received in evidence the prosecution must prove that it was a free and voluntary one, that is to say, that it was not made from fear, or induced by a promise of favour. The use of physical violence, of course, renders a confession procured by it quite inadmissible, and so does any threat or promise held out by any person having power to influence the proceedings in respect of which the confession is made. Indeed, so strict is the law in its protection of prisoners, that once a threat or promise has been made, any confession by the prisoner thereafter is inadmissible unless it be shewn that the effect of the threat or promise has been completely removed from his or her mind.

In order to ensure that statements made by prisoners on their arrest are legally admissible in evidence, it has been judicially laid down that a police officer, on formally charging a prisoner, should use to him the following form of words, "Do you wish to say anything in answer to the charge? You need not say anything if you do not wish, but if you do say anything it will be taken down and may be used in evidence." (*See* SPECIAL SUPPLEMENT "POLICE.")

CONFIDENCE TRICK.—The confidence trick is a form of obtaining money by false pretences. It is practised in many ways but in essence it is usually the same. Two or more confederates get into conversation with some stranger, usually one who is unfamiliar with the country and who appears to be in possession of money. They then inform him that they know of some means of obtaining easily some large sum of money. A familiar form is to tell him that they are entitled under some legacy to receive a large payment. They suggest to him that he might perhaps come into the venture which will entitle them to receive this fortune. They then raise the question of confidence. Confederate A says that really he does not know Confederate B any more than he knows their intended victim, and they discuss methods of testing the honesty of all of them. They suggest that the victim's honesty should be tested by their allowing him to hold in his possession for a short time some large sum of money or valuable thing. They hand to him for safe custody a package which they declare to contain bank notes or something else of a valuable kind, and then they leave him for a short period. The victim, glad to have his honesty tested in this way, duly meets them at an appointed place with the package, which he of course believes to be valuable but which in fact usually contains nothing more than useless pieces of paper.

It is then suggested that the victim having been entrusted by the confederates with valuables should return the compliment and entrust his valuables to them. If the trick succeeds, the victim will then hand his note case to the confederates and arrange to meet them a short time later. Of course he arrives there but the confederates do not. It is always a matter of comment that this trick, though so patently obvious when described and so well known, nevertheless persists and is frequently successful. Anyone who is approached with a trick of this kind should at once inform the police.

CONFIRMATION OF JUSTICES' LICENCE.—All new justices' licences, whether on or off, all provisional grants of such licences, all ordinary removals (*see* INTOXICATING LIQUOR), and provisional ordinary removals will require confirmation after being granted by the local justices. The Confirming Authority is the Quarter Sessions who must delegate their power to a committee appointed by them. In boroughs the Confirming Authority is the whole body of borough justices; but if there are less than ten such justices then the Authority is a joint committee of three borough and three county justices.

The procedure before the Authority is really a re-hearing of the application, but licences may not be granted to persons other than the original grantee. Only those who opposed the grant before the licensing justices can oppose on confirmation. The application for confirmation cannot be heard till twenty-one days at least have expired since the grant of the licence. (*See* INTOXICATING LIQUOR.)

CONFLICT OF LAWS.—It sometimes happens that a case which comes before an English Court has a certain foreign element in it; as, for example, where one or both of the parties are foreigners, or the case has to do with some transaction carried out, or wrong done, in a foreign country. In such a case the Judge has to answer two, and sometimes three, questions, namely:

1. Is the case one which the English Courts, according to English law, have the right to try?

2. If so, which country's laws are to be referred to in deciding the case?

and, in cases where a foreign Court has already given a judgment on the matter:

3. Had the Court which gave judgment the right, according to English law, to do so?

Such a state of affairs is said to give rise to a "conflict of laws," and the rules by which a Judge in such a case comes to a decision, together make up the body of law known as Private International Law. The reason for the word "Private" in this name is to distinguish this body of law from Public International Law (usually called simply International Law), which deals largely with the relations between foreign states (through their governments) rather than those between individuals of different nationalities.

Six Main Principles.—There are six main principles which guide the English Courts when considering question of Private International Law, namely:—

1. Any right which has been duly acquired under the law of any civilized country is recognized in the English Courts, but no other so-called rights.

2. A right which is recognized under [1] (above) will not be enforced if:

(a) it runs counter to any Act passed by Parliament in which it is stated that it to have effect outside England, or

(b) it is inconsistent with the principles of English law or with moral rules which are upheld by English law, or would interfere with the maintenance of English political or judicial institutions, or

(c) it involves interfering with the authority of a foreign state within its own borders.

3. The Courts of any country may only deal with those matters on which they can give an effective judgment, and the country whose courts can give the most effective judgment has the right to hear the case.

4. The Courts of any country have juris-

diction over any person who voluntarily submits to the jurisdiction.

5. When a right under foreign law is recognized by the English Courts, the effects of that right must be decided according to the law of the country where the right was acquired.

6. When persons have entered into a transaction with the intention that it shall be governed by the law of a particular country, then the legal effect of that transaction must be decided according to the law which they agreed should be binding.

These are the general principles, though there are numerous detailed rules which have grown up around them. (*See also* INTERNATIONAL LAW.)

CONJUGAL RIGHTS; CONNIVANCE. — (*See* SPECIAL SUPPLEMENT "DIVORCE.")

CONSENT, Age Of.—If a man is accused of committing a sexual offence against a girl under sixteen or of enticing her away from her parents, it is no defence for him to say that she consented to the act. The law does not regard a girl as competent to have a will of her own in these matters until she has reached the age of sixteen. Hence sixteen is known as the age of consent. But even above that age her consent is no defence for the man if he obtained it by deceiving her as to the nature of the act.

CONSIDERATION.—It is a principle of English law that unless an agreement is made under seal (*see* DEEDS), it is not a valid contract or enforceable in law unless each of the parties to the contract receives a benefit in return for the promise that he makes.

A promise in return for which the person making the promise does not receive a benefit, is called a "gratuitous promise," and it creates no rights or obligations unless it has been fully carried out or "executed." Thus a mere gratuitous promise to pay £100 is not enforceable by the person to whom the promise is made, unless in return for that promise he also promises to confer a benefit upon the person who makes the promise. Naturally, if the promise to pay £100 is followed by the actual handing over of the £100, this is a perfectly valid gift and the person who received the £100 cannot be compelled to hand it back; but until it has been actually handed over there is no enforceable obligation upon the person who has made the promise to do so.

The benefit which each party to a valid contract receives from the contract is known in law as "consideration," and it is an essential of every valid contract which is not under seal that there should be consideration for the promise made by each party to the contract.

Consideration in law may take many forms. It may be a right, profit, interest or any other benefit accruing to one party, or a forbearance, or loss, or a responsibility undertaken by the other. A few examples may make this more clear. In a contract for the sale of goods the consideration given by the seller is the goods themselves, the consideration given by the buyer is the price to be paid for the goods. In a contract for doing work, such as gardening, the consideration given by the gardener is the work that he does, the consideration given by the employer the wages given for the work done. In a contract of fire insurance the consideration given by the policy holder is the premiums on the policy; by the insurance company it is the responsibility that they undertake to pay for any damage that may be done by fire. In an agreement whereby a claim under the Workmen's Compensation Act (q.v.) is settled without going to court, the consideration given by the employer is the sum of money offered as compensation, the consideration given by the injured workman is the forbearance to bring his claim in the ordinary way before a County Court Judge.

In every valid contract, it is easy to see that there is consideration given by both parties to the contract, but there are some cases which are at first sight confusing, because of the view that the law takes as to what is, and what is not, good consideration.

In the first place it must be noticed that the consideration must be between the parties to the contract. Suppose that A says to B: "I will give you £50, if C pays me the debt that he owes me." This is a mere unenforceable promise since B has given no consideration for it. Again, if A says to B: "If you will give me £50, I will let C off his debt of £100 which he owes me." This is a promise which B may accept, and may insist that A shall release

C from his debt because he has given consideration for it, but C himself cannot enforce it against A even if B does pay the £50, because C has not given any consideration for the promise to release his debt.

In the second place the consideration must be of some legal value. It is not necessary that it should be of a reasonable value compared with the promise, but it must be some value which is measurable. If the consideration be money, it may be the smallest coin in the realm. Thus a promise of A to B: "I will give you a motor-car if you will give me a farthing" will be a contract, if accepted by B, because B is giving a farthing as consideration, and this is valuable consideration in the eyes of the law.

The consideration need not be money or goods: it may be the doing of an act or the forbearance to do something. Thus a promise of A to B: "I will give you £100 if you will walk down the road with me" will be a valid contract if B accepts, for by walking down the road he is doing something which he is not already legally bound to do, and that, in the eyes of the law, is valuable consideration.

On the other hand, a mere moral motive, however admirable, is not consideration valuable in the eyes of the law. Cases of this kind arise where a person wishes to reward another person for services which have been rendered in the past. If A, being under a strong moral obligation to his brother, promises to pay him money, the brother cannot enforce that promise because the mere moral obligation is not enough, and if, for example, A dies before he pays over the money, the brother cannot, in law, recover it from the executors.

So also, the consideration must be a present consideration. If A has performed a great service for B, such as saving his life, and B promises to give A a sum of money for having done so, nevertheless A cannot enforce the promise if B fails to pay over the money because the consideration is past. Naturally, once the money has been paid over it is a valid gift, but until it is paid over, it is a mere unenforceable promise, for the law takes no account of past benefits.

Further, the consideration must be the doing or the promise to do something more than .the promisor was already legally bound to do. If A promises to accept the sum of £50 in settlement of B's debt to him of £100, and B accepts the offer and pays his £50, A can still continue to sue for the extra £50, because the only consideration for A's offer to accept £50 in settlement of B's debt was the payment of the £50 which B was already legally obliged to pay; and the performance of a legal obligation that is already present is not consideration in the eyes of the law. It would be otherwise if B promised to pay the sum of £50 even one day earlier than the debt of £100 was due, for in that case B would be doing something which he was not already under a legal obligation to do. (*See* Contract.)

CONSISTORY COURT.—A Consistory Court is the Ecclesiastical Court of a diocese; the Chancellor of the diocese is the Judge, holding office for life (*see also* Diocese). In some cases, the Bishop is entitled to take a matter out of the hands of the Chancellor, and himself act as Judge. A Surrogate may be appointed by the Chancellor as his substitute. The Court has various functions, including the trial of ecclesiastical offences under the Clergy Discipline Act, 1892, and the hearing of petitions for faculties (*see* Faculty). For the trial of the above-mentioned offences, a body of five "assessors" may be required by either party to act in much the same capacity as a jury in any ordinary civil Court. Appeal lies in such cases to the Provincial Court, but frequently they are sent by the Bishop directly to the Provincial Court before they have time to come on for hearing in the Consistory Court.

The Chancellor holds his Court in public, unlike the tribunals of the dissenting churches in similar cases. This much-criticized procedure is followed on the ground that the Church of England is the Established Church of this country to which every person has the right to belong, and to the disciplinary proceedings of which every person should, in the interests of justice, have a right of entry. (*See* Church of England; Diocese; Provincial Court; Surrogate.)

CONSOLIDATION OF ACTIONS. —Where two separate actions are brought which concern the same matter and arise out of the same set of circumstances, the Court may order them to be tried at the same time, that is, to be consolidated. This is an obvious saving of time and money, for if the actions were not consolidated, the same evidence would have to be called and the same legal points considered on two separate occasions. Thus, if A and B collide in their motor cars, and A sues B for the damage he has suffered in one action and B sues A for his damage in another action, the two actions would be consolidated, for the same questions would have to be considered in each, namely, who was responsible for the accident?

CONSOLIDATION OF MORTGAGES.—This is a right which is given by Equity to a mortgagee of land who holds more than one mortgage on different properties from the same mortgagor. It enables him to refuse to permit the mortgagor to redeem (by repaying the money borrowed) one of the mortgages unless, at the same time, he redeems the other or others.

Originally to prevent hardship.— It was originally introduced as a concession in hard cases. If A borrowed £500 on a mortgage of Black Acre and £500 on a mortgage of White Acre from B (the mortgagee), and Black Acre then increased in value till it was worth £800 while White Acre decreased until it was only worth £250, A would naturally be anxious to redeem the mortgage on Black Acre by paying off the £500 he had borrowed on it and becoming unfettered owner; he would also be very loath to redeem White Acre for he would in effect be paying £500 for a property which was only worth £250. This would be a great hardship to B because he would be left with White Acre, valued at £250, as security for a debt of £500; so it was decided that, if A tried to redeem Black Acre, B can refuse to allow him to do so unless at the same time he redeems White Acre. B is said to consolidate the mortgages on Black and White Acres.

Not a question of hardship now.— For many years now, the right to consolidate has been held to exist without any reference being made to the hardships of individual cases; B, in the case set out above, would be just as much entitled to consolidate Black Acre with White Acre—that is, to refuse to allow A to redeem the latter unless he also redeemed the former—though here it is obvious that all the hardship would be on A. The right to consolidate is confined to cases where the mortgages were all made *by* the same person, but it is not necessary that they should all have been made *to* the same person or should not have changed hands since then. It exists in two classes of cases:

(*a*) Where all the mortgages were made between the parties and have not changed hands since.

(*b*) Where the mortgages were made between the same parties but at some later date have changed hands. The first class of case has already been discussed; the second may give rise to great complications. There are two important points: the person who seeks to consolidate two or more mortgages must himself be the owner of them at the time when he does so, but on the other hand it is not necessary that the person against whom the mortgages are consolidated should still be (or have ever been) the owner of all the equities of redemption—as the mortgagor's interest is called.

Where mortgages have changed hands.—Class (*b*) can therefore be subdivided into two further classes, namely:—

(i) Where all the mortgages are held by one person and all the equities of redemption by another. Thus, if A mortgages Black Acre to B and then also mortgages White Acre to B, and A subsequently sells both his equities of redemption to X, and B sells both his mortgages to Y, Y can consolidate Black Acre with White Acre or vice versa against X—can force him, that is, if he wishes to redeem one, to redeem the other at the same time.

(ii) Where all the mortgages are held by one person but the equities of redemption are now held by different persons.

If, instead of selling both his equities of redemption to X, A had only sold him one and had retained the other, or had sold it to W, Y's right to consolidate would still remain for the mortgages are still held by one person (Y), and, though the equities of redemption are *now* held by different persons (X and W), they have both been held at the same time by *one* person and that is all that the rule requires. The result is curious; if X wishes to redeem the property he has bought from A, Y can refuse to permit him to do so unless he also redeems the mortgage on the property which was sold to W, although

it is not X but W who is the owner of the equity of redemption over it. Similarly, if W tries to redeem his mortgage he may be forced to redeem X's as well. If either of them is forced to redeem the other's mortgage in order to be able to redeem his own, he will, so far as the other is concerned, step into the shoes of the mortgagee—Y; if W tries to redeem his mortgage and Y consolidates X's against him, then, if W decides to pay them both off to redeem his own, W will become X's mortgagee in the place of Y who will drop out altogether.

The cardinal rule for all questions of consolidation has been stated by the House of Lords, "Consolidation is only allowed if, at the date when redemption is sought, all the mortgages, having originally been made by one person, are vested in one person and all the equities (of redemption) in one person, or if, after these two things have once happened, the equities of redemption have become separated."

The right to consolidate cannot now be asserted unless it is expressly mentioned in at least one of the mortgages concerned; it need not, however, be mentioned in them all. (*See* MORTGAGE.)

CONSPIRACY, CRIMINAL. — If two or more persons agree together to do an act which is unlawful or to do a lawful act by unlawful means, such an agreement constitutes the offence of Conspiracy in the eyes of the criminal law. The essence of the offence is the conspiring or agreeing together to do some unlawful act, or to do a lawful act by unlawful means, and the offence is still committed even if no actual step is taken in furtherance of the agreement, or, as the law says, even if the conspiracy is not "evidenced by an overt act."

The offence cannot exist without the agreement together of two or more persons, and it is interesting and important to note that a husband and wife, without the addition of any other person, cannot be charged with conspiracy, because the law regards them as one person. If two persons are charged with conspiring together they must both be convicted or both acquitted, and this is true even if one of them has pleaded guilty. One may be convicted and one acquitted, however, if they are charged with conspiring with other persons unknown, and the jury find that one prisoner did conspire with a person unknown.

Conspiracy is what is called an "indictable misdemeanour" that is to say it is an offence which is only triable by a jury and not a magistrate. This is so even if the conspiracy was to commit an offence which is triable by a magistrate.

An agreement by two or more persons to do *any* act which is unlawful is a conspiracy. An important form of conspiracy is to cheat and defraud, such as the recent conspiracy to defraud insurance companies by setting fire to business premises. Other forms are conspiracy to defeat the ends of justice by preventing an important witness from attending a trial; conspiracy to coerce employers or workmen into adopting a particular course of action; conspiracy to murder; conspiracy to injure an individual by wrongful acts otherwise than by actual fraud, for example, conspiring to make pirated music and sell it, and so obtain the profits to which the conspirators have no right.

The most serious is a conspiracy to murder or to incite to murder, and persons who are found guilty of such an offence are liable to be sent to penal servitude for ten years. The offence of inciting to murder was held to have been committed by writing newspaper articles exulting in the assassination of a king and commending the example to other revolutionists.

It is important to observe that persons may be charged with the offence of conspiracy even if the act, which they agreed together to do, would not have been an offence if done by an individual. The facts of an interesting case will make this clear. A woman was charged with conspiring with other persons to administer drugs to herself with intent to procure abortion, she believing that she was pregnant. In actual fact she was not pregnant and therefore could not have been charged with attempting herself to procure abortion, yet she was rightly charged for conspiring with others to commit the offence, the conspiracy itself being the unlawful act.

The most difficult class of conspiracy to decide is that in which workmen or employers have combined together to do an injury to a third party to further what they consider to be their trade interest.

Since the year 1871 it has been legal for workmen to protect their interests by forming unions in order to make terms with their employers. In pursuance of this object the workmen may employ the weapon of a strike, but they must not use it in such a way as to interfere with workmen who desire to remain outside the union, nor to interfere with the right of such men to dispose of their labour as they think fit. There are, of necessity, certain limits set by the law to what the workmen may do in combination, and if they accompany their lawful actions such as strikes or picketing by violence or threats, then they may find themselves charged with conspiracy. A large measure of immunity for acts done in furtherance of a trade dispute has been granted to trade unions by various Acts of Parliament; and the cases where combinations of persons have been charged with conspiracy to commit an offence during a trade disturbance have nearly always been cases where the conspiracy charged was that of doing an unlawful act, for example an assault. The Criminal Law governing the subject of conspiracy is more straightforward, and presents much less difficulty in practice, than the law relating to conspiracy as a civil wrong which entitles the injured person to claim damages. (*See* COMBINATION ACTS.)

Civil.—A doubtful point.—The Criminal Law knows the offence of conspiracy, but the Civil Courts have not yet decided whether conspiring together to inflict an injury on a third person can be the subject of an action. The question which has not yet been decided is this—"Can two or more persons ever be joint wrong-doers and liable to an action by the person injured, by doing an act together in accordance with an agreement previously made between them, if such act, without any agreement to act jointly, would have been perfectly lawful for them to do?" That is to say, can the act of combining to do an act be wrongful, when the act, if done by a single individual, would be lawful. The cases which have been decided go to show that it is the aggravated damage caused by the combination, and not the actual combining, which has influenced the Courts.

The majority of the cases upon the subject have been cases in which an individual trader has brought an action against a trade combine for damages for conspiring together to ruin him in his business. The trade combine defend themselves by saying that their action was taken to protect their trade interests, and the individual trader has then to prove that their real purpose was to ruin him and not to protect their trade interests; or, put in another way, he must prove that the combine was actuated by malice against him.

This distinction is not an easy one and it will be more easily understood by the example of two contrasting cases. Robinson was a baker who employed among others a non-union man. The union of which his other employees were members requested him to dismiss the non-union employee. Robinson, refused, whereupon the union induced Smith, the best customer of Robinson to cease to deal with him by the threat that if he did not do so, they would call his (Smith's) men out on strike. This was an unlawful action since it deprived Smith and Robinson of freedom of action in the conduct of their business, and the motive of the union was the malicious one of ruining Robinson. Robinson recovered damages from the members of the union.

In the other case, three owners of steamships wishing to cut out a rival who was affecting their trade with an eastern country, offered special cheap rates to shippers who used only their ships. This action was successful in putting the rival out of business, but his claim for damages was unsuccessful, as there was nothing unlawful in what the three traders had combined to do, and what they had done was held to be in furtherance of their trade interests.

Trade Unions enjoy a special protection against law suits brought against them for damages, where the act for which damages are claimed was done in furtherance of a Trade Dispute. This subject is dealt with fully under Trade Union and Trade Dispute. (*See also* BLACK LIST; COMBINATION ACTS; TRADE DISPUTE; TRADE UNION.)

CONSTABLE.—Any member of the police force below the rank of sergeant is a police constable. He is required to be of certain standards of education and physique. He is not sworn in to service for any definite period. His pay normally varies, according to his length of service, from 70/- to 90/- a week.

Any branch of the force may be supplemented, if necessary, by constables from another branch. In addition, ordinary citizens of respectable character may be sworn in as special constables in emergencies, and a reserve of special constables can be maintained permanently in any district. When on duty they have the same powers as ordinary constables. Whether he has a warrant or not, a constable may arrest anyone actually committing or suspected of committing a felony. He may also arrest anyone whom he reasonably suspects of being about to do so, or anyone obstructing him in his duty. There are certain other offences also for which he can arrest without a warrant, but he must state that he is a police constable and name the offence. He can search a house if he has a search warrant. (*See* SPECIAL SUPPLEMENT "POLICE.")

CONSTRUCTION OF DOCUMENTS.—When documents have to be considered in Courts of Law disputes frequently arise as to what they mean. In order to decide these disputes there are certain recognised rules of construction. (*See* MEANING OF DOCUMENTS.)

CONSTRUCTIVE CRIME.—There are many cases in which a person may lawfully be convicted of a crime even though he has no intention of committing that particular crime. In general it may be said that a person sets out to commit a crime at his peril, and if the consequences of his acts turn out to be more serious than he intended he must be held liable for them. For instance, anyone who commits a felony of a violent nature and who, in the course of committing that felony unintentionally kills another, may be convicted of murder. This principle would be applied in the case of a man who, in attempting to kill himself, accidentally killed someone else. Similarly, bandits engaged on a smash and grab raid could, in strict law, be convicted of murder if their motor ran over and killed anyone in the course of the raid.

The principles of constructive crime are not confined to murder. They are applied in the same way to manslaughter. If a person in the course of committing any dangerous crime short of felony unintentionally kills another he may be convicted of manslaughter even though he is not guilty of negligence. (*See* MURDER; MANSLAUGHTER.)

CONSULTATION.—A meeting between two or more barristers to consult in regard to a case is called a "consultation." At a consultation the solicitor who is instructing the barristers attends and in some cases he is accompanied by his client. A consultation usually takes place at the chambers of the senior barrister concerned. (*See* CONFERENCE.)

CONTINGENT REMAINDERS.—

A remainder was a particular kind of estate in land which entitled the person to whom it was given (and who was called the remainder-man) to take the land for life or in fee simple at some time in the future. Thus a gift of land to A for life and then to B gave B a (vested) remainder, i.e. the right to take the land when A's estate, which was called the "particular estate," determines at his death.

A contingent remainder was opposed to a vested remainder and was a gift of a future interest, which might or might not take effect according to whether the condition on which it depended was fulfilled. If the gift in the above case had been to A for life, and then to B (if he is twenty-one), B would have got a contingent remainder until he reached 21; for until then it is not certain whether he will be ready to take the land when A dies. Similarly "to A for life remainder to the heir of B" gives a contingent remainder so long as B is alive, for until his death it is impossible to say who is his heir. The remainder becomes a vested remainder as soon as B reaches 21 in the first case or dies in the latter. Remainders no longer exist as a separate class of estate and the rules relating to them are now obsolete. (*See* REMAINDERS.)

CONTEMPT OF COURT.—There

are many kinds of Contempt of Court. In general—any wilful act or omission calculated to impede the proceedings of a Court or the carrying out of its orders is Contempt of Court. Any person who interrupts proceedings by shouting or other noisy conduct is guilty of Contempt of Court. For a man wilfully to keep his hat on in Court or to smoke is conduct which may amount to contempt. A witness who refuses to give evidence or to answer any proper question is guilty of Contempt of Court.

Contempt may be committed away from the Court building itself. Publicly commenting on the merits of a case before it has been tried and finished, attempting to influence witnesses or members of the jury are examples

of this. Similarly, any interference with an officer of the Court in executing a judgment or order or any wilful refusal to comply with an order amounts to contempt.

Contempt of Court is punishable with a fine and imprisonment. If it is committed in the face of the Court, that is to say, in the presence of the tribunal, the punishment may be inflicted without formal enquiry. If it is not committed in the face of the Court, or if the Court in question is not one having power to punish for contempt, the conduct complained of is investigated by the appropriate Court and an order is then made as to the punishment. In general, inferior Courts have power to deal with contempts in the face of the Court and superior Courts have jurisdiction over any form of contempt.

A person is said to be "committed" or "attached" when sent to prison for contempt. When he earns his release he is said to have "purged his contempt."

CONTRACT.—A contract is the legal

term which describes an agreement between two or more persons whereby rights and obligations are created that are binding in law.

It is not every agreement that is a contract. If A asks B out to dinner and B accepts the invitation, this is not a contract, though it is an agreement; but it was never intended by either party that A should be entitled to damages if B failed to attend the dinner party, and accordingly the agreement lacks that essential characteristic of a contract that it should create rights and obligations that are enforceable in law. In the same way a husband may agree to hand over to his wife a certain portion of his wages each week for the housekeeping, but if he fails to do so the wife cannot enforce the payment of that sum by an action at law, for the agreement is not a contract.

In all these cases it is the intention of the parties that is the vital matter, and as a general rule it may be said that an agreement is not a contract unless the parties to the agreement intend that it shall be enforceable, in the last resort, by the assistance of a Court of Justice. This is far from meaning that, when a person enters into an agreement, it is not enforceable as a contract, merely because he did not think of the possibility that it might end in the Law Courts.

It does mean, however, that the person entering into a contract should intend that he should be bound by the rights that that contract creates.

Requirements of a Contract.—
Under English law there are two factors which must be present in every contract:
(1) An agreement consisting of a communicated offer and acceptance between the parties to the contract.
(2) Form or consideration.

These two factors are technical terms which require further study, and wherever they are present there is the material for a binding legal contract, which may however be unenforceable for one or more of several reasons which are dealt with hereafter.

Offer and Acceptance.—
A contract, whatever kind of, is always made by an offer and an acceptance. One of the parties to the contract, called the promisor, makes an offer to do something, or to refrain from doing something, and the other party to the contract called the promisee, accepts that offer.

The simplest and commonest kind of contract is of the form: "Will you buy my bicycle for £5?" which is the offer; "Yes, I will," which is the acceptance; and a completed contract has been made. More complicated forms of contract involve mutual promises between the parties, as where two men enter into an agreement for partnership which may be contained in a document running into dozens of pages, regulating the whole course of the business which they intend to carry on; but when such a contract has been analysed it will be found to consist of whole series of simple offers and acceptances such as that mentioned above: "Will you do something, if I do something?" the offer; "Yes, I will," the acceptance. Similarly there may be a large number of parties to a contract, as where a member joins a club or benevolent society. In such a case each member is in fact entering into a contract with all the other members to do all those things which the rules lay down, and to abide by the decisions of the rules.

Nature of an Offer.—
An offer which when accepted results in a contract may be made in many different ways. Very frequently it is made by word of mouth, (though certain contracts must be in writing [see below]) as when a housewife offers to engage a servant or a bootmaker to mend a pair of boots.

In most commercial contracts the offer is made in writing, generally by letters passing between the parties. Examples of this are letters written to shops ordering goods, quotations sent in response to enquiries, offers of rewards in advertisements and all the hundred and one agreements that are made in every business.

Perhaps the commonest form of offer in everyday life is the offer that is made, not by word of mouth or by writing, but by conduct or implication. Every time a person steps on to an omnibus he is accepting the implied offer of the bus company to carry him to a destination at the price of the fare. By putting an automatic machine outside his door, the tobacconist is making an implied offer to sell cigarettes to any person who accepts the offer by placing the appropriate coin in the machine, and as a consequence any person who puts a coin in the machine without receiving the goods is entitled to recover his coin from the owner of the machine by an action at law if necessary. Other examples of implied offers are where a doctor or any other person is called in to perform a service which it must be obvious he did not intend to do for nothing. In such a case there is an implied offer to pay a reasonable price for the service, if it is rendered. It must be remembered, however, that the mere doing of a service without the knowledge of the person to whom it is rendered, cannot amount to acceptance of an offer and accordingly create a right to payment, because in such a case there cannot possibly be an offer to accept.

Communication of an Offer.—
It is not sufficient that an offer, whether verbal or in writing, should be made. It must be communicated to the person to whom it is made. This would appear to be merely common sense, but cases occasionally arise where it is a little difficult to determine. Supposing for example that a doctor offered to treat A if A's brother would pay the fee, and A accepted that offer without making any enquiry from his brother, the brother would not be liable for the fees because the offer had not been communicated to him. Another and better example is given by the offer of a reward in a newspaper. If A offers in the newspaper to pay a reward of £10 to the finder of a watch that he has lost, and B who has *not* seen the advertisement

finds the watch and returns it to A, B is not entitled to the reward because the offer has not been communicated to him.

In the same way the whole of the offer must be communicated and it is not sufficient that merely a part should be so. If part of the offer is not communicated, the person who accepts the offer is not bound by the part that he has not seen. An example will make this more clear. Many railway companies issue tickets in which their liability in case of accident is greatly limited by conditions of bye-laws which are not printed on the ticket, but which are referred to in some such words as "Issued subject to the conditions contained in the Company's Bye-laws." If the purchaser of a railway ticket, which is merely a contract between the railway company and the passenger to carry the passenger, reads this notice or ought, if he were reasonably alert, to have read this notice, he will be affected by the bye-laws which he should in such cases read. But if the notice is too obscure for the reasonable man to read, *and* the passenger has not actually seen it, then that part of the offer which limits the liability of the railway company has not been communicated to him and he is not bound by the terms and conditions referred to.

It is perhaps unnecessary to add that the time at which an offer is communicated is the actual time at which it comes to the knowledge of the other party to the contract, or his agent, and thus an offer sent by post is not communicated until it has actually been seen by the promisee or his agent.

Revocation of an Offer.—Until an offer has been accepted there can be no contract, and accordingly the person making the offer can withdraw it at any time before the acceptance without incurring any penalties. Once an acceptance has been made, however, if the promisor wishes to withdraw his offer, even though nothing has been done under the contract, such withdrawal is a breach of contract and renders him liable to what penalties the law decrees.

It is important to remember the possibility that in English law an offer may be withdrawn at any time before acceptance, particularly in cases where the offer is in the nature of a quotation. A quotation of a price is merely an offer to sell goods or to do work at that price and like any other offer can be withdrawn. Accordingly, no person who has received a quotation should enter into another contract, such as a contract for resale, with a third party on reliance on the figures contained in the quotation; for the person who made the quotation is perfectly entitled to withdraw it at any moment before it has been accepted.

It is sometimes of importance in cases where offers are made by correspondence to appreciate the time at which the revocation is made. A revocation, like an offer itself, is not made until it has been communicated to the person to whom the offer was made, or to his agent, or, in the case of a letter, has been delivered at his office during office hours. The importance of this will be appreciated when it is realised that an acceptance of any offer by post dates from the moment that the letter of acceptance passes into the possession of the postman, and accordingly since acceptance puts an end to the possibility of revoking an offer, a revocation may be actually posted before the acceptance, and yet be too late to prevent a valid contract from being made.

It is not necessary that the revocation of the offer should be directly communicated by the person who made the offer. It is sufficient, if before the offer was accepted the promisee knew that it was revoked. For example, if X offers to sell Y a house for £750 and before Y accepts the offer he sells the house to Z and Y knows of this. Y cannot then accept the offer on the grounds that X did not give him notice that the offer has been withdrawn.

Lapse of an Offer.—Although as a general rule an offer remains open until it is either revoked or accepted there are certain cases where it may be said to lapse. Wherever the offeror—i.e. the person making the offer —dies before the acceptance of the offer, it ceases to be binding upon his executors— i.e. those who take his property after his death—while in every case it is safe to say that if an offer is not accepted within a reasonable time the offer lapses—i.e. can no longer be accepted. As to what is a reasonable time naturally depends upon the nature of the contract and a tender or offer to sell perishable foodstuffs would be held to have lapsed earlier than an offer to sell a house. Very often, the time at which an offer will lapse is stated in the offer itself, as, for example, where it is stated "If I do not hear from you by return of post, I shall dispose of the goods elsewhere" or "this offer to remain open for a fortnight."

Quotations and Tenders.—It is important to distinguish between what is an offer and what is merely an invitation to submit an offer. An enquiry as to the price of goods or for a tender from a contractor is merely an invitation to the seller or the contractor to make an offer, and the fact that the seller gives a quotation or the contractor a tender, does not constitute a contract but a mere offer, which can be accepted by the person to whom the quotation or tender is given.

Acceptance.—An offer remains open until it is revoked, lapsed or accepted. The acceptance turns the offer into a contract which creates rights and liabilities which may be enforced by law.

The first essential of an acceptance is that it should correspond with the terms of the offer, otherwise it is not an acceptance but a counter-offer. An example will make this clear. A offers to sell B a motor car for £50. B replies, "I will give you £45." This is clearly not an acceptance but a new offer on the part of B and he can withdraw it until it has been accepted by A.

Again the acceptance must not add a new term to the intended agreement. If A offers to sell the motor car for £50 and B replies "I accept your offer if you will guarantee that its brakes are in good order." This again is not an acceptance even though A is quite willing to guarantee that its brakes are in good order. It is a counter-offer and may be withdrawn at any time before A has accepted it.

Possibly the most difficult question that arises in considering whether a reply to an offer is an acceptance is where there is a reply to the possibility of a formal written contract being drawn up. Most important contracts are drawn up in a formal written instrument after negotiations have been carried out between the parties. In such a case the offer may be thought of as being made by the party who first puts his signature to the final document, and the acceptance as being made by the persons who sign afterwards. At the same time, however, a binding agreement may have been entered into before the written contract was drawn up and this

will be a contract quite independently of the final written document. The difficult question therefore often arises when an acceptance refers to a written document to be drawn up, as to whether it constitutes an acceptance of the offer or a counter offer only. The rule by which this question is decided is simply an application of the general rule that the acceptance must be in the same terms as the offer.

The problem as to what is an acceptance generally arises where a contract is made by correspondence. In such a case the negotiations may continue through many scores of letters, the first being generally enquiries, the later letters being offers and counter-offers. Whether the whole of the correspondence taken together will amount to a contract will depend on whether it is possible to find in the letters a moment at which it is clear that the parties have agreed on all the terms.

Methods of Acceptance.—Just as there are several methods of making an offer, so there are different methods of accepting an offer. It must be remembered, however, that a person making an offer is entitled to stipulate the manner in which it must be accepted as for example "in writing," and a verbal acceptance in such a case would not be an acceptance of the contract. Very often, however, the method of acceptance indicated in the offer is a mere suggestion and if an acceptance is made in some other method before the offer has been revoked the contract will be a binding one.

Where a person stipulates some special method of accepting an offer he must take the risk that such a method involves, and if a person asks that an offer shall be accepted by post he will be bound by the acceptance once it is posted, even if it is never delivered to him.

Except in those cases where the offeror stipulates the manner in which the offer must be accepted, the only necessity is that the acceptance should be communicated to the offeror.

Communication of Acceptance.— An acceptance, like an offer dates from the moment that it is communicated to the offeror. Thus where goods are priced in a shop, the acceptance which creates the completed contract dates from the moment where the customer says, "I'll have that, please," or in the case of a passenger getting on a bus the acceptance and the binding contract date from the moment that he steps on to the bus, for at that moment he accepts the offer of the bus company to carry him for the price of his fare.

There are, however, certain apparent exceptions to the rule that the acceptance must be communicated, and the first of these is where the offeror states, either expressly or by implication, in his offer that he does not require assent to be communicated to him. Examples of this are where rewards are offered in newspapers. Here the offeror does not expect anybody to write to tell him that they accept the offer of the reward. He expects such an offer to be accepted by the person carrying out the conditions of the offer, e.g. finding the missing property, and acceptance of such an offer is made when the conditions have been performed. An equally common example is where a housewife sends a note asking the sweep to call to sweep the chimneys. To this offer to employ the sweep, for that is what it amounts to, she does not expect an acceptance to be communicated to her, but she expects the offer to be accepted by the arrival of the sweep upon her doorstep, and the binding contract dates from that moment.

Careful distinction must be drawn between this case where an offer may be accepted without communication to the offeror, and those cases where the offeror attempts to stipulate that, unless the offer is refused, it will be assumed to be accepted. The motto "silence gives consent" is never true of a contract and in a case where A writes to B—"I will sell you my dog for 40/-. Unless I hear from you I will assume that you will buy it."—B's failure to write to A refusing the offer does not make him liable to buy the dog.

Such cases often arise where a hawker leaves goods at a house on approval with a note to say, that, unless the goods are returned within a week, the householder will be presumed to have bought them. In such a case nothing can make the householder liable to pay for the goods unless he writes and accepts them, or refuses to hand them back to the owner when he calls for them.

Contract by Correspondence.— Another apparent exception to the rule that the acceptance must be communicated to the offeror is where the offer has been made in various letters. Here if the offeror either expressly or impliedly authorises the other party to accept by post, the offer is accepted from the moment that the letter of acceptance is collected in the pillar box in which it is posted. The explanation of this rather strange rule is that the offeror is presumed to have made the post office his agent or servant to receive the acceptance, and the communication of the acceptance dates from the moment that the letter gets into the hands of the collecting postman. The vital importance of this rule will be realized when it is remembered that an offer can be withdrawn at any time before it is accepted, and that the withdrawal of an offer dates from the time that it actually reaches the acceptor. Accordingly it is possible for A to post an acceptance of B's offer at 12 midnight, although B has already posted a letter withdrawing his offer which reached A at 7 a.m. next morning, and the contract will be binding although B withdrew his offer before he knew that A had accepted it.

Consideration.—Although an offer followed by an acceptance generally constitutes a contract, this is only so because, as a general rule, there is present in the contract another element known in law as Consideration (q.v.).

It is a principle of English law that if a person enters into an agreement which, if carried out, will confer a benefit on the other party to the agreement, but will not confer any benefit upon himself, the agreement is not binding, unless it has been fully carried out. The name given to the benefit to be conferred upon each party to an agreement is "consideration," and the rule is that, before a contract becomes enforceable each party must obtain consideration for the promise that he makes. The only exception to this rule arises where the agreement is made under seal, accompanied by the ceremony that is involved in the making of a Deed. (q.v.)

An example may make this clear: if A says to B "I will give you £100," and B accepts the offer, but does not promise to do anything in return for the £100, this is not a contract which is enforceable, because A does not receive any benefit from his promise or in other words B does not give any consideration for the promise of A. Of course, if A goes on to present B with the £100, that is valid, and A cannot recover the money back from B. But until the £100 has been handed over and the agreement has been fully carried out or "executed," B has no means in law of enforcing the fulfilment of the promise.

The rules as to what the law considers to be valid consideration are somewhat complicated and are set out under the title CONSIDERATION (q.v.).

Options.—An option may be an example of a contract in which there is no consideration. Where A offers to sell goods to B at a fixed price and to hold the offer open for a certain period of time, this is an option to B to purchase the goods at the price fixed. But if B acts on reliance of this option he is likely to find that he cannot enforce it, since he has given no consideration to A for keeping the offer open, and despite his promise to keep it open A is entitled in law to revoke his offer at any moment that he pleases. For this reason it is usual to provide some nominal consideration for the option and B promises, for example, to pay A 1/– in consideration of his keeping the offer open for a certain period of time. In such a case there is a proper contract legally enforceable, B can obtain damages if A revokes it before the time arranged has elapsed.

Executed and Executory Contracts.—A contract is called either executory or executed according as to whether the parties to it have not yet done all that they are obliged to do under the contract, or whether their duties and obligations under the contract have been fully performed. Thus a contract to buy goods is executed when the seller has handed over the goods and the buyer has paid the price. A contract to marry is executed when the parties marry one another. A contract to buy goods is wholly executory on the other hand, when the buyer has done nothing more than to offer to buy the goods and the seller has done nothing more than to accept the offer. A contract to marry is wholly executory until the marriage takes place.

Just as the contract may be executory or executed, so the consideration given by either party may be executory or executed. Where in a contract for the sale of goods the seller has handed over the goods to the buyer, the seller has done all that is needed by him under the contract, and his consideration is executed; if the buyer on the other hand has not yet paid the price of the goods, the consideration on his part is still executory.

The importance of whether a contract is executed or executory lies in the effect that it has upon the doctrine of consideration. It has already been stated that if a promise is made without consideration it is unenforceable as long as it is executory; but once it is executed, the person who has performed the gratuitous service or paid money as a gift cannot recover it back.

In the same way while a contract is wholly executory the parties can put an end to it by mutual consent, for the forbearance of one of them to enforce his rights under the contract is valuable consideration for the forbearance of another. But if one of the parties to the contract has executed his consideration (e.g. if a gardener has done the work that he promised to do), his promise to dispense with part of the payment is not binding upon him, because such a promise amounts to a new contract, in which the only consideration given by the employer is a promise to pay a sum less than he was already bound to pay under the original contract; and as we have seen before this is not sufficient consideration in the eyes of the law. On the other hand, if there is a genuine dispute between the gardener and the employer as to the efficiency of the work that has been done, there is good consideration for the promise to pay only a part of the agreed price, for the employer in such a case foregoes his legal right to obtain a decision of his dispute in the Courts and that as we have already seen is good consideration. To sum up then: every contract that is not made by deed, must consist of an offer and an acceptance communicated between the parties, and each party must give consideration to the other party, such consideration being present and not past, and consisting of something more than the party was already legally bound to do apart from the contract.

Form of a Contract.—Although most contracts in which consideration is present are binding whether they are made in writing, verbally or by implication, or by a mixture of all these methods, there are certain contracts which the law says shall not be binding unless they are made in a particular form, either under seal, i.e. by deed, or in writing.

Contracts under Seal.—The following contracts must be made under seal:

(1) A gratuitous promise, if it is to be binding.

(2) A transfer of a British Ship or of a share in a ship.

(3) A lease of land for a period of more than 3 years.

(4) A contract entered into by a corporation, except for everyday matters of small importance and the contracts of trading companies which relate to the business for which the company was formed.

These special contracts are dealt with under DEEDS; LEASES; AND SHIPPING.

When Contract must be set out in Writing.—There are a large number of contracts which are not enforceable unless they are made in writing, and the chief of these are:

(1) Bills of Exchange (q.v.).

(2) Assignments of shares. (*See* SHARES.)

(3) Marine Insurance Contracts. (*See* MARINE INSURANCE.)

(4) Promises by executors to pay damages out of their own pockets. (*See* EXECUTORS.)

(5) Promises to guarantee the debt or the performance of a contract made by another person. (*See* GUARANTEE.)

(6) Agreements made in consideration of marriage. (*See* HUSBAND AND WIFE.)

(7) A contract for the sale of lands or interest in land. (*See* LAND.)

(8) A contract not to be performed within a year.

(9) A contract for the sale of goods of a value greater than £10, except in certain circumstances. (*See* SALE OF GOODS.)

The rule of English law which requires that the above-mentioned contracts shall be in writing before they are enforceable in a Court of Law, is subject to certain technical details and exceptions which are set out more fully under the title WRITTEN CONTRACTS (q.v.).

Void and Voidable Contracts.—A contract which fulfils the requirements of offer and acceptance, form and consideration, which have been dealt with above, may

yet be unenforceable for a number of reasons which require some comment. The following are the chief reasons tending to make a contract unenforceable:

(1) Where one or more of the parties were not capable in law of entering into the contract. (*See below.*)

(2) Where one or more of the parties entered into the contract owing to misrepresentations made by the other party. (*See* MISREPRESENTATION.)

(3) Where one or more of the parties entered into the contract under a vital mistake. (*See* MISTAKE.)

(4) Where one of the parties was induced to enter into the contract by the fraud of another party. (*See* FRAUD.)

(5) Where one of the parties to a contract was induced to enter into the contract by force. (*See* DURESS.)

(6) Where the contract, or the consideration for the contract, is illegal. (*See* ILLEGAL CONTRACTS; RESTRAINT OF TRADE.)

(7) Where a party has lost his rights to enforce the contract owing to lapse of time. (*See below* STATUTE OF LIMITATIONS.)

The effect of the existence of any of these factors will make the contract unenforceable, but there are three different ways in which a contract may be unenforceable. It may be void, it may be voidable, or it may be merely unenforceable in a Court of Law. The distinction between these three things should be borne in mind for many differences flow from them.

A contract is said to be void when it is treated as if it had never been made at all. Neither party has the option of treating it as valid, and all the acts which they may have done under the contract are treated as if they had been done without the existence of a contract at all. Examples of this are illegal contracts and contracts entered into under a vital mistake of fact.

Voidable contracts are contracts which one party is entitled to treat either as void or as valid at his option. If he decides to treat the contract as void, it becomes void from the moment that it was made. If he elects to treat it as valid, it has all the characteristics of a valid contract. Examples of this kind of contract are contracts entered into by reason of a misrepresentation of the other party or by force.

When a contract is neither void nor voidable but merely unenforceable, it simply means that neither of the parties to the contract can obtain their rights through the help of a Court of Law. Examples of such contracts are the contracts which ought to be in writing and are not, and contracts where one of the parties has lost his rights through lapse of time.

The difference between a void and an unenforceable contract is best shown by an example. If A agrees to pay B a sum of £100 if he will commit a burglary, and gives B a cheque for the amount, the contract is illegal and therefore void, and A need not pay the amount of the cheque when B presents it at the Bank. But if A agrees to pay B £100 to be his servant for two years and gives B a cheque for that sum, the contract is unenforceable because it is not in writing; but B is entitled to recover the amount of the cheque when he presents it at the bank, and if A refuses to pay he can sue him for the amount.

It is therefore important to discover whether the presence of one of the six factors mentioned above makes the contract void, voidable, or merely unenforceable.

(1) The chief instances of contracts being affected by the incapacity of the parties entering into them are as follows:

(a) **Alien Enemies.**—Whereas in times of peace an alien has the same rights of entering into, and enforcing contract, as a British subject (except that he cannot become owner or part owner of a British ship), in times of war an enemy subject or any person, even if he is a British subject, who voluntarily lives in enemy territory, is an alien enemy and cannot enter into a contract with a British subject during the continuance of the war. Naturally this does not apply to persons who are interned or involuntarily detained in the enemy country. Such contracts are thus void.

If a contract has been entered into before the war between a British subject and an enemy alien, which would involve intercourse with the enemy during the war, it is automatically dissolved and all obligations put an end to.

If a contract has been entered into before the war between a British subject and an enemy alien, which does not involve intercourse with the enemy during the war, it is rendered unenforceable during the continuance of the war, i.e. neither party can sue in the Courts upon the contract. But when the war is over the contract revives, and either party can sue upon it in the Courts again.

If a contract has been made before the war between a British subject and an alien enemy, and there has been a breach of that contract before the war, the enemy alien cannot sue for that breach during the war, though his right to do so revives after the war. The British subject on the other hand can sue during the war, and if he does so the enemy alien is entitled to defend the action.

(b) **Foreign Sovereigns.** — Foreign Sovereigns and Governments, and Ambassadors of Foreign States can enter into and enforce contracts in the same way as anyone else, but, unless they consent to an action being brought against them in the English Courts, the persons entering into contracts with them cannot enforce the provisions of the contracts by process of law. Such contracts are therefore unenforceable by the person entering into the contract.

(c) **Barristers.**—Barristers cannot sue for their fees and thus contracts made by barristers for fees are unenforceable by them.

(d) **Physicians.**— Although ordinary doctors are entitled to sue for their fees, Fellows of the Royal College of Physicians are not entitled to do so, and are thus in the same position as barristers.

(e) **Lunatics.**—A contract entered into by a lunatic or by any person of unsound mind is binding both upon him and the person contracting with him, unless it can be shewn that the lunatic was incapable of understanding the terms of the contract, and the other person knew that the mental state of the lunatic was such that he did not understand what he was doing. If both those conditions are fulfilled the contract entered into becomes voidable at the option of the lunatic, of his committee or trustees.

(f) **Drunkards.**—If a person enters into a contract when he is drunk, under the influence of drugs, or in any other similar condition, it is binding upon him, unless he can shew, as in the case of the lunatic, that he was so drunk that he could not understand the terms of the contract, and that the other party to the contract was aware of his state. In such a case the contract is voidable at his option.

(g) **Married Women.**—(*See* MARRIED WOMEN'S CONTRACTS.)

(h) **Infants.**—(*See* INFANT.)

(2) **Misrepresentation.**—Where one party to a contract during the course of negotiations makes to the other party a statement which he innocently believes to be true, but which is in fact false, and the other party enters into the contract on the faith of the truth of that statement, such a statement is called a misrepresentation (q.v.), and the person to whom it is made is entitled to be freed from the contract, in certain circumstances, upon finding out its falsity. Contracts induced by misrepresentation are thus voidable.

(3) **Mistake.**—Where either both or one of the parties to a contract enters into it under the influence of a vital mistake of fact, the contract is treated as if there had never been any real agreement between the parties at all, and it is accordingly void. Not all mistakes of fact have this effect, and cases where the mistake is only on the part of one of the parties to the contract are often considered not as mistakes but as innocent misrepresentation (q.v.), and render the contract not void but voidable. (*See* MISTAKE.)

(4) **Fraud.**—Where a party enters into a contract as a result of an untrue statement made by the other party during the course of the negotiations, which statement the other party either knew to be false, or made recklessly, not caring whether it were true or false, this is said to amount to Fraud (q.v.) and entitles the injured party not only to repudiate the contract but also to recover damages for any loss which he has suffered as a result of that untrue statement. Such contracts are therefore voidable at the option of the injured person.

Where, after a contract has been honestly made, and one of the parties indulges in a course of dishonest dealing, this also is considered as amounting to fraud, and the injured party is entitled to put an end to the contract when he discovers the dishonesty. (*See* FRAUD; MISREPRESENTATION.)

(5) **Duress and Undue Influence.**—Where actual physical force or undue influence is employed to compel a party to

enter into a contract, the person so compelled is entitled to repudiate the contract at his option. The contract is accordingly voidable. (*See* DURESS; UNDUE INFLUENCE.)

(6) **Illegal Contracts.**—Where a contract is made with an illegal object, or would involve in its performance a breach of the law of the land, it is void. (*See* ILLEGAL CONTRACTS.)

(7) **Statute of Limitations.**—As a general rule, if a party to a contract allows six years to elapse before exercising his rights under the contract, his rights lapse and the contract becomes unenforceable in the Courts of Law. In certain contracts, particularly those relating to land, the period before which his rights lapse is extended to 12 or 20 years.

Liability under a Contract.—Once a valid contract has been made it is the duty of the parties to the contract to do all those things which they have promised to do. A man who has promised to sell goods must sell the goods that he has promised, and if he has promised that they shall be of a certain kind or a certain quality, he must see that they are of that kind or of that quality. Thus, if A contracts to sell Kenya Coffee to B, he must supply B with Kenya Coffee, and it is no compliance with the contract if he supplies B with coffee that does not come from Kenya, even though he can prove that the actual coffee that he has supplied is better and worth a higher price than the Kenya Coffee. In the same way, if A calls in a plumber to mend a broken pipe, and the plumber instead of mending the broken pipe clears a drain, this is not a compliance with the contract, and the plumber must either mend the pipe as he contracted, or he will be liable to pay damages to A. Any failure to comply with the terms of a contract is known as a breach of contract

This liability continues until the contract is "discharged," that being the usual legal term used to indicate that the obligations have been fulfilled and are no longer subsisting.

Discharge of a Contract.—There are a number of ways in which a contract may be discharged, i.e. the obligations under the contract put an end to. The first and by far the commonest way is by performance. In most contracts made between two persons, both of them fulfil the promises that they have made and accordingly the matter there ends. Thus where A sells goods to B, the contract is discharged by performance, when A has delivered the goods to B and B has paid the price of them to A. Where A contracts to do work for B the contract is discharged by performance when A finishes the work to the satisfaction of B, and B pays the promised price to A.

Many contracts fix a definite time at which the contract shall be discharged. Thus, if A agrees to employ B as his secretary for one year, the contract is discharged when B has worked as secretary for one year and been paid his agreed wage. If B continues to act as secretary after the end of the year, it is not under the old contract that B is entitled to his wages but under a new implied contract that A shall pay him a reasonable sum for his services.

Sometimes contracts instead of fixing a time at which they will be discharged fix a certain condition which will render the liabilities at an end. For example, if A books a passage in B's ship to go for a sail, "weather permitting," if the weather is too rough for sailing, B's obligation to take A for the sail ceases, as does A's obligation to pay for his seat in the ship. The parties are thus in the same position as if the contract had never been made.

Discharge by Agreement.—Just as contractual liabilities may be created by a legally binding agreement, so they may be put an end to in the same manner; but it is important to notice that an agreement discharging a contract must possess the same characteristics as a contract itself. It is made by an offer and an acceptance communicated between the parties, and it must have either form (i.e. it must be under seal), or it must have consideration.

Wherever in a contract there is some liability left undischarged by both parties, then if they decide to release each other from the remaining liabilities, there is ample consideration for the discharge of the contract, since the consideration offered by each party is a forbearance to insist upon the performance of the contract.

Thus supposing A engages B, a plumber, to mend two burst pipes for 15/-, and B mends one of them only; then at that stage, if A and B agree that B need not finish the contract and A need pay him nothing, the contract is discharged by

agreement, because in return for B's loss of his eventual right to 15/- he is being excused the obligation to mend the other pipe. It is otherwise if B has already mended both pipes satisfactorily. In such a case he has discharged all his liabilities by performance while A has not discharged his liability to pay the 15/-. If B agrees to accept the sum of 14/- instead of 15/- there is no consideration for this new agreement, because B gets nothing in return for the loss of his right to the extra shilling.

Novation of Contracts.—Another example of discharge of a contract by agreement is where A and B at some time before a contract is discharged by performance agree to cancel it and to enter into a new agreement. This happens dozens of times a day in ordinary life. If A, a housewife, orders vegetables from B, a greengrocer, and pays for them on the spot, but before the vegetables are delivered A rings up B and asks B to send flowers instead, and B agrees—this amounts to a discharge of the old contract to deliver vegetables and the making of a new contract to deliver flowers. A process such as this is called novation and no question as to consideration applies. For although in the above case, if A and B simply agreed to cancel the order for vegetables, this would not be a discharge for there is no consideration for A foregoing his right to delivery of the vegetables; yet when the new order for flowers is substituted, then A receives as consideration for foregoing his right to receive the vegetables, the fresh promise of B to deliver flowers.

Thus any contract may be discharged by agreement when in addition to cancelling the old contract, the parties enter into a new one.

Discharge by Tender.—Occasionally there are cases that arise where one party is willing to fulfil his liabilities but the other refuses to accept that fulfilment. Cases of this kind generally arise where there is a dispute either as to the quality of goods supplied under a contract, or the proper price to be paid for goods or services. If A a doctor treats B during his illness, without mentioning the price that he is going to charge, B, as has been mentioned before, is presumed to have agreed to pay a reasonable price for the treatment. A's view as to what is a reasonable price may differ from B's, and in such a case when A sends in his bill, B may offer to pay him a lower amount on the grounds that that is a reasonable amount. This offer if made in cash is called a tender (q.v.), and, if A refuses it on the ground that it is too little, B is entitled to consider himself discharged from the contract, for he has attempted to discharge his liability and has been prevented from doing so by the fault of A. In such a case however it is important to realise that, if B tenders too small a sum, this is not a discharge of the contract since his liability was to pay a larger sum. And in point of fact, in such a case, no one can tell whether the sum tendered amounts to a discharge until a Court of Law has decided whether it was the reasonable amount or not. The importance of tender arises when an action for breach of contract is brought.

Another example of tender arises where A, having sold goods to B, attempts to deliver them to B, who for some reason or other refuses them. In such a case A by tender of the goods in this manner has done all that is within his power to discharge his liabilities, and has been prevented from doing so by B's fault. He is accordingly discharged from his liability by tender.

Discharge by Impossibility. — In the ordinary way the law adopts two attitudes towards persons who make a contract that is impossible of performance. If the contract is obviously impossible to perform, such as where A contracts with B to jump over the moon, it is not a contract at all, since the law will never assume that the parties intended it to be serious. Again, if a contract is impossible to perform because of something that has happened unknown to the parties before the contract is made, it is avoided because it was entered into under the mutual mistake that it was possible. An example of this is where A agrees to insure B's ship against loss by tempest, when in fact unknown to both of them the ship has already been sunk.

But there are other cases where the impossibility takes place after the contract has been entered into, and in such cases the subsequent impossibility of performing the contract may discharge each party from his obligations. The distinction to bear in mind in deciding whether impossibility discharges

a contract, is this. If it is quite obvious that it was intended by both parties that the contract should not be carried out, if the event which renders it impossible takes place, then the happening of that event discharges the contract. Examples will make this clearer. If A agrees to transport B's goods from Carlisle to Newcastle by Tuesday, and a snowstorm takes place which makes it impossible for the goods to be transported, A's liability is not discharged because that was a risk which he ought to have taken into consideration when he entered into the contract.

But if A agrees to transport B's cattle from Carlisle to Newcastle, and owing to an outbreak of foot and mouth disease it becomes unlawful to move them from Carlisle, then A's liability is discharged because the law presumes that when two parties enter into a contract they intend that it should not be discharged if the performance becomes illegal.

Again if A agrees to hire out to B a seat in his window to watch the Lord Mayor's Show and for some reason the Lord Mayor's Show is not held, this is assumed to discharge the contract, for it was clearly not the intention of the parties that B should pay for a seat if the show was not held.

It is perhaps hardly necessary to add that if A agrees to serve B as a servant, clerk or secretary, and either A or B dies, the contract is discharged, because it is quite clear that neither party intended that wages should continue to be payable, or services to be rendered, after the death of one of them.

When a contract is discharged by impossibility in this manner, the effect is that it is put an end to at the very moment that the impossibility takes place, and all the rights and obligations up to that moment are subsisting and valid. Thus, in the example of the Lord Mayor's Show, if B were obliged by the contract to pay for his seat in advance, then he must pay for his seat in spite of the impossibility, for the obligation to pay arose before the impossibility took place.

Discharge by Breach of Contract. — The final way in which the liabilities under a contract may be discharged are by breach of the contract. A breach of contract (q.v.) is any failure on the part of either party to the contract to fulfil its terms, but of course it is not every breach of contract that discharges it.

There are however a number of different kinds of breaches of contract, which, if committed by one party, give to the innocent party a right to treat the contract, and his own liabilities under it, as at an end.

Of these the chief are the following:—

(1) If one party to a contract definitely refuses to be bound by it at all, the other party is discharged from his obligations under it. It is important to realize that the refusal must be to be bound by the contract at all. It is not sufficient that one party should refuse to comply with one small term in it. Thus, if A engages a plumber to mend a burst pipe for 7/6, and the plumber at any time says: "I will not mend the pipe," A is discharged from his liability both to pay the 7/6 or to give the plumber an opportunity of mending the pipe. The contract is discharged by the plumber's refusal to be bound by it.

Supposing however that the plumber does mend the pipe but refuses to turn on the water at the main, as was his duty under the contract, this refusal is not a refusal to be bound by the whole of the contract, but merely a refusal to perform a part of it, and A is not discharged from his liability to pay the 7/6, subject however to his right to recover damages for breach of contract from the plumber.

(2) If one party by his own fault, makes it impossible for the contract to be performed, the other party is discharged from his liabilities under it. Thus, if A agrees to marry B, and then marries C, B is no longer bound by her promise to marry A since A has made it impossible for her to do so.

Again, if A agrees to sell B his house and before he does so sells the same house to C, then B is under no obligation to tender the purchase price, for the contract has been discharged by A making it impossible for it to be fulfilled.

(3) In certain circumstances a failure on the part of one of the parties to a contract discharges the other from his liabilities under it. It is not every failure to perform one of the terms of a contract that discharges the other party from all his liabilities under it. The failure must be of a drastic nature and mere non-compliance in some small particular will not give rise to a right in the other party to consider the contract at an end, but will merely give him a right

to damages for the loss which the failure has occasioned.

It is a useful general rule to remember that common sense is the best judge as to whether a contract is discharged by a breach committed by one party or not. If it seems likely that both the parties intended that the term which one of them has failed to fulfil should go to the root of the contract, then the contract is discharged. If it seems probable that both the parties only intended that a failure to fulfil the term should only give to the other a right to pay a smaller price, or to recover some money compensation, then the contract is not discharged.

For example, A agrees to build a wall for B and to finish the wall by a certain date If A fails to finish the wall by the stated date, but finishes it shortly after, then B is not entitled to refuse to allow him to finish it or to refuse to pay for it merely because A has not fulfilled the term as to finishing the wall in time. B is only entitled to recover from A such damage as he has suffered by reason of the delay.

On the other hand if A, instead of building a brick wall as ordered, were to build a wall of concrete slabs, then B would be entitled to treat this breach of contract as putting an end to his liability to pay for the wall at all, and the contract would be discharged by reason of A's breach. B would also be allowed to recover damages for the harm he had suffered by the building of the concrete wall instead of the brick wall.

Again if A lets a house to B promising to keep it in repair and fails to do so, B cannot move out of the house and refuse to pay rent any longer, because A's breach of contract does not go to the root of the contract of letting. What B must do is to sue for damages for the failure to repair the house.

Those terms in the contract which are not regarded as going to the root of the contract in this manner are called warranties; while those which do go to the root of the contract (and which entitle the person to consider the contract at an end if they are not fulfilled) are called conditions. But, since the theory underlying this distinction is the intention of the parties to the contract, it is always open to them to decide when making the contract whether a particular term shall be a condition or a warranty (q.v.). An excellent example of this is contained in insurance contracts where the insurance company nearly always makes it a condition of the policy that the insured person shall give notice of claims within a certain specified time. If the insured person fails to give notice of a claim within that time, the insurance company is discharged from its liability to pay the claim, although in fact the failure to give notice of the claim has not prejudiced them in any way at all. This is because it is stated in the contract that the term shall be a condition and not a warranty.

Effects of Discharge.—When a contract has been discharged in any of the ways mentioned above, the various rights and liabilities of the parties to the contract come to an end, and the parties are no longer bound to fulfil its terms.

Any rights, however, that arose during the course of the contract, such as rights arising in an injured party by the failure of the other party to keep to its terms, still continue and can be enforced in the Courts. Rights so arising out of breaches of contract continue to exist until they have been lost either through lapse of time, or through the recovery·of damages for the breach of contract (q.v.) in the Law Courts. (*See* ASSIGNMENT; BILL OF EXCHANGE; COMPANIES; CONSIDERATION; DAMAGES; DEEDS; SALE OF GOODS; UNDUE INFLUENCE; WRITTEN CONTRACTS.)

CONTRACT (SCOTS LAW).—A great many of the rules of contracts in Scots Law are the same as those in English Law. The most important distinction is that Scots Law does not require any consideration in the contract. Thus, a promise which a man has given may be enforced although the person to whom he has given it has not promised anything in return. The greatest practical difference it makes is in cases where parties are negotiating for the sale of property or of goods and one of them makes to the other an offer to sell the property for a certain price. The other may desire time to consider whether or not he will buy at that price, and accordingly may ask the intending seller to keep the offer open for a week, which the seller may promise to do. In English law the seller is not bound by his promise to keep the offer open and may sell the goods

to some other person before the week has elapsed, unless at the time when the promise is given, the intending purchaser gives to the intending seller some consideration, that is, some promise in return. It does not matter how small this consideration is, e.g. it may be a shilling but something must be given. In Scotland such a promise would be enforced without consideration and the seller would be compelled by law to stand by his bargain.

It is recognised,however, in Scotland that it would be unfair to hold a man to every promise which he had given for which he was to receive nothing, and therefore the law will not allow such promises to be enforced unless they can be proved in a certain way. The method of proof must be either by producing some written document, in which the person making the gratuitous promise has set out the promise in writing, or by requiring the person who has promised to admit his promise on oath. Thus a mere oral promise cannot easily be enforced.

Persons under 21.—The capacity of persons to contract is also slightly different in Scotland from in England. For legal purposes persons under 21 are divided into two classes, those who are pupils, and those who are minors; a boy is a pupil until he is 14 and a girl until she is 12. Both are minors from the end of the period of pupillarity until they are 21.

A pupil cannot under any circumstances contract on his own behalf. All his contracts are made for him by his tutor, who will normally be his guardian. The contractual powers of a minor are wider. He does not have a tutor but he may have a curator who again will normally be his guardian. The minor contracts on his own behalf although, if he has a curator, he must obtain the curator's consent. If he has a curator and makes a contract without his consent, the contract is void. If, however,he has no curator,or if he has one and obtains his consent, the contract is good. All contracts by a minor, with a few exceptions, whether he has a curator or not may be disowned by him at any time before he reaches 25. This period is known as the *quadriennium utile*. Before the minor can disown them, however, he must show what is called "lesion," that is, that the bargain was an unfair one and that he has suffered loss. A gift by a minor could obviously be disowned in this way.

The minor cannot disown contracts even on the grounds of lesion if he pretended that he was of full age when he entered into the contract and was believed by the other party, or if he was engaged in business or trade and the contract was made for the purposes of his business, or if, after he became 21, he ratified the contract with knowledge of his legal rights.

Two important distinctions should be noticed between the Law of Scotland and that of England. In England the person under 21 is not bound by a contract even though he has said, and though the person with whom he has contracted has believed, that he was over 21; nor is he bound in cases where he has carried on a business with persons who may not meet him personally at all and so may not have an opportunity of judging his age. In England it does not matter how advantageous to the infant the contract may be. He is entitled to snap his fingers at his creditors who cannot make him bankrupt or enforce the contract. In Scotland creditors are protected in both these cases.

The Form of Contracts. — The form in which a contract has to be expressed differs in some cases in Scots Law. There is no document in Scots Law executed by a private person with a seal as is the Deed in English Law. The most formal document in Scots Law is known as a *probative writ*. This may be made in either of two ways. It may either be written throughout its length or at any rate in its main clauses by the person granting it, in which case it is said to be holograph, or it may be an attested Deed signed by the person granting it and witnessed by two witnesses (*see* ATTESTATION [SCOTS LAW]). A document will have the effect of a holograph writ even if it is not written by the grantor, if he has written "adopted as holograph" and signed his name. No witnesses are required. Probative Writs of this kind are required only for certain purposes, e.g. contracts relating to land; contracts of service for more than a year; or contracts for cautionary obligations, i.e. guarantees. For all ordinary business transactions these formalities are not necessary.

Where a transaction of the above kind has not been entered into by a probative writ the contract may be enforceable if one or other of the parties has done something on the strength of the contract, such as altering his position or incurring expense. When this has happened the other party will be bound and cannot rely on the absence of the proper document. This doctrine is similar to the English specific performance and is known as *rei interventus*. Thus, if A and B agree in a written document which is not probative that A should grant B a lease of land for 3 years, and B enters the land and erects expensive buildings to the knowledge of A, he will be entitled to enforce the lease for 3 years.

In addition to those contracts which require to be made in writing there are also certain others which, although they may be made orally, can only be enforced in a Court of Law if some written document setting out the terms and signed by the party against whom the contract is being enforced can be produced, or unless that party admits on his oath that he entered into the contract.

The writing for this purpose need not be probative, and need not have come into existence until after the contract has been made. Contracts of this kind are said to require proof by the writ or oath. The party suing on the contract is entitled as a preliminary to compel the other party to go into the witness box under oath and to answer questions in the nature of cross-examination, in order to secure an admission that the contract was made.

Contracts which must be proved in this way are gratuitous obligations, promises to pay the debts of another, trusts and contracts of an unusual kind. These contracts correspond to a large extent to those of which written evidence is required in English Law; but it should be noticed that the alternative of obtaining the sworn statement of the other party is not open in English Law. The requirement in English Law that contracts for the sale of goods over £10 in value must be evidenced by writing does not exist in Scots Law.

The other rules of contract in Scots Law are on the whole similar to the rules of England: other differences which exist are noted under Special headings.

CONTRACTING OUT.—This is the technical name given to the action of two parties who make a contract that the provisions of some Act of Parliament which would otherwise bind them, shall not apply to them. Thus the Employers' Liability Act provides for the payment of compensation to a workman under certain circumstances, but the employer and his workman may agree together that the provisions of the Act shall not apply to them.

Contracting out is not permitted in two very important cases. It is not permissible to contract out of the Rent Restriction Acts, nor the Workmen's Compensation Acts except by way of what is called a Certified Scheme, and any contract which attempts to put the parties outside the scope of either of these Acts is void and has no effect in law.

Many Acts of Parliament expressly provide that contracting out of their provisions shall not be permissible. (*See* CERTIFIED SCHEME; EMPLOYERS' LIABILITY; WORKMEN'S COMPENSATION ACT *and also* SPECIAL SUPPLEMENT "RENT RESTRICTION.")

CONTRIBUTION (GUARANTEE).

—Whenever two or more persons have become guarantors for the performance of some act or payment of some money by a principal debtor, any one who pays more than his share on the default of the principal debtor will be entitled to claim the excess from the other sureties. This is called the right of contribution.

Where one surety is insolvent he is not counted and the others may each therefore be required to pay his share as well as their own. Thus, if the sum of £1,000 is due and there are 5 sureties, any one paying the full amount can recover £200 from each of the other four, if they are solvent; (£800 in all) but if one of them is insolvent the one paying the full amount can recover £250 from each of the other three (£750 in all).

Notice that this right of contribution only exists as between the sureties themselves. The creditor is entitled to claim the full amount from any of them unless the contract expressly provides to the contrary. (*See* GUARANTEE.)

CONTRIBUTORIES.

—The contributories of a Company are those persons who are liable when the company is wound up, to pay money for shares that have been issued by the company. Persons who have paid all that is due on their shares—i.e. who hold fully paid shares, cannot be called on to pay anything more. When the holder of a share which is not fully paid transfers it to someone else, the person to whom the share is transferred will thereafter be liable in the first place for any money due; but the person transferring may still be liable to pay if the company is wound up within a year of the transfer. In that event, if the person who is the present holder of the share has not enough money to pay what is due, the original holder will have to make up the deficiency if the money is required to pay debts which were owing when he was a shareholder. Thus, suppose A B sells his £1 shares, on which the company has only required him as yet to pay 10/- to X Y on the 1st of October, and the company is wound up on the 30th of September following, XY will first of all be required to pay to the company the 10/- still due, but if he cannot pay, A B will be called on to do so. (*See* CALLS; SHARES; WINDING-UP.)

CONTRIBUTORY NEGLIGENCE.

—This phrase is almost self-explanatory. When an accident occurs, and someone has been injured, in order to recover damages against another, the victim must prove:

(1) That the other person was negligent, and

(2) That that negligence was the cause of his injuries.

But sometimes more than one person is to blame, and there may be several people, including the injured person, who have by their negligence contributed to cause the accident. In other words, each has been guilty of contributory negligence. It then becomes necessary to discover which of them, if any, are liable in law. At first sight this may seem a difficult task, but it becomes simple when a well known legal principle is applied. The principle expressed in non-legal terms is simply this: Of all the people who have been negligent in the case under consideration whose negligence was the proximate or decisive cause of the accident? By "person whose negligence was the proximate cause of the accident" is meant the person but for whose negligence the injury might never have occurred—in other words, the person who had the last opportunity of avoiding the accident.

Should that person be the plaintiff then he will not be able to recover even though he can prove the defendant also was negligent.

This principle is well illustrated by the following two examples:—

The plaintiff was riding his horse violently in the dusk, when he came against a pole left by the defendant in the highway and was thrown from his horse and injured. In this case the defendant was negligent in leaving the pole in the road. The plaintiff also was guilty of negligence contributing to the accident in that he was riding his horse at a rapid pace in the dusk. But the plaintiff's negligence was the proximate cause of the accident, and it was he who had the last chance of avoiding it—therefore he was debarred from recovering.

In the second example the plaintiff left his donkey, with its legs tied, in the public highway. The defendant drove into it and killed it. In this case again both were negligent—the plaintiff for leaving his donkey in the road with its legs tied and the defendant for running it down. But here it was held that the plaintiff could recover, because the defendant was the person who had the last opportunity of avoiding the accident, and by being ordinarily careful he might have avoided the consequence of the plaintiff's negligence.

If, however, a third person's negligence is the proximate cause of the accident, the plaintiff will not be prevented from recovering, provided the defendant's negligence was a substantial cause of the accident.

A child can be guilty of contributory negligence, but of course he must be judged as a child and cannot be expected to exercise the amount of care an adult would. Thus, if a child is plaintiff in an action where the defendant has been proved to be negligent, in considering whether the child was negligent as well, and if so, whether its negligence was the proximate cause of the accident, the child must not be judged too harshly, but proper allowance must be made for the irresponsible nature of children. (*See* ACCIDENT; COLLISION; NEGLIGENCE.)

CONVERSION.—Conversion means the appropriation by one person of the property of another. It may constitute both a crime and a civil wrong. When it is a crime it is larceny, embezzlement or fraudulent conversion. As a civil wrong however it is described simply as conversion.

If the goods of another come into a person's possession the person receiving them must in general return them to the true owner, and he is liable for damages to the true owner if he uses them as his own. This is so even though he does not know the owner. Thus, suppose A steals B's property and sells it to C, even though C may honestly believe that he had purchased the property from A, he can be made to return it to the true owner, B, when B finds out where it is; and if C has himself disposed of it he must pay damages to B. There is one exception to this rule. Where the stolen goods have been sold in market overt, that is to say a place treated by the law as an open market, the true owner cannot in general recover them from anybody who acquired them honestly, after such sale; but even to this rule there is an exception which enables the true owner in some circumstances to get them back. If he manages to discover the thief, and prosecutes him and gets him convicted of the theft, then the protection given to the person in possession by virtue of the sale in market overt (q.v.) disappears, and the true owner can get back the goods or their value if he can find the person in possession of them. (*See* FRAUDULENT CONVERSION.)

CONVEYANCING.—The methods by which land and certain rights therein are transferred and the law relating thereto which involve the use of a document are termed "Conveyancing." One of the branches relates to the sale of land. Others are Leases, Mortgages, Settlements, gifts by Will and "inter vivos" (q.v.) and several other forms of transactions known to the law. (*See also* LANDLORD AND TENANT; MORTGAGE; SALE OF LAND.)

CONVICTION.—A conviction is any finding recorded by a Court exercising criminal jurisdiction that a person has been found guilty of a criminal offence. In certain circumstances, however, although it is known that the accused person is guilty, a Court has the power to take the course of discharging him, with or without an order that he pay the costs of the prosecution, without recording a conviction. This course is often adopted in the Police Court for first offenders who are charged with

An aerial view of Dartmoor, the chief convict prison of this country.

minor offences. The effect is that a person's record is thereby preserved from the stigma of a conviction.

CONVICT.—A convict is a person who has been sentenced to penal servitude. In former times a person sentenced to this punishment forfeited all his property, but modern legislation has abolished this result. It has, however, been found necessary to provide convicts with some means by which their property can be looked after while they are undergoing sentence. A convict, therefore, owning property may have an administrator appointed to look after it. The administrator has extensive powers, and can receive money owing to the convict, and make payments on his behalf from his funds. If there is no administrator appointed, any person interested in a convict's property can apply to the Police Court for an interim curator to be appointed. The interim curator has very similar powers to those exercised by the administrator, but for certain matters has to obtain the sanction of the Court that appointed him before he may deal with the convict's property.

If a convict goes to serve his sentence without having made provisions for his wife and children, his wife or the guardian of his children may require a curator to make an allowance for them out of his property. If no curator has been appointed, then the person desiring money should apply to the Police Court for one to be appointed.

For treatment of convicts whilst undergoing sentence, *see* Penal Servitude.

CO-PARCENERS.—Before the Administration of Estates Act in 1925 coparceny could arise in two ways; on the intestacy of the owner of a fee simple estate (q.v.) in land, and on the death of a tenant in tail (*see* Estate Tail) who left no sons alive but only female heirs. A fee simple is the most extensive kind of ownership of land known to the law. 'Fee' implies that it will descend to the owner's heirs, and "simple" that there is no provision for bringing it to an end. If the owner of such an estate died intestate before 1926 and left only female heirs, these heirs all inherited the land together as co-parceners. A similar rule prevailed for estates tail save that, since a tenant in tail could not before 1926 dispose of his interest by will, it was immaterial whether he made a will or not, for if all his male heirs failed his daughters would take as co-parceners.

Since 1926 co-parceny has been restricted to the latter class and, since a tenant in tail can now dispose of his interest by will, it is only on the death of such a tenant intestate that any question of co-parceny can now arise. Co-parceners are each owners of a proportionate part of the whole, but till they divide the land voluntarily or by proceedings at law they do not individually own any particular area, and they have the right to go upon, use and enjoy the whole. A co-parcener may sell her share to a stranger who will then become not a co-parcener but a tenant in common, and she may leave it by will in which case the same principle applies. If she dies intestate her share does not go to her sisters but to her heirs.

CO-OPERATIVE SOCIETIES.—

A co-operative society is a society of persons who join together for the purpose either of manufacture or (more commonly) of distribution in such a way as to confer upon the members of the society the profit that would otherwise go elsewhere. The co-operative movement was founded in Great Britain, where it can be traced back to the middle of the eighteenth century. The movement started primarily with the idea of co-operative manufacture for the benefit of the *producer*, but it gradually veered round, with the establishment of retail shops and the payment of "dividends" to consumers, until the major part of the movement is nowadays directed in favour of cheapening distribution for the benefit of the *consumer*.

In 1860 an Act was passed which enabled the various individual co-operative retailing societies to found a wholesale federation which afterwards became known as the Co-operative Wholesale Society, or more generally "C.W.S." From this federation, the retailing societies were enabled to purchase their supplies on the same basis as their own individual members purchased goods from them.

It is a remarkable thing that co-operative or consumers' society is a name unknown to the law. The first Act of Parliament which dealt with societies of this kind was the Friendly Societies Act, 1834, which, as amended in 1846, divided co-operative societies into two kinds. To these two branches were given the names "industrial" (i.e. the producers' society) and "provident" (i.e. the consumers' society). These are the names which the law has attached to co-operative societies. As a result of their early connection with, and resemblance to, Friendly Societies, the law relating to co-operative societies very closely resembles that relating to Friendly Societies (*see* FRIENDLY SOCIETIES), and it bears a similar but less close resemblance to the law relating to Building Societies, which, after all, are but another manifestation of the co-operative movement (*compare* BUILDING SOCIETIES).

The activities of co-operative societies are probably more far-reaching than those of any other single organization in the country. The manufacture of their own stock by their own factories is taking a position of far greater importance than formerly, and the competition between co-operative manufacturers and independent manufacturers is keen. The movement has an enormous banking business, with an annual turn-over of about £700,000,000. It is estimated that their members, who total almost eleven millions, buy nearly £30 of goods per head per year.

Of the profit made, a part is distributed as interest to the persons who originally supplied capital, a part is distributed among the members in proportion to the amount of their purchases during the year, and the remainder is applied to reserves. The original shareholders bear income-tax on their dividends as if they were ordinary shareholders in an ordinary company; the members, however, do not bear income-tax on their "dividends," which are regarded merely as a refund of discount on the goods they have purchased, and not as income. The remainder of the annual profits is put to reserve, being invested either in the business or in securities. Until 1933 all Co-operative societies were exempt from income-tax under schedules C and D, and they were the only trading companies which were so exempt. They are now, however, liable to pay income-tax on the same basis as other trading companies, and the amount of annual profits put to reserve, as well as the income arising from such reserves, is now taxable.

COPYHOLD.—Copyhold tenure was the method by which the villeins (labourers) of the lord of a Manor used to hold their land, and the land itself came to be called copyhold land. The name is derived from the fact that the tenants' title and the past dealings with the land were recorded in, and proved by, the Manor Rolls which were kept by the Steward. In 1925 copyhold tenure and another very similar type of land holding—customary tenure—were abolished and all the differences between them and the ordinary ownership of land were removed.

The respective rights of tenant and lord varied from manor to manor. A few have been retained unaltered; any rights to timber, quarries, sport or commons which either party used to enjoy are still reserved to them as before. Some have been temporarily retained whilst provision is being made for the adequate compensation of each side: examples are the "fines" or money payments which the tenant was sometimes bound to make at certain times; but the rest, including the custom that land should descend to the youngest son, and the tenant's duty to get his lord's consent before parting with the land, have been abolished.

COPYRIGHT.—What Copyright is. —Copyright is the sole right to reproduce or perform in public an original literary, dramatic, musical or artistic work, or any substantial part thereof, in any material form. There can be no copyright in ideas, but only in the actual form in which the idea is clothed. The only way in which a mere idea can be protected is by registering it as a patent, if it is of such a kind that it can be so registered. (*See* PATENTS.) There is, therefore, no copyright in a piece of news published in a newspaper, but if the actual words in which it was written were copied out word for word, the newspaper's copyright would have been infringed, and the newspaper would be entitled to bring an action against the person who reproduced

it. On the other hand, if Smith independently writes or designs a work, for example a map, and, by mere coincidence, it turns out to be identical with a work of Robinson's that has already been published, Robinson cannot prevent Smith from publishing it, and both Robinson and Smith have copyright in it. There is no copyright in illegal, immoral or libellous works.

Who is entitled to Copyright.— Since 1911 no registration or other formalities are required to give a right to copyright. The mere creation of a work suffices to entitle its creator to the protection of the law. But where a work is created by an employee or apprentice in the course of his duties, the copyright belongs to his employer.

How long Copyright lasts.—Copyright continues for the lifetime of the author plus fifty years, except in a few cases which are mentioned below, e.g. photographs. Where the work was created by joint authors, copyright continues for fifty years from the date of the death of the author who first dies or until the death of the author who last dies, whichever happens to be the longer. This was enacted in the Copyright Act, 1911, and there are special provisions for works in which copyright existed before 1911.

Unpublished Works.—Copyright may exist in all unpublished works just as in published works, provided the author was, when he made the work, a British subject or resident within the Empire. If the author dies before publication, copyright will expire fifty years after the date of publication in the case of literary, dramatic or musical works; in the case of drawings or paintings, fifty years after the death; and, in the case of photographs, fifty years after the original negative was made.

Death of Owner of Copyright.— Copyright is property, and can therefore be left by will, or, if there is no will, it passes to the owner's heirs. If the author of an unpublished work leaves the manuscripts or canvas etc. as a legacy, it is presumed that he has intended the legatee to have the copyright as well.

Transfer of Copyright.—Transfer may be for a limited period, or for a limited purpose, e.g. photographic rights, and ought to be in writing signed by the owner of the copyright. It must be stamped to the following values: where the price does not exceed £5—6d.; £10—1/-; £15—1/6; £20—2/-; £25—2/6; thereafter adding 2/6 for every £25 up to £300; and thereafter 5/- for every £50 or any fractional part thereof. Transfer will be effective even though the writing be contained only in letters, and a mere receipt may suffice. At the end of 25 years after the death of the author, notwithstanding any contract to the contrary, the copyright will revert to the author's heirs, except in the case of encyclopædias and other collective works.

Royalties.—A royalty is a sum that is agreed to be paid to an author of a work for every copy that is sold, or for every performance of the work; or it may be for a share of the profits. It should always be made clear in such an agreement who is to be the owner of the copyright, and it is better for the author that the copyright should be expressed to be his.

Joint Authors.—Joint authors are entitled to copyright in their work in equal shares, and when one of them dies, his share passes to his heirs. A joint author (or his heirs) must obtain the consent of the other joint authors (or their heirs) before he can publish the work or allow others to publish it. But he does not need such consent in order to take proceedings to prevent infringement.

Foreign Works.—Nearly all works first published within the Empire are protected in England. Agreements have also been reached with most foreign countries (excluding U.S.A.) that, in exchange for reciprocal rights, English copyright will be extended to works first published abroad, and in the majority of cases the period of protection is the same as if the work had been first published in England. The law of copyright in U.S.A. is very different from that in England; it provides, amongst other things, that two copies of the best edition of the work must be deposited, and that no book written in English is to have the benefit of copyright unless it was printed and bound, and its type set within the limits of the United States. These rules are only slightly relaxed in favour of British authors, who are therefore compelled to have their books separately published in the United States in order to obtain copyright. A British subject may, however, obtain an "ad interim" protection by depositing a copy of the book not more than sixty days after its publication in England: the book will then be protected for four months after it was deposited. But the protection expires at the end of four months, unless meanwhile the book has been published in U.S.A. in accordance with the rules mentioned above. These restrictions apply to most, but not all, books, e.g. certain artistic, dramatic and musical works are exempted; but, even there, the rules are complicated, and expert advice should always be taken before any attempt is made to reserve American copyright.

Right to publish in spite of Copyright.—When, after the author has been dead for twenty-five years, the owner of the copyright refuses either to publish, or to consent to the publication of, a work that has already been published, it may be republished without the consent of the owner of the copyright subject to certain conditions and formalities (e.g. a royalty of 10% on the price at which the work is published must be paid to the owner of the copyright). If the author has died before the first publication of the work, the twenty-five years runs from the date of such publication.

Books.—Maps, plans, charts, tables, and compilations are all protected in the same way as books, so that there may be copyright in a list of brood mares with their sires, or a selection from English literature. There is no copyright in the title of a book unless it indicates some intellectual effort, e.g. it was decided that no copyright existed in the title "Splendid Misery" since it was a common phrase. But if people are deceived into buying a book or newspaper because the title of it bears a resemblance to that of another book or newspaper, the use of such a name or title may be prevented. The rule is really a branch of the law known as the law of "passing off," which aims at preventing one man from unfairly reaping the benefit of trade connections and custom worked up by another man; for example, if a firm of publishers published a series of half a dozen "Manuals for the Young Scientist," and another publisher then published a "Manual for the Young Scientist, No. 7," he would be guilty of passing off, since his real object

8

was to pretend that his Manual was a continuation of the series, in order to attract the custom of those members of the public who had admired the original series. The publisher of the original series would be entitled to claim all the profits made on the sale of No. 7, and to confiscate the copies that remained unsold, and to obtain an order from the Court prohibiting the passer off from printing or selling any more copies under that name. New editions, if they substantially differ from the old editions, and abridgments are entitled to copyright.

Encyclopaedias, Newspapers, and other Collective Works.—The "author" of a collective work is the person who edits it, and he owns the copyright. At the same time, each of the various contributors owns copyright independently in each of his contributions unless he has transferred it. But as it is possible that they may be deemed to have transferred it by sending it in to the editor, it is safer for him to reserve his copyright expressly, so that he may use his contribution as he likes afterwards. Apart from the actual words in which it is clothed, there is no copyright in a piece of news, unless there is an express contract to that effect between the person supplying the news and the person supplied, e.g. the buyer of a newspaper enters into no such contract, and is therefore entitled to use the news therein as he pleases.

Translation of Books.—If a work is entitled to copyright it is an infringement to publish a translation of it. Copyright exists in an original translation as in any other work. If A's English book is translated into French, and B then retranslates the French edition back into English, A can sue B for infringement.

Dramatization and Film Rights.—The author is entitled to sue for infringement any person who dramatizes and performs his book in public, even though the infringer has stolen merely the situations, and has not copied a single sentence word for word. The author of a literary, dramatic or musical work has an action for infringement against any person who either makes a film of his work, or exhibits or authorizes the exhibition of such a film in public. Persons snapped in a news film cannot prevent its exhibition, and the person who took the film has copyright in it.

Plays.—All kinds of stage entertainments are protected, including dancing and entertainments in dumb show, provided that the way in which they are to be acted is "fixed in writing or otherwise," e.g. stage directions suffice. There is probably no copyright in "gags." An adaptation of an old play may be copyright, e.g. a special production of Shakespeare. The music of a musical play is copyright. To constitute infringement of a dramatic work it is not necessary that the actual words should have been copied but merely the situations. Films have the same protection as plays.

Poems.—Copyright in poems is exactly the same as in books and other literary works. An anthology of poems, though each individual poem be non-copyright, is entitled to protection from infringement if it is made as the result of careful reading, study and comparison.

Lectures and Sermons.—Copyright in a lecture is the sole right to deliver or print it. It exists even though the lecture was purely extempore and no manuscript copy was made of it by the author. Newspapers are entitled to print even a verbatim report of a lecture, unless such report is prohibited by conspicuous notices displayed during the lecture at the main entrance and near the lecturer.

Paintings and Drawings.—Where the author of a painting or drawing has sold it and any person makes an alteration in either it, or any reproduction of it, during the author's life, such person shall be liable to certain penalties. The object of this provision is to protect artists' reputations which might be injured if their works were open to unauthorized alteration. Unauthorized photographs, engravings or other reproductions of copyright paintings or drawings infringe copyright.

Sculpture and Architecture.—Sculptural and architectural works are protected like other works of art, except that it has not yet been decided whether photographs and engravings may be made of them with impunity. Works of sculpture, architecture or artistic craftsmanship may be copied by painting, drawing, photographing or engraving if they are permanently situated in a public place or building.

Music.—Any unauthorized publication

or public performance, even with a fresh setting, of copyright music is an infringement of the copyright. If the owner of musical copyright has ever consented to the making of mechanical contrivances for the reproduction of it, any person may, without obtaining consent and on payment of royalties, make similar mechanical contrivances.

Photographs.—Copyright in photographs and works produced by similar processes lasts for fifty years from the making of the original negative. The person entitled to copyright is the person who owned the original negative when it was made. Where an order is given for a photograph, the copyright belongs to the person giving the order. But where the photographer himself solicits a sitting the copyright is his, although he is not entitled, it seems, to use such photographs either for sale or for advertising, unless it was a part of the arrangement that he should be allowed to. On the other hand, no person can prevent the use of snapshots taken of him, even though they were taken without his consent, unless they were libellous.

Engravings, Lithographs, etc.—As with photographs, the copyright in all etchings, engravings, lithographs, woodcuts, prints, etc., that are ordered for valuable consideration belongs to the person who gave the order. The copyright continues for the life of the author plus fifty years. A public exhibition of such works or of any artistic works does not infringe copyright.

Gramophones.—The copyright in records, perforated rolls, or other contrivances to reproduce sound continues for fifty years from the making of the original plate. Copyright belongs to the person who owned the plate when it was first made. It was said by two Judges in the House of Lords in 1929 that if a gramophone record of copyright music is played in public, that constitutes a public performance, and infringes the copyright. Gramophone records of copyright music are made only for private use. As to right to make musical records, *see* "Music" above.

Broadcasting.—In 1927 it was decided that if any copyright work was broadcast, such broadcasting constituted a public performance, and therefore was an infringement of copyright unless the express leave

of the owner of the copyright had been obtained. And in 1933 it was further decided that even if the broadcaster had the leave of the copyright owner to transmit the work, still no person is entitled to use his loud speaker for the purpose of entertaining members of the public with such broadcast. He may use his wireless set only for private domestic purposes, and cannot use it even to entertain the guests in his hotel, since they are, for this purpose, deemed to be members of the public.

Damages, Injunctions, etc.—The remedies for infringement are numerous. (1) Damages: the plaintiff, i.e. the person whose copyright has been infringed, has a right to be compensated by damages for the injury done by the infringement. (2) Injunction: an injunction is an order of the Court to cease infringing, and disobedience of the order involves imprisonment. (3) Accounts: the Court may order that the defendant shall pay the plaintiff all the profits he has made by infringing. (4) Delivery to the plaintiff of all infringing copies, negatives, plates and records. Generally speaking, it is no defence to say, "I did not know the work was copyright."

Fines and Imprisonment.—Magistrates may summarily impose a fine of 40/- per copy (not more than £50 in all), and for subsequent offences imprisonment, for knowingly making, selling, hiring, distributing, exhibiting or importing for the purpose of trade any infringing copy of a work in which copyright exists. They may also order constables to search for and seize pirated copies of music. There are various other punishments that may be imposed in connection with copyright, including penalties for making or dealing with false signatures on works of art, and for making records for the purposes of trade of dramatic or musical performances without the written consent of the performers. (*See also* DESIGNS; PATENTS; TRADE MARKS.)

CORONER.—The office of Coroner is a very ancient one. He is a representative of the King and is charged with enquiring into the cause of deaths. He also has the further duty of ascertaining the owners, if any, of alleged treasure trove. In the City of London the coroner carries out enquiries into the cause of fires that have taken place in the City. A coroner holds a Court known as an Inquest. In cases where there is a suspicion of murder or manslaughter, or where the death arose in an accident on the road, or in circumstances the possible recurrence of which would be injurious to public health or safety, the coroner sits with a jury. In other cases he sits alone. A coroner has to view the body of the deceased either at, or before, the first sitting of an inquest, and if the jury so wish he has to allow them to see it also.

Coroners are appointed for counties and boroughs. They must be barristers, solicitors or legally qualified medical practitioners of not less than 5 years' standing in their profession. They receive payment varying according to the nature of their appointment. They may appoint as their deputies persons who are themselves qualified to be coroners. In most cases coroners are only employed in a part-time capacity, but in London and some of the big cities they are whole time officials. (*See* SPECIAL SUPPLEMENT "POLICE.")

CORPORATION.—A corporation or corporate body is an artificial person, i.e. not a human being, which is nevertheless capable of having legal rights and liabilities. The type of corporation best known to-day is a company registered under a Companies Act. (*See* COMPANIES.) A corporation however may be of other kinds.

Corporation Sole.—There may be what is known as a corporation sole, that is, an artificial legal person consisting of only one individual. In such a case there are really two legal personalities, one belonging to the individual as a private person, and the other belonging to him as the corporation sole. There will accordingly be two entirely distinct sets of rights and liabilities. The most common type of corporation of this kind is an ecclesiastic such as a Bishop, or Vicar of a Parish. As a corporation sole the Vicar will have certain rights, e.g. the parish churchyard belongs to him, and money may also have been left payable each year to the "Vicar of the Parish." He will also have rights and liabilities as an ordinary individual, e.g. he may own shares or a motor car or owe money to his butcher. During his lifetime it may not be easy to see that those rights are separate, but when he dies the distinction will be clear. His rights as a corporation sole will not go to

his personal representatives, e.g. his executor, but to the person who may succeed him as Vicar of the Parish and who will then be the corporation sole. His personal rights as an individual will go to his executor. The executor therefore could not sell the churchyard to pay the butcher's bill.

Corporations Aggregate.—Corporations which do not consist of one person only are known as corporations aggregate. Examples of these are the members of a Municipal Corporation. These corporations are brought into existence by a Royal Charter or by Acts of Parliament. Corporations aggregate, like corporations sole, are not affected by the private rights and liabilities of the persons who may be members of the corporations from time to time, nor are these persons affected by the rights and liabilities of the corporation. They neither own its property nor are they liable for its debts. When the members of a corporation change e.g. by death or by an election—the rights and liabilities of the corporation remain unaltered.

A corporation has, as has been seen, an artificial personality and can only do the acts which the law has given it power to do. (*See* COMPANIES.) These Acts will be contained in the charter or other document which created the corporation. If it attempts to do any act which it has not power to do the act is said to be "ultra vires," i.e. beyond its powers, and is of no effect. The members of the corporation who have used the corporation property for an ultra vires purpose can be compelled to replace it. (*See* COMPANIES.)

CORROBORATION. — Where the evidence of one witness supports that of another, or where certain facts support what is said by a witness or witnesses, there is said to be corroboration. In most cases the evidence of a single witness is sufficient for a tribunal to decide any fact in issue in a case. There are however certain exceptions to this rule. For instance no person may be convicted of perjury unless two or more witnesses speak to the falsity of the accused's alleged untrue evidence. Again the evidence of young children in practice has to be corroborated. Judges always warn juries of the need for this to be done before they accept the evidence of a child. Accomplices also provide a further exception. In practice juries are only allowed to convict a person on the evidence of accomplices if there is some corroboration of the accomplices' story.

CORRUPTION.—The name given to all classes of bribery. In general it is a punishable offence to offer or to receive a bribe in respect of the performance of a person's duty. This is so whether the duty is towards a public body or a private individual. Corruption by private agents is punishable by two years' imprisonment and a fine of £500. Penal servitude may be inflicted for corrupt offences in relation to contracts with Government departments. In the latter class of offence there is an important provision whereby, once it is proved that any present has been given to a Government servant by anyone holding or seeking to obtain a contract with a Government department, the present is to be treated as given and received corruptly until the contrary is proved. Prosecutions for corruption cannot be commenced without the consent of the Attorney General. (*See* BRIBERY.)

COSTS IN COUNTY COURT.— Included in his judgment the Judge will make an order as to the costs of the action. The Judge is entitled to make whatever order he pleases as to who is to pay the costs, and in what proportion they are to be paid. As a general rule, however, the costs are awarded to the party who is successful in the action. If the plaintiff is successful he will be awarded the amount of his claim with costs. If the defendant is successful he will generally be given judgment for his costs.

The amount of costs which will be awarded against the unsuccessful litigant depends, where the plaintiff is successful, upon the amount which he recovers; and where the defendant is successful, upon the amount which the plaintiff unsuccessfully attempted to recover in the action. There are four different scales upon which costs are taxed according as whether the amount recovered or sought to be recovered is (1) less than £10; (2) between £10 and £20; (3) between £20 and £50; and (4) between £50 and £100.

Naturally the greater the amount recovered the greater the costs, and for this reason litigants who are claiming general

damages must limit the amount of damages that they claim, in order to keep down the amount of costs that may be awarded against them in the event of their being unsuccessful.

In all cases where the amount recovered exceeds £2 the scale of costs allows for the employment of a solicitor, and where the amount recovered is more than £10 for the employment of a barrister as well, while in many cases under this limit the Judge will give a certificate to the successful litigant permitting his costs in employing a barrister to be paid by his unsuccessful opponent.

These provisions will apply also to a defendant, if successful, where the amount claimed in the action falls within the limits mentioned above. Thus, if a County Court action is not conducted upon an extravagant scale, a litigant, if he is successful, may be confident of having all his expenses (except perhaps for a few shillings) paid by his opponent out of the costs allowed by the Judge in his judgment; and in view of the technical pitfalls that beset the layman, it is always advisable to take advantage of these provisions and to employ a solicitor.

Where a solicitor is not employed, the successful litigant is naturally not allowed to charge his opponents with the costs that would have been occasioned by his employment; and the costs which he will recover will be limited practically to the Court fees that he has been obliged to pay and the allowances permitted for witnesses. In some, though by no means in all, cases, a litigant who appears in person is allowed to include his travelling expenses to and from the Court and his hotel expenses as part of the costs that he may recover.

In the simplest kind of action where the litigants conduct their cases in person, the fees payable by the plaintiff will be restricted to the Plaint Fee payable upon entering a plaint and issuing a summons, and the Hearing Fee payable before the trial of the action starts. While if the defendant fails to appear, instead of a hearing fee the plaintiff may pay a fee on entering judgment, which fee will be one half of the appropriate hearing fee.

The plaint fee and hearing fee are of the same amount and vary according to the amount claimed in the action as follows:

For a claim not exceeding 10/- the Fee is 1/-

do.	£1	do.	1/6
do.	£2	do.	3/-
do.	£3	do.	4/6
do.	£4	do.	6/-
do.	£5	do.	7/6
do.	£6	do.	9/-

Thereafter the amount of the fee rises by 1/- for every £1 of the amount of the claim up to £30, for which the appropriate fee is 33/-, and thereafter rises fairly regularly to 40/- where the amount claimed does not exceed £50, and 59/- where the amount claimed does not exceed £100.

The witness fees allowed include their reasonable travelling expenses to the Court together with an additional sum which varies from £1 1s. for a person of independent means or a professional man to 6/- for a manual labourer.

In addition to these fees small additional fees are payable in respect of interlocutory proceedings, while for the issuing of a subpœna to serve upon witnesses a further fee of 2/- if the subpœna is to be served by the bailiff, or 1/- if to be served otherwise, must be paid.

In those cases where a defendant brings a counterclaim against the plaintiff he must pay a hearing fee calculated upon the amount of the counterclaim, and, if his counterclaim exceeds the amount claimed by the plaintiff he must pay the extra amount of the plaint fee when he enters notice of his counterclaim. (*See* COUNTY COURT PROCEDURE.)

COSTS IN HIGH COURT.—An important part of the judgment in an action relates to Costs. Costs, in their technical sense do not mean the out-of-pocket expenses of litigants, but such portion of the expenses of an action as the Court allows through its appropriate official the Taxing Master. This is an official who, after an action has been heard and judgment given, goes through the statements of expenses of the solicitors to the litigants and taxes, and allows and disallows certain portions of them. The judgment will lay down the proportion of the costs of the successful litigant which must be paid by the unsuccessful litigant. It may also lay down the Scale upon which such costs shall be allowed. There are several different scales in the High Court, the lowest being ordinary

costs, the next Costs as Between Solicitor and Client, and the highest Costs as Between Solicitor and Own Client. It is only when the successful litigant is awarded costs upon this latter scale that the amount which he receives from his unsuccessful opponent upon taxation will cover the expenses which he has incurred.

When costs have been taxed by the taxing master, they are added to the amount of the money claim granted in the judgment, and the person entitled to costs may recover them as taxed, together with such other sums as may be recoverable by him on the judgment. (*See* HIGH COURT PROCEDURE; SOLICITOR.)

COUNSEL.—"Counsel" in England means a barrister and includes both King's Counsel and Junior Counsel. (*See* BARRISTER.)

COUNT.—A Count is a single charge in an indictment. An indictment may consist of many counts but no count may allege more than one offence. For instance a man may be charged with a series of frauds committed on various days. In the absence of any special reason to the contrary all these frauds may be placed in one indictment, but each fraud must be made the subject of a separate count in that indictment. Usually the whole of an indictment is tried at once by a jury, though of course they differentiate between the various counts contained in it when giving their verdict. (*See* INDICTMENT.)

COUNTERCLAIM.—A Counterclaim is a claim or cause of action which a defendant in an action in the High Court or County Court makes against the plaintiff. He is entitled upon giving notice to the plaintiff to have the counterclaim tried at the same time as the plaintiff's action unless this is manifestly inconvenient. It will be tried by the same Court, and as far as costs and judgment are concerned it is treated in much the same way as if it were an independent action between. the defendant and the plaintiff. In the County Court, if the counterclaim is larger in amount than the plaintiff's claim, the defendant must pay a hearing fee equal to the difference between the hearing fee already paid by the plaintiff and the hearing fee appropriate to an ordinary action for the amount of the counterclaim. Defendants who have a claim against the plaintiff and some other person, may join the other person as a defendant to counterclaim, and the counterclaim will be tried at the same time as the plaintiff's claim.

The name counterclaim is also given to that part of the pleadings which contains the defendant's claim against the plaintiff. (*See* COUNTY COURT PROCEDURE; HIGH COURT PROCEDURE; PLEADING.)

COUNTERFEIT COIN.—This is false coin intended to pass for current coin of the realm, or coin altered in any way to pass for coin of a higher value. (*See* COINING.)

COUNTERPART.—When a landlord grants a lease to a tenant two copies are usually drawn up, one being the lease itself which is signed by the landlord, and the other being called the Counterpart and signed by the tenant. The lease is given by the landlord to the tenant and kept by him while the counterpart is kept by the landlord. (*See* LANDLORD AND TENANT; LEASE.)

COUNTY COUNCIL.—A County Council is composed of a chairman, county aldermen and county councillors. It is the body in general control of the affairs of the county, and is the most considerable authority in the hierarchy of local government. For its powers, duties and constitution, *see* LOCAL GOVERNMENT.

COUNTY COURT.—Throughout the country, in nearly every town of any size, there are County Courts presided over by a County Court Judge, and in these the greater part of the judicial business of the Kingdom is done. Practically all forms of actions, where the sum involved is not greater than £100, can be brought and tried in the County Court at small expense. The exceptions to this are actions for libel and slander, and for breach of promise of marriage and seduction. Further, wherever in an action the right or title to real property is concerned, the action cannot be tried in the County Court unless the annual value of the land or the rent received for the land is less than £100 per annum; nor can an action be tried in a County Court at all if a toll, fair, market or franchise is in question.

In addition to such actions as these which may be started in the County Court, actions for small amounts which have been started in the High Court are often remitted to the County Court for trial; and in cases where the plaintiff is a person of small means, who would be unlikely to be able to pay his opponent's costs in the event of his losing the action in the High Court, such action is often remitted to the County Court.

Administration Actions where the estate is of a value of less than £500 are heard in the County Court and also suits for the recovery of legacies of not more than £100.

Actions by and against Trustees in respect of their trusts are dealt with by the County Court if the amount of the trust fund or estate is not greater than £500.

Another important branch of the work of the County Court is in connection with the administration of funds for the benefit of infants, which are dealt with where the amount of the fund is not greater than £500; while, if an infant recovers damages in an action in the High Court, (e.g. for personal injuries), the money may be transferred to the convenient County Court, where the guardian must in future make application if he wishes to withdraw part of the money for the infant's benefit.

Under the Workmen's Compensation Acts, the Judge of the County Court is the Arbitrator appointed to decide questions under those acts; but although in such case he sits in the same Court as when sitting for other matters and often takes such cases at the same time as others, he is not actually sitting as a County Court Judge, and the duties which he performs are not part of the business of the County Court.

Although a claim for a sum greater than £100 cannot be started in the County Court, yet any person claiming a sum greater than that may yet bring his action in the County Court if he waives or abandons his right to receive a sum greater than £100 in the action. He cannot however split up a larger claim into several actions in order to give the County Court jurisdiction to hear the case.

There is one other limitation upon the powers of a County Court. Whereas in the High Court it is possible for a plaintiff to claim merely an injunction, (i.e. an order of the Court forbidding the other party to do something which he is not entitled to do, which order will be enforced by imprisonment on disobedience), or a declaration, (i.e. an authoritative pronouncement upon the rights of the parties to the action), such relief cannot be obtained in the County Court unless it is accompanied by a money claim. For the purpose of the work of County Courts the whole country is divided into a number of districts in which Courts must be held at least once a month, the hour and date of which sitting must be placed on a notice in the Court House and the Registrar's office three months before the sitting. Actually the Country Districts are divided into circuits presided over by a County Court Judge, and he arranges to visit each Court at regular intervals, at least once a month, with the exception of a month's vacation in August or September. In London there are a number of districts, viz., Bloomsbury, Bow, Clerkenwell, Lambeth, Marylebone, Shoreditch, Southwark, Westminster, Whitechapel and West London. The Mayor's and City of London Court sitting at the Guildhall, has jurisdiction where the whole cause of Action arises in the City of London to an unlimited amount, but otherwise as an ordinary County Court. The London Courts sit at very frequent intervals as do those in the other large cities.

At the County Court House, the office of the County Court is open from 10 a.m. to 4 p.m. each day except Sundays and certain holidays, and from 9 a.m. to 12 noon or from 10 a.m. to 1 p.m. on Saturdays, and in some places there are County Court offices in towns where, although there is no County Court, business may be done in respect of action brought in the County Court of the district.

Each County Court is presided over by a Judge, of whom as at Westminster there may be more than one for a district or, as in many country districts, one Judge will act for several districts.

In addition to the Judge every County Court has a Registrar, who must be a solicitor of seven years' standing or may be a barrister. The Registrar is in charge of the office of the County Court and issues writs, summonses, warrants, writs of execution, etc., and deals generally with all fees and business of the Court before and after the actual trial. He has also jurisdiction that will be mentioned later to try certain of the cases in the Court.

Another important member of the staff of the County Court is the High Bailiff and he, together with his assistants, is responsible for serving summonses, warrants, etc., upon defendants and other litigants and for levying execution upon County Court Judgments. In connection with the duties of the High Bailiff in which he is assisted by assistant Bailiffs it is important to note that any person who interferes with an officer of the County Court in the execution of his duties is liable to a fine of £5, and he may be arrested by the Bailiff and fined either by the Judge of the County Court or through the medium of police proceedings. This is in addition to any other criminal proceedings as may be brought against the offender. (*See* ACTION; COUNTY COURT PROCEDURE; PARTIES.)

COUNTY COURT PROCEDURE. —A person who has a cause of action properly triable in the County Court, must first decide upon the district in which he is entitled to bring the action. The general rule is that the action must be started in the County Court of the district in which the defendant lives or has his place of business, or, in the case of an action against a Company, the place where its principal business is conducted—which need not necessarily be the registered offices of the company. But leave may be obtained to commence an action in the Court of the district where the defendant dwelt or carried on business within six months of the start of the action, or in the district where the cause of the action in whole or in part arose. This latter provision is often taken advantage of by persons who have made contracts by correspondence for delivery of goods by post, but leave will not be granted where the defendant is an agricultural or manual labourer or a miner, unless it is shewn either that the defendant is unlikely to defend the action or that he was present in the district when the cause of action arose, or when the Judge is of opinion that the proposed place of trial will not be less convenient to the defendant than the proper district.

Commencement of an Action. — An action in the County Court is started by the entry of a Plaint. The plaintiff, or his solicitor, must attend at the Registrar's office of the County Court in the appropriate district and file at that office a form, a copy of which will be handed to him, called a Praecipe. In this he must insert

(1) his Christian name and surname, occupation and address; (2) the surname, occupation and address of the defendant and whether he is male or female; (3) a short statement of the cause of action, e.g. "The plaintiff's claim is for £10 lent to the defendant." Particulars of the way in which the claim arises must be filed at the same time if the amount claimed is greater than £2.

He will then be given a note sealed with the seal of the Court showing that he has fulfilled these formalities, and must pay a fee varying from 1/- to £2 10s. according to the amount of money he wishes to recover. If, in order to reduce the amount of costs payable should he lose, he wishes to limit his claim to a lower amount than its true value, he must state so on the praecipe and he will then be charged the lower fee. If the claim is greater than £100, but the parties have agreed to allow the County Court to try the question at issue, the document giving such consent must be filed at the office.

In those cases where leave to commence an action is necessary, because the action is being brought in a different district, the plaintiff must make an affidavit, properly sworn before a commissioner for oaths, explaining why he asks for permission to issue the plaint outside the usual district.

If, as so frequently happens, the proper district being that in which the proposed defendant resides, the action is started in a district where the plaintiff does not himself reside, he need not attend at the office of the County Court himself but can send by ordinary post to the Registrar a praecipe containing the necessary information together with a postal order for the amount of the fee. This useful rule is only available if the plaintiff does not reside in the district, and if he is not represented in the action by a solicitor who has an office in that district.

When the plaint has been entered in the above manner it is generally the duty of the Registrar to issue and seal a summons, which is a document addressed to the defendant calling upon him to appear at the Court. The summons states the nature of the action and basis of the claim, the name of the plaintiff etc.

If the action is for a debt or for a liquidated sum of money, (i.e. is not for general damages) it is quicker and more convenient to issue a Default Summons, if the amount claimed is less than £10, or a Special Default summons if the amount claimed is greater than £10.

In order to issue such a summons, the plaintiff must at the time of entry of the Plaint, file particulars in writing, or in the case of a special default summons, file an affidavit, containing a brief account of the manner in which the claim arose and stating his belief that there is no defence to the claim. The summons which is issued upon this informs the defendant that, if within 8 days of the service of the summons he fails to give notice, (in writing in the case of a default summons, and by way of an affidavit in the case of a special default summons), to the Registrar of the Court that he intends to defend the action, the plaintiff will be entitled to judgment against him. The notice of intention to defend may be given by post either personally by the defendant or through his solicitor. Alternatively the defendant may send a notice in writing to the Registrar offering to pay the debt in instalments.

This is the usual summons that should be issued if the plaintif has a claim for a liquidated sum of money, as the procedure is speedy and efficacious as long as there is no substantial defence to the claim.

Service of Summons.—A summons in a County Court action is served as a general rule by the Bailiff of the Court to whom the Registrar delivers the summons. It must be served at least 10 days before the date of hearing of the action, and it should be handed to the Bailiff at least 15 days before the action if the defendant lives within the district of the County Court that is to hear the action, or 18 days before if the defendant lives outside that district. The Bailiff serves the summons by handing it to the defendant personally or by handing it to some other person not less than 16 years of age at the defendant's dwelling place, or at his place of business if he is one of the masters of the business. Where the summons is for recovery of possession of a tenement, the service may be effected, if the defendant cannot be found, by fixing a copy of the summons to a conspicuous part of the tenement. In many cases the defendant's solicitor will already have expressed his

8*

willingness to accept service of the summons on behalf of his client, in which case the Bailiff must obtain the signature of the solicitor to the copy of the summons which the Bailiff retains.

If any one refuses to accept service of a summons by a Bailiff, then the Bailiff may leave it near the person refusing to accept service.

A summons upon an infant should be served upon the guardian of the infant or the person with whom he resides: a summons upon a partnership business may be served upon any partner or it may be left at the principal place of business, as may be done when a defendant carries on business in a name other than his own.

There is nothing to prevent a plaintiff himself serving the summons instead of getting the Bailiff to do so, but it is always wiser to do this through the Bailiff.

If it is impossible to serve the summons in any of the ways mentioned above, the plaintiff may go to the Registrar's Office, and after making an affidavit shewing that service as above has proved impossible, the Registrar will grant permission for the service of the summons to be made in some other way, such as by advertising it in the local newspapers or forwarding it by registered post.

Default and Special Default summonses must be served upon the defendant personally within twelve months of their issue. They may—and should for choice—be served by a Bailiff, but they may also be served by the plaintiff or some person in his employ or by the plaintiff's solicitors, but in such case the person making the service must make an affidavit that the summons has been properly served, and must file this at the Court within three days of making such service.

Where, in those cases where the action is brought in some district other than that in which the defendant dwells, it is necessary for him to be served in another district, the summons will be served by the High Bailiff of the Court where the defendant lives, and notice of the service will be transmitted to the Registrar of the Court where the action is to be heard.

Many difficulties may arise where the defendant is abroad or where he has died without appointing any executors. and in such cases a solicitor should always be consulted.

Procedure after service of summons.—Where an ordinary summons has been served a defendant need not take any further steps until the day mentioned in the summons when he can appear in Court and defend the action. But where a default or special default summons has been served upon him, it is vital that he should within eight days forward to the Registrar a statement in writing, or an affidavit, in the case of a special default summons, setting out the fact that he intents to contest the claim, and also setting out concisely the grounds of his defence. In the case of a special default summons he must also send to the Registrar a copy of the affidavit for the information of the plaintiff.

It is always wise for a defendant to write to the plaintiff for further particulars of the claim, and this applies whether the summons is an ordinary one or a default one. With this request the plaintiff must comply and must at the same time file a copy of the particulars which he sends, with the Registrar of the County Court.

This notice to the plaintiff asking for further particulars must be given at least 5 days before the trial or, where the claim is for more than £50, at least 15 days before the trial. Failure to comply with the request by the plaintiff renders him liable to be prevented by the Court on the day of the trial from proceeding with his action until the particulars have been given, and being mulcted in costs for the delay caused by his neglect.

Although the defendant to an ordinary summons need not file any defence, he can be forced to by the plaintiff, in cases when the claim exceeds £20, if the plaintiff sends to him in writing 7 clear days before the trial, or 12 clear days if the claim is for more than £50, notice asking for the nature of his defence. The defendant must then, within four days of receiving the notice, file with the Registrar a written statement of the grounds of his defence and must forward a copy of it to the plaintiff. A failure to do this is visited with the same disadvantages as apply to the plaintiff when he fails to file particulars of his claim upon demand by the defendant.

In addition to this, if the defendant intends to rely upon the defences that are set out below, or any one of them, he must give particulars of the defence, whether he has been asked to do so or not, and in default of his so doing he will not be allowed to rely upon such defence when the case comes on for trial:

(1) Where he intends to allege fraud or misrepresentation.

(2) Where infancy or coverture—i.e. where the defendant is a married woman—is relied upon.

(3) Where the defendant intends to rely upon a defence founded on statute.

(4) Where in the case of an action for libel or slander the defendant intends to shew that the words are true.

(5) Where the defendant intends to rely upon any equitable defence or upon a defence that he tendered the money before action was brought.

In addition the defendant is entitled, if he wishes, to include with his notice of particulars of defence any counterclaim which he may have against the plaintiff, and such counterclaim will be tried at the same time as the main action. Such notice must be given at least 5 clear days before the trial.

Similarly, if the counterclaim is against the plaintiff and some other person as well, the defendant may go to the Registrar's office and apply to add the other person as plaintiff as well. If the Registrar permits this a notice will be served upon the other person by the usual officers of the Court.

A like procedure is available, if the defendant has a right to be indemnified by a third party in respect of the subject matter of the action, and the Registrar, upon application being made to him by the defendant, will arrange for a notice of this being served upon the third party, who will thereafter be treated as if he were defendant in an action between the defendant and himself, and must appear at court when the case is tried and must deliver particulars of his defence, etc., in exactly the same way as mentioned above.

Interlocutory proceedings.—In the simplest kind of County Court action there will be no necessity to take any further steps other than the above before the case comes on for trial; but where the action is for a considerable sum and the facts of the case are obscure, either party may seek the assistance of the Court in preparing for it.

A defendant, for instance, may decide for the sake of peace and quiet to pay some part of the plaintiff's claim together with the costs incurred, and in order to do this he must take or forward the sum which he wishes to pay in to the court to the Registrar. Unless he specifically states so on an appropriate form, the amount which he pays in will be presumed to be an admission of the plaintiff's claim to the extent of the sum paid in. But if he still denies liability and files a form saying so at the time that he pays it in, the plaintiff has either the choice of taking the money out of Court and abandoning the action (in which case he will be entitled to receive his costs up to the date at which the money was paid in, even if these costs are greater than the amount that the defendant has paid in in respect of them), or continuing with his action and leaving the money in Court. In such a case, if the plaintiff fails at the trial to recover more than the sum paid in by the defendant, he will be obliged to pay the defendant's costs incurred after the date that the payment was made. If the plaintiff recovers more than the sum paid in, he is entitled to all his costs.

Where the defendant pays the money into Court without denying his liability, the plaintiff is entitled either to take the money out and continue or abandon his action, or to leave the money in and continue it. The same provisions as to costs will apply.

The Registrar must give notice within 24 hours to the plaintiff of any money paid into Court, stating whether it is paid with or without denial of liability. The plaintiff can then call at the Registrar's office to take the money out, producing the copy of the plaint note as evidence of his right to it, or if he lives outside the district of the County Court he may apply in writing to the Registrar forwarding the necessary copy of the plaint note, and the money will be sent to him by post at his own risk. It is thus important to pay any money into Court as early as possible so as to save unnecessary costs.

Other matters which either party to an action may wish to have decided will be whether a jury is to be used at the trial, and a demand for a jury may be made by either party to the Registrar at least 10 days before the day set down for trial.

Notices to the other side to produce

documents at trial may also be given at least 5 days before the trial, and similarly notices to admit that documents in possession of one party are what they purport to be. These notices are given on forms obtainable at any law stationers, and their effect is to make the cost of proving any documents contained in the notices the expense of the party refusing to admit them, whatever may be the result of the main action. A notice to produce documents permits the side serving the notice to give secondary evidence of their contents, if the party served with the notice fails to produce them. (*See* EVIDENCE.) The other possible interlocutory proceedings (which include a right to administer questions to be answered on oath by the opposite party and known as interrogatories, and a right to be informed of, and to inspect, all relevant documents in the possession of the other party), are so many and varied that it is unwise to attempt to deal with them without the assistance of a solicitor.

Admissions by Defendants.—In a great many County Court cases, particularly those for which default and special default summonses are suitable, the defendant has no defence to the action but is merely not in a financial position to pay the amount owing. In such a case if the amount claimed is less than £20 he may send a notice in writing to the Registrar, admitting that he owes the money and making an offer to pay by instalments. This he should do at least 5 days before the case comes on for trial, for although he may do so later, he may find himself liable for greater costs.

The Registrar then notifies the plaintiff of the admission and the offer of payment, and the plaintiff, if he wishes, may then send a notice of acceptance of the offer to the Registrar and the defendant; in which case the Registrar will forthwith enter up judgment for the amount admitted and for the Court fees and costs, and will make an order for these to be paid by the defendant in the instalments that he has offered.

The plaintiff may leave it until the last moment to accept the offer, accepting actually in Court at the time the action is called on, if he so wishes.

If the plaintiff does not accept the offer for payment by instalments, he must either attend at Court on the day fixed for trial and pay the Court fee for hearing (in which case he may move by calling witnesses or giving evidence of facts within his knowledge that the defendant's means are sufficient to enable him to pay the whole debt at once or by larger instalments), or he may send the Hearing Fee by post to the Registrar. In either case the Registrar will be guided by his own discretion as to the order that he makes for payment of the amount admitted to be owing, the costs, Court fees, etc. In such cases, however, it is always wiser for the plaintiff to appear, either himself or by his solicitor, to give the reasons for thinking that the defendant is in a position to pay instalments larger than those which he has offered. No judgment for payment by instalments, however, may be given without the plaintiff's consent, if the amount claimed exceeds £20.

Trial of Action.—It is a very good rule for intending litigants in the County Court never to attempt to conduct their cases themselves, unless the cases are of the kind suitable for the issue of default or special default summonses, where it is unlikely that the defendant has any defence.

Litigants should remember that the Judge can only take account of such facts as are proved to him and in this connection the rules of evidence are important.

In different County Courts different rules prevail as to calling over cases. The litigant whose case is down for hearing on the return day should attend at the Court and should ascertain by enquiry at the office of the Registrar, in what Court his case will be heard, and then from the attendant in the Court in question the order in which the various cases are being taken. The Hearing Fee must be paid by the plaintiff at the office of the Court before the action is tried.

Where barristers or solicitors are employed the proceedings are conducted with greater formality than where the litigants appear in person. Generally speaking, no person may address the County Court on behalf of any party unless he is a barrister or a solicitor, though in certain cases the Judge will permit the wife or husband of a litigant, or some close relative to appear, if the litigant himself is unable to be present.

Where no legal advisers are employed the plaintiff is generally required to step into the witness box on the right hand side of the Judge and the defendant into the witness box on the left hand side. In theory the plaintiff is allowed first to state the nature of his case and then to call any evidence that he may require to prove it. In actions for money owing by the defendant, he should be in a position to call into the witness box the person who actually dealt with the defendant in the matter, and it is useless to go to Court without such evidence. Mere hearsay i.e. a statement which has been made to the plaintiff by someone not present, cannot be admitted. All the relevant documents should be produced and shown to the Court.

When the plaintiff has addressed the Court and called his witnesses the turn of the defendant, who has so far only been permitted to question the witnesses called by the plaintiff, arrives to call any witness that he may have. These witnesses the plaintiff is in turn allowed to question. The defendant is not usually allowed to address the Judge before calling his witnesses as he is in the High Court.

Then the defendant is allowed to address the Court while the last word is reserved for the plaintiff. The Judge then gives judgment.

It is important to distinguish between the speeches made by the parties to the action and the evidence which they call. If solicitors or barristers are employed there will be no difficulties as to this, but where the litigants conduct their cases in person difficulties occasionally arise.

The initial speech of the plaintiff in which he explains shortly the facts of his case is not made on oath, and no interruption by the defendant is permitted. But if, after the plaintiff has opened his case in this manner, he goes into the witness box to give evidence on oath to prove his case, the defendant is allowed to question or cross-examine him. Cross-examination, however, must consist solely of questions and not of speeches made by the defendant. The plaintiff, if he calls other witnesses to give evidence, must extract their evidence by question and answer, and must not by the way he puts the question even hint at the answer which he requires. A question framed in such a manner is known as a "leading question" and will not be permitted. The defendant is entitled to cross-examine the plaintiff's witnesses in the same manner and

subject to the same limitations as his cross-examination of the plaintiff.

When the plaintiff has called all his evidence, the defendant then calls his evidence, going into the witness-box to give evidence on oath himself, if necessary, and examining by question and answer the witnesses whom he wishes to call. The plaintiff has the right to cross-examine the defendant's witnesses.

The defendant then makes his final speech, not on oath and free from interruption from the plaintiff, urging every fact that has been proved in favour of his case; and the plaintiff then follows on with his own final speech.

Careful attention to these simple rules will avoid a great deal of trouble in the County Court, and will meet with the approval of the Judge who is trying the case.

Registrar's Court.—In many Courts the Registrar takes the place of the Judge in deciding and giving judgment upon actions where both parties consent and the amount claimed is less than £5, and in other cases with leave from the Judge. This is in addition to the functions of the Registrar who hears and decides upon all of those default and special default summonses, where the defendant has no real defence to the facts of the dispute but makes an offer to pay the money owing by instalments. In many County Courts also, where a case has been started by a default or special default summons, the case is called on first before the Registrar and is then sent over to be tried by the Judge in those cases where the defendant proposes to defend the action. (*See* APPEAL FROM COUNTY COURT; COSTS IN COUNTY COURT; COUNTY COURT; JUDGMENT IN COUNTY COURT.)

COUNTY PALATINE.—The Counties Palatine are Lancashire and Durham. Originally the lord of each of these Palatinates had almost kingly power within his boundaries, and the whole area was controlled by its own officers and courts. The Chancellor of the Duchy of Lancaster is now no longer a judicial officer, though he still nominally controls the crown property belonging to the Duchy, whether or not such property be situated in Lancashire. The Lancaster Palatine Court of Chancery still functions, having the same duties as the Chancery Division of the High Court. The revenues of both the Counties Palatine now belong to the crown in its personal capacity, and do not pass into the public funds.

COURSE OF EMPLOYMENT.— A master is liable for any damage done to a stranger by a servant acting in the course of his employment. This means that a master is liable for the negligence of his servant so long as his servant was doing that which he was employed to do, but the master is not responsible if the servant was doing something he was not employed to do at all. (*See* MASTER AND SERVANT.)

COURSING.—The killing of hares is a sport for which there is no close season, except in the case of moorlands and unenclosed non-arable lands, when there is a close season for killing ground game (including hares) from 1st April to 10th December. If, however, guns are not used, this close season extends only from 1st April to 31st August, i.e. the season for coursing hares is close on moorlands etc., only between 1st April and 31st August. Hares (unlike rabbits) may not be killed on Sundays or Christmas Days. Since hares are ground game, a landlord cannot agree with the occupier of his land wholly to deprive him of the right to kill them, but he can agree with him that the only person who shall be entitled to kill such game *with firearms* shall be the occupier himself and *one* person authorized by the occupier in writing, such person to be a member of his household or employed by him on the land. But if no firearms are used (e.g. in the case of coursing) the occupier cannot be limited to one person but may authorize as many persons as he likes, provided they are members of his household or employed by him on the land. Even if they are not so resident or employed, he may invite as many persons as he likes to be spectators of the coursing. Any agreement between a landlord and the occupier that the occupier shall not exercise these limited rights is null and void. (*See also* GAME.)

COURT.—It is one of the functions of the government of a country to provide tribunals before which disputes between subject and subject may be decided peaceably by due process of law.

The right that a Court has to try an action is known as its Jurisdiction, and Courts are divided into Superior and Inferior Courts

The Main Entrance of the High Courts of Justice, Strand, London.

according as to whether their jurisdiction is unlimited or limited in any manner, either as to the area in which the actions which it may hear arose, or by reason of their nature or amount.

The Superior Courts include the various branches of the Supreme Court of Judicature (q.v.), i.e. The House of Lords, the Court of Appeal, the High Court of Justice; and the Inferior Courts include such Courts as County Courts, Petty Sessional Courts, Sheriffs' Courts, Coroners' Courts, etc. which are limited by law as to the nature of the actions which they may try and the areas within which the cause of action arose.

The Jurisdiction of a Court may be either Original or Appellate. The Original Jurisdiction is the right to hear and determine an action which has been started in the Court hearing it, and which has not already been decided upon by another Court. The Appellate Jurisdiction is a right to rehear an action which has already been tried in another

Court, and to override or to confirm the decision of the previous Court.

Every Court, subject in the Inferior Courts to certain conditions, has the right to insist upon the presence of persons to give evidence upon oath before it, and to enforce their presence by punishment, if need be; to visit with punishment and imprisonment, if necessary, those who disobey its lawful orders; to enforce the decisions that it may give; while persons practising in the Court are entitled to immunity from the usual consequences of the law of libel and slander, etc., if properly engaged upon the business of the Court. (*See* ACTION; COUNTY COURT; HIGH COURT OF JUSTICE.)

COURT OF APPEAL.—This Court is part of the Supreme Court of Judicature and consists of the Lord Chancellor, the Lord Chief Justice, the Master of the Rolls, the President of the Probate, Divorce and Admiralty Division and five Lords Justices of Appeal. It is a Court of Appeal from all divisions of the High Court of Justice, from decisions of the County Court, after hearing by a Divisional Court by way of appeal, and from the decisions of the Judge in Chambers on preliminary points that arise in the course of an action, and from the decisions of a County Court Judge in Workmen's Compensation cases. It generally sits in two Courts and three members of the Court are necessary to hear appeals. (*See* APPEAL IN HIGH COURT; SUPREME COURT OF JUDICATURE.)

COURT MARTIAL.—A Court Martial is a special court which is set up from time to time for the trial of offences alleged to have been committed by persons subject to Naval, Military or Air Force law. Naval Courts Martial sit under the Naval Discipline Act, Military Courts Martial under the Army Act, and Air Force Courts Martial under the Air Force Act. They consist of bodies of officers who are appointed to sit specially for the trial of the cases brought before them. They are of various kinds and exercise varying powers.

In the Army and Royal Air Force there are two kinds, General Courts Martial and District Courts Martial. A General Court Martial is the only service tribunal that can try an officer. It can also try persons of lower rank. It exercises the highest powers as regards punishment and may award any sentence allowed by law for any particular offence. Thus, if it is trying a case of murder it may award a death penalty. It consists of five or more officers presided over by a Colonel or a General, and it invariably has a Judge Advocate as legal adviser. District Courts Martial on the other hand cannot try officers and may in no case inflict punishment greater than two years' imprisonment with hard labour. They consist of not less than three officers and are usually presided over by a Major, and in cases of legal difficulty they usually, in Great Britain, have the assistance of a Judge Advocate.

Another form of Court Martial is known as Field General Court Martial. This kind of Court sits when troops are on active service, and also for the trial of certain classes of cases abroad though the troops are not on active service. Its procedure is very flexible and its powers of punishment are limited only by the maximum powers permitted in the case of any particular offence. It can consist of two or more officers, and it may not pass sentence of death unless all the members concur in such a sentence.

Courts Martial, although sitting under special codes of law, are subject to the ordinary law of the land as regards the admissibility of evidence. Their procedure is very similar to that of ordinary criminal courts. Any person charged may be represented by counsel or by a solicitor.

All Courts Martial are held in public, and the press have a right of access and may report the proceedings. The only qualification to the public's right of access is the power of the Court in exceptional circumstances, such as the interests of the State or public decency, to sit in camera.

COURT OF SESSION.—The Court of Session is the Supreme Civil Court of Scotland. Its decisions are, however, subject to appeal to the House of Lords, which in hearing them sits as a Scots Court of Appeal and applies the rules of Scots Law. It consists of an Outer and an Inner House. The Judges in the Outer House are called Lords Ordinary and hear cases in the first instance. The Inner House sits in divisions presided over by the Lord President or the Lord Justice Clerk, and is a Court of Appeal from the Outer House and from decisions of the Sheriff Courts.

COURTESY (SCOTS LAW).—In Scotland a husband is still entitled to a liferent of any heritable property, i.e. land, belonging to his wife at the time of her death, provided that there has been a child born of the marriage and "heard to cry," i.e. born alive, who, if he or she had lived, would have been the wife's heir. A second husband will not be entitled to courtesy if there is an heir of the first marriage. This is one of the "legal rights" which spouses enjoy in the property of one another, and which children have against the property of their parents and of which they cannot be deprived by will. The policy of English law has always been opposed to any restrictions on the freedom of a man to dispose as he pleases of his property on his death, without regard to the moral claims which members of his family may have on him. This is one of the most important distinctions between Scots and English Law. (*See* HUSBAND AND WIFE [SCOTS LAW].)

COVENANT.—Where a deed contains a clause which creates some obligation to do, or refrain from doing, some act by one of the parties to the deed, it is called a Covenant. There are important distinctions between negative or merely restrictive covenants and positive covenants or those creating a duty actually to do something. Where there are several parties to the deed, they may each enter into Covenants. In addition there may be "Mutual Covenants" in which all or several of the parties join. (*See* SALE OF LAND.)

COVER NOTE.—In connection with most policies of insurance, insurance companies issue a Cover Note to a person taking out a policy, which operates as a sort of provisional insurance until the proper policy is issued.

An applicant for an insurance policy, particularly an insurance policy against Third Party Risks in connection with a motor vehicle, often wishes to be insured immediately instead of waiting to fill up a proposal form and to permit the insurance company to make those inquiries as to his standing, etc., which they generally require to make before issuing a formal policy. To meet such cases as these insurance companies issue to the applicant a document called a Cover Note, or in some cases a Slip, which operates as a policy of insurance upon the same terms as the policy intended eventually to be taken out, for a certain fixed period of time,

generally 14 days. If at the end of that period of time the insurance company refuses to issue the policy, the insurance lapses. But if the contingency insured against, e.g. an accident, takes place during the period for which the cover note is issued, then the insurance company must pay the policy moneys, even though they had intended to refuse to issue a policy when the period of time had expired. For example, if A wishes to insure his car against Third Party Risks and applies to an insurance company for a policy of insurance, the company will issue him a cover note for 14 days pending the filling up of a proposal form. The insurance company may demand as a condition of issuing the policy that A shall obtain an engineer's report upon the car that will satisfy the insurance company. Then, if an accident occurs during the 14 days, the insurance company must pay the policy moneys, although in fact A would not have been able to obtain a satisfactory engineer's report. On the other hand, if the 14 days had elapsed before the accident took place, and A had not yet obtained from the insurance company his policy of insurance, he would not be covered. If the risk is not accepted the premium is returned less a proportionate part in respect of the period covered by the cover note. (*See* FIRE INSURANCE; INSURANCE; MARINE INSURANCE; MOTOR VEHICLE INSURANCE.)

COVERTURE.—Coverture is a technical legal expression meaning the status involved by marriage. A woman is said to be in a state of coverture during the lifetime of her husband. As such, of course, while entitled to certain legal advantages, she is also under certain legal limitations. Thus while she cannot be sued by her husband for civil wrongs, her remedy against her husband for similar wrongs, though not non-existent, is subject to certain special rules. (*See* MARRIED WOMEN.)

CREDITORS' MEETING.—In the winding-up of a Company and in the administration of the estate of a person who has become bankrupt, the creditors of the Company or of the bankrupt meet from time to time to decide various matters relating to the collection and distribution of the assets. In most cases the creditors act through a committee of inspection appointed by themselves from their number. The creditors appoint the liquidator and trustee in bankruptcy and exercise a control over these officers throughout the realization of the estate. In most cases a bare majority in number and value of the creditors present and voting will be sufficient to carry any resolution, but for some purposes a larger majority is required. The value of a creditor's vote is the amount of money of his admitted claim against the estate. If a creditor holds some security for his debt he must, if he wishes to rely on it, put a value upon it and claim only in respect of the amount (if any) by which the money due to him exceeds the value of the security. (*See* BANKRUPTCY; SECURED CREDITOR; WINDING-UP.)

CREMATION.—Disposal of a dead body by burning is recognized and regulated by the provisions of the Cremation Act, 1902. A Burial Authority may provide a crematorium in the burial ground or cemetery, but the approval of the Ministry of Health as to the situation and plans must be obtained before cremations can take place. Further, the crematorium must be built "strictly to the plans and properly fitted to dispose of bodies by cremation and certified to the Secretary of State as being so built and fitted." The Burial Authority have no power to build a crematorium instead of a cemetery and, of course, they are under no obligation to provide one in the cemetery, but may if they wish.

A crematorium must be kept in proper condition under the Regulations authorized by the Statute and must likewise be open to inspection by the person appointed by virtue of such Regulations. The Burial Authority has power, however, to close it by proper notice in accordance with the Regulations.

It is not lawful to cremate the body of a person who is known to have left written directions as to his or her desire not to be cremated. No cremation of a person dying in England can take place until the death has been duly registered, or a certificate obtained that the death is not required by law to be so registered in England, unless a Coroner's certificate has been obtained that an inquest or post mortem examination has taken place. Nor can a body be cremated unless an application supported by a statutory declaration be made, and a certificate obtained of the cause of the death by a registered medical practitioner who attended the last illness of the deceased, confirmed by another medical practitioner duly qualified, as laid down by the Regulations under the Statute referred to above. In the alternative to the latter requirement, however, a certificate may be given by an expert pathological medical practitioner (duly appointed by the proper authority) that he has held a post mortem examination, if such be the case: or in like case the cause of death may be certified by the Coroner, or an inquest held and a certificate given by the Coroner. The Coroner, in certain cases, if he is satisfied that death was due to an accident, may give a modified certificate in the statutory form before the completion of the inquest.

Applications for cremation should be made by an executor or nearest surviving relative of the deceased. In certain circumstances some other person interested may make the application if he gives some satisfactory reason therefor. The application, statutory declaration and any certificates required, as above, have to be examined by the Medical Referee who must be nominated by the Burial Authority. His appointment is made by the Secretary of State and his duty is to see that the Regulations are observed and to permit or refuse cremations. He need give no reason for refusing to allow cremation.

In the case of bodies that have been already buried for not less than one year the formalities above set out do not apply, but the Secretary of State may impose formalities as a condition of cremation. In the case of a still-born child the formalities are also modified, and substantially it is only necessary to obtain a certificate that the child is still-born from a registered medical practitioner after he has examined the body, and, unless there has been an inquest on the body, a certificate of registration of the still-birth in accordance with the law.

The ashes of a deceased person after cremation must be given to the person who applied for the cremation, if such person so desires. Otherwise they must be retained by the Burial Authority and decently disposed of by burial or by scattering in the ground reserved for that purpose. If the ashes after cremation are not removed by the person entitled to them within a reasonable time, a fortnight's notice to such person of intention to dispose of them in the manner already mentioned must be given by the Burial Authority. (*See* BURIAL; CEMETERIES.)

CRIME.—An important division in law is that between criminal and civil cases. In civil actions the dispute is between two or more of His Majesty's subjects in regard to their property or rights. Criminal cases on the other hand are those in which a person is prosecuted for some breach of the criminal law.

A prosecution is carried on in the name of the King, because all crimes are regarded as being offences against the King's peace. They take place in Courts having criminal jurisdiction and not in the ordinary civil Courts. If a person is found guilty of a crime he is subject to punishment, unlike the unsuccessful defendant in a civil case who can only be made to effect restitution. Punishments, of course, vary enormously according to the nature of the various crimes. In some cases death can be inflicted (*see* CAPITAL PUNISHMENT). Other forms of punishment are penal servitude, whipping, imprisonment and fines. (*See* the various crimes, e.g. MURDER, BURGLARY.)

CRIMINAL CONVERSATION.—This is the name of the action a husband could formerly bring against a man who committed adultery with his wife. It was for damages only. Since the introduction of the right to sue for divorce, this action has been abolished. A husband who desires damages now makes his claim for damages part of the relief he asks for in his divorce suit. (*See* SPECIAL SUPPLEMENT "DIVORCE.")

CRIMINAL APPEAL, COURT OF. —The Court of Criminal Appeal was created in 1907. It was in substitution for the ancient practice in the King's Bench Division of hearing appeals by means of writ of error, and in fact took the place of the old Court for Crown Cases Reserved. The Court of Criminal Appeal consists of the Lord Chief Justice of England and all the Judges of the King's Bench Division of the High Court of Justice. In practice, however, only three Judges sit, though in exceptional cases five or more may do so for the determination of points of great difficulty. The Court of Criminal Appeal sits in the High Court of Justice, usually in the Court of

the Lord Chief Justice. The Court hears appeals from persons who have been convicted upon indictment, that is to say before a jury. Persons convicted in the Police Court have no right of appeal to this Court, there being other machinery for hearing their appeals. A person may appeal to this Court against his conviction or against his sentence. He has a right to appeal against his conviction on any ground involving a question of law alone. Where the ground of his appeal involves a question of fact alone, or of mixed law and fact, he may only appeal with the leave of the Court of Criminal Appeal or upon the certificate of the Judge who tried him. Where he wishes to appeal against his sentence he must first obtain the leave of the Court of Criminal Appeal. Where the sentence is fixed by law, as for instance the death sentence in murder, he has no right of appeal against sentence. A person who desires to appeal must give notice of appeal, or of his application for leave to appeal, within ten days of his conviction.

Notice must be given in writing and a form of notice can be obtained from the governor of the prison to which he has been committed. When the date is fixed for his appeal, or for his application to appeal, his counsel is allowed to argue the matter before the Court. If he is without money he may in a proper case obtain the services of counsel free of charge. The Court may grant permission for him to be present in person during the hearing of his appeal should he wish to do so. In a proper case the Court of Criminal Appeal may admit a prisoner to bail pending the hearing of his appeal.

In almost all cases the Court of Criminal Appeal is the final court of appeal in criminal matters. The only superior Court is the House of Lords, and there is no right of appeal to this Court. Where, however, the Attorney-General certifies that a point of law of exceptional public importance is involved and it is desirable in the public interest that a further appeal should be brought, the House of Lords will hear an appeal from the Court of Criminal Appeal. It is important to note that in such cases the prosecutor may appeal as well as the prisoner. (*See* APPEAL IN CRIMINAL CASES.)

CRIMINAL LAW AMENDMENT ACT, 1885.—This Act is intended to protect women and young girls from the practice known as "white slavery" and from similar dangers. It imposes heavy penalties on anyone procuring women for immoral purposes, or taking advantage of them by means of threats, fraud or drugs. Violation of girls under 16 and abduction of them under 18 are other offences under this Act. There is also a clause dealing with acts of gross indecency between males. Provision is made for punishing anyone who allows these offences to be committed on his premises or organizes his house as a place of immoral entertainment.

CRIPPEN.—The name of Crippen awakens feelings of horror in almost every mind. Yet Lord Birkenhead could give him the epitaph: "He was at least a brave man and a true lover." Perhaps his notoriety depends upon the contrast of the appearance of this mild bespectacled little doctor from the U.S.A. with the revolting and gruesome nature of his crime.

Circumstances of the Crime.—The facts that led up to Crippen's trial at the Old Bailey were briefly—an unhappy marriage with a flamboyant Polish-German woman who was known on the stage as Belle Elmore; a romantic affection for a refined and delicate girl typist in his office, Ethel le Neve; the disappearance of Belle Elmore and the answer of Crippen to enquiries by her friends that she had gone to America; the dramatic flight by liner across the Atlantic of Crippen and Ethel le Neve dressed as a boy; the discovery under some loose bricks in the cellar of the Crippens' house in London of pieces of human flesh wrapped in pyjamas; the arrest of the fugitives on landing in Canada. An interesting point in the Crippen case is that wireless was used for the first time from land to a ship at sea. Without that wireless message, Crippen would have landed unchallenged, and probably made good his escape.

The Trial.—Crippen was tried for the murder of his wife at the Old Bailey in October, 1910, before the Lord Chief Justice Lord Alverstone. Mr. (later Sir) Richard Muir led for the prosecution and Mr. Tobin, K.C. (now a County Court Judge)for the defence. The Crown set out to prove that the remains found in the cellar were those of Belle Elmore and that her death had been wilfully caused by Crippen. The defence was that Crippen denied any

knowledge of the remains found, and said that his wife had left him for another man. Slowly and with wonderful ingenuity the great prosecuting counsel, Mr. Muir, forged the links of circumstantial evidence that proved the prisoner's guilt. The pyjamas were proved to be his, and the medical evidence given with remarkable force and clarity by Dr. (now Sir) Bernard Spilsbury, proved conclusively that the remains were those of Mrs. Crippen, and that they contained a new and virulent poison named hyoscine. Crippen's demeanour in the witness box under the detailed and searching cross-examination of Mr. Muir made his conviction assured. The jury were only absent 27 minutes before returning their verdict of guilty.

A sequel was the trial of Miss le Neve at the Old Bailey for being an accessory to the murder. She was defended by F. E. Smith (later Lord Birkenhead), who made one of the most famous speeches of his career, and was acquitted.

CROSS-EXAMINATION.—In any trial one party may cross-examine each witness called by the opposing side. The purpose of cross-examination is to test the veracity of the witness and to bring out any points not brought out in his examination by the side that called him. It is permissible to attack the credit of a witness by cross-examining him as to his motives, record and character. Leading questions, whilst forbidden in examination in chief, may be put in cross-examination. An important rule is that, whenever it is intended to call evidence to contradict an account of any incident given by a witness, that witness must in cross-examination be challenged on every point in which it is intended to contradict him.

CROWN, THE. Succession to.— The King's title to the crown is derived from the Act of Settlement, 1701, and by that Act the succession to the crown is determined on the hereditary principle in the same manner as lands descended before the Real Property Acts, 1925. Thus to-day the heir-apparent is the Prince of Wales: unmarried, he would be succeeded by his younger brother the Duke of York, next by the latter's eldest child, Princess Elizabeth, who would succeed before her uncles. The King in Parliament may at any time alter the successions.

The King succeeds to the throne immediately upon the death of his predecessor; there is no interregnum and because of this there is the saying "The King is dead. Long live the King." Two ceremonies mark the accession of a new King. First he is proclaimed Sovereign and later, after an interval of time, there is the coronation ceremony where the people formally accept their King, and he takes the oath in the prescribed form declaring that he is a faithful Protestant and will uphold the Act of Settlement. He also signs a declaration prescribed by the Bill of Rights. Then comes the religious ceremony of anointing and crowning, and finally homage is rendered to the new King in person by the Lords and Bishops.

Duties of the Crown.—Besides the valuable and active part which the King and his Consort play in the social and ceremonial life of the country, he has many and varied duties which occupy a great deal of time. He is the Commander in Chief of his forces. He receives the credentials of foreign diplomatic representatives, appoints Judges and colonial governors, confers honours and gives audiences to those engaged in the legislative and executive business of the country. He attends meetings of his Council—summons prorogues and dissolves Parliament—and has to make himself acquainted with the contents of innumerable State papers and attach thereto the Royal Signature.

Crown Lands.—In Feudal times the King was lord paramount of all the land in England, and the lords and citizens held their estates of him.

Since the reign of Queen Anne all the hereditary landed property of the King—except the duchies of Lancaster and Cornwall which are retained for the private income of the King and Prince of Wales, has become Crown Lands. By the Civil List Act, 1715, the Crown is restrained from ever alienating these lands. A Civil List Act is passed at the beginning of each reign—and on its authority the hereditary revenues are paid into the Consolidated Fund and a fixed sum allowed to the King in consideration of his assigning his rights to his lands. The present King receives £470,000 per annum.

Revenues of the Crown.—Crown Revenues come from two sources—the Ordinary and Extraordinary. Extraordinary revenues are those which have been created by Statute as Customs, Excise—various Taxes and Suez Canal Shares. The Ordinary Revenues are derived from certain rights to Treasure Trove, etc., but principally from Crown Lands.

CRUELTY TO ANIMALS.—There are a number of criminal offences which may be grouped generally under the heading cruelty to animals. For the purposes of the criminal offence the word "animals" applies only to domestic or tame animals and animals which have been brought into captivity, but as in fact practically any wild animal which has been wounded comes into the possession of the wounder, it covers nearly all possible forms of cruelty to animals of all kinds.

Cruelty consists of beating, kicking, ill-treating, over-riding, over-driving, torturing, infuriating or terrifying an animal in such a manner as to cause it unnecessary pain and suffering. The mere infliction of pain, which may be necessary for the purposes of correction, or which may occur by accident, does not amount to cruelty, though there may be cruelty by neglect as, for example, where an animal is underfed, kept in insanitary conditions or without proper shelter. In order to constitute the crime of cruelty it is necessary to shew that the offender knew that he was inflicting the pain or that the pain was being inflicted. An owner of an animal who permits the cruelty is also guilty of an offence.

Other offences of cruelty consist of carrying or transporting animals in such a way as to cause them unnecessary suffering, and railway companies are under a duty to provide food and water for animals carried by rail. Administering poisonous drugs or performing operations without due care and humanity are also offences, though there are exceptions to this under the strict rules relating to vivisection (q.v.).

Cock-fighting or the baiting of any other animals is strictly forbidden, and it is an offence even to attend a cock-fight or to keep a place where a cock-fight is held.

The coursing or hunting of captive animals is not illegal provided that the captive animal is not liberated in an injured or exhausted condition; but this does not apply where the animal is liberated in an enclosed space, such as coursing rabbits in an enclosure from which they cannot escape. The penalty for any of these offences is a fine not exceeding £25 and imprisonment not exceeding 3 months, though the owner of an animal whose offence consists only in not having shewn sufficient care in preventing the cruelty is liable only to the fine.

Where a conviction for cruelty has taken place the Court may order that the animal in question shall be destroyed, and in such case the cost of its destruction may be recovered from the owner in a Court of Summary Jurisdiction. Unless the owner of the animal consents, however, the animal cannot be destroyed unless a veterinary surgeon has given a certificate to that effect.

Instead of ordering the animal to be destroyed the Court may deprive the owner of it and may order it to be disposed of in any manner the Court thinks fit. This, however, it is not entitled to do, unless it has reason to think that by reason of the owner's character, which may be shewn by a previous conviction, the animal is likely to be exposed to further cruelty if left in the possession of the owner.

Such an order does not prevent the owner who has been convicted of cruelty from subsequently obtaining another animal, but in the case of cruelty to a dog, the Court may make a special order that a person convicted of cruelty to a dog shall be deprived in future of his right to own dogs at all. This order also can only be made where the Court has reason to think that the person convicted of cruelty is not a fit person to own a dog at all.

Poison.—It is an offence for any person to lay down poison upon land except for the purpose of killing insects, rats, mice and other small vermin, or for manuring the land, and in any case reasonable precautions must be taken to prevent dogs, cats, etc., being damaged by the poison. The penalty for this is a maximum of £10.

Traps, Hooks, etc.—The use of pole-traps for the capture of wild birds, or the taking of birds with hooks is forbidden under a penalty of 40/- for the first offence and £5 for subsequent offences.

The use of spring traps, except in rabbit-holes, is forbidden entirely, and in the case of every trap or snare intended for catching rabbits, any person setting such a snare must visit it without fail at least once every twenty-four hours between sunrise and sunset upon a penalty not exceeding £5.

The use of tethered, or blinded, or injured birds as a decoy in the taking of wild birds is forbidden, as is the use of bird-lime for the purpose of catching wild-birds.

Pigeon Shooting.—It is forbidden to take part in any way in the shooting of captive birds liberated from a trap. The penalty for each of the last two offences is a fine not exceeding £25 and 3 months' imprisonment.

Performing Animals.—Anyone who trains or exhibits performing animals must be registered. Police constables are entitled to inspect all the provisions made for the training and performance of animals, though they may not go behind the scenes during a public performance in order to do so. If upon complaint being made to a Court of Summary Jurisdiction, either that a person registered as a trainer or exhibitor of performing animals has been guilty of cruelty, or that the training necessarily involves cruelty, the Court may order that his name be erased from the register either permanently or temporarily, or that the training or exhibition should take place only under certain specified conditions.

Any person who trains or exhibits animals without being registered, or who does not comply with an order of the Court as to the conditions under which the training or exhibition may take place, or who prevents a police constable or inspector from examining the conditions under which the animal is kept, is liable to a fine not exceeding £50. If convicted of cruelty to an animal under his charge, he is of course liable also to the ordinary penalties for that offence.

Destruction of Injured Animals.—Wherever an animal is injured so badly that it is impossible to remove it without inflicting further cruelty, a police constable may arrange for it to be slaughtered there and then; and the cost of destroying it can be recovered from the owner by proceedings in a Court of Summary Jurisdiction. The police constable, however, is not allowed to arrange for the animal to be destroyed unless either the owner has consented, or if the owner cannot be found or refuses to permit it to be slaughtered, a certificate from a veterinary surgeon has been obtained.

R.S.P.C.A.—The Royal Society for Prevention of Cruelty to Animals is a charitable society whose constitution is regulated by Act of Parliament, and exists for the purpose of promoting kindness and preventing cruelty to all animals. It provides and pays the wages of uniformed inspectors in most parts of the country with the object of seeing that cruelty to animals is prevented; but the inspectors of the R.S.P.C.A. do not occupy any privileged position and their rights in law are no greater than those of any other private citizen. They are not entitled to arrest persons for committing offences of cruelty, nor to enter the houses or yards of any one who they think may be committing an offence of cruelty. Their right, like that of other citizens, is to complain to a police constable and to permit him to take the appropriate steps to bring the offender to justice.

The R.S.P.C.A., in addition to providing inspectors, frequently institutes and bears the cost of proceedings in the Courts where cases of cruelty to animals are suspected. This is a right which any private individual possesses of laying any information before the magistrates, but it is wiser, as well as cheaper in cases of suspected cruelty, to make a complaint to the local inspector of the R.S.P.C.A. The Society will then take the case up and bear the expenses, if it thinks it to be a proper case in which to institute proceedings. (*See* ANIMAL; DOG; VIVISECTION.)

CRUELTY TO CHILDREN.—At Common Law a child has the same redress for ill-usage as an adult citizen, subject to the right possessed by a person in whose legal custody he is to inflict reasonable chastisement upon him.

The Children's Acts, 1908 and 1933.—These provide that anyone over sixteen years of age having custody of a child under sixteen who wilfully assaults, illtreats, neglects, abandons or exposes him in a manner likely to cause him unnecessary suffering or injury to his health, shall be guilty of an offence. It further provides that "neglect" is to cover the failure to provide adequate food, clothes, medical aid or shelter, or, if unable to provide it, to procure them under the Poor Law Acts. A person guilty of any form of cruelty as defined by the Act commits a misdemeanour and is liable to a fine and/or imprisonment. A person who knows of a case of cruelty

should go before a Justice of the Peace and give information on oath that there is reasonable cause to suspect that an offence under the act is being committed; and the J.P. will, if satisfied, issue a search warrant or order the child to be removed to a place of safety.

Punishment of Children. — The Common Law right of a parent, teacher or other person in lawful control of a child to administer corporal punishment is preserved. But this right must be exercised solely for the purpose of correction and not from motives of passion or rage, and the punishment must be reasonable and moderate in extent, in the nature of the instrument used, and having regard to the age and understanding of the child. A schoolmaster or prefect may punish a child for the breach of reasonable rules, but an elder brother is not, as such, in lawful control of his younger brother.

If punishment is excessive it may result in a prosecution or a civil action for assault, or, if death results, in a prosecution for murder or manslaughter.

CRUELTY TO A WIFE.—(*See* ASSAULT; *and* SPECIAL SUPPLEMENT "DIVORCE.")

CUM DIVIDEND.—When shares are bought and at the time of the purchase the company has declared a dividend on the shares but has not yet paid it, the transaction is said to be cum dividend, if the parties agree that the purchaser of the shares shall be entitled to the dividend when paid. As the seller will still be the registered shareholder the dividend will be paid to him in the first place, and he will require to hand it over to the purchaser. (*See* SHARES.)

CUM TESTAMENTO ANNEXO.— When a person dies without leaving a will or without appointing an executor by will, on application to the Court an order will be made appointing some person as administrator to perform the duties of executor. The authority issued by the Court to an administrator is called "letters of administration." Where there is a will, but no executor appointed in it, the Court issue "letters of administration" with the will annexed. Such letters are described with the Latin name of Cum Testamento Annexo. (*See* WILLS; EXECUTORS; LETTERS OF ADMINISTRATION.)

CURATOR (SCOTS LAW).—A curator is a person appointed to supervise the legal transactions of persons who for some reason are unable to look after their own affairs. Thus a curator may be appointed to a minor, i.e. a person under 21, or to an insane person.

A curator is distinguished from a tutor who acts for a pupil, that is, a person under 12 in the case of girls, or 14 in the case of boys, for the tutor enters into contracts himself on behalf of the pupil, whereas a curator merely consents to contracts which the minor himself has made.

Sir Henry Curtis Bennett.

Where the father is alive he will act as curator, unless he has neglected his duty, when another curator may be appointed by the Court. A father may appoint a curator to act after his death. A minor need not have a curator, but if he wishes to have one and has not already got one, he may bring an action for that purpose. (*See* CONTRACT [SCOTS LAW].)

CURTESY OF ENGLAND.— Curtesy has since 1925 been abolished except in one very rare case, but before then it was a right which a widower had to claim an estate for life as tenant by the curtesy in all the lands which his wife owned at her death. The husband's right only arose in certain circumstances; thus he had to shew that his wife's interest in the property was such

that it could have been inherited by their children, and also that a child who was capable of inheriting the particular property had in fact been born alive; provided that the child was born alive, it did not matter if it never lived to grow up, or indeed even if it died immediately. The husband had also to shew that his wife was the sole owner of the property.

Tenancy by the curtesy could only be claimed over land which was not the separate property of the wife in its legal sense. The Married Women's Property Act of 1882 contains provisions the result of which is that all property acquired by a married woman after 1882 is her separate property. Thus the abolition of curtesy in 1925 did not make any real change.

CURTILAGE.—This word means the land belonging to a dwelling house and surrounding or immediately adjacent to it.

CURTIS BENNETT, Sir Henry (1879–).—A successful advocate in criminal cases. He defended Armstrong the poisoner, Patrick Mahon, and Mrs. Thompson in the Bywaters case. He was in the Secret Service during the War where his skill in cross-examination was of great use in interviewing spies and suspects. He is the Recorder of Colchester, a post he has occupied since 1929.

CUSTOM.—The English common law is based on the immemorial custom of the King's Court. In certain parts of the country there are immemorial customs which differ from the common law but have the force of it in their particular localities. If a custom dates from the reign of Richard I., or at least if there is no reason for supposing it does not, it is regarded as immemorial and the Courts recognise it as being the law for that locality. For this reason no modern practice can acquire the force of customary law. A custom is usually assumed to be immemorial if the oldest inhabitants of the district cannot remember a time when it did not exist. Only a reasonable custom can have the force of law and it can be abolished by Act of Parliament like the common law, but by nothing else. Custom should be distinguished from prescription, which is the right belonging to individuals, such as the lord of the manor. It is also different from usage which is a particular mode of dealing confined to some trade or profession. Customary law is essentially connected with a particular district and is most frequently met with in relation to land. **CUSTOMS DUTIES.**—Customs duties are duties payable on the import or export of goods into, or out of, Great Britain, though until recently duties on exports have been rare. The original purpose of customs duties was purely to bring in revenue, but nowadays they are often imposed to

drugs; arms and ammunition; vaccines, serums, toxins and other such substances; explosives; dyestuffs; etc. They also enforce quarantine regulations.

When dutiable goods arrive at a port, and before they are unshipped, the importer must make "entry" of them on the appropriate entry-form. They may then be unshipped, and, when the duty has been paid, may be removed. Alternatively, they may be placed in a duty-free warehouse, and the

An example of clever smuggling. Opium hidden in a Bible.

foster home industries by excluding foreign produce.

The control of customs is vested in the Commissioners of Customs and Excise, who also have been given various other powers in relation to goods whose importation requires, from public policy, careful control or prevention. For instance, it is their duty to prevent the importation of obscene literature; pirated editions of copyright works; the plumage of certain birds (*see* PLUMAGE); gold or silver plate not of standard quality; goods made in foreign prisons; seal-skins taken in contravention of certain regulations; opium prepared for smoking; lottery advertisements; matches made with white phosphorus; hay or straw from almost every country; etc. It also is their duty to see that the necessary licences have been obtained for the importation of morphine, cocaine, heroin and other

duty then becomes payable only when they are removed from it for home use; if they are again exported, the duty is not payable at all.

Any person making a false declaration or answering questions untruly is liable to a penalty of £100.

Passengers to Great Britain must unship their baggage only with the authority and in the presence of a customs officer, and the responsibility for unpacking and repacking luggage rests on the passenger. The passenger must declare to the officer all prohibited or dutiable articles, however small their quantity. Duty should, strictly, be paid on all dutiable goods, but, for the convenience of passengers, the authorities will permit the import of certain small quantities provided they are declared. If they exceed the amount so permitted, duty is charged on the whole quantity. This concession is granted only at the port of entry, and therefore dutiable goods contained in luggage registered through to an inland town will have to pay duty however small their quantity (except in the case of personal silks or laces). Articles intended to be sold may not be imported in personal luggage. If dutiable or prohibited goods are not declared, the offender is liable to considerable penalties, and the goods will be confiscated. Private motor-cars are, on security being given, admitted duty free into Great Britain for a limited period.

Parcels posted abroad or in the Channel Islands for delivery in Great Britain must be accompanied by a declaration of the contents, and the duty (if any) is collected on delivery by the Post Office unless it has been prepaid. If the declarations are found to be untrue, the parcel may be confiscated or may be retained to secure a conviction. The same rules apply to parcels posted in Great Britain for delivery abroad or to the Channel Islands.

Any goods manufactured more than a hundred years before being imported (except wines and spirits) may be imported duty free.

Several kinds of goods may be unshipped only at certain ports, e.g. saccharine. All goods brought by air, whether dutiable or not, must be landed at certain specified air-ports and nowhere else.

Duties are either "specific," i.e. so much per unit, whether it be a unit of weight, number or volume, or "ad valorem," i.e. so much per cent. of the value. For example, on unused cinematograph films the duty is $\frac{1}{2}$d. per foot, while on musical instruments, clocks or motor-cars it is $33\frac{1}{3}\%$. All goods are now subject to a 10% import duty as from 31st March, 1932, except certain specified goods, e.g. gold, wheat, maize, meat, live quadrupeds, tea, wool, skins, wood pulp, raw rubber, metallic ores, pit props, coal and cork. The Treasury may also recommend increased duties on luxury articles or articles likely to be soon produced in the United Kingdom in substantial quantities, and they have exercised this right in many cases.

In fixing these additional duties, preference may be given to the Dominions and Southern Rhodesia. The Board of Trade may impose additional duties against foreign countries that discriminate in tariffs against this country.

Imperial preference is regulated by a series of Acts of Parliament, commencing in 1919 and culminating in the Ottawa Agreements Act, 1932.

By the Safeguarding of Industries Act, 1921, a $33\frac{1}{3}\%$ duty was imposed upon certain imports to protect certain industries known as the "Key Industries." It includes optical glass and instruments, scientific instruments, wireless valves and ignition magnetos.

CY PRÈS.—When the intention of a donor or testator is incapable of being literally acted upon, or where its literal performance would be unreasonable, or in excess of what the law allows, or in the case of a charity where the object of a gift fails or is insufficiently described—the Courts will often allow the intention to be carried into effect cy près, that is, as nearly as may be practicable, or reasonable, or consistent with law; as when a testator attempts to settle his property on future generations beyond the bounds allowed by law, or where a sum of money is found to be too large for a charitable purpose to which it has been devoted, or for some other reason cannot be applied thereto. (*See* CHARITY.)

D**.O.R.A.**—The Defence of the Realm Acts were a series of enactments passed during the War to meet wartime emergencies of various kinds. The majority of such Acts, and the Regulations made thereunder by the Home Secretary, have now expired. Certain of the Acts, however, still remain in force—e.g. a small part of the Defence of the Realm (Acquisition of Land) Act, 1916, but only so far as regards such matters as selling off land compulsorily acquired by the Government during the War. The spirit of some of the Defence of the Realm Acts has been preserved in subsequent legislation, e.g. the Shops (Hours of Closing) Act, 1928, preserves the bulk of the war-time Regulations in that respect (see EARLY CLOSING), and the restrictions on hours imposed by D.O.R.A. have been maintained in the Licensing Act, 1921. But, apart from a few survivals of this nature, this vast and intricate body of statutory enactments and administrative Regulations has ceased to be effective, and "Dora" is virtually dead.

DAMAGE FEASANT.—If animals are found trespassing on land and damaging it, they are said to be trespassing "damage feasant." The owner of the land may seize them and keep them until their owner has made good the damage they have done, and also paid the cost of keeping them.

Most domestic animals can be so seized except when actually in use. Thus a ridden horse may not be distrained. Animals when so seized may not be sold or used. While the animals are in the possession of the distrainor he cannot bring an action for trespass, for by law you can bring an action for trespass or distrain, but not both together. (See TRESPASS.)

DAMAGES.—When a person has suffered injury by the fault of another, the law will make that person restore the injured one to the position he originally occupied. If, for some reason, this is not possible, the injured man will be entitled to some monetary compensation and that compensation is known as damages.

Tort.—Damages are of two kinds "general" and "special." General are those which the tribunal itself assesses as proper. Special damage is the amount which an individual plaintiff can prove that he has actually lost owing to the particular circumstances of the case. For instance, a person having been knocked down and injured by a motor-car will probably be able to prove that he has had to pay a doctor a fee to attend to his injuries, and also perhaps that he has been unable to follow his trade, and so has lost his wages. These are the special damages peculiar to his case, but besides this he will be entitled to a sum for the pain of his injury and the general inconvenience he has suffered. These are general damages.

How the Amount of Damages is Determined.—Everyone is entitled to

damages which arise naturally and directly from the injury complained of. All other damages are too remote and are not recoverable. In actions for tort everyone is liable for the consequences which flow naturally from the wrongful act, whether one could have anticipated the consequences or not. Suppose a cyclist bumps lightly into a pedestrian who falls to the ground and, because he has an abnormally thin skull, is killed—the cyclist will be responsible in damages for killing him, though he might never have anticipated such woeful consequences from a light push. On the other hand there may be a breach of duty to a person which results in no injury; only nominal damages would then be recovered. These must be distinguished from contemptuous damages, often one farthing, which are awarded when the jury think the action ought never to have been brought. Sometimes a plaintiff is entitled to "exemplary" damages. This is when it is desired not only to recompense the plaintiff, but to punish the defendant for his conduct. It is most usually found in cases of libel where the defendant has sought to justify the libel and failed. Finally, there is "Damnum sine Injuria," where damage is suffered but there is no legal redress.

Breach of Contract.—Wherever a party to a contract fails to observe its terms, the party wronged by that failure is entitled (in addition to any other remedy which he may have, such as a right to consider a contract at an end, or an injunction or specific performance) to bring an action to recover full compensation for all the pecuniary loss he has suffered owing to the breach. Thus, if A promises to make a suit of clothes for B, and makes them badly, this is a breach of contract and B is entitled to recover the amount which he would have to pay in order to have them altered; or if they cannot be altered, he is entitled to recover the difference in value of the suit as it should have been, and as it actually is.

Again if A promises to sell B potatoes at £9 a ton and fails to deliver them, then B is entitled to recover from A as damages the difference between the contract price of the potatoes and the price which he has been obliged to give for the potatoes elsewhere—say £12. Thus in this case the damages recoverable would be £3 per ton.

Further, all the damage that naturally results from the breach of contract is, subject to certain exceptions mentioned below, recoverable in this manner. Thus, if A, a plumber, agrees to mend a pipe for B, and as a result of his inefficient work the water overflows, and destroys the wall-paper in the room below, so that it will cost £25 to put it right—the amount of damages which B can recover from A will include not only the cost of putting the pipe right but also the cost of the wall-paper, which has been destroyed by reason of A's inefficient work.

The mere fact that the damages are difficult to assess does not preclude the right to recover them. Let us suppose that A has entered for a beauty competition and has been selected among the last ten competitors for a final trial, and the organiser of the competition sends to A a notice to attend the final trial, in which notice he inserts the wrong date. A misses the final trial and loses her chance of winning the competition. In such a case A is entitled to recover damages, though it is extremely difficult to suggest any manner in which those damages could be fairly calculated. The calculation in a case like that is a matter for the jury, or if there is no jury, for the Judge.

Limits on the Right to Damages.—There are two methods in which the rights of an injured party to a contract to recover damages against the party in default are limited. As a general rule all the damage naturally flowing from the breach of the contract may be recovered, but only so much damage may be recovered as is the sort of damage that both parties would expect to result from the breach at the time that the contract was entered into.

An example will make this clear. If A agrees to supply B with certain machinery by a certain date and fails to deliver it upon the date fixed by the contract, then B is entitled to recover damages for the lateness of delivery. But if B happens, unknown to A, to have an order to use the machinery, and by reason of the lateness of delivery of the machinery he loses this important order on which he would have made a profit of £200, B cannot recover the £200 as damages from A, because, at the time of the contract, A could not have foreseen that such damages

would result from his failure to deliver. If on the other hand A had at the time of the making of the contract been told of the important order, A would have been liable for the damage resulting and would be obliged to pay B the £200 which he had lost.

As to what is the sort of damage naturally flowing from a breach of contract, and therefore recoverable as damages in an action, the best test is: Is the damage that has resulted of a kind which an ordinary man would have expected would result, if he had considered the matter at the time at which he entered into the contract?

Mitigation of Damages.—There is another doctrine of English law that limits the amount of damages which may be recovered for a breach of contract. Although a party not in default is entitled to recover the loss that he has suffered, he is not entitled to sit back and watch that loss grow larger in reliance upon the other party paying for it. It is his duty to do all that is reasonably possible to keep the damages within bounds. If he fails to do so he will be unable to recover them from the party in default.

Let us suppose that A agrees to sell B a ton of potatoes at £10, and B intends to re-sell them for £15 so making a profit of £5. If A fails to deliver the potatoes, B cannot sit back and claim £5 damages, as the profit that he has lost upon the re-sale; but must, if potatoes can be bought elsewhere for £12 a ton, buy them and so make a profit of £3 instead of £5, and in such case he can recover the extra £2 profit which he has lost as damages. Even if B does not, although he could, buy the other potatoes elsewhere, he cannot make A pay for his laziness or lack of foresight, but will only be able to recover the sum of £2 which would have been his actual loss if he had performed his duty of keeping the damages resulting from the breach as low as possible.

So again if A, a plumber, undertakes to mend a pipe for B and does so badly, B is not entitled to sit back and leave the pipe in the state in which A left it, thus allowing it to ruin his wall-paper, but must get the pipe repaired as quickly as possible, and so mitigate the damage which it causes. If he does not do this he cannot recover the cost of replacing the wall-paper from A, unless he can prove to the satisfaction of the

Court that the damage was in no way increased by his failure to take all reasonable steps to get the pipe repaired by someone else, when he appreciated that more damage would ensue.

This duty of the injured party to take all reasonable steps to prevent the damages being increased is known as mitigation of damages.

Liquidated Damages.—Sometimes where the damages resulting, or likely to result, from breaches of a contract are difficult to assess, the parties to the contract may make provision in the contract itself for an agreed sum of damages to be payable upon breach of the contract. The commonest examples of this occur in building contracts where the contractor agrees to pay a penalty of so many pounds per day for every day (after the date fixed in the contract for completion) during which the building is unfinished.

Where the penalty clause represents a fair and bona fide attempt on the part of the parties to the contract to assess the amount of damages resulting from the breach, the Court will adopt that measure, and will give damages for the breach to that amount. But where the Court is of the opinion that the penalty provided in the contract is not in fact a bona fide attempt on the part of the parties to the contract to assess the damages likely to result from the breach, but is of the nature of a penalty or fine inflicted by one party upon the other, the Court in construing the contract will ignore the penalty clause altogether, and will give damage according to the ordinary rules as if such clause did not exist. The damages which the Court gives when it ignores a penalty clause are generally less than the amount of the penalty provided for in the contract; but there is no reason why they should not be greater and in certain circumstances they will be so.

Where the clause is not a bona-fide attempt to assess the damages it is known as a penalty clause; where it is such an attempt it is known as a clause providing for liquidated damages.

It is often difficult to decide whether the clause in question is a penalty clause or a liquidated damage clause; but as a general rule it cannot be the latter if it provides that the same penalty shall be payable for a number of different breaches which are clearly not all of the same importance. (*See* COMPENSATION; CONTRACT.)

DAMAGES (SCOTS LAW).—The principles by which damages are calculated in Scots Law are to a large extent the same as in English Law. The most important distinction arises in the law of reparation—i.e. tort or civil wrong. In English law the amount which may be recovered in respect of the death of any person is limited to the financial loss which has been suffered by those who were dependent upon him. It thus follows in English law that no damages will be payable where the person who has been killed is a child. In Scots law, however, there are no such limits, and damages may be recovered in excess of the amount of financial loss, and in respect of mental suffering caused to a relation, e.g. when a parent is suing for the death of his child. This applies to any person suing for the death of a relative.

DANCING.—The law as to the licensing of dance halls varies with the place in which the hall is situated.

1. **When the hall or place is situated within twenty miles of London and Westminster but outside Middlesex and the places to which the Home Counties Licensing Act 1826 (Section 2) apply.**—In this area no person may keep any place for public dancing without a licence from the County Council. Whether a place is "kept for public dancing" is a question of fact, but an open place enclosed by ropes has been held to require a licence. The fact that a place is habitually used for dancing, and that anyone is allowed in who cares to pay an entrance fee, is strong evidence that the place is kept for public dancing. It does not matter whether the dancing is by the public or by performers for their entertainment. Naval and military recreation rooms are, however, not required to be licensed.

The London County Council hear applications for these licences and in hearing them must act judicially, but there is no appeal from their decisions.

When a licence is granted the following inscription must be affixed over the door in large capital letters—"Licensed pursuant to Act of Parliament of the twenty-fifth of King George the Second." The hours during which such a place may be kept open are noon to midnight unless a special order of exemption is granted by the Commissioner of Police (*see* SPECIAL EXEMPTION ORDER). Any place kept for public dancing without a licence will be treated as a disorderly house.

2. **When the hall or place is situated within the districts to which the Home Counties Licensing Act applies.**—This area consists of so much of Buckinghamshire, Essex, Hertfordshire and Kent as lies within twenty miles of the City of London or Westminster whichever be nearer, and the County Boroughs of Croydon, East Ham and West Ham. In this area, as in the London area, no person may keep any place for public dancing without a licence from the local County or Borough Council. Such a licence can be granted for any term not exceeding thirteen months, but the Council's power to grant a licence is discretionary and may be subject to such terms and conditions as they think fit. On renewal no notices need be given. If such premises are kept without a licence the penalty is £5 per diem. Unless by consent of the Council, a place so licensed must not be used between midnight and midday, and must while licensed display the words "Licensed in pursuance of Act of Parliament for . . ."

3. **When the hall is situated in Middlesex.**—In Middlesex the Music and Dancing Licences (Middlesex) Act 1894 applies. This enacts that a place must not be kept for public dancing without a licence from the County Council on pain of £5 per diem penalty. The licence costs five shillings and may be granted subject to conditions, but the Council has complete discretion in granting licences and there is no appeal from its decision. Fourteen days' notice of applications for a new grant must be given to the Council and to the Police but no notice is required for a renewal.

4. **When the hall is situated in any other part of England.**—Licences are not necessary unless required by a local Act, or unless Part V of the Public Health Acts Amendment Act 1890 is in force. If this Act is in force its provisions are in most respects identical with the Music and Dancing Licences (Middlesex) Act 1894 which is in force in Middlesex. But the licences are granted by the licensing justices at the general annual licensing meeting and not by the County Council. (*See* INTOXICATING LIQUOR.)

DANGEROUS ARTICLES.—The law imposes upon everyone a duty to use care in his activities so that harm or injury to another does not arise from them. If, therefore, a person has in his possession an article such as a firearm or an explosive, he is under a duty to exercise the highest possible degree of care in regard to it. If an accident occurs from the use or possession of such an article, which would not, with the use of ordinary care, have occurred, then the law holds that a prima facie case of negligence has been established against the user or possessor, and it is for him to shew that the accident was not due to any lack of care on his part. Thus, if a man lets off a firework, and it explodes and injures someone, he will be held liable, unless he can shew that he took every precaution to see that no injury was caused by letting it off.

A person who sells or supplies goods which he knows to be dangerous must warn the person to whom they are sold or supplied of their dangerous nature, unless he knows for certain that the purchaser is already aware of it. If a person is not warned that goods are dangerous, and while using them in a reasonable manner is injured or suffers damage, the seller or supplier of the goods will be liable to him. The seller or supplier is usually under a duty to warn of danger only the person to whom he sells or supplies goods, or, as the law puts it, to warn the person with whom he contracts; if, however, he knows that the goods are going to be used by a third person, and fails to give any warning of their nature, or sells an article with a hidden defect, he will be liable to the third person.

The sale of several kinds of dangerous articles is governed by strict statutory provisions and any sale which contravenes such provisions is an offence. The most important of such articles whose sale is regulated are Explosives, Drugs and Petrol.

Quite apart from these special regulations, anyone who sells goods, sells them with an implied warranty that they are fit for the purpose for which they are to be used. That is to say he guarantees them, and, if damage is caused by them to the person to whom they are sold when he has used them for their proper purpose, the seller is liable. A good example of such an article is hair dye which is impliedly guaranteed as harmless. In some cases the seller or even the manufacturer of goods may be liable to pay damages to a person who is injured by the use of them, even although the seller or manufacturer did not deal direct with the injured person, and could not therefore be held to have given him any guarantee.

If a person gives or lends a dangerous thing to another he is not liable for any damage which may result, unless he knows that the thing is dangerous and fails to warn the person to whom it was given or lent.

Carriage of Dangerous Articles.— When a person sends goods by a private or a common carrier he must warn the carrier that they are dangerous, otherwise he will be held by the law to have guaranteed to the carrier that they are fit to be carried in the ordinary way and are not dangerous. If damage results from the carriage of goods the person sending them is liable for it, whether he knew or did not know that the goods were in fact dangerous. If he has warned the carrier that they are dangerous, and the carrier still undertakes to carry them, then the sender will not be liable.

Special provisions with regard to the carriage of dangerous goods apply to railway companies and they may refuse, and cannot be required to carry, anything of a corrosive or explosive nature which in the opinion of the company's officials is dangerous. If any person sends such goods by rail without giving the company written notice of the nature of the goods, he commits an offence and is liable to forfeit a fine of £20 to the railway company. If a company consents to carry dangerous goods, they must be carried at either company's risk rates or owner's risk rates.

Explosive and dangerous substances must not be sent by post, nor must any living creature which is likely to do damage to other postal packets or any officer of the post office service. If any sharp instrument or article is sent by post, it must be securely wrapped up so that it will not do damage to any person or thing. Failure to observe any of these regulations is an offence punishable by a maximum fine of £10.

Storage of Dangerous Articles.— If a person brings on to his land and keeps there a thing which would be dangerous if

it escaped, such as a lion or a tiger, he keeps it at his own risk, and is liable for all the consequences should it escape, even although it does so without any fault upon his part.

A famous case.—The case of Rylands v. Fletcher is known to every lawyer, and it lays down the rule just quoted about keeping dangerous articles on one's land. In that case Rylands had a reservoir constructed on his land and filled it with water. The water escaped from the reservoir through an old mine shaft and flooded Fletcher's mines. The escape was caused by reason of the negligence of the workmen who constructed the reservoir in not securely sealing up the old mine shafts, and Rylands personally was in no way responsible. The House of Lords said that he had caused the water to be brought on to his land and he must keep it there or be liable for the damage caused by its escape, and he therefore had to pay damages to Fletcher.

If a man brings a dangerous thing on to his land because he is authorised to do so by some Act of Parliament, then, unless the Act also lays down that he must keep it secure, he is not liable if, without fault on his part, it escapes and does damage. An example of such a case is a water board authorised by Act of Parliament to construct a reservoir.

Special precautions must be taken by persons possessing dangerous things to see that they are not left about in such a way that children can meddle with them, since children are liable to meddle with anything that comes within their reach. Thus a railway company was held liable for injuries sustained by a child who was playing with a turn-table on the railway company's premises. The company had allowed a gap in the fence surrounding its yard to remain unclosed and had taken no precautions to warn the children or chase them away as trespassers.

In the same way if a person uses dangerous machinery or carries out dangerous operations, such as blasting in a quarry, he must take every proper precaution to see that no one is injured. If the employer fails to exercise the necessary degree of care, or fails to take all proper precautions, he will be liable if someone is injured by the machinery either while operating, or if he is in the proximity of the machinery in the course of his employment. (*See also* Dangerous Articles; Dangerous Premises; Master and Servant; Railways.)

DANGEROUS PREMISES.—A person who owns premises has a right to use them in the natural and ordinary way, but he must use them in such a way that he does not interfere with any right of another person which is recognised by law. If premises are in a dangerous condition the interference with a legal right may be either a breach of contract, or a breach of the duty to take care not to injure persons using the premises. They may also constitute a nuisance, and if a person is injured or suffers damage by reason of the nuisance, breach of contract, or breach of duty, the owner or occupier will in most cases be liable to compensate him for his injury or damage.

An owner who lets premises in a dangerous condition, if he is under no obligation to do the repairs, is not liable for any injury sustained by the tenant, or his family, or guests by reason of the defective condition of the premises. If he has undertaken to do the repairs, he will not be liable to any person other than his tenant, unless the accident happened on a part of the premises over which he has retained control, such as a common stairway; and even then only if the danger was in the nature of a trap which the person injured could not observe.

The person usually liable, therefore, for any injury caused by premises being dangerous is the occupier, since he owes a duty to persons using the premises. The law divides persons using premises into three different categories, namely, Invitees, Licensees, and Trespassers, and the occupier of premises owes a different degree of duty to each of these types of persons.

Who is an Invitee?—An invitee is a person who comes upon premises upon business which concerns the occupier at his invitation, express or implied. The term invitee is apt to be a little confusing because it does not include a guest who in the ordinary way comes by invitation of the occupier, but does not come upon business concerning the occupier. A guest at an hotel paying for his accommodation is an invitee, but a guest staying at a private house and paying nothing is only a licensee. Examples of invitees are, customers at a shop, intending passengers on a railway station, and persons attending a performance at a theatre who have paid for their seats. The duty owed by an occupier of premises to an invitee is to have the premises reasonably safe for him, to take precautions to prevent injury to him, and to warn him of dangers which are concealed but of whose existence the occupier is, or ought to be, aware.

Who is a Licensee?—A licensee is a person who comes upon premises with the permission of the occupier, but who has no common interest with the occupier in coming upon the premises. Such a person is sometimes called a bare licensee as distinct from a person who pays to come upon the premises, who is called a licensee with an interest, and is to all intents and purposes identical with an invitee.

A licensee has to take the premises as he finds them with all their dangers and traps, and the owner or occupier is under no liability to him if he is injured by a defect in the premises which has been in existence for some time. He must not, however, intentionally set a trap for the licensee, nor must he allow a new danger to arise without taking precautions to protect a licensee from injury from it.

Who is a Trespasser?—A trespasser is a person who comes upon premises without invitation or permission from the occupier or owner. In fact he is a person who has no right to be there, and to him the occupier owes no duty to warn of dangers or to keep the premises safe for him. The only duty he owes is not wilfully to injure the trespasser, either intentionally or by acting with reckless disregard for his safety. That is to say, he must not set a trap for him like a spring gun, or do some dangerous operation when he is aware that the trespasser is upon the premises.

The duty of the occupier of premises is not confined simply to protecting persons coming upon them from injury by reason of their dangerous condition. If his premises adjoin a highway he must keep the premises in a safe condition, so that no injury arises from them to a member of the public using the highway. For example, if he has a balcony or lamp suspended from the building and projecting over the highway he must keep it in good repair. If it becomes dangerous, he must see that warning is given to persons using the highway, while it is being repaired, and he will be liable if no warning is given of the danger and a passer-by is injured.

An occupier of premises has also a duty towards the occupiers of neighbouring premises, and must not use his premises in such a way that damage is sustained by neighbouring owners, nor must he allow his premises to get into such a condition that they are dangerous to adjoining premises. If he fails to carry out this duty he will be liable for any damage caused by his neglect to the adjoining premises. If the owner has undertaken with his tenant to do the outside repairs and an accident happens to a passer-by because of his failure to do the necesssary repairs, then he, and not the occupier, will be liable.

Local Authorities, if they receive a report from their surveyor that a building is dangerous, may serve a Dangerous Structure Notice upon the owner or the occupier, requiring him to repair the building. (*See also* ACCIDENT; DANGEROUS STRUCTURE NOTICE; LANDLORD; NUISANCE.)

DANGEROUS STRUCTURE NOTICE.—If a building, or a wall, or any part of a building is in a ruinous state and dangerous to passers-by, or to the occupiers of neighbouring buildings, the surveyor of the local authority must give written notice to the owner requiring him to repair the dangerous structure. A copy of the notice must be served on the occupier or affixed to the building if it is unoccupied. The owner or occupier is required to commence the work within three days, and if he does not do so he may be ordered to do the work by two justices acting upon the complaint of the surveyor. If he fails to comply with this order, then the local authority must themselves do the work, and recover the expenses from the owner.

If anyone is aggrieved by a notice served upon him in this way by a surveyor of a local authority, he may raise objections to the notice when he is summoned before the magistrate for an order to be made. (*See* BUILDING; HOUSING; LOCAL AUTHORITY.)

DANGEROUS TRADES.—If the Home Secretary is satisfied that any manufacturing process, plant or machinery used in factories or workshops is injurious to health or dangerous to the workers, he may certify that manufacturing process, plant or machinery to be a dangerous trade and may make special regulations governing the trade. Before these regulations are made, notice of the proposal to make them, and of the place where copies of the draft regulations are obtainable, must be published. The time within which objections to the proposed regulations may be made must also be specified. If the Home Secretary does not amend or withdraw the draft regulations objected to, he must direct any enquiry to be held in public regarding them. When the regulations are made they must be laid before both Houses of Parliament, and either House may within forty days resolve to annul all or any of them.

Copies of the regulations must be posted up in conspicuous places in all factories and workshops to which they apply, and failure to do so renders the occupier of the factory liable to a penalty of £10. Any person pulling down or defacing such regulations is liable to a fine of £5.

The following is a list of the trades which have been certified as dangerous and in respect of which regulations have been made:—

List of Dangerous Trades.
Manufacture of : Bichromate or chromate of potassium or sodium.
Asbestos.
China and earthenware.
Cinematograph films.
Electric accumulators.
Lucifer matches.
India rubber.
Paints in which dry carbonate of lead is used.
Cutlery.
Red, yellow, orange or white lead.
Nitro- and amido- derivatives of benzine.
Explosives with the use of dinitrobenzol or dinitrotoluol.
Hollow ware and iron drums by tinning.
Felt hats.
Process of : Bronzing with dry metallic powders in letterpress printing.
Lithographic printing and coating of metal sheets.
Cleaning of castings.
Grinding and glazing of metals.
Spinning by self-acting mules.
Spinning and weaving flax and tow.

Lord Darling.

Sorting, washing, combing and carding wool and hair.

Heading of a yarn dyed by means of a lead compound.

Spinning and weaving hemp and jute.

Using horsehair from China, Siberia or Russia.

Casting of bronze or any alloy of copper and zinc.

Vitreous enamelling on metal or glass.

Generation, transformation, distribution and use of electricity.

Smelting of lead.

Mixing and casting of brass, gun metal, bell metal, white metal, delta metal.

Metal, phosphor bronze and manilla mixture.

Bottling of aerated waters.

Vulcanising india rubber.

Sorting foreign skins and hides.

Loading and unloading ships.

Moving of rolling stock in a factory railway siding.

Enamelling of iron plates.

File cutting by hand.

Painting of vehicles.

Film stripping.

Chromium plating.

Ship building. (*See* FACTORY.)

DARLING, Lord. (1849–).—Noted for his brilliant wit Lord Darling was made

a Judge at the early age of 48. On his retirement in 1923 he was made a peer. He presided at the trial of the poisoner Armstrong.

DEAD'S PART (SCOTS LAW).— This is the name given to the part of a man's or a woman's movable estate, which they are allowed to dispose of freely by will, or which descends according to the rules of intestacy if there is no will. Before the Dead's Part can be calculated it is necessary to deduct from the total movable estate all claims by a widow (or widower) and children in respect of their "legal rights" i.e. jus relictae or jus relicti and legitim (q.v.). A simple example will make this clear. John Smith has a wife and two children and his movable property amounts to £21,000; in making his will he must bear in mind that of this money his widow will be entitled to one third (£7,000), and his children among them to another third (£7,000). This will leave £7,000 of which he may dispose as he pleases and it is this last £7,000 that is known as "Dead's Part." If a man has no widow or children with legal rights, the whole of his property after his creditors have been paid is Dead's Part. (*See* HUSBAND AND WIFE [SCOTS LAW] ; INTESTACY [SCOTS LAW] ; LEGITIM [SCOTS LAW].)

DEAFNESS (Education).—Provision is made for the education of deaf children at special schools on the same lines as provision is made for blind children (*see* BLINDNESS). For this purpose, "deaf" means too deaf to be taught in a class of hearing children in an elementary school.

Motor Cars.—A deaf person applying for a driving licence should disclose his deafness on the form of application, and should claim a test of his fitness to drive. The fee for the test is ten shillings.

DEAN.—The term Dean is applied to many different offices, chiefly ecclesiastical, though there is the exception of the Dean of a University, college or faculty, who is generally a layman. Ecclesiastical Deans are of four classes: (i) *The Dean of a chapter, or Cathedral Dean*, is the head of the Chapter and is bound to reside in his Cathedral for at least eight months in every year, his duties being concerned mainly with the management of the Cathedral; in some new dioceses the Bishop acts also as dean;

(ii) *The Rural Dean* is not a cathedral officer but is the chief officer of a Rural Deanery, which may be regarded either as a sub-division of an Archdeaconry or as a group of parishes. Usually some clergyman having a living in the deanery is appointed Rural Dean; his immediate superior is the Archdeacon. His duties are mainly to report to the Bishop on all ecclesiastical matters within the area of the Deanery, e.g. as to vacancies. In most Rural Deaneries, a periodical meeting is held, known as the Ruri-decanal Conference; it is composed of the clergy residing in the Deanery and certain laymen elected by the Parochial Church Meeting (*see* PARISH, ECCLESIASTICAL); it is presided over by the Rural Dean. (iii) *"Deans of Peculiars,"* i.e. a Dean having no Chapter, e.g. the Dean of Arches (*see* ARCHES, COURT OF); and (iv) *Honorary Deans*, e.g. the Dean of a Royal Chapel. Sub-deans are officers appointed in Cathedrals to assist the Dean or to act when no Dean has been appointed.

DEATH.—When a death occurs, notice of it must be given personally to the local Registrar of Births and Deaths by a relative present at the death, or in attendance during the last illness. Failing him, the notice must be given by any other relative, or, failing him, a person present at the death, or the occupier of the premises where it occurred, or, failing them, a person present in the house or the person who makes the funeral arrangements. The personal attendance on the registrar must be made within five days, unless notice of the death is sent to him with a medical certificate of the cause of death, when the time is extended to fourteen days (penalty for failure, 40/–). On failure to register within fourteen days, the registrar may require any of the above-mentioned persons to attend (penalty for failure, a further 40/–). After twelve months, no death can be registered without the consent of the Registrar-General (fee 10/–).

The registrar must give a certificate of registration which must be delivered to the person effecting the disposal of the body (usually, the person performing the funeral service). The person effecting the disposal must give notice thereof to the registrar within 96 hours. The doctor (if any) who attended the deceased must send a certificate of the cause of death to the registrar, and must hand a notice that he has signed such certificate to one of the persons whose duty it is to effect the registration; such notice must be produced to the registrar when registration is effected.

In the case of a sudden, violent or unnatural death, it is the duty of the occupier of the house in which it occurred to inform the police in order that a coroner's inquest may be held. In the majority of cases, the inquest is purely formal, and the coroner does not normally call a jury unless it appears that the death was due to murder, or manslaughter, or to an accident, poisoning, or disease which should have been notified, or to a street accident. When the birth of a stillborn child is registered (*see* BIRTH), the registrar will, if so required, give a certificate of registration which must be produced to the person effecting the disposal of the body. Death certificates may be obtained in the same way and at the same charges as birth certificates. (*See* BIRTH; BIRTH CERTIFICATE.)

DEATH DUTIES.—Death duties are taxes levied on the property of persons when they die. There have been, in all, seven different kinds of death duties, but three of these are now virtually extinct since they can be levied only in connection with deaths that occurred before 2nd August, 1894; they were called Probate Duty, Account Duty, and Temporary Estate Duty. For the modern death duties *see* ESTATE DUTY; LEGACY DUTY; AND SUCCESSION DUTY.

DEBENTURE.—Every trading company is entitled by law to borrow money, whether or not there is any clause in its Memorandum of Association expressly giving it power to do so; and it is also authorised to give any charge over its property in security for the loan. This power of borrowing is widely used by companies and often provides them with the working capital they require.

Strictly speaking a debenture is the name applied to a document by which a company undertakes to repay money it has borrowed, whether there is some security for the loan or not; but in practice it is usually applied to cases in which a company gives some security over the whole or a part of its property in return for the loan made to it. Sometimes a debenture may be issued to one creditor only, e.g. to a bank to secure an overdraft, but more often the company makes what is called an issue of debentures. This means that the company invites members of the public to lend it money in return for which it (usually) undertakes to repay the money on a certain date, and meantime to pay interest at a fixed rate, and in addition gives the lenders a charge over its property or some part of it, in security for the loan. The effect of such a charge is that, if the company does not carry out its obligations as set out in the debenture, the persons who have lent money, called debenture holders, can take and sell the property charged and pay themselves out of the proceeds what is due to them, in preference to any of the other creditors of the company.

Debentures and Shares.—In some respects a debenture resembles a share. Thus debentures may be transferred from one person to another in very much the same way as shares, and may be bought and sold on the Stock Exchange, the exact formalities necessary for the transfer depending on the terms of the conditions written on the back of the debenture document. Any buyer will have the same rights to payment of principal and interest as the person from whom he bought.

Debentures may be either payable to registered holder or payable to bearer. If they are payable to registered holder they are transferred by a document registered with the company, and the only person who is entitled to them is the person whose name appears as the holder on the register kept by the company. If they are payable to bearer, then they are what is known as Negotiable Instruments (q.v.), that is to say, they can be transferred from one person to another by the simple process of handing over the debenture document without any registration. The former type of debentures resembles ordinary shares in these respects and the latter resembles share warrants.

Although debentures thus have some resemblances to shares, yet the money lent by debenture holders is in a very different position from the money paid or owing by shareholders. The debenture holders are creditors of the company whereas the shareholders, although they may be creditors when a dividend has been declared or when, on the winding up of the company, there is some money left after all the other creditors have been paid, are yet not so much

creditors of the company as its members, that is, the persons of whom it consists. Whereas the law requires that shares should not, except in very special cases, be issued for less than their nominal value, i.e. a share of the value of £1 must not be issued by the company to a shareholder as fully paid for 15/–, there is nothing to prevent a debenture for £100 being issued for £80. Indeed this is frequently done, a company issuing a £100 4% debenture for £80 with the result of course that the holder really receives 5% interest on the money actually lent, and when the debenture is repaid will get £100 for the £80 originally paid by him. To allow such a transaction to take place in the case of shares would have the effect of making the capital of the company less than it appeared to be, and the law always insists that where a company is stated to have a capital of a certain amount the full amount of the money must either have been paid, or at any rate be liable to be paid if calls are made in respect of the shares.

This ruling is intended to protect persons trading with the company, for otherwise a company might be stated to have a capital of £100, indicating that that sum had at one time been in the possession of the company; whereas all the £1 shares might in fact have been issued for 10/– and treated as fully paid, with the result that the company would never have had more than £50 in its possession. This, of course, does not prevent shares being issued as "£1 shares, 10/– paid" if 10/– has in fact been paid for them, and if the shareholder is liable to pay the further 10/– when a call is made.

Irredeemable Debentures—A Recent Danger.—A debenture is frequently issued on the terms that the company can never insist on paying it back, and such a debenture is said to be irredeemable. This has many advantages to the lender of the money, one of the chief being that whatever may be the normal rate of interest at which money can be borrowed in future times, he is sure that the money he has invested in the debenture will bring in the same return; for the company will not be able to pay off the debenture with money obtained by borrowing at a lower rate when money becomes cheaper, thus leaving the debenture holder to find another investment for his money, which will, of course, also be at a lower rate. During the last few years when it has been possible to borrow money very cheaply, many companies have evaded this intended effect of irredeemable debentures by having themselves "wound up." On the winding up, the debenture, like every other debt of the company, becomes payable and those controlling the company can therefore pay back the debenture, form another company, and borrow the money required at the lower rate of interest prevailing.

Registration.—All debentures are required to be registered in a book kept by the company. In England they must also be registered within 21 days of their creation with the Registrar of Companies at Somerset House, and if this is not done, the debenture is void, that is to say, the person who has lent money cannot claim any of the security given by the debenture, although he is at once entitled to reclaim the money lent as an ordinary creditor, that is, without having any right to be paid before the other creditors. In Scotland no such special registration is necessary, for the reason that all documents giving a charge over property in Scotland must be registered in other registries.

A "Floating Charge."—One of the most usual forms of debenture is that which gives what is called a floating charge over the property of the company. This is very useful to a company, for it enables it to obtain an additional amount of credit without preventing it from dealing with its assets in the ordinary way of business. A floating charge is one which attaches to all the property of a company which may belong to it at any given moment, but which ceases to attach as soon as the company sells the property. It is to be distinguished from a fixed charge, which is granted by the company over some particular part of its property, for example, a mortgage over its land, in which case the charge will continue to apply to the land even although it is sold by the company.

Where a floating charge is granted, it will usually cover all the property of the company including any stock in trade the company may have, and any sums of money that may be owed to it, but it will not prevent the company from carrying on its business in the ordinary way, selling its stock and collecting its debts.

When the company buys more stock or gets any new property the charge automatically attaches to that property, so long as it belongs to the company.

"Crystallizing." — When anything happens which, under the terms of the debenture, makes the principal amount of the debenture repayable, e.g. when interest is in arrears, or, when the company is wound up, the debenture is said to crystallize, that is to say, instead of "floating" over the assets of the company it becomes a fixed charge on whatever property the company may have at the time when the crystallization takes place. The company can then no longer get rid of its property, and if it tries to do so, the property still remains subject to the debenture. This system of borrowing money is sometimes rather hard on the ordinary creditors who find that when they have been dealing with the company and giving it credit, all the property of the company is taken by debenture holders.

How to enforce a Debenture.—When a debenture becomes repayable in this way the most usual remedy of the debenture holders is to appoint a receiver, that is to say some person who enters into possession of the property of the company which is covered by the charge, and who sells it if necessary and repays to the debenture holders what is due on their debentures, returning any balance to the company. The debenture holders may also petition the Court to have the company wound up. When a debenture creating a floating charge is issued within six months before the date of the winding up (q.v.) of a company, the debenture will be void unless the money for which it gives security was actually paid at the time the debenture was issued, or else the company was solvent at the date.

Thus, if the company owes its bank £1,000 for money already advanced, and then gives a security over its property to the bank to cover that loan, if the company is wound up within six months of that time, the bank will not be entitled to rely on the security—unless it can be shewn that the company had enough money to pay all its debts at the time when the debenture was given. It will, of course, be entitled to claim repayment of the money lent, but will have to share equally with the other creditors in the property of the company. The preferred creditors (q.v.) are also entitled to be paid before debenture holders with a floating (but not a fixed) charge, if there is not enough money to pay both the preferred creditors and the debenture holders.

Trust Deed.—In some cases, the money lent by the debenture holders is secured by a trust deed in favour of certain trustees by which the company charges its property in favour of the trustees for the repayment of the money. This method has the advantage that it is more easy for the trustees than for individual debenture holders to take the necessary steps if the company makes default in its obligations. (*See* COMPANY; RECEIVER; SHARES; WINDING-UP.)

DEBENTURE (SCOTS LAW).— In Scots law a company has much less power to give security for loans than in English law, for what is called a floating charge (*see* DEBENTURE) is not recognised. If security is given for a loan, a company is in no different position from any private individual, and the property given in security must be conveyed in the way required by the general law, which will usually make it necessary that possession of the property is transferred to the lender, or else that the transaction is registered.

DECEASED WIFE'S SISTER.— A man is allowed by statute to marry his deceased wife's sister, or his brother's widow, or his niece by marriage. A clergyman cannot forbid the use of his church for the ceremony, but he need not perform it himself. If he does act, he is still liable to ecclesiastical censure.

DECEIT.—In all actions for misrepresentation it is necessary for the plaintiff to prove that the defendant persuaded him by some representation, which was in fact false, to act in a certain way. But before bringing an action of deceit he must be able not only to shew all these things, but also to prove that the defendant deliberately set out to deceive him, and that he himself was really deceived and was led by the defendant's wilful misrepresentation to act in some way which resulted in actual loss to himself. These two things, which are technically known as fraud and damage, are essential to the action and it will fail unless

both can be proved. In an action of deceit the accusation of fraud must be made perfectly plain, as a person against whom fraud is alleged, may have the case tried by a jury.

DECREE ABSOLUTE.— When a marriage is finally dissolved or declared null and void, a decree absolute is pronounced by the Court. A decree absolute must in all cases be preceded by a decree nisi. (*See* SPECIAL SUPPLEMENT " DIVORCE.")

DECREE NISI.—In divorce and nullity suits the relief asked for is granted in two parts. At the end of the hearing of the case a decree nisi may be pronounced, that is to say a provisional decree of dissolution or nullity. At the end of six months, or such period as the court may determine, this decree may be made into a decree absolute. Until this is done the marriage in respect of which the decree nisi was declared remains in existence. The purpose of this interval of time is to allow of the intervention of the King's Proctor, or any other matter relevant to the suit being brought before the court. (*See* SPECIAL SUPPLEMENT " DIVORCE.")

DEED.—A Deed is a written document bearing the seal of the person or persons who are parties to it. It is this sealing which is the essential part of a deed, and historically when persons were frequently unable to write, they contracted by a deed to which their seals where affixed. It is now necessary to sign a deed as well as to seal it, and the process of sealing consists merely of touching a wafer which has already been placed on the deed or the space marked on a deed for a wafer, at the same time stating that the person making the deed delivers it "as his act and deed."

A deed may be either an Indenture or a Deed Poll. An indenture is a deed to which there is more than one party—i.e. where there is a contract under which the parties to the deed each undertake liabilities. A deed poll is where there is only one party, as where one person binds himself to do something, e.g. to pay an annuity to someone else. The origin of these terms is that a deed poll had a clean or shaved edge because it was written on one entire piece of paper. When an indenture was made it was made in two copies, one for each of the parties, and the paper was divided and had in consequence a torn or wavy edge.

A contract made by a deed does not require any consideration (q.v.), that is, it may be enforced although the obligations under it are undertaken solely by one party, and although he receives no promise or other act from the person who is the other party to the contract. Thus, a promise to give something as a present must be by deed. (*See* GIFT.) A deed is not binding until it has been delivered. This delivery may be either actual or constructive. It is actual when the paper is physically handed over to the other party, and is constructive when the words—"I deliver this as my act and deed"—are used by the person making it, showing he intends to deliver. When he uses these words the deed is enforceable even though he himself retains it. A deed may be delivered on the terms that it is only to become effective on a certain event happening; it is then known as an Escrow. A deed cannot be delivered as an escrow to a person who is a party to it.

Where a contract is made by seal, the right of action under it is not barred at the end of 6 years, as is the case when the contract is verbal or merely in writing, but extends for 20 or in some cases 12 years.

The form of a deed will depend upon the purpose for which it is made. Any contract may be expressed in a deed but certain contracts will not be valid unless they are made by deed. These are:

1. Contracts without consideration—i.e. promises to give as a present;

2. Contracts by corporations, except contracts entered into in the ordinary course of their business;

3. Leases of land for more than 3 years, but an agreement for a lease may be valid if the tenant has entered into possession (*see* LANDLORD AND TENANT); and

4. The transfer of a British ship or any share in it. (*See* ATTESTATION; BILL OF SALE [SHIP]; CONTRACT.)

DEED (SCOTS LAW).—A distinction between a document in writing and a document under seal is not known in Scots Law, except in the case of companies. All written documents are called deeds, but in some cases the term is applied particularly to documents which are probative writs. (*See* CONTRACT [SCOTS LAW].)

DEED OF ARRANGEMENT.— When a man is in financial difficulties, he is liable in certain cases to be made bankrupt by his creditors. If he is made bankrupt, his estate and property will be given to a Trustee for his creditors who will have to administer the estate in the formal and public way required by the Bankruptcy Acts. It is always possible, however, for a man, instead of going bankrupt, to make an arrangement with his creditors. If the creditors accept the suggested arrangement, then the debtor's property will be disposed of according to the arrangement for payment of the creditors' debts and the debtor will not be made bankrupt. The real distinction is that there is, when an estate is administered under a Deed of Arrangement, very much less publicity and very much less official interference from the Court than when it is administered in bankruptcy.

Composition or Assignment.—The arrangement most usually proposed by a debtor to his creditors is either a composition or an assignment. When a debtor makes a composition, he proposes to his creditors, or some of them, that they shall accept a certain amount in the £ in full settlement of their debts.

The debtor most usually agrees to pay the composition in cash by instalments on certain dates, and he usually obtains guarantees from other persons to make payment of the instalments should he himself fail to do so. In some cases the debtor, in security for the payment of the instalments, will assign his property to a trustee, on trust to sell it if the instalments are not kept up, and use the proceeds to pay them. If the debtor pays the instalments, then he is released from the debts in respect of which the composition has been made. It should be noticed that a composition may be made with some only of the debtor's creditors. If a debtor fails to pay the instalments, or any of them, the effect may be that the creditors are entitled only to sue for the balance of the composition agreed, or it may be that they are then entitled to claim the full amount of the debt and to ignore the composition agreement. Which is the case will depend on the terms of the composition deed.

Another very usual method of making an arrangement with one's creditors is by an assignment, that is, by assigning the debtor's property to some trustee to divide among the debtor's creditors. Any creditor who wishes to come into the arrangement must assent to it, and only creditors who do consent are bound by the arrangement. An assignment may be made either by a debtor transferring his property to a trustee without telling the creditors about it and then getting their assent, or by the debtor first calling a meeting of these creditors and getting their assent beforehand to the proposed assignment to a trustee.

The important distinction between the composition and an assignment is that the second is an act of bankruptcy (q.v.) whereas the first is usually not. If the assignment is to trustees for the benefit of the debtor's creditors generally, whether of all or part of his property, it will be an act of bankruptcy; but if the assignment is only for some, and not all, of his creditors, then it will not necessarily be an act of bankruptcy. A composition may be an act of bankruptcy if it involves notice by the debtor that he intends to suspend payment of his debts.

Registration.—Any deed of arrangement must be registered within 7 days of its execution. For this purpose the expression deed of arrangement includes certain documents when made by a debtor for the benefit of his creditors generally, whether the debtor was insolvent or not, or when made by a debtor who was insolvent at the time of executing the document for the benefit of any 3 or more of his creditors. The documents in question are:

1. An Assignment of the debtor's property;
2. A Composition Agreement;
3. A Deed of Inspectorship entered into for the purpose of carrying on or winding up in business;
4. A Letter of Licence authorising the debtor or any other person to manage, carry on, realise, or dispose of a business with a view to the payment of debts;
5. An Agreement entered into for the purpose of carrying on or winding up the debtor's business, or authorising the debtor or some person to manage, carry on, realise, or dispose of his business with a view to the payment of his debts.

Any one of these documents must be registered with a Registrar appointed by the Board of Trade within 7 days from the date when the debtor or any creditor first signs it, or, if it is executed out of England, then within 7 clear days of the time at which it would in the ordinary course of post reach England if posted within one week after the execution thereof. Registration is effected by sending a true copy of the deed, and of every schedule or inventory to it, to the Registrar together with an affidavit varying the time of execution and describing the residence and occupation of the debtor and the place or places where his business is carried on. There must also be included an affidavit by the debtor stating the total estimated property and liabilities under the deed, the amount of the composition, if any, and the name and addresses of the creditors. The original of the deed must be produced to the Registrar at the same time to show that it is properly stamped.

The Register kept is open to the inspection of any person at any reasonable time on payment of the fee of 1/-. A person inspecting may not only examine the register but may also see and take copies of any deed that may be registered there. Any person is entitled to do this without being required to make a written application, or to specify any particulars, e.g. to give any reasons why he wishes to inspect.

If a deed of arrangement is not registered within 7 days as above, it is void, and this is so whether the deed is for the benefit of creditors generally, or for the benefit of 3 or more creditors only. The effect is that the creditors who have assented to the deed cannot be held to its terms, but may use any methods to recover their debts.

Consents of Creditors.—As soon as a deed has been made, it is to the interest of the debtor to obtain the consent of as many creditors as possible to it. Where it is for the benefit of his creditors generally, the deed will become void if the consent of a majority in number and value of the creditors has not been obtained within 21 days after it has been registered. In order to assent to a deed a creditor must either sign the deed of arrangement or send to the trustee his assent in writing attested by a witness. The trustee has got to file within 28 days after registration a statutory declaration that the necessary majority of the creditors has assented,

For the purpose of calculating majority, a secured creditor is reckoned in respect of any balance left after deducting the value of the security from the debt, and creditors whose debts are under £10 are counted in the majority in value but not in the majority in number.

Where the deed is not for the benefit of creditors generally, but for 3 or more creditors, it still requires to be registered as seen above, but obviously it does not require to get the assent of any majority of the creditors since it is not for their benefit.

An Act of Bankruptcy.—It has been stated above that a deed of arrangement may be an act of bankruptcy, e.g. if it is an assignment of the whole or part of the property to some or all of the creditors. It would obviously be useless for a creditor to assent to a deed of arrangement as a substitute for bankruptcy proceedings if he were at once able to upset the deed by relying on it as an act of bankruptcy, and presenting a petition to have the debtor made bankrupt. Accordingly, no creditor who has assented to the deed can rely on it as an act of bankruptcy unless it becomes void. Where a creditor has not assented he can treat the deed as an act of bankruptcy and present a petition within 3 months as in the case of any other act of bankruptcy; but the trustee under a deed which is expressed to be, or is in fact, for the benefit of creditors generally, may serve on any creditor notice of the fact that the deed has been made, and the creditor then has only *one* month after that notice to present his petition unless the deed becomes void, e.g. because the majority of the creditors do not assent to it.

Operation of Deed.—Until the deed has been intimated to the creditors it may at any time be revoked by the debtor. When a trustee has been appointed under the deed—e.g. where it is an assignment— he is usually empowered to realise the estate, to pay himself a remuneration, to pay all preference claims payable under the rules of bankruptcy, and to pay to the other creditors dividends on the amount of their debts. If there is a surplus, he must hand that back to the person making the deed, that is, the debtor.

A clause is frequently added enabling the trustee to pay off in full creditors for small amounts who do not assent to the deed, and so to prevent them upsetting the whole arrangement by presenting a bankruptcy petition.

When a deed is avoided and the debtor is made bankrupt, none of the creditors is bound by the deed and may prove for their debts in the ordinary way. Where, before the deed becomes void, the trustee has acted under it and has dealt in any way with the debtor's property at a time when he did not know the deed had been made void, he cannot be called upon to account to any trustee later appointed in the debtor's bankruptcy for his dealings with the property.

Trustee's Accounts.—The trustee must give security and must prepare accounts every six months, which he must verify by affidavit and send to the Board of Trade who may audit these accounts. Any money received by him under the deed must be paid into an account to be opened in the name of the debtor's estate. As soon as any deed becomes void for any other reason than failure to register within the time required, the trustee must give notice in writing to each creditor of the debtor. If he acts as trustee at a time when he knows the deed has become void he will be liable to a fine not exceeding £5 a day.

Arrangements in Bankruptcy.— Even after a debtor has had a receiving order (q.v.) made against him, or after he has been adjudicated bankrupt, he may still make some arrangement with his creditors. An arrangement made at this time is governed by the rules of bankruptcy, and not by the rules mentioned above. Thus it will always require the approval of the Court. If this approval is given, the bankruptcy proceedings will be brought to an end and the receiving order or adjudicating order will be annulled, that is, will be set aside. Any scheme or arrangement made after bankruptcy proceedings have commenced requires a majority in number and three fourths in value of the creditors, and not a bare majority in number and value as in the case of a deed of arrangement made prior to bankruptcy proceedings ; but on the other hand, the minority of creditors who do not consent, are bound by the arrangement when it is made in the course of the bankruptcy proceedings, but only those who have consented are in any way bound when the arrangement is made outside bankruptcy. (*See* BANKRUPTCY.)

DEER.—A game licence is required for the killing of deer (*see* GAME), except in hunting with hounds or in enclosed lands. Heavy penalties may be inflicted on persons who hunt or kill deer unlawfully, or who have venison in their possession without being able to shew that they came by it lawfully. (*See* GAME; GAMEKEEPER.)

DEFAMATION.—Defamation is the wrong caused by the publication of a defamatory statement concerning some person without lawful justification or cause.

What is a Defamatory Statement? Libel and Slander.—A defamatory statement is a statement concerning any person which has a tendency to diminish the good opinion which others have of that person, and tends to expose him to public hatred, ridicule or contempt, or to injure him in any office, profession or business. A defamatory statement may be either a libel or a slander. A libel is a defamatory statement made in some permanent form, such as writing, printing or pictures. A slander is a defamatory statement made in some transitory form, such as spoken words or gestures, and not in a permanent form as in the case of libel. A libel may be a criminal offence as well as a civil one, but unlike a slander it is in all cases actionable without proof of special damage, that is to say, an action will lie for libel although the person complaining of the statement cannot prove he has suffered actual financial loss as a result of the publication of the libel. (*See* LIBEL.)

A slander, unlike a libel, is a civil offence only, and cannot be a crime unless the slander is also seditious, i.e. a treasonable or blasphemous statement. An action for libel must be brought within six years of its publication, and an action for slander must be brought within two years of the time the defamatory words were spoken.

When slander is actionable although no financial loss is proved.—To the rule that slander is only actionable on proof of special damages there are four exceptions:—

(1) *Where the slander is a statement charging a person with having committed a crime.*—The statement must charge a person with a crime which is punishable by imprisonment, not merely a fine or a penalty;

so that to charge a person with being drunk, is not actionable with proof of special damages, for it is an offence which is punishable only by a fine or penalty; but on the other hand to call a man a thief is clearly to charge him with an offence punishable corporally, for a thief may be imprisoned.

(2) *Where the slander imputes that a person is suffering from a contagious disease of a particular kind, namely from venereal disease or leprosy.*—The statement must imply that a person is actually suffering from the disease at the time the statement was made.

(3) *Where the defamatory statement imputes unchastity or adultery to any woman.*

(4) *Defamatory statements which are made in relation to a person's office, profession or trade.*—The person complaining of the slander must prove, in order to succeed without proof of special damage, that at the time the words were spoken he held such office, profession or trade, and also that the words do relate to his conduct, connected with his office, profession or trade. It is not enough to say that the statement tends to injure a person in his trade, office or profession; it must be a charge against him *in* his office, trade or profession; thus it is not actionable without proof of special damages to accuse a grocer of being a drunkard, because that does not mean he is a bad grocer. But it would be actionable to say that he gives short weight.

Defamation generally.—Defamatory statements must be distinguished from (1) statements which are merely injurious without being defamatory; (2) mere vulgar abuse. Thus it would not (1) be defamatory if one shopkeeper said falsely of another that he had closed his shop for the day, though if such a statement should actually cause a financial loss to the shopkeeper, another remedy known as an action for injurious falsehood might lie against the person making the statement. (2) To abuse another by calling him a villain, a rogue, a scoundrel or a rascal is not defamatory in the ordinary way. Such general words are not accusing a person of a definite crime, but are the sort of words likely to be used by a person in a temper. When words are spoken in heat, the fact that they were so spoken is taken into consideration, in order to determine their true meaning and to ascertain whether they are defamatory or not. In order to be defamatory the statement must affect the person complaining of it. It must affect his character, his business or his office, and not merely his goods or title to property; if, however, a person disparages another's goods or title to property, an action for slander of goods or title may lie (*see* INJURIOUS FALSEHOOD). However, a statement which disparages another's goods may also amount to a libel or slander as well as an injurious falsehood, if besides disparaging a person's goods it casts aspersions upon the manner in which that person conducts his business. For instance, if a person said of a certain fishmonger that he habitually sold fish that was bad and unfit for human consumption, such a statement would be a libellous statement, because it reflected upon the fishmonger in the conduct of his business, and so reflected upon the fishmonger personally, and not merely his goods.

Words must refer to person complaining.—The words or matter complained of must also refer to the person who complains of them. The whole world need not be able to understand them to refer to him, so long as some person reasonably understood them in that way. It is no defence in an action for libel or slander for a person to say that he did not intend to refer to the person complaining of the statement or matter. For instance, if a person writes a work of fiction with a character called Y and, in fact, the name the author invented is the name of a real person, even if the author has never heard of him, then the author will be liable to that person in an action for libel, if that person, can shew that some persons reading the book reasonably thought it referred to him. It most cases the mere similarity of name would not be enough, but the whole story in the book will be taken into account, and even if the name is different, an action may lie if from other circumstances, e.g. the locality, the character in the book can reasonably be taken for the person complaining. Of course no action can be brought unless the character is defamatory in the sense set out above.

The Innuendo.—Although a statement may not be defamatory in its primary sense, that is to say in its plain ordinary meaning, it may be defamatory in its special meaning, that is the meaning which it bore in the circumstances in which it was made, and in which it was understood by persons to whom it was made. Such a secondary meaning which a statement may bear is known as an innuendo; for instance, if a person identifies Y by referring to him as the man in a red motor car, quite clearly such a statement is not defamatory in its ordinary, primary meaning; but if at the time the statement was made, a murder had been committed in the neighbourhood and the murderer had not been identified, but had been seen driving a red motor car, under such circumstances a statement identifying Y as the man in a red motor car, might well be a statement defamatory of Y. Any person who alleges that a statement not defamatory in its primary sense bears a defamatory innuendo, must establish that a reasonable person aware of all the circumstances could understand the words in the secondary sense, which he alleges that they bear.

Publication.—A defamatory statement is not actionable unless it has been published to some third person. The publication of a defamatory statement does not mean making public in the ordinary sense. A defamatory statement is published as soon as it has been made known to any person other than the person complaining of it. It is sufficient to constitute publication if it has been written on a postcard or in a telegram (but not in a letter) to the person complaining of it, as some other person will, in law, be presumed to have read the telegram or postcard. In the case of a slander it is sufficient if it has been spoken in the hearing of persons other than the person complaining of it.

The repetition of a defamatory statement.—It is no defence to an action for libel or slander for the person who has published the libel or slander to say that he was merely repeating that which somebody else had said: but in certain circumstances the fact that the person publishing the defamatory statement was merely repeating a statement, what he had been told, or a statement he had seen in a newspaper, may reduce the amount of damages recoverable from him.

A husband's liability for a wife's libel or slander.—A husband is liable for a defamatory statement made by his wife so long as there is not a divorce or separation order in existence at the time of the action brought: it is usual, therefore, to sue both husband and wife as defendants in an action for defamation published by the wife. As a general rule, no action for defamation will lie by a husband against his wife, or a wife against her husband, as for most purposes a husband and wife are still one in law, but where they are living apart under a separation order, or where a wife is carrying on a separate business and the defamatory statement is upon her in the way of her business, she may have a right of action against her husband.

Liabilities of Principal and Agent and Master and Servant.—A master is liable for any defamatory statement published by his servant within the scope of his employment. At the same time the servant is also personally liable for the publication of the defamatory statement. A principal is also liable for the publication of a libel within the scope of the agent's authority. (*See* MASTER AND SERVANT; PRINCIPAL AND AGENT.)

The principal defences to an action for libel or slander are:—

(1) Justification.
(2) Privilege.
(3) Fair Comment.
(4) Apology.

(1) **Justification.**—It is a good defence in a civil action for libel or slander for the defendant to say that the alleged defamatory statement was true. By so doing, the defendant is said to justify the defamatory statement, and such a defence is known as the defence of justification (q.v.).

(2) **Privilege.**—Though the general rule is that, if a person makes a defamatory statement of another he does so at his peril, in certain cases on the ground of public policy the person who makes it is relieved from liability, even though the statement is defamatory. The occasion on which they are made is said to be privileged. Privileged occasions may be classed as being of two kinds: occasions (*a*) of Absolute privilege and (*b*) of Qualified privilege.

(*a*) ABSOLUTE PRIVILEGE.— There are certain occasions upon which a person is absolutely protected from the consequences of any statement he makes, however false the statement may be, and however maliciously that statement is made: but quite naturally such occasions are exceptional in character and are not likely to be abused. This absolute privilege is given to:

(1) Any statement made during the course of any judicial proceedings by any person taking part, that is to say, statements made during a case in Court by the Judge, a witness or counsel, or any member of the jury or any party to such proceedings. This privilege extends to judicial proceedings in any recognized Court of Law whether civil, naval, or military, and it extends not only to statements made in the Court but also to any statement made to a solicitor by a witness or party in the case in the course of the preparation of the case by the solicitor.

(2) Any statement made by one officer of state to another officer of state in the course of his official duties. For instance, a communication by the Home Secretary to an Under-Secretary of State, or of a naval or military officer to his inferior in the course of an official enquiry.

(3) Any statement made in either House of Parliament by a member of that House, but this protection does not extend to statements made by members outside the Houses of Parliament.

(4) Any contemporaneous report by a newspaper of any judicial proceedings, or any proceedings in either House of Parliament are absolutely privileged, so long as they are a fair and accurate report of those proceedings. If a newspaper report of such proceedings consisted merely of extracts of such proceedings or contained comment, such a report would not be protected by absolute privilege, but by qualified privilege only. (*See* NEWSPAPER.)

(5) Reports published by order of Parliament are protected by absolute privilege. The findings of a Royal Commission set up to enquire into some matter is an instance of such a report.

(*b*) QUALIFIED PRIVILEGE.—There are certain occasions upon which, ". . . . for the common convenience and welfare of society," persons making statements are given some measure of protection from the consequences of making a statement which may in fact be defamatory, so long as the statement is made honestly. Such occasions are known as occasions of qualified privilege, and a statement made on such an occasion is conditionally privileged. That is to say, if on such an occasion of qualified privilege the statement is made maliciously, the privilege is destroyed, and the person making the statement is no longer protected from the consequences of his statement. To put it in another way, malice destroys the privilege attached to the occasion.

Malice in law is a very wide term and therefore difficult to define. It has been defined as any wrong feeling in a man's mind. Thus any statement made out of spite or made by a person who knows it to be untrue is a statement made maliciously, and such a statement would not be protected by qualified privilege.

There are very many occasions upon which a statement may be qualifiedly privileged, and it is not possible here to enumerate them. The chief instances fall under the following heads:

(a) STATEMENTS MADE IN THE PRO-TECTION OF A COMMON INTEREST.—Any member of the public may make a complaint against a servant of the Crown, and so long as the charge is honestly made and made to some person who has control of the official and may be able to investigate the matter, the communication would be privileged. If the statement or any statement which is qualifiedly privileged is made to more persons than is necessary, such publication might amount to malice and so destroy the privilege attached to the occasion. It may be safely said that any statement is privileged if it is made by a person concerning a wrong done, or on the possibility of another doing a wrong to others, and made to some person capable of preventing the occurrence of the wrong, and made for the purpose of protecting society generally or the person to whom it was made, so long as the statement were honestly made. As a further example of such statements, a communication made to a woman, by a relation or connection, as to the character of the man she proposed to marry was held to be qualifiedly privileged, and so also have been communications made by one director of a company to another concerning an official of the company.

(b) STATEMENTS MADE IN THE PERFORM-ANCE OF A DUTY.—If a master who answers questions put to him concerning a servant who has been in his employ, by a prospective employer, or some person who has an interest in the matter and therefore is doing so under a duty, and provided he answers them honestly, then the occasion upon which the master makes the statements is privileged. In fact any statement made in the performance of a duty (which need not be a legal duty, but may be a moral or social duty) is qualifiedly privileged. A communication made by the secretary of a charitable organization as to the character of an applicant for charity, and a statement by a curate as to the character of his parishioner are examples of such statements.

(c) Fair and accurate reports contained in any newspaper of any public meetings held for the furtherance of matters of public concern, such as the meetings of a public board of guardians or of a vestry meeting, are qualifiedly privileged so long as the publication of the report of any such proceeding is made for the public benefit, that is to say, it must be the report of some matter the publication of which is, or would be, of benefit to the public. (*See* PRIVILEGE.)

(3) **Fair Comment on a Matter of Public Interest.**—An action for defamation will not lie for a statement which is fair comment upon a matter of public interest. It must be comment and not statements of fact, for statements of fact, unless they are protected by privilege, must be proved to be true and justified. A statement though defamatory is not actionable, so long as it is comment made fairly, that is, without malice, upon a matter of public interest. Fair comment is really only a statement of opinion, and therefore, if a person who stated his opinion were called upon by the law to prove his opinion were true, it would clearly be an obligation almost impossible for him to fulfil. So long as the comment is made honestly, that is to say, the person who makes it believes what he says, and the matter is of interest to the public, no action for defamation will lie against the person making the statement.

(4) **Apology.**—In an action for libel contained in a newspaper or other periodical publication, no action will lie if the defendant prove that the words complained of were put in the newspaper without malice or negligence, and that at the earliest opportunity an

apology was inserted in the newspaper and payment of a sum of money to the plaintiff was made by way of amends. (*See* NEWSPAPER.)

Libel as a Crime.—Libel, unlike slander, may be the subject of criminal proceedings, and every statement which amounts to a libel may constitute a crime if its publication is liable to cause a breach of the peace. The reason for ranking libel among criminal offences is, it has been said, "because of its supposed tendency to arouse angry passions, provoke revenge and thus endanger the public peace." Thus a person libelled may either pursue his civil remedy, or may institute criminal proceedings, but of course criminal proceedings will not lie if the libel be a mere personal squabble, unless the libel or its repetition is likely to cause a disturbance of the public peace.

A person complaining of a libel may, if he desires to prosecute, proceed either by way of an indictment or by way of information.

The usual method of proceeding is by way of indictment, and the first step that the prosecutor must take is to charge the defendant before two justices or a stipendiary magistrate. However, in the case of a libel published in a newspaper, before he can begin proceedings to prosecute he must obtain leave of a Judge in chambers. The Judge will not give leave to prosecute, unless he is satisfied that the case will not be met by civil proceedings, and there is no appeal from his decision.

The course of instituting proceedings for libel by way of an information is only adopted in very serious and pressing cases of a public nature, where the libel is upon a person in an official or judicial position, and it is in the public interest that action should be taken. In a civil action for libel the defences of "Privilege" and of "Fair Comment" are good defences to a charge of criminal libel, and in a civil action for libel "Justification" is a good defence; that is to say, no action will lie if the defendant can prove that the words are true. But in a criminal action for libel it is no defence for the defendant to prove that the statement complained of was true, unless the defendant can also prove that the publication of the statement was for the public benefit. It is also a good defence

to an action for criminal libel for the defendant to prove that the publication of the words was made without the defendant's knowledge or consent, and that their publication did not arise through want of care or caution on the defendant's part. (*See* JUSTIFICATION.)

DEFAMATION (SCOTS LAW).—The Scots Law Defamation is in many respects the same as the English. There are, however, three important differences.

Firstly there is no distinction in effect between a spoken defamatory statement, i.e. slander in English law, and a written defamatory statement, i.e. libel. Both are equally actionable in Scots Law. Again, it is not necessary in Scots law that the defamatory statement should be published to some third person, and an action will lie and damages may be recovered for the injury to feelings caused by a defamatory statement, even though it was made only to the person to whose character it relates and not to any third party.

Finally defamation is not a crime in Scots law.

DEFAULT SUMMONS.—Where a plaintiff in a County Court action has a claim against a defendant for a debt or liquidated, i.e. ascertained, or agreed sum of money of an amount less than £10, he may at the time of entering the plaint file particulars in writing of his claim and issue a Default Summons. If the defendant fails within 8 days of service of such default summons to give notice in writing to the Registrar that he intends to defend the action, the plaintiff will be entitled forthwith to sign judgment against him. (*See* COUNTY COURT PROCEDURE; SPECIAL DEFAULT SUMMONS.)

DEFENCE.—A Defence is a document in which the defendant in an action sets out the facts upon which he relies as constituting an answer to the plaintiff's claim. It is most important to bear in mind that if, in his defence, the defendant fails to contradict any of the facts set out by the plaintiff in the Statement of Claim he is presumed to admit those facts. It is also important to bear in mind that the defendant must set out in the defence the exact grounds upon which he relies, and must not rest content with merely denying, for example, that he is indebted to the plaintiff at all.

If the defendant fails to deliver a defence within the times set out in the rules, he is liable to have judgment entered against him in default of defence. (*See* COUNTY COURT PROCEDURE; HIGH COURT PROCEDURE; PLEADING.)

DEFENDANT.—In cases in the Chancery and King's Bench Divisions of the High Court of Justice in probate cases, and in actions in the County Courts, the person against whom the action is brought is called the defendant. The person bringing the action is called the plaintiff. In divorce matters it is otherwise, the parties being named the petitioner and the respondent. In criminal cases it is usual to describe the person charged with any offence, less than a felony, as the defendant.

DEFERRED CREDITORS.—In bankruptcy and in the winding-up of a company, just as there are certain debts which are paid before all others, known as "preferred debts," so also there are certain debts which are not paid until all others have been satisfied, known as "deferred debts." In the case of bankruptcy the following debts are deferred;

(1) Any loan made by a wife to her husband, who has become bankrupt, for the purposes of his business;

(2) Any loan by a husband to his wife, who has become bankrupt, for the purposes of her business;

(3) Any loan made to the bankrupt on the terms that the rate of interest shall vary with the profits of the bankrupt's business; and

(4) Any sum due in respect of a sale of the goodwill of a business for a share of the profits, whether by way of annuity or otherwise.

In the case of companies the only debts which are deferred are those which are due to a shareholder in the company in his capacity as shareholder, e.g. dividend. (*See* BANKRUPTCY; WINDING-UP.)

DEL CREDERE AGENT.—A Del Credere agent is a person who undertakes to sell goods for another on the terms that, if the person who purchases the goods does not pay for them, the Del Credere agent will do so. He makes himself responsible only for the payment for the goods, and does not guarantee that the purchaser will accept the goods or will fulfil the obligations under

the contract in any way. He only guarantees his solvency. The contract which makes a person a Del Credere agent is not strictly a contract of guarantee, because the agent has an interest in the contract since he negotiates it, and the rules of guarantee do not apply where the person undertaking that the payment will be made—i.e. the guarantor—has such an interest. The contract therefore is not required to be in writing. (*See* GUARANTEE; PRINCIPAL AND AGENT.)

DELICT (SCOTS LAW).—The deliberate infringements of rights arising apart from contract, e.g. the making of a defamatory statement, is called a delict. When the infringement is not deliberate but arises from the failure to exercise proper care, it is said to be "quasi-delictual." Delict and quasi-delict thus correspond to the tort of English Law, and the English term tort is frequently used in Scotland. (*See* REPARATION [SCOTS LAW].)

DEMESNE.—When part of a manor was in the actual occupation of the Lord of the Manor it was said to constitute the demesne. Since the abolition of copyhold tenure the importance of this term has disappeared.

DEMISE.—When premises are let under a lease they are sometimes said to be demised. Originally the term demised covered the transfer of any kind of right, but now it is confined to the grant of leases.

DEMURRAGE.—Demurrage is the amount payable by the shipper to the shipowner for delay in loading or unloading the cargo.

When goods are carried at sea, either under a charter party or under a bill of lading, it is necessary to calculate the time likely to be occupied in loading and unloading in order to determine the amount of freight, because obviously, if the ship were detained for an unreasonable period in any port by the delay of the person sending or receiving the goods in loading or unloading, a loss would fall upon the shipowner. The period fixed for the operations of loading and unloading is known as the "lay days," and these run from the time when the ship arrives at the place at which she is bound to proceed under the charter party, and the charterer has been informed of her arrival there. If no "lay days" are mentioned, the charterer will still be liable if he keeps the ship beyond a reasonable time, and his liability will be the same even though the delay was not due to his own fault but to circumstances beyond his control, e.g. by bad weather or strikes. He will not, however, be liable where the delay is caused by the fault of the owner of the ship, or where the ship is loaded within the lay days but is afterwards prevented from leaving port by storms.

It is usually provided in the charter party what sum per day shall be paid by the ship-owner as demurrage, but if no provision is made, the ship-owner will still be entitled to claim damages, the amount of which will be the loss to which he has been put by the delay.

It is frequently provided that the charterer shall not be liable for delay caused by strikes or other similar causes; and where it is desired that the charterer should not be liable for delay through bad weather which had made it impossible to load, he should be required to load at a certain rate per "weather-working" day.

Although the original use of the term demurrage was confined to cases of carriage by sea it is now applied also to carriage by land. Thus, if goods are carried by a railway in trucks not belonging to the company, the trader to whom the trucks belong is entitled to recover a reasonable sum as demurrage if his trucks are detained beyond a reasonable period. Demurrage here is due not in respect of delay in loading or unloading as at sea, but in respect of delay in the actual journey. A similar claim could be made by the railway company where trucks belonging to it are detained un-duly by a trader in loading or unloading.

DEMURRER.—An old form of plead-ing whereby one party alleged that the other party to an action in his pleading had shewn no case in law. In other words the defendant would say that, assuming every fact pleaded by the plaintiff were true, nevertheless these facts did not constitute in law a good cause of action. Demurrers have been abolished, and the modern pro-cedure is to apply to strike out the pleading of the opposite party.

DENMAN, Lord (1779-1854).—Starting practice at the Chancery Bar, he won renown by his defence of the Luddites, when he became the popular hero of the hour. After being out of favour with the Court for his impassioned defence of Queen Caroline he was made Lord Chief Justice in 1832. On the bench, his most sensa-tional trial was that of O'Connell, who came before him and the four other Law Lords as a final Tribunal. By his vote O'Connell was set free by three to two.

DENTISTS.—The position of dentists, their rights and obligations are very similar to those of doctors (q.v.). It is illegal for unqualified and unregistered persons to practise as dentists, and no person whose name does not appear upon the Register of Dentists, which is kept by the General Medical Council, may recover his fees in a Court of Law, although the fitting of artificial teeth does not amount to dental surgery, and the cost of their fitting and the materials contained in them can be recovered by an unqualified practitioner. Further, any unqualified person who practises as a dentist, or who describes himself in such a manner as wilfully to induce the public to be-lieve that he is duly registered, when he is not so registered, is liable to a penalty of £20. The use of the word "dentist" or "dental surgeon" amounts to such an offence.

Any person who has passed the requisite examination in an approved medical school is entitled to have his name placed upon the Register, as are persons who are qualified abroad as foreign or colonial dentists.

The General Medical Council exercises over Registered Dentists a control similar to that which it exercises over Registered Medical Practitioners (q.v.), and is entitled to hold enquiries and to punish registered dentists by erasure of their names from the register or otherwise.

No registered dentist is entitled to assume a name or title which would induce the public to believe that he is entitled to practise ordinary medicine, or surgery or midwifery. (*See* DOCTOR; NATIONAL HEALTH INSURANCE; REGISTERED MEDICAL PRACTITIONER.)

DEPONENT.—Any person who swears to a statement such as affidavit, is called a deponent. A familiar example is the case of any person who gives evidence at the Police Court on the preliminary hearing of some indictable crime. Witnesses in such cases are required to sign a written record of their evidence, which is called a deposition.

DEPORTATION ORDER. — Any alien who has been convicted of any offence punishable with imprisonment without option of a fine may be recommended by the Court that convicted him for deportation from the country. This is a recommendation only and is examined by the Home Secretary. The latter may then, on such recommendation, actually order the deportation of the alien. Any alien who is in receipt of poor relief, or has no means of living, or who has been convicted of a crime in a foreign country, can be deported in a similar manner. The Home Secretary also has the power to deport where in his view deportation is necessary in the public interest, even though none of the previous considerations is present. Any person who appears in this country in breach of a deportation order is liable to be imprisoned for six months. Any police officer has the right of arresting without warrant any person whom he reasonably suspects of committing an offence against a deportation order. (*See* ALIENS.)

DEPOSITION. — When indictable offences are being enquired into in a Police Court, the statements of witnesses are written down and signed by them. These written statements are called depositions. They must be taken in the presence and the hearing of the prisoner, and they must be read over and signed by the witness, and also signed by one of the magistrates before whom they are taken. They are actually written down by the magistrates' clerk and should set out as far as possible the actual words of the witness.

Depositions may be used at the trial of a prisoner before a jury in the following circumstances:—If a witness is dead or unable to attend the trial by reason of illness, then his deposition can be read in his absence. Also a witness can be cross-examined upon the deposition which he swore to and signed at the Police Court, if there is any variation between his evidence at the trial and that at the Police Court. Sometimes where witnesses are dangerously ill and it is essential that their evidence shall be obtained and recorded for future use, a magistrate attends at their home or the hospital at which they are and takes the deposition there. Provided that the accused person either was present when such a deposition was taken, or had an opportunity of being there, then the deposition, if the witness should be dead or permanently unable to travel, may be read at the subsequent trial.

DESERTER. — Desertion is the act of a sailor, soldier or airman absenting himself without leave from his unit with the intention of permanently avoiding future service in His Majesty's forces. It is desertion for a man to absent himself with the intention of avoiding some special duty, such as proceeding with his unit on active service, even though he may intend eventually to return to the service.

Any police officer, if he suspects on reasonable grounds that a man is a deserter or absentee, may arrest him without a warrant. He must at once bring him before a Police Court. It is the duty of a Police Court, if satisfied that a man is a deserter, to make arrangements for him to be handed back to an escort from his unit. Any person, even though not a member of the armed forces, who knowingly assists a deserter to remain in concealment, commits a criminal offence.

DESERTION. — Desertion is a matrimonial offence which consists of the withdrawal of one spouse from cohabitation with the other without reasonable excuse. The essence of desertion is that there shall be a parting without mutual consent. If a husband and wife mutually agree to live separate and apart, and one of them later on regrets this agreement, he or she cannot legally complain of the other if that other persists in his or her refusal to return. Of course this parting by mutual consent must be intended to be a separation. Where a husband or wife for the purpose of their work or for some similar reason cease to live together for a time, but intend to return to each other when the reason for the separation has passed, then the act of separating does not constitute a separation by mutual consent, and the failure of one to return to the other may constitute desertion.

In deciding who is guilty of desertion, it must be remembered that in English law it is for the husband to decide where the matrimonial home is to be. He it is who usually pays for it, and it is a recognized principle that he shall decide where it shall be and what form it shall take. Further, it is for the husband to decide on the standard of living which he and his wife shall adopt. On the other hand if a wife shews that her husband conducted himself unreasonably in regard to the choice of home or the method of living in order to force her to leave him, she is held in law to be justified in leaving him. Indeed this principle is of even wider application. The law does not require a husband or wife to live with his or her spouse if the conduct of the other party is such as to make it impossible or dangerous to do so. This is interpreted in a common-sense way by the Courts, and it is not every act of unkindness or unpleasant behaviour that justifies the withdrawal of one spouse from the other. In order to justify this there must be the commission by the other of some recognized matrimonial offence such as adultery, cruelty or wilful failure to provide reasonable maintenance.

A husband or wife complaining of desertion may petition in the Divorce Division of the High Court of Justice for a decree of judicial separation. (See JUDICIAL SEPARATION.) The grant of such decree will, in the case of a wife, entitle her in a proper case to an order for alimony. (See ALIMONY.) A deserted wife has the alternative and cheaper remedy in the Police Court. She may go to the Police Court for the area in which she is when deserted, and complain that her husband has deserted her. If she establishes this at the hearing, she may be granted a separation order forbidding her husband to return to her, and also if the facts justify it, a maintenance order. (See SEPARATION ORDER.) This remedy of the Police Court is, of course, a cheap and quick method, but it should be noted that the Police Court can only order a payment of £2 per week and 10/- for each child. In both the High Court of Justice and the Police Court, orders may be made for the custody of the children of the marriage. As a general rule the innocent party will be granted the custody of the children, though, in the case of very young infants, a guilty wife may in some cases be allowed their custody, or at any rate their care and control during their early years. (See SPECIAL SUPPLEMENT "DIVORCE.")

DESIGNS.—It is possible in certain circumstances to acquire the copyright in a design for a limited period of years by means of registration. The Patents and Designs Act defines a design as "only those features of shapes, configuration, pattern or ornament applied to any article . . . which in the finished article appeal to and are judged by the eye." It is the shape, form or ornamentation of the finished article which constitutes the design and may be registered under the act as such; the mechanical process by which the design is attained is not in itself the design, and if the inventor or proprietor wishes to protect the process as distinct from the result he must do so by registering it as a patent (q.v.).

What is a Design?—The essence of a design is that it should appeal to the eye, and its object is æsthetic rather than indicative of origin. It must be distinguished from a trade mark (q.v.). A design is something which is incorporated in, and forms part of, the article to which it is applied, as for instance the mouldings upon the door of an oven, the pattern of a cloth, carpet or wallpaper or the shape of an ash tray; it need not necessarily consist of the configuration of the whole of the article. In the case of the oven door the design is not the shape of the oven or even of the door, but only of the mouldings upon it, whereas in the case of an ash tray shaped like an elephant, it is the outward appearance of the article as a whole. A trade-mark on the other hand is usually a very unimportant part of the article, and is placed upon it for the sole purpose of indicating its origin. Furthermore, the right to copyright by registration of a design has been created by Act of Parliament in order to protect and reward the creator or designer; there must therefore be some degree of invention or creation. Far more invention than this is required before a process of manufacture can be patented (see PATENTS), but very much less will justify the registration of a trade-mark (q.v.). Lastly, as is explained below, the period for which copyright may exist in a design is limited to a maximum of fifteen years, but a registered trade-mark may be kept alive indefinitely.

When is a Design Original?—The only designs which can be registered are those which are "new or original"; but in this connection regard must be had not merely to the design itself but to the completed effect of the design upon the article. A design for the manufacture of money boxes in the shape of Roman galleys would be new and original, not because the shape of the galleys was first conceived by the designer, but because he first applied the old shape to the new purposes. Similarly the fact that a particular design has been used in the past, and has even acquired copyright by registration in connection with one article does not prevent it from being "new or original," and so registrable again when applied to a totally different article. An application to register the design of a motor car shaped like a galley would not be invalidated by the earlier registration of a similar design for money boxes or ash trays; but the two articles must be so entirely different in their nature that no confusion can arise. If there is not sufficient difference between them, as there would not be in the case of a design on silk and the same design on other cloth, the only person who will be allowed to register the design in its new connection will be its registered owner in the old, and an application by a newcomer to register it for cloth would be refused.

Previous Use of Design.—The right to acquire copyright in a design by registration is lost if the design has been previously published. Publication in this legal sense, as in the law of copyright in artistic and literary works (*see* COPYRIGHT), has a specialized meaning; it includes the use of the design by anyone, including the designer himself, in connection with the article for which registration is sought, the exhibition of the design as applied to the article or its manufacture and sale, and the publication of the plans, drawings and specifications. The hardship that follows from holding all of these acts to be publications of the design, any of which render any attempt to acquire copyright by registration at a later date impossible, is mitigated by the provision of exceptions. The Patents and Designs Acts provide that the confidential disclosure of a design, and the placing and execution of a confidential first order shall not constitute publication of the design in the legal sense.

Period of Registration.—The period for which copyright in a design may be obtained by registration is a short one; in the first place it is only for five years (from the date of the application for registration);

but if the registered proprietor gives notice to the Patent Office before the five years expire he is entitled to have his copyright extended for a further five years. At the end of this total period of ten years, the registered proprietor may again apply for yet another extension of five years, but he is not entitled to this, and the Comptroller of the Patent Office may in his discretion refuse it. Prescribed fees are payable on registration or renewal.

Effect of Registration.—During the period throughout which any person is the registered owner of the copyright in a design, he has the exclusive right to apply the design to any article of the class or classes for which it was registered, and may prevent any other person from so using it: but this right only extends to the use of the registered design in connection with the article for which it was registered. It does not confer upon him the exclusive right or monopoly of making it; nor can he prevent any other person from making the same article in the same way and for the same purpose provided only that it has a different form. All articles bearing the design must also be marked with the word "registered." It is an offence to mark articles in this way after the copyright has expired.

The registered proprietor of a design can enforce his copyright against anyone who infringes it by means of an action. This may take one of two forms; for the proprietor may either rely on the statutory right of action given by the Patents and Designs Acts, by which he can recover a penalty not exceeding £50 for each infringement of the design (though in no case can he recover more than £100 at a time in respect of any one design by this action), or he may bring an ordinary action for damages in which he will be entitled to recover the amount he has lost, and will probably be able to compel the infringer to hand over any profits he may have made. To an action of the latter type the proprietor of a design may also join a claim for an injunction to restrain the infringer from repeating the infringement: alternatively, he may ask for such an injunction alone. It is a good defence to any action to shew that the articles made by the registered proprietor in accordance with his registered design were not marked with the word "registered," and the proprietor will then only be able to succeed if he can shew either that the infringer already knew that the design had been registered, or that all reasonable care had been exercised, or the Board of Trade's consent obtained.

How to Register.—The only person who may apply to register a design is its proprietor; he is defined as either:

(a) the author of the design; or

(b) the person under whose direction or orders, or in whose service the author prepared the design; or

(c) Any person to whom the author or his employer, may have transferred the ownership of the design.

Application for registration must be made by the proprietor (either personally or through a solicitor or patent agent) to the Comptroller of the Patent Office (from whom particulars and forms can be obtained). Fully detailed plans and specifications of the design must be submitted as well as a clear statement of the articles to which it is to be applied. This application and disclosure are confidential, and if for any reason registration is not obtained, no unauthorized person may inspect the documents. Any delay on the part of the applicant in pursuing his claim to registration is regarded as tantamount to an abandonment of it.

The Comptroller may only refuse to register a design on certain grounds, viz:

(i) That it is contrary to law or morality;

(ii) That the design is not new or original in the sense already explained;

(iii) That the design has been previously published.

If the Comptroller bases his refusal to permit registration on ground (i) the applicant may appeal to the Law Officers; but if he bases it on grounds (ii) and (iii) appeal lies to the High Court. If the Comptroller decides to permit registration he gives a certificate to the applicant. A register is kept at the Patent office of all registered designs and their owners. In the event of the registered owner dying or assigning his rights, application must be made to insert the new owner's name in the register; but this can only be done when there is a complete transfer of ownership, as trusts, etc., can never be entered on the register. In order to prevent piracy, the right to inspect this register is slightly confined. During the first two years after registration the only

persons who are permitted to inspect it are the registered proprietor and his agent, or any person ordered to do so by the Court or the Comptroller; but any person whose application for registration has been refused on the ground that his design has already been registered by some one else may claim to see particulars of the registered design.

At all other times the register is open to all, and certified copies of the contents may be obtained. The Comptroller is also bound to state whether any particular design is still registered, and to what classes of goods it has been applied.

Anybody who is—or would be—affected by the registration of a design may apply to the Comptroller at any time to cancel or vary the registration on the ground that it ought never to have been allowed. The Comptroller must hear both sides and an appeal lies from his decision to the High Court.

DETENTION OF LUNATICS.— Great care has obviously to be taken in securing the detention of any person as a lunatic. The first step is the obtaining of a certificate by a doctor that the person is insane. (*See* CERTIFICATION OF LUNATICS.) When this has been done it is next necessary to obtain an order from some judicial authority.

The most usual method by which a person is detained is by a reception order (*see* below) but in three cases persons may lawfully be detained without a reception order following on some kind of judicial inquiry.

(a) Idiots and imbeciles. The parent or guardian of a person who falls within either of these two classes may place him in an institution or with an approved guardian, provided he first obtains two medical certificates, of which one is from a doctor approved by the Board of Control or the Local Authority.

(b) Mental defectives (idiot, imbecile, feeble-minded person or moral imbecile), if found in a neglected condition, or abandoned, or cruelly treated, may be detained until a petition for a reception order can be presented.

(c) Dangerous persons. An "urgency order" may be made by the husband, or wife, or near relative (or failing them a friend) of any person whom it is necessary to restrain either for his own safety or for that of the public. Such an order will only justify restraint if it is accompanied by a medical certificate given not more than two days previously. It operates for seven days, or if a petition for a reception order is applied for, until this has been heard.

Procuring Certification.—Except in these three cases no person may lawfully be detained unless his sanity has first been inquired into by some judicial authority and a reception order justifying detention made. The old method was by an inquisition in lunacy tried by a Jury in the High Court, but this is almost obsolete (a person declared insane by an inquisition is called a "person of unsound mind so found" and the person in whose charge he is placed "the committee of the person").

The normal method of procuring certification and a reception order is now by petition to a judicial authority.

Parliament has declared that the following persons shall each be a judicial authority:

(1) A County Court Judge (but in practice he seldom acts).

(2) A Stipendiary or Metropolitan Police Magistrate.

(3) A Justice of the Peace specially appointed by Quarter Sessions or the Lord Chancellor.

In the case of rate aided persons of unsound mind and lunatics found wandering at large, a summary order (i.e. without a petition) may be made by any Magistrate. Police Constables are bound to report all cases of neglected or cruelly treated persons of unsound mind, and summary orders may be made against them by a judicial authority. If the relatives or friends of the patient apply and can satisfy the Magistrate that he will be properly treated, they may take the patient away. In other cases the procedure is as follows: A petition is addressed to the judicial authority and notice of it served on the patient. Wherever possible the husband, wife or near relative should be the petitioner; if anybody else petitions, the Court will inquire into his reasons. The petitioner must have seen the patient within 21 days and must present two medical certificates, one from a doctor approved by the Board of Control. Any person interested may require the proceedings to be private. The patient himself must be given written notice that he is entitled to be seen in person by the judicial authority making the order, and

may demand that he be so seen. But the authority need not see him before making the order and if no demand is made, or the medical officer certifies that it would be bad for the patient, he need never see him at all. There is no appeal from the decision of a judicial authority (but there are many checks on unjustified detention). If he refuses an order he must send his reasons to the Board of Control; if a reception order is granted it only justifies the reception of the patient into a hospital, etc., within seven days; it then lasts for one year. At the end of that time the Board of Control may extend the order for two years, and so on indefinitely.

Treatment and Care of Patients.— In addition to exercising general supervision over all places in which persons of unsound mind are detained, the Board of Control have made specific regulations for the treatment and care of patients. Managers of such places must submit regular and detailed reports of all patients admitted and discharged; of the treatment given to them and its results. No form of mechanical restraint (strait waistcoat, padded room, etc.) may be employed unless a medical certificate has first been obtained to state that it is necessary. On any occasion in which a certificate is given a report must be made to the Board of Control. In general, the manager of a hospital has a discretionary power to refuse to post letters written by a patient under his charge; but letters to the Lord Chancellor, the Board of Control, the person who presented the petition for the reception order, and the person who signed the order, must be posted without being opened under penalty of a fine.

Regular visits have to be made by the Lunacy Commissioners and their Inspectors and the local Visiting Committee (if any). Every patient has the right, of which notice must be given to him, to an interview alone with the Commissioners. If relatives or friends wish to visit a patient, or to have him medically inspected, they should apply to the Board of Control who can give them an order for admission, and can also order that the doctor be allowed to examine the patient. Indeed any person may apply to the Board to have a patient examined by two doctors; the doctors will report to the Board who may then order the patient's release. Quite apart from any such examination, any two Commissioners of the Board of Control may at any time order the release of the patient, and so, in most cases, may the local Visiting Committee. The release of a patient may also be obtained (provided that the medical officer of the hospital does not certify that it would be dangerous) by the person who presented the petition for the reception order (or in the case of mental defectives detained without a reception order by their parent or guardian); if he is dead any near relative may apply. A friend, however, if he wishes to secure the release of a patient would have to apply to the Board of Control. If he does not know where the patient is he may demand that a search be made in the records of the Board of Control to discover whether, and if so where, a patient is detained.

If a Patient Escapes.—If a patient (including a temporary patient, but not a voluntary patient) escapes, whether while actually detained or when out on licence, he may be retaken by any constable, or by the manager of his hospital or any person authorized in writing by him; but in all cases except that of mental defectives, the recapture must be within fourteen days of the escape. If a patient is at liberty for more than a fortnight he cannot be detained under the old reception order. Proceedings for a new order must therefore be started.

When discharged, a patient may apply to the Board of Control for copies of the petition, certificates and reception order relating to his case; these must be supplied to him free of charge.

Any person who has fraudulently obtained the certification of a person of sound mind and any person who has wrongfully detained him, may be sued in an action of trespass to the person and false imprisonment and may be ordered to pay very heavy damages. If he acted knowingly he will also be guilty of a criminal offence. But Parliament has declared that no person shall be liable in any way for any petition, report, or reception order, or act done in carrying out such order, unless it can be proved that he acted in bad faith and without reasonable care. (*See* CERTIFICATION OF LUNATICS.)

DEVILLING.—Assistance given by one barrister to another is popularly described as devilling. If a barrister holds the brief of another, that is to say, does a case for him he is said to devil for him. If he looks up points of law for him such work is also called "devilling." The practice amongst barristers as to payment for this kind of work varies. Sometimes fees are shared, but frequently the work is done gratuitously.

DICKENS, Sir Henry Fielding (1849-1933).—Sir Henry Dickens was Common Sergeant at the Central Criminal Court from 1917-1932. He was the sixth and last surviving son of the great Charles Dickens and was one of the most popular figures on the Bench.

DICING.—All games of dice except backgammon are illegal games. Any person who keeps any house or place for the purpose of illegal games being played there may on summary conviction be subjected to a fine of £500. (*See* SPECIAL SUPPLEMENT "GAMBLING.")

DIES NON.—This is a Latin expression meaning a day on which legal transactions do not take place. Sundays are dies non.

DILAPIDATIONS.—This is the name applied to the tenant's liability to repair premises which have been let to him. The exact extent of his liability will depend upon the terms of the letting. The word is also used to indicate the tenant's claim against the landlord where the landlord has failed to do repairs for which he is liable. In practice, when premises are let on a long lease a schedule of dilapidations, that is, a list of all the repairs which the landlord thinks the tenant is bound to do, is served upon the tenant some months before the end of his tenancy. (*See* LANDLORD AND TENANT.)

DILIGENCE (SCOTS LAW).—In Scots Law diligence, in addition to its ordinary meaning of carefulness, is used to denote all the processes of law by which a creditor seizes the property or person of a debtor, with the object of forcing him either to appear in court to answer an action which the creditor has brought, or to find security for the satisfaction of some judgment which may be pronounced against him in the action, or again to carry out a judgment already pronounced. This diligence takes several forms:

1. *Imprisonment for debt* has now been largely abolished but still exists in certain cases. (*See* IMPRISONMENT.)

2. *Arrestment.* This involves the seizure

either of property belonging to the debtor which is in the hands of some other party, or of some debts which some third party owes to the debtor. (*See* ARRESTMENT.)

3. *Poinding.* This is the method by which goods belonging to the debtor in his own hands and possession are seized. (*See* POINDING.)

4. *Adjudication.* Adjudication is a diligence by which heritable property, i.e. the debtor's land, may be taken by his creditors. (*See* ADJUDICATION [SCOTS LAW].)

5. *Inhibition.* Inhibition acts not against the debtor's property but against him personally. Its effect is to prohibit him from making any contracts or executing any documents which have the effect of transferring any part of his estate to some other person. Its object is to preserve the debtor's property in the state in which it is in the time of the inhibition. (*See* INHIBITION.)

6. *Poinding of the Ground.* This is a type of action by which creditors who are owed money in relation to some land, or which is considered to arise out of the land, or be secured on it, may enforce their rights. (*See* POINDING OF THE GROUND.)

7. *Maills and Duties.* Where a creditor has lent money on a security of land he may compel the tenants of the land to pay their rent to him instead of to their landlord by what is called an action of Maills and Duties.

8. *Sequestration for Rent.* This is the method by which a landlord causes the goods of a tenant to be sold in payment of his rent. (*See* LANDLORD AND TENANT [SCOTS LAW].)

DIOCESE.—A diocese is an area entrusted to the care of a Bishop in matters ecclesiastical. There are thirty dioceses in the Province of Canterbury and thirteen in the Province of York. A diocese is sub-divided into archdeaconries (*see* ARCH-DEACONRY). A Diocesan Conference must be held at least once a year in every diocese; the Bishop is president of the Conference, which is composed of a Chamber of Clergy and a Chamber of Laity. The Chamber of Laity is composed of some *ex officio* members (e.g. lay members of the National Assembly elected for the diocese); members elected (unless the Conference otherwise decides) at the annual Parochial Church Meetings;

not more than fifteen representatives of education in the diocese; and not more than ten of the Bishop's nominees. The powers of the Conference in relation to the management of the diocese and its finances are extensive.

The Chancellor of a diocese is usually appointed (for life) by the Bishop. He then acts as the Judge of the Consistory Court, being answerable only to the King, and dealing with all ecclesiastical cases arising within the diocese, except that he cannot depose from holy orders, but all cases where that would seem to be the appropriate punishment, he must refer to the Bishop. The office of Chancellor is usually held by a layman possessed of knowledge of ecclesiastical law. The Surrogate is a substitute appointed by the Chancellor to hold courts on his behalf. (*See* CONSISTORY COURT.)

DIRECTORS.—The persons who are usually appointed to manage the affairs of the company are known as its directors. The law requires that each public company should have two directors at least, and almost all companies, public and private alike, in fact have directors, although the private company is not by law required to do so. The exact position of the directors in a company will depend on the terms of the company's Articles of Association, which will fix the manner in which they may be appointed and removed, and their remuneration.

Directors as Trustees.—The directors, being in possession and control of money which has been entrusted to them by other people, i.e. the shareholders, are regarded in many respects as trustees of that money, and must exercise any powers given to them for the best interests of the company. For example, they must not make calls on shares unless it is in the interests of the company to do so, and in one case where they made calls for the purpose of getting money with which to pay their own fees, there being no other money available, the call was held to be void. It should be noticed, however, that directors are not trustees so far as individual shareholders are concerned. Therefore, if, to the knowledge of the directors, the company has had a very good year, and is about to declare a large dividend which will increase the market value of its shares, there is nothing wrong in a director buying shares from a shareholder without giving him this information.

Directors as Agents. Ultra Vires. —Directors are also to a very large extent the agents of the company, for the company, being an artificial person, cannot act except through human agents. As agents, the directors have the authority given to them by the Articles of Association and it is only within the limits of the authority there set out that they can bind the company in contracts which they enter into on its behalf. If they do any act which is outside their authority, the company will not be bound by it. Such an act is said to be ultra vires (q.v.)—i.e. beyond the powers of the directors—and can only be made binding on the company if it is ratified, i.e. approved, by all the shareholders.

There is a further rule that where the directors are given power to do an act by the articles, provided that some internal step has been taken in the company, any person dealing with them is entitled to assume that that internal step has been taken. For example, if directors are given power to sell the company's land, provided that they have been authorized by an ordinary resolution of the company, and if they do in fact make a contract to sell the land, without any such resolution having been passed, to someone who is either unaware that an ordinary resolution is required or, if he knows that, is not aware that it has not been passed, then the contract nevertheless binds the company, because the person dealing with it is not required by law to find out matters relating to the internal management of the company, such as the passing of resolutions.

Director May be Liable to Pay Damages.—In cases where a director has entered into a contract in such a way that the company is not bound, he will, like any other agent in like circumstances, be liable to an action for damages, which is called an action for breach of warranty of authority. It should be clearly understood that a director will not himself be liable on the contract even when he has acted without authority; for no person can be liable on a contract which he has entered into expressly as agent for someone else. In practice the distinction is not perhaps very clear in cases where the contract which has been

entered into has been one under which the company agreed to pay money, for in that case the damages recovered against the director will be the same as would have been recovered against the company had they been bound by the contract and had broken it.

In cases, however, where the contract is to do something other than pay money— for example, where the contract is one under which the company undertakes to build a house—the distinction is more obvious, for there the person who has contracted with the company could not compel the director to build the house (which, of course, he would have been able to do had the director been liable on the contract) but can only get from the director as damages the amount which he has lost through the company's failure to build the house.

Only in two cases may a director be liable on the contracts of the company. Where a company is wound up, and it is then discovered that it has been carrying on its business and trading in a fraudulent way, the Court has got the power to order the directors responsible to pay all the debts that have been incurred. In some cases also directors are appointed whose liability for the company's debts is expressly stated to be unlimited, but this is not now usual.

Contracts in which Directors are Interested.—Directors being persons who are, as has been seen, in a sense trustees for the company, they are not allowed to make any contract between themselves, or any firm or company in which they are financially interested, and the company. If they were allowed to do so, there would be a conflict between their own private interests, which would incline them to make as much money out of the contract as they could, and the interests of the company for whom they were acting. If they make such a contract it will be void, quite apart from any question as to whether or not it is fair to the company. There are two exceptions to this. Firstly, a director can agree to take shares in the company, and, secondly, the Articles of Association may, and usually do, provide that a director may make contracts with the company so long as he discloses to his co-directors or to the company that the contract is one in which he is interested. The articles usually provide in such a case that the director must not vote at the meeting of directors at which the question of entering into the contract is considered. No director may under any circumstances make any profit out of any of the company's transactions unless the fact that he is about to do so is known to, and approved by, the company, i.e. the other directors or the shareholders.

Directors' Shares.—As it is very desirable in the interests of the shareholders that directors should have a financial stake in the company, it is almost invariably provided by the articles that they must hold a certain number of shares in order to qualify them to act. These are known as Qualification Shares, and must be taken up by the directors within two months of their appointment or else the appointment will lapse. When a company is first formed it cannot begin to carry on its business until the directors have taken up, or agreed to take up, their qualification shares and have paid on them the same amount as has been paid by the holders of shares issued to the public. The directors must not receive these shares as a present from their promoters (the persons who have brought the company into existence).

Duties.—A director cannot appoint someone else to act for him at board meetings or to do acts which he should do personally on behalf of the company. He is not bound to attend every board meeting, but if he fails to attend a reasonable number he may be removed from office. If he agrees without enquiry to acts which his other directors have decided upon at board meetings, he cannot escape liability for these acts, if they turn out to be criminal or fraudulent, by merely saying that he acted on the advice of his co-directors. He must give the company's affairs proper consideration and make up his own mind. A director must always remember that he is bound to act in the interests of the company. For example, if a director is contemplating leaving the company and setting up another business in competition with the company, there is nothing to prevent his doing so provided that he does not do anything during the time he is a director which conflicts with the interests of the company. He must not, therefore, approach the company's customers while he is interviewing

them on the company's business, and ask them if they would be prepared to transfer their custom to him in the event of his setting up in competition with the company. This would be a breach of trust and would make him liable to pay damages to the company.

As the company cannot act for itself, the law requires the many acts which a company must do, such as filing documents or sending returns, to be done by its directors on its behalf; and if they fail to do so they will be liable to penalties, which may be fines, or in more serious cases, imprisonment.

Fees.—The remuneration of a director is fixed by the articles. The total amount of directors' fees must be disclosed in the company's balance sheet. If, however, the director is also a servant of the company, e.g. managing director, and receives a salary in addition to his director's fees, there is no obligation to disclose the amount of this salary in the balance sheet, but persons who hold a quarter of the voting power of the company can compel the auditors to state what has been paid to the directors as salary in addition to their fees during the last 3 years. The auditors are bound to give this information unless a resolution of the company is passed to the effect that it is to be withheld.

False Statements in Prospectus.—When a company issues a prospectus inviting the public to subscribe money for shares or debentures, the prospectus will usually be drawn up by the directors, each of whom is required to sign it; and if the prospectus contains any untrue statement the directors will be liable for damages. If a person is induced to take shares by a statement in the prospectus which turns out to be untrue, he may either sue the directors responsible for damages for fraud, or else claim compensation against them as provided by the Companies Act. If he takes the first course, he must prove not only that the statement he complains about is untrue, but also that the director knew it to be untrue, or else made it recklessly without any knowledge as to its truth or untruth one way or the other. This will be a very difficult matter to prove, and usually the shareholder will prefer to claim compensation. In order to do this he does not need to prove that the statement was known to be untrue by the director, and when he has proved the statement to be untrue will be entitled to succeed, unless the director can prove either that he had reasonable grounds for thinking the statement to be true, or that it was made on the authority of the report of some expert who he had reasonable grounds to think was reliable, or else was a correct copy of some official document, for example, a government report. It should be noticed that these powers of claiming damages and compensation are in addition to the right of a shareholder to cancel his shares and claim back his money from the company. (*See* Prospectus.)

Directors' names.—The law is very anxious that persons who have a disreputable trading reputation, and with whom people would not willingly deal if they traded under their real names, should not be able to trade as directors of a company without disclosing the fact that the company is controlled by them. For that purpose the law requires that in the case of every company registered after 1916 the names of the directors must appear on all the catalogues, letters and circulars of the company, together with a statement of any previous names held by them, and also their nationality if that is not British. A document containing full particulars of the names of directors must also be lodged at Somerset House in London, or the Office of the Registrar of Companies in Edinburgh in the case of companies registered in Scotland, when the company is formed or when a new director is appointed.

Compensation for loss of office.—It has long been the practice when a company is being taken over by another concern, in such a way that the directors of the first company lose their office and remuneration, for the directors to require that certain compensation will be paid to them by the concern which is taking over. There is no objection at all to this, but the amount of the compensation must be fully disclosed to the shareholders. (*See* Companies; Prospectus; Shares.)

DISABLEMENT BENEFIT.—A person insured under the National Health Insurance Scheme who is incapacitated from work by sickness or disease, is entitled to benefit known as disablement benefit after the 26 weeks period, during which he draws sickness benefit, expires. It is not payable where the insured person is entitled to compensation under the Workmen's Compensation Acts, and it is in any case payable only upon a certificate given by the panel doctor. (*See* National Health Insurance.)

DISBAR.—When a barrister is no longer allowed to practise he is said to be disbarred. His status as a barrister is taken away by the Inn of which he is a member.

DISCHARGE. Bill of Exchange.—A bill of exchange is a contract to which there may be many parties:—the drawer, acceptor, indorsers and final holder; any of these parties may be discharged from liability under the bill before the bill becomes mature, e.g. if the holder of a bill intentionally cancels the signature of a party to the bill, such party is freed from all liability under it. The bill itself, on the other hand, will remain valid as between the other parties, and will be said to be discharged only when it ceases to be of any effect at all, e.g. when it has been duly honoured. (*See* Bill of Exchange.)

Bond.—A bond may be discharged (or rendered ineffectual) in a number of ways, the chief of which is, of course, the performance of the condition to secure performance of which the bond was made; or, if the condition has been broken, by the payment of the amount which was agreed to be paid in such an event.

Contract.—A contract is said to be discharged, like a bill of exchange or a bond, when it becomes no longer operative. As in the case of a bill of exchange, it is possible that, where there are more than two parties to a contract, one of them may be discharged while the others remain bound; in other words, the contract may be rendered no longer operative as regards that one person. Discharge of one party in this way will arise usually by agreement between all the parties that the individual in question shall be no longer bound by the contract. Discharge of the whole contract, whereby every party is released from any further liability thereunder, arises in one of four ways:

(i) The parties may agree between themselves that the contract shall be terminated. Even though the contract was written or under seal, it may be terminated by a verbal agreement, provided each party stands to gain something by the agreement, this gain being known as "consideration." If Jones covenanted to pay Robinson £100 and subsequently Robinson and Jones agreed by word of mouth that Jones should not pay, such subsequent agreement would be void for lack of consideration, since Robinson stands to gain nothing as a result of it. The only way to make it binding would be to have it under seal. If, on the other hand, they agreed that, in consideration of Jones supplying Robinson with a box of matches, Robinson would let Jones off his debt, that agreement would be binding on both parties, for the box of matches would be "consideration" sufficient to satisfy the law.

(ii) The contract may be fully performed and, when each has done what he agreed to do, the contract will be discharged.

(iii) It may become impossible to perform the contract, e.g. if A contracts with B to hire him a hall for a concert, and the hall is struck by lightning before the date fixed, the contract will terminate. But it is no excuse if the impossibility arises from the party's own fault or imperfections, e.g. if a man contracts to make a machine, and then finds he is not skilful enough to perform his contract, he will not be excused from performing it, but will be liable for damages.

(iv) The contract may be broken by one of the parties. If it is broken before the time fixed for performance, e.g. if A writes to B to say that he is not prepared to do what he agreed to do, the injured party, B, may, if he likes, treat the contract as at an end and sue for damages for breach. Except when this happens, a contract usually continues in existence, in spite of breaches, until the injured party has sued the other for damages in the Courts. When he obtains judgment, the original contract is discharged.

Jury.—A jury is usually discharged when their verdict has been given, and may not thereafter be recalled to rectify or explain their verdict. Members of a jury do not, on discharge, receive exemption from future service unless the Judge expressly exempts them, which he often will do (for a period, usually, of five years) after a lengthy case. A jury will usually be discharged if any member of it is guilty of

misconduct, e.g. if he talks to one of the parties after having been sworn, or if a verdict is arrived at by casting lots. Juries are also discharged if there appears to be no probability of their arriving at a verdict. A single juror may be discharged by consent of the parties in any trial, and this is usually the course adopted in civil cases when it appears that one of the jury is interested in the result of the case.

Lunatic.—The discharge of a pauper lunatic from a hospital or home may be ordered by the authority liable to maintain him. The discharge of a private patient from an institution may be directed by the petitioner for the reception order, or, in the case of his incapacity, by certain other persons. In neither case will the patient be discharged if his medical officer or attendant certifies that he is dangerous and unfit to be at large. Three visitors of an asylum or two Commissioners, however, may visit any patient and order discharge.

Prisoner.—When a person is detained in prison for failure to pay a fine he may be released as soon as he pays the governor the whole of the fine and proper charges; if he pays a part, his term will be proportionately reduced. In other cases, the only means by which a prisoner may obtain discharge before expiry of his term are:— (i) by obtaining a Royal Pardon; or (ii) by obtaining remission marks. A person sentenced to penal servitude may obtain liberation on licence after serving three-quarters of the sentence if male, and after serving two-thirds if female. A sentence of penal servitude for life is specially considered at the end of twenty years. If the sentence was imprisonment for more than one month, one sixth of the term may be remitted, and the prisoner then receives unconditional discharge. The amount of remission in either case is calculated by remission marks. If a prisoner is sentenced for a year, he will have to earn (if a male) 2190 marks (i.e. six for each day of the sentence) in order to obtain the maximum remission. Those marks he may earn for industry and good conduct at the rate of eight per day.

Seamen.—Seamen of British foreigngoing ships must, when discharged at a home port, be discharged in the presence of a superintendent, and the master must then and there sign a report on his qualifications, conduct and character or must make a signed statement that he refused to do so. Every seaman of every British ship is entitled to a certificate of discharge shewing the time and place of discharge and his period of service, and such certificate must be given to him by the master when he is discharged or paid off under penalty of not more than £10. A similar certificate must be given when a seaman is discharged abroad unless he was shipped in the country where discharged or, if not shipped there, unless the authority of the British consular office is obtained (in British Possessions, the authority of the superintendent or chief officer of customs).

Army.—Discharge from the Territorials is usually not difficult to procure, but certain conditions may be imposed at the discretion of the county association, e.g. the person applying for discharge may be required to give up to three months' notice; to pay up to £5; and to deliver up all government property or to pay for same. Territorials may be discharged on certain grounds, e.g. of medical unfitness, or inefficiency, or merely because their services are no longer required. Members of the regular forces may purchase their discharge within three months after attestation (i.e. enlistment) on payment of a sum not exceeding £20. It is a condition of their service that they serve only so long as their services are required, and it is therefore open to the authorities to discharge soldiers, either with or without cause, whenever they desire to do so, and they will have no cause of complaint that notice has not been given. On discharge, a soldier is entitled to a certificate of discharge. Discharge takes effect from the date of the confirmation of the discharge, and not from the date of the delivery of the certificate to the soldier.

Navy.—Discharge from the navy is governed by similar, but by no means identical, rules. Application for discharge must be made through the commanding officer, and generally can be obtained only by purchase, unless there are "compassionate grounds," i.e. unless the applicant can shew that his dependents are suffering pecuniarily from his retention in the service. In the case of men who entered service at the age of 16 years, discharge is free. Otherwise

the payments for discharge vary from £20 to £75 according to length of service, etc. (*See* BANKRUPTCY AND DISCHARGE [OF BANKRUPT.])

DISCLAIMER.—When an individual becomes bankrupt or a company is wound up, it often happens that the property which comes into the hands of the liquidator, or trustee in bankruptcy, or liquidators, has attached to it a legal obligation requiring the performance of some act. For example, where a company is the holder of a lease it will be required normally to pay the rent and to spend money in some cases on carrying out repairs. When this is so, the trustee in bankruptcy or liquidation is entitled to repudiate the property, and to refuse to carry out the obligations. This act of repudiation is known as Disclaimer. The person who was entitled to have the obligations carried out will, of course, be entitled to sue the bankrupt or company for damages.

DISCOVERT.—An unmarried woman or widow is sometimes in legal phraseology described as discovert. Her position in law differs in many respects from that of a married woman. Thus she can be made bankrupt, and may be committed to prison under judgment summonses in the same way as a man can be.

DISCOVERY.—Discovery means the duty of each party to give a list to the other of the documents—i.e. letters, etc., in his possession.

When an action is brought in the High Court or the County Court, the parties are entitled, if they wish, to be informed upon oath by affidavit what documents dealing with the questions in dispute are in the possession of the other side, and to inspect and take copies of these documents. Certain documents, such as documents prepared by a legal adviser for the purposes of the action, are privileged from discovery in this way, but as a general rule each side is entitled to see every document which is in any way relevant to the case.

In High Court actions the disclosure of documents is generally provided for in the Summons of Directions, which orders each side within a certain time to make upon oath a list of documents relevant to the case, and to permit the other side to inspect, and to take copies of them. In the same affidavit of documents each side sets out those documents which it claims are privileged from inspection, and, provided that the claim of privilege is a proper one, these will not be open to inspection.

If one party thinks that the other party has failed to disclose some relevant documents, he may take out a summons for a further and better affidavit of documents, or for an order that the other party shall produce a certain document to the Master for him to decide whether it is privileged from production; and the master may order it to be produced or not as he thinks fit.

In the County Court discovery of documents does not take place as a matter of course, but it may be obtained in proper cases by applying to the Registrar. (See COUNTY COURT PROCEDURE; HIGH COURT PROCEDURE.)

DISCRETION.—Wherever a tribunal has a discretion in any matter, it must use that discretion judicially, that is to say not arbitrarily or from improper motives. For instance, a Judge usually has a discretion as to granting costs to one party or another in an action, but he may not deprive a successful party of costs simply because he does not like him as an individual, or because he does not care for his behaviour. There are certain limits beyond which a Judge cannot go in the exercise of his discretion, and if he does do so, then a Superior Court can say he has exercised it unjudicially and reverse his decision.

In divorce cases the judicial discretion has frequently to be exercised. A petitioner, although proving that the respondent has been guilty of some matrimonial offence, may have himself or herself to admit a matrimonial offence. In such circumstances the Court has to decide whether it will exercise its discretion in favour of the party who has to make these admissions. Sometimes, of course, where there are cross petitions, both parties will ask for discretion, that is to say, both admit their own wrongdoing but say that their own case is specially deserving of consideration and that the Judge's discretion should be exercised in their favour. Here the Judge has to decide where the balance of wrong lies. (See SPECIAL SUPPLEMENT "DIVORCE.")

DISGUISE AT NIGHT.—It is a misdemeanour to be found at night wearing a disguise with the intention to commit a felony. Thus, if a man is found in such circumstances wearing a mask, or with his face blackened, he may be convicted even though he has not actually started to commit the felony he has in mind. Anyone, not necessarily a policeman, may arrest a person in these circumstances.

DISHONOURED CHEQUES.—A cheque is dishonoured when the Banker on whom it is drawn refuses to pay it. The usual method of refusal is for the banker to write "R.D." or "Refer to Drawer" upon the face of the cheque, and return it to the person who presented it for payment. The person to whom it is then returned has no rights or cause of action against the Bank, but he can sue the drawer or any indorser for the amount of the cheque.

Lack of funds in the drawer's account is the usual cause of dishonour. If this is the reason, notice of dishonour need not be given by the bank to its customer, the drawer. Where the account is in funds every bank is under a duty to honour its customer's cheques. If it fails to do so the customer may sue the bank for breach of contract or, where the cheque has been marked "R.D.," for libel, for his credit may be damaged by the bank's action.

DISINFECTION.—Many local authorities provide places equipped with apparatus and attendants for the free disinfection of articles of clothing, infected bedding and other articles. The Medical Officer of Health of each district is usually empowered by the local authority to require the owner of an infected article to deliver it up for disinfection to an officer of the authority. Written notice must be given and failure to comply with the notice entails a maximum penalty of £10. (See INFECTIOUS DISEASE; PUBLIC HEALTH.)

DISORDERLY HOUSES.—Any brothel, or gaming house or other house of a disorderly character is a disorderly house. It is not essential that noise or similar disorder should be apparent. A person who manages a disorderly house is liable to be fined or imprisoned. (See BROTHEL; GAMING HOUSE.)

DISSOLUTION (COMPANIES).—As the law has allowed a new legal person to be brought into existence when a company is formed, it has also been necessary for it to make provisions for that legal person ceasing to exist. In the case of a private individual the legal personality will cease on death, but in the case of a company this could not apply for "a company can never die." A company does not cease to exist when it is wound up, but only when it is dissolved. Winding up is merely a preliminary step for distributing the assets of the company among the persons entitled to them. When the winding up is complete and all the property of the company has been distributed to creditors or shareholders, the Court may make an order that the company be dissolved. If this order is not made the company will be dissolved by the registrar of companies.

When a company is dissolved, any property which is in its possession and is not claimed by anyone will become what is known as "bona vacantia" and pass to the State. Usually, of course, the shareholders or creditors will have taken all the property, but it often happens that a shareholder or a creditor to whom money is due cannot be found, and this money therefore will still remain the property of the company. After the dissolution, if the shareholder or creditor is discovered, he may take steps to have the dissolution set aside and to obtain the money.

DISTRESS FOR RENT.—By common law a landlord has got a right to distrain for his rent, that is, to seize certain goods which are on the land let, and ultimately to sell them in payment of the rent.

How Distress is made.—The distress may be made either by the landlord himself or by a bailiff with a certificate from the County Court. If the landlord is a limited company the distress can only be made by a bailiff, and in practice this is the most usual method. The bailiff in such cases receives from the landlord a written authority called a warrant of distress.

It is, of course, necessary that rent should be due before any distress can be levied, but the landlord may not have made any demand for the rent, and he must not have brought an action and recovered judgment for it before distraint. The distress must be made in the day-time and cannot be made on Sunday. The entry to distrain must not be made by force, and accordingly it is illegal to break open an

outer door, but if entry is once obtained peaceably, inner doors may be broken open.

What Rent may be Distrained for.—The distress must be for rent due within 6 years before the distress, but rent due before that time may be distrained for, if some written acknowledgment of the indebtedness has been made by the tenant within the 6 years. Where the premises for which the rent is due are an agricultural holding, not more than one year's rent may be distrained for, except, where by the ordinary course of dealing between the landlord and tenant, the payment has been allowed to be deferred until the expiration of a quarter or half year after the date when it was legally due. In this case it is deemed to have become due at the expiration of that quarter or half-year, that is, the year in respect of which rent can be taken does not commence to run until the end of that quarter or half-year. Where the tenant becomes bankrupt, or if a company is wound up, the landlord's right of distress is subject to special rules.

What Goods may be Taken.—The principle of distress is that the landlord may take, with certain exceptions noted below, all goods on the premises let, whether they belong to the tenant or not. But he can take only goods which are *on* the premises let and cannot take goods elsewhere. Thus, if a landlord has let the premises to one tenant by separate lettings with two lots of rent, and if the rent due on the first premises is paid, but the rent on the second is not, the landlord cannot distrain on any goods on the first premises for the rent due for the second. The tenant may, however, agree in his leases to allow the landlord to distrain on goods not on the premises let. Distress is therefore distinguished from execution, which entitles a creditor to take goods which belong to his debtor wherever they may be, but not to take goods which belong to others. Where goods have been fraudulently or secretly removed from his premises to avoid a distress they may be taken. (*See below.*)

Certain goods can never be taken in distress and others can only be taken if there are not sufficient other goods available to pay the amount due. There is still a third class of goods which may be taken in distress in the first place, but which may be claimed back from the landlord by the persons to whom they really belong.

The goods which can never be taken are:—

1. Goods belonging to the Crown;
2. Fixtures (q.v.);
3. Goods delivered to the tenant to be dealt with in his business, e.g. shoes sent to a shoemaker to be soled, or a car sent to a garage to be repaired or kept;
4. The goods of a guest at an hotel or inn;
5. Wild animals;
6. Perishable goods, such as butcher's meat;
7. Money;
8. Things actually in use; thus, a motor car in the garage of a house could lawfully be taken, but not if the owner was sitting in it and about to drive at the time. The object of the law here is to prevent a breach of the peace, because it is considered that if the landlord or his bailiff attempted to take goods actually in physical use, they would probably be resisted with violence;
9. Goods which have been taken in execution;
10. The wearing apparel and bedding of the tenant or his family, and the tools and implements of his trade to a total value of £5. If £5 worth of goods of this class are left, any excess may be taken. This protection does not apply where (i) the tenancy has expired; and (ii) the landlord has demanded possession; and (iii) the distress is made within seven days after the demand of possession. Bedding includes the bedstead and whatever is used for sleeping purposes. Implements and tools mean something to be worked with in a trade—not, for example, samples. Where goods of this class are taken which should have been exempt, the tenant may recover them by applying to the Police Court;
11. Goods of an ambassador;
12. Railway rolling stock;
13. Gas, water, and electric light meters and fittings.

Goods Privileged if other Goods Available.—If there are other goods which can be taken and which are sufficient to satisfy the distress, tools and implements of trade, even over the value of £5, must not be taken.

Goods which may be taken but which must be Released if Claim Made.—When a landlord distrains on premises which the tenant has sub-let, and takes goods which belong to an under-tenant or a lodger, or to some stranger who has no tenancy in any part of the premises whether he lives there or not, that person should serve on the landlord a notice in writing stating that the tenant has no property in the goods distrained, and that they belong to him, or are in his lawful possession, and are not goods or live stock of the kind set out below. (*See* GOODS NOT PROTECTED, *below*.) A person whose tenancy is for shorter periods than a quarter is not an "under-tenant" but may be a "lodger." Where this declaration is made it should be given to the landlord or the bailiff who is levying the distress, and afterwards the landlord has no right to distrain on those goods or proceed with the distress if he has already distrained, but must release them. If he does not do so he is guilty of an illegal distress (*see below*) for which damages may be recovered, and the under-tenant, lodger, or other person to whom the goods belong may apply to the Police Court for an order compelling the landlord to restore his goods to him. The declaration must have attached to it a correct Inventory or the declaration. Where the declaration list of the goods signed by the person making it is made by an under-tenant or lodger it must also state what amount of rent, if any, he owes to the tenant, the times when rent is usually due, and it must contain an undertaking by him to pay the future rents to the landlord instead of to the tenant until all the arrears have been paid off.

Goods Not Protected.—Certain goods are still liable to distress, although they do not belong to the tenant. These are (i) goods belonging to the husband or wife of the tenant as the case may be; (ii) goods over which the tenant has granted a bill of sale, or which he has on hire purchase, or which are included in any settlement made by him; (iii) goods in the possession order or disposition of the tenant by the consent and permission of the true owner under such circumstances that the tenant is the reputed owner thereof (*see* REPUTED OWNERSHIP); (iv) goods of the tenant's partner; (v) goods belonging to an under-tenant on premises where any trade or business is carried on in which both the tenant and under-tenant are interested; (vi) goods belonging to, and in the offices of, any company on premises where the tenant of the premises is a director or officer of the company.

Loss of Right to Distrain.—The right to distrain will clearly be lost where rent is paid or tendered, but it is interesting to note that it will also be lost if the landlord obtains a judgment for the rent, or if he has already distrained for the same rent. Thus, if he distrains and, finding plenty of goods, does not take sufficient to cover the rent, he cannot distrain again for the same rent unless he has been induced to take too little by the tenant. If, however, he takes all there is when he first distrains, but that is insufficient, he may distrain a second time.

Procedure after Distraint.—After goods have been distrained, it is the landlord's duty to impound them in order to keep them safely, and impounding involves placing the goods in the custody of the law. Formerly goods were removed to a pound off the premises but usually to-day they are impounded on the premises. A detailed inventory of the goods must be made at once and served on the tenant or left on the premises with a written notice of the distress, stating the total amount due for rent and costs and that the goods will be sold unless replevied (*see below*) or the amount paid. The goods are usually placed in a room on the premises and locked up there, but it will be a sufficient impounding if the tenant consents to the goods remaining in their ordinary position. The goods must be kept impounded for 5 days, and if, before the end of that time, the tenant or owner of the goods requests the landlord in writing to extend the time, they must be kept for a further 10 days. If at the end of five or fifteen days, as the case may be, no steps have been taken by the tenant either to pay the amount due or to replevy the goods, they must be sold either privately or preferably by public auction. The sale should be advertised and every effort made to procure a good price. Any surplus should be returned to the tenant.

Wrongful Distress.—A distress may be wrongful in any three ways. It may be illegal, irregular, or excessive. The rights of the tenant or owner of goods taken will differ in each of these cases. *Illegal*

Distress.—A distress is illegal when it should never have been made at all. Thus a distress will be illegal if no rent is due; or the rent has been tendered; or it is a second distress for the same rent (*see above*); or the goods are privileged from distress (*see above*); or they are the goods of an under-tenant, lodger or stranger (*see above*), and the distress is proceeded with after the owner has claimed them in the manner provided above. When the distress is illegal, the tenant (or the owner of the goods if the tenant is not the owner) may bring an action for damages for illegal distress, or may obtain the goods back by replevying. Where the goods do not belong to the tenant but to some under-tenant, lodger, or other person, a special method of recovering the goods by making application to the Police Court is provided. (*See above.*)

When the person complaining replevies, the procedure is called replevin. The effect is that the goods are delivered back to the owner on his giving security and undertaking to bring an action against the person levying the distress to test its validity. The more usual method is to bring an action for damages against the landlord.

Replevin.—Where the person claiming the goods wishes to replevy, he must take this step within the 5 or 15 days during which the landlord holds the goods and before they are sold. He must go to the County Court and give notice there to the Registrar furnishing also the names of two persons who will be his sureties, and enter into a bond to bring the action. The Registrar of the County Court then gives the landlord notice of the replevin, and asks him if he objects to the sureties; if he does not, the security will be accepted and the goods returned to the person claiming them. Thereafter the action for replevin will be heard. If the landlord is successful, the goods are returned to him.

Irregular and Excessive Distress.—A distress which is legal in the first place may become irregular by reason of some act of the landlord after, or during, the levy of the distress, e.g. failure to give to the tenant a proper list of articles taken before selling, or selling too soon. Again, even if the proceedings are regular the distress will be wrongful if it is excessive, that is, if the amount of goods taken is grossly disproportionate to the amount of rent due. The mere fact that the value of the goods taken is in excess of the rent due will not make the distress excessive unless this excess is very large.

Damages.—Where the distress is illegal, irregular, or excessive, the tenant may sue for damages. Where the distress is illegal, the person to be sued is the bailiff unless the landlord knew of the illegality. Where the distress is irregular or excessive, the landlord may be sued in any case. For an illegal distress the damages will be the value of the goods, and if the goods have actually been sold for rent pretended to be due but not in fact due, the tenant may recover double the value of the goods. No action can be brought for an irregular distress unless the tenant has suffered actual financial loss. In an excessive distress the value of the goods lost may be recovered. If the landlord or other person responsible for an irregular or excessive distress, tenders amends, i.e. money compensation, no action can be brought against him.

Special Provisions in London.—When any form of wrong has been committed during a distress in London in the Metropolitan Police District, and the tenancy is weekly or monthly or the rent is under £15 a year, the tenant may complain to the Police Court which may order the goods to be returned to the tenant or, if they have been sold, order their value to be paid to him.

Pound Breach and Rescue.—If the tenant or any other person removes goods after they have been impounded, even though the impounding was wrongful, he is said to commit pound breach. When goods have been removed in this way the landlord may take them wherever he can find them and may sue the tenant for treble damages, that is, three times the amount of the loss he has sustained. Rescue takes place when goods are seized by any person after distress but before impounding. As distress and impounding now usually take place at the same time rescue can now rarely happen. Both pound breach and rescue are criminal offences.

Removing Goods to avoid Distress.—Although normally goods can only be distrained if they are on the premises, yet if a tenant fraudulently or secretly removes his goods from the premises to prevent the landlord from distraining on them, the landlord may take them wherever they may be by distress within 30 days after the removal, provided that they have not before then been sold to an innocent person, who was not aware of what the tenant was doing, and provided that sufficient goods to satisfy the distress are not left on the premises. A tenant who removes his goods in this way, or any person who assists him knowingly to remove them or conceal them, may be sued by the landlord for double the value of the goods.

Rent Acts.—Special provisions very materially reducing the landlord's right of distress apply to premises controlled by the Rent Acts. (*See* SPECIAL SUPPLEMENT "RENT RESTRICTIONS"; DISTRESS [BANKRUPTCY]; DISTRESS [COMPANIES]; REPUTED OWNERSHIP.)

DISTRICT COUNCIL.—District Councils may be either urban or rural; for an explanation of their constitution, powers and duties, *see* LOCAL GOVERNMENT.

DISTRICT REGISTRY.—A plaintiff may take out a writ for an action in most provincial towns at the district registry, but a defendant who does not reside or carry on business within the district registry's area may, if he desires, enter his appearance at the Central Office in London instead of in the district registry. The District Registrar performs the duties of a Master of the Supreme Court.

DISTURBANCE.—Compensation for disturbance, i.e. being put out of possession, is awarded under the Agricultural Holdings Act to a tenant who has been given notice to quit by his landlord. (*See* AGRICULTURAL HOLDINGS.)

DIVIDEND.—The method by which the profits of a company are transferred to its shareholders is by the payment of dividends which are declared by the company in general meeting, usually on the recommendation of the directors in their report. A company cannot be compelled by a shareholder to pay dividends even though it has made profits.

Dividends must be paid out of profits and not out of capital. This means that if there are no profits available, no dividends can be paid. It is not always easy to say what money is profits for this purpose. Where the company's accounts shew that the circulating capital, i.e. the stock in trade—has depreciated in value during the year, the loss must be made up before the amount of profits can be calculated; but where there is a depreciation in the value of the fixed capital, that is, property owned by the company, not for the purpose of sale but for the purpose of carrying on its business, e.g. its factory premises, this loss is not required by law to be taken into account before the amount of money available as profits is calculated. It is, however, wise business policy to write off this loss or some part of it. In the same way when there has been a gain in the value of fixed or circulating capital this may be used to increase the profits, at any rate if the gain has been realized and turned into cash.

The dividends may be paid either as interim or final, an interim dividend being paid during the trading year in anticipation of what the final profits will be. Dividends are paid less income tax, and a dividend warrant is issued certifying that the tax payable has been deducted. The shareholder is thus not liable for the income tax on his dividends but he is liable for sur-tax. (*See* CUM DIVIDEND; EX DIVIDEND; SHARES.)

DIVIDEND WARRANT.—This is the name of the document by which dividends are paid. The warrant is in two parts, one being the actual authority to pay, and the other being a certificate to the effect that the income tax has been deducted. If the first part of the warrant is lost, the shareholder can still recover the amount due from the company. The certificate of deduction of income tax should be kept by the shareholder and sent to the income tax authorities if required.

When the company's capital is divided into share warrants (q.v.) and not into registered shares, dividend coupons are attached to the warrant and should be sent to the company when a dividend is declared.

DIVEST.—Where any right is actually vested, the act of taking away that right is called "divesting."

DIVIDING SOCIETY.—A Dividing Society is a friendly society which, in addition to providing benefits for its members out of the society's funds, also carries out a division of the surplus funds at certain fixed periods among the members. It is very much the same as a slate club, save that a

dividing society usually is intended to be more permanent, and does not exist solely from year to year like a slate club.

A dividing society can be registered with the Registrar of Friendly Societies if the rules contain an express provision that all claims must be met before any division takes place. (*See* FRIENDLY SOCIETY.)

DIVISIONAL COURT.—Two Judges of the King's Bench Division when sitting together may constitute a Divisional Court. This Court hears appeals from County Courts, as well as criminal appeals by way of Case Stated from the Magistrates' Courts. It is the Court that grants Writs of Mandamus, calling upon judicial officers of inferior courts, or any person who has a judicial duty to perform, to do such duty; Writs of Prohibition, which call upon judicial officers or persons having judicial duties not to act in breach of their duty; and Writs of Certiorari removing cases from the inferior to the superior Courts, all of which are known as prerogative writs since they are part of the old prerogative of the Crown as the fountain of all justice.

Two Judges of the Chancery Division form a similar Divisional Court for hearing appeals from County Courts on the Chancery side, while two Judges of the Probate, Admiralty and Divorce Division form a Divisional Court on this side. (*See* APPEAL FROM COUNTY COURT.)

DIVORCE.—(*See* SPECIAL SUPPLEMENT "DIVORCE.")

DIVORCE (SCOTS LAW).—The grounds upon which Divorce may be granted in Scots Law are wider than in English law. Divorce may be granted not only for adultery but also for desertion for 4 years. Divorce has also important effects upon the rights of the parties to the property of one or other of them, and in some respects the divorced party is treated, so far as rights of property are concerned, as if he had died at the time when the divorce was granted. (*See* HUSBAND AND WIFE [SCOTS LAW]; SPECIAL SUPPLEMENT "DIVORCE.")

DOCK.—The place in any criminal court where the prisoner remains whilst being tried is called the dock. Most Judges permit the prisoner to be seated in the dock during trials of any length. In the Police Court it is customary only to place in the dock those persons who are accused of crimes punishable with imprisonment on first conviction. In other cases, such as minor motor matters, disputes between husband and wife, and affiliation summonses, the defendant is permitted to stand or sit outside the dock.

DOCK BRIEF.—Any person who is about to be tried on indictment for a criminal offence may secure the services of a barrister for the fee of one guinea. He is required to select his counsel from among the barristers actually in Court. Having made his selection he gives to the barrister the sum of one guinea together with half a crown for his clerk. He is then entitled to instruct the barrister as to the facts of his defence, and it becomes the duty of the barrister to conduct the case on his behalf.

DOCK WARRANT.—A dock warrant is similar to a bill of lading. It is a document issued by a dock company describing certain goods, and stating that the person named in the warrant, or anyone to whom he has indorsed it, is entitled to them on presenting the warrant at the dock.

DOCTOR.—A doctor who treats patients for illness, or undertakes surgical operations upon patients, is subject to the ordinary laws governing persons who hold themselves out as possessing skill in any particular subject, and, in addition, is subject to various provisions which have been enacted with a view to safeguarding the public against treatment by unqualified persons.

Although any person, whether qualified or not, may offer advice or assistance as to the curing of diseases, no person may recover fees for medical or dental advice or treatment unless he is registered as a Medical Practitioner or a Dentist respectively. (*See* REGISTERED MEDICAL PRACTITIONER.) This does not apply to masseurs or osteopaths who may sue for their fees in respect of treatment they may have given, but they cannot recover any fees for diagnosis or advice.

Any person who calls in a registered medical practitioner is liable to pay a reasonable fee for the service and treatment of the doctor, and these fees the doctor can recover by an action in the Courts unless he is a Fellow of the Royal College of Physicians, none of whom is allowed to sue for fees, although they are entitled to charge for attendance. Also anyone who calls in a

doctor to treat a servant, is himself liable for the doctor's fees and cannot deduct them from the servant's wages unless the servant has agreed to this. A master or mistress of a domestic servant, however, is under an obligation to call in a doctor to treat the servant, and if the servant is insured, as practically all servants are, the panel doctor should be called in, and he is under an obligation to treat the servant free of charge. (*See* NATIONAL HEALTH INSURANCE.)

Consent Needed for Operations.—A doctor is not entitled to undertake an operation upon a patient without the consent of the patient, or, if the patient is a child, without the consent of the parent or guardian of the child, or person responsible for the child. But if a patient submits to an operation, and during the course of the operation the doctor comes to the conclusion that it is necessary to undertake a more drastic operation in order to safeguard the patient's life or health, the patient will be presumed to have consented to the more drastic operation unless he has specifically forbidden it. It is also probable that, where a patient is unconscious and unable to state whether he consents to an operation or not, the doctor is entitled to perform any operation which is in his view necessary to safeguard life or limb. The same principles apply when a patient goes into a hospital or nursing home for an operation, though generally in these cases the patient is asked to sign a form consenting to the performance of any operation that the medical adviser may consider necessary.

A Doctor Must Use Care.—A doctor who undertakes to give medical advice must give that medical advice without negligence, i.e. he must shew a proper skill in the practise of his profession. If he fails to do so, he is liable to the patient for any damage which may have been caused by his unskilful treatment. But it must be remembered that a doctor need only show a reasonable amount of skill, and that mistakes of judgment or diagnosis, which any medical man might make, will not render him liable, nor will the fact that other medical men with greater skill in one particular branch would have performed the treatment differently or more efficiently. Nothing less than gross negligence is sufficient to make a doctor liable in damages, and only the patient is entitled to recover these, unless the injury results in death, in which case the near relatives may recover for the monetary loss as in other cases where a breadwinner is killed by negligence. In addition to being liable in damages for negligence, a negligent doctor cannot recover his fees in respect of the treatment over which he was negligent. These rules as to negligence apply to a person who undertakes to cure diseases whether he is a registered medical practitioner or not, though the latter are never entitled to recover their fees in a Court of Law.

Where an operation is performed negligently in a hospital or nursing home, the hospital or nursing home is not liable for the negligent performance of any operation, unless it can be shewn that the damage was due to their not having taken sufficient precautions to provide a competent staff. Even if the damage is due to the negligence of the nurses in the operating theatre itself, it is still the surgeon who is liable, though if the damage is due to the negligent treatment by the hospital staff after the patient has returned to the wards, the hospital or nursing-home authorities are liable.

Infectious Diseases. — Whenever a doctor is called in to visit a patient suffering from certain infectious diseases, chief among which are smallpox, cholera, diphtheria, scarlet fever, typhus, typhoid, erysipelas, enteric, membraneous croup, relapsing, continued or puerperal fevers, he must send a certificate of this to the Medical Officer of Health for the District in which the patient lives. In some areas he is also obliged to give notice of the birth of any child at which he has been present, and in all areas, if the father and mother of the child and occupier of the house where the child was born fail to give notice to the Registrar of Births within 42 days, the medical practitioner who was present at the birth must do so. He is also under an obligation to sign a death certificate in respect of every patient whom he attends during the last illness, stating to the best of his belief and knowledge the cause of the death. If the doctor fails to do so, it is the duty of any other person who was present at the death to give the best information that he can to the Registrar of Deaths within five days of the death. (*See* BIRTH; DEATH; HOSPITALS; PANEL; REGISTERED MEDICAL PRACTITIONER.)

DOCUMENTS. — This is not an expression of any particularly legal meaning. Any piece of paper containing any writing or inscription is a document.

DOE, JOHN. — Until the 19th century in order to effect the transfer of land held on certain conditions it was the practice to go through a legal fiction involving the use of the names of two imaginary persons. These two persons were called John Doe and Richard Roe. This is why many old cases bear the name Doe d. before the name of one of the parties, thus, Doe d. (i.e. on the demise of) Jones *v.* Brown. (*See* ROE, RICHARD.)

DOG. — Every person, with a few exceptions, who keeps a dog which is more than 6 months old must take out a licence for it. A dog licence which costs 7/6 can be taken out at any post office and is current until the 31st December of the year in which it was taken out. This means that if a puppy reaches the age of six months in the month of December, the owner must take out a licence which must be renewed again on the 1st January. The cost of renewal of licences is also 7/6. A licence is needed in respect of every dog kept, and though the owner of the dog is liable to take out the licence, any person in whose custody, or on whose premises, the dog is found is presumed to be the owner unless he can prove the contrary. The penalty for failure to take out a dog licence is a maximum of £5. Persons convicted of cruelty to dogs may be deprived of their right to take out a dog licence. (*See* CRUELTY TO ANIMALS.)

The exceptions to this rule are: blind persons who are entitled to keep a dog to lead them about, without the necessity for a licence; hound puppies up to the age of 12 months, provided they have not yet hunted with the pack; and farmers or shepherds who are entitled to obtain a certificate of exemption from a Petty Sessional Court for two dogs which are to be used for tending sheep or cattle. A farmer who owns more than 400 sheep may obtain exemption in respect of 3 dogs, 1,000 in respect of 4 dogs and an extra dog for every 500 sheep up to a maximum of 8 exempted dogs.

In order to obtain this exemption, the farmer or shepherd must fill up a declaration form, which can be obtained from the Clerk to the Justices of the area in which the dog is kept, and until a certificate has been obtained the farmer or shepherd is not entitled to do without the usual licence.

It is not a defence, if charged with keeping a dog without a licence, to take out a licence after being caught. If the defence is that the dog was under age, the onus of proving its age lies upon the person charged.

,The possession of a dog licence does not permit the owner to use the dog for the purpose of killing game, and in order to do this he must take out a Game Licence (q.v.).

Every dog of whatever age must wear a collar bearing the name and address of its owner when it is on a highway or place of public resort. This does not apply to packs of hounds, dogs being used for sporting purposes or dogs being used for tending sheep or cattle. The maximum penalty for this offence is £50 and the police and inspectors appointed under the Diseases of Animals Acts are entitled to seize dogs which do not wear a collar as required.

If the owner of a dog suspects that it is suffering from rabies he must at once inform a policeman, and keep the dog separate from other dogs and human beings. The local authority may order that the dog suspected shall be slaughtered or may isolate the dog, or order the owner to do so, and disinfect the places where the suspected dog has been.

No dog can be imported into the country without a licence from the Ministry of Agriculture, and it must, as a general rule, be isolated at the expense of the importer for six months after its arrival; exceptions may be made for performing animals or dogs imported for breeding or other special purposes. The penalty for breach of any of these regulations is a maximum of £50.

Stray Dogs.—If a dog strays from its owner any policeman may seize it, if it is on a highway or in a place of public resort, and detain it at the police station or send it to a dogs' home. If the dog has a collar with a name and address on it, the police must send written notice of its having been found to the owner and warn him that, unless he reclaims it within 7 days and pays the expenses of its seizure and keep, it will be sold or destroyed. Dogs seized in this way are generally sent to a dogs' home where they are kept for a further time and, if valuable, are sold, if valueless are painlessly destroyed. They may not be sold for vivisection purposes.

Any person other than a police constable finding a stray dog must either send it back to its owner, if there is a name and address on the collar, or take it to the police station and report where it was found. If he wishes to keep it he may give his name and address to the police, and if the dog is not reclaimed by the owner he will be entitled to retain it. He must in any case keep it for at least one month unless it is reclaimed before that time. If he does not wish to keep it, it will be dealt with by the police like any other stray dog.

The police in most towns keep a register of all dogs found which contains a description of the dog, and the date and place it was found and the manner it was disposed of. The public are entitled to inspect such register on payment of 1/-. All dogs' homes to which the police send stray dogs must keep a register which may similarly be inspected.

In England and Wales no dog may be used for drawing any barrow or cart under a maximum penalty of 40/- for the first offence and £5 for subsequent offences.

Dangerous Dogs.—In the ordinary way a dog is not assumed to be a dangerous animal. (*See* ANIMAL.) Accordingly, if a dog bites a human being, the owner of the dog is not liable to pay damages unless it can be shewn that he knew that the dog was liable to bite humans. The commonest way of shewing this is to prove that the dog has attacked human beings before, hence it is often said that a dog is entitled to his "first bite." But once a dog has attacked human beings to the knowledge of its owner, the owner will be liable for any subsequent damage which it inflicts, and he keeps it at his peril. To shew that the dog was known to be savage in this respect it is not enough to shew that he is savage towards other dogs, but that he has been savage to human beings.

A dog that attacks cattle, sheep or poultry, however, is not entitled to its "first bite," and the owner of the dog is liable for any damage that it may do in this respect. The occupier of the house where the dog is kept is presumed to be the owner until he can prove the contrary. If the damage done by the dog is less than £5, it can be recovered against the owner in the Police Court. If it is greater than £5, there must be an ordinary action in the County Court or High Court.

In addition to being civilly liable for the damage done by a dangerous dog, any Court of Summary Jurisdiction, if complaint is made, may adjudge a dog to be dangerous and may order the owner to keep it under proper control, and if he does not do so, may order it to be destroyed. They may even order it to be destroyed without giving the option of keeping it under proper control. A person making a complaint of this nature does so by taking out a summons in the ordinary way on application to the magistrates. A dog that has worried sheep or cattle is a dangerous dog and may be ordered to be destroyed by this procedure.

Besides the remedy through an action at law or in the Police Court, any person who is actually being attacked by a ferocious dog is entitled to kill it, provided that it was reasonably necessary to do so in self-defence and he does not do so with unnecessary cruelty. He may also kill a dog that is attacking his property, but the property must be valuable, such as sheep or cattle or poultry, and probably no one is entitled to shoot a dog merely because it is destroying game. In any case no one may shoot a dog merely because it is trespassing, and notice-boards which state "Dogs will be Shot" will not affect the fact that a person shooting a trespassing dog will be liable in damages for doing so.

In the same way, although a landowner may take steps to protect his game by setting traps, etc., which are reasonably necessary for preserving his game from loss, he must not set a trap in such a way either by baiting or otherwise, as to attract dogs from a highway or from other land. If he does so, he will be liable for any injury done to the dog.

An owner of a dog is not generally liable if it trespasses upon someone else's land, even if it does damage, but as in the case of dogs biting human beings, if he either encourages it to trespass after game, or allows it to trespass knowing that it is likely to kill game, he is liable for the damage that it does.

To steal a dog is a criminal offence. (*See* ANIMALS; CRUELTY TO ANIMALS; GAME; POACHING.)

DOG-RACING.—By the Racecourse Betting Act, 1928, totalizators were permitted to be installed on approved racecourses, i.e. upon racecourses that have been granted a certificate by the Racecourse Betting Control Board. Such certificates cannot, however, be granted in respect of racecourses used for purposes other than horse-racing, and totalizators on dog-racing tracks are therefore illegal. The provisions in that act, that (under penalty of £50) no bets may be made with persons appearing to be under seventeen, also applies only to approved racecourses, and not, therefore, to dog-tracks. Similarly, the Racecourses Licensing Act, 1879 requiring licences for the holding of horse races within ten miles of Charing Cross, applies only to horse-racing, and dog-tracks need no licence and are subject to no control by authority, unless they should become public nuisances or should offend against the ordinary laws relating to betting.

The duties on bookmakers' certificates and entry certificates were abolished in 1930. (*See also* BETTING and SPECIAL SUPPLEMENT "GAMBLING.")

DOLE (SCOTS LAW).—Dole is the corrupt and evil intention which, in almost all cases, must accompany the doing of any act before it can be criminal. It corresponds to the *mens rea* of English law.

DOMESTIC SERVANTS. — They have been defined as servants whose main or general function is to be about their employers' persons or establishments, residential or quasi-residential, for the purpose of ministering to their employers' personal needs, or to the needs or wants of those who are members of such establishments, including guests. They generally reside in the master's house.

Unemployment Benefit cannot be drawn by domestics, for they do not come within the provisions of the Unemployment Insurance Acts. Several other acts including the Shops Act, 1912, do not apply to domestics.

Who is a domestic servant is a question of fact. It becomes important when a gift is left by will to "my domestic servants," and in considering the length of notice necessary.

Theft.—If a domestic feloniously gives away his or her master's food or other property, it is theft. A search warrant should always be obtained from a magistrate before searching servants' boxes for supposedly stolen goods.

Livery.—On leaving, a domestic is not entitled to keep livery, including caps and aprons, or mourning provided by the master, in the absence of a special agreement or unless it was given as a gift.

Medical Attention.—A master must supply board and lodgings, but there is no duty upon him to provide medicine or medical attention. If, however, the master does pay the doctor or the chemist, the money cannot be deducted from wages unless the servant agrees—although the servant of course owes it to the master.

Pregnancy.—In general a maidservant may be summarily dismissed if she is pregnant. She cannot be examined against her will.

A licence is required for a male domestic.

DOMICILE.—A person may be resident in several countries at the same time, but be can be domiciled only in one, for a person's domicile is the country in which he has his permanent home. In many cases a man's rights differ according to whether he is domiciled in one country or in another, and for this reason it is often of importance that his domicile should be ascertained, e.g. in questions of succession on death to movable property as opposed to immovable property (i.e. land), the law of the place of domicile at the date of his death applies. There are serious differences in this respect between the law of England and that of the continental countries. Similarly, the English courts will not decree a divorce except when both parties are domiciled within the area over which the courts have jurisdiction, even though the parties should agree to be bound by the decision. A co-respondent, however, need not be domiciled in England for the divorce to be valid. Again, English law will not in general recognize the validity of a divorce decreed in a country where the parties were not domiciled.

The first domicile a person acquires is that obtained by birth; a child is deemed to have the domicile of its father, or, if it is posthumous or a bastard, of its mother; this is known as "domicile of origin." It follows, therefore, that a child may be born and may reside in France, yet have an English domicile. Domicile of origin may be lost, and a new domicile acquired by subsequent conduct, this being known as "domicile of choice." In order to change his domicile, a man must take up actual residence in the

country where he intends to acquire domicile, and must have the intention of remaining permanently there. The domicile of a wife, however, is—and always must be—that of her husband so long as the marriage continues effective. When the marriage terminates, the wife is free to take a new domicile.

DONATIO MORTIS CAUSA.—Where a person believes that he is dying from an illness from which he is then suffering, he may make a gift of property to take effect on his death. In order to render such a gift effective, it is essential that he should deliver the property itself to the donee at the time of making the gift. Such a gift is called Donatio Mortis Causa.

DOORBELL.—It is an offence wilfully and wantonly to disturb any householder by ringing the doorbell or knocking at the door without reasonable excuse. The offence is punishable with a fine not exceeding 40/-.

DOWER.—In order to protect widows, the Common Law of England long ago provided that in certain circumstances a widow should be entitled to an estate for her life in a certain proportion of her husband's land. In many large estates there still exists a dower house which was formerly used for this purpose. Originally the widow was entitled for her life to one-third of all the land of which her deceased husband had ever been the legal owner during their marriage, provided that she could shew that his interest in the land had been such that any children who might have been born of the marriage would have inherited it. She did not have to prove that such children had been born; but her right was not affected if they had, and were still alive.

The right to a dower was an exceedingly troublesome one and several ways of circumventing it were discovered. In addition power was given to the husband by the Dower Act of 1833 to defeat any claim his wife might have.

Dower is no longer of any importance, as it can now only be claimed out of property which belonged to the deceased husband in tail (*see* ENTAIL), and then only if he has not disposed of it during his life, or by will.

A husband used to have a similar right in his wife's land called curtesy (q.v.). (*See* CURTESY; ENTAIL.)

DRAFT.—Before a legal document is finally agreed between the two parties to it, it is prepared first in a rough form. Copies of this are then exchanged between the parties, so that they may criticise and discuss its contents. This rough document is called a draft.

DRAINS.—It is part of the duty of a local authority to see that houses in its district have a proper drainage system, and that all the drains within its district are so constructed and kept in order that they are not a nuisance or a danger to health.

Since the year 1875 all main sewers have been taken over by the local authorities, and they are responsible for the upkeep of them. Every house built since 1875 must have a covered drain draining into a sewer, provided or maintained by the local authority, if there is one within a hundred feet of the house. If there is no such sewer within a hundred feet, then the house must be provided with a cesspool. The penalty for non-compliance with these provisions is a fine of £50.

If a house was built before 1875 and the local authority are of opinion that it is not supplied with a sufficient drainage system, they may serve a notice upon the owner requiring him to connect the house with one of their sewers or else provide a cesspool. If the owner neglects to comply with such a notice, the local authority may themselves carry out the necessary works and recover the amount of the expense from the owner. Every house must be provided with a sufficient water closet or earth closet, and an ashpit covered with proper doors and coverings; and if a house is without sufficient accommodation of this kind, then the local authority may serve a written notice upon the owner or occupier requiring him to provide such accommodation. It should be noted that the provision of a water-closet may not fulfil the requirement of providing a "sufficient" water-closet, because it has been held that a water-closet with a soil pipe which was insufficiently ventilated was not a "sufficient" one.

In London all new houses, and all houses pulled down to the ground floor and rebuilt, must have a sufficient water-closet, and it is only in exceptional circumstances where sewerage or water supply is not reasonably available that any such house will be permitted to have an earth-closet.

All drains, water-closets, earth-closets,

privies and ashpits must be kept so as not to be a nuisance or injurious to health. It is an offence punishable by a penalty to allow the contents of any water-closet or cesspool to overflow or soak away from it, and if any such overflow is permitted, the local authority may do the repairs necessary to stop it and recover the expenses from the owner of the premises.

In London the sanitary authorities have power to enter at all reasonable times, after giving twenty-four hours' notice, any premises within their districts and inspect any water-closet or cesspool or any part of the drainage system of a house. If any part of the drainage system is in a bad condition, the owner or occupier of the premises may be required to repair it, and if he fails to do so the local authority may themselves do the work and recover the expense of so doing from the owner. A tenant of a house whose landlord has contracted to do the repairs should call in the sanitary inspector for the district if the drains appear to be out of order and the landlord refuses to remedy them. The sanitary inspector can then report to the local authority and they may serve a notice upon the landlord requiring him to repair the drains.

Any person may however complain to the local authority of the condition of any drains in their district, irrespective of whether he has any interest in the premises or not. The local authority must then send their sanitary inspector to the premises.

Sewers and drains are protected by special statutory provisions, the most important of which are those which impose penalties upon persons who erect any building over a sewer without permission of the local authority, or who allow any mud or solid matter apart from ordinary house sewage to pass down the drains into the sewers of a local authority. (*See* HOUSING; PUBLIC HEALTH; SANITARY INSPECTOR.)

DRAWEE.—A Bill of Exchange is always addressed by the person who draws it to another person called the drawee. (*See* BILL OF EXCHANGE.)

DRAWER.—The person who makes a Bill of Exchange and addresses it to the drawee. (*See* BILL OF EXCHANGE.)

DRILLING, ILLEGAL.—It is illegal for people to meet together for the purpose of military training or drilling without lawful authority. All persons who are present at any such meeting for the purpose of giving instruction in military training may be sentenced to penal servitude for a period not exceeding seven years. If they attend for the purpose of themselves being trained then the maximum sentence is two years' imprisonment. Any Secretary of State may authorise meetings of persons for drilling or military training if he thinks it proper. Meetings at which unlawful drilling takes place may be broken up by the police, and any persons present may be arrested by them without warrant.

DRUGS.—In order to protect the health of the community the law lays down certain strict rules about the sale or supply of drugs to the public. These rules are directed mainly to ensure that a standard of purity in drugs sold to the public shall be preserved, and that purchasers of drugs get what they ask for, and not some substituted or adulterated article.

It is an offence, except where it is necessary for compounding purposes, to mix, stain, colour, or powder any drug with an ingredient which is dangerous or injurious to health. Similarly it is an offence to sell any drug which has been thus mixed, stained or coloured. The penalty for both these offences is a maximum fine of £50 for a first offence and for a second offence a maximum of six months imprisonment. A person who is charged with either of these offences may escape from liability if he shews that he was not aware, and could not have, by the exercise of care, discovered that the drug in question was so mixed, stained or coloured. This provision applies to all drugs, and the law defines a drug as any medicine for internal or external use.

Every drug sold must be of the nature and quality demanded by the purchaser, and must contain only the ingredients which he has demanded.

It is an offence to sell a drug which is not of the nature and quality demanded, the penalty being a fine of £20 for a first offence.

No offence is however committed in the following cases:

(1) Where some ingredient which is not injurious to health, is added to make the drug fit for consumption or carriage, and not for any fraudulent purpose such as to increase the weight.

(2) Where the drug is what is called a proprietary or patent medicine and is supplied in accordance with the specification of the patent.

(3) Where the drug is unavoidably mixed with some other matter during the process of collection or preparation.

If a drug which is mixed is sold to a purchaser with a label attached stating clearly and readably that it is a mixed preparation, then the seller is protected from any liability to which he might otherwise be subject for selling a mixed article.

The purchaser of any drug is entitled to take it to the public analyst for the district in which he purchased it and ask him to analyse it. The public analyst may charge any sum up to 10/6 for making the analysis, and must give the person submitting the drug a certificate of analysis setting out the results of his analysing it. Any medical officer of health, sanitary inspector, or inspector for weights and measures may procure any sample of a drug from a shop in his district if he has reason to suspect that the drug is being sold contrary to the law. If a seller of drugs refuses to allow a sample to be taken, he may be liable to a penalty of £10, and in this case it should be noted that the employer can be held liable for the penalty if the refusal to sell, or allow a sample to be taken, was made by his employee. Similarly it is an offence to refuse to sell an article to an inspector who offers the price of it, and the penalty for such refusal is £10.

When any public officer, such as an inspector, purchases a drug intending to have it analysed, he must tell the person who sells it to him at the time of the sale that it is his intention to have it analysed. He must then divide the sample or drug wherever it is possible to do so, into three parts, leave one with the seller, give one to the public analyst, and keep the third himself for future comparison. He must seal up or fasten with string each of the three parts in such a way that the samples cannot be tampered with, without interfering with the sealing or fastening. If the inspector does not tell the seller that he is going to have the sample analysed, then the seller cannot be prosecuted.

The Defence of a Warranty.—If any one is prosecuted for selling a drug which is adulterated, or impure, or mixed, it is a good defence to the charge if he proves that he bought the drug in question from another person, and that he received from that person a written warranty stating that the drug was the same in nature, substance and quality as that which was asked for by the purchaser, and that he sold it in the state in which he received it. A warranty is a sort of legal guarantee given to protect purchasers from getting something different from that which they want. But in order to use a warranty as a defence, the person charged must, within seven days after getting a summons, send a copy of the warranty to the prosecutor, who will usually be the inspector, and with it he must send a written notice saying that he is going to use it as his defence, and containing the name and address of the person who gave him the warranty. He must also give notice to the person who gave him the warranty that he has been charged with an offence in respect of that drug, and that he is going to rely upon the warranty for his defence. (*See* FOOD; LOCAL GOVERNMENT; PUBLIC HEALTH.)

DRUNKENNESS.—This is not of itself an offence, but may become so if accompanied by some other circumstance, such as drunk and incapable, drunk and disorderly, etc. The offences of which drunkenness forms a component part are numerous. Besides the two cases already mentioned there are "being drunk in a highway or public place," the latter would of course include licensed premises; "being drunk in a public place while having charge of a child apparently under the age of seven." The penalty for the former offence may range from 2/6 to 40/–, but when the drunken person is in charge of a child, they range from 40/– to one month's hard labour. If a drunken person refuses to quit any licensed premises he makes himself liable to a further fine of £5.

Habitual Drunkard.—Of course no one can be confined in a home unless he or she is a certified lunatic. But if a person is charged with one of the above offences and it is at the same time found that he has been convicted before of three similar offences, and also that he is a person who through habitual drinking is dangerous to himself or others, or is incapable of looking after himself, then the magistrates can have him put in an inebriates' home for not longer than three years. They can also send particulars of the conviction to the local police authority, so

that it will be an offence for the convicted person to buy intoxicating liquor, and also for anyone knowingly to sell it to him. Every person can insist on being tried by a jury on such a charge.

DUELLING.—Duelling is illegal in English law. It is a misdemeanour punishable with imprisonment or a fine, or both, to challenge a person to fight a duel. No amount of provocation will legalise such a challenge. If anyone is killed in a duel, all persons taking part in it are guilty of murder.

DURESS.—Duress is a technical term which means a threat of actual physical violence offered to a person, his wife, parent or child, and if anyone is forced to enter into a contract by such a threat, he is entitled to refuse to be bound by it if he wishes. In other words the contract entered into is voidable if the party threatened by the duress renounces it, but is perfectly valid if he wishes to be bound by it. Such cases are very rare in civilized communities, since the threat must be actually of physical violence to the person, and it is not sufficient that the contract should be induced merely by a threat to retain goods, or some threat of that description. The most likely to occur is where A says to B, "I will not let you out of this room until you agree." In such a case the threat amounts to duress and is voidable at B's option. An example may make the operation of this clear. If A says to B, "I will not let you out of this room unless you agree to purchase my land for £1,000," and B agrees to purchase the land, B may subsequently either insist upon purchasing the land, if he wishes to, or refuse to buy it, on the grounds that he was induced to enter into the contract by duress. (*See* CONTRACT; FRAUD; UNDUE INFLUENCE.)

DYING DECLARATION.—A statement made by a dying person in circumstances which allow its contents to be proved in evidence at the trial of anyone charged with killing the person who made it. The rules of evidence exclude testimony as to statements made in the absence of prisoners. In this case, however, such a statement is allowed, as it is thought that the chances of falsehood are remote at a moment of such solemnity. It must, however, be proved that at the time of making the statement the person making it knew that he was dying and that there was no chance of recovery.

10*

EARLY CLOSING.—All shops, with the exception of those where one of the businesses specified below is carried on, must by law be closed for the serving of customers not later than one o'clock in the afternoon on one day every week. This is called the Early Closing Day and the particular day for each district is fixed by the local authority. The early closing day may be the same for all shops or different days for different kinds of shops, and it may be on a different day of the week at different periods of the year to suit the requirements of the shop-keepers.

Shops carrying on any of the following trades or businesses are not required to have an early closing day:

The sale of: intoxicating liquors by retail; refreshments; motor, cycle and aircraft supplies and accessories to travellers; newspapers and periodicals; meat, fish, milk, cream, bread, confectionery, fruit, flowers, and other perishable articles; tobacco and smokers' requisites; medicines, medical and surgical appliances; and businesses carried on at an exhibition or show, provided the local authority gives a certificate stating that such trade is only subsidiary to the main purpose of the exhibition. (*See* SHOP.)

EASEMENT.—Easement is the legal name for a particular kind of right which one man may have over the land of another; examples of easements are the right to light (Ancient Lights), private rights of way or to draw water, and the right to have a house supported by an adjoining property.

An easement is a very peculiar right because it is not attached to a particular man (as is the ordinary right which arises out of a contract) but to a particular plot of ground (called the dominant tenement) for the benefit of the owner for the time being of that plot. On a sale or other transfer of the dominant tenement the right to the easement passes with the land from the old owner to the new, whereas if the right were only contractual it would not pass to the new owner. In a similar way it binds not a particular person but the owner for the time being of the land over which it is exercisable; this latter land is called the servient tenement. The fact that easements attach to land in this way is important because otherwise they would soon become extinct; if an ordinary contract is made between two persons it does not (save in a few cases) affect their property

directly at all, even though it is concerned with it; and if they, or either of them, sell their property the purchaser will neither be bound by, nor able to enforce the contract. An exception to this is to be found in restrictive covenants (q.v.)

How an Easement is Created.— There is a legal rule which says that every easement must have been created by a deed; this does not now mean that in fact there must have been a deed actually executed, for (as will be seen) the law is prepared to assume that this was so even though it is perfectly clear that it was not, but it does mean that no right can be an easement unless it *could* be created by a deed. There are a number of rather vague and indefinite rights which the law holds cannot be created by a deed and it follows, therefore, that they cannot exist as easements. It is as a result of this that one cannot acquire an easement to have the view from one's house left unspoilt, the sun allowed to fall on one's garden or the wind to create a draught for one's chimneys. Though rights such as these may be created by contract they cannot be easements, and therefore do not attach to, and bind, the land. The easement of light is an exception introduced for convenience. On the sale of any particular piece of land all the existing easements connected with it pass to the purchaser automatically, unless they are expressly excepted in the conveyance.

Easements may be created by express contract or by uninterrupted user over a long period, from which the law will infer that there must have been a contract and a deed at some time in the past. In order to create a proper legal easement by means of an express contract a deed under seal must be used. If the contract is not under seal it does not have quite the same effect; for it will only create an equitable easement, which, like all equitable rights, will not be enforceable against any person who buys the legal ownership of the servient tenement, unless he knew of the existence of the easement at the time. Equitable easements created after 1925 should be registered as such at the Land Registry, for it is now the law that no purchaser of the servient tenement can be held to have known of the existence of such equitable easements at the time of his purchase unless they had been registered.

There are some circumstances in which,

although the parties to a contract for the sale of land did not make any express stipulations about easements, they will be in the same position in law as if they had, for one of the rules of English contract law is that, if the parties would obviously have inserted a particular provision in the contract had they ever directed their minds to it, then they must be treated as if they had actually inserted it. The law will imply it as a term of the contract. Thus in every conveyance there is implied a grant of all easements connected with the property. It is on the same principle that when an owner of two adjoining properties sells one and nothing is said in the conveyance about easements, the purchaser may acquire easements over the land retained by the vendor. Any rights which the vendor had been in the habit of exercising himself over that half of his own land which he has retained for the benefit of the half which he has sold, will be implied by law as easements in favour of the purchaser, provided it was obvious that they were being exercised.

The position is the same where the owner of two adjoining properties sells them both at substantially the same time to different purchasers. If, however, he sells them at different times, the later of the two purchasers will step into the shoes of the vendor and the law will only imply in his favour such easements as are absolutely necessary for the enjoyment of the land, i.e. a right of way to an otherwise land-locked plot. These are called easements of necessity.

Easement by prescription.—The uninterrupted exercise of a right over a long period may convert it into an easement which will bind the land over which it has been exercised. This is known as prescription. The theory of the law is that if the right has been exercised for so long without being objected to, it must have had a proper legal origin. The period for which uninterrupted user is necessary in order to create an easement varies according to the circumstances; special rules apply to the easement of light (see ANCIENT LIGHTS). The most usual period is twenty years. If it can be shewn in any proceedings that the owner or occupier of a plot of land has enjoyed and exercised a right which could be an easement over a plot of land belonging to another throughout the last twenty years,

he will have gone a long way towards establishing his right to be considered as the legal owner of an easement. But there are several ways in which he may be defeated.— It is a defence to such a claim to shew that he was only allowed to exercise the right because of an agreement with the owner of the servient tenement; that the latter persisted for at least a year in attempts to prevent the enjoyment of the right; or that it had only been exercised secretly. If uninterrupted enjoyment for forty years can be proved, the mere fact that verbal permission had been given will not prevent an easement from being created; though the existence of a written or sealed permission (i.e. by deed) would, as also would secrecy or a year's obstruction. It is important to notice that the twenty (or forty) years during which the right has been uninterruptedly enjoyed must be the twenty years immediately before the date on which the proceedings commenced.

If it is impossible to comply with the above requirements, it is still sometimes possible to acquire an easement by prescription. If it can be shewn that for a long time past the right has been fairly regularly exercised (interruption for a year or so before the proceedings were commenced would not be fatal here) the Court will presume that there must have been a grant under seal. Sixty years is the sort of period on which such a presumption can be raised. (*See* ANCIENT LIGHTS; RIGHT OF WAY.)

EASTER.—Easter is a movable feast, being held always on the first Sunday after the full moon which happens upon, or next after, the 21st day of March, and, as a result, Easter may fall on any date between 22nd March and 25th April. By the Easter Act, 1928, it is provided that Easter shall always fall on the first Sunday after the 2nd Saturday in April, as a result of which Easter will fall between 9th and 15th April. This Act, however, cannot come into force until agreement has been reached with foreign countries and the churches, and a date is fixed for its commencement by an Order of His Majesty in Council to be approved by both Houses of Parliament.

ECCLESIASTICAL COMMISSIONERS.—The Ecclesiastical Commissioners are a corporate body with power to purchase and hold lands notwithstanding the statutes of Mortmain (*see* MORTMAIN).

It is constituted thus: the Archbishop of Canterbury, who is chairman ex-officio, and the Archbishop of York; the Bishops; the Deans of St. Paul's, Canterbury, and Westminster; the Lord Chancellor; the Lord Chief Justice; the Chancellor of the Exchequer; the First Lord of the Treasury; a Secretary of State nominated by the Crown; the Lord President of the Council; the Master of the Rolls; seven laymen appointed by the Crown; two laymen appointed by the Archbishop of Canterbury; and the three Church Estate Commissioners.

The Commissioners from time to time prepare and lay before the King in council such schemes as they think fit, such as union of benefices and so forth. Objections to such schemes are heard before the Privy Council on the part of anyone aggrieved. If the scheme is approved, it is ratified by order of His Majesty, and an insertion in *The London Gazette* has the same force and effect as an Act of Parliament.

ECCLESIASTICAL LAW. — The term ecclesiastical law is applied to that branch of English law which deals with ecclesiastical matters, and, more especially, with matters relating to the Church of England. It includes, therefore, the law regarding exchange and plurality of benefices, offences by clergymen and their punishment, the peculiar rights and duties of clergymen, and the constitution of ecclesiastical courts. Ecclesiastical law is derived, to some extent, from the papal canon law, but mainly from English parliamentary enactments. The National Assembly is now able to pass measures equivalent to Acts of Parliament. For the various branches of ecclesiastical law, *see* separate titles, e.g. BENEFICE; BISHOP; CHURCH OF ENGLAND; CLERGYMAN; NATIONAL ASSEMBLY.

EDUCATION.—At Common Law there is no obligation upon a parent to educate his child. The law relating to education is, therefore, for the greatest part statutory, and dates from the early 19th century. In earlier times educational institutions were founded and maintained by private benefactors and by voluntary organizations. In the late 19th century, however, there came an immense mass of legislation, providing for the reform and reorganization of existing educational es-

tablishments, and in the Education Acts for the setting up of free and compulsory elementary education. Provision has been made for the education of children in the case of Poor Law Authorities, or children who have been convicted of crime, or who associate with criminals, while the Factory Acts protect children engaged in industry.

Compulsory Education.—Beginning with the Elementary Education Act, 1870, successive statutes dealing with Elementary Education have been passed culminating in the Education Act, 1921, which repealed and consolidated most of the statutes dealing with education. The purpose of these Acts was to provide a national system of education for all persons capable of profiting thereby.

The Central Authority charged with the superintendence of education in England and Wales is the Board of Education. Poor Law Schools, however, are under the Ministry of Health; Industrial and Reformatory and Approved Schools are under the Home Office, while the Universities are under the supervision of the University Grants Committee of the Treasury. The money voted annually by Parliament for educational purposes is mostly distributed by the Board, and by imposing conditions upon the grant of sums in aid of local education authorities. The Board maintains a strict supervision over State aided education, and by its grant of certificates to teachers and moneys to College and Universities ensures the adequate and efficient staffing of elementary schools throughout the country. In the same way the Board controls the provision of Higher Education. In many matters, local authorities can only exercise their statutory powers subject to the consent and approval of the Board, and in case of default on the part of local authorities the Board can take action.

The local authorities for elementary and higher education are the County, County Borough, Borough, and Urban District Councils. The powers of these authorities in respect of education (except the power of raising a rate or borrowing money) are exercised by education committees appointed partly by the authorities and approved by the Board. It is the duty of the local authorities to provide for the progressive development and comprehensive organization of education in their areas, and for this purpose schemes may be submitted by, or may be required from, the local authority for the approval of the Board.

Elementary Education.—The local authority must provide and maintain adequate elementary school accommodation and efficient elementary education for all children resident in the area; and for this purpose they have powers to purchase land and erect or take over buildings. Any ten ratepayers in the area, however, may, within three months of notice given of the proposed building of a new elementary school, object thereto to the Board of Education.

Public elementary schools may be of two types:—

(a) Provided or council schools. These are provided and maintained by the local education authority. The teachers are appointed and dismissed by the authority. They are supervised by a body of four managers appointed by the authority.

(b) Non-provided or voluntary schools. These are schools provided by persons other than the education authority. They are carried on by four foundation managers, together with two managers appointed by the authority. The schools, are, however, under the supervision of the local authority, which is responsible for their efficiency and conduct. Teachers are appointed and dismissed by the managers subject to the consent of the local authority.

In neither case can fees or charges of any kind be asked or made, except in respect of payments for the provision of meals, or medical treatment of children, or in respect of blind, deaf, defective or epileptic children.

All elementary schools must be open to inspection by H.M. Inspectors.

Duties of Parents. School Attendance.—Parents are under various statutory duties in respect to the education of their children.

1. The parents of a child between the ages of 5 and 14 or, if a bye-law so provides, between 6 and 14, must cause that child to receive efficient elementary instruction in reading, writing and arithmetic, and so must

cause him to attend at an elementary school. Failure to do this duty will be excused if:—

(a) The child is prevented from attending by sickness or other unavoidable cause.

(b) There is no school within three miles from the child's residence. This will not be an excuse if the authority provides a conveyance.

(c) The child is receiving efficient education elsewhere.

Where the parents fail to perform this duty, after due warning, the local authority must take proceedings before the Petty Sessional Court of the district to enforce it. The Court may grant a school attendance order ordering the child to attend an efficient school selected by the parent. If the order is not complied with the parent may be fined and the child may be ordered to be sent to an approved school.

Local authorities must make bye-laws providing for school attendance by children.

2. The duty to educate extends to parents of a child who live in a canal boat. Where the boat is registered under the Canal Boats Act, the child and his parent are considered to be living in the place to which the boat is registered as belonging, and are subject to the bye-laws of that place. If the parent satisfies the local authority that the child is receiving proper elementary education in some other area, the local authority must grant, without charge, a certificate to that effect, and the parent and child will be considered as living in the area where the child is being educated. The certificate may be cancelled or altered if the child is not being educated properly.

3. The parent of a blind or deaf child must cause his child to receive not only efficient instruction as set out above, but also education suitable to such child. Except where the child is under 7 years of age, deafness and blindness or distance from an elementary school will not be sufficient excuse for neglecting this duty. The local authority must make proper provision for the education of such children.

4. The parent of a defective or epileptic child over 7 years of age in any place where there is a certified class or school, must cause the child to attend such class or school; and he will not be excused by reason only that a guide or conveyance is necessary.

The local authority, if satisfied that the parent is not making suitable provision for the child's education, may require the child to be sent to a suitable class or school, and if the parent fails to do so, may obtain an order from the Court.

The local authority must ascertain what children are defective or epileptic, and make proper provision for their education.

The period of compulsory education for blind, deaf, defective or epileptic children extends until the child attains 16 years of

(b) Who are over 16 years of age and have passed a University Matriculation examination, or who up to 16 years of age have been under full-time instruction in an efficient school recognized by the board.

(c) Who are under full-time instruction at an efficient recognized school.

(d) Who are under efficient part-time instruction for a period similar to that which is required for attendance at a continuation school.

The children of bargemen must go to school. Where no school is available, classes are held actually on a barge moored in a quiet backwater of the canal.

age. The parent must contribute a weekiy sum towards the expenses of the local authority in providing for such children, and if such sum cannot be agreed upon, it may be fixed by the Court.

Higher Education.—Local authorities must make such provision for Higher Education and spend such sums thereon as they think fit. They may take over schools or institutions for science and art, may help research and may provide for evening classes.

' The local authorities must provide for continuation schools, which must be attended, without payment of fees at such times as may be prescribed, by all young persons under the age of 18 in the area, for 320 hours in the year. Regard must be had to any preference shewn by the young person or his parent. The obligation does not extend to young persons:—

(a) Who have completed a course of training for service on the sea.

Religious Instruction.—It shall not be a condition of the admittance of any child to a public elementary school or school of Higher Education that he shall, or shall not, attend any place of religious worship, or that he shall attend any religious service or instruction at the school. He may be withdrawn from such instruction by his parent, and if his parent so desires, need not attend the school on any day exclusively set apart for religious observance by the religious body to which his parent belongs.

In provided elementary and higher education schools, no religious instruction distinctive of any particular denomination shall be given in the school. In non-provided schools, however, the religious instruction shall be in accordance with the provisions of the trust deed, and shall be under the control of the managers. H.M. Inspectors cannot enquire into the religious instruction given at any of these schools.

Where a blind, dumb, deaf or epileptic child is required to attend any school, he is not to be compelled to receive religious instruction contrary to the wishes of his parent. As far as possible, he is to receive religious instruction, and to attend religious services according with the religious creed of the parent, which is to be registered when the child is admitted to the school.

Schools for Children instead of Prison.—Prior to 1932, reformatory and industrial schools were set up for the compulsory detention and industrial training of youthful offenders or children, which provided lodging, clothing, food and instruction and which were under the supervision of the Home Office. Reformatory schools provided for youthful offenders between the ages of 12 and 16 years convicted of certain offences. Industrial schools provided for children under the age of 12 years convicted of similar offences, and for children under the age of 14 years who were found begging, destitute or consorting with criminal or immoral persons.

The protection and welfare of the young and the treatment of young offenders is now governed by the Children and Young Persons Act, 1933.

A Juvenile Court may now order to be sent to a school approved by the Home Office any child under the age of 14 years, or any young person between the ages of 14 and 17 years:—

(a) Who through lack of care, is falling into bad associations or is exposed to moral dangers, e.g. where the child is destitute or found begging, or wandering without a settled home.

(b) Who is being subjected to cruel treatment, or is a member of the same household as a child against whom an offence has been committed, or a person who has committed such an offence.

(c) Who is brought before the Court by a parent or guardian who is unable to control the child or young person.

(d) Who is under the care of the Poor Law Authority and is proved to be refractory.

(e) Who has been convicted of certain offences.

The Home Secretary also has power to send young offenders to such schools.

The order shall be an authority to detain the child at the school for three years or until he attains the age of 15. If he is a young person over 14 but under 16 years of age, he is to be detained for 3 years, and if over 16, until he attains the age of 19 years.

The parents or persons responsible for the child must make contributions to the expense of maintaining the child at the school.

Existing reformatory and industrial schools are to be approved schools, and local authorities with the approval of the Home Secretary have power to build such schools.

The managers of approved schools are under an obligation to provide for the clothing, maintenance and education of the persons under their care. The schools are to be under the supervision of the Home Office and its inspectors.

Religious Instruction.—In determining the approved school to which a person is to be sent, the Court or the Home Secretary shall take into consideration the religious belief of the person, and shall, when practicable, send the person to a school for persons of the religious persuasion to which he belongs. If this is not done, the parent or guardian may apply to send the child or young person to an approved school for persons of his religious persuasion, and if practicable, this is to be done. To give the child religious instruction and assistance, a minister of the religious persuasion to which the child belongs shall attend at the school at such times as may be fixed by the Home Secretary.

Poor Law Education.—The Central Authority for Poor Law Education is the Minister of Health. The local authorities are the County and County Borough Councils who have now superseded the guardians. The Councils act in this connection through their public assistance and education committees. Certain Borough Urban District Councils also have power in regard to Education.

The Minister has power to make such rules as may be necessary for the government of workhouses, the education of children therein, and the apprenticing of children of poor persons. The Minister may require the local authority to provide schools for the relief and management of the children of poor persons, and may regulate such schools as though they were workhouses. The Minister may also certify for this purpose schools supported by voluntary contributions.

The local authority may send the children of poor persons to certified schools and may pay the reasonable expense of their maintenance at such schools. The consent of the parents, or, if the child is illegitimate, the mother, is necessary before this can be done except, e.g. where the child is an orphan or has been deserted by his parents. The child may not be kept at such a school against his will if over the age of 14, or against the will of his parents. Local authorities also have power to send poor deaf, dumb, and blind children to special schools.

Religious Instruction.—In every workhouse and separate school a register is to be kept of the religious creed of every inmate, and in the case of every child under 12, the entry is to be of the creed of the father, and if that is not known, of the mother; and the child may receive religious instruction from a minister of his denomination who may visit for that purpose. No child who is so visited may receive instruction in any other creed if the parent or the minister makes a request to that effect. The child may, on the application of the parents, be sent to a certified school established for children of the religious creed to which the child belongs.

Endowed Schools.—Where property has been vested in charities subject to trusts for the purpose of education at school of boys and girls, or for the purpose of providing scholarships at school or university, such charities with certain exceptions come under a special and wide jurisdiction conferred upon the Board of Education by the Endowed Schools Acts.

These Acts do not relate to the seven Public Schools of Eton, Harrow, Rugby, Winchester, Westminster, Charterhouse and Shrewsbury. The purpose of this jurisdiction is to obtain the utmost educational advantages from the charities, and the Board has power to alter, modify, and extend trusts and charities. These powers are to be exercised through schemes which must follow the procedure prescribed by the acts, which confer certain rights of appeal against any changes or extensions proposed to be made.

Under such schemes all teachers and officers are to be in the employment of the governing body, and except in cases of misconduct, are to be entitled to notice on dismissal.

No person is to be disqualified from being a teacher, and no teacher or pupil is to be under any disadvantage on grounds of religious belief. On the request of parents or guardians, children may be excused from attending religious instruction or services.

Welsh Intermediate Education.—For the purpose of providing for technical and secondary education in Wales under various acts schemes have been passed for reorganizing certain endowments and providing new endowments out of rates assisted by Parliamentary grants.

With the consent of the local authorities a scheme may provide for endowments by the levy of a rate to provide scholarships or annual contributions to pupils. The local authority may also contribute sums received from certain Exchequer grants. Such a scheme must comply with the conditions as to religious instruction set out above, and no catechism distinctive of any particular religious denomination may be taught. The supervision of Welsh Secondary Education is by the Central Welsh Board, which is responsible to the Board of Education.

EFFECTS.—A man's goods and chattels, e.g. motor-cars and furniture, are called his effects. The term does not include land which may belong to him, nor money or securities.

EGGS.—To take the eggs of wild birds on another's land is not theft unless the owner of the land has "reduced them into possession," i.e. collected them or otherwise specially protected them. The eggs of game-birds are, however, protected by the Game Act, 1831, which imposes penalties for destroying or taking without authority eggs of game (including black game and bustards) and of swans, wild duck, teal or widgeon. The same penalties (5/– per egg) are imposed on persons knowingly possessing such eggs. (*See also* BIRDS.)

Premises intended to be used by way of trade, or for purposes of gain, for the cold storage or chemical storage of eggs may be registered with the County Council or County Borough, and, in certain circumstances, must be so registered. It is illegal to sell or expose for sale any preserved egg (fine, £5 for first offence and £20 for subsequent offences) unless it is marked with the word "preserved" in letters not less than a sixteenth of an inch high, enclosed in a circle of not less than a half-inch in diameter. The Ministry of Agriculture and Fisheries has prescribed "trade designations" for eggs, and, as a result, eggs may be marked "special,"< "standard," "medium" or "pullet"; if so marked, they must come up to the standard prescribed by the Ministry, e.g. if an egg is marked "special," it must weigh 2¼ ozs., the shell must be clean and sound, the white must be translucent and firm, etc.

EJECTION FROM PREMISES.—

An owner or occupier of premises has the right to eject from them any person who comes upon them without any right to do so or without his permission. He may also eject a person who is on the premises with his permission or by right, if such a person misbehaves himself or is disorderly. If a trespasser enters upon premises in a peaceable manner, the person in possession, or entitled to the possession, of them, may request him to leave, and in the event of refusal may use reasonable force to eject him. If the trespasser enters with force and violence he may be removed by force without a previous request to depart being made to him.

The force used must not be excessive, otherwise it will amount to a trespass upon the person removed. If the trespasser is in actual possession of the premises, the rightful owner may enter and eject him using such force as is necessary, but he must take care not to injure the trespasser, his goods, or his family.

When a person is given permission to enter upon premises he is called a licensee, and cannot be treated as a trespasser until the licence is revoked. A bare licence may be revoked at any time without a reason being given, but if the licence is accompanied by an interest it cannot be revoked arbitrarily by the person granting it. For example, permission given by a landowner to a person to use his private road may be withdrawn at any time, but the permission given to a person to enter a theatre upon payment for his ticket cannot be withdrawn without good reason, such as misbehaviour upon the part of the ticket-holder. When a person

purchases a ticket for a seat at a theatre, or other similar entertainment, he has the right to stay and see the whole performance, provided he behaves properly and complies with the rules of the management. If he interrupts the performance or is disorderly he may be ejected.

Ejection from Places of Worship.— Public worship in churches and chapels, public meetings and games are protected by the law from the actions of persons who create disturbances at them. The stewards of a public meeting may eject any person who creates a disturbance or prevents the transaction of the business for which the meeting was called.

Ejection from Public Houses.— The licensee of a public house or place of refreshment may eject from the premises any person who is drunken, violent, quarrelsome or disorderly. He must first request him to leave, and, if he refuses, a policeman may be called to assist in removing the offender. The licensee is not liable even if the policeman uses unnecessary force in ejecting any person from his public house. A person refusing to leave at the request of the licensee may be fined forty shillings. A public-house keeper is not allowed by the law to let prostitutes remain upon his premises for a longer period than is necessary for them to be served with, and to consume, refreshments, and if a prostitute refuses to leave after finishing her refreshment he may eject her.

An innkeeper is bound to receive and entertain travellers unless his inn is already full, and he cannot eject a guest as a trespasser because he has not paid or refuses to pay his bill. At the same time, if a guest annoys the other guests in any room in the inn and refuses upon request to leave that room, he may be ejected from the room by the innkeeper.

In all cases where an occupier of premises exercises his right of ejecting persons from them, he must only use such force as is reasonably necessary, and if he employs excessive force he may render himself liable to an action for assault at the instance of the person who has been ejected. (See also DANGEROUS PREMISES; LANDLORD AND TENANT; PUBLICAN.)

EJECTMENT.—Ejectment is the name applied to the action brought by a person claiming that land which is in the possession of some other person belongs to him. In strict law there is now no such action, as its place has been taken as an action for possession. The action of ejectment was originally used to protect a person who held land upon a lease from being deprived wrongfully of the possession of the land, and was not originally intended to decide questions of ownership of land. The only method for deciding, as between two claimants which was the true owner of the land, was extremely cumbersome and full of formalities, and accordingly the action of ejectment was used by means of a legal fiction to decide the question of ownership of land. The procedure was as follows: Suppose that A claimed as his some land that was in the possession of B. A, the person claiming the land, granted a lease of the land, or pretended that he had granted a lease of it, to some third person. In practice in later times, no such third person ever existed, but the lease was assumed to have been granted to a fictitious person always known as John Doe.

In early times the lessee, John Doe, went on to the land and was at once physically put out of the land by a person, known as the "casual ejector," who claimed that he was entitled to the land through rights obtained from B. John Doe then called upon A to make good the lease which had been granted to him, and A then commenced an action of ejectment against B. In later times none of these events actually took place, but were assumed to have taken place by a legal fiction. The question apparently for decision in the action was whether John Doe had been wrongfully ejected or not! But as this would depend on whether A or B was the owner of the land the question of ownership would thus be decided.

ELDON, Lord (1751-1838).—After a large practice in Chancery and at the Parliamentary Bar, John Scott was made Chief Justice of the Common Pleas as Lord Eldon. Later he became Lord Chancellor. A high Tory, he fought innovations of any kind and it was under his presidency that the Chancery developed into the scandalous state which was exposed by Charles Dickens.

ELECTION. **Parliamentary Elections.** **General Elections.**—A General Election takes place whenever the King orders by Royal proclamation that writs be issued for the summoning of a new Parliament.

For the purposes of Parliamentary elections, England and Wales, Scotland, and Northern Ireland are divided into borough and county constituencies, most of which return only one member. There are also four University constituencies in England, as well as one each in Wales, Scotland and Northern Ireland. (*See below.*)

A writ is issued to the Returning Officer of each constituency. He is in county and borough constituencies respectively the sheriff and mayor or their deputies and he is responsible for the management of the election.

At a time fixed (any 2 hours between 10 and 3) on the eighth day after the summoning of Parliament (nomination day), every person wishing to become a candidate must present to the Returning Officer, either in person or through his proposer or seconder, one or more nomination papers each signed by ten electors in the constituency, and must at the same time pay a deposit of £150 in cash (or with the consent of the Returning Officer in any other manner, e.g. by cheque), which deposit is forfeited if the candidate fails to obtain an eighth of the total amount of votes polled. Candidates usually hand in a large number of nomination papers although one is sufficient.

Anyone can stand as a candidate although certain people are disqualified from being elected (*see* MEMBERS OF PARLIAMENT). Most candidates are, however, selected by the local associations of one of the political parties, comparatively few independent candidates standing.

If only one candidate is nominated in a constituency, he is forthwith declared elected. If more than one candidate is nominated, then a poll takes place on the ninth day after nomination day. (If that is a Sunday, Monday is fixed as polling day.)

The election campaign of a candidate is deemed to start when the election is reasonably imminent. Each candidate must, before nomination day, appoint an election agent (he may appoint himself) who is responsible for the management of the election campaign particularly in regard to expenses. The appointment of an election agent is one of the first tasks of a candidate, as until this is

ELECTIONEERING IN THE EIGHTEENTH CENTURY.
These two prints by Hogarth show (above) polling day and (below) chairing the
successful candidate.

done no expenditure can be incurred (*see* ELECTION AGENT). There are numerous restrictions governing the conduct of an election campaign (i.e. as to what are illegal and corrupt practices), which the candidate should know and be careful not to infringe. If they are infringed, the candidate's election may be upset and he may be liable to other penalties. (*See* ELECTION PETITIONS *below*.)

On the day of the poll, candidates tour the polling booths and they and their agents are entitled to be present at the counting of the votes. As to who may vote, and the law as to one method of voting, *see* VOTING. Immediately polling hours have ended, the ballot boxes are sealed and sent to the Returning Officer. In almost every constituency the votes are counted that night or the next day. The counting must be continuous, and the candidate is entitled to be present, together with a counting agent if he appoints one. All invalid ballot papers must be rejected. (*See* VOTING.) When the counting is completed the Returning Officer publicly announces the result, declaring the candidate with the most votes to be elected. If there is a tie, the Returning Officer has the casting vote.

Bye-Elections.—A Bye-Election takes place whenever a seat becomes vacant owing to a Member of Parliament resigning, becoming ineligible, or dying.

If the House is sitting when a bye-election becomes necessary, a motion is moved by an M.P., usually the Whip of the late member's party, and the Speaker then issues a writ. If the House is not sitting a notice is inserted in the *London Gazette*. Nomination day must be within nine and seven days of the receipt of the writ by the Returning Officer in county and borough constituencies respectively, and polling day, if that is necessary, between six and eight days thereafter. A bye-election must be conducted in the same way as a general election.

University Elections.—The following English Universities return Members of Parliament elected by their graduates:— Oxford, Cambridge, London, Combined English Universities. The Scottish and Welsh Universities return one member respectively.

As to the method of voting in University elections *see* VOTING.

It is an illegal practice corruptly to pay any person's graduation fees in order to enable that person to vote at a University election.

Election Petitions.—Any defeated candidate or elector in a constituency can bring a petition to have an election declared void on any of the following grounds:—

(i) That a successful candidate or his agents were guilty of, or knew, or consented to, any corrupt or illegal practices. (*See* ELECTION AGENT.)

(ii) That the successful candidate was ineligible for election. (*See* MEMBERS OF PARLIAMENT.)

(iii) That the successful candidate did not poll the largest number of lawful votes. Under this head the petitioner can claim that persons were wrongfully allowed to vote; or he can claim a recount on shewing reasonable grounds.

(iv) That the election was not a real one because the result was effected by an irregularity committed by the Returning Officer or one of his officials, or because general bribery, treating or undue influence affected the views of a large number of the electors. (*See* ELECTION AGENT.)

The petition must be presented within 21 days of the announcement of the result unless it relates to election expenses, when it may be made within 14 days of their return. The petitioner must provide security for costs to the amount of £1,000. The petition is tried by two High Court Judges nominated for that purpose.

If the allegations in a petition based on (ii), (iii) or (iv) above are proved, the election will be declared void and a new one must be held. If the petition is based on any of the grounds under (i) above, then if any corrupt or illegal practice is found to have been committed by the candidate or with his knowledge or consent, or if any of his agents are found guilty of bribery, the election is automatically declared void. If the election is voided for a corrupt practice, the candidate can never be elected for that constituency again or for any other constituency for seven years. If it is voided for an illegal practice, or for the corrupt practice of treating, or if undue influence is only committed by one of the candidate's agents, he will, in certain circumstances (broadly speaking when he is really not to blame), be excused and the election may not be declared void. In any event the candidate will only be ineligible for that constituency for that Parliament, or seven years respectively.

Local Government Elections.—A local government election is an election for any County Council, Municipal or Metropolitan Borough Council, District or Parish Council.

Anyone who is a British subject over the age of 21 and is not subject to any legal disability is qualified to be elected as a member of any local government body provided he or she is either:—

(i) Registered as a local government elector in the area;

(ii) An owner of freehold or leasehold land within the area;

(iii) Resident in the area during the whole of the preceding 12 months.

The members are elected by local government electors. (*See* VOTING.)

The following are ineligible for election, or are unable to retain their seats if already elected before coming under the disability:—

(i) Persons found guilty of corrupt and illegal practices. (*See* ELECTION AGENT and ELECTION PETITIONS *above*.)

(ii) Persons holding any paid office other than that of Mayor, Chairman or Sheriff at the disposal of the local authority or one of its committees.

(iii) Persons adjudicated bankrupt until their discharge (or five years later if found guilty of any misconduct), or who have made a composition with their creditors.

(iv) Persons who have, within 12 months before their election or since election, received poor relief.

(v) Persons surcharged over £500 by the district auditor.

(vi) Persons who have, within 5 years before their election, or since election, been sentenced to more than 3 months' imprisonment without the option of a fine.

(vii) Coroners, Recorders and certain other officials in respect of their own districts.

Clergymen are now no longer ineligible.

Persons who fail to attend council meetings for 6 months, unless it is on account of illness, lose their seat.

County and Borough Elections.—The Borough and County Council elections are the most important local government elections.

County Council elections take place every third year on some date between 1st and 8th of March. Each county is divided into divisions returning one member each, with the exception of the county of London where there are two members to a division.

Borough Council elections take place every year on November 1st. One-third of the members retire every year, the term of office being three years. Most Boroughs are divided into Wards for the purpose of elections.

County and Borough elections are conducted under substantially similar law to Parliamentary elections with the following modifications:—

(i) Nomination papers must be handed in before 5 o'clock on nomination day which is 12 and 8 days before polling day in county and borough elections respectively. No deposit is required.

(ii) There are no election agents, so the candidate is himself responsible for the expenses and management of his campaign. He must, therefore, make a return of all expenses with the statutory declaration himself and must vouch all payments over 20/-. The return must be made within 28, instead of 35, days.

(iii) A candidate's expenditure is limited to £25 and 2d. extra for every elector over 500, e.g. £35 may be spent if there are 1,700 electors. If there are two or more joint candidates, each of them is only allowed to spend three-quarters or two-thirds of the maximum respectively.

(iv) A candidate may employ two clerks and two messengers and, in addition, one of each extra in respect of every 1,000 electors over 2,000.

(v) A candidate may have one committee room and, in addition, one extra for every 1,000 electors over

2,000. The same restrictions as to what premises may be used apply except that public elementary school premises may be used. In local government elections, premises that may not be used as committee rooms may not be used for meetings either.

(vi) The hours of voting are always from 8 a.m. to 8 p.m., and no proxy voting is allowed.

(vii) Bye-elections must take place within 30 days of a vacancy occurring, unless the vacancy occurs within six months of the date when the member would normally retire, when the seat remains vacant until the election.

(viii) In regard to election petitions:—

(a) The petition must be brought by a defeated candidate or by four or more of the electors.

(b) A deposit of between £300 and £500 is required.

(c) The petition is tried by a commissioner appointed annually by the election judges and he must be a barrister of 15 years' standing.

In addition to the councillors elected as above, County and Borough councils have aldermen members. Their term of office is six years, half of them retiring every three years. They are elected by the council at its first meeting. Councillors or persons qualified for election as councillors are eligible; a councillor who is elected as an alderman ceases to be a councillor. The number of aldermen is one-third of the total number of councillors.

The Mayor and Chairman of Borough and County Councils respectively are elected by the Borough and County Council before the election of aldermen, if there is one, so that any new aldermen cannot vote. Their election is annual.

Urban and Rural District Council elections take place annually on April 15th when one-third of the members retire. Parish Council elections take place every third year on April 15th when all the members retire. (*See* ELECTION AGENT; MEMBERS OF PARLIAMENT; VOTING.)

ELECTION AGENT.—Every candidate in a Parliamentary election must appoint an Election Agent. He can appoint himself or any person except the Returning Officer, one of his officials, or a person whom he knows to have been convicted of corrupt practices at an election within the previous seven years.

Great care should be taken to select a suitable agent, as the candidate is absolutely responsible for all the acts of his agent, who has to observe a number of election rules, mostly dealing with what expenditure is allowed. Moreover, the agent is largely responsible for the successful management of the campaign.

The appointment of an election agent should be the candidate's first step in a campaign, as he alone can pay the election expenses. The candidate must give notice in writing of the appointment to the Returning Officer on or before Nomination Day, stating the name, office and address of the agent. The address must be in the constituency or in an adjoining one.

The appointment may be revoked at any time, but, on revocation or death of an agent, a new one must be appointed forthwith and the same notice given to the Returning Officer. A candidate may not have more than one election agent, but in a county constituency he may appoint sub-agents for each polling district who, in relation to their respective districts, are in the same position as the agent, except that they are not concerned with the return of election expenses. Notice of their appointment must similarly be given to the Returning Officer.

The election agent is responsible for the management of the campaign, in which work he is assisted by a limited number of paid helpers, and also unpaid workers who do clerical work, canvass individual electors and address public meetings.

The election agent is personally responsible for the control of all election expenditure and, with the following exceptions, no sum can be paid in respect of an election campaign by anyone except him:—

(i) The candidate can pay up to £100 for his personal expenses, i.e. his reasonable travelling and subsistence expenses. He must, however, send to the election agent a written statement of any amount so paid within 14 days of the declaration of the result. Any sums over the £100 must be paid out by the agent.

(ii) Any helper can pay for his own petty expenses provided he is not repaid the money so spent.

(iii) Anyone can pay the £150 deposit to the Returning Officer on behalf of the candidate.

Not only must the election agent pay all the accounts and keep all accounts and receipts—he should keep a complete set of books shewing all sums received and expended, the names of all persons employed, etc.—but he must also see that the total expenditure does not exceed the total amount allowed and is only incurred in respect of allowed purposes.

The total amount that may be spent in an election campaign, excluding the three items excepted below, is limited to 6d. and 5d. per elector on the register in county and borough constituencies respectively. Thus, if there are 40,000 electors in a county constituency, not more than £1,000 can be spent. The three exceptions are as follows:—

(i) The personal expenses of the candidate, (*see above*).

(ii) £75 and £50 in a county and borough constituency respectively out of the remuneration of the election agent.

(iii) Sums spent on conveying voters across the sea, if this is the only way they can reach their polling stations.

This total amount of 6d and 5d per elector respectively may only be spent for the following purposes:—

1. The employment of (*a*) sub-agents, (*b*) clerks and messengers, (*c*) polling agents.

(*a*) Sub-agents are only allowed in county constituencies and are limited to one for each polling district.

(*b*) One clerk and one messenger for each 500 electors, and additionally in a county constituency, one clerk and one messenger for the Central Committee room for each 5,000 electors.

(*c*) One polling agent for each polling station whose name must be sent to the returning officer before polling day, and whose main duty is to prevent impersonation at the poll. All other helpers, e.g. canvassers and speakers, must be unpaid.

2. The hiring of committee rooms. One committee room is allowed for each 500 electors and an additional central committee room is allowed in the case of county constituencies.

3. Stationery, messages, postage and telegrams. Every candidate can send one free postal communication to each elector provided it does not weigh more than two ounces.

4. Printing, publishing and distributing of bills, posters, notices, etc.

5. Holding of public meetings.

6. Miscellaneous objects not otherwise disallowed. Not more than £200 may be spent under this heading.

No expenditure is allowed for the following purposes:—

(i) To anyone for conveying voters to the poll except across the sea if that is necessary.

(ii) To an elector for exhibiting bills, notices, etc. unless it is his ordinary business to let out the site.

(iii) To anyone for bands of music, torches, flags, banners, cockades, ribbons or other marks of distinction.

Another important duty of the agent is to see that no corrupt or illegal practices are committed by himself, the candidate or anyone on his behalf.

An illegal practice is one forbidden by law; a corrupt practice, which is a more serious offence, is one forbidden by law if done for an improper purpose, or which the law implies to have been so done.

A person found guilty of an illegal practice at an election is liable to a maximum fine of £100, and he loses the right to vote in that constituency for 5 years.

A person found guilty of a corrupt practice at an election is liable to a fine of £200 and loses:

(i) The right to vote in any election for 7 years.

(ii) Any public or judicial office he may hold.

(iii) The right to stand as a candidate in any constituency for 7 years or in that constituency for ever.

For the result of illegal and corrupt practices committed by, or with the knowledge and consent of, the candidate or his agents, *see* ELECTIONS *under* ELECTION PETITIONS.

Illegal Practices.—It is illegal:

1. To exceed the total maximum expenditure allowed, *see above*.

2. To make excessive expenditure for the allowed purposes, *see above*.

3. To spend money for a disallowed purpose, *see above*.

4. To do any of the following things:—

(a) To publish any bill, notice, etc. without its having the name of the publisher, i.e. the election agent, and of the printer on it.

(b) To use as a committee room any licensed premises, any premises where intoxicating liquor is sold, (except a permanent political club), any premises where ordinarily food or drink is sold for consumption thereon, or any premises which are used as a public elementary school. A separate part of the last mentioned buildings, other than the actual school premises, may be used if it has a separate entrance and is ordinarily hired out as offices or for public meetings.

(c) To employ for a candidate any stage or hackney carriage for the purpose of conveying voters to the poll. Stage and hackney carriages include taxi-cabs, buses and charabancs.

(d) To make, without reasonable belief in its truth, any derogatory false statement about the personal (as distinct from the political) character of a candidate.

(e) To make a statement, knowing it to be false, that a candidate has withdrawn.

(f) To make any payment for election expenses unless one is an election agent. (The three exceptions are given above).

(g) To pay money to anyone except the election agent for use in the election. A candidate is not bound by this rule.

(h) To bribe any candidate to withdraw.

(i) To disturb any political meeting after the writs for election have been issued. (This rule is scarcely ever enforced).

As to other illegal practices, *see below* under "After the election" and *see* VOTING.

Corrupt Practices.—It is a corrupt practice for anyone to bribe, treat or exercise undue influence over an elector with the object of inducing him to vote, or abstain from voting, for a candidate. A bribe may be offered directly or indirectly; it may be a promise to give, or the giving of, money or anything of value, or the offer of employment. Payment of the travelling expenses of an elector may be a bribe. Payment for food, drink or entertainment of an elector is considered as treating. To intimidate any elector by the use or threat of violence or by inflicting, or threatening to inflict, any loss or damage, is included under the heading of undue influence.

It is also a corrupt practice for:

(i) Anyone, other than the agent, to incur expenses on account of holding public meetings, or issuing circulars, posters, etc. without the written authority of the agent;

(ii) Anyone to attempt to obtain a ballot paper by personation (*see* VOTING);

(iii) A candidate or an agent to make a false declaration as to expenses, (*see below*).

After the Election.—After the election result is announced, the agent must, within 35 days, send to the returning officer a full and detailed statement of all sums spent and received for the purpose of the election, the personal expenses of the candidate and of any disputed claims, together with all accounts and receipts in respect of the election. He must at the same time provide the returning officer with a declaration, sworn before a Justice of the Peace, stating that to the best of his knowledge and belief the return of the election expenses is a true one. The candidate must forward a similar declaration within the same period unless he is abroad, when he is allowed until 14 days after his return.

A member may not vote or sit in the House of Commons if he or his agent are in breach of the above rule, and he is liable to a heavy fine if he does so.

The agent must not, without an order of the High Court, pay any claim sent in more than 14 days after the result is announced, or any claim after 28 days.

There are no election agents in local government elections. (*See* ELECTION; VOTING.)

ELECTION, DOCTRINE OF.—This is an equitable doctrine to the effect that, if a person has got a choice between taking one or other of two rights, he must take one or the other with all conditions that attach to it, and cannot attempt to take both or to ignore the conditions. Thus, if A by his will gives to B property belonging to C, and also gives some other property belonging to himself to C, C cannot take the property given to him unless he is prepared to give up *his* property to B. He is not bound, of course, to give up his property, but if he does not do so he cannot take the property left to him by A. If C refuses to give up his property he will not necessarily lose all his rights to the legacy from A, but will only lose them to the extent necessary to compensate B for his (C's) refusal. Thus, if A gave to B an estate belonging to C worth £5,000 and at the same time gave to C a legacy of £15,000, C, if he were unwilling to give up his estate, could nevertheless claim £10,000 of the legacy and allow the other £5,000 to go to B in compensation for the loss of the estate.

ELECTRICITY.—The first Act of Parliament relating to electricity was the Electric Lighting Act, 1882. During the War, however, the use of electricity for power as well as for lighting purposes was so vastly increased, that it was realized that the supply of electricity was of national importance; and an Act of 1919 shewed a marked advance in the control of supply by the creation of the Electricity Commissioners, whose duty it was to promote, regulate and supervise the supply of electricity, and by the creation of joint electricity authorities, each of whom was to administer a large area. Since the Act conferred no compulsory powers, the activities of the Commissioners could not be very extensive, and it was not until the Electricity (Supply) Act, 1925, was passed that any real advance could be made. By that Act, the Central Electricity Board was created, with very wide powers to compel conformity from the supply companies, which still remain, to some extent, independent.

The Board is an independent and non-profit corporation, having control over the whole country, but owning few, if any, power-stations. The principle of this new arrangement is that the Board shall buy electricity from selected undertakers (or manufacturers) at a fixed price; the major part of the electric supply of the country will thus be pooled and will then be sold for distribution at a fixed price to the undertakers as and when they require power. The Board will provide main transmission lines for connecting one undertaker with another in order to meet the requirements of distribution. Companies that have not been selected by the Board will still continue in existence, and the Board may purchase electricity from them, but, generally speaking, may not sell it to them. But the Board has very extensive powers to order the closing of unselected undertakers if their existence is uneconomic. The effect of the organization will, therefore, be to close all unnecessary power-stations and, by the erection of new stations and the enlargement of old stations, all smaller stations will finally be closed down and electricity for the whole of the country will be produced from a limited number of large stations with a free interchange of standardized power between stations when required. The selected companies will continue in existence, subject to control by the Board, and will, of course, continue to distribute their profits among their shareholders. The Act makes special provision for the compensation of regular employees who have lost their employment as a result of the economies effected by the Board, e.g. on the closing down of redundant stations.

Inspectors and Meters.—Electric inspectors are appointed by local authorities or the Board of Trade, whose duties are to inspect and test undertakers' lines and works and the supply of electricity given by them; to certify and examine meters, etc. Hired meters must be kept in order by the undertaker, and the undertaker or the consumer may call in an inspector (on paying his fee) to certify the meter and its manner of fixing, or to test the current supplied. No meter may be connected or disconnected without forty-eight hours' notice on either side.

Trees and Hedges.—Trees and hedges may be lopped, cut or felled by the undertakers when they interfere with electric lines, subject to compensation being paid to the owner thereof. (*See also* LARCENY.)

ELEGIT.—In those cases where a judgment debtor is the owner of land or real property, or is in possession of leasehold interests, a judgment creditor can obtain satisfaction of his debt by issuing execution by means of what is called a Writ of Elegit.

The writ of elegit, which is issued in the same manner as a Writ of Fi. Fa. (q.v.), imposes upon the sheriff, through his officer the under-sheriff, the duty of inquiring as to the lands in the county which are held by the judgment debtor. This he must do with the aid of a jury of twelve persons entitled to serve upon a jury at assizes.

When the inquisition as to the judgment debtor's lands has been held, the judgment creditor becomes entitled to possession of all the lands which may be either freehold or leasehold of the debtor, and may enforce his right to possession by taking legal proceedings for it if he cannot obtain it peaceably. He is entitled to take the income of the lands until he has received from them the amount of the judgment debt and costs, and, upon application by originating summons to the Chancery Division, he may obtain an order for the sale of the debtor's interest in the land. After the return of the inquisition and before sale of the land, he is known as the tenant by elegit, and he must cause this fact to be registered in the Land Registry.

The interest of the tenant by elegit in the land ends when either the judgment debtor tenders to him the amount of the judgment debt, together with the costs of execution, or when the judgment creditor has received out of the income of the lands the amount of the debt and costs.

It will be seen that execution by means of a writ of elegit is a cumbrous method of procedure, and it cannot be recommended when other methods are available. (*See* EXECUTION.)

EMBEZZLEMENT. — Embezzlement is a term which is very loosely applied in popular speech. In law it has a very precise meaning and is confined to offences by clerks and servants who fraudulently keep or dispose of goods or money that they have received for, or in the name of, or on account of, their masters or employers. Thus, if a servant is paid money in settlement of a debt due to his master, and keeps it with intent to defraud his master of it, he is guilty of the crime of embezzlement. Embezzlement is a felony punishable with penal servitude.

Difficult questions often arise on points connected with the ingredients of this offence. The Courts have had on many occasions to decide exactly what type of employment creates a clerk or servant. For instance, a son who lives with his father and does clerical duties for his father has been held to be a clerk for the purpose of embezzlement, and this is so although he receives no pay and is not bound to perform any of his duties. Again, the employment can be of a purely temporary nature. Where a man allowed another to carry parcels when the latter had nothing to do, and paid him what were really merely gratuities, the man carrying the parcels was held to be a servant for this purpose. Even a man who on a single occasion drove two cows for their owner to sell to somebody else and who, having received the purchase money, kept it, was held rightly convicted of embezzlement.

Where a person is a clerk or servant to a society which is illegal, he cannot be convicted of this offence since the law does not recognize such a person as clerk or servant. Questions of great difficulty have arisen in the case of commercial travellers. It has been laid down that a commercial traveller who is under the orders of an employer as to the times when he will work and as to the routes that he will take, is a clerk or servant. On the other hand, a person who is acting as an agent for somebody else on a commission basis, and who is allowed to select whatever times he likes for travelling, and in fact need not, so far as his principal is concerned, travel at all, is not a clerk or servant for the purpose of embezzlement.

It is important to note that in order to convict a person of embezzlement it must be shewn that he embezzled some particular sum and not merely that he was short in his accounts. In an important case on this point, it was laid down that it is not sufficient to prove at the trial a general deficiency in an account: a particular sum must be proved to have been embezzled, just as in larceny a particular article must be proved to have been stolen. This rule does not, however, mean that a general deficiency in accounts is not triable under the criminal law. Such cases can frequently be dealt with as fraudulent conversion of money or as falsification of accounts. (*See* FALSIFICATION OF ACCOUNTS; FRAUDULENT CONVERSION.)

EMBLEMENTS.—The right to emblements was one given by the Common

Law to any tenant of land whose tenancy came to an end without his fault at an unpredictable time, to re-enter upon the land, after his tenancy had ceased, to cultivate and reap any crops sown during the tenancy which reached maturity during the next year. It applies therefore to wheat, oats, roots, etc., but not to fruit trees or to a second crop of clover.

As it can only arise where the termination of the tenancy was not known in advance, it cannot apply to an ordinary lease for a fixed term of years. It is now rendered of no importance in all other cases except agricultural tenancies at will (tenancies which may be terminated by either party without notice, usually the result of a holding over by a tenant after his proper tenancy has run out) by the Agricultural Holdings Act, 1923, which provides that one year's notice to quit must always be given. (See AGRICULTURAL HOLDINGS.)

EMBRACERY. — This is the name given to the bribing or attempted corruption of members of a jury. It is an indictable offence and is punishable with fine and imprisonment. Prosecutions for this offence seldom take place nowadays, as attachment for contempt of court is a more suitable method of dealing with people who attempt improperly to interfere with juries.

EMPLOYER'S LIABILITY. Liability of a Master for his Servant's Acts.—As the servant is usually "a man of straw" (q.v.), it is only justice that the master should be responsible for what is done by the servant in the performance of his duties. That is known as vicarious liability and is sometimes referred to as the doctrine of Respondeat Superior. The liability differs slightly according to the kind of act the servant does.

Contracts by a servant for his master make the latter alone liable if he has expressly authorized the servant to make them, or if their making falls within the general authority conferred by the nature of the employment. The master is liable on any contract made within the apparent scope of the servant's employment even though he has expressly forbidden the servant to make it. So long as the master has capacity to make the contract any servant can do it for him.

Where the master has acquiesced in previous contracts of a similar kind he is liable, for example, where the cook has been in the habit of ordering the household provisions. This is called ostensible authority.

The question is treated more fully under PRINCIPAL AND AGENT, but two matters are of special interest to employers: a master is not liable if the third party knew that the servant was exceeding his actual authority; and where a servant is acting within his express, implied or ostensible authority it matters not that he is making the contract for his own benefit and in fraud of the master, the master is still liable.

Crimes committed by a servant make the master liable to a criminal prosecution if he orders or allows them, or participates in their proceeds.

There is an increasing number of statutes by which the master is absolutely liable for his servant's crime, even though he has expressly forbidden the act and is entirely unaware of it. A well-known example is provided by recent legislation relating to Food and Drugs by which the master is absolutely liable if his servant sells an article not of the nature and quality demanded by the customer.

Nuisances render the master liable to prosecution if they are committed by the servant in the course of his employment, and the master will be liable in a civil action for damages if the nuisance amounts to a tort.

Torts.—For these the master is liable, if at all, in addition to, and not, as in contract, instead of the servant. In the majority of cases which arise in practice the master is liable for his servant's torts, because in nine cases out of ten they are committed while properly about his master's business. Thus, the employers of a lorry driver are liable for damage caused by his negligent driving while upon their business.

Bearing in mind that it is the exception for the employer to escape liability in practice, we can examine the specific cases in which liability arises. Obviously if the master expressly authorizes a tort or conduct which must inevitably result in injury being done, he is liable. This applies also to ratification by the master after the act. But by far the greatest number of torts for which masters are responsible are those committed by servants in the course of their employment and within the apparent scope of their authority. It can, of course, be said that a servant has no authority to commit a tort. This is quite true, but the master may even go so far as to prohibit expressly the act and yet be liable. The explanation is that the master, expressly or impliedly, puts his servant in a position to do certain acts or pursue a course of conduct, and he is responsible for the manner in which the servant, acting as such, performs the prescribed duties, and for all acts done in the discharge of those duties. Thus, a master is liable if his chauffeur drives his car negligently, unless the chauffeur is using the car for his own purposes; and a railway company if a stationmaster arrests someone who he mistakenly thinks has not paid his fare.

It has been said that masters have a duty to employ competent servants. They are not, however, insurers. A master does not have to pay for damage by a servant simply because the relationship of master and servant exists. The master is not always liable.

Thus, when a servant is engaged upon his own business and his act has no connection with his employment, as when he libels his neighbour; when a servant does something beyond that which he is employed to do, as when a conductor drives an omnibus; when a servant does an unnecessary wrongful act, as shooting a trespasser; or an act entirely independent of his employment, though in the course thereof, like the carpenter who lit his pipe while at work and threw the match among shavings, thus starting a fire—in each of these cases the master escapes liability. Very difficult questions arise as to what is, and what is not, in the course of a servant's employment and within the scope of his authority. No guide save common sense can be suggested, for each case depends upon its own facts.

Forbidding the act will not of itself relieve the master from liability.

Exemptions.—Trade Unions and Public Authorities are exempt from liability in certain cases (*see* TRADE UNIONS; PUBLIC AUTHORITIES), and the Crown cannot be sued for its servants' torts for "The Crown can do no wrong." Ministers of the Crown (e.g. the Postmaster-General), and government officials are not responsible for the acts of subordinates, for they are not their servants but servants of the Crown.

Liability of Master when Servant is Injured or Killed.—Apart from the duties imposed upon him by statute, a master is not liable for injury to his servant simply because he is the master, any more than he is to a stranger. Indeed, a master's liability to his servant is much narrower than his liability to a stranger because of the doctrine of common employment (*see* MASTER AND SERVANT), which leaves the servant without any remedy against his master, apart from remedies given him by Acts of Parliament, when his injury results from the negligence of a fellow servant. Moreover, it is open to the master to say (as he often does in practice), that the servant voluntarily undertook the risk of the injury. This is known as the defence of Volenti Non Fit Injuria, which means that no actionable wrong can be done to one who willingly subjects himself to known risks.

To look at the other side of the picture, it is clear that a servant cannot be injured with impunity by the master even at Common Law (i.e. apart from statute). The master is often liable to an action for negligence, for he must not subject his servants to unreasonable risks. He must see that all his servants are competent, for if he negligently employs one who is not, the defence of common employment will be defeated. He must see that all his machinery and plant are, and are kept, in proper condition and free from defect, and that the system of work and methods of control are proper and reasonable. This appears to put a wide duty upon a master but it is not so, for he escapes liability if he has delegated his duties to a competent subordinate.

A master is, of course, liable for his personal wrongful or negligent acts, and if the employment is of a dangerous nature he must use all reasonable precautions for the safety of his servant. This includes telling the servant of any defect of which the master knows or ought to know.

Duties Imposed on Master by Statute.—The best-known duties are those imposed by the Factory Acts and the Regulations thereunder requiring the master to fence dangerous machinery and holes. The acts relating to the master's trade or business have to be looked at in each case to ascertain what, if any, is the duty; and further to see if the servant is expressly or impliedly given a remedy if injured by a breach of the duty.

Often the master is liable both criminally and civilly.

The duty imposed by statute is absolute. It is no defence for the master to say that fencing is commercially impracticable, or for him to prove that he has not been himself guilty of personal negligence, or that he has delegated the duty. For the same reason "common employment" is no defence nor can the master say the servant undertook the risk (i.e. plead "volenti"). This has been recently affirmed by the Court of Appeal. Contributory negligence by the servant has recently been held to be a good defence. It is submitted that it is not.

Another recent decision lays down that a breach of statutory duty is the "personal negligence or wilful act of the employer," so that an action for such breach lies independently of the Workmen's Compensation Act, 1925.

Death and the Fatal Accidents (Lord Campbell's) Act.—No action can be brought at Common Law by the representatives of a servant killed while at work, but by Lord Campbell's Act, right of action is given to certain dependants of the deceased in respect of the loss of pecuniary help; or the expectation thereof, which they actually suffer by the death. Thus, if the servant is killed in such circumstances that the master would have been liable had the deceased been injured only, the widow, if she was dependent upon her late husband's financial support, can recover damages from the master.

Employer's Liability Act, 1880.—The result of this Act is broadly that a workman who has been injured is given the same rights against his employer as a stranger would have. In other words the defence of "Common Employment" is made unavailable to the master in certain cases. The Act applies only to "Workmen," by which is meant those employed in manual labour and railway servants. Domestic servants and menials are expressly excluded.

In order to bring a successful action under the Act the workman must have been injured through one of the five specific causes set out in the Act. These are : defective machinery or plant which the employer, or some person to whom he has delegated the duty, has negligently failed to discover or to remedy; the negligence of any person

entrusted with superintendence by the employer; the negligence of any person to whose orders the workman was bound to, and did, conform at the time of injury; the act or omission of any servant in obedience to rules, bye-laws or the particular instructions of his employer or his employer's delegate; and the negligence of certain fellow servants upon a railway.

Actions under this Act are seldom met in practice because the master may rely successfully upon any defence which would be good against a stranger, and because the damages recoverable are limited to the estimated earnings, during the three years preceding the injury, of a person in the same grade employed during those years in like employment and in the district. Earnings, however, include payments in kind and overtime for another employer. The workman may contract out of the Act, that is, he may expressly agree to forego its benefits.

Notice of injury must be given to the employer within six weeks except in cases of death, and the action must be brought within six months of the injury and brought in the County Court.

Workmen's Compensation Act.—Valuable protection is given to servants by the Workmen's Compensation Act (q.v.). This act imposes a wide statutory obligation on a master to compensate his servant for any personal injury he sustains by accident arising out of, and in the course of, the employment. The Act applies notwithstanding a contract to the contrary.

By section 29 the master is not liable to any proceedings independently of the Act, except where the injury has been caused by his personal negligence or wilful act (including, so it has been decided by the House of Lords, breach of statutory duty), or by that of some person for whose act or default the employer is liable. The employer cannot be liable both under the Workmen's Compensation Act and independently of it; but if the servant brings an action at Common Law, or under some other Act, and fails, the Court may, with his consent, assess compensation under the Workmen's Compensation Act, deducting therefrom some or all of the costs of the other proceedings.

It will be apparent to the reader that it is usually safer to proceed under the Workmen's Compensation Act, although the lure of substantial damages, and not merely assessed compensation, may be very great. Most employers insure against liability. (*See* WORKMEN'S COMPENSATION for a full account and *see* MASTER AND SERVANT; PRINCIPAL AND AGENT.)

EMPLOYMENT AGENCY.—Every person who carries on for the purpose of gain the business of keeping a female domestic servants' registry must register his name, address and premises where the business is carried on with the local council. Bye-laws may be made by the local council prescribing the books which must be kept and regulating the conduct of the business. The council are entitled to send Inspectors to the premises to examine the books. Failure to register or to keep proper books is a criminal offence punishable by fine, and the Court has power to suspend or cancel the registration.

In London, all employment agencies, whether for domestic servants or not, must obtain a licence from the London County Council (or Corporation of the City of London in the City area). The licence costs £2 2s. 0d., is valid for one year and may be renewed at a fee of £1 0s. 0d. Bye-laws have been made relating to the books which must be kept and regulating generally the carrying on of the business.

ENCLOSED PREMISES.—Any person who is found on any enclosed premises for an unlawful purpose may be convicted and sentenced to six months' imprisonment. Enclosed premises include dwelling-houses, warehouses, stables or other outhouses and also any yard or garden. In order for this offence to be committed it is essential that the accused person shall be there for the purpose of committing some crime, although he may not actually intend to commit the crime on that particular occasion.

ENDOWED SCHOOLS.—(*See* EDUCATION.)

ENGAGEMENT RING.—It is curious that it was not until 1926 that the English Courts were asked to decide the rights of the parties to an engagement ring after an engagement has been broken off. The point came up for decision in a case tried in that year, before (appropriately enough) the famous bachelor Judge, Mr. Justice McCardie. The action was brought by a young lady for breach of promise of mar-

riage. The defendant, whilst admitting the engagement, said it was the plaintiff herself who broke it off, and he counterclaimed for the return of the engagement ring. The jury found that it was the defendant and not the plaintiff who broke off the engagement, and awarded the latter damages.

As to the ring, Mr. Justice McCardie delivered a considered judgment in which he said, "It is curious that, after the centuries in which so many engagements to marry have been made in hope, but dissolved in disillusion, the questions now before me have not been long ago determined by direct decision."

After reviewing the cases bearing on the point he went on, "If a woman who has received a ring refuses to fulfil the conditions of the gift she must return it. So, on the other hand, I think that if the man has without a recognized legal justification refused to carry out his promise of marriage, he cannot demand the return of the engagement ring. It matters not in law that the repudiation of the promise may turn out to the ultimate advantage of both parties. . . . If the engagement to marry be dissolved by mutual consent, then, in the absence of agreement to the contrary, the engagement ring and like gifts must, I think, be returned by each party to the other. . . . If the marriage does not take place either through the death of, or through a disability recognized by law on the part of the person giving the ring or other conditional gift, then I take the view that in such case the condition is to be implied that the gift shall be returned." In this illuminating judgment Mr. Justice McCardie, with his usual thoroughness and clarity, laid down the law applicable to the various contingencies that can arise in such cases.

ENGINE SPARKS.—If a steam engine is used, whether on road or rail, and throws out sparks which set fire to neighbouring property, or do any other damage, the owner of the engine will be liable for the damage so caused, even though he took every care to prevent the escape of the sparks. He may use a dangerous machine of this kind if he likes, but if it causes damage he will have no excuse, unless he can say the damage was caused by something beyond his control, e.g. that the spark was thrown out as a result of unauthorized interference with the machine by a third person. If, however, the owner of the engine is authorized to use it by statute (as most railways are), he will not be liable for damage done by sparks if he can shew that the engines were carefully constructed and that, even so, it was impossible to prevent the escape of sparks. This avoidance of liability seemed to bear particularly hard on farmers whose lands adjoined railways and it was, therefore, provided in the Railway Fire Acts, 1905 and 1923, that railway companies shall be liable for the first £200 of damage done by sparks or cinders from their locomotives to agricultural land or crops, even though the railway had taken every precaution to prevent their escape. (*See also* CHIMNEY; FIRE.)

ENGROSS.—When a deed is copied out from a draft so that it may be ready for execution by the parties, it is said to be engrossed. In order that such documents may be preserved for some considerable time they are usually engrossed upon parchment or some other durable substance. The name engrossment is applied to the copy of the legal document which is prepared from the draft as agreed between the parties to such document, or their respective solicitors. After being signed (if the document is to be under hand only), or executed (signed, sealed and delivered), if it is to be under seal, it becomes the Conveyance, Lease, Mortgage, Assignment, or other form of legal document, according to the nature of transaction affected. (*See also* SALE OF LAND; LANDLORD AND TENANT; MORTGAGES.)

ENTAILS.—The original conception of an estate tail was an estate in land which could not be disposed of by its owner for the time being, but which would descend in the direct line from father to son independently of any attempted alienation or devise. For over four hundred years, however, it has been possible for the owner of property which was subject to an entail to get rid of the restrictions and "bar" or disentail it. The effect of so doing was to bring the entail to an end, to deprive the owner's heirs of their rights in the land and to make the owner himself the absolute unfettered owner. It has become progressively easier to bar an entail, and the position now is that

the tenant in tail (as the owner is called) can do so by any conveyance of the property during his life and even by devising it in his will. It is not necessary for him to insert any special provisions, as disentailment will follow automatically.

The results which it was sought to obtain by means of the entail can still be procured to a certain extent, and property can still be retained in the one family by means of settlements (q.v.), provided that at the end of the period permitted by the rule against perpetuities (roughly 75 years) all the restraints on alienation have come to an end and there is some person who is the absolute unfettered owner. (*See* PERPETUITIES.)

Despite its comparative impotence, the estate tail is still commonly used in settlements in company with other provisions; the usual practice in a marriage settlement being to give an estate tail to the eldest (unborn) son of the persons about to marry.

In order to create an estate tail, certain technical words must be employed in the deed or will. The only effective expressions are ". . . to A in tail," or " . . . to A and the heirs of his body." If any other words are used they will create not an estate tail but an estate in fee simple (unfettered ownership). By the addition of certain words it is possible to narrow the class of persons to whom the property will descend, if the entail is not barred by the tenant in tail during his life, or by will. Thus, if the expression was ". . . to A and the heirs of his body begotten upon X," then only the joint children of A and X could succeed. The children of either of them by another marriage could have no claim. Again, ". . . to A and the heirs male of his body" or "to A in tail male" limits the possible successors to the male descendants of A. If no such provision is inserted and A dies without having barred the entail leaving no male descendants but only daughters, all these daughters will take the property together. In 1926 it became possible for the first time to create an estate tail in personal property; previously they had been confined to realty, i.e. property in land except leases. (*See* PERPETUITIES; REAL PROPERTY; SETTLEMENTS.)

ENTERTAINMENTS DUTY.—Entertainments Duty is charged on all payments for admission to an entertainment.

It was first imposed as a war-time measure in 1916.

An entertainment is defined as including an exhibition, performance, amusement, game or sport to which persons are admitted for payment. It has been decided that where a man lets a room so that people may watch a procession from its windows, he must pay entertainments duty on the rent he so receives. So too, if a subscription to a sports club entitles the subscriber to watch matches and tournaments provided by the club, entertainments duty must be paid on a proportion of the subscriptions, at any rate in cases where ordinary members of the public are admitted only on payment. A public dinner, whist drive or dance is not an entertainment, though it may become so if a concert is combined with it in such a way as to become an important part of what the public paid to enjoy. Even where admission is free, duty may be payable on seats that, for the convenience of the public, are reserved at a fee.

There are a number of entertainments for which duty is not payable, e.g. (i) where the whole of the receipts are devoted to philanthropic or charitable purposes, without any deduction being made for expenses (but if the Commissioners are satisfied that the deducted expenses do not exceed 50% of the takings, and that such net proceeds were all devoted to philanthropic or charitable purposes, they may refund the duty paid); (ii) where the purpose of the entertainment is wholly educational, or where, if the entertainment is provided by a society not established for profit, its purpose is partly educational and partly scientific; (iii) entertainments provided by schools or other educational institutions where the performers are past or present members of the school; (iv) exhibitions by societies not established for profit.

The tax is collected by means of stamps, unless some other method is approved by the Commissioners, e.g. mechanical registers or the furnishing of returns by the proprietor.

Any person admitted for payment without paying duty is liable to a penalty of £5, and the proprietor to a penalty of £50. Numerous "Entertainments Duty Regulations" were made in August, 1921, and may be purchased from the Stationery Office or through any stationer. They provide, for example, that on admission the ticket and duty-stamp shall be torn in half and one half given to the person admitted, the other half to be retained by the proprietor until noon the next day.

ENTICEMENT.—The right of action for enticement of a wife is a curious relic of a distant past—a past when the position of married women was very different from what it is now; yet some of the causes of action evolved in those days still survive. A husband can by an action for enticement recover damages against anyone who without lawful justification persuades his wife to cease to reside with him.

Mr. Justice McCardie's Judgment. —The present law on the subject of enticement was defined by the Court of Appeal in 1932 in the well-known case of Place v. Searle. The plaintiff was a grocer's assistant at Cambridge. His wife lived with him and took in lodgers. The defendant was a doctor practising in Cambridge. He had been on terms of friendship with the plaintiff's wife for several years before 1931; he had made her gifts of flowers and fruit; he had provided a horse for her from time to time so that they could ride together; and they had shot together at some rough shooting he rented near Cambridge. To quote Mr. Justice McCardie, who tried the case: "It is only just to point out here in the clearest way that there was no allegation of adultery against the defendant nor was there the slightest evidence of it."

One evening in the summer of 1931 a violent scene took place between plaintiff and his wife. As the result of a telephone message the defendant came round to their house. Again to quote Mr. Justice McCardie as to what happened: "What was then actually said is, of course, in dispute, but I point out again that there is no suggestion that the defendant then said anything to the wife to persuade her to leave the plaintiff. The plaintiff then invited the defendant to fight him. The fight took place. The plaintiff was defeated. . . . Such was the state of affairs when the alleged 'enticement' took place. . . . The defendant then took the wife's arm and said: 'Come on, Gwen. We will go. . . .' The defendant escorted the wife to his motor-car and took her to spend the rest of the night with one of her old family friends."

At the trial of the case at Cambridge Assizes the jury disagreed. Mr. Justice McCardie adjourned the case for legal argument in London, and eventually held that there was no evidence on which the jury could find in favour of the plaintiff. In the course of a remarkable judgment he said: "It seems to me that the only inference on the whole of the above circumstances is that, when the defendant said: 'Come on, Gwen. We will go,' he merely recognized the obvious fact that it was useless further to oppose the wife's intention to leave her husband. So far from the circumstances tending to shew that it was the defendant's wish to induce the wife to leave the house against her own desire, they tend most strongly, and indeed inevitably, to the opposite conclusion."

Later in his judgment he said: "I should like to add three things, in view of several questions raised in the speeches or arguments of counsel. First, it seems to be clear that the position as between husbands and wives and third parties calls for reconsideration by the law in view of the new status of married women. Secondly, the rights of a married woman to form her independent friendships and enjoy her own amusements can never be solved by the law but must be determined by the standards of loyalty, of courtesy, and of good sense; and, thirdly, that the comfort and happiness of married life rest not on statutes or decisions but on matters that lie beyond and above the realm of law."

The Appeal.—The plaintiff appealed to the Court of Appeal, where the matter was considered by Lords Justices Scrutton, Greer and Slesser. The Court overruled Mr. Justice McCardie and ordered a new trial.

Lord Justice Scrutton said: "It seems to be clear that at the present day a husband has a right to the consortium of his wife, and the wife to the consortium of her husband, and that each has a cause of action against a third party who, without justification, destroys that consortium. The old law has been altered to this extent, that the means of enforcing the right to consortium have been materially weakened. There are dicta in the old cases to the effect that a husband has the dominion and property over his wife; but . . . it is clear that whatever rights the husband may

possess he cannot enforce them by the physical confinement of his wife; he cannot seize her if she attempts to leave the consortium and lock her up. But there are still means of enforcing the right of the husband and the right of the wife. . . .

There being such a right it follows, and it has been so decided in numerous cases, that any person who, without justification, interferes with that right is liable to an action in tort. . . . It is quite sufficient to support the action if a wife of equal will with that of the defendant is persuaded to depart from the consortium of the husband. . . . That being so, the question on the facts is whether there was evidence on which the jury could reasonably come to the conclusion that the defendant's conduct offended against the rule of law I have stated. In considering the question, I agree that it is not enough to find one statement in the plaintiff's evidence which, if believed, would constitute a breach of his right; we have to look at the whole of the evidence, and unless we can say that the statement of the plaintiff cannot be accepted, because all the evidence is the other way, the case must be left to the jury."

Lord Justices Greer and Slesser in substance agreed with the views of Lord Justice Scrutton, and the plaintiff obtained judgment for £500 damages.

EQUITY.—The expression Equity in ordinary speech usually means that which is right in fairness, or in moral or natural justice, as distinct from that which is right according to strict law. When the expression is used in its legal technical sense, however, it has a very different meaning and may be defined as those legal rules which until the Courts of Equity and Common Law were united were administered solely in the Courts of Equity. This definition may seem an unsatisfactory one, but it should be made clear that the difference between the rules of law and the rules of equity has nothing to do with natural justice but is purely a matter of history. Equitable rules are not necessarily more fair or more in accordance with natural justice than legal rules.

Historical Distinction.—It is impossible to understand the division of Equity in English law without some consideration of English legal history. From the Norman Conquest until the 13th or 14th

11

century all law was administered by the King's Courts, known as the Courts of King's Bench, Common Pleas, and Exchequer. When the Judges of these Courts first came to hear cases there was practically no statute law or previous decisions to guide them, and they had to make up their minds in most cases simply by what they considered fair and reasonable, and in accordance so far as possible with the local customs and rule of the district where the case was heard.

The endeavour of these Judges was to make the law throughout the country uniform. Gradually, however, as a result of their decisions, a rigid system of common law grew up, and in early times we come across one of the most significant features of early law in all countries, namely, that any change in the law was undesirable. It is difficult for us to-day to understand this feeling when our Parliament has its full time taken up in dealing with masses of new legislation each year, but in the times of which we are talking, one of the features for which the law relied for its force was that it was right, and any deliberate and conscious alteration would have amounted to an admission that the law previously had been wrong and therefore would have weakened its force.

Thus we find that the common law when it had developed became a very harsh and rigid system not easily capable of change. It had been built up, as we have seen, in the period from the 11th to the 14th centuries and no doubt presented sufficiently well the public opinion and legal requirements of the country during those times. When, however, alterations in the mode of life of persons and the departure from the purely military organization of the early feudal system introduced at the Norman Conquest made some alteration necessary in the law, the common law was too rigid to admit of any change or to recognize any new rights which were made necessary or desirable.

Equity and the Chancellor.—At that time the idea that the King was the fountain head of Justice had still a real practical meaning, and persons who had been unable to obtain their rights from the ordinary Courts had long been accustomed to petition the King asking him to give them the redress which they were unable to get elsewhere. The King and his Council at an early date referred these petitions to the Chancellor, who was at the time usually a Churchman and trained in the Canon Law of the Church and in Roman Law. At first he decided these cases without any fixed rule simply on the natural justice of each, but gradually after about 1600, a system of precedents grew up, and definite rules were propounded and followed by the Chancellors in giving their decisions, so that by the 18th century the rules of equity which the Chancellor administered had become as fixed and definite as the rules of common law. The Common Law Courts had developed to some extent but still very largely represented the public morality and requirements of the period of their early growth, that is to say, from the Norman Conquest to the 14th century.

The rules of equity, having become equally fixed and rigid, represented the requirements and public morality of the 15th to 17th centuries. Any change in the law now required had to be made by legislation, and gave rise to the enormous number of statutes touching every part of the law which have been passed from the beginning of the 19th century to the present time.

Up to the last quarter of the 19th century the position with regard to law and equity was that the two systems existed side by side, the principles of each being administered in different courts. The common law recognized and protected certain rights, and equity recognized and protected other rights, and if a person, wishing to enforce or protect an equitable right, went to a Court of Common Law, the Court would not be able to assist him and he would lose his case.

This was obviously a very unsatisfactory state of affairs and gave rise to what now would appear ridiculous situations. Thus a plaintiff might obtain a judgment in a Common Law Court, relying on the principles of the common law; the defendant might have some defence which would be recognized in an Equity Court but not in a Common Law Court. The defendant would then go to the Equity Court and obtain an order to prevent the plaintiff from enforcing the common law judgment, and so the equitable rules would be recognized. Such an order was called a Common Injunction. Another weakness in the division lay in the fact that even when a Common Law Court recognized the rights of the plaintiff, i.e. when they were common law rights—and was willing to help him—there were several important remedies which could only be given by a Court of Equity. Thus, a Common Law Court had no power to order a person who had broken a contract to fulfil his obligations under the contract—i.e. to order specific performance—nor could it make an order forbidding a person from doing some act which would injure some other person— i.e. an injunction. All the Common Law Court could do was to order one party to pay *money damages* to the other. Thus, if a party wished to obtain specific performance or an injunction, it was necessary to go to a Court of Equity. When he was there, however, he could not in addition claim damages, which was purely a common law remedy.

The Judicature Act.—It is a remarkable fact that this state of affairs existed practically unchanged until 1873. In that year the Judicature Act was passed which amalgamated all the Courts of Law and Equity into the Supreme Court of Judicature, and declared that any principles, whether legal or equitable, should be reorganized and any remedy should be available in any division of this new Court. All that the Act did was to provide that both law and equity should be administered in the same Court. It did not, however, affect the distinction between legal and equitable rules and this distinction still exists. It is frequently of considerable importance to decide whether a person has a legal or merely an equitable right.

The importance of the distinction between legal and equitable rights will be seen from the following example. If A wishes to borrow money from his bank on the security of some land, he may give the bank either a legal mortgage of the land or merely an equitable mortgage. If he signs a deed transferring the property to the bank, that will be a legal mortgage. If, however, he merely hands over to the bank the title deeds of the land without signing any transfer, this is merely an equitable mortgage, that is, it would have been recognized before 1873 in a Court of Equity but not in a Court of Common Law. Any Court will now recognize it by reason of the Judicature Act, but will recognize it only to the extent to which it would have been recognized by a Court of Equity before 1873—i.e. as an equitable mortgage. Whether the mortgage be legal or equitable the bank is entitled to have the debt paid out of the land. If, however, A fraudulently gets back the title deeds from the bank under some pretext, and transfers the land by a proper transfer to some other person who does not know of the mortgage, that person will have a legal right to the property, which will prevail over the bank's right, if that is equitable, but will not prevail if the bank has a legal right.

In addition to merging the administration of the two principles the Judicature Act declared that where the rules of law and equity were in conflict the rules of equity should prevail.

Matters Controlled by Equity.—The matters which were governed by equitable rules are still usually considered by the Chancery Division of the High Court of Justice. The most important of these is undoubtedly the Doctrine of Trusts. The Common Law never recognized the rule that, if property is given to one person to be used by him on behalf of some other person, i.e. on trust—he is bound to use it for that purpose. This had always been recognized by equity. Other important matters within the province of equity are the dissolution of partnerships, the administration of the property of deceased persons, the redemption of foreclosure of mortgages, and the specific performance of contracts. (*See* EXECUTORS AND ADMINISTRATORS; MORTGAGES; PARTNERSHIP; SPECIFIC PERFORMANCE: TRUSTS.)

EQUITY OF REDEMPTION.—When one person transfers to another land in security for payment of money which has been lent to him, i.e. mortgages his property, it is usually provided in the deed that if the money is not paid on a certain date the property shall belong in future to the mortgagee, i.e. the lender. This was the rule of common law, but equity always allowed the mortgagor, i.e. the borrower, to get his land back on repaying the amount of the loan even after the day fixed for payment by the contract, and although the estate had therefore become forfeited at law. Even where the transaction under which the property is transferred is not stated on the face of it to be a mortgage, but appears as an out and out sale, equity would always allow evidence to be admitted for the purpose of shewing that the transaction really was a mortgage and would allow the borrower of the money to have the land back again. Equity gives the borrower this right even though the contract states in express terms that he shall not be entitled to redeem after the date fixed.

This right, which the mortgagor has, to recover the land on payment of the money, is known as the Equity of Redemption and is an estate, i.e. a right, in the land which can be transferred by the mortgagor like any other estate, e.g. by sale or by being mortgaged.

The mortgagee has the legal title, i.e. the title recognized by the Common Law—whereas the mortgagor had the "equitable" title of redemption.

Clogs.—In order to secure to the mortgagor his right to redeem, equity always holds that any conditions limiting the right are void. Thus, any provision which acts as a penalty on the mortgagor, making it more expensive for him to redeem, or is unfair as between mortgagee and mortgagor, would be held to be void. Such a provision is said to be a "clog" on the equity. The mortgagee may stipulate for some benefit to himself from the mortgage in addition to the payment of principal and interest without this being regarded as a clog, provided that when the money is finally repaid, the mortgagee gets the property free from any restrictions.

Thus, brewers may lend money to the licensee of a public-house on mortgage of the public-house and stipulate, in addition, that during the continuance of the mortgage the licensee shall buy his beer from the mortgagees and from no one else. This is valid. If, however, the terms were that even *after* the mortgage had been paid off the licensee should continue to buy his beer exclusively from the mortgagees for a fixed period, the stipulation would be void and would be disregarded as being a clog on the equity. (*See* FORECLOSURE; MORTGAGE.)

ERSKINE, Lord (1750-1823).—Lord Erskine started his career in the Navy, but owing to a chance interview with Lord Mansfield he entered for the Law and became one of the greatest advocates England has ever seen. He was an immediate success and he displayed great courage and eloquence in all the principal political trials of the time. He defended Lord George Gordon, Thomas Paine, author of the "Rights of Man," and Queen Caroline as her Attorney-General. He was later made Lord Chancellor.

ESCAPE.—It is a misdemeanour for a prisoner in lawful custody to escape. The offence is committed not only by the prisoner himself but also by any persons who assist in the escape. It is, of course, no defence to show that the prisoner was innocent of the crime for which he was in custody. Any gaoler or other custodian who, from neglect of duty, allows a prisoner to escape can be convicted of a misdemeanour.

ESCAPED LUNATIC.—When a lunatic has escaped from an asylum he may be retaken at any time within 14 days of his escape. If, however, he retains his freedom for a longer time than this a new order certifying him insane must be made. (*See* DETENTION OF LUNATICS; LUNATICS.)

ESCHEAT.—Ever since the Norman Conquest it has been the fundamental theory of the English Common Law that the ultimate ownership of all land is in the King, who has irrevocably granted parts of it to his different subjects whilst retaining at the same time a residual interest in it. If the owner of land dies without disposing of his property by his will, and without leaving any next of kin (*see* INTESTACY) to succeed to him, the land was said to escheat to the King in virtue of this residual interest. In a few very rare cases where land had been held by one family since before 1290 it might, on that family becoming extinct, have escheated to the descendants of the man who had sold it to them before 1290.

Both varieties of escheat were abolished in 1925. The right of the Crown to claim property in land was extended to all cases where a man dies intestate without next of kin, and is now identical with its right to take other kinds of property in similar circumstances as *bona vacantia*. (*See* INTESTACY.)

ESCROW.—When a Deed or other document, such as a bill of exchange, is delivered to a person on the terms that it is only to become effective on a certain event happening, it is said to be delivered as an escrow. When the event happens the person holding the deed hands it over to the other party to it and it thereupon becomes effective. If the event never happens the deed never comes into force. A deed cannot be held in escrow by a person who is a party to it. Delivery to such a person will probably amount to effective delivery, although it is stated to be subject to a condition. (*See* DEED.)

ESTATE.—In connection with the law of Real Property (land) the word estate means one of the different kinds of ownership of land which may exist. The origin of this use of the word is probably to be found in the fact that in feudal times a man's status was determined by his ownership of land, so that the ownership itself came to be called his status or estate.

The different kinds of estate may be divided into freehold and leasehold estates. The former were "real property," the latter only "personal property," though they were called "chattels real" to distinguish them from pure personalty. (For the difference between real and personal property *see* REAL PROPERTY.)

The possible freehold estates in land are the estate in fee simple or absolute unfettered ownership, the fee tail or estate tail (*see* ENTAIL), the estate for life (*see* LIFE INTERESTS), and the estate *pur autre vie* (old law French for "for somebody else's life.") (*See* REAL PROPERTY.)

ESTATE AGENT.—An estate agent is a person who carries on the business of negotiating sales of property, both land and dwelling-houses. The scope of his business also includes the negotiation of leases of property. An estate agent has no authority to make a contract of sale if only authorized to procure a purchaser. If he is authorized to sell he may sign an agreement so as to bind his principal, but his authority does not extend to the making of conditions about the title, nor to the receiving of the purchase money. The scale of fees or commission authorized to be charged by an estate agent was laid down by the Institute of Auctioneers and Estate Agents in 1929. (*See also* HOUSE AGENT; PRINCIPAL AND AGENT.)

ESTATE DUTY.—All property that passes on the death of any person after 1894 is liable for estate duty. But it is often difficult to decide what property can be said to pass on a death—e.g. life-insurance money (but not workmen's compensation) is deemed to be property passing at the death, and is liable to pay duty. It is specially provided that a gift made by the deceased less than three years before his death is subject to death duties as if it had been part of his estate, except if it was a gift for a public or charitable purpose when the period is only a year. Even then, it must have been an out and out gift made in good faith, and not such as might have been regarded as a mere loan: for instance, the person to whom the gift was made ought to have taken it away and used it exclusively as his own. A declaration of trust is equivalent to a gift for this purpose. Gifts made in consideration of marriage are not chargeable, nor gifts made in the normal course of the deceased's expenditure. Property held by the deceased as trustee is not chargeable with duty. Where duty has been paid on an estate on the death of a husband, no further duty is payable on the death of his wife, and vice versa.

In arriving at the *rate* (or percentage) at which the various items in the estate will be liable for estate duties, all the different properties are valued and aggregated together. From this aggregate certain deductions may be made, e.g. in respect of debts, funeral expenses and duties paid in foreign countries. When the aggregate value of the estate so arrived at exceeds £100 but does not exceed £500, the rate is 1 %; when it does not exceed £1,000, 2 %; £5,000, 3 %; £10,000, 4 %; £12,500, 5 %; £15,000, 6 %; and so on, by gradual steps, until the limit is reached at 50 % for £2,000,000 or over. But estates worth only £300 or £500 may pay a fixed sum of 30/- or 50/- respectively. Very considerable reductions in the amount to be paid (sometimes amounting to 50 %) are made when deaths occur at short intervals in the one family.

Generally, the duty on all personal property and leaseholds is to be paid by the executors or administrators out of the residue (i.e. out of whatever is left of the estate after distributing legacies and land specifically mentioned in the will). In the case of land other than leaseholds, the duty is to be paid by the person to whom the land devolves, and such duties may be paid by instalments. The duty on personalty and leaseholds, however, must be paid by the executor or administrator when he delivers the Inland Revenue affidavit, which is the list of the deceased's property with values, and which is delivered when application is made for probate. Interest at 4% is payable on the duty as from the date of death. But in the case of lands other than leaseholds, the duty should be paid before the expiration of six months from the death (or by instalments), and interest runs similarly.

The whole management of estate duty is controlled by the Commissioners of Inland Revenue, who have considerable powers conferred upon them, in order to ensure that they can recover the amounts properly due to them. Appeal lies from them to the High Court or County Court.

ESTOPPEL.—An estoppel is a rule by which a person is prevented from denying the existence of some state of facts which he has previously asserted. Estoppels may be of four kinds.

1. *Estoppel by Record.*—This is where a judgment has already been given by the Court between the same parties and on the same facts. Neither of the parties is allowed to prove that the facts were otherwise than as found by the judgment.

2. *Estoppel by Deed.*—Where a person has entered into an engagement or contract by deed, and has set out in the deed certain facts, he will not at any later time be allowed to deny that these facts are as they are stated, or to contradict the deed, even though the facts are wrongly stated in the deed. This estoppel, like the first, only applies as between the parties to the deed or those to whom the rights of the parties have been transferred, e.g. their executors or assignees. The estoppel cannot be relied upon by a person who knew at the time that the statements were untrue, or where the deed has been obtained by fraud, and can be set aside for that reason.

3. *Estoppel by Agreement.*—This is much the same as the last, but arises in cases where the agreement is not by deed but is in writing or verbal. The most frequent example of it arises where a landlord has let premises to a tenant. The tenant is estopped from denying that the landlord had a title to the premises at the time he let them. Thus, if the tenant is interfered

with in the possession of the premises by someone who alleges that the landlord had no right to let them, his remedy is to sue the landlord for breach of the covenant for "quiet enjoyment" (*see* LANDLORD AND TENANT); and *he* cannot deny that the landlord had a right to the premises when let. Another example of the same principle arises between Bailor and Bailee, that is, where any person (the bailor) delivers goods into the possession of some other person (the bailee) for some purpose, such as safe custody or for the purpose of having something done to the goods. The bailee cannot deny that the bailor had a right to the goods at the time when they were delivered to him.

4. *Estoppel by Conduct.*—Where a person has made a clear and unambiguous statement of fact to some other person with the intention that the other person should act on that statement, and where the other person has so acted and has suffered some detriment through doing so, the first person will be estopped from denying the proof of the statement made even though he made the statement innocently believing it to be true. The same principle applies where a person acts in such a way as to lead others to believe that a certain state of affairs exists. (*See* EVIDENCE; LANDLORD AND TENANT.)

ESTREAT.—When persons go bail for prisoners they enter into recognisances for the appearance of the prisoner when required. If the prisoner fails to appear they may forfeit their recognisances and be required to pay to the Crown the amount of them. When this happens the recognisances are said to be estreated. The term is also applied to the forfeiture of recognisances entered into by people to be of good behaviour or to keep the peace.

EVICTION.—Eviction means the turning out of a person from premises of which he is in occupation, by a person having a right to the possession of them. Actual physical expulsion of the occupier from the premises is not necessary in order to constitute an eviction in the eyes of the law, for if the landlord enters and uses the premises while the tenant is still in possession, that will amount to an eviction of the tenant.

A landlord has the right to enter premises occupied by his tenant, at the end of the time limited in the lease, or after the expiry of a notice to quit if there is no written agreement showing the terms of the tenancy. From the expiry of the tenancy, a tenant remaining in occupation of the premises becomes a trespasser unless he is in occupation of a dwelling house controlled by the Rent Restriction Acts. (*See* SPECIAL SUPPLEMENT "RENT RESTRICTIONS.") In that event he remains on after the expiry of the notice to quit as a statutory tenant, and cannot be evicted except under an order for possession granted by a County Court. Such an order will only be granted if certain statutory conditions are complied with.

When a tenant remains on as a trespasser the landlord has the choice of two methods of removing him:—

(i) He may take legal proceedings if he is in any doubt as to his rights, and obtain a judgment for possession of the premises within a specified time. If the tenant remains in possession after the time fixed in the order of the Court, the landlord may, by filing an affidavit stating that the order has not been obeyed, obtain a writ for possession of the premises which will be enforced by the officers of the Court.

(ii) If the landlord does not wish to go through the somewhat slow process of obtaining an order for possession from the Court, he may himself remove the tenant, using only such force as is necessary. He must take care that he does not use more force than is necessary, otherwise he may render himself liable to an action by the tenant for damages for assault.

Any person seeking to evict another from premises must himself have a legal right to the possession of the premises, before he takes any steps to evict the occupier. Thus, if a landlord re-enters premises with the intention of taking possession of them because the tenant has broken one of the covenants in the lease, he must do so under an express right of re-entry given to him in the lease. If such right of re-entry is not reserved in the lease, and the landlord re-enters before the expiry of the tenancy, he will himself be a trespasser, and may be sued for damages by the tenant.

When a tenant has been evicted from premises, he is no longer liable to pay rent, even if the eviction takes the form of the landlord coming into the premises and remaining there while the tenant is still in occupation.

When a person has entered and remained upon premises without the consent of the owner, paying nothing for the use and occupation of them, he is called a "squatter" and may be evicted by the owner at any time, since he has no right to possession. (*See also* DANGEROUS PREMISES; EJECTION FROM PREMISES; and SPECIAL SUPPLEMENT "RENT RESTRICTIONS.")

EVIDENCE.—Whoever alleges anything as a fact at any trial must prove it by means of evidence. There are, however, many rules governing the way in which matters can be proved, and these are called rules of evidence. These rules are necessary in order to keep a case within reasonable limits and to prevent the attention of the Judge and jury from being distracted from those matters which are really vital to the issue.

The Rule of Relevancy.—The first and, perhaps, the most important rule of evidence is that nothing shall be said in evidence which is not relevant to the actual point which has to be decided in the case. This is called the rule of relevancy. Thus, evidence may not be given, in general, as to transactions or matters which are not the actual subject of the enquiry which is being conducted at the time. In a criminal case, for instance, the fact that an accused person has committed some other crime, either before or after the occasion on which he is alleged to have committed the crime for which he is being tried, is not, in general, regarded as relevant. Of course, where the commission of some other crime has a definite bearing upon the question as to whether the prisoner committed the crime with which he is charged, then it may be gone into. For instance, suppose a man who is proved to have been in possession of poison is charged with murdering a person by means of it, then, if he says that he had the poison for an innocent purpose, such as killing the weeds in his garden, it would be open to the prosecution to show that he had used this poison, not as he said for an innocent purpose, but in order to kill or attempt to kill some person. Great care has to be exercised in deciding whether or not evidence of this kind really does tend to shew that the accused person is guilty of the crime for which he is being tried. There is always a danger that such evidence will tend to discredit the accused person and shew him to be a bad character, without, at the same time, really proving or assisting to prove that he committed the actual crime he is then charged with.

The rule of relevancy forbids the prosecution to shew that a person is of a bad character, unless the evidence as to his character is otherwise admissible. This question is also governed by the provisions of the Criminal Evidence Act (1898), which forbids the prosecution to ask any question of a prisoner who gives evidence tending to shew that he has a bad character, unless he has given evidence as to his good character, or has atttacked the character of the witnesses for the prosecution or any other person charged jointly with him.

Opinion.—Another example of the rule of relevancy is that which excludes in general the opinions of witnesses in evidence. Witnesses are only allowed to testify to what they saw or heard, not what they thought. That this should be so is clear, because it is for the Court to decide what the effect of acts or words are, and the opinions of witnesses are clearly irrelevant. There are certain important exceptions to this rule. On matters of science or art, expert witnesses can be called and are allowed to give their opinion on questions as to which they are experts. In some cases, even the opinions of persons who are not experts may be received. These are confined to matters where it is really impossible to convey to the Court the facts upon which they can base an opinion. Thus, where the issue is whether a person was or was not drunk, a witness, even although he is not a medical man, is allowed to state his opinion as to whether the accused was drunk or not.

What is Hearsay?—Another important rule of evidence is that which provides that only the best available evidence as to any matter may be given. The most important of this is the rule excluding hearsay. This rule is frequently misunderstood, but may be shortly stated thus:—

A witness may not say what he has been told about some fact in issue. He may only testify to what he saw happen, not to what he heard a third party say did happen. Thus,

on the trial of a person for dangerous driving, a policeman is not allowed to say that he was told about the conduct of the accused by some spectator or other. It is necessary for that spectator himself to attend at the Court and say what he saw. Of course, in such a case, a policeman could say what the accused himself said, because the statements of the accused are relevant to the issue. Again, what is said in the presence of the accused person is relevant, in so far as it draws an answer from him, or if it is made in circumstances which would lead one to expect an answer. Here the object of such evidence is to shew, not the truth of the statement, but the effect upon the accused person, and to explain his answers or his silence.

There are several exceptions to the rule of hearsay. The most important of these is that which allows evidence to be given as to what a person, who, when dying, said as to the cause of his or her death. For instance, if a man is charged with murder, a witness may be called to prove what was said by the murdered person when dying as to who caused his injuries. But this can only be done if the murdered person at the time of making the statement knew that he was dying. The reason for this rule is that it is thought that a person in such a condition is likely to tell the truth. Another exception to the rule, including hearsay, is that which allows evidence to be given as to statements made by other people as to their bodily or mental feelings. It is important to note that this evidence must be confined to those feelings, and cannot be extended to the cause of them.

Documents.—A second important branch of the rule requiring the best evidence to be given at trials is that relating to the proof of documents. In general, a copy or verbal account of a document may not be given in evidence, unless the absence of the original documents has been satisfactorily accounted for. Suppose, therefore, in a breach of promise action, the plaintiff desires to prove the contents of letters written by the defendant, she must either produce the actual letters themselves or, before she can give a description of what they contained, she must explain what has happened to the originals. Once an explanation has been given, such as the destruction or loss of the original, either copies or a verbal account based upon the witness's recollection can be received in evidence. There are important exceptions to this rule laid down by Act of Parliament. It was so inconvenient, for instance, to carry all over the country bankers' books in order to prove their contents at various trials, that an act was passed, called the Bankers' Books Evidence Act, entitling certified copies of bankers' books to be produced in evidence.

Confessions.—A further important rule of evidence is that relating to confessions alleged to have been made by persons accused of criminal offences. The prosecution, before giving evidence as to the contents of an alleged confession, must prove that the confession was made freely and voluntarily. If a confession has been made as a result of any threat or any promise made by any person in authority, it is not regarded as free and voluntary and is excluded from evidence. Moreover, once a threat or promise of this kind has been made, anything said by the accused person is rendered inadmissible, until it has been proved that, at the time it was said, the effect of the threat or promise had been entirely removed.

In general, there is no rule governing the number of witnesses necessary to prove any particular point. A murder charge, for instance, can be proved by the evidence of a single witness, that is to say, it is open to a jury to convict of murder, if they are satisfied with the evidence of that one witness. There are, however, certain exceptions to this rule. In cases of perjury, the law requires the testimony of two witnesses as to the falsity of what was sworn. When accomplices are called for the prosecution in a criminal case the Judge always reminds the jury that no one should be convicted on the uncorroborated testimony of an accomplice.

Who may give Evidence?—Formerly there were very many restrictions governing persons who were allowed to give evidence. At one time, in civil actions the parties themselves were not even permitted to give evidence. It will be remembered that in the famous case of Bardell *v.* Pickwick, Mr. Pickwick did not go into the witness box to contradict the case that was made out by the plaintiff's witnesses. This was so because at that time the parties were excluded from giving evidence. Now, however, there are really no restrictions as to the competency of witnesses. A person, who is being tried for a crime, may give evidence on his own behalf, and so may his wife. A person who is deaf and dumb may be called as a witness, if he can communicate his evidence in some intelligible form. Children may be called as witnesses, subject to the discretion of the presiding Judge as to whether they are old enough for their testimony to be of any value. In the case of young children, they may give evidence without being sworn, and it is customary for the Judge to examine them before deciding whether they should give evidence, or whether they should take the oath as to their knowledge between right and wrong. Persons, however, who are definitely of unsound mind, and, in the opinion of the Judge, incapable of giving any intelligible evidence, will not be allowed to do so.

Privilege of Witnesses.—In some circumstances witnesses may claim privilege from answering questions. Thus a witness may always object to answering a question, the answer to which would tend to shew that he had committed a criminal offence for which he could be tried. In divorce cases also, no one may be asked a question tending to shew that he or she has committed adultery, unless he or she has already denied adultery on oath.

Method of Examining Witnesses.—Witnesses when giving evidence orally are examined in the first place by the counsel for the side that called them. As they are presumed to be favourable to him, he is not allowed to ask them leading questions, that is to say, he may not ask them questions in a form which suggests the answer. He cannot say, "Did you then do so and so?" He must say, "What did you then do?" After their examination is over, they may be cross-examined by counsel for the opposing side. Here, of course, there is no presumption that they are friendly to him and he may put his question in as leading and as forcible a way as he likes. The purpose of cross-examination is to test the accuracy and memory of a witness, and to communicate to the witness the case put forward by the side for whom the cross-examining counsel appears. After cross-examination is concluded, the witness may be re-examined by counsel who called him, in order that any matters left uncertain as a result of the cross-examination may be cleared up. It should be noted that a cross-examination is often of a ruthless and searching nature. This is perfectly permissible and proper conduct on the part of the cross-examining counsel, as he is bound to put to the witnesses called on the other side the case upon which he is relying, and also, if he thinks proper, to impeach their credit and to attack their character. (*See* EVIDENCE ON COMMISSION; OATH; PERJURY.)

EVIDENCE (SCOTS LAW).— Rules of Evidence in Scots Law are to a large extent the same as the rules of English law. The greatest difference arises in the case of contracts which require to be proved either by writing or by the admission on oath of the person who is being sued. In Scots law the contracts which require to be proved in this way are gratuitous obligations; trusts and loans of money. (*See* CONTRACT [SCOTS LAW].)

EVIDENCE ON COMMISSION.— The taking of evidence upon commission is a method of taking evidence outside the Court in which the case is to be heard, the witness being examined and cross-examined before a commissioner and his evidence being taken down in order that it may be read to the Court at the trial. Only in a limited number of cases may evidence be given in this way: (i) when the witness is very old or dangerously ill; (ii) when he is so ill that he cannot safely attend the Court; (iii) when he is going abroad. If a material witness is actually abroad, it is impossible for the English Courts to compel him to come to the Court, and commissions are sometimes issued to take the evidence of such persons in the place abroad where they live. But many countries will not permit the execution of commissions within their territory; and in such cases, letters of request are issued through diplomatic channels requesting the foreign government in question to permit one of its judicial officials to take the evidence and to remit it to the English Courts. Commissions to take evidence are now seldom used even within the jurisdiction, since it is a cumbersome and expensive method of procedure. It has

been replaced to a very large extent by the appointment of official examiners, to whom Judges refer the taking of evidence of aged or sick persons, or of persons about to go abroad. (*See also* EXAMINER TO THE COURT.)

EX-DIVIDEND.— When shares are sold "ex-dividend" the person selling retains any dividend that may have been declared at the date of the sale although it has not yet been paid. (*See* CUM DIVIDEND; DIVIDENDS.)

EX PARTE.— This means that an application to the Court has been made in the presence only of the persons making it, and not of any other parties who may be interested. Thus any order made in such circumstances is said to be made ex parte, that is, on hearing one side only. Such an order is sometimes made temporarily in cases of great urgency, as where it is necessary to prevent some act being done and where the time available is so short that it is not possible to bring before the Court the person threatening to do the act. Such an order might be made preventing a newspaper from publishing a libellous statement when it is just about to go to print.

Ex parte is sometimes used in another meaning. When in the course of proceedings an application is made to the Court by one of the parties to the proceedings, the application is said to be "ex parte" that person.

EXAMINATION.— When a witness gives evidence he may be asked questions by various people. He may be asked questions by the counsel for the side that has called him, and by the counsel for the opposing side or sides. Again, he may be interrogated by the Judge or Magistrates before whom the case is tried. Questioning by the first is called "examination in chief." Questioning by the second is called "cross-examination," and when the tribunal questions him, he is said to be "examined by the Court."

There are some forms of judicial enquiry where the procedure is different. For instance, in bankruptcy the debtor is examined in the first place by an official called the "Official Receiver." (*See* BANKRUPTCY.)

EXAMINER TO THE COURT.— When it is desired to take the evidence of a witness out of Court by reason of his age or illness, or by reason of the fact that he is about to go abroad or is abroad, the evidence is usually taken (by order of the Court) on oath before an examiner of the Court. An official examiner must be a barrister of not less than three years' standing appointed by the Lord Chancellor. The parties may, however, agree that the examiner shall be a person of their own choice, who is then known as a special examiner, as opposed to the official examiner. The evidence is taken as if in Court, both parties being present and being entitled to cross-examine each other's witnesses. The examiner records the evidence given, which may then be read out in Court. (*See also* EVIDENCE ON COMMISSION.)

EXCISE.—The powers in relation to excise of the Commissioners of Customs and Excise are in two parts. They collect the duties on excisable goods, and they grant licences known as excise licences. Such licences may be either for the manufacture of goods or for the carrying on of certain trades and businesses. From the combination of these branches about £120,000,000 results annually.

Excise Duties.—The rules relating to excise duties differ according to the article dutiable, and no general rules can be laid down. The amounts payable by way of duty are subject to frequent alteration. The duty is payable by the manufacturer, and the products dutiable are: certain kinds of artificial silk; beer; playing cards; coffee substitutes and mixtures; glucose and saccharine; matches; mechanical lighters; patent medicines; spirits; sugar, molasses and sugar extracts; unsweetened table-waters; home grown tobacco; and wines made in England.

Excise Licences.—Except in the case of valuers, auctioneers and hawkers, who may carry on their business at any place they choose, these licences are granted in respect of the premises specified in the licence. Except where a justices' licence is necessary (*see* LICENSING), licences may be transferred by indorsement to the new occupier when its original holder moves his premises, or to his executors, administrators, widow or child when he dies.

Licences for manufacturing must be taken out for: artificial silk yarn and waste; beer brewed for sale and in most cases where it is not brewed for sale; playing cards; glucose and saccharine; matches; patent medicines; British sugar; spirits; unsweetened table-waters; tobacco; vinegar; and British wines. In addition to these, licences must be taken out for dealing in or retailing: beer; cider; patent medicines; silver and gold plate; spirits; tobacco; and wines.

Licences are also necessary for the keeping and using of stills and retorts by chemists and others, and for the refining of gold and silver.

For the licences required to carry on a trade or business, *see* separate articles, e.g. AUCTIONEERS; GAME; HAWKERS; PETROL; PAWNBROKERS; TOBACCO. There are also other licences that used to be known as excise licences, but are now known as Local Taxation Licences. (*See* ARMS, COAT OF; DOG; GAME; GUN LICENCES.)

EXECUTION.—Execution is the name given to the process whereby a person, who has been successful in obtaining a judgment or order against his opponent in an action, can enforce the obedience of that judgment or order. The ordinary form of judgment in both High Court and County Court is for the payment of money by one party (known as the judgment debtor) to the other party (known as the judgment creditor).

Where a judgment has been given against the judgment debtor and has not been satisfied, the judgment creditor can apply for a writ of execution.

In the High Court, if the judgment is for the payment of a sum of money and costs, the judgment creditor may apply for his writ of execution immediately; while in the County Court, in the ordinary way, he is not entitled to his writ of execution until the judgment debtor has been allowed 14 days in which to pay. It very frequently happens, however, that the judgment makes conditions before a writ of execution can be issued, and in such cases the writ will not be issued until leave has been obtained from the Court. This sometimes happens in County Courts where an order has been made for payment of money by instalments, with a provision for the levying of execution if default is made in payment of any of the instalments.

In order to obtain the issue of a writ of

execution, the judgment creditor must forward to the Central Office of the High Court of Justice, Strand, London, if the judgment was made in the High Court, or to the Registrar of the County Court, if the judgment was made there, a copy of the judgment and a document known as a praecipe which sets out the title of the action, the record of the judgment and its date, the name of the person against whom execution is to be levied, and the nature of execution desired.

How Execution is Levied.—On receipt of these documents a writ of execution is issued in the name of the King addressed to the Sheriff of the County, in which the judgment debtor resides, calling upon the Sheriff to levy execution in the manner set out in the writ. In fact, of course, the Sheriff knows nothing about the writ which is delivered to the under-sheriff, who in turn after writing the date on which he receives the writ upon it, issues another document known as a Warrant to a Bailiff authorising him to levy execution. A Bailiff is generally a regular officer of the Sheriff, but any person may be a special Bailiff for the purpose of levying execution provided that the under-sheriff issues a warrant authorizing him to do so.

Writs of execution are of various kinds, of which the most important are Writs of Fieri Facias (known as Fi. Fa.), Elegit, and Possession, while an important process analogous to execution is provided by proceedings for attachment of debts, known as Garnishee Proceedings. All these should be referred to under their respective headings.

On receipt of the warrant the duty of the Bailiff is forthwith to levy execution, i.e. to take possession of sufficient of the judgment debtor's goods or land, etc., to satisfy the judgment; and if any person interferes with him in the execution of his duties he may arrest the person interfering, who is guilty of a misdemeanour and may be fined or imprisoned.

When execution has been levied as fully as is possible the under-sheriff should make a "return" to the writ by sending a document to the Court informing it what has been done under the writ. In actual practice he seldom does so, but may be called upon to do so if required.

The Fees Payable.—For levying execution the Sheriff is entitled to certain fees which may be recovered by the judgment creditor from the judgment debtor and added to the amount of the judgment for which he is levying execution. The judgment creditor is however liable to pay the Sheriff's fees, whether in fact the execution results in the recovery of any money or not. The fees consist of certain statutory fees for the various duties which the Sheriff performs and for poundage upon the amount recovered under the writ of execution. (*See* ELEGIT; FI. FA.; GARNISHEE PROCEEDINGS; JUDGMENT IN COUNTY COURT; JUDGMENT IN HIGH COURT; STAY OF EXECUTION.)

EXECUTOR DE SON TORT.—No person is entitled in law to deal in any way with the property of a deceased person unless he has been previously authorized to do so, by the obtaining of a grant of probate or letters of administration (q.v.) from one or other of the Probate Registries.

If before probate or administration has been obtained any person meddles with the estate of the deceased, e.g. pays or demands debts owing to the deceased, distributes any of the property or pays for funeral expenses, he becomes an executor de son tort, and if he has made any payments improperly he is liable to be sued by the proper executor or administrator, or by a beneficiary under the will or intestacy. It is, however, a good defence for him that the payments would have had to be made by the executor or administrator himself in any event, and he cannot in any case be made liable for more of the property than actually passed through his hands or was dealt with by him.

In fact, in nearly every case where there is an intestacy, someone or other becomes an executor de son tort, for there is nearly always some money, such as funeral expenses, which must come out of the estate before administration can, in the nature of things, be obtained.

Although there is no objection to the next of kin paying such expenses, it is wise to avoid any payments, if possible, until probate or administration has been granted, and if executors have been appointed by the will, all such urgent payments should be made by the executors and not by any other person; since, when probate has been obtained by them, their appointment dates back to the death of the testator. (*See* EXECUTORS AND ADMINISTRATORS; PROBATE OF WILLS; WILLS.)

EXECUTORS AND ADMINIS-TRATORS. Executors.

—An executor is a person who, alone or in conjunction with other executors, is appointed by the deceased in his will or codicil to distribute the estate of the deceased after his death to the persons named in the will, to pay funeral and testamentary expenses, to pay debts to creditors and receive payment from debtors of the deceased, and to bring or defend actions affecting the estate of the deceased. The method of appointment of executors and the obtaining of grants of probate by executors is dealt with under the title WILLS. When an executor dies, his own executor steps into his shoes as executor of the original will also.

Administrators.—When a testator by his will fails to appoint any executors, or where he appoints an executor who predeceases the testator, or where the deceased dies without having made a valid will at all, the estate is administered by an administrator instead who performs the functions of the executor appointed by a will. The same applies where an executor duly appointed survives the testator but dies before taking probate of the will, or being cited to take out probate of the will, fails to do so, or renounces his right to obtain probate and to act as executor.

Rights and Duties.—Upon the death of any person all his property rights and interests pass to his personal representatives, i.e. his executors or administrators. This does not happen automatically, but only when a grant of probate or of administration is obtained.

When probate or administration has been duly granted the position of the executors or administrators is regularised, but in the case of executors the probate dates back to the death of the deceased and they are treated as if they had been appointed upon the day of the deceased's death. The appointment of administrators dates only from the actual date upon which administration was in fact granted.

Executors and administrators are collectively called personal representatives and all the property of the deceased passes to them together with the right to sue for debts due on contracts made with the deceased or to defend proceedings brought upon such contracts. They cannot, however, sue for any personal injury done to the deceased unless it has resulted in an actual pecuniary loss to the personal estate of the deceased, or, if the injury happened within six months of the death, an injury to the real estate of the deceased. Further, they are not liable to be sued for any injury which the deceased has inflicted upon another person, unless that injury has resulted in a direct pecuniary loss to the property of that other person, and the action has been started within six months of the granting of probate or administration.

It is also as well to remember that if the deceased was in partnership with any other person, the personal representative is entitled to recover the share of the deceased in the assets including the goodwill of the partnership business: and, unless the partnership deeds provide otherwise, a partnership is automatically dissolved by the death of any partner and the whole business must be sold.

(1) The first duty of the personal representative is to arrange for the funeral of the deceased if this has not been already done. Their duty is to bury the deceased in a decent manner and they are not bound to, though they generally will, follow the directions of the deceased as to manner of burial, unless the deceased has willed that his body shall be disposed of for anatomical research. The amount to be spent upon the funeral depends upon the station of the deceased in his lifetime, but if the estate is insolvent no more than a reasonable amount for decent burial is permitted. A tombstone is not part of the funeral expenses unless the testator has given directions to his executors to erect one; and they are not entitled to pay for one, in any case, if the estate is insolvent, neither may they pay for mourning garments for relatives.

If, as so often happens, a relative of the deceased has made the arrangements and payments for the funeral, the executors must pay the costs of these, if reasonable, to the relative who has paid them. Insurance against the costs of funerals may be obtained through many Friendly Societies.

(2) The personal representative must, if called upon to do so, make an inventory of the estate of the deceased. He will, of

course, already have made a rough inventory for the Inland Revenue authorities when obtaining the grant and will have sworn to the gross value of the estate. But any person who is interested in the estate of the deceased may apply for a summons at the principal registry calling upon the executor or administrator to make out a full inventory. The Registrar can refuse the application at his discretion.

(3) The personal representative is under a duty forthwith to get in and finally distribute the whole of the property of the deceased. All the real estate will be held upon trust for sale (*see* LAND) and all personal property which has not been specifically bequeathed must be sold; but personal chattels such as furniture, motor cars, horses, etc., should not be sold unless they are needed to pay debts, etc., and the personal representative has in any case a discretion to postpone sale until such time as he thinks proper. As a general rule, however, he should be chary about exercising this right, and it is as well to remember that when getting in debts owing to the deceased he ought to get them in or sue for them before the end of a year. If he is unduly careless or slack in this respect he may become liable for them himself.

When Estate is Insolvent.—Out of the money so obtained the personal representative must first pay the funeral expenses referred to above, next all the debts of the deceased and other liabilities and distribute the rest according to the rules that are set out hereunder. But if the estate is insolvent, then the personal representatives must pay the debts in the following order:

(1) Funeral expenses, and costs of obtaining administration.

(2) (*a*) One year's rates and taxes.

    (*b*) Wages of clerks and servants due for four months before death of the deceased but not exceeding £50 per head.

    (*c*) Wages of labourer or workman due for two months before death of the deceased but not exceeding £25.

    (*d*) Any amount due under the Workmen's Compensation Acts.

    (*e*) Any amount due for employer's contributions under the National Health Insurance Acts.

These debts have an equal right among themselves to be paid, and if the assets are not enough to pay them fully the same proportion of each must be paid.

(3) All other debts and liabilities except those included under (4).

(4) Any claims by a wife or husband for money lent to each other, or loans at an interest varying with profits, or a partnership or partnership debts.

The personal representative, whether the estate is solvent or not, ought to safeguard himself by advertising for claims in a newspaper. An advertisement should be put in the *London Gazette* and at least once in a newspaper circulating in the area where the deceased lived. If the personal representative does this, he cannot be personally liable for non-payment of any debts of which he has not received notice, although the creditor can follow the property into the hands of the beneficiaries. All personal representatives are entitled to employ solicitors, accountants, auctioneers, clerks, etc., and to pay them reasonable fees out of the estate. They are not entitled to charge for their own time and trouble unless specifically authorized to do so by the will. The Public Trustee may always charge.

Duties where Estate is Solvent.—Having paid off the debts and liabilities of a solvent estate the duties of executors and administrators vary according to whether the deceased died intestate or not, and must be dealt with separately.

The duties of an executor under a will, or of an administrator who obtains administration of a will, failing the appointments of executors, are limited by the terms of the will. After paying death duties and funeral expenses and any other liabilities, the executors hold the balance of the estate under an obligation to sell the estate and distribute it to the persons entitled under the will, but subject to their right to postpone such sale for a reasonable time if they think fit. There are, however, certain rules which apply to all wills.

If the testator leaves a business, the executors have no implied right to carry on the business unless they are authorized to do so by the will, except for such short period as may be needed for the purpose of winding it up or selling it as part of the estate. If an executor does do so, even for this short period, he is personally liable for any debts which the business may contract, but he is entitled, if he carried on the business bona fide for the purpose of winding it up or selling it, to be indemnified out of the estate even in priority to the creditors. If he carries it on for a period longer than is necessary he loses his right to be repaid out of the estate.

Where, however, the testator leaves in the will a power to the executors to carry on the business, the executors may use, for that purpose and for the purpose of paying debts incurred in carrying on the business, those funds, and only those funds, which the testator has specifically said shall be liable for the debts of the business; but even this does not give him a prior right over other creditors upon these funds or any other funds of the estate unless the creditors of the business have consented, and even then it only gives the executors priority over such creditors as have consented. If the funds are not enough the executors are personally liable for the balance.

For these reasons executors would be well advised to exercise the greatest caution in continuing the business of the testator after his death, and in no case should they undertake to do so for any period longer than the minimum period required for winding up or sale, unless the testator has left ample funds to be used for this purpose.

Application of Assets.—It often happens that although an estate is solvent, i.e. sufficient to pay the debts of the testator, the amount remaining to pay the debts is not sufficient to satisfy all the legacies and bequests contained in the will. In such circumstances the executors must pay the debts from the various portions of the estate in the following order, exhausting completely one class of property before having recourse to the next.

(1) The property of the deceased undisposed of by will.

(2) Any property included in a residuary gift, i.e. where the testator leaves the residue of his property to some person.

(3) Any property which the testator has bequeathed specifically for the payment of debts.

(4) Any property bequeathed subject to a charge for the payments of debts.

(5) The fund retained for the payment of pecuniary legacies.

(6) Property specifically bequeathed.

(7) Property appointed under a general power of appointment.

The effect of these rules is that the duty of the executors is to pay the debts out of the property, having recourse to the various portions of it in the order set out above, and the amount payable to the beneficiaries of the various portions of the property will be diminished in proportion. The testator, however, may by his will alter the order in which such property is to be liable for debts, and it is important to remember that, if land which is subject to a charge is bequeathed, the charge is prima facie repayable out of the land.

Death Duties.—These include estate, succession and legacy duties and it is one of the duties of executors and administrators to set aside a fund sufficient for, and to pay, these duties. (*See* DEATH DUTIES.)

Privileges of Personal Representatives.—As against their very onerous duties personal representatives have certain rights and privileges, among the most important of which is the right of preferring creditors and the right to retainer. That is to say an executor or an administrator, who has not obtained a grant of administration as a creditor, is entitled to pay debts in what order he thinks fit. Thus he can pay creditor A before he pays creditor B, and if the estate is not sufficient to pay both creditor A and creditor B, creditor A will receive payment in full while creditor B will receive only partial payment, and this is so even if the debt of creditor A is too old to be sued upon, i.e. is barred by the statute of limitations. Further, the personal representative can, if he himself is a creditor, pay himself his own debt before paying the debts of other creditors. Thus, in cases where the estate is insolvent it may be very advantageous to be executor, but the executor is not entitled to make any profit by preferring a creditor, and he loses his right to prefer when an order for administration by the Court is obtained, and his right to retain his own debt when a receiver is appointed by the Court.

Another privilege of a personal representative is to appeal to the Court for its assistance or protection when any case of doubt or difficulty arises, and it is reasonable that he should do so. The costs of any such action will come out of the estate of the deceased.

Termination of Duties of Personal Representatives. — The duties of the personal representative end only when he has either fully administered the estate by paying all debts and expenses and distributing the residue to the persons entitled, or when he has been relieved of his duties either by paying the balance of the money into Court or by the making of an administration order together with the appointment of a receiver. If any creditor sues him for a debt against the estate of the deceased after he has fully and properly administered the estate, the personal representative can plead that his duties are at an end, and in such case the creditor must sue the beneficiaries to recover the money from them, for the liability of the personal representative has ceased. This, however, will not be so if the executor has been negligent in the discharge of his duties or has been fraudulent, and in such a case he will be personally liable to either creditors or beneficiaries who have suffered loss through his negligence or fraud, though the Court, if it thinks that the executor or administrator is not morally to blame, may relieve him from this liability at its discretion.

It will be seen, therefore, that in all but the simplest cases the duties of an executor or administrator involve points of complicated law, and except in the simplest cases no person should attempt to perform the duties of executor without the constant advice of a competent solicitor whose costs the personal representative is entitled to pay out of the estate. (*See* ADMINISTRATION ACTION; INTESTACY; LEGACIES; LETTERS OF ADMINISTRATION; PROBATE OF WILLS; WILLS.)

EXECUTORS (SCOTS LAW).— Executors are usually appointed by the Will of the person whose estate they have to control. Where the testator in his will has omitted to appoint any person to act as his executor, or where the person appointed fails to act, any persons who are appointed trustees by the testator in his will shall act; and if none such have been appointed then the executor is any person to whom the testator has left all his property, or the

person to whom the residue has been left if there are specific bequests to other persons. All these persons are known as "executors nominate" and have the powers of trustees.

Executors Dative.—If there are no executors nominate it is necessary to have executors appointed by the Sheriff. Such executors are known as "executors dative." The Sheriff in his appointment will consider the claims of the following persons in the following order (1) a universal disponee, that is, a person to whom under the will all property of the testator has been left; (2) the next of kin (*see* INTESTACY [SCOTS LAW]); (3) the widow or widower of the testator; (4) a creditor; (5) any person to whom a legacy has been left. In default of any of these persons being available or being willing to accept the office, the Court will appoint a judicial factor, who is an officer of the Court, to administer the estate. An executor-nominant corresponds to an executor in English law and an executor-dative corresponds to an administrator.

Confirmation of Executors.—An executor before he can act must be confirmed, and the act of confirmation gives him authority to deal with all the personal property of the deceased person. The confirmation is granted by the Sheriff of the district in which the deceased person was domiciled, or, if he was not domiciled in Scotland or in any particular place in Scotland, by the Sheriff of the Lothians and Peebles at Edinburgh.

The practical steps are as follows. The executor lodges with the Sheriff Clerk of the appropriate district an Inventory—i.e. a list of all the movable property of the deceased. At the same time he lodges the will or other document containing his appointment. He then takes an oath, firstly that the will is the only testamentary document left by the deceased, and secondly that the inventory contains all the movable property of the deceased. The inventory, oath and will are then recorded and a copy of the confirmation given. This is called the Testament Testamentar.

Duties of Executors.—The main duty of the executor is to collect the estate of the deceased person and to pay his debts. His position should be distinguished from that of a trustee whose duty is to hold the property for the benefit of other persons, whereas it is the executor's duty, once the debts have been paid, to transfer the property to the persons entitled to it. The distinction is frequently not easy to see because a man may by his will direct his trustees and executors to hold the property in trust after the debts have been paid, and in this case it will be very difficult to say at what point they cease to act as executors and begin to act as trustees.

Payment of Debts.—Debts of a deceased person become payable six months after his death, and the executor is not bound to pay before that time. He may, if he wishes, pay certain preferable debts earlier, but in that event he must take care to see that there are ample funds remaining to pay debts of an equal preference, or otherwise he may become liable personally in respect of these other debts. Executors invariably advertise in a newspaper for claims, and when this has been done and the period of six months has elapsed, all the claims then known to exist may be paid. If a claim is doubtful the creditor may be required to bring an action for the purpose of proving it.

Order of Payment.—The first claim on the estate is the expenses of confirmation and of administering the estate. This includes Law Agent's fees. When these have been paid the executor must see that the other debts are paid in the proper order, for if he pays a debt out of order or pays a debt not due, or a debt to the wrong person, he will be personally liable. The order of payment is.

(1) Death-bed expenses, that is, fees payable to doctors and nurses, and for medicines, etc., in connection with the last illness of the deceased.

(2) Reasonable funeral and burial expenses. What is reasonable will depend on the station in life of the deceased person.

(3) Suitable mourning for the deceased's family. This also will depend on the station in life.

(4) A reasonable sum of money to enable the widow and family to live and supply themselves with necessities, until the exact amount due to them under the will has been ascertained.

(5) The rent of the house in which the deceased was living at the time of his death for the term during which he died.

(6) Wages of farm and domestic servants for the term during which he died. Notice that this preference does not extend to wages of servants employed by the deceased in his business.

(7) Crown taxes and rates.

The executors must pay to the Crown the proper amount of Estate Duty (q.v.). This is calculated on the value of all property which passes on the death of the deceased from him to some other person, except property which he held merely as a trustee. Before the total value of his property is arrived at, death-bed and funeral expenses and all other debts of the deceased are deducted from the gross amount.

Order of Liability of Assets.—The executor in paying the debts cannot pay them out of such assets as he pleases but must observe the legal order. If any debt is secured over some particular asset, e.g. if money has been borrowed by the deceased on the security of a house, that debt will in the first place be paid out of the sum realized by that particular asset. The testator may direct that his estate shall be liable for debts in any order that he pleases, but in the absence of any particular direction the order is as follows: (1) The movable estate which has not been disposed of by the testator to any specific person, e.g. by a specific legacy. (2) The heritable estate which has not been given by the testator to any specific person. (3) Movable estate which has been specifically bequeathed. (4) Heritable estate which has been specifically bequeathed.

Of course, if the first of these is sufficient to pay all the debts it will not be necessary to have recourse to the second or any later one.

When the debts have been paid the deceased's executors must then dispose of the property according to the law. Their first duty will be to pay any claims in respect of their legal rights which the widow or children may have. These will be claims for *jus relictæ* in the case of the widow and for *legitim* in the case of the children. (*See* MARRIED WOMEN [SCOTS LAW]; INTESTACY [SCOTS LAW]; LEGITIM.) After that the executors must dispose of any property which has been specifically given to a beneficiary, e.g. a specified horse or motor-

Exhibit   [338]   Expiring Laws

car. Next special legacies must be paid, that is legacies of a special fixed sum of money, e.g. £100, and finally residuary legacies will be paid, that is, the rest of the money and movable property will be transferred to the person who is the residuary legatee under the will.

If the deceased person has not left a will the executor must dispose of the property according to the rules of intestacy after the above-mentioned legal rights of the widow and children have been satisfied. (*See* MARRIED WOMEN [SCOTS LAW]; INTESTACY [SCOTS LAW]; LEGITIM.)

EXHIBIT.—In most cases tried in the Courts documents and other articles are produced by the witnesses. These are called exhibits. The practice in criminal cases is that, whenever an exhibit is produced by the witness, it is given a serial number so that it may later be referred to easily by that number. This practice is sometimes followed in civil actions as well. It is customary to retain exhibits in the custody of the Court until the conclusion of the case in which they have been produced.

EXHIBITION.—It is an offence to exhibit in a caravan or otherwise in any street any show or public entertainment in such a manner as to cause obstruction, annoyance or danger to the residents or passers-by. "Street" for this purpose includes not only roads and thoroughfares but also any place to which the public have a right of access, including footpaths.

EXPENSES (SCOTS LAW).—The word expenses is used to denote what in England are called costs in litigation.

EXPERT EVIDENCE.—There are many matters for decision in the Courts of such a technical or scientific nature that it is necessary for Judges or juries to have the assistance of expert witnesses. For instance, if a person is injured in a motor accident and claims damages for his injuries, the evidence of doctors as to the extent of his injuries is usually regarded as necessary in order to enable the tribunal to decide what damages should be awarded. Again, questions on disputed handwriting are often decided upon as a result of the evidence given by experts in handwriting. An expert witness is treated in some matters slightly differently from other witnesses. It is usual for expert witnesses to be allowed to remain in Court throughout the trial, so that they may hear the whole of the evidence given in regard to the facts of the case thereby rendering themselves better able to give expert evidence. Counsel when examining expert witnesses called by him can, if he thinks proper, put leading questions to them, a thing he is not allowed to do in the case of ordinary witnesses. The reason for this is that it is assumed that expert witnesses are persons of such character and education that they will not be influenced by suggestions made to them by their own counsel in the way that other witnesses might.

There are certain limits placed upon expert evidence. It is for the Court or jury as the case may be to decide what facts have been proved and it is for the expert witnesses to say what, assuming such facts to be true, their effect in their particular science would be. Thus, if the issue is whether a man was insane at the time that he committed a crime, doctors who are called on one side or the other are not strictly allowed to say that he was or was not insane at that time. They can only be asked to what extent, assuming certain facts to be true, those facts indicate insanity.

EXPIRING LAWS.—Ordinarily, Acts of Parliament remain perpetually in force until repealed. In some cases, however, the Act will be expressed to be effective only for a limited time, e.g. "until 1940" or "until the termination of the present war." When a temporary Act expires, no further proceedings may be taken under it. In one case, an appeal was lodged in the High Court against a Munitions Tribunal's decision, but, before the appeal came on for hearing, the Act which gave the High Court power to deal with such appeals expired, and the Judge held that he had no authority to hear the appeal. A large number of temporary Acts are re-enacted every time they expire in what is known as the "Expiring Laws Continuance Act," which is passed in each parliamentary session. About 15 or 20 acts are annually renewed in this way, and a few have carried on quite a lengthy existence; the Wireless Telegraphy Act, 1904, for example, has been annually renewed since it was first passed. The Expiring Laws Continuance Act usually provides that all amendments to the act, whose existence it continues, shall also be continued with it.

EXPLOSIVES.—"Explosives" includes every substance used or made to produce a practical effect by explosion or a pyrotechnic effect, and thus covers gunpowder, dynamite, fog signals, fireworks, cartridges, and similar substances.

It is a criminal offence unlawfully and maliciously to cause an explosion of a nature likely to endanger life, or to cause serious injury to property whether such injury is in fact caused or not, or even unlawfully and maliciously to make or have in one's possession or control any explosive substance with intent to endanger life or cause serious injury to property in the United Kingdom, or to enable others to do those things by means of the explosives. Where a person has in his possession any explosive substance under such circumstances as to give rise to a reasonable suspicion that it is not for a lawful object, he will be guilty of an offence unless he can prove that his object was a lawful one.

Gunpowder must not be exposed or sold on any street or public place, nor sold to any child under 13. When it is sold or exposed for sale in quantities over 1 pound in weight, it must be contained in a substantial receptacle and labelled "Gunpowder."

Other explosives to which special regulations apply are petrol (q.v.), celluloid and cinematograph films (q.v.), bisulphide of carbon, which must be in steel or iron containers or in bottles specially marked, and cylinders containing compressed gas, which must be in containers specially constructed and tested.

A common carrier is not bound to carry dangerous loads, and if such goods are sent by rail they must be dispatched and packed in accordance with special regulations. (*See* CINEMATOGRAPH FILMS; GUNPOWDER; PETROL.)

EXTRA-TERRITORIALITY.—The Sovereign or his ambassador is regarded by the law as being always resident in his own country. This is the legal fiction known as extra-territoriality or exterritoriality. It is so called because the person or residence of the Sovereign when he is abroad is treated as if it was still in his native land and outside (extra) the territory where it really is.

It is provided by statute (The Diplomatic Privileges Act, 1708) that all process against the person or property of an ambassador shall be void, and the same privilege attaches to any of his servants who have been properly registered as such.

Although a Sovereign or ambassador is thus regarded as being outside the jurisdiction of any foreign country in which he is staying, he can waive his privilege and can consent to be sued within its jurisdiction. But he cannot be held liable for any of his acts without this consent, even though he has been living incognito and making contracts with private persons as if he was a fellow countryman of theirs.

The fiction does not extend to consuls, but they are allowed certain immunities and privileges. (*See* AMBASSADORS; CONSULAR OFFICER.)

EXTRADITION.—Extradition is the delivery by one state to another of persons who have been accused or convicted of crimes, in order that they may be brought to justice in the state where the crimes were committed. When an offender is required to be brought to justice from one part of the British dominions to another, he is known as a fugitive offender. Cases of that kind are governed by rather different considerations from cases where the offender is to be taken from British dominions to a foreign state or vice versa. (*See* FUGITIVE OFFENDERS.) This article deals only with the latter class of cases.

The English law of extradition depends entirely upon Act of Parliament, and no person, whether British or alien, can be extradited except in accordance with the Acts. The first and main Act was that of 1870. This Act lays down the general rules according to which extradition is to be conducted, but it provides that it is to come into force only when an extradition treaty is made between Great Britain and a foreign state; in other words, extradition can be effected between Britain and State X only if a treaty is made between the two countries to that effect. Treaties have in fact been entered into with the majority of foreign states, but there are a few exceptions, e.g. Venezuela and Paraguay. The Act provides a list of the crimes which are extraditable, including blackmail; crimes by bankrupts; criminal frauds by bailees, bankers, agents, trustees, directors, etc.; and most felonies. The following were added later: kidnapping; bribery; offences relating to dangerous drugs; indictable offences under the Malicious

Damage Act, Coinage Offences Act, Offences against the Person Act, and Forgery Act. Accessories to offences may be extradited like principals. Many treaties, however, do not include all the offences mentioned in the Act, and it is not unusual for a treaty to stipulate that the parties shall not be bound to deliver up their own nationals, e.g. no "native-born" British subject may be delivered up to France for crimes committed in France. All treaties include the chief offences, including frauds by bankers, agents, etc., and bankruptcy offences. Portugal will not give up a person accused of a capital crime.

Procedure.—The usual procedure to obtain the surrender of a prisoner by Great Britain is for the diplomatic representative of the foreign country to send a requisition to the Secretary of State, who then requires the police magistrate of the district where the criminal is believed to be to issue a warrant for his arrest. The criminal is then arrested and brought before the Bow Street magistrate.

The Secretary of State will not order the arrest of a person for extradition for any political offence, and may at any time order the release of an arrested person if it turns out that his offence was of a political character, extradition in respect of such offences being illegal. Arrest may, however, be made without a warrant (though that course is seldom taken), or a warrant may be issued without an order of the Secretary of State.

Trial.—When the offender is brought before the magistrate at Bow Street, the case is heard in the same manner as if the prisoner were charged with an indictable offence committed in England. Before the magistrate will commit the prisoner for extradition, it must be proved (i) that a treaty is in force which makes the alleged crime extraditable; (ii) that the foreign state has applied for extradition; (iii) that the foreign state has issued a warrant authorizing his arrest; (iv) that the person arrested is the person accused by the foreign state; (v) that the crime was committed within the jurisdiction of the state applying for extradition; (vi) that the crime was one which would have been punishable by English law if it had been committed in England; (vii) that there is such evidence as would have entitled the magistrate to have committed the prisoner

for trial if the crime had been committed in England (i.e. that there appears to be a good case against the prisoner). The prisoner may call evidence to shew that the crime is of a political character, or that extradition is being asked for in order to punish him for a political offence.

It is a rigid rule that extradition will never be granted to a state which does not undertake that the extradited person shall not be tried for any offence (other than the offence in respect of which extradition is granted) without giving him an opportunity of returning to British dominions. This means that if he ultimately proves to be innocent of the crime imputed to him, he cannot be convicted while still abroad of another crime, but that he may first return to England, and, if the foreign state desires to prefer additional charges against him, fresh extradition proceedings must be taken. If the magistrate is satisfied that the prisoner should be extradited, he commits him to prison to await surrender.

Transportation.—When the accused has been committed to prison by the magistrate, the Secretary of State will issue a warrant to a person authorized by the foreign state. This warrant authorizes the person to whom it is granted to convey the prisoner to the state which obtained his extradition, and such person has all the powers of the ordinary police over the prisoner. But no prisoner may be surrendered to such person until fifteen days have expired after the date of his committal, and, during that time, he or some person on his behalf is entitled to take out a writ of habeas corpus by which the case will be brought before the King's Bench Division of the High Court. (*See* HABEAS CORPUS.)

Extradition from British Dominions.—The method of extraditing criminals out of other parts of the British Empire (including all the dominions except Canada) is much the same as regards England. The Canadian law of extradition is governed by special Canadian statutes.

Extradition from a Foreign State. —When it is desired to obtain the trial in England of a criminal who has fled abroad, application should be made to the Home Secretary, together with all particulars and the warrant for his arrest. If a private individual applies, he is usually required to give an indemnity in respect of expenses which may be incurred. (*See also* FUGITIVE OFFENDERS.)

EXTRAORDINARY MEETING.— A Company is required to hold an Annual General Meeting and it is usual to transact at that meeting all the business of the company for the year. If, however, any matter comes up between the two Annual General Meetings which has to be immediately dealt with, an Extraordinary General Meeting will be called. (*See* MEETINGS.)

EXTRAORDINARY RESOLUTION (COMPANIES).—An extraordinary resolution may be passed at any meeting, but there must be a three-quarters' majority of the members entitled to vote and voting in favour of it; and notice must have been given that it was intended to propose the resolution as an extraordinary resolution. It is used for the purpose of winding-up a company voluntarily when it cannot continue its business by reason of its debts and is the usual way of removing directors from office.

F**.O.B.—**A sale of goods is said to be F.O.B. (Free on Board) or F.O.R. (Free on Rail) when the seller undertakes to deliver the goods free of charge, either on board a ship provided by the buyer, or to the railway company for delivery to the buyer. A sale of this kind is distinguished from a sale C.I.F. (Cost, Insurance and Freight). (*See* SALE OF GOODS.)

FACILITY (SCOTS LAW).—This is a state of mind that is recognized by the law of Scotland which indicates a weakness not amounting to insanity but which nevertheless renders a person, whether he is making a contract or a will, more pliable to the suggestions and influences of others. The Court will find that there has been undue influence exercised in such cases more easily than where the person, on whom the influence is alleged to have been exerted, was in full possession of his mental faculties. Facility may be due to natural disposition, to ill-health or to age. (*See* UNDUE INFLUENCE.)

FACTOR.—A factor is an agent who is employed to sell on behalf of another person, called the principal, goods which have been delivered to him by the principal. As consideration for the sale he receives a commission. He is distinguished from a broker because a broker has not possession of the goods which he sells, and cannot sell in his own name but only in the name of his principal, whereas a factor sells in his own name and has possession of the goods.

A factor has usually authority to receive payment for his principal and therefore a receipt given by him is valid. If he is owed money by his principal he has a lien over the goods in his possession, or over the proceeds of sale if the goods have been sold for the amount due. He may also pledge goods for the purpose of raising money.

Factors, as they deal in their own name with other person's goods, could do very grave harm in the trading community if it were possible for the true owner of the goods (i.e. the principal of the factor) to claim back the goods after the factor had sold them, on the ground that the factor had no authority to do so. It has therefore been provided by a statute (The Factors Act, 1889) that if a factor has possession of goods or of the document of title to goods with the consent of the owner, then any sale, pledge or other disposition of them made by the factor in the ordinary course of his business is binding on the owner, whether the transaction was authorized by him or not. This will not, of course, apply in cases where the person taking the goods does not act in good faith or, for example, if he knew at the time of taking the goods that the transaction was not authorized by the true owner.

"Documents of Title" include such documents as Bills of Lading, Dock Warrants, Warehouse-keeper's Certificates, Delivery Orders, or any other documents used in the ordinary course of business as proof of the possession of goods.

This principle is illustrated by the following example:

A owns a motor-car and hands it to B, who is a factor, with instructions to sell it, but fixes the minimum price at £500. B dishonestly sells the car to C for £300. C buys the car in good faith and does not know B was acting fraudulently. B misappropriates the £300 and A attempts to recover the car from C. As B has been in possession of the car *with A's consent*, he gave a good title to the car to C by reason of the Factor's Act and therefore A cannot recover the car from C. He could, of course, recover from B if he could be found. (*See* PRINCIPAL AND AGENT.)

FACTOR (SCOTS LAW).—In Scots law factor, in addition to the meaning of agent as in English law, has a further meaning, denoting an officer appointed by the Court to exercise the functions of a trustee in certain cases. A factor of this kind is more usually known as a judicial factor. (*See* JUDICIAL FACTOR [SCOTS LAW].)

FACTORY.—The series of Acts which have been passed by Parliament during the last century, dealing with factories and workshops, have had for their main object the protection of the health of the workers and the elimination of unnecessary danger from their employment. Most of the legislation is directed towards the regulating of the conditions of work of women and young persons, the legislature apparently presuming that men were able to look after themselves, and could to some extent secure their own conditions.

The law relating to factories and workshops was consolidated by the Act of 1901, and although several acts have since been passed dealing with various parts of the subject, the Act of 1901 is still the principal Act.

Since the Education Act, 1921, and the Children and Young Persons Act, 1932, the possibilities of children being employed in factories and workshops are so very much narrowed that for all practical purposes it may be taken that the special regulations with regard to hours of employment of women, young persons and children now apply to persons between the ages of sixteen and eighteen if male, and from sixteen upwards if female.

In order more easily to understand the legal provisions relating to factories and workshops it is necessary to define and explain some terms which are constantly used throughout the Act of 1901. A *factory* must be distinguished from a *workshop*, and, although the definition is by no means water-

tight, it may be laid down broadly that a factory is a place where mechanical power is used in the manufacturing process, and a workshop is a place where no mechanical power is used.

There are certain places which may be factories although no mechanical power is used to assist in the process of manufacture.

There are two kinds of factory: (*a*) textile, (*b*) non-textile. The distinction between the two types is of importance, because the provisions in the Acts with regard to hours of work and overtime in textile factories are more stringent than those relating to non-textile factories.

Textile Factory is the name given to premises where mechanical power is used to work machinery employed in preparing, making, or finishing, cotton, wool, hair, silk, flax, hemp, jute, tow, china grass, coco-nut fibre, or other similar material, or any fabric made of these materials, or any process incidental to the manufacturing of them.

There are one or two exceptions to this definition of which the following are the principal: print works, bleaching and dyeing works, lace warehouses, paper mills, flax scutch mills, rope works and hat works, are not textile factories.

Non-Textile Factories.—The following places are non-textile factories, and they are regarded as factories whether or not any mechanical power is used to assist the process of manufacture:

Print works, bleaching and dyeing works, earthenware works, lucifer match works, percussion cap works, cartridge works, paper-staining works, fustian-cutting works, blast furnaces, copper mills, iron mills, foundries, metal and india-rubber works, paper mills, glass works, tobacco factories, letterpress printing works, book-binding works, flax scutch mills and electrical stations.

The following places are non-textile factories provided mechanical power is used to assist the process of manufacture:

Hat works, rope works, bakehouses, lace warehouses, shipbuilding yards, quarries, pit-banks, dry cleaning, carpet beating, and bottle-washing works and laundries.

There are two other types of factories known to the law: Domestic Factories, and Tenement Factories.

A Domestic Factory is a private house, where work is carried on by members of the family living in the house, and where no mechanical power is employed to assist in the manufacturing process. The type of work done must be such as is usually done in a factory.

A **Tenement Factory** is a factory where mechanical power is supplied from a common source to different parts of the same building occupied by different persons, and used for the purpose of a manufacturing process.

A **Workshop** is the name given to premises where such trades as hat-making, baking, lace-making, are carried on without the aid of mechanical power; premises wherein manual labour is exercised in the making, altering, repairing, or finishing of any article, are also workshops.

A **Domestic Workshop** is a private house wherein certain work is also carried on. If the work is of the nature described above under workshop, then it is a domestic workshop. The persons employed therein must be members of the family who live in the house, and no mechanical power must be used.

A **Tenement Workshop** is the name given to premises in which persons work with the permission of the occupier or owner thereof, but are not in his employment. They must be engaged upon work which would make the place a workshop, if they were in fact employed by the occupier or owner.

Men's Workshops are workshops in which no woman or young person is employed.

Women's Workshops are workshops in which no young person is employed.

The Provisions of the Factory Acts are divided into three main categories: (1) Health, (2) Safety, (3) Employment and Wages.

1. (a) *Overcrowding.*—A factory, workshop, or workplace is deemed to be dangerously overcrowded unless there are at least 250 cubic feet of space per person in a room where work is being done. There must be fixed in every factory and workshop a notice specifying the number of persons who may be employed in each room.

(b) *Temperature.*—Adequate measures must be taken for securing and maintaining a reasonable temperature in each room in which a person is employed. In cotton cloth factories and textile factories in which

the air is made moist artificially by steam, the amount of moisture permissible in the air is fixed by regulations made by the Secretary of State, and the temperature must not be raised above 70° F., except when it is necessary to do so in order to make the atmosphere sufficiently moist for the manufacturing process. There must be provided and kept in order in every such cotton cloth and textile factory two sets of standardized wet and dry bulb thermometers. The occupier, or the manager, or the person in charge of the factory must read the thermometers daily, record the readings at the time of taking them, and at the end of each month send the special form with the readings recorded to the factory inspector of the district.

(c) *Limewashing, painting and washing.*— In all factories other than domestic factories, all the inside walls, the ceilings, the passages and staircases, must be limewashed once at least in every fourteen months, unless they have been painted with oil or varnish; in the latter case they must be painted once every seven years, but they must be washed with soap and hot water every fourteen months.

(d) *Ventilation.* — Every factory and workshop must be provided with sufficient means of ventilation to render harmless all the gases, vapours and dust that may be produced by the process of manufacture being carried on; every factory and workshop must be kept free from any odour arising from drains or urinals.

(e) *Sanitary Conveniences.*—Every building used as a factory or workshop must be provided with sufficient and suitable sanitary conveniences, regard being had to the number of persons employed and whether they are of both sexes or only of one. (*See also* BAKING.)

(f) *Unhealthy Industries.*—If the Secretary of State is satisfied that any process of manufacture, or the machinery, or the plant used in any factory or workshop is injurious to the health, or dangerous to the life or limb of any class of persons employed therein, he may certify that the manufacturing process or plant is dangerous and may make special regulations in regard thereto. Copies of any regulations so made by him must be posted up in a conspicuous and accessible place in every factory or workshop to which they apply.

In a factory or workshop where there is

carried on some process by which dust, gas, or vapour is generated and inhaled by the workers to an injurious extent, a factory inspector may order that a fan be installed if he is of opinion that the installation of a fan would prevent such inhalation being necessary.

In factories or workshops where lead, arsenic, or any other poisonous substance is used, suitable washing places must be provided for the use of the workers and meals must not be taken in rooms where such substance is used.

Written notice of any case of lead, phosphorus, arsenical or mercurial poisoning, or anthrax occurring in a factory or workshop must be sent to the factory inspector and the certifying surgeon of the district.

If there is any contravention of any of these provisions relating to the health of the workers, then the factory will be deemed not to be kept in conformity with the Acts and the owner or occupier may be liable to certain penalties. (*See below.*)

2. (*a*) *Fencing of Machinery.*—In a factory every hoist or teagle and every fly-wheel connected with steam, water or other power must be securely fenced. This is an absolute duty and must be carried out whether or not the machinery in question is dangerous without fencing.

Every dangerous part of the machinery in a factory must be fenced, or if it is not fenced it must be in such a position and of such construction as to be as safe to everyone employed in the factory as if it were fenced. All fencing must be kept in an efficient state and in its proper position when the machinery is moving.

There are some special provisions in the Acts with regard to self-acting machines, the most important being that a person must not be allowed to be in the space between the fixed and traversing parts of a self-acting machine while the machine is moving; and he may only be allowed in the space when the machine is stopped with the traversing part at the outward end of its run.

Where grinding is carried on in a tenement factory the shafting and pulleys must be protected with drum-boards and guards must be provided for the driving belts. There must also be instantaneous communication between each of the rooms in which the work is being carried on, and both the engine-room and the boiler-house.

(*b*) *Cleaning of Machinery.*—A child must not be allowed to clean any part of any machinery while that machinery is moving by the aid of mechanical power.

A young person must not be allowed to clean dangerous parts of the machinery in a factory while the machinery is being moved by mechanical power.

(*c*) *Steam boilers* in factories and workshops must have a proper safety valve, steam gauge and water gauge, and the boiler must be examined by a competent person once in every fourteen months.

(*d*) *Fire-escapes* must be provided in every factory or workshop employing more than forty persons, and the owner or occupier must obtain a certificate from the Council of the district in which the factory is situate, stating that the means of escape provided are such as could be reasonably required. If any accident occurs in a factory or workshop, which causes death, or disablement for at least one day, to a person employed therein, and if the accident was caused by moving machinery, molten metal, hot liquid, explosion, escape of gas or steam or electricity, then a written notice must be sent on the special prescribed form to the factory inspector of the district. If such notice is not sent, the occupier of the factory or workshop is liable to a fine not exceeding £10.

If there is a serious accident, or if the circumstances render it expedient, the Secretary of State may direct that an inquiry be held into the accident by a court appointed by the Secretary of State; such court reports its findings to him.

Notice of a boiler explosion must be sent to the Board of Trade, and if the Board think fit they may direct an inquiry to be held. (*See also* WORKMEN'S COMPENSATION.)

3. There are no general restrictions in the Factory Acts with regard to the employment or the wages of adult men who work in factories or workshops. They are presumed by the law to be able to look after their own interests in such matters. (*See* TRADE UNION.)

The regulations are mainly concerned with the hours of employment of women, young persons and children. The restrictions upon the employment of children in factories and workshops, other than domestic factories and workshops, are very wide-spreading, and indeed the hours which a child could work in a factory, and the type of work which it is permitted to do, are so circumscribed by the law as almost to preclude their employment in such places altogether.

A child of twelve years of age and under may not be employed at all in a factory or workshop, not even a domestic one, and a child between twelve and fourteen years of age may not be employed before 6 a.m. nor after 8 p.m., nor may he be employed for more than two hours on any day on which he has to go to school. He must not be employed in such a way as to prevent his attending school.

No child or young person under the age of sixteen may be employed in a factory for more than a week unless the occupier has obtained from the certifying surgeon a certificate of the fitness of the child or young person to be employed in the factory or workshop.

No woman, young person, or child may be employed in a factory on Sunday; but an occupier of a factory who is a person of the Jewish religion may employ young persons or women of the Jewish religion on Sunday if the factory is closed on Saturday. The factory must not be open for traffic on the Sunday, but customers may deliver or fetch away things in accordance with an arrangement made the previous day.

Hours of Employment.—Women and young persons may only be employed in textile factories, print works, and bleaching and dyeing works between the hours of 6 a.m. and 6 p.m., or between 7 a.m. and 7 p.m. on week-days, and between the hours of 6 a.m. and 12 noon, or 7 a.m. and 1 p.m. on Saturdays. The longest stretch of employment without an interval for meals permissible for women and young persons in a textile factory is four and a half hours. In bleaching and dyeing works it may be five hours. There must then be an interval of at least half an hour for a meal. Half an hour must be allowed for meals on Saturdays, and two hours, of which one hour is to be before 3 p.m., must be allowed on week-days.

In non-textile factories and workshops the period of employment for women and young persons must begin between 6 a.m. and 8 a.m. and end between 6 p.m. and 8 p.m. on week-days, and on Saturday the period of employment must be between 6 a.m. and 2 p.m. or 7 a.m. and 3 p.m. or, 8 a.m. and 4 p.m. Half an hour must be allowed for meals on Saturday, and one and a half hours, of which one hour is to be before 3 p.m., on week-days. The maximum stretch of employment without an interval is five hours.

In women's workshops the period of employment may be a twelve hours' period between 6 a.m. and 10 p.m. with one and a half hours for meals on week-days, eight hours between 6 a.m. and 4 p.m. on Saturdays with half an hour for meals.

In a domestic factory or workshop, a young person may be employed between the hours of 6 a.m. and 9 p.m. with four and a half hours for meals and absence from work on week-days, and between the hours of 6 a.m. and 4 p.m. on Saturdays with two and a half hours for meals and absence from work.

All these periods are the limits permitted by the law as set out in the Factory Acts, and an owner or occupier of a factory or workshop may fix the periods of employment and the times allowed for meals within those limits. He must specify the conditions and hours of employment in a notice to be fixed in the factory or workshop. Any employment outside these limits is deemed to be employment contrary to the Acts and the occupier may be liable to a penalty for such contravention. All women and young persons employed in a factory or workshop, other than a domestic factory or workshop, are to have their meal times simultaneously, and they may not be employed nor allowed to remain in a room in which a manufacturing process is being carried on during any part of the meal times.

Holidays.—Women and young persons employed in a factory or workshop must be given a whole holiday on Christmas Day, Good Friday, and every Bank Holiday. If it is arranged to work on any of these days then another full day must be substituted for them.

Overtime.—Overtime is not permitted to be worked in any textile factory, and it is only permitted under certain exceptional circumstances in non-textile factories and workshops. Overtime may be worked for a maximum of two hours on a week-day—

(1) Where the material is liable to be

spoiled by the weather, e.g. flax scutch mills.

(2) Where press of work arises at certain recurring seasons of the year, e.g. makers of Christmas and Easter cards.

(3) Where the business is liable to a sudden press of orders.

(4) Overtime may be worked in any part of a factory either textile or non-textile in which the persons employed are engaged solely in polishing, cleaning, wrapping or packing goods.

There are limits imposed upon the number of days on which overtime may be worked, that is, there must not be more than three days in one week and not more than thirty days in a period of twelve months. Half an hour of the extra time must be reserved for meals.

Overtime may be permitted to factories whose machinery is driven by water power and which are liable to be stopped by flooding or drought. Factories liable to be stopped by flooding may work overtime on forty-eight days out of twelve months, and factories liable to be stopped by drought may work overtime on ninety-six days in every twelve months.

Night Work.—A male young person of sixteen years and upwards may be employed by night in blast furnaces, iron mills, letterpress printing works and paper mills, subject to the following conditions:

(a) He must not be employed for more than twelve hours.

(b) Meal times as in day work must be permitted.

(c) He must not be employed during any part of the twelve hours succeeding or preceding.

(d) He must not be employed by night for more than six nights in two weeks.

If it is necessary to the process in a non-textile factory or workshop that it should be carried on throughout the night, and that male young persons of sixteen years and upwards should be employed therein, the provisions of the Special Order relating to blast furnaces, etc., above may be extended to that factory or workshop.

Male young persons above the age of sixteen years may be employed in a *lace factory* between the hours of 4 a.m. and 10 p.m., but they must be allowed nine hours off for meals and absence from work in that time,

and must not be employed both before and after the ordinary period of employment on the same day.

Male young persons over the age of sixteen may be employed in a bakehouse in the period between 5 a.m. and 9 p.m. under the same conditions with regard to meal times and absence from work as are applicable to their employment in lace factories.

Wages.—The Factory Acts do not lay down any fixed scale of wages in particular trades, but they contain certain provisions with regard to the deductions which may lawfully be made from wages. Deductions may be made in respect of fuel, medicine, medical attendance, material, tools, victuals prepared under the employer's roof and consumed by the workmen there, and fines for damage to goods and materials. Such deductions in respect of tools and materials are not illegal as being payment otherwise than in coin.

No deduction may be made except in pursuance of a contract in writing signed by the workman, and he may recover any deductions made without his written consent. Full written particulars of the acts and omissions for which the deductions are made must be handed to the workman on the occasion of each deduction.

Fines may only be imposed in the case of some act or omission likely to cause damage or loss to the employer or interruption to his business. An employer must keep a register of fines and enter therein the amount of a fine and why it was imposed.

Penalties.—A contravention of most of these foregoing provisions makes the factory a factory not kept in conformity with the Acts, and the occupier is liable to a fine not exceeding £10 upon conviction for allowing the factory so to be kept.

If a person is killed or suffers bodily injury in consequence of the neglect of the occupier to observe the statutory provisions, the occupier is liable to a fine not exceeding £100, and the whole or any part of the fine may be applied for the benefit of the injured person or his family as the Secretary of State may determine.

Where an offence, for which the occupier of the factory or workshop is liable, has in fact been committed by some agent or servant or workman, then that person will be liable to the same fine as the occupier.

(*See also* HOME WORK; MASTER AND SERVANT; PIECE WORK; PUBLIC HEALTH; SHOP; TRUCK; WORKMEN'S COMPENSATION; WORKSHOP.)

FACULTY.—No ecclesiastical person of the Church of England may interfere with the fabric of his church or the ornamentation or decoration thereof without the permission of the Ordinary, granted by what is called a "faculty." Any alteration without a faculty is an offence. Application for a faculty is made by petition to the Consistory Court, and the expense of this procedure has been the subject of recent complaint. A crucifix, pyx, or other elaborate monument are the usual subjects of faculty.

Faculties are of three types: (1) Original, authorizing the doing of something; (2) Confirmatory, confirming something already done; and (3) Removal, authorizing the removal of something wrongly introduced into the church. Difficult cases arise where there are counter-petitions for confirmatory and removal faculties heard together.

FAIR.—A fair is a meeting of persons for the purpose of buying or selling goods. The right to hold a fair is a legal right conferred either by a grant of the Crown, or by prescription or by Act of Parliament. A fair is very little different from a market. In fact every fair is a market but not necessarily every market is a fair. The distinction really rests on the size or frequency of the gathering, a fair being understood to be a large market and held usually only once or twice a year, whereas a market may be held several times a week. (*See* MARKETS.)

FALSE WEIGHTS.—So many commodities are bought and sold by weight, that the law has had to impose severe penalties upon anyone who uses false or fake weights in the carrying on of his business. Many persons were cheated by shopkeepers and others who used inaccurate weights and scales, and an Act of Parliament therefore was passed in 1878 to prevent and punish such frauds. That Act provides that anyone who uses, or has in his possession, any false weight, measure, scale, balance or weighing machine shall be liable to a penalty of £5 for a first offence and £20 for a second offence. The same penalty is incurred by anyone wilfully using a weight or weighing appliance in a fraudulent way, and upon conviction for either of these offences, the weight or scale may be forfeited. Any maker or seller of weights or weighing appliances who knowingly sells one that is false is liable to a fine of £50.

An employer is liable for a fraud committed by his servant in the use of any weighing apparatus, unless he can satisfy the Court that he used every care to see that the legal provisions were complied with, and that the fraud was committed without any connivance or fault on his part. Every local authority has to appoint an inspector of weights and measures for its district, and such an inspector may at all reasonable times, if authorized by a general warrant of a justice of the peace, inspect and test all weights and weighing appliances belonging to, or used by, persons within his district. (*See also* FOOD, LOCAL GOVERNMENT; WEIGHTS AND MEASURES.)

FALSE IMPRISONMENT.—To keep any person in confinement without lawful excuse can be both a crime and a civil wrong. It is triable criminally as assault, because a person cannot usually be kept in confinement without his consent unless some degree of force be used to keep him there. Actions for false imprisonment, if successful, sometimes lead to heavy damages being payable by the defendant. They are frequently combined with claims for malicious persecution.

A person may be falsely imprisoned without being placed in a prison or indeed in any building at all. If he is prevented from living in a particular spot or a particular area by means of force or unlawful threats, he is held to have been imprisoned. Again the physical force used need not be that of the actual defendant. If a man calls upon a policeman to arrest somebody else, and the arrest turns out to be unjustifiable, the person who calls the policeman is held to be guilty of this offence, even though the actual imprisonment was effected by the police. Cases sometimes arise where the point for decision is whether a policeman effected an arrest as the result of information given him by the defendant, but in the exercise of his own judgment, or whether he acted solely on the information of the defendant. In the former case the defendant will not be liable for false imprisonment, in the latter case he will.

FALSE PRETENCES.—The offence of obtaining goods or money by false pretences is a misdemeanour punishable with imprisonment, with or without hard labour, for not more than two years. The offence consists of fraudulently making a misrepresentation of some existing fact knowing it to be untrue, in order to induce some other person to part with goods or money. Thus, if a man goes into a shop and represents himself to be a person bearing a well-known name, intending that the shopkeeper shall give him credit and let him take away goods without paying for them, he may, if he obtains those goods, be convicted of obtaining them by false pretences.

A person can commit this crime by means of conduct as well as by words. Thus, where a man who had no connection with the University went into a shop in Oxford wearing the gown of a member of the University, and obtained goods on credit, but made no verbal statement as to his identity, he was convicted of this crime. It was held that his wearing of the gown constituted a fraudulent misrepresentation by conduct and entitled the tribunal to find him guilty. It is important, however, to note that the crime is only committed where the false representation is as to some existing fact. It is not sufficient merely to promise that something shall be done. There must be a statement that something has already been done or some state of fact is already in existence. To say to a shopkeeper "If you will let me have these goods I will pay you in a month's time," is not a misrepresentation of any existing fact and does not constitute the crime of obtaining goods by false pretences.

FALSIFICATION OF ACCOUNTS.

—It is a criminal offence for any clerk or servant wilfully with intent to defraud, to destroy, or alter, or falsify, any document or book in the possession of his employer, or received on behalf of his employer. A similar offence is committed by any clerk or servant who fraudulently makes, or concurs in making, any false entry or omits any material particular from any such books or documents. It will be noted that this offence is very similar to the offence of forgery, but it covers certain other conduct, such, for instance, as fraudulent omission to make entries. The offence of falsification of accounts is a misdemeanour and is punishable with penal servitude for not more than

seven years. Any director or officer of any company, who, with intent to defraud, destroys or falsifies any document or book of the company or concurs in any of these things, commits a similar offence.

FARE.—The amount payable by a passenger on travelling by rail, road or sea is known as his Fare. In some cases the maximum fare which may be charged is limited by law. (*See* CARRIAGE BY LAND; RAILWAY TICKET AND SPECIAL SUPPLEMENT "ROAD TRAFFIC.")

FATAL ACCIDENTS ACT.—By the Common Law of England no civil action could be brought against a person who, by his wrongful act or default, caused the death of another person, because an action for damages for personal injuries is what is called a personal action and dies with the person. To remedy this state of affairs an Act of Parliament, called the Fatal Accidents Act or Lord Campbell's Act, was passed in 1846. This Act provides that an action may be brought for the benefit of the wife, husband, parent or child of the deceased person, if the deceased could, had he lived, have brought an action. The persons on whose behalf the action is brought must have sustained pecuniary loss by his death; so that if the wife and children were not dependent upon the deceased for their living they cannot recover anything. In assessing the amount of damages, the jury are not to take into account any sum which may be due to the relatives from an insurance policy on the life of the deceased. (*See* ACCIDENT; NEGLIGENCE.)

FATHER.—The powers and duties of a father over his child may be divided into the following heads:

As to the Child's Person.—The father of a child is its natural guardian, and as such is entitled to the custody of the child and has complete control over its education and religious training. He may keep the child under his own control, or may put it under the control of a third person, e.g. a foster-parent or a schoolmaster. The right of the father used to override even that of the mother, so that if the mother took the child away, its father could recover control of it either by taking out a writ of "habeas corpus" or by petitioning the Court. Proceedings can still be taken either by the father, or, if he is abroad, by the person to whom he has entrusted the child. But if the child is a boy of fourteen years of age or a girl of sixteen, the Court will not compel it to return to its father against its wishes, unless there is some very good reason.

A father may appoint guardians by deed or by will (see GUARDIANSHIP); his consent is required to the marriage of every child under twenty-one, unless the child is already a widower or widow (for further information on this point, see MARRIAGE). A father may agree to forego any rights to custody by consenting to the adoption of the child by a third person (see ADOPTION); he may also, when entering into a separation agreement with his wife, agree that she shall have exclusive control of the child: such an agreement will be enforced by the Court unless it is of the opinion that it would not be for the benefit of the child. If a father agrees to transfer the custody of a child in some way other than this, he is never bound by his agreement unless he has actually transferred the custody, and the Court is of the opinion that the child's welfare will be best promoted by leaving it where it is.

A father also has the right to punish a child corporally or otherwise to a *reasonable* extent, and he may authorize any other person to do so. He also has a right to the service of his children who live with him if they are under the age of twenty-one.

But so extensive, and, in many cases, so unjust were the rights of a father that considerable powers have (mostly within the last century) been vested in the Courts to reduce or destroy his authority and to increase the powers of the mother (see MOTHER). In the first place, the Judges have always taken the line that it is their duty to place the interests of the child in the forefront, and if it can be proved that the father has deserted the child or is unfit in character and conduct, e.g. if he is constantly drunk and blasphemous, or has been guilty of a criminal assault on his daughter, or is cruel to the children, then the Court will appoint a guardian for the child's person and property, and prohibit the father from interfering. The method usually adopted for this purpose is for some friend of the child to pay a small sum of money into Court upon trust for the child: the child then becomes a ward of Court, and it is the duty of the Court to consider the child's interests.

But this power was not nearly sufficient, and further powers were given to the Courts by a series of statutes, extending from 1839 to 1925. By these statutes, it is provided that the Court may, on the application of the child's mother, make such order as it thinks fit in respect of the custody of a child under sixteen in certain events, e.g. if the father has by persistent cruelty or neglect caused the mother to leave him and live separately. If a father is convicted of certain criminal offences, and it appears that he has caused or favoured the seduction or prostitution of his daughter, the Court may deprive him of the custody of the child and appoint a guardian. And if a father (or, indeed, any other person having the custody) of a child under sixteen is convicted of, or committed to trial for, offences of cruelty against the child, or is bound over to keep the peace towards the child, the Court may act similarly.

But a far wider power is conferred by the Guardianship of Infants Act, 1886. By that Act, the Court may, on the application of the mother, make any order as it thinks fit as to custody and the right of access, or may alter its previous orders. By an Act of 1925, when a mother makes such an application, she must be treated as if she had exactly the same rights to custody as the father; the interests of the child are paramount, i.e. when such orders are made, the Court cannot say, "On principle, the father has the right to the child, and we shall not interfere with his right unless for some very cogent reason." The Court may also make an order for weekly payment to the mother for the maintenance of the child, but the money is not payable so long as the mother continues to live with the father. The Court to which application should be made is either the High Court or County Court, or, to a limited extent in the case of children over sixteen, the Magistrate's Court.

A father may also be deprived of custody on a divorce. (*See* SPECIAL SUPPLEMENT "DIVORCE".)

Child Maintenance and Education. —There was in the older law no obligation upon a father to provide for the maintenance of his child. But he may now be criminally liable if he does not do so, e.g. if a parent who is liable to maintain a child wilfully neglects to provide adequate food, clothing or medical aid, or if, being too poor to provide it himself, he fails to take steps for such purpose under the Poor Law, he will be liable to fine or imprisonment. The mother living apart from the father and having custody of the child by order of the Court, is usually entitled to pledge her husband's credit for the purpose of maintaining the child up to the same station in life as the father. Under the Poor Law, the father and, on his death, the mother, and, whether or not the father is dead, the grandfather and grandmother are liable to maintain a child if they are able to do so, so long as the child is unable to support itself. If a mother has separate property, she is liable equally with her husband to maintain the children of the marriage. As to education of the child, *see* EDUCATION.

If a child incurs debts, the father is never liable for them, and if the money is expended on maintaining the child, the father cannot, generally, be asked to refund it, except where it was spent by the mother living apart from the father as mentioned in the last paragraph. A father may be charged with the fines imposed on a child who is under seventeen, unless the Court is satisfied that the father has not conduced to the commission of the offence by neglecting the child. In the same way, a father may sometimes be liable for the "torts" or civil injuries committed by his child, e.g. a parent has been held liable for the injury done by a child by the use of an air-gun.

Child's Property.—A father has no rights, except in a few cases of landed property, over the property of his child. He often, as guardian, controls the child's property, but any profits are the child's, and the father is not entitled to use them for the maintenance of the child (unless by order of the Court), since he is himself liable to maintain. He cannot give a valid receipt or discharge for money paid to him on behalf of the child. But he is entitled to the earnings of a child who is living with him and whom he maintains.

Dealings between Father and Child.—The father (or mother) stands in what is known as a fiduciary relationship towards his child; in other words, he must always treat the child perfectly fairly in any dealings that he has with him in relation to property. If there is any doubt whether a father has made a gift to a child, the child will have the benefit of the doubt, and if the child makes a gift to the father, the Court will often decide that it was invalid because it was made as a result of "undue influence." If a father purchases property in the name of the child, it will be presumed in the absence of good evidence to the contrary, that he did not intend to make the child his mere nominee, but that he intended a gift.

The rights and duties of a father continue until the child attains twenty-one or, in the case of a girl, marrying when under twenty-one, until the date of her marriage.

The father of an illegitimate child has no rights at all over the child until after the mother's death. (*See also* CHILDREN; EDUCATION; GUARDIANSHIP; LOCO PARENTIS; MOTHER; STEPCHILDREN.)

FATHER (SCOTS LAW).—In Scots law a father is recognized as exercising over his children authority which, by analogy with the rules of Roman law, is known as "patria potestas." While the child is a pupil, i.e. until it reaches the age of 12 if it is a girl, or 14 if a boy, the father is entitled to control the person of the child and to order its upbringing. When the child ceases to be a pupil the father does not lose entirely his power of control, but his rights are very considerably diminished. The exact nature of his rights has never been clearly defined, but it cannot be doubted that they would only be recognized in so far as they are used for the benefit and guidance of the child. The father may lose his rights if, for example, the child leaves the home to live an independent life on its own. All rights of this character end when the child reaches 21.

Custody of the Child.—Until recently the father was considered to have a supreme right to the custody of his children, but a great change has taken place in the attitude of the law. It is recognised to-day that the important consideration, where there is any dispute as to whether the father or mother should have the custody of the child, is not any rights that either of them may have, but the welfare of the child. Accordingly, even where there are no divorce proceedings and whether the mother and father are living together or not, the Court may order the mother to have custody of the child, and direct the father to pay her a reasonable allowance for its maintenance.

The same principles are applied where there is a divorce.

When a person is entitled to the custody he may obtain an order from the Court for the child to be handed over to him or her, as the case may be, but the Court may refuse to make an order when it thinks that the parent applying has abandoned or deserted his child, or has so conducted himself as to lose the right of the custody.

One of the most important rights of the father has always been to require the child to be brought up in any religion that he pleases, and even where the child is taken away from the custody of the father the Court will endeavour to give effect to his wishes in this matter.

Father as Tutor and Curator.— So long as the child is a pupil he has no legal personality, and requires a tutor to act for him in protecting his person and managing his property. When he ceases to be a pupil and becomes a minor (which will happen at the age of 12 for girls and 14 for boys) he has a legal personality and acts for himself, but in many cases he has a curator with whose consent he enters into contracts. The curator, however, does not act *for* the minor in the way that the tutor acts *for* the pupil, but merely consents to acts which the minor does for himself. The father is the proper person to be tutor and curator to his children, but he may be superseded by a person appointed by the Court called a judicial factor if his conduct is not satisfactory.

Death of Father.—The father may appoint some person to act as guardian to his children after his death. If he does not do so the mother becomes guardian of any pupil children. If the father has appointed a guardian the mother will act jointly with him and even when no guardian has been appointed by the father, the Court may appoint one to act jointly with the mother. When the mother dies she may appoint a person also to act after her death, and he will also act jointly with the father.

Where there is no tutor to a pupil, as is the case where both parents are dead and have not nominated anyone to take their place, or where the person nominated is unwilling to act, the Court will appoint a judicial factor to safeguard the interests of the child. Curators may always be claimed by a minor if he has none appointed, but he is not bound to have a curator unless he wishes, except where the father is alive, when he automatically is curator because of his relationship. If a minor wishes to have a curator he may apply to the Court.

Duty to support Children.—A father is bound to support his child in accordance with the social position in which he himself lives. In Scots law this obligation does not end when the child becomes 21 but will continue so long as he lives, although when he has taken up some profession or trade for himself, the Court will not usually make any order against the father to support the child, unless the child's misfortune and his inability to maintain himself is due to some physical or mental incapacity of his own. The father may always discharge his obligation by offering to maintain the child in his own home.

This right to support can be enforced not only against the father but, if the father is dead or himself cannot support the child, it may be enforced against other relatives. A father is also entitled to be supported by his child when he is in need.

Illegitimate Children.—A father has no right to the custody of an illegitimate child, but he is bound to maintain it. The mother is entitled to the custody, and is also bound equally with the father to maintain the child. When the child reaches the age of 7 in the case of girls and 10 in the case of boys, the father may, instead of paying the mother for his maintenance, offer to take the child into his own keeping, or to place it in a suitable home. If the mother does not accept this offer she cannot afterwards make any claim against the father in respect of the maintenances.

Rights in Property.—When a father dies the child has got certain rights in his movable property, i.e. chattels, goods, shares, of which he cannot be deprived by any provision in his father's will. There is no such right in the child with regard to heritable property, i.e. land. This right is known as legitim (q.v.). As to the rights of a child when his father dies intestate, *see* INTESTACY [SCOTS LAW].

A father has no similar rights in the property of his child if the child chooses to make a will leaving the property to other persons. (*See* WILL [SCOTS LAW].) If the child does not do so but dies intestate, and without children or descendants surviving him, the father may have certain rights in the heritable property (i.e. land) of the child, if there are no other children or children of children alive. With regard to movable property (i.e. property other than land), the father, where a child dies intestate leaving no issue, i.e. no children of his own or descendants (i.e. the children of children who have died), the father is entitled to one-half of the movable property in preference to the brothers and sisters of the deceased child or the other next of kin. (*See* INTESTACY [SCOTS LAW].)

FELO DE SE.—Self-murder. This term is applied to felonious suicide, in other words, suicide by a person whose reason is not impaired. Attempted suicide is, of course, a punishable offence. (*See* SUICIDE.)

FELONY.—Originally in England all kinds of crime involving forfeiture of goods were called felonies, and in the Middle Ages were punishable by death. In modern times, however, the death penalty has been removed from nearly all felonies. Felonies are different from misdemeanours, although there is no general rule distinguishing one from the other. It will usually be found that a felony is one of the more serious crimes, and a misdemeanour one of the less serious. There are very many exceptions to this. Perjury for example, though a misdemeanour, is punishable with penal servitude for life.

Conviction for felony does not now involve forfeiture of land or goods. The procedure followed on the trial of a felony differs very little from that applicable to a misdemeanour. Prisoners charged with felony can challenge, without giving any reason, any number of jurors up to twenty, a right not enjoyed by prisoners on trial for misdemeanour. (*See* CHALLENGE.) The oath taken by members of the jury on the trial of a felony is different from that taken on the trial of a misdemeanour. (*See also* MISDEMEANOUR.)

FENCE.—The owner of land is usually under no obligation to fence it unless it adjoins a highway and might be dangerous to persons using it. If, as a result of his failure to erect or maintain a fence, some other person's cattle (but not dogs or cats) stray on to his land he can sue that person for trespass; nor will the fact that his fences were inadequate be any defence to the action. A man's duty is to keep his own cattle in, not to keep his neighbour's cattle out.

The owner of cattle who permits them to escape through inadequate fencing is liable for any damage they may do. There is one curious qualification to this rule. If cattle are being driven along a road and they stray into property adjoining it, whether house, shop or field, the owner of that property will not be able to sue for any damage they may do unless he can shew that the drover was careless.

It does sometimes happen, however, that a man is bound to erect and maintain proper fences. Such an obligation may arise either from an express agreement to do so or as the result of habit and practice for some time past.

Certain bodies such as railway companies and colliery companies are bound by law to fence their properties.

Wherever a hedge and ditch are found between properties, the presumption is that the ditch belongs to the same person as the hedge.

Dividing or common walls may belong wholly to one owner or may be notionally divided down the centre, in which case each owner is bound to keep his half in repair so as to support his neighbour's half. (*See* ADJOINING OWNERS.) There is no right to go upon one's neighbour's land in order to cut a fence or repair a wall.

Care should be taken wherever dangerous trees such as yews grow near or in a hedge, for if they encroach on to a neighbour's land their owner may be liable for the death of cattle killed through eating them.

FENCING MACHINERY.—To protect workers from injury, the law requires that all machinery in factories must be securely fenced off or otherwise made safe for persons using it or working in proximity to it. Certain kinds of machinery must be fenced whether the machinery is dangerous without fencing or not. For example, a hoist, a fly-wheel and every part of an engine supplying motive power to a factory must be fenced, whereas other machinery need only be fenced if it would be dangerous without fencing. Thus, if a shaft is so high above the ground as to be clear of all persons working in the factory, it need not be fenced. All fencing must be constantly maintained in an efficient state and must not be removed except where it is essential for cleaning or oiling the machinery. (*See* FACTORY.)

FERÆ NATURÆ.—For legal purposes animals are divided into two groups, "Domitæ Naturæ," or annimals of a domesticated nature, and "Feræ Naturæ," or animals of a wild and untamed nature. The latter kind can only be the property of anybody by being taken into the possession of that person. So long as they are at large they do not belong to anybody, even to the owner of the land on which they may be; but once they are reduced to captivity they may be owned and treated as any other chattels. A person who has on his property wild animals, keeps them there at his own peril. Thus, if a man keeps a lion in his house and it escapes, he is liable for whatever damage it may do, even though he was not guilty of any negligence in allowing it to escape.

FERRIES.—A public ferry is in fact nothing more than a continuation of a public highway or road across a river or other piece of water. A person who has the sole exclusive right to carry goods or passengers over a river or other water is said to be the owner of the ferry. This right may be granted by Royal Grant, or by Act of Parliament or may be inferred from prescription, i.e. from the fact that the person exercising it has done so for a long period of time.

Duties of Ferry Owners.—As a ferry is a monopoly it is granted for the benefit of the public, not for that of the ferry-owner. He is therefore not allowed to charge more than a reasonable toll or to refuse to carry passengers or goods which he is asked to take across. He must also keep his ferry in readiness and in good repair. While goods are in his charge he is liable as a common carrier (q.v.), that is, he is an insurer of their safety. He must provide a safe landing-place, but it is not necessarily his duty to land the goods as well as to carry them.

When one person has a right of ferry no other person is allowed to set up in competition with him, and any person attempting to do so may be prevented by the Court.

FERTILISER.—If a person sells certain articles which are specified in the Fertilisers Act 1926 as a fertiliser of the soil, he must give the purchaser at the time of delivery or immediately afterwards a statement in writing called the statutory statement. This statement must contain the following particulars:—

(*a*) The name under which the article is sold.

(*b*) The nature, substance and quality of the article.

(*c*) The names of the ingredients used in the article.

This statement constitutes a warranty that the particulars contained in it are correct, and that the article is suitable to be used as a fertiliser. Anyone who refuses or fails to give a statutory statement is liable to a fine of £5 for a first offence. (*See* WARRANTY.)

FI. FA.—Fi. Fa. is the abbreviation generally used to indicate the Writ of Fieri Facias which is the writ of execution in commonest use for enforcing the payment of money due under a judgment or order.

It is issued in the manner set out under the title Execution (q.v.) and calls upon the Sheriff to seize sufficient of the goods and chattels of the judgment debtor to satisfy the amount of the judgment and the costs and expenses of execution, and to sell the goods and chattels seized.

The duty of the judgment creditor is finished when he has applied for, and obtained, the issue of the writ, and thereafter the execution of the writ is entrusted by the under-sheriff to the Bailiff.

The Bailiff will then seize and take possession of the goods of the judgment debtor of a value sufficient to satisfy the judgment and costs of execution. He can under this writ seize only goods and chattels, i.e. he cannot seize real property or fixtures, nor can he take possession of the judgment debtor's leasehold property though he may sell it without taking possession. He is not entitled to seize bedding or clothing of the judgment debtor or his family, nor the tools of his trade of a value not exceeding £5. He cannot seize anything that is on the person of the judgment debtor.

Naturally, only the property which belongs to the judgment debtor can be seized and the property of any other person, such as his wife or family, or property over which some third party has a Bill of Sale, is exempt from seizure.

Seizure when used in connection with a

Writ of Fi. Fa. is a technical term, and it is only necessary that the Bailiff should enter on the premises where the goods are lying and say that he has seized the goods. In order to seize the goods, the bailiff may enter the premises on which the goods are kept, but he cannot break open a door in order to do so, nor break open a window; but once he is inside, he may break open inner doors, or may break out of the premises if any attempt is made to stop him either leaving himself or removing the goods.

Once the goods have been seized in this formal way they are in the custody of the law, and no other person is entitled to remove them or to interfere with them. If the Bailiff abandons them, they revert to the judgment debtor; but the mere fact that the Bailiff has been obliged to leave them for a short while does not necessarily mean that they have been abandoned.

The Bailiff is not entitled to remain upon the premises indefinitely, but must remove the goods and arrange for their sale. He must not hand them over to the judgment creditor, but must sell them at the best price which they will fetch, and if they are more than £20 in value he must sell them by public auction.

Out of the moneys which he receives from the sale he must pay to the judgment creditor or his solicitor the amount of the judgment, retaining his own fees and poundage, and must hand over the balance to the judgment debtor.

At any time during execution, if the judgment debtor tenders to the Bailiff the amount of the judgment debt and costs, the Bailiff must withdraw from the execution and give to the judgment debtor a discharge for the amount of the judgment debt. The money he receives the bailiff must hand over to the judgment creditor after deducting his fees and poundage. (*See* EXECUTION; SHERIFF.)

FIAT.—Before certain proceedings can be taken it is necessary to obtain the consent of some official such as the Lord Chancellor or Attorney-General on behalf of the Crown, and the indorsement of that official on the proceedings is known as the fiat.

FILMS, INFLAMMABLE.—As to the licence required for the exhibition of inflammable films and the Home Office regulations for safety *see* CINEMATOGRAPH.

An inflammable film is a "dangerous thing" and imposes on its possessor extra duties of care. Where there is a covenant in a lease not to carry on any dangerous trade, that covenant is broken by the giving on the premises of an exhibition of inflammable films.

Cinematograph Film Act, 1922.—Besides these general duties of looking after dangerous things with great care a statute was passed in 1922 called the Celluloid and Cinematograph Film Act.

The Act does not apply to premises which have been licensed under the Cinematograph Act, 1909. It imposes certain requirements which must be complied with by the occupiers of premises where inflammable films are stored. It applies to premises where more than 80 lbs. weight or 20 reels of film are kept, unless each reel is kept in a properly closed metal box. The occupier must register his name, address and the nature of the business carried on. The premises must not be underneath a dwelling-house and adequate fire escapes must be provided. The Home Secretary's regulations with respect to the use of cinematographs as well as those set out in the Act must be observed. The Act does not apply to the County of London.

FINDING.—Articles found in a public place (including the public part of a shop) do not become the property of the finder unless the owner intended to abandon them. The finder, however, is entitled to pick up such article and to take it away, but he may not use it for his own purposes. He is in the same legal position as if the article had been lent to him by the true owner for the purpose of its being looked after, but not used. The owner may, at any time within six years, claim the property back, and, if the finder has used it for his own purposes or has parted with it, the owner may claim damages for wrongful "conversion." The finder has no right to compensation for the expense of maintaining the property while he held it. If a finder has reasonable grounds for believing that the owner can be found, but nevertheless appropriates the property to himself and uses it as if it were his own, he will be guilty of theft ("larceny by finding"). If property is sold and the buyer finds something contained in it, e.g. bank-notes in a secret drawer, the existence of which was unknown to the seller or the buyer, the buyer is in the position of a finder, and holds the property on behalf of the owner. A finder has every right of an owner in the property he finds except against the true owner, and therefore may bring an action if it is taken from him by some third person. When property is found, not in a public place, but upon A's land by B, A is deemed the finder, and can insist upon B's handing it over to him.

FIRE.—Fire is such a potentially dangerous thing that the law imposes a strict duty of care upon persons who are responsible for lighting one to keep it within bounds and prevent its spread beyond the limits of safety. A fire may be kindled deliberately, as for example a fire in the parlour grate, or it may be kindled accidentally as happens when a lighted cigarette end falls in a pool of petrol.

If a man lights a fire on his own premises he must see that it does not spread beyond the bounds of those premises and do damage to the property of his neighbour. If it spreads through his neglect to take the necessary precautions, he will be liable for the damage which is caused by it. If, however, he can prove that the spreading was caused by some accident which he could not have guarded against, or by the interference of some unauthorized stranger, he will escape liability.

Should a fire start accidentally upon a man's premises he will not be liable for any damage caused by it spreading to his neighbour's land, unless the latter can prove that, although the fire was an accidental one, yet the accident was caused by the negligence of the owner of the premises or his servants.

For example, if Jones has his house burned down by a fire which started in Robinson's house next door, and it transpires that the fire started accidentally through a fuse in Robinson's electric lighting system, Jones will have to prove that Robinson was negligent in allowing the wiring to become defective or dangerous, before he can recover damages from Robinson.

A fire started by lightning is held to be an Act of God, and the occupier of premises affected by it will not be liable if damage is caused to neighbouring property by such a fire. Railway companies are liable for damage caused by sparks and cinders emitted by their engines, and if the damage is done to agricultural lands, negligence upon the part of the company need not be proved.

A fire brigade established by statute or by a local authority in the exercise of its legal powers has power to take possession of premises when a fire breaks out within them, and if they are negligent in dealing with the premises, the authority having control over the brigade is liable. If premises are burnt down after they have been sold, and when the transaction has been completed, the loss falls upon the purchaser; while an occupier of premises who has undertaken to do repairs must rebuild them if they are destroyed by fire.

A tenant is not released from his obligation to pay rent if the premises are destroyed by fire, unless the terms of his lease expressly provide to the contrary. (*See* ACCIDENT; ACT OF GOD; CHIMNEY; ENGINE SPARKS; NEGLIGENCE.)

FIRE ALARMS.—Any person who gives a false alarm of fire to a fire brigade commits an offence punishable with a fine not exceeding £20. The offence is the same whether the alarm be effected by means of a fire alarm or a verbal message to the fire brigade authorities.

FIRE INSURANCE.—A person cannot insure property against loss or damage by fire unless he has an insurable interest in the property, and stands to lose by its damage or destruction, nor under such a policy can he recover a sum greater than his loss.

Any person who owns goods or house property is entitled to insure them against fire. The landlord of a house is always entitled to insure it for its full value, but a tenant, except in the cases mentioned below, may only insure against the loss which he may himself suffer by being unable to use the premises after a fire. This, however, is only so if the tenant is not under an obligation either to insure or to repair the house himself.

Generally speaking, a lease contains an agreement by the tenant to repair the house; and if this is so, he is liable to the landlord to the full extent of any damage by fire that may take place during his tenancy, and so is entitled to insure against this liability, which will amount to the full value of the house. Most leases also contain a clause insisting upon the tenant insuring the premises either in his own name or that of the landlord, and in such cases also he is entitled to insure the house for its full value, and is indeed bound to do so.

Similarly, if a house is mortgaged, the mortgagor is entitled to insure it for its full value, and he is generally under an obligation to the mortgagee to do so. The mortgagee also may insure it, but only for the amount of the mortgage debt, since that is the total loss that he will suffer if the house is destroyed.

In the case of both mortgagee and tenant, however, they may take out an insurance policy for the full amount of the value of the house if they intend that such insurance shall be for the benefit of the mortgagor or the landlord, and in this case if they recover under the policy they must pay over any sum greater than their actual personal loss to the mortgagor or to the landlord, as the case may be. This is an application of the rule that no person may make a profit out of an insurance policy.

A person wishing to insure against fire, generally fills up a proposal form. In this form he must set down specified facts or answer specified questions, and any failure, even if inadvertent, to do this accurately will make the policy void. The greatest care should therefore be taken in filling up this form. The form also states the maximum amount for which the insurance company shall be liable, and if the applicant fills in this amount for a sum very much greater than the true value of the property insured, the policy is liable to be avoided.

When the proposal form has been sent to the insurance company, generally with a small deposit upon the proposed premium, many companies send to the applicant a "Cover Note." This protects the applicant from loss or damage by fire during the period while the insurance company is deciding whether to issue a policy or not, and if the fire takes place during this period the applicant is entitled to recover on the policy even if the company had intended to refuse to issue a policy to him.

If the proposal is accepted the company then issues a policy. This is a document which must be stamped with an Inland Revenue stamp of a value depending upon the value of the property insured, and which contains a description of the property insured, the risk insured against, the maxi-

mum liability of the company, the amount of the premiums and the dates upon which they become due.

The property insured should be accurately described, and if necessary a "floating policy" should be taken out, which covers all goods which may, at any time during the currency of the policy, be upon the premises. The nature of the risk insured against should also be read carefully, since it is a common condition of fire insurance policies that no money shall be paid in respect of damage resulting from explosions, etc., and if it is desired to insure against this danger, special provision should be made for it. Most policies of fire insurance are valid for one year, and contain a provision for their renewal upon payment of a fresh premium upon the date upon which the insurance expires or within the days of grace allowed after that. Careful note should be made of this date and the premium should be sent promptly, if it is desired to renew the policy.

Other conditions which are common (and are generally printed upon the back of the policy) include a provision that the insured person shall notify the company of any loss, together with full particulars within a certain time of the date of the fire; that the insurance company shall be entitled to bring any legal proceedings in respect of the fire in the name of the insured person; and that the insured person shall give the company all the information and assistance in his power in bringing such proceedings. Another usual clause provides that if a fraudulent or over-valued claim is made the whole policy shall be voided. These conditions must, of course, be strictly complied with.

In addition to these, the insurance company always has a right to inspect premises and goods after a fire and to make all reasonable examinations and enquiries. The insurance company is also entitled at its option, instead of paying money under the policy, to make good the damage done itself, i.e. to rebuild the house or to repair the goods. Generally speaking, however, the insurance company sends its own valuer to estimate the loss, while an arbitration clause, which is usually included, provides that any disputes as to value of the property insured shall be referred to an independent arbitrator.

Since an insurance policy is a contract of

indemnity, an insured person cannot dispose of his rights under it, before a fire has taken place, except together with the property insured. In such a case the permission of the insurance company must be obtained; and after this has been done, the person who has acquired the policy together with the property has the same rights and liabilities as the original policy holder. (*See* INSURANCE.)

FIREARMS. Certificate Required. —Under the Firearms Act, 1920, no one (with the exceptions below) can lawfully have in his possession any firearm unless he holds a certificate. This certificate should be applied for to the Chief Officer of Police of the district in which the applicant resides. The police have a discretion in the grant of the certificate, and must not grant it to a person of unsound mind or to anyone who is otherwise unfitted. On a refusal by the police to grant a certificate, the applicant can appeal to a Court of Summary Jurisdiction. The certificate specifies the number and nature of the firearms to which it relates, and only entitles the holder to have possession of these particular arms. The fee for the certificate is 5/– and it lasts for three years. At the end of the three years it is renewable for a further period of three years at the rate of 2/6 a year.

Firearm Defined.—The Act defines "firearm" as any lethal firearm or other weapon from which any shot, bullet or other missile can be discharged. No certificate is required for a smooth bore shot-gun, air-gun or air-rifle (other than those air-guns which are declared by rules made by the Home Secretary to be specially dangerous).

Exceptions.—The Army and Navy are, of course, obvious exceptions to the rule that a certificate is required. Further, members of a rifle club or a cadet corps approved by the Secretary of State need not have certificates when using firearms in connection with drill or target practice. A responsible officer of these clubs or corps should apply for a certificate for which no fee is charged. Gunsmiths and their servants may use firearms for testing and otherwise in the ordinary course of their business. Also, a carrier who is just carrying them as goods needs no certificate for firearms carried by him. There are further exceptions set out

in Sec. 1 (8) of the Act. Any person having in his possession a firearm without a certificate, or failing to comply with the conditions of his certificate, commits an offence and is liable on summary conviction to a fine of £50 and/or 3 months' imprisonment, or on indictment, to 2 years' imprisonment.

Dealers in Firearms.—All dealers must be registered. They must not sell a firearm to any person other than a registered firearms dealer until he produces a certificate authorizing him to purchase the firearm, nor must they undertake to repair a firearm without seeing the certificate. Dealers must keep a register of transactions which must be open to inspection by any officer of police and an office of customs, or of a county council on production of a written authority. If any person fails to comply with these provisions he is liable on summary conviction to 3 months' imprisonment and/or a fine of £20.

No person under 14 is allowed to have possession of a firearm, nor must any person sell one to anyone he has reasonable grounds for believing is under that age. A pawnbroker must not take a firearm or ammunition in pawn. It is a criminal offence to use any imitation firearm for the purpose of avoiding lawful apprehension.

FIREWORKS.—It is an offence to throw, or let off, fireworks in any public place or street. The offence is punishable with a fine not exceeding £5.

FIRM.—The term "firm" is an alternative word for the term "partnership" and the "firm-name" is the collective name under which members of a partnership trade; a firm must always be distinguished from an incorporated company, which can never be known as a "firm." A firm composed of Smith, Jones and Robinson may call itself "Smith and Company," but that does not make them an incorporated company, "Smith and Company" being merely the firm-name. But if the word limited is added after the name, it shews that the name is not that of a firm or partnership but of a company incorporated under the Companies Act and registered at Somerset House. The differences between a firm and an incorporated company are numerous and of great importance, the primary distinction being that each member of a firm is liable personally for the firm's debts, while members (shareholders) of 'ncorporated companies are not personally liable at all, because the company is regarded as a wholly separate person and is liable for its own debts. For certain limited purposes a firm (or partnership) is also regarded as having an identity or personality distinct from the partners who compose it: for example, "John Smith and Son" may sue or be sued by their firm name. But this is really a concession; in strict legal theory, the name appearing on the writ or summons should be "John Smith and William Smith, trading as Smith and Son." If a writ or summons is issued against a firm, it must be made clear that the defendant is a firm, for, in many cases, a firm-name is used when all the original partners have died or sold out; the sole partners of "Robinson and Son" may well be Messrs. Smith and Jones, and the writ should therefore be in the form "Cooper v. Robinson and Son, sued as a firm." If the firm is the plaintiff, it should be "Robinson and Son, suing as a firm, v. Cooper."

All firm-names must be registered, in order that the public may be able to find out who are the real owners of the business, (see BUSINESS NAMES); and the names of all partners must appear on the firm's letters, circulars, show-cards and catalogues, together with the nationality of each partner if it is not British; and, if his present nationality is not his nationality of origin, it must also be stated. A firm-name may become protected as a trade-mark. (See also PARTNERSHIP; TRADE-MARKS.)

FIRST OFFENDERS.—In recent years much has been done to prevent the first offender from being sent to prison. The policy has been, whenever possible, to give a second chance to anyone who has committed a crime, by placing him or her upon probation. The effect of this second chance is that many persons, who, as a result of imprisonment, might have embarked upon a career of crime, have been saved from that; and after the lesson of their first conviction have turned out into good citizens. Every Court, therefore, has the power to take this course in the case of a first offender. But it must be remembered that some first offences are so serious that the Court is bound to inflict some imprisonment. Also, the prisoner may make his first appearance in the dock to answer not one charge, but a number of charges resulting

from a series of offences spread over a considerable time. Here it is difficult to say that he is a first offender, although, wherever possible, the Court will do its best to avoid sending him to prison. (See PROBATION.)

FISHING.—The only places in which members of the public have a general right to fish are tidal rivers and the open sea; and even in tidal rivers they have no right to use the banks for fishing, but are only entitled to fish from boats. In other rivers, lakes, streams and ponds, members of the public are entitled to fish only with the permission of the owner of the water, i.e. of the land bordering on the water; and the right of fishing in water is a valuable right which may be let on lease or sold in the same manner as sporting rights. (See GAME.) In many neighbourhoods local fishing or angling clubs rent waters in which members may fish, and in others hotels keep fishing for their guests. There are, however, a great many places throughout the country where the owners of fishing waters allow the members of the public to fish. Particulars of places where fishing is available may be obtained on payment of a small membership fee from the British Field Sports Society, St. Stephen's House, Westminster, S.W.1.

Certain methods of catching fish are illegal whether done on public or private waters. These include using lights, spears, foul-hooking devices, and fish-roe bait or explosives. Further, nets may not be used for catching salmon or trout, if they have a mesh of less than 2 inches, and no nets may extend more than three-quarters of the way across a river.

Fishery Boards.—In most rivers where there are any trout or salmon or other freshwater fish, there is a fishery board which has control over the fishing in the river. In such rivers no person may fish at all unless he is the holder of a fishing licence issued by the board, which are obtainable at post offices, fishing tackle dealers, etc. Most fishery boards issue licences for salmon and trout fishing, and some for freshwater fishing. Where there is no licence issued for freshwater fishing, no one need hold a licence for fishing for fish other than trout or salmon. The holder of a fishing licence is not entitled to fish in any private water without the permission of the owner of the water.

Fishery boards also appoint water-bailiffs to guard the fishing rights in the river, and any holder of a licence must show it to a water-bailiff or to any other holder of a licence upon demand.

Close Seasons.—The Fishery Board fixes the close season for the various fish in its rivers. These close seasons vary from place to place, but as a general rule they are as follows:—

Trout. From the 30th September to the 1st March.

Salmon. From the 31st October to the 1st February.

Other freshwater fish. From the 14th March to the 16th June.

These close seasons apply to fishing with rod and line. In the case of salmon and trout, fishing by some method other than by rod and line is prohibited one month earlier, and in addition there is a close time each week generally from 6 a.m. on Saturday to 6 a.m. on Monday, but this time may vary from district to district.

Any person who either fishes without licence, or fishes in some method other than that which his licence covers, or fishes during the close season, or catches and takes immature fish, is liable to a penalty not exceeding £50. (*See* GAME.)

FIXTURES.—When any chattel is fixed in any way, not merely resting by its own weight, to a house or land, it is said to be a fixture and becomes part of the freehold. According to the old law in every case it belonged to the owner of the land, and not to the person who had affixed the chattel, who received neither the chattel nor any compensation. A slight attachment is not enough to make a chattel a fixture. Thus a carpet nailed to the floor or a picture hanging on a nail on the wall is not a fixture. On the other hand, even articles which are not attached to the house or land may in exceptional cases be regarded as fixtures if they are specially adapted to the building or premises. Thus statues forming part of the architectural design of a house have been held to be "fixtures," although they were not attached. The rule was recognized to be a hardship in cases where a tenant put on the land some valuable chattel, e.g. panelling on the wall, or a piece of machinery built into the floor of a factory, and was not allowed to remove the property when his tenancy ceased. For this reason certain exceptions

have been made, the effect of which is to allow certain chattels which he has erected, and which have become fixtures, to be removed by the tenant at any time before he leaves the premises. Of course, if a chattel has never been affixed to the premises it never becomes a fixture (except in the rare cases mentioned above), and the tenant may remove it at any time. There are still many fixtures which cannot be removed, but when premises are used for trade or for agriculture, the tenant may now obtain compensation in respect of fixtures which he cannot take away on the ground that they are improvements. (*See below.*)

When Fixtures may be Removed.—Whether a fixture, as above defined, may be removed by the tenant will depend mainly on the purpose for which the chattel was used, but partly also on whether the fixture can be removed without great damage to the house or land. A tenant may remove fixtures when they have been brought on to the premises for the purpose of trade, agriculture, ornament or domestic convenience. These fixtures are known as "tenants'" fixtures, as distinct from "landlords'" fixtures, which are articles annexed to the premises by the tenant during the tenancy and which do not fall within the above classes and therefore cannot be removed.

Trade Fixtures.—Where the purpose for which the fixture has been put up is to enable the tenant to carry on some trade, he may remove the fixture so long as the removal does not injure the house or land. Thus an engine screwed on planks or a boiler fixed in brickwork could be removed, and a greenhouse erected by a market gardener. Notice, however, that if a greenhouse were erected on a brick foundation by a private person for his own pleasure and not for trade, he could not remove it.

Agricultural Fixtures.—The removal of agricultural fixtures is provided for by the Agricultural Holdings Acts, under which any engine, machinery, fencing or other fixtures which the tenant has affixed may be removed by the tenant (*see* AGRICULTURAL HOLDINGS), provided that he has paid all rent and performed his obligations under his tenancy, and that he removes the fixtures with as little damage as possible and makes good such damage as is done. The tenant must give the landlord a month's notice in writing and the landlord can then, if he pleases, purchase the fixture instead of allowing the tenant to remove it. These provisions do not apply to fixtures or buildings which are regarded as improvements. (*See* AGRICULTURAL HOLDINGS.)

Ornamental and Domestic Fixtures. —A tenant's rights to remove ornamental fixtures are less extensive than in the case of trade fixtures. The fixture must be ornamental and not merely put up to complete the house. Thus a fire-grate or a chimney-piece unless of a peculiarly ornamental character could never be removed. Again, fixtures which cannot be removed entire and which are not merely slightly fixed to the premises, but are built in so that their removal would cause damage, cannot be removed. The following have been held to be removable:—

Tapestry on the walls, wainscotting fixed by screws, book cases fixed by screws or nails, ornamental chimney-pieces, water tubs, and blinds. If, however, any of these were fixed in such a way that they could only be removed by breaking up the wall or the floor, e.g. if they were cemented in— they could not be removed.

When Tenant Must Remove.—Except in the case of agricultural fixtures, where the tenant is allowed a reasonable time after the end of the tenancy, all fixtures must be removed before the tenancy ends. Thus, if a tenant leaves linoleum nailed to the floor, or light brackets fixed to the wall at the end of his tenancy, he cannot later return and take them. Nor has he any right to sell them to any new tenant who may come to the premises, for they belong to the landlord.

Special Terms.—Special provisions are frequently made in leases with regard to the fixtures, and of course if this is done these special provisions will apply instead of the above rules. Sometimes the tenant renounces all his right to remove fixtures. And in other cases he agrees to leave the fixtures on being paid their value. It is probable that if the tenant agrees in his lease to yield up the premises in repair "with all erections or improvements," he will not be entitled to remove fixtures for they are regarded as "improvements."

If a tenant removes fixtures when he is not entitled to do so, he may be sued for damages, and where he is entitled to remove fixtures, but is prevented by the landlord, he may in his turn claim for the value of the fixtures.

Distress.—The landlord has no right to take fixtures by way of distress for rent. A creditor, however, who has obtained a judgment against the tenant may have the fixtures seized in execution to pay the amount due to him.

Mortgage of Premises.—Where a tenant mortgages his lease, the mortgagee will be entitled not only to the lease itself, if the tenant makes default, but also to all fixtures even though they may have been erected for the purpose of trade, or for one or other of the purposes set out above.

Sale of Land.—When land is sold the purchaser is entitled to all fixtures which are annexed to the land at the time of the sale.

Fixtures not removable treated as Improvements.—On agricultural holdings (q.v.) and in the case of premises let for trade the tenant at the end of his tenancy is entitled to be paid by his landlord compensation in respect of any improvement (including the re-erection of any building) which he is not entitled to remove as a trade fixture or ornamental or domestic fixture, if the improvement adds to the letting value of the premises, and if notice was given to the landlord of the intention to carry out the improvement as set out below.

No compensation is payable in respect of improvements erected before 25th March, 1928, or less than three years before the end of the tenancy, or in respect of improvements made in pursuance of some statutory duty. The landlord, instead of paying compensation, may offer the tenant a new lease of the premises, and if this is on terms and at a rent which is reasonable (to be decided, if the parties cannot agree, by a tribunal, usually the County Court), the tenant cannot claim compensation if he refuses the lease.

The tenant will not be entitled to any compensation unless he gives the landlord notice of his intention to make the improvement before it is erected. The landlord may object, and if he does so, the question as to whether the improvement is reasonable and will increase the value of the premises will be decided by the appropriate tribunal, usually the County Court. The Court, if satisfied, will grant a certificate that the improvement is a proper improvement. (*See* IMPROVEMENTS.)

Assignment of Fixtures.—If fixtures are assigned together with the land or premises on which they are situated, e.g. by a mortgage, the transaction is not a bill of sale (q.v.); but if the fixtures are assigned separately, the transaction is regarded as an assignment of personal chattels and must comply with the requirements of the Bills of Sale Acts. (*See* AGRICULTURAL HOLDINGS; BILL OF SALE; IMPROVEMENTS; LANDLORD AND TENANT.)

FLAG DAY.—Most police authorities have made regulations dealing with the collection of money or the sale of articles such as flags in streets and public places for the benefit of charity. These regulations usually provide:—

1. That a permit must be obtained from the police;

2. That every collector must have a written authority to collect;

3. That all money must be at once placed in a closed receptacle;

4. That no person must be rewarded for service out of the proceeds of the collection;

5. That an account of the money collected and of the expenses must be submitted to the police authority.

FLAT.—Flats, which are sets of rooms let separately and self-contained are, in law, separate houses, and the lease of a flat differs in very few respects from the lease of a house.

Certain differences arise, however, from the fact that when flats are let the tenant is entitled to the use of certain other parts of the house which are not actually let to him. Thus, in order to get access to his flat he must use the common doorway and common staircase, and these parts are regarded as being under the control of the landlord. The common roof of the premises is also regarded as being under the landlord's control. The effect is, that although the landlord is not bound (apart from special agreement) to keep the premises let by him to the tenant in repair, he is bound to see to the repair of the premises kept under his own control, and if he fails to repair them properly he will be liable to the tenant for any lack of repair. Thus, if through the neglect of the landlord the roof leaks, and in consequence the tenant's pictures or furniture are damaged, the landlord will be liable without any express provision being made in the agreement. The landlord would also be liable if the tenant were injured on the common staircase through lack of repair. The landlord, however, in the absence of express provisions is not bound to light the staircase. If a lift is provided in charge of some servant of the landlord, the landlord will be responsible if the servant leaves the door of the lift shaft open when the lift is not there, and in consequence some person is injured. The landlord will not, however, be liable for any action of the porter which he does, not as the landlord's servant, but at the request of a tenant and for the time being as his (the tenant's) servant.

Usual Terms.—Every tenant of a flat should take care not only that he has a written agreement with his landlord, but that he reads and understands the terms of the agreement. It is frequently provided that the tenant shall not carry on any trade or business on the premises, or keep any animal there. If the tenant wishes to keep a dog or cat, he should see that this clause, if it is in the draft lease submitted to him, is altered so as to prevent him from keeping such animals only when they amount to an annoyance to the other tenants. There is usually a general clause by which the tenant agrees "to do nothing which may annoy" the other tenants. This, however, will not give one tenant any right against another if some annoyance is caused, but will merely entitle the landlord to take action against the offending tenant. Where a tenant is subjected to annoyance from another tenant, he will nevertheless be well advised to ask the tenant to refrain from the annoyance before reporting the matter to the landlord.

What is annoyance will depend entirely upon the circumstances of the case. The mere fact that a tenant is annoyed by what takes place in the next flat will not necessarily entitle him to prevent it. Thus a wireless set may cause great annoyance to neighbouring tenants, but they cannot object so long as it is used at reasonable times. In the same way, a large and noisy party or dancing may cause much annoyance to a tenant underneath, but he cannot necessarily prevent it. If the premises were not strongly constructed, e.g. were in a converted house with thin floors and walls, conduct might amount to annoyance in law which would not be so regarded in premises more effectively isolated from one another.

A tenant is usually prohibited from assigning or subletting, but in most cases it is provided that he may do so with the consent of the landlord, and wherever this position is found the landlord will not be able to refuse his consent if the assignee or sublessee is a responsible person likely to be able to pay the rent and bears a good character.

Service Flats.—These are flats in which the landlord undertakes to provide for the tenants certain services, such as attendance or the supply of meals. In some cases tenants are bound to spend so much per week on meals in the restaurant provided by the landlord. (*See* LANDLORD AND TENANT; and SPECIAL SUPPLEMENT "RENT RESTRICTIONS.")

FLOATING CHARGE.—This is a form of security over property which may be given only by companies registered in England and not by private individuals or by companies registered in Scotland. It enables the company to dispose of the property covered by the charge so long as it does so in the ordinary way of business. The charge covers the property while owned by the company, but ceases to attach when the company disposes of the property. A floating charge is distinguished from a fixed charge, i.e. a mortgage, in which the property continues to be covered by the charge even after the company has parted with it. (*See* DEBENTURES.)

FLOTSAM.—Goods floating upon the surface of the sea which have been lost from a ship or cast overboard are called flotsam. If ownership cannot be established they become the property of the crown.

FOOD.—In the interests of public health the sale or supply of food is governed by certain provisions of the law as to its wholesomeness, fitness for human consumption and purity. To sell or expose for sale diseased or unwholesome food is a common law nuisance, quite apart from being an offence prohibited by any Act of Parliament, and if a person eats diseased meat or unwholesome food and thereby contracts a disease of which he dies, the seller may be charged with manslaughter and convicted if

it is proved that he sold the meat or food knowing that it was unwholesome.

The Public Health Acts provide for the appointment by local authorities of inspectors of nuisances, and these inspectors or the medical officer of health for the district have the right of examining and seizing any foods which are in their opinion diseased. They may at all reasonable times inspect any article of food intended for human consumption which is exposed for sale, and if they come to the conclusion that it is diseased or unfit for human consumption they may seize it and take it to a justice of the peace to be dealt with. Any obstruction of an officer carrying out these duties is punishable by a fine of £5.

When an article of food is seized, it is taken before a justice, and if it appears to him to be diseased or unsound he must condemn it and order it to be destroyed. When an article has been condemned, the person who sold it may be proceeded against and, if convicted, may be fined £20 or sent to prison for 3 months.

Adulteration.—Provision is made by an Act of 1928 for the prevention of the adulteration of food. The term food includes every article used for food or drink by man, other than drugs or water, and any article which ordinarily enters into, or is used in, the composition or preparation of human food. It is an offence to mix, stain, colour, or powder any article of food with any ingredient or material which will make the article injurious to health. It is also an offence to sell any article of food which has been so mixed, stained, coloured or powdered. The penalty for either of these offences is £50; for a second offence the penalty is 6 months' imprisonment.

A defendant may escape liability if he shews that he did not know, and could not have found out with reasonable care, that the article was so mixed, stained, etc. To abstract any part of an article of food in such a way as to affect its quality, substance, or nature, and not to give notice of such alteration is an offence punishable with a fine of £20.

It is an offence to supply a purchaser with any article of food which is not of the nature, substance, or quality demanded by the purchaser. No offence is, however, committed in the following cases: (1) When an ingredient has been added because it is required to make the article fit for consumption or carriage, and where such addition is not made fraudulently to increase the weight of the article; (2) where the food supplied is a patent food and it is supplied in the state required by the specification of the patent; (3) where the food is unavoidably mixed with some outside matter in the process of collection or preparation; (4) where the article is whisky, brandy, rum, or gin, and is not adulterated in any way except by the addition of water, and provided that the mixture has not reduced the spirit more than 35 degrees under proof.

Taking a Sample.—A purchaser of any article of food is entitled to submit it for analysis to the public analyst for the place within which it is purchased on payment to such analyst of a sum not exceeding 10/6, and to receive a certificate of such analysis. The public analyst of each district is appointed by the local authority with the approval of the Minister of Health.

Any medical officer of health, sanitary inspector, or inspector of weights and measures may procure any sample of food if he suspects it of having been sold, or exposed for sale, contrary to any of the provisions of the Food and Drugs Acts, and have it analysed by the public analyst of the district. A sample is usually taken at the shop or place of business of the seller, and if a seller refuses to allow a sample to be taken he is liable to a penalty of £10. A similar penalty is incurred by any person who refuses to sell an article of food to an inspector who tenders the price of it. When a public officer, such as an inspector, purchases an article with the intention of having it analysed he must, at the time the purchase is made, notify the seller that he intends to have it analysed by the public analyst; and he must then divide the sample into three parts, give one part to the seller, one to the public analyst and keep the third himself for future comparison. The three parts must be sealed up or fastened in such a way that the sample cannot be tampered with, without interfering with the sealing or fastening. Notification of intention to have it analysed must be given by the inspector, otherwise the seller cannot be prosecuted.

If food mixed with an ingredient not harmful to health is sold with a label legibly written or printed which states that the food is mixed, then the seller is protected from any liability which he might otherwise incur for having sold adulterated food. The label need only state that the food is a mixture, but it is advisable that it should contain sufficient information to make it absolutely clear to the purchaser that it is a mixture.

If a person is summoned for selling unwholesome, or adulterated or mixed food, he may defend himself by showing that he bought the article from another person who gave him a written warranty that it was the same in nature, substance, and quality, as that which was demanded by the purchaser. If, however, he wishes to avail himself of this defence he must within seven days after a summons has been served upon him send a copy of the warranty to the prosecutor and a written notice, stating that he intends to rely upon it, and giving the name and address of the person who gave him the warranty. He must also give notice to the person who gave the warranty that he has been summoned to answer a charge, and that he is relying upon the warranty as his defence.

Special provisions are made by the Food and Drugs Acts with regard to particular articles of food such as Bread, Margarine, and Milk and these are dealt with under their separate titles. (*See* BREAD; BUTTER; DRUGS; PUBLIC HEALTH; WARRANTY.)

FOOT AND MOUTH DISEASE.— This disease is so infectious and causes so much loss to farmers and cattle dealers that very strict regulations have been made by the Minister of Agriculture and Fisheries under various Acts of Parliament with regard to the notification and isolation of cases of animals infected with it. If a person has in his possession or under his charge an animal infected with foot and mouth disease, he must give notice of the infection to a police constable. The constable must thereupon immediately send a telegram to the Ministry of Agriculture and Fisheries informing them of the outbreak. The person in control of the diseased animal must take steps to isolate it from other animals as far as is practicable.

The Minister has power to make orders forbidding the movement of all animals in the area in which the infection has been discovered, and he may also make orders providing for the slaughter of infected animals and other animals which have been in contact with a diseased animal. A person who disobeys any of these orders commits an offence and is liable to a penalty of £50. If cattle are slaughtered by order of the Minister to prevent the spread of infection, compensation is payable to the owners unless they have been guilty of an offence against the Diseases of Animals Act, or if the slaughter has been necessitated by their own neglect to take the necessary precautions to isolate the cattle.

FOOTBALL BETTING. Cash Competitions.—The Ready Money Football Betting Act of 1920 was passed to prevent the writing, printing, publishing or circulating in the United Kingdom of advertisements, circulars or coupons of any ready money football betting business. A "ready money football business" is defined as any business or agency for the making of ready money bets or wagers, or for the receipt of any money or valuable thing, as the consideration for a bet or wager in connection with any football game. The essence of the business aimed at is that it is of a cash or ready money nature, i.e. the bet or contribution is sent up to the promoters with the entries and before the result. The fact that skill is required in forecasting the result does not avoid the operation of the statute. The act makes it an offence for anyone to participate in the carrying on of such business, punishable on summary conviction for the first offence by a fine of £25 or in default 1 month's imprisonment. For the second offence the penalty is a fine of £100 or 3 months' imprisonment.

All those who take part knowingly in the circulation are liable. For instance, if a newspaper contains coupons inviting the public to forecast a match result, offering money prizes, and it is shewn that some persons bought the paper partly to get the coupons, the owners and publishers of the paper may be convicted.

FOOTBALL IN THE STREET.— It is an offence punishable by a fine not exceeding forty shillings to play football or any other game on any part of the highway to the annoyance of passers by.

FOOTPATH.—When members of the public are entitled as a matter of right to use a footpath, the footpath is technically a highway (q.v.), and the public are said to have a right of way over it. Under the Rights of Way Act, 1932, maps are being prepared throughout the country shewing all public rights of way in existence.

If a motor vehicle mounts the footpath and injures any person or property, there is what the law calls "prima facie evidence" of negligence. This means that, whereas in the ordinary case it is for the person who has suffered loss or damage to show that the motorist was negligent, in this case it is for the motorist to prove that he was not negligent. (*See* HIGHWAYS; NEGLIGENCE.)

FORECLOSURE.—Where a person who has borrowed money on the security of property by means of a "Mortgage" has defaulted in the due payment of the debt after it has become due, or has not paid his interest, or failed to observe the covenants (which are the conditions), the lender may apply to the Court for a foreclosure order, whereby the borrower will lose his right to get back the property mortgaged on paying off the mortgage, and the mortgagee becomes the complete owner. In the first instance the Court makes an order "nisi" which remains in force for six months. It also orders that an account shall be taken, or prepared, shewing what is due from the borrower to the lender in respect of the mortgage, and if this is not paid within the six months, then the Court makes the Foreclosure Order Absolute.

If the lender exercises this right, he may not exercise any of his other rights in order to get his money, for example, sue for it under the personal covenant or undertaking contained in the Mortgage Deed, whereby the borrower, in addition to transferring the property to the lender as security, personally undertakes to repay the borrowed money and interest. Also the lender must not exercise the power of sale which he has under the mortgage, whilst the Foreclosure Order Nisi is in force, or the order will automatically come to an end. Furthermore, the lender under a foreclosure order absolute takes the property in full satisfaction of the borrower's indebtedness.

FORCIBLE ENTRY.—It is a misdemeanour to enter upon premises to recover possession of them by means of force. A person who is guilty of a forcible entry may also be guilty of assault and render himself liable to criminal proceedings for that or to a civil action. Of course, where the owner or occupier of land or building premises is in occupation and a trespasser gets in, he may eject him, using no more force than is necessary to effect this purpose.

FOREIGN ENLISTMENT.—British subjects are forbidden to join the armed forces of any foreign State when it is at war with any state with which the King is at peace. This was enacted by the Foreign Enlistment Act 1870 which makes a contravention of this provision an offence punishable with imprisonment and fine or either. This Act further makes it an offence for any person to fit out, or send, any expedition from His Majesty's Dominions to assist any foreign state which is at war with any friendly state. The Act does not affect British subjects who join foreign armies in times of peace.

FOREIGN LAW.—(*See* "CONFLICT OF LAWS.")

FOREIGNER. — The restrictions at present imposed upon the immigration of foreigners and their residence in England are chiefly the result of war-time and post-war legislation. As to these restrictions and other branches of the law relating to foreigners *see* ALIENS; EXTRADITION; NATURALISATION.

FORFEITURE.—Is the right of the lessor, who is the person who grants a lease, to re-enter on the leased premises and terminate the lease. Apart from a special provision in the lease, the right to forfeit the lease in respect of non-payment of rent can only be exercised after formal demand has been made by the lessor on the premises at a convenient hour before sunset. Leases, however, usually contain a "Covenant" or stipulation, that if the rent remains unpaid for twenty-one days, whether formally demanded or not, the lessor may enter on to the whole or any part of the premises and terminate the lease.

Leases usually also give a right of forfeiture to the lessor where other covenants have been broken, such as the covenant to repair, or to insure. But this right can only be exercised after the lessor has served a notice upon the lessee, or tenant, setting out the respects in which the terms of the lease have been broken, requiring the lessee to remedy them within a reasonable time and to pay compensation. If the lessee does not comply with the notice, then the lessor can put an end to the lease either by entering and taking possession, or taking proceedings in the Court and obtaining an order forfeiting the lease. The lessee may apply to the Court to be relieved from the consequences of having broken the terms of the lease, whether or not the lessor takes action; and the Court can grant relief or refuse relief, by declining to make a forfeiture order, or rescinding one already made, but subject to such terms as it thinks fit.

This will usually include the payment by the lessee of all expenses incurred by the lessor in the proceedings. Relief must be claimed by the lessee, however, before the lessor actually enters, otherwise he will probably be too late. No relief will be granted in certain circumstances, for example where the lessee becomes bankrupt, or where certain kinds of leases—e.g. where the letting was made to the particular lessee because of his peculiar fitness to be the lessee—are taken in execution to satisfy a judgment against the lessee. If the lessee whose lease is forfeited has himself let the premises by an underlease, the underlessee—i.e. the tenant of the underlease—may make application to the Court for relief, and the Court may make an order placing the under lessee in the position of the lessee whose lease has been forfeited. (*See* LANDLORD AND TENANT.)

FORGERY.—Forgery has always been a crime in English law. It was defined by Blackstone as the fraudulent making or alteration of a writing to the prejudice of any man's right, and this definition still holds good as regards most types of forgery. Forgery is not confined to the preparation of a wholly fictitious document. The slightest alteration of any document constitutes forgery if the intention of the person doing it is thereby to commit some fraud. It is therefore forgery to add to, or remove, a single letter of a word in a document. Indeed it is not essential that that which is added or removed should be part of a word. Fraudulent removal of the crossing on a cheque is sufficient to constitute a forgery.

The present law as to forgery is contained in the Forgery Act of 1913. This Act classifies forgery into various categories according to the document that is forged. It enacts that forgery with intent to defraud of any will, deed, bond or bank note, is punishable with penal servitude for life. Forgery, with a similar intent, of any valuable security, any document of title to goods or land, or of any policy of insurance, is made punishable with penal servitude for a period not exceeding 14 years. This Act also renders forgery of certain official documents, such as birth, death or marriage certificates punishable with penal servitude for 5 years, and of any document not specified in the Act punishable with imprisonment, with hard labour, for a period not exceeding 2 years.

All these offences involve an intention to defraud. In the case of public documents, however, a person may commit forgery, even though his intention is not to defraud, but merely to deceive. In this case the evidence is punishable with imprisonment, with or without hard labour, for a term not exceeding 2 years.

FORMA PAUPERIS.—A poor litigant can obtain a certificate authorizing him to sue or be sued under special rules as a Poor Person, or "in forma pauperis." (*See* LEGAL AID, POOR PERSONS' DEPARTMENT.)

FORTUNE TELLERS.—Any person who pretends to tell fortunes can be convicted as an idle and disorderly person under the Vagrancy Act, 1824. It does not matter whether the fortune teller really believes that he or she can foretell the future; the offence is committed whatever the belief of the fortune teller. Any means of telling fortunes is illegal, including pretending to obtain information about the future from the spirits of deceased persons. On the other hand it is normally no offence, by means of palmistry or otherwise, to read a person's character, as distinct from his fortune or future destiny.

FOSTER-PARENT.—This term has no special legal significance. It is usually used to denote a person who has placed himself in loco parentis to a child (*see* LOCO PARENTIS), or a person who has undertaken the care and maintenance of an infant. (*See* BABY-FARMING; GUARDIANSHIP.)

FOXHUNTING.—The Fox.—A fox is vermin and may be killed by anyone.

There are no statutory restrictions as to the times in which it can be hunted and killed, i.e. there is no close season. Since a fox is not game, it follows that a licence to hunt over another person's land is not in the nature of a sporting right which would entitle the person hunting to take away the animal when killed. A fox is feræ naturæ (*see* FERÆ NATURÆ), and no person can claim ownership or property in it unless it is enclosed or tame.

A hunt is under no duty to keep down the number of foxes in a locality, nor to pay compensation for poultry destroyed by them. But compensation is usually paid voluntarily by a special fund kept for that purpose.

Trespass while Hunting.—An Englishman's home is his castle, and it is no excuse for any person who comes on to the land of another against his will to plead that he was following hounds. Hunting exists through the goodwill of farmers and landowners, and if any of them warn the hunt to keep off, they must do so, or the aggrieved owner can sue the trespasser. He can sue individual members of the hunt who trespass on his land or he can sue the master. In the words of Lord Tenterden, "If a gentleman sends out his hounds and servants and invites other gentlemen to hunt with him, though he doesn't himself go on lands of another, but they do, he is answerable for any trespass they do unless he distinctly desires them not to go on those lands." In the old days the justification for the trespass was said to be that the sole object of the hunt was to pursue and kill a noxious animal, but no one would argue that that was the sole purpose of foxhunting to-day.

FRANCHISE.—A franchise is a royal privilege or right which has been transferred to a subject by grant, either express or implied, from immemorial usage. The most common franchise is the right to vote at the election of Members of Parliament and the term "franchise" is commonly used to cover this right only. Other franchises include the right to hold a market, or maintain a ferry or toll, etc. (*See* VOTING.).

FRAUD.—It is a fundamental principle of English law that common honesty should be maintained between the parties to a contract. A departure from such a standard is known in law as Fraud and gives rise in the party wronged to a right not only to repudiate any contract in which there has been fraudulent dealing by the other party, but also to recover damages for any loss which he has suffered by reason of such fraudulent dealing.

The commonest kind of fraud in English law is Fraudulent Misrepresentation.

Fraudulent Misrepresentation.—Wherever, during the course of negotiations leading up to a contract, one of the negotiating parties makes a false statement of fact which induces the other party to enter into the contract, such a statement is known as a misrepresentation (q.v.) which may give rise to a right in the deceived party to repudiate the contract.

Where the party who makes the statement is unaware of its untruth, it is known as an innocent misrepresentation, and the only right conferred upon the deceived party is a right to repudiate the contract. He does not receive any right to obtain damages for his deception. (*See* MISREPRESENTATION.)

Where the party who makes the statement, either knows that it is untrue, or makes it in a spirit of recklessness not caring whether it be true or false, such a statement is held to be fraudulent, and entitles the party deceived not only to repudiate the contract, upon discovering the fraud, but also to recover as damages any loss which he has suffered as a result of his acting on the faith of the fraudulent statement.

For a misrepresentation to be sufficient to amount to a cause of action in fraud, it must fulfil all the following conditions: It must be a positive statement of fact; it must have been made in order to induce the party to whom it was made to enter into the contract; and it must have formed part of the actual inducement to him to enter into the contract.

If those conditions are fulfilled, the party deceived is entitled to repudiate the contract upon discovering the fraud. However, as in the cases of innocent misrepresentation, he can only repudiate the contract as long as it is possible that all parties to the contract can be placed in the same position as though the contract had never been made. If the placing of such parties in the same position involves the violation of the rights of third parties, the person wronged must fall back on his right to recover damages for fraud.

In addition to his right to repudiate the contract, a person who has been induced to enter into a contract by reason of fraudulent misrepresentation is entitled to recover damages for fraud, which will include any loss which he may have suffered by reason of the fraud.

Thus, a person who has been induced to enter into a contract by fraud, can either repudiate the contract and refuse further to be bound by it, and in addition sue for damages, or he can adopt the contract and continue to be bound by it, and at the same time sue for damages for any loss that he has suffered as a result of the fraud.

Fraud During a Contract.—Fraud as a cause of action is not limited to fraudulent statements made by a person in the course of negotiations for a contract. Any form of dishonest dealing taking place during the continuance of a contract amounts to fraud. Thus, assuming that A employs B to purchase goods for him on the market, and B sells to A his own goods at a high price and conceals from A the fact that he has done so, such a course of conduct would amount to fraud, and would entitle A not only to sue B for damages, but to repudiate the purchase, and to insist upon B taking his own goods back and refunding the money.

Concealed Fraud.—Generally speaking, a right to repudiate a contract for misrepresentation or for any other reason is lost unless the right to repudiate the contract is exercised within a reasonable time. Where, however, a person who has a right to repudiate the contract is prevented from discovering his right because of the fraud of the other party to a contract, he does not lose his right to repudiate the contract merely because he has not acted promptly. His right to repudiate is treated as if it had not arisen until he had every opportunity of finding out the true facts, and he is accordingly granted a reasonable time to repudiate after that discovery.

Cases where one person has dishonestly prevented the other party to the contract from finding out the true facts are known as cases of concealed fraud.

Other Effects of Fraud.—The existence of fraud in a contract has many serious effects, all based upon the doctrine that no man is entitled to profit by reason of his own wrong. If we assume that A and

B have entered into a contract which B has broken, and that A had waived the breach of the contract, i.e. indicated that he does not intend to enforce his strict rights, A is entitled to withdraw his waiver, if he subsequently discovers that B's breach of contract is fraudulent.

In a similar manner, if, at the end of a long series of mutual dealings between A and B, a settlement is made of all outstanding differences, as a general rule such a settlement, which is known as Settled Account, will not be reopened by the Court. But if A subsequently discovers that B has been guilty of fraud and that the account was agreed between them in ignorance of this fact, the account may be reopened and the whole question of the mutual dealings between A and B can be gone into again.

Gravity of Fraud.—In view of the serious manner in which the law regards fraud, charges of fraud should not be made in any legal proceedings except after the most careful consideration. If a charge of fraud is made in an action it must be set out in the Pleadings (q.v.) in the greatest detail, setting out every allegation which is relied upon. (*See* CONTRACT; MISREPRESENTATION.)

FRAUDS, STATUTE OF. — This name is applied to a very famous Act of Parliament passed in 1677. It is entitled "An Act for the Prevention of Frauds and Perjuries." It provides that unless certain transactions are entered into by a written contract, or in other cases, although not made at the time in writing, can be proved by some document in writing, they will not be enforced by the law. Oral evidence of them will not be accepted. It is no doubt possible that, before the Act was passed, many frauds may have been committed by persons swearing verbally and untruly that others had entered into certain transactions with them; but it is difficult to think that these frauds can equal in number the injustices that the statute itself has brought about since that time.

The statute applies to a contract of guarantee to a sale of land or lease for over three years, to contracts which are not to be performed within a year from the date when they were made, and to certain other contracts. In some cases the statute requires that the transaction should be entered into in writing at the time when it was made,

e.g. sales of land or leases; but in other cases it is enough if written evidence of the contract can be produced even though the writing has only come into existence after the contract was made. Some of the sections of the Statutes of Fraud have now been repealed, but their provisions have been re-enacted in more modern statutes, e.g. the Sale of Goods Act and the Law of Property Act. (*See* CONTRACTS; GUARANTEE; SALE OF GOODS; SALE OF LAND.)

FRAUDULENT CONVERSION.— Any person who receives property for, or on account of, any other person, and who fraudulently converts it to his own use or to the use of somebody else, commits the crime of fraudulent conversion. It is not essential that the accused shall receive the property directly from the owner. The offence can be committed even though the owner of the property does not know of its existence and has not got any intention of entrusting the money to the accused person. There are various special forms of fraudulent conversion applicable to directors of companies, etc.

Trustees who fraudulently deal with their trust funds may be convicted of fraudulent conversion as a trustee. Again, if anyone is entrusted with a Power of Attorney and fraudulently uses it in order to convert the property covered by it to his own use, he can be convicted of this crime. The maximum punishment for fraudulent conversion is penal servitude for not more than 7 years. Prosecutions for offences by trustees cannot be commenced without the sanction of the Attorney-General or in certain cases of a Judge.

FRAUDULENT CONVEYANCE.— Any conveyance or transfer of property by a debtor, done with the intention of putting the property out of the reach of his creditors, will be liable to be set aside by the trustee in bankruptcy and the property reclaimed. Such a conveyance is also an act of bankruptcy (q.v.). This provision is intended to prevent a trader transferring his business to a friend, and then carrying it on without disclosing that he is no longer the owner of it. When he becomes bankrupt he cannot rely on this transfer but the business must be treated as his. The transfer of the whole of the debtor's property for the benefit of certain creditors will always be treated as void. But in cases where the debtor receives the reasonable equivalent of the property transferred in exchange for the property itself, the transfer will not be void unless it can be proved that it was done with the intention of defrauding his creditors, as it may be where the debtor sells his stock intending to abscond with the money which he gets for it, which is naturally more easily removed than the stock itself.

When property is not exchanged for anything else, either money or other property, but is given away, the transaction is known as a voluntary settlement. Such settlements may be set aside if they are made within 2 years before the bankruptcy, unless they are marriage settlements made before marriage either by a man on his future wife or by some other person on the husband and wife.

Where the settlement is made more than 2 years before the bankruptcy but less than 10, it may still be set aside unless it can be shewn that, when the person made the settlement, he had enough money and property to pay all his debts at that time without using the property which he disposed of in the settlement.

A settlement does not include every transfer of property but only one in which the property transferred is intended to be kept, and not used or otherwise got rid of. Thus a gift of jewellery would be a settlement but a gift of money normally would not. These provisions are intended to prevent creditors being injured by conduct such as that of a foolish man who makes large presents of jewellery to his wife at a time when he cannot afford to do so. Even though he had no intention of defrauding his creditors, the property would be recoverable by the trustee in bankruptcy. (*See* BANKRUPTCY; TRUSTEE IN BANKRUPTCY.)

FRAUDULENT PREFERENCE.— One of the conditions on which a debtor is allowed to become a bankrupt and so be free from all his debts is that his property should be divided fairly among his creditors according to the law. If therefore a debtor at a time when he is not yet bankrupt, but when he sees that he will not be able to carry on much longer, pays one of his creditors or gives him some security for a debt which is already due *with the intention* of putting that creditor in a better financial position than the other creditors,

the transaction will be contrary to the principles of the law of bankruptcy.

When this happens, the creditor will not be allowed to retain the money which he got in payment of his debt or the property over which he was given a security, but will have to hand it back to the trustee in bankruptcy to be used for the benefit of all the creditors. The creditor himself will, of course, not be prevented from claiming in the bankruptcy for his debt, but he will only get the same proportionate share of what he claims as will the other creditors, and will not be preferred. It does not matter whether or not the creditor knew, when he got the money or the security, that that was being given to him by the debtor with the intention of preferring him to the other creditors.

In order to make a transaction a fraudulent preference three things are necessary:

1. The debtor must be insolvent when he makes it, that is to say his debts must exceed his assets.

2. His main motive in making the payment to the creditor or giving him the security must be to prefer him and to put him in a better position than the other creditors; and:

3. The transaction must take place within 3 months before a petition is presented to make the debtor bankrupt. If the creditor is pressing the debtor to pay—for example, is threatening to bring an action against him for the money—the preference will not be considered fraudulent, but the Court will always be ready to suspect that a debtor may have arranged with a creditor to have an action brought against him so that the transaction may appear not to be fraudulent to the other creditors, whereas it is in fact fraudulent.

A fraudulent preference is also an act of bankruptcy and this is important, for the trustee's title will "relate back" and enable him to claim everything that was the property of the debtor at the time of the earliest act of bankruptcy within 3 months before the presentation of the petition. (*See* BANKRUPTCY.)

FREEHOLD.—The adjective freehold is used to describe the different kinds of ownership of land—a lawyer would say the different estates in land—the length or duration of which is uncertain. It signifies that one cannot foretell in advance how long a particular ownership will continue. There were four varieties of freehold estate: the fee simple, the fee tail, the life estate, and the estate *pur autre vie*. The latter expression is old law French for "for the life of another.": In all these estates it is impossible to say in advance at exactly what moment they will come to an end. Some will obviously last much longer than the others; the first two, the fee simple and the fee tail, will descend to the owner's heirs; hence they are called freehold estates in fee, for fee means inheritable.

In contrast to the freehold estates are the leasehold estates. A leasehold is any interest in land which is created for a fixed number of years. Its duration can therefore always be calculated. This distinction between freehold and leasehold may be put in another form, for freehold estates are "real" property whereas leaseholds are not technically "real" at all but are only personal property or chattels. (*See* REAL PROPERTY.)

The distinction arises from the fact that for some time after the Norman Conquest, leasehold estates were not recognised at all by the law; and when they were at last permitted the legal characteristics of freehold or real estates had become too firmly established to admit of any expansion.

There were also reasons of policy. It was not until well into the fourteenth century that it became possible to leave real property by will. As leaseholds were principally used as investments it followed that the investor was not anxious to have them treated like realty. The results of the distinction have become less and less until now it is only of academic importance, but until 1700 the actions available for the recovery of land from a wrongful possessor varied according to whether the plaintiff's estate in the land was freehold or leasehold.

Indeed it was not till about the same time that a dispossessed leaseholder could claim to be put back into possession or recover more than mere damages if he were ejected. One set of rules now govern the distribution of all the property of a man who dies intestate, but until 1925 there was one set for freeholds, another for leaseholds and other kinds of property. (*See* INTESTACY; REAL PROPERTY.)

FREIGHT.—Freight is money payable by a person who sends goods to be carried at sea either under a bill of lading, when the whole capacity of the ship is not taken, or under a charter party, when the whole of the ship or some specific part of its capacity is taken. The carrier is not entitled to any freight unless he delivers the goods at the place where he is bound to take them, under his contract, except in cases where his failure to deliver them is due to the fault of the person who is sending them, or of the consignee, i.e. the person to whom they are sent. Thus, if goods are to be taken to a port, the carrier cannot claim any freight if he only takes them to the mouth of the river on which the port is situated. Even in cases where the carrier is unable to deliver the goods because they have been destroyed by one of the causes for which he is expressly stated not to be liable under the charter party or bill of lading (e.g. by fire), he is not entitled to any freight—the effect of the clause being merely to *prevent* him from being liable for the *loss* of the goods. If the goods are damaged when delivered, he is entitled to freight although he may be liable for having allowed them to become damaged.

Cesser Clause.—The person liable for freight will usually be the person who has shipped the goods, but his liability may be removed by the terms of the charter party or the bill of lading, and the person entitled to the goods at the place of delivery may be liable instead. This will be the case where there is what is known as a "Cesser Clause," by which the person shipping the goods is released from all liability once the goods are delivered on board ship, and, when this is so, the carrier will recover the freight from the consignee by means of his lien (q.v.)—that is, he will refuse to hand over the goods until the freight is paid. Where goods are shipped under a bill of lading, every person to whom the bill of lading may be transferred will be liable to the carrier to pay the freight. Where a bill of lading has passed through several hands the person who will ultimately have to pay on the freight as between the various holders of the bill will, of course, be the ultimate holder who receives the goods.

Advance Freight.—Freight may be payable, if the contract has so provided, before the goods are delivered, and in this case it will be known as "Advance Freight." Advance freight is due even though the goods are never delivered at all but are lost through one of the perils for which the carrier is not responsible.

Lump Sum Freight.—It may be arranged that a lump sum, known as "Lump Freight," shall be paid as freight for the sum use of the ship for a certain voyage or period, and if this is so the money must be paid if the carrier is ready to carry out his bargain, although, in fact, no goods are even shipped. Further, the carrier will be entitled to freight if he delivers any of the goods, so long as the others are lost through some cause for which he is not responsible; but he will not be entitled to any freight if the whole cargo is lost.

Although it is the case that if the carrier does not deliver the goods at the place appointed, he is not entitled to any freight except in the case of advance freight or lump sum freight, even though he may have taken them some considerable distance on their way, yet it is possible for the carrier and the consignor to arrange that the goods shall not be delivered at the place originally agreed, but at some point short of their original destination. In such a case a proportionate part of the freight may be paid. This is known as pro rata freight.

When a charterer has taken a ship for a voyage on the terms that he shall load a cargo of a certain amount and pay on it a freight calculated at so much per ton, he is under a duty to provide a cargo of that amount, and if he does not do so will be liable for damages. These damages are known as "dead freight" and will be the amount which would have been payable had a full cargo been shipped. (*See* CARRIAGE BY SEA.)

FRIENDLY SOCIETY.—A Friendly Society is the name given to an association of persons voluntarily formed, having for its purpose the raising of funds by subscriptions from members, to enable it to make advances to members for their maintenance during sickness, old age, widowhood and kindred circumstances.

A society may be registered or unregistered. It is better for a society to be registered because the law gives certain valuable privileges to a registered society that are not available to an unregistered one. An unregistered society resembles a club in its position in the eyes of the law, and it may in certain circumstances be illegal for lack of registration as a company. Moreover an unregistered society is absolutely prohibited by law from carrying on the business of life insurance.

How to Register a Society.—If a friendly society wishes to become registered it must have at least seven members. A society desiring to be registered must send an application to the Chief Registrar of Friendly Societies whose office is at 17, North Audley Street, London, W.1. The application must be signed by seven members of the society, and it must be accompanied by two printed copies of the rules of the society, together with a list of the names of the trustees and the secretary. If the registrar is satisfied that all the legal requirements have been complied with, he will send the society an acknowledgment of the application, and such acknowledgment is then conclusive evidence that the society has been registered.

Legal Requirements.—The rules of the society desiring to be registered must contain the name of the society and the address of its registered office. A registered society must have a registered office.

The Rules must also state the objects of the society, how its funds are to be applied, the conditions entitling a member to receive a benefit, the fines and forfeitures which can be imposed upon a member, and the manner of appointing and removing the office bearers of the society.

Provision must be made in the rules for the investment of the society's funds, and these may be invested in authorised trustee investment stocks or upon the purchase of any security which is expressly authorised by the rules.

Certain obligations are imposed by statute upon all registered friendly societies and these must be complied with. The society must have its assets and liabilities valued once in every five years, either by a valuer appointed by the society, or, if the society so desires, it may send all the necessary particulars to the registrar and request him to have the valuation carried out. The accounts of a society must be audited every year and the accounts, when audited, must be sent to the registrar.

Necessary Officers of a Society.— A registered friendly society must have one or more trustees and a secretary, a treasurer and a committee of management.

The Trustees are the persons who have the duty of investing the funds of the society. They hold any land or other property belonging to the society, and they distribute money payable upon the death of a member not leaving a will to the persons who appear to them to be entitled to it.

A trustee is personally liable for any money actually received by him on behalf of the society but not for a deficiency which may arise in the general funds. The trustees are the persons to bring a law suit on behalf of a friendly society and they are the persons who defend an action brought against it. If, therefore, a member wishes to sue the society in respect of a benefit which he alleges to be due to him, he must bring his action against the trustees.

The Treasurer is the person who will usually have charge of the funds, and it is very advisable, when he is appointed, to require him to give either a bond with at least one person to stand as surety for him, or else the security of a guarantee society; this is done to secure the rendering by him of accounts, and the payment by him of all sums which may be due from him.

A registered society has the first claim upon the assets of one of its officers who has died or become bankrupt, in respect of any debt due to it by the officer, but it loses this special privilege of first claim if it neglects to take a bond from the officer.

The Committee of Management of a society must be consulted about the investment of the society's funds and their consent is necessary before an investment can be made. They are the people to prosecute an official of the society for misappropriating the funds of the society, and they should immediately inform the police if any irregularity or defalcation is discovered.

The Object of Friendly Societies.— There are three main classes of objects for which a friendly society may be formed. These are:—

(1) Mutual relief and maintenance of members, and the payment to them of benefits upon the happening of certain contingencies: This class includes the following objects:—

(a) Maintaining or helping a member or his relatives during sickness, old age, and widowhood; and in the case of

orphan children of a member, maintaining them until they reach full age.

(b) The endowment of members at any age. This is usually done by securing for them the payment of an annuity.

(c) The insuring against fire to an amount not exceeding £15 of the tools or implements of trade of a member.

A society formed for any of these objects is capable of being registered.

(2) **Insuring the Life of a Member.—** A society which undertakes the insurance of life must be registered, and if it is a collecting society it must deposit £20,000 security with the Industrial Commissioner who is the chief registrar, and the security must be maintained as long as the society carries on life insurance. (*See* COLLECTING SOCIETY; INSURANCE.)

(3) **Lending Money to a Member.—** If a society wishes to include in its objects the lending of money to members, then it must have a separate loan fund created by subscriptions specially made to that fund. Loans may only be made up to £50, and may not be made to non-members on personal security only, because such a loan constitutes a breach of trust on the part of the trustees.

Membership.—A Society may have any number of members, and anyone may be a member, there being no fixed minimum age limit unless the rules so provide. A married woman may be a member of a society and, unless it is proved to the contrary, her interest in the society is to be regarded as her separate property.

Contributions.—All subscriptions by members of registered friendly societies are voluntary payments, and the society cannot sue a member for arrears or for current subscriptions. Fines imposed by the rules of the society can be recovered by the society in a court of summary jurisdiction, that is, before a magistrate.

Benefits.—Members who pay subscriptions to a friendly society become entitled, according to the rules, to certain benefits. There are certain limits imposed by the law upon the amounts which may be paid out to a member. Thus the maximum lump sum which any one member can receive by way of benefit from a society is £300, and the largest sum payable as an annuity is £52 per annum. No society, whether registered or unregistered, may pay out more than £6 in respect of the death of a child under six years, and more than £15 in respect of the death of a child under ten years.

Nomination of a Successor to Benefits.—A member of a registered society over the age of sixteen can dispose of sums of money not exceeding £100, payable by the society in the event of the member's death, by nominating some person who is to receive them.

He must make his nomination in writing, and it must be sent to the registered office of the society and recorded there before the death of the member. If the member marries after making a nomination, then that nomination is cancelled. When the death of the member thus nominating is satisfactorily proved, the society must pay over the amount due to the person thus nominated.

Forfeiture of a benefit may be incurred by a member if he falls in arrears with his subscriptions and the rules of the society so provide. A member cannot be deprived of his benefit by forfeiture unless he receives notice from the society stating the amount due by him, and informing him that his benefit will be forfeited in case of non-payment within a reasonable time; that time must not be less than fourteen days.

If it is a rule of the society that a member must make a certain number of contributions before qualifying for a benefit, and a member ceases to contribute before he has made the required number of subscriptions, then no notice is required and forfeiture may be automatic.

How Disputes are Settled.—Registered friendly societies must provide in their rules for the means whereby disputes relating to questions of membership, loss of membership, payment of benefits, the repayment of deposits made by members, and kindred subjects, are to be settled. Usually the rules provide for the adjudication of the rights of the parties by an arbitrator, and the ordinary law Courts cannot entertain any action by a member until the case has been heard and decided in accordance with the provisions of the society's rules. If, however, the society or the member is dissatisfied with the finding of the arbitrator, they may request the arbitrator to state a case, that is, set out the facts and his findings, for the opinion of the High Court. If the rules provide for the settlement of disputes in a certain way, and a decision is given in accordance with those rules, then such decision is binding on all parties and cannot be appealed from. (*See* COLLECTING SOCIETY; INSURANCE; SLATE CLUB.)

FUGITIVE OFFENDERS.—Where a person is accused of having committed, in any part of His Majesty's Dominions, any offence punishable with twelve months' imprisonment or any greater punishment, and goes to any other part, he can be arrested there and taken back to stand his trial in the part he left. (*See* EXTRADITION.)

FUNERAL.—An order to an undertaker for a funeral constitutes a contract. Therefore, if the undertaker fails to carry out any essential part of the funeral arrangements, he is considered to have committed a breach of the whole contract. In such a case he might not be entitled to payment for any portion of the contract. This would not be so, however, if he could prove that the failure was not due to any default on his part.

Funeral expenses, so far as they are proper, are due from the estate of the deceased. They take precedence over any other charges.

FURNISHED HOUSES. — A lease of a furnished or unfurnished house must, if the tenancy is for more than three years, be by deed. If the tenancy is for less than this period a deed is not required, and the agreement need not even be in writing, although a written agreement is always preferable. An agreement to take a lease of a house, as distinct from an actual tenancy agreement, must, however, be in writing whatever the period, so that anyone who merely gives a verbal promise to take a lease is not bound thereby.

At the commencement of a tenancy an inventory should be made of all the furniture, which should be carefully checked by lessor and lessee or their representatives. The inventory is often added to the lease as a schedule. Any blemishes in the furniture should be noted, as the lessee is responsible for any damage suffered by the furniture during his tenancy, fair wear and tear excepted.

On the letting of a furnished house, there is an implied covenant by the lessor that the house is reasonably fit for human habitation.

A furnished house has been held to be unfit for human habitation because it was infested by bugs, the drains were defective, or there was a reasonable danger of it still being infectious because of a recent occupier having had an infectious disease there.

It is no excuse that the lessor honestly and reasonably thought the house was all right. There is only a warranty that the house shall be fit for habitation at the beginning of the tenancy, not that it should remain so throughout. If the house is not fit, the tenant can leave without notice, refuse to pay any rent, recover anything paid in advance and sue the lessor for any damage he has suffered, e.g. in respect of commission paid to an estate agent or costs incurred in the preparation of the lease.

There is no implied covenant by the tenant that he is a fit and proper person to occupy the house or that he is not himself infectious.

Furnished houses are not affected by the Rent Restrictions Acts except for the provision that the lessor of a furnished house, otherwise within the scope of the Act, is only entitled to receive, and the lessee need only pay (he can recover any sum he has paid in excess) such rent as gives the lessor a profit which is 25 % more than that which he might reasonably have expected to have made from letting the house furnished on August 3rd, 1914, i.e. before the outbreak of the War. A lessor charging extortionate rent for furnished premises is liable to a fine of £100.

In order that a house should be held to be furnished for the purpose of the Rent Restrictions Acts, formerly only a minimum of furniture was necessary, e.g. linoleum has been held sufficient; but now a substantial part of the rent must be attributable to the furniture. (*See* RENT RESTRICTIONS.)

FURNITURE.—Furniture has been described as everything that contributes to the use or convenience of the house. The question of what is furniture arises frequently in disputes over legacies of "furniture" in wills. The above definition is rather wide as fixtures, e.g. mantelpieces and shelves, are not furniture. It has been held that plate, pictures, linen and cabinet wireless sets are furniture, but not books, wine or other consumable possessions. If a will bequeaths only the furniture in a particular

house, the furniture which is permanently kept there is alone included, e.g. not such plate as is moved whenever wanted elsewhere.

Anyone wishing to have his furniture moved should be careful to ascertain the terms of the contract with the furniture removers, as they are normally not common carriers since they do not undertake to move "everyone's goods." They only enter into specific contracts with each customer and are, therefore, not absolutely liable for the safety of the goods. Moreover, the terms of the contract which the owner is asked to sign are sometimes very hard, e.g. the removal contractor agrees to accept no liability for loss by theft or fire even if caused by his own negligence.

A railway company which carries furniture for a passenger as his luggage is not absolutely liable for its safety, as it is only a common carrier of personal baggage which does not include furniture.

If furniture stored in a depository is damaged or destroyed, the person or company with whom it is deposited is liable to the owner for such damage or loss if caused by his or its failure to take reasonable care in looking after it. Anyone storing furniture gratuitously is also bound to use reasonable care, but the standard of care required is, of course, not quite so high.

A landlord can seize a tenant's furniture by way of distress for unpaid rent, except bedding, including actual bed, up to the value of £5. Furniture on hire purchase may be thus seized, but not furniture that belongs to anyone other than the tenant. The furniture can only be seized while actually in the house, except that if it is fraudulently removed to avoid distress, the landlord can seize it anywhere within 30 days of removal unless it has already been sold. A policeman can stop any vehicle moving furniture between the hours of 8 p.m. and 6 a.m. and detain it, or at any time if, on enquiry, he reasonably suspects the furniture is being moved to evade distress for unpaid rent. (*See* DISTRESS.)

Furniture obtained on the ordinary hire-purchase system does not become the property of the hirer until the last instalment is paid, and it is usually a term of the contract that, on default in the payment of an instalment, the hirer loses the right to retain the furniture. Until the last instalment is paid the hirer cannot sell the furniture but he can transfer his rights in it. (*See* HIRE PURCHASE.)

If the hirer goes bankrupt the furniture may, nevertheless, if used for business purposes, be deemed to be his property for the benefit of his creditors, by the doctrine of reputed ownership. This doctrine may also apply to any other business furniture which the owner allows the bankrupt to use as if it were his own. This doctrine never applies to hotel furniture, since it is customary for it to be hired. (*See* BANKRUPTCY.)

It is now necessary that a house should be substantially furnished to be outside the scope of the Rent Restrictions Acts. (*See* APARTMENTS; FURNISHED HOUSES.)

GAMBLING.—For a full account of the law relating to this subject, *see* SPECIAL SUPPLEMENT "GAMBLING."

GAME.—Certain wild animals and birds which are used for food and for sporting purposes are classified as game, and a series of laws, known as the Game Laws, apply to them.

Game includes hares, pheasants, partridges, grouse, heath or moor game, black game and bustards.

Certain other animals and birds such as woodcock, snipe, quail and rabbits count as game in certain provisions applying to poaching (q.v.), but as a general rule game comprises only the animals and birds mentioned above.

Close Times and Seasons.—It is illegal to kill or take any game either by shooting or snaring, or in any other way, on Sunday or Christmas Day, and this applies to snares that are set on Saturday and left out over Sunday.

It is also illegal to kill or take any particular species of game during the close season in each year, or for game dealers (q.v.) to sell or have in their possession game after 10 days after the first day of the close season, or for other persons to buy or sell game after 10 days, or have game in their possession, after 40 days after the first day of the close season, except for the purposes of breeding.

The close seasons for game are:
Grouse, 10th December to 12th August.
Black Game, 10th December to 20th August.
Partridges, 1st February to 1st September.
Pheasants, 1st February to 1st October.
Bustards, 1st March to 1st September.

In addition to this there are close seasons for many wild birds (q.v.). There is no close season for hares, although between the months of March and July inclusive, it is illegal to expose hares for sale unless they have been imported. There is no close season for rabbits except on moorlands and unenclosed lands in certain circumstances.

The penalty for contravening these provisions is a fine not exceeding £1 for every head of game killed or taken.

In addition to these close days and seasons it is not permitted to shoot any game or rabbits at night time, though they may be taken by snares or any other method.

It is also forbidden to put down poison for game, though poison may be used for the purpose of killing ground vermin. (*See* CRUELTY TO ANIMALS.)

No game may be killed or taken by any person who does not possess a game licence (q.v.), with the exception of farmers who are entitled to shoot hares upon their lands as outlined below. (*See* ANIMALS.)

Sporting Rights.—The right to kill game over land is generally called shooting or sporting rights, and is a valuable property in the land which can be disposed of by the owner. A landowner may let the sporting rights on his land to a shooting tenant, in which case all the rights of shooting game pass to the shooting tenant, who may enforce them by an action in the Civil Courts, or by prosecution in the Criminal Courts. If a landowner leases land to a tenant without making any mention of the sporting rights, the tenant becomes the tenant of the sporting rights as well, but a landowner may let land while reserving the sporting rights for himself, or may let the land to one tenant and the sporting rights to another tenant. In such a case, the tenant of the land is not entitled to kill or take the game on the land except to the extent mentioned under RIGHTS OF FARMERS; and he can be sued or prosecuted for breaking the law in this respect, as can a landowner who lets the shooting rights of land in his own occupation to a shooting tenant.

Rights of Farmers.—Every tenant or owner of land who is in actual occupation of the land is entitled to take and kill rabbits and hares on the land, whether he has the shooting rights or not, and no agreement, even if he enters into it himself, can take away this right from him. He cannot, however, use a firearm at night, nor can he use poison at any time of day or night, or set any spring traps except in rabbit-holes, i.e. not above ground. The occupier himself can exercise this right, and he can authorize in writing one other person who must be a member of his household or a person in his service, or someone employed for reward by him for the purpose. This right applies to ordinary persons in occupation of land as well as farmers. No game licence is required for shooting hares in pursuance of this right.

In addition to this, a farmer or tenant of an agricultural holding who does not also possess sporting rights, is entitled to be paid compensation by his landlord for any damage done to his land or crops by deer, pheasants, partridges, grouse or black game, provided that the damage is greater than 1/– per acre over the area on which the damage is done. The amount of compensation if not settled by agreement must be settled by arbitration, and the landlord is entitled to recover the amount of the compensation he is obliged to pay from the shooting tenant in those cases where the landlord has not himself retained the shooting rights.

The only exceptions to this right of compensation are where the tenant has the shooting rights himself, or has let them to someone else, or where the rent of the holding has been specially fixed to allow for damage done by game. (*See* ANIMAL; GAME LICENCES; GUN LICENCE; POACHING; WILD BIRDS.)

GAME LICENCES.—No person, except in the cases mentioned below, is entitled to take or kill game (q.v.), woodcock, snipe, quail, rabbits or deer, either with a firearm, or any sort of machine, net, snare, trap or dog, unless he is in possession of a game licence current for the time at which he kills or takes the game.

The only exceptions to this rule are:

1. Woodcock and snipe may be taken with nets or springs in Great Britain without a game licence.
2. Rabbits may be taken and killed without a game licence by the occupier of the land or by anyone authorized by him. As a general rule anyone shooting rabbits does so by permission of the occupier of the land and so does not need a game licence, though a gun licence (q.v.) may be required.
3. Occupiers and persons authorized by them may kill hares on the lands in their occupation without a game licence. (*See* GAME.)
4. Hares may be coursed by greyhounds or hunted by beagles or other hounds without a game licence.
5. Deer may be hunted or, enclosed in a park, may be killed without a licence.
6. Members of the Royal Family and their servants need no licence, and gamekeepers and servants of other persons may assist their masters in the taking or killing of game without themselves possessing a game licence, but they must only assist and must not themselves shoot the game.

Cost of Licences.—Game Licences may be obtained at any post office and are current from the date of their issue until the 31st October or the 5th April in each year.

A licence taken out between the 5th April and the 1st November to expire on the 5th April of the following year costs £3, or £2 for a gamekeeper.

A licence taken out between the 5th April and the 1st November to expire on the 31st October of the same year costs £2.

A licence taken out after the 1st November to expire on the 5th April of the following year costs £2.

A gamekeeper's licence does not permit the gamekeeper to kill or take game except on the land of which he is in charge.

Game licences available for 14 days are issued at £1.

A list of holders of game licences is published by the local authority either in the local newspaper or exhibited publicly in the post offices or on the church doors.

Penalties.—Any person who takes or kills game without a licence is subject to a penalty not exceeding £20, and any person who is asked to produce his game licence by the owner, or occupier or gamekeeper of the land on which he is taking or killing game, and refuses either to do so or to give his name and address, is also liable to a penalty not exceeding £20.

Persons who deal in game must take out a licence to deal in game (q.v.). (*See* GAME; GUN LICENCE; POACHING.)

GAMING HOUSE.—It is an offence for anyone who is the owner or occupier of any premises to use, or knowingly permit others to use, them for the business of unlawful gaming. (*See* SPECIAL SUPPLEMENT "GAMBLING.")

GAOL DELIVERY.—This is one of the commissions issued to Judges of Assize. It requires them to deliver and try all persons who are in prison in the counties they are visiting. (*See* ASSIZE; OYER AND TERMINER.)

GARNISHEE PROCEEDINGS.— Where a creditor has obtained a judgment against his debtor ordering the debtor to pay money, and the creditor knows that the debtor is entitled to some payment from a third person, he may take proceedings known as garnishee proceedings to enforce payment of the debt by the third party to him, the creditor, instead of to the judgment debtor.

GAS.—Any person or company may undertake the supply of gas in a particular area, but unless the undertaking is performed by a company authorized by Act of Parliament, or by a local authority as part of its activities, the company has no power to dig up streets or highways even with the consent of the local authority, and may be prosecuted for doing so.

For this reason the supply of gas is usually undertaken by a local authority which is authorized to do so by a private Act of Parliament.

When a company is authorized by Parliament it is given express powers to lay pipes in the streets, and to break up streets and bridges for the purpose of laying the pipes. Even if such express power is omitted from the special Act, it will be implied where a general power is given to light the streets within the area of the undertaking. If a company desires to break up a street it must give at least three days' notice of its intention to do so to the local authority, unless the breaking open is necessitated by an emergency such as a leak.

When they have taken up a street they must complete the work upon the pipes with all possible speed and replace the street as soon as possible. They must keep in good repair for three months any portion of the street which they have dug up and replaced, and, while the street is opened up, they must fence off the excavations and light them at night.

The Gas Meter.—If a gas company requires a consumer to do so, he must use a meter to measure the amount of gas which he consumes, such meter to be supplied by the company. It may hire the meter to him or sell it to him, and if it is hired the company have to keep it in proper order at its expense, but if it is sold to the consumer he must keep it in order at his own expense.

Every meter used for the measurement of gas supplied must be examined and tested, and, if found to be correct, it must be stamped. The testing and stamping is done by an official of the local authority, and once a meter has been stamped it becomes a legal meter.

A meter which is found upon testing to register more than two per cent. off the true standard in favour of the seller of gas, or more than three per cent. in favour of the consumer, must not be stamped. Any person who uses an unstamped meter, or who alters or tampers with a stamped one so as to make it register incorrectly, is liable to a penalty of five pounds.

A "Slot-meter" is called a prepayment meter because the consumer has to insert his penny or his shilling into the meter before he receives any gas, and therefore pays in advance for his supply. Usually the gas company retains the key of the coin box in its possession, and if the money is stolen from the box without any negligence of the consumer, the company cannot recover the sum from him. The register of a meter is prima facie evidence of the quantity of gas consumed and it therefore shows how much a company may charge. The company sends an official to read the meter at regular intervals, and the bill is worked out from the amount of cubic feet of gas consumed. Officials of gas companies must be permitted to read meters and inspect the gas fittings at all reasonable times during the day.

If a dispute arises between a consumer and a supplier respecting the correctness of a meter, the meter may be tested by two meter-inspectors of neighbouring districts, and if they come to an unanimous decision, then that decision is to be regarded as final.

The Unpaid Gas Bill.—If a consumer does not pay the bill for the gas he has received, the gas company has several remedies against him. It may cut off his supply after giving him notice of its intention to do so, or it may apply to a justice of the peace for authorization to distrain upon his goods to an amount sufficient to satisfy their charges. It may proceed in a Court of Summary Jurisdiction to recover the sum as a penalty, or it may sue for the money in the County Court or the High Court according to the amount due.

A gas company may require a consumer to enter into a contract with it to take a certain minimum quantity of gas within a specified limit of time, and it may also require him to give it security for the payment of its charges.

If it has already supplied him with gas for some time, it may still demand a security as a condition of the continuance of his supply. But if he fails to give such security it may cut off his supply until he complies with its demand.

A consumer who is leaving his premises must give the gas company notice of his intended departure, otherwise he will be liable for the amount which becomes due the next time the meter is read. If, however, another tenant comes in, he will only be liable for the amount due at the time when the new tenant asked for a supply. An incoming tenant is not required to pay any gas bill left unpaid by the outgoing tenant before he receives a supply, unless he has expressly agreed with the outgoing tenant that he will pay it.

Nuisance from Gas.—Gas companies are not usually exempted by the special Act creating them from an action for nuisance caused during the construction of their works, or during the manufacturing of the gas, and therefore they must take precautions to see that their business is carried on without

damaging neighbouring property. A heavy penalty of two hundred pounds is incurred by a gas company which allows a stream to become fouled by washings from the making of their gas. It must take immediate steps to stop any escape from its mains when it is reported to it, and it will be liable for any injuries sustained in an explosion where such explosion is caused by the negligence of the company's servants. (*See also* LOCAL AUTHORITY AND NEGLIGENCE.)

GENERAL EXEMPTION ORDER. —This is an order which allows the holder of an on-licence to keep open outside the permitted hours, if he can shew the local authorities that it would accommodate a number of persons attending a market or following some particular trade in the vicinity. Thus the public houses in the neighbourhood of Covent Garden will be found open in the early morning under such an order. (*See* SPECIAL EXEMPTION ORDER AND PERMITTED HOURS.)

GENERAL MEDICAL COUNCIL. —The General Medical Council is the body entrusted with the control of medical education and of the registration of medical practitioners throughout the United Kingdom. It consists of the following persons:—five persons nominated from time to time by the Crown, three for England, one for Scotland and one for Ireland; one person selected by each of twenty-one Medical Societies and Universities; three persons elected from time to time by registered medical practitioners resident in England, one by those resident in Scotland, and one by those resident in Ireland.

All members must be themselves registered medical practitioners. They are elected for a period of five years and they may be re-elected. The President is elected by the Council itself for a period not exceeding five years.

Disciplinary Powers.—The Registrar of the General Medical Council publishes annually a Medical Register containing the names and addresses of all persons appearing in the General Register on January the first of each year. The fact that a person's name appears in this register is prima facie evidence that he is a registered medical practitioner, that is, unless it is disproved.

The General Medical Council has power to exercise disciplinary control over registered medical practitioners for professional misconduct or "infamous conduct in a professional respect," and may direct the registrar to erase from the register the name of any practitioner who, after proper enquiry, has been found guilty. There is a similar power where any practitioner has been convicted of any felony or misdemeanour in England or Ireland or of any crime or offence in Scotland. The council is the sole judge of these matters, and so long as it has come to its decision fairly, and has not offended against the rules of natural justice, there is no method by which its decision may be attacked or reviewed. When a practitioner has been removed from the register it is always open to him to apply to have his name restored at a later time. (*See* DOCTOR.)

GENERAL MEETING.—A Company must hold a General Meeting once in every calendar year and not more than 15 months after the previous meeting. At this meeting the accounts of the company must be laid before the shareholders together with the reports of the Directors and Auditors.

GIFT.—A gift takes place when any property is transferred from one person to another gratuitously. A gift should be distinguished from a mere promise or contract to give. Such a contract, being gratuitous —i.e. without consideration—would not be binding in law, unless made by deed (i.e. by a document under seal) so that if A promises verbally, or in writing, to give B £100, he cannot be compelled to do so. Where, however, the property is actually transferred, the transaction is a gift and binding, so that if A gives B £100 he cannot claim it back again.

Gifts of Goods or Money.—To complete the gift, the possession of the articles must be handed by the donor (i.e. the giver) to the donee (i.e. the person to whom the gift is made). When this transfer of possession is made, there is said to be actual delivery and little difficulty can arise in such cases. It is not necessary in all cases, however, that the donee should receive the goods himself or that the donor should have them in his physical possession at the time of the gift. The donor, for example, may send them to the warehouse to be stored in the name of the donee. If the goods are under lock and key there

will be an actual delivery of the possession of them by the handing over of the key. Where goods are in the hands of a third party who holds them on behalf of the donor, e.g. a warehouseman, the possession of them may be transferred, without the goods being moved in any way, by the donor and donee and the third party agreeing that in future the goods shall be held on behalf of the donee.

Gift of Choses in Action.—In order to complete the gift, all steps must be taken necessary at law to transfer the property from the donor to the donee. Thus, if shares are given a transfer must be executed. If a man draws a cheque in favour of another in his own bank, the gift is not complete until the cheque has been presented and the money drawn out, so that if the donor repents of his generosity and stops the cheque the donee cannot complain. If, however, a Bill of Exchange or cheque drawn by one person in favour of another is transferred by the person in whose favour it is drawn either by delivery (if it is payable to bearer), or by delivery and endorsement (if it is payable to order), to some other person even without consideration, that other person may sue on the document and the gift is good. Thus, if A draws a cheque in favour of "B or order," and gives it to B who in his turn endorses it to C as a gift and delivers it to C, C may sue on the cheque and the gift is irrevocable.

Gift of Land.—A gift of land is not complete until it has been conveyed from one person to another by the proper deeds and the deed has been delivered.

Declaration of Trust.—In some cases a transaction not valid as a gift, because the property has not been transferred, may be valid as a declaration of trust. Where the property is land the declaration must be proved by writing signed by the donor before it can be enforced against him: but if the property is personal property, i.e. goods, it will be enough if it can be proved that the donor used words indicating that he intended to hold the property on trust for the donee.

When Gifts may be set aside.—In certain cases gifts may be set aside on the ground that the person who gave the property did not act of his own free will, but was under the undue influence of the donee.

In some cases it may be presumed, from the very relationship of the parties, that the gift was made by undue influence, and it will there be set aside unless the donee can prove that no improper influence was used. This arises in cases of gifts to a trustee by a beneficiary, to a solicitor from a client, to a doctor from a patient or to the vicar of the parish from a parishioner. In other cases undue influence must not be presumed but must be proved.

When a man gives away property and later becomes bankrupt, the transaction may be avoided either as a fraudulent conveyance (q.v.) or as a voluntary settlement (q.v.).

Gifts to avoid Death Duties.— Persons who wish to avoid the payment of death duty on their estate used formerly to give away their property in their lifetime to the persons they wished to benefit instead of leaving it by will. It is still possible to do this, but if the person making the gift dies before the elapse of three years from the date of the gift, death duties must still be paid on the property.

A gift may be either *inter vivos*, that is, made and intended to operate when both donor and donee are alive, or it may be by will, that is, intended to operate only after the death of the donor, or, thirdly, it may be a *donatio mortis causa*, that is, made when the donor is ill and in anticipation of death. (*See* Donatio Mortis Causa.)

A Promise to Give.—This must in all cases be made by a document under seal, i.e. a deed, for it will not otherwise be enforceable as there is no consideration for the promise. A promise by deed will not necessarily be valid, for if there is some illegal or immoral consideration for it the law will not enforce it. So if A promises by deed to pay an annuity to B, who has been his mistress, the law would not enforce the promise. The ground here for its refusal is not that there is no consideration or that the consideration is past—that is, has already been performed for that is immaterial in a contract by deed—but that the consideration is immoral. (*See* Consideration; Death Duties; Donatio Mortis Causa; Fraudulent Conveyance; Marriage Settlement; Undue Influence; Voluntary Settlement.)

GIFT (SCOTS LAW).—A promise to make a gift may be enforceable in Scots law since Scots law does not recognize the English doctrine of consideration (q.v.), and will enforce contracts even though the person who has made the promise has not received from the other person any consideration or promise in return. The existence of such a contract, however, can only be proved by producing some document signed by the person who alleges the promise to make the gift, or by obtaining from him an admission on oath that he did promise to make the gift.

GLEBE.—The land which is actually retained for the support of an ecclesiastical living is called glebeland. The rents and profits of glebeland are normally paid to the incumbent of the living.

GOLD.—Where found in a natural state in the British Isles gold belongs to the Crown as it is a Royal Metal. But where the ore is mixed with another metal, this is not so, although the Crown has the right to purchase it at the market rate.

GOOD BEHAVIOUR.—Persons who disturb the public peace or who have been convicted of any crime can be required to find sureties for their good behaviour. It is to be observed that this course can be followed in the case of any persons who misbehave themselves in such a way that the public peace is broken, so that if the person in respect of whom they are bound over disturbs the peace during the term of their undertaking, they forfeit their recognisances. If the person required to find the sureties cannot find them, he can be committed to prison.

GOODWILL.—The goodwill of a business has been defined as being the probability that the "old customers will return to the old place." It may be a very valuable asset and its value will depend on the reputation and connection of the firm. In some businesses goodwill is personal, that is, arises solely from the reputation of the person carrying on the business. This is usually the case with the business of a doctor or of a solicitor. In other cases the goodwill is attached to some particular place, such as a grocer's shop situated in a good position in a busy street.

When a business is sold, the property which really passes includes not only the stock in trade and any debts that may be due to the business, but also the goodwill and

 made the First day of
September One thousand
nine hundred and
thirty ——— BETWEEN
HENRY HOOD of 976 High
Street Barchester
(hereinafter referred to as the Vendor) of the one part and GEORGE
BLAKE of 193 Forth Street Barchester (hereinafter referred to as the
Purchaser) of the other part N O W THESE PRESENTS W I T N E S S
AND IT IS HEREBY AGREED between the parties hereto:

1.   T H E Vendor shall sell and the Purchaser shall purchase the
goodwill of the business of a grocer now carried on by the Purchaser
at No. 976 High Street Barchester aforesaid together with all
implements and fixtures in the said shop (as set out in the Schedule
hereto) and all the stock in trade and book debts of the Vendor for
the sum of ONE HUNDRED POUNDS

2.   T H E Vendor hereby acknowledges the receipt of a deposit of
Twenty pounds on account of and in part payment of the said purchase
price The balance of the purchase price shall be paid by weekly
instalments of Eight pounds the first of such instalments to be paid
on the Eighth September One thousand nine hundred and thirty
If default shall be made in the payment of any instalment the full
amount of the instalments unpaid shall immediately become due and
payable

3.   O N the said Eighth September One thousand nine hundred and
thirty ——— the Vendor shall execute an assignment of the tenancy
from year to year which he holds of the said premises and of the
said goodwill and shall deliver to the Purchaser the said implements
fixtures and stock in trade

4.   T H E Vendor shall recommend the Purchaser to the customers of
the Vendor and shall personally assist the Purchaser in the carrying
on of the said business for one week from the Eighth September One
thousand nine hundred and thirty The Vendor shall not trade or
deal in the business of a grocer directly or indirectly by himself or
in partnership with any other person or persons within one mile of
the said premises at No. 976 High Street Barchester for the space
of one year of the date hereof

5.   T H E transaction hereby effected does not form part of a
larger transaction or of a series of transactions in respect of which
the amount or value or the aggregate amount or value of the considera
tion exceeds Five hundred pounds

    I N W I T N E S S whereof the parties hereto have hereunto set
their hands the day and year first above written

T H E   S C H E D U L E

[Here set out the implements and fixtures]

S I G N E D by the above-named HENRY)
HOOD in the presence of :-)
    Henry Hood.

John Gray,
   975 High Street, Barchester
    Grocers.

S I G N E D by the above-named GEORGE)
BLAKE in the presence of :-)
    George Blake

Frank H. Bennett.
  190 Forth Street Barchester
    Clerk

Agreement for the Purchase of a Business.

this may be the most valuable asset of all. Where the goodwill is of a personal kind it will tend to be less valuable, for once the person through whose skill the goodwill has been created has left the business, the probability that the old customers will return is much less than where the goodwill attaches to the premises which can be taken over by the purchaser of the business.

Protection of Purchaser.—When the goodwill of a business is sold, the purchaser should see that he obtains an undertaking from the seller that the seller will not set up in competition, for unless this undertaking is given, there is nothing to prevent the seller from setting up in opposition even next door to the premises where the old business is being carried on. The purchaser is not, however, entitled to impose on the seller any conditions as to competition which restrict his right to trade as he wishes more than is necessary to enable the purchaser to get the benefit of the goodwill which he has bought. What is reasonable in the circumstances will depend on the nature and extent of the business which is being sold. In the case of a small local business it is usually enough if the seller undertakes not to carry on any business in competition within a certain area around the old business premises. (*See* RESTRAINT OF TRADE.)

Where there is no express provision, the seller, as has been stated, may compete, with the purchaser, but he must not use the old firm name or state that he is carrying on the old business. Further, he must not canvass the customers of the old business or ask them to deal with him, but if they come of their own free will he is not prevented from serving them. The seller must not use any name which amounts to a representation that he is carrying on the old business.

) When a man becomes bankrupt and his business is sold by his trustee in bankruptcy, the situation is somewhat different, for he is not prevented from soliciting his old customers and starting business in competition. It follows, therefore, that the goodwill of a business bought from the trustee of a bankrupt is less valuable than the goodwill of other businesses.

Goodwill of a Tenant.—Until recently it was frequently a great hardship that a tenant should build up in his premises —such as a draper's shop—a valuable goodwill, and then find that when his lease expires he is unable to have it renewed and loses entirely the value of the goodwill he has built up. In order to prevent this hardship, it is now the law that any tenant is entitled at the end of the tenancy to claim from the landlord compensation for goodwill, if he proves that by reason of the carrying on by him, or by his predecessors in title at the premises of a trade or business for not less than 5 years, goodwill has become attached to the premises, which would therefore be let at a higher rent than they would have realized without it.

The seller of the goodwill, if he takes as part of the price a share in the profits, is a deferred creditor.

When, on the transfer of the goodwill of a business, the general book-debts are assigned, the transaction does not require to be registered. (*See* ASSIGNMENT; LANDLORD AND TENANT; PARTNERSHIP.)

GRAHAM-CAMPBELL, Sir Rollo (1868–).—After a successful career at the Bar, Sir Rollo Graham-Campbell has been Chief Magistrate of the Police Courts of the Metropolis since 1933.

GRAND JURY.—Grand Juries have now been abolished in England. Their function was to present at Assizes and Quarter Sessions persons they thought should be tried before a Judge and a Petty Jury. At the beginning of each Session all the Bills of Indictment against all the persons to be charged were presented to the Grand Jury; the Grand Jury examined these and the evidence that the prosecution intended to call to support them. If the Grand Jury was satisfied that an accused person on this evidence should stand his trial, they found what was called a True Bill. If they did not think the evidence sufficient, they threw out the bill.

Grand Juries consisted of not less than twenty-three members who were selected on a property qualification. They were a very ancient institution, and in the Middle Ages were a most important cog in the machinery of government. Of recent years they lost their value because their functions were really discharged by the Magistrates, and a Magistrate's Court now decides whether or not a person shall be tried.

GRAVEYARD. — (*See* BURIAL and CEMETERIES.)

GRAY'S INN. — One of the four Inns of Court in London. It is situated some distance from the other Inns of Court and the Law Courts, in the angle formed by Holborn and Gray's Inn Road. The original site was in the de Grey family, but the freehold was purchased by the benchers of Gray's Inn in 1733.

Among many famous members who

that such marriages can take place at Gretna Green only, and even in Scotland persons frequently come from other parts of the country to Gretna Green in order to be married. In fact, marriage in this form may take place in any part of Scotland, and the special reputation of Gretna Green is due solely to the fact that it is the nearest point in Scotland on the old coach road from England, and accordingly was the most suitable place for marriage for persons

The Smithy at Gretna Green as it is to-day.

played an important part in the life of the Inn were Nicholas Bacon and Lord Birkenhead.

GRETNA GREEN MARRIAGE. — This is the name applied to a marriage taking place in Gretna Green, just over the Scottish Border. The marriage is governed by the rules of Scots Law (*see* MARRIAGE [SCOTS LAW]) and it is not therefore necessary that the consent of the parents should be obtained if one of the parties is under 21 years of age as is the case in England. The marriage is not celebrated in a church, but is what is known in Scotland as an "irregular" marriage constituted by a solemn statement of the two parties of their intention to marry at that time.

There is a general impression in England

who had run away from England to get married without the consent of their parents.

There is also a very general impression that it is still possible for two persons to go to Gretna Green and to be married there in this way. It should be clearly understood that this is not now the case and that such run-away marriages are illegal and of no effect whatsoever. This is by reason of a Statute which was passed to prevent these run-away marriages, and which provides that the marriage shall not be valid unless one of the parties had at the time his or her usual residence in Scotland, or else had resided there for the twenty-one days immediately before the date of the marriage. If either of these conditions is fulfilled the marriage is as legal and binding as any marriage performed in any other way, but in other cases the marriage is of no effect.

Where a Gretna Green marriage has taken place and where there has been the necessary residence, it is very advisable to obtain a record of the marriage by registration as otherwise it may at a later time be very difficult to prove that it ever took place. (*See* MARRIAGE [SCOTS LAW]).

GROUND RENT.—When vacant land is being developed for building, the usual practice is for the owner of the land to grant a lease of it to a person, usually a builder, who undertakes to erect buildings on the land and to pay a rent. This rent is known as ground rent and is usually small in amount.

The lease is for a long term of years, e.g. 99 years—and at the end of the lease the land with the buildings on it will belong to the person who let it, or to the persons to whom he has transferred his title. (*See* LANDLORD AND TENANT.)

GUARANTEE.—When one person A undertakes to pay some money to, or do some act for B, and another person C agrees with B that if A does not pay the money or do the act, he (C) will do so, the contract between A and C is called a contract of guarantee. It is technically described as a promise to answer for the "debt, default or miscarriage" of another. It should be noticed that it is essential to a contract of guarantee that there should be some other person who is primarily liable to do the act and whose performance of it is being guaranteed.

Thus, if A and B go into a shop and A tells B to select some goods and informs the shopkeeper that he (A) will pay for them, this is not a guarantee by A, for B is never liable to pay for the goods and A is undertaking a liability of his own, and is not guaranteeing a liability of B. If, however, B orders the goods for himself and, the shopkeeper being unwilling to supply them to him without payment, A then says "let him have the goods; if he does not pay you, I will," this is a guarantee by A that B will pay for the goods; for there are two contracts, one by B to pay for the goods and another by A, promising to pay for them *if B does not*. In such a case the shopkeeper is called the creditor,

B is called the principal debtor, and A is called the guarantor or surety.

Any contract of guarantee must be evidenced in writing before it can be enforced by action, that is, there must be some written memorandum of the terms signed by the parties to be made liable. The contract may not be made in writing. It will be enough if at the time when action is brought there is in existence some written memorandum signed by the party being sued, even though the memorandum was not written out until after the time when the contract was made. The memorandum need not contain the consideration. Consideration is necessary to a guarantee but usually will be provided by the promise of the creditor to sell the goods to the debtor or grant him a loan in return for the guarantee of the surety.

Liability of Surety.—The surety will only be liable if the principal makes fault, and he will then be liable in accordance with the term of the contract. It is not necessary for the creditor to sue the debtor, or even to call on him to pay the debt before he proceeds against the surety, nor if there are several sureties, each bound jointly, can one of them refuse to pay because the others are not sued also. He must pay the full amount to the creditor and recover the excess from the other sureties. The exact liability of the surety will depend on the terms of the contract.

Rights of Surety.—The creditor must give the surety all information which he possesses as to the debtor, and if he fraudulently fails to do so or conceals any information, the surety will not be liable but will be entitled to avoid the contract.

When the surety pays the amount of the debt he is entitled to have assigned to him any judgment which the creditor has against the debtor in respect of the debt, or any security given by the debtor to the creditor, e.g. shares transferred. When the debt has become due, the surety, before he is himself asked to pay, can require the creditor to sue the principal debtor for the debt. Were this not the case, the creditor might not press the debtor to pay but might delay. The result might be that, when he ultimately took steps to recover the money, the debtor might be unable to pay although he might have been able to pay had he been required to do so when the money was first due. The creditor can, of course, sue the surety for the debt instead of the debtor, but the surety can then call on the debtor to indemnify him. In either case delay is avoided. If the surety himself is sued by the creditor he may rely on any set off or any counterclaim which the debtor possesses against the creditor, and when he has paid he is entitled to all relief and rights of action which the creditor has against the debtor.

As against the debtor the creditor has also certain rights. As soon as the debt is due and before payment has been even demanded he may compel the debtor to pay off the debt to the creditor. If the surety has paid the debt, he is entitled to be indemnified by the debtor. When he is sued by the principal debtor, the surety can issue a third party notice claiming an indemnity against the principal debtor.

If there are several persons all of whom have become sureties of the debtor (called co-sureties), any one who has paid more than his share is entitled to call on the others to repay him the excess. If, however, one surety is insolvent he is not taken into account in calculating the property share of each surety, but the total debt due is divided among the solvent sureties. This is called the right of contribution.

How the Surety may be discharged. —The surety will of course be discharged from liability if the principal debtor pays the debt. He will also be discharged if the creditor alters the terms of his contract with the principal debtor. Thus, where A guaranteed the repayment of a loan made by B to C, and where C later obtained further advances of money and entered into a new obligation to repay the money originally lent and the new advances by executing a deed, A was held to be discharged from liability. C's obligation to repay has been altered. It does not matter whether or not the alteration is in any way prejudicial to the surety.

Where the creditor agrees by a binding contract to give the debtor further time the surety is also released. Notice that this must be by a binding contract, i.e. a contract with consideration, and mere omission on the part of the creditor to press the debtor for payment would not be enough. The creditor may avoid releasing the surety if he

expressly provides in his contract with the debtor that his rights against the surety are "reserved." Thus, if A is surety for £100 lent by B to C repayable in 3 months, and if after 1 month has elapsed B agrees with C for proper consideration to extend the period of payment, A will be released from liability unless B expressly states in the contract, under which he extends the period, that he reserves his rights against A.

Any discharge or release by the debtor of the creditor will release the surety, as also will the doing of any act which by implication releases the debtor from his liability. The same applies to a guarantee of rent due under a lease. If the leasor forfeits the lease, the guarantor is released.

If the creditor gives up to the debtor any security held by him he will release the surety even though he receives some other security in exchange. The same will apply if he discharges from liability any co-sureties, for then the other sureties, if they remained liable, would have their share of the total liability increased.

Where a guarantee is a continuing one it can be revoked as to future transactions by notice given of the revocation or by notice of the death of the surety. Bankruptcy of the debtor will not release the surety although, by the discharge of the debtor in bankruptcy, he is himself released from liability for the debt.

Bank Guarantees.—Although these rules apply in cases where there is no special provisions to the contrary, it is almost invariably the practice, when a guarantee is given to a Bank, for special provisions to be inserted which deprive the surety of much of the protection given by these rules. Thus he may be bound liable as principal debtor and not merely a surety just as if the money had been paid to him; and it is usually also provided that the bank may make such arrangements as they please with the principal debtor without releasing the surety.

Guarantee is frequently used in an entirely different sense, as when the seller of goods "guarantees" that his goods are of a certain quality. When used in this sense the word means no more than a "promise" or "warranty" and this use is not recognised as having any special meaning in law.

GUARANTEE INSURANCE.— Some Insurance Companies are prepared to guarantee the fulfilment by employees of their duties to their employers, and in particular that they will not make default in paying over to their employers money which comes into their hands in the course of their employment. This insurance is also known as Fidelity Insurance.

GUARDIANS COMMITTEE.—A Guardians Committee is a sub-committee of a Public Assistance Committee, and is constituted for the purpose of administering certain portions of the Poor Law. A guardians committee consists of not more than thirty-six members and not less than twelve, of which two-thirds must be members of the County Council for their area or of the County District Council. A third of the members may be co-opted from non-members by the County Council. A guardians committee have to examine all claims for relief which are made in their area, and having examined the claim they then have to decide how much relief should be given. They act upon the report of the local relieving officer to whom all applications for relief must originally be made.

The guardians committee are also entrusted with the duty of visiting, inspecting and managing any poor law institution such as a workhouse or children's home which is situated within their area. In the area administered by the London County Council, the work of guardians committees is performed by area sub-committees of the Public Assistance Committee. (*See also* MEANS TEST; POOR LAW; PUBLIC ASSISTANCE COMMITTEE; WORKHOUSE.)

GUARDIANSHIP. — Guardians of children are of many various kinds, and may be appointed for various purposes, e.g. a guardian "ad litem" is a guardian appointed to act for a child in any action brought against the child; his duties relate only to the litigation and cease as soon as the action is concluded.

Again, for the purposes of the Children and Young Persons Act, 1933, guardian means any person who has for the time being the charge of, or control over, the child or young person (*see* CHILDREN). But generally a guardian means the guardian of the child's person (who also has incidental duties in relation to the child's property).

If a surviving father or mother objects to acting jointly with a guardian so appointed, such guardian cannot act. But in such a case the guardian may apply to the Court and the Court may order that the parent shall be the sole guardian, or that they shall act jointly, or that the guardian shall be the sole guardian. Any one of these orders may also be made when the guardian considers that the surviving parent is unfit to have the custody of the child. When a guardian is in this way appointed sole guardian, the Court may also order the surviving parent to pay a weekly sum for the maintenance of the child.

Where guardians cannot agree regarding any question relating to the welfare of the infant, any of them may apply to the Court to settle the dispute. Guardians may be removed by the Court whether they were appointed by the Court or by a parent, and new guardians may be appointed in their place. The Court in which these powers are vested is either the Chancery Division of the High Court, or the County Court of the district in which resides the person against whom the order is sought to be obtained, or the Magistrate's Court. But the latter Court may not deal with any case except applications to vary or discharge orders relating to a child who has attained sixteen years of age. Nor may it, in any case, deal with orders relating to trust properties or sums exceeding 20/- weekly payable for the maintenance of the child. Guardians may also be appointed by the Chancery Division of the High Court in other cases (e.g. when there has never been a previous guardian), but this is usually done only when there is property at stake. Such guardians may be appointed either for the property or for the person of the child, or for both.

A guardian has the custody and control of his ward, and may put the child in the custody of other persons, e.g. a schoolmaster. He must see that the child is maintained and educated in a way suitable to its rank and according to its religious persuasion, having the greatest regard to its parents' wishes in all respects. In questions of religion, the wishes of the father exclusively must be considered, and, if he expressed no wish, the child must be brought up in the same religion as its father, unless it would be of an irreligious or immoral tendency.

The guardian's consent is required to the marriage of his ward, and the guardian should endeavour to prevent any unsuitable match;

if necessary, he may call in the assistance of the Court. But a marriage contracted without the guardian's consent is nevertheless valid, although the failure to obtain consent may deprive the couple of any rights to the ward's property.

The guardian is under no obligation to spend his own money on the child, but must, when necessary, use the income belonging to the child (if any). He may never use the child's capital unless authorized by deed or will, or by the Court. A guardian appointed by will may receive all the ward's income, and may manage the ward's personal estate by investing, selling investments, etc. But as he is to be regarded as trustee, he must take the greatest care never to benefit from his rights of management, and any profit he makes will belong to the child. He must exercise the diligence of a trustee in the performance of his duties, or he will be guilty of breach of trust and liable to make good to the child all the damage he has done to the property. A guardian is not entitled to remuneration unless expressly authorized. His duties cease when the child attains twenty-one, or when the time for which he was appointed expires. (*See* BASTARDY; CHILD; FATHER; LOCO PARENTIS; MOTHER.)

GUILTY BUT INSANE.—Strictly speaking insanity is no defence to a charge of crime. It is, however, open to the jury to find that the prisoner, when he or she committed the crime, was insane at the time of so doing. The actual form of such a verdict is "Guilty but insane." The jury, however, may not find such a verdict unless the insanity is of a kind sufficient to come within certain well defined rules. These rules were laid down by the Judges in 1843.

In recent years attempts have been made to extend verdicts of insanity to cases of so called "irresistible impulse." These have always failed. It has been not inaptly said that an irresistible impulse is only really an impulse that is not resisted: in other words, would the prisoner have managed to resist the impulse had a policeman been standing at his shoulder at the time of committing the crime?

Prisoners who have been found "Guilty but insane" are not sentenced to any punishment, but are ordered to be detained in a criminal lunatic asylum. The period they remain in such confinement is due to the

progress, or otherwise of their mental condition.

GUN LICENCES.—No person, under penalty of £10, may use or carry a gun outside his own house and garden unless he holds a gun licence (ten shillings) or a licence to kill game (*see* GAME). But the occupier of lands may use a gun without a licence for killing vermin (but not rabbits) or scaring birds; and if he has a gun licence he may direct other persons to do the same even though they are themselves unlicensed. Air-guns and pistols require gun licences. Firearms Certificates are required for all firearms (5/-; renewal 2/6 every third year). (*See* FIREARMS; GAME.)

GUNPOWDER, Manufacture of.—For the setting up of any new factory or magazine for the manufacture of gunpowder a licence is required by the Explosives Act, 1875.

Retail sale of.—Premises on which gunpowder is kept for sale must have a licence. It is obtainable as of right from the local authority, who have no discretion in its issue, and is renewable on payment of an annual fee. The amount stored, if kept in a dwelling-house, must not exceed 50 lbs. Hawking gunpowder in the streets is forbidden, nor can it lawfully be sold to children under thirteen. (*See* EXPLOSIVES.)

GUTTERIDGE MURDER, THE.—Early on the morning of September 26th, 1927, the dead body of a police-constable was found beside a part of the Romford-Ongar Road in Essex. His notebook was lying by his side and his pencil clutched in his hand. He had evidently been in the act of taking a note, and as it was dark and his torch was in his pocket, presumably he was about to write by the light of a car. He had been shot four times, and on close inspection there appeared the ghastly detail that he had been shot through each eye whilst lying on the ground.

Directly the police were informed they made enquiries as to cars using the road on that night and they found that a Morris-Cowley saloon had been stolen from a doctor's house at Billericay close by. This car was discovered in Brixton at 7 a.m. abandoned—there were marks of blood on the running boards and a spent cartridge case inside.

The police then investigated the records

and movements of all criminals known to be car thieves and who were in the habit of carrying a gun—and as a result of their detailed research, four months later Browne was arrested at his garage in Catford, and later Kennedy in Liverpool, both being well-known criminals with terrible records. They came up for trial before Mr. Justice Avory at the Old Bailey and were prosecuted by the Solicitor-General, Sir Boyd Merriman. Browne was defended by Mr. Lever and Kennedy by Mr. Frank Powell.

Evidence at the Trial. When the case opened on April the 23rd, the two counsel for the prisoners applied to the Judge for a separate trial on the ground that a statement made by Kennedy to the police would prejudice the trial of Browne —but Mr. Justice Avory used his discretion in refusing the application. This statement by Kennedy gave an account of the murder in which he said that they were stopped in a stolen car by a suspicious policeman who was about to take particulars when Browne shot him. Browne then drove on whilst Kennedy reloaded the revolver. This statement was not evidence against Browne—but on his arrest the police had found several revolvers, one of which was proved con-

clusively to have fired the fatal shot—also medical instruments which had come from the doctor's stolen car. Browne went in the box, and swore that he was not with Kennedy on the night of the murder. Kennedy made a statement from the dock not on oath and so exempted himself from cross-examination. In this statement he threw the whole of the responsibility for the shooting on to Browne.

The Judge's Summing Up.—On the fifth and last day of the trial, Mr. Justice Avory in summing up to the Jury put four questions to them.

(1) Was P.C. Gutteridge murdered by some person or persons on the night of September 26th, 1927?

(2) Was the murder committed by the person or persons who stole Dr. Lovell's car?

(3) Were there two persons in the car when the murder was committed?

(4) If so, which of them shot him and, if only one, were they acting together with a common purpose to prevent their detention and arrest?

After an absence of $2\frac{1}{4}$ hours the jury returned a verdict of guilty, against both the prisoners who were condemned to death.

HABEAS CORPUS.—The Writ of Habeas Corpus is a writ directed by a Judge of the High Court to any individual ordering the production of the body of any person, whom the Court has reason to believe is imprisoned or confined by such individual, in order that the Court may enquire into the legality of such imprisonment or confinement. No person, of whatever rank or office, may refuse obedience to the writ without rendering himself liable to imprisonment for contempt of court until such time as he shall have "purged his contempt," i.e. obeyed the writ and undergone whatever other penalty the Court may see fit to impose. The process is, moreover, available to relieve any person who is entitled to the King's protection, and therefore will protect aliens present resident in England, Wales, Northern Ireland, the Channel Islands, the

Isle of Man or Berwick-upon-Tweed. The writ may be obtained even by a wife against her husband if he forcibly detains her. (*See also* PREROGATIVE WRITS.)

HABITUAL CRIMINAL.—When a person, after being convicted on indictment of a crime, is found by the jury to be an habitual criminal or admits that he is one, the Court, after sentencing him to penal servitude, may order him to be kept for an additional period in preventive detention. This is a form of imprisonment served in a different place and under less rigorous conditions than penal servitude, and it is intended for the protection of the public rather than for the punishment of the offender.

No one can be charged with being an habitual criminal without the consent of the Director of Public Prosecutions, and at least seven days' notice of the charge must be given to the Court and to the offender himself. Before he can be convicted he must be proved to have been previously convicted of a crime at least three times since the age of sixteen, or to have been convicted and sentenced as an habitual criminal. In all cases, however, even when these things have been proved, the jury must be satisfied that up to the time of his arrest he has been living a persistently dishonest or criminal life.

HABITUAL DRUNKARD is a person who, because of habitual intemperate drinking of intoxicating liquors, is dangerous to himself or others, or incapable of managing himself or his affairs. If a person is convicted of an offence and the Court holds that upon the evidence, the offence was committed under the influence of drink, he may be sentenced to a maximum period of three years' detention in an inebriates' reformatory. Before this can be done, either the offender must admit that he is an habitual drunkard or the jury must find him to be so. A person may be sent to a reformatory if guilty of cruelty to his children by reason of his habitual drunkenness, and the wife of an habitual drunkard may obtain a judicial separation and an order for maintenance.

A local authority may grant to an applicant a licence to keep a retreat for inebriates, but the licence must not be granted for a longer period than two years. Any habitual drunkard who wishes to be admitted into a retreat may apply in writing to the licensee of the retreat stating how long he undertakes to remain there. This application must be accompanied by a statutory declaration made by two persons that the applicant is an habitual drunkard. The applicant's own signature must be attested by a justice of the peace, who must satisfy himself that the applicant fully understands what is the effect of his application.

If any person who is detained in an inebriates' reformatory has sufficient property to maintain his family, an application may be made to a county Court Judge for an order directing that the expenses of keeping the inebriate shall be paid out of his property.

HACKNEY CARRIAGES.— Whereas previous licensing Acts applied indiscriminately to omnibuses (or stage carriages) and hackney carriages, the Road Traffic Act of 1930 (*see* SPECIAL SUPPLEMENT ON ROAD TRAFFIC) draws a sharp distinction between public service vehicles, which consist of all vehicles used for the carriages of passengers for hire if capable of seating eight or more persons, and hackney carriages which consist of all similar vehicles of a smaller seating capacity. The Road Traffic Act applies to public service vehicles only, and makes no changes in the law regarding hackney carriages, for which therefore one must look to the old Hackney Carriage Acts and the regulations made thereunder. These Acts provide for the registration of all cabs, and for the licensing of their proprietors and of the persons employed to drive them; and they empower local authorities in the provinces and the Secretary of State for Home Affairs in London to make regulations on matters of detail.

Proprietor's Taxi Licence.—Any person who wishes to put a hackney carriage upon the road within the Metropolitan Police Area (q.v.) of the City of London, must in the first place apply to the Metropolitan Police Commissioner or, if he is outside this area and the City, to the local licensing authority (viz. the County or Borough Council) for a proprietor's licence. The applicant must be over twenty-one years of age and the Commissioner has discretionary power to refuse to grant him a licence, if he has previously held a licence which has been suspended, if his character or financial reputation is doubtful, or if the cab in question is not certified by the Inspector of Public Carriages as complying with the regulations. There is a right of appeal from such a refusal to the Minister of Transport. Where the proprietor is a firm or a limited company, the application must be made by the senior partner or by the manager or secretary respectively; in all such cases the person who made the application will be held personally responsible for any breach of the regulations.

How application is made.—When an application for a proprietor's licence is made the applicant must produce to the Police Commissioner the Revenue Licence for the cab. This licence is obtained like any other vehicle licence, and in the case of all mechanically propelled cabs the price is £10 if the vehicle is to seat not more than four persons, and £12 if it is to seat between four and eight (if it seats more than eight it is not a hackney carriage at all but a public service vehicle). The price for a proprietor's cab licence is £2, but this is included in the revenue licence and therefore, if the latter has been paid for, no further sum need be paid.

The Police Commissioner may revoke or withdraw a licence, but, if he does so for a reason which existed at the time the licence was granted, he must repay to the applicant the cost of the licence. If an application is granted the applicant is handed a licence on which are written his name and address and particulars of the vehicle, at the same time a plate, in addition to the ordinary number plate, is affixed at the rear of the vehicle bearing its licenced number. Notice of any change of address must be given to the Police within seven days of the change, and the licence must be produced on demand to any agent of the Police Commissioner's. These officers also have the right to inspect the cab and the premises where it is kept. It is an offence rendering the licence void to alter or deface it, or to conceal the hackney carriage plate, and both plate and licence must be delivered up to the Commissioner within three days of notice or of the expiry of the licence.

Although a licenced proprietor may employ drivers, he may not sub-let the cab unless he gives the name and address of the sub-lessee to the Commissioner at least one day beforehand. The Police Commissioner has power to order the cancellation of the sub-lease, and in any case it may not be for more than twenty-one days. Hackney carriages may not be let to any electioneering agent for the carriage of electors to the polling booths, but they may be hired to groups of electors provided they pay for themselves, and there is of course no objection to a single elector taking a cab for himself and his family.

A proprietor need not take out a male servant licence for his drivers, but they are deemed to be his servants in law and therefore he is responsible for all their acts, e.g. he will be liable for damages if they drive negligently and cause an accident. A number of other obligations are laid upon him. Thus he must keep in his own possession the licences of his drivers and must enter upon them his own name and address, and the dates on which the drivers entered and left his employment: but he must surrender them when the driver is dismissed or gives notice, or, if there is a dispute, must take them within 24 hours to a police station. He must also give to every driver a sufficient number of tickets bearing the proprietor's name and address legibly written, and a statement that magistrates have power to settle disputes between drivers and their fares (one of these tickets must be given to any passenger who asks for it).

On the death of the holder of a proprietor's licence the licence should be taken to the Police Commissioner who may transfer it to the deceased's widow, children or personal representatives. On the marriage of a female licensee notice must also be given.

How a Taxi Must be Constructed.— Before a proprietor's licence for a cab can be obtained the cab itself must first be inspected and passed by the Inspector of Public Carriages (whose office is at 109, Lambeth Rd., S.W.), who will only give his certificate if it complies with the detailed regulations of the Police Commissioner and the Home Secretary. The proprietor must then cause to be painted upon the back of the cab the number of persons it is licensed to carry; no other notice or advertisement may be displayed on any part of the cab without the consent of the Commissioner.

Every motor cab must be fitted with a taximeter and the contract of hiring does not commence till this is set in motion (as to extras, however, *see below*). After dark the meter must be clearly illuminated by a lamp. It is sealed by the police after being set to record the fares then in force under the warrant of the Home Secretary, and it is an offence to interfere with it. If any change is made in the schedule of fares the driver is entitled to charge the new fare and that alone, but he is bound to display a notice of the change in his cab until the meter can be altered.

Drivers.—Before any man can lawfully drive a hackney carriage he must first take out a special driver's licence at a cost of 5/–. This is issued by the Police Commissioner to suitable applicants of not less than 21 years.

The licence itself must be handed to the proprietor of the cab to keep, unless the driver is an owner driver, but a copy must be carried by the driver himself who must also wear on his breast the metal ticket which

Lord Hailsham

is issued at the same time and bears the same number. He is bound to let any person read what is written on this ticket. If summoned to appear before a magistrate, the driver must take his copy of his licence with him. The licence can be revoked by a Police Commissioner or a magistrate.

Offences by Taxi Drivers.—It is an offence for any driver to be drunk, to allow any person not authorized by the proprietor to drive, to allow any person upon the driving seat, to make an offensive gesture, to cause an obstruction by loitering, to refuse to drive at a reasonable speed, to deceive any person about the fare of the journey, or to take more than the proper fare.

Lost Property.—At the end of every hiring the driver of a cab must make a search to see if anything has been left behind. If he finds anything which is not claimed he must take it within twenty-four hours to a police station. The owner of the property should apply to the police, but he is only entitled to get it back on payment to the driver of a reasonable sum for his time and trouble. It should, however, be noted that if no claim is made within three months the property may be sold and a share of the proceeds given to the driver.

Driver Cannot Refuse a Fare or Luggage.—Hackney carriages may lawfully ply for hire on Sundays and are subject to the same regulations as on other days. The driver of such a carriage is not entitled to refuse to carry any person who requests him to do so unless his cab is already hired; but he cannot be required to drive more than six miles or for more than one hour. He must not allow more than the authorized number of passengers to enter his cab; but he cannot refuse to carry up to this number, though he may charge extra for carrying more than two. He is bound to carry a reasonable amount of luggage free but may charge extra for anything carried outside.

Extras.—Such extra charges must be paid even though they are not entered on the meter. The proper remuneration is the fare shewn upon the taximeter, which has to be fitted to all motor cabs, and the extras set out above the hire do not officially begin until the meter is set. These meters usually register both time and distance, but, if they do not do so, a hiring is presumed to be by distance only unless the driver is asked to wait for more than fifteen minutes.

A driver is never entitled to ask for more than his legal fare and an agreement by a passenger to pay more is void and cannot be enforced. If paid, any excess can be recovered in a Police Court; the driver would also be liable to a forty shilling fine. On the other hand an agreement to pay less than the lawful fare is perfectly good, as also is an agreement to drive an indefinite distance at the will of the driver for a fixed fare.

On his part, a passenger must pay the proper fare including any extras (even though not recorded on the taximeter). It is an offence to hire a cab with the knowledge that one cannot pay for it or fraudulently to avoid payment in any other way. If by inadvertence a passenger is unable to pay, he must give the driver his true name and address under penalty of a forty shilling fine.

Disputes.—Any Police Court magistrate has authority to settle all disputes between drivers and their fares; in addition he has power to order the passenger to compensate the driver for his time and the journey to the Court if he decides that the passenger was in the wrong. (*See* CARRIERS.)

HAILSHAM, Lord (1872–).—The Secretary of State for War in the National

Government. As Sir Douglas Hogg he was one of the leading advocates at the Bar. He was Attorney-General (1922-28) when he was given the Woolsack as Lord Hailsham by the Conservative Government.

HALL, MARSHALL, Sir Edward (1858-1927).—Possessed of all the acknowledged attributes of the great advocate—courage, presence, eloquence and a sense of the dramatic, Marshall Hall was the most sensational and popular advocate of his day. His first great case was the defence of Marie Hermann at the Old Bailey. When his practice was at its height it suddenly fell away partly because of a series of indiscreet and angry scenes in Court with Judges. Marshall Hall, however, returned to fame and prosperity with the Camden Town Murder Case, where he secured a wonderful personal triumph in the acquittal of Wood. He regarded his greatest effort in a criminal case to be his defence of Ronald Light and, in the Civil Courts, the Russell divorce. The longest capital case in which Marshall Hall was concerned was the trial of the poisoner Seddon which lasted for ten days.

Among his other famous acquittals were Madame Fahmy, Greenwood the Kidwelly solicitor, and Smith of the Stella Maris case. He defended Smith, the Brides of the Bath murderer, and Bennet in the dramatic Yarmouth murder trial.

His wonderful knowledge of firearms,

Sir Edward Marshall Hall.

which were his hobby, and of medicine imparted into him by his father, a doctor, enabled him to fight on equal terms with the experts in these matters. It was by his human qualities rather than knowledge of the law that he attained the heights of his fame.

HALL MARKS.—Hall marks are the marks on gold and silver which indicate that the metal is of the requisite standard of purity, and which also state the date and place where it was tested. Gold and silver domestic plate, watch cases and gold weddings rings of 22 carats must be tested and hall marked in this way. Gold and silver watch chains need not be stamped. Offices have been set up where the metal may be tested and the hall mark stamped on, and these are called assay offices. They are situated at London, Birmingham, Chester, Sheffield, Glasgow, Edinburgh and Dublin.

Gold and silver are very soft metals and for practical use always require to be mixed with an alloy. Gold plate may be either 9, 14, 18, or 22 carat. 12 and 15 carat were formerly used instead of 14 carat. Carat is not a weight but denotes the quality. Pure gold is 24 carat; 22 carat means that the metal is a mixture of gold and some alloy in the proportion of 22 parts gold to 2 parts alloy; 9 carat indicates a mixture 9 parts pure gold to 15 parts alloy. There are two standards for silver, known as sterling and Britannia. Sterling silver is 11 oz. 2 dwt. fine silver to the pound troy (12 ounces one pound; 20 pennyweights [dwt.] one ounce) that is, 11 oz. 2 dwt. silver to 18 dwts alloy or ·925 pure silver. Britannia silver is 11 oz. 10 dwt. pure silver to 10 dwt. alloy or ·959 pure silver. From 1697 to 1720 Britannia silver was the only standard allowed, but silver of this kind is now rarely found as it is too soft for practical purposes.

It is a serious criminal offence to counterfeit any of these marks, or to erase or obliterate them. When plate is imported it must be marked on entry into this country and if it is not up to the proper standard it will not be allowed into the country. This does not apply to plate which has been brought in for private use and not for sale, but such plate must be marked and tested if it is sold at any time.

HAND-WRITING.—It is frequently important to prove in whose hand-writing

Sir Patrick Hastings.

HARES.—It is lawful for any person in the occupation of land, or for the owner of any land who has the right of killing game on it, to kill hares without obtaining a game licence. (*See* GAME.)

HASTINGS, Sir Patrick (1880-).—Is one of our leading advocates. A born fighter, Sir Patrick has been in many of the *causes célèbres* of the 20th century. He was Attorney-General to the Labour Government in 1924.

HAWKE, Mr. Justice (1869-).—After a distinguished career at the Bar in London and on the Western Circuit he was made a Judge of the High Court in 1928. He was formerly Recorder of Plymouth.

HAWKERS.—A hawker is a person who travels with a horse or other beast of burden, and goes from place to place or house to house exposing goods for sale; or any person who travels to places other than where he resides by any means of locomotion and there exposes goods for sale in any shop, stall or other hired place. Hawkers must take out annual excise licences (£2) and, under pain of fine or imprisonment, must produce a current licence upon demand.

Exemptions: (i) Commercial travellers; (ii) the original maker of the goods hawked and his children, or servants residing in the same house as himself; (iii) sellers of victuals and coal; (iv) sellers in public and legally established markets or fairs.

The licence is first granted only on the production of a certificate of good character

certain documents are. Thus in cases of forgery the fact that the hand-writing of the forged document is that of the prisoner is of the first importance. Hand-writing can be proved in several ways. Anyone who is acquainted with the prisoner's hand-writing, through having seen him write or through having corresponded with him can, after examining the disputed hand-writing, testify as to his opinion as whether or not they are the same. Again, experts in hand-writing can be called to give their opinion on the similarity or otherwise between the disputed hand-writing and any writing proved by other means to have been written by the prisoner. Yet again, the jury may themselves compare the disputed hand-writing with any other writing proved to be that of the prisoner, and come to a decision.

The value of experts in hand-writing lies, perhaps, not so much in their opinions, but in the assistance they give the tribunal in indicating points of similarity. To this end, hand-writing experts usually make photographic enlargements of the specimens of hand-writing which are to be produced at a trial and use them for pointing out the characteristics that are thus shewn.

13*

Mr. Justice Hawke.

from a local inspector of police, justice of the peace or clergyman. A hawker must have the words "licensed hawker" on each of his vehicles, shops, boxes or handbills. (*See* PEDLARS.)

HEARSAY.—The English Law of Evidence restricts witnesses from giving evidence as to many points. One of the most important of these restrictions is the rule preventing a witness from giving evidence from hearsay. The rule may shortly be stated in this way: A witness may not say what has been told to him in the absence of the opposite party. Thus, suppose a burglar is surprised by a householder and runs away. If the householder reports to a policeman what happened, the policeman cannot, at the subsequent trial of the burglar if caught, inform the Court of what the householder told him.

The object of this rule is to ensure that the best possible evidence shall be given as to any particular fact. In the example just given, clearly the best possible evidence would be the testimony of the householder himself as to what he saw of the burglar. If witnesses were allowed to say what they had been told by other people, cases might be decided and persons convicted on the testimony of people who were not present at Court to be cross-examined. Further, it is desirable that Judge and jury should see witnesses for themselves, so that some opinion can be formed as to their honesty and credibility by means of watching their demeanour.

The rule excluding hearsay is not confined to shutting out second-hand verbal statements, it extends also to written documents. The fact that a statement has been made in writing to somebody or other does not make that statement any the more acceptable in evidence. Thus, to take the example just given, the policeman could no more give an account of a written statement from the householder than he could give an account of the householder's verbal statement.

Statements made in the presence of the opposite party are usually admissible in evidence. Thus, if the householder referred to above had arrived on the scene of the arrest of the burglar and in his presence had said: "That is the man I saw in my house," a policeman or any other person who was present at the interview, could at the subsequent trial say what he had heard said. This is so because the fact of what is said in the presence of the opposite party, in this case the prisoner, is relevant to the issue. It would, for instance, be most important to shew that the prisoner, after such an accusation had been made, did not deny it.

Similarly, any statement made by the opposite party to the side tendering the evidence can in general be accepted. In criminal cases, for instance, any person who heard the prisoner say anything connected with the alleged crime, can in evidence say what he heard said. There is an important qualification to this rule, namely that in criminal cases statements by a prisoner cannot be proved if they amount to a confession, until it has first been shewn that they were made freely and voluntarily. (*See* EVIDENCE.)

HEIR.—Heir really means the person who was before 1925 entitled to succeed to the real property (land, except leases) of a man who had died without making a will. The person entitled to land under a will is not an heir but a devisee; the person entitled to property other than land is a legatee.

For old law of inheritance *see* DESCENT. For new law *see* INTESTACY.

HEIR (SCOTS LAW).—A man's heir is strictly the person who is entitled to succeed to his heritable property on his death, in the event of his dying without leaving a will. The heir is thus distinguished from the next of kin, who is the person entitled to succeed to a movable property of another on intestacy. (*See* INTESTACY [SCOTS LAW].)

HEIRLOOMS.—An heirloom is an article which is so closely connected with a family's estate in land that it is treated as part of that estate. Before 1925 this meant that it descended on the death of the owner to his heir along with his land; and not, as did the rest of his property, to the next of kin. They could be sold but not disposed of by will. Wild deer parks, or letters patent ennobling a family are probably heirlooms. In modern times heirlooms in this strictly legal sense are never met with.

There is, however, another class of articles to which the word heirloom is frequently applied. These are articles of personal property such as plate, jewels, pictures, armour, furniture, etc., which have been settled in such a way that they pass to whoever is the owner for the time being of the family estate. Like the settled land itself they cannot be disposed of by such an owner for his own benefit; but he has certain powers to sell them for the benefit of the family. If the leave of the Chancery Division of the High Court can be obtained, heirlooms may be sold; but the purchase price must either be invested in new heirlooms or be treated as capital under the settlement.

HEREDITAMENT.—Hereditament signifies something which is "inheritable"; something, that is, which could on death descend to the owner's heirs. It is only used in connection with the ownership of, or rights in, land.

The different kinds of interest or right in land which are inheritable, and are therefore properly described as hereditaments, may be divided into corporeal and incorporeal hereditaments. A corporeal hereditament is one which entitles the owner of it to take exclusive possession of the land; an incorporeal hereditament is either one which does not yet entitle the owner of it to take exclusive possession but may do so in the future (i.e. a future interest or remainder); or it is a right over land which can never entitle the owner to take exclusive possession of the land (i.e. advowsons, rent, charges and easements).

HERIOT.—Under the system of land holding known as copyhold (q.v.), examples of which used to be found scattered all over England, the possessor of the land was deemed to be the tenant of the lord of the manor in which it was situated.

The system was very old, and numerous antiquated customs survived; amongst them was the right of the lord to claim the best live beast or piece of movable property, e.g. goods, belonging to the tenant on the

Lord Hewart.

latter's death, and sometimes also on any alienation of · the land. The animal or property seized was called a heriot. Originally it was a payment made by the heir to the lord of the manor in return for being allowed to succeed to the land.

In 1925 copyhold tenure was abolished; but the lord's right to claim a heriot was preserved until 1935. He can, however, now only claim the value in money of the heriot. On December 31, 1935, the right will cease altogether, but until 1940 the tenant will be liable to be called upon to pay compensation to the lord of the manor.

HERITABLE PROPERTY (SCOTS LAW).—All property in Scots Law is divided into heritable and movable. Although heritable corresponds to a large extent to land and to real property in English law, it originally meant all property which passed to the "heir" of a person on his death instead of to his executors who represent his next-of-kin. Movable property always passes to the executors for the next-of-kin of a person, upon death and originally included all property which could be "moved," such as goods.

Heritable property includes not only land but also all fixtures and rights connected with land, such as leases and servitudes, i.e. rights over land such as a right to light. When money is borrowed on land by a bond and disposition, i.e. when a heritable security is created, the right both of the creditor to the money and of the debtor to the land when the debt is paid off were originally heritable, that is, passed to the heir and not to the next-of-kin; but now the creditor's rights pass to his executors for his next-of-kin.

Heritable securities still remain heritable to this extent, that the spouse or children of the creditor on his death are not entitled to their legal rights out of the property which they would have were it movable property.

The High Court of Justice, Strand, London.

So far as the debtor is concerned the property still remains heritable, and so after his death the obligation to pay must be discharged in the first place by the heir, that is, out of other heritable property and not out of the movable property. (*See* HUSBAND AND WIFE [SCOTS LAW]; INTESTACY [SCOTS LAW]).

HEWART, Lord (1870–).—The present Lord Chief Justice is well known for his classical learning and the purity of his English style. He started life as a reporter, and he was one of the few lawyers who have been a real success in the House of Commons.

HIGH BAILIFF.—This is an officer appointed for the purpose of serving summonses and executing warrants in the County Court. (*See* BAILIFF.)

HIGH COURT OF JUSTICE.— The High Court of Justice is the name given to that part of the Supreme Court of Judicature which does not comprise the Court of Appeal. It is the proper Court in which all actions in England and Wales may be commenced, and no action is too large and none too small to be heard by it, though in the case of certain small actions the

High Court of Justice has the power of remitting the actions to the appropriate County Court to be heard.

In addition to this, which is its Original Jurisdiction, the High Court of Justice has a certain Appellate Jurisdiction which it exercises when sitting as Divisional Courts (q.v.).

The Courts of the High Court of Justice are housed in the permanent buildings of the Royal Courts of Justice, Strand, London, but in addition to sitting in London, certain of the Judges of the High Court of Justice travel from county to county holding Assize Courts in the various towns of England and Wales, and these Assize Courts are part of the High Court of Justice, and have the same powers within certain territorial limits as the High Court of Justice when sitting in London.

The High Court of Justice is divided into three divisions for the purposes of convenience. These divisions are known as the King's Bench Division, the Chancery Division and the Probate, Divorce and Admiralty Division, and the various types of legal actions are divided between them.

In the same buildings as the Court Rooms in the Royal Courts of Justice, Strand, London, is the Central Office of the High Court of Justice, from which writs of summons, by means of which actions in the High Court are usually started, and all the other necessary summons, notices, etc., may be obtained and where the clerical and other business of the Courts is conducted.

There exist offices known as District Registries in most Assize Towns, where similar business is done in respect of actions to be heard at Assizes. These offices are under the charge of District Registrars.

The officers of the High Court consist of the puisne Judges, known as Mr. Justice ——, and addressed as "My Lord," the Masters who deal with interlocutory business of the Court, i.e. the proceedings that take place between the commencement of the action and its hearing before a Judge with or without a jury. In the Probate, Divorce and Admiralty Division, the place of the Master is taken by a Registrar, as it is in the District Registries in the provincial towns. (See ACTION; CHANCERY DIVISION; COURT; HIGH COURT PROCEDURE; KING'S BENCH DIVISION; PROBATE; DIVORCE AND ADMIRALTY DIVISION; SUPREME COURT OF JUDICATURE.)

HIGH COURT PROCEDURE.—

The various stages through which an action passes in the High Court of Justice are of a highly technical nature. There is no procedure comparable to that of a County Court where a litigant may obtain service of the necessary documents upon his opponent by the Court Bailiff; and in general the assistance that an amateur litigant can obtain in the County Court is not available in the High Court. For this reason, therefore, no one should attempt to start or to conduct an action in the High Court without professional advice and assistance throughout, and this assistance in cases of extreme poverty may be obtained free of charge through the agency of Poor Persons' Committees which administer the Poor Persons' Procedure (q.v.) (See ACTION; APPEAL IN HIGH COURT; COSTS IN HIGH COURT; DISCOVERY; EXECUTION; HIGH COURT OF JUSTICE; INTERROGATORIES; JUDGMENT IN HIGH COURT; PARTIES; PAYMENT INTO COURT; PAYMENT OUT OF COURT; PLEADINGS; TRANSFER OF ACTION; SUMMONS; WRIT OF SUMMONS.)

HIGH TREASON.—

The law of High Treason is mainly that set out in a statute passed in the reign of Edward III, namely, the Treason Act, 1351. The main provisions are: "When a man doth compass or imagine the death of our Lord the King or of our Lady his Queen, or of their eldest son and heir; or if a man do violate the King's companion, or the King's eldest daughter unmarried, or the wife of the King's eldest son and heir; or if a man do levy war against our Lord the King in his realm, or be adherent to the King's enemies in his realm, giving to them aid and comfort in the realm, or elsewhere, and thereof be . . . attainted by open deed by the people of their condition," he shall be guilty of High Treason. The exact meaning of this ancient statute has frequently given rise to questions in the Courts. The most important case in modern times in which it has been examined was that of Sir Roger Casement in 1916.

The Case of Sir Roger Casement.— Sir Roger Casement was charged with "High Treason by adhering to the King's enemies elsewhere than in the King's realm, to wit, in the Empire of Germany, contrary to the Treason Act, 1351." It was alleged that he had, whilst in Germany, incited certain British prisoners of war there to forsake their allegiance to the King and join the armed forces of the enemy. Counsel for the prisoner took the point that the charge was bad because the Act in question did not make treasonable "adhering to the King's enemies elsewhere than in the King's realm." They argued that the words "or elsewhere" referred only to "giving aid and comfort" and not to the "adhering to the King's enemies." After exhaustive hearings before three Judges of the King's Bench Division and the Court of Criminal Appeal this argument was rejected, and it was definitely laid down that the acts proved against the prisoner constituted high treason.

High Treason is punishable with death. It is usually not tried in the ordinary Criminal Courts but before a specially convened tribunal of three Judges and a jury. When so tried it is called a trial "at bar." In cases of high treason the prisoner is entitled to the services of two counsel to conduct his defence.

HIGHWAYS.—

At Common Law a highway is a way, whether a road or path,

over which all members of the public have the right to pass and repass whether on business or for pleasure. All ways which are open to the public are highways, even though they may only be used subject to restrictions, so long as those restrictions apply to the public generally, e.g. a footpath open to the public generally is a highway even though it cannot be used as a carriage-way. Thus a highway may be a carriage and cartway, a horseway, a driftway, i.e. a way for driving cattle, or a footpath. Further, a way may still be a highway even though it is a cul-de-sac, i.e. it is not necessary that the way should be a thoroughfare.

Creation of Highways.—Public rights of way may be created by "dedication" or by statute. At Common Law where land is dedicated, i.e. "given" to the use of the public for the purposes of passage, it becomes a highway when the public has accepted it for such purposes. There must be an intention to dedicate on the part of the landowner, which may be expressed in words or writing, or may be deduced by a jury from his conduct and from all the circumstances of the case, e.g. repair of the way at the public expense is strong evidence of dedication. The landowner must have the power to dedicate, i.e. he must have absolute control and in general be owner of the land and not a tenant.

Thus, a lessee cannot dedicate without the consent of the owner. Acceptance by the public of the dedication is to be inferred from evidence of use by the public. Such use must be open, i.e. known to the landowner and not secret, and "as of right," i.e. not exercised merely by some licence or permission granted by the landowner which he can withdraw at his pleasure. Further, such use must not have been obstructed by the landowner, e.g. by closing the way for one day in the year, and must have been indulged in for a substantial time. By the Rights of Way Act, 1932 (which came into force on January 1st, 1934), where a way has been enjoyed by the public for 20 years, it is presumed to have been dedicated as a highway, unless there is sufficient contrary evidence, or unless at any time during the 20 years there was some person in possession of the land who did not have the power to dedicate. Where it has been enjoyed for

40 years, it is presumed to have been dedicated to the public unless the contrary is shewn. A notice stating that the path or road is private, displayed by the landowner and visible to those using the land, will indicate that there was no intention to dedicate, and if the notice is torn down the landowner can give written notice to the local authority.

Public Highways may also be created by statute, e.g. the Minister of Transport may with the approval of the Treasury construct any new road that may be required. Local highway authorities also may construct new roads.

Highway Rights.—The public has the right to pass and repass on the highway and to use it for purposes reasonably incidental to the right of passage, e.g. resting, waiting for buses, etc. The public, however, has no right to remain on the highway for other purposes, so that, for example, if a person used the highway to watch trials of race horses taking place on adjoining private land, or to annoy and molest the owner of adjoining land, he will be guilty of trespass and may be removed by force.

Since the public has only a right of passage, the person dedicating retains at Common Law his ownership of the soil of the highway. The owner of adjoining land is, in the absence of contrary evidence, presumed to own the soil of the highway up to the middle. He can, therefore, take out the minerals below the surface of the highway; he owns trees, etc., growing along the road; he can sue in trespass any person who uses the road otherwise than for passage or who wrongfully places any obstruction thereon. He must not, however, exercise his rights so as to interfere with the rights of the public, e.g. by breaking up the road to lay pipes. County roads, however, their materials, drains, etc., are now vested in the County Councils or, where claimed, in the Urban District Councils, so that highway authorities now have control over so much of the actual soil beneath the surface and the air above as may be necessary for their purposes.

Highway Authorities.—Highways are controlled in part by a central authority and in part by local authorities. The central authority for highways, streets and bridges is the Minister of Transport and to him have been transferred nearly all the powers and duties of government departments in regard to highways. Certain powers in regard to highways are retained by the Board of Trade and Minister of Health, e.g. before money can be borrowed by local authorities the consent of the Minister of Health is necessary.

The Road Fund.—The Minister of Transport has control and management of this fund which was established by the Roads Act, 1920. Every year there is paid into the road fund all duties payable to the Exchequer under the Roads Act, 1920. These duties are the licensing duties for motor vehicles and other carriages which are levied by the county councils and paid into the Exchequer. Also, there is to be paid into the road fund fines imposed under the Road Transport Lighting Act, and fines and licensing fees received under the Road Traffic Act, 1930, and Road and Rail Transport Act, 1933. Temporary loans may also be made to the road fund out of the Consolidated Fund, which is the name applied to the account of the national exchequer.

At the present time the fund is not devoted solely to highway purposes, as was originally intended; e.g. under the Local Government Act, provision is made for the payment of sums from the fund as General Exchequer Contributions. These sums are used to meet the ordinary expenses of governing the country.

Local Authorities.—The functions of maintenance, repair and improvement of county roads are, in general, now vested in the county council as highway authority.

Maintenance and Repair of Highways.—At Common Law the liability to repair highways in the first place falls upon the shoulders of the "inhabitants at large," i.e. inhabitants of each parish through which the highways run. Under statute this liability now falls on the highway authorities which are set out above, though the ultimate liability rests upon the inhabitants at large.

Duties of Highway Authorities.— It is the duty of highway authorities to maintain and keep in repair all highways; and urban authorities must pave, metal and flag all streets. It is their duty to remove obstruction by snow or the collapse of roadside banks etc., but there is no duty on the authority to fence a highway, though it has power to do so if it so desires. If, however, it fails to maintain a fence erected by it or its predecessors the authority may be liable for ensuing damage. If any tree, hedge or shrub overhangs any street or footpath, and so obstructs the flow of light from a public lamp and interferes with the passage of vehicles or pedestrians, or obstructs the view of drivers of vehicles, the authority may serve a notice requiring the person responsible to cut or lop the tree in 14 days. When it is considered necessary or desirable for the safety of pedestrians, cattle, etc., the authority must provide footpaths or grass margins on roads under their control.

Lighting.—Highway authorities have no power or duty at common law to light highways, and the duty to maintain and repair does not include lighting. Under statute, however, certain local authorities are granted powers of lighting roads in their districts. Under the Public Health Act, 1875, urban authorities or rural authorities with certain urban powers may contract for the lighting of roads in their districts and may generate their own electricity or gas for this purpose.

Such a power, however, is discretionary, so that there is no compulsion under this act on the authority to light the streets. If they do light, they will be liable in damages for negligence in lighting, e.g. for allowing gas or electricity to escape, or putting up lamp-posts etc., in the highway without warning. If, however, the authority does not itself create a source of danger, it will not be liable for any damage resulting from its complete or partial failure to light.

Under the Metropolis Management Act, however, in London the local authority is bound to light, so that it will be liable not only for negligence in lighting as above, but also for failure properly to light.

Where the above acts do not apply, lighting may be carried out under the Lighting and Watching Act which must be adopted by a two-thirds majority at a meeting of parochial electors. The authority charged with the lighting will be the parish council or inspectors elected under the acts; they have powers of contracting for the supply of lighting, of erecting lamps, etc.

The maximum expenditure on the lighting of highways is to be fixed at the parish meeting.

Non-repair of Roads.—No action for damages will lie against a highway authority for damage suffered as a result of the failure of the authority to carry out their duty to maintain a highway in repair.

If, however, the highway is rendered dangerous by some wrongful act, as opposed to omission, of the highway authority, and damage results, an action can be brought against the authority.

The proper method to compel the person or body responsible to repair the highway is by indictment, i.e. criminal prosecution, or, if a statute requires certain works to be carried out, procedure known as a Writ of Mandamus will be issued. Further, summary proceedings in a Police Court may be brought under the Highway Acts.

Nuisance.—Any person who, without lawful justification, obstructs or renders dangerous the right of passage of the public along the highway commits a public nuisance and a misdemeanour. Obstruction may consist, e.g. in erecting a fence across a highway, leaving vehicles standing upon it for an unreasonable time and in unreasonable numbers, or causing crowds to collect. The highway may be rendered dangerous, e.g. by allowing adjoining buildings, or fences or trees to become dangerous, leaving unguarded piles of road material on the highway, sweeping fallen snow into heaps or melting snow by means of salt etc., so as to be dangerous to passing traffic; making dangerous excavations near the highway without adequate fencing or protection of passers-by

Footpaths.—Public footpaths are highways and generally the law of highways applies to them. Footpaths are commonly dedicated subject to rights reserved in the landowner, e.g. to erect stiles and to plough over the path. When the footpath runs by the side of a road, the person liable to repair the road is liable to repair the footpath. When a person occupies land over which a footpath runs, unless he is liable for the repair of the path as a whole, he is not liable to repair gates, stiles and bridges. If the footpath crosses a stream a bridge cannot be built by the highway authority without the consent of the owner. The Rights of Way Act, 1932, referred to above, protects landowners against the acquisition by the public of rights of way over his land.

HIRE.—A Contract of Hire is one under which the owner of goods allows some person to use the goods for a money payment. The goods remain the property of the owner and must be returned to him when the contract is at an end.

Making the Contract.—As a general rule, a contract of hire does not require to be in writing, but if it is for more than a year, there must be some written note of its terms signed by the party against whom the contract is to be enforced. Where the contract is for an indefinite time, that is, may be put an end to at any time by the hirer returning the goods or in any other way, it is not considered to be for more than one year.

Where the contract is in writing, it must be stamped with a 6d. stamp. If instalments of hire are not payable in advance, and with an ad valorem duty stamp if they are payable in advance, a 6d. stamp may either be on the agreement at the time when it is signed (in which case an adhesive stamp may be used), or it may be an impressed stamp obtained at the Inland Revenue Office at any time within 14 days of the agreement. Where an ad valorem stamp is required it may be impressed on the paper by the Inland Revenue Office at any time within 30 days after the agreement has been made.

Duties of Owner.—Any person who lets an article out for hire, e.g. a motor-car, is taken to promise that the goods hired are as suitable for the purpose for which they are hired as reasonable care and skill can make for them. Thus, if when a car has been hired a wheel comes off or some other accident happens, the person who has let the car for hire will be liable if he could have discovered the defect, if he had inspected the car properly, or if the defect would never have existed if the car had been properly looked after. Thus, if an accident occurs under these circumstances, not only will the hirer not be liable for the damage to the car but he will be able to recover from the owner of the car any damage that he may himself suffer.

If no provision is made as to who is to keep the article in repair the owner will usually be bound to do so, except in cases where the lack of repair is due to the carelessness of the hirer. Thus, if the hiring is for a definite period the owner is taken to warrant that the goods hired will remain in good order and condition during the period, and if they do not he is bound to repair them. In practice, when a motor-car is hired, the owner, at any rate if the hiring is for a short period, assumes responsibility for its upkeep. If a breakdown occurs the hirer should not, however, order any repairs to be done without first getting in touch with the owner. The owner will then usually make his own arrangements for the repairs to be carried out. Thus he may, if there is a puncture and a tyre must be replaced, despatch a new tyre himself by rail or otherwise to the place where the car has broken down.

Duties of Hirer.—The hirer must pay the agreed rent, take reasonable care of the goods and return them to the owner in good condition at the end of the hiring period. The hirer will not be liable for damage to the goods which is caused without any fault on his part, but if they have been damaged in his possession it is for him to shew that he was in no way to blame. (*See* BAILMENT.)

HIRE PURCHASE.—The object of Hire Purchase Agreements is to enable a person to have the use of goods before he has paid for them. The person to whom the goods belong and to whom the instalments are paid is called the "owner," and the person who wishes to buy the goods is called the "hirer," or "hire purchaser." The instalments paid are called "hire," or "hire rent," or in some cases "rent." The goods usually sold in this way are motor-cars, and articles of furniture. The term hire purchase agreement has no definite meaning in law and is used to indicate all agreements which carry out the above purpose.

Sales on the Deferred Payments.— In an agreement of this kind the intending purchaser buys the goods, or agrees to buy them, on the terms that he will pay the price by instalments spread over a period of time. It may be provided by the agreement that until he has paid all his instalments the goods do not become his property. This is an "agreement to buy or sell." If it is not so provided, the effect of the agreement will be that the goods become his

property as soon as the contract is made and even though the price is not paid. This is a sale as distinct from a mere "agreement to sell." The distinction between these two is important, for if the goods do not become his property until all instalments have been paid, the intending purchaser commits a breach of the agreement if he attempts to sell or pledge the goods before he has paid all instalments, and they may be taken from him by the owner. If the agreement contains no such provision, the hire purchaser can do what he pleases with the goods for they belong to him; and if he sells them or attempts to sell them he cannot be prevented, his only liability being to pay the amount of the price for which he may be sued. Notice that even when the agreement provides that the goods shall not belong to the hire purchaser until he has paid all the instalments, anyone who buys them from him without knowing that the hire purchaser has no right to sell, gets a good title—i.e., can keep them and cannot be compelled to hand them back to the owner. (*See below.*)

Hire Agreement with Option to Purchase.—This is the most usual agreement in practice, and under this the hire purchaser agrees to take the goods for a period and to pay during that period a fixed sum for their hire. He is not bound under the agreement ever to buy the goods, although in practice it will almost invariably be his intention to do so. Under the agreement he acquires merely an option, i.e. a right to buy the goods *if he pleases* when he has paid all the hire rent. Usually this option is for a very small sum such as 5/-. When this form of agreement is used, the hirer must not under any circumstances dispose of the goods to any other person before he has exercised the option to buy, and if he attempts to do so, the goods may be taken from him. It is usually provided by agreements of this kind that the hirer may terminate the hiring by returning the goods after he has paid say one half of the instalments. Unless there is some provision of this kind the hirer, if he finds that he cannot keep up the instalments, will have to return the goods, and will receive none of his money back, even though he may have paid three-quarters or more of the instalments. Hire-purchase agreements are usually contained

𝔐𝔢𝔪𝔬𝔯𝔞𝔫𝔡𝔲𝔪 𝔬𝔣 𝔄𝔤𝔯𝔢𝔢𝔪𝔢𝔫𝔱 made the *ten th*

Leave date blank.

day of *October* 193- BETWEEN UNITED MOTOR FINANCE CORPORATION LIMITED, whose registered office is situate at 6, Great Marlborough Street, London, W.1 (hereinafter called "the Owners" which expression shall include also its successors and assigns) of the one part and *Herbert Black,* of *976, Luton Road, Dalewinton, Insurance Agent* (hereinafter called "the Hirer") of the other part WHEREBY IT IS AGREED as follows :—

1. THE OWNERS (who are Owners of the Vehicle and Accessories described in the Schedule hereto) agree to let and the Hirer agrees to hire the same (hereinafter called the "Vehicle" which expression shall include besides the said Vehicle and Accessories any replacements renewals or additions thereto) upon and subject to terms hereinafter appearing.

2. THE HIRER agrees as follows:—

    (A) On the signing hereof to pay to the Owners at United Building, Trading Estate, Slough the amount of the first payment set out in the Schedule hereto in consideration of the option to purchase hereinafter given. In the event of purchase being effected under Clause 3 (A) hereof credit shall be given for such payment but not otherwise.

    (B) So long as the hiring shall continue to pay to the Owners at United Building, Trading Estate, Slough on the due dates an amount equal to the amount of the monthly payments set out in the Schedule hereto and in default of punctual payment thereof (but without prejudice to the Owners' other rights hereunder) to pay interest on any overdue hire rents or other payments at the rate of 10 per cent. per annum and provided always that any sums received hereunder may be appropriated by the Owners in reimbursement of any payments made by them under Clauses 2 (D), 2 (F) and 6.

    (C) To keep the Vehicle in good repair and working condition (but this obligation shall not authorise or entitle the Hirer to create any lien or charge on the said Vehicle).

    (D) To pay all licence duties, fees, insurance premiums and registration charges payable in respect of the Vehicle whilst this Agreement is in force and if any such duties, fees, premiums or charges shall be paid by the Owners (the Owners being entitled to pay same on behalf of the Hirer) to repay same to the Owners forthwith.

    (E) Not to use or permit or suffer the Vehicle to be used contrary to any Statutes or Regulations or to the Law ; not to take send or permit same out of Great Britain unless and until a purchase has been finally completed in accordance with the terms hereof.

    (F) To repay to the Owners forthwith all expenses costs or charges incurred in ascertaining the whereabouts of the Hirer or the Vehicle or in recovering or endeavouring to recover possession thereof from the Hirer or any other person firm or company.

3. THE OWNERS agree:—

    (A) If the Hirer shall duly make the said payments and strictly observe and perform all the terms and conditions on his part herein contained then the Hirer shall thereupon have the option of purchasing the Vehicle for the sum of Five Shillings.

    (B) Without prejudice to any Claim which the Owners may have against the Hirer in respect of any breach of this Agreement or in respect of any sum payable hereunder, and providing the Hirer shall not be in arrears with any payment under Clause 2 (B), he shall be at liberty voluntarily to return the Vehicle and to terminate the hiring without the option to purchase being exercised. In the event of such voluntary return and termination by the Hirer taking place within the first half of the full period of hiring the Vehicle shall be returned free of expense to the Owners to such address as shall be appointed by the Owners at the request of the Hirer and the Hirer shall pay to the Owners such sums by way of agreed compensation for hiring and for depreciation which with the amounts previously paid as hire-rents under Clause 2 (B) shall equal the amount which would have been payable as hire for such first half of the full period of hiring. In the event of the voluntary return and termination by the Hirer taking place after the first half of the full period of hiring the Vehicle shall be returned to the Owners free of expense to the Owners to such address as may be appointed by the Owners at the request of the Hirer.

4. IF during the hiring the Hirer shall:—

    (A) Make default in punctually paying any of the hire-rents provided by Clause 2 (B) ;

    (B) Be adjudicated Bankrupt or have a Receiving Order made against him or if the Hirer shall convene any Meeting of Creditors or make a Deed of Assignment or Arrangement or compound with his Creditors or (being a Company) shall pass a resolution for winding-up or have a petition for winding-up presented or have a Receiver appointed ;

    (C) Have any execution or distress levied or should the Vehicle be seized under any distress execution or other process ;

    (D) Fail to observe and perform all the terms conditions and stipulations on his part herein contained ;

    (E) Do any act or thing which may prejudice or jeopardise the Owners' interests or right of ownership ;

it shall be lawful for the Owners (but without prejudice to any other rights hereunder) to put an end to the hiring immediately and re-take possession of the Vehicle and (if necessary) for that purpose by their Agents or Representatives to enter upon premises and break open gates doors and other entrances. A demand by the Owners for the return of the Vehicle given orally by their duly appointed Representative or in writing left at or sent by prepaid post addressed to the Hirer at his last known address or the address set out in the preamble to this Agreement shall be sufficient notice of termination of this Agreement by the Owners.

A Specimen Hire Purchase Agreement.

In the event of the hiring being determined under this Clause the Hirer shall pay to the Owners the balance of all rent which would have become due if the hiring had continued for the full period and all damages (if any) for breaches of this Agreement and all other sums payable hereunder but credit will be given for such an amount as shall actually be received by the Owners as sale price of the Vehicle after deducting therefrom the costs of taking possession removal and sale of the Vehicle ; any surplus to the Hirer's credit will be returned to him by the Owners.

5. UNLESS and until the whole of the sums due under Clauses 2 (A) and 2 (B) hereof shall have been paid and purchase been made under Clause 3 (A) hereof the Vehicle shall remain the absolute property of the Owners and the Hirer shall not have any right or interest in the same other than that of Hirer under this Agreement. In particular, and without prejudice to the foregoing, the Hirer shall not represent or hold himself out as, or do or suffer anything whereby he may be reputed to be, the Owner of the said Vehicle ; and any implied consent of the Owners is also hereby expressly excluded.

6. THE Hirer agrees to indemnify the Owners against damage to loss or destruction of the Vehicle by any cause during the continuance of this Agreement or until such time as the option referred to in Clause 3 (A) hereof shall have been exercised or until the Vehicle has been returned to the Owners in terms of Clause 3 (B) hereof. Further and without in any way restricting the generality of the foregoing the Hirer shall insure the Vehicle under a full comprehensive policy of an "authorised insurer" as defined in Part 2 of the Road Traffic Act 1930. Any expense or monetary loss made or suffered by the Owners as a result of damage to loss or destruction of the Vehicle and/or the failure for any cause of the Hirer to insure the same shall be payable by the Hirer to the Owners upon demand and recoverable as a debt or liquidated demand.

7. IF the Hirer shall fail to insure or keep the said Vehicle insured as provided by Clause 6 hereof he shall be liable to the Owners for any damage to or loss of the said Vehicle. In the event of such failure to insure the Owners shall be entitled to insure on their own behalf against any loss to the Owners which may arise from the Hirer's neglect or failure to discharge his said liability. Such insurance as the Owners may effect under this clause shall not be for the benefit of the Hirer ; but the amount of any premium or premiums paid by the Owners in respect of such insurance shall be payable by the Hirer to the Owners on demand, and the Hirer shall not be entitled to exercise his option under this Agreement to purchase the said Vehicle while such amount remains unpaid.

8. IF the Owners think fit to grant time or other forbearance their rights or remedies under this Agreement shall be in no way affected or prejudiced thereby. In particular no extension shall be deemed thereby to have been made of the periods contemplated in Clause 3 (B).

9. THE Owners do not give any guarantee warranty or condition whatsoever as to the state or quality of the Vehicle or as to fitness for any purpose or as to road-worthiness and any implied guarantee warranty or condition is also hereby expressly excluded.

10. THIS Agreement is personal to the Hirer and the rights and/or obligations of the Hirer shall not be assignable or chargeable by him.

11. IT is expressly agreed and declared that any Motor Agent or Dealer by or through whom this transaction may have been introduced negotiated or conducted is not an authorised Agent of the Owners and that the Owners have no liability for any representations or statements not made directly by them to the Hirer and that should the word "Agent" have been or be used in connection with this transaction it shall be construed in a complimentary sense only.

AS WITNESS the hands of the parties the day and year aforesaid.

FOR UNITED MOTOR FINANCE CORPORATION LIMITED.

......................................_General Manager._

Signature of Hirer........_Herbert Black_...... over a 6d. adhesive stamp.

WITNESS to Signature of Hirer

Hugh Ash

Address..._975 Luton Road, Dalswinton_

THE SCHEDULE WITHIN REFERRED TO :

Vehicle ....

Type of Body...

Maker's No. ....

Registered No..

Accessories included..

Down Payment ... ... £ *55* : — : —
Balance payable (by *12* monthly payments of £ *15* : 3 : *2*
each) on the   day of each month commencing in the month
of   19 ... ... £*181* : *18* : —

Total amount payable if hiring continued for full period ... ... £*236* : *18* : —

(2)   No. 9.

A Specimen Hire Purchase Agreement (cont.).

in printed documents which set out a great many terms governing the contract, and every person should read these carefully and endeavour to appreciate what the terms under the contract are.

Third Parties.—Unless the agreement provides to the contrary, the hirer may always assign his rights under the agreement to some third party, but in practice this is almost invariably forbidden by the terms of the agreement. This does not mean that he can sell the goods, but merely that he may transfer such rights as he himself has under the agreement—i.e. a right to use the goods on paying the instalments. Where such an assignment is possible, however, the person to whom the rights are assigned must, of course, comply with the terms of the hire-purchase agreement. It happens much more frequently that persons who have goods on hire purchase attempt, not to assign the contract, but to sell or pledge the goods without informing the persons to whom they sell or pledge them that the goods are only on hire purchase. The rights of a person who buys or lends money on goods in this way in good faith will depend on the terms of the hire-purchase agreement.

If the agreement is in the form first referred to above, that is, a sale on deferred terms, the third person will get a good title to the goods and may refuse to hand them back to the owner, so long as the third person does not know that the goods are on hire purchase and acts in good faith. Thus, provided that the hire purchaser under the agreement has either "bought" the goods (when they become his property so soon as the contract is made), or has "agreed to buy" them (when he is *bound* to buy them although they do not become his property until the final instalment has been paid), a purchaser from him gets a good title.

The fact that the sale or pledge by the hire purchaser is a breach of the terms of the agreement does not matter to the third person in these cases, for a person who has "agreed to buy" goods and who is placed in possession of the goods by the seller before the goods have become his property is able to give a good title to the goods, even when he sells wrongfully. This is intended to protect persons who

assume when they see others in possession of goods that they have a right to sell them. (*See* SALE OF GOODS.)

If, however, under the hire-purchase agreement, the hire purchaser never "agrees to buy" the goods,—i.e. is not *bound* to buy them, but is merely given an *option* to buy them; then a purchaser from him is not protected by the above provisions and acquires no rights to the goods, but will have to give them up to the owner when called upon without receiving any compensation. He will, of course, be entitled to claim damages from the person who sold him the goods but in practice this right will be of little value to him, for that person will usually either have disappeared or will have no money to pay compensation. If the person who has purchased the goods from the hire purchaser himself sells the goods to another innocent third person, he is guilty of what is called a conversion, that is, wrongfully dealing with the goods; and if sued by the true owner, will be liable for damages, that is, the value of the goods, even though he no longer has them.

Every person, therefore, who purchases goods secondhand should satisfy himself that the person selling them to him has got a right to do so. It is in most cases very difficult to do this, and it should be particularly borne in mind in the case of second-hand cars that the fact that the registration book is in the name of the person selling the car does not mean that he is the owner, for where a car is obtained on hire purchase the registration book is always made out in the name of the hire purchaser.

An exception to this rule exists in all cases where sales take place in "market overt" (q.v.). A buyer, who buys in "market overt" in good faith and does not know that the seller has not got any right to sell, acquires a good title to the goods. "Market overt" means an open public and legally constituted market, and by a special rule every shop in the City of London is a market overt for things usually sold there.

Bill of Sale.—The hirer has got no right as against the owner to raise money on a Bill of Sale (q.v.) over the hired goods and the granting on a bill of sale is a breach of the agreement of hire. So far, however, as third parties are concerned, that is, the person who pays the money and takes the bill of sale over the goods, the bill of sale will be valid where the hire purchase agreement is in the form first set out above, namely, a sale on deferred payments. Where, however, the agreement gives merely an option to buy, then the bill of sale, if it is in security, will be no protection to the grantee, that is, the person lending the money; but it will be valid against the grantor. Where the bill of sale is absolute it will transfer no property to the grantee. (*See* BILL OF SALE.)

Execution.—When a judgment has been obtained in Court against the hire purchaser it may be enforced by the sheriff seizing his goods under a writ known as Fi. Fa. (*See* EXECUTION; FI. FA.) The sheriff is entitled to take goods held on hire purchase to the extent of the interest which the hire purchaser has in them, i.e. the right under the agreement to acquire the goods on paying the instalments, but not the whole property in the goods. Thus the owners of the goods will not lose them but can hold any person who bought them from the sheriff to the terms of the hire-purchase agreement. In practice, however, agreements almost invariably provide that the interest of the hirer ceases if the goods are taken on execution, and when this happens the sheriff has no interest which he can seize in the goods, and the owners can take them back.

Distress.—Goods held under a hire-purchase agreement can, as a rule, be taken by the landlord of the hire purchaser if he distrains for rent. (*See* DISTRESS FOR RENT.) In some cases where the owners have got power under the agreement to determine it, i.e. put an end to it—e.g. when instalments are in arrear—by serving a notice on the hire purchaser, the goods will not be liable to distress if the notice has been served and the agreement thereby terminated before the distress. Goods held under a hire-purchase agreement with the tenant's wife and not with himself are protected from distress.

The landlord may also take the goods if they are in the reputed ownership of the hire purchaser, that is, are in his possession with the consent and permission of the owner. Thus goods on hire purchase may be taken in distress unless the agreement has been brought to an end by some act of the owner of the goods before the distress.

Bankruptcy.—If the hirer becomes bankrupt, the rights of the hire purchase under the agreement will pass to his trustee. In most cases, however, the trustee will not wish to make the payments under the agreement and he may avoid doing so by disclaiming it. (*See* DISCLAIMER.) It may be that the goods themselves will pass as having been in the "possession, order, or disposition" of the bankrupt in his trade or business. (*See* REPUTED OWNERSHIP.)

Usual Clauses.—After reciting the names of the parties and referring to the goods covered by the agreement the document usually contains the following clauses:

1. The hirer undertakes to pay a deposit on signing the agreement and thereafter during the continuance of the hiring a rent payable monthly or at other periods.

2. The hirer undertakes to keep the goods in his own possession and in good repair and not to sell, pledge or otherwise deal with them, or to assign his rights under the agreement. He usually also undertakes responsibility for all damage to the goods, whether caused by accident or by his own lack of care.

3. The hirer shall pay all rent, rates and taxes punctually in respect of the premises where the goods are, and shall allow the owner to enter the premises to inspect the goods at any reasonable time.

4. The hirer shall insure the goods.

5. Occasionally the hirer undertakes to give bills of exchange as collateral security for the amount due under his agreement.

6. When the hirer has paid all the instalments of rent as they fall due and has observed all the other terms of the agreement, he is given a right to purchase the goods for some small additional payment. He may buy them sooner by making a larger payment.

7. The hirer may put an end to the hiring by giving the goods back to the owner, but if he does this before he has paid a certain number of instalments he must pay an additional amount by way of compensation.

8. If the hirer commits any breach of the agreement or any act of bankruptcy (q.v.) or, being a company, is wound up (*see* WINDING UP), or if a distress (q.v.) is levied or threatened, or if the goods are taken in execution (q.v.), or if a judgment against the hirer is obtained by any creditor and is not

paid, the owners may either without notice put an end to the agreement and take back the goods, or by notice to the hirer put an end to the agreement. In either case they may sue the hirer for instalments of hire in arrears, and if they adopt the first course they may sue the hirer for damages for breach of the agreement. The second course is usually adopted when a hirer fails to pay, as this, by putting an end to the agreement, prevents the goods being taken by the landlord as a distress or by the sheriff in execution. (*See above.*)

9. If the agreement is brought to an end by the owners under the first of these powers the hirer must return the goods, and if he does not, the owner is given power to enter on any premises of the hirer in order to take the goods.

Finance Companies.—The hire-purchase transaction is frequently complicated, particularly in the case of motor cars, by the fact that the hire purchaser does not obtain the car from the motor dealer nor pay the rents to him, but enters into the hire-purchase agreement with some finance company who put up the money to buy the car. In such cases the intending hire purchaser fills up a proposal form which he gives to a motor-car dealer. The dealer then sends the proposal form to some finance company. If they approve of the proposal, they buy the car from the manufacturers through the dealer and then let the car on hire purchase to the intending hire purchaser, and for that purpose enter into a hire-purchase agreement with him. When this procedure is followed the dealer drops out of the transaction, receiving his commission on his sale, and the hire purchaser deals in future entirely with the finance company who are the owners of the car.

HIRE PURCHASE (SCOTS LAW). —No hire-purchase contract for an article which does not exceed £20 in value is valid in Scotland—unless the contract is signed by the person hiring the article, and either a copy is sent to him at the time of his signature, and acknowledgment of the receipt of the copy is endorsed on the contract and signed by him, or a copy is sent to him by registered post within 14 days after he has signed the contract. The agreement in such cases must comply with these provisions.

The hirer must be entitled at any time before the final payment is due to put an end to the contract by returning the article hired in as good a state of repair as it was when he received it, due allowance being made for wear and tear. If he does this he must also pay any instalments due at that date and an additional sum, being the amount necessary to bring the total payments by him up to one third of the total amount due under the contract.

Any term in an agreement which gives the owner of the goods authority to enter any premises for the purpose of taking possession of any article hired is void. When the article is required to be delivered up, delivery may be made to any person (specified by the owner in a notice given to the hirer) residing or carrying on business within a radius of two miles from the place where any person who acted on behalf of the owner in connection with the contract resided or carried on business. Where the owner of an article has obtained an order on default being made in the contract for delivery to him of the article, the hirer, in spite of that order, is entitled to keep the article; or, in the case where he has already handed over possession to the owner, to recover the article from him, if, within fourteen days after the date of the order, he pays the owner the total amount of instalments due under the agreement together with any expenses to which the owner may have been put.

Any provision in a contract which infringes any of the rights set out above is void.

HOLDER IN DUE COURSE.— In practice nearly every holder of a bill is a holder in due course, and in law there is a presumption that this is so. A holder in due course is a person who holds what appears on its face to be a perfectly good bill which is not overdue and has not been dishonoured, and who does not know of any fraud, illegality, or similar vice affecting the title of the person from whom he gets the bill. Further, he must have taken the bill in good faith and have given value for it.

A holder in due course may sue all persons who are liable on the bill, that is, the acceptor, the drawer, and the indorsers. Neither a personal defence, for example, a set off which the acceptor has against the payee, nor any defect such as the theft or fraud occurring between the time when the bill was in the hands of the person sued and the time when it came into the hands of the holder in due course, will avail the person sued to defeat the claim. Any person who derives his title to a bill through a holder in due course has all the rights of that holder provided he is not a party to any fraud or illegality. (*See also* BILL OF EXCHANGE; CHEQUES; HOLDER FOR VALUE; INDORSEMENT.)

HOLDER FOR VALUE.—A

"holder" is the legal term for any person who has in his lawful possession a bill of exchange, including a cheque, or a promissory note, which is either expressed to be payable to him, or which has been indorsed over to him, or which is payable to bearer. When such a possessor has, in addition, given valuable consideration for the bill or note, or when value has at some time or other been given for it by a previous holder, then he is called a "holder for value." There is a presumption that every person whose name appears on a bill has given value for it. (*See* BILL OF EXCHANGE; CHEQUES; INDORSEMENT.)

HOLOGRAPH (SCOTS LAW).—

A holograph document is one which is written out wholly or in its main parts by the person who is making the document— i.e. the granter—in his own hand and signed by him. No witnesses are required. A document in this form is as effective for all purposes as a document made with witnesses. It may be used to create rights *inter vivos*, that is, between persons who are alive, or else to make a will.

A writing will also be considered holograph if it is typed or written by some person other than the granter, so long as the words "adopted as holograph" are written by the granter before his signature. The document, even when it is written throughout by the granter, should state in terms that it is so written. Holograph documents are not recognised in English Law as substitutes for deeds or other document with witnesses. (*See* ATTESTATION [SCOTS LAW]; DEED [SCOTS LAW]; WILL [SCOTS LAW].)

HOLT, Chief Justice (1642-1710).

—Known as the first of the modern Judges, Sir John Holt exercised his great skill and learning in applying the old principles of the law to the changing circumstances of his time. He incorporated the customs and habits of merchants in building up the Mercantile Law. He was the first Judge to adopt a strictly impartial judicial attitude in criminal trials; he would not allow the prisoner to be brought before him in irons, and disallowed evidence of previous convictions.

Among his many classic judgments are the cases of Price *v*. Torrington, and Coggs *v*. Bernard. The latter is still the leading authority on bailment.

HOME WORK.—Where the occupier

of a factory or workshop gives out work to be done at a place other than the factory or workshop, then that work is called "Home Work." Home work may be done in a building by a number of persons or it may be done in the dwelling-houses of the workers themselves. If the occupier of a factory or workshop, or any contractor employed by him, allows wearing apparel to be made, cleaned, or repaired in a dwelling-house or building whilst any inmate of that dwelling-house or building is suffering from small pox or scarlet fever, he is liable to a fine not exceeding £10.

He is excused if he proves that he was not aware of the existence of the illness and could not reasonably have been expected to have known about it. (*See* FACTORY; INFECTIOUS DISEASE.)

HOMICIDE.—The killing of a human

being. In law homicide may be felonious, justifiable, or excusable, according to the circumstances in which the death takes place. Homicide is only criminal when it is felonious. Felonious homicide may either be murder or manslaughter. Homicide is justifiable where, in law, the killing of another is permitted, as in the case of the execution of a criminal according to law. It is excusable where, though not permitted by law, there is present some reason which renders it not punishable. The most familiar example of this is accidental death caused in a collision where there is no criminal negligence on the part of anyone. (*See* MURDER AND MANSLAUGHTER.)

HORRIDGE, Mr. Justice. (1857-).

—One of the senior Judges of the King's Bench, he has presided at many famous trials. In January, 1911, the first mixed jury of men and women was sworn in before

Mr. Justice Horridge in a case in which Sir E. Marshall Hall was appearing.

HORSE DEALER.—When a horse-dealer, acting as agent for the owner, warrants that a horse is free from any particular vice or disease, the buyer may rely upon the warranty, and, if the horse turns out not to comply with the warranty, may sue the owner for damages for breach of warranty. Knackers may in no circumstances act as horse-dealers. (*See also* KNACKER'S YARD.)

HORSES. Damage caused by Horses.—If the owner of a horse knows that it is vicious and it causes damage as a result of its vice (e.g. by biting or kicking), the owner will be liable. But he will not be liable if he had no knowledge of the horse's vice. If a horse trespasses upon another person's land, the owner will be liable for all damage that could reasonably be expected to result from such trespass, e.g. the trampling down of crops. It has been decided that if a horse trespasses into a field in which is another horse and should kick that other horse, then the owner of the trespassing horse will be liable for such damage. Even kicking through a wire fence amounts to trespass.

Export.—Horses, asses or mules must, before exportation to ports outside the British Isles, be certified (the certificate to be delivered to the ship's master) by an inspector as being fit to be conveyed and disembarked without cruelty, and as being fit to work without suffering.

Glanders.—If a horse, ass or mule suffers from glanders, the Local Authority may slaughter it subject to payment of compensation to the owner. If, however, the value of a horse exceeds £80 (or of a mule or ass, £20), or if the owner objects, the local authority must obtain the authorization of the Ministry.

Hiring.—When a horse is hired out, the hirer impliedly warrants that it is suitable for the purpose for which it is required, provided he knew what it was required for. The person who hires it is obliged to provide it with proper fodder and drink, and may use it only for the purpose for which it was hired out; if, for example, it had been hired out for hacking and was used for hunting, whereby it was injured, the person who hired it would be liable for farrier's expenses

Mr. Justice Horridge.

and for the depreciation in the horse's value. He will be similarly liable if it falls ill and he negligently fails to call in veterinary assistance.

Sales and Warranties.—When a buyer buys a horse, he is entitled to assume that it belongs to the seller or that the seller has authority to sell it, and, if the seller turns out to have been unauthorized, he will have an action for damages against him. When, to the seller's knowledge, the horse is bought for a specific purpose, the seller is held to warrant that it is suitable for that purpose, e.g. if X says, "I want a horse suitable for a child," and the horse turns out not to be reasonably quiet or to be in any other way unsuitable, he will be entitled to damages for breach of warranty from the seller. But, beyond that, the buyer must take care of himself, and if the horse turns out to be unsound or vicious, he cannot complain. Every buyer should, therefore, insist upon obtaining a specific warranty (i.e. undertaking) that the horse possesses the virtues he desires. Such warranty need not be written, but must be made before the buyer agrees to buy the horse. It can refer to specific matters or may be quite general, e.g. "warranted sound and quiet in all respects."

Any defect or disease which has diminished

the ordinary usefulness of a horse constitutes unsoundness, even though only temporary; but the warranty will not cover defects which the buyer could see for himself, e.g. if a horse has only one eye and is warranted sound, the warranty will mean only that the horse is sound in all other respects. If the warranty is broken, the buyer cannot reject the horse or refuse to pay the price, but he may bring an action for damages or may even deduct an appropriate amount from the price. It is wise, therefore, to agree specifically that the horse shall be returnable if it does not comply with the warranty.

When a horse is sold by the seller's agent or servant, the buyer should always make certain that the agent or servant has authority to give a warranty, for, if he has no authority, the warranty will not bind the master. When, however, the horse is sold through a dealer, such dealer is always implied to have authority, even though in fact he has not such authority.

Shoeing.—There is no duty to shoe a horse, but, if it is not shod, there is a danger that its feet may become so injured that the owner would be guilty of cruelty in working it. When a smith shoes a horse, he impliedly warrants that he has sufficient skill to do so, and, if he causes injury through not having such skill or through negligence, he will be liable for the damage caused.

Slaughter.—Any person may slaughter his own horse provided he does not perform it in such a way as to render himself guilty of cruelty. Persons carrying on the trade or business of slaughtering cattle or horses are, however, subject to strict regulations (*see* KNACKERS). As to export of horses for slaughter, *see* EXPORT *above*.

Rule of the Road, etc.—Horses and horse vehicles must follow the ordinary rule of the road, except in the case of an unmounted horse which is being led, whether it is being led by a pedestrian or by a mounted person; such unmounted horses usually keep to the right-hand side of the road. In many cases it will amount to negligence to leave a horse unattended in a highway, and the owner will usually be liable for injuries resulting from such conduct. In one case, a horse left unattended by the owner's servant was struck by a stranger, and it was held that the owner was liable for damage resulting from its running away. As to various offences in relation to horse traffic, *see* CARRIAGES (CARTS).

HOSPITAL.—Every County Council is under a duty to provide for adequate accommodation within the county for persons suffering from an infectious disease. A hospital used for the treatment of infectious disease is called an Isolation Hospital, and is usually controlled by the local authority through a hospital committee. (*See* INFECTIOUS DISEASES; PUBLIC HEALTH.)

HOSTILE WITNESS.—In general a witness when examined by the counsel for the side calling him may not be asked leading questions. This is so because it is assumed that he is favourably inclined towards that side. If, however, it becomes clear from the demeanour of the witness that he is hostile to that side the Judge may give leave to the counsel examining him to treat him as a hostile witness. He may then be treated in the same way as he could had he been called by the opposing side, that is to say he may be cross-examined and questions in a leading form may be put to him. The counsel who called him, however, may not, as he can do with other witnesses, cross-examine him to shew that he is unworthy to be believed on oath, because it is assumed that counsel would not have called him unless he could be put forward as a witness of truth. (*See* EVIDENCE.)

HOTCHPOT.—The meaning of this is the putting together into a common fund of property to be divided equally among certain claimants. It is usual when a marriage settlement is made for the parents to be given a power of distributing the property contained in the settlement among their children, or giving it all to one or more to the exclusion of the others. It is also provided that in default of appointment the property is divided equally. In order to make sure that the persons to whom the appointments have been made do not receive more than their share, what is called a Hotchpot clause is generally introduced. This provides that any child who receives anything under the appointment cannot claim any share of the portion not appointed, unless he is willing to divide what he has received equally with the other children.

HOTELS.—Hotels are, in law, divided into two main classes, only the first of which is dealt with under this heading:—

(1) Those which are, in law, called "inns," the business of which is to provide board and lodging for anyone who is willing to pay a reasonable price and is in a fit condition to be received. Most hotels fall within this class, whether they are temperance hotels or not and whatever their size or style. One feature is, however, essential in every case: that there should be sleeping accommodation.

(2) Those which are, in law, regarded only as boarding-houses, the business of which is to let a room or suite of rooms to approved visitors, usually for a long period. In other words they are residential hotels as distinct from those which cater for travellers. The law applying to "inns" does not apply to this class of hotel. (*See* BOARDING-HOUSES.)

It is a question of fact in each case as to whether a hotel is an "inn" or a "boarding-house," and the mere use of the title "private hotel" is not conclusive evidence either way. The policy of the management, including the advertisements issued, is the main factor to be considered, e.g. an advertisement "bed and breakfast from 7/6" indicates that anyone willing to pay that price will be received and that the place is therefore an "inn."

The duties and liabilities of Hotel Proprietors are as follows:

1. **To receive Travellers.**—The first duty of a hotel proprietor is to receive all "travellers" who apply at his hotel at any time of the day or night (including Sunday), and to provide them at a reasonable price with such board and/or lodging as they require. For all practical purposes every person who arrives at an hotel asking for food or drink, or accommodation, is a "traveller" in law. This general rule is, however, subject to limitations as the proprietor need not receive visitors in the following circumstances:—

(*a*) If the bedrooms are all occupied—as the proprietor is only bound to offer such proper accommodation as he possesses, and he is not bound to allow visitors to sleep elsewhere in the hotel.

(*b*) If, on request, the visitor refuses to pay a reasonable sum in advance to cover his bill.

(*c*) If the visitor is not in a fit condition to be received, e.g. because he is drunk, or disorderly, or improperly clothed.

(*d*) If the visitor, by reason of his behaviour or reputation can reasonably be said to be objectionable or dangerous to other visitors, e.g. a notorious person with an enemy-alien name in time of war.

(*e*) If the visitor insists on bringing a dog or other animal into the hotel.

The mere fact that the visitor is ill is probably not a sufficient ground for refusing to receive him; but in the case of certain infectious diseases, the hotel proprietor must notify in writing the local medical officer of health, and the visitor can be removed to hospital at the expense of the local authorities. If a visitor suffering from an infectious disease occupies any room in an hotel, the proprietor must have that room and its contents disinfected to the satisfaction of a legally qualified medical practitioner, and must obtain a certificate from him to that effect before he allows that room to be occupied by anyone else. The maximum penalty for a breach of this regulation is a fine of £20.

The proprietor is only bound to provide reasonable accommodation, so that the visitor cannot insist on any particular room.

If a hotel proprietor refuses to receive a traveller without justification, the traveller has a right of action against him for any damage suffered and the proprietor is also guilty of a criminal offence. It is also a criminal offence to charge an excessive price.

The duty to receive any traveller extends to receiving his luggage, his horse and carriage (and therefore presumably his motor-car, although this has not yet been actually decided) if there is accommodation.

Not only must the proprietor receive any traveller, but he must continue to provide board and lodging as long as it is required until the latter ceases to be a traveller. It is a question of fact in each case when a visitor has ceased to be a traveller and has become a boarder, i.e. is using the hotel as a home instead of as a resting-place. The length of the stay, although an important factor is not conclusive, e.g. if caused by illness. When a visitor ceases to be a traveller, the proprietor can give him reasonable notice to leave, as he is in the position of a boarder. (*See* BOARDING-HOUSES.)

2. For Loss of Visitor's Property.—

An hotel proprietor is, subject to the Innkeepers' Liability Act (*see below*), in the position of being an insurer of his visitor's property against loss. He is therefore liable to pay the full value of any property lost in the hotel unless—

(*a*) The negligence of the visitor was the cause of the loss. (It is for the proprietor to show that the loss would not have occurred but for the visitor's own negligence, and the fact that the visitor failed to lock his door is not, by itself, sufficient evidence of negligence.)

(*b*) The visitor states that he will look after the property himself.

(*c*) The loss was caused by the act of enemy-aliens or by an Act of God, i.e. some natural cause without human intervention, which could not have been prevented by reasonable care on the part of anyone, e.g. an earthquake.

This stringent rule originated at the time when many hotel keepers were in league with highwaymen and it was modified by the Innkeepers' Liability Act of 1863. By this Act the proprietor is not liable for more than £30 in respect of any loss unless—

(*a*) The loss was due to the wilful act or negligence of the hotel proprietor or of one of his servants.

(*b*) The visitor had handed over the property to the proprietor, expressly stating that it was being entrusted to him for safe custody. The proprietor can, in such case, require the property to be placed in a box or some other receptacle fastened by the guest.

(*c*) He (the proprietor) refuses to receive the property into safe custody or, through his default, the visitor is unable so to deposit it.

The proprietor can only avail himself of the protection of this Act if a notice containing Section 1 of the Act printed in plain type is exhibited in a conspicuous place in the hall or entrance to the hotel.

3. For Damage to Visitor's Property.

—The proprietor is not the insurer of a visitor's property against mere damage; he is only liable if the damage is caused by the wilful act or negligence of himself or one of his servants. He and his servants must use due and reasonable care, and the property must be accommodated as well as can be done. It has been decided that a hotel proprietor is not liable for damage to a car left by the visitor in the hotel garage, when such damage was caused by the water in the radiator freezing, because the hotel garage was not heated; the reason for this decision being that an hotel proprietor is only bound to provide the best accommodation that he possesses.

4. For Injury to Visitors.—

It is the duty of an hotel proprietor to take reasonable care to ensure the safety of his visitors:—

He must keep the premises as safe as reasonable care and skill on the part of anyone can make them, but he is not liable for injury caused by defects which could not have been discovered by reasonable care or skill on the part of anyone responsible for the construction, alteration, repairs or maintenance of the premises. He must, moreover, warn visitors of dangers which are not easily seen.

He must provide visitors with food and drink that is harmless. He is deemed to warrant that all food and drink supplied is reasonably fit for human consumption and is liable if it is not and if a visitor is thereby harmed, e.g. if a harmful foreign substance is served up to a visitor in his food.

5. To Keep a Register.—

The proprietor must keep a register showing the name, address and nationality of every visitor.

He must also keep a register for alien visitors over the age of 16. This register must give the name of the visitor, the date on which, and the place from which, he arrived and must then be signed by him. On the visitor's departure, the date and his destination must be entered and he must then sign the register again.

This register must be kept for two years and produced to the police on request.

It is an offence for a hotel proprietor to fail to keep such a register and also for a visitor to refuse to give any of the above particulars. (*See* ALIENS.)

Remedies of Proprietor.—

An hotel proprietor has three remedies in respect of money due to him for unpaid hotel bills:—

(1) He can sue the visitor for the amount that is due to him, or again he can sue anyone who has promised to pay him the bill.

(2) He has a lien on all the property brought to the hotel by the visitor except the clothes which he is wearing, i.e. he can detain the property until the bill is paid. He has, however, no right to detain the visitor. This right of detention extends to all property brought to the hotel by the visitor whether it belongs to him or not, unless the proprietor knew it did not belong to him when he received it into the hotel. The right remains as long as the proprietor retains possession of the property, but is lost when possession is lost unless, of course, possession was obtained from him by fraud or violence.

The proprietor cannot charge for storing property thus detained, but if the property is an animal, he is bound to feed it and can charge the visitor with the cost of the food. He must take reasonable care to ensure the safety of the property and is liable for the loss of, or damage to it if caused by the negligence or wilful act of himself or one of his servants.

(3) He can sell any property brought to the hotel by a visitor after it has been in his (the proprietor's) possession for 6 weeks. The sale must be advertised in a London newspaper and in a local newspaper at least a month previously. The advertisement must describe the property to be sold and must give the name of the owner or visitor if known. The sale must be by public auction.

The proprietor must, on request, pay over to the visitor the balance (if any) of the proceeds of sale after deducting the amount of the bill and the expenses of the sale. (*See* ALIENS; BOARDING-HOUSES; INTOXICATING LIQUOR.)

HOUSE.—The law as it affects householders is of infinite variety; innumerable incidental questions arise as to insurance, rates, liability for the bursting of pipes or for the disrepair of fences, etc., as well as the more important matters with which this article will broadly deal.

Renting a House.—A house may be leased for any length of time, depending upon the terms agreed between the landlord and the tenant.

Buying a House.—Strictly speaking, a house can be purchased only by purchasing the freehold; but the term is sometimes applied to the purchase of a long lease at a low ground-rent. The existence of a lease of this kind means that the owner of the land originally leased the land on a long lease and that the house was subsequently erected by the tenant. The landlord will be entitled to the house as well as to the land when the lease falls in, but until that time he is entitled only to the ground-rent, which, in ordinary cases of moderate-sized residential houses, is usually between £4 and £20 a year. When a lease of this kind is sold, the owner assigns his lease to the new tenant.

When, however, the vendor disposes of a *freehold*, a wholly different procedure is adopted. It is not necessary that the transfer of the property should be effected by a formal document in writing, but that course is always adopted, since the purchaser would find it practically impossible to dispose of the property at a future date if he could not produce such a document (the "conveyance"). This formal "conveyance," then, marks the final completion of the transaction, and is therefore known to lawyers as the "completion."

The course of dealing is this: the parties negotiate until they have finally agreed terms; they then embody these terms in a written "contract"; when the contract has been signed and, almost invariably, when a deposit of 10% of the price has been paid, all that remains to be done is for the seller to shew that he has a good title to the property, and, when this has been done, for the purchaser to prepare, and the seller to sign and hand to the purchaser, the conveyance. The conveyance is usually handed over in exchange for the balance of the purchase-price, which is generally in the form of a banker's draft. A seller would be foolish to hand over the conveyance in exchange merely for a cheque, since the cheque might be dishonoured; while at the same time the seller would have lost his ownership of the land and would be in the position of an ordinary debtor whose only right would be to sue for the price. When the conveyance is handed over, the property becomes the buyer's. The golden rule during negotiations is never to commit yourself in writing until you are quite sure you are going to get exactly and precisely what you want. During negotiations it is useful to remember the words "subject to contract"; it is quite safe to write "I will buy your house subject to contract," for this simply means "I would like your house if we can agree on details." It is usual, and always advisable, before taking a house, to have it inspected by an architect or surveyor, who should be instructed to pay particular attention to the structure of the house and the drains: the fees are moderate, and expert advice of this kind may avoid very heavy financial loss.

An Open Contract.—If no conditions are arranged before the contract of purchase is made (e.g. if A writes to B, "I will sell you my house 'Mon Repos' for £1000, " and B replies "I will buy your house as offered") the parties are said to have made an "open contract." A contract of this kind must be in writing. When it is made, both parties will be bound by a large number of implied conditions, e.g. the contract must be completed within seven weeks, and, if it is not then completed, the purchaser is to pay 5 % on the unpaid purchase-money; the vendor must prove that he is the owner of the property by shewing that there are no flaws in his title for the past thirty years; the purchaser must prepare the conveyance, etc. If all these conditions are satisfactorily complied with, the vendor signs and seals the conveyance and hands it to the purchaser in exchange for the balance of the purchase-price. The purchaser then becomes the legal owner of the property.

There are numerous ways of purchasing a house without the purchaser having to pay the whole purchase-price out of his own pocket at once. For example, the purchaser may borrow the money from a third person in order to pay the vendor, on condition that the house shall be mortgaged to the lender as soon as the conveyance is signed. He may even grant a mortgage to the vendor himself, or, in other words, the vendor may be willing to accept payment by instalments on condition that he shall have the right to sell the house ("foreclose") if the purchaser falls into arrears with his payments. An intending purchaser may become a tenant in the house at a heavy rent on condition that, at the end of a number of years, the house shall become his.

He may become a member of a building society from whom he will be able to borrow the money for the purchase on giving a mortgage to the society as security for his repaying the sum borrowed (see BUILDING SOCIETIES). The vendor may even agree to take the purchase-price in instalments without any security.

Deposits.—When a contract for the sale of land is signed, the purchaser is usually required to pay part of the purchase-price as a deposit, the remainder of the purchase-price to be paid on completion, i.e. when the conveyance is executed by the vendor. A deposit is almost invariably 10 % of the full price. When a deposit has been paid, and the purchaser subsequently elects, as he is entitled to do, to rescind the contract on the grounds that the vendor has failed to prove his title to the property for the past thirty years (see above), the purchaser will be entitled to recover his deposit. When the contract, however, falls through by the fault of the purchaser who paid the deposit, he cannot recover it, but it is forfeited to the vendor, e.g. when a purchaser fails to pay the remainder of the purchase-price so that the whole contract falls through, he cannot then say that he wants his deposit back. A deposit is usually held by the estate agent or solicitor as a stake-holder.

Renting or Buying Building Plots. —The owner of vacant land may decide to lease the land out in plots in order that it may be built on. Leases of this kind are usually for 99 years or longer, and a small annual rental ("ground-rent") is payable by the tenant. The lease is usually granted on the terms that a house shall be built on the plot by the tenant within a specified time, and it is not uncommon for the landlord to stipulate as to the size, quality and character of the house. When a large area is being sold off in this way, the tenant of a plot can almost invariably be sure that after he has built his house he will not find that the adjoining land on the estate is to be utilized for factories, or gipsy encampments or other undesirable purposes. The landlord will draw his annual ground-rent until the end of the 99 years. As soon as the 99 years expire, the land and all that is on it, including the house, become the absolute property of the landlord; and it is therefore to the landlord's interest to see that every house built on the estate conforms with his conditions as to size and quality.

When an estate is developed in this way,

covenants as to the design of the buildings, the use to which they are to be put etc., are usually enforceable not only by the landlord but also by each tenant against the other, for the restrictions were imposed as much for the benefit of the tenants as for the ultimate benefit of the landlord. If, therefore, there is a covenant in each of the ground-leases that no house shall be converted into a factory, and one of the tenants does so convert his house, any of his neighbours may take action to prevent him from doing so, and for damages for any injury he may have caused by his breach of covenant. Exactly the same principles apply if the land is sold for building and not merely leased, except, of course, that no ground-rent is payable, and the property does not revert to a landlord at the end of the 99 years. As to the actual building of a house and the duties and rights of a builder, see BUILDING CONTRACTS.

Building Regulations.—Before any house is built, or before any additions are made to a house, or even before any serious alterations are made, careful enquiry should be made as to local building regulations.

Solicitors.—The above brief summary of the chief rules of law relating to houses will shew that an ordinary man cannot expect to understand the intricacies of the law and the pitfalls that are to be avoided. Any person who intends to do more than to take a weekly tenancy is strongly advised to consult a solicitor before he binds himself in any way in writing. The simplest words in a document may impose upon him onerous liabilities which he had never for a moment contemplated, and a slight mistake or oversight may render his property valueless for the purposes for which he wished to use it. In the case of tenancies for a period up to three years, a solicitor's services need not be engaged, provided a reputable estate agent is employed to assure the prospective tenant that he is not being imposed upon in any way.

Rates.—In cases of weekly tenancies and in the cases of maisonettes and flats, the landlord usually agrees to pay the rates, but in longer leases of houses it is usually the tenant who bears them. But even when a landlord has agreed to pay them, the tenant may find that he in fact must pay them, for, if the landlord fails to pay them the authorities

are entitled to compel the occupier to meet the deficiency. In fact it is the occupier who is primarily liable, and it is only for convenience that the authorities accept payments from the landlords. If a tenant is compelled to pay rates which his landlord should have paid, he may deduct the amount so paid from future rent to the landlord.

Miscellaneous.—The innumerable other matters which arise in connection with houses are dealt with under separate heads, e.g. as to the liability of an occupier for damage caused to his neighbours by the bursting of pipes, see PIPES; for the circumstances in which a house may be compulsorily closed or destroyed see DANGEROUS PREMISES. (See also BUILDING CONTRACTS; BUILDING SOCIETIES; LANDLORD AND TENANT; LEASE; MORTGAGES, etc.)

HOUSE AGENT.—A house agent is a person who carries on the business of negotiating sales and lettings of house property, acting as a go-between for buyer and seller, and for lessor and lessee. If a person advertises himself as carrying on the business of an agent for selling or letting furnished houses, he must take out a house-agent's licence each year. If he carries on such a business without a licence he is liable to a penalty of £20. If, however, his business is confined to the letting of furnished houses at an annual rent of less than £25, or if he is employed as an agent in the management of landed estates, he may act without a licence.

A house agent has very much the same authority as any other kind of agent, but several important cases have defined the limits of it. His general authority is only to get offers and communicate them to his principal, and he cannot without special authority enter into a contract. If he is given authority to find a purchaser and to sell at a definite price, that empowers him to make a binding agreement and sign a contract on behalf of the principal, but it does not authorise him to make conditions as to title, nor to receive the purchase-money.

If a house agent is instructed to find a tenant he must exercise reasonable care in ascertaining the fitness and suitability of a proposed tenant. (See HOUSE; LANDLORD AND TENANT; PRINCIPAL AND AGENT.)

HOUSE BREAKING. — House breaking is the felony of breaking and entering a dwelling-house in order to commit a felony. When this offence takes place at night it is called burglary. There need not of course be any breaking of anything. The turning of a key in order to gain admittance to a house constitutes a breaking in law just as much as would battering down a door. (*See* BURGLARY.) The essence of the crime is a felonious intention, and a person cannot be convicted of this offence unless he had an intention to commit a felony whilst in the house. The maximum punishment for house breaking is penal servitude for not more than 14 years.

HOUSING.—The law is concerned with housing from the point of view of building regulations to ensure the safety of the buildings which are in existence or are being built. But by far the greater number of the provisions of the law relating to housing are concerned with the promotion and safeguarding of the health of the inhabitants of houses. The body mainly responsible for enforcing these provisions is described in the legislation on the subject as "The Local Authority." This means for this purpose the County Council or County Borough Council.

The duty of keeping house property in a condition fit for human habitation rests, in the first place, upon the owner of the property, but if he fails to carry out this duty, then the local authority for the district may usurp his functions and take the necessary steps for safeguarding the health of the inhabitants. The local authorities are responsible to the Minister of Health for the general housing conditions in their districts and they have been given very wide powers by a series of Acts of Parliament to enable them to fulfil their responsibilities.

The Owner's Duty to Repair.— The owner of property is the person to whom the law looks to keep it in a habitable condition and in a proper state of repair, and if he fails to perform his legal obligations there are several means whereby the local authority can compel him to do so, or at least to pay for the expense of having them carried out.

The local authority in each district must arrange for a periodic inspection of all the dwelling-houses in their district which are used for, or are of a type suitable for occupation by, persons of the working classes with a view to ascertaining whether any of these houses is in such a condition as to be unfit for human habitation.

If, as the result of such inspection, the local authority is of opinion that any such dwelling-house in the district is unfit for human habitation, it may serve a notice upon the person who has control of the house, requiring him to execute works specified in the notice which are sufficient to render the house fit for human habitation. The person who is regarded for this purpose as having control of the house is the person who receives the "rack rent," either for himself or as agent for any other person; and the "rack rent" means a rent which is not less than two-thirds of the full net annual value of the house.

If any such notice is not complied with by the person having control of the house, then the local authority may enter upon the premises and do the work required to be done. The period for compliance with the notice may be fixed by the local authority, but it must not be less than twenty-one days.

When the local authority has done the work it may recover the expense of the work from the person having control of the house. If, however, such person proves that he was receiving the rent merely as agent or trustee for some other person, and has not since the date of the notice demanding payment received sufficient money to meet the requirements of the local authority's demand, then he is only held liable up to the amount which he has in fact received.

Repairs and Demolition Orders.— The local authority will only serve a notice requiring a house to be repaired if satisfied that it can be made in all respects fit for human habitation at a reasonable expense. If the authority decides that a house is unfit for human habitation, but the cost of putting it in habitable repair would be excessive or unreasonable, then it must serve a notice upon the person having control of the house, telling him where and when he may appear before them to make some offer about it, e.g. with regard to putting it in repair. The owner may then appear and make an offer to the local authority, and, if this offer is accepted, he is usually required to give an undertaking that the work necessary to render the house fit for human habitation will be carried out.

If the owner makes no offer, or gives no undertaking, or having given one fails to observe the terms of it, then the local authority must make a demolition order requiring that the house shall be vacated.

Who is an Owner?—It sometimes happens that there is more than one person who can be regarded as the owner of a dwelling-house for the purposes of the Housing Acts, because a person who is tenant of the house under a lease, which was originally granted to him for a longer period than twenty-one years, is held to be an owner for the purpose of serving notices with regard to repairs, and such other steps as the local authority may take against an owner of property. In such a case, the notice requiring repairs would probably be served upon the leaseholder, and if he did not comply with it the local authority could proceed as already outlined. Such a course might prejudice the freeholder, who might be quite willing to carry out the required repairs rather than have the house demolished or the work carried out by the local authority.

In order to safeguard all owners of property or persons having an interest in the property, such as a mortgagee, it is provided that any person who is an owner of a dwelling-house, but is not the person receiving the rents and profits, may give notice of his interest in the house to the local authority; and the local authority must send him notices relating to any proceedings which it proposes to take in the exercise of its powers under the Housing Acts.

When an owner of a dwelling-house has been prejudiced by a closing order made through the default in repairing the house by another owner, he may apply to the County Court for an order empowering him to enter the house and carry out the repairs required by the local authority. The closing order is then suspended and removed, if the works are carried out to the satisfaction of the local authority.

A similar remedy is available to a landlord whose tenant has covenanted by his lease to do the repairs and has failed to do so. The landlord may apply to the Court for an order allowing him to enter upon the premises and execute such works as are necessary to prevent them becoming in-

jurious to health or unfit for human habitation. If such an order is granted, then any lease held from the person applying in respect of the premises about which he seeks an order, comes to an end and the landlord must pay to the tenant compensation for the loss of the lease. The landlord may recover from the tenant the cost of doing the repairs.

The procedure of serving notices to repair upon landlords or owners of individual dwelling-houses, and the making of closing or demolition orders in respect of single dwelling-houses is usually only applied in cases where one house among a group or block is injurious to health or unfit for human habitation. It does not greatly avail when a whole area of houses is, either because of their overcrowding or the narrowness of the streets, injurious to the health of the inmates or unfit for human habitation.

The local authorities are entrusted with wide powers to enable them to make a clean sweep of such areas by resolving that they shall be made a clearance area or an improvement area.

What is a Clearance Area?—If a local authority is satisfied that the dwelling-houses comprised in an area in its district are dangerous to health because of disrepair, sanitary defects, bad arrangement, or narrowness of the streets, and that the most satisfactory method of dealing with them is to demolish all the buildings in the area, then it shall declare by a resolution that that area is to be a clearance area.

If no objections are lodged, the Minister may confirm the order made by the resolution, but if there are objections then he must hold a public local inquiry to consider such objections and modify the order if he thinks fit. The order when made and confirmed becomes a Clearance Order, and when it comes into effect the owner of any building to which it applies must demolish the building within six weeks from the date when it is vacated by the inmates in compliance with the clearance order. If any building is not demolished by the owner within that period, the local authority may enter and demolish the building and sell the materials. The expense of doing such demolition may be recovered by the local authority from the owner after giving him credit for any amount realized by the sale of the materials. If there is more than one owner they may recover the amount in such shares as seem fair to the County Court Judge.

When a clearance order has become operative, the land to which it applies must not be used for building purposes except subject to the conditions which a local authority may impose, and any person who starts any work in contravention of such conditions commits an offence and is liable to a penalty of 40/-.

There is an alternative method of dealing with a clearance area open to a local authority. Instead of making a clearance order imposing upon the owners of the buildings the duty of demolishing them, it may purchase the land comprised in the area and demolish the buildings.

If it is necessary for the securing of a clearance area of convenient shape and size, the local authority may also exercise its powers of purchase in respect of any land which is surrounded by the clearance area or which adjoins it.

What is an Improvement Area?— When the same conditions of disrepair, or overcrowding, are apparent, but the local authority is satisfied that the danger to health is remediable by repairing the houses, or by pulling some down to reduce the overcrowding, or by purchasing land to open out the area, then it may pass a resolution declaring that area to be an improvement area.

The Position of Controlled Tenants.— It is very important to note that in the case of a clearance order and a consequent order to vacate a dwelling-house, the protection against dispossession given by the Rent Restriction Acts to a controlled tenant no longer applies, and if the house is to be demolished he must vacate his premises. (*See* SPECIAL SUPPLEMENT ''RENT RESTRICTIONS.'')

If, however, his dwelling-house is comprised in an improvement area, and in order that the required repairs be carried out it is necessary for the tenant to leave the premises, they do not become decontrolled by reason of the landlord obtaining possession to carry out the repairs. If the tenant returns to the house when the repairs have been done, he resumes occupation as a controlled tenant.

Compulsory Purchase of Land.— If a local authority decides to purchase land for the purpose of furthering a clearance or improvement scheme, it may do so by agreement with the owner, or it may be authorized to purchase compulsorily by means of an order confirmed by the Minister of Health.

If the land is sought to be purchased for a clearance area, then the order must be submitted to the Minister of Health within six months, but if it is to be purchased for an improvement area, then the period is twelve months, each period commencing from the date of the passing of the respective resolutions.

What Compensation is Payable?— If the land which is compulsorily purchased is comprised in a clearance area, then the compensation is to be the value at the time the valuation is made of the land as a site cleared of buildings and available for development. If the land thus cleared is required for building houses for the occupation of the working classes, then the compensation is reduced by an amount which is calculated under the Housing Acts.

If land is acquired for any purpose other than that of a clearance area, then the compensation payable is determined by an arbitrator.

Compensation for Removal.— If any person is displaced from a dwelling-house or any other building to which a clearance, demolition or closing order applies, the local authority may make him a grant towards the expenses of his removal.

Using Condemned Premises.— Any person who, while aware that a clearance or demolition order applies to any building, himself enters into occupation of that building, or allows any other person to occupy it after the date fixed by the order when it must be vacated, commits an offence and is liable to a penalty of £20 and a further penalty of £5 for every day that the occupation continues after his conviction for the offence.

If any person remains in occupation of any dwelling-house or building after the date fixed by the order for its vacation, then the owner or the local authority may make a complaint to the local magistrates, and they must then make an order that possession is to be given up to the person complaining within four weeks from the date of their order.

Working-class Houses.—A local authority carrying out its duties with regard to the provision of suitable houses for persons of the working classes, may, in addition to such measures as declaring an area to be a clearance or improvement area, undertake the task of providing the necessary accommodation.

How the Owner may get a Loan.—If the owner of a dwelling house wishes to do repairs to it to make it habitable, or if he wishes to carry out structural alterations which will render the building or dwelling-house suitable for occupation by persons of the working classes, he may request a loan for these purposes from the local authority. The local authority may thereupon make the owner a loan to enable him to carry out the work, if it is satisfied that when it is completed the dwelling-house will be suitable for the purpose for which the loan is requested, and that in its adapted state it will not contravene the regulations of the Minister of Health.

The loan with the interest must be secured by mortgage, and the amount of the loan must not exceed 90 % of the value of the interest which the mortgagor has in the property. (*See* LOCAL GOVERNMENT; PUBLIC HEALTH; SLUM.)

HUMANE KILLER.—As from the beginning of 1934, animals, such as horses, cattle, sheep, pigs and goats must not be slaughtered in a slaughter house or knacker's yard unless they are instantaneously slaughtered or stunned before death by a mechanical humane killer. No person can act as a slaughterman unless he has obtained a licence from the local authority and is over 18 years of age. Any local authority may provide, in spite of the Act, that the provisions shall not apply to sheep or goats, and in any event it does not apply to animals which are killed in accordance with the methods required by the Jewish and Mohammedan religions. A person who has a humane killer for the slaughter of the animal does not require a firearms licence. Notice that none of the provisions applies where animals are killed elsewhere than in a slaughter house or knacker's yard. They would not therefore apply to animals destroyed on a farm. (*See also* CRUELTY TO ANIMALS.)

Mr. Justice Humphreys.

HUMPHREYS, Mr. Justice (1867–).—There was practically no criminal *cause célèbre* of the last thirty years in which Sir Travers Humphreys did not figure. He was senior Treasury Counsel before his appointment to the Bench, where he is regarded as one of the greatest Criminal Judges of the day. He presided at the trials of Mrs. Barney and the Hatry frauds.

HUSBAND.—The liabilities of a husband are many. He is, in the first place, required to provide reasonable maintenance for his wife. His means are not conclusive as to the standard of living which he should provide for his wife. Provided he does not place his wife in a worse position than his own, she cannot complain in law. In the event of a husband failing to provide reasonable maintenance for his wife, she may proceed against him in the Police Court for an order requiring him to do so. The Police Court order, however, can in no case exceed a weekly payment of £2 for the wife and smaller amounts for any children of the marriage. Should failure to provide maintenance amount to cruelty, a wife can commence proceedings in the High Court of Justice for a judicial separation. Should she succeed in such a suit, she may become entitled to an order for alimony if the circumstances justify it.

A husband cannot be forced to reside with his wife, but if, without due cause, he fails to do so, he may be guilty of desertion. A deserted wife may proceed in either the Police Court or the High Court of Justice, and may obtain orders for money payment on a similar basis to those previously mentioned.

Since 1882 the property of the wife has ceased to pass to her husband on her marriage. A wife is now entitled to her separate estate over which her husband has no claim. On the other hand, a husband, in certain circumstances, is liable for the debts of his wife. Where she has purchased things as his agent or where she has purchased articles which she found to be necessaries, the husband has to pay for them. In cases of civil wrongs not arising out of contracts (e.g. libel), a husband is still liable jointly with his wife for her acts. Thus, if a married woman, whilst driving a motor-car negligently, injures another person, her husband, even though he may not be present at the time of the accident or may have expressly forbidden his wife to drive, is responsible for the damage that she does. (See SPECIAL SUPPLEMENT "DIVORCE.")

HYPOTHEC (SCOTS LAW).—A hypothec is the name applied to a right in security for payment of a debt over property which is not in the possession of the creditor—but remains in the possession of the debtor.

Landlord's Hypothec, or his rights in premises within the Rent Act, is discussed in the SPECIAL SUPPLEMENT "RENT RESTRICTIONS."

Maritime Hypothec.—This is the name applied in Scots law to a Maritime lien. (See LIEN.)

Solicitor's Hypothec.—A solicitor may obtain payment of money due to him by his client out of money or property which the client has recovered in the action.

I.O.U.—An I.O.U. is an acknowledgment of debt, and means no more than that the person signing it admits that he owes the person named in the I.O.U. the sum set out upon it. This is a specimen I.O.U.:—

I.O.U.
£25 (Twenty-five pounds).
Sgd. HARRY SMEE.
1st April, 1934.
To JOHN BROWN, Esq.

An I.O.U., not being a receipt or a promissory note, does not require to be stamped, but if there is added to the above specimen the words "which I promise to pay in one month's time," then it becomes a promissory note and must be stamped. If the name of the creditor does not appear upon the I.O.U. then any holder of it can produce it as evidence of a debt owing to him. (See PROMISSORY NOTE.)

IDENTIFICATION PARADES.—When a person is suspected of having committed a crime the proof of his guilt or innocence frequently depends upon whether he is identified or not by the spectators of the crime. As mistakes as to identity are so easily made, one safeguard against error is to require the witnesses to identify the accused from amongst a number of other persons. The value of the identification so obtained is obviously far greater than that where the witness is merely shewn one man and asked whether that is the man whom he identifies.

The modern practice is for the suspected person to be placed with a number of other persons of similar age, height and appearance. He is permitted to select his own position amongst them and is usually asked whether he is satisfied with the arrangements made. When all is ready the witnesses are brought in, one by one, and are asked whether amongst the persons on the parade there is anybody they identify. If a witness identifies one of them he is required to go up and touch him. Care is taken to prevent any communication passing between the detective officers engaged in the case, and any of the witnesses after the parade has started.

IDIOT.—In law an idiot is not a lunatic (q.v.), but a mental defective (q.v.). He is defined as a person who from an early age has been unable to guard against common physical dangers—someone, that is, who needs constant care and supervision for his own safety. Special treatment is provided for such persons. (*See* LUNATICS; MENTAL DEFECTIVE.)

ILLEGAL CONTRACTS.—No person is allowed by law to contract to do something which is illegal or contrary to public policy, and this is so whether the actual thing which he promises to do under the contract is illegal or whether the consideration for the contract is illegal. An example may make this clearer. It is contrary to public policy that a man should have a mistress. Accordingly if A enters into an agreement to become B's mistress if B will give her £100, the contract is completely void and A cannot enforce the payment of £100; nor can B, even if he has paid the £100, force A to become his mistress. This is a case where the object of the contract is illegal.

Suppose, however, that A and B have entered into that contract and B gives A a cheque for £100, the cheque is a new contract in which B promises to pay A £100. Yet B can, if he wishes, stop the cheque at any time before it is paid, whether A has become his mistress or not, because the consideration for his new contract on the cheque was the illegal consideration that A should become his mistress.

The doctrine as to illegality goes even further than this. Any contract which has as its indirect object something illegal is void in this manner. Thus, if C lets a flat to B this is a perfectly legal contract, but if C lets a flat to B knowing that B is going to use the flat for an immoral purpose, the contract is illegal and void.

There are a number of different contracts which are, in the view of the law, illegal either on the ground that their object is a crime or on the ground that they are contrary to public policy. Of these the most important are the following:

(1) A contract to commit a crime. Such a contract is illegal however mild the crime may be. Thus a contract to publish a criminal libel or a seditious book is an illegal contract.

(2) Certain contracts are made illegal by statute. Examples of these are wagering contracts (*see* BETTING); contracts whereby tenants are deprived of their rights to kill ground game (*see* GAME); lotteries (q.v.).

(3) A contract to commit a tort (q.v.). Examples of this are contracts intended to defraud the public, such as a contract to buy shares with the intention merely of making the public believe that there is a market for the shares, or any other agreement involving the commission of a fraud.

(4) A contract with an alien enemy. If during a time of war a British subject enters into a contract with an alien enemy, the contract is illegal and void.

(5) A contract which tends to interfere with the performance of the duties of public servants. Examples of this are agreements with civil servants to induce them to use their influence to the advantage of the person making the contract, i.e. bribery, or an agreement by which a public servant assigns a portion of his salary to another person. (*See* ASSIGNMENT.)

(6) A contract tending to pervert the course of justice. This sort of contract arises where A agrees not to prosecute B on condition that B pays him a sum of money; or where B has stolen money from A and A agrees that, if B pays it back, he will not prosecute; or even where A having lost his watch advertises for its return and puts in his advertisement "No questions asked—" for such an advertisement is an encouragement to crime. A similar illegal agreement is where A promises to pay B the amount of his bail where B goes bail for A.

(7) A contract for maintenance or champerty (q.v.).

(8) An agreement tending to immorality. This applies not only to an agreement between A and B to commit immorality together, but also to any agreement between A and some other person C, which aids immorality between A and B, such as the letting of a flat, etc.

(9) A marriage broking contract is illegal and anyone who pays a fee to a marriage broker for an introduction to another person with a view to marriage can recover the fee by an action at law.

(10) An agreement providing for a future separation between husband and wife.

(11) An agreement in restraint of trade. (*See* RESTRAINT OF TRADE.)

Results of Illegality.—The results of a contract being illegal vary according to a number of different circumstances. In the first place, if a contract is wholly illegal it is void and neither party can enforce it against the other. But an illegal contract differs from a contract which is void for some reason other than illegality such as mistake. For a party to an illegal contract cannot recover any money that he has paid under it, because the law will not assist a wrong doer. Thus, if A agrees to become the mistress of B for the sum of £100 which B pays to her, B cannot in any circumstances recover the £100, because he is a wrongdoer and the law will not assist him. The only exception to this is where the parties to the contract are not equally to blame. If, for instance, A enters into an agreement with B to commit a crime, such as to publish a seditious libel, and B, not knowing that it is a seditious libel, pays him for it, B can recover his money because he is not equally guilty with A; but if both of them knew it was a seditious libel, B could not recover his money back, and A could rightly refuse to publish the libel on the grounds that the contract is illegal.

This is the rule when the contract is wholly illegal, but there are many cases where the contract is only partly illegal, as where A enters into a contract with B to become B's servant, and the contract contains a clause which is illegal because it is in restraint of trade. In such a case where the contract can be said to consist of two parts, the contract of service which is perfectly legal, and the agreement in restraint of trade which is illegal, then the contract is treated as if the illegal part of it were not present and the contract of service is enforceable, while the covenant in restraint of trade is ignored.

This sort of case where there is partial illegality must be distinguished from a contract which is made for an illegal consideration, as where C lets to B a flat which he knows B is intending to use for immoral purposes. Here the contract is wholly unenforceable. (*See* BETTING; CONTRACT; GAME; LOTTERIES; RESTRAINT OF TRADE; WAGERS.)

ILLEGITIMATE CHILDREN.—

An illegitimate child, or bastard, is a child not born in lawful wedlock, i.e. the child either of an unmarried woman or conceived by a married woman in adultery. It makes no difference that the mother has gone through the ceremony of marriage with the father before the birth of the child if it afterwards (perhaps many years later) turns out that the marriage was invalid. When a marriage is annulled, all the children are thereby declared illegitimate, but divorce does not have the same effect.

It is a principle of English law that a child born in wedlock is the legitimate child of its mother's husband, and for this purpose the date of conception is irrelevant; a child born the day after the marriage is presumed legitimate. Similarly a child born within about nine months after the death of the husband is presumed to have been his child. There are three ways in which this presumption can be rebutted and the child proved to be illegitimate: (i) the father must be proved to have had no access to the mother, e.g. if he was abroad during the time when the child must have been conceived, or (ii) he must be proved to have been incapable of begetting children, or (iii) it must be proved that husband and wife were living apart under a decree of judicial separation, or under the order of a Magistrate's Court, or under a deed of separation. In the latter cases, a child born more than nine months after the separation will be presumed illegitimate until the contrary be proved.

The husband and wife are barred from personally giving any evidence proving, or tending to disprove, that they had intercourse. Anybody else may be called as a witness for this purpose except the husband and wife. Suppose, for example, that a husband never visited his wife except in company with a friend, and then, about nine months after the visits, a child was born: the friend could be called as a witness to say that no intercourse took place between the husband and the wife, but neither the husband nor the wife would be allowed to give similar evidence. On all other points except this their evidence is admissible, e.g. to prove that the marriage itself was a nullity. Where, however, the child was conceived before the marriage, the husband is free to give evidence that he had no connection with his wife at the date of the conception.

It is clear from the above principles that the child of a marriage is always legitimate unless it be proved that it was quite impossible for the husband to have been its father.

A person desiring to test whether he is legitimate or not, may apply to the High Court for a declaration of legitimacy, but nobody can ask the Court to declare a person illegitimate. Such a declaration will be made only if some property is involved, the title to which depends upon the legitimacy of that person. Since 1925 a bastard may become legitimate by the subsequent marriage of his parents (*see* LEGITIMATION). As to the rights and duties of the parents of illegitimate children, *see* BASTARDY and AFFILIATION ORDERS.

IMPEACHMENT. — Impeachment is the prosecution of an individual for a crime before the House of Lords at the instance of the House of Commons. (*Compare* ATTAINDER.)

IMPEACHMENT OF WASTE.— In England Land Law Waste as applied to land had a very wide meaning, denoting not only acts which injured the premises but also those which altered it in any way, although they might in reality be for the benefit of the land. When a person was intended to hold land without being liable for waste his holding was said to be "without impeachment of waste." (*See* WASTE.)

IMPLIED CONTRACT.— When two persons make a contract it will usually happen that they do not state in words if the contract is verbal, or in writing if it is contained in a document, all the terms which they wish to include in it. It is in practice almost impossible for them to do so, for it is impossible to contemplate all the circumstances which may arise. The law, however, will always imply into a contract any provisions which it thinks the parties must both have intended as reasonable persons, and will enforce those terms just as if they had been expressly stated by the parties. Thus where goods are bought it is an implied term that they are of merchantable quality. (*See* SALE OF GOODS.)

In some cases the circumstances will be such that very few terms of the contract have been expressed and nearly all have been left by the parties to be implied. Thus, if A takes his shoes to a shoemaker to be soled there will probably be nothing in writing between them, and all that will be said is that A will ask the shoemaker "Will you sole these shoes?" and the shoemaker will reply "Yes." Into this contract to sole the shoes the law, however, will imply many terms. It will assume that A intended to pay a reasonable price for the work, and will compel him to do so. If, however, the price charged is excessive A will not be bound to pay it. The law will also imply terms that the shoemaker is a reasonably competent shoemaker and will use reasonable skill and good materials. Further, he must do the work within a reasonable time.

The contract may state that no terms are to be implied, and, if it does so, the law will keep the parties to the express terms which they have set out without implying any additional terms. A provision excluding all implied terms is frequently found in forms of contracts for sale of goods. This will exclude all implied warranties as to the quality of the goods and will seriously reduce the rights of the buyer against the seller. (*See* CONTRACT; SALE OF GOODS.)

IMPOSSIBILITY OF PERFORM-ANCE.— In certain cases when one party under a contract finds it impossible to do what he has agreed to do he is excused from performance of the contract and no action can be brought against him. This is not, however, a general rule, and it is only when the contract becomes impossible for certain specific reasons that the principle applies. If a man promised to make a suit of clothes in ten minutes he could not escape liability when he failed to do so by proving that such a feat was impossible. Still less can a contract be said to be impossible of performance merely because it cannot be performed so as to give one of the parties the profit he expected or any profit at all. Thus, if a man agrees to sell to another 1,000 tons of coal on a certain day at a certain price, and before the time for delivery a coal strike takes place so that coal costs three times as much as the price mentioned in the contract, he must fulfil his contract or pay damages.

When impossibility excuses performance.— When the parties have contemplated at the time of making the contract that a certain state of things would continue, and this state of things has ceased and has made the performance of the contract impossible, then performance is excused. Thus, the parties may have contemplated that it would continue to be legal to perform the contract, and if, owing to the passing of some **Act of** Parliament, it becomes illegal, the parties will not be bound. Thus, if A agrees to sell B some coal, but before the date for delivery all coal is taken over by the Government and private sales are made illegal, performance will be excused. (*See* CONTRACT.)

IMPRISONMENT.—A prisoner may be confined in a convict prison, a local prison, a preventive detention prison or a Borstal institution. Convict prisons are set apart for those sentenced to penal servitude, preventive detention prisons are for habitual

deal with all the matters affecting the admission, treatment and discharge of prisoners.

A term of imprisonment other than penal servitude may be served in one of these divisions. Offenders of the first division are kept separate from other prisoners and are allowed to provide their own clothing, food, furniture and literature if they wish. They may be visited and receive letters from not more than three friends at intervals of a fortnight. This is only ordered in exceptional

A Debtors' Prison of last century. The well-known illustration in "The Pickwick Papers" where Mr. Pickwick discovers Jingle in the Fleet Prison.

criminals, and Borstal institutions for juvenile offenders. Prisoners sentenced to death or to ordinary imprisonment, debtors, persons committed to prison under civil process and persons awaiting trial or sentence are confined in local prisons. All these are superintended by the Prison Commissioners and are under the control of the Home Secretary.

The details of prison discipline are laid down in a statutory code of rules. These

cases. Offenders of the second division are also kept apart from other prisoners, but they must eat the prison food and wear prison dress. They are employed at industrial work and may thus earn remission of sentence. They may receive a letter and a visit once a month. Offenders not sentenced to hard labour, nor ordered to the first or second division, are placed in the third. They are treated under the general prison rules. They may write and receive a letter and a visit after two months of their sentence and subsequently at monthly intervals.

A sentence of imprisonment with hard labour is served under conditions similar to those of the third division, except that for the first twenty-eight days offenders are employed for from six to ten hours a day on hard manual labour in strict separation. After this they are employed in association with other prisoners on industrial work.

Prisoners under sentence of death are confined in strict separation in the constant charge of an officer. Their food and exercise are prescribed by the governor.

Debtors and persons imprisoned for non-criminal offences, together with those awaiting trial or sentence in custody, may receive treatment and privileges similar to those of offenders of the first division. (*See* PENAL SERVITUDE.)

IMPRISONMENT FOR DEBT (SCOTS LAW).—(For English Law, *see* JUDGMENT SUMMONS.) Imprisonment for debt in Scotland is now only possible where the debt is in respect of taxes or fines due to the Crown or where it is for aliment, that is an obligation to pay money for the support of some person whom the debtor is bound to support, e.g. a wife. Imprisonment is still possible where the debtor disobeys an Order not to pay money but to do some act called an Order ad Factum Præstandum. In the case of aliment the debtor cannot be sent to prison for more than six weeks, and only then if it is proved that he wilfully refuses to pay the money. If he has in fact failed to pay, his refusal will be deemed to be wilful unless he himself proves that it was not, i.e. that he has not had any money. The serving of the sentence of imprisonment does not extinguish the debt.

Owing to the large number of debtors who were sent to prison because they had failed to deliver up some goods held by them under hire-purchase agreements (on the agreements being forfeited when default in payment was made), it was necessary in 1932 to provide that no person should be imprisoned for failure to hand over any goods, unless special application had been made to the Court after notice to him, and unless it could be shewn that he was wilfully refusing to comply with the Order. Even in that case the Court has power to order the debtor to pay a sum of money instead of handing over the goods. (*See* HIRE PURCHASE [SCOTS LAW].)

IMPROVEMENTS.—Where an agricultural tenant quits his holding at the termination of his tenancy, he will be entitled to compensation under the Agricultural Holdings Act for improvements. (*See* AGRICULTURAL HOLDINGS; FIXTURES.)

IN REM.—Rights in law are divided into rights "in rem" and rights "in personam." The first kind is one which is available against the whole world. The second kind is one which is available only against certain persons. Thus the owner of property is said to have a right in that property in rem. A person on the other hand who merely has a right against somebody else, by reason of an agreement between them, has a right in personam, that is to say he cannot enforce that right against everybody, but only against the person with whom he has the agreement.

INCEST.—The Punishment of Incest Act, 1908, rendered incest punishable by penal servitude for a period not exceeding seven years or by imprisonment with hard labour for not more than two years. Both males and females may be convicted of the crime. All trials for incest must be held in camera. Except where proceedings are instituted by the Director of Public Prosecutions no prosecution for incest may be commenced without the sanction of the Attorney General.

INCORRIGIBLE ROGUE. — The Vagrancy Act provides that persons convicted of certain types of offences may be punished as incorrigible rogues. The punishment is imprisonment up to one year. Amongst other offences resisting lawful arrest on a charge of being a rogue and a vagabond renders the person who so resists punishable as an incorrigible rogue.

INDECENT PUBLICATIONS.—It is an offence punishable with a fine of forty shillings or imprisonment for not exceeding one month for any person to exhibit or distribute in any public place any picture, printing or writing of an indecent or obscene nature. A police constable may arrest for this offence without warrant.

Where it is reasonably believed that any obscene books or papers are being kept on any premises for the purpose of sale, distribution or exhibition for gain, and that one of such articles has already been sold or published, a search warrant may be issued. This may be granted by any Metropolitan, or stipendiary magistrate or by two justices. It empowers the police to enter, if necessary by force, and seize any such articles. The magistrate or justices may, after hearing anyone claiming to own any such articles which are seized, order their destruction.

It is an offence to send through the post any indecent matter whether entirely wrapped up or not. It is a similar offence to send through the post any packet having on the cover any words or designs of an indecent, obscene, or grossly offensive character. Anyone who commits either of these offences may, on summary conviction, be fined £10, or, if convicted on indictment, be sentenced to imprisonment with or without hard labour for a period not exceeding 12 months.

INDEMNITY, CONTRACT OF.— A contract of indemnity arises when one person agrees with another that he will pay any loss which the other may suffer on a certain event happening. The best known example of a contract of indemnity is a contract of fire or accident insurance. There the insurance company undertakes to pay the person insured any money which he may lose as a result of the risk insured against e.g. fire or accident.

A contract of indemnity is frequently confused with a contract of guarantee (q.v.), and it is sometimes important to decide whether a contract is an indemnity or guarantee, for a guarantee requires to be "evidenced by writing," i.e. either made or at a later time set out in writing; and if the parties have made a verbal contract only, it will be invalid if it is a guarantee, but fully binding if it is a contract of indemnity. A contract of guarantee arises when a man promises another that, if some person does not fulfil some obligations towards the other, he, the first person, will do so.

Thus, if a bank lends money to A, and B promises the bank that if A does not pay it he will, here A is primarily liable to the bank and B is only liable in the event of A not paying. This is a contract of guarantee and not indemnity. There are two contracts in the transaction, one by A to pay the bank, and the other by B to pay in the event of A defaulting. B's contract is a guarantee.

Indemnity between wrongdoers.— When one person asks another to do an act for him which is a civil wrong or tort (q.v.), and therefore renders that other liable to an action for damages, the question may arise as to whether the person who is liable can claim to be indemnified by the person at whose request he has acted.

The general rule is that one wrongdoer is not entitled to claim from a fellow wrongdoer any part of the damages he has had to pay (as a contribution), or to expect the wrongdoer, under whose instructions he has acted, to bear the whole loss (indemnity).

Enforcement of Indemnity.— To avoid unnecessary litigation, procedure has been provided by which, if a man is sued in Court in respect of a claim in respect of which he alleges he is entitled to be indemnified by some third person, he may bring that third person into the proceedings and have the question of his rights to indemnity determined at the same time as the question of his liability.

Cases frequently arise when goods sold by a retailer are manufactured by a manufacturer, sold by him to a wholesaler, by the wholesaler to a retailer, and by a retailer to a customer. If the goods turn out to be defective the customer will sue the retailer, who will claim an indemnity from the wholesaler, who in his turn will claim an indemnity from the manufacturer.

In a recent case an action was brought by a customer who had suffered injury through wearing a fur which had been treated with some harmful dye. She sued the shop which sold the fur to her. They brought the wholesalers in as third parties, and the wholesaler brought in the manufacturer of the dye as a fourth party.

In another recent case a similar series of claims arose out of the eating of bad oysters in an hotel.

INDENTURE.— An indenture or deed of indenture is a deed executed by several different parties and binding upon each of them, as opposed to a deed poll. (*See* POLL, DEED OF.) It is so called because originally such deeds were copied out in duplicate or triplicate on the same parchment, and the different copies were then cut apart from each other, and each party was provided with one copy. The cutting was irregular, so that if any dispute arose as to the deed having been

14*

forged, the different parts could be assembled together, and, if the irregular edge of one fitted exactly into the others, there would be some evidence that it was not forged.

INDICTMENT.—When a person is to be tried before the jury, he is said to be presented for trial on an indictment. The indictment actually is a written or printed document setting out the offences with which he is charged. (*See* COUNT.)

INDORSEMENT.—This is the signing of his name by the payee on a bill of exchange, cheque or promissory note so that it may be negotiable, that is, so that it may be payable to the person to whom it is given. The signature is usually on the back of the bill, and it may be in pencil.

When Required.—Only instruments payable to particular persons or to order require indorsement, for others are already payable to bearer and are consequently negotiable by mere delivery.

Indorsement in Blank.—Where a bill or cheque is payable to John Smith and he indorses it, it then becomes payable to any person into whose hands it falls. Legally Smith could take the cheque to the bank and demand payment without indorsing it, but in practice, most banks require his indorsement by way of receipt. The reader will doubtless remember that he is generally required to indorse a cheque drawn payable to "self."

Special Indorsement.—A may sign his name on the back and say, in addition, "pay B." This is called a special indorsement and the bill or cheque is payable to B or his order. In effect A becomes a new drawer and B is a new payee. They are called the indorser and the indorsee. Now the cheque will be paid only to B, so if he (B) wants anyone else to get payment he must again indorse either specially or in blank, and so the process may go on. There is no limit to the number of indorsements. Any holder may convert a blank indorsement into a special indorsement by writing above the indorser's signature a direction to pay the bill or cheque to, or to the order of, some other person.

Indorsement must be of the whole bill; where there are several payees all must indorse.

Delivery to the indorsee is necessary to complete his title to the bill. Delivery without indorsement gives the transferee all the rights of the transferor and the right to have his indorsement.

Restrictions.—Conditions in an indorsement may be disregarded, but it may contain terms making it restrictive, as, e.g. a term restraining further negotiations.

Errors.—Where the payee or indorsee is wrongly designated or his name is misspelt, he may indorse the bill or cheque as therein described, adding, if he thinks fit, his proper signature.

Forgery.—Where a banker pays a cheque in good faith and in the ordinary course of business relying on a forged indorsement, he incurs no liability.

Liability of Indorser.—An indorser undertakes that the bill will be paid on due presentment, and that, if it is dishonoured, he will compensate the holder or any subsequent indorser who has to pay, provided all the necessary steps are taken on dishonour. He cannot deny to the holder that the signatures of the drawer and of the previous indorsers are regular and genuine. He is also precluded from denying to later indorsers that the bill was valid, and that he had a good title to it at the time of his indorsement. (*See* BILL OF EXCHANGE; CHEQUES.)

INDUSTRIAL DISEASES.— There are certain forms of employment in which persons working are susceptible to particular diseases by reason of the nature of their work or the manufacturing process carried on in that trade or business. Diseases of this kind are as much an incident of the workman's employment as injuries caused by accident, and for this reason the contracting of a disease is regarded as an accident arising out of, and in the course of, his employment, and compensation is payable under the same rules as for personal injury.

A workman is entitled to compensation

(1) If he is certified by a certifying surgeon to be suffering from one of the diseases set out in the list below and that he is thereby disabled from earning full wages.

(2) If under any rule or regulation made under the Factory and Workshops Act, 1901, he is suspended from his usual employment because he has contracted any such disease.

If the workman dies from any of these diseases then his dependants are entitled to compensation. The disease must be due to the nature of the employment in which the workman was employed during the twelve months previous to the date of his disablement or suspension. Compensation for an industrial disease is recoverable from the employer who last employed the workman during the twelve months in the employment to the nature of which the disease was due.

If, however, the last employer alleges that the disease was contracted while the workman was in the employment of some other employer and not whilst in his employment, he may add such other employer as a party when the question is decided by the arbitrator. If he proves this allegation, then the workman or his dependants may recover compensation from the earlier employer.

If the acquiring of the disease is a gradual process, then any other employers who may have employed the workman during the previous twelve months are liable to refund to the employer actually paying compensation such amounts as may be agreed as their rightful contributions, and if they cannot agree then the amounts are to be settled by arbitration.

A workman or his dependants must, if they are requested to do so, furnish the employer with the names and addresses of all the other employers who employed him in the same kind of employment during the preceding twelve months.

Compensation is calculated from the earnings of the workman under the employer who has to pay the compensation, and it is payable from the date of disablement. The date of disablement is the date which the certifying surgeon certifies as the date when disablement commenced, or, if he is unable to state such date, then the date upon which the certificate is given. If a workman dies of an industrial disease without having obtained a certificate of disablement, or if not at the time of his death receiving weekly payments by way of compensation, then the date of disablement is held to be the date of his death.

A workman forfeits his right to compensation if it is proved that at the time of entering the employment he wilfully and falsely stated in writing that he had not previously suffered from the disease.

There is a special provision in favour of a workman who is suffering from an industrial disease. If the workman before his disablement or suspension was employed in one of the processes mentioned below and the disease contracted by him is the corresponding disease to that process, then it is assumed in his favour that the disease was due to the nature of his employment and the burden of proving the contrary rests upon the employer.

If either the workman or the employer is dissatisfied by the refusal or the granting of a certificate by a certifying surgeon, he may apply to have the matter referred to a medical referee and the decision of the referee is final.

It is important to note that a workman can recover compensation if he is suffering from a disease which is not included in the list below, provided that he proves that he contracted the disease as the result of an accident which arose out of, and in the course of, his employment. (*See* FACTORY; WORKMEN'S COMPENSATION.)

TABLE OF INDUSTRIAL DISEASES

Nature of Process of Employment.	*Corresponding Disease.*
Handling of wool, hair, bristles, hides and skins.	Anthrax.
Any process involving the use of lead or its preparations or compounds.	Lead poisoning.
Any process involving the use of mercury or its preparations or compounds.	Mercury poisoning.
Any process involving the use of phosphorus or its preparations or compounds.	Phosphorus poisoning.
Any process involving the use of arsenic or its preparations or compounds.	Arsenic poisoning.

Mining.	Ankylostomiasis.
	Miners' nystagmus.
	Subcutaneous cellulitis of the hand (Beat Hand).
	Subcutaneous cellulitis or acute bursitis arising at or about the knee (Beat Knee).
	Subcutaneous cellulitis or acute bursitis over the elbow (Beat Elbow).
	Inflammation of the synovial lining of the wrist-joint and tendon sheaths.
Handling benzene or any of its homologues.	Poisoning by benzene and its homologues.
Handling any nitro- or amido-derivative of benzene or of any of its homologues or any process in the manufacture or involving the use thereof.	Poisoning by nitro- and amido-derivatives of benzene.
Handling dinitrophenol or any process in the manufacture or involving the use thereof.	Poisoning by dinitrophenol.
Any process in which nitrous fumes are involved.	Poisoning by nitrous fumes.
Any process in the manufacture of aircraft.	Dope poisoning.
Any process involving the use of carbon bisulphide or its compounds.	Carbon bisulphide poisoning.
Any process in the manufacture or involving the use of tetrachlorethane.	Poisoning by tetrachlorethane.
Any process in which nickel carbonyl gas is involved.	Poisoning by nickel carbonyl.
Any process in the manufacture of articles from African boxwood.	African boxwood poisoning.
Handling or use of tar, pitch, bitumen, mineral oil or paraffin or any compound or products of any of these.	(a) Epitheliomatous cancer or ulceration of the skin due to tar, bitumen, etc.
	(b) Ulceration of the corneal surface of the eye, due to tar, pitch, bitumen, or paraffin, etc.
Any process involving the use of chromic acid or bichromate of ammonium, potassium or sodium or their preparations.	Chrome ulceration.
Chimney-sweeping.	Scrotal epithelioma (chimney-sweeps' cancer).
Any process carried on in compressed air.	Compressed air illness.
Processes in the manufacture of glass involving exposure to the glare of molten glass.	Cataract in glassworkers.
Any process in the manufacture of iron or steel normally involving exposure to rays from molten or red-hot metal.	Cataract caused by exposure to rays.
Care of any equine animal suffering from glanders, handling the carcass of such animal.	Glanders.
Use of telegraphic instruments.	Telegraphists' cramp.
Twisting cotton or woollen yarns.	Twisters' cramp.

No particular process.	*Industrial Disease.*
	Dermatitis produced by dust or liquids. Ulceration of the skin produced by dust or liquids. Ulceration of the mucous membrane of the nose or mouth produced by dust. Writers' cramp. Inflammation, ulceration, or malignant disease of the skin and subcutaneous tissues due to exposure to X-rays or radio-active substances.

INDUSTRIAL INSURANCE.

What It Is.—Industrial Insurance is a particular class of insurance business governed by the Industrial Insurance Act of 1923. Generally, it consists of life insurances at small weekly premiums made to cover funeral expenses of a relative. It is defined by the Act as the business of effecting assurances upon human life, premiums in respect of which being received by means of collectors. Assurances, the premiums in respect of which are payable at intervals of two months or more, are not included.

The Policy must set out all the provisions of the Act relating to forfeiture, disputes, transfers, etc., but with the consent of the Commissioner or Chief Registrar of Friendly Societies, the policy may contain a statement in lieu of the actual provisions which in his opinion sufficiently sets forth their effect.

Every policy except (*a*) where it is taken out on the life and on behalf of a child under 16, or (*b*) one which assures a payment for funeral expenses of a near relative, or (*c*) where the person whose life is to be assured is a person in whom the proposer has an insurable interest (*see* INSURANCE), must contain a declaration by the person whose life is to be assured that the policy is to be taken out by him and the premiums are to be paid by him. And where the policy is of class (*c*) above, it must contain a statement of the nature of the interest.

Policies on Children's Lives.—The provisions of the Friendly Societies Act, 1896, extend to payments on the death of children made by industrial assurance companies (*see* FRIENDLY SOCIETIES), except that the rates of payment are altered to £6 for children under three, £10 for children up to six, and £15 for children up to ten years of age.

The payment must be made to the person who took out the policy or his legal representative, or failing him such next-of-kin as proves he has defrayed the funeral expenses of the child.

Illegal Policies.—Where a society or company has issued an illegal policy or one which is not within their legal powers, they are liable to pay the owner of the policy a sum equal to its surrender value where it was effected before the Act of 1923, and where issued after the Act, a sum equal to the amount of the premiums paid, unless it is proved that the society or company were deceived by some false representation by the proposer which caused them to be ignorant of its illegality.

Surrender Values of Policies.—Rules are laid down for the calculation of the value of a policy at any given time. The surrender value of a policy is an amount equal to 75% of the value of the policy as calculated by these rules.

Forfeiture Notice.—No forfeiture shall be incurred by a person assured if he fails to pay any premium until after (*a*) notice has been served on him, stating the amount due, and informing him that unless he pays that amount within 28 days his benefit will be forfeited, and (*b*) default has been made by him in complying with that notice.

Paid-up Policy.—Where notice of the forfeiture of a policy as above has been served on the owner, and has provided (a) that if the policy is for 50 years or upwards, the person whose life is assured is over 15, and not less than 5 years' premiums have been paid up on the policy; or (b) if the policy is for 25 years or upwards, not less than 5 years' premiums have been paid; or (c) the policy is one for a term less than 25 years and not less than 3 years' premiums have been paid— the owner, if he makes application within one year of the notice is entitled to a free paid-up policy calculated under certain rules. The amount must not exceed the difference between the amount of the forfeited policy and the amount which would be assured by a corresponding policy at the same premium, effected on the life of the same person according to his age at his next birthday following the date of the forfeiture.

Substitution.—Where the owner of a policy agrees to accept a new policy in place of his existing one, the assurance society must pay him the surrender value of the old policy, or issue to him a free paid-up policy of equivalent value; unless the value of the substituted policy, calculated according to certain rules, equals, or is greater than, the surrender value at the date of the substitution. In such a case, the society must furnish the owner with a statement containing a certified account of the respective values of the old and new policy.

Transfers.—Should a person wish to transfer his assurance from one society or company to another, he must give his written consent in a prescribed form—and no society can transfer his assurance without that consent. The society or company, to which the assured is to be transferred, must furnish the owner with a signed copy of the consent and of the document in prescribed form annexed thereto, and must give notice within seven days of the proposed transfer containing full particulars and the consent to the society or company from which the assured is seeking to be transferred. And from the date of that notice the society from which the person is being transferred ceases to be under any liability under the policy.

Societies and Companies, Deposit.—Industrial assurance counts as a separate class of assurance business for the purposes of the Assurance Companies Act 1909, and a separate deposit is required of £20,000 with the Supreme Court from societies and companies in respect of it.

Meetings.—At least one general meeting must be held every year, and except where the day, hour and place of the meeting is fixed by the rules—notice must be given to members by advertisement in the papers or served upon every member individually, at least a fortnight before the appointed meeting. A notice of the meeting, must be kept during that time, in or outside every office where business is carried on.

Disputes.—In all disputes with his society or company, a member or person assured may, notwithstanding any of the rules of the society or company to the contrary, apply to the County Court, or to a court of summary jurisdiction (if the amount of the claim does not exceed £25, and not less than 14 days' notice of the application is given to the society or company), who may settle that dispute according to the provisions of the Friendly Societies Act, 1896.

As an alternative, the dispute may be referred to the commissioner by the company, or society or the private member, if the amount of the claim does not exceed £50 and the legality of the policy is not questioned, nor fraud or misrepresentation alleged. By consent of both parties it may be referred to the commissioner without any of the restrictions above.

INDUSTRIAL SCHOOL.—An industrial school was a school to which children who had committed offences were sent for education and correction. The Children and Young Persons Act of 1933 abolished Industrial Schools and Reformatory Schools and replaced them with what are called Approved Schools. (*See* APPROVED SCHOOLS.)

INFANT.—In law any person under 21 years of age is an infant The law recognises that an infant is not fully capable of managing his own affairs or looking after his own interests, and for that reason has provided a very large measure of protection for him. This protection extends to limit his power to bind himself by contract and also to dispose of his property by will. He is also provided with guardians to look after his interests and himself personally and see to his upbringing, support and education.

Contracts.—The contracts of an infant may be either (a) binding on him; (b) binding unless he repudiates them within a reasonable time of his reaching 21; (c) void and of no effect; and (d) unenforceable against him.

Binding Contracts.—A large number of contracts are binding on any infant because they are for necessaries, that is, for things which are required by him.

Necessaries do not merely include sufficient food, drink and clothing to keep the infant alive, but will depend in the first place on the social position in life which the infant occupies. Thus the 20-year-old son of a millionaire who ordered a motor-car which was delivered to him, would be compelled to pay for it because it was reasonably necessary to his state of life; but the same motor-car sold and delivered to a person in a less wealthy position would not bind him to pay for it. Not only, however, must the article sold in itself be necessary with the above meaning but it must also be shewn that the infant was not already sufficiently provided with the article. Thus, if the infant already has three motor-cars a fourth one would clearly not be necessary for him.

Persons dealing with an infant do so, it will be seen, at some considerable risk to themselves, for even if the article is necessary to the infant so far as his social position is concerned, if it should turn out that the infant is already well supplied with the article in question, it would not be considered necessary to him and the price could not be recoverable. In one case a University undergraduate ordered eleven fancy waistcoats from a tailor. It was held that, although one or two waistcoats might be necessary to him, eleven could not be. The position would be the same if an infant who already had, say, eleven pull-overs ordered one more. That one by itself would no doubt have been necessary, but the fact that he had eleven already would prevent it being so, even though this fact was not known to the shopkeeper.

Contracts which an infant makes for his benefit are also binding on him. These are usually confined to contracts for his education and for apprenticeship or service. It is recognized that, even though the service contract or apprenticeship contract may contain clauses which are of themselves against his interests, e.g. which prevent him trading after he has left the employment in competition with his employer—yet if such clauses were not binding no one would be willing to take an infant into their employment at all, for they would not be able adequately to protect themselves, and therefore the contract as a whole is considered to be for the infant's benefit.

Contracts binding unless repudiated.—In some cases an infant may acquire some right of property which, although it is of value, yet imposes on him certain obligations. Thus he may become a tenant under a lease and will be bound to pay the rent and perform the other obligations of the lease, e.g. to keep the premises in repair. Again an infant may become a shareholder in a company and hold shares which are partly unpaid. In this case he will be called upon to pay the further amount due on the shares when calls are made by the company. In both these cases the infant has a choice when he becomes 21 as to whether he shall remain bound by the contract or not. If he does not wish to be bound he must repudiate the contract within a reasonable time of becoming 21 by giving notice to his landlord or to the company; and if he does this the contract will cease to be binding upon him so that he will not be liable for further rent in the case of the lease, nor for calls to be made in the case of the shares.

Void Contracts.—Certain contracts entered into by an infant are, for his protection declared by law to be absolutely void and of no effect. The most important of these is a contract for the repayment of money lent. No person who lends money to any infant can recover it from him. Even if the infant after he becomes 21 promises by what would otherwise be a binding contract to repay the money borrowed before he is 21, he will not be bound to do so. Contracts for goods supplied other than necessaries and all accounts stated by infants are also void. An account stated arises when two parties who have accounts between them agree that on balance a certain amount is due by the one to the other.

Even if the infant has induced the other party to the contract to lend him the money or supply the goods by deliberately stating that he is over 21, and if the other party has believed this statement and relied on it, the infant will not be liable. Where the infant has paid the money due under the contract he can always recover it back if he is prepared to give up what he received in exchange, but he cannot claim the money back and also retain the goods or whatever else it may be that he has obtained.

Where an infant has obtained goods without paying for them he may be ordered to return them if he has obtained them by fraud, e.g. by stating that he is over 21; but where he has obtained them without any fraud, he may refuse either to pay for the goods or to return them. It is obvious, therefore, that it is very risky for any person to trade with an infant and supply him with goods on credit, for the infant may refuse either to pay for the goods or to hand them back. When it is remembered that persons of 20 years of age are, for the purposes of the law, classed as infants, it will be seen the protection afforded to them is possibly more than circumstances require.

New Contract after Infancy.—Even though an infant when he becomes 21 makes a new contract for fresh consideration (q.v.) to do what he has contracted to do during infancy, this new promise by him will not be binding. Thus, if an infant trader has contracted a debt while an infant for goods supplied to him, and later after becoming 21 agrees with the person who has supplied the goods that, if he will supply more, the infant will pay for those and also for the goods which were supplied previously, the infant cannot be compelled to pay for the goods supplied before he was 21.

It should be especially noticed that a father is not liable to pay a debt incurred by his son, unless he has agreed with the person to whom the debt is owed that he will pay the money, or has authorised the son to incur the debt. This rule applies whether or not the debt is for necessaries, and the ordinary rules of principal and agent apply. (*See* Principal and Agent.)

Bankruptcy.—As an infant is not liable so he cannot be made bankrupt.

INFANT (PROPERTY).—An infant cannot own a legal estate in land but any land may be held in trust for him. An infant can own goods or shares in a company. He can become a shareholder by applying for shares when a company is formed and having shares allotted to him. He cannot transfer any of his property except possibly chattels, which he may dispose of by gift or otherwise, but the transaction is always liable to be set aside on the ground of undue influence (q.v.).

An infant cannot make a will but he can dispose of money belonging to him in the Post Office Savings Bank by a document equivalent to a will and in certain cases, when he marries before reaching 21, he may at the age of 20, if a male, and 17 if a female, make a binding marriage settlement with the permission of the Court.

INFANTICIDE.—Until 1922 whenever it was proved that a woman had murdered her child, whatever the circumstances of the crime, sentence of death had to be passed in the same way as in any other murder. The Infanticide Act 1922, however, provided, that whenever a woman is tried for the murder of her new-born child the jury may, if they think that by reason of her state of health following the birth of the child the balance of her mind was disturbed, return a verdict of infanticide and not of murder or manslaughter. It also provided that where the circumstances warrant it, a woman need not even be charged with murder, but merely for the lesser offence of Infanticide. It is a misdemeanour, punishable by a term of imprisonment not exceeding 2 years or by a fine.

INFECTIOUS DISEASE.—There are certain infectious complaints which are called notifiable diseases, because the local medical officer of health must be notified of any case of infection. The following diseases or complaints are notifiable:—Smallpox, diphtheria, cholera, scarlet-fever, membraneous croup, erysipelas, typhus, typhoid and enteric fever, malaria, dysentery, trench fever and acute primary pneumonia, cerebro-spinal fever, acute encephalitis lethargica and acute polio-encephalitis, tuberculosis, and puerperal fever. The term infectious diseases includes all the above complaints.

Notification and how it is done.—If an inmate of any house, ship, tent, shed, or van, or other human habitation is suffering from an infectious disease, the head of the family to which the sick person belongs must, whenever he becomes aware that the person is suffering from an infectious disease, send notice of the illness to the medical officer of health for the district.

If there is no relative of the patient residing in the house, then the notice must be given by someone in attendance upon the patient, or failing such person, the occupier of the building in which the patient lies. The occupier in the case of a lodging-house where all the rooms are let to lodgers is the person who receives the rent from the lodgers. When a doctor is called to the patient he must send a certificate to the medical officer of health stating the name of the patient, the address of the place where he is, and the disease from which he diagnoses him to be suffering. A person responsible for giving the notice who fails to do so is liable to a penalty of 40/-.

What is Exposure?—It is an offence for a person suffering from an infectious complaint to expose himself, without taking proper precautions to prevent the spread of infection, in a street, or shop, or in any public conveyance.

If a person in charge of a sufferer from an infectious complaint allows him so to expose himself he commits an offence. Similarly any person who gives away, or sells, or exposes without previously disinfecting them, any bedding, clothes, or other things which have been exposed to infection, commits an offence. The penalty in each case is a maximum fine of £5.

Clothes or bedding which have been exposed to infection must not be sent to a laundry or to any public wash-house, unless they have been disinfected to the satisfaction of the local authority, or unless they are sent with proper precautions for the purposes of disinfection and the laundry is informed that they have been exposed to infection.

A person suffering from an infectious complaint must not take away or use any book from a public or circulating library, nor must he return or cause to be returned any book which he knows to have been exposed to infection. He must give notice to the local authority that the book has been so exposed and the authority must then have it disinfected or destroyed. If the authority

orders the book to be destroyed it must pay the value of the book to the proprietor.

Exposure in Public Vehicles.—The owner or driver of a public vehicle may refuse to carry a person who is suffering from an infectious complaint, unless he has been paid sufficient to cover the costs of disinfecting the vehicle subsequently. If he has knowingly carried an infectious person in his vehicle he must immediately have it disinfected or be liable to a penalty of £5.

This provision applies more particularly to taxi-cabs and hackney carriages for, in the case of conveyances used by the public at different fares, e.g. an omnibus, the owner or driver in charge must not knowingly permit anyone suffering from an infectious complaint to use the vehicle, and a person who is so suffering must not enter such a vehicle.

School Attendance.—A child who has been exposed to infection or who is suffering from an infectious disease must not be sent to school after a notice has been received from the medical officer forbidding the child to be sent. The parent or person in charge of such child, who permits the child to attend school after receiving such a notice, is liable to a penalty of £2.

The local authority acting on the advice of the medical officer may require that a public elementary school shall be closed or that certain children shall be excluded from it from a certain time, with a view to checking the spread of an infectious disease.

Disinfection of Houses and Articles.—If the medical officer of health or any other legally qualified doctor certifies that the disinfection of a house or any of the articles in it would tend to prevent or check the spread of any infectious disease, the local authority must serve a notice on the occupier, or if the house is unoccupied, the owner, that the disinfection of the house and the articles will be carried out by the authority, unless the occupier or owner informs the authority that he will carry out the disinfecting to the satisfaction of the medical officer. If he does not undertake to do so then the local authority must carry out the disinfection and pay compensation for any unnecessary damage caused by their action.

If a person ceases to occupy any room or

house in which within six weeks previously there has been an infectious person, he must disinfect the room and all the articles in it to the satisfaction of a doctor, or else he must give notice of the previous existence of such infectious disease to the owner of the house or room. Failure to give such notice or carry out such disinfection renders him liable to a penalty of £10.

If, when he has ceased to occupy a house, he is questioned by the owner as to the existence of any infection during the previous six weeks and knowingly makes a false answer, he is liable to a penalty of £10. Similarly any person who lets a house without having it disinfected after an infectious person has resided in it, or makes any false answer to a question by an intending tenant about previous infection, is liable to a penalty not exceeding £20. (*See also* HOSPITAL; PUBLIC HEALTH; VACCINATION.)

INFORMATION.—In order to get anybody before a Police Court on a charge it is necessary to obtain from a Justice of the Peace either a summons directing him to attend, or else a warrant directing a police constable to arrest him and bring him to the Court. Summonses and warrants, however, are only issued after information has been made before the justice to whom the application has been made. The information may be verbal or it may be written. Where a warrant is applied for, it is customary to require it to be in writing, and for the person who is making it to swear on oath that it is true.

INHIBITION (SCOTS LAW).—Inhibition is an order of the Court directed against some particular person by a creditor, prohibiting him from contracting any debts or doing any act which may affect his lands contrary to the interests of some creditor.

INJUNCTION.—An injunction is very like specific performance (q.v.), except that it is an order of the Court forbidding the person against whom it is made from doing some act. It is not only restricted to preventing breaches of contract, but may deal also with nuisances (q.v.), breaches of copyright (q.v.), infringement of patents (q.v.), trespass, libel and a great many other matters.

INNER TEMPLE.—The largest of the four Inns of Court, situated south of Fleet Street with gardens running down to the Embankment. Founded by the Knights Templar who were suppressed in 1312, practically all its buildings were destroyed by the Great Fire, only the famous Temple Church and the Priests' Hall being saved. The Temple Church is round in shape as were all those built by the Templars and is shared by the Inner and Middle Temples—members of the latter sitting to the left of the aisle and those of the Inner sitting to the right. Among the many celebrated members of the Inner Temple were Coke, Selden and Littleton.

INNS.—*See* INTOXICATING LIQUOR AND PUBLIC HOUSES.

INNS OF COURT.—All barristers in England derive their rank as such from being members of one of the four Inns of Court. No one who is not a member can practice at the Bar. These Inns are situated in London (*see* GRAY'S INN; INNER TEMPLE; LINCOLN'S INN), and are voluntary, independent unincorporated societies. Membership is of three categories—students, barristers and benchers.

The Bench.—The governing body of each Inn are the benchers, who are drawn from barrister members of the Inn. All barristers in practice are subject to the supervision of the benchers of their Inn. They determine who shall be admitted as a student, who shall be called to the Bar, and the call of members of their Inn is made by them. They form a domestic tribunal to enquire into any alleged professional misconduct by a member and they have the power of disbarring or disbenching him, subject to an appeal to the Visitors, who are the Lord Chancellor and all the Judges of the High Court. No action by a member of an Inn which is brought against the benchers for anything done by them in their official capacity will be heard by the High Court.

INNUENDO.—A statement is often capable of more than one meaning. An innuendo is the term applied in law to that meaning of a defamatory statement which is not clear on the face of the statement, that is to say, the secondary meaning which the person complaining of an alleged libellous or slanderous statement himself puts upon the statement. Thus a statement which could not in its plain ordinary meaning be defamatory, may, in the circumstances in which it was made, be capable of bearing a

THE INNER TEMPLE

Above is the Great Hall and below, the interior of the Temple Church.

special meaning. Thus, to say that A is a bad swimmer would be a statement which could not in its ordinary meaning be said to be a defamatory statement, but if such a statement was made to persons who knew that A was a professional life-saver, then the statement would probably be defamatory of A. Under such circumstances the statement could be said to bear an innuendo.

In every action for libel or slander the person suing must be careful to specify the meaning in which he alleges the words have been understood, and it is for the plaintiff to prove that a reasonable person, in all the circumstances in which the statement was made, could understand the defamatory statement in the sense alleged in the innuendo. (*See* DEFAMATION.)

INQUEST.—An inquest is an enquiry carried out by a coroner. An inquest may be for several purposes. Usually, of course, it is to ascertain the cause of death of a person, but coroners hold inquests as to treasure trove, and the coroner of the City of London holds inquests as to the causes of fires in the City.

In certain cases coroners are required to have juries to arrive at verdicts. They have to do this in all cases where murder or manslaughter is suspected, or where death has resulted from an accident on the highway. Where there is a jury the coroner acts rather as a Judge does and sums up the evidence to the jury. The jury then give a verdict as to the cause of death, and they are usually allowed, if they wish, to add a rider blaming or exonerating individuals. Where there is no jury the coroner arrives at a verdict himself.

Inquests are, compared with ordinary Courts of law, rather informal in their procedure. Evidence is freely admitted which would contravene certain of the rules as to evidence in the ordinary Courts. Interested parties can be legally represented; but it is left to the discretion of the coroner as to whether he will allow legal representatives to take any part in the enquiry. The usual practice is to allow them to cross-examine witnesses but not to address the jury.

Witnesses are summoned by the coroner's officer, though other persons may tender themselves to give evidence if they so desire. Witnesses are entitled to receive proper travelling expenses and are usually

Sir Thomas Inskip.

paid on the spot by the coroner or his officer. A person cannot decline to give evidence at an inquest, but if there is any possibility that he may be charged with a criminal offence arising out of the inquest, he may be warned by the coroner that he need not give evidence if he does not wish to do so.

INQUISITION IN LUNACY.—A lunatic may be either of unsound mind "so found," or a lunatic not "so found." Before a person can be a lunatic "so found" there must be a trial in the High Court of Justice—usually before a jury—to determine the state of his mind. This procedure is rarely adopted now. (*See* LUNATIC.)

INSANITY.—Persons who are afflicted with mental disease may be either lunatics or mental-defectives. An insane person is not responsible for crimes committed by him. (*See* DETENTION OF LUNATICS; LUNATIC; MENTAL-DEFECTIVE.)

INSKIP, Sir Thomas (1876-).—The present Attorney-General has occupied that post once before and has twice been Solicitor-General to Conservative Governments. He is the Recorder of Kingston. He is a most respected and trusted member of the House of Commons.

INSOLVENCY.—The word insolvency

is used somewhat loosely in two senses. Firstly it may mean inability to pay one's debts as they arise, i.e. shortage of ready money. Secondly, it may mean that one's liabilities exceed one's assets. A person may be insolvent in the first of these senses without being insolvent in the second, and vice versa, for it is quite frequent for a man to be unable to meet his liabilities because his debtors are slow in paying him what they owe, and it is equally frequent for a man to be able to meet all his debtors who come to him for payment of their debts, although in fact his liabilities are far greater than his assets.

Insolvency of itself has no very great legal significance in either sense. Both in England and in Scotland it is not enough to make a man bankrupt merely to prove that he is insolvent, in the sense that his liabilities exceed his assets. Insolvency in the first sense will, however, in England enable a petition to be brought if it is made clear by the debtor's failure to comply with a bankruptcy notice calling on him to pay the debt, and in Scotland it has a similar effect. Insolvency in the second sense has considerable effect on a man's right to dispose of his property as he pleases. This, it must be admitted, is reasonable, for if his liabilities exceed his assets it will follow that all his property in fairness, although not in law, belongs to his creditors and should not be used or dealt with by him in any way which injures their interests. Thus any gifts made by a man of his property when he is insolvent may be set aside, or any acts by which he interferes with the legal order of distribution of his assets among his creditors by creating a fraudulent preference in favour of one of them, i.e. by paying him before the others. (*See* BANKRUPTCY.)

INSPECTION OF DOCUMENTS.
—When two parties are litigating they are each entitled to know the documents in the possession of the other on which that other is relying in the action. For this purpose each party is usually required to make an Affidavit stating the documents which he has in his possession or has had in his possession relating to the matters in the action.

INSTRUMENT.—Any formal document having a definite legal effect is called an Instrument. Thus a deed conveying property is frequently described in this way.

INSULTING LANGUAGE.—The use of insulting language may in some circumstances lead to an action for slander. (*See* SLANDER.) It is punishable criminally in many boroughs under local bye-laws, providing it occurs in some street or other public place.

INSURANCE.—Insurance has as its object the making of provision against death or injury, loss or damage to property or the incurring of pecuniary liabilities to third parties.

A person may, and generally does, take most risks upon his own shoulders, but it is becoming more and more common for persons to insure themselves against death, accident, damage or loss by fire or theft, liability to third persons, etc. In certain cases, such as National Health and Unemployment Insurance and insurance of motorists against Third Party Risks, insurance is madec ompulsory by law.

A policy of insurance is an ordinary contract by which, in return for paying a premium or series of premiums, the insurance company binds itself to indemnify the person insured for any loss or damage which he may suffer by reason of the risk which he insures against. It is thus subject to the ordinary law of contracts, with the addition of certain rules of law which apply to this particular form of contract.

Insurable Interest.—Before a person is entitled to take out an insurance policy against any risk, he must be in a position to shew that he will suffer an actual pecuniary loss if the risk that he insures against takes place. Thus a man may insure his own house against fire, since if it is burnt he will be a loser. But he cannot insure the house of a stranger, since if it is burnt down the loss will not fall upon him.

If he attempts to insure against some loss which will not fall upon himself, the policy will be illegal and he will not be able to recover the money provided for by the policy or even any premiums that he may have paid, for the law looks upon such contracts as mere bets, which is in actual fact exactly what they are.

An apparent exception to this occurs in the case of life and accident insurance (q.v.), but in these cases the law presumes that a man has an insurable interest without any limit in his own life or his own limbs or health.

Indemnity.—Just as a person must have an insurable interest before he can take out an insurance policy, so also, in the event of his recovering money under the policy, he is not permitted to make a profit out of his mishap. A contract of insurance, except in the case of life and accident insurance, is an agreement by the insurance company to put the person insured as far as possible in the same position as he would have been in, had the event against which he has insured not taken place. Thus, if damage be done by fire to the extent of £5, the insured person can recover £5 and no more from the insurance company, whatever the maximum amount payable under the policy may be. This is merely another application of the general law against wagering, for if a person were entitled to recover say £100 whatever damage were done by the fire, the policy would be a mere bet between himself and the insurance company upon the likelihood of the fire taking place and the damage that it would do.

But although a person may never recover under an insurance policy a sum greater than his actual pecuniary loss, it is often provided by the terms of the policy that the insurance company shall not be liable to pay more than a certain maximum sum, however great the loss may be. In such cases, if the loss is greater than the maximum amount for which the insurance company is liable, they will pay only the maximum; while if it is less they will pay only the actual amount of the damage. Certain policies of insurance contain a clause providing for "average." (*See* MARINE INSURANCE.)

Good Faith.—A contract of insurance also differs from many other forms of contract in that the utmost good faith must be observed between the parties. In an ordinary contract there is no obligation on either party to disclose to the other any facts which might influence him in entering into the contract. There is only an obligation not to make positive statements that are untrue. But when a person is negotiating for a policy of insurance it is his duty to make a full and frank disclosure of every fact which might influence the insurance company either to refuse the policy or to increase the premium, and this he must do whether he is asked specifically or not. Further, if he answers a

relevant question inaccurately, through innocent lack of knowledge of the fact enquired about, the insurance company is entitled to consider the policy void. In such a case the person insured is entitled to a return of his premiums, whereas, if any of his answers has been knowingly untruthful, or if he has deliberately refrained from disclosing to the company a material fact, he is not even entitled to a return of his premiums if the company choose to consider the policy as void.

For this reason it is vitally important that anyone taking out a policy of insurance should be meticulously careful in any answers that he makes to enquiries from the insurance company, and should endeavour to put before them every fact which he thinks might influence them in granting him the policy.

Conditions.—Policies of insurance are almost invariably made subject to conditions which are printed upon the back. These should be read with the greatest care, for in a contract of insurance, a failure to observe any of the conditions of the policy will make the whole of the policy void. The commonest conditions in the various kinds of insurance policies will be dealt with under their separate headings, but among those common to all insurance policies is a condition that the insured person shall give notice of any claim to the insurance company within a fixed period (often fourteen days): another that unless the premiums are paid upon the due date or within the "days of grace" immediately following the due date, the policy shall lapse: and another that if a claim is made fraudulently or if a claim is made for a sum much greater than the actual damage, the policy shall become void. If these conditions are not observed strictly, the insured person will be unable to recover on his policy, and it is therefore necessary for a policy holder to acquaint himself with and observe strictly the conditions printed upon his policy.

An insurance policy of any kind is part of the insured person's "estate" and accordingly upon his death his rights under it will pass to his executors or administrators with the rest of his property, and in the event of his bankruptcy it passes to his trustee in bankruptcy and is dealt with by him for the benefit of the creditors.

The most important kinds of insurance are

Fire and Burglary Insurance, Motor Vehicle Insurance, Marine Insurance, Life and Accident Insurance and National Health Insurance, each of which is dealt with in a special article herein, but in addition to these there is practically no risk against which an insurance policy cannot be taken out. Professional men usually insure against liability for negligence in their professional duties: one may insure against a wet holiday or a fall in foreign exchange, but to all these the principles outlined above and the principles dealt with under Fire and Burglary Insurance apply. (*See* ACCIDENT INSURANCE; BURGLARY INSURANCE; FIRE INSURANCE; NATIONAL HEALTH INSURANCE; LIFE INSURANCE; MARINE INSURANCE; *and also* SPECIAL SUPPLEMENT "ROAD TRAFFIC.")

INSURRECTION.— Any violent attempt to achieve a political end by violent means is an insurrection. If it amounts to "levying war against the King" it becomes High Treason. (*See* HIGH TREASON.)

INTER VIVOS.—This is the name applied to transactions taking place between two living persons as distinct from those which are only intended to be effected after the death of one of the parties to the transaction.

Thus a sale of shares or a gift of shares by a man in his lifetime is a transaction inter vivos; but if shares are left by will the transaction is only to have effect after the death of the person leaving the shares and is therefore not inter vivos.

INTEREST.—Interest is a word which, in law, has many significations. For example, persons acting in a judicial capacity should have no "interest" in the matter they are trying; in one case, a conviction for riding on a railway without a ticket was upset on the grounds that one of the magistrates who tried the case held shares in the prosecuting company. Similarly, no person may be elected as Municipal Councillor if he has an "interest" in any contract or employment with the Council.

INTERDICT (SCOTS LAW).—An interdict is an Order of the Court forbidding some person from doing some act which he is doing or threatening to do. It corresponds to an injunction in English law. (*See* INJUNCTION.)

INTERLOCUTORY PROCEEDINGS.—During the course of any litigation it is necessary and inevitable that many preliminary matters should be dealt with before the actual trial of the action. Thus one party may have in his possession certain documents which he claims should not be shewn to his opponent, and the opponent may make an application to the Court for an order that these documents should be shewn to him. Such an application is known as an interlocutory application.

INTERNATIONAL LAW. — International law has two main branches known as "public" and "private" international law. Public international law is the Law of Nations or legal relation of one state with another, and includes such matters as the interpretation and enforcement of treaties, definitions of boundaries, etc. (*See also* ADMIRALTY JURISDICTION.) The term is also often used to include the relationship of a state with foreign individuals, e.g. questions of nationality, extradition, patents and trademarks. Private international law, on the other hand, is the law applied to the relationships of an individual member of one state with an individual member of another state, e.g. when Smith and Schmidt make a contract together, it may be of great importance to decide whether that contract is to be governed by English or by German law; this question is determined by the rules of private international law, which is also, therefore, known as "Conflict of Laws."

INTERPLEADER.—When any person is the holder of goods or money etc., to which he makes no claim himself but to which two or more other persons are making rival claims, he is entitled to go to the Central Office of the Royal Courts of Justice, Strand, and take out an Interpleader Summons calling upon the rival claimants to appear before the Court and to state the nature of their claims. (*See* COUNTY COURT PROCEDURE; EXECUTION; HIGH COURT PROCEDURE.)

INTERPRETER.—Whenever any person is charged with any offence in any Court and is unable to understand English properly, an interpreter must be supplied by the Court.

The duty of an interpreter is to translate the evidence that is given. He must be careful to translate the exact words used, however foolish these words may be, and must avoid any tendency to attempt merely to reproduce the gist of the witnesses' statements. An interpreter must always be sworn faithfully to translate. The interpreter who wilfully misstates any evidence given is liable to be convicted of perjury, just as any witness who makes a false statement.

INTERROGATORIES.—In actions in the High Court and very occasionally in actions in the County Court, it is sometimes convenient for a party to obtain the written answers of his opponent on oath to various questions relevant to the matters in issue before the actual trial. In this way the party asking the questions may discover what is admitted and what is disputed in the action, and may save the costs of calling evidence upon points that are not in dispute.

Questions asked in this manner are known as Interrogatories. (*See* COUNTY COURT PROCEDURE; HIGH COURT PROCEDURE.)

INTERVENER.—An intervener is a person who, though not primarily a party to a suit, intervenes in it. In the Probate, Divorce, and Admiralty division of the High Court, the most common form of intervention is in divorce suits where a wife petitions for divorce on the grounds of her husband's adultery. She is required to name the woman in question. The woman so named is always permitted to intervene and become a party of the suit, if she so desires.

INTESTACY.—In the ordinary way every person should make a will before his death, and his property will then be left according to his desires. A person who dies without having made a will is called an intestate, and in such cases the law lays down a general rule as to who shall benefit from his property after his death.

Duties of Personal Representative. —Where a person dies having made no will or having made a will which for some reason is not valid, the duty of the personal representatives after they have paid all the funeral expenses and all the debts of the deceased is relatively simple. The right to take the property falls upon the following persons:

(1) If the deceased leaves a husband or wife, the husband or wife is entitled to all the personal chattels and to a sum of £1000 free of death duties together with interest at 5 % from the date of the death. The

surviving husband or wife is also entitled, if there is any balance of the estate, to a life interest in that balance if there are no children, and to a life interest in half the balance if there are surviving children—in which case the children are entitled to the other half of the balance absolutely subject to the trusts which are referred to below.

(2) Subject to the above rights of the surviving spouse the residue of the estate after the death of the surviving spouse, or, if there is no surviving spouse, immediately will pass:

(*a*) To the children of the deceased in equal shares, and if any of the children have predeceased the deceased themselves leaving children, such grandchildren take their parent's share equally among them; or failing any children or grandchildren

(*b*) to the parents of the deceased in equal shares or, if only one is alive, to the surviving parent; or failing any parents still living

(*c*) to the brothers and sisters of the deceased in equal shares; or failing them

(*d*) to the brothers and sisters of the half-blood of the deceased; or failing them

(*e*) to the uncles and aunts of the deceased in equal shares; or failing them

(*f*) to the uncles and aunts of the half-blood of the deceased in equal shares.

In each of these cases, if any of the persons entitled to succeed to the property has died before the intestate, leaving children, the latter are entitled to their parent's share divided equally among them.

(*g*) Failing any of these the property passes absolutely to the surviving spouse.

The Rights of the Crown.— Finally, if none of these persons is alive to receive the property, it will pass to the Crown, or if the deceased lived in the Duchy of Cornwall or Lancaster to those Duchies, though generally, if there is some person who has a moral claim to receive some of the property of the deceased, the Crown or the Duchies will make a compassionate allowance to such persons.

It is also important to remember that an adopted child who has been adopted with the usual formalities does not count as a child of its *adoptive* parents for the purpose of receiving property under an intestacy, but remains a child of its *natural* parents as far as receiving property under their intestacy is concerned; and this applies to the adopted children of the brothers and sisters and uncles and aunts of the deceased as fully as it applies to any adopted children of the deceased himself.

If any of the beneficiaries under these provisions are under 21 at the time of the death of the intestate, they cannot receive their share outright, but the personal representatives must hold it on trust for them, investing it in authorized trust securities, just as any other trustees, until the infant reaches the age of 21 when he or she will be entitled to it absolutely. In the meantime the personal representatives have the usual powers to pay out portions of the money for the maintenance of the infant for living expenses and education, and if the income from the property is greater than is needed for this purpose, to accumulate the income for the benefit of the child; but if the child marries while under 21 he is entitled to the income and to any accumulations, though he is not entitled to the property absolutely until he or she attains the age of 21.

If any child entitled to property in this manner dies before he or she reaches the age of 21, the property which would have passed to that child on attaining majority passes to the person or persons who would be next entitled under the rules set out above.

So far as the interest of the surviving spouse is concerned, their rights to the sum of £1,000 absolutely is a first charge on the property, and if the estate does not exceed this sum the whole of the estate will pass to the surviving spouse. But if the estate is larger than this sum, the personal representative is entitled to raise this sum on the security of the whole of the estate and further, with the consent of the surviving spouse, may raise from the estate a sufficient capital sum to purchase an annuity to pay off the life interest, so that the rest of the estate may pass to the other persons entitled free from the life interest. This is always the most advisable way to deal with such an interest.

Partial Intestacy.—These rules also apply to cases where the testator has made a will but has failed to dispose of the whole of his property, e.g. where he has bequeathed legacies and has failed to dispose of the residue, or where he has disposed of the residue to some person who predeceases him and the gift fails. In such cases the residue undisposed of by will must be

dealt with by the executor in exactly the same way as if there were a total intestacy, with the distinction that any children of the deceased who have received benefits under the will must count those benefits as part of their share in calculating the amount which they are entitled to receive out of the undisposed-of residue. (*See* EXECUTORS AND ADMINISTRATORS; LETTERS OF ADMINISTRATION.)

INTESTACY (SCOTS LAW).— When a man or woman dies without leaving a will, part of his or her property will be disposed of according to the law of intestate succession. In England in similar circumstances all of the property is disposed of in this way, but in Scotland certain legal rights, vested in the widow (or widower) and children have first to be satisfied, and it is only the balance left after these rights have been satisfied that is distributed according to the rules of intestacy. This balance is known as "Dead's Part." (*See* MARRIAGE [SCOTS LAW].)

Heritable Property. — Heritable property means strictly property which goes to the "heir" as distinct from movable property which goes not to the heir, but to the executors for the "next of kin." For purposes of succession, this distinction has now been abolished in England but it still exists in Scotland, and in Scotland it may happen on a man's death intestate that one person is entitled to his heritable property and another to his movable property. Heritable property consists of land.

The legal rights which have got to be satisfied in heritable property before the rules of intestate succession can be applied are terce, when a man dies leaving a widow, and curtesy, when a woman dies leaving a widower. These rights do not entitle the widow or widower to any part of the capital value of the heritable estate, but only to an interest for their life in one-third of the income in the case of a widow and in the whole of it in the case of a widower. Subject to these rights, the heritable property will pass to the heir of the deceased person.

The problem of ascertaining the heir is governed by extremely intricate and complicated rules. Males always take in preference to females of the same degree, i.e. equally closely related to the deceased, and the first persons entitled to succeed are lineal descendants of the deceased person, that is, sons and daughters, grandchildren, etc. Thus, if a man has two sons and a daughter, the eldest son will take the heritage to the exclusion of his younger brother and his sister. This is the case even though the sister be the eldest of the family. If this eldest son has died before his father, the heir will be found among any children of his. If he has a son or sons living, that son, or the eldest of them, will be the heir. If he has a daughter and no sons she will be the heir. If, however, the deceased has left no sons but one or more daughters it is not the eldest daughter who takes the property, but all take equally no division being made.

A Strange Rule.—If the deceased has left no children, his heir must be found in the first place among any brothers or sisters of his. There is here a somewhat surprising rule. If the deceased had two elder brothers and two younger brothers, it might be expected that it would be his eldest brother who would succeed him, but in fact the person entitled is the immediate younger brother, i.e. the eldest of the two younger brothers. If *he* is dead he will be succeeded by any children, but if he has no children alive his younger brother or *his* children will succeed in default. If the younger brother is dead without children the property then passes to the immediate elder brother of the deceased, and if he is dead to his eldest brother. These complicated rules may be illustrated as follows: A, B, C, D, and E, are five brothers in that order of age; C dies and it is necessary to find out his heir; he has no children; the first heir will be D. If he has died before C, E will be the heir; if he is also dead, B will be the heir; and if he is dead A will be the heir.

Where there are no brothers alive nor children of brothers, but there are sisters, these will take all equally and not according to their age.

If there are no brothers or sisters, or descendants of brothers or sisters, alive, the property will pass to the father of the deceased, if alive. If he is dead, an heir must be sought among any brothers or sisters of his, i.e. uncles or aunts of the deceased, or their children or other descendants, i.e. first cousins or first cousins removed of the deceased. If none of these is

available, the succession will go one stage further back to the grandfather of the deceased, and heirs will then be sought on exactly the same principles among *his* brothers or sisters or their descendants. The same process is repeated through great-grandfathers, etc., until a surviving relative is found. If no relative can be found on these principles the Crown takes the property as "ultimus haeres."

Relationships for all these purposes can only be traced through legitimate children. In the case of illegitimate children there is no right to succeed to the father, but they have the same right to succeed to the mother's property as they would have had if they had been legitimate.

Movable Property.—Movable property includes such things as furniture, goods, shares, etc., and also, for the purposes of intestate succession, what are called "heritable bonds," that is, money which has been lent by the deceased on the security of land, or, in English, money lent by him on mortgage. The legal rights which have to be satisfied before the property to be dealt with under the rules of intestacy can be determined are the jus relictae of the widow (or jus relicti of the widower as the case may be) (*see* MARRIAGE [SCOTS LAW]), and the legitim (q.v.) claims of any children. If there is a widow (or widower) and children, the widow (or widower) will be entitled to one third of the movable property (this is the right called jus relictae or jus relicti) and the children to another third, in respect of legitim, so that only the remaining third can descend according to the law of intestacy. If there is no widow (or widower) but children, or no children but a widow (or a widower), the children or the widow (or widower), as the case may be, may claim a half of the movable property and the remaining half will descend according to the rules of intestacy.

If the deceased has left neither widow (or widower), nor any children, the whole of the property will descend according to the rules of intestacy

What the Rules are.—The person or persons entitled to the movable property is known as the "next-of-kin," just as the person entitled to the heritable property is known as the "heir." The rules of succession to movable property differ very considerably from those relating to heritable property. In the first place there is no preference for males over females, nor is there any rule that the eldest child succeeds before his younger brothers or sisters. The first persons to succeed are any children of the deceased, whether sons or daughters, and they all take equally, dividing the property among them. If any of them is dead, leaving children, these children take the share which their deceased parent would have taken had he or she been alive. If the person whose property is being disposed of had no children, or descendants of children, alive at his death, his widow is entitled to £500 in addition to her legal rights mentioned above, but will not take any other part of the estate. In such a case the property will be divided equally among all the brothers and sisters of the deceased. If any of these brothers or sisters has died, their children take the share among them which their parent would have had. If the father of the deceased or his mother is alive, he or she takes one-half of the deceased's property in preference to his brothers or sisters or other next of kin, who only take the remaining half of the property. If there are no brothers or sisters the father takes all the property if he is alive, or if he is dead the mother takes all. If all these persons are dead the property will pass to brothers and sisters of the father equally among them, then, if none of them is alive, to their children, then to the grandfather, then to his brothers and sisters and then to their children and descendants. It will be noticed that the mother may take a larger share of the property in movable succession than in heritable succession. (*See* MARRIAGE [SCOTS LAW]; LEGITIM.)

INTOXICATING LIQUOR.—Intoxicating liquor is defined by the Licensing Act, 1910, as meaning "spirits, wine, beer, porter, cider, perry, and sweets (or British wines), and any fermented, distilled, or spirituous liquor, which cannot, according to the law for the time being in force, be legally sold without an excise licence." In other words, for the sale of any intoxicating liquor an excise licence is required. These can be obtained upon payment of the appropriate duty to the excise authorities and are usually annual licences. .

Justices' Licences—When they are Required and how they are Applied

For.—In certain cases, however, in addition to an excise licence a justices' licence is required. When such licences are required they must be applied for and obtained before the excise licence will be granted.

When they are Required.—These are required in all cases where it is desired to retail intoxicating liquor for consumption on the premises, and in certain cases when it is required to retail intoxicating liquor for consumption off the premises.

The first of these two groups is known as "on-licences," and it is composed of four different kinds of licences.

Firstly, the Spirits or Publican's Licence which is the licence held in respect of "fully licensed premises." The holder of such a licence is authorized to sell by retail, spirits, wines, sweets (or British wines), beer or cider, in any quantity up to four and a half gallons or two dozen reputed quart bottles in the case of beer and cider, or two gallons or one dozen reputed quart bottles in the case of the other liquors, for consumption on or off the premises.

Secondly, there is the beer on-licence or the "beerhouse licence" which, as its name implies, is held by the licensees of beerhouses. It authorises its holder to sell by retail beer and cider only, up to four and a half gallons or two dozen reputed quart bottles for consumption on or off the premises. Then there is the retailer's wine on-licence, which authorises the sale of wine or sweets up to two gallons or one dozen reputed quart bottles for consumption on or off the premises. Lastly, there is the sweets on-licence authorising the sale by retail of sweets only up to two gallons or one dozen reputed quart bottles for consumption on or off the premises, and the cider on-licence authorising the sale by retail of cider only for consumption on or off the premises, but in quantities up to four and a half gallons or two dozen reputed quart bottles.

Off-Licences.—It will be seen, then, that the publican's licence contains, as it were, all the other licences in this group: while the beerhouse licence contains the cider on-licence, the wine on-licence and the sweets on-licence.

The second group contains all the "off-licences," which are retail licences to sell intoxicating liquor for consumption off the premises only. There are five such licences.

Firstly, the retailer's spirits off-licence authorizing the holder to sell by retail spirits in shut vessels of not less than one pint pot in capacity, for consumption off the premises. In other words off-licences can sell spirits by the half-bottle.

Secondly, the retailer's wine off-licence allowing sale by retail of wine or sweets for consumption off the premises only in shut vessels of not less than one pint capacity.

Thirdly, the retailer's beer off-licence authorising the sale by retail of beer or cider for consumption off the premises.

Fourthly, the retailer's cider off-licence which is similar to the previous licence but authorises the sale of cider only.

Fifthly, the retailer's sweets off-licence authorising the sale by retail of sweets for consumption off the premises only.

This last group being, like the first group, composed of retail licences the holders, as in the case of the "on-licences" mentioned above, cannot sell at any one time to one person more than two gallons or one dozen reputed quart bottles in the case of spirits, wine or sweets, or four and a half gallons or two dozen reputed quart bottles in the case of beer or cider.

All the licences enumerated above require a justices' licence before an excise licence will be granted. But a justices' licence is not required for a retailer's spirit off-licence or a retailer's wine off-licence taken out by a spirit dealer or wine dealer, whose premises are exclusively used for the sale of intoxicating liquors, or of intoxicating liquors and mineral waters or other non-intoxicating drinks, and have no internal communication with the premises of any person who is carrying on any other trade or business, unless it is desired to sell spirits by the half-bottle.

For such a sale a justices' licence is essential. Justices' licences are applied for at the Brewster Sessions which are usually held about February of each year, though no special time for holding them is laid down.

The licensing justices then sit to hear applications, and, if all the business is not finished at the first meeting, the justices have power to adjourn the meeting from time to time.

How to renew a Justices' Licence.— No formal notice is required to be given by a person for the renewal of his licence.

How and when a Licence should be transferred.—It very often happens that a licence holder dies, becomes bankrupt, leaves the premises, becomes infirm, forfeits his licence, or fails to renew it. Should any of these events happen it becomes permissible to transfer the licence to another person, usually the new tenant or occupier. Application for permission to do this must be made at the Transfer Sessions.

How and when a Licence can be removed.—Whereas the transfer of a licence means the transfer of a licence from holder to holder, removal means the removal of a licence from house to house. Thus, where a public house becomes unsuitable, either because it is structurally bad or for any other reason, and it is desired to abandon it and take over a new house, the licence can be removed from the old house to the new. There are two types of removal: ordinary and special. A special removal is where the old premises are to be pulled down for public purposes or where they have been rendered unfit for use because of fire, tempest, or some unavoidable calamity.

An ordinary removal is where the licence is to be removed for some other reason. (*See also* BREWSTER SESSION; CANTEENS; COMPENSATION OF JUSTICES' LICENCES; CONFIRMATION OF JUSTICES' LICENCES; DRUNKENNESS; HOTELS; LONG PULL; MONOPOLY VALUE; OCCASIONAL LICENCES; OFF - LICENCE; ON - LICENCE; PERMITTED HOURS; PROTECTION ORDER; PUBLICAN; PUBLIC HOUSES; REDUNDANCY LIST; RENEWAL; RESTAURANT; SHIPS; SPECIAL AND GENERAL EXEMPTION ORDER; SWEETS; THEATRES; TRANSFER.)

INVENTION.—*See* PATENT.

INVOICE.—This is a written document sent with goods on their delivery and states particulars of the quantity, weight, and price of the goods. If the person receiving the invoice does not find that the goods are as there described, or does not agree that the price set out in the invoice is the proper contract price, he should make his objection at once.

IRREDEEMABLE DEBENTURE. When a company borrows money on the terms that the company is never entitled to repay the money, but must continue merely to pay the interest, the document stating this transaction is known as an irredeemable debenture. The advantage of this form of loan is that, if the lender lends money at a time when the rate of interest payable is high, he is not in any danger of the company repaying him the money at a later time when the rate of interest is low, and thereupon borrowing more money elsewhere at the lower rate. Companies have recently been able totally to destroy the effect of an irredeemable debenture by having themselves "wound up." When this happens all the debts of the company are paid including, of course, the debentures, and the company, or those interested in it, may form a new company to take over the assets of the old and avail themselves of the lower rate of interest at which money may be borrowed. (*See* DEBENTURE.)

ISSUE.—When any action is brought into Court the object of all the preliminary proceedings, such as the pleadings, is to discover on what points the parties are agreed and what points are in dispute between them. The points in dispute between them are known as the issue in the case, and it is these which the Judge or jury have to decide. The word issue is used in another sense in law. It may either mean a man's children or his descendants generally, i.e. including grandchildren, etc. The exact meaning to be given to it, e.g. in a will, will depend on the surrounding circumstances and the terms of the will.

JACTITATION OF MARRIAGE.— This is an old form of petition previously in use in the Ecclesiastical Courts, but it can still be brought in the Divorce Court. If anyone falsely boasts persistently that he or she is married to another person, the latter may petition the Court to order that the individual against whom the petition is directed shall be perpetually silent.

JEFFREYS, Judge (1648-1689).— Though he has become almost a legendary figure of the brutal, unjust Judge, the case against Jeffreys has been overstated. In his time judges did not adopt a strictly impartial attitude in criminal cases. Many of them acted as prosecutors from the Bench and Jeffreys was among that number. It is his conduct on the Western Circuit of 1685 which has become known as the "Bloody Assize" which aroused the great hostility. Shortly after the Duke of Monmouth's rebellion Jeffreys dealt with the utmost severity with the rebels, sentencing over 300 to be executed and many hundreds to transportation to the Indies. His bullying, furious manner on the Bench was seen at its worst, but it must not be forgotten that he was acting as the servant and under the will of James II, who approved so highly of his conduct as to make him Lord Chancellor on his return.

His career in the Law was brilliant. Common Sergeant at the early age of 23, he was made Recorder and later Lord Chief Justice at the age of 35. When he died at 41, in the Tower of London, he had occupied the Woolsack, the highest legal office in the Kingdom.

JESUITS.—Members of the Society of Jesus and other kindred religious orders are not allowed to enter the country without a special licence from a Secretary of State. The licence only runs for six months, and may be withdrawn at any time. A person in this country who embraces one of these religious orders is liable to be banished for life. If he remains at large in this country

Judge Jeffreys.

without lawful cause for three months after the order is made, he is liable on conviction to penal servitude for life.

JETSAM.—Goods which have been thrown overboard or otherwise lost from a ship or wreck, and which sink and do not float, are called jetsam.

JEWS.—Jews are now under no political disabilities. A marriage solemnised according to Jewish Usage is specifically recognised by the law. An oath should be administered to a Jew as to a Christian, save that the Old is substituted for the New Testament. A Jew wears his hat while taking the oath.

The Minister of a registered Jewish synagogue is exempted from service on a jury but is otherwise not specially privileged by English Law. Certain concessions are made in view of the Jews' Sabbath being held on a Saturday, e.g. cases coming on for hearing on a Saturday may be postponed. (*See also* SYNAGOGUE.)

JOBBER.—A jobber is a person on the Stock Exchange who buys and sells shares, not as agent for anyone else, as a broker does, but on his own behalf. When a broker is instructed by his client to buy shares acting on his client's instructions and as his client's agent, he buys them from a jobber. Jobbers deal mostly only with brokers, but they may deal with the public directly but not in the Stock Exchange. (*See* STOCK EXCHANGE.)

JOINT ACCOUNT.—A joint account is a banking account in the names of two or more persons, as for example a partnership account. An account in the names of two or more persons may only be drawn upon by a cheque signed by each and all of them, unless special instructions have been given to the banker authorising him to pay money over on cheques signed by one of them.

When an account is in the name of a firm trading in partnership, one partner will usually have an implied authority to sign cheques, drawn upon the bankers of the firm, in the partnership name. This implied authority may, of course, be negatived by express instructions to the contrary being given to the banker. When one of two persons having a joint account with a bank dies, the banker is entitled to pay over the balance remaining to the survivor. (*See also* BANK; CHEQUES; PARTNERSHIP.)

JOINT AND SEVERAL.—When two or more persons are liable under con-

tract, their liability may be either joint, or joint and several. If A and B promise to pay £100 to C, the liability will be presumed to be joint and not joint and several. The distinction between the two types of liability is not very great, for, whether the liability be joint or joint and several, C can only recover one sum of £100 in all. Further, in either case he may recover the whole £100 from *either* A or B, or may sue them both together, and is not bound to claim £50 from A and £50 from B. The distinction is largely a matter of legal theory, for where persons are liable jointly there is only one cause of action against them both, but where they are liable jointly and severally there is a cause of action against each— i.e. two causes of action altogether. The effect is that, if the creditor sues one only of two persons who are liable jointly only but not jointly and severally, and recovers judgment against that one, he cannot afterwards, if he finds that the person he has sued has not enough money to pay the amount of the judgment, bring another action for the balance of the amount due against the other joint debtor. He had only one cause of action and that has been exhausted by bringing the action. If he wished to make both debtors liable to him, he should have sued them both in the one action. If, however, the debtors are liable jointly and severally, the creditor may sue one of them and recover judgment, and may then go on and sue the other and recover from him any balance which he was unable to obtain from the first, because he has two causes of action, one against each debtor.

Partners in England are liable jointly for the partnership debts in contract, but jointly and severally for debts arising out of tortious (i.e. wrongful) acts—e.g. negligence in driving the partnership car on partnership business. In Scotland their liability is joint and several in both cases.

Contribution.—When a joint debtor is sued he is entitled to apply to the Court to have all other persons jointly liable with him made defendants also in the action. If judgment is then obtained, the creditor, if he pleases, may enforce it and recover all the money due from one only of the joint debtors, but that joint debtor will be entitled to call on the others to bear the proper proportion of the debt. This rule does not apply when

Sir William Jowitt.

the action is brought in respect of a tort or civil wrong. Persons who commit torts are jointly and severally liable for all the amount of damages, and have no right to claim any contribution from one another if the creditor calls upon one of them to pay the full amount. Thus, if a libel is published in a newspaper, damages may be obtained against the printer of the paper, the editor, and the proprietor, and, if the creditor enforces his judgment against one of those persons only, that one has no right to recover any part of the damages from the others but must bear the full share himself. This is expressed legally by saying that there is no contribution between "joint-tortfeasors."

JOINT OWNERS.—Two or more persons are said to own property jointly when they have one undivided right to the whole of it and where neither of them owns any specific part of the property. Joint ownership corresponds to joint tenancy in land. Partners own jointly all the partnership property but the mere fact that two persons own property jointly does not of itself make them partners in that property. (See JOINT TENANTS; PARTNERSHIP.)

JOINT TENANTS.—When two or more persons own the same land at the same time they may do so either as joint tenants or

as tenants in common. There are several differences between these two classes; the most important of them are that, on the death of one joint tenant, his share of the land passes to the other joint tenants and not to his relatives, and that joint tenants have one common title to the land whereas each tenant in common has a separate title.

JOINTURE.—This is the name applied to the property which is settled upon a husband and wife, or more usually upon the wife only before marriage with the object of preventing her from claiming her right of dower. Since dower has been abolished jointure is now of little importance.

JOWITT, Sir William (1885-).—One of the most able and distinguished members of the Bar to-day, Sir William Jowitt was Attorney-General from 1929-32. In that capacity he led for the prosecution in Rex v. Kylsant at the Central Criminal Court.

JUDGE.—In England there are two grades of Judges: Judges of the Supreme Court of Judicature and Judges of County Courts. The duties of these two grades of Judges are similar in that both sit to try judicially the cases brought before them.

Judges of the Supreme Court are appointed by the Crown on the recommendation of the Lord Chancellor. They are selected from distinguished practising barristers of not less than fifteen years' standing. They are entitled to a salary based upon £5,000 a year. They hold office for life and can only be removed by the Crown on an address from both Houses of Parliament. This provision is designed to render them secure in office and free from all fear or favour from the Government of the day.

Judges of County Courts are appointed in the same way as Judges of the Supreme Court but have not the same absolute security of tenure. They are appointed from practising barristers of not less than seven years' standing and receive a salary of £1,500 a year.

JUDGE ADVOCATE.—A person appointed to sit on a Court Martial as legal adviser. His duties are to advise the Court on all points of law and procedure, to keep the record of the proceedings and to sum up. He may be either an officer or a civilian but should have legal knowledge and experience. He does not vote on the

The Procession of the Judges on the opening of the Law Courts after vacation.

finding or sentence. In the Army and Royal Air Force a Judge Advocate must be appointed to every General Court Martial.

JUDGE ADVOCATE OF THE FLEET.—This is a permanent official whose duties are to supervise the proceedings of Naval Court Martial and to advise the Admiralty of matters of naval discipline and procedure. The appointment is usually held by a barrister practising at the Admiralty Bar.

JUDGE ADVOCATE-GENERAL.—The Judge Advocate-General is a permanent official. His duty it is to advise the Secretary of State for War and the Secretary of State for Air on matters of Military or Air Force discipline. His duties include studying the record of all Courts Martial with a view to finding out whether they are in order from a legal point of view. In cases where serious legal errors have occurred at trials by Court Martial, or where persons subject to Military or Air Force law have been unfairly or illegally treated by Courts Martial, he has to advise the proper authority that the proceedings should be quashed or the sentences reduced. Whenever a soldier or airman petitions on any point of law it is the duty of the Judge Advocate-General to advise as to what action should be taken on the petition. (*See* COURT MARTIAL.)

JUDGES' RULES.—In order that statements made to the police by persons suspected of, or charged with, crime, may be admissible in evidence, the Judges of the King's Bench Division have laid down certain rules for the guidance of the police known as the Judges' Rules.

Persons suspected of Crime.—A police officer who is investigating a crime is entitled to put questions to any person he pleases, whether he suspects him or not, if he thinks that any useful information can be obtained. Persons are not as a rule required to answer these questions but will usually be well advised to do so, in their own interests. When a police officer as a result of his enquiries has made up his mind to charge a person with the crime, he should not ask him any questions at all until he has first administered a caution (q.v.).

Prisoners.—Before any statement is taken from a prisoner he should be cautioned. This caution is usually given at the time when the prisoner is charged, and usually takes the form: "Do you wish to say anything in answer to the charge? You are not obliged to say anything unless you wish to do so, but whatever you say will be taken down in writing and may be given in evidence." It is wrong to add to the caution the words "against you," for this is apt to lead the prisoner to assume that he can do himself no good but only harm by making a statement, and may therefore deter an innocent man from saying anything at all.

When a prisoner makes a voluntary statement he must not be asked questions about it except for the purpose of clearing up what he has actually said. If he makes this statement before there has been time to caution him, it may be still admissible in evidence but he must be cautioned as soon as possible. Persons in custody should not be asked questions in the nature of cross-examination at any time and more especially before they have been cautioned. When a statement has been made it should, wherever possible, be taken down in writing and signed by the person who makes it, after it has been read to him and he has had an opportunity of making any alterations that he wishes to make. (*See* CONFESSIONS; EVIDENCE.)

JUDGMENT IN COUNTY COURT.—The judgment is the final decision of the Court in any action and must be drawn up by the Registrar and entered in a minute book. The registrar prepares a copy of the judgment and hands it to the Bailiff who, within twenty-four hours, must send it to the party against whom judgment is given. If the judgment is for payment of money and costs, or for costs only, it may be sent by post, but if it is a judgment, like an injunction which orders the party to do or to refrain from doing something upon penalty of imprisonment for contempt of Court, it must be served personally upon that party in the same manner as a Default or Special Default Summons.

Any party to an action may obtain a copy of the judgment from the Registrar by making application for it, and for this purpose he must state whether he wants the judgment for proceedings in another court, such as the Bankruptcy Court, or merely for using as evidence of the judgment.

Judgment by Default.—In many cases a County Court plaintiff can obtain judgment against the defendant by default without proceeding to the hearing of the Action.

In all those cases where a Default or a Special Default Summons (q.v.) has been issued and the defendant has failed to give notice in writing or by affidavit respectively within 8 days of the service of the summons that he intends to defend the action, or where it is plain from his notice of intention to defend that he has no real defence to the action, the plaintiff is entitled to obtain judgment forthwith by default. In such a case the plaintiff or his solicitor may call at the office of the Registrar, bringing with him the plaint note, the præcipe and the money for the requisite fees upon entering judgment, and can have judgment entered against the defendant. Alternatively, he or his solicitor, if he has no office in the County Court district, may send the above-mentioned documents and the fees by post to the Registrar together with a stamped addressed envelope directed to himself, and judgment will be entered without any necessity for his attendance at the office of the Court.

In a similar manner, if in an action commenced by an Ordinary or a Default Summons, the defendant fails to appear at the Court on the day fixed for hearing, the plaintiff is entitled to judgment upon proof of his claim and that the summons was properly served. If the action is founded upon a contract, the hearing of the plaintiff's case will, with the leave of the Judge, be sent over to the Registrar's Court and the Registrar will enter up judgment. If the action is not founded upon contract the Judge must hear the plaintiff's case and decide upon it himself.

In those cases where the plaintiff fails to appear at the hearing of the case, the defendant is entitled to enter up judgment against the plaintiff for such sum by way of costs as the Judge thinks fit.

Judgment upon Admissions.—Where the defendant, either at or before the hearing of the case, admits that he has no defence and makes an offer to pay by instalments, if the plaintiff accepts before the hearing and sends notice of his acceptance to the Registrar, the Registrar may enter judgment for payment by instalments immediately.

If, however, the plaintiff does not accept before the hearing, or the admission or offer is not made before the hearing, the case with the consent of the Judge will be sent over to the Registrar's Court for him to enter up judgment, without further proof, or he may enter up judgment for payment by instalments, if the amount claimed is less than £20, or, if being over £20, the plaintiff agrees to accept payment by instalments. (*See* COUNTY COURT PROCEDURE.)

Setting aside Judgment.—In every case, after judgment has been delivered or signed the unsuccessful party is entitled to make an application to have the judgment set aside. The application may be made verbally on the same day as the trial if both the parties are present, or it may be made at the first Court held after the expiration of 12 days after the trial, though in this case 7 clear days' notice of intention to apply for a new trial must be given to the registrar of the Court and to the opposite party. This applies, however, only to those cases where the unsuccessful party was present at the hearing of the action. If the judgment was given against a defendant in his absence, or in default of his giving a notice of intention to defend when served with a Default Summons (q.v.), the application need not be made at the next Court sitting after the expiry of 12 clear days, nor is it strictly necessary that notice is given, though it is extremely advisable to do so.

It is very much easier to get a judgment by default set aside than where the judgment has been given in the presence of both parties. Proof of misunderstanding is often sufficient in the former case, while in the latter it is generally necessary to shew, either that the verdict was so wrong that no reasonable jury could have given it, or that there was some mistake or perjury in the evidence.

An appeal (q.v.) is the more common remedy in cases where judgment has been given after a full hearing.

Enforcement of Judgment.—An ordinary judgment for money must be paid within 14 days of the judgment, but where an order has been made for the payment of the amount due by instalments, the sum due must be paid punctually in instalments at the times ordered in the judgment.

The usual order is that the money be paid into Court, but it may be varied by ordering that it should be paid to the successful litigant or to his solicitor.

The person against whom a judgment is entered in a County Court is known as the Judgment Debtor, and, if he fails to pay the amount of the judgment within the 14 days allowed (or fails to keep up the instalments, if payment by instalments has been ordered), there are a number of remedies open to the Judgment Creditor.

The judgment creditor may apply to the Court for a warrant of execution, for which purpose he must forward to the Registrar a copy of the plaint note and a document, known as a præcipe, identifying the judgment debtor. Execution is then levied on the goods of the judgment debtor, but not upon his lands, in the manner described under the title Execution.

An alternative procedure is to apply to the Registrar for an order for payment by instalments. This application may be made in writing to the Registrar or at any sitting of the Court, and it may also be made by the judgment debtor if he so wishes.

Usually the next step taken by a judgment creditor, where he has failed to recover the money payable under the judgment, is to apply at the office of the Registrar for an order that the debtor shall be examined orally as to his means, liabilities, etc., and to produce documents, books, etc. A copy of this order is served by the Bailiff personally upon the judgment debtor, who must appear upon the day named for his examination on oath, which generally takes places before the Registrar, who takes a note of any evidence then given for use in subsequent proceedings. The debtor may be ordered to produce his books of account, bank-books etc., and the evidence of other persons having knowledge of the debtor's affairs may be taken.

The result of this examination may be that the creditor will discover some goods upon which execution can be levied, but more usually it will show that the debtor has no property which may be taken by the ordinary processes of execution, and in such case the creditor's next step is to apply for a Judgment Summons.

Application for this must be made to the Registrar, to whom the same information and documents must be supplied as when an order for examination of the judgment debtor is desired. The Registrar must issue it at least 10 days before the hearing of the Judgment Summons and it must be served upon the judgment debtor at least 5 days before. The object of a judgment summons is to obtain committal of the debtor to prison, but the Judge will not make an order for this unless he has reason to believe that the debtor is capable of paying the debt but is avoiding so doing.

At the time of hearing of the judgment summons, the debtor must appear in Court (if he does not do so he is liable to fine or imprisonment for contempt of Court) and give his explanation of his reasons for non-payment of the judgment debt. Generally the judgment summons is issued without any previous examination of the debtor before the Registrar, but there are some County Court Judges who will refuse to allow the debtor to be cross-examined upon a judgment summons unless he has been previously examined before the Registrar.

Although upon a judgment summons the Judge is entitled to order the committal of the debtor forthwith, it is usual for him to make a new order for payment of the judgment debt by instalments, either greater or smaller than the instalments, if any, already ordered. If the debtor fails to pay those instalments, the judgment creditor after waiting for a decent interval may take out another judgment summons—and in this case, unless the debtor can prove to the Judge that the instalments are more than he can pay, an order will be made for the payment of the instalments, and, in default of their payment, for the committal of the judgment debtor to prison without any necessity for further proceedings.

By this cumbrous process a judgment of the County Court may be eventually enforced by the most severe penalty, but it is possible for a debtor of small means to delay payment of his judgment debt, even by instalments, for very many months, since there is the greatest reluctance on the part of most County Court Judges to use the very drastic persuasion of a committal order. (*See* COUNTY COURT PROCEDURE; EXECUTION.)

JUDGMENT IN THE HIGH COURT.—In a civil action the judgment of the High Court or any other Court is the decision of the Court which sets out the rights and remedies of the parties to the action. The word is often used loosely to denote the actual words used by the Judge in stating his reasons for the decision that he makes, but these words are, strictly speaking, only the directions of the Judge as to what judgment is to be entered in writing upon the records of the Court. The actual judgment is the written record of the decision.

Final Judgment.—A final judgment is a judgment which settles substantially all the questions that are in dispute between the parties to the action, as far as the Court that is trying the action is concerned. It is not final in the sense that there cannot be an appeal to a higher Court if the appeal is made within the proper time; nor is it final in the sense that in proper cases it cannot be set aside. It is, however, final in the sense that, unless within the appropriate time one of the parties takes the proper steps either to appeal against it or to set it aside, it establishes once and for all what the rights and liabilities of the parties to the action are.

Interlocutory Judgment.—There are a number of cases where a judgment may be given which does not dispose of all the questions in dispute between the parties to an action, but disposes only of some of them.

The commonest of these is where A brings an action against B for damages which require to be estimated, e.g. for damages for personal injuries due to a motor-accident. In such cases there are really two points in dispute, the first whether B caused the accident and is so liable to pay some damages, and the second how much damages B ought to pay. If B enters an appearance and the case is tried in Court both these questions are decided at the same time, and accordingly final judgment can be entered. But if B fails to appear, or appears but admits that he is liable to pay some damages, one of the questions is disposed of while the other still remains outstanding.

In such a case A can enter interlocutory judgment, which is the decision of the Court that B is liable to pay A damages, and B, except by getting this interlocutory judgment set aside for one of the reasons mentioned above, cannot thereafter dispute that he is liable to pay some damages. The question as to how much damages B ought tô pay is then sent to be tried by a Sheriff's jury in the Sheriff's Court (q.v.), and, when the Sheriff's Court has decided upon the amount of damages payable, A can file at the Central Office the result of the findings of the Sheriff's Court and enter final judgment for that amount.

Terms of Judgments.—The terms in which a judgment whether final or interlocutory may be made, and the results which flow from the judgment, will differ according to the remedy for which the parties to the action have asked the Court to give them. A judgment may be, and generally is, for a sum of money which includes the cost of the action, but it may be also for an injunction, a decree of specific performance, a declaration of rights or for an account, as well as costs.

Effects of a Judgment.—The mere entry of a judgment of whatever kind does no more than to prevent the parties to the action from bringing any other action upon the same set of facts as resulted in the judgment. The rule is that, once a matter has been finally decided upon in a Court of Law, none of the persons who have been parties to the action may again call in question either the facts or decision in the action. This, however, only applies to those persons who are parties to the action, and whose names appear in the action; and a previous judgment upon the same set of facts will not bar the right of any person who was not a party to the first action from bringing a fresh action if he wishes—though his prospects of success may be small. At the same time, if there are a large number of possible actions between a great many parties which are all based upon the same or similar sets of facts, it is possible to bring a Representative Action in which, although there are only certain named parties to the action itself, all the other persons who are interested in the same set of facts bind themselves to abide by the decision of the Court; and in such a Representative Action all the other persons will also be bound by the decision.

It is also important to bear in mind that criminal proceedings brought against a defendant are no bar usually to subsequent civil proceedings even by the person who has launched the criminal proceedings, since in criminal proceedings the prosecutor is in every case technically the Crown.

Although the mere entry of a judgment has this effect of barring subsequent actions between the parties, it does not, without further steps being taken, put any pressure upon the party, against whom it has been entered, to comply with its terms. If it is a money judgment, however, it bears interest from the date upon which it was entered. (*See* APPEAL IN HIGH COURT; EXECUTION; HIGH COURT PROCEDURE.)

JUDGMENT SUMMONS.—Where in a County Court or in the High Court a judgment debtor has failed to pay the amount of any judgment or order, the judgment creditor may apply to the Registrar of the County Court, or to the Central Office of the High Court of Justice, for a Judgment Summons calling upon the judgment debtor to appear before the Court to explain why the judgment or order has not been satisfied.

A Judgment Summons in the County Court is heard by the County Court Judge prior to the ordinary business of the day. In the High Court it is heard by a Judge of the Chancery Division, or where the judgment in respect of which the Judgment Summons was taken out was a judgment of the Probate, Admiralty and Divorce Division, by a Judge of that Court.

The object of a Judgment Summons is to enforce payment of the judgment debt by committing the judgment debtor to prison, if it can be proved that he has been in a position to pay the amount of the judgment, and yet has failed to do so. (*See* COUNTY COURT PROCEDURE; EXECUTION; JUDGMENT IN COUNTY COURT.)

JUDICATURE ACTS.—This is the name applied to several Acts of Parliament which lay down the procedure to be followed in the Supreme Court of Judicature, and provide generally for the administration of the law. By far the most important of these acts are the Judicature Acts 1873 and 1875, which set up as one Court the Supreme Court of Judicature in England and amalgamated the separate Courts of Chancery, Queen's Bench, Common Pleas, Exchequer, Admiralty, Probate, Divorce, and Bankruptcy, into one High Court of Justice with separate divisions, dealing with different classes of work.

JUDICIAL COMMITTEE OF THE PRIVY COUNCIL.—The Judicial Committee of the Privy Council consists of all

Privy Councillors who have held high judicial office together with a number of Colonial and Dominion Judges, though the latter seldom sit as members of the Judicial Committee until after they have retired from their judgeships in the colonies or dominions. When the Judicial Committee sits as a Court it is composed of practically the same personnel as the House of Lords, i.e., the Lords of Appeal in Ordinary.

The Judicial Committee of the Privy Council sits in its own Court Rooms in the Privy Council Office in Downing Street, a few doors from the Prime Minister's residence. It is the final Court of Appeal of the Empire with the exception of England, Wales, Scotland and Northern Ireland, and has the largest jurisdiction of any Court in the world. Members of the legal profession in every part of the Empire are allowed to appear and argue their cases before it.

The Judicial Committee of the Privy Council does not administer the law of England, but administers the law of the country from which the appeal comes. Thus it is possible for the Judicial Committee of the Privy Council to deliver judgments based upon Hindu-Mohammedan law on appeals from India, Roman Dutch law on appeals from South Africa, and French law on appeals from Mauritius, all in the course of the same week. Thus, in addition to having the largest jurisdiction in the world, the Judicial Committee of the Privy Council administers the largest variety of law in the world. (*See* COURTS.)

JUDICIAL FACTOR (SCOTS LAW).—A judicial factor is a person appointed by the Court of Session in Scotland to look after property in cases where, for some reason or other, it is necessary to protect the property from loss. He therefore corresponds to some extent to the English Receiver.

JUDICIAL NOTICE.—In general, any person who alleges any matter in a Court, must prove what he alleges. There are, however, certain matters which are regarded as being so well-known that the law does not require proof to be given of them. Judges are said to take "judicial notice" of such matters Thus, the meaning of English words, the ordinary course of nature, the recognized division of time and the contents of the Calendar, are assumed to be known by

every Judge, and need not be proved. (*See* EVIDENCE.)

JUDICIAL PROCEEDINGS, REPORTS OF.—Newspapers do not incur any liability for fair and accurate accounts of cases tried in Court, provided they do not publish any blasphemous, seditious or indecent matter, or anything the publishing of which is prohibited by the Court. Even if that which is said in Court was defamatory, newspapers cannot be rendered liable in libel for publishing it, if they publish it contemporaneously with the proceedings. Thus, if a newspaper publishes a report of something said by a witness in Court, anybody injured has no redress against the newspaper, in the same way as he has no redress against the person who said it.

For this absolute protection to be enjoyed by a newspaper, however, the publication must be made in the issue of the paper next after the events dealt with in the publication. If a considerable period of time elapses between the trial and the publication in the newspaper of what was said at the trial, then the newspaper can only escape liability if its editor was not actuated by malice.

Divorce Cases.—In 1926 an Act of Parliament was passed to regulate publication in newspapers of accounts of divorce cases. This act applies not only to divorce suits proper, but also to those for nullity of marriage, judicial separation and restitution of conjugal rights. It provides that no one may publish any report in regard to any such case except the following particulars:—the names, addresses and occupations of parties and witnesses; a concise statement of the pleadings; submissions on points of law and the decision of the Court thereon; and finally the summing up of the Judge, the decision of the jury and any observation made by the Judge in giving judgment. It will be noticed that this allows newspapers to publish in such cases the Judge's own comments; sometimes when Judges feel that publicity should be given to the conduct of parties in such cases, they comment on such conduct in their judgments. Publicity so approved of by the Judges is thereby effected. Any breach of this Act renders an offender liable to imprisonment for not more than 4 months, and to a fine not exceeding £500.

JUDICIAL SEPARATION.—A judicial separation can only be granted in the High Court of Justice. A very similar order can be made in the Police Court, but in that case it is called a separation order. (*See* SEPARATION ORDER.)

A judicial separation may be granted to either a husband or a wife on any of the following grounds:—adultery, cruelty, desertion for over two years, failure to return to cohabitation contrary to a decree for restitution of conjugal rights. (*See* CONJUGAL RIGHTS; AND SPECIAL SUPPLEMENT "DIVORCE.")

JUNIOR. Whenever two barristers appear in Court on the same side one is described as the "Leader" and one as the "Junior." A King's Counsel must always have a junior barrister briefed with him. It is customary for a junior barrister to receive a fee equal to two-thirds of that of his leader.

JURAT.—An Affidavit contains at its end a memorandum setting out the date and place where it is sworn, together with a description of the Commissioner for Oaths before whom it is sworn. This is called the Jurat of the Affidavit.

JURISDICTION.—The jurisdiction of a Court is the extent of the right of that Court to determine issues that are brought before it. Some Courts have a right to deal only with certain classes of people. For instance, a Court Martial can only try persons subject to the law of the service under which that Court Martial is sitting. Even Courts Martial themselves have limits to their respective jurisdictions. A District Court Martial in the Army, for instance, cannot try an officer. Again, Courts are limited as to the territorial area over which they have jurisdiction.

The Mayor's and City of London Court can only deal with cases arising in the City of London. Other Courts are limited as to the nature of the cases they can deal with. County Courts, for instance, cannot, in general, deal with actions of contract involving more than £100. Courts of Petty Sessions cannot try cases of any of the more serious criminal offences. The High Court of Justice, on the other hand, can try any civil action whatever the amount at issue, while the Central Criminal Court can try any indictable offence however serious.

JURISPRUDENCE. — Jurisprudence has been defined by a famous classical writer as the "Science of the just and unjust." It deals with the fundamental qualities of law, with the idea of justice in the abstract. Jurisprudence is not directly concerned with existing law except so far as it provides examples and material for the study of abstract principles of general law.

JURY.—In English law one of the most ancient features has been the decision of all questions of fact by a body of laymen called a Jury. The most common use of juries is in Civil or Criminal cases where they hear the evidence and at the end of the case are directed and assisted by the Judge in arriving at their decision, which is called their verdict. Sometimes special questions are left to them by the Judge to which they have to answer "yes" or "no," and in other cases they are simply required to state whether they find for the one party or the other.

Juries are used for deciding questions of fact not only in ordinary Civil and Criminal trials but also at Coroners' inquests, and in assessing damages in a Sheriff's Court in a civil case where liability is not denied. They are also available for the purpose of having a person declared a lunatic, and such a person is called a lunatic so found by inquisition.

Kinds of Juries.—Juries may be classified as "grand" or "petty." Grand Juries, which have now been abolished, were formerly used in all criminal trials at assizes or at the Central Criminal Court, i.e. the Old Bailey. It was their duty to hear the evidence of the prosecution only before the trial proper began. If they considered that there was some evidence on which the prisoner might be found guilty, they found a "true bill," and the trial of the prisoner before a new jury proceeded in the ordinary way. If they did not consider that there was any evidence on which he could be found guilty, they found "no bill" and in that case the prisoner was discharged without a trial.

These grand juries were of very great antiquity and it was through them in the early days that all prisoners were brought to trial, for it was their duty, when the King's Judges came into the county on circuit, to present to them persons who were suspected of crime for the purpose of having them tried. At the present time, however, all charges are investigated by a bench of Magistrates or by a Police Magistrate before they are tried at the assizes or at the Old Bailey; and the additional safeguard for the prisoner provided by the grand jury is not now considered necessary. Petty Juries are those which try some question of fact. After a grand jury had presented a prisoner for trial he was then tried by a petty jury.

Special Juries and Common Juries both sit to hear and decide questions of fact in ordinary civil trials, and the only distinction between them is that the class of persons eligible to serve upon special juries is more limited than the class of persons who serve on common juries.

Qualification of Jurors.—All British subjects, and aliens who have been domiciled in England for 10 years, are liable to serve on juries, if they are between the ages of 21 and 60, and if they have £10 a year worth of land or rents or £20 a year leasehold, or are assessed for poor rates at not less than £30 in the Metropolitan Area and £20 elsewhere, or occupy a house with not less than 15 windows. Such persons are not only eligible but may also be compelled to serve on a jury. The qualifications for a special juror are somewhat higher. Women are equally liable with men to serve on any jury but a Judge has power to order that the jury for any particular case shall be composed of men only, or of women only, and he may also release a woman from a jury if he thinks it desirable.

Exemption.—Aliens who have not been 10 years domiciled in England or Wales are disqualified and so also are lunatics, imbeciles and persons affected by deafness, blindness or other permanent bodily infirmity. There is a large class of persons who, although they are not disqualified in the above way, are yet exempted from service. These include peers, M.P.s, clergymen, Judges, barristers and solicitors if actually practising, magistrates of Metropolitan Police Courts, and persons employed in their Courts, Justices of the Peace, members of Municipal Corporations, doctors, chemists and dentists, officers of the Army or Navy while on full pay, soldiers in the regular forces, officers and men of the Territorial Army, persons engaged in the carrying on the business of Post Office, or the management or collection of customs or in the Indian Revenue. No person can be summoned to serve on a jury more than once in every year unless all the other jurors on the list have already been summoned to serve.

Persons who are liable to serve on juries must attend if they are summoned to do so. The list of persons liable to serve is now contained in the Electoral Lists of Voters. Against the name of each person there contained the letter "J" will be placed if he is liable as a common juror, and the letters "S.J." if he is liable as a special juror. A person who is entitled to be exempted, but whose name appears on the list, should claim exemption before he is summoned to attend. A juror who does not attend when summoned may be fined £10 in the High Court or £5 in the County Court or Coroner's Court; but a juror is not required to attend unless he receives a summons 6 days at least before the date on which his services are required.

Right of Challenge.—Any party may object to the jury either as a whole ("Challenge to the Array") or as to individual members of it ("Challenge to the polls"). Challenge is now rarely used. Challenge to the Array arises when the person summoning the jury has not done so fairly but has selected a jury likely to be favourable to one party or to the other. Challenge to the polls is exception taken to individual members of the jury. It may either be peremptory, that is, without any reason being given, or "for cause," when it is necessary to shew some ground indicating that the person challenged will not try the case fairly or is not properly qualified. On a charge of treason there is a peremptory right to challenge 35 jurors; on a charge of felony the number is 20; in the case of misdemeanour there is no peremptory challenge.

Conduct during Trial.—Persons serving on a jury should be very careful during the trial to hold no communication with any persons engaged in the case or appearing in it as a party or a witness, nor should a juror make any statement to any representative of the Press, or in any way disclose, either during or after the trial, what was said or done in the jury room by himself or any other juror. Except in trials for murder, treason, or treason felony, jurors are not now prevented from separating or going to their own homes. All jurors are now allowed the use of a fire when out of Court and reasonable refreshments at their own expense. In former times jurors were allowed no comforts of any kind until they had given their verdict.

Remuneration.—In civil cases special jurors usually receive 21/- each for each action that they try, but if the case lasts some time the parties may agree to increase the payment. If it is necessary for the jury to have a view, that is, to inspect the locality connected with the action for the purposes of the trial, they receive an extra guinea. Common jurors receive a shilling for each case in the High Court in London and 8d. for cases on circuit. In County Courts the fee is a shilling for each case. Juries in criminal cases never receive any payment.

Trial by Jury.—All criminal cases except those minor offences heard at Police Courts must be tried before a jury. In civil cases, juries are much less commonly used than formerly. No person can insist on the case being tried by jury except when charges of fraud are made, or where the claim is for libel, slander, malicious prosecution, seduction or breach of promise in marriage or in divorce cases.

When a jury is required, a panel is prepared of persons summoned to attend, and the necessary twelve persons for the jury are taken at random from this list by the clerk of the Court. In coroners' juries the number of persons who sit is not twelve but varies, but must not be less than seven nor more than eleven. In the County Court there are eight jurors. In all cases except Coroners' Courts the jury must be unanimous in their verdict. If they cannot agree the parties may be willing to accept the decision of the majority, but otherwise the jury must be discharged and the case must begin again. In Coroners' Courts the coroner may accept the verdict of a majority so long as the minority is not greater than two. If a juror becomes ill during the hearing of the case or dies, the case must be tried again with a fresh jury, unless both sides assent in writing and the number of jurors left is not less than ten. In this case the reduced jury may continue and decide the case.

Judge and Jury.—While the jury are the sole jury on all questions of fact and while the Judge's only duty is to explain the law

to them, it frequently happens that Judges in summing up to juries indicate in very strong terms what they themselves consider are the proper view of the facts. It is perfectly proper for a Judge to do this, so long as he makes it quite clear to the jury that they are not bound to agree with his view in their verdict.

JURY (SCOTS LAW).—The Scots Law relating to juries is very similar to that in England. In criminal cases there are fifteen jurors instead of twelve. In both civil and criminal cases the jury are not required to be unanimous but may return a verdict which is supported by the majority of them. This provision gives less protection to a prisoner than the English rule requiring a unanimous verdict, but on the other hand juries in Scotland instead of finding a prisoner "guilty" or "not guilty" may bring in a verdict of "not proven." The effect of this is the same as "not guilty," but obviously indicates that the jury, although uncertain, have been inclined to think the guilt of the prisoner has been made out. This verdict is not entirely satisfactory for, since it is the law that unless the prosecution succeed in proving the prisoner to be guilty then he ought to be acquitted, there should be no room for an intermediate verdict. If the prosecution have failed to prove their case the prisoner should be entitled to be found "not guilty."

JURY OF MATRONS.—This was a jury impanelled in former times when a woman who was being tried pleaded that she was pregnant. It was for this jury to decide the question. The effect of a plea of pregnancy was to defer the execution. Nowadays such matters can normally be determined by medical evidence.

JUS RELICTÆ.—This is the right enjoyed by a married woman in the movable property of her husband at his death. She cannot be deprived of this by any provision in her husband's will. (*See* MARRIED WOMAN [SCOTS LAW].)

JUS RELICTI.—This is the right enjoyed by a husband in the movable property belonging to his wife at the time of her death and corresponds to the Jus Relictæ which a wife enjoys. There is one important distinction between those rights, for, whereas the wife's right to jus relictæ arises not only when her husband dies but also if she divorces him, the husband's right to jus relicti does not arise if he divorces his wife but only on her death. (*See* MARRIED WOMAN [SCOTS LAW].)

JUSTICE OF THE PEACE.— Justices of the Peace are appointed for every county and for those boroughs to which separate commissions of the peace have been granted. In counties The Lord Lieutenant recommends the names of candidates to the Lord Chancellor, and the appointments are then made by the Crown. In boroughs, recommendations are made by the Borough Council, and these recommendations are acted upon, or not, as the Lord Chancellor thinks fit.

The duties of Justices of the Peace are very varied. They investigate charges of indictable offences, and if they think that the evidence is sufficient they commit persons so charged to Assizes or Quarter Sessions for trial before a jury. Also they themselves try all summary or minor offences, and certain less serious indictable offences which can with the consent of the accused be dealt with summarily. They exercise jurisdiction in regard to various licensing matters (*see* INTOXICATING LIQUOR) and perform other ministerial duties.

A Justice of the Peace before entering upon his duties is required to take an oath of allegiance. He must, at the time of his appointment, in the case of a county appointment, reside in the county, or within seven miles of its boundary, and in the case of the borough, he must reside in the borough, or within seven miles of it, or occupy some property in the borough.

The Mayor of any borough automatically becomes the presiding Justice of the Peace for the borough. (*See* PETTY SESSIONS.)

JUSTICIARY, COURT OF.—This is the supreme criminal Court of Scotland and consists of the Lord President of the Court of Session (who, when sitting in the Court of Justiciary, takes the title of Lord Justice General), the Lord Justice Clerk and other Judges of the Court of Session. The Court sits permanently in Edinburgh but Judges of it occasionally go on circuit.

JUSTIFICATION.—When a person is being sued for having made some defamatory statement about another person, it is always a good defence if he can shew that

15*

the statement is true. If this is so it does not matter whether, when he made this statement, he was acting spitefully and maliciously or not. The principle on which this rests is that, if a man has a bad character, the law will not allow him to recover damages in respect of an injury which merely states the character which he really has. Notice, however, that this does not mean that, if a man has got a bad character in one respect, he is not entitled to recover damages if persons make defamatory statements about his character in other respects. Thus if a man is called a forger, it is no defence to an action for defamation to prove that he is a thief.

Criminal Libel.—The rule about justification does not apply to criminal prosecutions but only to civil actions. In criminal cases the principle is "the greater the truth the greater the libel." If, however, the person charged with the crime of libel can prove not only that the statement is true but that it is in the public interest that it should be made known, this will be a defence. The reason why justification of itself is no defence to a criminal charge is that the criminal law of libel has for its object the prevention of breach of the peace or assault; and it has been not unreasonably thought that a person is perhaps even more likely to assault anyone who makes a defamatory statement about him if the statement is true than if it was false.

It is for the person who has made the defamatory statement to prove that it is true, and he must prove it is true not merely in any narrow sense which the words may bear, but in the ordinary meaning which any reasonable person might take from them. He need not, however, prove the truth of the statement in every detail so long as he proves that it is true in substance. He must justify what is called the "sting" of the libel. Thus, where the defendant had said the plaintiff had been convicted of travelling in a train without a ticket and had been fined £1 with *three weeks'* imprisonment in default of payment, it was held that he justified the statement sufficiently by proving that the plaintiff had been guilty of the offence and had been fined £1 with a *fortnight's* imprisonment in default.

Repeating Rumours.—It is no defence to an action for libel that the person who made the statement only stated that he had heard it reported and did not vouch himself for the truth of the statement. If he wishes to justify, he must prove not only that there was such a report but that it was true. In the same way, if it is stated that a man is "suspected" of a crime, it is not enough justification to prove that he was suspected, but the defendant to justify his statement must prove he actually committed the crime.

Honest Belief.—As a general rule it is no defence to prove that the defendant really believed the story to be true and was not really actuated by any evil purpose in spreading the report. In certain cases when the statement is made on what is known as a privileged occasion, this may be a defence (*See* DEFAMATION; LIBEL; PRIVILEGE.)

JUSTINIAN (483-565).—One of the most famous of the Roman Emperors, he was called "the Great." He is best known to modern civilization for his magnificent work in consolidating Roman Law. Under his direction and through the medium of Commissions appointed by him, the four books of the "Corpus Juris" were published.

JUVENILE COURT.—A Juvenile Court is a Court specially constituted to hear charges against children and young persons, and the rules relating to its constitution and procedure are laid down in the famous "Children's Charter," which is the well-chosen name given to the Children's and Young Persons Act, 1933. (*See also* APPROVED SCHOOL; CHILDREN.)

K EEPING HOUSE.—When a debtor begins to "keep house," that is, to stay indoors so as to avoid his creditors, he is guilty of an act of bankruptcy. A debtor who gives orders that creditors who called to see him are not to be admitted will be "keeping house." (*See* ACT OF BANKRUPTCY.)

KING.—In the Statute of Westminster, 1931, the Crown is defined as "the symbol of the free association of the members of the British Commonwealth of Nations," who are "united by a common allegiance to the Crown." The King in his official capacity is, therefore, the keystone of the British Empire. The powers of the Crown are so extensive and in many cases so vague as hardly to be capable of enumeration. The major part of public officials are nominally appointed by the Crown and are the servants of the Crown; the major part of the public services are conducted in the King's name; the King is the head of the Church of England; the Cabinet is selected and Parliament itself is summoned by the King. But, by the growth of constitutional customs and understandings, the Crown's original autocracy has been broken down, and the powers nominally and legally vested in Crown are now in fact exercised by other persons, e.g. Archbishops an Bishops are nominally appointed by the King, but in fact owe their office to the Prime Minister in power at the time of a vacancy; the right of Royal pardon is in fact controlled and exercised by the Home Secretary. But it is clear that, when all matters of this kind have to pass through the King's hands, his influence must be by no means small; Cabinets are continually re-organized and dismissed, and the King is the only high officer of state who remains perpetually in power and who will probably, therefore, remain perpetually disinterested as a result of his perpetual security. It is therefore unavoidable that his influence and experience should be both valuable and extensive. But the actual extent of his influence cannot be estimated, since it depends upon the sentiments of the public and upon the character of the Sovereign himself.

Apart from what may be called his public or official legal position, the King's personal legal status is peculiar. For example, since the King is regarded as the fountain of all justice, and since the Judges are therefore only his own servants, he can never be compelled to attend the Courts. The King is, furthermore, protected by the maxim that "the King can do no wrong." The joint effect is that, if the King were to commit a crime, he could not be punished, and if he were to commit a civil wrong he could not be sued. In certain cases, when servants of the Crown have committed civil wrongs in the name of the Crown, the subject is entitled to launch a "petition of right," and the Courts then look into the matter as if it were a dispute between two subjects.

The right to succession to the Crown is laid down in the Act of Settlement, 1700; by the Statute of Westminster, 1931, it is provided that any alteration in the law regarding the succession to the Throne and the Royal Style and Titles requires the assent of all the Dominion Parliaments. Any marriage contracted by any descendant, male or female, of George II without the consent of the Sovereign is null and void (except in the case of children of princesses married into foreign families). Such descendant may, however, if over twenty-five years of age, give a year's notice to the Privy Council of his or her intention to marry without consent, and such marriage will be valid unless both Houses of Parliament declare their disapprobation. (*See also* CROWN; PETITION OF RIGHT.)

KING'S BENCH DIVISION.—

This Division consists of the Lord Chief Justice, who is the President of it, and some fifteen or sixteen other Judges. In the Royal Courts of Justice, Strand, there are eight court-rooms set aside for the work of this Division, and in addition, three, or in places four times a year, Judges of this Division travel from county town to county town throughout the country holding Assize Courts for the various counties. Although Assizes are largely devoted to criminal proceedings, civil actions are heard at them also, and a Judge sitting in an Assize Court is as much a part of the High Court of Justice and has the same powers as if he were sitting in Court in London.

The King's Bench Division deals with all ordinary actions in which the person who is bringing the action is seeking to recover monetary compensation for an infringement of his rights, except in so far as some of these matters are reserved from the Chancery Division. It also hears Petitions of Right, Applications for Habeas Corpus, etc.

Two Judges of the King's Bench Division when sitting together may constitute a Divisional Court (q.v.). (*See* HIGH COURT OF JUSTICE; HIGH COURT PROCEDURE; and also SUPREME COURT OF JUDICATURE.)

KING'S COUNSEL.—

Barristers are divided into King's Counsel and Junior Counsel. A King's Counsel is really the holder of a title of honour and a person so appointed is in theory supposed to be available primarily for conducting cases on behalf of the King. He is entitled to sit in Court within the Bar (that is to say the front row of seats for Counsel) and he wears a silk gown. K.C.s may not appear in a case unless they are also briefed with junior barristers. When a junior barrister becomes a K.C. he is said "to take silk." This expression arises from the fact that on appointment he changes his stuff gown for a silk one. K.C.s are appointed by the Lord Chancellor; and a junior barrister, who considers that his practice is sufficiently large to justify him in becoming a K.C., informs the Lord Chancellor that he desires to be so appointed. If the Lord Chancellor thinks that his standing is sufficient to merit the honour he grants it to him.

On appointment as King's Counsel he has to go through the ceremony of being called "within the Bar." The new K.C. has to appear before each Judge sitting in the High Court of Justice. On his entering the Court the Judge says to him: "It having pleased his Majesty to make you one of his counsel learned of the law, will you take your seat within the Bar?" The new K.C. then enters the seats within the Bar, bows to the Judge and other members of the Bar in Court, and then passes on to repeat the ceremony before the next Judge.

KING'S EVIDENCE. —

When an accomplice in a crime, in order to avoid being punished for it himself, gives evidence against other persons he is said to turn King's evidence. The evidence of such witnesses, of course, has to be taken with reserve and scrutinised with great care because from their own lips they have to admit they are themselves as guilty as the persons whom they are accusing.

It is the duty of a Judge to point out to the jury in his summing-up, in cases where the evidence of an accomplice is tendered by the prosecution, that it is always dangerous to convict on the uncorroborated evidence of an accomplice or accomplices. In practice, juries do not convict on such evidence unless it is corroborated in material particulars by facts or witnesses whose credit is not impeached. (*See* ACCOMPLICES; APPROVERS).

KING'S PEACE.—In the early Middle Ages the King was able only by degrees to establish his authority over the whole of the kingdom. Wherever his power was in force he was said to enforce his peace in that area. In areas remote from the royal seat of government, local lords would exercise their own authority—in other words, they would have their own peace.

For many centuries, of course, the King has exercised jurisdiction over the whole of the Kingdom, and the King's Peace, therefore, has been the effective peace. Criminal offences (*see* CRIME) are, in theory, treated as offences against the King's peace, and it is for this reason that the King is always the nominal prosecutor in criminal cases.

KING'S PROCTOR.—An official whose duty it is to represent the Crown in matrimonial and probate cases. The need for this official is often discussed but it must be remembered that in probably the majority of divorce cases both the parties are anxious that a divorce shall be granted. Divorce therefore differs from all other causes of action. For this reason it has been found necessary that there shall be somebody to scrutinise divorce cases with a view to bringing to light any facts that the Court should know of, such as collusion between the parties. When the King's Proctor finds anything which the parties have concealed or

which otherwise justifies the Court in taking action, he is said to "intervene." He usually does this during the time between the making of a decree nisi and a decree absolute. Indeed, one of the reasons for this interval is to allow him to conduct enquiries and, if necessary, intervene.

The King's Proctor is a permanent official who is a barrister. It is usual for him to combine with it the duties of Treasury Solicitor. He has a staff of lawyers and his office is at the Law Courts, Strand. (*See* SPECIAL SUPPLEMENT "DIVORCE.")

KING'S REGULATIONS. — The King's Regulations for the Army and Army Reserve are contained in a book bearing this title. Though they do not strictly constitute law, nevertheless on any point that is not dealt with by law they provide a code of discipline for members of the Army and Army Reserve.

KING'S REMEMBRANCER.—This is a very old office at present held by the Senior Master of the Supreme Court. His duties nowadays are little more than nominal, being mainly ceremonial. In former times, however, he had important duties to perform in connection with the recovery of Crown debts.

KNACKERS.—A knacker is a person who carries on the business of slaughtering cattle (including sheep, goats, pigs and horses), when the flesh of such animals is not to be used and sold as butcher's meat. He requires a licence. (*See also* HORSES.)

L.S. —These letters stand for the Latin expression "Locus Sigilli." They are placed on deeds in order to indicate the spot on which the seal is to be placed.

LABOUR EXCHANGE.—Labour Exchanges were first officially recognised by the State in 1909, and at that time they were intended for the purpose of furnishing information to employers desiring workmen, and to workmen desiring employment. They have been renamed Employment Exchanges and their full title is "Ministry of Labour Employment Bureau."

With the establishment of a comprehensive scheme of Unemployment Insurance in 1920 the Labour Exchanges were given the

additional task of paying out benefit to claimants. Workmen may register at the Employment Exchange in their district and they will then be supplied with information relating to employment which may be suitable for them. A contributor to the Unemployment Insurance Scheme who desires to claim benefit during unemployment must usually attend at the Local Labour Exchange every working day and sign the register, unless he lives more than two miles from an exchange, in which case he need only sign on alternate days. He must fill up the appropriate form claiming benefit and deposit his unemployment insurance cards with the officials at the Exchange. In certain cases unemployment benefit may be paid through the Post Office with the consent of the Post-master-General, but in all cases it is paid once a week on a fixed day. (*See also* SPECIAL SUPPLEMENT "UNEMPLOYMENT INSURANCE.")

LACHES.—One of the maxims of equity is that "equity aids the vigilant but not the indolent," or "delay defeats equity." Delay of this type is technically known as laches.

There is no fixed period which will amount to laches. The following questions have to be considered: Has the delay in making the claim been such that documents, or other evidence which might have been available to defeat the claim, had it been made in proper time, may have been lost? Is it possible to imply an agreement not to enforce the claim? Has the person against whom the claim is made done some act to his detriment, which he would not have done had he not thought the claim was being abandoned? (*See* STATUTES OF LIMITATIONS.)

LADY DAY.—Lady Day is the 25th of March and one of the four quarter days of the year for the payment of rent and determination of tenancies in England.

LAND.—Until modern times land was the only form of wealth known, and the law relating to the ownership of land shows to this day many traces of those times and of its origin in the feudal system. No one can be the absolute owner of land except the Crown; all other persons are tenants of one kind or another. The chief tenant is the tenant in fee simple who for all practical purposes is the absolute owner of the land. His ownership of the land is said to extend downwards to the centre of the earth and upwards to the sky, and therefore, unless he or some predecessor in title of his has transferred the mineral rights, he will be entitled to anything that may be discovered beneath the surface. Since 1925 it is no longer possible to hold a legal estate in land except a freehold estate in fee simple, and a lease for a term of years, but all other forms of interest in land may still be created as equitable interests.

Land has been considered so important a form of property that anything which is placed on the land so as to be fixed to it becomes the property of the person who owns the land. Many exceptions have been made to this rule, in particular with regard to fixtures which a tenant puts upon the land for his own purposes during his tenancy. (*See* FIXTURES.)

The sale of land and the conveyance of interest in the land is subject to special rules, as to which, *see* SALE OF LAND. Provisions have also recently been introduced for simplifying the transfer of land by means of registration of title. Under these provisions the title to land consists merely in a certificate issued by the appropriate registration office.

LAND CHARGES.—Land Charges are rights and interests of a particular kind which may be held by one person over the land of another. For purposes of convenience a number of these rights are grouped together under the collective name of land charges, which expression includes:

(*a*) Puisne mortgages, i.e. legal mortgages in which the mortgagee does not get possession of the title deeds to the mortgaged property.

(*b*) General Equitable Charges, i.e. equitable mortgages in which the mortgagee does not get the title deeds.

(*c*) Estate Contracts, i.e. agreements to sell the legal ownership of land.

(*d*) Restrictive Covenants (q.v.), e.g. covenants limiting the free use of the land.

(*e*) Equitable Easements (*see* EASEMENT).

(*f*) Death Duty Charges.

All these are rights which a person who is not the owner of a particular piece of land may have over it. In order to protect purchasers of that land from finding themselves unexpectedly burdened with such rights, it is provided that they must all be registered in the Land Charges Register at the Land Registry in London. Anyone who is contemplating the purchase of land should make a search in this registry (as well as in other registries for other classes of rights) to find out to what burdens the land is subjected. He may do so himself on payment of a small fee, or may have an official search made for him on payment of a slightly larger one. Such an official search is conclusive, and the purchaser will not be affected by any charges which were in fact registered but were not reported to him in the official report.

Any land charge which was first created *after* 1925 and has not been registered will not be effective against any purchaser of the land, even though he actually knew of the existence of the charge when he bought it; as regards charges created before 1926 the position is slightly different; restrictive covenants (q.v.) and equitable easements (see EASEMENT) need never be registered and will remain effective against purchasers of the land; but puisne mortgages (see above), though they need not be registered so long as they do not change hands, will cease to bind purchasers of the land if they have been transferred to a new owner and he has neglected to register them.

There are also certain circumstances in which puisne mortgages and general equitable charges will not affect the purchaser even though they are registered. (See SALE OF LAND.)

LAND (COMPULSORY PURCHASE).—When at the beginning of the nineteenth century the development of the railway system began, it was necessary for the railway companies to buy land over which to run their lines. Many owners of land were unwilling to sell to the railways because of prejudice, or else were willing to sell only at an exorbitant price. It was, therefore, necessary to provide powers enabling the railway companies to purchase land compulsorily, that is, against the will of the owner. This principle of compulsory purchase then introduced has been very largely developed since that time, and is now used to enable housing authorities to clear districts on which slum property is situated and for public purposes generally. Powers are now contained in many public and private acts.

LAND TAX.—The modern form of Land Tax first appeared in 1692 "for carrying on a vigorous war against France." The tax was 4/– a year on every 20/– for which the land so taxed could have been honestly leased. By a series of statutes extending to 1798 the system was brought almost to the condition in which it is found at the present day. In that year it was declared that a definite and fixed sum was to be raised by each parish or other defined area by means of rates to be assessed on the above principle. The result is that parish rates for this purpose have now become very unequal because, even though the value of land in one of the areas has greatly increased, still only the same fixed quota is to be paid by that area.

The tax is controlled by the Land Tax Commissioners appointed for each area, and all justices of the peace and mayors are entitled to sit on the Commission. (Compare LAND VALUE TAX; LAND VALUES DUTIES.)

LAND VALUE DUTIES.—These duties or taxes were imposed by the Finance Act of 1910, which levied taxes of four different kinds, known as Increment Value Duty, Reversion Duty, Undeveloped Land Duty and Mineral Rights Duty. All these taxes except the last mentioned were abolished in 1920. (See MINERAL RIGHTS DUTY; compare LAND TAX; LAND VALUE TAX.)

LANDLORD AND TENANT.—The relationship of landlord and tenant arises when one person, the landlord, allows another person, the tenant, to use land for some period of time. The period may be either long or short, but it must necessarily be shorter than the time for which the landlord himself is entitled to use the land. Thus, if the landlord is the freeholder, that is, the owner of the land for all time, he may grant a lease to the tenant for as many years as he pleases. If, on the other hand, the landlord has himself only the right to use the land for a limited period, e.g. is himself a tenant for a number of years, he may only allow another person to use the land for a lesser period. The period may be less than the landlord's right to enjoy the land by as little as a day.

The period for which the tenant is to have the land may either be a fixed period or a period ending on some future event. An illustration of the first type is a tenancy for a term of years and a tenancy may be granted from year to year. Apart from express grant, a tenancy from year to year will arise whenever a person in possession of the land pays rent which is measured by reference to a year, e.g. "quarterly." Thus, where a tenant has had a lease for a number of years which has expired, and stays on in possession of the premises and pays rent on a yearly basis, he will be a tenant from year to year. This type of tenancy may be brought to an end by six months' notice expiring on the day in the year before the anniversary of the commencement of the tenancy. The parties may, however, make other arrangements for the termination of the tenancy which should be clearly set out.

Tenancy at Will.—This is a tenancy not of great practical importance, under which the tenant only holds the land for such time as the landlord allows him to do so. No notice to put an end to this type of tenancy is required, and it comes to an end on the death of either party. Tenancies of this kind occasionally arise where a tenant under a lease retains possession of the premises after the period of his lease has come to an end. When he pays rent he will become a tenant from year to year, but until that time he is only a tenant at will. Where a person is allowed to live in a house rent free, or for no fixed period, he is a tenant at will.

Creation of Tenancy.—When a tenancy is for a long period of time it is almost invariably made by the grant of a lease, which is a document by which the landlord conveys to the tenant the land for a period of time. A lease need not be made by deed, that is by a document not only signed but also sealed by the landlord, if it is for three years or less; but if it is for more than three years, or if the rent is less than the best rent which can reasonably be obtained, it must, in strict law, be made by deed. When it is not required to be by deed it may be either orally or in writing, although it is very unwise to enter into a tenancy without having all the terms fairly set out in writing. In practice it is very usual, instead of a lease being granted which actually conveys the land to the tenant for a period, that there should only be an *agreement* by the landlord that he will convey the land to the tenant. The distinction may appear to be very slight, but in the past it has had very great importance, although to-day there is little difference between a person who holds land under a lease and one who holds under an agreement for a lease.

What makes a Lease Binding.—Where an actual lease has been granted, whether it be orally, or by a written agreement or by deed, it will be binding subject to what has been said above about leases for over three years. Where, however, the transaction is merely an agreement for a lease, it cannot be enforced by either the landlord or the tenant unless there is some written note of the terms of it signed by the party against whom it is sought to enforce it. It follows, therefore, that agreements for leases must always be proved by written evidence

whether they are for three years or less, or not. This applies not only to houses or land but also to a flat or furnished lodgings if any specific rooms are let. It does not follow from this that the agreement must *originally* be made in writing. It is enough if, at some time before it is desired to enforce it, the party against whom the action is to be brought has signed a document setting out the following matters:

1. The names of the parties.
2. The premises which have been let.
3. The time for which they are to be let.
4. The day on which the letting is to commence.
5. The amount of the rent.

These particulars may not be contained in any one document but may be scattered about through various letters which may have passed between the parties. It will be seen that it may be possible for one person to enforce the agreement but not the other. If, for example, the landlord has written a letter setting out the terms of the agreement the tenant can enforce it against the landlord: but unless the tenant had himself signed some document the landlord cannot enforce it against him. The document need not be signed by the landlord or tenant himself but will be equally valid if signed by some authorised agent. A house agent who has merely been instructed to find a tenant has no authority to enter into a contract with the tenant.

Part Performance.—The effect of what has been set out above is very much reduced by what is called the doctrine of part performance. This means that, although (where there is not written evidence as required above) neither party may be able to compel the other to carry out their bargain, yet if one or other of them has done any act on the faith of the agreement he may enforce it even although it is verbal. The act relied upon must be an act which clearly shows that some agreement was made. Where the tenant has gone into possession of the premises, this will be conclusive, but where the tenant is already in possession at the time of the agreement, e.g. under a lease which is due to expire—the mere continuing in possession will not be sufficient part performance.

During the negotiations which are bound to take place between the parties before they come to a fixed agreement, many propositions may be discussed by the one or the other, but neither will be bound until they have come to an agreement on all points. That is, they must have made a contract (q.v.).

Very frequently one party or the other accepts "subject to formal contract," and it may be stated that the contract must be approved by the solicitor of one party. As a general rule, if they make this provision, they are not bound until their formal contract has been drawn up and signed by them.

Preparation of Documents.— Where the letting is for three years or less, a lease, which is a document under seal (i.e. a deed, q.v.) is not required and a written document not under seal is sufficient. It is quite proper and usual for such agreements to be drawn up by persons who are not solicitors (such as Estate Agents) and they may receive payment for the work. In the case of lettings for periods over three years, the documents can also be drawn up by persons who are not solicitors, but they cannot take payment for doing so.

Unless the parties make a special agreement to the contrary in the contract for a lease, a person taking a lease from a person who owns the freehold of the land cannot insist on the latter proving his title, i.e. that he owns the land and is entitled to lease it, but must assume he has the right to grant a lease. The parties can agree at the outset that the Lessor must prove his title. A person taking a sub-lease will be entitled to inspect the lease under which his Lessor derives his title (i.e. owns the land), and also all Assignments thereof (which are transfers) since the lease was first granted. This lease is called the "Head Lease." If the head lease has been in existence for more than thirty years, then the sub-Lessee will be entitled to inspect the head lease and all Assignments thereof during the thirty years preceding the agreement to create the sub-lease. It is very desirable for the sub-Lessee to inspect the head lease as it may contain covenants (which is the name given to terms in a deed) relating to the use of the land which will bind the sub-Lessee whether or not he is actually aware of them.

In order to facilitate his investigation of the Lessor's title, where the parties have agreed that the Lessee shall be entitled to call for proof of title, they may further agree that the Lessor shall supply the Lessee with an "Abstract of Title" (q.v.), which is an epitome of the documents and facts proving the Lessor's title to the property. This is prepared by the Lessor's solicitor and sent by him to the Lessee's solicitor, who investigates the title, makes searches, prepares and delivers Requisitions on Title (which are queries arising out of his investigations) and receives replies thereto from the Lessor's solicitor, exactly as in the case of a sale of land.

The next step is for the Lessor's solicitor to draft the proposed lease, which he submits to the Lessee's solicitor for approval. After the wording has been agreed, the lease is engrossed in duplicate, i.e. two fair copies are made, one of which is executed by the Lessor. This is the lease. The other part is executed by the Lessee. This is the Counterpart Lease. An appointment is made and the solicitors exchange the two parts.

The lease will be stamped by means of an impressed stamp, the amount of the stamp depending on the rent and other terms of the lease. The Counterpart Lease will be stamped 5/–. As it is the duty of the Lessor's solicitor to satisfy himself that the two parts are properly stamped, he usually prepares the engrossment of both the lease and the counterpart lease, and stamps them before sending the counterpart lease to the Lessee's solicitor for execution.

If a person buys an already existing lease, he is said to take an "Assignment" of the lease. His investigations will extend back for thirty years, subject to any agreement to the contrary, and the lease itself. The seller is called the "Assignor" and the purchaser the "Assignee." The procedure follows the lines already described with reference to the granting of a lease.

In the counties of Middlesex and Yorkshire all leases for terms exceeding twenty-one years, or assignments of leases which have still more than twenty-one years to run, must be registered in an Official Registry. In Middlesex the Registry is at the Land Registry in Lincoln's Inn Fields, London. There are three registries in Yorkshire for the different Ridings of that county.

Matters to be Considered.— A tenant entering into a tenancy should consider carefully each of the following matters:

Repairs.—It is a remarkable fact in English law that there is no obligation on the landlord to do repairs to a house that he has let, unless he has expressly agreed to do so in the contract creating the tenancy. Exceptions occur to this rule which are of great importance in the case of premises let as flats (q.v.) and all premises let as dwelling houses at a rent not over £40 a year in London or £26 elsewhere. In the last case the landlord cannot by any terms of the agreement escape from his liability to repair. Special rules also apply in the case of furnished lettings.

Apart from these exceptions, the landlord may allow the house to fall to pieces so that it becomes uninhabitable, and the tenant will still be liable to pay the rent. A tenant should make sure that the tenancy agreement requires the landlord to do repairs. A usual provision is that the landlord shall be liable for structural and exterior repairs.

The tenant without any agreement or special terms will be liable to carry out proper repairs to the premises. He must not allow them to deteriorate more than is natural as a result of fair wear and tear, and subject to this he must at the end of the term hand back the premises to the landlord in the same condition as they were at the commencement. The exact amount of repair required will depend on the condition of the premises at the commencement of his occupation, and also on the district in which they are situated. The most usual expression is that the tenant shall be liable to put the house into "good tenantable repair," and this means that he must make it reasonably fit for the occupation of a tenant of the type who is likely to live in the district, having regard to the age and locality of the house.

Apart from express agreement, the tenant is liable to keep the property in a proper and workmanlike way and must, for example, repair windows which have been broken during his occupation, or any other damage that has been caused by himself or his family. The tenant is not bound to do decorative or ornamental repairs unless there is some clause in his agreement. Where he has been required by the agreement to do internal decorative repairs, he may apply to the Court to be exempted from his obligation on the grounds that it is unreasonable in the circumstances, and in particular, in view of the length of time which has yet to expire of his lease.

Where the landlord intends to pull down the premises at the end of the tenancy, he cannot complain or recover damages for any breach of covenant by the tenant to leave them in good repair. In almost all leases it is provided that, if the tenant fails to carry out his obligations, one of which is to repair, the landlord may put an end to the lease by re-entering on the premises. Before he can do this, however, it is necessary for him to serve on the tenant a notice specifying the exact nature of the breach of covenant and calling on the tenant to remedy it. This is called a Schedule of Dilapidations. The tenant must carry out the work in two months. The landlord must also give the tenant an opportunity of paying money compensation instead of having the lease forfeited. When this has been done the tenant may always apply to the Court for relief against the forfeiture, and the Court will usually make this order on the terms that the tenant makes good the breach of covenant which he has committed. (*See* FORFEITURE.)

In some cases a covenant to repair only requires the landlord or tenant to repair after notice, and the landlord is never liable for lack of repair until the fact that repair is required has been brought to his attention.

Fire.—If the premises are destroyed or rendered uninhabitable by fire, the tenant will not be relieved from his duty to pay the rent for the rest of the term, nor is the landlord bound to rebuild the house. The tenant should, therefore, have a clause inserted to the effect that if the premises are destroyed in whole or in part by fire, the tenant's liability for the rent shall come to an end until he is able to occupy them again. Where the tenancy is for a short time, e.g. a weekly tenancy, it may be determined by a weekly notice, and in such a case any provision against fire is not necessary, but in the case of long leases for a number of years some provision reducing the tenant's liability should always be inserted.

Where the tenant has not made any covenant to repair, he is not liable to build the house again if it is burnt down, but where there is a covenant to repair and keep in repair, he will be liable to rebuild the premises even if the fire was accidental, or was due to the malicious act of some third person.

Use of Premises.—Most leases provide that a tenant shall not use the premises for certain purposes, or in a certain way. It is frequently stated, where the landlord is himself a tenant, that the tenant shall observe the covenants contained in the landlord's lease. Where this occurs the tenant should make himself acquainted with the covenants contained in that lease. Where the tenant agrees to use a house as a private residence or dwelling house only, he cannot carry on any business there, or receive any orders, nor can he use it as a boarding house, or for the purpose of giving music lessons. It is also frequently provided that the tenant shall not permit any sale by auction, and that he shall not carry on any trade of business, or permit any outward show of business to be affixed to the premises. In some cases the tenant merely covenants not to carry on certain specified trades, e.g. public house, and in this case he will be entitled to use the premises for other trade purposes. The exact effect of a covenant not to carry on an offensive or noisome trade will depend to some extent on the nature of the premises and of the district where they are situated.

Animals.—Leases frequently contain provisions that the tenant shall not keep on the premises any animals. The object of the clause will usually be equally well obtained if the clause merely prohibits the tenant from keeping any animal in such a way as to be a nuisance or annoyance to other tenants or persons.

Alterations.—The tenant is usually forbidden to make any alterations on the premises, or to remove partitions, or doors, or cupboards, or other fixtures, or in any way to cut or injure any of the walls, floors, or timber. He is usually permitted to make these alterations if he gets the written consent of the landlord beforehand. But if the tenant contemplates making any alterations he should obtain permission from the landlord to do so before concluding his tenancy agreement.

Insurance.—A lease frequently contains a covenant on the part of the lessee to keep the premises insured against loss or damage by fire, and he is usually required to produce the insurance policy and receipts for the premiums when called upon to do so. When the insurance is done by the landlord and not by the tenant, the tenant usually agrees not to do anything which may render the insurance policy void or cause the company to increase the premium, and further agrees that, if by any act or default of his the insurance money is not payable on the house being burnt down, he should be liable for the amount. Thus, if the tenant were to keep on the premises any particularly inflammable materials, he might find that the insurance company would increase the premium, and he would be liable under this covenant.

Assignment and Sub-letting.—A tenant assigns the premises held by him when he transfers them for the whole of the remainder of the period of his lease to some other person. He sub-lets or under-lets the premises when he transfers them to some other person for a period shorter than the remainder of the period of his lease. In the absence of any provision in the agreement, a tenant is entitled either to assign or underlet without obtaining any permission from the landlord; but it is almost invariably provided in the agreement that the tenant is not to assign, sub-let or part with the possession of the whole or part of the premises without the previous written consent of the landlord. It is usual to add that the landlord's consent is not to be unreasonably withheld on proof being furnished of the respectability and financial responsibility of the proposed assignee or sub-tenant, but even if this is not expressly included such a provision is now implied in every letting. If the lease merely provides that the tenant is not to assign, sub-let, etc., without stating that the landlord's consent may be obtained, then the tenant cannot do so, nor can he require the landlord to give his consent even in the case of a respectable and responsible assignee.

When a tenant assigns, he remains liable for the rent and for the other obligations of the tenancy in the event of his assignee failing to carry them out. Where he sublets he remains himself primarily liable, and the sub-lessee is bound to pay the rent and fulfil the other obligations of the letting to the tenant and not to the landlord. Where the tenant is himself an assignee, i.e. where the original lease was not granted to him but to someone else by whom it was transferred to him—he remains liable for all the obligations of the lease during the time he is tenant; but if he assigns his interest, his liability

 made the Tenth day of
November One thousand
nine hundred and thirt.
———— B E T W E E N
ROBERT BROWN of 642
Hood Street Hampstead
(hereinafter called the landlord) and ELIZABETH QUEEN of 859 Rodney
Street Harrow (hereinafter called the Tenant) of the other part
W H E R E B Y IT IS A G R E E D as follows :-

1.   T H E Landlord shall let and the Tenant shall take the two
front rooms on the Ground floor at 642 Hood Street aforesaid on a
monthly tenancy from the Fourth December One thousand nine hundred
and thirty———   at a rent of FIVE POUNDS per month payable monthly
in advance on the Fourth day of each month

2.   DURING the said tenancy the Tenant shall be entitled to the use
(in common with the other tenants in the said house) of the entrance
hall common stairs bathrooms and lavatories in the said house

3.   T H E Landlord shall keep the said rooms in good tenantable
repair and in as good a state of decoration as the same are now in

4.   T H E Tenant shall not at any time assign or sublet the said
rooms or any part thereof without the previous written consent of
the Landlord but such consent shall not be unreasonably withheld in
the case of a responsible and respectable person

5.   T H E Tenant shall not use the said rooms or any part thereof
for any purpose other than that of private residence

6.   I F at any time the rent or any part thereof shall not be paid
within seven days of the date when it shall be due, whether legally
demanded or not or if the Tenant shall commit a breach of any of the
terms of this agreement the Landlord may determine the tenancy at
any time   Either party may determine the tenancy on the Fourth day
of any month by giving to the other one month's notice in writing of
such determination

        I N W I T N E S S whereof the parties hereto have hereunto
set their hands the day and year first before written

S I G N E D by the above-named)
ROBERT BROWN in the presence of:)   *Robert Brown.*

Eric Wilson,

927, Wolfe Street,

Hampstead, Clerk.

S I G N E D by the above-named)
ELIZABETH QUEEN in the presence)   *Bessie Queen*
of :   )

Frank H. Connett

500 Luton Road, Welyn,

Herts. "

Specimen Tenancy Agreement.

ceases altogether, irrespective of the fact whether or not the assignee carries out the terms of the lease. (*See* ASSIGNMENT [LEASES].)

Rent.—The amount of money which the tenant agrees to pay the landlord for the premises is called rent. This is due on the first moment of the morning of the day upon which it is payable under the agreement, but it is not in arrears until the end of that day, i.e. 24 hours later. It is usually the tenant's duty to send the rent to the landlord. If the rent is not paid, the landlord may, of course, sue the tenant for it; and it is also usually provided that, if it is unpaid for fifteen days after it is due, the landlord may re-enter the premises and determine the lease. This is called the "landlord's right of forfeiture" (*see* FORFEITURE), and the tenant is always entitled to apply to the Court for relief against the forfeiture which will usually be granted if the rent is paid. The fact that a power of forfeiture is given to the landlord after fifteen days does not mean that he cannot sue for the rent before that time.

The landlord has another very valuable right for the recovery of rent called "distress," which entitles him to go on the premises and seize goods which he may find there. This again may be exercised as soon as the rent is due, even though the lease does not give a power of re-entry to the landlord until the rent is fifteen days overdue. (*See* DISTRESS.)

When a lease is made by deed, that is by a document under seal, rent may be recovered even though it may be twenty years in arrear, and in other cases rent may be recovered for six years in arrear.

Rates and Taxes.—Whether the landlord or the tenant is to pay the rates and taxes will depend on the terms of the actual arrangement made between them. In small premises it is usual for the landlord to pay the rates and taxes, and thus the amount paid by the tenant to the landlord is paid partly in respect of rent and partly in respect of the rates.

Certain taxes are frequently called "Landlord's Taxes," and, when a tenant pays these, he is entitled in the absence of any agreement to the contrary to recover them from his landlord or to deduct them from the next rent. The most important of these is what is

called "Property Tax," that is income tax on the premises under Schedule A.

Normally the tenant pays the amount of the tax to the Inland Revenue and he is entitled to deduct the amount paid from the first payment thereafter made in respect of rent to the landlord. Any landlord who refuses to allow the deduction is liable to a penalty, and any agreement for the payment of the rent in full, without deduction on the terms that the landlord will repay the amount of the tax to the tenant, is void.

Assessment on Landlord.—In the case of (*a*) dwelling-houses of less annual value than £10 a year; (*b*) lands and buildings let for less than a year; (*c*) or houses let in different apartments or tenements and occupied by several persons—e.g. houses let in flats—the assessment is made on the landlord and the tenant pays his rent without any deduction. If the landlord fails to pay, the tax may be levied on the tenant.

In addition to the Property Tax the landlord in the absence of any agreement is also liable for Land Tax, Sewers Rates and Tithe Rent Charge, and if the tenant pays these he may recover them from the landlord.

Tenant's Taxes.—In the absence of any agreement to the contrary, the tenant must pay all other rates such as Inhabited House Duty and General Rates, and he is not entitled to make any deduction from the rent in respect of these. In practice the liability for the landlord's taxes is placed upon the tenant by the terms of the lease. A liability to pay "taxes" does not include "rates."

Quiet Enjoyment.—This covenant by the landlord that the tenant shall "quietly enjoy" the premises is one of the most important in the whole lease from the tenant's point of view. It means that the tenant is entitled to have the use of the property free from any interference from the landlord or from anyone else claiming under him. Even if no covenant for quiet enjoyment is stated, it is always implied. It protects the tenant not only against anyone to whom the landlord may have let the premises contrary to the rights of the tenant, but also against all disturbances committed or authorised by the landlord, that is acts of the landlord which prevent the tenant from enjoying the premises, even though they are not the assertion of any legal right but acts of physical interference. The covenant is only broken if the acts are done by the landlord or someone authorised by him; and if the person committing the acts is a stranger the landlord cannot be made liable.

End of the Tenancy.—Where the tenancy is for a fixed period of time it will come to an end at the end of that time, but if the tenant remains on in possession of the premises after the end of his tenancy and pays rent he will become a tenant from year to year. Until he pays rent he may be required to leave the premises and is not a tenant.

Where a tenant wishes to be relieved of the lease before it comes to an end, he may arrange with the landlord to surrender it to him. If he does this he will cease to be liable on any of the future obligations of the tenancy.

A surrender sometimes takes place where a tenant wishes to take a new lease before the end of his old one. The tenancy may also be terminated by the forfeiture of the landlord on the tenant committing a breach of covenant, which entitles the landlord to re-enter under the terms of the lease. The tenant here may nearly always obtain relief against the forfeiture.

Notice to Quit.—Where a tenancy is not for a fixed period of time but is a continuing tenancy, e.g. yearly, monthly or weekly—it will be brought to an end by a notice to quit given by either landlord or tenant. If the occupation is to cease on a certain day, e.g. in the case of a lease for three years—there is no need to give a notice. A notice to quit should always be in writing, and should be served on the person to whom it is addressed. It is not necessary to give it to the tenant himself, but it may be left with his wife, or servant, or other person on the premises. It will be sufficient if the notice is sent by post but it should be registered. The exact form of the notice is immaterial so long as it states clearly the intention of the person giving it to put an end to the tenancy at a certain date. It should state the premises in respect of which it is given. It need not specify the particular day on which the tenant's tenancy is to end, but, if a day is named, it must be the correct one. It may be given either by the landlord or tenant or by an agent of theirs, and again it may be given to an agent in the same way.

The length of the notice will depend upon the terms and length of the tenancy. The agreement may provide for some specific period of notice, and this period must be given. Where there is no express agreement, the notice will depend upon the length and nature of the tenancy. Thus, in a tenancy from year to year, the notice must be a half year's notice expiring with some current year of the tenancy. The half-year must be not merely six months but a full period of 182 days. If, however, the tenancy commenced on one of the usual quarter days, the notice must be given on the quarter day next but one before that on which the tenancy is to terminate. Thus, if a tenancy commenced on Christmas Day, it may be terminated in any year by notice given on or before Midsummer, June 24th.

In quarterly tenancies and monthly tenancies, a quarter or month's notice respectively must be given expiring at the end of one complete quarter or month from the day when the tenancy began. Thus, if the tenancy commenced on the tenth of a month it must be ended on the tenth of some later month. In weekly tenancies a week's notice is required, and this must expire on the day the rent becomes due. Most weekly tenancies run either from Saturday to Saturday or from Monday to Monday, and the notice should accordingly be given on or before the previous Friday or Sunday as the case may be. The notice may be served on a Sunday.

A notice which is given for too short a time or for the wrong day is bad and of no effect, and does not put an end to the tenancy. It should be observed that, if it is served too late for one day on which the tenancy might be ended, it is not considered as being effective for a later day. If the exact date on which the tenancy ends is doubtful, it would probably be good to require the tenant to quit "At the earliest possible moment." Even if the notice is not bad originally it may be waived, that is, withdrawn by mutual consent or by the act of the party giving it. In particular, if the landlord either distrains for or receives rent *due* after the expiration of the notice, he will be considered to have waived the notice. The important date is, however, not the date when the notice is given but the date when it expires, and so the landlord may accept rent due in the period

NOTICE TO QUIT.

WEEKLY TENANT - NOTICE BY LANDLORD.

To, Mr. James Black
I hereby give you notice to quit and deliver up on Monday the 14th day of June 193-, the rooms in my house at No 276, Trafalgar Road which you hold of me.

Yours faithfully,
Arthur Rowlands

1st June 193-.

WEEKLY TENANT - NOTICE BY TENANT

To. Mr. Arthur Whitacre.
I hereby give you notice of my intention to quit and give up possession on Monday the 14th day of June 1934, the rooms which I now hold of you in your house No 1001. Blake Street

Yours faithfully
Sarah Gray.

1st June 193-

NOTICE
TO
QUIT.
By the landlord to the tenant (above), and by the tenant to the landlord (right).

When there is any doubt as to the day of the week on which a weekly tenancy ends the following words may be used:-

To Mr Adam Brown,

I hereby give you notice to quit and deliver up to me at the end of the next complete week of the tenancy after the date hereof the possession of the premises at No 999 helcon Street, which you now hold of me.

Yours faithfully,

John Smith

1 St. June 193—

between the giving of the notice and the date when the tenancy comes to an end. He may also, of course, accept rent paid after the expiry of the notice so long as it was *due* before the notice expired.

Tenant refusing to leave.—If the tenant refuses to leave at the end of his tenancy the landlord is entitled to enter into possession of the premises without legal formality, provided that he can do so without committing a breach of the peace. In all cases, however, he should bring an action for ejectment against the tenant. This may be brought either in the High Court, or the County Court, or in the Police Court. The proper Court will be determined by the value of the premises. Where the premises are let for a term not exceeding seven years at a rent not exceeding £20 a year, and the

tenancy has been brought to an end, the landlord, if the tenant refuses to go out, may serve on him seven clear days' notice, e.g. given on a Tuesday to expire on the following Wednesday, and may then apply to the Police Court for a warrant for possession.

In the case of premises where neither the annual value not the rent exceeds £100 a year, and on which there has been no fine or premium, the landlord, when the term has expired or been determined by a notice to quit and the tenant refuses to go out, may bring proceedings in the local County Court. He may claim not only arrears of rent, but also an amount equivalent to what would be due for rent since the tenancy expired and up to the date of the proceedings. The legal name for this claim is "mesne profits."

In premises over this amount in value, or not complying with the above provisions, proceedings must be taken in the High Court.

Forfeiture.—Forfeiture takes place when the landlord puts an end to the tenancy and re-enters on the ground that the tenant has broken some term of the lease. The landlord is not bound to put an end to the tenancy in such a case, but may allow the tenancy to continue and may sue for damages. The lease usually provides that, if the rent shall at any time be in arrears for twenty-one days, or if the tenant shall make default in regard to any other condition of the lease, the landlord shall be entitled to re-enter on the premises and to retake possession. The effect of this is that the tenant has no more rights under the lease, nor is he bound to fulfil any further liabilities under it, but he remains liable for all breaches of covenant which have taken place before the landlord re-enters.

The landlord may deprive himself of his right of re-entering by waiver, that is, by doing some act, after he is aware of the breach of covenant, which recognises that the tenancy is still in existence. Such acts would be the acceptance of rent that accrued *due* after the date when the landlord is entitled to forfeit, or even taking proceedings to recover such rent by distraining or otherwise. The landlord, however, will not be taken to have waived the breach by anything he does after he has once clearly shewn that he intends to rely on the forfeiture.

The Tenant's Right to Relief.— The law will not enforce a forfeiture of a lease at the will of the landlord, but will always give to the tenant an opportunity of being relieved from the forfeiture on applying to the Court. Further, the landlord must always serve the tenant with a notice pointing out the breach of covenant which has taken place, and requiring him to remedy the breach or pay damages, and he cannot re-enter until a reasonable time has elapsed after that notice. (*See* AGRICULTURAL HOLDING; ASSIGNMENT; FORFEITURE; *and* SPECIAL SUPPLEMENT "RENT RESTRICTIONS.")

LANDLORD AND TENANT (SCOTS LAW).—The law of Scotland on this subject differs in many respects from that of England. In order to give the tenant any

right to the property, the contract for the lease, if it is for more than a year, must be entered into by a document in proper legal form known as a "Probative Writ." Leases for a period not exceeding a year may be verbal. If, however, a lease for a longer period is granted verbally, it may nevertheless be enforced in much the same manner as in English law if the party against whom it is desired to enforce it has done some act shewing that the lease has been made, or if the party desiring to enforce it has himself done some act which he would not have done had there not been a lease. Thus, if the tenant goes into possession or pays the rent, the lease may be proved, or again, if, where he is already in possession under an earlier lease, and wishes to prove that he has been granted a new lease, he makes such alterations to the premises which it is not conceivable he would have made had the lease been coming to an end, and had he not had rights to the property in addition to those under his old lease. This is known as Rei Interventus.

Rights of Tenant.—There is an implied warranty, i.e. promise, by the landlord that the premises let are reasonably fit for the purpose for which they are let, and if they are not, the tenant may claim damages. In the lease of a house the landlord is bound to execute repairs during the tenancy, and will be liable for damages if he does not. He is not bound, however, to do any repairs until he has been notified by the tenant that the repairs are needed. In the case of houses let for £26 a year or less, as in England, the landlord's liability is greater, and he is there liable for failure to repair even though he has not received notice. In Scotland the tenant is not bound to go on paying rent if the premises are destroyed, and even if the destruction is only partial he is entitled to a proportionate deduction from the rent. The relationship of landlord and tenant in Scotland is thus much less one-sided than in England in all these respects. If the landlord fails to carry out repairs, with the result that the premises are no longer fit for the purpose for which they were let, the tenant is no longer bound by the lease, but may leave the premises and terminate his liability. In England in the same position the tenant has no rights at all to claim damages or to leave the premises, unless the agreement expressly requires the landlord to repair, and even then the tenant's right is one of damages only. In Scotland, if the lack of repair is slight, the tenant cannot abandon the lease, but can only claim damages from the landlord. If he continues in the premises he is entitled to withhold his rent until any material defects in the premises have been repaired.

Duties of Tenant.—The tenant in his turn must use reasonable care of the premises. For example, he must not leave them in winter, when pipes are liable to burst, without turning off the water or giving notice to the landlord; and if he does so, and in consequence of pipes bursting the premises are damaged, he will be liable. Again, where the landlord has a right of hypothec, that is, a right to take the tenant's goods in payment of his rent, the tenant is bound to furnish the premises and keep them furnished. Rates in Scotland are divided into two portions, one being payable by the tenant and the other by the landlord.

Hypothec.—This is the landlord's right equivalent to the English remedy of distress. It is, however, a much less effective right, for he cannot exercise it except after an application to the Court, and further, it is only available for one year's rent and cannot be used unless it is put in force by applying to the Court for an order called sequestration within three months of the last term of payment of the rent, the payment of which is to be enforced. Hypothec has, in many cases, been abolished but still exists in leases of houses or shops. The goods which may be taken include the furniture in the house and the stock in the shop, and are known as "Invecta et Illata." Tools of trade are exempt. The hypothec covers goods which are on the premises even although they do not belong to the tenant, provided that they are not there merely for a temporary purpose. It does not cover goods which are the property of a lodger or of some member of the tenant's family.

Rent.—The landlord and tenant may agree on such terms, i.e. periods of payment of the rent, as they please, and if they do so agree the terms are to be called "conventional" terms. If no specified terms are agreed the "legal" terms will apply. In the case of houses these are the Martinmas after entry, i.e. the 11th November, and the Whitsun Day following, i.e. 15th May. The normal term of entering into a house in Scotland is 28th May.

Assignation.—As a general rule the tenant may assign his lease unless it expressly forbids him to do so. It is sometimes provided that the tenant shall not assign without the landlord's consent, and if there is such a provision in the lease the landlord may refuse to assent in all cases. When the assignation is complete the tenant ceases to be liable for anything except for arrears of rent up to the day of assignation. The assignee becomes liable for all future rents. Where the premises are not assigned but are sublet by the tenant to a sub-tenant, the tenant remains liable for all the rent, and must pay it whether or not his sub-tenant defaults in payment of the rent to him under the sub-lease.

The period of notice will vary with the length of the lease. Where land is let for agriculture or pasture, and is over two acres in extent, and the lease is for more than two years, notice must be given not less than one, or more than two years before its termination. If it is for less than two years, the notice must be six months before the termination. When houses are let, the notice must be given at least forty days before the end of the lease, except in cases where the lease is for less than four months, when the period of notice must be one-third of the total lease.

Small Houses.—Special provisions apply to small houses used as dwelling houses only and not let with a shop. What is a "small" dwelling house will depend on the population of the burgh in which the house is situated. When premises of this type are let, it is illegal to make the agreement more than two months before the let is to commence, and agreements made contrary to this provision are of no effect. All lets for a month or more must terminate only at noon on the 28th of the month, and lets for less than a month must terminate at noon on a Monday. If the lease is for three months or more, forty days' notice is required, and if for less than that time, the notice must be one-third of the total time of the let. The owner is liable in such houses for the share of the rates which in Scotland is borne by the occupier, known as the occupier's rates. A summary method is also provided for compelling a tenant to remove, who fails to do so on being given notice. All these provisions are very considerably affected by the provisions of the Rent Restriction Acts. (*See* SPECIAL SUPPLEMENT "RENT RESTRICTIONS.")

LAPSE.—A legacy of money or devise (i.e. gift by will), of land is said to lapse when it becomes ineffective, either because it is contrary to law or because the person to whom the money has been left (i.e. the legatee), has died before the testator. A legacy or devise will lapse in this way even though it is expressly given to the legatee "his executors, administrators, and assigns," or to the devisee and "his heirs." When a legacy is left to a person who is a child of the testator or other issue, e.g. grandchild, of his, and that child dies leaving children before the testator himself, there is an exception and the legacy or devise does not lapse. The gift takes effect as if the death of the legatee or devisee had taken place *immediately* after the death of the testator. The result of this is that if the legatee has left a will, the legacy which would have come to him from his parent had he lived is considered to be covered by the terms of the will, and will pass to any residuary legatee named in the will or otherwise according to its terms. If there is no will, the property will pass according to rules of succession on intestacy.

When a legacy lapses it will pass to the person appointed as a residuary legatee, if any, under the will of the person giving it; and if there is no residuary legatee or if the legacy which has lapsed was one given to a residuary legatee, the property will pass to the persons entitled according to the laws of intestacy. (*See* INTESTACY.)

LAPWINGS.—It is illegal for anyone between March 1st and August 31st to sell any Lapwing or Lapwings' eggs for human consumption, or to have either of these in his possession for the purpose of sale. This is enforceable by a fine not exceeding £5.

LARCENY.—Larceny is stealing. Anyone steals, who, without lawful excuse, takes and carries away the property of another person with the intention of permanently depriving that person of it. For the offence to be committed all these matters must be present; if any one of them is absent there is no larceny. If a man takes and carries away the goods of another believing that they are his, or that he has a legal right to take them, he does not commit larceny however wrong he may be in his belief as to his rights. Again, if he merely touches the thing he intends to steal but does not move it, he does not commit larceny, though his conduct may well amount to the offence of attempting to steal. Yet again, he may, without any kind of excuse at all, take and carry away another's property with the intention merely of using it for a particular purpose and then returning it. Here he will not be guilty of larceny because he did not, when he took it, intend to deprive the owner of it permanently. So frequently did cases occur of persons taking motor cars away for a short time but without any intention of really stealing them, that the Road Traffic Act, 1930, created a special offence of taking away a motor car without the consent of the owner.

What may be stolen.—Anything that is the property of another is capable of being stolen. At common law this was confined to personal chattels as distinct from land or things growing on, or forming part of, the land. Modern statutes, however, have made many things other than personal property capable of being stolen. Thus trees, cultivated roots, plants, fruits, or vegetables, though actually growing, are now articles in respect of which the offence of larceny may be committed. Gas and electricity, if fraudulently obtained by secret pipes or connections, are also property the unlawful taking of which constitutes larceny.

There are, of course, many things that are incapable of being stolen. Wild birds are not the property of anyone. A poacher may commit offences against the poaching laws but he does not actually steal the birds he obtains. This is so also with animals except those of a domestic kind, such as horses and dogs, or wild animals that are kept in captivity.

Who may commit Larceny.—Any person over eight years of age who has sufficient intelligence to form an intention to steal, can commit larceny. There are, however, special rules applying to thefts by husbands of their wives' property or vice versa. Husband or wife cannot in law steal the other's property while living together. But it is otherwise if they are living apart or if one is deserting or about to desert, the other. In such circumstances the ordinary law of larceny applies. ;

Larceny by Finding.—When a thing is found it does not by any means follow that the finder may lawfully keep it. Indeed he may commit larceny if he does so. If the article bears some mark showing who the owner is, and yet the finder when he takes it decides to appropriate to his own use and does so, he is guilty of larceny. Similarly, though the article itself may not bear any mark showing the owner, it may be found in circumstances which point to the owner, or at any rate to the possessor, sufficiently to make the finder guilty of larceny if he keeps it. Similar principles have been applied to cases where persons have been paid money, such as change, or given goods, by mistake. If it is clear that the person receiving the money or goods knew at the time of receiving them that the amount was wrong, and yet fraudulently took and kept them, he can be convicted of larceny.

Larceny by Servants.—A servant steals the property of his master when he unlawfully takes it out of his master's possession. This does not mean that he must actually remove it from his master's premises; if, with intent to deprive his master of it, the servant without lawful excuse places it in his own trunk or in some other hiding-place he has stolen it just as though he had already sold or pawned it.

Larceny by a Bailee.—When goods are placed in the temporary custody of another for a particular purpose they are said to be "bailed" and the custodian of them is called a "bailee." If, in such a case, the bailee fraudulently sells or pawns the goods he becomes guilty of "larceny as a bailee." An example of this would be theft by a carrier of goods entrusted to him.

Larceny by a Trick.—Larceny is not confined to cases of stealing property during the absence of the owner or in defiance of him. What of the man who, by means of some fraudulent trick, gets the owner of goods to let him have temporary possession of them? What of the bicycle thief who hires a bicycle for an hour and, so far from returning it to the owner, disappears and sells it for his own advantage? In such cases the law holds that the consent of the owner to parting with the possession of the thing lent is not a true consent, and that there is a taking without his consent. This is called "larceny by a trick." It is, of course, essential that the thief has an intention of stealing throughout. If he gets the goods honestly and later decides to keep them or dispose of them, he does not commit the crime of larceny by a trick, because in such circumstances it follows that the means he used to get them could not have been a fraudulent trick.

There are many well-known examples of larceny by a trick. The most persistent is perhaps some variation or other of the time-honoured confidence trick. The methods of thieves practising the confidence trick vary, but the basis of it is usually the same. The thief or thieves gain possession of some article of value from their victim, ostensibly as proof of his confidence in their honesty, and then make off with it so that he never sees it again.

The growth of the use of automatic machines in recent years has provided a new form of larceny. Obtaining goods from these machines by means of discs or worthless coins is, of course, as much stealing as is shoplifting.

The maximum punishments allowed by law for larceny vary according to the nature of the offence and the previous convictions of the offender. In some cases penal servitude for ten years may be imposed.

LATENT AMBIGUITY.—When, in a written document, there is some uncertainty as to the exact meaning of the words used in the document, these words are said to be ambiguous. This ambiguity may be either patent or latent. A patent ambiguity arises where there is an obvious discrepancy—as where a sum expressed in words does not agree with the sum expressed in figures, or where a blank has been left for a name. A latent ambiguity arises where the document appears at first sight to be perfectly clear but where, owing to some external circumstances, it is, in fact, not clear.

Thus, if in a will a gift is made of "my gold watch" there is at first sight no ambiguity in the document. If, however, it should be the case that the person making the will had two gold watches the document will be ambiguous.

The importance of the distinction lies in the rule that where there is a patent ambiguity in a document, verbal evidence is not allowed to shew the real meaning of the document, but where there is a latent ambiguity, verbal evidence of the circumstances relating to the document is admissible.

If it is stated in a will, "I leave a hundred pounds to my niece........," the name of the legatee not being inserted and the testator having had several nieces, there is a patent ambiguity, and no evidence would be admitted to show which niece he meant; but if he had said "I leave all my money to my niece Jane", and there had been two nieces of that name, evidence would be admitted to shew, for example, that the testator knew only one of these nieces, or that, from some other circumstances, he must have intended to refer particularly to one.

LATENT DEFECT.—A latent defect is one which cannot be discovered by the exercise of reasonable care and skill. The best example is that of a latent flaw in metal which no amount of testing would discover. As a general rule, when an accident occurs by reason of a latent defect, the injured person cannot recover damages, because the law does not impose a duty to protect people against dangers which cannot be discovered by the exercise of reasonable care and skill. (*See* DANGEROUS ARTICLES; DANGEROUS PREMISES.)

LAW.—The word law is used in many senses, as when we talk of a "law of nature" or "natural law" or of "moral laws." The law which is considered in the Courts is not a law of this kind but may be defined as "rules of conduct which may be enforced by the State." In former times jurists have given great attention to theoretical considerations of how law first came into being. Law, it is said, involves the giving up by each citizen of certain of his natural rights in return for a similar action on the part of his fellow citizens and it is this theory which gave rise to the idea of the "social contract." Under this theory law arises from a voluntary restriction of the liberty of each person, as where A is willing to agree to give up, his rights to strike B and receives in exchange the giving up by B of his right to strike A.

Law is also used in a rather special sense in England to distinguish it, as Common Law, from Equity. Both the rules of equity and

of common law are part of the law of the land and the distinction between them is largely historical. Another division is sometimes made between substantive and adjective law. Substantive law consists of the rights which each citizen has, while adjective law consists of the rules of procedure and practice in the Courts which are necessary to enable effect to be given to the rights created by substantive law. Thus, if A sells B goods, the substantive law gives to each of them certain rights. If either fails to observe the rights of the other, e.g. fails to take the goods or pay for them, or fails to deliver them, the substantive rights have been broken. It would, however, be of little use to a man to have rights unless he could enforce them, and the party whose rights have been infringed in the above example would take proceedings in the Courts to recover damages or other remedy for the breach of his rights. The rules which govern the method in which he will bring the matter before the Courts, e.g. the issue of the Writ and the pleadings in the action—are part of the adjective law.

LAW AGENT (SCOTS LAW).—This is the name applied in Scotland to a Solicitor. (*See* SOLICITOR [SCOTS LAW].)

LAW LIST.—The annual publication containing the names and professional addresses of Barristers and Solicitors. It also contains lists of members of the circuits, and other details.

LAW OFFICERS.—The Crown has two law officers in England and two in Scotland. In England the officers are known respectively as the Attorney-General and Solicitor-General and in Scotland as the Lord Advocate and Solicitor-General. It is the duty of these officers to advise the Crown on all legal questions arising in any part of the business of Government and to appear for it in prosecutions when instructed. Each officer receives a salary and additional fees for the actual work that he does when he is required to go into Court.

LAW REPORTS.—Reports of the decisions on law of High Court Judges have been made for many centuries. There are in existence numerous series of these reports compiled by lawyers. They are quoted in the Courts in the course of arguments by Counsel. Since 1865, a series known as the Law Reports has been published annually containing decisions of the High Court of Justice and The House of Lords in all branches of the law.

LAW SOCIETY.—The Law Society is an institution charged with the control of solicitors in their professional capacity. The committee of the Society, known as the Disciplinary Committee, has power to enquire into complaints about the conduct of solicitors, and where required, to strike solicitors off the rolls. The Law Society also conducts the admittance of solicitors to the profession, and superintends professional examinations. It was first formed in 1825. (*See* SOLICITOR.)

LAWYER.—Barristers and solicitors are both included in the general word "lawyer." It has not any technical significance; it merely means any qualified person who follows the profession of the law.

LAY-DAY.—When a ship is chartered the amount of time allowed to her in which to load and unload her cargo is usually stated. If she is occupied beyond the time fixed demurrage will be paid. The time fixed is usually called the "Lay-days" or "Running days." (*See* DEMURRAGE.)

LEADING CASE.—In English law the decisions of the Judges on questions of principle are cited in subsequent cases in order to ascertain what is the law on any particular point. Where a case decides the principles of a particular subject or branch of the law it is said to be a leading case.

LEADING QUESTION.—A leading question is one which suggests to a witness the answer that is expected. For instance, "Did you then leave the room?" is a leading question as distinct from, "What did you do then?", which is not. Counsel, when examining their own witnesses, are not generally permitted to put leading questions, but when cross-examining witnesses called by their opponents they may do so. In practice, counsel only refrain from putting leading questions to their own witnesses when they are asking about some point really in dispute.

LEASE.—A lease is the grant or "demise" of land and certain interests in land from one person to another for a smaller interest than a freehold, which is a right to land for ever. The person who grants the Lease is called the "Lessor," and the person who takes the Lease, the "Lessee."

The lessor may be the owner of the freehold, or he may himself be a Leaseholder holding the land under what is termed a "Superior Lease," in which event, the demise must be an interest which is less than the lessor's interest in the Superior Lease. It may be of such a nature that it can be put an end to at any time. This is called a "Tenancy at Will." Or it may be a tenancy which will continue until either party gives to the other six months' notice expiring at the end of any completed year. This is a "Tenancy from Year to Year." It may be for a fixed period, called a "Tenancy for Years." A lease is an estate "carved out" of the lessor's estate in the land. What is left to the lessor is called the "Reversion"—indicating that the land will revert to him at the end of the lease. (*See* LANDLORD AND TENANT.)

LEAVE AND LICENCE.—If anyone trespasses on land, or damages another's property or person, it is always a good defence to him in an action by the injured party to shew that what he did was done with the permission of the latter. When this plea is made it is described as one of Leave or Licence. A familiar example is when a person is injured in the course of taking part in some lawful sport or game such as football. If a player is sued for accidentally injuring another player the first can always say, "I was not guilty of any rough handling of the plaintiff over and above the normal handling which he had by implication agreed to receive when he consented to play the game. In other words, what I did was done with the leave and licence of the plaintiff." (*See* TRESPASS.)

LEGACIES.—All gifts left by a testator to his relatives, friends and to institutions are known as legacies, and the persons who are entitled to receive them are called legatees.

Legacies may be of several different kinds and it is important to distinguish between them, as the rights of the legatees differ in various respects according to which kind of legacy has been left to them.

General Legacies.—A general legacy is usually a gift of a definite sum of money such as: "I give and bequeath to my friend A the sum of £50." It need not necessarily be money, however, but may be a gift of anything of a particular kind, such as £100 stock, or a ring, or motor car, provided that the legacy does not refer to any specific stock, ring or motor car. It may also be cast in the form, "I give and bequeath the sum of £100 to my friend A to be spent on books." This is a general legacy because A, if he chooses, can accept the £100 in cash instead of in books. General legacies of sums of money are sometimes called pecuniary legacies, to distinguish them from general legacies which are not of sums of money.

Demonstrative Legacies.—A demonstrative legacy is a legacy of a sum of money where a particular fund is pointed out to satisfy it, e.g. "£100 to be paid out of the $3\frac{1}{2}\%$ Conversion Stock now standing in my name."

It would have been a general legacy if it has been the mere gift of £100. It would have been a specific legacy if it had been "the £100 $3\frac{1}{2}\%$ Conversion Stock now standing in my name." Therefore, to constitute a demonstrative legacy, there must be a gift of money and an indication of a specific piece of property from which the gift is to be paid.

Specific Legacies.—A specific legacy is a gift of a particular thing such as a specific ring or a specific motor car or specific shares. Thus "I give and bequeath to my friend A my house called Birch View." Or "I give and bequeath to my dear wife my mahogany book case," or "I give and bequeath to my son Rupert, my shares in the X Company"; all these are specific legacies.

Residuary Legacy. — A residuary legacy is a gift of a share in the residue of the estate of the deceased after the specific, demonstrative and general legacies have been paid. Thus "I give and bequeath to my two daughters A and B the whole of the residue of my property real and personal whatsoever in equal shares" is a residuary legacy, and A and B are the residuary legatees.

The importance of the distinction between the various kinds of legacies is due to the fact that when the time comes for payment the different classes of legatees have different rights as to payment of their legacies.

How the Terms of a Will are Observed.—When a person dies the property he leaves must be used to pay his debts and legacies in the following order:

1. The testamentary and funeral expenses must be paid. These include the costs of a decent funeral, the cost of taking out probate of his will, etc., and, if the whole of the estate is exhausted in this way, then neither his debtors nor his legatees will receive anything at all.

2. After testamentary and funeral expenses have been paid, then all the debts of the deceased must be paid and, if the payment of these exhausts the whole of the estate, then none of the legatees will receive a penny.

3. The two former items having been paid, it is the duty of the executors to pay the specific legacies even if the payment of these exhausts the whole of the remainder of the estate and none of the other legatees gets anything. Supposing that the amount of the estate remaining, after testamentary and funeral expenses and all debts have been paid, is not sufficient to satisfy all the specific legacies, then each specific legatee will receive only a portion of the value of his legacy, and all the specific legacies will abate, i.e. be reduced, in the same proportion.

There is, however, one very important exception to this. If the testator has disposed of the subject of the specific legacy during his life time, then the specific legatee gets nothing at all; e.g. if A is bequeathed "my diamond ring," and the testator sells the diamond ring before he dies, then A will receive nothing at all.

4. Next in priority of payment come general legacies. These will not be paid at all unless the estate has proved sufficient to pay all the specific legacies which are payable, but, this having been done, each of the general legatees has an equal right to the payment of his legacy, and if the estate is not sufficient for all to be paid in full then all will abate (be reduced) in the same proportion.

5. Demonstrative legacies occupy an anomalous position between pecuniary and general legacies. If the fund out of which the demonstrative legacy is to be paid is still in existence, then the demonstrative legatee is entitled to payment in full as if his legacy were a specific legacy, and it will not abate with the rest of the general legacies. If the fund out of which it was to be paid is no longer in existence, the legacy is not treated as a specific legacy (as in that case it would not be paid at all) but as a general

legacy, and the demonstrative legatee is entitled to his legacy as a general legatee, and if the general legacies abate, the demonstrative legacy will abate in the same proportion.

6. The last legacies to be paid are the residuary legacies, and until funeral and testamentary expenses, specific, demonstrative and general legacies have been all paid in full, the residuary legatees are not entitled to any payment at all.

Payment of Legacies.—The executors are under a duty to pay over the legacy to the legatee, but they are entitled to a reasonable time in which to do this, and cannot generally be forced to pay over the legacies until the end of a year after the death of the testator, though often they will do so long before this.

No legatee is entitled to his legacy until the executors have assented to his receiving it. Thus, if A has been bequeathed the house and furniture of the testator, he cannot insist upon going into possession until the executors assent to his doing so, and they may take a reasonable time to give their assent. The assent to the vesting of the legacy in the legatee may be given in writing, or verbally, or merely by handing over the property or money to the legatee. If the executors delay unduly in handing over the legacy, the legatee's rights are restricted to compelling them to do so by an administration action (q.v.), and he must not take the law into his own hands by seizing the property himself.

Legacies to Infants.—It should be remembered that the executors cannot pay a legacy over to an infant, but should appoint trustees for the infant who should hold the fund for the infant until he reaches the age of 21 years.

Another point that must be borne in mind by executors when a father or person in loco parentis gives a legacy to a child, is, that if after making the will he subsequently makes a gift to, or a settlement upon, that child for the purpose of setting him or her up in life, the gift or settlement is presumed to be in place of the legacy, and the legacy to the child will be adeemed or diminished by the amount of the gift or settlement. In order that this may happen, the following three conditions must be fulfilled. (1) The testator must be in loco parentis, i.e. he must either actually be the father or have undertaken the obligations of father by adoption or otherwise towards the child. (2) The gift or settlement must be made after the date of the will and: (3) It must be of the nature of a "portion," i.e. for the purpose of setting the child up in life, by purchasing a business or partnership, etc., but not merely by paying debts for the child. The doctrine does not apply to anyone who is not a child or quasi-child of the testator.

A similar position may arise where a settlement is made upon children before the will is made, leaving legacies to the children. In such a case if it is clear that the legacy was intended to take the place of the settlement for that child, the child has a right to elect whether he or she will take the legacy and forfeit the right under the settlement, or will forfeit the legacy and take the right under the settlement. In either of such cases, however, it is vitally important to consult a solicitor as to the position.

Double Legacies.—Further, where two legacies are left to the same person, each being of the same amount, and either no motive or the same motive is expressed for each, and both are left in the same will or codicil, the legatee will only take one legacy. If they are contained in different instruments, e.g. a will and a codicil, the legatee will take both unless both are of the same amount and expressed to be made for the same motive. This will never apply if the legacies are of different amounts.

Thus, supposing a testator leaves at two different places in his will "£100 to A," then A will receive not £200 but £100, because it will be assumed that the second legacy of £100 was put in by mistake. But if one of the £100 legacies was left in a will and the other in a codicil, A will be entitled to receive them both. If, on the other hand, both the legacy in the will and the legacy in the codicil were couched in some such form as "I give and bequeath the sum of £100 to A in recognition of the many years faithful service which he has rendered to me in the capacity of head gardener," then A will receive only £100, because the motive expressed is the same in both cases.

Legacies to Executors.—Where a testator leaves a legacy to one or more of his executors it is assumed that this legacy is by way of payment for the trouble caused him by being executor, and accordingly it will not be payable if the person named does not undertake the duties of executor. Accordingly, where a testator wishes the person named as executor to take the legacy whether he consents to act as executor or not, he should state so definitely in the will.

It is also worth while remembering that if one of the executors is a solicitor, and the testator expressly authorises him to charge for his professional services when acting as executor, this is a legacy.

Legacies to Attesting Witnesses.— Any legacy left to a person who witnesses a will is void, and the attesting witness is entitled to receive nothing.

Legacies to Charities.—A legacy to a charitable institution is treated in much the same way as an ordinary legacy, except in two respects. Apart from these differences it will abate in the ordinary way with the other legacies according to whether it is specific, demonstrative or general. The respects in which it differs are:

1. A testator leaving his money to a charitable institution can tie it up in a manner which he could not employ if the charity were an ordinary person. Thus he is not concerned with the rule that states that property cannot be tied up for more than twenty-one years after the death of a person who is alive at the time of the death of the testator, and he can, therefore, if he wishes, leave a sum of money to be invested for ever, and the income to be applied to some charitable purpose such as the provision of scholarships, the relief of the poor, etc.

2. If a testator leaves his money to a charity, and makes it clear that his intention was exclusively charitable, the legacy will not lapse because he has either described the charity by the wrong name, or because the charity has gone out of existence. The bequest, in such an event will go to a charity or charities whose objects are nearest to those of the charity described in the will. This is known as the cy-près doctrine. (*See* CHARITY.)

Lapse of Legacies.—Where for any reason a legacy given by a will is not payable, it is said to lapse and the property which would have been devoted to the legacy is treated as part of the residuary estate —i.e. it is treated as if it had never been made.

The chief causes for lapse of legacies in this manner, is where the beneficiary pre-

deceases the testator. Thus, if A leaves money to B, and B dies before A, the legacy to B lapses, and B's family or legatees receive nothing.

If, on the other hand, A dies before B, then although B dies before he receives the amount of the legacy, the legacy does not lapse, but forms part of B's estate and goes to the beneficiaries under his will, or under his intestacy.

This is why it is sometimes very important when two persons have died within a short time of each other, to know the exact time at which they died, for the important question as to whether a legacy lapses or not depends entirely upon whether the beneficiary has died before or after the testator. (*See* ADMINISTRATION ACTION; DEATH DUTIES; EXECUTORS AND ADMINISTRATORS; WILLS.)

LEGACY DUTY.—Legacy duty is a duty payable on all personalty, including within that term anything left by a deceased person except lands or leaseholds, and for this purpose a legacy need not have been specifically mentioned in the will; it is still a legacy even though it is only a share in residue, or even property passing to the next of kin on an intestacy. But the duty is payable only if the legacy is a pure gift, e.g. not if money was left by will to pay a debt. On the other hand, the forgiveness of a debt owed to the testator is equivalent to a legacy, and the person whose debt was forgiven is liable to pay legacy duty on it. A share in a partnership is a legacy even though the partnership property included land.

The rate of duty payable on a legacy depends upon the closeness of the relationship between the testator and the legatee. Where the relationship between them was that of husband or wife, or was lineal (i.e. where the testator was a grandson, granddaughter, son, daughter, father, mother, grandfather or grandmother), the rate is 1%. Where the relationship is that of brother or sister to the deceased, or their descendants (e.g. a relationship of uncle and nephew), 5%. In any other case, 10%. There are numerous exemptions from legacy duty, of which the chief are: (i) where the whole value of the personal estate, (i.e. excluding land) is less than £100; (ii) where the whole value of the estate that is liable to estate duty (including lands) is less than £1,000 and the estate duty has been paid thereon; (iii) the 1 % is not payable where the legacy in question is chargeable with estate duty, nor where the value of the estate for estate duty purposes is less than £15,000, nor where the total number of legacies left by the deceased do not exceed £1,000 in value or, if the legatee is the testator's widow or infant child, £2,000.

The value of the legacy for the purpose of computing the amount of duty payable is to be taken at the time that the payment is made, and not as at the time of the testator's death. This may be important in the case of stocks and shares.

It is generally the obligation of the executor to pay the duty, and he then deducts it from the legacy when he hands it over. But if the legacy is not money, so that a deduction cannot be made, the executor usually pays and the legatee reimburses him, though the Crown is at liberty to sue either of them. Until payment, interest on the legacy duty runs at 4 %. (*See* ESTATE DUTY; SUCCESSION DUTY.)

LEGAL AID.—Free legal aid can now be obtained by anyone who cannot afford to pay for it himself. In criminal cases tried on indictment the accused can, in certain circumstances, obtain a "defence certificate" entitling him to free legal assistance or he may by means of a dock brief (q.v.) himself engage any barrister present in court.

In civil proceedings, in the Supreme Court, and in Divorce proceedings, assistance is provided free for those who need it by the Poor Persons Committees administered by the Law Society.

Since, however, the majority of cases in which the poor man needs assistance are those dealt with by County Courts, a number of charitable societies have been formed to play the same part in these as the Poor Persons Committees do in the High Court and Assizes. Professional lawyers attend these Poor Man's Lawyer societies and give free advice and, if necessary, conduct the case in Court free of charge. If the case has to be dealt with in the High Court the applicant is sent to the Poor Persons Committee. Information about local Poor Man's Lawyers in London can be obtained from the Bentham Committee, 1, Lincoln's Inn Fields, W.C.2.

It sometimes happens that poor people who are injured in street accidents find that the first person they see on recovering consciousness is someone who offers to take their case to court and obtain heavy damages for them. There are also societies with imposing names who offer to do the same on condition that they receive 10 % of the money recovered. The consequences of going to such people who, if they are solicitors, are making themselves liable to be struck off the roll, are, that the unfortunate client gets either less than he is entitled to or else nothing but a heavy bill of costs. (*See* POOR PERSONS COMMITTEE; POOR PRISONERS.)

LEGAL EDUCATION, COUNCIL OF.—This is the body which conducts the education of students, who are intending to be called to the Bar, and examines them as to their legal qualifications. The Council has a staff of lecturers in various subjects and also a director of studies, who advises students as to the various courses they should pursue. Any student of any of the four Inns of Court is allowed to attend the lectures arranged for by the Council.

LEGAL ESTATE.—Under the doctrine of Trusts as established in English law it is possible to have either a legal estate or an equitable estate in land. Where land is held on trust, the legal estate is vested in the trustee and the equitable estate or beneficial ownership is vested in the person for whom the trustee holds the property. Since 1925 it is now possible to have legal estates of only two kinds—either an estate in fee simple or an estate for a term of years—i.e. a number of years. All other interests in land may still be created and take effect as equitable interests.

LEGAL RIGHTS (SCOTS LAW). The rights which a husband has in the property of his wife on her death and vice versa, and the rights of children in the property of their parents on death are known as legal rights. (*See* MARRIAGE [SCOTS LAW]; LEGITIM.)

LEGAL TENDER.—Legal tender is such coinage and Bank of England notes as, when offered separately or together in discharge of an obligation, are regarded in law as objects which the creditor is obliged to accept by way of payment.

The following are good legal tender:—
(i) Gold coins up to any amount.

16

(ii) Silver coins up to 40/-.

(iii) Copper coins up to 1/-.

(iv) Bank of England notes up to any amount, except that notes of £5 or more are not legal tender by the Bank of England itself or any of its branches.

Notes issued by a bank other than the Bank of England, e.g. the Bank of Scotland, cheques and bills of exchange are not good legal tender either in England or Scotland. If the tender is of a greater amount than is due, the debtor is not entitled to demand change. If a tender is bad in form, the payee will be deemed to have waived the irregularity if he refuses to accept the tender on some other ground without raising this objection. (*See* TENDER.)

LEGITIM (SCOTS LAW).—This is the name applied to the right which every child has in Scotland to succeed to a portion of the movable property—i.e. money, shares, goods, etc.—belonging to his or her father or mother at the time of the death of either. The amount of legitim will be either one third or one half of the movable estate, and it will be divided among all the children entitled to legitim. If there is a surviving spouse claiming his or her legal rights, i.e. jus relictae or jus relicti (*see* MARRIAGE [SCOTS LAW]), the legitim fund will be one third of the movable property, but if there is no surviving spouse, or if he or she has released all claim to legal rights, the legitim fund will be one half.

This may be illustrated by the following example. Suppose that John Smith dies leaving a widow and two sons, and his estate consists of heritable property, i.e. land, worth £1,000 and movable property worth £12,000. The widow will be entitled to claim one third of the movable property (£4,000) as her jus relictæ, and the two sons between them will be entitled to claim another third as legitim, i.e. £2,000 each.

How Right is Lost.—A child may be deprived of his right to legitim either by the terms of his parents' marriage contract (which gives some money to him expressly in place of legitim), or by his own express renunciation, or after his parent's death by the acceptance by him of some provision made for him in his parent's will and stated to be in place of legitim. When the claim of one child to legitim is discharged before the death, the result is that the full amount of legitim can be claimed by other children whose claim has not been discharged, and so their share is increased; but where the discharge of legitim by one child takes place after the death, e.g. by accepting a provision in place of legitim, the share of the other children is not increased, but the amount released by the discharge must be disposed of either according to the terms of any will of the deceased or according to the law of intestate succession if there is no will. (*See* INTESTACY [SCOTS LAW].)

The portion of the man's estate which he can dispose of by will or which, if no will is made, will be dealt with according to the rules of intestacy is known as "Dead's Part."

Collatio inter Liberos.—When the father has made advances to a child during his lifetime, e.g. for the purpose of setting him up in business, the child will not be allowed to claim his share in the legitim fund unless he is prepared to give credit for the amount which has been advanced to him. Thus, if there are two children, A and B, and A has received £5,000 during his father's life, and the legitim fund is £8,000; A cannot claim any part of that unless he is prepared to give credit for the £5,000 already received. This would then increase the legitim fund to £13,000 of which B would receive £6,500 and A would receive £1,500 in addition to the £5,000 he received during his father's life-time.

LEGITIMACY.—A child is legitimate when it was born of parents who were married to each other, or whose parents, in certain circumstances, subsequently married each other (*see* LEGITIMATION OF CHILDREN). The law also assumes that, until the contrary be proved, every child born of a married woman is the child of her husband, and, therefore, due to the difficulty of proving other paternity, many children in fact illegitimate are treated as if they were legitimate. (*See* BASTARDY; ILLEGITIMATE CHILDREN; LEGITIMATION OF CHILDREN.)

LEGITIMATION OF CHILDREN.—Before the Legitimacy Act of 1926, there was no means by which a bastard could be legitimated unless at the enormous expense of a special Act of Parliament. There was one exception to this rule: if the parents of the child subsequently got married, and it happened that the father of the child was, both at the time of the birth and at the time of the marriage, domiciled in a country by the law of which the subsequent marriage legitimated the child, then the child would be recognized in England and Wales as legitimate. Such cases were naturally very rare.

In 1926 an Act was passed which brings the law of England into line with that of Scotland and of most continental countries. It provides that where the parents of an illegitimate person marry (whether before or after the date of the Act), the illegitimate person, if living, shall be rendered legitimate. But he is not to be deemed to have been legitimate before the date of the marriage or before 1st January, 1927, which is the date when the Act came into operation, whichever is the later date. This latter provision may be of importance in relation to property, and especially in relation to succession on death; for example, Smith dies leaving £50 to each of Robinson's children, and then, a week later, Robinson marries a woman whose son John thereby becomes legitimate: John will have no claim to the £50, for a gift in a will to a "child" nearly always means to a legitimate child, and John was not legitimate at the date of Smith's death; he became so a week too late.

The only exception to this rule is that no child will become legitimate by the subsequent marriage of its parents if, at the time when it was born, one of its parents was married to a third person. In other words, a child born as the result of adultery must always remain illegitimate. In this connection, it is useful to remember that if a married woman living with her husband bears a child, that child will always be presumed to be the legitimate offspring of herself and her husband until the contrary is proved, and it is only very rarely that such proof can be obtained.

It is the duty of the parents of a child who has been legitimated by their subsequent marriage, to re-register the birth of the child. For this purpose, certain information must be furnished by both parents to the Registrar of births, deaths and marriages. Information as to these requirements should be obtained from the registrar, who is usually to be found at the local town hall.

Information need be furnished by only *one* parent when (i) the father's name was signed in the register on the original registration of the birth, or (ii) an affiliation order or other order establishing the paternity of the child has been made. The information must be furnished within three months after the date of the marriage. If the information is not furnished within that time, a fee of not more than ten shillings will be charged for registration, which otherwise is free. Even if the parents fail to re-register the child, he will nevertheless become automatically legitimate. (*Compare* ADOPTION *and see* BASTARDY; FATHER; MOTHER.)

LEGITIMATION OF CHILDREN (SCOTS LAW).—An illegitimate child will become legitimate if its parents marry after it has been born, so long as they were free to marry at the time when it was conceived. Thus, if either was married at that time to some third party, the subsequent marriage to the father or mother of the child will not make that child legitimate.

LETTER OF CREDIT.—This is the name applied to a letter written by one person to another requesting that other to advance money to a named person, and pledging the writer's credit for the repayment. It is thus a form of guarantee but it is not a negotiable instrument.

LETTERS OF ADMINISTRA- TION.—Where there are no executors to take probate of the will, letters of administration of the estate must be taken out. The person who takes them out is known as the administrator.

A person wishing to take out letters of administration should apply at the Principal Probate Registry at Somerset House or at the District Registry (as in the case of an executor). He must make out and leave at the Registry an ordinary affidavit for Inland Revenue purposes, setting out the full amount of the estate of the deceased. Like the executor also, he must make an "oath" in which he must set out his right to become administrator, viz., as a legatee under a will, or as next of kin, etc., and must account for the absence of any persons who may have a prior right to be administrators. He must also identify and describe the deceased, and state the gross value of the estate.

In addition to this, he must enter also into an "Administrator's Bond" (q.v.).

Records of all public documents, such as Letters Patent, and all State Documents—among them, Domesday Book—are kept in the Public Records Office, the interior of which is shown here.

When these formalities have been complied with the administrator is entitled to receive the letters of administration duly sealed from the registry. It is, however, always advisable to employ a solicitor in applying for letters of administration.

As with executors, administration will not be granted to more than four, or, if there is an infant beneficiary or any life interest under the intestacy, less than two.

As in the case of applications for grant of probate of wills, so in applications for administration, any person objecting may enter a caveat and the person applying for administration must serve a warning upon the caveator. If the caveator enters an appearance, a probate action must be started by writ in the High Court, or if the estate is less than £200 of personal property and £300 of real estate, by plaint and summons in the County Court having jurisdiction in the area where the deceased resided.

District Probate Registries in which Probate of Wills and Grants of Letters of Administration can be obtained exist in the following towns in England and Wales: Bangor, Birmingham, Blandford, Bodmin, Bristol, Carlisle, Carmarthen, Chester, Durham, Exeter, Gloucester, Ipswich, Lancaster, Leicester, Lewes, Lincoln, Liverpool, Llandaff, Manchester, Newcastle, Norwich, Nottingham, Oxford, Peterborough, Shrewsbury, Taunton, Wakefield, Winchester, York. (*See* ADMINISTRATION ACTION; ADMINISTRATOR'S BOND; EXECUTORS AND ADMINISTRATORS; INTESTACY; WILLS.)

LETTERS OF MARQUE.—When it is intended to use merchant ships for belligerent purposes against an enemy at sea, the Admiralty issue an authority for them so to act. The documents in which this authority is so contained are called Letters of Marque.

LETTERS PATENT.—When the Crown grants land or makes an appointment in the nature of an office, it does so by means of a document sealed with the Great Seal. These documents are not closed up, but left so that the Great Seal is visible. This is done because the document is in the nature of a public one, for information for all the King's subjects. Such documents are described as "Letters Patent."

LETTING.—The word letting is applied usually when a tenant agrees with a landlord to take premises for a certain period of time. It is also applied to goods which are held under a hire-purchase agreement. (*See* HIRE PURCHASE; LANDLORD AND TENANT.)

LEVANT AND COUCHANT.—Where a right to pasture so many cattle on common land is enjoyed by some person in respect of a piece of land occupied by him, the number of cattle which can be maintained during the winter by the produce of his land are said to be levant and couchant on the land.

LIBEL.—A libel is a statement concerning some person, which has a tendency to diminish the good opinion which others have of that person, and to expose him to public ridicule, hatred or contempt. A libel is a defamatory statement made in some permanent form, such as words, writing or pictures. An action for libel must be brought within six years of the publication of the libel. A libel may be a criminal as well as a civil offence. (*See* DEFAMATION.)

LIBRARIES.—Public Libraries are under the control of the Library Authority, which is a body of commissioners appointed by the local authority for that purpose. The local library authorities are under the general control of the Board of Education. The expenses of public libraries are paid out of the rates.

The Library Authority may make byelaws to regulate the use of the library and to prevent injury to, or destruction of, the books.

Anyone who maliciously destroys or damages any book belonging to a library open to the public, whether free or not, is guilty of an offence for which the maximum penalty is 6 months' hard labour, and, if the offender is a male under 16 years of age, whipping may be added.

It is also an offence with the same maximum penalty for any person to

(i) take out or use any book belonging to a public or circulating library if he knows that he is suffering from an infectious disease,

(ii) allow any such book to be used by any person known to be infected,

(iii) return any such book knowing it has been used by an infected person. Notice should be given to the local authority who will take steps to disinfect or destroy the book.

The library authority may not make any charge to inhabitants of the district for entering the library or borrowing books from it, but non-inhabitants when allowed to borrow books may be required to pay for so doing. Public libraries are not bound to lend books to non-inhabitants.

Any person who is not a householder or ratepayer wishing to take out a book must, before obtaining a reader's ticket entitling him to do so, produce a written guarantee from a householder or ratepayer accepting liability for loss of, or injury to books taken out, and for any fines that may be incurred. The guarantor can cancel his guarantee at any time if there is no liability existing thereunder.

In addition to acting as a lending library, public libraries contain reference books, papers and magazines which may be read on the premises.

The provision of a public library—but not a library for private subscribers—is a charitable purpose in law, e.g. in respect of charitable trusts.

Public libraries are exempt from property tax as literary institutions, but are not exempt from rates.

The publisher of every book, newspaper and magazine must, within one month, deliver a copy to the British Museum, which therefore contains a copy of everything that is published. The publisher must also, within one month of demand, deliver a copy to the libraries of Oxford, Cambridge and Dublin Universities, and of the Faculty of Advocates in Edinburgh and of the National Library of Wales. The demand must be made within 12 months of publication.

LICENCES.—For the carrying on of many trades, businesses or other activities, licences must be obtained from a proper authority. Licences are of two kinds: a licence may be issued for the purpose of obtaining revenue and is then usually known as an excise licence (e.g. for motor cars), or it may be required for the purpose of controlling the activity for which the licence is required (e.g. driving licences). Of the latter class, some are issued at the discretion of the authority who grants them, although that discretion must usually be exercised according to well-defined rules (e.g. licences to sell intoxicants); others may be claimed as of right by any subject, and the issuing authority has no *discretion*, while, at the same time, the issue of the licence may be refused on proper grounds (e.g. driving licences can be refused only if the right to obtain the licence has been suspended by a Court of Law, or if the applicant is physically unfit to drive). Licences are dealt with under the following separate titles:

"A" Licence;
Arms, Coat of;
Auctioneers;
"B" Licence;
Beer Dealers, see Excise; Intoxicating Liquors;
Beer Houses;
Betting;
Bookmakers;
Brewers, see Excise; Intoxicating Liquors;
"C" Licence;
Carriage and Carts;
Children Giving Public Entertainments, see Children;
Cider, see Intoxicating Liquors;
Cinematograph;
Dancing;
Distillers, see Excise;
Dogs;
Estate Agents;
Firearms, see Gun Licences;
Fishing;
Films;
Game Licences;
Glucose, see Excise;
Gun Licences;
Hackney Carriages;
Hawkers;
Horses, see Knackers;
House Agents;
Knackers;
Liqueurs, see Excise; Intoxicating Liquors;

Locomotives, see Special Supplement "Road Traffic";
Manservant;
Marriage;
Match Manufacturers, see Excise;
Methylated Spirits;
Moneylenders;
Motor and Motor Drivers, see Special Supplement "Road Traffic";
Music, see Dancing;
Patent Medicines, see Excise;
Pawnbrokers;
Pedlars;
Playing Cards, see Poisons; [Excise;
Railway Restaurant Cars, see Intoxicating Liquors;
Saccharine, see Excise;
Silk Yarn and Waste Manufacturers, see Excise;
Spirits, see Excise; Intoxicating Liquors;
Stills or Retorts, see Excise;
Sweets, see Excise, Intoxicating Liquors;
Sugar, see Excise;
Table Waters, see Excise;

TOBACCO;
THEATRES;
VALUERS, *see* ESTATE
    AGENTS;
VINEGAR MAKERS,
    see EXCISE;

WINE, *see* EXCISE;
INTOXICATING
    LIQUORS;
WIRELESS.

The word licence has also a variety of meanings in law, since, by derivation, it means only "permission." Thus a tenant may obtain a "licence" to assign his tenancy (*see* LANDLORD AND TENANT); the owner of water may give a fishing licence; the owner of land may give a "licence" to another person to use the land for a certain purpose, e.g. for the purpose of walking over it or parking his car on it; a convict may be released on "licence," i.e. by permission subject to conditions; the owner of copyright may give a "licence" to another person to publish the work. (*See* COPYRIGHT.)

LICENSED PREMISES. (*See* PUBLIC HOUSES.)

LICENSEE. (*See* PUBLICAN.)

LICENSING. *See* INTOXICATING LIQUOR.

LIEN.—When money is owed by one person to another, and the creditor has in his possession some property belonging to the debtor, he may in certain cases be entitled to refuse to hand over the property to the debtor until the debt has been paid. It should particularly be noticed that this does not in every case give the creditor a right to *sell* the property. He is merely entitled to hold it and although in certain cases (e.g. a hotel-keeper) a right to sell is also given, this is an exception to the general rule.

Possessory Lien.—A lien of this kind may be either general or particular. A general lien arises when the creditor is entitled to retain possession of the debtor's property until the debtor has paid him not only what may be due in respect of that property but also all sums owed to the creditor. A particular lien entitles the creditor only to retain the goods until money due in respect of those particular goods had been paid. Thus, suppose that A sends his suit of clothes to be cleaned by a tailor. The tailor may refuse to hand the clothes back to A until the amount due for cleaning has been paid. If, however, A owes the tailor not only in respect of these clothes, but also for the cleaning of other clothes which have already been returned to him,

the tailor cannot claim to refuse delivery of the suit of clothes he now has until the money due to him for work previously done has been paid He has only a particular lien. If he had a general lien he would be entitled to refuse delivery of the suit of clothes until everything due has been paid to him. A general lien may be created by virtue of some well-known custom, or else by the express terms of some agreement. It is recognised that solicitors, bankers, factors, and stockbrokers have a general lien.

A particular lien arises whenever work has been done or money expended on a chattel, provided that the chattel has been improved by the spending of the money or the doing of the work. Thus, if a car is taken to a garage to be repaired, and the repairs are done, the proprietor may refuse to hand over the car until the money has been paid. He would not, however, be entitled to retain the car on a lien for money which was due for garaging it or for petrol supplied, because in neither of these cases has the car been improved by what he has done.

How Lien is enforced.—As a general rule, the right of lien does not entitle the creditor to sell the goods, but he must hold them until the money is paid. Such a right is clearly of no very great value, and accordingly in some cases a right is given to sell. Thus, innkeepers, railway companies, shipowners, dock companies and persons who have held goods and not been paid, are entitled to enforce the lien by selling.

Loss of Lien.—A lien is lost if the possession of the goods is once given by the creditor to the debtor, even though the goods may afterwards again pass into the possession of the creditor. Thus, if A owes a garage £20 for repairs for his car, and the garage owner allows him, after the repairs have been done and the money is due, to take out his car and use it as he pleases, he loses his lien and does not recover it again when A brings the car back to the garage to be kept there.

Instances of Lien. Hotels.—Hotel proprietors have a lien on the goods belonging to a guest for the amount of his bill. This does not apply to boarding houses. Hotel proprietors have also a right of sale. (*See* HOTEL.)

Carriers.—A carrier has a lien over

goods for the amount due for their carriage. This is a particular lien. (*See* CARRIER.)

Solicitors.—Solicitors are entitled to retain all papers belonging to a client until a client has paid money due by him to the solicitors, whether the money became due for work done in connection with the papers detained or not (i.e. a general lien).

Seller of Goods.—When goods are being sold, and there is no agreement to give credit, the seller may refuse to hand over the goods until the price has been paid. Where he has agreed to give the buyer credit, he cannot exercise his lien unless the goods are still in his hands after the period of credit has expired, or unless the buyer becomes insolvent.

Warehouseman.—A warehouseman is entitled to retain goods until charges due for storing them are paid. This is a particular lien.

Maritime Lien.—This is a special right in maritime law which enables certain persons to claim payment of a debt out of the proceeds of a ship, cargo or freight. Seamen have this right for their wages, and the Master of a ship for his wages and disbursements. Such a lien is quite independent of possession, and merely means that the person entitled to it is in the position of a secured creditor and entitled to have his debt paid out of the ship, and to have the amount realized on the sale of the ship applied first in payment of his debt before it can be available for any other debts.

Equitable Lien.—A lien of this kind is also quite distinct from possession. A person who has sold land has an equitable lien over the land for the amount of the purchase money, that is, if the purchaser cannot pay the money or all of it, the seller may sell the land and pay himself what is due, even though the land has ceased to be his property and has been transferred to the purchaser.

LIFE INSURANCE.—There is a great variety of different forms of life insurance, some providing merely for the payment of a fixed sum upon the death of the policy holder, others known as "endowment policies" providing for the payment of a lump sum or a fixed permanent income for the remainder of his life upon a person attaining a certain age, together with a lump sum if he dies before reaching that age. In some policies, known as "with profits" policies, periodical bonuses are paid to the policy holder which may be cashed without affecting the principal moneys due under the policy. The exact terms of insurance, of course, differ with different policies, but both life and endowment policies are governed by the same rules.

A life insurance policy is unlike any other form of insurance except accident insurance in that it is not strictly a contract of indemnity. Thus any person is entitled to insure his own life for as great a sum as he pleases, and a husband can insure the life of his wife, or a wife the life of her husband in the same way; for the law assumes that everyone has an insurable interest in his own life, and that spouses have an insurable interest in the life of one another. This, however, is the limit to which the law will go, and no person is entitled to insure the life of another person for his own benefit except to the extent of his pecuniary interest in the life of the person insured.

Thus a father cannot insure his son's life for the father's benefit, but a creditor can insure the life of his debtor for an amount no greater than the amount of his debt, or an employee can insure the life of his employer if his employment will end upon the employer's death, but only to the extent of the wages due to him on the unexpired period of the contract of employment.

There is, however, a further variety of life insurance in which a husband or wife insures his or her life expressly for the benefit of the surviving spouse and children. This has a similar effect to making a settlement upon the spouse and children, and the insured person is considered as being a trustee for the persons who will eventually benefit under the policy, which is not considered as being part of the estate of the insured person. Thus, this sort of policy does not pass to the trustee in bankruptcy of the insured person unless it is the sort of settlement that would be void on bankruptcy (q.v.).

An applicant for a life insurance policy must fill up a proposal form. This generally asks questions as to age, general health, sobriety, employment, family history, etc. all of which questions must be answered with the most meticulous accuracy. If the applicant does not himself know the information required, he should not state it as a fact but should state it as a belief, as in that case the insurance company, if it cares to issue the policy on the strength of that answer, will not be able to declare it void if the answer subsequently proves to be inaccurate.

Further, the insurance company generally requires the names of two friends from whom enquiries may be made, and if the conditions of the policy provide that the applicant shall be liable for any misstatements made by the friends, the utmost care must be taken that their answers, too, are strictly accurate.

Finally, the applicant is generally examined by the medical officer of the company, and as this doctor will be an agent of the society, the applicant should take care that any statements made by him in the course of such examination are frank and true.

Very often the policy provides that the statements made in the proposal form and at the medical examination shall form part of the contract of insurance, and the most meticulous care must be taken throughout the whole negotiations.

Upon acceptance of the proposal the policy is usually issued forthwith, though a "cover note" may be given as in the case of fire insurance.

Life insurance policies besides the conditions common to other policies of insurance, generally contain a condition that the policy shall lapse unless the premiums are duly paid upon the dates on which they are due, or within the days of grace (generally thirty days) immediately after. There is sometimes a further clause which provides that in the event of the policy lapsing for this cause, it may be taken up again on certain conditions later, if arrears of premiums are paid.

They also frequently contain a condition that the policy shall become void if the insured person dies on the high seas or goes outside the limits of Europe without the licence of the directors of the insurance company, or if he dies by his own hand. Further, by the common law of England, no money will be payable if the insured person commits suicide, provided that the suicide does not take place during temporary insanity, or if he dies at the hands of justice, i.e. capital punishment. But there is a condition in most policies against the insured person dying by his own hand, and this applies whether the suicide is during temporary insanity or not.

Most modern insurance policies contain a large variety of alternative benefits to which the holder may become entitled, either by paying some additional premium or by indicating to the insurance company that he wishes to transfer to another kind of policy. In every case the exact terms of the policy must be looked at, and any explanatory booklets issued by the insurance company should be read with the greatest care, while most insurance companies and their agents are only too pleased to explain to policy holders the various types of policy which they may obtain. Persons contemplating insurance can obtain a comparison of the premiums charged by different companies from The Insurance Agents' Vade Mecum, (Waterlow & Sons, Ltd.)

Surrender Values.—Most modern insurance policies contain a provision that the holder may, if he wishes, either at any time, or after a fixed number of years, exchange his policy for an immediate cash payment known as its surrender value. If this is done, of course, the policy lapses, and no further sum is payable upon the death of the holder.

Even where the insurance policy does not give the holder a right to surrender the policy for a cash payment, a knowledge of the surrender value of the policy is useful as a rough indication of the amount of money which a lender would advance on the security of the policy. A lender, such as a bank, will generally advance an amount varying from two-thirds to three-quarters of the calculated surrender value.

Fully Paid-up Policies.—As an alternative to surrendering the policy in exchange for a cash payment of its surrender value, most insurance companies now permit the holder, after payment of a certain number of premiums, to exchange his ordinary policy for a fully paid-up policy. This ensures the payment of a lump sum upon death without the necessity of paying further premiums. Of course the total sum payable upon death where an ordinary policy has been exchanged for a fully paid-up policy is less than the amount which would otherwise have been payable, and a rough indication of the amount payable on a fully paid-up policy may be obtained by adding to the surrender value of the policy at the date of the exchange an allowance for interest on that sum up to the date upon which the policy moneys will become payable. Insurance companies also

16*

issue tables giving the paid-up values of their policies.

In the Case of Bankruptcy.—The rights under an insurance policy pass to the trustee in bankruptcy on the bankruptcy of the policy holder, to be applied for the benefit of his creditors, but this does not occur when the policy has been taken out by the policy holder for the benefit of his wife or children except where it is void as a voluntary settlement (q.v.).

An advantage of life insurance as a means of providing for dependants after death, or for making provision for old age under an endowment policy, is that a deduction in respect of the premiums payable may be made from the insured person's income for the purposes of income tax assessment. (*See* SPECIAL SUPPLEMENT "INCOME TAX.")

Although apart from husband and wife a person may not insure the life of another person in whom he has no insurable interest, once a policy has been taken out by a person upon his own life, he may assign, sell, transfer or otherwise deal with it as he pleases, this right being a noteworthy difference between life and fire insurance.

Assignment.—Anyone who acquires by assignment, by purchase or otherwise, an insurance policy upon the life of another, must give a written notice to the insurance company; and this should be given immediately, as his rights date from the receipt of the notice. After such notice, he is entitled to sue the insurance company in his own name, and has the same rights as to payment of premiums, taking a paid-up policy, etc. as the original policy holder, while the insurance company has the same rights against him as it would have had against the first policy holder, and can refuse to pay the policy moneys on the grounds of non-disclosure, etc. as if the policy were still held by the person whose life it insures.

Instead of selling or assigning the policy outright a policy holder may mortgage it to another person as a security for an advance, and this is the commonest way of dealing with an insurance policy. The effect is much the same as an assignment, and the person to whom the policy is mortgaged must give notice to the insurance company, and his rights will date from the receipt of such notice by them. In such cases the insurance policy is almost invariably deposited with the

person making the advance. The mortgage differs from an ordinary assignment, however, in that although, if the policy money becomes payable during the existence of the mortgage, the insurance company must pay it to the mortgagee who holds the policy, yet the mortgagee cannot retain all the money himself, but is under a duty, after deducting the amount owed to him by the mortgagor, to pay the balance to the mortgagor. Further, if during the currency of the policy the mortgagor pays off his debt, he is entitled to have the policy returned to him, and should give notice of this to the insurance company.

If, in such cases, the debtor fails to keep up the premiums upon the policy, the mortgagee, if holding the policy, may pay the premiums himself and add them to the amount of the debt, while in addition, if nothing is said to the contrary, any further advances made by the mortgagee to the mortgagor are presumed to be intended to be added to the debt secured by the policy.

As a general rule also, a person who pays premiums upon an insurance policy at the request of the policy holder, or a trustee who pays premiums in order to prevent the policy from lapsing, has a right to be recouped from the policy moneys, and should give notice of this to the insurance company. He has also a right, if the policy is in his possession, to retain it until the premiums have been repaid to him.

Another common transaction is for insurance companies, when themselves lending money, to insist that the borrower should take out an insurance policy upon his own life as security for the loan. In such a case the company may retain the policy until the loan is paid off, and if the borrower fails to keep up the premiums upon it, the company is entitled to declare the policy void and to sue for the full amount of the debt as if no premiums at all had been paid by the borrower.

Upon the death of the person whose life is insured by the policy the persons entitled to the policy money, i.e. the executors, or if the policy has been assigned the assignees, must prove the death to the satisfaction of the insurance company. In ordinary cases there is no difficulty as to this, and the insurance company is in any case only entitled to such proof as should satisfy a reasonable man. A death certificate is normally the most that can be required. If, however, a person disappears without leaving any information as to his whereabouts, and is not heard of for seven years, he is presumed to be dead and the policy moneys become payable.

A contract of life insurance must bear a sixpenny stamp. (*See* INSURANCE.)

LIGHTING OF HIGHWAYS.— Outside London the highway authorities are not bound to light the highways, although they have power to do so if they desire.

In London, street lighting is compulsory. (*See* HIGHWAYS.)

LIMITATIONS, STATUTES OF. —It is very common to hear such remarks as "The law never forgets" or "The long arm of the law," when a criminal is at last apprehended for a crime committed many years before. But it is only when his wrongful act is criminal that a man need always fear its consequences. At civil law, when a certain number of years have elapsed after the commission of an injury, the right of the injured person to his legal redress is barred. The length of time varies with the nature of the illegal act and with the position of the person who has committed the injury.

In any case, where the injury is committed by a public authority, such as a district or county council, proceedings must be started within six months under the Public Authorities (Protection) Act. Again, if you wish to sue the personal representatives of a deceased person for a wrong committed by the deceased against your property within six months before his death, you must start proceedings within six months after his death.

In addition to cases, however, where the plaintiffs belong to a class of persons specially protected, every person is protected by statute against law suits in which the right of action first accrued many years ago. The statute giving this protection is the Limitation Act of 1623, and applies to all actions of tort and simple contract, thus including an action to recover a simple debt.

Time within which Action must be brought.—The time laid down by the Statute of Limitations within which most actions of tort and simple contract must be brought is six years from the time when the cause of action first accrued. This is an important point, and one which is frequently imperfectly comprehended. Thus, if a contract is made on the 1st May to repay borrowed money on the 1st of August, the six years will run from the date when the cause of action first accrued, i.e. 1st of August, not from the date of the contract, the 1st May. The six-year term, however, does not apply to all actions in tort. In actions of slander (q.v.) where the words are actionable "per se," the period is two years. In actions for trespass to the person, it is four.

The periods are rather different in the case of actions founded on claims for land and actions for the recovery of debts due under deeds. Such cases are not governed by the Statute of Limitations, 1623, but by the Real Property Limitation Act of 1874 and the Civil Procedure Act, 1833; and the periods are twenty years in the cases of debts due under a deed and twelve in the case of claims to land or to monies charged on land.

Some Exceptions to the Rule.— These periods of time will not run where the person to whom the cause of action accrues is insane, or under age, or out of the country. So soon, however, as he becomes sound in mind, attains the age of twenty-one, or returns, the time begins to run.

If, however, time has begun to run, it will not be stopped by the occurrence of a subsequent disability. Again, if the person to whom the right of action has accrued is prevented from suing by some fraud on the part of another person, he is allowed to count the time as running from the date on which he discovered, or ought to have discovered, the fraud.

There is another matter which affects the date from which time will begin to run, and that is an acknowledgment of the debt or an unconditional promise to pay. Time begins to run afresh from the date of such acknowledgment. The acknowledgment must, however, be in writing and must be signed by the debtor. If the acknowledgment is only conditional it will still be quite sufficient if the condition is fulfilled within six years, but it will not be enough if accompanied by a refusal to pay.

Another method by which the effect of the Limitation Act, 1623, may be avoided is by part payment of the debt for which action is taken or by payment of interest. The circumstances should shew that it is improbable that the payment is made for any other purpose. (*See* ACTION; SLANDER; TORT.)

LIQUIDATED DAMAGES.
—*See* DAMAGES.

LIQUIDATOR.—When a Company is being wound up it is necessary to appoint some person known as a liquidator to divide its assets fairly and according to law among the creditors and shareholders. When he is appointed, he replaces the Directors in the control of the company's affairs.

A liquidator is usually an accountant and is entitled, as remuneration for his services, to a percentage calculated on the amount of property that comes into his hands. If any person, whether shareholder or creditor is dissatisfied with the liquidator's decisions he may appeal to the Court.

The liquidator works usually in close co-operation with the Board of Trade, and further is entitled to obtain the advice of the Court on all matters in which he wishes assistance relating to the winding up. When all the property has been distributed the winding-up is then complete, and the liquidator applies for his release.

The liquidator is also assisted by a committee of inspection of the creditors or shareholders. (*See* COMPANIES; WINDING-UP.)

LIQUOR LAWS.—*See* INTOXICATING LIQUOR.

LIS PENDENS.—Any action which is pending and has not been tried is Lis Pendens (a pending suit). Where such an action relates to land, it may be registered so that intending purchasers may know of the existence of the dispute.

LITTLETON, Sir Thomas (1407-1481).—A Judge of the Common Pleas, his Treatise on Tenures was the earliest treatise on the English law ever published. It is an exposition of the land law of the Middle Ages, and is perhaps better known in the form of the "First Book of Coke's Institutes," which is a commentary upon it.

LIVING.—A popular term applied to a Church of England benefice. (*See* BENEFICE.)

LOAN.—A loan may take either one or other of two forms: Firstly, it may be a loan for use of some article which is to be returned when the period of use has come to an end. An example of this type of loan is to be found when books are borrowed from a library. The contract of loan in this shape gives rise to the relationship known as a bailment (q.v.), the person borrowing the book being known as the bailee. The loan may or may not be gratuitous. In any case, the bailee's duty is to take reasonable care of the goods, but he is not liable for damage caused to them through ordinary wear and tear. When a loan is for value or other legal consideration it is called "hire" (q.v.) and where it is gratuitous the term "loan" is used.

The second form of loan takes place when the parties do not intend that the identical article which has been lent should be returned. Thus, if one man lends another a pound note he does not expect to have returned to him that identical note, but merely to receive the equivalent of a pound in value. Loans of this kind consist almost entirely of loans of money and are dealt with under the heading "Money-lending."

LOAN SOCIETY.—*See* DIVIDING SOCIETY.

LOCAL AUTHORITY.—"Local authority" is a term that is frequently used in Acts of Parliament, and its meaning is usually defined at the end of the Act in which it is used. It means either the County Council, the County Borough Council, the Borough Council, the Rural District Council or the Urban District Council. Therefore, when any application or communication has to be sent to a "local authority" it should be sent either to the Town Hall or to the County Hall of the area. (*See* LOCAL GOVERNMENT.)

LOCAL GOVERNMENT. — Local Government is that part of the government of the country which is not carried on directly by the central bodies, most of which are situated at Westminster. The chief bodies that have local administrative and legislative powers are mentioned below.

Parishes.—For local government purposes, the parish means the poor law parish, and must not be confused with the ecclesiastical parish. Only about 6,000 out of a total of about 13,500 English parishes have the same boundaries for both purposes.

Parishes may be urban or rural. A parish in a rural sanitary district is a rural parish. Urban parishes are not as important as rural parishes: they have no parish council and their powers are exercised by the vestry, but most of those powers have now been transferred to the Urban District Council.

Poor Law Unions.—These were amalgamations of parishes for the purpose of administering the Poor Law, and were controlled by Guardians. But the work of the unions is, since 1st April, 1930, transferred to the county or county borough councils, and the guardians have been replaced by Public Assistance Committees. (*See* POOR LAW.)

Urban Districts.—The total number of urban districts in England is about 800. The members of the council are elected, and each member holds office for three years (*see* ELECTIONS). The council must meet at least once a month, and the chairman is, ex-officio, a justice of the peace. The public are not entitled to be admitted to the meetings, though the press generally is.

Rural Districts.—The rural district was originally called the rural sanitary district, and comprised the same area as the poor law union. The members of the council are elected by the local government electors, and each councillor holds office for three years. The council must meet at least once a month. The chairman is, ex officio, a justice of the peace.

Municipal Boroughs.—Municipal boroughs are towns so constituted by royal charter, but all boroughs are now subject to the same general statutory provisions except in the case of the City of London, which is still governed by its ancient charters. Every borough is an urban district.

The mayor and most recent ex-mayor are justices of the peace. Some boroughs have been given a Royal grant to hold separate quarter sessions, with a salaried Recorder.

County Boroughs.—County boroughs number about eighty-three, and, in addition to having all the powers of municipal boroughs, they also have almost every power of county councils except in relation to judicial, parliamentary or other matters that are not purely administrative. For most purposes they are regarded as separate counties from the county in which they are situated.

Counties.—There are two kinds of counties—the administrative, and what may be called the ancient or parliamentary counties. For parliamentary and most judicial purposes the fifty-two ancient counties are used, but for administrative purposes there are sixty-two counties, the

increase in number being due to the creation of the county of London, the division of Cambridgeshire, Hampshire, Northamptonshire, Suffolk and Sussex into two parts each, and of Lincolnshire and Yorkshire into three.

The chief officers of the parliamentary county are the Lord Lieutenant, the Sheriff and Under-Sheriff, the Justices, the Clerk of the Peace and the Coroners. The administrative county, on the other hand, is governed by a county council composed of a Chairman, County Aldermen and Councillors. The whole council is elected by the local government electors, and the aldermen are chosen by the councillors so elected. They hold office for six years, while the councillors hold office for only three years. The chairman is also chosen by the councillors, and becomes a justice of the peace. The council must meet at least four times a year, and the public have no right to admission.

London.—London is both a county and a city. The City is of comparatively small area, and is governed by the Court of Common Council, of which there are 206 elected members. The City has two sheriffs who, contrary to the general rule, are elected. The chief other officers are the Recorder, the Chamberlain, the Clerk and the Common Serjeant, all of whose offices date from the earliest times.

The County of London, on the other hand, is of very considerable size, extending over 117 square miles, and overlapping the neighbouring counties. It was originally created in 1888 almost entirely for the purposes of administration, and is controlled, much in the same way as any other county, by its county council. The whole of the county was divided in 1899 into twenty-eight metropolitan boroughs, each of which is governed by a borough council. The borough of Westminster was raised to the dignity of a City in 1900.

The London police are also in two divisions: the City Police which are controlled by the City Corporation, and the Metropolitan Police which are controlled, not by the county, but directly by the Home Office. For the various matters dealt with by local authorities, *see under* the separate titles, e.g. EDUCATION; ELECTION; PUBLIC HEALTH; LICENCES, ETC.

LOCK-OUT.—A lock-out is the closing of a place of employment, or the stopping

of work by an employer, or the refusal by
him to continue to employ any number of
persons employed by him, in consequence of
a dispute, when such closing is done with
the purpose of compelling these persons
to accept terms or conditions of employment. A general lock-out by employers
combining together to coerce the Government or to further a dispute between workmen and employers in another industry, is
illegal. (*See* STRIKE; TRADE DISPUTE.)

LOCO PARENTIS.—A person not the
father of a child may put himself in the
position of one in loco parentis to the child,
and so incur the obligation to make provision
for the child. Whether a person has put
himself in loco parentis depends entirely
upon the facts of the case. A man may
undertake to pay for the education of a
child or even to educate it himself, but he
does not thereby put himself in the position
of a parent: he must act in such a way as to
indicate that he wishes to undertake all the
duties and liabilities of a father as if the
child were his own. (*See* ADOPTION;
BASTARDY; CHILDREN; FATHER; MOTHER.)

LODGER.—A lodger is distinct from a
tenant. In order to decide whether a person
is a lodger or a tenant it is necessary to find
whether he has exclusive possession of
premises or not. Merely occupying a room
in a house does not necessarily give the
occupier of it exclusive possession. If the
landlord retains control of the room, the
occupier is a lodger only. Whether or
not the landlord is retaining control may
be ascertained in many ways. Can he or
his servants enter as of right? Does he
supply and maintain the furniture? Is he
responsible for cleaning? These are all
points indicating the nature of the agreement as to the premises. It will thus be
seen that a person may be a lodger only,
though he may have the right to use several
rooms, while another may be a tenant
though he has only a single room.

It has been held that where a lodger is
provided with accommodation in a house, he
is entitled, in the absence of any special
agreement to the contrary, to the use of the
general conveniences of the house. He
must, of course, also be provided with
facilities for entering and leaving at all
reasonable times. He cannot lawfully be
ejected without notice unless his behaviour

is such that it is reasonable so to do. The
notice to be given on either side is usually
fixed when he arrives, but if this is not done
he is nevertheless entitled to, and in his
turn must give, reasonable notice. What is
reasonable is usually decided by reference
to the period for which rent is payable.
If it is payable weekly a week's notice is
reasonable, if monthly, then a month's.

A landlord cannot lawfully detain any
of a lodger's luggage or other goods as
security for rent due unless the lodger
agrees to this. If any landlord in the
Metropolitan Police District unlawfully detains any property of a lodger not exceeding
£15 in value, the lodger can, on complaint
before a police magistrate, obtain an order
for its return. Outside the Metropolitan
Police District, proceedings should normally
be brought in the local County Court.

If distress is levied upon goods in a house,
a lodger may recover any of his own goods
that have been taken, or which have been
threatened. He may do this by serving
upon the person who has levied the distress,
or his agent, a declaration in writing stating
what goods are his, and also the amount of
rent he himself then owes and the amounts
and dates of payment of his future instalments
of rent. It is necessary to attach to this
declaration a detailed inventory setting forth
exactly what goods the lodger claims as his
own. If after these things have been done
the person levying the distress does not hand
over to the tenant his goods, the tenant may
complain to the police court and obtain
an order for the return of the goods.
(*See* APARTMENTS; DISTRESS.)

LODGING HOUSE.—The control of
lodging-houses is vested in the local
authority in each district, and they may
make regulations with regard to the keeping
of lodging-houses and the number of
persons who may reside therein. These
duties are part of a local authority's work as
the authority in charge of the public health
of the district.

A house may not be used as a public
lodging-house unless it is rated for poor
relief at a sum of at least £10 per annum,
and is registered as a lodging-house with
the local authority, which must keep a
register for the purpose.

Common Lodging-house is a house
in which persons are lodged for a single

night, or less than a week at a time and which is open to all-comers, so as not to exclude any who are dirty and possibly infectious, or who from their character or appearance are likely to disseminate anything offensive or dangerous amongst the other inmates. Every local authority has to keep a register and enter the name and address of those who keep common lodging-houses, the situation of each such lodging-house, and the number of lodgers authorized to be received therein. A local authority must not register a house as a common lodging-house unless the house has been inspected and approved by an officer of the local authority. If the local authority requires it, the keeper must report the names of every person who resorted to the lodging-house during the preceding day or night. No person may keep a common lodging-house in the County of London as controlled by the London County Council without a licence from the London County Council. Such a licence when granted specifies the number of people who may occupy the premises, and when granted lasts for a year. The person licensed to keep the lodging-house must reside constantly in the house and must remain there every night from 9 p.m. to 6 a.m.

If any case of infectious disease occurs in a common lodging-house, the keeper of the house must at once notify the medical officer of health for the district. (*See* INFECTIOUS DISEASE; PUBLIC HEALTH.)

LOITERING.—Loitering without any criminal intention is not a crime under the general law of the land. The bye-laws of various bodies such as railways, however, render it punishable on certain premises. Loitering with any criminal intention, however, is very stringently guarded against. Any suspected person found loitering with intent to commit a felony in any street or public resort may be arrested by any police constable without warrant, and may be sentenced to three months' imprisonment. Similar powers of arrest and punishment exist in the case of persons found in enclosed premises, such as gardens, for any unlawful purpose. If anyone is found inside a building with intent to commit a felony in it he may be arrested by any person, whether a constable or not. In such cases, if the offender has previously been convicted of felony or misdemeanour, he may be sentenced to penal servitude for ten years, otherwise to penal servitude for five years.

LONDON COUNTY COUNCIL.—The London County Council controls the administration of the whole of the County of London, in which are included the Cities of London and of Westminster, together with the twenty-seven metropolitan boroughs. The council is composed of a chairman, 20 aldermen and 124 councillors, all of whom are elected by the local government electors. The council meets regularly on every Tuesday at 2.30 p.m., and at any other time when a special meeting is called. For its powers and duties, *see* LOCAL GOVERNMENT. (*See also* COMMON COUNCIL.)

LONDON PASSENGER TRANSPORT BOARD.—The L.P.T.B. is a Board of six persons and a chairman who hold office for not more than seven years. They are appointed by an advisory committee which consists of a number of ex-officio members including the Chairman of the L.C.C., the Chairman of the Committee of London Clearing Bankers, the President of the Law Society and the President of the Institute of Chartered Accountants. The object of making the appointments in this way is to avoid as far as possible all political influence, and this is still further secured by a rule which prohibits any member of Parliament from holding office on the Board. The public are also protected by a provision that no member of the Board may hold any shares in any of the undertakings under its control, and that if any member has an interest in any contemplated contract, he must disclose it to the rest of the Board. Any member who absents himself without leave for more than six months is disqualified.

How the Board came into existence.—The Board was formed with the object of bringing under one control the numerous bodies—tubes, trams and buses—which had previously catered for the passenger traffic of London. A rough circle was drawn round the outskirts of London and provision was made for the taking over by the Board of all passenger services operating within it with the exception of the surburban services of the four great railway companies, and such services as are operated partly in and partly out of the area. In order to secure co-ordination between railway and road passenger transport, provision is made for discussion and exchange of views between the L.P.T.B. and the railway companies; and the Railway Rates Tribunal (q.v.) is given special powers to fix and vary fares both by rail and road within the London passenger area and, if necessary, to order the provision of special facilities. The Board are specially directed by the Act to consider the possibilities of utilising the Thames for passenger transport.

Notice has to be given by the Board of the withdrawal of any service, and local authorities may protest to the Minister of Transport.

Powers.—The special powers conferred upon the Board by the Act include all those things necessary for the management and maintenance of the different services transferred under it, but for the protection of private traders the Board are forbidden to act as garage proprietors (except at Morden), though they may provide and charge for open or covered car-parks and may sell old vehicles, etc.

They are also forbidden to undertake the manufacture of car bodies, chassis or engines, except in so far as the various concerns since transferred to them have done in the past.

LONG FIRM FRAUDS.—This is a name given to an ingenious method of obtaining goods by false pretences. Where a person sets up in business and gives out that his business is an established one and being carried on bona fide, and obtains on credit quantities of goods from other firms, never intending to pay for those goods, he may be convicted of obtaining them by false pretences, and the fraud that he has practised is described as a long firm fraud. The essence of the crime is that the business which is being carried on by the accused person is a fictitious one, and run solely as a cover for the fraud he is practising on the firms from whom he obtains the goods. (*See* FALSE PRETENCES.)

LONG PULL.—A licensee sometimes pumps into a receptacle a larger amount of intoxicating liquor than his customer has asked for. This is called giving the "long pull" and is illegal as a customer must not be served with an amount of intoxicating liquor exceeding the amount he has ordered.

LORD ADVOCATE.—The Lord Advocate is the principal law officer of the Crown in Scotland corresponding to the Attorney-General in England. He is appointed by the Crown, and his duty is to act as public prosecutor and to appear in all cases in which the Crown is interested. It is for him to decide whether the prosecution should take place in the case of crimes committed and brought to his notice, and in this he corresponds to the Director of Public Prosecutions in England.

LORD CHIEF JUSTICE.—*See* CHIEF JUSTICE.

LORD HIGH CHANCELLOR.—*See* CHANCELLOR.

LORD HIGH STEWARD.—When a peer is tried for felony before the House of Lords, a member of that House is appointed to preside at the trial. He is called the Lord High Steward. As such, he acts as the Judge as in any other criminal trial, and the other peers present perform the duties of the jury. If the House of Lords is not in session when the peer is indicted for felony, a special Court known as the "Court of the High Steward" is set up to try him.

LORD JUSTICE.—There are five Lord Justices appointed to sit in the Court of Appeal, together with the Master of the Rolls. They usually sit in two divisions. They are appointed from eminent members of the Bar or from other Judges.

LORD JUSTICE CLERK.—The Lord Justice Clerk is, in the absence of the Lord Justice General or Lord President, the presiding Judge in the Court of Justiciary, i.e. the Criminal Court of Scotland. He also sits in the Civil Court, the Court of Session, where he presides over one of the Courts of Appeal called the Second Division.

LORD LIEUTENANT.—The Lord Lieutenant is the King's Representative in a county. He is charged with the defence of the county, and also has the duty of recommending candidates for appointment as Justices of the Peace. Lords Lieutenant are appointed by the Crown, and the office is an honorary one.

LORD MAYOR.—Certain cities, such as the Cities of London, York and Norwich, have as the chief officer of the municipality a Lord Mayor. His duties are similar to those of Mayors of Corporations. (*See*

The Interior of the House of Lords.

MAYOR.) The addition of the "Lord" is really only a title of honour.

LORD OF APPEAL.—The House of Lords, when sitting for judicial business, has amongst it members a certain number of Lords of Appeal. These are eminent lawyers who have been created peers so that they may sit in this capacity. Lords of Appeal receive a salary of £5,000 a year.

LORD ORDINARY.—In the Court of Session, the Judge before whom a case first comes is known as the Lord Ordinary. Although always addressed as "Lord" he is not in fact a Peer of the Realm nor even a Peer of Scotland, and the title really corresponds to the English form of address "Mr. Justice."

LORD PRESIDENT (SCOTS LAW).—The offices of Lord President and the Lord Justice General are now combined in one person. The Lord President is the supreme judicial officer in Scotland and head of the civil court the Court of Session. As Lord Justice General he presides over the Criminal Court, i.e. the Justiciary.

LORDS, HOUSE OF.—The House of Lords is the final Court of Appeal from both English and Scots Courts, and any person may, in a civil action, appeal from the decision of the Court of Appeal to the House of Lords. Attempts to discourage appeals are made by making the procedure as expensive as possible, but still many appeals go each year to the House of Lords.

The House of Lords, when sitting to hear appeals from the English or Scots Courts, is a very different body from the ordinary House of Lords. Although the Court is held in the same chamber where the House of Peers sits at Westminster, the only persons allowed to sit as members of the Court are the Lord Chancellor, who is the president, peers of parliament who have held high judicial office, and the Lords of Appeal in Ordinary who are lawyers and have been appointed by the Crown, generally with a life peerage, for this purpose. The House of Lords is also the second chamber through which all bills (except in special cases) must pass before they become law. Its procedure is, in general, the same as that of the House of Commons. (*See* APPEAL FROM HIGH COURT; COMMONS, HOUSE OF; PARLIAMENT; SUPREME COURT OF JUDICATURE.)

LOST PROPERTY.—When property of any sort is lost or mislaid, the owner does not lose his rights of ownership over it. He loses possession, but not the right to possession. It follows that the finder of such property does not become full owner of it, and can be forced to return it to the true owner or to pay damages if it has been sold, even though at the time of the sale he had no idea that he himself was not the full owner. But there is a rule of the English Common Law which says that any person who is in possession of property must be considered to be the owner of it until some other person can prove that *he himself* (not a third person) is the real owner. It is not sufficient to shew that the possessor is not the owner; it is also necessary to shew that the person claiming the goods is himself the owner. The result of this rule is that the finder of property becomes the owner of it except so far as regards the true owner, to whom he can be forced to restore it.

Keeping may be Theft.—Not only can the finder be sued in a civil action by the true owner if he refuses to restore, but he can also, in certain circumstances, be prosecuted for theft; for it is theft to keep property if there was, to the knowledge of the finder, a reasonable chance of discovering who was the owner. If, therefore, property of any value is found in the streets, it is theft to keep it as the owner could probably be traced through the police. But a finder is not expected to go to the length of advertising or incurring expense. If property is taken to the police and is not claimed, the finder may demand to have it handed back to him as, under the rule explained above, he is the owner of it except so far as concerns the person who originally lost it.

Property found in 'Buses.—It is necessary, however, to add one large qualification; for the law says that where property is found on the land, or in the possession of a third party, the finder has no claim to it at all, as the third party is already in possession of it. If lost property is found in a house or shop it must be handed to the owner thereof, or the finder will commit theft, and the position is exactly the same if it is found in the carriages, or on the platforms or approaches of a railway company, in the omnibus of an omnibus company, or in a taxi. In every case the finder must hand the property over to the owner of the premises or thing in which it was found, to the servants of the railway company, the conductor of the 'bus or the driver of the taxi. These employees are, of course, bound to hand it over to their employers.

Taxicabs.—Special laws have been made for taxi drivers. The driver of every hackney carriage is bound to make a search of his cab at the end of every hiring, and must take all unclaimed property left therein to a police station. If it is not reclaimed within three months, the police have power to sell it and to pay part of the proceeds to the driver. If it is reclaimed within that time the owner must compensate the driver for his time and trouble. Railway companies, the London Passenger Transport Board and other similar bodies have their own lost property offices to which application should be made; they also have power to sell unclaimed property after a reasonable period.

LOTTERY.—Any distribution of prizes by chance or lot is a lottery. It is an offence to sell any tickets in lotteries or to publish schemes for lotteries. It is also an offence to keep any premises for conducting lotteries thereat. For a full account of the law relating to this subject, see SPECIAL SUPPLEMENT "GAMBLING."

LUGGAGE.—Although railway companies are not common carriers (q.v.) of passengers, they are common carriers of passengers' luggage. In return for the standard fare the company contracts to carry not only the passenger, but also a certain amount of personal luggage. For any loss or delay of or damage to such luggage the company is absolutely liable whether guilty of negligence or not, and even if it is stolen by some trespasser upon the railway property. The maximum amount of luggage which may be carried is 150 lbs. for a first- and 100 lbs. for a third-class ticket; for any excess an extra charge must be paid. As the company is not bound to carry anything which is not "luggage" it is important to know what this may consist of. The law on this point is not at all clear, but apparently anything is "luggage" which is "usually or ordinarily carried as such" and "which is intended for the use and convenience of the passenger during, or at the end of his journey."

A Rocking Horse not Personal Luggage.—Clothes, tools, books and shot-guns have been held to be personal luggage, whilst among those things which have been held to be excluded by the definition are trade samples, a bicycle and a rocking horse. The obligation is also confined to the personal luggage of the passenger; if the latter is travelling with another's luggage, he can be made to pay for the carriage of it and, if he does not, the company are only liable if the luggage is damaged by negligence, i.e. are not common carriers.

The Carriers' Act of 1830 applies to the carriage of luggage, and the company are not liable except for delay in respect of a number of valuable things, including coin, notes, silver, jewellery, lace, furs, clocks and watches, pictures and glass, the combined value of which in any one package exceeds £25, unless a declaration of value was made to the company when the ticket was purchased, and an extra charge—if demanded—paid, or the loss can be proved

to have been caused by the felonious, i.e. criminal, act of a servant of the railway.

Excursion Trains.—In addition, when granting exceptional facilities, such as cheap tickets, the railway companies generally limit their liability and often refuse to the passenger the right to take more than a very small amount of luggage with him. This course is usually adopted for excursion trains and cheap day returns. In order to encourage traffic, certain kinds of persons, such as commercial travellers and touring theatrical companies, etc., are allowed to take with them free of charge a certain amount of what is not, properly speaking, personal luggage. The Standard Conditions of Passenger Traffic issued by the companies now provide that wherever such a concession is made, the company is to be relieved from all liability.

The company's liability for personal luggage begins as soon as the luggage is first brought upon its premises, provided that this is done a reasonable time before the train starts (45 minutes to 1 hour has been held a reasonable time for catching an express from a London terminus) and continues until a reasonable time after the train has reached the station to which the passenger was travelling; but the passenger must be ready within a few minutes to receive his luggage from the van, though the company may remain liable until he has got it on a cab or out of the station. If luggage is left for an unreasonable time with a porter, the company are not liable. It should be left in a railway cloak-room (q.v.). Their liability, however, does extend throughout the journey; if luggage is lost, injured or stolen they are, subject to the exceptions set out above, bound to make good the loss; and this is so even though the passenger may have left it in one carriage whilst he went to sit in another or to take a meal in the restaurant car, or though he may have placed it in the corridor. It is the passenger's duty to see that any luggage which he had with him in the carriage is removed when he gets out, but the company are bound to unload anything in the van. (See RAILWAYS; RAILWAY PASSENGERS.)

LUNATICS.—Although it is still usual to speak of lunatics in ordinary conversation, this word is no longer recognised in law except in the case of persons detained as lunatics abroad and criminal lunatics (persons who have been found guilty but insane by a Criminal Court and have been sentenced to "be detained during His Majesty's pleasure"); the correct legal expression is "persons of unsound mind." In dealing with such persons, a distinction is drawn between those who were born mentally normal but have become insane through the growth of an hallucination or delusion, or from mental disease or decay, and those who were born abnormal or became so shortly after birth.

There is no legal definition of mental illness in the first sense, and it is a question rather for doctors than for lawyers or laymen, but it must be appreciated that mere eccentricities, even though very pronounced, do not of themselves constitute mental illness. There must be some delusion or belief which no reasonable man could possibly hold, and which the person suffering from it cannot be persuaded for any length of time is fallacious; or some serious deterioration of reasoning power as a result of mental disease or decay. Such persons are certifiable under the Lunacy Acts, 1890, as of unsound mind.

Mental Defectives.—In the second sense—persons abnormal from birth—mental illness has received a statutory definition in the Mental Deficiency Act of 1913. A mental defective is a person whose mental incapacity originated at birth or within a few years of birth. The Act divides them into four classes, idiots, imbeciles, feeble-minded persons and moral imbeciles. The distinctions between these classes are important, as the procedure on obtaining a certificate varies. It is easier to get a certificate where the patient can be described as an idiot or imbecile than if he can only be described as feeble minded or as a moral imbecile. (*See* DETENTION OF LUNATICS.) An idiot as defined by the act is a "person who from an early age has been unable to guard against common physical dangers;" some one, that is, who needs constant care and supervision for his own safety. Age is immaterial. No matter what his age, a person can be an idiot (or for that matter any other type of mental defective) provided that his disability dates from early childhood.

An imbecile is "a person who from an early age has been incapable of managing himself or his affairs, or of being taught to do so." To fall within this class a mental defective need not be as helpless as an idiot, but must nevertheless require a certain amount of supervision to keep him clean and healthy.

A feeble-minded person is very similar to an imbecile. He is defined as "a person who from an early age has required supervision, or who is incapable of deriving proper benefit from the ordinary schools." The amount of supervision necessary in such a case is less than that needed for imbeciles and the commonest cases are children who from some mental defect are unable to take advantage of the ordinary schooling provided for normal children, but could probably be educated to a certain limited extent if they were sent to schools which catered specially for their needs.

Moral imbeciles, the fourth and last class of mental defectives, are "persons suffering from some permanent mental defect, who in addition have strong, vicious or immoral habits or desires, and who cannot be restrained by punishment." No one can be a moral imbecile unless his mental defect dates from an early age, and is one which is not likely to improve.

A person who is unable to distinguish between right or wrong will almost certainly be a person of unsound mind within the Lunacy Acts, or in common speech, a lunatic; but it often happens that a person, though recognising that what he does is wrong, is impelled to do it by some mental urge so strong that the prospect of certain punishment will not deter him. Such a person is a moral imbecile. It would be senseless to punish him for his acts, for one, at any rate, of the objects of punishment is to deter the victim from repeating his offence in the future; nevertheless it would be clearly undesirable that he should not be subject to some restraint.

There is yet one more class of person who is affected by the different Lunacy and Mental Deficiency Acts: namely, persons whose mental affliction is of such a nature that in the opinion of two doctors it could probably be relieved by not more than six months' medical treatment.

Lunatics "So Found."—There is another and a different method of distinction which divides persons of unsound mind so found and those not so found. This distinction is founded on the two different methods of getting anybody declared a person of unsound mind. A person of unsound mind "so found" is a person who has been declared of unsound mind as the result of an inquisition in lunacy, i.e. a trial in the High Court of Justice, generally before a jury. A person not so found is a person against whom a reception order has been made (q.v.). Persons so found are incapable in law of doing any act, and cannot have lucid intervals, i.e. temporary sane periods; persons not so found may legally act during a lucid interval. The distinction is not of great importance, as inquisitions in lunacy are extremely rare. The only case in which they are at all likely to be necessary is where it is desired to prevent a person of unsound mind from marrying and so giving his wife a right to his property. Persons of unsound mind and mental defectives may be placed and detained in mental hospitals or houses approved by the Board of Control, or under the charge of an approved guardian. In some cases this can be done without getting an order from any Court, but it is usually necessary to get a reception order from a "judicial authority," which expression includes a County Court Judge, a J.P. specially elected by his fellows, or a Stipendiary or a Metropolitan Police Magistrate.

Release.—All detained persons suffering from mental illness must be visited regularly by the Inspectors and Members of the Lunacy Board of Control, and in the case of persons detained in any institution maintained by a Local Authority (such as a County Council or Borough Council), by members of its visiting committee. Almost any of these persons can procure a patient's release, and in most cases, except where a doctor certifies that it would be dangerous, the person who presented the petition for the reception order can also do so. (*See* ASYLUMS; CERTIFICATION OF LUNATICS; DETENTION OF LUNATICS.)

Remedies for Wrongful Detention. —Any person who presents a petition for a reception order when he actually knows that there is no possible ground for it, any doctor who signs a certificate which he knows to be false, and any Magistrate or official who acts in bad faith, can be sued for damages in an action for false imprisonment and will usually also be liable to be prosecuted for a criminal offence. But there is a special clause of an Act of Parliament which says that no person shall be liable either civilly (that is, to an action for damages) or criminally for presenting a petition for a reception order: in the case of a judicial authority, for making such an order; or in the case of officials, managers of mental institutes, etc., acting on and carrying out such an order, unless he acted in bad faith or without reasonable care. This means that only in the worst and most flagrant of cases will it ever be possible to bring an action. Before any action can be brought the leave of a High Court Judge must first be obtained.

Can a Lunatic Make a Contract or Marry ?—An ordinary contract made with a person suffering from mental illness is perfectly valid and enforceable unless the other party knew of the defect at the time when he entered into the contract. Where this knowledge existed, the mental patient, or those responsible for managing his affairs (the receiver or committee of his estate) have an option to treat the contract as valid or as void. Contracts for the purchase of things which were necessary for the mental patient (and, in determining what was necessary, one must have regard to his station and position in life, and to the extent to which he was already supplied), can be enforced against him even though the other party knew of his condition; but the price which the patient is liable to pay will not necessarily be the price agreed upon at the time of the sale. It will be what the Court considers a reasonable price for the goods in question.

A person of unsound mind so found, that is, who has been declared to be insane as the result of an "inquisition in lunacy" (*see* CERTIFICATION OF LUNATICS.), is incapable of contracting a valid marriage, and any ceremony he may go through will be of no effect, but in the far commoner case of persons of unsound mind who are not so found, a marriage will be perfectly good and legal unless he or she did not understand the nature of the ceremony and of the obligations assumed under it. Mental unsoundness subsequent to the marriage is not a ground for divorce nor for a judicial separation; but the sane party to a marriage has special rights with regard to the presentation of petitions for reception orders as well as the administration of the other party's property.

A Lunatic's Will.—A person of unsound mind so found is incapable of making a valid will even during a lucid interval; persons not so found can do so during a lucid interval, but it must be shewn that they fully appreciated their duties, obligations and family ties. Any person who believes that at the date when a will was made the testator was mentally unsound, can serve a notice, which may be obtained from any Registry of the High Court, on the executors of the will, called a caveat, which forces them to bring an action to have the question decided in the Probate Division of the High Court. Mere eccentricities, although very pronounced, and unreasonable dislikes or affections are not "insanity," and will not make a will void unless it can be shewn that they are the result of delusions.

A contract to act as agent is terminated by the insanity of the principal, even though the agent was not aware of it; but a contract of partnership is not, though insanity is one of the grounds on which a Judge may dissolve a partnership.

The Management of a Lunatic's Property.—It often happens that a person of unsound mind is entitled to certain property. Whether or not he is detained or certified as being of unsound mind, it will probably be undesirable in such a case that he should continue to manage it, or to have any power of disposition over it; and indeed, as will appear later, if a person of unsound mind does not enter into any contract with another person, the former (or his receiver) (*see below*) may avoid it (set it aside) if he can shew that the latter knew he was not normal at the time when the contract was made. It is not, however, permissible for the relatives, friends or agents of a person of unsound mind to administer his property for him without first getting an order from the Court authorizing them to do so. If they act without such an order, the patient and his property will not be in any way liable, while the person who acted will be liable to pay damages to anybody affected.

Appointment of a Receiver.—Applications for the appointment of a receiver should be made where possible by the husband or wife, or nearest relative of the patient, but they may also be made by the executors or trustees of any deed or will under which the patient is entitled to property. If no relative is in a position to act (as for instance if they are all abroad or under age), then application may be made by a friend of the patient, but he will have to explain to the Court why he, and not a relative is applying, and the Court will only proceed with caution. Applications may also be made by any creditor of the patient or by the Official Solicitor. The latter is a person who is appointed by the Court to look after the interests of persons of unsound mind and to represent them in Court, etc., when necessary. (*See* ASYLUMS; BOARD OF CONTROL; CERTIFICATION OF LUNATICS; DETENTION OF LUNATICS.)

McCARDIE, Mr. Justice (1869-1933).—At the Bar Sir Henry McCardie had a good commercial practice and the reputation of a sound lawyer, but it was on the Bench, which he ascended in 1916, that he became so widely known to the general public. His great legal knowledge and his practice of citing all relevant authorities made his judgments of the greatest use to lawyers for reference to the legal questions with which they dealt. He was an outspoken reformer of the Law, in fact he has been called "A Crusader on the Bench." In consequence he found himself sometimes in conflict with the more conservative legal points of view, as in his trial of the O'Dwyer libel action over the affair at Amritsar. He had modern views on birth control and matrimonial affairs, and many of his decisions, to which the greatest publicity was given, dealt with the status of married women.

MACMILLAN, Lord (1873-).—One of the soundest lawyers of the day, Lord Macmillan was formerly at the Scottish Bar. After occupying the post of Lord Advocate he was made a Lord of Appeal in 1930. He has been chairman of many committees, notably among them those to consider the law as to Lunacy, as to Street Offences and as to Income Tax Consolidation.

Mr. Justice McCardie.

MAGISTRATE.—(*See* JUSTICE OF THE PEACE.)

MAIM.—(*See* MAYHEM.)

MAINTENANCE.—Although it is impossible to recover damages from anyone who institutes civil proceedings against another party from malicious motives, the law looks askance upon those persons who, although a right of their own has not been infringed, support with money or legal assistance another person whose right has been infringed. It is still a criminal offence to support with money-gifts an action in which a person is not himself interested.

In the ordinary way this is the crime of Maintenance, but if the financial support is given in return for a promise of a share of the proceeds of the action, it becomes Champerty (q.v.). For this reason, agreements which are not uncommon nowadays, where a so-called legal aid society promises free legal assistance to the victims of street accidents, etc., in return for a percentage of the damages, if any, obtained, should be avoided.

The rule against maintaining another person in an action has certain important exceptions. Thus, if a person has an interest in an action inasmuch as he contemplates bringing an action himself against the defendant upon similar grounds, financial assistance given in such a case is not maintenance. Further, charity is an excuse, and legal assistance may be, and frequently is properly given by charitable organisations, but in such a case the person giving such assistance should have a bone fide opinion that the action is a just and proper one, and it is needless to say that any suspicion of an agreement to be paid a percentage of the proceeds of the action makes the assistance unlawful.

Besides charitable reasons, a person is entitled to assist in this manner a poor relation, a servant or a poor co-religionist, but unless the person bringing the action is poverty-stricken, caution should be observed in taking advantage of this exception.

In addition to being liable to criminal proceedings, the person who is guilty of maintenance or champerty is liable to a civil action at the suit of the person against whom the action has been maintained. (*See* ACTION; POOR PERSONS PROCEDURE.)

MAINTENANCE ORDER.—(*See* SEPARATION ORDER AND SPECIAL SUPPLEMENT " DIVORCE".)

MALFEASANCE.—A malfeasance is the doing of some act which is unlawful. It is distinguished from a misfeasance which is the doing of an act which is in itself lawful, in

Lord Macmillan.

an unlawful way, e.g. acting negligently, and from a nonfeasance which is the omission to do some act which a man is in law bound to do.

MALICE.—Malice has a special meaning in law. It does not necessarily involve any ill-will towards anyone. For instance, a person may lawfully be convicted of maliciously damaging property even though he does not know, and has never heard of, the owner. In this connection "maliciously" merely means intentionally and without lawful excuse.

᾿Malice is of great importance in connection with libel and slander (q.v.). Here it means any improper motive, or, as a great Judge has said, "Any indirect motive other than a sense of duty."

MALICIOUS DAMAGE.—It is a crime to do any malicious damage to any property whether publicly or privately owned. The word "malicious" has in law a special meaning. It does not necessarily involve ill-will or an intention to do some particular person an injury. It means wilful and intentional as distinct from negligent or accidental. Thus, a person who intentionally breaks a shop window may be convicted of malicious damage to property, though he has no particular malice towards the owner of it and may never have heard of him.

In the case of malicious damage to property for which no special punishment exists, the maximum punishment depends on the amount of the damage. Where the damage exceeds £5, the offender may be awarded imprisonment with or without hard labour for a period not exceeding two years, or if the offence took place at night time, penal servitude for not more than five years. Where the damage does not exceed £5, imprisonment for not more than two months or a fine up to £5 may be inflicted. There are also certain provisions under which a Court of Summary Jurisdiction can order compensation to be paid by the offending party to the party aggrieved.

MALICIOUS PROSECUTION.—Anyone who has been prosecuted without proper cause, and through the ill-will of the prosecutor, may, if he is acquitted of the charge, recover damages against the prosecutor for malicious prosecution. This right, however, is limited to cases where the following conditions are present:—

The case must have resulted in the acquittal of the accused person. Next, it must be shewn that the person to be made liable was actually responsible for starting the prosecution. Further, it must be shewn that he had no reasonable or probable cause for commencing the proceedings. Finally, it must be shewn that he was actuated by malice in what he did. It may be seen, therefore, that it is by no means every accused person who is acquitted who has a good cause of action for malicious prosecution. Before bringing any such action the plaintiff should be satisfied that all these matters can be established, as otherwise the action will fail.

MAN OF STRAW.—This is the term applied to a man of no substance or property. Consequently an agent or a servant is sometimes called a man of straw.

MAN TRAPS.—It is a punishable offence to set any man trap or other contrivance on any land calculated to do serious injury to anyone caught in it. This provision constitutes a protection for trespassers, Parliament according the landowner no right to imperil the lives even of trespassers in order to protect his land. A householder is permitted to set contrivances of this kind inside a dwelling-house between sunset and sunrise for protection against burglars. Such contrivances, however, must be released during the daytime.

MANDAMUS.—The writ of mandamus is a writ directed by a Judge of the High Court to any inferior Court or to any individual, person or other body ordering such person to perform any public duty he may be liable to perform. The writ is what is known as a prerogative writ, and it therefore will not be granted until good cause has been shewn that it is, or may be necessary (*see* PREROGATIVE WRITS). Furthermore, it is entirely at the discretion of the Judge whether he will issue it or not.

MANSERVANT.—Every person employing a male servant as, amongst other things, house-steward, valet, butler, under-butler, cook, footman, page, waiter, groom, chauffeur, gardener, gamekeeper, whipper-in, etc., must take out a licence (fifteen shillings) under penalty of £20. But it is only required if the servant is employed in a personal, domestic or menial capacity. For example, a page-boy employed at one's business premises will not require a licence.

MANSFIELD, Lord (1705-1793).— Handsome William Murray was known as the "silver tongued" in the Courts of Law and in the House of Commons. The great advocate on reaching the Bench was noted for his scrupulous fairness, as an instance of which, although during the Gordon Riots the mob had destroyed Lord Mansfield's house, Lord George Gordon chose the Chief Justice as his Judge.

Lord Mansfield was particularly interested in the Law of Evidence, and the doctrine of res gestæ (q.v.) is almost entirely his work.

MANSLAUGHTER.—The felonious killing of another without malice. It is distinguishable from murder by the absence of malice express, or implied. If, while doing any unlawful act not being a violent felony, a man kills another accidentally, he can be convicted of manslaughter. If the act is a violent felony he is guilty of murder, even though the killing be accidental. Again, if a man is doing a lawful act, but does it in a grossly negligent way, and death results, he is guilty of manslaughter.

The most familiar example of this class is the killing of persons by the negligent driving of vehicles. In such cases, though the act of driving is lawful, gross negligence in driving may amount to manslaughter if death result.

There is a further class which is on the borderline of murder, and great difficulty is sometimes experienced by juries in deciding whether the facts should lead to a verdict of murder or manslaughter. This class is sometimes described as "voluntary manslaughter," and includes cases of death resulting from a fight arising from a sudden quarrel, and killing under provocation.

Killing under provocation is also attended by subtle, though important, principles. Provocation cannot render homicide justifiable or excusable, but it may reduce it from murder to manslaughter. To have this effect the provocation must be very great indeed; it must be sufficient to deprive a reasonable man of the power of controlling himself.

In general, the provocation must be of a physical kind, that is to say, it must consist of violence to the person and not merely of words. Of course, words may increase the provocation afforded by the violence, but in themselves words probably cannot amount to sufficient provocation. As to what is popularly called "the unwritten law," this is neither more nor less than the application of the principle of provocation. Where a man finds his wife in adultery with another man, a jury may find that the shock was so great that it deprived him of his self control sufficiently to reduce a killing of the adulterer from murder to manslaughter. (*See* HOMICIDE; MURDER.)

MARGARINE.—Margarine is any article of food, whether mixed with butter or not, which resembles butter and is not milk-blended butter. It is unlawful to manufacture or sell margarine the fat of which contains more than ten per cent of fat derived from milk, or of which more than sixteen per cent is water. Preservatives which are forbidden by regulations made by the Minister of Health must not be used in the manufacture of margarine.

Every person dealing in margarine whether he be a manufacturer or importer, consignor, consignee or commission agent, a wholesaler or retailer must see to it that every package containing margarine has marked upon the top, bottom and both sides of it the word "Margarine" in capital letters not less than three-quarters of an inch square.

When margarine is sold by retail, not in a package as just described, but in small quantities, then it must be delivered to the purchaser in a wrapper, upon which is printed in capital letters at least half an inch long the word "Margarine." The same provisions apply to dealings with margarine cheese which is any substance prepared imitating cheese and which contains fat not derived from milk. (*See* FOOD.)

MARINE INSURANCE.—The term Marine Insurance is applied to insurance policies which are taken out to provide against risk of damage resulting from sea voyages, and the subjects of marine insurance are ships and their fittings, the cargoes of ships, profits, commissions, etc., earned by ship owners and charterers of ships, or by owners of the cargo or forwarding agents of cargo, and also the risk of pecuniary liability for negligent management of ships, in the same way as policies may be taken out against Third Party Risks in motor vehicle insurance.

Any one who has an insurable interest in a marine venture, i.e. a voyage by a ship, may insure that interest up to, but not exceeding its full amount. The chief types of persons who have such insurable interest are the shipowners who have an insurable interest in their ship even though it is let to a charterer who is responsible for its full value, and charterers who have either contracted to pay for the ship if it is lost, or who have contracted to insure it. These persons have an insurable interest up to the full value of the ship, and also in respect of any profits of which they would be deprived by the loss of the ship.

An insurable interest in the freight is possessed by shipowners, and charterers, but only if they put the ship up as a general ship or carry their own goods, and also to the extent of any dead freight which they are liable to pay under the charter-party (q.v.)

In the actual goods carried upon a ship the owner has an insurable interest as have carriers, warehousemen, and, in short, all persons who stand to lose by the loss of the goods, while all persons who would stand to make a profit by the carrying of the goods in the ship are entitled to insure that profit.

Shipowners may also insure against the liability which they may incur to other ships from the negligent navigation of the ship.

Lloyd's Policies.—Although any person or insurance company may issue policies of Marine Insurance, most policies are issued by underwriters who are members of Lloyd's and who issue a traditional form of policy couched in language which was framed a great many years ago, but which has been brought up to date, not by alteration in the actual words, but by the interpretations that have been put upon those words by the Court. Under a Lloyd's policy, a whole series of underwriters join in issuing the policy, and each member of the group undertakes to be liable for a certain proportion of the insurance, so that the effect of a Lloyd's policy is the same as if the insured person had taken out a very large number of insurance policies of small amounts with the individual underwriters.

Policies of marine insurance may take a number of different forms according to the manner in which the risk is insured against. All policies are either open policies or valued policies.

Open Policy.—A policy of marine insurance is known as an open policy where the value of the ship, goods, or interest insured is not stated in the policy. These are like the ordinary policies of fire insurance, and the insurable value, and thus the amount recoverable is the value of the ship, goods, etc. at the beginning of the voyage.

Valued Policy.—In a valued policy the insured and the insurers agree as to the value which is to be set upon the subject matter of the insurance, and state that amount in the policy. Unless the value is a fraudulent overvaluation, in all subsequent proceedings arising out of the policy, the full value of the subject matter of the insurance is assumed to be the value appearing in the policy.

Voyage Policy.—A voyage policy is a policy which insures the subject matter for one particular voyage from one named port to another named port, and if the ship deviates unnecessarily from the ordinary route between those two points, the insurance ceases to be effective.

Time Policy.—A time policy covers the subject matter of the insurance for a definite time and ceases to be effective at the end of that time. No time policy may be made for more than 12 months.

Mixed Policy.—Most policies of marine insurance are a mixture of time and voyage policy, being made for a definite voyage and for a certain number of days before the commencement, and after the close of the voyage.

Floating Policy.—It often happens that a ship owner or an owner of goods to be carried by ship wishes to insure them, but does not know at the time exactly the ship or the goods which will be the subject of the insurance. In such a case he may take out a floating policy which is a policy cast in general terms such as "on goods by ship or ships hereafter to be declared." If he does this he must, as soon as he knows on what ship the goods are to be carried, declare, generally by endorsement on the policy, the ship and goods which the insurance is to cover, and thereafter the policy is treated like an ordinary policy.

Sums Insured.—In all these policies, whether valued or unvalued, voyage, time, mixed or floating, the insured person and the underwriters settle a fixed sum which is the maximum for which each underwriter will be liable in the event of the subject matter of the insurance becoming a total loss. But this does not mean that in the event of there being a partial loss the underwriter will be liable for the full amount of the partial loss if it is less than the sum insured.

The theory underlying marine insurance is that the whole of the subject-matter of the insurance is fully covered, and if the insured person does not cover it by taking out a policy, he is assumed to be his own insurer to the extent of the value not covered by insurance. Thus, if a ship is valued at £20,000 and is insured with underwriters for £10,000 only, the owner is treated as being his own insurer for the other £10,000 of the ship's value, and accordingly if the partial loss to the ship amounts to £5,000 the underwriters are liable to pay him half that sum only, i.e. £2,500, while he himself is responsible for the other half of the loss. *This is a very important distinction between marine insurance and fire insurance*, where if the sum insured is £10,000 the insurer is liable for the whole of the loss up to that amount, though the actual value of the total property insured may be £20,000.

Loss and Abandonment.—Once the policy has been issued, the insurer is liable to pay for any loss which has been caused by the risks insured against. The loss that occurs may be a total loss or a partial loss, it being a total loss when the subject matter of the insurance is either destroyed or so damaged as to be useless, e.g. where a ship and cargo is sunk, or where the whole of a cargo of sugar is entirely ruined by sea-water owing to rough weather. A partial loss arises where either part of the subject matter of the insurance is lost or destroyed, or where either the whole or part is damaged but not destroyed.

Abandonment.—It sometimes happens that the subject matter of the insurance, although not lost or destroyed, is so much damaged that it would cost more to repair than it would be worth at the conclusion of the repairs. In such a case, the insured person is entitled to treat the loss as a partial loss and to retain the subject matter, or he can treat the loss as a total loss, in which case it is called a constructive total loss, and the insured person must give notice to the underwriters that he abandons the subject matter to them, and if they accept the notice of abandonment, the subject matter of the insurance will belong to the underwriters who can deal with it as

they like, e.g. salvage it. The underwriters, however, if they accept the notice of abandonment will be obliged to pay to an insured person the amount payable under the policy on a total loss.

Salvage.—Under maritime law a person who saves life or property of another at sea, is entitled to payment for the services which he renders, and may recover these payments from the persons liable, who may be either the owner of the property salvaged alone, or may be all the persons interested in a venture. In the first case the costs payable as salvage count as a particular average loss, and may be recovered from the underwriters by the insured person who is obliged to pay them. In the second case it counts as a general average loss, and is treated in the same way as any other loss made for the benefit of all the persons interested in the venture. (*See* FIRE INSURANCE; INSURANCE; SHIPPING.)

MARINE STORES DEALERS.— Every dealer in marine stores must keep a book and enter in it the particulars of every article of marine stores that he purchases. Further, he is prohibited from purchasing any such article from any person under sixteen years of age, and he may not cut up cables exceeding five fathoms in length without permission of a Justice of the Peace. Dealers in these articles must also have their names together with the words, "Dealer in Marine Stores" painted in large letters above their premises.

MARKET.—Strictly speaking, a market is a right enjoyed by some person to set up a place where buyers and sellers may come for the purpose of dealing in goods, but the term is also applied to the place itself, or to the concourse of buyers and sellers at that place. A market is very similar to a fair, but is distinguished from it usually by its size, a market being smaller, and by the frequency with which it takes place, a market being held once or twice a week, whereas a fair takes place usually on one or two occasions in a year.

Rights of Owner of Market.—The owner is entitled to have the buyers and sellers assembling in a manner which, but for his right, might amount to a nuisance, e.g. by obstructing traffic in a street, and he has a corresponding right of action against any persons who interfere with the holding of the market. He is also bound to provide a place for the market to be held of a size sufficient to accommodate all who wish to attend.

Creation of Market.—The right to hold the market may be obtained by a grant from the Crown or by some local Act of Parliament authorizing the holding of a market. In addition, every District Council has got a right to provide a market place within its area, and may make bye-laws regulating the sale and general conduct of the market. In every market there must be provided proper scales and balances and weights and measures, and the clerk of the market or the toll collector must weigh goods if he is required to do so. The owner of the market is entitled to charge such tolls as are authorized by the grant under which he holds the market. (*See* MARKET OVERT.)

MARKET GARDENS.—Market gardens up to a large extent are covered by the Agricultural Holdings Acts, for which purpose they mean any holding wholly or mainly cultivated for the purpose of the trade or business of market gardening. The right of a tenant at the end of his tenancy to claim for compensation for improvements he has carried out includes the following:

1. Planting standard, or other fruit trees permanently set out;
2. The planting of fruit bushes permanently set out;
3. The planting of strawberry plants;
4. The planting of asparagus, rhubarb and other vegetable crops which continue productive for two or more years;
5. The erection or enlargement of buildings for the purpose of the trade or business of a market gardener.

Where a tenant wishes to make any of the above improvements to his holding and the landlord refuses to agree to treat the holding as a market garden, the tenant may apply to the Agricultural Committee of the district, and this Committee, after hearing the parties, may order that the tenant be entitled to compensation, and that the provisions as to compensation for improvements shall apply to that holding. Thus, if a tenant of a farm wishes to turn part of it into a market garden, he must either obtain the landlord's consent, or a decision from the local Agricultural Committee.

Where the tenant himself gives notice to quit and so ends the tenancy, he will not be entitled to compensation for improvements unless, not later than one month after the date on which he gave his notice, he produces to the landlord an offer in writing by a substantial and otherwise suitable person (being an offer open for at least three months from the date on which it was produced) to accept a tenancy of the holding after the end of the existing tenancy, and to pay to the outgoing tenant all compensation payable by the landlord. It is only if the landlord fails to accept this offer within three months that the tenant has any right of compensation for improvements against him. If the landlord accepts the offer, the incoming tenant must pay to the landlord all sums payable to him by the outgoing tenant in respect of rent, or breach of contract, or otherwise in respect of the whole. The committee may attach conditions to their direction at the landlord's request, and if it relates to part only of the holding, may make it a condition that the holding shall be divided into parts to be held at rents settled by the committee in the default of agreement by the landlord and tenant.

The exact meaning of market garden is not very clear. An experimental bulb farm has been held not to be a market garden, but land covered with greenhouses for growing fruit and vegetables is a market garden. (*See* AGRICULTURAL HOLDINGS.)

MARKET OVERT.—Goods are said to be sold in market overt when the sale takes place in any public market on a market day. In the City of London, market overt includes any sale in a shop in which goods are exposed for sale, provided that the goods actually sold are those which are usually sold in that shop.

The importance of a sale in market overt is that any person who purchases the goods in this way in good faith, and without any knowledge that the person who sells them to him has no right to do so, gets a good title to the goods. Thus, if the goods have been stolen, a sale in market overt to an innocent purchaser would entitle the purchaser to retain the goods, although, had they been sold anywhere else, he could have been compelled to hand them back to the owner. Even in this case there is, however, an exception, for if the thief is prose-

must always be solemnized before 6 o'clock in the evening, and in the presence of two or more witnesses. Where the marriage is according to the rites of the Church of England, the wedding service contained in the Prayer Book is the only lawful form. It is interesting to note, however, that slight variations in that service do not render a marriage invalid; for instance, the intentional omission by a bride of the words "to obey" would not render the marriage invalid. In the case of marriages solemnized elsewhere, it is essential that at some part of the ceremony the following words (known as the contracting words) are used, namely, the bridegroom is required to say, "I call upon those persons here present to witness that I, A.B. do take thee, C.D. to be my lawful wedded wife," and in the case of the bride, "I, C.D. take thee, A.B. to be my lawful wedded husband."

Marriages Solemnized Outside England.—A lawful marriage may be contracted on a British merchant ship on the High Seas. If possible, the ceremony should be performed by a clergyman of the denomination to which one or both of the parties belong, but even though not so performed it is regarded as valid if there is evidence that the parties intended it to be a lawful marriage. All such marriages must be entered on the official log of the ship.

Marriages Abroad within the Empire.—These vary according to the law of the country in which they take place, but are recognized in England provided they are lawful where they are solemnized.

Marriages Outside the Empire.—English law regards as valid marriages by British subjects in foreign countries if they are lawful in the place in which they take place. There is, however, one exception. Polygamy is so opposed to the English conception of marriage that a polygamous marriage, though legal in the country where it takes place, is not recognized in English law.

Invalid Marriages.—Where there is doubt as to the validity of a marriage, or where there has been some informality not going to the root of the marriage, power exists for a Secretary of State to make an order provisionally declaring the marriage to be lawful. These provisional orders, if unopposed, are subsequently confirmed by Parliament, and such a marriage then becomes as lawful as if made with all proper forms and ceremonies. No order of this kind can be made where invalidity arises from consanguinity, want of consent, or similar vital cause.

How a Marriage may be Proved.—In England, registers of marriage are kept, and certified copies, known as marriage certificates, can be obtained on demand from the General Register Office. Where, for any reason, a marriage was not registered, proof can still be given as to its having taken place. In cases of deceased persons it is sometimes impossible to obtain proof that they were lawfully married. Evidence may then be given that they lived together in such circumstances that they were regarded as man and wife, and a Court is then entitled to presume a lawful marriage. Children of such marriages are presumed legitimate should the question of inheritance arise. Questions of doubt frequently arise in proving marriages solemnized abroad. The methods of proof vary according to the various countries, but in most cases a certificate from the person in charge of any marriage register abroad is proof of the marriage set out therein having taken place.

For Dissolution of Marriage *see* SPECIAL SUPPLEMENT "DIVORCE." *See also* MARRIED WOMEN'S PROPERTY; MARRIED WOMEN'S CONTRACTS; NULLITY OF MARRIAGE.

MARRIAGE (SCOTS LAW).—It is probably true to say that there are no matters in which Scots Law differs so widely from the law of England as in the rules relating to marriage, and the rights of succession enjoyed by husband and wife in one another's property, and by children in the property of their parents.

Form of Marriage: Regular Marriages.—Marriage in Scotland may be either a regular or an irregular marriage. Both are equally valid in the eyes of the law. A regular marriage must be celebrated by a minister of religion after banns have been proclaimed, or a notice of intention to marry has been given to the registrar of births, deaths and marriages in the Parish and published by him. The object of the proclamation of banns in Church is to enable any member of the congregation who knows of any reason why the parties should not be married, e.g. that one of them is already married—to state his objection and to prevent the marriage. The proclamation must be made in the Parish Church or in the Parish where the parties live, and if they reside in different parishes it must be made in the Churches of both.

The marriage is celebrated with a religious ceremony, but a certificate of the due proclamation of banns or of the publication of the notice to marry must be produced. The ceremony need not take place in a Church but may take place in any private house. When a marriage is celebrated with a religious ceremony by someone who is not a clergyman, or where no banns have been proclaimed, the marriage is still quite regular, but is called "clandestine" and the parties are liable to a penalty.

Irregular Marriages.—It is thus the absence of a religious ceremony that makes a marriage irregular. Irregular marriages may be of three kinds:—

Marriage By Declaration de Præsenti .—This is by the mutual consent of the parties to be married at that time. A promise given by them both to marry one another at a future time, i.e. a betrothal is not sufficient. It is not legally necessary that there should be any witnesses, and the parties may sign mutual declarations of marriage, but the ceremony usually takes place in front of witnesses, as otherwise it would be difficult to prove.

It is this type of marriage which is known as a Gretna Green marriage (q.v.).

Marriage by Habit and Repute.—If a man and a woman have lived together at bed and board, and are generally reputed husband and wife, and where this state of affairs has continued for some considerable period of time, they will be considered in Scots law as being legally married. It is necessary, of course, that neither of them should already be married to any other person.

A Promise followed by Intercourse.—Where two persons have promised to marry one another, and on the faith of the promise, intercourse takes place between them, this amounts in Scots law to a valid binding marriage. Certain strict rules of proof are required of the promise, and the person alleging it must shew either some document signed by the other party admitting the promise, or from which the promise can be inferred—e.g. a love letter referring to a contemplated marriage—or else there must be extracted from that person an admission on his oath. For that purpose he may be compelled to go into the witness box and answer questions and be cross-examined with the object of obtaining statements from him amounting to an admission.

Registration of Marriage.—In the case of regular marriages, particulars must be sent to the local Registrar within three days of the marriage. When the marriage is irregular the parties must now, within three months of the marriage, apply to the Sheriff or Sheriff Substitute of the County where the marriage took place for an order permitting them to register the marriage. When this Order is made the registration must take place in the ordinary way.

Position during Marriage: Duty of Support.—A husband is bound to support his wife, that is, to supply her with the means of livelihood. It is enough, however, if he offers to allow her to share his home, and if she leaves him without proper cause she cannot compel him to pay anything towards her maintenance.

Insurance Policies.—If a married man takes out an insurance policy on his own life which is expressed to be for the benefit of his wife, or children, or both, this policy cannot be touched by the trustee in bankruptcy if the husband later becomes bankrupt, nor can it be taken by his creditors in any way. If, however, it is proved that the policy was effected in order to defraud the creditors, or if the husband becomes bankrupt within two years of taking out the policy, the creditors may claim the amount of the premiums which have been paid.

Rights on Death.—Whether a husband makes a will or not, his wife will be entitled to a certain definite proportion of the property on his death, and in the same way a husband is entitled to a proportion of the property of his wife. The right is one which only arises on death, and therefore if the husband disposes of any property by gift or otherwise *before* his death, the wife has no claims against it. On the other hand, if the husband is possessed of any property at the time of his death, the wife cannot lose her rights by any provision the husband may make in his will. The protection which is thus given to the wife in Scots Law is one which she does not receive according to the law of England. A husband has similar rights in the property of his deceased wife. The various rights are known as terce, courtesy, jus relictæ, and jus relicti.

Terce.—Terce is a right enjoyed by a widow who receives a liferent—i.e. the revenue from the third of the heritable property, i.e. land which her husband owned at his death. She is not entitled to the capital value of the land, but only to the income, and the right ends on her death.

Courtesy.—This is the corresponding right enjoyed by the surviving husband in heritable property of his wife. It entitles him not merely to one-third of the revenue of the wife's land during his life, but to the whole of the revenue. He cannot claim it, however, unless a child has been born of the marriage and "heard to cry"—i.e. born alive.

Jus relictæ.—This is the right enjoyed by a widow in movable property, e.g. money, goods or shares—belonging to her husband. In this she is entitled not to the mere revenue, but actually to a proportion of the capital sum. The exact proportion will depend on whether or not there are any children of the marriage. If there are no children, the wife may claim one-half of the property, but if there are children, she can only claim one third.

Jus relicti.—This is the right of a husband in the movable property of his wife, but again the amount to which he is entitled will be one half if there are no children, and one third if there are children.

How Rights may be Lost.—These rights may all be lost during lifetime if the husband or wife, as the case may be, either expressly renounces them or accepts some provision, e.g. rights under a marriage settlement, given instead of them. In the same way, a man may in his will give to his wife some property stated to be in lieu of her other rights. She is not bound to accept this property, but if she does so she cannot also claim her other rights but must make up her mind between the two.

The wife's right to jus relictæ arises if she divorces her husband, as well as on his death, but the husband's right to jus relicti arises only when his wife dies, and not if he divorces her. (*See* INTESTACY [SCOTS LAW]; LEGITIM.)

MARRIAGE SETTLEMENT.—When a man and woman are about to marry, property is frequently settled on trustees either by the man or woman or by their relations, the interest of which is usually enjoyed by them during their lives and the capital of which they are usually given power to distribute among the children. (*See* SETTLEMENT.)

MARRIED WOMEN (BANKRUPTCY).—A married woman may now become bankrupt, but only if she is carrying on some trade, business, or profession or is separated from her husband under a judicial separation. When a married woman is living with her husband, the debts which she contracts will in most cases be his liability and not hers. (*See* BANKRUPTCY.)

MARRIED WOMEN'S CONTRACTS.—Although married women may now contract in their own right just as if they were unmarried, most contracts made by married women are in law regarded as having been made on behalf of their husbands. Marriage in itself does not make a wife the agent of her husband, but married life causes her to undertake this role on countless occasions. Whether or not in any particular case a wife is to be held to have pledged her own or her husband's credit is to be ascertained by the application of certain rules of law to the facts of each case.

The law presumes that a wife is the agent of her husband when ordering goods which are necessaries. This presumption only arises where they are living together, it being based on the probability of the wife being entrusted by the husband with the management of his home. The presumption can be shewn by a husband to be ill-founded. If he can prove that he had expressly forbidden his wife to order any goods on credit, he can avoid liability unless, of course, he has done anything to make the tradesman suppose that his wife was his agent. If, for instance, a man has paid without demur previous bills for goods ordered by his wife it would be idle for him to show that he had, unknown to the tradesman, revoked her authority. On the other hand, once he has informed a tradesman that he will not be responsible for debts incurred by his wife, the tradesman cannot look to him for payment.

It is always open to a husband to prove that he provided his wife with a sufficient allowance for the purchase of necessaries or that she already had a sufficient supply. In such circumstances there is no implied authority by the husband for the wife to exceed the allowance.

When Luxuries may be " Necessaries."—A word is desirable as to what the law regards as necessaries in this connection. Since there are many different standards of living, there are obviously as many standards of necessaries. The term "necessaries" does not mean "necessary to life" but necessary to the particular standard of living adopted by the husband. It is for the husband to decide what standard of living he wishes to adopt, and this is not necessarily dependent on his income. A man may live in a style exceeding that normal in his circumstances, or on the other hand he may desire to accumulate the greater part of his income, and may live on but a fraction of it. In both cases the decision as to what are necessaries or not will be determined by his style of living. But whatever the standard, a wife has no implied authority to pledge her husband's credit for articles of mere luxury, or for articles which are not necessary by reason of their exceeding the quantity normal in the circumstances. In every case it is a question of fact for the tribunal as to whether, in all the circumstances, the articles were necessaries or not.

Where a husband and wife are not living together there is no presumption that the wife is the agent of her husband.

Where, however, the husband has deserted his wife, or where the parties are living apart without any agreement by the husband to pay the wife maintenance, other considerations arise. Has the wife any means of support either in her own right or through her own efforts? If she has not, then in the absence of any adequate provision by her husband she becomes his "agent of necessity." As such, she is regarded by the law as having his authority to act as his agent in providing herself with necessaries suitable to his own standard of living. In such circumstances, this agency cannot be revoked by the husband so long as he fails adequately to make provision for his wife. Moreover, this agency extends to the provision of necessaries for the children if they are living with her.

MARRIED WOMEN'S PROPERTY ACTS.—It was not until the latter part of the last century that married women first acquired the right to own property.

In 1882 the Married Women's Property Act became law. It provided that any woman married after that year should be entitled to own property just as if she were unmarried. As far as women married before that year are concerned, they become entitled to any property they acquired after that year. As a result of this Act and subsequent legislation, married women have gained all the advantages in this respect that unmarried women possess. However, whilst the married woman is now able to enjoy her separate property irrespective of the control of her husband, the latter remains liable for the results of any wrongful action of which his wife may be guilty, such as slander or damage through negligence in the driving of a motor car.

A wife can sue her husband for the protection of her property just as if she were unmarried. There is a convenient method provided for disputes between husband and wife as to property by the Married Women's Property Act of 1882. That Act provides that any such dispute may be dealt with in a summary way by a judge of the High Court or County Court; such cases are usually held in private.

MARRIED WOMEN (SCOTS LAW).—The power of a married woman to enter into a contract in Scots Law which will be binding upon her is as full and complete as if she were not married, and her husband is not liable in respect of any contract entered into by her on her own behalf.

When husband and wife are living together, the wife has an implied authority, as in English Law, to pledge her husband's credit for household requirements.

A husband in Scots Law is not liable for wrongful acts committed by his wife—e.g. for slander spoken by her. In this respect he is in a better position than is a husband in English Law.

MARTIAL LAW.—Martial law has two meanings. In its older and more historical sense, it was applied to the law governing soldiers when on active service. In modern times, however, this meaning has been reserved for the expression "military law."

Martial law at the present time means the suspending of the ordinary law of the country, and the administration of justice by means of military force. When there is a state of rebellion, or, where civil disturbances reach such a state that the ordinary law can no longer be enforced, the Crown may declare martial law. This is done by means of a proclamation announcing that martial law will be enforced. Such a proclamation, however, is of no validity unless the state of affairs in the country is such that the Civil Law Courts can no longer administer justice. Once martial law has been proclaimed, the only law that remains is that which the military commanders, on behalf of the Crown, allow. It has been very aptly said, that martial law means government by the will of the military commander. The military commander may permit some of the Civil Courts to continue, or he may suspend them; he may set up tribunals of his own, which may enforce any regulations which he cares to make. These Courts usually consist of a body of officers and are described as Military Courts. As a matter of convenience they usually follow the procedure of Courts Martial. But they are not Courts Martial—they are in fact not Legal Courts at all, and are not subject to the control of any of the Civil Courts sitting outside the area in which martial law is enforced.

Martial Law in Force in the British Isles.—The most recent example of martial law in the British Isles was provided in the Irish rebellion in 1920–1921. The greater part of the south of Ireland was then, by reason of the disturbances there, placed under martial law. The military commander issued proclamations forbidding the possession of arms, imposing curfew regulations which required people to be indoors by certain times in the evening, and dealing with innumerable other matters. Anyone who committed any offence against these regulations or who took part in the armed resistance to the forces of the Crown, was charged before Military Courts set up by the military commander. These Courts inflicted death sentences for many matters which, under the civil law, were not punishable with death. Thus death sentences were passed for the unlawful possession of fire-arms. It is noteworthy that when complaint was made to the High Court of Justice outside the martial law area of sen-

tences inflicted by the Military Courts inside, the answer of the Judges was, "these Courts not being Legal Courts cannot be interfered with."

After martial law has been in force and order is restored, it is customary to pass through Parliament an Act of Indemnity. The purpose of this is to prevent persons aggrieved by the conduct of the military during the martial law period, from prosecuting or suing officers and other persons for acts done while martial law was in force.

MARTINMAS.—This is one of the two term days in Scotland on which rent is normally payable and tenancies begin or end. It falls on the 11th November. The other term day is Whitsun Day. The English Quarter Days are not recognized in Scotland.

MASTER AND SERVANT.—The relationship of master and servant usually depends upon a written or oral contract between the parties. The agreement may, however, be implied, as where a person performs work which is usually done by a servant. There is then a presumption that he is a servant till the contrary is shewn.

Anybody who can contract may agree to be a servant, but the terms of the agreement are restricted by law in many trades. (*See* FACTORY; SHOP; TRUCK.)

An infant, or person under 21, is bound by his agreement to serve if it is for his benefit. Most agreements by which wages are given for work are held so to be.

The Agreement, if for a year, or less, may be oral, though it is always wiser to have it in writing if possible. If the service is to last for more than a year from the date of the contract, the agreement must be written. Seamen's contracts must be in writing.

Stamp Duty must be paid by affixing a sixpenny stamp except where the agreement is for the hire of a labourer, artificer, manufacturer or menial servant. Clerks are not exempt.

Licence Duty at the rate of 15/- is payable upon an enumerated number of male servants. It is required for most menials, and expires at the end of December each year. Livery stable keepers, hackney carriage keepers, officers in the Army and Navy, hotel and refreshment house keepers and publicans are exempt. Others are liable to a penalty of £20 for failure to take out a licence. Application should be made to the Post Office.

Covenants are often put in the agreement limiting the servants' freedom to contract after leaving the employment. These may be invalid. (*See* RESTRAINT OF TRADE.)

Length of Service.—In the absence of any express or implied agreement or custom to the contrary, a contract of service is presumed to last for a year. In practice, however, it is most difficult to shew from all the circumstances of the agreement that the service is in fact a monthly, weekly or even daily one. The payment of wages at short periods affords some indication of the intended length of the service, but it is not conclusive. The length of notice necessary may also be taken into account.

Death of either master or servant ends the employment.

Dismissal of a servant without notice or wages in lieu of notice is justified where there is misbehaviour (*see* NOTICE). Conviction for crime does not justify summary dismissal unless the crime is connected with the employment. Notice, the length of which depends on the terms or type of service, must be given in other cases.

Two actions are open to a servant against his master: he may sue for wages due or he may claim damages for a wrongful dismissal.

A master need not give any reason for dismissal, and he may rely upon a reason which he discovers after dismissal and which is different from the reason given, provided it existed at the time of dismissal.

The servant can end his employment summarily when he has reasonable fear for his life or health, where the master fails to perform his part of the contract or ill-treats the servant. If the servant leaves before the end of the agreed period of service, or without given notice, it is a breach of contract giving the master the right to damages.

Failure to Employ.—Where a person engages a servant for a future date and then, before the date arrives, intimates that the services will not be required, this is a breach of contract for which the servant may bring an action for damages at once. There is no necessity for the servant to wait for the date to arrive, though he may do so if he wishes. The law gives the master similar rights where the servant says he will not perform the services when the day arrives.

Insurance. — Unemployment and National Health Insurance must be paid as required by the Acts. Both master and servant contribute. The master usually keeps the card, as it is primarily his duty to stamp it. The servant's contribution may be kept out of his or her wages, but any agreement to take the master's contributions out of wages is illegal. (*See* NATIONAL HEALTH INSURANCE; UNEMPLOYMENT INSURANCE.)

The Servant's Duty to the Master. —A servant must obey all his master's lawful orders and serve personally, honestly and faithfully. He must be careful when performing his duties and look after his master's property when necessary. After leaving employment a servant must not make use of information gained thereby. He cannot, for example, use the addresses of customers, but he may solicit customers and set up in business next door so long as there is no restrictive covenant to prevent him.

The Master's Duty to the Servant. —Apart from express agreements or duties imposed by statutes, a master, as such, does not have to take any special precautions to ensure the safety of his servant. An employer, however, is liable for personal negligence or wilful act, and it may well be that if he has dangerous or defective machinery unknown to the servant, he will be liable to the servant who is thereby injured. The master must take reasonable precautions against accidents.

The only duty put upon the master by law is to repay his servant for any outlays necessarily made by him in the course of his duty. He is not obliged to give a servant a character. (*See* CHARACTER OF SERVANTS.)

The Master's Rights against the Servant.—What then may a master safely do with an unsatisfactory servant? To summarise the position: he may dismiss without notice if the circumstances permit it, or he may give the servant notice or wages and possibly board-wages in lieu of notice when the service is terminable by notice. If the servant leaves wrongfully the master has an action for damages for any loss he may suffer, and he may obtain an injunction if at any time the servant should seek to break a restrictive covenant. No master has a right to administer corporal punishment to a servant.

 made the twelfth day
of July One thousand
nine hundred and
thirty ———— BETWEEN
ROBERT KNIGHT (trading
as Knight and Company)
(hereinafter called the Company) of the one part and JOSEPH DAY of
768 Whittingehame Drive Barchester (hereinafter called the traveller)
of the other part

WHEREBY IT IS AGREED as follows :-

1.   The Company shall employ the traveller and the traveller shall
serve the company as a traveller in their business of manufacturing
clothiers for the period of two years from the first August One
thousand nine hundred and thirty ——— and thereafter until the said
employment is determined as herein provided

2.   The traveller shall devote his whole time and best energies and
attention to the business of the company except when prevented by
sickness or unavoidable accident and shall in all respects obey the
orders and directions given to him and shall not disclose any of the
private concerns of the business of the company

3.   The traveller shall call upon persons and endeavour to obtain
orders for all goods dealt in by the Company and he shall make a
daily report to the company of business done and calls made by him
and shall keep proper accounts and books   He shall not collect any
money due to the company except when specially requested so to do by
the company

4.   The company shall pay to the traveller
(1) A salary at the rate of Three hundred pounds a year to be paid
weekly;
(2) Commission at the rate of two and a half per cent upon all
monies received by the company in respect of orders obtained by the
traveller and executed by the company   The company shall not be
required to pay commission upon repeat orders unless directly obtained
by the traveller and shall be entitled to refuse to execute any order
The said commission shall be payable on the fifteenth April and
fifteenth October in each year;
(3) reasonable travelling expenses and hotel bills incurred by the
traveller in connection with the business of the company

5.   The employment of the traveller may be determined at any time
after the first October One thousand nine hundred and thirty
by one month's notice in writing   In the event of the traveller
committing any breach of the terms of this agreement the company may
determine his employment without notice

6.   For the period of three years from the termination of his
employment the traveller shall not for or on account of any employer
or on his own behalf solicit orders in respect of any goods dealt in
by the company from any person who at the date of the determination
of the agreement is a customer of the company or call upon or transact business with any such person in respect of any such goods

     IN WITNESS whereof the parties hereto have hereunto set their
hands the day and year first above written

SIGNED by the above named ROBERT KNIGHT)
in the presence of :-   )   *Robert Knight.*

James Dewar,
     666, Grove Street,
          London E.C. Solicitors Clerk.

SIGNED by the above named JOSEPH DAY in)
the presence of :-   )   *Joseph Day.*

Charles John Hornsby
     560 Browning Road Barchester. — Furniture

A Specimen Employment Agreement for a Commercial Traveller.

Crimes by Servants.—Embezzlement by a servant, or theft of property given him for his master is perhaps the commonest form of crime by servants. It is a summary offence for a servant to steal, sell or pawn tools or materials given to him for his work.

A master is responsible for his servant's crime if he ordered or allowed it, but an authority to commit crimes cannot, except perhaps in the case of nuisance, be implied against the master.

Servant's Liability to Strangers.— *Contracts:* In making a contract for his master the servant is an agent, and his personal liability upon the contract depends upon the law of agency. (*See* PRINCIPAL AND AGENT.)

Torts.—That a servant is personally liable for any wrong done by him is based on the rule that the person committing a tort is always responsible for the damage. If the servant is sued, it is no defence that the master is also liable, or that he authorised or ordered the act, or that it was done in the course of employment. A contract of service never affects the servant's personal liability to the injured party. True, a master is often sued alone, but this is simply because the servant has no money, and an additional judgment against him would be worthless. If the servant has any money, it is often wise to sue him as well, and in actions arising out of motor car accidents the driver is sometimes sued, although only the servant of the owner. This, however, depends upon the attitude of the owner's insurance company and the terms of his policy. It is safer to sue the owner if you are reasonably sure the driver is his servant or agent. But if you are knocked down by a mail van, the driver and not the Postmaster-General is the person to sue, because the superiors in a government department are not responsible for their subordinates.

A servant may defend his master's person or property provided he uses only such force as is necessary. He may assist his master in carrying on a civil action without being guilty of the crime of maintenance (q.v.), and he can rely on the defence of qualified privilege if sued on account of a defamatory statement made to his master in the course of duty.

Master's Liability to Strangers.— This generally depends upon whether or not the act is within the scope of the servant's employment.

Wrongs by Strangers to Masters and Servants.—Encouraging a Breach of Contract by the master or by the servant without reasonable justification is actionable at the suit of the other party injured thereby. There must be a contract and a breach of contract, so the master has no right of action where the servant is induced to leave after the contract period of service is ended, or where the servant is persuaded to give notice, provided, of course, there is no conspiracy or coercion, for these are distinct actionable wrongs. (*See* CONSPIRACY.)

Justification probably means no more than the giving of advice by one who has a duty to do so. Thus, a father may persuade his daughter to break her engagement, a doctor may order his patient to stop work, and a lawyer may similarly advise his client.

Inducing Persons not to Serve, or not to employ, is governed by the law of Conspiracy.

Harbouring a Servant or employing or continuing to employ a servant with knowledge that there is a contract of service in existence is actionable, and the first master can recover from the second such damages as he has suffered, which in most cases will be nominal, for he can usually employ another servant. Where the servant is difficult to replace, as in the theatrical profession, the damage may be substantial.

"Blacklegging," or harbouring a master, does not appear to give the servant any right of action.

Personal Injury to the Servant, which prevents him from discharging his duties, gives the master a right to be compensated by the wrongdoer, even when the servant has himself recovered damages or where the wrongdoer has been prosecuted for assault or the like. Where the damage results from breach of contract the master has no remedy. If, for example, the servant is made ill by impure milk, he, the servant, has an action in contract against the seller, but in the absence of negligence the master has no right of action.

Seduction of a female servant and her consequent confinement gives the master an action for damages, for he is deprived of her services. As a daughter is assumed to be the servant of her parents this action is

Mr. Frederick Mead.

concerned in the case are not allowed to be present when cases are being heard. Masters in the King's Bench Division are usually barristers but they cannot practise once they have taken this office.

In the Chancery Division the Master occupies a somewhat different position. Each Judge has a Master attached to him, and the Master confines himself to the business which comes before that particular Judge. When it is desired to appeal from his decision to that of the Judge, the Master will adjourn the matter to the Judge. In the King's Bench Division the Masters are not attached to particular Judges, but any appeal from their decisions lies to the Judge in Chambers who is selected from among the Judges, each Judge taking his turn in sitting in this capacity.

MATERNITY BENEFIT.—A woman, or the wife or widow of a man who is insured under the National Health Insurance Scheme, is entitled to the payment of the sum of £2, or in some cases £4 upon confinement to cover the expenses of childbirth. This is in substitution for medical benefit under the scheme, and no woman is entitled to the attendance of a panel doctor, except upon payment of his fees for the purposes of attention during her confinement. (*See* NATIONAL HEALTH INSURANCE.)

MATERNITY HOME. *See* NURSING HOME.

MATS.—It is an offence, punishable with a fine of 40/-, in any street or public place in a town to shake any mat or carpet. This, however, does not apply to doormats if shaken before 8 a.m.

MAYHEM.—An obsolete legal term covering any injury to a man's body which might render him less able to defend himself. The expression is no longer of practical importance, as such injuries are included in the modern law governing wounding. (*See* WOUNDING.)

MAYOR.—The Mayor is the chief officer of a borough. As such he presides in the local police court.

MEAD, Mr. Frederick (1847-).—One of the best-known figures in London legal circles for half a century. He was made a Metropolitan Police Magistrate in 1889. He was formerly counsel to the Treasury.

MEANING OF DOCUMENTS.—When the meaning of a document is in

common. (*See* CHARACTER OF SERVANTS; DOMESTIC SERVANT; NOTICE; SERVANTS; WAGES; WORKMEN'S COMPENSATION; WRONGFUL DISMISSAL.)

MASTER OF THE ROLLS.—The Master of the Rolls is now the effective head of the Court of Appeal where he sits and presides. He occupies the third place in the order of legal seniority, coming next after the Lord Chancellor, the Lord Chief Justice, and before the President of the Probate, Divorce and Admiralty Division.

The Master of the Rolls admits all persons who are qualified to become solicitors. He also appoints the Disciplinary Committee of the Law Society whose duty it is to hear all applications to strike solicitors off the Rolls. (*See* SOLICITOR.)

MASTER OF THE SUPREME COURT.—A Master is an official of the Court who has control of all the preliminary proceedings which are necessary in an action before it can be brought to trial. Masters sit in rooms called "chambers." Their rooms in the King's Bench Division open on to an open hall colloquially known as the "Bear Garden." Members of the public not question, the duty of deciding its meaning falls upon the Judge and not upon the jury, except in the case of libel, where, as the result of an Act of Parliament passed specially for the purpose, the jury is to decide what the words mean, as well as whether they are defamatory.

In documents of all kinds, the ordinary and grammatical meaning of words will be adopted, unless such an interpretation would lead to an obvious absurdity or inconsistency. Ordinary words are to be interpreted according to their ordinary meaning, and technical words according to their technical meaning. An ordinary word may, however, have been used with some unusual meaning, and it will be interpreted according to the unusual meaning *if* it can be shewn that that meaning was intended, e.g. in one case, A agreed to sell rabbits to B at so much "per thousand"; a dispute having arisen, B proved that a "thousand" in that part of the country and in connection with rabbits was always understood to mean 1,200 (a sort of "baker's thousand"), and the Court adopted that interpretation.

Concurrently with the rule that documents must be construed according to their natural meaning unless custom varies that meaning, there is another rule that requires that a particular phrase or sentence must be construed in the light of the intention of the whole document. This really means that, if there is any ambiguity, the main intention of a document may be looked at to clear it up. Clerical errors and obvious omissions or mistakes will be rectified. When a document is on a printed form, partly in printing and partly in writing, the written part will usually prevail over the printed part in case of inconsistency; but if a construction can be found which will reconcile two apparently contradictory statements in such a document, it will be adopted, e.g. when a bill of lading contained in writing the exact weight, and in printing, the words "weight unknown," the Court adopted the suggestion that the words "weight unknown" meant "I have filled in what I think the weight is, but I will not be bound by my estimate"; it was therefore decided that there was no inconsistency.

When an ambiguity cannot be cleared up by the foregoing rules, the Court will adopt the meaning that is least favourable to the person who wrote the document, for it is his carelessness that has caused the trouble.

There is another rule of construction known as the *ejusdem generis* ("of the same kind") by which, if general words are used in the same context as special terms, the general words will be limited in their meaning, e.g. if a man assigns all his "tables, chairs, carpets, cabinets, pictures, china, cutlery and other property," the words "other property" will include only things of the same kind as the foregoing list (i.e. furniture); it will not include every kind of property he possesses, such as stocks and shares, or leases, or copyrights, or book-debts. (*See* CONTRACT; LEASE; WILL.)

MEANS TEST.—The Means Test was instituted to insure that persons who received assistance from public funds were actually in need of such assistance, and although it is looked upon as a modern creation, it is really as old as the Poor Law. As a general rule, the Means Test is applied in every case where a person is claiming relief as distinct from benefit, and it is not applied where a person is claiming a benefit to which he has become entitled by virtue of the contributions which he has made to a fund. The distinction is well illustrated by contrasting Unemployment Benefit with Transitional payment. Thus, an unemployed person who fulfils the necessary conditions, is entitled to twenty-six weeks of unemployment benefit in a benefit year without reference to his means. If, however, he exhausts his twenty-six weeks and then claims Transitional benefits, he must submit to an enquiry into his means when he claims.

The Public Assistance Committee of each local authority is charged with the duty of making the enquiries required by the law into the means of a person who claims either out-door relief under the Poor Law, or Transitional benefit under the Unemployment Insurance Scheme. Under the provisions of the new Unemployment Insurance Bill, however, they are to be relieved of the charge of the able-bodied unemployed, and will only have to administer the means test in relation to persons who are claiming poor relief. There are no fixed rules laid down by the law for the assessment of need, and the Public Assistance Committees have a discretion in the matter, but by an Act of 1932 they have to observe these regulations:

If a Committee take into account a wounds or disability pension when assessing need, they must disregard half the amount of it. Similarly, only half of any weekly payments by way of Workmen's Compensation received by an applicant for relief must be taken into account. If the committee takes into account any money or investments of an applicant, they must disregard the first £25 of such assets, and treat the weekly income derived from investments of a capital value between £25 and £300, as being 1/– per week for each £25.

These regulations apply when the committee is considering an application for either Transitional Benefit or Out-Door Relief under the Poor Law. (*See also* OLD AGE PENSION; OUT-DOOR RELIEF; POOR LAW; PUBLIC ASSISTANCE COMMITTEE; UNEMPLOYMENT INSURANCE.)

MEDALS.—It is an offence for any unauthorized person to wear any military decoration, medal or ribbon, or falsely to represent that he is entitled to wear them. Similarly it is an offence for any person without lawful excuse to supply any unauthorized person with any such articles. The offence is committed even though the article is only an imitation of the official article. But it is lawful on all occasions to wear ordinary regimental or similar ornaments.

MEDICAL BENEFIT.—Medical Benefit is the term applied to the right possessed by all persons who are insured under the National Health Insurance Scheme, to free medical and surgical treatment from panel doctors in case of illness. Medical benefit includes a right to attend and consult the panel doctor to whom the patient has been assigned during his normal panel consulting hours, and in cases of serious illness to receive visits from the doctor at the patient's own home. It also includes a right to the free provision of drugs and surgical appliances, an order for which must be obtained from the panel doctor, and the drugs and appliances obtained from a chemist who is registered under the scheme. (*See* APPROVED SOCIETIES; NATIONAL HEALTH INSURANCE; PANEL.)

MEDICAL JURISPRUDENCE.— The law makes very full use of medical and kindred sciences in determining questions tried in the Courts. In the detection of crime, the doctor is frequently an all important person. What time elapsed between the death of the deceased and the discovery of the body? What is the nature of the poison of which he died, and what symptoms would it produce when effecting its deadly work? With what kind of implement was this bruise produced? How far from the deceased was the pistol when it fired the fatal shot? These are but a very few of the questions on which the doctor comes to the help of Judge and jury in the work of the Courts. But his work is not confined to the detection of crime. His assistance is sought also whenever the mental condition of any person is at issue. Was the testator sufficiently sane to make a valid will? Is this person so mentally deficient that he can no longer be suffered to remain at large? On countless topics of this kind the mental specialist is heard as a witness.

MEDICAL REFEREE.—Certain selected medical practitioners are appointed as medical referees under the Workmen's Compensation Acts. On any dispute as to the physical condition of a workman who claims compensation under the Acts, if the parties cannot come to an agreement, one or both can cause the matter to be referred to a medical referee. If any workman refuses to submit himself for examination when a reference has been ordered, or in any way obstructs the referee, his right to compensation becomes thereby suspended. (*See* WORKMEN'S COMPENSATION.)

MEETINGS.—In general, persons may assemble together for any lawful purpose. But persons desiring to meet together have not thereby any right to interfere with other people's interests or convenience. They must not, for instance, meet on private land without the consent of the owner. Nor may they meet on land to which the public have access unless the public have a right to hold meetings thereon. For instance, the public have a right to pass along a highway, but that does not mean that they may assemble in a stationary body to the obstruction or inconvenience of other users of it.

The object of a meeting may render it unlawful even though it is held on private land. Thus, any gathering of three or more persons for the purpose of committing a

17*

violent crime or with the intention of carrying out any common purpose, even though a lawful one, in such a way as to give normal persons in the locality reasonable ground to suspect that the public peace will be broken becomes an unlawful assembly. Such an assembly may be dispersed, and persons taking part in it may be punished.

A seditious meeting is unlawful. Such a meeting is one held for the purpose of incitement to violence in political matters or for the creation of disaffection. Again meetings for the purpose of unlawful drilling may be dispersed and all persons taking part arrested and tried on indictment. (*See* DRILLING, ILLEGAL; SEDITION.)

MEETINGS, COMPANY.—While the immediate control of the affairs of the company is in the hands of its directors, it is necessary that the shareholders should meet from time to time and receive reports from the directors as to the success which has attended their administration.

The first and perhaps most important meeting of shareholders is known as the statutory meeting. This takes place as soon as a company is formed, and must be held not less than 1 month and not more than 3 months from the date at which it was entitled to commence its business (*see* COMPANIES). This is the first occasion on which the shareholders who have subscribed money to the company have had an opportunity of meeting, and it is very important to them to know what has been done with their money and how the company has progressed in the short time since its formation. A private company, since it does not issue shares to the public, is not required to hold a statutory meeting.

In every calendar year the company must hold an Annual General Meeting, which must be held not more than 15 months after the previous meeting. If any business of the company requires to be considered between two annual general meetings, an extraordinary meeting may be called for that purpose. At any time persons who hold not less than one tenth of the shares of the company may require the directors to call an extraordinary meeting to consider any matter which they think of importance. If the directors do not call the meeting within 21 days, one half of the persons who have required them to do so may call and hold the meeting themselves.

The voting at meetings is governed by the Articles of Association (q.v.) of the company, and very often some classes of shareholders are not entitled to vote. If there is no such provision, every member will, of course, be entitled to a vote. The quorum—i.e. smallest number of shareholders who must be present—is also usually fixed by the articles, but if no provision is made, the quorum will be two members in the case of a private company, and three in the case of a public company. The chairman of the meeting will either be appointed by the articles or elected by the meeting.

The voting may be of two kinds. Firstly on a show of hands, when each shareholder has one vote, and secondly on a poll when each shareholder has one vote for every share he holds. On each resolution the show of hands is first taken and the chairman states whether or not the resolution has been carried. A poll may then be demanded, the number of persons who can compel a poll being fixed by the Articles of Association of the company. In the cases of extraordinary or special resolutions, the articles may state that a poll cannot be demanded by fewer than 5 persons; and if the articles contain no provision, 3 persons—or even 1 person if he holds 15 per cent. of the capital—may demand a poll.

When a poll has been demanded, the chairman usually fixes the time and place where it is to be held. On the taking of the vote, each person signs a paper for or against the resolution, and each paper will count for the number of shares held by the person signing it. Votes may also be given on a poll by persons who are not present, by means of proxies. A proxy must be in writing and must authorize some person who is present to vote for the absent shareholder at a meeting. If the proxy is for one meeting only it requires a penny stamp, but if it is for a series of meetings it must have a 10/- stamp. Proxy papers should be deposited at the company's office before the meeting.

A company is bound to keep minutes of its meetings in proper minute books, and these books may be inspected at the registered office by any member without any charge. (*See* COMPANIES; RESOLUTIONS.)

MEMBERS OF PARLIAMENT.— There are 615 Members of Parliament who are elected to represent constituencies by almost universal adult suffrage (*see* VOTING.) They remain members until Parliament is dissolved (*see* DISSOLUTION OF PARLIAMENT), or they apply for the Chiltern Hundreds because they wish to resign (*see* CHILTERN HUNDREDS), or they become ineligible, falling within any of these classes.

Any man, or since 1919 any woman, can become a member of the House of Commons with the following exceptions:—

(i) Aliens.
(ii) Minors.
(iii) Peers.
(iv) Lunatics.
(v) Clergymen of the English or Scotch Established Churches, or of the Roman Catholic Church.
(vi) Judges, Magistrates and other legal officers.
(vii) Governors and other Government officials.
(viii) Undischarged bankrupts.
(ix) Persons convicted of treason.
(x) Persons convicted of a felony until they have served their sentence or been pardoned.
(xi) Persons guilty of corrupt practices at an election within the previous seven years.

Anyone falling within any of these classes is barred absolutely from taking his seat, or if he is already a member the seat is declared vacant.

MEMORANDUM OF ASSOCIATION.—This is the most important document relating to a company, and it has to be filed with the Registrar of Companies at the time of the formation of the company. The memorandum has five clauses.

1. The name of the company; (q.v.)
2. The Country in which the registered office is situated—i.e. England or Scotland;
3. The objects of the company; (*see* COMPANIES; ULTRA VIRES.)
4. A statement that the liability of the shareholders is limited; (*see* COMPANIES.)
5. The amount of the capital (q.v.) of the company, i.e. the total sum of money which it has power to raise in shares.

At the end of the document is set out what is called the subscription clause. In this the various persons who are forming the company sign their names and set out against them the numbers of shares which each proposes to take. (*See* ARTICLES OF ASSOCIATION; CAPITAL; COMPANIES; ULTRA VIRES; WINDING UP.)

MENACES.—Any person who commits the crime of obtaining, or attempting to obtain money by menaces commits blackmail. Anyone who sends a letter demanding money or property with menaces, or, with intent to extort money or property threatens to accuse some person of certain crimes, may on conviction be sentenced to penal servitude for life. Again, anyone who with menaces or by force demands any property with intent to steal it may be sentenced to five years penal servitude. Threatening to publish libels is a misdemeanour which may be punished by imprisonment for a period not exceeding two years.

MENS REA.—This is a Latin expression meaning a criminal intention. Most crimes involve such an intention. For instance, if A takes B's property thinking, though wrongly, that he is entitled to, he does not commit the crime of stealing; this is so because he had no criminal intention, or in legal phraseology there was no mens rea.

MENTAL DEFECTIVES.—A mental defective is a person whose mental incapacity originated at birth, as distinct from a lunatic, or person who has been born mentally normal but has become insane through the growth of a hallucination or delusion or mental disease or decay.

Special treatment is provided for such persons by the Mental Deficiency Act, 1913, which divides them into four classes—idiots, imbeciles, feeble-minded persons and moral imbeciles. (*See these headings, see also* LUNATICS.)

MERCHANDISE MARKS.—A series of Acts imposes penalties on any person who infringes a registered Trade Mark. Thus, any person who forges a trade mark or falsely applies it to goods, or applies to goods any mark so nearly resembling a trade mark as to be calculated to deceive, or applies any false trade description to goods, is guilty of an offence unless he can prove that he had no intention of defrauding in doing what he did. In the same way any person who sells or has in his possession for sale, or for any purpose of trade any goods to which any forged trade mark or false trade description is applied, or to which any trade mark or mark

Sir Boyd Merriman.

so nearly resembling a trade mark is falsely applied, is also guilty of an offence unless he can prove, (1) that he had taken all reasonable precautions and had no reason to suspect the genuineness of the mark or description, (2) that he gave all information in his power with respect to the persons from whom he obtained the goods and, (3) that he has acted innocently. The punishment for the offence varies from a fine not exceeding £50 to imprisonment for not more than two years. The article in relation to which the offence has been committed is forfeit to the Crown.

Watches.—Where a watch-case has on it any words or marks which are generally understood to amount to a description of the country in which the watch has been made, and the watch itself has no marks describing the country, the marks on the watch-case are taken to be a description of the country within which the watch was made, and if the watch was not in fact made in that country, an offence will have been committed. This is to prevent persons stamping watch-cases with an English mark and thereby leading purchasers to think that the whole watch, and not merely the case, was made in England.

Imported Goods.—By an act passed in 1926 it is made illegal to sell, or expose for sale any imported goods bearing a name or trade mark of any manufacturer or trader in the United Kingdom unless there is also added an indication of the country from which the goods have been imported. The Board of Trade have power to exempt from this provision goods of any class if there are special circumstances which make it difficult to comply with the provision, and if public interests in the country would not be materially affected by exempting these goods.

MERRIMAN, Sir Boyd (1880-).—The recently appointed President of the Probate, Divorce and Admiralty Division, who comes next in order of precedence to the Master of the Rolls. Sir Boyd Merriman was formerly Solicitor-General.

MERRIVALE, Lord (1855-).—After a period in journalism, Edward Duke was called to the Bar and made a great name on the Western Circuit. He entered the House of Commons and was recognized as an impressive speaker. On being made President of the Probate, Divorce and Admiralty Division he was raised to the peerage. He retired from the bench in 1933.

MESNE PROFITS.—When a tenant stays on in premises after the tenancy has been brought to an end, and against the wishes of the landlord, he may be sued for damages. The amount of the damages will be the rent which, if he had been a tenant, he would have paid for the period during which he has remained in the premises since

Lord Merrivale.

the lease came to an end, but this sum is always known as "mesne profits" and not as rent, for rent is only payable by a *tenant* to a landlord, and thus cannot be claimed or paid after the tenancy—and therefore the relationship of landlord and tenant—has ceased to exist. (*See* LANDLORD AND TENANT.)

MESSUAGE.—This word is normally used in all deeds transferring the property in land to denote a dwelling house, and will include not only the house itself but also any gardens or outbuildings attached to it.

METHYLATED SPIRIT.—Methylated spirits must not be sold between 10 p.m. on Saturday and 8 a.m. on the following Monday. Makers of methylated spirits, other than licensed distillers, must, subject to a penalty of £50, take out an excise licence to do so (10 guineas). The object of methylation is to make the spirits undrinkable, and regulations to enforce sufficient methylation are therefore numerous and strict, e.g. a surveyor and an excise officer must always be present.

A retailer of methylated spirits must also, under penalty of £50, take out a licence (ten shillings). No person licensed to distil or to retail beers, spirits or wines may take out either of the licences. No retailer may have more than 200 gallons on his premises at once, and may not sell more than four gallons at a time.

MICHAELMAS.—This is one of the four Quarter Days in England and Wales and falls on the 29th September.

MIDSUMMER.—This is one of the four Quarter Days in England and Wales and falls on the 24th June.

MIDWIVES.—No person is entitled to act as a midwife or to attend a woman in childbirth unless he or she has passed an examination and obtained a certificate in midwifery from the Central Midwives Board which is the controlling authority. There are certain exceptions to this, (1) in cases of emergency, when no certified midwife can be obtained, (2) when the attendance is given under the supervision of a registered medical practitioner, (3) when the attendance is given as part of a course of training either for medical practitioners or for midwives. The penalty for contravening these provisions is £10.

Throughout the country local supervising authorities constituted by County and Borough Councils and by District Councils, where Maternity and Child Welfare Clinics have been established, exercise control over the midwives in their area of whom a register must be kept. These bodies have the right to investigate any complaints made against certified midwives, to suspend the right to practise of any midwife of whose conduct complaint is made, or to order the erasure of the name of a midwife from the roll.

The legal rights of midwives to recover their fees, and of patients to recover damages for negligence against midwives are similar to, and governed by the same principles as apply to Doctors and Dentists. (*See* DENTIST; DOCTOR.)

MILITARY LAW.—Military law is that part of the law of England governing the discipline and disciplinary machinery of the Army. The Royal Navy is governed by Naval law, and the Royal Air Force by Air Force Law.

Law in the Army.—To-day military law is mainly contained in the Army Act. This is not a permanent part of the law but is brought into effect every year by the Army and Air Force (Annual) Act. It renders punishable the various offences against discipline, such as mutiny and desertion, and lays down the punishments that may be inflicted for them. It provides for the trial of such offences by Courts Martial or, in some minor matters, by summary disposal by commanding officers. It also deals with enlistment, billeting and other matters pertaining to the Army. In addition to the army act there is a collection of Rules of Procedure made under its authority whereby the method of working by military tribunals is provided for. The King's Regulations also contain rules as to the discipline of the army. There are also various acts dealing with the reserve and auxiliary forces such as the Reserve Forces Act, 1882, and the Territorial and Reserve Forces Act, 1907.

The tribunals at present exercising jurisdiction under military law are of two kinds. In the first place there is the commanding officer of a unit. He has authority to dispose of most minor charges against soldiers under his command. He may not, however, award more than twenty-eight days' detention. Moreover, a soldier has the right of electing to be tried by Court Martial whenever the punishment awarded will deprive him of any pay.

MILK.—Milk, being an article of food for human consumption, is protected from adulteration or dilution by the provisions of the Food and Drug Acts.

To put water in milk is to alter the nature and substance of it and make it something different from that which is demanded by the purchaser. Any person adding water to milk is liable to a penalty of £20 for the first offence, £50 for the second offence, and £100 for a third offence. To add any ingredient which is injurious to health is a more serious offence, entailing a penalty of £50 first offence, and six months imprisonment for a second offence.

There is a standard of purity for milk which is fixed by the Ministry of Agriculture and Fisheries, and the present standard is that milk sold for human consumption must contain at least three per cent. of milk fat and at least eight point five per cent. of milk solids other than milk fat. For skimmed and separated milk the standard is at least nine per cent. of milk solids. If milk, when analysed, is below these standards, then it is presumed not to be genuine milk, i.e. that it has been watered or mixed, and it is upon the person selling it to shew that it is genuine milk straight from the cow. If milk is found to be deficient in milk fat, but it is proved that it is genuine milk, then the supplier cannot be convicted of selling impure milk, even though he has fed his cows by a method which he knew would be likely to produce milk deficient in fat.

Abstraction of Cream.—It is an offence to sell milk from which the cream has been abstracted without giving notice of the abstraction to the purchaser at the time of the sale. Even accidental or careless removal of cream by neglecting to keep the milk stirred, and thus allowing it to be removed during the first sales, is sufficient to constitute the offence.

Artificial Cream is any substance resembling cream, but containing water or other non-injurious ingredient added to make the article fit for consumption or carriage. Artificial cream must not be sold as anything but artificial cream, and any receptacle used for containing it, either during conveyance or while it is displayed for sale, must be marked in large letters

"Artificial Cream." Premises used for the manufacture or sale of artificial cream must be registered with the local Food and Drugs Authority.

A contravention of these provisions is an offence against the Acts and the penalty is £5 for a first offence, and £50 for a second offence.

Condensed Milk.—Every tin or receptacle containing condensed, separated, or skimmed milk must bear a label clearly visible to the purchaser on which the words "Machine-skimmed Milk" or "Skimmed Milk" or "Condensed Milk" as the case may be, are printed in large and legible type.

MINERAL RIGHTS DUTY.—This tax is to be paid by any person who works his own mine or who leases a mine to somebody else to work. The rate is 1/- in the pound of the annual amount at which a mine either could be, or actually is leased. Any contract between the lessor and the lessee of a mine agreeing that the lessee shall pay the duty is void. (*See* LAND VALUES DUTIES.)

MINES AND MINERALS.—A mine means an underground excavation made for the purpose of getting minerals. "Minerals" means any substance that is part of the natural formation of the earth with the exception of the natural soil or rock of the country. A quarry is distinguished from a mine by being a working open to the surface.

Who owns Mines.—By the theory of English law the person who owns the surface of the land is also entitled to all that may be in the land underneath the surface, except mines of gold or silver which are royal mines and belong to the Crown. A person who owns land in fee simple, that is an absolute owner, may work a mine at his pleasure, but in most cases he will lease the mine to some person who will work it and pay to him a rent or royalty. Where such a lease is made, it will not entitle the lessee to do anything which will cause the surface of the land to subside unless express power is given to him. The lessee usually agrees to pay to the owner of the land both a fixed annual rent and a royalty on the amount of the minerals he obtains from the mine. The rent must be paid even though the mine is not worked, but it is frequently provided also that the lessee must work the mine during the lease, and if there is such a clause he is bound to, even though the working should be possible only at a loss.

Regulations.—A great many of the regulations applicable to coal mines apply also to other mines. A return must be made each year as to the amount of mineral worked and the number of persons employed. Notice of accidents must also be given. (*See* COAL MINE.)

MINIMUM SUBSCRIPTION.— When a company makes an issue of its shares to the public, i.e. invites members of the public to become shareholders, it may be that the public do not respond, and therefore all the shares offered are not applied for, i.e. the issue is not fully subscribed. When this happens it does not necessarily follow that the company allot shares to any of the applicants. Whether or not it can do so will depend on whether or not the "minimum subscription" has been applied for. The minimum subscription is the minimum amount of money which the company requires for certain preliminary purposes, and without which it will not be able to carry on its business successfully. Whenever an issue is made to the public the minimum subscription must be calculated beforehand and stated on the prospectus (q.v.). This provision of the law has been rendered necessary by the temptation which there is to persons who have promoted a company not to abandon their project, even when there has not been a sufficient amount of money subscribed to give the company any reasonable chance of success. In the calculation of this minimum subscription allowance must be made for the preliminary expenses of the company and for the working capital, so that there will be no risk of the company failing through lack of money in its early stages. (*See* PROSPECTUS; UNDERWRITING COMMISSION.)

MINOR (SCOTS LAW).—A minor is a person between the ages of twelve in the case of girls—fourteen in the case of boys—and twenty-one. He corresponds to an infant in English law. He is under the authority of his father, who is his guardian at common law and who may appoint persons to be curators after his death. If the father does not appoint curators the minor is not bound to take one, but if he wishes he may do so, and may bring an action for this purpose.

Power of Contract.—The minor has a much wider power of contract than has an infant under the law of England. If the minor has a curator, then he cannot make a valid contract without the curator's consent, except in cases (1) where he is carrying on business and the contract is made for the purposes of that business; (2) where the contract is to his advantage; and (3) where he pretends that he is of full age and so induces the other party to contract with him. Where a minor has no curators he can, himself enter into contracts without any restrictions.

In every case, whether a minor contracts with the consent of his curators or not, he may always set aside the contract before the end of what is called the quadriennium utile, that is between the ages of 21 and 25, within four years of attaining his majority if he can show that the bargain was an unfair one. A minor may make a will relating to his movable property, but not relating to his heritable property, i.e. land. He cannot give a valid receipt for moneys due to him, and where such a receipt is required, a curator should be appointed. A minor cannot marry until he is sixteen years of age.

MISADVENTURE.—A common verdict at inquests is "death through misadventure." This simply means that the death was caused through an accident, and not through the commission of some felony. If a man kills another through misadventure he cannot, of course, be convicted of murder or manslaughter. (*See* HOMICIDE; MANSLAUGHTER; MURDER.)

MISDEMEANOUR.—Any indictable crime other than treason and felony. Crimes are divided into treasons, felonies and misdemeanours, and in general the more serious crimes are felonies, the lesser misdemeanours. A prisoner charged with misdemeanour, if tried before a jury, has no right to peremptory challenge. If he wishes to exclude any person from the jury, he must give his reason to the Court. (*See* CHALLENGE; FELONY.)

MISDIRECTION.—When a Judge in summing up to a jury makes an error in law, or wrongly instructs them as to the facts of the case, he is said to have misdirected the jury. Misdirection is a frequent cause of appeal, because, if a Judge has seriously misdirected a jury on any point of law in a way which is prejudicial to the party against which the Jury has found, then that party can, on appeal, obtain either a reversal of the finding or an order for a fresh trial.

MISFEASANCE.—A misfeasance is the improper performance of a lawful act, as distinguished from a non-feasance which is the failure to do an act which one is under a duty to do. The distinction is of importance in the case of repair of the highway. If a highway authority omits to repair a road when it needs repair, that is a non-feasance; but if it attempts to repair the road and does so carelessly, that is a misfeasance. A highway authority is liable for a misfeasance but not for a nonfeasance. A director of a company who neglects his duties to the company is guilty of a misfeasance and may be sued for damages. (*See* DIRECTORS; HIGHWAYS.)

MISPRISION.—There are two forms of misprision, namely of treason or of felony. Misprision of treason consists of failure to give information to the public authorities of any impending treason. Misprision of felony is rather similar in its nature, but is not committed by a person who merely fails to give information about a felony. There must be some active concealing of the felony. Misprision of treason and of felony, however, are now only of historical interest, and prosecutions are not in modern times proffered for either.

MISREPRESENTATION.—When parties are negotiating for a contract there is except in special circumstances one golden rule for the bargainers. They must not make any statement of fact which is untrue. If they do so, however innocently, there is a danger that the other party if he has been induced to enter into the contract upon the faith of the statement of fact may repudiate the contract which is voidable at his option.

In order that a contract may be voidable for innocent misrepresentation, it is necessary that the misrepresentation should fulfil the following conditions: It must be a statement of fact. It must be material to the contract. It must have played a part in inducing the other party to enter into the contract. These conditions are worthy of detailed consideration:

Statement of Fact.—Except in certain cases dealt with below, there is no obligation on a party to a contract to warn the other party of things that he does not know. Suppose A sells a horse to B without making any statement as to its soundness, he is not under any obligation to inform B that the horse is lame in the off hind leg. On the other hand, no party to a contract may tell a lie to another party, and if, in the above case, A asks B whether the horse is sound in the legs and B answers "Yes," that is a positive statement of fact that the horse is not lame, and accordingly, if it fulfils the other conditions, is good reason for making the contract voidable at A's option.

The only case in which a mere failure to warn can be a misrepresentation in law is where a party has already made a truthful statement and circumstances have altered to make that statement untruthful. In such a case, the party who made the statement must correct it, or the contract will be voidable. Suppose that A who is selling a horse to B says truthfully that the horse is not lame, but that before the sale actually takes place the horse goes lame, then A must inform B that the horse has become lame, otherwise B on finding out that the horse is lame can repudiate the contract.

Materiality.—It is only common sense that it should be necessary that the representation should be material to the contract. Suppose that A, selling a horse to B, says quite untruthfully that there has been an earthquake in China, this is not material to the contract and naturally will not affect its validity.

Inducement.—Finally, although the representation may be positive and of fact and material to the contract, it will not render the contract voidable unless the person to whom it was made was induced by it to enter into the contract. Two cases may arise where he is not induced by the representation: (*a*) where he does not believe it and (*b*) where he would have entered into the contract whether it were true or not. Thus, if A in bargaining with B to sell him a motor-car, tells him that it has a self-changing gear, whereas B knows perfectly well that it has not; since B did not believe the misrepresentation, it does not avoid the contract because it clearly did not induce B to buy the car. On the other hand, if A tells B that the car has a self-changing gear and B replies that he does not care whether it has a self-changing gear or not; then, whether or not it had in fact a self-changing gear, the representation did not influence B to enter into the contract and hence it is valid.

For the purpose of deciding whether there has been a misrepresentation or not, it does not matter whether the person who made the statement, believed it to be true, or made it with the knowledge that it was false. But once it has been decided that a misrepresentation has been made, it becomes very important to discover whether the person who made the statement made it innocently, under the impression that it was true, or whether he made it, either knowing it to be false, or recklessly, not caring whether it were true or false, in which case the misrepresentation is known as fraud (q.v.). If the latter be the case, the person who was induced to enter into the contract because of the misrepresentation has additional remedies which are dealt with under the heading of Fraud.

In the absence of fraud, however, the effect of misrepresentation upon a contract is as follows:

Result of Misrepresentation.— Wherever a contract is induced by innocent misrepresentation, the party who has been deceived is entitled to repudiate the contract when he discovers its untruth, provided that he repudiates it at such a stage that the parties can be put back in the same position as if the contract had not been entered into. This is the general rule that governs voidable contracts and it is a very important one in practice. Thus, if A sells a horse to B having told B innocently but inaccurately that it has won the Newbury Cup, B is entitled to repudiate the contract at the moment that he finds out that this is untrue. Thus, if he finds out that it is untrue before he has either paid the money or received the horse, he can refuse to pay the money. If he has received the horse but not yet paid the money, he can return the horse and refuse to pay the money. But he cannot refuse to return the horse or pay the money, because of the rule that the parties to the contract must be put back into the same position as if the contract had not been made.

B can also lose his right to repudiate the contract in various other ways. If, after having found out the falsity of the representation, he does not repudiate the

contract immediately or within a reasonable time, he will lose his right to repudiate. Thus he cannot keep the horse for a week or so after the sale in order to see whether he can sell it at a profit. The moment for him to decide whether he wishes to repudiate the contract or not, is when he finds out the falsity. Again, supposing that he finds out the falsity after he has sold the horse, he cannot repudiate the contract because he is not in a position to return the horse to A, and hence the parties will not be placed in the same position as if no contract had been made.

It is needless to say that the person who makes the misrepresentation is never entitled to repudiate the contract, and A cannot demand the horse back from B on the ground that B entered into the contract owing to A's misrepresentation of fact.

It will be seen, therefore, that a situation may arise where B, although he has entered into a contract because of a misrepresentation by A, has no remedy. His only right is to repudiate the contract, and this right is lost wherever B delays unduly in exercising his right, or where the parties cannot be put back in the same situation as if the contract had never been made. This is the important difference between innocent misrepresentation and fraud (q.v.) (*See* BREACH OF CONTRACT; CONTRACT; FRAUD; GUARANTEE; INSURANCE.)

MISTAKE.—It is not the function of the Courts of Justice to save normal persons from the results of their own foolishness. Thus, the mere fact that a person has not turned his mind to all the terms of a contract, or has not realized the extent of the obligations that it places upon him, is not that special kind of mistake which alone in law may prevent a contract from being enforceable. A great many persons enter into contracts, such as hire-purchase agreements or agreements to pay for goods by instalments, without ever reading the terms of the contract that they are signing. In one respect it might be said that they enter into the contract under a mistake as to its terms, and they do frequently complain in County Courts that the written agreement was not the agreement that they thought they were making. None the less such a contract is enforceable, for the law assumes that every man intends the full consequences of what he does, and will not render unenforceable an otherwise valid contract because one of the parties has been careless.

Fundamental Mistakes.—There are, however, certain fundamental mistakes which will render a contract void or unenforceable. The basis upon which this may occur is where the mistake is a mistake of a fact, not of law, as to one of the essential parts of the contract, i.e. the subject matter of the contract, the parties to the contract, or obvious clerical errors.

These best appear by examples of the kind of mistake that renders a contract void or unenforceable.

(1) If A agrees to sell to B his motor-car, and at the time that the agreement is made the motor-car has in fact been destroyed. This is a mistake as to the existence of the subject matter of the contract and accordingly the contract is wholly void, so that if B has already paid for the motor-car he can recover his money from A.

(2) If A agrees to sell to B his motor-car when he has two motor-cars and A intends to sell one while B intends to buy the other. This is a mistake as to the subject matter of the contract which is accordingly void.

(3) If A enters into a contract by letter with B, believing him to be C, who perhaps lives at the same address, or who may have the same name. The contract is void because there is a mistake as to the parties to the contract, but if A enters into a verbal contract with B under the impression that he is C, the contract is not void because A intended to enter into the contract with the person he actually saw before him. If, however, B had lied to A about his identity, the contract would be not void but voidable for fraud, (q.v.).

(4) If A signs a cheque under the impression that it is not a cheque at all, but let us say, a reference or merely a specimen signature. He is not liable to pay on the cheque because this is such a mistake as to the essential nature of the contract that he is entering into that the contract is void. This is true wherever A signs a written contract under the impression that it is a contract of an entirely different kind, and whether his signature is due merely to his own carelessness or whether it is due to the dishonesty of B. It should be borne in mind, however, that A will have great difficulty in proving that he

made a mistake of this nature unless he is illiterate or stupid and there is some suspicion of a deliberate attempt to overreach him.

(5) CLERICAL ERRORS.—Wherever a party to a contract makes a clerical error and the other party knows that it is a clerical error, the party who made the error may refuse to be bound by the contract. If A by mistake puts up a price ticket that is obviously a mistake, as where A puts a price ticket of £10 on a new Rolls Royce car, although this is prima facie an offer to sell the car for that price, yet if B goes into the shop and accepts the offer, A, when he realizes his mistake can refuse to sell the car. In the same way, if A enters into a written agreement with B in which the price is inserted wrongly by a clerical error, and B knows that it was so inserted, A can either repudiate the contract or can have it carried out as if the proper price which was agreed upon had been inserted. The contract is thus voidable. The rule, however, does not apply where B does not know that there is a clerical error, and in such a case the contract is enforceable, though if the price is obviously absurd it will be extremely difficult for B to convince the Court that he did not know that it was a mistake. (*See* BREACH OF CONTRACT; CONTRACT; MISREPRESENTATION; FRAUD.)

MONEY-LENDING.—Under this heading only the law relating to persons who are not "money-lenders" in law will be dealt with. (For the definition of, and law relating to, "money-lenders" in law see MONEY-LENDERS.)

The loan of money by persons who are not money-lenders in law is governed by the general law of contract. The lender can recover the loan by an action for money lent or he can enforce the security, e.g. foreclose a mortgage (*see* MORTGAGES). If no date is fixed for repayment, the lender can sue at any time. (*See* MONEY-LENDERS; MORTGAGE.)

MONEY-LENDERS.—A money-lender in law is any person, firm or company (with a few exceptions given below) that carries on the business of money-lending or announces himself or itself as so doing. A person who only makes isolated loans to friends is not a money-lender in law even though he charges interest.

The exceptions are as follows:—

(i) Those carrying on businesses of

which money-lending is not the primary object, e.g. banking and insurance.

(ii) Pawnbrokers, provided they are acting within the scope of the Pawnbrokers Act.

(iii) Friendly, Loan or Building Societies incorporated by Act of Parliament.

(iv) Bodies empowered by Act of Parliament to lend money.

(v) Companies exempted by the Board of Trade.

Under certain circumstances pawnbrokers may be bound by some or all of the rules governing money-lenders. (*See* PAWNBROKERS.)

Under this heading only "money-lenders" in law are considered. Other persons, firms or companies, lending money are governed by the general law. (*See* MONEY-LENDING.)

Certificate.—Before carrying on business as a money-lender, a person or company must first obtain a Certificate. This certificate is obtained from the Petty Sessional Court of the district where the business is intended to be carried on, or in the Metropolitan Police district from a Police Magistrate. If the business is to be carried on at more than one address, a certificate must be obtained in respect of each address and, in the case of a partnership, each partner must obtain a certificate, application being made on the same day.

The certificate expires on the following July 31st and henceforth has to be renewed annually by means of the same procedure as on the obtaining of the first certificate, except that the newspaper notice is not required. If a money-lender is convicted of any money-lending offence, his certificate is endorsed and may be suspended or forfeited. There is a right of appeal against suspension or forfeiture. The certificate must be produced for endorsement on demand; failure to do so renders the holder liable to a fine of £5 for every day during which he is in default.

Licence.—Having obtained a Certificate, the prospective money-lender must next obtain a licence. A licence is obtained from the local collector of Customs and Excise to whom the certificate and licence fee must be sent or delivered. The fee is £10 if the licence is taken out after January 31st, or £15 if taken out before. It always expires

on July 31st and henceforth has to be renewed annually on payment of £15.

If a money-lender has already taken out a pawnbroker's licence in respect of his business address, an amount of the duty payable for a money-lender's licence, equal to the duty on the pawnbroker's licence, will be remitted, e.g., if a money-lender has already paid £7 10s. 0d. for a pawnbroker's licence, he will get £7 10s. 0d. remitted out of the £15 he has to pay for a money-lender's licence.

When the certificate is suspended or forfeited, the licence becomes suspended or void respectively. If a money-lender obtains a licence in any name other than his true name, or carries on a business without a licence, he is liable to a fine of £100 for the first offence and to three months' imprisonment for each subsequent offence, with or without a fine of £100, or, in the case of a company, to a fine of £500. Moreover, any contract entered into by him is in either of these circumstances void.

Having obtained a certificate and a licence, the money-lender can begin business, but there are several restrictions as to the way in which he can do so, which apply equally to companies and partnerships as to individuals, except where the contrary is stated.

All business must be carried on under the authorized name and at the authorized address, and all agreements must be entered into, and securities taken, in the authorized name. No document must be issued which suggests the business is a banking one. If any one of these rules is broken, the money-lending contract is void. The maximum penalties are the same as above. All documents issued by a money-lender must bear his authorized name; the maximum penalty for non-compliance with this regulation is £20 for each offence.

Advertising.—A money-lender may not circularise or send out to any person any document with the intention of obtaining clients except in response to a request, and then not if the person is an infant; nor is he allowed to employ agents or canvassers. Further, advertisements must only give his name, telephone number and address, any former business address, the date on which he started carrying on business, a statement that money is lent with or without security, the maximum and minimum amounts that will be lent, and the rate of interest that will be charged. (Interest must be expressed as so much per cent. per annum in advertisements and in all money-lenders' documents.)

Any transaction involving infringement of any of the above rules is void. The maximum penalty is three months' imprisonment or a fine of £100. A canvasser or agent is also liable to this penalty.

The Contract of Loan.—As to the loan itself, a memorandum or note containing all the terms of the contract, particularly the date of the loan, the amount lent and the rate of interest, must be signed by the borrower before any money is given or any security taken. A copy of this note or memorandum must be sent to the borrower within seven days. There is no criminal penalty for breach of this last rule but neither the sum lent nor interest can be recovered, nor can the security be enforced if the rule is broken, unless the breach consists of only a slight error or omission as to some immaterial detail.

Further, as to the contract itself, a money-lender is not allowed to make any charge for his expenses. An agreement to pay any such sum is void, and any sum so paid can be recovered by the borrower or set off against the sum lent. The charging of compound interest is not allowed, nor, if there is any default in the payment of any sum due, can an increased rate of interest be charged, but only simple interest at the ordinary rate on the sum in default until it is paid. Any agreement contrary to this rule is void, and any sum so paid can be recovered or set off by the borrower in the same way as sums paid for expenses.

After the loan is made, the following rules apply. A money-lender must, on written request and on payment of one shilling, supply the borrower with:

(i) A statement showing the date, amount and rate of interest of the loan.

(ii) The date and amount of all payments by the borrower.

(iii) The amount of all sums due but unpaid, with the date when they became due, and the amount of due and unpaid interest on them.

(iv) The amount and date of all future payments due from the borrower.

He must also, on written request and on payment of a reasonable sum for expenses, supply the borrower with copies of all documents. If a money-lender fails, without reasonable excuse, to comply with any of these requests within a month, he cannot sue for any sum due or charge interest until he has done so.

Transfer of Debt.—If a money-lender transfers to someone else a debt due to himself in respect of money lent, interest thereon, or any security received in respect of a loan, he must give notice to the transferee that the debt is a money-lender's debt, and must supply him with all the information he requires to fulfil the last mentioned conditions. If he fails to do so, he is liable to indemnify the transferee against all the results of his failure and is liable to 2 years' imprisonment with or without a fine of £500.

Moreover, if the transferee, not being another money-lender, is not aware that some rule has been broken before transfer, which breach either renders the transaction void or gives the borrower some other relief, the borrower cannot rely on the breach as against the transferee but is entitled to an indemnity from the money-lender against any loss he may thereby suffer.

Period of Limitation.—A money-lender can recover any sum due in respect of a loan, or interest thereon, as soon as it becomes due by means of an action for money lent. He must, however, begin the action within 12 months from when he first had the right to sue, except where payments become due from time to time in one transaction. In this case, the money-lender can sue any time within 12 months of the last instalment becoming due. If, during the 12 months, the debtor signs an acknowledgment of the amount due and gives a written undertaking to pay that amount, the money-lender has 12 months from then in which to sue. Further, if the money-lender becomes insane or the debtor is abroad, the 12 months does not begin until the former regains his sanity or the latter returns.

Harsh and Unconscionable Transactions.—The borrower may successfully resist the whole or part of the money-lender's claim if he can rely on such a breach of one of the above rules as either makes the transaction void or unenforceable or entitles him to some relief. In addition to defending the action on the ground of one or more of these breaches, a borrower can get the transaction re-opened if it is held to be harsh and unconscionable. The Court, if satisfied that this is so, may cancel the transaction or vary any of its terms and order an account to be taken on the basis of the new terms, e.g. on the basis of a lower rate of interest, and will order the borrower to pay the sum so found due. It may even be that it will be found that the borrower has paid too much, in which case the money-lender will be ordered to repay the excess amount to the borrower.

The borrower cannot only obtain this relief when sued, but can himself apply at any time to have the transaction re-opened on the ground that it is harsh and unconscionable. If it is so found, the money-lender's certificate is endorsed. A transaction may be held to be harsh and unconscionable solely on account of the excessive rate of interest, or because of the rate of interest together with other circumstances of the transaction.

Since the repeal of the Usury Laws, there is no absolute limit as to the rate of interest that may be charged, but if the rate exceeds 48% per annum there is a presumption that it is excessive, and the money-lender must show exceptional circumstances to justify such a rate. All the circumstances will be considered in deciding whether or not the rate of interest is reasonable. For example, the fact that no security was given or that the borrower was in a bad financial position with no prospects or that the loan was for a short period would justify a high rate of interest.

Among the factors which are considered, in addition to the rate of interest, in deciding whether or not relief shall be given are the following:

(i) That the borrower was an expectant heir.

(ii) That the money-lender made mis-statements during negotiations.

(iii) That the borrower was helpless and foolish or never understood the terms of the transaction.

In fact, anything may be relied on which goes to prove that the money-lender took advantage of the weak position of the borrower. (*See* PAWNING, PAWNBROKER.)

MONEY ORDERS.—Amongst the many powers conferred upon the Post-master-General by statute is that of issuing money orders for so long as the Treasury shall think fit. A money order is a document which may be purchased at a post office for the amount of money mentioned on its face (and an additional sum of poundage to pay for the expenses of the Post Office) and which authorises a particular Post Office to pay the sum mentioned on its face to the person named thereon. In certain cases no extra charge beyond the face value of the money order is made. Where it is drawn in favour of the Commissioners of Customs and Excise or of Inland Revenue no charge will be made if the payment is in respect of beer, corporation, customs, entertainment, Income, Land or succession taxes, or of money lenders license, or probate or estate duty.

Payment may be refused if the paying office is not satisfied that the person presenting the order is the person named on it or his agent, or if the order is more than twelve months old. In the latter case a new order less 6d. can be obtained. If the order is lost in the post a new one will be granted free of charge, but if it is lost in other way a fee of 6d. is charged.

MONOPOLY VALUE.—This is the difference between the value of premises licensed and their value unlicensed.

Duties which a Publican must pay. —When a licence is granted the justices must make it a condition that the Monopoly Value is paid into the Exchequer, but they may allow it to be paid by instalments. In addition, of course, to the monopoly value, the duty on the licence must be paid by the licensee, though of course this will be taken into consideration in calculating the mono-poly value. The revenue of course obtain also the proper duty on any intoxicating liquor which may be sold.

Conditions which may be attached to a Licence.—The justices may attach any other condition to a licence which they think proper in the interests of the public, but not for any interest unconnected with the public. (*See* INTOXICATING LIQUOR.)

MONTH.—The expression Month is interpreted in a different way in different connections. Wherever the rules of pro-cedure of the High Court of Justice refer to a month this expression is held to mean a calendar month. Where the expression is used in contracts, the old rule that it means the lunar month is still applied unless the context or surrounding circumstances indicates that a calendar month was intended. In the case, however, of documents made or coming into operation after 1925 the word month by virtue of the Law of Property Act, 1925, must be read as meaning a calendar month.

For ascertaining what is a calendar month the following is the general rule: The last day of a month is regarded as the day having the same number as that on which the month is to commence.

MOORE, Sir William (1864-).— Has been Lord Chief Justice of Northern Ireland since 1925.

MOOT.—In the Middle Ages it was customary for lawyers and law students to hold mock trials or legal debates. These were called Moots. They were used as a form of legal education and were, in fact, the chief method of training young men in the practice of the law. It was, of course, customary to select for argument difficult points of law. This is the origin of the expression "moot point" meaning a difficult legal question.

MORAL IMBECILE.—In law a moral imbecile is not a lunatic but a mental defective. He is defined as a person suffering from some permanent mental defect who, in addition, has strong vicious or immoral habits or desires, and who cannot be restrained by punishment. Special treatment is provided for such persons. (*See* LUNATICS; MENTAL DEFECTIVES.)

MORRISON, Steinie.—In March, 1911, before Mr. Justice Darling at the Old Bailey there took place one of the most remarkable and controversial trials in the criminal history of this country. Steinie Morrison, a Russian Jew, who claimed to have been born in Australia, was charged with the murder of Leon Beron, also a Russian Jew, who had spent most of his life in France.

Beron had met his death in melodramatic fashion. He was last seen by a cabman who had driven him in company with Morrison from Sydney Street at 2 a.m. on New Year's Day, walking off with his companion into the darkness of Clapham Common. He was found later in the morning lying dead in some bushes on the Common, killed by seven blows on the head, with the letter S slashed by a knife across each of his cheeks.

A week later, after extensive enquiries the police called at Morrison's address to find that he had left hurriedly, but they arrested him elsewhere later in the day. He was taken to Leman Street Police Station, and, it was alleged, before he had been told by any police officer why he was detained, volunteered the statement, "I understand I am here on a very serious charge, murder I am told."

The Case for the Prosecution.—At the trial it was the duty of Mr. (later Sir) Richard Muir, who appeared for the Crown, to connect the prisoner Morrison with the murder. There was no complicated medical evidence as is so often found in murder trials, but a series of witnesses was called by the prosecution to prove that Morrison had the opportunity of committing the crime and had been seen out and about in Whitechapel with the murdered man on the night of the murder. By far the most important of these witnesses were three cabmen who identified Morrison as a passenger in their different taxis on that evening. First there was the man who had driven Beron and Morrison from Sydney Street to Clapham at 2 a.m., then A. Stephens, who picked up a single fare at Clapham shortly after 3 a.m. and drove him to Kennington, and third, Castlen, who drove two men, one of whom he identified as the prisoner, from Kennington to Finsbury Park at 3.30 a.m. If their evidence of identification was believed, it was proved that Morrison came to the scene of the crime with the murdered man and about an hour later left alone.

Carrying Gold on Him.—Besides this evidence, it was proved that Morrison and Beron frequented the same restaurant in Whitechapel, where Beron was known as "the Landlord," and commonly regarded as a man of means who carried sums of gold upon him, that Morrison knew Clapham Common well having been previously employed by a baker there; finally, that shortly after the murder he was possessed of a large sum of money, which he accounted for by stating that it had been sent to him by his mother in Russia. The prosecution further stressed his flight from his home and alleged that he ceased to use the restaurant of which Beron and he were formerly habitués.

Finally, there was his alleged statement at the Police Station mentioning "murder" before any officer had told him the charge.

The Defence and Character of Accused.—Morrison, who was defended by Mr. Abinger, denied all knowledge of the crime, and swore that he was at home and in bed by midnight. To those crown witnesses who said they saw him in the restaurant with Beron he replied by an alibi, saying he was at the Shoreditch Empire and was seen by two young women. During his cross-examination of the witnesses for the prosecution, Mr. Abinger attacked the character of at least one of them. Now the Criminal Evidence Act, 1898, which allows a prisoner to give evidence on his own behalf, does not generally permit of questions being put to him to shew his previous bad character. But there are exceptions, and one is if the defence attack the character of prosecution witnesses. So by his attack, Mr. Abinger enabled Mr. Muir to cross-examine Morrison as to his prior history, and to shew him to be an ex-convict and professional burglar. The fairness of this rule has been much criticised, and in this case it probably played an important part in securing a conviction.

A Last-Minute Witness.—At the ninth day of the trial, when Mr. Muir was about to continue his final speech, a sensation was created in court by an application by Mr. Abinger to call fresh evidence. The witness was a P.C. Greaves, who swore he had heard a detective-sergeant tell Morrison he was wanted for murder. If believed, this disproved of one of the points for the prosecution. The witness was severely cross-examined, and Mr. Justice Darling told the jury he regarded this as a minor point in the trial.

The jury were absent only a little over half an hour and brought in a verdict of guilty.

Reprieve.—The Court of Criminal Appeal upheld the conviction, but the Home Secretary, Mr. Winston Churchill, commuted the sentence to penal servitude for life. Morrison died in 1921.

MORTGAGE.—A Mortgage is a conveyance of land, or an assignment of other property, as a security for the payment of a debt or the discharge of some other obligation for which it is given. The terms "conveyance" and "assignment" each mean transfer.

The person borrowing the money on the security of land is called the "Mortgagor" and the person lending it the "Mortgagee." The document whereby the land is transferred for this purpose is called the Mortgage Deed. It contains the terms subject to which the loan has been granted so far as they affect the security provided by the land. Notwithstanding the transfer, the mortgagor remains in possession and complete control over the land so long as he complies with the terms of the mortgage deed. Furthermore, on repaying the money borrowed, and interest, he is entitled to have the land conveyed back to him, or to anyone else at his request, free from the rights which he had given to the mortgagee for the purpose of the security.

The law governing mortgages is contained in a number of Acts of Parliament from 1925 onwards. The principal Act is the Law of Property Act, 1925. The contract to lend money and create a mortgage as security must be in writing.

As the sole object of a mortgage is to provide security for a loan, the mortgagee should have the land valued by a competent valuer, and the amount advanced should be a third or a quarter less than the full value of the land.

The next step is for the mortgagee's solicitor to make a very strict investigation of the title, i.e. of the mortgagor's right to the land and power of mortgaging it. The mortgagor's solicitor prepares an Abstract of Title, which is an epitome of the documents and facts constituting the mortgagor's title, which he sends to the mortgagee's solicitor, who makes precisely the same investigations, submits requisitions on title (which are queries arising out of the investigation), which are replied to by the mortgagee's solicitor, as in the case of a sale of land.

Terms of Deed.—The mortgagor undertakes in the mortgage deed to repay the money by a certain date, usually six months after the date of the deed, together with interest to the date of repayment at the stated rate; but if he does not repay at the expiration of such time, then to pay interest every six months on so much of the mortgage money as shall not have been repaid. In practice it is not intended that he should repay within the six months. There are numerous other conditions, some of which, if of a special nature, must be set out in full in the deed. Others will be implied by law. The term of three thousand years, or other term created by the mortgage deed can be terminated at any time by either party giving to the other six months' notice.

A mortgage can also be created by the mortgagor creating a "Charge" on the land in favour of the mortgagee. The deed is called a "Charge by way of Legal Mortgage," and in it the mortgagor charges the land with repayment of the borrowed money and interest. This has the same effect as if a term of years had been created as described above. The rights and liabilities of the parties are laid down by statute.

The draft mortgage deed, which is prepared, or drawn, by the mortgagee's solicitor is approved by the mortgagor's solicitor and is then engrossed and executed as in the case of a Conveyance in the sale of land) by the mortgagor. The mortgagor's solicitor hands the mortgage deed, together with all other documents in the mortgagor's possession which relate to the property (called the "Title Deeds"), to the mortgagee's solicitor, and receives in exchange the money agreed to be lent. In the case of a second or subsequent mortgage, the mortgagor will not have any title deeds to hand over, as they will all be in the possession of the first mortgagee. In such a case the solicitor acting for the second or subsequent mortgagee must register his client's mortgage at the Land Registry in Lincoln's Inn Fields, London, in accordance with the provisions of the Land Charges Act, 1925. Otherwise a person taking a later mortgage may register first, having lent his money without "Notice" of the second mortgage, and so gain priority in the way of security.

If the mortgagor fails to repay the loan and interest at the expiration of the six months' notice given him by the mortgagee, the latter may apply to the Court for a "Foreclosure Decree," which is an order that the mortgagee shall become the owner of the land, and that the mortgagor shall lose his right to redeem the mortgage. During the next six months, however, the mortgagor will still have the opportunity of paying off the mortgage money together with interest

and costs, in which event he will get back the land free of the mortgage and of the order of the Court. If the money is not paid, the mortgagee can enter into possession. He will then manage the property and collect the rents himself. By doing so, however, he will incur certain responsibilities in relation to the property which he can avoid by appointing a "Receiver" (q.v.) who will manage the property in his interest, whilst in law the Receiver will be regarded as the agent of the mortgagor. The mortgagee can also secure repayment by selling the property. But before doing so he must give the mortgagor three months' written notice of his intention to sell. This will give the mortgagor the opportunity to pay in the meantime.

Movables.—A mortgage of movables, such as household furniture, is created by a Bill of Sale by way of security if the property is to remain in the possession of the mortgagor, or by a pawn or pledge if the property is handed over to the lender of the money. (*See* BILL OF SALE; PAWNBROKER.)

Life Policies.—A mortgage of a Life Policy is effected by assigning (i.e. transferring) the policy to the lender for the purpose of providing him with a security for the money lent by him. (*See* LIFE INSURANCE.)

MORTMAIN.—For varying reasons it has always been the policy of the law to put restrictions on the ownership of land by corporations and gifts of land to them. These restrictions do not apply to other kinds of property. Mortmain is the word used to describe this ownership, and it signifies that the land has come into the hands of a being which, unlike an ordinary human being, cannot die; this was a very important fact in feudal times because on a man's death the King had certain rights in his property.

All trading corporations are now exempted from these restrictions, but it is still unlawful for most charitable corporations to hold more than two acres of land without a licence from the Board of Trade; there are, however, a number of exceptions. If the holding of a charity exceeds the authorized amount the surplus may be forfeited to the State.

MORTUARIES.—Any local authority under the Public Health Acts, and every Sanitary Authority in London must provide and fit up a Mortuary. The former need only do so, however, if required by the Minister of Health. Although they are not obliged to do so unless required, they may, if they wish, provide one.

MOTHER. — Until comparatively recently, the rights of a mother of a legitimate child over the child were small compared with those of a father, and her duties also were correspondingly small. For example, the father could, in the past, always recover the custody of his child from the mother, but now, if the mother has custody of the child, the Court will not deprive her of it in favour of the father unless it is convinced that it will be for the benefit of the child. On the application of a mother, the Court may make any order that seems fit as to the custody and maintenance of the child (*see* FATHER). In certain cases, the mother has a definite right to the custody, e.g. if her husband has by persistent cruelty and neglect caused her to leave him and live separately. On the death of a child's father, the mother is the sole guardian of the child, unless the father has appointed guardians to act with her, and she then has all the powers and duties of a father, e.g. over the marriage, education, custody, religion and maintenance of the child.

A mother is empowered by the Guardianship of Infants Act, 1925, to appoint guardians to act jointly with her husband after her death, and such appointment may be made either by deed or will. (*See* ADOPTION; BASTARDY; CHILDREN; EDUCATION ; FATHER ; GUARDIANSHIP ; LEGITIMATION OF CHILDREN; LOCO PARENTIS; STEP-CHILDREN.)

MOTHER (SCOTS LAW).—A mother is entitled on the death of her husband to be the guardian of any pupil children, i.e. boys under fourteen or girls under twelve. If the father has appointed a guardian she acts jointly with him, and even if no guardian has been appointed, the Court may appoint a guardian to act with the mother. The mother has a right to appoint a guardian of her pupil children after her death and, if she dies before her husband, this guardian will act jointly with the father.

In the case of illegitimate children the mother is alone entitled to the guardianship, and if the child dies intestate—i.e. without making a will—she will take the same rights

in his property as she would have done had the child been legitimate and she had been the only surviving parent. In the same way if she dies intestate leaving no legitimate issue, any illegitimate children take the same interest in her estate as they would have had if they had been legitimate.

MOTION.—This is the name applied to certain applications made in Court to a Judge asking the Court to make some order in favour of the applicant. In these cases the Court is said to be "moved."

MOTIVE.—A motive is that which actuates a person in adopting a particular course of conduct or doing a particular act. It must always be distinguished in law from intention. For instance, if a man shoots at another, his intention usually will be either to kill or injure him. His motive will be quite a different thing. It may be ill-will, revenge, or any of the countless causes of human behaviour. In the criminal law, motive is in general immaterial, though of course, intention is all important. If a man kills another without intention, it will, in general, not be murder, and frequently not even manslaughter. But whatever it is, it is idle for him, when the question of his guilt or innocence is being decided, to prove his motive. A motive is, however, frequently of importance in connection with the question of punishment. If a person does wrong through a good motive his punishment will normally be lighter than if he be actuated by a bad motive.

MOTOR-CAR.—Until 1930 there was no complete legislation for motor-cars in this country, but they were merely treated as a division of a much wider class of vehicles known as locomotives on the highway. Since 1930 special rules and regulations have been passed dealing with every conceivable aspect of the motor-car. These regulations relate to the equipment, construction, inspection and use of the motor-car. (*See* SPECIAL SUPPLEMENT "ROAD TRAFFIC.")

MOVABLES (SCOTS LAW).— Movables correspond to the personal property of English law and are distinguished from heritage or heritable property, which corresponds to the land or real property of English law. As heritage strictly means property which on a man's death passes to his heir, so movables strictly means property which passes to a man's executors for the

Sir Richard Muir

benefit of his next of kin.   In fact, however, movable property indicates almost every right other than land.   Thus simple debts, stocks and shares in public companies are movable.   Rights which have a tract of future time, i.e. rights which entitle the owner to have money paid to him for a period in the future, such as annuities, are considered to be heritable until they become due.   When they become due they are then considered to be movable rights.

MUIR, Sir Richard (1857-1924).— As Senior Counsel to the Treasury, Sir Richard prosecuted most of the more notorious criminals of the last generation, including Steinie Morrison and Seddon. He may be said to have abolished the Old Bailey style of advocacy, and was noted for his mastery of facts and scrupulous fairness. His cross-examination of Charles Crippen is regarded as a particularly fine piece of work.

MURDER.—The unlawful killing of a human either intentionally or in the course of committing some violent felony.   For a person to be guilty of murder he need not intend to kill the particular person he does kill.   If a man shoots at A and kills B, he is guilty of the murder of B.   Again, if he throws a bomb in a place where he knows people are likely to be, he is guilty of the murder of anyone killed by it, even though he really never intended to kill anyone at all. This is so because if a man wilfully takes the risk of killing others, not caring whether they are killed or not, his mind is really the same as that of someone who intends to kill.

Again, if two men set out to commit a crime, one having a loaded revolver and the other knowing that ne has and that he intends to use it to overcome resistance or to avoid arrest, both are equally guilty of murder if the revolver is used with fatal results.   Or if a motor bandit, held up by a policeman, drives straight at him and kills him, he can be convicted of murder.   In such a case it would be no defence to say that he thought the policeman would jump out of the way in time.

By the law of England sentence of death must be passed on every person convicted of murder, unless he is under the age of eighteen.   (*See* CAPITAL PUNISHMENT; HOMICIDE; MANSLAUGHTER.)

MUSIC.—*See* COPYRIGHT; DANCING; AND STREET MUSIC.

MUTINY.—Mutiny is an offence under the Naval Discipline Act, the Army Act, and the Air Force Act.   It means collective insubordination by persons subject to those Acts with the intention of resisting lawful superior service authority.

It is important to note that it is the combining together that is the essence of mutiny. A single individual cannot, generally speaking, be found guilty of the crime of mutiny.

NAME, CHANGE OF.—The law relating to changes of personal names is in an uncertain state, and it is impossible to define it with confidence.   It seems that, strictly speaking, a christian name (or baptismal name) may not be legally changed except at confirmation.   But any name that is not a baptismal name (e.g. a surname or the forename of a non-christian or even, perhaps, the christian name of a non-conformist) may be changed.   But, though that appears to be the strict rule, christian names are continually changed, and the discontinuance of the use of an original christian

Where the Great Murder Trials are staged. Above: No. 1 Court of the Old Bailey to-day, and below: the Old Bailey a hundred years ago.

name can seldom, if ever, prejudice the user. In any case, any number of additional names may be used at will.

Apart from the question of christian names, a person's name is the name by which he is commonly known, and, of course, generally speaking, a child is commonly known by the surname his father bore. An illegitimate child, on the other hand, is usually known by his mother's name; but nothing can prevent his using any other name (including that of his reputed father), and, when such use has caused him to be generally known by that name, it will actually be his name. A new name, therefore, may be acquired by persuading one's neighbours to call one by such new name. No formality of any kind is required; a name is merely a tag or label to be used for the purposes of identification. Any name may be adopted or used, and no objection can be raised by A if B takes it into his head to use his (A's) name. A divorced wife is, therefore, entitled to retain the name of her husband. The only limitation to the right to discard a former name is that it may not be discarded for the purpose of effecting a fraud.

Formalities.—Although no formalities are legally necessary, it is a common practice to accompany a change of name either by the insertion of an advertisement in a local and/or national newspaper, or by the execution of a deed poll. The purpose of such a course is to preserve evidence (so that if any question arises as to identity at a later date, the advertisement or deed may be produced to set all doubts at rest), and to induce one's neighbours and friends to adopt and use one's new name, for, until they do so, no change of name has been effected, the change depending entirely upon repute. But, as advertisements or deeds may be lost, there is a procedure whereby a deed poll may be enrolled in the Central Office of the Supreme Court. Before this facility will be given, various requirements must be complied with, e.g. a British birth certificate or naturalization certificate must be produced (for further particulars, apply to Room 106, Royal Courts of Justice, London, W.C.2). The fee for enrolment is £2.

Aliens.—By the Aliens Restriction Amendment Act, 1919, an alien "shall not for any purpose assume or use, or purport to assume or use, or continue, after the commencement of this Act, the assumption or use of any name other than that by which he was ordinarily known on the fourth day of August, nineteen hundred and fourteen." The effect of this section appears to be that every alien must use the name he used in 1914, even though he visits England for the first time twenty years later for a short holiday, and even though he had changed his name by the law of his own country twenty years previously.

NATIONAL ASSEMBLY.—The National Assembly or Church Assembly was endowed in 1919 by the Church of England Assembly (Powers) Act, with considerable powers in relation to church legislation. It is composed of a House of Bishops (which is an amalgamation of the upper houses of Convocation); a House of Clergy (which is an amalgamation of the lower houses of Convocation); and a House of Laity (which is elected by the Diocesan Conferences). The Assembly must meet at least once a year under the chairmanship of the Archbishop of Canterbury, or, failing him, of the Archbishop of York. Any of the three houses may sit separately, and, in some cases, are bound so to do.

The purpose of the Assembly is to act as a Parliament for the church, to consider Measures (legislation) relating to ecclesiastical matters. After having passed such a Measure, which is always in a form similar to an Act of Parliament, the Assembly then presents it to Parliament for approval. The Measure must either be accepted or rejected by Parliament as a whole: it is not possible for Parliament to amend or to reject only part of a Measure. By this procedure, the delay and unsuitability previously involved in the passing of ordinary Acts of Parliament in relation to church matters are very largely eliminated.

NATIONAL EMERGENCY.—The Emergency Powers Act, 1920, gives to the Crown power to proclaim that a state of emergency exists in Great Britain. This may only be done when action by a body of persons has been taken, or is immediately threatened on so extensive a scale as to be likely to interfere with the food, water, fuel, light, or transport services, to such an extent as to deprive the community, or any substantial portion of it, of the essentials of life.

A proclamation under this Act may only remain in force for a month, but fresh proclamations may be made from time to time as circumstances demand. If, when a proclamation is made, Parliament is not sitting, it must be assembled at once, and the proclamation communicated to it.

When a proclamation has been made, the Privy Council may make regulations having the force of law for securing the essentials of life to the community. These regulations may deal with the preservation of public order, the distribution of food, water, fuel and light, the maintenance of transport facilities, and any other matters essential to the public safety. They may not authorise any form of compulsory military service or industrial conscription, nor may they make it an offence for persons to take part in a strike or peacefully persuade others to do so. Every regulation must be laid before Parliament immediately it is made, and must be approved by a resolution of both Houses of Parliament within seven days of being so laid.

NATIONAL HEALTH INSURANCE.—Generally speaking, every person between the ages of 16 and 65 who is employed at a salary not greater than £250 per annum, and is not in business upon his own account, is required by law to be insured under the National Health Insurance scheme. This applies to domestic servants, etc., as much as to other employees. Members of the army, navy and air force, salaried railway servants and certificated school teachers have schemes of their own, and are exempted from the ordinary provisions of the scheme; while any person who possesses a pension or unearned income of more than £26 per year may obtain a certificate of exemption from the local insurance committee or approved society, and, after receiving such certificate, may claim to be exempted from the scheme.

Approved Societies.—The National Health Insurance is run through approved societies. There is a large number of these in different areas, providing for different trades, and all of them are subject to the control of the Minister of Health. They must not be run for profit, and must be controlled by the insured members of the society. Various provisions for their amalgamation and organisation by the Minister

of Health provide that members are in no danger of losing their benefit under the scheme by reason of the bad management or failure of an approved society.

Although most insured persons prefer to be insured through one or other of the approved societies, it is not necessary to be a member, and anyone who is not a member, or who has been expelled from membership is entitled to become a "deposit contributor." In such a case his contributions are paid direct to a fund administered by the government, and except that he does not obtain any additional benefits such as are referred to hereafter, he is, as far as benefits are concerned, in the same position as a member of an approved society.

Contributions.—The ordinary rate of contribution is 1/6 per week for men and 1/1 per week for women, but a voluntary contributor pays 3d. per week less if his income is greater than £250 per year. The contributions are not payable by the employee after the age of 65, but if he or she continues to be employed after that age, the employer must continue to pay 9d. per week for a man and 7d. a week for a woman. No contribution is payable during unemployment, nor during absence from work owing to sickness whether the insured person receives wages during the absence from sickness or not.

The whole of the contribution is payable by the employer, who must stamp a card at, or before the time of payment of the wages for the week. He may then deduct from the wages of the employee the sum of 9d. a week in the case of a man, and 6d. per week in the case of a woman, but where the wages are especially low, the workers' contribution is sometimes smaller. The worker is entitled to possession of his own card, but must hand it to his employer whenever the employer needs it for paying contributions, or to shew it to an Inspector, and the penalty for failing to do this is £10. It is most important that the cards should be stamped each week punctually, otherwise the employer is liable to penalties.

There are also severe penalties upon an employer for failing to stamp cards or for wilfully withholding them from the workman, the penalty in each case being £10 for each separate offence.

Voluntary Contributors.— Persons

who are not bound by law to contribute to the insurance scheme may become voluntary contributors and receive full benefit in the following cases:

(a) An insured person who ceases to be employed, provided that he has paid 104 contributions before he ceased to be employed.

(b) Persons in exempted employment, or who have been in exempted employment for at least 104 weeks and have ceased such employment.

(c) Uninsured men who marry insured women for whom 104 contributions have been paid, and various other persons.

If any of these voluntary contributors pays less than 45 contributions in the course of any one year, he cannot continue to be a voluntary contributor unless he makes up his contributions for the year to 45, but weeks of sickness will count as part of the 45 contributions.

Benefits.—The ordinary benefits under the scheme available to all members are Medical, Sickness, Disablement and Maternity Benefit, and if owing to the failure of an employer to stamp the card of a worker he can shew that he has been deprived of benefit which he would otherwise have obtained, he can recover the full amount of the benefit from the employer by Police Court proceedings, provided that he brings the proceedings within a year.

Medical Benefit.—Immediately an employee becomes insured, he is entitled to receive medical benefit, which consists of medical attendance and treatment, drugs and medicines, surgical appliances, treatment for consumption, etc. Medical attendance at childbirth is not included, nor is a voluntary contributor whose income exceeds £250, entitled to medical benefit at all.

Every area in the country has a local insurance committee which administers medical benefit, and a panel of doctors is provided from which the insured person may select his own doctor to whom he must thereafter go for treatment. For minor ailments, the panel patient must call upon the doctor during his usual panel consulting hours; but where urgent treatment is required, the doctor is obliged to call at the home of the patient, and if he fails to give such service as an ordinary paying patient is entitled to get, complaint may be made to the local insurance committee who may take what disciplinary steps they think fit.

Drugs, medicines and surgical appliances when prescribed by the panel doctor are obtainable free of charge, generally from chemists approved by the local insurance committee or from the doctor himself if he has been approved for this purpose. Full particulars of all of these arrangements in every area can be obtained through the approved society or direct from the Insurance Committee for the district, whose address may be obtained at any Post Office in the locality.

Sickness Benefit.—Sickness benefit consists of a weekly payment to an insured person direct from the approved society or from the deposit contributors fund through the local insurance committee, while the insured person is disabled from work by reason of sickness or disease for a period longer than 4 days.

It is payable after the fourth day of incapacity, provided that notice has been given to the approved society, and it continues during the incapacity but not for a longer period than 26 weeks. It is payable in respect of the period before the fourth day also.

No one is entitled to sickness benefit unless he has paid at least 26 weekly contributions before falling sick, nor is anyone over 65 so entitled since an old age pension is then payable.

In calculating the 26 weeks for this purpose, if the insured person falls ill again during the next twelve months after his recovery, his next illness is considered as a continuation of the first for the purpose of calculating the 26 weeks of sickness benefit.

The ordinary rate of sickness benefit is 15/- per week for men, 12/- for unmarried women and widows, and 10/- for married women; but if the insured person has been insured for more than 26, but less than 104 weeks, only the reduced benefit of 9/- for men and 7/6 for all women is payable.

However, any person who has paid less than 104 contributions and is ill, or unable to obtain employment, may himself pay contributions for his period of illness or unemployment until 104 contributions have been paid, when he will be entitled to full benefit.

Disablement Benefit.—After the 26

weeks of sickness benefit has expired an insured person, if still disabled from work, is entitled to draw disablement benefit, provided that 104 contributions have been paid; the normal rate of disablement benefit being 7/6 per week for men and 6/- per week for women if widows or unmarried, and 5/- per week for married women.

Sickness and disablement benefit is not payable when the insured person is entitled to benefit under the Workman's Compensation Act or in some other manner, unless the amount of compensation obtained by him in that manner is less than the benefit due under the Health Insurance scheme, in which case he is entitled to be paid the difference between the compensation he actually obtains and the benefit to which he would otherwise be entitled. In this case, if he falls ill again within 12 months of the first illness, only a period proportionate to the benefit actually paid counts in reckoning the 26 weeks for sickness benefit.

Discharged soldiers, sailors and airmen who are entitled to a pension in respect of disablement in the highest degree can obtain sickness benefit under the act at the rate of 7/6 per week, but only until they have been in subsequent insurable employment for at least 26 weeks; and they cannot obtain disablement benefit at all unless they have been in subsequent insurable employment for at least 104 weeks.

Maternity Benefit.—This consists of a payment of £2 when the wife or widow (if the child is posthumous), of an insured member gives birth to a child, or when an insured woman, whether married or unmarried, has a child. If both wife and husband are insured, the wife is entitled to two maternity benefits totalling £4, being one in respect of the husband and one in respect of her own contributions, while if she is an employed contributor and her husband is not insured, the wife is entitled to double benefit, i.e. £4.

No right to maternity benefit arises until at least 42 weekly contributions have been paid, and if the woman is herself insured, she is not entitled to sickness or disablement benefit for 4 weeks after her confinement. All approved societies have a rule that no woman must undertake remunerative work at all during the 4 weeks after confinement.

The maternity benefit is intended for the use of the mother and child, and must be employed for their benefit. It is not intended for the benefit of the husband.

Married Women.—When an employed contributor who is a woman is married, she must at once give notice to her approved society, and if she fails to do so, she is liable to a penalty.

A married woman who continues in employment after her marriage is entitled to the ordinary benefits of married women as if she were not married. But a woman who ceases to be a person normally in employment after her marriage (and for this purpose she ceases to be a person normally in employment if, during the eight weeks immediately before her marriage, or for eight consecutive weeks in the year after her marriage, she is unemployed), is entitled only to reduced benefit, viz.

(1) Six weeks sickness benefit during the year after her marriage.

(2) A single maternity benefit during the two years after her marriage.

(3) Medical benefit for one year after the expiry of the six months' period in which she ceased to be a person normally in employment, and (4) additional benefits for two years after marriage.

If, subsequent to having become a person not normally in employment, the married woman becomes permanently employed again, she is treated as if she were becoming insured for the first time for the purposes of ordinary benefits; but she is also entitled during the two years after her marriage to the reduced benefits referred to above until she is qualified again for full benefits.

If a married woman does not return to work for two years after marriage, she ceases to be insured, and no married woman can be a voluntary contributor during her husband's lifetime.

Soldiers, Sailors and Airmen, if they are members of an approved Society at the time when they enter the service of the Crown, continue members during their service. They are entitled to maternity benefit but not to medical, sickness or disablement benefit, and no deduction in respect of health insurance is made from their pay. On leaving the forces they become entitled to the full ordinary benefits.

Arrears and Unemployment.—

Since the contributions of an employed contributor are paid in the ordinary way by the employer, he cannot in the normal way get into arrears with his contributions when he is unemployed. A voluntary contributor, however, can fall into arrears by failing to keep up his contributions himself, and in such cases a member who falls into arrears is liable to a penalty in the form of reduction of benefit until the arrears are paid off. If the arrears arise because of the fault of the employer, the workman is entitled to recover the benefit he has lost through that default from the employer direct by Police Court proceedings.

If, however, an employed contributor becomes unemployed, or a voluntary contributor fails to keep up his contributions, he continues to be a member of the approved society until the 30th June or the 31st December which comes next before the expiry of two years after the date on which he became unemployed.

During this period he is entitled, without any payment, to full benefits under the scheme, and when this period has ended he is not entitled to any further benefits, and his membership lapses unless he can prove (1) that throughout the whole of the period of two years when he obtained free benefit he was genuinely seeking work (this he can generally do by shewing the society his unemployment card stamped by the local Labour Exchange); and (2) that he has been an employed contributor for 208 weeks before he was last employed, and had paid 160 contributions while last continuously insured under the act. If he can satisfy these conditions, he is entitled to full medical benefit and one half the ordinary sickness and disablement benefit for a further period of a year without paying any further contributions. Persons who are over 60 when entering upon this "extended year" can sometimes obtain benefit until they are 65. If the insured person was entitled to sickness benefit at the date at which he fell out of work—the two-year period for this purpose is reckoned from the end of the illness—and if, during the two-year period of free insurance or the extended year mentioned above, the insured person falls sick and is still sick at the date when his insurance would otherwise have expired, he

is entitled to continue his benefit until his disablement is completed, and continues to be insured until the end of the half-year period next after the date at which the disablement ceased. Any other illness during the two-year free period or the extended year does not increase the period of free insurance.

While an insured person is unemployed, he need not pay any contributions, though he is entitled, if he wishes to do so, to continue to pay up to 104 contributions himself in order to qualify himself for full sickness and disablement benefit, and after 104 contributions in all have been paid, whether while he was in employment or not, he can, on giving notice to his approved society, continue to pay the full contributions himself as a voluntary contributor.

If he has not paid contributions during his unemployment, and during the two-year period of free insurance he regains insurable employment, he must pay arrears of contributions in respect of one half of the number of weeks during which he was unemployed and genuinely seeking work, or his benefit will be reduced. In estimating the amount of the arrears, the full amount of the contribution without deduction of the employer's share is payable by the workman in arrears.

After the two years have expired and the workman has ceased, by reason of unemployment, to be a member of the approved society, he is treated, if he enters into insurable employment again, as if he were becoming insured for the first time; but if he becomes employed again within one year of having ceased to be a member of the approved society he is entitled of right to be re-admitted as a member of the same society. If he becomes employed again outside the year period he can only be re-admitted to his old society if the society consents. (See Approved Society; Disablement Benefit; Maternity Benefit; Medical Benefit; Panel; Sickness Benefit.)

NATIONALITY.—On account of the confusion and conflict of various national laws relating to nationality and naturalization, it is not an uncommon thing for a person to have, or to acquire a dual nationality. For example, a person may be naturalized in England, yet still retain his foreign nationality, and, indeed, may be wholly unable to throw off such foreign nationality. Similarly, a person born abroad of British parents who were born in England will be British by reason of his parentage; but he will also very probably be a national of the country in which he was born; and if military service is compulsory in that country, he will be liable to perform such service. In case of war, such a person could hardly avoid being a traitor to one state or the other. Until some international agreement is arrived at, there appears to be no way of avoiding such difficulties, and in recent times the difficulties have become by no means negligible.

Conversely, a person may lose all nationality, and become stateless; this is particularly noticeable in the case of women who marry citizens of the United States: by their marriage with an alien they become, by English law, aliens; yet, by the law of the United States, they do not acquire citizenship in the United States, but remain aliens there too. Similarly, a British subject naturalized, say, in France, thereby loses his British nationality; if, subsequently, his naturalization certificate is revoked by the French Government, he will not automatically become British by English law, even though French law may declare him to be so, with the result that he may be deemed British in France, yet an alien when he gets to England. The troubles of stateless persons are multifarious, the most striking being that, as they belong to no state, no state is able to issue them a passport. (*See also* ALIENS; BRITISH SUBJECT; DENIZENS; NATURALIZATION; PASSPORT.)

NATURALIZATION.—In 1901 the Naturalization Laws Committee issued a report which resulted in the British Nationality Act, 1914. This Act, with subsequent amendments, contains the whole code of naturalization.

Naturalization certificates are granted by the Home Secretary, and whether he will make such grant is entirely in his discretion; no appeal lies against his decision; and he need give no reason for giving or withholding the certificate. The applicant must satisfy the Home Secretary (i) that he has resided in His Majesty's dominions for not less than five years during the preceding eight years (of which at least the one year immediately preceding the application must have been passed within the United King-

dom); or that he has been in the service of the Crown for not less than five years within the preceding eight years; and (ii) that he intends, if the certificate is granted, to reside in His Majesty's dominions or to enter or continue in the service of the Crown; and (iii) that he is of good character and has an adequate knowledge of the English language. It is important to notice that the Home Office has taken the view that residence in the United Kingdom by virtue of a temporary licence is not residence such as is required by the Act. It follows that only in very few cases will an application for naturalization succeed, for the number of aliens possessing a licence permanently to reside in the United Kingdom is comparatively small.

A certificate of naturalization has no effect until the applicant has taken the oath of allegiance, and such oath must be taken within one month of the date of the certificate (*see* ALLEGIANCE). In certain circumstances, the requirements of residence will be relaxed, especially in the case of a woman who was originally British but lost her nationality by marrying an alien, and has subsequently become single by divorce or the death of her husband.

The effect of naturalization is to vest in the person naturalized all the rights and duties of a natural-born British subject with a few minor exceptions, e.g. there is still some limit on his holding shares in British ships. (*See* NAME, CHANGE OF.)

It is the duty of the Home Secretary to revoke the certificate if it appears to him that it had been obtained by false representations or fraud, or that the naturalized person has shewn himself, by act or speech, to be disaffected or disloyal to His Majesty; or has, during any war with His Majesty, unlawfully traded or communicated with the enemy; or has, within five years of the grant of the certificate, been sentenced by one of His Majesty's Courts to imprisonment of not less than one year, or to penal servitude, or to a fine of not less than £100; or was not of good character at the date of the grant of the certificate; or has, since the grant of the certificate, been for a period of not less than seven years ordinarily resident outside the Empire unless during that time he has (i) acted as a representative of a British subject, company or firm that carries on business within the Empire, or (ii) been in the service of the Crown, or (iii) maintained substantial connection with His Majesty's dominions. But in all these cases the Home Secretary must be satisfied that the continuance of the certificate is not conducive to the public good. In certain cases an enquiry must be held if application is made by the naturalized person, before the revocation of his certificate can be effected. In other cases the Home Secretary may order such enquiry if he thinks fit. The committee of enquiry has all the powers of a Court of Justice in such matters as compelling the attendance of witnesses, etc.

The wife and children of a person whose certificate has been revoked retain their British nationality unless the Home Secretary otherwise orders, or unless the wife makes a declaration of alienage within six months after the revocation. The original holder reverts (according to English law) to the nationality he formerly held: it is quite a different matter whether his state of origin will, by *its* law, accept him back again—if it will not, then he will find himself in the position of having no nationality at all. (*See* NATIONALITY.)

Numerous regulations as to the procedure to be adopted in order to obtain a naturalization certificate have been issued by the Home Office, to whom application should be made. The fee payable is £10, of which £1 must accompany the application, the balance being payable only if the certificate is granted. But when the certificate is granted to a woman who was originally British and became an alien by marriage, the whole amount of the fee is 5/-.

An alien may become a naturalized British subject in any British possession, but, except in the case of the Dominions and British India, the approval of the Home Secretary must be obtained for the grant of such certificate. (*See also* ALLEGIANCE; BRITISH SUBJECT; DENIZENS; NATIONALITY.)

NE EXEAT REGNO.—The writ "Ne exeat regno" is a prerogative writ (*see* PREROGATIVE WRITS), and was formerly considerably used for the purpose of preventing persons from leaving the kingdom, but it is now very rare, since it will be granted only (i) when the person seeking the writ is the plaintiff in an action against the person against whom the writ is sought; (ii) where the plaintiff's claim exceeds £50 and is in

respect of an ascertained and fixed debt (e.g. not for damages) (iii) where there is probable cause for believing that the defendant is about to quit England; and (iv) where the absence of the defendant from England will materially prejudice the plaintiff in his action. (*See also* PREROGATIVE WRITS.)

NEGLIGENCE.—Negligence is a term of the first importance in law. It figures in criminal matters where it is described usually as criminal negligence. If death results from criminal negligence the crime of manslaughter is committed. It occurs also in connection with contracts. Was there negligence in performing a contract? Again in trusts the question is frequently asked: Was this or that trustee negligent in the performance of his duties?

In the Law of Torts (q.v.) negligence constitutes a special cause of action usually invoked in connection with personal injuries or damage to property or if, through negligence, anyone injures the person, or to make good any damages for the injury that he has done. The most familiar example is that of negligence by the driver of a vehicle on the highway.

The question of whether a person is negligent or not, has to be decided by the application to each particular case of a general rule, namely "Did the defendant act as a reasonable man would have acted in the circumstances?" The standard of the "reasonable" man is not that of a man of exceptional skill or mental agility; just as it is not that of a man of subnormal skill or mentality. A person may fall short of the highest standard of care, and not be negligent in law. For instance, if a driver of a motor car is, through some circumstances which he could not reasonably foresee, placed in a position of great danger and, as between two courses of action, adopts the less wise one, he will not necessarily be guilty of negligence. In such a case an exceptionally skilled driver, or a person of exceptional mental quickness might have adopted the better course, but the question will be what would the ordinary reasonable man have done? So, also, it is no excuse for a driver to say: "I only started driving a car yesterday, consequently I do not know how to drive reasonable well, but I did drive as well as I could." (*See* CONTRIBUTORY NEGLIGENCE, AND SPECIAL SUPPLEMENT "ROAD TRAFFIC.")

NEW PROCEDURE.—In 1932 in order to accelerate the trial of cases, a new system was introduced for bringing cases to trial known as new procedure. This applies to all actions except actions for libel, slander, malicious prosecution, false imprisonment, seduction, breach of promise of marriage, actions in which fraud is alleged by the plaintiff, and actions in a District Registry other than the District Registries in Liverpool and Manchester. No case can be placed in the new procedure list unless the solicitor for the plaintiff certifies that it is fit for the list.

The main features of a case which is tried in the new procedure list are that a great deal of the preliminary work, i.e. interlocutory proceedings (q.v.) which were previously heard before Masters of the Court are now taken by one of two Judges who are in charge of the new procedure list and who will ultimately hear the case. Further, on the hearing of a summons, the Judge deals once and for all with the large number of matters which were otherwise dealt with piecemeal on various applications. Thus he will decide what particulars of pleadings are required and also whether any party wishes to administer interrogatories. The parties may also agree to limit the number of their witnesses or their right of appeal, i.e. that they will appeal only to the Court of Appeal, and not to the House of Lords.

NEW TRIAL.—Where an unsuccessful litigant in the High Court or a County Court wishes to appeal against the decision of the Court that tried the action, upon some ground such as misdirection of the jury by the Judge, or the admission or rejection of evidence improperly, or because the verdict is against the weight of the evidence, or the mistake or perjury of a witness, the proper application for him to make is for a new trial. If the original action was tried in the High Court, then the application for a new trial must be made to the Court of Appeal after giving 14 days' notice to the other litigant. If the original action was heard in the County Court, the application may be made to the County Court Judge immediately after the trial, or with seven days' notice to the other side, at the first Court held after the expiry of 12 clear days from the date of hearing.

The Court by which an appeal is heard, is entitled always to order a new trial if it thinks proper. (See APPEAL IN COUNTY COURT; APPEAL IN HIGH COURT.)

NEWGATE CALENDAR.—The Newgate Calendar is a series of unofficial publications commenced in 1773, containing the lives and trials of many notorious murderers, thieves, and forgers who have been

---

EXECUTION
OF FRANCIS WARNE,
For the Murder of AMELIA BLUNT, at Chadwell Heath.

This morning, Francis Warne expiated his crime on the scaffold at Springfield County Goal. There was a large concourse of people to witness the sad spectacle. At an early hour the worthy Chaplain, was engaged in prayer, and so sincere appeared the contriteness of the condemned man's spirit, that the Rev. Chaplain administered to him the Sacrament. The Culprit slept but little during the night, and he became very excited, which appeared to increase as the fatal hour drew near, and it was not till he had received consolation from the Chaplain that he became composed. Then it was that the prisoner wept bitterly, and while tears rolled down his cheeks, said to the Chaplain, "Oh, sir, it's very soon for me to part with life, and in a way so awful I now I deserve my fate, and I hope it will be a warning to other men." Here the colloquy was interrupted by the entrance into the condemned cell of Calcraft, who having shook hands with the Culprit, at once pinioned him. The mournful cavalcade then formed, the Chaplain commenced reading in a very impressive manner, the burial service for the dead, the Culprit praying fervently till they reached the gallows. Anon the drop fell with a heavy thud, and after a few struggles, Francis Warne ceased to exist. He fully confessed to his terrible crime.

On Wednesday, December 14, Francis Warne, alias Toddy, a great hulking fellow, was at the Chelmsford assizes, charged with the wilful murder of Amelia Blunt, on the 24th of September, by cutting her throat.

Mr. Poland and the Hon. Dudley Campbell conducted the prosecution on behalf of the Treasury, the prisoner was defended by Mr. Woollett.

The facts of the case were of a somewhat singular character, and there was not the least doubt as to the prisoner's guilt, the only question raised by his counsel being whether he was of sound mind at the time he did it. The deceased, a widow, with two children, consented some time since to live with the prisoner. Although he was a most ruffianly fellow, she cohabited with him for some months, but at last his brutality compelled her to leave him. She then went as housekeeper to an old man named Warren. He had a son who had formed an intimacy with the deceased, and they were to have been married within a week after the murder was committed. The prisoner, who was very angry at the deceased for leaving him. About six weeks before the murder, the deceased had been to a public-house, which is a short distance from the cottage where she resided, and she saw the prisoner there. He called her out, and asked her whether there was any chance of their coming together again. She told him there was not, and said that she was going to get married to another man. The prisoner upon this said to her, "Milly, then you must die." The deceased rejoined, "If I do, you will have to die too;" and they then parted. On the 24th of September, the old man, Warren, went out about half-past ten to fetch some beer, leaving the deceased in a wash-house adjoining the cottage; He returned in a very short time, and went into the wash-house when he found the woman partly in the act of taking some clothes out of the copper and leaning over it. He went to her and put his arm round her, and to his horror she fell upon him and forced him to the ground. He then observed that her throat was cut, and she gave one sigh and died. As soon as he had recovered from the shock, he gave an alarm, and Mr. Bowen, surgeon was soon on the spot, and discovered that she had received three frightful wounds upon the throat, one of which divided the carotid artery. Suspicion at once fell upon the prisoner. Shortly before the murder was committed the prisoner met a man named Turner; and after some conversation had passed between them, the prisoner made use of the observation that he would hear of something presently; and he then went to a hedge and cut his throat. The evidence left no doubt that he must have proceeded almost immediately to the cottage, and waited until the old man left, and then rushed upon the unfortunate woman while in the act of washing, and cut her throat. He then made his escape. The police easily traced the prisoner after he fled from the wash-house. He had very singular "clump" feet, and these marks led the police upon his track. After examining several witnesses confirming the above particulars, the jury almost immediately found the prisoner Guilty. The learned judge sentenced him to death in the usual form.

Behold a sad and wretched man,
In Springfield's gallows high,
I a murder did on Chadwell Heath,
And for the same I die.
It was there I killed Amelia Blunt,—
She would not live with me,
My life a forfeit I must pay,
Alas! at Springfield's tree.

On Chadwell Heath I did her kill,—
Left her weltering in her gore,
The twenty-fourth day of September,
Eighteen hundred and sixty-four.

She once lived with me as my wife,
But I ill-used her sore,
She told me would never live,
With me for evermore;
Then I resolved to murder her,
West with a knife in hand,
And I did her so she should not live
With any other man.

She was shortly to be married
To James Warren, who did dwell,
At Chadwell Heath, near Romford,
Where they were respected well,
But Warne was fill'd with jealousy,
And vowed he'd take her life.
He determined was she should not be
Un north, another's wife.

Poor old Warren went to get his beer,
And while that he was gone,
The murderer went unto the house
Where this sad deed was done,
And when he killed Amelia Blunt,
No help of any was nigh—
And on the gallows, Francis Warne,
A murderer must die.

The murderer soon was taken,
In a cell he did display,
His moments are approaching,
Eighteen hundred and sixty-four
For him there is no pity,
See the hangman standing by,
Waiting for the signal
For the wretched man to die.

Oh! fatal cursed jealousy,
The thou that was the cause,
Of this most dreadful tragedy
As everybody knows.
Warne dearly loved Amelia Blunt,
Although he took her life,
Determined was to kill her,
'Bec she was another's wife.

And when Warne any the Hangman,
On Springfield's gallows high,
He trembled when he heard him say,
Prepare, now you must die.
You are a cruel murderer,
No power can you save,
You are condemned to lay till the Judge
Whilst a murderer's grave.

That wretched man did trembling stand
On Springfield's drop so high;
And thousands flocked from far and near
To see the murderer die.
Henry, Printer, Chelmsford.

A leaf from the Original Newgate Calendar

confined in Newgate Prison. The books are usually illustrated with crude engravings depicting either the crimes, or the execution of the criminals.

NEWSPAPERS.—The Statute law governing newspapers has been directed towards fixing the responsibility for any breach of the law by a newspaper, and in making readily ascertainable those persons, namely the printers, publishers or proprietors, responsible for its publication.

A newspaper is defined by the Newspaper and Libel Registration Act of 1881 as "Any paper containing public news, intelligence or occurrences, and any remarks or observations therein printed for sale" and published in England and Ireland periodically, or in parts or numbers at intervals not exceeding 16 days between their publication, and also any paper made public weekly or at intervals not exceeding 26 days, containing only or principally advertisements.

Proprietors and Printers.—A registry of newspapers is now kept at Somerset House, and the printers and publishers of newspapers are required to make an annual return of the title of the newspaper, and the names, descriptions and addresses, of all the proprietors. When, however, in the opinion of the Board of Trade, inconvenience might arise by the registration of the names of all the proprietors, the Board of Trade may allow the registration in the name of one or more representative proprietors. If proper annual returns are not made by the printers, or publishers, or if an omission or wilful misrepresentation is made in making the annual return, then the person making the return, or the printer or the publisher, may be liable to a penalty of £20. All returns made must be registered in the "Register of Newspaper Proprietors" which may be searched by any member of the public who may obtain certified extracts from it.

In order to enable a person, who has been injured by a libel published in a newspaper, to discover who are the persons responsible for the publication of the libel, any person who prints any book or paper, whether it comes within one of the statutory definitions of a newspaper or not, must print on the first or last page of the book or paper his name and address. Certain papers are exempted from this rule. These are papers printed by the authority of, and for the use of either of the Houses of Parliament; or impressions of engravings, or circulars containing the name and address or business of any person, or the articles in which he deals, or any catalogue for the sale of goods, by auction or any other way. Exception is also made in respect of bank notes of the Bank of England, and certain commercial documents. In the case of books or papers printed at the University Presses of Oxford or Cambridge, the printer must print instead of the name and address of the printer, "Printed at the University Press, Oxford," or "The Pitt Press, Cambridge." If he fails, he may be liable to a penalty of £5 for each copy printed.

If any person desires to bring an action for the recovery of damages, which he alleges that he has sustained by reason of the publication of any defamatory matter contained in a newspaper, such person on application to the Court may compel any person concerned as printer, publisher, or proprietor of the newspaper, to disclose the name of any person concerned with the printing or publishing of the newspaper. Where a penalty is imposed upon the printer for failing to print his name on the paper or book he has printed, or for failing to make a proper return to the newspaper registry, the informer may recover half the penalty imposed on the printer.

Libels contained in Newspapers.— (*See* DEFAMATION.) Newspapers are given some measure of protection against proceedings for libel. Reports of any judicial proceedings heard publicly are absolutely privileged, so long as the reports are fair and accurate reports, and are published contemporaneously with such proceedings and are not seditious, indecent, or blasphemous. A fair and accurate report in any such newspaper of any public meeting, except one to which neither the public nor newspaper reporters are admitted, or of any public bodies (such as a vestry meeting or a meeting of the board of management of a school), are privileged so long as they are not made maliciously, and the report of the proceedings is for the public benefit. For instance, a report of some public meeting which set out the evidence of some of the witnesses for one side while omitting to set out fully the evidence of witnesses for the other side, would in all probability make the report unfair, for it would not be a fair account of what took place and would destroy the statutory protection given to newspapers. (*See* PRIVILEGE.)

Divorce Proceedings.—By the Judicial Proceedings Act of 1926 it is not now lawful to publish in a newspaper any indecent matter the publication of which would be liable to injure public morals. This prohibition is a wide one. In particular it is not now lawful for a newspaper to publish any particulars of divorce or nullity proceedings, other than the names and addresses of the parties and the witnesses, and a concise statement of the charges and counter charges, a report of any questions of law arising, and the decision of the Court on them, the summing up of the Judge and the findings of the jury, the judgment of the Court and observations made by the Judge in giving judgment.

Criminal Libels contained in Newspapers.—A criminal prosecution for libel, may not be brought against any proprietor, publisher or person responsible for the publication of a newspaper libel alleged to be contained in it without the leave of a Judge of the High Court.

NEXT FRIEND.—Certain persons are not able to prosecute actions in the Court of their own accord and in their own name, but must do so through someone technically called a "next friend." Formerly, married women could only sue through a next friend, but to-day infants, that is persons under twenty-one, lunatics, and other persons of unsound mind are the only persons who are subject to this disability.

The next friend is usually, in the case of an infant, the nearest relation, such as the mother or father. The next friend is liable for the costs of the action, although he may recover them from the property of the infant if he has any. For this reason no one can be appointed a next friend unless he consents in writing to allow his name to be used. When an action is commenced by a next friend the form is John Brown, (an infant), by Robert Brown his next friend, plaintiff.

NEXT OF KIN.—The next of kin of a person are those who on his death would, before 1926, have been entitled to his personal property. They are distinguished from the heir, who would be entitled to the real property or land, and the rules for calculation were different. Since 1925, both real and personal property descend according to the same rules, and the distinction between the next of kin and the heir is no longer preserved. The distinction still exists in Scotland.

NISI.—"Nisi" (pron. nye sye) is a Latin word often used in the law, meaning "unless." An order nisi, therefore, is a declaration that unless good reason is shewn to the Court why it should not make the proposed order, it will proceed to do so. The object of such a declaration is to enable the person against whom the order will be made to look into the facts, and object to its being made if he sees fit. Similarly, a decree nisi in a divorce suit is a declaration that the Court will, at the expiration of six months or such shorter period as may be mentioned in the order, give a decree of dissolution or nullity of marriage unless, before that time, evidence is produced to shew why such a decree should not be made. At the end of the time fixed in the order, decree or judgment, the Court will, unless reason has been shewn why it should not, make the order "absolute," i.e. operative.

"Nisi Prius" means "at assize," because in theory every provincial case is to be tried in London at a fixed date in the future, *unless before* that date a judge should happen to come on circuit to the assize town of the district.

NOISE.—Where the occupier of premises is seriously disturbed in the enjoyment of his possession by noise on adjoining premises, he can apply for an injunction to restrain the persons guilty of the nuisance from continuing it. In order to obtain an injunction, however, it is necessary to prove that the noise is really substantial, and the complaint something more than merely fanciful. In considering whether an injunction should be granted or not, the Court is allowed to take into account the nature of the locality. For instance, a noise in a remote country district is a different matter from a noise in the centre of a busy part of London.

It is an offence to cause excessive noise by means of a motor-car. This may be done through unnecessary hooting or through friction with the road. It is the duty of all drivers of motor-cars to ensure that their vehicles are in such a state of repair, or so adjusted that they do not cause unnecessary noise when running. It is the duty of a driver of a vehicle to stop the engine when the vehicle is stationary. Noise caused through faulty silencers is also punishable.

Passengers on public service vehicles who cause unnecessary noise to the annoyance of other passengers or to persons on the highway commit an offence which may be punished in Courts of Summary Jurisdiction.

It is also an offence for any person in any urban district to annoy people by loud singing, or shouting, or other unnecessary noise.

NOMINAL DAMAGES.—Where a plaintiff succeeds in an action for damages but proves merely the violation of a legal right as distinct from substantial damage, he is entitled only to nominal damages. For instance, in a libel case if the jury think that the plaintiff has not really suffered any damage through the libel, they may award a sum such as 20/– as nominal damages. This is to be distinguished from contemptuous damages, such as $\frac{1}{4}$d., which is applicable only where the jury think that the plaintiff, though strictly speaking entitled to a verdict, should not have brought the action, or where his character is so bad that really no additional harm can have been caused to it by the matter complained of.

NONCONFORMISTS.—Members of nonconforming churches are under no disabilities of any sort or kind, save that the King himself must be in communion with the Church of England. Nonconformist ministers enjoy the same civil rights as laymen, and may sit in either House of Parliament, except that they may not become borough councillors while holding a pastoral charge.

The appointment of a Nonconformist minister to a pastorate, and his tenure thereof, are dependent upon the terms of the trust deed by virtue of which the church to which he belongs was formed and is governed. If there is no trust deed, then usage is the test. But where the pastorate is supported by voluntary contribution, the congregation have the right of election. He holds office at the will of those who have appointed him, and he may be removed without notice

at any time. Almost all property belonging to Nonconformist bodies is vested in trustees, successors to whom are, in the absence of provision in the trust deed, chosen by the congregation or body in question.

It is unlawful for more than twenty persons to meet together for the purpose of nonconforming religious worship unless the place in which they meet

(i) has been registered by the Registrar General; or

(ii) is in a private dwelling house; or

(iii) is in a building not usually appropriated to the purposes of religious worship.

Registration also carries with it certain other advantages, e.g. freedom from rates. Registration is also required for the meeting places of Roman Catholics and Jews. (*See also* QUAKERS; ROMAN CATHOLICS.)

NONFEASANCE.—A nonfeasance is the failure to do an act which one is bound to do, as distinguished from a misfeasance, which is the doing in an improper way of an act which would be legal if properly done. (*See* HIGHWAYS; MISFEASANCE.)

NON-PROVIDED SCHOOL.—A school which is not-provided—i.e. which does not belong to and is not maintained entirely by the local education authority, but which belongs to some private persons (usually under an educational trust) is called a non-provided school. (*See* EDUCATION; SCHOOL.)

NONSUIT.—When a plaintiff has presented the whole of his evidence and the Judge holds that he has not made out a case requiring the defendant to answer it, he nonsuits the plaintiff.

NOT GUILTY.—When a person is tried on indictment the jury have to return a verdict of "guilty" or "not guilty." A verdict of "not guilty" prevents the person charged from being tried again on the same facts.

NOT PROVEN (SCOTS LAW).—In Scots law a jury in a criminal case is not compelled to find a prisoner "guilty" or "not guilty," but may adopt a third choice of finding the charge not proven. As it is the law in Scotland just as in England that it is the duty of the prosecution to prove a prisoner guilty, and that if they fail to do this the prisoner is entitled to be found "not guilty", the verdict of "not proven" cannot be logically supported. Since, if the jury come to the conclusion that the facts necessary to establish the prisoner's guilt have not been made up, they should find him "not guilty." In practice, however, the verdict is used to indicate that the jury, although satisfied that the prosecution have failed to prove the prisoner guilty, are not yet satisfied that the prisoner has established his innocence. The verdict is not frequently used, and its effects, so far as the prisoner's legal position is concerned, are exactly the same as a verdict of "not guilty."

NOTARY PUBLIC.—A notary public is an office usually held by a solicitor. The holder is entitled to draw, attest or certify deeds in order to make them valid abroad. When a bill of exchange has been dishonoured on presentment for acceptance or payment, the holder may note and protest it in front of a notary public. A notary may also take and draw up protests by the master of a ship, made for the purpose of exonerating the master and owners from blame for damage to the ship or her cargo during a voyage. (*See* BILL OF EXCHANGE; SHIPPING.)

NOTE OF HAND.—This is the name occasionally applied to a promissory note. The expression promissory note is more often used in law. (*See* PROMISSORY NOTE.)

NOTICE.—A person is said to have notice of a fact when its existence has been brought to his knowledge, and in many cases the person's rights over property which he has acquired will be affected by notice of any defect in the title in the person from whom he has acquired it. Thus, if A takes a bill of exchange from B for value, he normally would have a good title to it even though B himself had no title, e.g. he stole it. If, however, A *knew* that B had stolen the bill of exchange—i.e. if he had notice of the defect in B's title— he would not be able to acquire a good title himself.

Constructive Notice.—Notice of the kind indicated above is called express notice, but there has grown up a doctrine that a man will be considered to have notice of a fact even though he had in reality no knowledge of it if he did in fact know of certain other facts which should have led him to make enquiries, and so discover the facts of which

he is deemed to have notice. Notice of this kind is known as constructive notice. It is commonly met with in the case of limited companies, for every person dealing with a company is deemed to have notice of the contents of the company's Memorandum and Articles which are lodged in Somerset House, even though he may not in fact have troubled to find out what they contain. Thus, if A makes a contract with a company through the directors for the sale to the company of certain land, and it is provided in the Articles that the directors have no power to buy land for the company, but that any purchase of land must be carried out and approved by the company in General Meeting, A cannot hold the company to the bargain because he is deemed to have constructive notice of the contents of the Articles.

NOTICE TO ADMIT.—This is the name given to one of the notices served during the proceedings before an action comes for trial. The notice may be either to admit documents or to admit facts. A notice to admit documents requires the other party to the action to admit that the documents were written and signed by the persons by whom they purport to be written and signed. When such an admission is made it will obviously save the necessity of giving formal proof of the writing and signature of the documents, and thus may save considerable time and expense. The other party by admitting the documents does not prevent himself from contending that the documents are not properly admissible as evidence in the case.

A notice to admit facts is used in cases where certain facts are not in reality in dispute between the parties, and where the expense of proving those facts would be considerable. Thus, suppose that it was desired to prove that there was a long period of hot weather in a certain place during the summer of 1934 and that a certain temperature was reached on a certain date. To prove this strictly would involve calling the persons from the meteorological offices to give evidence as to the readings of their instruments on the relevant dates, and this would be an expensive proceeding. In such a case the other party to the action should be asked to admit the fact. If a party is asked to admit a fact or to admit documents and refuses to do so, except in cases where the Judge decides that he could not reasonably be expected to admit them, he will be ordered to pay the costs to which the party giving the notice has been put in proving those facts, even though the party refusing to admit them should ultimately win the action.

NOTICE TO PRODUCE.—To prevent one party being taken by surprise by the production in Court against him of copies of documents of which he himself has the original, without his being aware of the intention of the other party to produce them, a rule has been made which requires any party who wishes to rely on a document in the possession of his opponent, to give to his opponent a notice to produce that document. If he fails to do so it should be remembered that this does not entitle the party giving the notice to dispense with proving the document, nor does it compel the other party to produce the document. Its only effect is that, if the notice is not obeyed, the party giving it is entitled to give what is called "secondary evidence" of the document—e.g. to produce a copy of it.

Thus, if A is suing B for a suit of clothes supplied to him and wishes to prove that on a certain date he wrote to B demanding payment and that B did not reply, he cannot put in evidence a copy of the letter which he wrote unless, before the action is tried, he sent a notice to B requiring him to produce the original letter. The notice to produce must be given a reasonable time before the action is tried so as to enable the person on whom it is served to find the original document. When it is desired to compel a person to produce a document in Court, he should be served with a "subpœna duces tecum" (q.v.).

NOTICE TO QUIT.—When either a landlord or a tenant wishes to put an end to a tenancy he must serve a notice to quit. The length of the notice will depend upon the nature of the tenancy. A tenancy cannot be terminated by a notice to quit when it is for a fixed period—e.g. one year—but only when it is a continuing tenancy—e.g. weekly or monthly. (*See* LANDLORD AND TENANT.)

NOTICE TO SERVANTS.—The general rule is that where a contract of service, whether written or unwritten, fails to state expressly or by implication the period for which it is to last, it is presumed to be a hiring for a year, and in the absence of any arrangement about notice or of any custom relating to the particular employment (for example, the custom in the theatrical world that the engagement is for the run of the piece), such a yearly hiring can be ended only at the conclusion of the year, provided, of course, no occasion arises to justify instant dismissal without notice, as explained later. Other hirings can be ended by reasonable notice, and what is "reasonable notice" is a question of fact to be decided from the circumstances of each case. As this is a matter over which master and servant can easily differ, some arrangement as to the length of notice should always be made at the time of hiring.

Sometimes a custom in a particular trade to give notice of some definite length can be proved, but it is always very difficult to do so. There are, however, some types of employment where the custom is so well known that no evidence about it is necessary, and the most important of these is:—

Domestic Service where the employment may be ended by a month's (not a fortnight's as is popularly supposed) notice on either side, or by a calendar month's wages, without board wages, by the master or mistress in lieu of notice. There is a further recognized custom that at, or before the end of the first fortnight of employment, notice may be given to terminate the engagement at the end of the first month. In domestic service, as elsewhere, an agreement as to the length of notice can be, and often is, made at the time of engagement. Such an agreement, of course, overrides the custom. A point which all mistresses should remember is that domestic servants are entitled to all wages which have accrued due, that is, to all wages up to their last pay day, even if they depart without giving any notice. Thus, if the cook who is engaged by the month leaves suddenly of her own accord to-day, she is entitled to wages up to the end of her last month's employment, which was perhaps yesterday. The mistress, in such a case, has no right to withhold wages, and must resort to an action for damages for breach of contract if she has suffered loss.

When Notice is Unnecessary.—Civil and Military servants of the Crown can be dismissed without notice notwithstanding any agreement to the contrary. Servants who wilfully disobey the lawful orders of their masters, provided such orders are connected with their ordinary duties; servants who are guilty of pecuniary or other misconduct inconsistent with the fulfilment of the express or implied conditions of service, or prejudicial to the master's business; servants who are habitually or grossly negligent or incompetent, or who are permanently disabled by illness—all may be dismissed without notice, and here again the servant is entitled to wages up to the last pay day only. A servant can leave without notice where he is in fear of danger to life or of personal injury, and where the master has failed to carry out his part of the contract or has ill-treated the servant.

Notice to Quit need not be given to a servant on dismissal provided the occupation of the house was necessary for the performance of the service and not merely permissive. (*See also* MASTER AND SERVANT; WRONGFUL DISMISSAL.)

NOVATION.—Novation is said to take place when the parties to an agreement arrange that they shall give up their rights under the old agreement and shall accept instead rights under a new agreement into which they enter. The old agreement is replaced by the new one. Novation may also take place when a new party is brought into the agreement. One of the most common examples of novation arises when a new Bill of Exchange is given in place of an old Bill which is about to expire owing to the lapse of time. (*See* ACCORD AND SATISFACTION; CONTRACT.)

NUISANCE.—The word nuisance has a very much wider meaning in law than in ordinary speech, and includes a great many offences and wrongs which have no logical connection with one another.

Public Nuisance.—A public nuisance includes a large number of acts injurious to the public at large, such as the keeping of a common gaming house, or the obstruction of a highway. Nuisances of this kind are criminal offences. They may also give rise to an action for damages as civil wrongs, but only where some member of the public has suffered some specific financial damage through the nuisance.

Private Nuisance.—Private nuisances are not crimes, but give rise to an action for damages which may be brought by the person who has suffered loss. In this case also the term nuisance is applied to a variety of wrongs between which there is no very clear logical connection. Thus, the interference with an easement such as the blocking up of a right to light enjoyed by the window of a house would be an act of nuisance. Further, nuisance is also used in the popular sense to include the act of wrongfully allowing the escape of harmful things on to another person's land—e.g. smoke, smells, noise, or water. Thus, if a person establishes a factory on land with the result that poisonous or unpleasant fumes or smoke pass from his land on to the land of another, he will be liable to an action for nuisance.

Nuisance is distinguished from trespass. An act will be a nuisance if it does not involve any direct physical interference with the land of another, and a trespass if it does involve this physical interference. Thus, if A allows his trees to grow so that their branches overhang his neighbour's land, this may amount to a nuisance, but if he plants a tree in such a position that its branches *when planted* overhang his neighbour's land, his act is a trespass. The importance of the distinction is that no action can be brought for a nuisance unless actual damage—i.e. financial loss—is suffered, but an action will always lie for trespass without proof of any damage.

Interference with Personal Comfort.—It will thus be an important question in all cases of nuisance whether damage has been incurred by the person complaining—i.e. the plaintiff—sufficient to entitle him to sue. The damage may be either some physical injury to the plaintiff's property or some interference with his enjoyment of it. The question will, therefore, arise in cases where the nuisance is based on mere discomfort as to what degree of discomfort is required, and it is clear that the discomfort must not be merely trifling. Thus, persons living in a thickly populated district cannot complain if, while sitting in their houses or flats, they hear the gramophones or wireless sets of their neighbours, so long as the noise is not unduly loud, or at unreasonable hours. In the same way a man who lives in a busy street cannot complain of the noise of

18*

traffic. It has been said that he who dislikes a noise should not live in a locality devoted to the business of making boilers or steamships. He is, however, entitled to the standard of reasonable comfort which an average man would expect in the locality in which he is living. What is a nuisance in Belgrave Square would not necessarily be so in Bermondsey.

The special circumstances under which a person lives will not entitle him to claim any additional freedom from noise or other nuisance. Thus, if an author is prevented from working in his home by noises which would not annoy other persons, or if he establishes delicate instruments which are upset by vibrations which would not otherwise do any harm, he cannot complain.

" Coming to the Nuisance."—It was at one time thought that if a man came to a district in which there was some nuisance such as noise or smoke already in existence he could not complain, because, as it was said, he had "come to the nuisance." This is not, however, the case, and if the disturbance in fact amounts to a nuisance, i.e. is unreasonable in *all the circumstances* of the locality, the fact that it has been in existence for some time and before the plaintiff came to the district will be no defence.

The fact that all possible care has been taken to minimise the noise or smoke, will be no justification for continuing it, and will not prevent it being a nuisance if it is in fact excessive. Thus, if a factory discharges poisonous fumes into the air so as to affect the comfort of the persons living near it, it is no defence to prove that all the most modern devices for the reduction in the volume of the fumes have been used. If the manufacturing process cannot be carried on without causing the fumes then it must be stopped.

Statutory Authorities.—A distinction arises in the case of acts which have been authorised by Act of Parliament. When public works have to be erected, their erection is usually authorized by some Statute, and if in the carrying out of the works a nuisance is caused, it will frequently happen that persons suffering damage from the nuisance will be unable to claim compensation. A distinction must be made, however, between cases in which the Statute authorises the doing of the act *notwithstand-*

ing the fact that it may cause a nuisance and cases in which the act is merely authorized *provided* that it can be carried out *without* causing a nuisance. An example of the first class arises where the building of a railway is authorized. It is impossible to run a railway without causing considerable inconvenience to persons living near the railway line from smoke, noise, and vibration, and no degree of care exercised by those in charge of the railway will prevent these results. Accordingly no action will lie for nuisances caused in those circumstances. On the other hand, when a public authority is authorized to do some act, it may be possible for it to do it without causing a nuisance, and in such a case it will be liable if, through lack of sufficient care, a nuisance is caused. Thus, an authority authorized to establish a fever hospital must not place it in such a district where it would be a source of danger to the residents. Whether the act is authorized, even though it be a nuisance or is merely authorized provided that no nuisance is caused, will depend on the construction of the particular Act of Parliament authorizing the act.

Who is Liable.—Where a nuisance exists on land, the person who is liable is the occupier of the land whether he is also the owner or not. He is bound not merely to refrain from creating any nuisance himself but also to put a stop, so soon as he knows of it, to any nuisance created by any other person on his land, even though that person had no authority from the occupier to do the act creating the nuisance, but was a mere trespasser.

Remedy for Nuisance.—A person who is suffering from a nuisance has three courses open to him. He may put an end to the nuisance himself, e.g. by cutting off the branch of an overhanging tree. When a person takes the law into his own hands and puts a stop to the nuisance himself he is said to abate it. Instead, he may bring an action in the Courts claiming an injunction, i.e. an order requiring the person responsible for the nuisance to abate it (put a stop to it), or he may bring an action claiming damages. No one to-day should attempt to abate the nuisance, but should apply to the Court. (*See* EASEMENT.)

NULLITY OF MARRIAGE. — A decree of nullity of marriage is quite different from one of dissolution of marriage. In the first case the marriage is annulled on the ground that there never was really a marriage at all, in the second a marriage, perfectly lawful and complete, is dissolved.

Marriages which can be annulled are divided into two groups—those that have been void from the beginning, and those which are voidable at the option of one party. A marriage is void from the beginning if it was bigamous, i.e. if one of the parties was at the time of the ceremony lawfully married to someone else who was still alive. It is also void if it is between parties who are within the prohibited degrees, or if it was not celebrated according to law. Finally, if one of the parties by reason of insanity, duress, or fraud, was not a willing and understanding party to the ceremony, the marriage is void.

A marriage is voidable if it has not and cannot be consummated, or if one of the parties, if married before 10th May, 1929, was at the time of the ceremony under the then lawful age for marriage. The first of these grounds, of course, involves more than mere non-consummation. It is necessary to shew that at the time of the marriage one of the parties was incapable of it, and remains incapable of cure. Invincible repugnance can constitute such a disability, but mere unjustifiable refusal does not. Sterility, of course, is not a ground for a decree of nullity. (*See* SPECIAL SUPPLEMENT "DIVORCE.")

NURSES.—No one may hold herself out to be a registered nurse unless actually on the Nurses' Register. This is a register kept by the General Nursing Council for England and Wales. A similar system of registration exists for nurses in Scotland. No person may be registered unless she has undergone the training prescribed. Persons may be removed from the register by the General Nursing Council.

NURSING HOMES. — All nursing homes must be registered with the local authority. The local authority may, at its discretion, refuse to accept any nursing home for registration; may cancel existing registrations, and may cause nursing homes to be inspected. Every nursing home must exhibit in a conspicuous place on the premises its certificate of registration. Mental institutions are dealt with by other regulations.

OATH—A witness is required to take an oath, or, if he objects on conscientious grounds, he may affirm (*see* AFFIRMATION). A witness is allowed to take the form of oath proper to his religious belief. The usual form for a Christian is upon the New Testament, but a Roman Catholic can require the version approved by the Roman Catholic Church. A Jew swears on the Old Testament and covers his head while swearing.

If a witness is so young as to be unable to understand the nature of an oath, yet of a sufficient age to give evidence, the oath is dispensed with. The Judge or presiding magistrate may examine child witnesses to ascertain their understanding in order to decide whether an oath should be administered.

There are very many more occasions when oaths are taken. Jurors are sworn before trying a case, and so are interpreters before interpreting in Courts of law. Judges, magistrates, and many public officials are required to take various kinds of oaths on appointment. (*See* AFFIDAVIT; PERPETUATION OF TESTIMONY.)

OBITER DICTUM.—It frequently happens that the Judge in giving judgment will state some legal proposition which is not necessary for the decision of the case which he is trying, but which arises incidentally or "by the way" (ob iter). Such a statement is called an obiter dictum, and has not the same authority binding on later Judges trying similar cases as it would have had if it had been necessary for the purpose of deciding the case.

OBSCENE LANGUAGE.—Any person who uses any obscene language, or sings any obscene song in any street or in any public place in a town may be apprehended by a constable and on summary conviction punished by a fine of 40/- or 14 days' imprisonment. Any language of a filthy or disgusting kind is regarded as obscene.

Mr. Ingleby Oddie.

OBSTRUCTION.—Any conduct intended to obstruct or prevent the course of public justice constitutes a misdemeanour punishable by imprisonment. Interference with witnesses in cases which are to be tried or are being tried in the Courts also constitutes obstruction punishable by imprisonment. Any person who obstructs any clergyman from officiating in any church, chapel, or other place of divine worship, or in any churchyard may be convicted of a misdemeanour.

Obstruction of the police in the execution of their duty constitutes a serious offence for which imprisonment may be awarded. Obstruction of this kind includes not merely physical resistance, but also any conduct which has the effect of preventing police officers from carrying out their lawful duty. Thus it is obstruction to warn a motorist who is committing an unlawful act of the existence of a police trap. It has, however, been decided by the High Court that it is not obstruction to warn a motorist unless the motorist is at the time committing an offence.

Obstruction of the highways is dealt with by various regulations. A common form is obstruction caused by leaving motor-cars in a road. It is important to note that though one motor-car may not in itself very much interfere with the passage of others along the highway, if the road is of such a kind that the presence of many stationary cars will cause obstruction, the driver of any one such car can be convicted of obstruction. Obstruction of the footpath by placing any objects such as chairs on it is an offence for which the fine is 40/-.

OCCASIONAL LICENCES.—Very often, on occasions such as cricket matches, shows and dinners, it is decided to sell intoxicating liquor upon premises not ordinarily licensed. To meet this difficulty an occasional licence can be applied for. It will be granted only to a person who already holds an on-licence, and only for a period not exceeding three consecutive days. The licence is granted by the Excise Authority, but the consent of a Petty Sessional Court is necessary. The application to the Court is made in the following way. Notice of intention to apply, setting out the name and address of the applicant and the place, occasion and period for which the licence is required, should be served upon the superintendent of police for the district. It should also shew the hours during which it is proposed to sell intoxicating liquor, which must be between sunrise and 10 p.m. except in the case of a public dinner or ball. (*See* PUBLIC HOUSES; PUBLICANS; INTOXICATING LIQUOR.)

ODDIE, Ingleby.—The Westminster Coroner who has presided over many interesting inquests. At the Bar he was noted for his medical knowledge. He assisted in the prosecution of Crippen and Steinie Morrison.

OFF-LICENCES.—As the name implies, these are licences to retail intoxicating liquor for consumption off the premises. They consist of the spirit off-licence, the wine off-licence, and the beer off-licence. Justices' licences are required for all of them. But a spirit dealer or a wine dealer does not require a justices' licence to sell by retail spirits or wine for consumption off the premises where the premises are exclusively used for the sale of intoxicating liquors, and have no internal communication with the premises of any person carrying on any other trade. The owner of such premises, however, even though he requires no justices' licence, is still subject to the general provisions of the Licensing Act, and cannot therefore sell by retail intoxicating liquor outside the permitted hours, nor can he sell by non-standard measures (see PERMITTED HOURS.) On the other hand, however, as the premises have no justices' licence, a constable has no right of entry. (See INTOXICATING LIQUOR AND PUBLIC HOUSES.)

OFFENCE.—Any kind of crime or contravention of the criminal law is called an offence. The term, therefore, includes every such act from the most minor to the greatest crimes known to the law. In practice the term is usually confined to minor matters dealt with in the Police Court which do not amount to felonies or misdemeanours.

OFFICE COPY.—An Office Copy is the name applied to copies of judicial documents—e.g. an order of the Court or a writ—made by the officer having charge of the original document and bearing the seal of the office in which the document is lodged. The proper method by which to produce in evidence any document filed in the Court is by an office copy of the document.

OFFICIAL RECEIVER.—The Official Receiver is an officer of the Board of Trade who acts in England and Wales in cases of bankruptcy and in the winding-up of companies. The property of the bankrupt or of the company is placed under his control after a receiving order has been made in the case of the bankruptcy, or a winding-up order in the case of a company. When, at a later stage, a trustee or liquidator is appointed, the property passes out of the control of the official receiver. He nevertheless retains a general control over the proceedings.

It is his duty in bankruptcy to investigate the conduct of the debtor and to make a report to the Court, particularly on the occasion of the debtor's application for discharge, stating to what causes his bankruptcy must be attributed, e.g. misfortune or extravagant living, and also whether the debtor has committed any offence of a criminal character or any act which would justify the Court in refusing or suspending his discharge. The official receiver also takes part in the public examination of the debtor, and will act as trustee if at any time the office of trustee should become vacant. In many cases the creditors do not appoint a trustee, but leave the official receiver to act as trustee. (See BANKRUPTCY; WINDING-UP.)

OFFICIAL REFEREE.—An Official Referee is a permanent officer attached to the Supreme Court, and is appointed by the Lord Chancellor. At present there are three official referees. Subject to any right to have a particular case tried by jury, any question arising in the course of any legal proceedings, except criminal proceedings, may be submitted by order of the Court or Judge to the official referee for enquiry or report; and in any legal proceedings—other than criminal proceedings—the Court or Judge, if all the parties consent, may order the whole matter, or any question of fact arising from it, to be tried by an official referee. This procedure is usually adopted when complicated accounts have to be considered.

In certain exceptional cases where the matter or question to be tried requires prolonged investigation, or the examination of scientific documents, the Court or Judge may compel the parties to refer the matter to an official referee. The report or award of the official referee, unless it is set aside by the Court or Judge, is equivalent to, and may be enforced, as though it were the verdict of a jury. Where matters are remitted to an official referee by the Court or Judge, for report or enquiry, the duty of the referee is not to make an award, but to report upon specific questions, or to ascertain, where the facts are in dispute, what the true facts are.

OFFICIAL SECRETS.—Official secrets are protected by two quite recent acts of Parliament—the Official Secrets Acts of 1911 and 1920. These acts are designed to prevent the disclosure to unauthorised persons of official information which, in the public interest, it is not desirable to disclose. The matters covered include spying and collecting information calculated to be useful to an enemy, the publication of official documents and the unlawful use of military and naval uniforms. The acts give the police very far-reaching powers in respect of offences or suspected offences against these acts. Failure to give information on demand to senior police officers is an offence, while in cases of emergency a police superintendent may himself issue a search warrant.

The punishments authorized for certain of the graver offences against the Official

Secrets Acts are very severe, and in some cases amount to penal servitude for not more than 14 years.

OIL.—If any oil is discharged or allowed to escape either directly or indirectly from any vessel, or from any place on land, or from any apparatus used for the purpose of transferring oil from or to any vessel, and is allowed to escape into any water which is part of the territorial waters of Great Britain and Northern Ireland, or the water of any harbour in that area, the person responsible for allowing the oil to be discharged is guilty of an offence, and is liable on summary conviction to a fine not exceeding £100. The person charged will, however, have a good defence if he can shew in cases where he is the owner or master of the vessel, that the escape of the oil was due to, or that it was necessary to discharge the oil by reason of the vessel being in collision, or the happening of some damage or accident; and also that he took all reasonable means to prevent the escape in cases where he is charged with allowing oil to escape, and not with discharging it deliberately. In other cases it is a good defence where oil has been allowed to escape to shew that all reasonable means were taken to prevent the escape.

OLD AGE PENSION.—Since the year 1918, all persons upon attaining the age of seventy have been entitled to an old age pension, provided that they can prove to the Pension Authorities that in their case certain conditions imposed by the Pension Acts are satisfied. To obtain an Old Age Pension under the Old Age Pensions Scheme, the claimant must be seventy years of age, but there are two other forms of Old Age Pensions which are payable under different schemes, a Blind Person's Pension for which the age is fifty, and the pension under the National Health Insurance Scheme for which the age is sixty-five.

How to qualify for a pension.—Before a pension can be obtained a claimant must fulfil the following conditions:—

(a) He must have attained the age of seventy.

(b) He must satisfy the pension authorities that for at least ten years up to the date when he receives any sum by way of pension he has been a British subject. If the claimant is a woman, married to an alien, she is only required to prove that but for her marriage she would be a British subject.

(c) That his yearly income does not exceed £49 17s. 6d. A deduction of £39 is permitted if that income is derived from a source other than actual earnings.

(d) That if a natural born British subject, he has, since attaining the age of fifty, had his residence in the United Kingdom for an aggregate period of twelve years; if a naturalized British subject the period is twenty years.

Certain periods not actually spent in the United Kingdom are counted as residence in the United Kingdom for the purposes of the Pension Acts:—

(a) Any period spent in the service of the Crown, or as the wife or servant of a person so employed.

(b) Any periods spent in the Channel Islands or the Isle of Man by a person born in the United Kingdon.

(c) Any period spent abroad during which the person has assisted in the maintenance of a dependant in the United Kingdom.

(d) Any periods spent in service on a ship which is registered in the United Kingdom, by a person who, before his absence on that service, was living in the United Kingdom.

(e) Any periods of temporary absence not exceeding three months in duration at any one time.

How means are calculated.—A person is not entitled to an Old Age Pension if his income exceeds £49 17s. 6d., and there are certain rules laid down for the calculation of the means of a claimant. Account is to be taken of:—

(a) The yearly value of any property which is invested or put to profitable use, or which though not invested is capable of investment.

The yearly value is to be calculated according to the following rules:—

(i) The first £25 of the capital value of the property is to be excluded.

(ii) The annual value of the next £375 of the capital value is to be taken to be one-twentieth of that value.

(iii) The annual value of so much of the capital value as exceeds £400 is to be taken as being one-tenth of that value.

(b) Any cash income which is expected to be received during the year excluding income from any property as detailed in (a) above.

No account is to be taken of any sickness benefit received from a Trade Union, Friendly Society, or National Health Insurance, unless more than three months' benefit has been received.

(c) No account is to be taken of the furniture or personal effects, such as clothing or jewellery, whatever the value may be.

(d) The means of one of a married couple living together are to be taken to be half the total means of the couple.

(e) If a husband is separated from his wife under a Court Separation Order, then the sum which he has to pay under that order is to be deducted before calculating his means.

The table beneath indicates the amount of pension payable to persons of varying incomes who pass the "means test."

be obtained at any Post Office, and when it is filled up it must be delivered to the postmaster at the Post Office at which the claimant wishes the pension to be paid, or to the local pension officer with instructions as to which Post Office the claimant desires the pension to be paid. The postmasters have instructions to give assistance to anyone in the filling-up of the forms, and in any difficulty, his assistance should be requested.

It is an offence to make any false statement or representation to obtain a pension for oneself or anyone else, and the offender is liable to 6 months' imprisonment with hard labour.

The Health Insurance Old Age Pension.—When a person who was insured under the National Health Insurance Scheme reaches the age of sixty-five, he is entitled to an Old Age Pension of ten shillings per week without any enquiry into his means. The only conditions to be fulfilled are that the person claiming must have been insured for five years prior to the time when he becomes eligible; that one hundred and four contributions have been paid on his account; that he has been resident in Great Britain for a period of two years

		£ s. d.			£ s. d.		
Where the income exceeds		49 17 6	.	. . .	.	. .	No pension
"	"	47 5 0	but does not exceed	49 17 6	.	.	1/– per week
"	"	42 0 0	"	"	47 5 0	.	2/– "
"	"	36 15 0	"	"	42 0 0	.	4/– "
"	"	31 10 0	"	"	36 15 0	.	6/– "
"	"	26 5 0	"	"	31 10 0	.	8/– "
Where the income does not exceed		. . . . .		26 5 0	.	10/– "

How a Person may be Disqualified. —A person may be qualified by fulfilling the conditions relating to age, means, and residence, and yet he may not be entitled to a pension because of the special disqualifications laid down in the acts. A person is not entitled to an Old Age Pension if he is an inmate of a workhouse or other poor law institution. This provision does not apply if the period spent in the workhouse is for the purpose of receiving medical treatment, and does not last longer than three months; if a pensioner is sent to prison for an offence, he is disqualified during imprisonment.

How to make a Claim.—In order to obtain an Old Age Pension it is necessary to fill up a claim form. The proper form can

immediately prior to attaining the age of sixty-five, and that his last employment was in Great Britain.

When a person receives a pension at the age of sixty-five, he no longer has to pay any contributions to the insurance fund, but his employer has to continue to make payments until he attains the age of seventy. When a person who is receiving an Old Age Pension under the National Health Insurance Scheme reaches the age of seventy, he goes over to the Old Age Pension Scheme and receives a pension of ten shillings per week without any enquiry into his means, and without having to satisfy any of the conditions relating to nationality or residence.

If the pensioner is a woman, and becomes

entitled to a widow's pension, then she ceases to be entitled to an Old Age Pension under the National Health Insurance. A wife who has attained the age of sixty-five but not seventy, is entitled to an Old Age Pension payable in accordance with the Health Insurance Scheme if her husband reached seventy before the 2nd January, 1928, and is entitled to an Old Age Pension under the Old Age Pensions Acts. The couple must have been married for three years before the wife attains sixty-five.

Who Decides Claims.—When the claim form has been filled up and delivered, it is referred to the local pension committee for the district. A local pension committee is appointed for every borough and urban district which has a population of twenty thousand or over, and for every county. The committee is appointed by the borough, district, or county council as the case may be, and must consist of not less than seven persons and not more than the number of members in the council by which it is appointed. The local committee may appoint sub-committees consisting wholly or partly of members of the committee, and delegate powers to them. When the committee have a claim delivered to them, they refer the claim to the local pension officer who makes enquiries and then reports to the committee. The committee then give their decision upon the claim. If a question arises about the increase or diminishing of an existing pension, that question is also referred to the local committee. There is an appeal from the local committee to the central pension authority which in England and Wales is the Minister of Health. If complaint is made to the central pension authority that the local committee refuses to decide a question or claim, and the central authority find that the complaint is justified, then they may themselves decide the question or claim.

It is not possible to assign or place a charge on an Old Age Pension, and any such assignment or charge is void and of no effect. The benefit of an Old Age Pension does not pass to the trustee for the creditors upon the bankruptcy of the pensioner. (*See also* NATIONAL HEALTH INSURANCE; PENSION; WIDOW'S PENSION.)

OLD METAL DEALERS.— Restrictions apply to the manner in which dealers in old metals carry on their trade. Thus they may not purchase certain metals, such as copper and brass, at any one time of less weight than 56 lbs. If a dealer is found to be in possession of stolen old metal he may be required to register with the police and to keep a book recording all his transactions in old metal. A registered dealer must keep all purchases for 48 hours before he disposes of them, and he must not buy metal during the night time.

OMNIBUS.—Omnibuses are now public service vehicles and require the various licences necessary for such vehicles. (*See* SPECIAL SUPPLEMENT "ROAD TRAFFIC.")

ONE-MAN COMPANY.—This expression is sometimes applied to companies in which a very large number of shares are held by one person who thus controls the company. It is not legally possible for a company to consist of one man only, but there is no objection to one man holding as many shares in the company as he pleases while the other shareholders hold only one share each. The person who controls the company in this way is quite a distinct legal person from the company itself, and in no way liable for its debts. For example, if he lends money to the company on a mortgage, he is entitled to be repaid before creditors who have got no security just as if he had no connection with the company whatsoever. (*See* COMPANIES.)

ON-LICENCES.—As the name implies, these are licences which permit intoxicating liquor to be sold for consumption on the premises so licensed. They expire in every case upon 30th September of each year and all require a justices' licence as well as an excise licence. (*See* INTOXICATING LIQUOR.)

The various on-licences are as follows:—

(1) Publican's or full licence, authorizing the sale by retail of spirits, wines, and beer, for consumption on or off the premises.

(2) Beerhouse licence, authorizing the sale by retail of beer, for consumption on or off the premises.

(3) Wine on-licence, authorizing the sale of wine by retail, for consumption on or off the premises.

There is no on-licence to retail spirits

alone. Thus it can be seen that on-licences allow the sale of intoxicating liquor for consumption on or off the premises, while off licences allow sale for consumption off the premises only. The holder of a publican's licence does not require either a beerhouse licence or a wine on-licence as it includes both of them.

When a Licence Becomes Void.— A licence will be void and of no effect under the following circumstances:—

(1) Where it has been granted to a disqualified person or premises. (*See* PUBLIC HOUSES AND PUBLICANS.)

(2) Where it has been renewed in the name of a dead man.

(3) Where it has been granted, all the parties and the justices acting in mistake of law on the notion that an enactment was repealed when in fact it was not.

(4) When forfeited because the holder has been convicted of using the premises as a brothel, it will be void from the moment of conviction, as will the licence of a beerhouse keeper convicted of selling spirits without a licence.

A person holding a licence which has become void for any of the above reasons can, if he sells intoxicating liquor, be convicted of doing so without a licence. (*See* INTOXICATING LIQUOR.)

OPEN CONTRACT.—Where, in agreeing upon certain transactions in relation to land and the sale of goods, the parties thereto do not impose on each other any particular conditions, but are content to rely on the law relating to such transactions, they are said to enter into an "open contract." The rights and obligations of the parties are then said to be "implied." The implied rights and obligations in relation to the selling, leasing and mortgaging of land, which are the most common forms of transactions, are contained for the most part in the Law of Property Act, 1925. In the case of the sale of goods, they are dealt with by the Sale of Goods Act, 1893. (*See* SALE OF LAND; SALE OF GOODS; LANDLORD AND TENANT; MORTGAGE.)

OPTION.—The general rule of English law is that if a person wishes to have time to consider a purchase of some property and wishes to have a right to purchase that property at a certain price, he must acquire that right by a contract which complies with the general law, i.e. for which there must be consideration. Thus, A is interested in the purchase of a house and is quoted £2,000 as the price at which the seller is prepared to sell; he wishes, however, to make certain investigations before he agrees to buy the house, or it may be that he intends to resell the house as soon as he gets it, and does not wish to buy it until he has himself secured a contract from the person to whom he proposes to sell. In such a case he would enter into a contract for an option for a stated period of time, e.g. a week, to buy the house at £2,000.

There must be some consideration for this contract, that is, the person acquiring the option must give something in exchange for it. What he gives need not be of great value—e.g. it may be one shilling—but, of course, in many cases an option is an extremely valuable thing, and a large sum of money may be paid for it. Once the option has been obtained, the person acquiring it has the time allowed by the option within which to decide whether he will exercise the option or not. If he decides to exercise it, he must indicate his intention within the time given by the option. If he does not wish to exercise it, he may simply allow the time given by the option to elapse, and his only liability will be to pay the money or other consideration which he agreed to give for the option.

Stock Exchange.—The purchase of options is a frequent method of speculation on the Stock Exchange. The person intending to speculate acquires the right to purchase or sell a certain number of specified shares at a certain price at any time within, say, three months; if he has bought a right to buy certain shares, the transaction is termed a "call," and if the right acquired is to sell the shares, the transaction is termed a "put." If the person has obtained an option to buy at a certain price, he will, of course, make a profit if the shares go above that price within the period of the option, because he may then call for delivery of the shares at the price named in the option, and sell the shares at the higher market cost. In the same way, a person who has taken an option to sell shares will make money if the shares fall in value. The holder of the option cannot compel the other party to deliver or accept the shares, as the case may be, until the time fixed by the option contract arrives. The following illustration will make the transaction clear. A, in June takes an option on the shares of the "XYZ" Company Ltd. at 25/– for the end of August. For this he may pay 2/– a share. The shares at the present time may be standing at a price either higher or lower than the option figure. When the end of August arrives the holder of the option, if the shares are over 25/– in value, will exercise his option and call for delivery of the shares. He will, of course, have to pay 25/– each for them. If the shares have fallen in value below 25/– it will not pay him to exercise the option, and he will allow it to lapse. (*See* STOCK EXCHANGE.)

ORDER IN COUNCIL.—An Order in Council is an order made by the Privy Council. Modern acts of parliament display a tendency to lay down merely the outlines of legislation and leave the details to the Privy Council to deal with by Order in Council. There must, of course, be authority provided by Parliament for the Privy Council to make orders, and if the Council exceeds the authority granted it, its orders are not enforceable in the Courts.

ORDINARY.—An Ordinary in ecclesiastical law is one having jurisdiction to hear ecclesiastical cases in his own right and not by deputation, e.g. the Archbishop is the Bishop's Ordinary and hears cases brought against Bishops for ecclesiastical offences; again, the Bishop is the Ordinary of the inferior clergy. The jurisdiction of the Ordinary is usually exercised by a delegate, e.g. the Judge of the Bishop's Court is the Chancellor (*see* CONSISTORY COURT), and the Judge in the Archbishop of Canterbury's Court is the Dean of Arches. (*See* ARCHES, COURT OF.)

ORDINATION.—No person may be admitted a deacon of the Church of England until he is twenty-three, or a priest until he is twenty-four years of age. Every candidate must produce testimonials of conduct, must have some certain place where he may use his function as a minister of God; i.e. generally he must shew that some person is willing to employ him in his church; must satisfy the Archdeacon in an examination as to his learning, and must make and

subscribe the declaration of assent and the oath of allegiance. (*See* ALLEGIANCE.) By the former the declarant solemnly assents to the 39 Articles and the Prayer Book. Ordination takes place on the Sunday next following the Ember weeks. There are three orders in the Church, deacons, priests and bishops; the first ordination is, therefore, ordination to the rank of deacon, followed (at least a year later) by ordination to the rank of priest. A Bishop is not "ordained" but "consecrated." (*See also* CLERGYMAN, ORDINATION; DEACON; PRIEST.)

ORGANIST.—An organist is not a church official but is generally employed by the Parochial Church Council as their servant. He, therefore, has no rights in relation to the church except such as may be a term of his contract with his employers.

ORIGINATING SUMMONS.—In certain cases where a person desires the decision of the Court upon some such matter as the construction of a legal document, etc., or as to which of two rival claimants to money is really entitled to it, he may instead of issuing a Writ of Summons obtain an Originating Summons, which is served in the same manner as a Writ, and which calls upon any parties concerned to attend in Chambers upon the day fixed for the determination of the question in issue. (*See* ADMINISTRATION ACTION; HIGH COURT PROCEDURE.)

ORPHAN'S PENSION.—Since the 4th January, 1926, an orphan child, both of whose parents are dead, has been entitled to receive an orphan's pension if the father was an insured person under the National Health Insurance Scheme, or if the mother before her death had been receiving a Widow's Pension under the Widows', Orphans' and Old Age Contributory Pensions Act, 1925. In order to entitle an orphan child to an orphan's pension through the insurance of his or her father, it is necessary that the following conditions should be satisfied:—

(a) One hundred and four weeks must have elapsed, and one hundred and four contributions must have been paid by him or on his behalf since the time when he first became insured.

(b) Where two hundred and eight weeks or more have elapsed since the date of his entry into insurance, the number of contributions paid during the three contribution years before his death must represent an average of at least twenty-six contributions per year.

(c) The father must have been resident in Great Britain for a period of two years immediately prior to the date of his death, and his last employment must have been in Great Britain.

The Orphan's Pension is seven and sixpence a week, and is payable until the child reaches the age of fourteen, or if under full instruction in a day school, until the date of leaving school, or the 31st of July in the year in which the child became sixteen, whichever of these dates is the earlier. The pension is paid to the guardian or other person who has charge of the child.

The Children's Allowance.—If a child is left fatherless but the mother is still alive and receiving a widow's pension, then an additional allowance is paid to the mother for the maintenance of the child. This additional allowance is only payable if the conditions entitling a child to an orphan's pension are satisfied, and the amount of the allowance is five shillings for the eldest or only child, and three shillings for each other child. The age limit for the payment of a children's allowance is the same as in the case of an orphan's pension. If the mother who is receiving the widow's pension and the additional allowance dies, then the child becomes entitled to a full orphan's pension of seven and sixpence per week, which is paid to the person having charge of the child. If a child is removed from the custody of the person receiving the additional allowance by the order of any Court, and placed in the charge of some other person, then the full amount of seven and sixpence per week is paid to the child's guardian.

OUT-DOOR RELIEF.—Relief may, in certain cases, be given by a council to able-bodied persons or to their families without requiring them to enter a workhouse or other institution; but the amount and nature of the relief must be in accordance with the regulations made by the Minister of Health.

A Court of Summary Jurisdiction may direct that relief is to be given to an adult person who by reason of old age or infirmity of body is wholly unable to work, without his being required to reside in the work-house. One of the justices constituting the Court must however certify of his own knowledge that the person is unable to work.

If out-door relief is granted to an able-bodied person, at least half of it must be "relief in kind"—that is food and clothing, and the order granting relief must not be made for a longer period than eight weeks. The relieving officer may make a report within four weeks after the order for relief is made, and the council may vary the order if they think it necessary. Out-door relief must be administered at least once a week.

The relieving officer for each public assistance committee must make out a Case Paper in respect of every application for relief which is made to him.

The case paper must contain the following information:—

(a) The name, age and address of (i) the applicant, (ii) the members of the applicant's family resident with him and dependent upon him for support, (iii) the relatives who are liable to contribute towards the applicant's maintenance.

(b) The date, nature and cause of the application.

(c) Particulars of the home of the applicant.

(d) Length of residence in the area.

(e) The occupation, earnings and other income of: (i) the applicant, (ii) the members of the applicant's family and relations residing with him, (iii) the other relatives liable to contribute.

The case paper, when completed, is put before the Committee of the Council in charge of Relief, and they must endorse upon it the order, if any, which is made by them. The council must keep a register of the names of every person who is receiving out-door relief in their area.

Relief without any conditions may be given to an able-bodied poor person requiring it:—

(a) On account of sickness, or accident, or bodily or mental infirmity affecting himself or any member of his family who is dependent upon him for support.

(b) For the purpose of defraying expenses of burial of any member of his family.

When the council grant relief to a member of a friendly society, they are not to take into account any sum received by the applicant from the society by way of sick pay, except so far as that sum exceeds five shillings per week. Similarly, no account is to be taken of any sum received by the applicant under the National Health Insurance Scheme except so far as that sum exceeds seven and sixpence per week.

If a council departs from the regulations made by the Minister of Health when granting relief, then any sum improperly paid will be disallowed by the auditor of the council's accounts. If, however, the regulations are departed from in a case of emergency, and such departure is reported to the Minister within fifteen days and approved by him, the amount irregularly spent will be allowed in the accounts.

Relief by way of Loan.—Relief given to a person over the age of twenty-one may be considered to be a loan to that person if it is given in accordance with a rule or regulation of the Minister of Health which lays down that it may be so considered. No undertaking to repay is necessary nor need a receipt be given by the person receiving the money, to enable the council to take legal proceedings for it in the County Court. If the person receiving such relief secures employment, the council may summon him and his employer to the local Court of Summary Jurisdiction, and an order may be made directing that part of the wages should be paid over to the council. (*See* FRIENDLY SOCIETY; POOR LAW.)

OVERT ACT.—An overt act is one which is part of the carrying into execution of any criminal project. In treason, for instance, though there may be a treasonable intention, it does not become punishable until the offender commits an overt act towards the attainment of his object. In order to convict a person of an attempt to commit a crime, it is always necessary to prove that he commited some overt act.

OYER AND TERMINER.—This is one of the commissions issued to Judges of Assize. It requires them "to inquire, hear and determine" all treasons, felonies and misdemeanours for which indictments are presented in the counties they happen to be visiting on circuit. (*See also* ASSIZE.)

PALATINE COURT OF LANCASTER.—The County of Lancaster falls within the limits of the old Duchy of Lancaster, and one of its privileges is to hold a Court of Chancery. It has the same right to hear actions as the Chancery Division of the High Court of Justice, though this right is limited to cases where the persons who are parties to the action reside within the limits of the county. The Court is presided over by the Vice-Chancellor of the Duchy of Lancaster, as the Chancellor of that Duchy is a politician who is a member of the Government. Appeals from this Court go direct to the Court of Appeal.

A somewhat similar Court exists in the County of Durham which was also originally a County Palatine. (*See* HIGH COURT OF JUSTICE.)

PALMISTRY.—In order to ascertain whether palmistry constitutes a criminal offence or not, it is necessary to ascertain whether the person pursuing it professes to tell fortunes, that is to say, to foretell the future, by means of it. If he does, this constitutes fortune-telling. (*See* FORTUNE-TELLERS.) Where, however, palmistry is merely used in order to indicate the character of the person whose hand is being read it does not constitute an offence.

PANEL.—Under the National Health Insurance Scheme it is the duty of local Insurance Committees to provide a list or Panel of registered medical practitioners who will give medical attendance and treatment to which persons are entitled under the National Health Insurance Acts. This list is published in the local newspapers, and can be obtained by any insured person from the local insurance committee.

Any person duly insured under the scheme is entitled to select from the panel the practitioner by whom he wishes to be treated, and thereafter to be treated by that doctor. But the doctor's consent must be obtained beforehand, and no one can insist upon being treated by a doctor who does not wish to accept him as a panel patient. Persons who have no particular preference as to which doctor shall treat them are distributed by the committee among the doctors on the panel.

Where a panel patient removes from one neighbourhood to another, he is entitled to be transferred to the panel doctor in the new neighbourhood.

Changing Doctors.—If a panel patient wishes to change his doctor for another practising in the same neighbourhood, he can do so at the end of each year provided that he gives notice to the local insurance committee before the 1st December in the preceding year, and the transfer will take place on the following 1st January. If a patient, however, wishes to change his panel doctor during the course of the year, he cannot do so without the consent of that doctor, and the doctor to whom he transfers must give notice of the transfer to the local insurance committee.

Most panel practitioners arrange certain hours each day upon which panel patients may consult them, but in the event of a serious illness the doctor must visit the patient at his home, provided that it is within a certain distance, and as a general rule it may be said that a panel doctor is obliged to give to his panel patients as much attention as he would give to an ordinary patient.

Panel practitioners must also order for their patients the requisite drugs and appliances which are obtainable from pharmacists whose names appear upon a separate panel. As very few doctors nowadays do their own dispensing, the panel doctor generally hands to the patient an order form for the drug or appliance required, and the patient takes this to one of the panel chemists. Panel doctors must also give the requisite certificates which entitle the patients to sickness or disablement benefit, but, of course, must not give these unless the condition of the patient justifies it.

No panel doctor need give treatment for a confinement (for which maternity benefit is payable), or for any diseases which would entitle the panel patient to sanatorium benefit. If the panel doctor does attend one of his panel patients during a confinement, etc., he is entitled to charge his ordinary fees.

If the Doctor Fails in his Duty.— Any patient or other person who has reason

to complain that a panel doctor is failing in his duty to any of his panel patients may complain to the local insurance committee, which will hear and determine the complaint subject to a right of appeal to the Minister of Health. The local insurance committee is empowered to punish a panel doctor either by reducing the amount of his remuneration or by striking him off the panel. They may also recover from the doctor in default in this manner any costs and expenses which may have been incurred by the committee, or any money of which the committee or patient has been deprived by the default. (*See* DOCTOR; NATIONAL HEALTH INSURANCE.)

PANEL (JURORS).—The list of persons who have been summoned to attend Court as jurors is called the panel. When a jury is sworn twelve names are called from the panel.

PARDON.—In nearly all cases the Crown alone can pardon persons convicted of criminal offences. In modern times this right is exercised through the Home Secretary. The exercise by the Crown of this right cannot be challenged, e.g. by aggrieved parties. A pardon carries with it a revocation of the conviction, in the sense that a pardoned criminal can obtain damages from anyone who described him as a criminal. In some cases a money grant is given to a pardoned person as compensation for the imprisonment he has undergone.

An interesting exception to the right of the Crown to pardon is the provision in the Habeas Corpus Act depriving the Crown of the power to pardon the crime of unlawfully sending any prisoner out of the country. This, of course, is a relic of the days when the powers of the sovereign were frequently used oppressively against his subjects.

PARENT.—The word parent normally means the father or mother; but where the word is used in an Act of Parliament, it is usually defined at the end of the Act, and may include persons other than the father or mother, e.g. in the Elementary Education Act, 1870, it includes the guardian, and every person who is liable to maintain, or has the actual custody of any child. The rights of a father differ from those of a mother in some respects; as to such rights, *see* FATHER; MOTHER. (*See also* ADOPTION; CHILDREN; LEGITIMATION OF CHILDREN; etc.)

PARI PASSU. — Where a certain

amount of money has to be divided among persons who have claims against it, and there is not enough money to pay all those persons in full, each may be required to accept the same proportion of his total claim, and in this case they are said to take the money pari passu. Thus, if creditors of a debtor have claims amounting in all to £10,000 and all the money the debtor has is £5,000, each of the creditors will receive 10/– in the £, or half of the amount he claims. In some cases certain creditors will be preferred, and will be entitled to be paid, not pari passu, but in full before any of the other creditors. Thus, if in the case put there were creditors who were preferred in this way with claims for £2,000, they would be entitled to receive their money in full, and the remaining creditors for £8,000 would share equally in the £3,000 that was left over. This principle also applies in cases where money has been left by will to certain legatees and there is not enough money to pay all the legacies in full. Here also, the shares taken by each of the persons entitled to a legacy will be reduced in equal proportions.

PARISH. — Parishes are the smallest units of local government, and every part of England is contained in a parish. They vary in population from less than a hundred to almost a million. For their powers, constitution, etc., see LOCAL GOVERNMENT.

PARISH, ECCLESIASTICAL.— The ecclesiastical parish is the smallest territorial unit in the church, and is defined as "the district committed to the charge of one incumbent having the cure of souls therein." Parishes are formed into groups known as Rural Deaneries, the Rural Dean being the immediate superior of the incumbent. The parish is now represented by two bodies, the Vestry (see VESTRY) and the Parochial Church Council. The council is composed principally of elected residents of the parish, who must have attained the age of twenty-one, and who must be communicating members of the Church of England. The election takes place every year at the annual parochial church meeting (see below), usually by a show of hands; if, however, one-fifth of the voters present demand a poll, then a poll must be taken at a later date.

Parish Officers.—The chief officers of the parish, apart from the incumbent and his curate(s), are the churchwardens. (See CHURCHWARDENS). They are sometimes assisted in their duties by sidesmen, who also are elected at the parochial church meeting and approved by the incumbent. The other officers are the Beadles, Organists, Parish Clerks, Sextons and Vergers (for each of these see separate titles).

Parochial Church Electors.—Every person is entitled to become a parochial church elector if he is a baptized member of the Church of England, of eighteen years of age or older, and is resident within the parish, or has attended services in the parish for the six months prior to enrolment as an elector. No person may vote at parochial church meetings until he has been entered in the electoral roll, for which purpose he must send application to the Parochial Church Council, by whom the roll is kept.

Parochial Church Meetings.—The Parochial Church Meeting is the meeting of the parochial church electors, held annually in Easter Week.

PARISH CLERK.—The parish clerk is appointed and dismissed by the incumbent and the parochial church council acting jointly. He may be a layman or in Holy Orders. If a layman he must be at least 20 years of age, and may be removed by the Archdeacon for misbehaviour. He may sue the incumbent or churchwardens for the fees due to him on marriages or burials.

PARKING.—(See SPECIAL SUPPLEMENT "ROAD TRAFFIC.")

PARLIAMENT.—Parliament is composed of two bodies, the House of Commons and the House of Lords. Their main duty is legislation, but no bill becomes law until it has received the assent of the King. The Royal Assent, however, is now in practice never refused. (See further, ACT OF PARLIAMENT; PREROGATIVE OF THE CROWN.) Apart from legislative functions, Parliament has certain important rights, some of which are frequently exercised. For example, the House of Lords acts as supreme Court of Appeal from the Royal Court. In 1876 the office of "Lord of Appeal in Ordinary" was created for the purpose of ensuring that the House of Lords should contain lawyers of sufficient ability to act as Judges of the supreme appeal Court. Although ordinary members of the House of Lords are entitled to sit and vote in such cases, they do not in fact do so; the procedure, however, in an appeal to the Lords is almost exactly the same as if the House were sitting to consider and debate upon any non-legal matter, e.g. the Lords do not deliver "judgments" but "speeches."

Each House of Parliament has the right to commit any person to custody who is guilty of contempt to the House, e.g. for the writing of libels on Parliament; and the House itself is judge of whether or not a contempt has been committed. Any person so arrested must be released at the prorogation of Parliament.

By the Parliament Act, 1911, the powers of the Lords were considerably cut down by a provision that, after certain necessary delays and formalities, a bill may become a binding Act of Parliament without the consent of the Lords. (*See* BILL; PARLIAMENTARY COURTS; SUPREME COURT OF JUDICATURE.)

PAROL EVIDENCE.—Evidence which is given verbally is called parol evidence, as distinguished from written or documentary evidence. In general, where an agreement has been reduced to writing, Court, in determining its meaning, can only look at the document itself and cannot listen to verbal accounts given by the parties as to what they may, or may not, have agreed verbally. Where, however, the written document does not deal with some subsidiary question, and it is reasonable to suppose that an agreement must have been come to as regards that question, then parol evidence can be admitted as to what was agreed by them as to it. Also, when there is some ambiguity on the face of a written contract, the parties are allowed to explain verbally the ambiguity. (*See* EVIDENCE.)

PARSON.—This is another name for the incumbent of a Church of England living. The parson of a parish has the control, during the time that he holds the living, of the glebe lands of the parish.

PARTICULARS.—If, in any action in the High Court or the County Court, one of the parties fails to set out in his pleadings or, in the County Court, in his summons or affidavit of defence, etc., the facts upon which he relies in sufficiently precise form, the other party may demand particulars of the allegations contained in his pleadings, etc. This should be done in the first place by

letter, and if the request is not complied with, or is insufficiently complied with, the party aggrieved may take out a summons calling upon the other party to give in more precise form the particulars required. (*See* COUNTY COURT PROCEDURE; HIGH COURT PROCEDURE; PLEADINGS.)

PARTICULARS OF SALE.—On a sale of land by auction, the seller, or "Vendor" must set out in detail a full description of the property to be sold. The Particulars are printed in one document with the "Conditions of Sale," which deal with the title to the property and any matters which might be of importance to an intending purchaser. After having bought the property the purchaser signs one copy of this document, which is called the "Particulars and Conditions of Sale," and hands it, with a deposit on the purchase price, to the auctioneer, who hands him in return another copy signed and receipted by himself as agent for the vendor. If it subsequently transpires that the property does not correspond in any material respect with the description as set out in the Particulars, the purchaser may have the right to "rescind" the Contract, that is, refuse to go on with the sale, or to claim damages. (*See also* SALE OF LAND.)

PARTIES.—Generally speaking, any person may bring an action, unless he is an alien enemy during a time of war, or a bankrupt. The prohibition against enemy aliens bringing actions is absolute and lasts as long as the war continues, but after its close the enemy alien is as free to bring an action as anyone else. As far as a bankrupt is concerned, his right to bring an action is transferred to his trustee in bankruptcy, though there are exceptions—such as actions brought in respect of personal injuries to himself, or injuries by defamation on which he is entitled to sue personally. Infants also, though they are entitled to bring actions, are subject to special rules of procedure, and must bring them in the name of a person, generally the father or guardian, but who can be appointed by the Court if necessary, who is known as the "next friend" (q.v.) of the infant. Persons of unsound mind who have had a committee appointed must sue through their committee, or if no committee has been appointed, they, too, must sue in the name of a "next friend."

The parties to an action are known by

different names according to the nature of the action which is being brought, and the part which they are taking in it.

The person who starts an action claiming redress for an infringement of his rights is known as the Plaintiff, and if two or more persons bring an action together they are called Co-plaintiffs. The person against whom the action is brought is called the Defendant, and if more than one defendant appears in an action they are Co-defendants.

Where the defendant has a counterclaim against the plaintiff, the latter is still referred to as the plaintiff in the action, though he is, in fact, the defendant in the counterclaim; but if the defendant brings a counterclaim against the plaintiff and another person who is not a plaintiff, the latter is called the defendant to counterclaim.

In matrimonial cases, i.e. Divorce, Nullity Suits, petitions for Judicial Separation, etc., the applicant is known as the Petitioner, and the person against whom the right to divorce, etc. is claimed is called the Respondent. A man cited as having committed adultery with a married woman is known as a Co-respondent, while a woman cited as having committed adultery with a husband is, if she appears to answer the charge, known as an Intervener.

In Bankruptcy proceedings or in proceedings for the winding-up of a company, the person who initiates the proceedings is known as the Petitioning Creditor, if it is, in fact, a creditor who institutes the proceedings.

Where cases are taken to a Higher Court in appealing against the decision of a Lower Court, the party making the appeal is called the Appellant, and the other party the Respondent.

When an action is referred to, the name of the plaintiff, petitioner or appellant is mentioned first. Thus, an action in which Smith is plaintiff and Jones defendant is referred to as Smith v. Jones. If Jones brings a counterclaim against Smith and Robinson, the action is referred to as Smith v. Jones, Jones v. Smith and Robinson. If Jones brings third party proceedings against Brown the action is referred to as Smith v. Jones, Jones v. Brown. If, in the action of Smith v. Jones, Jones is unsuccessful and appeals against the decision of the Court, the appeal is referred to as Jones v. Smith. (*See* ACTION; COUNTY COURT PROCEDURE; HIGH COURT PROCEDURE.)

PARTNERSHIP.—The law of partnership is contained in the Partnership Act, 1890, and in a large body of cases.

What Partnership is.—Partnership is defined as the relationship which subsists between persons carrying on a business in common with a view to profit.

The best evidence that a partnership exists is that profits are shared; but this is not an infallible test, for employees in a firm often share profits, but they are not partners, since they have no share in the control of the business and the business is not carried on for them. A partnership may be formed in any trade, business or profession with certain well-defined exceptions, e.g. barristers may never work in partnership, and a partnership composed of more than ten persons for banking, or of more than twenty persons for any other purpose is illegal. Apart from these exceptions, there are no fixed rules as to when a partnership exists or does not exist, but all the facts of the relationship between the parties must be looked at. The mere fact that they own property jointly, or that they share joint returns will not, of itself, prove them to be partners, although it may help.

As has been mentioned, the best test is whether they share net profits; but the mere fact that a creditor is to receive payment of his debt by instalments varying with profits does not constitute him a partner; nor is the widow or child of a deceased partner necessarily a partner because of receiving a share of profits; nor is a man a partner merely because he lends money the interest upon which is to vary with profits, provided that the contract of loan is in writing and signed. If it is not in writing and signed, the lender will probably be deemed to be a partner. Nor is a person who has transferred the goodwill of his business to another person to be deemed to be that other person's partner merely because he chooses to take the purchase-price in the form of an annual share in the profits. But in all other cases, a person sharing profits will be assumed to be the partner of the person with whom he shares them, unless he can prove the contrary. A person who lends money and receives a share of the profits as mentioned above, although not a partner, is in a rather peculiar position, for, if the person to whom he lent the money is adjudged bankrupt, or arranges with his creditors to pay them less than 20/– in the pound, or dies insolvent, the lender can recover nothing in respect of his loan. A person who has transferred his goodwill, as mentioned above, is in the same position.

Firms and Firm-Names.—A partnership is often known as a "firm," which is a shorter term for "partnership." (*See* FIRM.) On the formation of a firm, a name must be chosen, and, although fanciful names are often taken, in the majority of cases the firm-name is composed of the names of the partners or of the chief partners; for example, if there are a dozen partners, it would be more convenient to adopt the abbreviation "and Co." or "and Sons." The fact that a firm is called "Smith and Sons" does not necessarily shew that any Mr. Smith is a partner: there may never have been a Mr. Smith, or he and his sons may have died or retired long ago. In order to see who are the real partners, it is necessary to inspect the Register of Business Names, where all business names must be registered if they differ from those of the real proprietors. (*See* BUSINESS NAMES.)

How to Form a Partnership.—From the above description of what a partnership is, it is clear that a partnership can be formed without any formalities at all; indeed, when entering into close business relationships with another person it is often wise to make it clear that there is no intention to form a partnership; for, as will be explained, one partner has very wide powers to bind another. When, however, a partnership is expected to transact a considerable amount of business, a usual precaution is to define the rights and duties of the partners towards each other in what are known as "articles of partnership."

Who may become Partners.—Any person may become a partner provided he is sane and twenty-one years of age, unless he is a convict or an alien enemy. Infants (i.e. persons under 21) may become partners, but usually will be under no liability either to the firm's creditors or to the other partners. An infant partner may at any time before he attains twenty-one, or within a reasonable time thereafter, repudiate his liabilities; an infant has no right to share in the partner-

ship property until all creditors have been paid off, nor may he claim to share profits without sharing losses; he may claim back the premium he paid on entering the partnership, except when he has derived benefits under the contract. Even a lunatic may become a partner if the other partners did not know he was a lunatic at the time the agreement was made. Married as well as single women may be partners, and their separate property will be liable for debts incurred by the partnership; a husband is not liable for his wife's partnership debts, unless, of course, he also was one of the partners.

Relation of Partners with Persons Dealing With Them.—*Power of single partner to bind the firm.*—One of the essential rules to remember in relation to partnership is that each partner has full authority to act as agent for the firm in all matters connected with the firm's business. This means that he is capable of making a contract that will be binding on his co-partners. Such a contract may be binding on the co-partners even in spite of the fact that it has been agreed between the partners that he is to have no authority to make contracts.

This implied authority for each member of a partnership to bind the firm extends only to contracts that are usual in a business of the kind carried on. For example, in a grocery business it is usual for supplies of groceries to be ordered, but it is not usual to purchase agricultural lands or to order suits of clothes. Innumerable cases have been decided on this question, and each case, of course, depends upon its peculiar facts, but it is safe to say that in all trading partnerships, one partner will bind the others (i) in selling goods belonging to the firm; (ii) in buying goods to be used in the firm's business; (iii) in employing servants for the business; (iv) in receiving payment of debts or releasing debts; (v) in borrowing money for the firm and pledging the firm's goods, or depositing title-deeds as security for such money; (vi) in making or accepting bills of exchange or cheques in the firm's name. In non-trading (e.g. professional) partnerships the list is not so comprehensive. But in either case the customary course of dealing of the partnership may have conferred a power upon a partner to bind the partnership by a contract concerned with matters not necessarily related to the business. Apart from such a customary course of dealing, the fact that a contract made by an individual partner is prudent or necessary does not of itself bind the partnership if it was not also usual. For example, where the borrowing of money is not usually necessary for the carrying on of the firm's business (e.g. in the case of a professional partnership), a partner who borrows money in the firm's name will not make the firm liable to repay it, even though he took that course to save the firm from ruin. It would be necessary for all the partners to consent expressly to the taking of such a loan. The borrowing of money on the firm's credit is, however, a usual part of the business of an ordinary trading company. A document under seal must always be executed by each partner personally. A partner may always bind the firm, however unusual the contract, if he has been specially authorized by the other partners to do so, even if the other party to the contract was unaware that such special authorization had in fact been given.

Liability of Partners for the Firm's Debts, etc.

Every partner is liable for the firm's debts to the same extent as if they had been his own personal debts, and this applies even to a sleeping partner. A partnership is not a limited liability company. The greatest care should therefore be taken to ascertain the reliability of a person with whom it is intended to enter into partnership, since each partner may make contracts which the other partners may be called upon to fulfil. All partners should be sued together at the same time, and judgment will then be obtained against all of the partners, and if it is found that one of them is unable to pay, execution may be levied against any of the others.

In the case of wrongs as distinguished from contracts (e.g. libel, trespass, negligence, etc.), each partner is liable for the acts of the others provided the wrong was done in the ordinary course of business. For example, in one case A and B were partners in competition with C, and it was the ordinary course of their business to obtain information as to their competitors' methods; A bribed one of C's clerks wrongfully to disclose C's trade-secrets, here B no less than A, is liable to pay C damages.

Misappropriation by Partners of Money entrusted to the Firm.

Every partner is liable if one partner receives a third person's money or property and misapplies it, provided he received the money within the scope of his apparent authority, e.g. it would not be within the scope of the apparent authority of a partner in a grocery business to receive money for the purpose of investing it for a third person. If the firm receives money in the ordinary course of business and one partner misappropriates it, all the partners are liable to the person to whom it belonged, for when a firm (e.g. a firm of bankers) receives another person's money, it is the duty of every partner to see that the money is taken care of.

Liability of Persons who seem to be Partners.

If a man, by conduct or by words, represents that he is a partner in a firm, and a third person gives credit to the firm on the faith of that representation, he will be liable to such third person as if he actually had been a partner. He will be similarly liable if he knowingly allows others to represent that he was a partner.

Liabilities of New or Retiring Partners.

When a new partner is introduced into a firm he does not become liable to the firm's creditors for anything done before he became a partner, nor does a retiring partner cease to be liable for debts or obligations incurred before his retirement. An agreement may, however, be made to the contrary in either case between the partners and the creditors, and such agreement may be implied from conduct. The addition of a new partner, or the retirement of an old partner makes a new firm; and if the creditors, knowing of the reconstruction, continue to deal with the new firm, they can usually be taken to have agreed to discharge the old firm from all liabilities and to have accepted the new firm as the debtors. If a firm is given a continuing guarantee or if a third person is giving a continuing guarantee, or if a third person is giving a continuing guarantee in respect of transactions with the firm, that guarantee will terminate when any change is made in the constitution of the firm, e.g. if A says to a bank, "I will guarantee B and Co.'s account until further notice," and a partner subsequently retires from B and Co. or a new partner is taken in, the guarantee then terminates.

Partnership Property.

Partnership property consists of all property, and rights

and interests in property originally brought into the partnership stock, or subsequently acquired for the firm. The partners may use such property only for the purposes of the partnership business, and not for their own purposes. When a firm occupies land or buildings as tenant of one of the partners without the lease containing a specific period, it is assumed that the firm's tenancy will expire only when the partnership is dissolved. Any property bought with the firm's money is partnership property. For example a partner bought railway shares in his own name out of the partnership funds, but without the authority of the other partners; such shares were deemed to be the property of the partnership.

Partners' Shares in Partnership Property.—Each partner has an equal share in the profits of a partnership, even though he has himself contributed no capital. The Articles usually, therefore, provide the proportions in which partners are to share profits, usually giving a larger share to partners of longer standing. If the business makes losses, the partners must bear such losses equally, unless otherwise agreed. When any payment is made by a partner, or when any personal liability is undertaken by him in the ordinary conduct of the firm's business, or for the preservation of the firm's business or property, the firm must indemnify him, i.e. such a loss is shared equally. As to each partner's right to share in the partnership's capital, *see below*, DISTRIBUTION OF PROPERTY ON DISSOLUTION.

Partner's Right to Take Part in the Business.—Every partner has a right to share in the management of the business, but no partner is entitled to remuneration for his service (apart, of course, from special agreement between the partners). No new partner may be introduced without the consent of all the existing partners. Every partner may inspect the accounts, which are always to be kept at the principal place of business.

When any dispute arises between the partners as to ordinary matters connected with the partnership business, the opinion of the majority will prevail, but any change in the nature of the business to be carried on must have the consent of all partners. No partner may be expelled by the other partners (unless, of course, special terms exist to that effect).

Retirement—Unless a period has been fixed for the duration of the partnership, it may be terminated by any partner at any time by his giving notice to the other partners. If the notice specifies no date, it will take effect immediately upon the date when it was communicated to the other partners. A partnership to be terminated "by mutual arrangement only" can be terminated only by the consent of all partners, or by the death of one. If the partnership was entered into by deed, the notice must be in writing. It is to be noted that retirement necessarily involves a dissolution of the whole partnership. If the remaining partners continue the business, they are a new firm. Where a fixed period of duration has expired, and the partnership is still carried on, the partnership is governed as far as possible by the terms and conditions governing it at the time when the period expired. If a retiring partner does not withdraw his share of the assets on retirement, he is entitled to profits made thereafter which are attributable to the retention of his capital, or, if he chooses, he may claim 5 % per annum on such capital; a dead partner's representatives have the same right.

Partner's Duty to Disclose and Render Accounts.—Partners are bound to render true accounts and full information of all things affecting the partnership to any partner, or to his executors or administrators. Any benefit derived by a partner without the other partners' consent from transactions concerning the partnership, or from his use of the partnership property, or partnership name or business connection, belongs to the partnership. If a partner, without the consent of the other partners, carries on a business competing with the firm's business, he must pay over all the profits so made to the partnership.

Transfer of a Partner's Share.—A partner may, with the other partners' consent, transfer his share of the partnership to another person who is to be admitted as a partner. This is equivalent to the resignation of the old partner and the admission of a new one (*see above*), i.e. the firm is dissolved and a new firm is created. A partner may, however, without the consent of the other partners, assign his

made the tenth day of October One
thousand nine hundred and thirty——
B E T W E E N   ALBERT GREEN of Number
2800 Whitestock Road Clapham of the
one part and ROBERT SCARLETT of Number 564 Browning Road Clapham of
the other part

WITNESSETH that it is mutually agreed between the said parties
as follows :-

1.   The said parties shall become partners in the business of Sanitary   engineers plumbers and gas fitters and shall carry on business
at Number 2800 Whitestock Road Clapham or at such other place or
places as they may from time to time agree upon

2.   The said partnership shall commence from the date hereof and
shall continue for five years from the date hereof if the parties
shall so long live

3.   The said business shall be carried on under the name of the
Whitestock Plumbing Co.

4.   The capital of the said partnership shall be the sum of FIFTY
POUNDS to be contributed by the said partners in equal shares (or
shall be the net value of the stock in trade book debts and other
assets less any present liabilities of the business of sanitary
engineer plumber and gas fitter carried on until this time by the
said Albert Green at Number 2800 Whitestock Road and the sum of
Twenty five pounds to be contributed by the said Robert Scarlett
The net value of the said stock in trade book debts and other assets
less the said liabilities shall be taken to be Twenty five pounds
and that sum shall be credited to the said Albert Green as his share
of the capital)

5.   The partners shall be entitled to share equally in the net
profits of the said business and shall share equally in any losses

6.   Each partner shall be at liberty to draw out of the said business
for his own use the weekly sum of Three pounds on account of his
share of profits

7.   Each partner shall keep proper records of all his transactions
in connection with the partnership business and of all moneys
received and paid by him on behalf of the partnership Neither
partner shall transact any business or give credit to any person
after he has been requested not to do so by the other partner

8.   As soon as conveniently may be after the tenth day of October
in every year during the partnership there shall be prepared an
account of all the assets and liabilities of the partnership and a
profit and loss account for the past year Each partner shall sign
the said accounts and shall thereupon be bound thereby Any net
profits shown by the said profit and loss account shall be divided
between the partners provided that the drawings of either partner
under clause 6 hereof shall be taken into account before division
of the said net profits and if either partner has drawn a sum larger
than his share of the said net profits he shall forthwith refund
the difference

9.   Each partner shall diligently attend to the business of the
partnership and devote his whole time thereto Neither shall during
the continuance of the partnership without the consent of the other
either separately or in partnership with any other person engage in
or carry on any other trade or business

10. If either partner shall commit an act of bankruptcy or shall do or suffer anything whereby his partnership share becomes liable to be taken in execution or to be sold or shall assign his said share or any part thereof or commit any breach of this agreement the other partner may within one month after becoming aware thereof by notice in writing terminate the partnership The partner giving such notice shall have the option (to be exercised at the time the said notice is given) to purchase the share of the other partner at a valuation The valuation shall be made by two valuers, one selected by each partner or his representatives and in case the two valuers shall be unable to agree they shall appoint a third valuer whose valuation shall be final

11. If either partner shall die the partnership shall be dissolved and the surviving partner shall have an option (to be exercised within three months of the death) to purchase the share of the deceased partner at a price to be fixed by valuation in the manner set out under clause 10 hereof

12. In the event of the share of either partner being purchased by the other under the provisions of clauses 10 or 11 hereof the purchasing partner shall have an option to pay the sum due for the said share in equal monthly payments over a period of not more than twenty four months

I N WITNESS whereof the parties to these presents have hereunto set their hands and seals the day and year first before written

SIGNED SEALED AND DELIVERED by the above)
named ALBERT GREEN in the presence of :-)

Albert Green.

James White,
3660, Redford Lane, Clapham S.W.
Bank Clerk.

SIGNED SEALED AND DELIVERED by the above)
named ROBERT SCARLETT in the presence of:-)

Robert Scarlett.

Frank H. Connett
300 Blackpool Road
Clapham. S.W.
Builder

A Specimen Deed of Partnership.

share in the partnership, either absolutely or by way of mortgage, but the assignee has no right to interfere with the management of the partnership business, or to require accounts, or to inspect the books; his only right is to take the share of the profits that the partner would otherwise have been entitled to, and he must accept the remaining partners' word as to the amount of such profits. He has no share in deciding what profits shall be declared, i.e. he has no share in deciding how much of the actual profits are to be put to reserve. Such an assignment does not relieve the assigning partner of his duties and liabilities, which remain the same as if he had not assigned. When the partnership is finally dissolved, the assignee has a right to his proper share in the partnership property, and for that purpose may see the accounts.

Dissolution of Partnership.—A partnership becomes dissolved (subject, of course, to other agreed terms): (i) At the expiration of the period (if any) during which it was agreed to run; (ii) by notice given by one partner to the other (see "RETIREMENT" above); (iii) by the death or bankruptcy of any partner; (iv) at the option of any partner, if another partner allows his share to be charged; (v) by the happening of any event which makes it unlawful for the firm's business to be carried on, e.g. on the outbreak of war English partnerships between friends and alien enemies are dissolved; (vi) when the Court decrees dissolution. The Court may decree dissolution (1) when a partner is found lunatic by inquisition, or is shewn to be of permanently unsound mind; or (2) when a partner, other than the partner suing, becomes in any other way permanently incapable of performing his partnership duties; or (3) when a partner, other than the partner suing, has been guilty of such conduct as is calculated prejudicially to affect the carrying on of the business; or (4) when a partner, other than the partner suing, wilfully or persistently commits breaches of the partnership agreement or otherwise so conducts himself in the partnership business that it is not reasonably practicable for the other partners to carry on business in partnership with him; or (5) when the partnership can be carried on only at a loss; or (6) whenever circumstances have arisen which render it just and equitable that the partnership be dissolved.

Effect of Dissolution.—When, after the dissolution of a partnership, a new partnership continues with the old firm's name (e.g. when one partner retires), the old customers of the firm are entitled to assume that they are dealing with the old firm, and may hold the members of the old firm liable until they have had it brought to their notice that the old firm is dissolved. It is, therefore, desirable for retiring partners, or partners selling their business to a person who is to carry it on under the old name, to circularize their old customers as to the dissolution. Even new customers who knew of the old firm's existence and membership are in the same position, and may assume that the old partners are still members of the firm until an advertisement has been inserted in the *London Gazette* as to the change in the firm's constitution, or until they have received actual notice of the change. But when a partner dies, no customer may assume that he is still a partner, and his estate will not therefore be liable for partnership debts contracted after his death even with persons who knew nothing of his death. After dissolution, one partner is still able to bind the other partners in all matters necessary to be done to wind up the firm's affairs.

Distribution of Property on Dissolution.—Every partner is entitled to have the partnership property applied to the settlement of the firm's liabilities, and to have any surplus divided in the same proportions between the partners as profits are divisible. If, however, the partners have contributed to the capital of the partnership in unequal shares, each partner is entitled to have repaid to him the capital he subscribed before any distribution is made.

This rule often works very harshly on partners who have been taken into the firm for their skill and not for the capital they could provide, e.g. suppose A had supplied no capital, and after a month's trading the firm failed for £2,000; A would have to find not only his share of the £2,000 but also his share of the lost capital. When a partnership is wound up, all the partnership property must be sold, and the term "property" includes the goodwill. When the goodwill is sold, only the buyer is entitled to use the firm's name, and ex-partners may not use it, although there is nothing to prevent them from carrying on a competing business. The buyer of the goodwill may, however, use the old firm-name only provided it will not lead old customers to believe that the old partners are still members of the firm.

When a partner has paid a premium on becoming a partner, and the partnership comes to an end before the agreed date (if any) otherwise than as the result of the death of a partner, the Court may order repayment of the premium or a part thereof.

Limited Partnerships.—By the Limited Partnerships Act, 1907, a special form of partnership was authorized in which there must be one or more active partners who have the same rights and duties as partners in an ordinary partnership, and in which there are also one or more "limited partners."

PARTNERSHIP (SCOTS LAW).—The Scots law of partnership is in most respects the same as the law of England. Two differences, however, should be noted. Firstly, in Scotland the partnership is a legal person capable of having rights and duties of its own, and quite distinct from the legal personalities of the individual parties. In England a partnership has no legal personality. Secondly, in Scotland every partner is liable jointly and severally for all the debts of the firm, whereas in England he is liable jointly and severally in respect of all debts arising from tort, i.e. wrongful acts, but is only jointly liable with his co-partners in respect of contracts. (*See* JOINT AND SEVERAL.)

PARTY WALL.—A party wall is one which separates one property from another and at the same time forms part of a building on both properties. The duty of maintaining it may rest on either of the owners of the two properties, or on both of them equally. Where there is no agreement of any kind, the wall is deemed to be divided vertically into two parts, and each owner is bound to maintain his own part so as to support the other. (*See* ADJOINING OWNERS; FENCE; WALL.)

PASSENGERS.—The liability of carriers of passengers is not so great as the liability of carriers of goods. The carrier of passengers is not liable unless he has failed to take reasonable care in carrying out his contract. (*See* RAILWAY PASSENGERS AND SHIPPING.)

PASSPORT.—A passport is a permit to pass into or out of a state. It is popularly understood to be the document issued by the Government of the state of which an individual is a national entitling him to leave and return to that state, and requesting and requiring all those whom it may concern to allow him to pass freely, and to afford him every assistance and protection of which he may stand in need.

A passport is required for persons travelling to any part of the British Dominions, except to Canada, or from the United Kingdom to the Irish Free State, or from the United Kingdom to Newfoundland; but passengers intending to return to the United Kingdom should provide themselves with passports. If a person having a passport desires to travel to a country the name of which is not included in his passport, he must, in addition to obtaining any requisite visa, apply to the Passport Office for the inclusion of that country in the passport. It is, therefore, advisable on first applying for a passport to see that it is endorsed for all countries that the applicant may ever desire to visit.

Passports are obtainable at the Passport Office, Queen Anne's Gate Buildings, West-

minster, S.W.1, or at the Branch Passport Office, 36 Dale Street, Liverpool. Application may be made by post, and should be made four days or more before the passport is required. Application forms may be obtained from the same address, together with copies of the regulations. All passports expire after five years from the date of issue, and must then be renewed. After ten years from the date of issue, or when there is no more space left for visas, an entirely new passport must be obtained. (See specimen form on pages 592-3). (*See also* ALIENS; BRITISH SUBJECT; NATURALIZATION.)

PATENT MEDICINE.—A patent medicine is, strictly speaking, any medicine in the shape of a pill, powder, lozenge or potion, which is prepared or sold under letters patent, but the term is commonly used to describe what are known as Proprietary Medicines. A proprietary medicine is a preparation which the makers or sellers claim to have the secret of manufacturing, or which they advertise to the public as being specially beneficial towards the prevention, cure, or relief, of any ailment. Such medicines, both patent and proprietary, are subject to special duties, and the bottle or box must have a stamp attached to it which is broken by the opening of the bottle or box. The duty payable varies from 3*d.*, when the price of the article is 1*s.* 0*d.*, to £1 when the price is £2 10*s.* 0*d.* The scale of the duty is as follows:—

PRICE						DUTY		
s. d.						£	*s.*	*d.*
1 0	.	.	.	.	.	—	—	3
2 6	.	.	.	.	.	—	—	6
4 0	.	.	.	.	.	—	1	0
10 0	.	.	.	.	.	—	2	0
20 0	.	.	.	.	.	—	4	0
30 0	.	.	.	.	.	—	6	0
50 0	.	.	.	.	.	1	0	0

Ginger and peppermint lozenges, sold as confectionery, are not subject to duty, but if they are sold as beneficial for the prevention, cure, or relief of any ailment, then duty must be paid upon them.

PATENTS.—The only person who may apply for a patent is "the true and first inventor." This expression has a very much wider meaning than laymen might suspect, for since the object of the law is to promote the dissemination of knowledge in Great Britain, the first person to introduce a foreign invention into England is as much the first inventor of it and entitled to apply for a patent as if he had conceived the idea himself. This rule used to be of much greater effect than it is now, as it has now been enacted that no person may apply for an English patent in respect of a foreign invention unless he is either resident in Great Britain or represents the foreign inventor. Further, as a result of international conventions with a number of other countries, it has been agreed that any inventor who has applied for protection in his own country may also apply in England. Provided he applies within twelve months of his application abroad, such a foreign inventor will be entitled to the grant of a patent in England, notwithstanding the fact that in the interval between the two applications someone else has introduced the invention into England.

Inventions by Servants.—If a servant acts under the orders or direction of his employer, his inventions and patents belong to the latter; but inventions arrived at independently by the servant, even though in his employer's laboratories, etc., do not necessarily belong to the employer unless there is a contract express or implied to assign them.

What is an Invention?—A patent may only be applied for in respect of an invention; that is, either a new and original method of making an article which is already known, a method of making an article which has not been previously known, or the discovery of a new use to which a known article may be put. It used to be said that a patent could only be obtained for a process of manufacture. This is too narrow a statement of the law as it now stands, but it is still true to say that every invention must be related to manufacture in order to be patentable. A mere idea independent of any manufacture or creation can never be patented. New methods of musical notation or of indexing, etc., are ideas, whereas a new method of printing musical scores or a new kind of filing cabinet would be manufactures. A principle as such is not a manufacture, but a mode of carrying it into effect is; a man who conceived the idea of having cars driven by air propellers would be unable to obtain a patent for it unless he also worked out a proper method of putting his idea to practical effect.

Grant of Patent.—A patent may only be granted in respect of an invention which was not previously known within the British Isles, for protection is only given in return for the disclosure of something new. If, therefore, the invention has already been made by somebody else, and has been communicated by him to some portion of the public, no matter how small, no patent may be obtained by a later inventor, even though he reached his conclusions entirely unaided. But if the first inventor kept his knowledge to himself and did not communicate it to the public, then the second inventor (provided that he worked independently and did not obtain his material from the former) may obtain a patent, for he will have something to offer the public in exchange for it, namely, the disclosure of something which they do not yet know.

Publication.—It follows from this necessity for disclosure in return for protection by patent, that there must have been no previous disclosure—publication is the legal expression—by the inventor. Publication is the communication of the principle of the invention except under conditions of confidence and secrecy. It includes (subject to what is said below) speeches, papers, articles, etc., describing the invention, demonstrations of its working or the manufacture and marketing of the invented article or of materials, etc., constructed by it. The application for a patent must, therefore, be made while the invention is still unknown. Publication after the date of the application but before the grant of a patent does not invalidate it.

There are certain exceptions to the rule that any disclosure constitutes publication. If the information was obtained in fraud of the inventor, or was communicated by him in confidence, disclosure of it will not be legal publication, and applications by the thief for a patent for himself will not affect the rights of the inventor. The working of the machine may be demonstrated and the machine itself may be constructed and worked, provided that this is done in confidence and that it is not worked commercially, without there being any publication in law. Lastly, the exhibition of the invention at certain kinds of exhibitions is, in some circumstances, declared not to be publication, and the inventor who describes his invention to a earned society may apply within six months for a patent, provided he gave notice to the Comptroller of Patents before he read his paper.

Length of Grant.—The maximum period for which a patent may be granted is twenty-six years; the initial period is always sixteen years, but it may be extended on application for a further five, and occasionally ten years on payment of the prescribed fees. In deciding whether to extend the life of a patent beyond sixteen years, the Comptroller will consider the nature and merits of the invention from the point of view of the public, and the profits which the inventor has made. The broad principle is that, provided the patentee has done his best to develop the invention, he is entitled to a reasonable re-numeration, and if it is one which does not give a quick return he deserves an extension of the term.

Rights of Patentee.—The grant of a patent dates back to the filing of the pro-visional specification, and gives the patentee the sole and exclusive right of working his invention within Great Britain and the Isle of Man, and to restrain any other person from working it except under a licence.

The patentee may enforce his rights against infringers by means of an action for damages and by injunctions. He must not, however, threaten proceedings or make allegations of infringements which he is not prepared to bring or substantiate, as the person threatened or anyone injured by the threats (i.e. a rival trader) may bring what is called a threats action, claiming damages, unless the patentee proceeds with his action for infringement. Infringement includes the manufacture, importation, sale, offer for sale or use of a patented article except under licence. The patentee may grant licences to other persons to work his invention (if the patent is endorsed "licences as of right" he must do so). Within certain limits he has a free hand in dictating his terms, but he must not attempt to fetter the licensee too severely or he will be guilty of an abuse of monopoly rights, nor can he bind the licensee beyond the life of the patent. He may also assign the benefit of his patent. A register of assignments is kept at the Patent Office.

A patent will expire naturally at the end of its period; but it may also be revoked earlier by the Comptroller, and it will lapse if fees are not paid, though in the latter case it may be revived by payment.

Procedure.—Application for a patent must be made to the Comptroller at the Patent Office from whom detailed instructions may be obtained. Heavy fees are payable on application and renewal, but the latter may be reduced if the patent is endorsed "licences as of right." A complete explanation and specification of the invention must be given though the applicant may, if he chooses, send a provisional (less detailed) description first. This will be handed to an examiner whose duty it is to see whether it is really new or has been patented before. The examiner is not liable in law for his report, and there is no guarantee that it is accurate. An appeal lies from his decision to the Law Officers (Attorney- and Solicitor-General). The Comptroller next advertises the application in the *Patent Gazette* and the drawings are thrown open to public inspection. Anybody interested may come forward and object to a grant of a patent on the ground that:—

(i) the invention was obtained from him;

(ii) it had been published within the last fifty years; or

(iii) it is not properly described in the specification.

The same grounds may be adduced for revoking a patent which has been granted within the last two years, but there is a further cause for which revocation may be sought, namely, an abuse of monopoly rights (*see above*).

PAUPER.—A pauper is a person who is receiving relief from the Poor Law Authorities under the provisions of the Poor Law, either as an inmate of a Poor Law Institution or by way of out-door relief. The term is also applied to a person who prosecutes or defends an action "in forma pauperis," and who receives the free assistance of counsel and solicitors in the conduct of his case. In order to receive such assistance he must be worth less than fifty pounds and have an income not exceeding two pounds per week, or, in exceptional cases, four pounds per week.

Residence in a workhouse or other poor law institution does not constitute a residential qualification for the purpose of being placed on the registry of voters, and a pauper in receipt of parish relief is disqualified while receiving such relief from holding certain local offices. The councils of counties and county boroughs are bound by law to bury any pauper who dies while residing in one of their institutions. There is no obligation upon them to bury paupers not resident in an institution, but it is lawful for them to bury any pauper who dies in their area, and to pay the expenses out of the county fund.

Relatives of paupers are, in certain circumstances, liable to maintain them or contribute towards their maintenance, and the amount of their contribution may be assessed by the magistrates in the area in which the pauper is relieved. (*See* BURIAL; ELECTIONS; LOCAL GOVERNMENT; POOR LAW; VOTING.)

PAWNBROKERS.—A Pawnbroker is a person who carries on the business of lending money on the security of articles of personal property delivered to him.

Under this heading, only the law relating to licensed pawnbrokers will be dealt with.

If the pawnbroker only lends sums in excess of £10, the pawning is governed, with a few exceptions, by the law applying to money-lenders (*see* PAWNING) and nothing appearing hereafter under this heading is applicable to the transaction.

If, however, a person intends to carry on the business of pawnbroker in respect of loans of £10 or under, he must become a licensed pawnbroker, and the special provisions of the Pawnbrokers Act apply, but the law applying to money-lenders does not.

Certificate.—In order to obtain a licence, a certificate must first be obtained from the Justices of the Peace of the local Petty Sessional Court sitting as a District Council for that purpose, or, in London and other big towns where they exist, from a Stipendiary Magistrate.

If the certificate is refused, there is a right of appeal to Quarter Sessions.

The certificate remains in force for one year from its date of issue, and henceforth has to be renewed annually by further applications, but no further notices are required.

Licence.—Having obtained a certificate, a licence can be got from the Commissioners of Inland Revenue on production of the certificate and on payment of a fee of £7 10s. 0d.

Having become a licensed pawnbroker, loans of £10 and under may be made, but

the following rules must be observed. (The ordinary rules of Pawning [q.v.] also apply except where they are inconsistent with the following rules.)

Pawnbrokers' Duties.—A pawnbroker must exhibit in large letters over the outer door of his shop his full names, together with the word "Pawnbroker." He must also exhibit in a conspicuous place in the shop, so that it is legible to all his clients, a notice containing all the information that is required to be printed on pawn-tickets.

He must keep and use in his business a pledge book which sets out all the details of every transaction. These must be entered up on the day of the pawning or within four hours of the end of the day.

He must keep a supply of pawn-tickets, forms of the statutory declarations for use when the pledge is claimed by the true owner or when the pawn-ticket is lost, forms of special contracts, and a sales book in which all the particulars of sales must be entered.

Failure to observe any of the above rules is an offence, and a pawnbroker is also guilty of an offence if he does any of the following things:

(i) Takes an article in pawn from any person appearing to be intoxicated or under the age of 14. (The age limit is under 16 in the Metropolitan police district and in Liverpool.)

(ii) Purchases or takes in pawn or exchange a pawn-ticket issued by another pawnbroker.

(iii) Employs anyone under the age of 16 to take pledges in pawn.

(iv) Carries on business on Sunday, Good Friday or Christmas Day.

(v) Under any pretence purchases, except at a public auction, a pledge pawned with him, or allows a pledge to be redeemed from him so that he can purchase it, or makes any agreement with the owner or pawner of a pledge to purchase it from him within the period of redemption.

(vi) Sells or disposes of a pledge in any way other than is authorized.

(vii) Accepts as a pledge certain forbidden articles. (*See* PAWNING.)

(viii) Refuses to deliver a pledge to anyone who is entitled to it unless, of course, he can shew he had a good and reasonable excuse for refusing.

Though the law does not compel it, every pawn-broker uses the sign of the three golden balls. This is the crest of the Medici family, one branch of which were the first money-lenders in England. The three balls actually represent three pills, for the Medicis were formerly famous for the knowledge of medicine.

The penalty for the commission of any of the above offences is a fine of not more than £10.

In regard to the actual contract of pawning, the pawnbroker must at the time give the pawner a pawn-ticket.

Interest.—On loans of 40/- or under, the rate of interest that may be charged is limited to ½d. per 2/- or fraction thereof per month or part thereof, provided that if the loan lasts for more than a month and is repaid during the first half of any subsequent month, only ¼d. per 2/- or fraction thereof may be charged in respect of that month.

On loans of over 40/-, the maximum rate is ½d. per 2/6 or fraction thereof per month or part thereof (without the proviso mentioned above).

A charge of ½d. if the loan is 10/- or under, or 1d. if the loan is over 10/-, may be made for the pawn-ticket. A further charge of ½d. for every 5/- or fraction thereof may be made if the loan is not more than 40/-.

If a pawnbroker insists on receiving a higher rate of interest or any other charge for expenses, the pawner can recover any sum so paid.

Redemption of Pledge.—The pledge is always redeemable, i.e. recoverable, at any time within a year and seven days of its being pawned and, if the loan is over 10/-, it is redeemable at any time thereafter until it is sold. It is redeemable on payment to the pawnbroker of the amount of the loan and of all sums due for interest and charges. The pawnbroker must, if requested, give a receipt for the payment, but the receipt need not be stamped unless he has received over 40/- in interest.

The person seeking to redeem the pledge must, as well as paying the amount due, produce the pawn-ticket. If it has been lost or mislaid the claimant can obtain a form of declaration from the pawnbroker stating that he is entitled to the pledge, and that the pawn-ticket has been lost or mislaid. This form must be signed on oath by the claimant in the presence of a Justice of the Peace or a Commissioner for Oaths, and in the presence of a person who can identify him. If the declaration is sworn before a Commissioner for Oaths, it requires a 2/6 stamp.

The declaration must be returned to the pawnbroker not later than three days after it was obtained from him, and it then takes the place of the pawn-ticket. During those three days the pawnbroker is not liable to deliver the pledge to anyone else and only does so at his own risk. A person making a false declaration is guilty of perjury. A pawnbroker who has in good faith delivered the pledge to a holder of a pawn-ticket, or to a person who has made the above declaration, is not liable to anyone who subsequently claims to be entitled to the pledge.

Sale of Pledge.—If the loan was for 10/- or under, the pledge becomes the absolute property of the pawnbroker after a year and seven days have expired.

If it was for over 10/-, the pawnbroker only has a right of sale after that period. The sale of any pledge must be by public auction.

The holder of the pawn-ticket has a right at any time within the three years to inspect the entry of sale in the pawnbroker's sale book and the catalogue of the auction, which must be filled in and signed by the auctioneer and kept for three years by the pawnbroker for that purpose. A charge of 1/- may be made for inspecting the sale book.

Damage or Loss of Pledge.—If the pledge is damaged or lost through the pawnbroker's negligence, default or wilful misbehaviour, the latter will be ordered to pay the pawner a sum to cover the damage suffered, or to deduct such sum from the amount due to him from the pawner. This relief can be obtained from a Court of summary jurisdiction, but the pawner must be entitled to redeem the pledge, and must offer to do so.

If the pledge is damaged or destroyed by fire caused by any reason whatsoever, the pawnbroker is liable to pay to the pawner the value of the pledge, less what is due to him, if the pawner applies at any time before his right to redeem has expired. For this purpose, the value of the pledge is deemed to be 25 % more than the amount of the loan and interest. A pawnbroker is at liberty to insure any pledge for this amount.

Offences by Pawner.—It is an offence for a pawner:—

(i) To pawn anything belonging to someone else unless he has the owner's consent;

(ii) To offer a pledge without giving a satisfactory explanation of how he obtained it if requested to do so;

(iii) To give false information as to his name and address, or that of the true owner;

(iv) To attempt to redeem a pledge without any right to it;

(v) To forge a pawn-ticket;

(vi) To pawn certain forbidden articles. (*See* PAWNING.)

Rights of True Owner.—The true owner of a pledge can obtain it from a pawnbroker without the pawn-ticket (if someone has wrongfully pawned the pledge) by signing a declaration on the form supplied by the pawnbroker stating that the pledge is his own property. The procedure and rules are the same as those governing a declaration made by a person who has lost his pawn-ticket. (*See* above under "REDEMPTION OF PLEDGE.")

Special Contracts.—Notwithstanding any of the above rules, a pawnbroker can, if the loan exceeds 40/-, always make a special contract with the pawner. By the contract special terms may be arranged as to rate of interest, charges for pawn-tickets, inspection of sales book, storage and the period of redemption (which, however, must not be less than three months). The ordinary rules will apply except in so far as they are excluded by these express terms.

To create a special contract it is essential that at the time of the pawning the pawnbroker should deliver a special contract pawn-ticket signed by himself, and that a duplicate should be signed by the pawner. Neither of these documents requires a stamp unless the loan is over £10, when a 6d. stamp is required. Any rate of interest and any sum for expenses may be agreed on, but the transaction may be reopened by the Court if it is held to be harsh and unconscionable in the same way as if it were a money-lender's transaction. The other rules in regard to money-lenders do not apply. (*See* MONEY-LENDERS; MONEY-LENDING; PAWNING.)

PAWNING.—Pawning is the depositing of some article of personal property as a security for money lent. The essence of pawning is that the property pawned, called the pledge, shall either actually be delivered to the pawnbroker or constructively delivered, i.e. the right to possession given to him, e.g. by delivery of the key of the warehouse where the pledge is kept, or of documents of title. The loan and the delivery of the article pawned need not be contemporaneous, but delivery must follow as a result, and within a reasonable time, of the loan.

Under this heading only the law relating to unlicensed pawnbrokers will be dealt with.

The law in regard to pawning is divided into that applying only to loans of £10 or under, and that applying to loans of over £10.

If the sum lent is £10 or under, the pawnbroker, unless it is an isolated transaction, must be a licensed pawnbroker, and special rules apply. (*See* PAWNBROKERS.) In this case nothing appearing hereafter under this heading is applicable to the transaction.

If the sum lent is over £10, the pawnbroker is not bound by these special rules, but must take out a money-lender's licence and is bound by the rules with regard to licensed money-lenders, with some exceptions for which *see* MONEY-LENDERS. Any article may be pawned with the following exceptions:—

(i) Naval and military equipment or decorations.

(ii) Documents giving the right to naval or military pay or pension.

(iii) Naval, military or public stores.

(iv) Seamen's or police clothing.

(v) Workhouse property.

(vi) Pawn-tickets.

(vii) Linen, apparel, materials or unfinished goods entrusted to persons to be washed, scoured, ironed, mended, worked up, or finished, etc.

(viii) Hosiery materials.

(ix) Firearms or ammunition.

(x) Savings Bank books.

It is a criminal offence to pawn any of these articles or to accept any of them as a pledge.

Position of Pawner.—The pawner, at the time of the pawning, is deemed to warrant either that he is the owner of the pledge, or that he has the owner's authority to pawn it. He is not, however, deemed to make any warranty as to its quality, although he is guilty of a criminal offence if he intentionally makes false statements as to the quality of the pledge in order to raise money on it. This offence is called "duffing."

The pawner has an absolute right to redeem, i.e. get back, the pledge at any time before its sale by the pawnbroker (*see* below) on repayment of the loan and payment of the full sum due for interest charges and expenses.

Any term agreed to by the pawner at the time of the pawning, which deprives him of his right to redeem, is void; but he can agree that the pledge shall not be redeemable within a certain period—not longer than three months.

If the pawnbroker refuses to deliver up the pledge on tender of the amount due, the pawner can sue him to recover it, and can recover any damage he may thereby have suffered. He can also sue the pawnbroker for damage, loss or destruction of the pledge caused by the latter's negligence.

The pawner may transfer his right to redeem to someone else, who then has the same rights against the pawnbroker as the pawner himself.

On the sale of the pledge, the pawner is entitled to an account of the amount received by the pawnbroker and to payment of any balance remaining after deduction of what is due, including the expenses of the sale.

Position of Pawnbroker.—The pawnbroker must use ordinary care to restore the pledge undamaged, but if it is lost through no fault of his own, he can recover the sum due to him although he is unable to deliver up the pledge. If, however, he delivers the pledge to a person not entitled to it, he remains liable to the pawner. The pawnbroker usually safeguards himself by a term in the agreement that he shall not be liable if he delivers the pledge to a person producing the pawn-ticket.

The pawnbroker may transfer the pledge to someone else, but he remains liable to the pawner for its safe return. The third person has the same, and only the same rights against the pawner as the pawnbroker himself.

The pawnbroker may sell the pledge when the time fixed for repayment has expired. If no time has been fixed, he may sell within a reasonable time after he has demanded payment, provided he gives notice to the pawner of his intention to do so. He may sell privately or by public auction provided the sale is an honest one, but he cannot buy the pledge himself. If the sale does not realize the amount of the debt, the pawnbroker can sue for the balance; he can indeed, always sue instead of sell.

The pawnbroker is not, on the sale of the pledge, deemed to warrant his title to it, but only that it has been pawned with him. He cannot obtain a better title to the pledge than the pawner had; so that if the article has been pawned without the authority of the true owner, e.g. by a thief, the former can recover the pledge from the pawnbroker free from liability.

Moreover, in the Metropolitan Police district, a pawnbroker, who is in possession of goods pawned by someone without the owner's authority, may be ordered to appear before a magistrate and may then be ordered to deliver up the goods to the true owner— but in this case, with or without a condition that the latter shall pay him the amount of the loan. (*See* MONEY-LENDERS; MONEY-LENDING; PAWNBROKERS.)

PAYMENT INTO COURT.—In any action, whether in the High Court or the County Court, the party against whom a claim is made is entitled, at any time before the action is tried, to pay money into the Court in order to satisfy the other party's claim.

Claim Settled by Payment.—If the other party decides to accept the sum paid in in satisfaction of his claim, he must drop the rest of his action and send a notice to the solicitors of the party paying the money in, within 7 days, that he has accepted the sum paid in. He then fills up a form addressed to the Accountant-General, Royal Courts of Justice, Strand, stating that he has accepted the money in satisfaction of his claim, and has given due notice of that fact to the solicitors of the party paying the money in, within 7 days; he may also add to this form a request for payment of the amount by post, or he may take the form round and obtain payment personally.

The great importance of paying money into Court in this manner is that if money is paid into Court, the party making the claim must decide there and then whether he will take the money out or not. If he does take it out of Court, he is entitled to the costs that he has incurred up to the moment of the payment into Court but cannot continue his action. If he does continue his action, he must leave the money in Court, and when the action comes to trial, if he receives a verdict for an amount greater than the sum paid into Court he is, generally speaking, entitled to the whole of his costs, but where he receives a verdict for a sum less than the amount which has been paid in, he will generally be liable to pay all the costs incurred both by himself and his opponent since the date when the money was paid into Court. These costs may be very considerable, and it is thus important for the party making the claim to weigh carefully his chances in the action before deciding whether to take the money out or not. (See PAYMENT OUT OF COURT; HIGH COURT PROCEDURE; COUNTY COURT PROCEDURE.)

PAYMENT OUT OF COURT.— Where money has been paid into Court by a defendant in an action either in the High Court or the County Court, the plaintiff is in certain circumstances allowed to take it out.

If the money has been paid without denying liability, the plaintiff may take it out by applying on the appropriate form to the Accountant-General, Royal Courts of Justice, Strand, in the case of a High Court action, or to the Registrar in the case of a County Court action, without any further formalities, and may abandon or continue his action as he thinks fit.

If the money has been paid in with a denial of liability, the plaintiff may take it out in the same manner within 7 days and discontinue his action, or he may leave it in Court and continue his action in the hopes that he will be awarded a greater sum at the trial.

In the County Court the Registrar must give notice to the plaintiff of any money paid in by the defendant. (See COUNTY COURT PROCEDURE; HIGH COURT PROCEDURE; PAYMENT INTO COURT.)

PEDLARS— A pedlar is a person who travels on foot from town to town or house to house exposing goods for sale or barter, or obtaining orders for immediate delivery, or offering his skill in handicraft (e.g. tinkers and chairmenders are pedlars). A pedlar must obtain a police certificate (five shillings) by application to the chief police officer of the district in which he has resided for at least one month. He must shew his certificate on demand to any constable or person to whom he offers his goods for sale.

The following persons do not require a certificate to act as pedlars: (i) Commercial travellers; (ii) sellers of victuals; (iii) sellers in public or legally constituted markets or fairs. (Compare HAWKERS.)

PEERAGE.— There are five classes of peers:—dukes, marquesses, earls, viscounts, and barons. All peers have the right to be summoned to sit in the House of Lords except peers of Scotland and Ireland, who are represented there by certain peers of their own number elected by them. Peers are created by the Crown by letters patent and there is no limit to the number who may be created.

A peer is not entitled to sit in the House of Lords if he is a bankrupt, an alien, a traitor or felon who has not served his sentence. A peer may be tried for felony only in the House of Lords, though this privilege does not apply to misdemeanours.

PENAL ACTION.— Certain Acts of Parliament provide that any person who does what is rendered illegal by it, shall be liable for a sum of money to any persons who care to sue for it. This sum of money is called a penalty, and an action to recover the penalty is called a penal action.

PENAL SERVITUDE.— This is the modern method of dealing with criminals whose offences merit long periods of detention in custody. It is the successor of the old system of transportation to convict

The Central Criminal Court, called the Old Bailey, where most of the important criminal cases are tried.

settlements in Australia. The change was effected in 1853, when the Penal Servitude Act substituted penal servitude for transportation.

Penal servitude must be distinguished from imprisonment. The former is designed for long sentences, and the latter for short. Indeed, no sentence of penal servitude can be for less than three years, while no individual sentence of imprisonment can be for more than two.

Sentences of penal servitude are served in convict prisons. These are controlled by the Home Office and the Prison Commissioners. After being sentenced convicts are classified as follows: The Star class for first offenders, or persons not habitually criminal; the intermediate class for persons not suitable for the Star class and yet without bad criminal records; and the Recidivist class for habitual offenders. Care is taken to ensure that convicts of a particular class do not come in contact with those of another class.

PENALTY.—Parties frequently provide in a contract that if either of them should break the contract he should pay a certain sum of money to the other. If this sum has been calculated by the parties, and is a genuine estimate of the extent of damage likely to be suffered in the event of the contract being broken, it is known as liquidated damages and the obligation to pay it may be enforced. If, on the other hand, it is merely a sum in the nature of a fine which has no relation to the amount of loss likely to be suffered by a breach of contract, but is merely inserted in order to make any breach of contract very expensive, it will be a penalty and will not be enforced by the Court.

The word penalty is also used to mean the fine which may be imposed for a breach of the law, and also the money which may be recovered by a common informer in a penal action. (*See* LIQUIDATED DAMAGES.)

PENDENTE LITE. — This means pending the conclusion of the suit. It is usually used in connection with alimony. (*See* ALIMONY.) In matrimonial cases, once a suit has been commenced, the wife can in general petition for an order for alimony pendente lite. Money ordered as a result of such petitions is payable until the suit has been determined.

PENSION.—A pension is the name given to the payment made to a person who retires from his employment through ill-health, or age, or because he has reached a fixed retiring age. There are a great variety of pensions, the most important being Service Pensions, Old Age Pensions and Widows' Pensions. Pensions are paid to persons who have served in the Crown forces, the Police forces, the Post Office and various statutory bodies such as the Metropolitan Water Board.

Pensions in the Army, Navy and Air Force.—Pensions in the army are granted according to the terms of a Royal Warrant which is called the Pay Warrant. Non-commissioned officers and men receive a pension, while officers receive what is called Retired Pay. Non-commissioned officers and men receive a pension after fourteen years' service if they are then invalided out of the army, or discharged because of a reduction in the establishment; otherwise their period of service must be twenty-one years.

A non-commissioned officer's pension varies from 2/9 per day to 2/- per day according to the number of years during which he has occupied the rank of sergeant. A private soldier's pension varies from 1/1 per day for twenty-one years' service to 10d. for fourteen to eighteen years' service. Disability pensions are also payable to soldiers who are injured or wounded during their service, and these vary according to the earning capacity, if any, of the disabled man.

An officer in the army is not entitled to receive any retired pay until he has completed fifteen years' service. All ranks from a second lieutenant to a captain receive a retired pay of £80 per year after fifteen years, rising to £200 per year after twenty-four years' service. A retired major receives £225 per year after twenty-five years' service, while the retired pay of the higher ranks varies according to their period of service, as they have to retire at a fixed age. Officers are granted wounds pensions if they have lost an eye, a limb, or the use of a limb, and with these pensions they receive gratuity of a fixed sum according to their rank. Wounds pensions may, in certain circumstances, be commuted by the payment of a lump sum.

Naval Pensions are paid in accordance with Orders in Council made by the King, and the regulations and rate of pensions are set out in the Appendix to the Navy List which is published by H.M. Stationery Office in June and December each year.

Retired pay of Naval Officers varies from £1,800 per annum for an Admiral of the Fleet to £300 per annum for a Captain, Commander or Lieutenant retiring at the age of forty after seventeen years' service. The Admiral of the Fleet's pension is fixed, but the other officers' retired pay varies according to the length of their service. This retired pay is only paid during good behaviour, and may be forfeited if the officer brings discredit upon the Service. Petty-Officers and other ratings must serve for a period of twenty-two years from the age of eighteen, or the date of entry into the Service if that is later, in order to qualify for a pension. These twenty-two years of service must be completed within thirty years from the time when the seaman reached twenty years of age, which allows for breaks in the period of service; but such breaks must not exceed five years at a time. Disablement pensions similar to those paid to soldiers are paid to naval officers and men.

Air Force Pensions are paid under regulations made by way of an Order of the King, and are provided for on similar lines to those of the Army and Navy. Airmen below the rank of an officer have to complete twenty-four years' service normally before they become entitled to a pension, while an officer has to complete seventeen years' service. Disability pensions are paid to the rank and file of the Air Force in accordance with the extent of their disability, and special provision has been made with regard to the widows of airmen, owing to the dangerous nature of the service, and the likelihood of death ensuing after a crash.

Police Pensions.—Every member of every police force throughout the country receives a pension if he retires after completing a specified period of service.

The scale of police pensions is graded according to the pay which the policeman was receiving immediately prior to his retirement, and rises from half-pay after twenty-five years' service to two-thirds of his pay after thirty years' service.

If a policeman retires after ten years' service with a medical certificate stating that he is no longer fit for duty, he receives a pension rising from one-sixth of his pay if he has completed ten years' service to two-thirds

of his pay if he has completed thirty years' service before his retirement. If he retires with a medical certificate after less than ten years' service, he receives a gratuity. Policemen who are totally disabled, either accidentally or non-accidentally by an injury received in the execution of their duty receive a disability pension.

Deductions are made by the police authority of every police force of two and a half per cent per annum of the pay of all the members of the force, and these are used to provide the pension fund.

A pensioned policeman forfeits his pension if he is convicted of any offence and is sent to prison for more than three months, or if he associates with reputed criminals or carries on an illegal employment after his retirement from the force.

The widow of a policeman who dies after five years' service receives a widow's pension; and the widow of a policeman who dies as the result of an injury received in the execution of his duty receives a special widow's pension. Pensions may be granted by the King to any person in recognition of his or her political services. These pensions are divided into three classes: first, second and third—the first class being payable to a person who has held a political office remunerated at the rate of £5,000 per annum. This pension must not exceed £2,000 per annum, and four years' service is the minimum qualifying period. A second-class pension not exceeding £1,200 per annum is payable in respect of service of not less than six years in an office for which the salary is not less than £2,000. A third class pension not exceeding £800 per annum is payable in respect of service of not less than ten years in a political office for which the salary is not less than £1,000 per annum. If a person receiving one of these pensions becomes entitled to some salary payable out of moneys raised by taxation, then his pension may be suspended or diminished in accordance with the amount of salary which he is receiving.

Any person who is receiving a pension from the Crown, either during the pleasure of the Crown or for a fixed term of years is disqualified from being elected to, or sitting, or voting in the House of Commons. This disqualification does not apply to pensioners who receive their pension from any source other than the Crown nor does it apply to

Civil Service or Diplomatic Service pensioners. (*See* OLD AGE PENSION; ORPHANS' PENSION; WIDOWS' PENSION.)

PER CAPITA.—Distribution of property "per capita" is distinguished from distribution "per stirpes." When property is distributed "per capita," each person of those entitled takes a share in his own right. Thus, if property had to be divided between two children of a deceased person and two grandchildren who were themselves children of a child who was dead, if the distribution were "per capita," each of the four claimants would take one-fourth part of the total property; but if the distribution were "per stirpes" then the property would be divided among them according to the number of *branches* of the family, not according to the number of individuals, and so each of the children living would take one-third, and the two grand-children would take one-third between them, i.e. one-sixth each.

PERFORMING ANIMALS. — No person is allowed to exhibit any performing animal at any entertainment to which the public are admitted, whether on payment or not, or to train any animal for public exhibition, unless he is registered with the local authority of the district where he lives. This provision does not apply to the training of animals for military, police, agricultural or sporting purposes—e.g. not to the training of a sheepdog. Any police officer is entitled to enter at all reasonable times any premises on which performing animals are trained, exhibited or kept for the purpose of inspecting the premises or the animals. He is not, however, entitled to go on to the stage or go behind the stage during any public performance. The Court has power, on being satisfied that cruelty is involved in any performance, to make an order prohibiting the training or imposing conditions on the trainer preventing the cruelty. Any person who infringes any of the provisions, e.g. fails to register, or obstructs any police officer desiring to inspect his premises, or conceals an animal so as to avoid inspection, may be prosecuted in the Police Court, and, if convicted, may have his registration cancelled or be disqualified from registration.

PERJURY.—Any person lawfully sworn as a witness in any judicial proceeding who wilfully makes any material statement which he knows to be false, or does not believe to

be true, is guilty of perjury. It is important to note that the statement must be a material one, that is to say, that it has a bearing on the issue the Court is trying. It has been decided that questions put in cross-examination to a witness simply to discredit him are questions material to the proceeding, and therefore that false answers to them constitute perjury.

It will be observed that a person may be convicted of perjury in falsely swearing, not merely what he knows to be false, but also what he does not believe to be true. For instance, if A swears that he is certain B was with him on a particular day, though really he does not know whether B was with him or not, this is as much perjury as if he knew for certain that B were not with him.

Other False Statements.—It is not only in judicial proceedings that false statements are punishable. Whenever anyone is required or authorized by law to make any statement on oath for any purpose, and wilfully swears falsely, he may be punished as if he had committed perjury in a judicial proceeding.

It is also an offence to make a false oath or to sign any false declaration under any Act of Parliament relating to marriage or to make any false entry in any marriage licence. Again, anyone who forbids the issue of a marriage licence by falsely and wilfully representing himself to be a person whose consent to the marriage is required by law, commits a similar offence.

It is also punishable wilfully to give false information to any registrar as to any birth or death, or the cause of any death, or any false statement as to a child born alive being still-born, or as to the body of a deceased person or a still-born child in any coffin.

Any of the offences set out above may be punished by penal servitude for not more than seven years, or by imprisonment, with or without hard labour, for a period not exceeding two years, or a fine.

PERMITTED HOURS.—These are the hours during which intoxicating liquor may be sold or supplied in any licensed premises or club, for consumption either on or off the premises. Save during such hours, intoxicating liquor may not be sold or supplied or even consumed or taken away from licensed premises or clubs. The permitted hours are different inside and outside the metropolis. (*See also* SPECIAL EXEMPTION ORDER; GENERAL EXEMPTION ORDER; INTOXICATING LIQUOR.)

PERPETUATION OF TESTIMONY.—It sometimes happens that a person has not at the moment any right to claim some estate or right, his right so to claim not accruing until some event has occurred, such as the death of another person. In such cases it is always possible that essential witnesses may die before the right to prove the claim accrues, thereby rendering the claimant unable to proceed. In circumstances such as these he may at once bring an action to place on record his case, and to perpetuate the testimony his witnesses can give.

PERPETUITIES.—English law permits the owner of both land and money to settle it in such a way that no one can interfere with the property itself or the capital, but can only dispose of the actual occupation of the land or the interest from the money. But it sets limits to this power. In the interests of free alienation it provides that all settlements must be drawn up in such a way that at the end of a certain period of time the restrictions on alienation will come to an end. This period is called the perpetuity period. Any provision in a settlement which might result in the identity of the persons entitled to the land being uncertain, or their powers of alienation restricted at the end of that period, is called a perpetuity, and is completely void.

Length of Period.—The perpetuity period during which the law permits the alienation of land to be restricted and its ownership to be uncertain is a curious one, the result of slow historical development. It has now been settled to be the duration of the life, or lives, of any person or persons alive at the date of the deed or (in the case of a will) the death of the testator, and twenty-one years after the death of the last life.

The rule against perpetuities applies to all kinds of disposition of land or money except gifts to charity. Thus, a gift of money to provide capital for the upkeep of a tomb for ever is void for infringing the rule (though the same result may be obtained in other ways).

A very much stricter set of rules than the above applies to all directions for the accumulation of money. (*See* ACCUMULATION.)

PERSON.—Legal persons are of two kinds—natural and artificial persons. A natural person is a human being, whereas an artificial person is somebody on which the law has conferred the capacity to acquire rights and duties, e.g. a limited company, or corporation. Person thus means something which the law recognises as capable of having rights and duties.

When the word person occurs in an Act of Parliament, it is taken to include an artificial person as well as an individual, unless it is obvious that that cannot be the meaning.

Entities which are not legal persons cannot have rights or duties. Thus, a collection of individuals engaged in some project—e.g. a club—does not constitute a legal person and can have no rights or duties. The separate individuals may themselves acquire rights and duties each for himself, but the unit formed by them is not a legal person unless it is registered as a company. Animals are not legal persons, and therefore it is not possible for anyone to leave property to a pet dog by will. If the owner of the pet dog wishes to have it provided for after his death, he may leave property to some natural person on condition that that person looks after the pet dog.

PERSONAL PROPERTY.—All property in England is divided into personal property and real property. Originally, as a general rule, personal property consisted of things which could be moved, such as chattels, and real property consisted of immovable things, i.e. land. This distinction, however, is not completely accurate for the division in English law into real and personal property does not correspond exactly with the division into movable and immovable property found in other countries.

The basis of the distinction in English law originally consisted not in the nature of the property itself, but depended on whether or not it was possible for the person who owned the property to bring an action to recover back the property if he were deprived of it. At the present time it is usually possible to recover all property in this way, but formerly the only property which was specifically recoverable was land. In this case, the person owning the property could recover the thing itself, and so property of this kind came to be known as real property. (*See* INTESTACY; REAL PROPERTY.)

PETITION.—A petition means some request made by an inferior to a superior. A petition is usually only made for a matter which cannot be claimed as of right, but may be granted or not at the discretion of the person petitioned as a matter of grace. Petitions are frequently made to the King or to Parliament, and every subject has a right to petition the Sovereign or Parliament so long as he does so in an orderly manner.

In law a petition is a method of commencing certain legal proceedings, e.g. in bankruptcy or for a divorce; and proceedings commenced in this way differ very little in practice from proceedings commenced by action. A petition is also the proper method for attacking the validity of the election of any member of Parliament. All appeals to the House of Lords are also made in the form of a petition.

PETITION OF RIGHT.—By the rules of English law it is not possible for the King to be sued by an action in his own Courts, and therefore all proceedings against the Crown must be brought by a Petition of Right. In effect this follows in many respects the same procedure as an ordinary action. No petition of right, however, can be brought in respect of any tort—i.e. wrongful act—and the right is therefore limited to cases in which some subject desires to enforce a contract entered into with the Crown, or to recover from the Crown some property which has been taken from him wrongly, and is in the possession of the Crown. The reason why no petition can be brought in respect of a tort is probably to be found in the doctrine of English law that the King can do no wrong.

Before a petition can be brought, it must receive the fiat, i.e. the permission, of the Attorney-General. This is now granted almost as a matter of course, unless the petition is frivolous.

PETROL.—No person is entitled to keep petrol except under a petroleum spirit licence authorising it to be kept. This does not apply to petroleum spirit kept either for private use or for sale so long as:—

(a) It is kept in separate glass, earthenware or metal vessels securely stoppered and containing not more than one pint in each; and

(b) The aggregate amount kept by the person does not exceed three gallons.

Motor Vehicles.—The Secretary of State has made certain regulations as to the keeping and use of petroleum spirit by persons intending to use it for the purpose of any motor vehicles, motor boats, aircraft, or petrol engines, and has exempted such persons from certain provisions of the Act applicable to the keeping of petrol. These regulations provide that the amount of petroleum spirit to be kept in any one storehouse must not exceed 60 gallons at a time, and that the fuel must be kept in metal vessels of not more than two gallons capacity provided with a screwed stopper. Storehouses in the same occupation which are within twenty feet of one another are to be regarded as one storehouse, and therefore must not contain more than 60 gallons in all. The storehouses must be properly ventilated, and the spirit must be kept in vessels from which there is no leakage. If the building in which the petrol is kept is within twenty feet of any other building, notice must be given to the local council in January of each year, and if they please they are entitled to inspect the premises. For the purposes of these regulations any inflammable goods or material such as timber is considered to be a building. Fire extinguishing apparatus must be kept in all places where petrol is stored, and it should be noticed that when petrol is kept in the tank of a private motor car in a private garage it is considered to be in a "place" within the meaning of the regulations, and an extinguisher is required. Where petrol is kept under these conditions and for the purpose of motor vehicles, no licence under the Petroleum Act as set out above is required.

Accidents.—Whenever any accident which occasions loss of life, or personal injury occurs by explosion or by fire in or about, or in connection with any premises licensed for the storage of petrol, the occupier must, if the explosion or fire involved petroleum spirit, send notice to the Secretary of State of the accident and of the loss of life or personal injury. In the same way when an accident which occasioned loss of life or personal injury occurs by explosion or fire in, about, or in connection with any vehicle on which petroleum spirit is being conveyed, loaded, or unloaded, notice must also be sent, unless the spirit was being used only for the purpose of fuelling that vehicle.

Powers of Inspection.—A government inspector is entitled to enter, inspect, and examine at all reasonable times, all licensed premises, and also any premises in which petroleum is kept or is suspected to be kept in contravention of the Act; and may require the occupier or any person employed by the occupier to give him samples of any petroleum on the premises. Any person failing to permit an inspector to enter, or to inspect, or examine, or obstructing an inspector in any way is liable on summary conviction to a fine not exceeding £50, or, on conviction on indictment, to a fine not exceeding £100.

Protection of Health.—The Secretary of State, if he is satisfied that any class of petroleum spirit is likely to be dangerous to health, may make regulations prescribing precautions for the protection of persons handling the spirit; for requiring persons selling to the public spirit of that class to give warning of the danger, and of the precautions required; and for prohibiting the sale or use of petroleum spirit if he considers it to be so dangerous or injurious to health that precautions for the protection of the persons employed or engaged in handling or using it are impracticable.

Definition.—Petroleum spirit means petroleum which, when tested in a manner prescribed by the Act, gives off an inflammable vapour at a temperature of less than seventy-three degrees Farenheit.

PETROL FILLING STATIONS.—

For the purpose of preserving the amenities of any rural scenery, or any place of beauty or historic interest, or any public park or pleasure promenade, or place which is of interest by reason of its picturesque character, any County Council or Borough Council may make regulations and bye-laws regulating the appearance of filling stations, or prohibiting the establishment of filling stations, and in particular, may prescribe the position, design, size, colour, and screening of such stations. They cannot, however, prevent the use of any pump or other apparatus approved for use in such places by the Secretary of State, and they must make provision for exempting any filling station established at the time of making the bye-laws from any restrictions requiring structural alteration for such period, not being less than two years from that time, as they think fit. All bye-laws under this section must be confirmed by the Secretary of State, and must be published, together with a notice of the place where the plans may be inspected.

Definition. — Petrol Filling Station means any premises or place used or intended to be used by way of trade, or for purposes of gain, for fuelling motor vehicles with petrol, and includes any building, advertisement, pump or other apparatus in, or used in connection with, any such premises.

PETTY SESSIONS. — Magistrates'

Courts are of two kinds: Petty Sessions (Police Court), and Quarter Sessions. A Court of Petty Sessions consists of two or more Justices, or of one Metropolitan Police or Stipendiary Magistrate, or, in the City of London, of the Lord Mayor or an Alderman sitting alone. The work of Petty Sessions is mainly connected with criminal cases. They try small offences in a summary way, such as obstruction of the highways, and they also investigate the more serious offences with the view to ascertaining whether they should be sent for trial before a jury. They have power to deal in a summary way with certain of these more serious offences if they think that no good purpose would be served by sending them to a higher Court, and if the accused person agrees to accept their jurisdiction.

In addition to dealing with criminal matters, Petty Sessions have to dispose of great masses of civil and semi-civil cases. Thus, a wife can summon her husband before Petty Sessions for wilful failure to maintain her. They also deal with summonses for non-payment of rates, applications for ejectment from small tenements and with affiliation summonses.

The magistrates sitting in Petty Sessions are appointed by the Lord Chancellor, and usually are not lawyers. They are, however, advised on legal points by their clerk, who is almost invariably a solicitor. Metropolitan police and stipendiary magistrates, on the other hand, are invariably barristers. (*See* MAGISTRATES.)

PICKETING.—Picketing is the posting of persons, either by themselves or in groups, in the vicinity of a factory or place of business while the workers in that factory or place of business are engaged in a strike; such pickets may be posted for the purpose of peacefully obtaining or communicating information, or for the purpose of peacefully persuading a person to work or to abstain from working.

If the persons forming the picket, either by the greatness of their numbers or by the threatening nature of their behaviour, cause any person in the place picketed fear for his safety or apprehension of damage being done to property, or if they obstruct the approach to the place, then their action becomes unlawful, and they may be fined a maximum of £20 or imprisoned for three months. It is unlawful for pickets to use violence in their attempts to persuade persons to work or abstain from working. (*See* STRIKE; TRADE DISPUTE; TRADE UNION.)

PIECE WORK.—Piece work is the name given to the method of calculating wages by the amount of work done. An occupier of a textile factory is required, for the purpose of enabling a piece worker to reckon up the amount of wages due to him, to publish particulars of the rates of wages applicable to the work done.

Workers engaged in weaving in the worsted and woollen trades, but not the hosiery trade, must be supplied with particulars in writing of the rate of wages applicable to the work done by him, at the time when the work is given out to him. (*See* FACTORY.)

PILLION RIDING. — *See* SPECIAL SUPPLEMENT "ROAD TRAFFIC."

PIN-MONEY.—If a husband makes an allowance to his wife for the purpose of personal adornment it is in law described as pin-money. The wife is required to spend this money for the purpose for which it was given and cannot assign it, nor after her death have her executors any claim for arrears of it.

PIPES. Damage caused by Bursting Pipes.—The liability of an occupier of property for damage caused by the breaking or leaking of supply pipes on his premises is very inadequately provided for by English law. It is certain that if the occupier's negligence was the cause of the damage, he will be liable to compensate the person injured. But it has never yet been clearly decided whether any liability arises apart from negli-

gence. Perhaps the best view is that if the pipes were used for ordinary domestic purposes, no liability will result, but if they were used for other purposes, the person using them would be liable for any damage caused by them, unless he can prove that the damage resulted from "Act of God" (q.v.), the King's enemies, or the interference of an unauthorized person. For example, if A uses a domestic water-supply and, without any negligence on his part, the pipes leak and injure his neighbour's furniture, he will not be liable for the damage; but if he had been using the water for some unusual purpose (e.g. if he had a special supply of water for a large refrigerating machine), then he would have to pay for the damage, unless he could prove that the cause of the damage was, for instance, that the house had been struck by lightning.

How to Compel Companies to Lay Pipes.—Every water-supply company has an area allotted to it, and must supply water to houses within that area when a sufficient number of owners or occupiers apply. A sufficient number has been obtained when the aggregate amount of the water-rate that will be payable by them annually is not less than a tenth of the expense of providing laying down the pipes. (*See also* GAS.)

PIRACY.—Piracy is robbery on the High Seas. It is punishable by death. Piracy may be tried at the Central Criminal Court though it be committed in any part of the High Seas. The High Seas include the sea, except in rivers above bridges. It does not matter whether the offender is a British subject or not, or whether the ship attacked is British or foreign.

PIRATING.—Pirating is the selling of copies of musical, literary, dramatic or artistic works that infringe copyright. (*See* COPYRIGHT.)

PLAINT NOTE.—A County Court action is, in the ordinary way, started by a Plaint and Summons. When an intending Plaintiff has filed with the Registrar of the County Court a Præcipe setting out the nature of his claim, and particulars of his claim if the amount claimed is more than £2, and has paid the appropriate fee, he is handed a document known as a Plaint Note, which is sealed with the seal of the Court, and which shews that he has fulfilled the necessary formalities. (*See* COUNTY COURT PROCEDURE.)

PLAINTIFF.—A plaintiff is a person who brings an action. The name is applied with this meaning in most cases in the High Court and in the County Courts. In divorce matters heard in the High Court, however, a person bringing the suit is described as a petitioner, the reason being that the suit is commenced by a petition.

PLEADINGS.—Pleadings is the name given to the written statements cast in a formal style which are made by the parties to an action, and in which they set out the facts on which they rely as constituting their case.

The object of a pleading is to narrow down the issues that are in dispute, and every pleading should contain a concise summary in chronological order of the facts upon which the party intends to rely and the nature of the redress that he seeks. Each pleading must be filed at the appropriate office of the Court and a copy of it delivered to the other parties to the action.

The plaintiff's pleading is known as a Statement of Claim in the High Court, Points of Claim in actions in the Commercial List, and Particulars of Claim in the County Court.

The defendant's pleading is known as the Defence and if, as often happens, he has a claim against the plaintiff, he may include this claim in his defence, in which case it is known as a Counterclaim, and in the ordinary way the counterclaim will be tried at the same time as, and in a similar manner to, the plaintiff's claim, without the necessity of the defendant starting separate action in respect of it.

The plaintiff, if he wishes to contradict or to explain fresh facts which have been set out in the defence, or, if a counterclaim has been raised by the defendant, to defend such counterclaim, is then entitled by leave of the Court to file an answer to the defence, which document is known as a Reply, or if it is in answer to the counterclaim, a Reply and Defence to Counterclaim.

If the defendant instead of having a counterclaim against the plaintiff, or in addition to his counterclaim is able to point to another person as being the person liable to the plaintiff, he may make that other person a party to the action by means of

Third Party Proceedings (q.v.). (*See* COUNTERCLAIM; DEFENCE; HIGH COURT PROCEDURE; PARTICULARS; REPLY; SPECIAL DEFENCE; STATEMENT OF CLAIM.)

PLUMAGE.—By Act of Parliament of 1921 it was provided that, with a few exceptions, no plumage of birds might be imported into the United Kingdom unless it happened to form part of the personal wearing-apparel of a passenger. The list of exceptions includes the plumage of eiderducks, African ostriches, jays, magpies, starlings, golden pheasants and cormorants, and of any bird that is ordinarily used in the United Kingdom as an article of diet.

PLURALITY.—Plurality is the possession by one and the same clergyman of two or more benefices in the Church of England with the cure of souls at one and the same time.

This is an offence, unless a licence or dispensation has been obtained from the Archbishop of Canterbury, from whose decision there is a right to appeal to the Privy Council.

POACHING.—Poaching is the term popularly employed to cover the various offences of trespass in pursuit of game, and which are punishable as crimes.

To amount to the offence of poaching, the poacher must enter on the actual land of some other person with the object of taking game, woodcock, snipe, quails or rabbits with a dog, gun, snare or by any other method.

It is not poaching to shoot from the highway (except at night), or from one's own land, but it is poaching to go on to private land to pick up the birds shot, unless the bird has risen on the shooter's own ground and has fallen dead or clearly wounded on the land of another owner. But a person who shoots from a highway or from his own land birds which a confederate has put up from private land, is guilty of poaching as much as his confederate.

Poaching by day is visited with less severe penalties than when done by night. A person convicted of poaching by day may be fined up to a maximum of £2, but if five or more people are poaching together the penalty is £5, and if any of the five is armed with a gun, and he or any other of them uses violence or intimidation to anyone who calls upon them to quit the land, or to give their

The whole of the Declaration and Marginal Particulars snould be in the Applicant's ow

| This space is reserved for official use. | ✳ Surname in Block Capitals. | Declaration to |

(a) Insert Date and Town where staying when filling in the form.

(b) Christian Names and Surname of the applicant in full. (Surname in BLOCK CAPITALS.)

(c) In the case of a MARRIED WOMAN or WIDOW, the particulars of birth required are those of her HUSBAND or LATE HUSBAND— not of the applicant herself.

(d) State exact national status, e.g., a British Subject by Birth or a British Subject by naturalisation, British-protected Person, &c. IN THE CASE OF A BRITISH SUBJECT BY NATURALISATION SEE RULE 5 AT BACK.

(e) Wife $\frac{and}{or}$ children should only be included if they do not possess separate passports. Strike out the words in brackets in other cases.

(f) [Strike out and initial which-
(g) [ever is not applicable.]

NOTE.—All previous passports must be accounted for.

(h) Signature of applicant.

The applicant must also write a specimen of his signature on the pink slip attached below marked✳✳.

(i) Name and Qualification of person verifying the Declaration (see Rule 4 at back), viz. :—

Mayor, Magistrate, Provost, Justice of the Peace, Minister of Religion, Barrister-at-Law, Physician, Surgeon, Solicitor, Notary Public, &c., giving professional or business address.

Recommendations from members or officials of Banking Firms should bear the printed stamp of the Bank here below.

CAUTION.

† The attention of persons who are asked to sign this declaration is specially called to the fact that it can only be signed from personal knowledge of the applicant and not from information obtained from other persons.

9703

(In the case of children under the age of parent or guardian in a

(a) _____

✳I, the Undersigned, (b) ____

at present residing at *Rose Cotta*

(c) { For A MARRIED WOMAN OR WID

the *wife* of *widow*

a (d) *British Subjec*

at *Poprings Sussex*.

{ FOR PERSONS BORN ABROAD
born within His

my (his) *father* paternal gra
at ____

and not having lost the status of Bri

to *France Belgium*

for the purpose of *Holiday*

(e) [accompanied by my wife (and chi separate Passports].

(f) I declare that I have no
have made no oth

(g) [I declare that all previ
cancellation to
F.O. No. *39642/24*
made no other ap
issued to me.

†AND I, the Undersigned (i

of *St Johns Vicarag*

personal knowledge and belief the above

_____ is true,

as a fit and proper person to receive a

PHOTOGRAPHS: Two small unmounted dupli which should be certified and signed on th likeness of ____

Sign your name on the pink slip, which will be detached and affixed to the Passport when issued.

Specimen signature of wife if to be included on the Passport.

M. Ravel

J. A. Ravel.

‡ Appli
warned th
in their r
the conseq

A Specimen Passport Application Form Correctly Filled in.

(A.)

by Applicant for Passport.†

a separate Passport, the Declaration must be made by the child's
...ained upon application to the Passport Office.)

...arket. 29ᵗʰ June. 1934.

...Ravel. (RAVEL)

...ee Court. Stowmarket. Suffolk hereby declare that I am
out in other cases). Particulars of HUSBAND'S birth to follow.
and that my husband is
...tt _____ late husband was
_____ having been born

the 3Rd day of April 1897.

...h nationality from a father or paternal grandfather
...us. (To be struck out in other cases.)

...been born within His Majesty's Dominions
_____ day of _____

...as acquired, I hereby apply for a Passport for travelling
...erland

...age of 16), as indicated in the margin, who do not possess

...n granted any Passport whatever, and that I (f)
...for a Passport.

...granted to me have been surrendered for
...t or Consular Officer, other than Passport
...attached for cancellation, and that I have (g)
...Passport since the attached Passport was

...igned S. Ravel.

...ohite Clerk – Holy Orders
...owmarket hereby declare that to the best of my
Mr. & Mrs.
...tion and Description of the said Mrs. J. Ravel
Miss

...from my personal knowledge of him them him
her vouch her
...ort. I have known the applicants for 8 years.

...ed ‡ Chas White

...of the applicant (and wife if to be included) must be sent, one of
...aarantor, as follows : "I certify that this photograph is a true
_____"

...PORTANT.

...ersons recommending them, are
...ny of the statements contained
...clarations prove to be untrue,
...em may be serious.

Description of Applicant.

Age 34

Profession Schoolmaster.

Whether married or single Married.

Domicile or ordinary place of residence
Stowmarket

Place of birth Poynings Sussex

Date of birth 3Rd April 1894.

Height 5 feet 11 inches.

Colour of Eyes Grey

Colour of Hair Dark Brown

Visible distinguishing marks Scar on Right Temple
or peculiarities.

Maiden name of widow or married woman (in Block
Capitals) _____

CHANGE OF NAME.

If name has been changed by Deed Poll or otherwise the
original name must be stated here.

If there has been no change of name the word "None" must
be written here None.

Signature of S. Ravel.
applicant.

**Description of wife of Applicant, if to be
included on the Passport.**

Name in full Joan Alice Ravel.

Age 36

Profession None.

Place of birth Brighton Sussex

Date of birth 10ᵗʰ October 1898

Height 5 feet 7 inches.

Colour of Eyes Blue

Colour of Hair Light Brown

Visible distinguishing marks None.
or peculiarities.

Maiden name LEWIS
(in Block Capitals)

Signature of wife J. A. Ravel.
of applicant.

Children under the age of 16 if to be included on this Passport.

CHRISTIAN NAMES.	SURNAME.	DATE OF BIRTH.	SEX.
George.	Ravel.	6ᵗʰ February 1924.	M.

(By courtesy of the Passport Office.)

names and addresses, all of them are liable to an additional penalty of £5. Day, for the purposes of the game laws, means from an hour before sunrise to an hour after sunset.

Poaching by night includes killing game on the highway as well as on private land, provided that the game do not come from the land of the person killing them, and in any case it is an offence to *shoot* game at night. (*See* GAME.)

The penalty for poaching by night is a maximum of three months' imprisonment, six months for the second offence and seven years' penal servitude or imprisonment for two years for the third and subsequent offences. In addition to the penalties for first and second offences, the poacher may be bound over for a year or two years.

The police are entitled to search people whom they suspect of being guilty of this offence, and seize the game and implements of poaching which may be confiscated on conviction of the offender who is also liable to a maximum fine of £5.

Gamekeepers.—A gamekeeper whose duty it is to preserve the game for the use of the owner of the shooting rights is entitled to order any person whom he finds poaching on his master's land, to produce his game licence, if he is doing anything for which a game licence is required, to call upon him to quit the land, and to give his name and address. If the poacher fails to do so, the gamekeeper may arrest him.

This, however, only applies during the daytime, and at night time no gamekeeper of a mere shooting tenant is entitled to arrest any poacher unless he is committing one of the offences that are punishable with seven years' penal servitude.

At night a gamekeeper who is the servant of the owner or occupier of the land may arrest any poacher whom he finds on the land under his charge, and may chase him and arrest him elsewhere if he runs away. The gamekeeper of a tenant who possesses only the shooting rights may do none of these things. (*See* GAME; GAME LICENCES; GUN LICENCES.

POINDING (SCOTS LAW).— This is a form of execution by which the creditor who has obtained a decree or judgment requiring some person to pay him money seizes goods belonging to his debtor in order to get the money which is due to him.

POINDING OF THE GROUND (SCOTS LAW).—This is a form of diligence, i.e. English execution available in Scotland to enable a person who has got certain rights over land—e.g. a heritable creditor, i.e. mortgagee, who has lent money on the security of the land—to seize all goods situated on the land and belonging to the owner.

POISON.—In order to protect the public from injury, either wilful or accidental, the sale of poisons has had to be strictly regulated by the law, and no person, unless he be an apothecary or a veterinary surgeon, is permitted to sell poisons by retail without being registered as a pharmaceutical chemist. A contravention of this provision is an offence punishable with a fine of £5. Certain poisons are specially scheduled by an Act of Parliament of 1908 and others have been added to the list since the passing of that Act. It is unlawful to sell any of the poisons so scheduled, unless the box, bottle, or other container is clearly labelled with the name and address of the seller, the name of the article, and the word "Poison" in conspicuous letters.

A seller of poisons must not sell them to a person who is unknown to him, unless the would-be purchaser is introduced to him by some person who is known to him. He must enter in a special book the purchaser's name and address, the purpose for which the poison is required, and the name and quantity of the poison sold. This entry must be signed by the purchaser. If the purchaser is a registered medical practitioner buying the poison for the purposes of his profession, he need not sign the poison register, provided he gives the seller a signed order containing his name and address, and the name and quantity of the article purchased. Failure to make an entry is an offence punishable with a fine of £5.

No entry need be made when the poison is supplied in accordance with a prescription given by a registered medical practitioner under the National Health Insurance Act, 1923.

Poisons which are to be used for agricultural purposes, such as weed-killing, may be sold by any person who is licensed by the local authority.

Arsenic.—Special precautions are

required by the law to be observed in the sale of arsenic. The poison if colourless must be mixed with soot or indigo so as to colour it; the person to whom it is sold must be of mature age, and his occupation must be given in addition to his name and address in the poison register kept by the seller.

POLICE.—*See* SPECIAL SUPPLEMENT "THE POLICE."

POLICE COURT.—This is the popular term applied to Courts of summary jurisdiction. (*See* PETTY SESSIONS.)

POLITICAL OFFENDERS.—It is an invariable rule that persons cannot be extradited from this country for trial upon political charges. This rule is applied by most civilized countries.

POLL (COMPANIES).—(*See* MEETING; COMPANY.)

POLL, DEED.—A Deed Poll or Deed of Poll is a deed executed only by one person, and binding only upon that one person. The term is most generally used in connection with deeds executed by persons intending to change their names. (*See* NAME, CHANGE OF; INDENTURE.)

POOR LAW.—The Poor Law is now administered by each county council or county borough council within its own district, and they are subject to the supervision and control of the Ministry of Health. In special cases county councils may combine for the purpose of administering poor relief if such a combination will promote greater efficiency or save expense.

The Public Assistance Committee. —Every council is required to appoint a Public Assistance Committee and such committee may consist entirely of members of the council, or its number may be made up by co-opting additional members who are not members of the council. Two-thirds of the committee must be members of the council.

The Forms of Poor Relief.—County councils are entrusted with the task of setting to work all persons within their area who have no means of maintaining themselves and use no ordinary trade to get their living; of providing relief for the lame, impotent, old and blind poor who are unable to work; to apprentice children who are orphans, or whose parents are unable to maintain them; to assist in the emigration of poor persons. There are many other activities which are comprised under the heading of poor relief, such as medical relief, boarding out of children, and assisting in the burial of poor persons. All these duties are imposed upon the county and county borough councils, and they are responsible for seeing that they are carried out. These functions are undertaken by the Public Assistance Committee and a certain portion of the duties are done by the Guardians Committees.

If a poor or destitute person desires to obtain relief he must apply to the Relieving Officer of the district. The Relieving Officer investigates the claim and reports to the Guardians Committee. The committee consider the report and makes the order for the relief if they are of opinion that the applicant's claim is substantiated.

The Relieving Officer cannot himself give any relief except in cases of urgent necessity. In such cases he may give relief, not in money, to any poor person even though he is not settled in the county or county borough for which the Relieving Officer acts.

In cases of sudden illness, a justice of the peace may order the Relieving Officer to give medical relief to the sick person, and the Relieving Officer must obey the order, otherwise he is liable to a fine of £5.

The Liability of the Relatives.—If a person becomes chargeable to the council of a county or borough, and they have to expend money on his relief, they may obtain an order for his maintenance upon the relatives who are liable to maintain him.

It is the duty of the father, grandfather, mother, grandmother, husband or child, of any poor, old, blind, lame or impotent person, or person not able to work, if possessed of sufficient means to maintain that person.

The mother of an illegitimate child so long as she is unmarried or a widow is bound to maintain the child until it reaches the age of sixteen, and a married woman who has separate property of her own is liable for the maintenance of her husband, her children and her parents. If a married woman is relieved without her husband or removed to a lunatic asylum, a maintenance order may be obtained upon the husband.

A notification is sent to the relatives who are presumably liable to maintain a person who has become chargeable, and they are required to send particulars of their means to the council and to make an offer of a contribution towards the maintenance of that person. The council applies to a Petty Sessional Court for an order upon the relatives, and the magistrate, before making the order, must be satisfied that the person relieved is unable to work or maintain himself, and that the relatives are able to contribute. A council may re-imburse themselves for relief given out of any property, money or valuable security for money, which a recipient of relief may have in his possession or belonging to him. It is an offence for an applicant for relief not to make full disclosure of any property which he may have. Any person guilty of such non-disclosure is deemed to be an idle and disorderly person. (*See* CASUAL WARD; LOCAL GOVERNMENT; MEANS TEST; OUT-DOOR RELIEF; SETTLEMENT; WORKHOUSE.)

POOR PERSONS COMMITTEE. —The system by which poor persons can obtain free legal aid in High Court proceedings is administered by the Law Society through a number of Committees. The London Committee is at Room 785 Royal Court of Justice, W.C.2, and others are situated throughout the provinces.

A poor person's certificate, entitling the holder to a solicitor and counsel without charge, is obtainable from any of these Committees. To qualify for it the applicant must have a reasonable cause of action and must be worth not more than £50, exclusive of wearing apparel and trade tools, and his income must not exceed £2 per week. In certain circumstances these figures may be raised to £100 and £4. He may have to deposit up to £5 in the first instance to cover the solicitor's out-of-pocket expenses but he does not have to pay anything else.

Criminal matters are dealt with officially under the Poor Prisoners' Defence Act and County Court matters unofficially by charitable societies. (See LEGAL AID; POOR PRISONERS.)

POOR PRISONERS.—A poor person who is committed for trial is entitled to free legal aid at Quarter Sessions and Assizes and to have a solicitor and counsel assigned to him if he can get a "defence certificate." This certificate may be granted by the

justices who commit him for trial, or by a Judge of Assize or Chairman of Quarter Sessions if it appears that the accused has a reasonable defence. A certificate is only granted where the accused is too poor to obtain his own legal aid. It must always be granted in case of murder. (*See* DOCK BRIEF.)

PORT.—It is not every place where a ship may discharge that is a port in law. A port can only be created by the exercise of the Royal prerogative and by a grant of the rights to a certain district. The persons who are the owners of the port are entitled to charge certain dues for ships coming to the port and are also under certain duties with regard to the maintenance of the port in such a condition that it is safe for ships to enter, and for the provision of docking and other facilities. Frequently the rights of a port and its duties are controlled by a private Act of Parliament as is the case in the Port of London.

PORT OF LONDON AUTHOR-ITY.—This is an authority set up in 1908 which controls the river Thames from Teddington to the sea. It consists of twenty-eight members, eighteen of whom are elected and ten appointed.

POSSESSION.—In considering any property in law, two questions may arise, firstly who owns it, and secondly, who is in possession of it. The question of ownership will depend on certain legal rules which will vary with the particular nature of the type of property concerned. There are certain types of property in which it is not possible to separate the ownership from the possession. These are properties which are incorporeal—i.e. have no physical existence, or, as it has been said, cannot be "sat upon," e.g. shares, rights to receive money—as distinct from corporeal property such as goods or land.

While ownership is thus a question of law, possession is largely a question of fact and, with certain exceptions, a man possesses any property if he exercises physical control over it. Thus the driver of a motor car possesses the car while he is driving it. Possession itself however, has several meanings in law:—

1. **Bare Physical Possession or Detention.**—This is a pure question of fact, and a person may have physical posses-

The Pool of London, which is under the control of the Port of London Authority.

sion of some goods although he is not entitled to retain that possession, but must deliver up the goods to some other person on being requested to do so. Thus a guest at a dinner has physical possession of the knives and forks he uses to eat it, but he cannot claim to take them away with him after the dinner.

2. **Legal Possession.**—This is a mixed question of law and fact, for a person may have legal possession of some goods although he has not physical possession of them, but in most cases a person who has physical possession has also legal possession. The essence of legal possession is that the possessor should have control of the goods physically either by himself, or through some servant of his, and should also intend to exercise the control over the goods "against all the world," as it is said. This means that his physical possession of the goods is for himself, and that he cannot be required to hand over the goods to any other person. He need not, however, be the owner of them. Thus a person who has hired a car for a week is entitled to possession of that car during that time, and may refuse to hand it back to the person from whom he has hired it until the end of the week, although he may make no claim to ownership.

3. **The Right to Possession.**—This is the right claimed by a person who allows another for a period of time to have legal possession of some property to the possession of which he himself is entitled.

Trespass.—Another important aspect of possession is that it is the possessor who is entitled to protect his rights by bringing an action for trespass. Thus, if A lets a house to B, and C trespasses on the land, C may be sued by B for the trespass because B is in legal possession, and trespass is an offence against possession. The same applies in the case of possession of goods so that if A hires his motor-car to B and C then takes away the motor-car B is entitled to sue C for damages.

Possession Nine-Tenths of the Law. —This popular phrase is to a very large extent justified by the rules of law. Its real meaning is that if a person is in possession of land or goods, he is presumed to be the owner until some other person can prove that he in fact is the owner and not the person in possession. It is not for the person in possession to prove that he is the owner, but for the person claiming the property to prove his title. In former days any matter of proof was always very difficult to establish, and even to-day although this difficulty has been considerably reduced, the fact that the onus—i.e. burden of proof, is put on the person not in possession is in most cases a considerable advantage to the possessor.

POST-MORTEM.—The examination by dissection or otherwise, of a body after death, carried out by a medical man to ascertain the cause of death or other matter. A coroner may direct a post-mortem to be carried out whenever he deems it advisable.

POST-NUPTIAL SETTLEMENT.

—A post-nuptial settlement is a settlement of property made by a husband on his wife or a wife on her husband after marriage, and it is distinguished from an ante-nuptial settlement which takes place before the marriage. The distinction is important, for a settlement taking place before marriage and in consideration of marriage is not a voluntary settlement, and therefore cannot be upset even though the person making the settlement (called the settlor) should go bankrupt, but a settlement after marriage is voluntary, i.e. made for no consideration, and if the person making the settlement goes bankrupt, the settlement may become void and the trustee in bankruptcy can reclaim the property. (See TRUSTEE IN BANKRUPTCY; VOLUNTARY SETTLEMENT.)

POST OFFICE.

—The Post Office is a Government Department which has been created by Acts of Parliament. At its head is an official known as the Postmaster-General who is always a Member of Parliament on the government side, and is usually a member of the Ministry in power though he is not often in the Cabinet. The Post Office has the sole right and monopoly of collecting, carrying and delivering letters; there are only three cases in which this monopoly is not enforced:—

(*a*) Letters may be given to a friend on a journey to deliver at places which he passes, provided he is not paid anything for delivering them.

(*b*) Letters may be sent by a special messenger, but not by common carriers (such as Railway Companies or Omnibus Companies), unless they are sent together with goods to which they relate, and no extra charge is made for carrying them. The Post Office do, however, arrange for stamped letters to be sent by train and posted at the town of destination for delivery there.

(*c*) Summonses, writs and other documents coming from a Court of Justice need not be sent by post. The Post-

master-General has also a monopoly of the sale of stamps, but may grant a licence to a private person or Company to deal in them.

Employees may carry Revolvers.

—The employees of the Post Office are civil servants and can therefore be dismissed without notice or reason at any time; such an employee, no matter how unjustifiable his dismissal may have been, has no right of action against the Postmaster-General or the King. In recompense for this he has the privilege, if he is ordered to do so by his superiors, of being entitled to carry a revolver without having a licence for it! (See LETTERS; MONEY ORDERS; POST OFFICE SAVINGS BANK; TELEGRAPH; TELEPHONE.)

POST OFFICE SAVINGS BANK.

—The Postmaster-General has statutory authority with the consent of the Treasury to administer a Post Office Savings Bank which is managed by an official called the Comptroller.

Accounts may be opened in this Bank at almost any post office by any person over the age of seven (including a married woman), either in his own name

or in the name of any child under the age of seven, in which case the money can only be withdrawn on the child's signature after it attains the age of seven years, though it can be invested in Government Stock through the Post-Office;

or by two or more persons jointly;

or by one or more persons in trust for another person or persons;

or by the Committee of a lunatic so found;

or by Friendly, Industrial, Provident or Charitable Societies;

or by Corporate bodies if the Postmaster-General approves;

or by Vicars and Rectors of English Parishes in their official capacity;

or by the Registrar of a County Court;

or by the Public Trustee.

No sum less than 1/- may be accepted, and no fractions of a shilling except where the deposit is made by cheque or money order. Interest at the rate of $2\frac{1}{2}\%$ per annum is paid on all deposits. When the initial deposit is made, the depositor is handed a book in which are recorded all his dealings with the Bank. By presenting this book at any post office he can withdraw any sum up to £3 provided he does so not less than four days after the deposit was made (or eight if the deposit was made by cheque).

Larger sums can only be withdrawn under a warrant to be obtained from the Comptroller, though amounts up to £10 can, in some circumstances, be withdrawn by telegram. The bank book itself is in no sense a security, for the amount deposited for payment can never be made except to the depositor himself.

Money which is deposited in the name of a child under seven years of age cannot be withdrawn until he or she reaches the age of seven, and then only on the child's signature; but money which is deposited by an adult as trustee can be withdrawn by him though he is, of course, bound by law only to apply it for the benefit of the cestui que trust (q.v.).

On marriage a female depositor must inform the Comptroller, but need not send him her certificate. All deposits in the name of a married woman are presumed to be her separate property to deal with as she likes unless the contrary is shewn. Depositors who are over sixteen years of age can nominate one or more persons to whom any balance in the Savings Bank is to be paid on the death of the depositor, but such a nomination must be sent to the Comptroller of the Bank to be registered during the life of the depositor.

If this has not been done application must be made to the Comptroller; payment will only be made to the executors if there is a will, or to the administrators if there is none. On application the Comptroller will supply information as to the obtaining of probate of a will or the grant of letters of administration.

Deposits in the Post Office Savings Bank are not liable to be attached for the judgment debts of the depositor. In order to protect customers, the Post Office are put under an obligation of secrecy with regard to the names and accounts of depositors. Any dispute which may arise cannot be made the subject of an action, but must be submitted for arbitration to the Registrar of Friendly Societies. Finally it is an offence to alter any Post Office Savings Bank Book, to withdraw more than is deposited or

to forge the signature or impersonate the person of a depositor. (*See* POST OFFICE.)

POSTAL ORDERS.—A postal order is a money-order for any sum from sixpence up to, and including one guinea. It is not negotiable. The Post Office is not liable for any loss or damage caused by the delay or non-payment of a postal-order; post office officials can only be sued if they were actually responsible for the delay and then only if they acted fraudulently or wilfully. (*See* MONEY ORDER; POST OFFICE.)

POSTAL PACKETS.—The Post Office has the complete monopoly of the collecting, carrying and delivering of letters (though not of parcels).

The sending of anything by post which, owing to its nature or the way in which it is packed, is likely to injure other letters or parcels is prohibited; this applies in particular to the following things:—explosives or dangerous substances, sharp instruments improperly packed, live animals, unless the Postmaster-General's consent is first obtained (except that live bees and leeches may be posted if they are properly packed), and any indecent literature or picture. It is also an offence to place in, or near a letter box anything likely to injure the letters.

It is illegal to send through the post:— Any lottery tickets or advertisements, fortune tellers' advertisements, advertisements or coupons referring to any illegal betting business, literature or medicine for the cure or prevention of venereal disease except to doctors and chemists, any unsolicited money-lending advertisements or any contraband articles. The Post Office officials may refuse to accept letters or parcels containing any of these things; or if they are discovered in the post, may open and keep them, or return them to the sender at the ordinary rate of postage, though, in the latter case, the sender may be prosecuted just as if they had been delivered. It is also an offence to send in one letter an enclosure addressed to another person at another address; such an enclosure may be taken out and sent on surcharged with the full amount of postage. Special regulations set out in the current Post Office guide apply to the contents of letters for foreign countries. Letters or parcels containing coin or jewellery not packed according to the regulations, or found open in the post will be compulsorily registered by the Post Office and an additional fee of 6d. charged.

Secrecy in the Post.—A number of provisions have been made in order to secure, as far as possible, the safety and secrecy of the post. It is an offence for any one employed to carry letters to leave them unattended, to get drunk, to endanger the safety of the mails by negligence, to collect or deliver letters without authority and outside the ordinary course of the post, to give false information of any attempt to rob him, or not to do everything reasonable to secure speedy delivery. Post Office officials must not embezzle or destroy any letter; the penalty is imprisonment for life; neither must they delay or open letters except those which cannot for some proper reason be delivered, or letters which contain prohibited articles; but any letter may be obtained or opened under the authority of a warrant from a Secretary of State. It is possible that a civil action would lie for the damage caused by the delay or non-delivery of a letter against the official who unlawfully delayed it. There is no right of action in such a case against the Postmaster-General or by Petition of Right against the King.

It is an offence for any person not an employee of the Post Office fraudulently to retain, or wilfully to secrete, or refuse to deliver up on demand any letter which ought to have been delivered to some other person; and there is a penalty of £50 or 6 months for anybody who opens or causes any delay in the delivery of a letter; parents and guardians are excepted apparently without any reference to the age of the child. Once a letter has been posted it must be delivered; it cannot be recalled. If delivery is impossible, the Post Office is under no legal obligation to return a letter, though in practice letters and parcels are returned to the sender without extra charge; postcards and other specially cheap communications are not returned unless there is an express request on the outside, in which case the sender may be charged a second postage.

Delivery of a communication may only be made to the addressee at the place to which it was addressed, though in country districts and by special arrangements in towns letters may be collected at a Post Office by the addressee. Arrangements may also be made for letters to be forwarded from the Post Office if there is no one at the address to receive and forward them, or on a change of address, though in the latter case a charge is made after one year.

In towns, all letters must be posted in boxes or handed over the counter of a Post Office, but in the country it is the duty of a postman to accept letters and parcels within reason both registered and unregistered unless they are offered to him near to a box or office in which they could be posted. The drivers of mail vans may not collect parcels or letters from private persons on their route, except at pillar boxes which are too small to admit them.

Lost Letters.—The Post Office are under no legal liability whatsoever for the loss of, or delay or damage to, any letter or thing sent through the post (though it may be that the individual official responsible for the delay might be liable personally). It is important to realize that this rule applies not only to letters and parcels sent by ordinary post but also to registered packets. The Postmaster-General, however, does as a matter of grace pay compensation up to but not exceeding £2 for any loss or damage to any unregistered parcel unless it contained money or jewellery; he also pays compensation on registered packets up to a maximum figure which varies according to the additional fee paid by the sender at the time of posting. Care should be taken to make sure that the fee paid on registration is sufficient to cover the value of the packet. Fragile goods must be clearly marked and in no case will more than £5 be paid by way of compensation in respect of coin as distinct from notes.

POUND BREACH.—If cattle are impounded it is a misdemeanour to rescue them, without lawful excuse, from the pound. This applies whether they are cattle in the pound or are being taken to it.

POWER OF APPOINTMENT.— A Power of Appointment is a right to give to some person called the appointee an estate or interest of which the person who exercises the right and makes the appointment need not himself be the owner. Thus on the marriage of A and B, property might be settled on B for life and a power of appointment given to A to appoint the property on B's death amongst their children.

General and Special Powers.—
Powers of appointment are divided into general and special powers. The distinction depends on the nature of the persons to whom an appointment may be made. A general power is one by which the donee of the power may appoint the property to anybody including himself. A special power is one by which the persons who may be appointed the possible appointees are restricted so that the donee can only appoint amongst a limited class—as "amongst the children of X."

POWER OF ATTORNEY.—When
it is necessary for one man to appoint another as his agent to do acts for him which include the execution of documents under seal, the appointment of the agent must be made itself under seal, i.e. by a deed—and the document creating the appointment is known as a Power of Attorney. The person appointed will usually execute all deeds on behalf of his principal by signing the name of the *principal*, but he may, if he thinks fit, execute the deed in his own name and a deed executed in that way is as fully binding as if it had been executed in the name of the Principal.

PRÆMUNIRE.—An offence against
the "Statute of Præmunire" (1351) is the paying to a foreign sovereign or power that obedience which is due to the King alone; the statute was originally aimed at the suppression of the papal power in England.

PRAYER BOOK. — The Book of
Common Prayer serves two main purposes. It contains the ceremonies and prayers that may be used in the Established Church, and it provides the main source to which the Courts look for information when any doctrinal or liturgical point respecting that Church has to be decided. Such variations from the Book of Common Prayer as are legally permissible are laid down by law. Thus on certain special occasions other forms of service may with proper ecclesiastical authority be used, but they may not contain anything, except hymns or anthems, not in the Holy Scriptures or Book of Common Prayer.

The Book of Common Prayer cannot be altered save under the authority of an Act of Parliament. Since the Enabling Act, the National Assembly of the Church of England has had power to promote changes in the Prayer Book, but a resolution of both Houses of Parliament is necessary before such changes can be of legal effect.

PREAMBLE.—Any Act of Parliament
has at the beginning a short statement of the reasons of the passing of the act. This is known as the Preamble.

PRECEDENT.—Whenever the Court
of Superior Authority has decided a point of law the decision may be cited in subsequent cases. It is referred to as a Precedent. Precedents are contained in various series of law reports, but any report of a case if vouched for by a barrister can be treated as a precedent. (*See* LAW REPORTS.)

PRECOGNITION (Scots Law).—
A precognition is a statement of a witness in a case. The word is applied both to the statement taken by a solicitor before the case is heard and for the purposes of the hearing, and also to the statement taken by the Procurator Fiscal from witnesses and others when he is investigating some criminal act with a view to considering whether or not a prosecution should be instituted.

PREFERENCE SHARES. — Shares
may be either preference, ordinary, or deferred. A preference shareholder is entitled to a fixed percentage of dividends out of the profits before anything is paid on the ordinary shares. He may be entitled to a larger percentage if the Company has a large amount of profits to distribute, and in this case his shares are said to be participating. He is not entitled to dividends for any year unless there are profits during the year available to pay him, i.e. he cannot be paid out of capital. When he has not received a dividend in any year, he may in the next year be entitled to receive the dividend which had been missed, as well as the dividend for the current year before anything is paid to the ordinary shareholders. If he is so entitled, his shares are said to be cumulative as distinct from non-cumulative. Preference shares are usually taken to be cumulative unless the Articles indicate they are not.

It sometimes happens that when a company is wound up there are not sufficient assets to pay back the capital due on the ordinary and preference shares—i.e. one pound for each pound share—and the question arises as to whether the preference shareholders are entitled to be paid in full before the ordinary shareholders get anything, or whether they must all share and share alike. This will depend on the proper meaning of the clauses in the articles or memorandum which specify the rights of the shareholders, but usually preference shareholders are not entitled to preferential repayment of capital.

Preference shares may be issued on the terms that the company may cancel them by paying to the shareholders the amount of the shares out of profits or out of the new issue. Such shares are called Redeemable Preference Shares. (*See* SHARES.)

PREFERRED CREDITORS.—Although one of the objects in bankruptcy (q.v.) and in winding up an insolvent company is to secure that all the money available shall be divided fairly among all persons claiming it, this does not mean that these persons are entitled to claim equal amounts. Where there is not enough to pay all in full the law recognises that certain creditors—i.e. preferred creditors—should be paid in full before the others receive anything. Debts that are regarded as being entitled to be paid before the others in this way are the following:—

1. Rates and taxes owing by the bankrupt or insolvent company for not more than a year;
2. Wages of a clerk or servant for not more than 4 months before the bankruptcy or winding up and not exceeding £50 for each clerk or servant;
3. Wages of a workman for not more than 2 months before the bankruptcy or winding up and not exceeding £25 for each workman;
4. Compensation payable to an employee under the Workmen's Compensation Act in respect of injuries received by him while engaged in his employment;
5. The amount of money which the bankrupt or company should have paid under the National Insurance, Pensions and Unemployment Insurance Acts in respect of employees.

(*See* BANKRUPTCY; SECURED CREDITORS; TRUSTEE IN BANKRUPTCY; WINDING-UP.)

PREJUDICE, WITHOUT.—Whenever there is a dispute between two parties, it is convenient to have some method, whereby negotiations with a view to settlement out of Court can be carried on with-

out prejudicing the position of one or the other of them by being read in Court should negotiations break down. If one party wishes that negotiations shall be treated as being without prejudice, he should mark all letters written in the course of negotiations with the words, "Without Prejudice" at the top. Once a letter has been written with this title, the reply to it also acquires the privilege of non-disclosure in Court.

PREROGATIVE OF THE CROWN.—The Royal Prerogative is the special privilege or pre-eminence which the King has to act outside the ordinary law of the land. These privileges are nowadays chiefly operated by the Ministry, although in theory the King is entirely unfettered in the exercise of his prerogative powers in all cases when they have not actually been cut down by Statute. The Ministry, in turn, is controlled as to the direction in which it advises the Crown to exercise the prerogative by the people in accordance with the general principles of English Constitutional government. (*See also* CROWN; KING; PARLIAMENT.)

PREROGATIVE WRITS.—A prerogative writ is a writ to the issue of which a subject has no absolute right, but which is issued only on the order of the King acting through his Judges. Its purpose is to provide a remedy where process by the ordinary course of law would be inadequate, and the use of the prerogative writ is therefore relatively uncommon. The prerogative writs now in use are Habeas Corpus, Certiorari, Mandamus, Ne exeat regno and Procedendo, the old writ of Quo Warranto being now obsolete (for the purpose and effect peculiar to each of these writs, see separate titles). None of these writs can be issued except by a Judge of the High Court; in no case will a Judge issue the writ on mere demand, but will require that probable cause be shewn why it should be issued; in some cases, even when cause has been shewn, the issue is still in the discretion of the Judge, but in other cases (e.g. habeas corpus) the Judge is bound to grant the application.

PRESCRIPTION.—This is the legal name for certain rules of law which provide for the creations of rights by mere lapse of time. Prescription has a very limited scope as it only affects the acquisition of easements (q.v.) and profits a prendre (q.v.). It is quite distinct from the Statutes of Limitation. Under prescription lapse of time creates a new right; under the statutes of limitation it merely extinguishes and destroys an already existing right. The doctrine of prescription is based partly on the assumption that every act which is not challenged within a reasonable time must be presumed to be lawful, and partly on the theory that it is the function of law to help those who assert their rights in the proper way, and not to encourage people to wait a long time before raising a complaint. If, therefore, one finds that a man and his predecessors in title have enjoyed and exercised an easement or profit for a great many years without any protest or objection being made, one is entitled to assume that he has a right to that easement or profit, and that at some time in the past it was formally conferred upon him or his predecessors. The result of the use coupled with the lapse of years is to create in law the right which has in actual fact been exercised, even though there can be found no other proof that such a right ever was created.

It has already been pointed out that prescription only applies to the acquisition of easements and profits à prendre (and in certain cases to customary rights). An easement is a right enjoyed by one owner of land over the property of an adjoining owner, such as a right of way or light (*see* ANCIENT LIGHTS; EASEMENT); a profit à prendre is a right in one owner of land to take something, such as gravel, grass, turf or wood from adjoining land. (*See* PROFITS À PRENDRE.)

User as of right.—Since prescription rests on unchallenged use of the right in question, it is, of course, necessary, in order that the right may be shewn to have been acquired by prescription, that it should have been exercised regularly for some time in the past. It is also necessary to shew that it was exercised "as of right;" that is, in such a way as to leave no doubt that the person who exercised it believed himself entitled to do so, and was prepared to assert his claim. If the right has only been exercised furtively after dark, or when it was known that those who were likely to object were safely out of the way, then the user is not "as of right" and the presumption of lawful origin is rebutted. Similarly, if the user was by permission of the owner of the property

affected and a payment of money or some other consideration was made in return for it, there can be no prescription. Even although there has been long use in the past which was genuinely believed by the person claiming to prescribe the right to be lawful, it will not nevertheless be "user as of right" if protests or attempts were made by the occupiers of the property over which it was exercised.

Length of User.—The period of time during which user of the right must be shewn to have existed, in order that the right may be prescribed for, varies according to the kind of prescription which is relied upon and the nature of the right to be prescribed.

There are three kinds of prescription; common law prescription, prescription under the doctrine of the lost modern grant and prescription under the Prescription Act of 1833.

Common law prescription was the earliest. It is now by far the most unusual, for in order to succeed under it the person who claims to prescribe for a right must shew that he and his predecessors have used and enjoyed that right from before 1189, i.e. from "time immemorial" (q.v.). In practice it is seldom necessary for him to produce actual proof of such user; it would almost always be impossible for him to do so. It is usually sufficient to produce proof of user during the last fifty to seventy years, for the Court will infer from that, if no evidence to the contrary is produced, that there has been continuous user since 1189. But it is always open to an opponent to prove that, in fact, the user of the right did not commence until after 1189. This would be fatal.

" Lost Grant."—It will readily be appreciated that this kind of prescription cannot often be relied upon with success, and it was because of this fact that the doctrine of the lost modern grant was developed. Under this kind of prescription it is sufficient to shew that the right has been exercised for some time in the past—fifty years is about the normal period. From this user the Court will infer that at some fairly recent date a grant of the right was made under seal, and that this grant has been lost. Hence the name of the prescription—'the doctrine of the lost modern grant."

Prescription Act.—The Prescription Act provides a third method of prescription whilst at the same time leaving the two older methods unaffected. It enacts that if uninterrupted user as of right for twenty years can be proved, the right shall be deemed to be established. But it is necessary, in order to comply with the provisions of the act, to shew that the twenty years' user extends right down to the date on which the action concerning the right was started. It is not enough to prove twenty years' user at some date in the past.

Similarly, the user must have been continuous throughout the twenty years; it must not have been interrupted by any objector. Nothing, however, is deemed to be an objection unless it is persisted in for at least a year. It follows from this that if nineteen years and six months' user can be proved followed by six months' objections immediately before action was brought, a claim to prescribe will succeed.

The Prescription Act goes on to provide that if only twenty years' user is proved, then proof of verbal consent to the exercise of the right shall be sufficient to prevent prescription, but if forty years' user is proved, then mere verbal consent will not suffice, and a written or sealed consent must be produced if prescription is to be prevented.

These periods apply to easements; for profits the periods are thirty and sixty years respectively. Special rules apply to the easement of light. (*See* ANCIENT LIGHTS; PROFITS À PRENDRE.)

PRESCRIPTION (SCOTS LAW).
—Prescription corresponds to what is known as the limitation of actions in English law, and by it an obligation may be extinguished or may be made capable of being enforced only if proved in a special manner. Prescriptions are of several kinds.

(1) Triennial Prescription. Debts such as ordinary shop accounts, law agents' accounts, servants' and workmen's wages, or house rents, where the transaction has been purely verbal, must be sued for within three years. If the creditor does not sue within this period, he may still sue if he can prove his debt either by producing some written document signed by the debtor in which he acknowledges the debt, and the fact that it is still owing, or by obtaining from the debtor an admission on oath of the debt.

(2) Quinquennial Prescription. Contracts concerning movables or sums of money which do not require by law to be made in writing, prescribe within five years. After that time the creditor may still sue, but again he can only do so if he can produce some writing by the debtor or secure from him an admission on oath. Contracts which fall under this heading are those of loan, pledge, and sale of movables.

(3) Sexennial Prescription. Bills of Exchange and Promissory Notes must be sued on within six years after they become due. Any action after this time can only be enforced, as in the other cases, by proof by the writ or oath of the debtor.

(4) Septennial Prescription. Cautionary obligations (i.e. contracts of guarantee) in which the cautioner (i.e. the guarantor) is clearly stated in the document which binds the principal debtor to be a cautioner prescribe within seven years. In this case it is not merely the right of proof which is altered by the delay, but the liability itself is extinguished, and so it is not possible for the creditor to prove the debt after seven years even by the writ or oath of the debtor.

(5) Decennial Prescription. This applies to actions by pupils and minors (i.e. persons under twenty-one) against their tutors and curators (i.e. those who have had charge of their property before they came of age). Any action calling a tutor or curator to account for his dealing with the property must be brought within ten years.

(6) Vicennial Prescription. Holograph bonds and subscriptions in account books without witnesses prescribe within twenty years. This applies to all binding contracts executed without witnesses.

(7) Forty Years' Prescription. Any right is lost if the person in whom it is vested fails to prosecute or execute it for forty years. Thus, a contract entered into by probative writing with witnesses would endure for forty years. In the same way, rights over land or obligations relating to land may be lost, but here the period is twenty years.

PRESENT.—(*See* GIFT; UNDUE INFLUENCE.)

PRESUMPTION OF DEATH.—
If a person has not been heard of for more than seven years by those who in all the circumstances would expect to hear of him, there is a presumption that he is dead. This

is a very general rule, and will not be acted upon if there is any reason other than his death to account for his not having been heard of. On the other hand, if the circumstances of the disappearance justify it, an order to presume death can be made before the expiration of seven years. Orders of this kind are made on application to the High Court of Justice.

Questions of great difficulty sometimes arise where it is important, for purposes affecting the inheritance of property, to decide which of two persons killed in the same disaster died first. If two such persons have left wills leaving property to each other, the exact moment of death will obviously affect the ultimate disposal of such property. If there is no evidence either way on the point the Court will not presume that one died first.

PRESUMPTION OF LIFE (SCOTS LAW).—Where a person has disappeared and has not been heard of for seven years or more, the Court may hold that he died at some specified date, or, where there is not sufficient evidence that he died at any definite date, may declare that he is to be presumed to have died seven years after the date on which he was last known to be alive. These provisions will be of value in the case where one person is entitled to succeed to a property on the death of another, and where that other disappears and cannot be found. If the person who has been presumed to be dead returns, he may recover the estate from the person who has obtained it, or if he has sold it he may recover the price at any time within thirteen years from the date at which the title to the estate, if it is capable of being registered in a public register, was so registered; and in other cases from the date on which possession of the estate was in fact taken. After the end of the thirteen years the right to recover the estate is lost.

PREVENTIVE DETENTION.—A person who is convicted as an habitual criminal (*see* HABITUAL CRIMINAL) may receive, in addition to penal servitude, a sentence of Preventive Detention. This last may only be inflicted if the Court is satisfied that, by reason of the offender's criminal habits and mode of life, it is necessary for the protection of the public that he should be kept in custody for a period longer than the sentence of penal servitude awarded.

Preventive detention must be for more than five years and less than ten years. It is divided into three grades: ordinary, special and disciplinary. A prisoner starts in the ordinary grade, but if he gains sufficient certificates of good conduct he may be promoted to the special grade. This grade carries certain privileges. If, on the other hand, a prisoner conducts himself badly, the governor may order that he be placed in the disciplinary grade. The restrictions in this are more severe than in the other grades. Prisoners whilst undergoing preventive detention are employed at useful trades and, if in the ordinary or special grades, they earn remuneration for their work. Money so earned may be spent on buying special food, or remitted to their families or allowed to accumulate until they are discharged.

PREVIOUS CONVICTIONS.—In general, the previous convictions of a prisoner cannot be made known in Court until after he has either pleaded guilty to all the charges against him, or been found guilty after a trial. It is customary then for the Court to be informed of the criminal record, if any, of the prisoner with a view to ascertaining what is the proper sentence that should be inflicted.

There are, however, certain cases in which previous convictions may be referred to during the course of the trial. Where, for instance, a person is charged with receiving stolen property, the prosecutor may, providing he has given proper notice, bring evidence of previous convictions of the prisoner during the preceding five years. Also, where a prisoner goes into the witness box and attempts to set up his own good character, or attacks the character of witnesses for the prosecution or other persons charged at the same time, he may be cross-examined as to his previous convictions, and if he denies them, witnesses may be called to prove them. (*See* CRIMINAL EVIDENCE ACT.)

PRIEST.—No person may be ordained a priest of the Church of England until he has attained twenty-four years of age, and until he has been ordained at least a year as deacon. On ordination, he becomes entitled to administer the sacrament and to preach the Word of God. No person may, under pain of a fine of £100 for each offence, administer the sacrament or take any benefice or preferment without having been ordained a priest. (*See* DEACON.)

PRIMA FACIE.—This is an expression in constant legal use, and is applied to evidence which, on the face of it, makes out a case for the side that tenders it. A "prima facie" case is one which, if there is no evidence to contradict it given by the other side, would entitle the side making it out to win the case.

PRINCIPAL AND AGENT.—There are many acts which a man may appoint another to do on his behalf so that the act, when done, has the same effect as if it had been done by the man personally. The person appointed to act is known as the agent, and the person appointing him is known as the principal. Where, however, the act to be done is one of some public character, it is not possible to do it through an agent. Thus, a man cannot, except in very special cases, vote through an agent at an election but must record his vote in person.

Again, when a man has been entrusted with certain powers and duties, he will not be able to appoint an agent to do them for him in cases where he has himself been appointed on account of his personal qualifications for the doing of the acts. This principle is the source of the rule of agency expressed in the Latin maxim "delegatus non potest delegare" ("a person to whom a duty has been delegated cannot himself delegate that to another").

How Agents are Appointed.—There is no special form required for the appointment of an agent, and the authority may either be given by words or in writing. If, however, the agent will be required to enter into some contract under Seal—i.e. a deed—on behalf of his principal, then his appointment also must be under seal, and will be known as a Power of Attorney. The relationship of principal and agent will be implied in certain cases even although there is no express arrangement creating it. Thus, an agent appointed for one purpose will be held to have implied authority to do all acts necessary to carry out the purpose of his appointment. The most frequent example of this type of agency arises where a husband and wife are living together and where, as is usual, the wife orders on behalf of the household such things as are necessary.

Estoppel.—This arises in cases where the person alleged to be the principal has not in fact given any authority to the agent, or where the authority has been brought to an end, but is prevented from denying that he has given authority by some conduct on his part. Thus, if a wife has been in the habit of dealing with a particular tradesman, and if the husband has paid the bills to that particular tradesman, he cannot at a later time refuse to pay a bill on the ground that he has withdrawn his wife's authority to buy goods on his credit unless he has informed the tradesman of this withdrawal of authority. Until this time he is said to hold out his wife as his agent to that tradesman, and will be bound by her acts by reason of this doctrine of holding out, even though the agency has in fact come to an end.

Ratification.—Even though an agent has no authority to contract on behalf of the principal at the time when he does so, the principal may later adopt the act, and this adoption is known as ratification. When this takes place, the principal is as fully liable on the contract as if the agent had been authorized at the time when he entered into it.

Duties of Principal.—It is the duty of the principal to pay to the agent the remuneration agreed upon. This remuneration is frequently expressed as a commission at a certain rate on the price of the goods or other articles sold. What the agent has to do in order to earn this commission will depend upon the exact terms of his contract. Normally, where he is to be paid a commission when a sale is effected, he will be entitled to his commission if he introduces someone to his principal who is ready, willing and able to buy the property, even though no sale takes place owing to some act of the principal himself. Where an agent selling goods on commission acts for several principals, he will not usually be entitled to complain although no goods are sent to him for sale, but where he is acting for one principal only, in fact, as a servant, he will be entitled to notice of the termination of his employment, and to damages if he is not given reasonable facilities by his employer to enable him to earn his commission. In some agencies commission may be payable, not only on orders obtained by an agent, but also on all repeat orders at a later time received from the same customer, and in such a case commission may still be payable on orders received after the death of the agent. Agencies of this kind are not frequently found, and in most cases an agency may be brought to an end by reasonable notice or the expiry of a fixed period if the contract has been originally for a fixed period.

A principal is also bound to indemnify the agent against all sums of money properly expended on the principal's behalf. Thus, a partner who has incurred liabilities, or spent money in looking after the firm's interests, is entitled to be indemnified by the other partners.

Duties of Agent.—An agent must use proper skill and care in carrying out his duties and must at all times be prepared to render an account to his principal of the transactions he has entered into and the amounts due. The limit to the right to delegate his authority has already been noted. An agent is not entitled to accept any profit out of the transaction other than that which is being paid to him by his principal. Thus, it would be very improper and illegal for an agent who is employed to buy property to accept a sum of money from a supplier who promises it to him if he places the order. Secret profits of this kind are very frequent, but it should be realized that they are illegal, and render both the agent and the person paying the profit guilty of a criminal offence. In addition, the principal is entitled to claim from the agent the amount of the profit, and may, in addition, dismiss the agent without notice and refuse to pay him his commission on the transaction. Thus, if X is a large buyer for B & Company, who are restaurant proprietors, he may well receive an offer from some supplier that if he, X, will place with the supplier all orders for meat required by B & Company, the supplier will give him $2\frac{1}{2}\%$ on the amount of the orders. It should be clearly understood that this transaction is illegal, and renders both X and the supplier liable to criminal punishment.

Third Parties.—An agent in contracting may do so in any one of the following three ways.

1. He may contract expressly as agent for a named principal, e.g., A buys one hundred sacks of flour "on behalf of B." In this case the agent can never be liable on the contract, unless the principal does not exist, or unless there is a special custom of the trade making the agent liable.

2. Where the agent states that he acts for a principal, but does not say who that principal is. Here also the agent will not be liable in the contract, and the principal will be the only person entitled to sue or liable to be sued.

3. Where neither the existence of the principal or his name is disclosed, e.g. where A enters into a contract with X in his own name, but is in fact acting for B, although X is not aware of this. Here there is nothing to prevent B suing on the contract that has been made, but A is also entitled to sue. When X discovers that A was not the principal but was acting on behalf of B, he may equally sue B, but he must make up his mind whether he intends to sue A or B. He cannot sue both, and if he obtains judgment against one and does not succeed in getting the money on the judgment, he cannot later sue the other.

Liability for Wrongs.—A principal may be liable for the acts of his agent even though he has not authorized them but has in fact forbidden the agent to do the acts complained of. Thus, if an agent is employed to sell goods for a principal, and in doing so makes untrue statements about the goods so that an action for fraud will lie against him, the principal may also be sued for the fraud. The test is whether or not the principal authorized the agent to do in a proper way the thing which he has done in an improper way.

How Agency is Ended.—Just as the parties may make a contract commencing the agency so they may, by their agreement, put an end to it. Even apart from this, however, a principal is entitled to put an end to the agent's authority at any time. This may be a breach of contract so far as the agent is concerned, and he may, therefore, be entitled to claim damages from the principal, but it will nevertheless put an end to his authority and prevent him from binding his principal by transactions he may enter into with third parties. Thus, if A is employed for a period of seven years as the buyer for an hotel owned by Y, Y may at any time dismiss A. A will be entitled to damages, but if after that time he places any orders on behalf of Y, Y will not be liable upon them. It should be noticed that, as pointed out above, Y might be liable on the orders if they were given to persons who had previously dealt with A as the agent of Y, but this is not on the ground that A has any authority to bind Y, but on the ground that Y has held out A as his agent to those particular persons by reason of the previous transactions, and so is estopped i.e. prevented, from denying the authority. Y in such cases must inform all previous customers that A no longer has his authority to place orders.

Agency will also come to an end apart from the acts of the parties by what is called the operation of law, that is, on the happening of certain events. Thus, on the death or bankruptcy of either the principal or agent the authority automatically comes to an end, and the same result takes place if the principal becomes insane or if the country of which the agent is a citizen goes to war with the country of the principal so that the principal becomes an alien enemy. In most cases it is of no consequence whether the agent knew or did not know that his principal was dead or had become insane; he will be liable to an action for damages brought by the person with whom he has contracted. In the case of bankers, however, the banker is considered to have authority to pay cheques drawn by his customer even after the customer's death until notice of the death has actually been given to him.

Liability of Agent.—Where a person enters into a contract as an agent for another he is said to "warrant his authority;" that is to say, he undertakes that he is authorized to enter into the contract in question by the principal for whom he purports to be acting.

If, in fact, he has no authority or if he has exceeded his authority, the third party with whom he has contracted may bring an action against him for the damages he has suffered in not being able to hold the principal liable on the contract. An agent will be liable, even though he has acted perfectly innocently, and honestly thought his authority was still good, e.g. was unaware of his principal's death. But he will not, of course, be liable if the third party was aware that he had no authority or if the agent stated at the time that he was not certain that his authority still held good.

PRISONER.—The term "prisoner"

covers all persons who are in custody, whether awaiting trial or undergoing sentence. It is a crime to rescue any prisoner or to assist one to escape from custody. (*See* IMPRISONMENT; PENAL SERVITUDE.)

PRISONS.—There are various kinds of prisons. Convict prisons are those in which convicts or persons undergoing penal servitude serve their sentences. Prisons in which persons undergoing imprisonment, as distinct from penal servitude, are confined are called local prisons. Prisoners awaiting trial or execution, and debtors and others imprisoned for Contempt of Court are confined in local prisons.

Anyone who, by any means, sends, or attempts to send to a prisoner any intoxicating liquor, tobacco, money, foodstuff, papers or other articles, unless authorized by the governor, commits a punishable offence. If the offender is actually a prison officer, he is liable to dismissal and forfeiture of emoluments due. (*See* IMPRISONMENT; PENAL SERVITUDE.)

PRIVATE BILL.—When it is desired to obtain the authority of Parliament in a matter affecting some individual or corporation as distinct from the public, it is necessary to promote a private Bill in Parliament. When passed, it becomes an act, and of equal validity to any other act. Railway companies and similar corporations frequently find it necessary to resort to private bills.

PRIVATE HOUSE.—A not unusual covenant in a lease of domestic premises is that the premises shall be used as a private dwelling house only. Such a covenant is interpreted strictly, and excludes the use of the house for taking in paying guests even though the guests be the friends of the occupier. Conversion of a house into flats also constitutes a breach of such a covenant.

PRIVATE ROAD.—In law, a private road means a road upon which the public have no right. It is occasionally used also to mean a road which is not repaired at the public expense. (*See* HIGHWAYS: RIGHT OF WAY; "TRESPASSERS WILL BE PROSECUTED.")

PRIVILEGE. Privilege in Defamation.—The most common use of the word privilege is to indicate an occasion on which a person may make an untrue statement defamatory of another, and untrue without being liable to have an action brought against him for defamation. The occasion is said to be a privileged occasion and the statement a privileged statement.

Absolute Privilege.—Privilege in this sense may be either absolute or qualified. A statement is absolutely privileged when no action can be brought upon it however untrue it may be and even though it is made spitefully and with intent to injure the person to whom it relates. Absolute privilege exists only in the following cases:—

1. Statements made in judicial proceedings by a Judge, juryman, party, witness, or advocate;

2. Statements in Parliament;

3. Statements made by one officer of State to another in the course of his official duty—e.g. an official communication by one minister to another; and

4. Parliamentary papers published by the direction of either House of Parliament—e.g. a Parliamentary Blue Book.

Qualified Privilege.—A statement is said to possess a qualified privilege when it is made on a privileged occasion without any malice or improper motive, even though it is untrue and defamatory. The chief instances of qualified privilege are:—

1. Statements made in pursuance of a duty;

2. Statements made in protection of an interest;

3. Fair comment on matters of public interest;

4. Reports of Parliamentary and other public proceedings.

Within the first class would fall statements made by an employer of a servant as to the character of that servant to some person who was contemplating taking him into his employment. The employer giving the character will not be liable, even though he says what is untrue, so long as he, in fact, believes that it is true and so long as he is not acting with the intention of injuring the servant. Thus, if A has employed B and during his employment found that sums of money were constantly being missed in such circumstances that suspicion attached strongly to B, though nothing was ever proved, A would not be liable to any action for damages by B if he stated that he did not consider B to be honest.

Fair Comment.—A statement is said to be fair comment when it relates to some matter of public interest and expresses an opinion which, whether it be right or wrong, is one that is generally held. Thus, a person who publishes a book must submit to reviews of it even though they are adverse.

Privileged Report.—Fair and accurate reports of public proceedings, whether they are judicial proceedings or Parliamentary proceedings or public meetings, are entitled to qualified privilege. (*See* DEFAMATION.)

Privilege in Litigation.—In certain cases, persons are entitled to refuse to disclose to the Court statements made to them or documents brought into existence under privilege. The best known of these privileges is that which protects professional confidence. No legal adviser, whether he is a barrister, or solicitor or clerk, can be compelled, without the express consent of his client, to disclose statements made to him by his client in professional confidence or to produce documents made in the same circumstances. It should be noticed that this does not extend to confidential communications made to priests or ministers of religion or doctors.

Matrimonial Communications.—It is an elementary rule of English law, to which great importance is attached, that at no time should either husband or wife be required to make public statements made by the one to the other during the marriage. (*See* DEFAMATION.)

PRIVY.—As distinguished from a party to any transaction, the word privy indicates a person who, without being a party to a transaction, is bound by it. Privies may be either in estate or in blood. Privity in estate exists where two or more persons are legally bound together by the same estate in lands—for example, lessor and lessee. Privity in blood exists between the persons who take property either on intestacy or under a will. The result of this is that an heir of a deceased person who takes land has only the same title to the property as had the person from whom he received it.

PRIVY COUNCIL.—The Privy Council is the nominal executive governing body of the United Kingdom. It exercises a great variety of functions, most of which have been entrusted to it by Acts of Parliament. Its orders are set out usually in Orders in Council or Proclamations. The

members of the Council are appointed by
the Crown from among persons distinguished
in various walks of public life. Many high
official appointments carry membership
almost as a matter of course. Members
receive the title of Privy Councillor, with
the prefix "Right Honourable" before their
names. (*See* JUDICIAL COMMITTEE.)

PRIZE FIGHT.—Prize-fighting is
unlawful in England. It must not, however,
be confused with a boxing-match. The
distinction between the two is whether
victory is gained by means of skill rather
than through the causing of injuries or ex-
haustion. One indication on this point is
whether or not boxing gloves are used.
Persons who attend as spectators at a prize-
fight may be convicted as well as the principals if they are present aiding and abetting.

**PROBATE, DIVORCE, AND
ADMIRALTY DIVISION.**—To this
Division are assigned all petitions for
divorce, nullity of marriage, restitution
of conjugal rights, judicial separation,
legitimacy declarations, suits for jactitation
of marriage, etc.; all actions arising out of
applications for probate and administration
(but not actual administration by the Court);
actions for salvage and/or possession of
ships; actions arising out of collisions at sea;
and in general all matters that arise in
connection with shipping or prize. (*See*
COURTS; HIGH COURT OF JUSTICE; SUPREME
COURT OF JUDICATURE.)

PROBATE OF WILLS.—After the
death of a testator his will does not take effect
immediately, but must first be "proved,"
i.e. the law must be satisfied that the will has
been properly made and that the executors
have been properly appointed and that
death duties have been paid. This is
done by the executors obtaining a Grant
of Probate.

It is the duty of the executors of a will
to obtain a grant of probate.

Probate cannot be obtained until at least
seven days after the death of the testator.
It may be obtained at any time after that, but
if there is a delay of more than three years
in applying for it, proof of some excuse for
the delay must be given. The only person
who is entitled to a grant of probate of a will
is an executor, if any have been appointed;
but anyone else who is interested in the will
may go to the principal probate registry,

which is at Somerset House, Strand, London,
and demand a document called a "citation,"
calling upon the executor to apply for a
grant of probate, if he delays in doing so.

Where a will is made with a proper
attestation clause (q.v.), and where there
are no difficulties about it, the executor may
obtain a grant of probate by proving the
will in Common Form.

In nearly every large town in the country
there is an office known as a District Probate
Registry under the charge of a District
Registrar (for a list of these *see* ADMINISTRA-
TION, LETTERS OF). These officers, as well as
the Registrar of the principal probate registry
at Somerset House, are entitled to give grants
of probate where a will is proved in Common
Form. In addition to this, if the estate of
the deceased does not exceed £500, a grant
of probate may be obtained from the Inland
Revenue Officer, one of whom exists in
practically every town. All these persons
may make grants of probate of testators who
were domiciled in England and Wales, or
who, being domiciled elsewhere, leave
property situated in England and Wales.
If a testator dies domiciled in Scotland or
Northern Ireland, the will should first be
proved in the Scots or Northern Irish
Court and may then be produced to the
Registrar at Somerset House, who will
reseal it and make an English grant of
probate.

An executor may apply for probate of a
will either personally or through a solicitor.
He must swear an affidavit called the
"oath" in which he swears to the date of
the testator's death, the truth of the will, i.e.
that it was properly executed and that he will
perform the duties of executor. This document must contain a sufficient description
of the testator, the number of codicils, and
the gross amount of the estate left by the
testator. He must also swear another
affidavit for the Inland Revenue Authorities
in which he must set out to the best of
his knowledge, together with the proper
accounts, the amount of the estate for the
purpose of death duties.

These documents, together with the
actual will, must be taken to the District or
Principal Registry. The original of the will
is filed at Somerset House and another copy
of it may be inspected there by anyone
demanding to see it upon payment of a

small fee, generally 1/-. This process is known as proving a will in Common Form.

Proof in Solemn Form.—When there is any doubt as to the validity of the will, or when the executor thinks that there is a likelihood of some person opposing the grant of probate on one of the grounds referred to in the succeeding sub-section, probate should be obtained not in Common, but in Solemn Form.

Proof in solemn form is of the nature of an action at law. If the executor is applying for it, he must go to the Principal Probate Registry and make an affidavit confirming that he is executor, stating the name and residence of the testator and the fact that he requires the will to be proved in solemn form.

The Registrar will then issue a certificate permitting the executor to issue a writ in the High Court, or if the estate is a small one, as mentioned above, to issue a plaint in the County Court in the area where the deceased resided; but before the plaint in the County Court is issued, the executor must leave a copy of the registrar's certificate at the office of the County Court, and he must also file particulars, when he issues the plaint, stating concisely the nature of his demands. The plaint and summons should be addressed to, and served on, the person who proposes to contest the will, and notice of it should be served on any person who will be interested in the result.

In the normal way, if an executor successfully proves the will in solemn form, the costs of so proving it will come out of the estate, and as a general rule the costs of all persons concerned in the action will come out of the estate, if either the necessity for proving the will in solemn form was due to the fault of the testator, e.g. in making a careless will, or if the unsuccessful litigant or intervener had a good and sufficient reason for bringing or defending the action.

The advantage of proof in solemn form over proof in common form is that after proof in solemn form, no person who has been a party to, or has been present at, the proceedings can afterwards attempt to upset the will, whereas if the will is proved only in common form, any person can afterwards, by the process referred to below, start proceedings to revoke a grant of probate.

Opposition to a Grant of Probate. —Any person may object to probate of a will being granted to the executors. In order to do so, he must go either himself or by his solicitor to the principal registry or any district registry and apply for a caveat. This will prevent the grant being given until he has had a chance to oppose it, and remains in force for six months, after which it can be renewed from time to time for another six months. The executor applying for probate after a caveat has been issued must in turn issue a "warning," which he can obtain only from the Principal Registry at Somerset House. The warning must be signed by the Registrar and must state the name and interest of the person making the application for a grant of probate, the date of the will, and codicils, and must give an address, usually the address of the executors' solicitors, within three miles of the G.P.O. at London, where notices may be received. A copy of the warning must be left at the address of the person who obtained the caveat, who must, within 6 days of receiving the warning, enter an appearance at the principal registry and set out his reasons for objecting to the will. If he does not do so, the application will be granted after the executor has proved that the warning was served.

The caveator can withdraw his caveat at any time before he receives the warning or within 6 days after that, but he cannot afterwards withdraw it without leave of the Court, which will probably insist upon his paying costs as a term of the withdrawal. It must be withdrawn at the same registry as that at which it was entered.

A grant of probate may be opposed upon a number of grounds, but it should be remembered that a person who opposes the grant of probate should be in a position to shew (a) that he or she will be in a better position by opposing the grant of probate; and (b) that he or she has a good and sufficient reason for so doing, otherwise costs may be awarded against the caveator instead of coming out of the estate. (*See* ADMINISTRATION ACTION; ADMINISTRATION, LETTERS OF; ADMINISTRATOR; CAVEAT; EXECUTORS AND ADMINISTRATORS; WILLS.)

PROBATION.—When a court convicts anybody, but is of opinion that having regard to the character, age, health or mental condition of the accused, or the trivial nature of the offence, or the circumstances under which it was committed, it is desirable not to punish the offender but to place him on probation, the Court may make an order accordingly. In such circumstances, the offender may be placed upon probation for a period not exceeding three years. The effect of such an order is that if the offender remains of good behaviour and complies with the conditions of the order, he is not punished for the offence for which he has been convicted. If, however, he commits another offence or breaks the conditions of the probation order, he may be brought up and punished for the original offence.

PROCEDENDO.—The writ of procedendo is an order directed by the High Court to an inferior Court or other body or person exercising judicial functions ordering them to continue proceedings which have been stopped by a writ of certiorari (*see* CERTIORARI). It is what is known as a prerogative writ. (*See* PREROGATIVE WRITS.)

PROCESS.—This is the name applied to any writs or orders issued in legal proceedings as distinct from proceedings taking place outside the Court. The person authorized to serve any of these documents is known as a process server.

PROCURATION.—This is popularly described as the White Slave Traffic. Anyone who procures or attempts to procure any girl under twenty-one years of age who is not of known immoral character for an immoral purpose with some other person, commits an offence under the Criminal Law Amendment Act, 1885. A similar offence is committed in attempting to procure any woman or girl to leave the United Kingdom for any purpose connected with the white slave traffic. Anyone convicted of these offences may be sentenced to imprisonment for not more than two years and to be privately whipped.

PROCURATOR FISCAL (SCOTS LAW).—The Procurator Fiscal is an official appointed in each district in Scotland who acts as a public prosecutor in criminal cases and also fulfils some of the duties carried out in England by a coroner. Coroner's inquests are unknown in Scotland and are replaced by an enquiry by the Procurator Fiscal in cases where he thinks enquiry necessary. It is also his duty when any serious crime has been committed to take a precognition of the facts, that is,

to obtain statements from persons who have knowledge as to the circumstances of the crime.

When the Procurator Fiscal has obtained the statements he will consider whether or not it is possible to bring any prosecution against any person in respect of the crime.

PROFANE LANGUAGE.—The use of profane language in any street or public place, or in any town, to the annoyance of residents or passers-by is punishable on summary conviction by a fine of forty shillings or fourteen days' imprisonment. A police constable may arrest an offender on such a charge without a warrant. Profane language includes songs or ballads of a blasphemous or unpleasant type.

PROFITS À PRENDRE.—A profit is a right, conferred upon the owner for the time being of one particular plot of land, to take away, for the benefit and use of that particular plot, something which is part of or grows upon another plot of land. Examples of profits are the right to cut turf, to cut timber and the right to graze and pasture cattle, pigs, etc. A profit attaches not to a particular man but to a particular plot of *land* and can only be exercised by the owner or occupier for the time being of that particular plot.

Profits are now rarely met with except where there are extensive areas of common land, as, for instance, in the New Forest. Profits may be acquired by an express grant under seal, or by prescription, that is, undisturbed user and enjoyment over a long period (usually forty years for profits). (*See* EASEMENT; PRESCRIPTION.)

PROHIBITION, WRIT OF.—The writ of prohibition is a writ directed by a Judge of the High Court to an inferior Court (including an Ecclesiastical Court), ordering such inferior Court to discontinue the proceedings mentioned in the writ by reason of their illegality. It is what is known as a prerogative writ. (*See* PREROGATIVE WRITS.) It will be issued only when proper cause is shewn that it is necessary, but once such cause has been shewn to the satisfaction of the Judge, to whom application is made, he may not refuse to grant the writ. Its purpose is to prevent inferior Courts from acting outside the powers legally conferred upon them, or to prevent a Judge, Magistrate or other person or body exercising judicial functions, from continuing to act in any case in which he has an interest such as will bias him, e.g. if he has a pecuniary interest in the result of the case. (*See also* PREROGATIVE WRITS.)

PROMISSORY NOTE.—A promissory note is defined as "an unconditional promise in writing made by one person to another signed by the maker, engaging to pay, on demand or at a fixed or determinable future time, a certain sum in money to, or to the order of, a specified person or to bearer." A Bank Note is a form of promissory note. No precise words are necessary, but there must be a promise, and for this reason an I.O.U., which is a mere statement of debt, does not amount to a promissory note. (*See also* BILL OF EXCHANGE; HOLDER FOR VALUE; HOLDER IN DUE COURSE; INDORSEMENT.)

PROMOTER.—A person who is engaged in the formation of a limited company is known as a promoter. Promoters are not prevented from selling their own property to the company when it does come into existence or from making any profit they please out of their transactions with the company, but they must disclose this profit to the shareholders or directors.

Promoters who induce any persons to subscribe for shares in a company by fraudulent statements are liable to damages at the action of the persons defrauded. (*See* COMPANY.)

Common Informers.—The term promoter is also used to indicate persons who prosecute offenders under penal actions as common informers, but in this connection the word has fallen into disuse. It is still, however, used to indicate persons who desire to have some private Act of Parliament passed for such purposes as the acquiring of land by a railway company or for other public purposes. Such persons are called "promoters of the undertaking."

PROPERTY.—The word property is used in several senses in law. Firstly, it is used to indicate the right of ownership of goods or land or anything else which is capable of ownership. Thus it might be said of a particular piece of land that the property in it belonged to X, meaning that he was the owner. Sometimes the word property is used to mean not the full ownership but some lesser right in the goods or land.

In such a case the person enjoying the right over the goods, etc., is said to have a special property in them, e.g. a pawnbroker with whom goods have been pawned has a special property in them.

Another use of the word property arises when it is applied not to the rights which may exist, but to the things over which the rights may be exercised, as when one uses the expression "a man of property," meaning a man who owns much wealth. Here the word means the actual land, houses or goods, which he owns.

Ownership.—A person who has the property in anything, i.e. owns it, is not entitled to use it absolutely as he wishes. He must not, for example, use it in any way that may injure another. Thus, the owner of land may normally build a house on it, and the house may be as large or as ugly as he pleases, but if his next-door neighbour has got rights of ancient lights, i.e. is entitled to have an uninterrupted flow of light to one of his windows, the house must not be built so as to interfere with the right. In the same way, a man would probably be entitled to excavate in his land as much as he pleases, but if the excavation causes any part of his neighbour's land to fall in, it may be stopped. Statutes prescribing maximum heights for buildings, and building and town planning schemes have considerably limited the right of property in land so far as building is concerned; and in addition, the land may be subject to what are called restrictive covenants, i.e. agreements preventing the owner from using the land for certain purposes. This may make it illegal for him to build houses other than of a certain character or to carry on certain trades. (*See* PERSONAL PROPERTY; REAL PROPERTY.)

PROPERTY TAX.—This is the name applied to the tax payable under Schedule A as Income Tax from ownership of land. (*See* SPECIAL SUPPLEMENT "INCOME TAX.")

PROSECUTION.—Prosecution is a process by which criminal proceedings are carried on against persons charged with offences. Prosecutions are usually carried on with the King as the nominal prosecutor. They are, therefore, described under the title of Rex versus the name of the person charged. Actually a prosecution may be carried on by anybody. When a private individual prosecutes, the prosecution is called a private one.

The costs of a prosecution are normally borne by local funds, and this is so in the case of private prosecutions, provided the costs are not disallowed by the Judge who tries the case. (*See* PUBLIC PROSECUTOR.)

PROSPECTUS.—When a Company is being formed and it is intended that members of the public should be asked to invest their money in it by subscribing for shares, those responsible for promoting the Company prepare a document known as the prospectus, which is sent round to persons likely to subscribe, and which gives them such information about the Company as will be likely to induce them to take up shares. It is obvious, therefore, that there is a great temptation for those who are preparing this document to state only what is in favour of the Company, and to paint its prospects in the most glowing colours, and it has been by no means infrequent to find that the statements in the prospectus contain many untruths, inserted with the object of procuring subscriptions for shares. It has therefore been necessary for the law to protect intending shareholders as far as possible against the effects of untrue statements in prospectuses, and to make sure, so far as it can, that the prospectus gives information and true information about all the important facts relating to the Company, and also that it contains nothing which is not true. (*See* SHARES.)

" Issuing Houses."—These provisions were, until recently, frequently evaded by shares being issued not to the public, but to what was known as an "issuing house," namely, two or three persons or a Company who subscribed for the shares and who then sold them to the public. As this was not an "issue to the public" but a "sale," the provisions relating to prospectuses did not apply; but it is now provided that where shares are issued and then offered for sale to the public in this way, a prospectus must be prepared and filed if the offer for sale to the public is made within 6 months of the allotment to the issuing house, or if all the money which is due from the issuing house in respect of the allotment is not paid to the Company before the offer for sale is made.

When the Prospectus is Untrue.—While the law has thus provided that certain statements should be inserted in a prospectus,

it is yet necessary for it to make provision for cases where the complaint is not that anything has been omitted from the prospectus which is required to be inserted, but that untrue statements have been made. In such cases, the shareholder who has bought his shares on the faith of these statements will have remedies against both the Company and the directors who sign the prospectus. As against the Company he may firstly apply for rescission of his contract to take shares, that is to say, he may call on the Company to take back his shares and pay him back the money he has paid for them. He must, however, do this before any proceedings to wind up the Company have been commenced, and within a reasonable time of the date when the shares were allotted to him. In order to succeed here, he will have to prove that the statements made were untrue, but he need not prove that they were known to be untrue by the persons who made them on behalf of the Company. In legal language, he may succeed if he proves "innocent" misrepresentation. In cases where he can shew that the statements were made "fraudulently," i.e. were known to be untrue, he may sue the Company for damages for fraud, but he cannot both sue for fraud and retain the shares. He must choose which course he wishes to adopt.

The shareholder has also certain rights against the directors who have signed the prospectus. (*See* DIRECTORS.) It is very important to remember that all these rights apply only to cases where the shareholder has been induced to subscribe for shares from the Company or to buy them from an issuing house in the circumstances set out above. They do not apply to cases where the shareholder has bought the shares on the market from some other holder of them, even although he may have been induced to buy them by reason of the statements which he saw in the prospectus. (*See* COMPANIES.)

PROTECTION ORDER. — Sometimes the holder of a Justices' licence wants to get rid of his licence at once and does not want to have to wait till next transfer sessions to transfer it to the new holder. For example, it may be more convenient for a new tenant to come in at once instead of waiting for the next transfer sessions; or the holder may have forfeited his licence and it is desired to put in a new man at once so as to save shutting up the house until a transfer is effected and so losing trade. In such cases a Protection Order must be applied for. This is an order authorizing the proposed new holder to carry on the business and sell intoxicating liquor until the next transfer sessions.

Such an order should be applied for by the new holder, and the application will be heard by the ordinary justices at petty sessions.

PROTEST.—A protest is the method of establishing certain facts before a Notary Public. The most usual instance of a protest arises when a Bill of Exchange is dishonoured either by non-acceptance or by non-payment. When this happens, the holder should take the document to a Notary Public to have the fact of dishonour recorded.

It is not necessary to protest the dishonour of an inland bill but a foreign bill must be noted and protested. If the holder fails to protest a bill when required to do so, he cannot afterwards make the drawers or endorsers of the bill liable.

When a Notary Public is not available, a bill may be protested by a householder or a substantial resident in the presence of two witnesses. A protest must bear a stamp which may be either an adhesive postage stamp or an impressed stamp. The amount of the stamp will depend on the duty on the bill itself. Where that does not exceed one shilling the stamp must be of the same value as the stamp on the bill, and in any other case the stamp must be a shilling. (*See* NOTARY PUBLIC.)

PROTEST (SHIPPING). — After every voyage the Master of a ship attends before a Notary Public and makes a protest stating the damage which has been sustained during the voyage. In practice, a protest is of little value when it merely relates that bad weather and rough seas were encountered; but if any exceptional accident or weather has taken place to cause damage, the protest may later be of value in determining the question as to whether the underwriters are responsible for damage. (*See* SHIPPING.)

PROTEST, PAYMENT UNDER.— A trader may frequently desire to pay a debt, although he contends he does not owe

it, in cases where the person claiming the money has got some hold over the trader, e.g. of a railway company claming to withhold goods until the carriage due on them is paid. Payment in these circumstances does not amount to an admission by the trader that the claim by the railway company is a valid one, and he will be able to recover it at a later time if he can shew that the claim was not in fact valid. He should be careful to make quite clear the terms on which payment is being made.

PROVIDED SCHOOL.—A school provided—i.e. entirely maintained—by the local education authority is known as a provided school to distinguish it from a school which, although controlled by the local education authority, draws its funds in whole or in part from some other source, such as a bequest of money for educational purposes. (*See* EDUCATION; SCHOOL.)

PROVINCIAL COURT.—There are two Provincial Courts in England, the Court of Arches (for the province of Canterbury), and the Chancery Court of York (for the province of York). These Courts are the Archbishops' Courts for the trial of ecclesiastical cases. Primarily, they are Courts of Appeal from the Consistory Courts in the province, but they also have power to hear cases in the first instance if the Bishop makes a request to that effect, and, in such circumstances, the case is not heard by the Consistory Court at all. (*See also* CHURCH OF ENGLAND.)

PROVOCATION. — Provocation is chiefly of importance in cases of homicide and assault. Words alone do not constitute provocation. Where, however, grossly insulting words or gestures are accompanied by blows, even though the blows are not very serious, there may be sufficient provocation to reduce the result of a fatal struggle from murder to manslaughter. The question in such cases is whether the provocation was sufficiently great to deprive a reasonable man of his self-control. If it is, a person who kills under the effect of it may be convicted of manslaughter only. In no case, however, can provocation excuse a killing altogether, the utmost result it can produce is a reduction from murder to manslaughter.

The Unwritten Law.—There is really no such thing as the so-called Unwritten

Law. When a man discovers his wife in adultery with another, such discovery can be regarded as sufficient provocation to deprive him of his self-control just as other forms of provocation. If it has that effect and he kills the adulterer on the spot, it is open to the jury to convict of manslaughter only. If, however, there is any interval during which his anger should have cooled, the provocation cannot be regarded as sufficient to reduce the killing from the capital crime.

Provocation in Assault.—It is only actions that can justify an assault. Insulting words or gestures are not sufficient, though of course they may have a bearing on the appropriate punishment. A blow or even the threat of a blow, however, may justify a person in striking his assailant in self-defence. (*See* ASSAULT; HOMICIDE.)

PROXY.—A Proxy is a person appointed to vote for another. The document appointing the proxy is itself also called a proxy or a proxy paper.

Proxies in Parliamentary Elections.—Anyone who is on the Absent Voters' List is entitled to vote either by post or by proxy at a general election or a bye-election. Any person on the register of voters is entitled to have his or her name put on the Absent Voters' List (which is supplemental to the register) who (i) by reason of his or her occupation, service or employment may be debarred from voting at an election while that register is in force, i.e. that year, or (ii) is either a serving member on full pay of the Army, Navy or Air Force, or (iii) is engaged in war work, and would otherwise have had the necessary residential qualification.

An elector wishing to be put on the Absent Voters' List should, before August 18th in any year, notify the Registration Officer of the constituency, who is the clerk to the council or the town clerk in a county or borough constituency respectively. Anyone can get his name removed by giving notice to the registration officer at any time.

An elector wishing to vote by proxy at any election must, one clear day before nomination day, send to the registration officer an application for the appointment of the proxy giving the proxy's full name and address. The application must be witnessed. The prescribed form of application is obtainable from the registration officer.

He will then issue a proxy paper to the proxy. It does not require a stamp.

The proxy, when voting, must produce the proxy paper to obtain a ballot paper.

The person appointed proxy either must be the wife, husband, parent or brother or sister of full age of the elector, or must be himself an elector in the constituency who is not already acting as proxy for more than one other person.

Other Proxies.—There is no voting by proxy in Local Government elections.

Company Meetings.—(*See* BANKRUPTCY; COMPANIES; MEETINGS.)

PUBLIC ANALYST.—Local Authorities have to administer the provisions of the law relating to the sale of Food and Drugs, and as one of the most common offences against the law is the selling of impure, mixed, watered, or adulterated food and drugs, it is necessary that some person should be available to analyse specimens of food and drugs which are sold.

In order to fulfil this duty, the local authority must appoint a person who has the necessary skill and technical knowledge as the public analyst for their district.

Any person who has purchased a drug or an article of food may submit it to the public analyst for the district in which he bought it and request him to analyse it. The analyst may charge a fee up to a maximum of 10/6, and must give the person who submitted the sample a certificate stating the results of his analysis. The name and address of the public analyst for each district is obtainable at the offices of the local authority or at a police station in the district. (*See* DRUG; FOOD; LOCAL GOVERNMENT; PUBLIC HEALTH.)

PUBLIC ASSISTANCE COMMITTEE.—The duty of relieving and maintaining the poor is placed upon the County Councils and County Borough Councils, and to enable them to carry out this work, they are required to appoint a Public Assistance Committee. (*See also* GUARDIANS COMMITTEE; MEANS TEST; POOR LAW AND SPECIAL SUPPLEMENT "UNEMPLOYMENT INSURANCE.")

PUBLIC AUTHORITIES PROTECTION ACT.—Persons acting on behalf of a public authority have certain protection against legal proceedings instituted against them by persons complaining of their conduct in their official capacity. This protection is set out in the Public Authorities Protection Act, 1893. This Act provides that no action shall be commenced against anybody for any act done in execution of any Act of Parliament or any public duty, unless the action is commenced within six months of the act or neglect complained of. Furthermore, if any person who is sued in respect of his conduct arising out of the public duties is successful in his action, he is entitled to his costs as between solicitor and client (*see* SOLICITOR), and not, as is customary in other cases, merely as between party and party.

PUBLIC HEALTH.—The law relating to Public Health is almost exclusively contained in a series of Acts of Parliament, and the bye-laws and regulations made under those Acts by the local authorities, who are entrusted with the duty of enforcing the provisions of the Statutes, and who are responsible for the various health services and the preservation of healthy living conditions in their district.

Verminous Persons, Houses and Articles.—Any local authority may permit any person who applies to them, on the ground that he is infested with vermin, to have the use, without charge, of any apparatus which they possess for cleansing the person and his clothing from vermin.

If the sanitary inspector of a local authority reports to the authority that any premises used for human habitation in the district are infested with vermin, the local authority may give a written notice to the occupier of the premises requiring him within a specified time to cleanse the premises so as to remove or destroy the vermin. If the occupier is a tenant and by the terms of his tenancy the owner is required to carry out such work, then the notice should be served upon the owner.

If the person on whom such notice is served fails within the specified time to comply with its requirements, then he becomes liable to a penalty not exceeding £5 and to a daily penalty of 10/– so long as he fails to comply with the notice.

The local authority upon the expiration of the time specified in the notice may themselves do the necessary cleansing and may recover all the expenses from the person who was required by the notice to do it.

Offensive Trades.—If a person wishes to carry on what is known as an "offensive" trade in certain premises, he must obtain the written consent of the local authority to use them for such a purpose, and if he uses the premises for an offensive trade without obtaining the consent of the local authority he is liable to a penalty of £50. The following trades are laid down by the law as being offensive:—

Blood-boiler, tallow-melter, soap-boiler, bone-boiler, fellmonger and tripe-boiler. (*See* FOOD; DRUGS; HOUSING; HOSPITAL; INFECTIOUS DISEASE; SLUM; VACCINATION; WATER; ETC.)

PUBLIC HOUSES.—This is the name popularly applied to places at which intoxicating liquor can be sold and drunk upon the premises. All such premises require to be licensed (*see* INTOXICATING LIQUOR), and so one often hears them called licensed premises though, in fact, many other premises also require licences. As they require licences, it follows that public houses are under the strict surveillance of justices, both as to the construction and condition of their premises and as to the manner in which they are carried on; for instance, when public houses are built their structure must be approved by the licensing justices before a licence will be granted; also, a constable can at any time enter upon licensed premises to see that the law is being complied with, and it is a serious matter to try and prevent him coming in. But, of course, he cannot enter unless the premises hold a justices' licence.

When a new licence is applied for (for procedure *see* INTOXICATING LIQUOR), plans must be produced before the justices who, unless they approve of them, will not grant the licence.

Four Important Points for Publicans.—In considering these plans what the justices chiefly look for and desire are:—

(*a*) Good supervision of all his customers by the publican.

(*b*) Good opportunity for observation by the police—for instance, "cosies" and "nooks" are frowned upon.

(*c*) Decent living quarters for the licensee, and

(*d*) Modern sanitary arrangements for both sexes.

Publicans must be careful not to alter any part of the premises used for drinking, so as either to give increased facilities for the sale of liquor or to conceal any part of the premises, without the consent of the justices. If he does so, the justices may declare his licence to be forfeit or make him restore the premises to their original structural condition.

a whole are adversely affected. A familiar example of this class of offence is making false reports to the police of imaginary crimes.

PUBLIC POLICY.—While the law, so far as it can, has laid down special rules as to what it will, and what it will not, permit the citizens of the State to do with their

Offences Relating to Public Houses	Penalty
1. Found drunk in a public house.	1st offence .. 10/- 2nd offence .. 20/- if within 1 year. 3rd offence .. 40/- if within 1 year.
2. Drunk or disorderly persons refusing to quit refreshment houses.	40/-
3. Refusing to allow a policeman to enter premises which have a justices' licence.	1st offence .. £5 Subsequent offence .. £10
4. Persons found on premises refusing to give name and address on entry of a policeman.	£5
5. Paying or allowing wages to be paid in a public house.	£10
6. Forging a justices' licence.	£20, or six months' hard labour and disqualification.
7. Causing or allowing a child to be in a bar of licensed premises.	1st offence .. £2 Subsequent offences .. £5
8. Causing or allowing a child to be on licensed premises for purpose of singing or offering anything for sale.	£25, or, alternatively, imprisonment.
9. Causing or allowing a child to obtain intoxicating liquor in uncorked vessel.	1st offence .. 40/- Subsequent offences .. £5
10. Procuring or attempting to procure intoxicating liquor on licensed premises for a drunken person.	40/- or one month's imprisonment.
11. Selling intoxicating liquor on credit.	£30
12. Selling intoxicating liquor to person under eighteen years of age or allowing them to consume such liquor.	1st offence .. £1 Subsequent offence .. £2

Disqualified Premises.—If they are not of a certain required annual value or not structurally adapted in the justices' opinion to hold a licence then they become disqualified to receive an on-licence. (*See* INTOXICATING LIQUOR; ON-LICENCES; PERMITTED HOURS; PUBLICAN AND RENEWAL.)

PUBLIC MISCHIEF.—It is a misdemeanour to commit an act tending to the public mischief. The test to be applied is whether the interests of the community as

property and rights, there yet remains a large number of cases which fall within none of these precise rules in which the Courts have stated that some act is not permissible because it offends against "public policy, meaning that it is against the public interest. (*See* RESTRAINT OF TRADE.)

PUBLIC PROSECUTOR.—The Director of Public Prosecutions is a permanent official whose duty it is to initiate and conduct prosecutions for murder and any crime of public importance. The Director is a barrister of standing and he has a staff of barristers and solicitors to conduct prosecutions in the lower Courts.

PUBLIC RECORD OFFICE.— The Public Record Office has been established with the object of preserving for future generations many documents which would otherwise have been lost. In it are collected many government and legal records which were previously distributed in other places. The Record Office is under the control of the Master of the Rolls, who may make orders necessary for the cleaning, preserving and arranging of the records. Copies may be made of any records in the Record Office at the request of the person making the copy. A copy when made is examined and certified as a true authentic copy by the Deputy Keeper and is then capable of being received as evidence in any Court.

PUBLIC SCHOOLS.—The seven Public Schools of Eton, Harrow, Winchester, Rugby, Westminster, Shrewsbury and Charterhouse have been reorganized by various statutes which provide for the government of the schools and regulate their endowments and properties. The term Public School includes any school represented on the Headmasters' Conference, an annual meeting of headmasters. (*See* EDUCATION; TEACHERS.)

PUBLIC TRUSTEE.—The Public Trustee is an officer appointed by the Lord Chancellor under the Public Trustee Act, 1906, on such terms as the Treasury determines.

The Public Trustee may act as a custodian trustee (*see under* TRUSTEE), or as an ordinary trustee, or as a judicial trustee (*see under* TRUSTEE), and may act alone or jointly with another person or persons; he may decline to accept any trust, but he must not decline solely on the grounds of the smallness of the trust property; he cannot accept a trust exclusively for religious or charitable purposes, or a trust which involves the management or carrying on of a business (except to the extent to which he is authorized to do so under the rules laid under the Act), or a trust under a deed of arrangement (q.v.) for the benefit of creditors, or the administration of an estate known or believed by him to be insolvent.

Nor can he accept the trusteeship of any settlements other than English ones.

The Public Trustee thus meets the case where there is difficulty in finding a person willing to act as trustee. There are two important advantages from his employment as trustee:—firstly, he never dies, the office of public trustee being a corporation sole; and secondly, the state is responsible for any loss to the trust estate caused by his breaches of trust.

The estate of a deceased person may be administered by the public trustee if the gross capital value is less than £1,000. Applications for administration by the public trustee can be made by the same persons who can apply for administration in the Chancery Division of the High Court of Justice, that is to say by a creditor or any person interested in the estate as legatee, divisee, next-of-kin or heir, or by the personal representative of the estate himself. (*See* TRUSTEE.)

PUBLICAN.—A publican is the name popularly given to a person who holds a licence to sell intoxicating liquor. He is also known as a licensee. (For the law relating to applications for licences and licensing generally, *see* INTOXICATING LIQUOR.)

People who are disqualified from holding a licence are:—

1. A sheriff or officer executing the legal process of any Court of Justice in England while he is such an officer.
2. Any person convicted of felony is disqualified for life.
3. Any person forging or using, knowing it to have been forged, a justices' licence is disqualified for life.
4. Any holder of a justices' licence who has permitted his premises to be used as a brothel is disqualified for life.
5. Any person convicted of selling intoxicating liquor without a justices' licence and who has consequently been ordered to be disqualified, the disqualification to continue for the time mentioned in the order.
6. Any person who by virtue of any other Act is disqualified for holding a justices' licence for the time provided under the Act.

Sex, infancy, bankruptcy, and nationality do not necessarily disqualify a person from holding a licence to sell intoxicating liquor.

Offences by Licensed Persons	Offence	Penalty
1. Selling or exposing for sale unauthorized liquor in an unauthorized place . .	1st 2nd	£50 or 1 month. £100 or 3 months. Possible forfeiture of licence and disqualification for five years.
	3rd	£100 or 6 months; permanent disqualification.
2. Allowing customers to drink liquor on highway or on unlicensed premises .	1st 2nd	£10 [qualification. £20
3. Taking liquor from premises not licensed for consumption to premises so licensed there to be sold for his benefit . .	1st 2nd	£10 £20
4. Allowing person under eighteen to consume intoxicants in a bar on the premises	1st 2nd	20/- 40/-
5. Possession of liquor not authorized for sale and not satisfactorily accounted for .	1st 2nd	£10 and forfeiture of liquor and £20 [vessels.
6. Not affixing name and description of licence to premises	1st 2nd	£10 £20
7. Permitting drunkenness or riotous conduct, or selling liquor to a drunken person	1st 2nd	£10 £20
8. Permitting premises to be a brothel . .		£20. Forfeiture of licence and permanent disqualification.
9. Bribing or supplying liquor to a constable on duty	1st 2nd	£10 £20
10. Allowing gaming or gambling. . .	1st 2nd	£10 £20
11. Keeping open where ordered to be closed by Justices in case of riot . . .		£50. House may be closed by force.
12. Refusing to admit a constable . . .	1st 2nd	£5 £10
13. Not producing licence or exemption order on demand		£10
14. Person licensed to sell beer or cider allowing wine, spirits, sweets, etc., to be brought into or consumed on his premises .		£20
15. Harbouring thieves or reputed thieves .		£10, or 4 months and/or bound over in £20 for 3 months.
16. Not producing licence on hearing of charge of last offence (15)		£5
17. Selling or delivering to child under fourteen intoxicating liquor save not less than one pint in a corked and sealed vessel .	1st 2nd	40/- £5
18. Procuring or attempting to procure intoxicating liquor for a drunken person.		40/- or 1 month.
19. Allowing child in a bar	1st 2nd	£2 £5
20. Forging or knowingly tending forged justices' licence		£20 or 6 months.
21. Selling or supplying intoxicating liquor to be consumed either on or off the premises outside permitted hours . .		£30
22. Offences contrary to condition as to distribution of intoxicating liquor .		£30

(For other offences against the licensing laws *see* Long Pull; Public Houses; Dance Halls; Drunkenness; Permitted Hours. *See also* Intoxicating Liquor.)

PUISNE JUDGE.—The term literally means younger and is applied to all Judges of the High Court who have no other distinctive title.

PUNISHMENT (IN SCHOOLS).—(*See* Education; Teacher.)

PUPIL.—(*See* Education; Teacher.)

PURCHASER.—Means in law, not only the person who acquires property for money or money's worth but also one who inherits property, under a will, or on an intestacy (that is to say, on the death of a relative without leaving a will) or who acquires property from any living person by the various means known in law. (*See also* Sale of Land; Landlord and Tenant.)

PUTATIVE FATHER.—The name given to the father of an illegitimate child when he has been so found by the Magistrates Court. (*See* Affiliation Orders.)

QUAKERS.—The Quakers are a privileged body of nonconformists. They cannot be required to make the declaration of faith which can be, although in point of fact it never is, demanded from a nonconformist minister. Nor are they forbidden, as are other nonconformist bodies, to hold meetings behind locked doors. Quakers enjoy peculiar privileges with regard to marriage, and a marriage solemnized according to Quaker custom is valid even though neither party is a Quaker.

QUALIFICATION SHARES.—It is frequently provided by the Articles of a company that directors must hold certain shares in order to qualify them to act. The Articles need not so provide. The directors must take up their qualification shares within one month of their appointment, and the amount of the qualification must be set out in the prospectus. (*See* COMPANY.)

QUANTITY SURVEYORS.—When an architect has prepared plans and specifications, he will have to give them to a quantity surveyor if the work to be done is very large. The plans and specifications by themselves are not enough to enable a contractor to decide what tender he can send in. The quantity surveyor therefore prepares bills of quantities. These give exact calculations of the amount of material and labour needed. Quantity surveyors usually charge a percentage on the contract price and are paid by the first progress certificate granted by the architect. (*See* ARCHITECTS; BUILDING CONTRACTS.)

QUANTUM MERUIT.—Very frequently no fixed scale of remuneration is made before a person is hired to carry out certain services. When this is so, the person who has rendered the services can sue the person who hired him for the fair and reasonable sum due for the services. What is fair and reasonable is, of course, for the tribunal before whom the case is brought to decide. The person suing in this way is said to sue on a "quantum meruit," that is to say, he sues for as much as he merits.

QUARANTINE.—There is power to require passengers on ships arriving in British ports to remain in quarantine to prevent the spread of certain contagious diseases. Cholera and yellow fever are the chief diseases against which such powers are exercised. There are similar powers as to animals and a period of six months' quarantine is usual in the case of dogs.

QUARTER DAY.—By English law the year is divided into four quarters which are not, however, of equal length. The four quarter days are:—

1. Lady Day, March 25th, which is the feast of the Annunciation of the Blessed Virgin Mary;
2. Midsummer Day, June 24th, which is the feast of St. John the Baptist;
3. Michaelmas Day, September 29th, which is the feast of St. Michael and All Angels; and
4. Christmas Day, December 25th.

In Scotland these quarter days are not recognized and the appropriate days are:—

Candlemas, February 2nd;
Whitsunday, which is May 15th and not, it should be noted, necessarily a Sunday;
Lammas, August 1st; and
Martinmas, November 11th.

QUARTER SESSIONS.—There are two kinds of Quarter Sessions—County and Borough. In the former, justices from all parts of the county sit and the proceedings are presided over by a chairman elected by them. In Borough Quarter Sessions the sole Judge is the Recorder (q.v.).

Quarter Sessions deal with certain administrative business arising in the County or Borough and also with criminal cases. The latter are of two classes—appeals from petty sessions in summary cases and trials on indictment. Appeals are heard by the justices or Recorder as the case may be. Trials are decided by juries, the Chairman or Recorder acting as Judge.

QUASH.—When any order or conviction is, on appeal, set aside it is said to be quashed. Thus, the Court of Criminal Appeal, when it decides that a conviction cannot be upheld, makes an order quashing the conviction.

QUEEN ANNE'S BOUNTY.—In the reign of King John the Papal Legate Pandulf introduced into England the custom of paying to the Pope the first fruits (i.e. the first year's income), and tenths (i.e. a tenth part of every subsequent year's income), of every ecclesiastical preferment or benefice. In 1535 an Act was passed at the instance of Henry VIII transferring these revenues from the Pope to the Crown.

In 1704 the income of this tax upon the Church was restored to the Church by the creation of Queen Anne's Bounty, which is a body whose full title is "the Governors of the Bounty of Queen Anne for the Augmentation of the Maintenance of the Poor Clergy"; and to this body all first-fruits and tenths were in future to be paid for distribution among the poorer clergy. In 1852 these fluctuating payments were fixed and commuted for an annual payment of £1 17s. 6d. for every £100 annual value of the benefice or preferment. By virtue of the First Fruits and Tenths Measure, 1926, all such first-fruits and tenths have ceased to be payable except in respect of certain sinecure offices. But although this vast source of revenue has been abolished, Queen Anne's Bounty still continues to exercise important functions; it is still entitled to accept gifts and legacies on trust for Church purposes, and its capital is considerable, the income distributed among the poorer clergy amounting to over £20,000 annually; the distribution is made in the form of relief from dilapidation assessments on benefices of not more than £300 net annual value. But the corporation has recently had conferred upon it perhaps more important duties than those it used to perform. Under the Ecclesiastical Dilapidations Measure, 1923, it is the "Central Authority" for the purposes of the Measure, and therefore bears a very important share of the control of all ecclesiastical property in England. Under the Tithe Act, 1925, all tithe rent-charge is vested in Queen Anne's Bounty, who is to collect all money due thereunder in order to distribute it to the persons formerly entitled to receive it. (See TITHE.)

QUIET ENJOYMENT.—When land is sold or when a tenancy is created by a landlord letting land to a tenant, there is always implied a convenant, that is, promise, by the person selling or by the landlord that the purchaser or tenant shall have "quiet enjoyment" of the premises. (See LANDLORD AND TENANT.)

QUINQUENNIAL VALUATION LIST.—An assessment area has to have a new valuation list every five years. This rule only applied to the Metropolis until 1925, when it was extended to the rest of England and Wales. (See RATES.)

QUOTA.—It is required by certain Acts of Parliament for the protection of British Industries that a percentage only of foreign products should be allowed to enter the country. Thus in the case of cinematograph films, every film renter or exhibitor must include a certain percentage of registered British films in his programmes. (See CINEMATOGRAPH FILMS.)

QUO WARRANTO.—The writ of Quo Warranto is now obsolete, its place having been taken by similar proceedings known as "an information in the nature of a quo warranto." Their purpose is to question the right by which a person exercises the functions of an independent crown official whose duties are of a public nature, e.g. a coroner or vestry-clerk, but not a rate-collector or a treasurer to a District Council. (See also PREROGATIVE WRITS.)

RABBITS.—Rabbits and hares are known as "ground game," but only hares are "game" within the meaning of most of the Game Acts. This distinction often has important consequences, e.g. licences are required for dealing in hares but not rabbits. But the owners of sporting rights, or their gamekeepers, have the same rights of arrest, etc., over those trespassing in pursuit of rabbits as over those pursuing game.

If rabbits stray out of Smith's land and injure Robinson's crops, Robinson cannot sue Smith for the damage unless he can prove that Smith has done something deliberately to encourage their breeding or spreading.

No tenant who has the shooting rights incidental to his tenancy may, at night, either shoot rabbits with a gun or use traps, unless they are set actually inside the rabbit-holes. But the landlord who occupies his own lands, or the tenant who has had sporting rights specifically granted to him, may shoot or trap rabbits at any time, and does not require a game licence to do so though any outsiders must have such a licence. Gun licences are required for the shooting of rabbits. (*See* GAME; GUN LICENCES.)

RABIES.—Any person having in his possession any animal suffering from, or suspected of suffering from rabies must take immediate steps to isolate the animal, with a view to preventing it from infecting others, or doing harm to human beings. Notification to the police must also be made at the earliest moment of any case of rabies.

The Minister of Agriculture and Fisheries has power to make orders when rabies is prevalent, and such orders may include one requiring the muzzling of dogs.

RACECOURSE.—The prohibition of betting in public places does not apply to racecourses on the days on which racing takes place. To be a racecourse for this purpose, however, the premises must be laid out for horse racing and permanently used for that purpose. (*See* SPECIAL SUPPLEMENT "GAMBLING.")

RACK RENT.—Where the rent of premises is equal to the full annual value of the premises, the rent is said to be a Rack Rent. The amount of the rent is important in some cases because, where a verbal agreement for the letting of land has been made, it can be enforced in cases where the rent under the agreement is two-thirds of a rack rent. (*See* LANDLORD AND TENANT.)

RAFFLES.—Raffles, strictly speaking, are illegal. A raffle is really a lottery, since the prizes are drawn by lots or chance. In the case of smaller raffles run under private auspices, it is not usual for prosecutions to be undertaken, but if they are on a larger scale, prosecutions under the Gaming Acts can be, and frequently are, instituted. (*See* SPECIAL SUPPLEMENT "GAMBLING.")

RAG AND BONE DEALER.—No dealer in rags and bones may sell from the vehicle or premises which he uses for that business any foodstuff or toys.

RAILWAY COMPANIES.—Since a railway must necessarily interfere with private rights by causing noise and smoke, it may only be lawfully created (except in very rare and limited cases where it is a completely private line) under the authority of an Act of Parliament. The modern railway companies are regulated in part by their own private Acts, in part by the private Acts of the Companies with which they have amalgamated, and in part by Public Acts of Parliament intended to lay down general rules for them all with regard to their constitutions, powers and obligations.

Railways Running Buses.—A railway company may not engage in any work or trade which is not authorized by these Acts; to do so is ultra vires, i.e. it is outside the powers of the company, and it could be prevented from so acting by an order of the Court. It was for this reason that it was necessary in 1928 for the companies to secure the passing of a number of private Acts in order to make it possible for them legally to engage in road transport on a large scale.

Excessive Smoke.—The authority conferred upon railways both by their Private Acts and the Public Acts is, in general, only an enabling authority. This means that they are entitled to run rail and road services and to use engines, locomotives and motor buses, etc., but must do their best to do so without infringing any private right. They are bound to take advantage of all scientific discoveries and improvements which may make their property safer; this has been decided in a number of cases which turned on the escape of sparks from the funnels of engines. The result of them is that unless it is almost impossible to prevent the escape of sparks, the company will be liable for any injury which they may cause. In the same way, it is impossible to get an injunction or damages against a railway company for causing annoyance by smoke or noise unless it can be shewn that the company could reasonably carry on their business without making so much smoke or noise.

Private Trains.—When railways were first built it was intended that private persons should be able to put their own trains or carriages on to the companies' lines. The companies are still legally under an obligation to allow such private trains to be run on payment of a reasonable toll, but apparently the Courts will no longer enforce this obligation on account of the great danger to other persons.

Duties.—In exchange for the virtual monopoly which they originally enjoyed, railway companies have had certain duties laid upon them by statute and by Ministerial regulations. These duties are for the most part enforced by the Railway Rates Tribunal (q.v.) who can order a railway to extend or alter stations, sidings, or docks to accommodate increased traffic, to provide reasonable facilities for passengers—such as smoking compartments, roofs over platforms, waiting-rooms, etc., to arrange for through booking and for the through carriage of goods and passenger traffic over different lines, or to provide workmen's trains at special rates.

Accidents.—Notice must be given of every accident to the Minister of Transport, who appoints an official to hold an enquiry into its causes and to report on what changes, if any, ought to be made to the company's practice or regulations. Returns must now also be made of all suburban traffic as and when the Minister may require. (*See* RAIL-WAY GOODS TRAFFIC; RAILWAY PASSENGERS.)

RAILWAY GOODS TRAFFIC.—

The Railway Rates Tribunal which was set up by the Railways Act of 1921 has drawn up a set of standard terms and conditions for the carriage of goods by rail. There are two sets of such conditions for the carriage of ordinary goods; the principal difference between them being that under one it is for the company to satisfy the Court that it was not guilty of negligence, while under the other it is for the customer to prove affirmatively that the damage was the direct result of the company's negligence.

Company's Risk.—Under the set of conditions known as the Companies' Risk Conditions, and contained in Form A, the company are liable as common carriers (q.v.) For his part the consignor must pay a standard rate which is called the ordinary rate and which is fixed by the Railway Rates Tribunal for each class of goods after hearing representatives of the companies, the traders concerned, the public, etc. Wherever nothing to the contrary is said, it is presumed that any contract for the carriage of goods is made at these ordinary rates under the company's risk conditions; the company is then liable for any loss, or misdelivery of, or damage to goods in transit unless it can prove that reasonable care was used and that the cause of the loss, etc., was:

(i) An act of God. Which "untheological expression" means any unusual natural phenomenon such as a violent snow or thunder-storm, an earth-quake or landslide, a fog or flood.

(ii) An act of the King's enemies. This does not include rioters or mere revolutionaries, but only foreign states at war with this country.

(iii) The seizure of the goods by legal process.

(iv) The orders of restrictions imposed from time to time by the government.

(v) Any act or omission of the consignor or consignee of the goods which in itself occasioned the loss.

(vi) The inherent liability of the goods in question to waste by evaporation, leakage, etc.; or the inherent vice or natural defect of the thing itself.

(vii) Casualty. This term has never been defined but it appears to include accidental fire or explosion, and possibly an entirely unavoidable accident.

Owner's Risk.—The second set of conditions is known as the Owner's Risk Conditions and is contained in Form B; the fare charged is proportionately lower than under Form A to compensate the trader for the increased risk. No goods may be accepted for carriage at this rate unless there is a written request by the consignor to the company to do so.

The company is then not liable for any loss, delay or detention unless it can be proved to have been caused by the wilful misconduct of the company's servants. But it is expressly provided that the company is to be liable (unless it can shew that the loss was not caused by the wilful default of its servants or was due to accident or fire) for the non-delivery of any package which was properly addressed; or for thefts from any package which was properly packed, provided that the attention of the company's servants was drawn to them on arrival, or for misdelivery, where this results in a delay of at least 28 days in the case of ordinary goods, or an unreasonable time in the case of perishables.

Animals.—With regard to the carriage of animals the railway companies have had certain obligations laid upon them by the Board of Trade and the Ministry of Agriculture. As in the case of ordinary goods, there are two sets of conditions, contained in Forms C and D. Under Form C— the Company's Risk Conditions—the company is liable for any loss due to misdelivery, delay, etc., unless this is proved by the company not to have been caused by the neglect or default of its employees; but it is only liable for injury to the animal consigned if the consignor can prove that it was due to their negligence.

Under Form D—the Owner's Risk Conditions—the company's liability is limited to loss which can be shewn to have been caused by wilful misconduct.

Limits on Claims.—The standard conditions also provide that in neither case is the company to be liable for more than £2 in respect of any dog, deer, or goat; 7/6 for any rabbit, bird or poultry; £50 for each head of cattle; £100 for every horse and £5 for any other domestic animal unless a declaration of value was made to the company.

Carriage on Special Terms.—There is nothing to prevent the company from entering into a special contract of carriage with any person, but such a contract falls within the Railways Act of 1854 and must be in writing.

RAILWAY PASSENGERS. — Railway companies are not common carriers of passengers, but though this means that their liability for passengers is not so extensive as in the case of goods, they are not entitled to refuse to carry any person who is ready and willing to pay his fare, unless there is some good reason, such as infectious disease, drunkenness or filth, to justify them. The maximum fare (called the standard fare) which a company is entitled to charge for any particular journey is fixed by a body called the Railway Rates Tribunal; but the company may charge exceptionally low fares. These must be submitted to the Minister of Transport for his approval, and if this is not forthcoming they have to be considered by the Rates Tribunal.

Taking a Ticket.—The legal relationship between a railway company and its passenger depends on the contract into which they have entered and which confers rights and duties on each of them. The ticket which is invariably given to a passenger in return for his fare is not the contract itself, though it is evidence and acts as a receipt. It follows from this that the only person who is entitled to use a ticket is the person for whom, or on whose behalf, it was bought. Nearly all railway tickets are non-transferable and a passenger who has bought his ticket from someone who is not the accredited agent of the company has not entered into a contract with the company at all, and is in exactly the same position as if he had no ticket. The duties of a passenger are fairly simple; he must conform to the company's bye-laws and regulations which are exhibited on boards at every station, and when requested to do so by any servant of the company he must produce and deliver up his ticket. If he is unable for any reason to do so, he must either pay the full fare for the journey he is making or must give his name and address.

If he refuses to do either of these things, the company may arrest him until he can be charged before a magistrate for a breach of the bye-laws. If the address or name is false he may also be arrested, though if he is arrested on suspicion of giving a false name or address and this suspicion turns out to have been unfounded, he can sue the company and get damages for false imprisonment and assault (provided that the servant who ordered his arrest was someone whose duty it was to do so, i.e. a ticket inspector and not a mere porter).

If a passenger has never had a ticket (and this would apply to the case of a man who has bought a non-transferable ticket from a friend), he is bound on demand to pay the fare for his journey; if he refuses to do so he can be ejected—though only of course if the train is stationary. But if he has had a ticket and has only lost it, then he may either pay his fare again or may give his name and address. If he chooses to give his name and address and the company's servants eject him on suspicion of never having paid his fare, he can sue the company.

Passengers' Rights.—The companies are bound to carry the passenger between the places mentioned on the ticket, to allow him to take a certain amount of luggage free of charge for which they assume complete responsibility (*see* PASSENGER; LUGGAGE), and to use all reasonable care to make their premises safe and to prevent the passenger coming to any harm during his journey. Unless there is any special contract to the contrary the latter duty continues even when the passenger is being carried over the lines of another railway.

When a Train is Late.—But a railway company does not bind itself to carry a passenger by any particular train; nor is it bound to run trains at any particular times. If it publishes a time-table, this does amount to a promise that its trains will keep to it, and a passenger who bought his ticket in reliance upon the time-table could sue the company for breach of contract if its train were late; but every company has inserted in its time-tables and in the standard conditions of passenger carriage a clause to the effect that it will not be liable for any loss or delay or any failure to connect with other trains on the same or another line caused by accidental departure from the advertised times. For any delay caused by the wilful misconduct of its servants it would be liable; but the passenger in such a case is only entitled to recover his reasonable expenses directly caused by the delay. Thus, he would probably be able to recover his hotel-bills and perhaps the hire of a car, but he could not claim damages for loss of business or for the curtailment of his holiday.

No Right to a Seat.—Neither does the company undertake when they sell a ticket that there will be a seat or even standing-room for the passenger on any particular train or in any particular class, except in the case of trains departing from main line termini, when it is probably bound to provide additional coaches if necessary; it reserves the right to discriminate between the persons whom it will carry if the accommodation is insufficient, and it states, though without binding itself in any way legally, that it will give preference to persons travelling the greater distances. In the same way, when a company sells a first-class ticket, the purchaser cannot complain if the carriage becomes crowded or if persons with third-class tickets are allowed into it.

Liability for Accidents.—As stated above, the obligation of railway companies towards their passengers is to use reasonable care; they are not liable for accidents caused by *hidden* defects in their rolling stock or permanent way, nor would they be liable for accidents caused by the illness of an employee or the malicious act of a third person. Railway companies are not insurers of passengers (though they are of passengers' luggage [q.v.]) and goods; they are only liable for damage which is the result of the negligence of their employees. Neg-

ligence is acting in an unreasonable way and has been judicially defined as "doing what a reasonable man would not do, or omitting to do what a reasonable man would do." A company will not be liable unless the passenger can prove that the damage is the result of negligence. This is not always easy, but in certain cases the law helps the passenger by laying down a rule which says that if he can shew that the accident which caused the damage was probably the result of negligence, and that the company and its servants are the only people who can really say whether it was so or not, then he is taken to have proved negligence unless the company can shew that in fact there was none. If two trains collide on the same line this rule comes into play, and the company must explain how the accident happened, as it was forced to do where a brick fell from a bridge on to the head of a person underneath.

Platform Tickets.—It has been recognized that many persons come to stations without actually intending to travel—to see their friends off or to meet them. The company is not bound to admit such persons to its premises or platforms and may, if it chooses, charge them a small fee, generally by means of the sale of platform tickets (the law as to these is the same as for ordinary tickets except that the price need not appear on them). Where such a charge is made all persons who pay it are in the same position as if they were passengers, but even where there is no such charge the duties of the company are to all intents and purposes exactly the same.

When Company not Liable.—There is nothing to prevent a passenger from agreeing with the company that the latter's duties are to be cut down, nor need such a contract be in writing. Some such limitation of liability is usually stipulated for in return for the special terms granted for workmen's tickets, excursion tickets and cheap return tickets. No limitation, however, is valid unless the company can shew that the passenger had the option of travelling on payment of a higher fare without any limitation of liability. The company must also shew that any condition limiting their liability was brought to the notice of the passenger. This does not mean that the passenger must be actually told of the existence of the conditions and of its effect; it is enough if they are printed clearly on the back of the ticket or on some handbill and there is some reference to them on the front (as for instance "for conditions see back"). Where this is done, the passenger is presumed to have read and assented to the conditions whether he actually knew of their existence or not; it is not even a defence for him to prove that he cannot read. (*See* PASSENGER; LUGGAGE.)

RAILWAY RATES TRIBUNAL.— This is a body set up by the Railways Act of 1921. It is composed of an experienced lawyer, an experienced business man and an experienced railway official. It has had large powers conferred upon it. It fixes the standard terms and conditions for the carriage of passengers and goods, both by rail and by road, and it has power to alter any exceptional charges or rates which a railway company may make, if they appear to the Minister of Transport to prejudice unduly the interests of others.

RAPE.— Rape is the crime of carnally knowing a woman without her consent. The crime is committed whether effected by force or fraud. The consent of the woman is, of course, a defence to a charge of rape, but this consent must not have been obtained by threats. In the case of a feeble-minded woman a man may be convicted of rape if she was incapable of giving consent. In general, a husband cannot rape his wife. A boy under the age of fourteen is by law regarded as incapable of rape. A man may be convicted of rape if he obtains the consent of a woman by impersonating her husband. Rape is punishable with penal servitude for life.

RATES. — Rates are a Personal Liability.— It is convenient to speak of land or buildings as being rateable, but in fact rates are not a liability attaching to land. It is the occupier who is under a personal liability to pay the rates in respect of the land or buildings that he occupies, and if the rates are not paid, it is he who is in default, and who remains liable for the rates he should have paid. The liability does not attach to the land, so subsequent occupiers cannot be made liable for any outstanding rates.

The Person to be Rated.— Rates must be paid by the occupiers of lands and buildings that are situated in the assessment area. There is now no liability attaching to personal property, and an occupier is, of course, only liable to be rated for lands and buildings that are situated in the particular rating area, and not in respect of all property that he may occupy anywhere. One need hardly say that in the absence of special provisions the liability attaches to all occupiers equally. To discover if there is anyone to be rated in respect of particular premises, it is necessary to discover if there is an occupier.

Occupation.— Anyone who can be described as an occupier in the ordinary sense of the word may be said to be liable. The first important distinction to be kept in mind is that between occupation and ownership. An owner may, or may not, be an occupier, but mere ownership without occupation is not a ground of liability. The owner of premises or land will, of course, be presumed to be also the occupier, but he may be able to shew that someone else is—he may have leased them to a tenant. Also, he may have allowed them to remain vacant. If a house is really left vacant, the owner is not in occupation, and there is no liability, but it is not sufficient for the owner merely to say that he is not in residence. If he keeps the house furnished and ready to occupy whenever he wishes, he will be deemed to be in occupation. But if an owner goes so far as to remove his furniture and exhibits a sign saying that the house is for sale so that the house is genuinely vacant, he will not be deemed to be in occupation.

It may be said that if a servant merely has a house provided for him in order that he may perform his duties as a servant better, then he will only reside there as a servant and the master will be the rateable occupier. If, however, the residence of the servant in that house has no direct connection with the better performance of his duties, but is merely provided incidentally or, for example, by way of part-payment of his wages or salary, then he is the occupier and is rateable. The use of the house must be a use for the master and not merely his own residence in order that the servant may escape liability. A lodger does not occupy his room from the point of view of rating. A tenant of a flat, however, does, and it is difficult in some cases to distinguish between such a tenant and a lodger.

As rateable liability depends on the mere

fact of occupation, no question as to the right or title of the occupier is material, and a trespasser in occupation is under full liability as long as his occupation continues. Title may, of course, become material if the owner wishes to shew that in fact he has leased the premises to a tenant.

As has already been said, a house that is left empty cannot be described as occupied in this connection because it is not occupied as a house. Cases may arise in which an empty house is left with a caretaker in charge of it. The caretaker himself cannot be rated as he is a servant of the owner. In these cases it is the general practice not to rate the owner either. But this exemption from liability will only arise when the house is empty; the owner not having left any furniture in it. Nor must the caretaker be put in for any other reason than to protect the premises.

The Rateable Value of Premises.— It is only when it has been decided that there is an occupier that any enquiry can be made as to the amount that he shall pay. The questions whether anyone is rateable and what the rateable value of premises is, are quite distinct. It is the latter question that must now be considered. The rateable value determines the amount that an occupier must pay in rates. Broadly speaking, the rateable value is arrived at by estimating the rent that the particular house or land would command. One must imagine that it is vacant and then consider the rent a tenant might reasonably be expected to give for it. This amount that a tenant would be willing to pay yearly is the basis of the rateable value. The tenant is taken to be a tenant from year to year. Such a tenant only holds for a period of one year though of course he may continue in occupation for several successive years. But it is important to note that the tenant is not assumed to be holding for a term of years.

Gross Value and Rateable Value.— In practice the rateable value is not arrived at quite so simply. It is necessary in some cases to find what is known as the gross annual value. This is estimated on the basis of the rent that a tenant would be willing to pay, but in making the estimate, it is assumed that the landlord has agreed to bear the cost of repairs and other expenses necessary to keep the premises in such a state that they can command the rent they do, and the insurance. (It is assumed that the tenant will pay the usual tenant's rates and taxes.) In these circumstances, the tenant would be willing or compelled to offer to pay a higher rent. After this gross annual value has been arrived at, varying amounts, that are set out in a schedule to the Rating and Valuation Act, 1925, must be deducted from it.

The Estimated Rent that a Tenant would Pay.— It must be understood that this estimate of rent that a tenant might reasonably be expected to pay is pure rating machinery. In a sense it is an artificial process for the calculation may be made without regard to the existing circumstances. There may be a tenant in occupation of property, but the rent that he pays is not necessarily to be taken as the rateable value. The rent actually paid may be the same as the yearly rent at which the property should be valued but the calculation must always be made.

As this process is based on an imaginary tenant, it makes no difference that the occupier is in fact the owner; the rateable value is still estimated on what rent a tenant might reasonably be expected to pay.

Rateable Value and Profits of a Trade.— It may be that the premises to be rated are used for trading. But it must not be thought that the rateable value is related in any way to the question whether the particular trade is being carried on at a profit or not. As emphasized above the inquiry is solely directed to estimating the rent that an imaginary tenant might pay. The object or motive of a particular tenant in taking the premises makes no difference, and premises are often taken over by occupiers who cannot possibly make any pecuniary profit out of their occupation. A local government board may have to occupy premises at a loss in the discharge of some statutory duty. But the rateable value of premises is a question of fact, and all the surrounding circumstances must be taken into account including anything that might affect the mind of a tenant.

Interest on Cost.— If the property is of such a kind that it will never be let from year to year, some other measure has to be adopted to provide evidence on which the rateable value can be established. This exception to the general rule does not affect the rating of ordinary private property and its scope is limited to buildings like libraries, etc. The annual value of such buildings is arrived at on these lines. The present owners have thought it worth their while to purchase the property for a certain sum. If this sum had been invested, it would have brought in so much a year. They have given up this annual sum in order to buy the property, and this sum is taken to be evidence of the amount of rent that they would have been willing to pay yearly if in fact they had rented the property instead of buying it. As there is no other available evidence, this interest on the cost price is regarded as the rateable value. It is not quite accurate to say that it is the actual cost in these cases; the starting point should be the value of the building, for this may be somewhat lower than the price paid for the building which may have been a bad bargain.

General Rates.—The rating authority can raise the whole of the money that is needed for their expenditure by means of a general rate. After the expenditure for the coming year has been estimated a rate is fixed that will bring in sufficient to meet it. This rate is an amount per pound value of all property in the area. The rateable value is that which is given in the valuation list that is in force at the time of making the rate. A rate comes into force by a resolution being passed by the rating authority approving the amount of the rate and it dates from the passing of the resolution. The rate is then in force for a period of a year or less but the period must always end on the 31st March of each year. If more money is needed a supplementary rate can be approved.

Rating Authorities and Committees.—(a) In an urban rating area the rating authority is the council of the county borough, borough or urban district.

(b) In a rural area the rural district council is the rating authority and each parish council appoints two persons to act with it for matters touching that parish.

(c) There is an assessment committee in every assessment area. County boroughs are usually separate areas. (*See* ASSESSMENT COMMITTEE.)

(d) The county valuation committee.

These have been set up to take every possible step to ensure that rating within their area is carried out on uniform principles.

(e) Similar to the county valuation committees is the Central Valuation Committee for the whole of England and Wales.

Valuation Lists.—The rating authority has to prepare a valuation list containing every property in the area and giving its rateable value and particulars of it. The procedure is to issue notices requiring returns; then from the returns to prepare a draft list, and then to send the draft list to the assessment committee for their approval. Each occupier will be rated in accordance with the rateable value of his property given in the valuation list. All properties must be entered in the valuation list, other than agricultural holdings, even though they are exempted or are at present unoccupied, and so only liable to become rateable in the future.

Rating in the Metropolis.—This requires separate mention as rating in London is regulated by statutes other than those dealing with the country as a whole. The two systems must be distinguished, but the general principles applied are the same although there may be variations in the practice followed. The City of London and every Metropolitan borough is an area with an assessment committee. The rating authority of an area makes and deposits a valuation list, and sends a copy to the surveyor of taxes of the district before it is sent to the assessment committee. There is a right of objection if anything in the list is considered to be unfair or incorrect.

Enforcing Payment of Rates.—After a demand has been made for the payment of rates that are overdue, the rating authority makes a complaint before the justices and takes out a summons. Evidence must be given that the defaulter has neglected to pay for seven days after the demand for payment. A distress warrant will then be issued and the defaulter's goods seized. If there is not sufficient goods, the defaulter may be committed for a period of not more than three months. He will not be committed if the justices are satisfied that the failure to pay is due to circumstances beyond his control; but the justices cannot refuse to issue the distress warrant on account of the poverty of the defaulter.

At the hearing of any of these proceedings before the justices, the person said to be in default can raise objections to the validity of the rate or his assessment, e.g. he can shew that he is not the occupier or that he occupies as a servant. (*See* AGRICULTURAL RATES; ASSESSMENT COMMITTEE.)

RATIFICATION.—One person may enter into a contract or do some act purporting at the time to be acting not on his own behalf but as agent for another. If in fact he has no authority from that other person to do the act, it is possible for the other person at a later time to ratify the act, and when this has been done the effect is exactly the same as if the agent had had authority in the first place. Before an act can be ratified, however, it is necessary that the agent should purport to contract as agent. If he does not state at the time that he is contracting as agent, ratification is not possible. (*See* COMPANIES; PRINCIPAL AND AGENT.)

READING, Lord (1860-).—Starting his career in the City and on the Stock Exchange, Rufus Isaacs found his commercial experience of the greatest value at the Bar, and no one was his equal over a complicated mass of figures. It was said of him that he never made a mistake. As Attorney-General he prosecuted Whitaker Wright and the Seddons. He was made Lord Chief Justice and given the title of the Marquis of Reading.

REAL PROPERTY.—Although the words "real property" are frequently used in a loose sense to include all kinds of ownership of, or rights in, land, their proper meaning is much narrower. They are never used except in connection with land, for the only kind of property that can be "real" is property in land. In their strict sense they denote only a particular class of interests in land, for "real" is synonymous with "freehold" property. (*See* FREEHOLD.) The words real property do not include leasehold interests. A leasehold is the interest which a tenant of land under a lease for a definite period has in that land; it is not real but personal property and therefore in legal parlance it is a chattel. In order, however, to distinguish it from other kinds of personal property and because of its close connection with land, a leasehold is called a chattel real. Real property, there-

Lord Reading.

fore, since it includes all interests in land which are not held under a lease for a period of years, consists of fees simple, fees tail, and estates for life. (*See* FEE; ENTAIL.)

There is no longer any important difference in the rules of law applying to real and personal property. Until quite recently there were several, the most important being that on the death of their owner intestate (without making a will), his real property descended to his eldest son, whereas his personal property was divided equally amongst all his children. Since 1925, however, this has no longer been the case; real property as well as personalty is now so distributed. (*See* INTESTACY.)

REBEL.—A rebel is a person who takes part in a rebellion, i.e. any armed resistance to the Crown in the British Dominions. A rebel is usually guilty of High Treason (q.v.). Any degree of force may be necessary to be used to suppress a rebellion. Rebels who surrender may not be killed but must be brought to trial before the proper tribunals.

REBUTTAL.—When a defendant in a case calls evidence dealing with a fresh matter which the plaintiff could not reasonably foresee, the plaintiff is allowed to call evidence at the close of the defendant's case in reply to the fresh matter proved by the defendant. This evidence is said to be given in rebuttal.

RECEIPT.—A receipt is an acknowledgment that the sum of money set out on it has been paid to the person signing it. If it is for over £2, it must be stamped with a 2d. stamp by the person who gives the receipt. A receipt that is given unstamped may be stamped with an impressed stamp on the following terms: within 14 days on payment of the duty and a penalty of £5; within one month on payment of duty and penalty of £10. A fine of £10 will be incurred by any person who gives an unstamped receipt, refuses to give a stamped receipt, or divides the amount payable with intent to evade the duty. A receipt is not conclusive evidence of payment, though naturally a person who gives a receipt for money without having received it has much to explain and in most cases would have much difficulty in doing so. Strictly speaking, a receipt cannot lawfully be demanded.

RECEIVER.—This is the name applied to a person appointed for the purpose of protecting property from some danger which threatens it, or for the purpose of enabling some creditor to have his debt paid out of some property belonging to the debtor which he cannot seize by any of the ordinary means of legal execution. A Receiver of the last kind is known as a receiver by way of equitable execution.

If two persons are disputing as to which of them is entitled to certain property which is in the possession of one of them, the Court may be asked to take the property out of the possession of the person who now has it and place it in the hands of a receiver until the question of the rights of the parties has been determined.

Where the property in dispute is not goods but money, a receiver will be more readily granted. Further, where none of the parties claiming the property are in possession of it, so that none can claim that he will suffer hardship if a receiver is appointed, the appointment will usually be made.

Receivers may also be appointed in the case of partnerships where the partners are claiming the dissolution of their partnership and where one of them is alleging that the other will waste the partnership assets if they are left in his hands. Another instance where a receiver would be appointed is where a person has become a lunatic or where a trust has lapsed, i.e. where the trustees have all died—and there is no one to look after the property until new trustees have been appointed.

Receivers of Mortgages.—When a person lends money to another on the security of the land belonging to that other, i.e. on a mortgage of the land, he has many remedies for recovering his money should the debtor fail to pay principal or interest. One of these is to appoint a receiver. The receiver will enter into possession of the debtor's property and will collect the rents due on it and pay outgoings. Out of the balance of the money he will hand over to the mortgagee what is due to him and any remaining balance will be handed to the mortgagor.

Receiver for Debenture Holders.—When persons have lent money to a company on the security of debentures, power is usually given to them by the debenture deed to appoint a receiver if the interest on the debenture is in arrear or if the security is otherwise in jeopardy, i.e. if there is a risk that the property over which the debt is secured will be lost. In such cases, the receiver is usually also made a manager and this gives him the power to carry on the business of the company. It is his duty to realise the assets of the company for the benefit of the debenture holders. The effect of his appointment in cases where there is a floating charge (q.v.) is to crystallise the security and make the charge a fixed one.

Receiver Appointed by the Court.—In all cases considered above, except that of the receiver appointed in the case of a mortgage or in the case of a debenture, the appointment of a receiver is made by the Court on some person applying to the Court for that purpose. A receiver appointed by the Court is not considered to be an agent of any person, but is personally responsible for all contracts into which he enters in the course of his duties. He is, of course, entitled to be repaid out of any assets to which his appointment extends, but it may be that in fact these assets are not sufficient to meet the liabilities which he has incurred and in such a case he will have to bear the loss himself.

Receiver Appointed out of Court.—In the case of mortgages and debentures, the mortgagee or debenture holder can, if he wishes, apply to the Court for the appointment of the receiver, but usually he has the power to appoint himself without application to the Court. When he does make that appointment, the person appointed will be in a very different position from the receiver appointed by the Court. In the first place he will only have the powers which are conferred on him by the document giving authority to appoint him, that is, by the mortgage or the debenture. By statute, however, he is entitled to receive and collect the income on the property and to take a commission of 5%.

RECEIVING ORDER.—This is the order made by the Court on a petition presenting to make a debtor bankrupt. It does not deprive the debtor of his property but merely preserves the property until a later adjudication order vests it in a trustee for the creditors of the bankrupt, or the receiving order is discharged. (*See* BANKRUPTCY; TRUSTEE IN BANKRUPTCY.)

RECEIVING STOLEN PROPERTY.—It is a felony punishable with penal servitude for fourteen years to receive stolen property knowing it to have been stolen. The guilty knowledge of the receiver may be proved by inference arising from such facts as his concealment of the goods, paying an extremely low price for them, etc. On an indictment of receiving stolen property on proof that the prisoner had the goods in his possession, the prosecution may prove against him any previous conviction for fraud or dishonesty during the preceding five years.

RECEPTION ORDER.—This is the usual method by which a person who is insane is put under restraint. The order is made by some judicial authority on proof that the person whom it is desired to detain is in fact of unsound mind. (*See* DETENTION OF LUNATICS.)

RECITAL.—The first part of a deed usually sets out in legal language the reasons why the deed is being made. This part is called the recital.

RECOGNIZANCE.—An undertaking to pay the Crown some fixed sum of money unless certain conditions are satisfied. A person who is the prosecutor in a criminal case may be required to enter into a recognizance to appear at the trial. Should he fail to appear he may forfeit the amount set out in the recognizance. Recognizances are also used for the purpose of binding people over to keep the peace or to be of good behaviour; failure to comply with the specified conditions leading to forfeiture of the amounts fixed in each case.

RECORDER.—Judges of borough Quarter Sessions are called Recorders. They are appointed by the Crown from among practising barristers of standing. Their salaries are paid by the boroughs for which they act. As their duties only involve a few days' attendance a year they usually continue in practice after appointment. The Recorder of London is a whole-time appointment, the salary being £4000 a year. He sits at the Central Criminal Court for the trial of criminal cases, and also at the Mayor's and City of London Court to dispose of civil actions. His duties include attendance at various civic functions of the City.

RECTOR.—A rector is a person who is entitled to the tithes (*q.v.*) of a parish; it is possible that such a person should not be in holy orders, and he is then known as a "lay rector." Usually, however, the incumbent of the living is entitled to the tithes.

RED CROSS.—No person may use for the purposes of trade, the words "Red Cross" or "Geneva Cross" or the representation of a red cross on a white ground without the authority of the Army Council, unless he was the registered proprietor of such a trade mark before 1911.

REDEMPTION.—(*See* EQUITY OF REDEMPTION.)

REDENDUM.—In a lease there is a clause under which the landlord reserves to himself a certain rent which the tenant has to pay. This is known as the redendum.

REDUNDANCY LIST.— The licensing justices of a district may decide that there are too many licensed houses in their district, and that it is desirable to decrease the number. They then make a list of certain of the houses which they think are not required. Such houses are said to be redundant, and the list upon which they are placed is called the redundancy list. The justices have not themselves power to take away licences of redundant houses, but when such licences come up for renewal they should renew them provisionally and refer the matter to the Compensation Authority which decides whether their licences are to be taken away or not. (*See* COMPENSATION AUTHORITY; INTOXICATING LIQUOR.)

RE-ENTRY.—In a lease a condition is usually inserted entitling the landlord to re-enter on to premises in the event of the failure by the tenant to pay the rent or perform other obligations of the tenancy. (*See* LANDLORD AND TENANT.)

REFER TO DRAWER.—When a cheque is presented for payment at a bank and there are no funds in the hands of the banker to meet it and no arrangement has been made for an overdraft, the banker on whom the cheque is drawn will usually write the words "Refer to Drawer," or the letters "R.D." on the cheque.

REFEREE IN CASE OF NEED.—This is the person who may be named by the drawer of a bill of exchange by inserting his name on the bill as a person to whom the holder may resort in case of need, that is to say, in case the person named as drawee of the bill fails to accept it or to pay it. The holder is not bound to apply to the referee, but may treat the bill as dishonoured, and the referee is not liable until he has accepted for honour. (*See* BILL OF EXCHANGE.)

REFEREES, COURT OF.—Courts of Referees were constituted to decide claims for Unemployment and Transitional Benefits under the Unemployment Insurance Scheme.

A Court of Referees is composed of a chairman appointed by the Minister of Labour and two other members, one representing employers and one representing insured contributors. Every claim for benefit is first made to an Insurance Officer, and he may decide the claim in favour of the claimant. If, however, he decides against the claimant, he must refer the matter to a Court of Referees.

An appeal lies from the decision of a Court of Referees to an Umpire who is appointed by the Crown. An appeal may be brought by an Insurance Officer or by an Association of employed persons of which the claimant is a member. A claimant may also himself appeal but only if leave to appeal is given by the chairman of the Court of Referees, or if the decision of that Court is not unanimous. (*See also* MEANS TEST; UNEMPLOYMENT INSURANCE.)

REFORMATORY SCHOOLS.—This was the name formerly applied to State schools to which youthful criminals might be sent so that they might be trained for some career and prevented in particular from associating with other criminals and embarking on a life of crime. The best known of these institutions is Borstal. The name Reformatory School has now been abolished and such institutions are now known as Approved Schools.

REFRESHER.—When a case lasts more than one day the counsel engaged in the case are entitled to receive from their clients a further fee beyond the brief fee. This is called a refresher.

REFRESHING MEMORY.—A witness is not in general permitted to read his evidence in a Court of Law. He must speak from his recollection of the incidents he describes. But if he made a note when they were fresh in his memory he may look at this note in order to refresh it. He may only do this if he made the note himself or, if the note was made by someone else, he saw it when the matters were fresh in his memory and then knew it to be correct. Moreover, the note to which he refers must be the actual original note and not some subsequently prepared copy.

REGISTERED MEDICAL PRACTITIONER.—Before any person may practise in this country as a doctor his name must be registered upon the Register kept by the General Medical Council which is the governing body of the medical profession in the United Kingdom. The qualifications for regulation involve the passing of examinations in medicine, surgery and midwifery, generally called "conjoint," and no person is entitled to be registered unless he has qualified in each of these three subjects. Every person who is so qualified is entitled upon sending proof of his qualifications to the Registrar or to a Branch Registrar of the G.M.C. in one or other of the branch districts to have his name entered upon the register together with such other academic qualifications as he may possess. Both men and women may qualify as doctors but no one under the age of 21 may be registered.

A practitioner whose name is struck off the register, though still entitled to practise medicine, falls under all the disadvantages suffered by the quack. (*See* DENTIST; DOCTOR; HEALTH INSURANCE; PANEL.)

REGISTERED POST.—The post office may accept for transmission certain packets by registered post, but it should be understood that whether the package is registered or not there is no legal liability for loss. In practice, however, the Postmaster-General will pay compensation up to but not exceeding £2 for any loss or damage to any unregistered parcel, except in cases where it contained money or jewellery. Where the package is registered, the compensation will be paid even if the package contains money or jewellery, but no more than £5 will ever be paid by way of compensation in respect of actual coin. In any event the amount payable will depend on the registration fee paid at the time of registering, and great care should be taken to make sure that this is sufficient to cover the value of the packet. (*See* POSTAL PACKETS.)

REGISTRAR (COUNTY COURT).—The Registrar in the County Court is responsible for the general conduct of business there, and also sits in Court for the purpose of deciding cases where liability is admitted, or where the amount involved is under £5 and the parties consent. (*See* COUNTY COURT PROCEDURE.)

REGISTRAR GENERAL.—This is the official in charge of the registration of births, deaths and marriages. He is assisted by a local registrar in each district.

REGISTRAR IN BANKRUPTCY.—This official controls to a large extent all the proceedings in bankruptcy. In the High Court special registrars are appointed, and in such County Courts as have bankruptcy jurisdiction, the registrar of the County Court acts as registrar in bankruptcy.

Powers.—All registrars may hear bankruptcy petitions and make receiving orders and adjudication orders. In addition, it is part of their duty to hold a public examination of debtors; to grant orders of discharge where the application is not opposed; to approve compositions or schemes of arrangements when they are not opposed; and to summon and examine any person known or suspected to have in his possession any property of the debtor, or to owe the debtor any money, or to be capable of giving information respecting the debtor his dealings or property. A registrar has no power to commit for contempt of Court but must refer the matter to the Judge with a report of the occasion.

REGISTRAR OF COMPANIES.—This is the official at the head of the department controlling all matters dealing with joint stock companies. Anyone desiring to incorporate a company must take the necessary documents to the registrar who will issue a certificate of incorporation.

He also issues a certificate that the company is entitled to commence business and that all charges, e.g. debentures relating to the company must be registered with him. (*See* COMPANIES.)

REGISTRATION.—The following matters require registration, Bills of sale, births, deaths, marriages; the use of a business name by a trader, almost all matters relating to companies; designs, dentists, doctors, money lenders, patents; matters relating to ships; trade marks, voters, charges on land, and all debentures issued by a company.

REJOINDER.—This is one of the pleadings in an action in which the parties set out the facts upon which they rely. The first pleading is the statement of the claim by the plaintiff to which the defendant files his defence. If there are any matters in the defence which require the plaintiff to file a further pleading, this pleading is known as a reply. If there are any matters in the reply which require the defendant to deliver a further pleading, this further pleading is called a rejoinder.

RELIGIOUS INSTRUCTION.—(*See* EDUCATION.)

REMAINDER.—A remainder is an estate in land which does not entitle its owner to immediate possession of the land, but only confers upon him the possibility of becoming entitled to possession at some unknown time in the future. (*See* PERPETUITIES.)

REMAND. — An adjournment of a criminal charge is in the Police Court described as a remand.

REMITTED ACTION.—Actions which have been commenced in the High Court may, in certain cases, be sent to the County Court for trial. Where the claim is one on contract and is under £100, it will usually be remitted in this way, but where the claim is for damages for tort, e.g. negligence—and it is not therefore possible to say beforehand how much money the plaintiff will recover if he succeeds, the action will be remitted only if the defendant can prove that the plaintiff would not have enough money to pay the costs of the defendant should he, the plaintiff, lose the action. If the plaintiff can give some security for the costs, the action will not be remitted.

RENEWAL OF JUSTICES' LICENCES.—Justices' licences are either granted for a year running from the 5th April next after the grant, or for a term of years. If for a term of years the licence will require a re-grant at the end of the term, but if an annual licence, it will require only to be renewed at the end of the year. This is a formal matter and no notice need be given by the applicant, nor need he attend, though he should apply by letter, unless he has been served with grounds of opposition when it is, of course, advisable to attend. The justices can only refuse to renew a licence on certain specified grounds depending on the nature of the licence. (*See* INTOXICATING LIQUOR.) If they think the renewal should be refused on any other ground, then they should refer the matter to the Compensation Authority.

RENOUNCE.—This is the technical term used to indicate the act of an executor named in a Will who refuses to accept the office. He is said to renounce probate. (*See* COMPANIES.)

RENT.—Rent is a payment due at stated periods in respect of land. Rent need not necessarily, but to-day usually does, consist of the payment of money. (*See* LANDLORD AND TENANT; SPECIAL SUPPLEMENT "RENT RESTRICTIONS.")

RENT CHARGE.—A rent is a sum of money which is payable at regular intervals in respect of a particular plot of land, and the payment of which can be enforced by the re-entry on to that land of the person, called the proprietor, to whom the rent is payable.

Kinds of Rent.—There are two kinds of rents; rent services and rent charges.

Rent service is the legal name for all rents which are payable to a person who still retains some interest in the land in respect of which it is paid in addition to his right of re-entry. The commonest form of rent service is the rent paid by a tenant to his landlord.

A rent charge is a rent which is payable to a person who has no interest in the land except the rent itself. They are sometimes created by settlements, but it is more usual for them to be set up on the sale of the land. Instead of demanding a lump sum price from the purchaser the vendor stipulates for a rent charge.

If a rent charge is not paid, the proprietor has the right after forty days to re-enter and take possession of the land in order to raise the amount of the rent charge by taking any income which may accrue. He may not, however, sell. It is also possible in the same circumstances for the proprietor to hand the whole property over to a trustee by a lease. The trustee will then be able to mortgage or assign the lease in order to raise the necessary money. Lastly, in addition, of course, to bringing an action for the rent, the proprietor may distrain upon the land like a landlord. (*See* DISTRESS.)

REPAIRS.—In England a landlord is not bound to repair premises let by him (except in the one case mentioned below) unless he has made an agreement with his tenant binding him to do so. The exception arises where the house is let at a rent per annum not exceeding, in the case of a house in the county of London, £40 and, in the case of a house elsewhere, £56. In this case it is not possible for the landlord to provide by the terms of the tenancy that he shall not be liable for repairs. These provisions, however, do not apply where the house is let for a period of not less than three years upon the terms that it be put by the lessee into a condition reasonably fit for habitation, and the lease is not determinable at the option of either party before the end of three years. The landlord may at reasonable times of the day on 24 hours' notice in writing enter the premises to view the state of repair.

In Scotland the landlord is under a higher duty with regard to repairs than in England. He must keep the house wind and water tight and in reasonable repair, having regard to the locality. In most cases this obligation may be altered by agreement, but in cases corresponding to those mentioned above with regard to England, the landlord cannot escape these obligations by any agreement. (*See* LANDLORD AND TENANT.)

REPARATION (SCOTS LAW).—When any person has committed a wrongful or negligent act and has thereby caused damage, the party who has suffered the damage is entitled to claim reparation. The word, therefore, is equivalent to the duty in English law of paying damages when a tort has been committed. To a very large extent, the law of Scotland in this matter is the same as that of England. The most important exception is that the rule of English law by which no action can be brought for damages which have caused the death of any person except in special cases has no application in Scotland. Further, the law as to defamation differs considerably in the two countries.

REPEAL.—One Act of Parliament may have the effect of cancelling another previous one or part of it. When this happens, the earlier one or the part in question is said to be repealed. Repeal may either be expressly provided for in the repealing act or it may be the natural inference to be drawn from the new provisions.

REPLEVIN.—This is the name given to an action which a tenant may bring for the purpose of recovering the actual goods taken in distress when the distress is wholly illegal. (*See* DISTRESS.)

REPLY.—A Reply is a document in which the plaintiff, in an action in the High Court, replies to the contentions raised by the defendant in his defence (q.v.) or to the Counterclaim put forward by the defendant. (*See* HIGH COURT PROCEDURE; PLEADINGS.)

REPRIEVE.—A reprieve is the postponement of the carrying out of a sentence passed by a court in the exercise of criminal jurisdiction. In practice the word is confined to sentences of death. In the United Kingdom the right of reprieve is that of the Crown.

REPUTATION.—The law recognizes that a person's good name is an asset which he is entitled to have protected against attacks, and therefore it has enabled him to bring an action for slander or libel if statements are made against him injurious to his reputation. (*See* SLANDER; PRIVILEGE; DEFAMATION.)

REPUTED OWNERSHIP. — In bankruptcy where one person allows another to use the goods of the first person in his business in such a way that persons dealing with him will think the goods are his own property, the goods are said to be in the reputed ownership of the person using them, and the lender will not be allowed to claim them back should the person to whom he has lent them go bankrupt. This rule only applies to goods which are used in a business and not, for example, to furniture which is used in a private house. Further, if there is a recognized custom in the business that persons who carry it on should use goods belonging to others the rule will not apply, for persons dealing with them will be presumed to have known of it, and so not to have been misled. (*See* BANKRUPTCY; TRUSTEE IN BANKRUPTCY.)

REQUISITIONS ON TITLE.— These are the questions which are submitted in writing by the purchaser's solicitor to the vendor's solicitor after the latter has delivered to the former the abstract of title (which is the epitomized history of the documents and facts proving that the vendor is the owner and has the right to sell in accordance with his contract). These questions arise from the consideration by the purchaser's solicitor of the Abstract of Title and the investigations he makes in verification of the matters there set out. The various questions are set out on the left half of sheets of foolscap and are numbered consecutively. They are sent to the vendor's solicitor who writes his "Replies to Requisitions on Title" opposite the respective requisitions and returns the document to the purchaser's solicitor. The Contract of Sale usually specifies the time after the delivery of the Abstract of Title that the requisitions must be delivered and the replies sent. Unless such times are extended by agreement they must be adhered to, or they may prejudice the sale going through, or a proper investigation of the title. (*See also* SALE OF LAND; MORTGAGES.)

RES GESTÆ.—A statement which is made at the time of the occurrence in respect of which a trial takes place, and which is inseparably part of the occurrence, is termed part of the res gestæ and may be given in evidence. The rules of evidence in general reject testimony as to statements made in the absence of an accused person or opposite party, but, in the circumstances outlined above, such evidence is admissible. For instance, in a case arising out of an accident on the road, the cries of onlookers just before the accident would be admissible in evidence even though the drivers of the vehicles could not have heard them.

RES IPSA LOQUITUR.—This is a Latin expression meaning "the thing speaks for itself."

It is a maxim in English law that where something has happened which could not, on the face of it, happen normally without negligence on the part of the defendant, a plaintiff need prove only the happening of the thing itself. This is contrary to the usual rule which requires a plaintiff who alleges negligence to prove it. Where the maxim applies, it is for the defendant to shew that the event complained of happened without his negligence.

RES JUDICATA.—In order that a person may not be put continually to the expense of defending his rights, the law lays down that once a matter has been decided it is res judicata—"a matter on which judgment has been given." If any further action is brought on a matter which is res judicata, the Court will refuse to entertain it.

RESCISSION.—When two persons have made a contract, the contract may be put an end to, i.e. rescinded, in several ways. Firstly, the parties may agree each to give up his rights, and secondly, one party may be entitled, without the consent of the other, to repudiate the contract and have an order made by the Court for its rescission. This will arise where the party applying has been induced to enter into the contract by fraud, i.e. by some untrue statement of the other party. Rescission, however, will only be ordered in cases where the parties can be put back into the same position as they were before they made the contract.

RESERVE PRICE.—When property is put up for sale by auction, it may be sold either with or without reserve. When a reserve has been fixed, the amount of it is not made known before the auction, and each bid is therefore made conditionally on it being above the reserve price. If in fact the reserve price is not reached, no sale takes place. (*See* Upset Price.)

RESIDUARY LEGATEE. — When a man makes a will he frequently gives gifts of his personal property to various persons and thereafter leaves the rest of his property to some other person. Thus a man might give £100 to A "my motor-car to B, my shares to C and the rest of my personal property to D." D will hereupon be the residuary legatee. If a person does not appoint a residuary legatee, he will be considered to be intestate so far as the property not specifically dealt with in his will is concerned, and that property will go to the persons entitled on intestacy. The residue of property may be left to two or more residuary legatees. If half the property is left to A and the other half to B, and the gift to A lapses, e.g. he dies before the testator, B does not take all the property. The half which A would have had is distributed according to the rules of intestacy.

RESISTING ARREST.—Any person who resists lawful arrest by a police constable, or who assists another in resisting arrest, may be punished by a fine not exceeding £5, or imprisonment for not more than one month. Where resistance amounts to an assault, the fine may amount to £20, and the imprisonment to six months.

RESOLUTION.—A resolution is the expression of agreement on some matter by some majority of the persons present at a public meeting.

RESPITE.—This is the term applied to the postponement of a case from one session to a future one at Assizes or Quarter Sessions.

RESPONDENT.—When a case is brought before a superior Court on appeal, the party appealing is called the appellant and the other the respondent. The term respondent is also applied to defendants in divorce cases.

RESTAURANTS. — Restaurants are subject to the ordinary law as to the sale of intoxicating liquor, and will therefore require a justices' licence for such sales of intoxicants as a justices' licence is ordinarily required. They are also, of course, subject to the provisions of the Licensing Act, 1921, relating to permitted hours, and must not sell intoxicants outside such hours. The keeper of a restaurant will not be disqualified from receiving a licence because his premises are not a dwelling-house or because he does not live on the premises. He will also be entitled to receive a one hour extension on the permitted hours if the justices, being satisfied that his premises are bona fide for the purpose of supplying food to which the sale of intoxicants is ancillary, decide to grant such an extension. Ordinary public houses are not entitled to such an extension.

Drinking in Railway Restaurant Cars.—These do not require a justices' licence and are not subject to the permitted hours. A licence is, however, required on which the duty is £1 per annum. Such a licence granted in respect of a car in which passengers can be supplied with meals authorizes the sale by retail to passengers on the car of any intoxicating liquor for consumption in the car. (*See* PERMITTED HOURS; INTOXICATING LIQUOR.)

RESTITUTION OF CONJUGAL RIGHTS.—Any person whose husband or wife has deserted him or her may proceed by petition on the Probate, Divorce or Admiralty Division of the High Court of Justice for a decree for Restitution of Conjugal Rights.

On proof that the petitioner has been deserted without due cause, the Court may make an order requiring him or her to return to the petitioner within a time fixed by the Court. Disobedience of such an order entitles the petitioner to a decree of Judicial Separation on the ground of desertion. There is no power to enforce the order by making the party against whom it is directed return to cohabitation. (*See* SPECIAL SUPPLEMENT "DIVORCE.")

RESTITUTION OF PROPERTY.—If a thief is convicted of stealing or certain similar offences, the Court before whom he is tried may order the return to the owner of any property in respect of which he has been convicted. If property under such an order is taken from an innocent purchaser, the Court may compensate him out of any money found on the prisoner when arrested. There is a special provision in the case of stolen property which has been pawned. In making an order directing a pawnbroker to return to the owner stolen property received in pledge, the Court may, if it thinks fit, impose the condition that the owner shall pay to the pawnbroker the amount of the advance or a part of it. Whenever the police have received any property and there is a dispute as to who is the rightful owner, the police or any person claiming to be entitled to it may apply to a Court of summary jurisdiction for

an order as to its disposal. At the hearing of such an application all claimants are entitled to call evidence in support of their claims.

RESTRAINT OF MARRIAGE.—When property is left by will or settlement, conditions are sometimes imposed governing the marriage of the person for whom the property is left. The law does not, however, allow completely unrestricted discretion in such matters. It is regarded as contrary to public policy to make a person have to choose between forfeiting property and not marrying at all. Therefore any condition alienating property, if the beneficiary marries, is void and of no effect. But there is no objection to provide for forfeiture if he or she marries a particular person or even one of a class of persons, such as adherents of a particular form of religious belief.

RESTRAINT ON ANTICIPATION.—This is a device which has for long been used for the protection of married women. Where property is settled upon a married woman in trust, provision may be made in the trust instrument to prevent her from anticipating the income derived from it. The effect of this is that any contracts made by her cannot be enforced against future instalments of her income. Thus, if a married woman whose property is protected in this way orders goods and refuses to pay for them, her creditors cannot seize in execution any of the trust property, or any instalments of income not due at the time of ordering the goods.

RESTRAINT OF TRADE.—The law takes the view that every person should be given a reasonable opportunity to earn his living in the occupation for which he is most fitted, and a contract which restricts unreasonably a man's right to do this is illegal.

It is not easy to say what is, and what is not, a reasonable restriction. The question generally arises either when a man sells the goodwill of his business or when an employee of a firm enters their employment. In such a case it is usual for the seller of the goodwill or the employee to enter into an agreement not to carry on the same trade within a certain radius of his previous business or his previous employment. The rule is that any contract which restricts a man in any way from carrying on a trade or profession is illegal unless one of the parties to the contract can shew that the contract was both in the interest of the contracting parties and in the interest of the public.

Where an employee, however, enters into an agreement restricting his right to gain new employment, the test as to what is reasonable is much more strictly applied, and as a general rule an agreement by an employee not to serve another employer will be illegal unless it is restricted both as to the kind of employer whom he cannot serve, the area in which the restriction applies, and the time for which it applies.

This, of course, has nothing to do with an agreement not to pass on trade secrets or not to tout for the customers of his former employers, both of which agreements are always reasonable. (*See* CONTRACT; ILLEGAL CONTRACTS; TRADE UNIONS.)

RESTRICTIVE COVENANTS.— A restrictive covenant is an undertaking by an occupier of land not to do a particular act, i.e. not to build upon a particular spot, or not to carry on a particular or an offensive trade. Such covenants are frequently inserted into leases in order to prevent the tenant from lowering the tone of the neighbourhood. It is also common to find a covenant by the lessee that he will not assign without the leave of his landlord. The landlord must not withhold his consent unreasonably, and if he does so the lessee should proceed with the assignment. If the tenant assigns the lease, the assignee will himself be bound by any covenants contained in it; if he breaks them, the landlord can sue him for damages. But the landlord can also sue the original tenant, for nothing that he can do can relieve him of his original liability. If, instead of assigning the lease, the tenant were to make a sub-lease, the sub-lessee would not be bound by the covenants contained in the original lease, but the lessee would remain bound.

On Sale.— Restrictive covenants may also come into being on the sale of land. They are usually required by speculative builders who are developing residential estates. The person who actually covenants is, of course, bound by any such covenant and so are his heirs and representatives; but if he sells or transfers the land to a third person, that third person will only be bound

to observe the covenant if it is negative, that is, if it is an undertaking not to do something. An undertaking to do a positive act can be enforced against the person who actually gave it, but it cannot be enforced against persons into whose hands the land to which it relates may subsequently come by sale or gift. Negative covenants can be enforced against anybody who becomes entitled to the occupation of the property to which they relate unless he can shew that he knew nothing about them when he bought the land.

RETAINER.— The effect of giving a retainer to a person is to secure the services of that person. The word is most frequently used in the case of a solicitor or barrister.

Solicitors.— By giving the retainer to a solicitor the client gives him authority to act on his behalf and to bind him, and this authority will be sufficient to render the client liable for acts done or contracts made by the solicitor with third parties on the client's behalf. The retainer need not be in writing unless it is bound to continue for more than a year, but if given by a limited company or other corporation, it should be given under the seal of the company.

Barristers.— A retainer may be given to a barrister by a solicitor on behalf of a client. When the retainer is given, the barrister undertakes impliedly not to take a brief from the opponent but to act on behalf of the person retaining him. (*See* BARRISTER; SOLICITOR.)

RETAINER (EXECUTORS).— An executor to whom the deceased person owes money is entitled to pay himself out of assets before other creditors, except secured or preferred creditors, and this right is called his right of retainer.

REVERSION.— Where a person has let his land to another, he becomes the "Lessor" and the person taking the Lease, the "Lessee." The interest comprised in the lease, that is to say the period for which it is let and the conditions of the letting, form an "Estate" which is carved out of lessor's interest or "Estate" in the land. The lessor retains a certain right over the land during the continuation of the lease, including the right to have the land back free of the lease at the termination thereof in law. This right retained by the lessor is called the "Reversion." (*See* LANDLORD AND TENANT.)

REVOCATION OF APPOINTMENT.

MENT.—Where a person is given a power of appointment relating to certain property, the power may be either revocable or irrevocable. If it is irrevocable, the person exercising it must do so once and for all, i.e. he cannot make an appointment and then change his mind. (*See* POWER OF APPOINTMENT.)

REWARD.—It is illegal to offer a reward for the return of stolen or lost property if any suggestion is made that no questions will be asked. And it is a felony for anyone to accept any reward offered unless he has used his best endeavours to cause the thief to be arrested and tried.

Where a reward is offered for information leading to the arrest of a thief, the person who supplies such information can maintain an action for the amount against the person who offered it.

RIDER.—A rider is an addition made to a verdict by a jury. It is not uncommon for coroner's juries to add riders to their verdicts. A coroner's jury's verdict should be confined strictly to the cause of death, but a rider deals with such matters as praise or blame attaching to individuals connected with the fatality, and suggestions for the prevention of future accidents.

RIDING.—A person mounted on a horse has, of course, no greater right to pass over other people's land than a foot passenger. A horseman may not ride on any footpath reserved for the use of foot passengers. Contravention of this provision renders an offender liable to a fine not exceeding forty shillings. Riding to the common danger is punishable by a fine not exceeding £5.

RIGHT OF WAY.—A right of way is a right enjoyed by the public of using the land of another either as a carriage way, bridle way or footpath. Any road or way subject to such a right is called a highway (q.v.). The signs frequently seen on private property to the effect that "Trespassers will be prosecuted" are intended merely to shew that persons who enter the property do so against the wishes of the owner and so cannot, by using the path, establish a right of way. (*See* HIGHWAYS; TRESPASSERS WILL BE PROSECUTED.)

RING-DROPPING.—This is a form of confidence trick. The trickster produces to a passer-by a ring, which he says he has just picked up. He offers to deposit it with his victim if the latter will hand him some money as security. If the victim is foolish enough to agree, the trickster departs and needless to say the ring turns out to be quite valueless. The practice is, of course, a criminal one and is punishable as larceny by a trick. (*See* LARCENY.)

RINGING THE CHANGES.—This is a method of stealing money. The thief enters a shop and makes some small purchase, for which he tenders a note or silver coin. When change is given to him, he so manipulates it that the shopkeeper does not notice that the thief is getting in change not merely the change he is entitled to, but all, or part of, the money he has tendered. This is, of course, punishable as larceny. (*See* LARCENY.)

RIOT.—A riot is a tumultuous disturbance of the peace by three or more persons who are assembled together with the intention of helping each other against anyone who may oppose them in some enterprise, and who have actually started to carry out their enterprise in a violent manner to the terror of persons in the neighbourhood. To take part in a riot is a misdemeanour punishable with a fine and imprisonment for not more than two years.

The Riot Act.—This Act was passed in 1714 but is of great practical importance to-day. (*See* SPECIAL SUPPLEMENT "THE POLICE.")

RIVERS.—The law relating to rivers is, of course, extensive, and, in view of its exceptionally complicated nature, it is not intended to deal with it here in detail. In the first place, it should be remembered that nobody owns the water flowing in a river, for, if any person (e.g. a person owning land on the banks of the river, known as a "riparian owner") used the water for his own purposes and thereby injured its flow or its quality, persons entitled to use the same river lower down would have a legal cause of complaint.

A river may become a public highway, and most tidal navigable rivers are highways as far up as the effect of the tide is felt, the river-bed belonging usually to the Crown. The fact that a tidal river is a highway does not authorize landing on parts of its shores except where a customary landing place exists, or in the event of necessity; nor, similarly, is there necessarily a right to walk along the banks for towing. Every riparian owner is entitled to access to the water. Non-tidal rivers are in a similar position, except that (i) there is no absolute legal right to navigate, but the water must have been expressly or impliedly "dedicated" for use as a highway in the same way as right of way over land must be dedicated (see RIGHT OF WAY); after a long period of public navigation on a river, therefore, it becomes a public highway, and the same result follows if the river was originally made navigable at the public expense; (ii) the ownership of the bed of the river usually belongs to the riparian owners up to an imaginary line drawn half-way between the opposite banks.

ROAD.—A road may be either private or public. A private road is one which the public have no right to use, whereas a public road is a highway (q.v.). Another division of roads is into county roads and ordinary roads. County roads include all the "main roads." This division is important in determining on whom falls the liability for repair. County roads are repaired at the expense of the County Council. (See HIGHWAYS; RIGHT OF WAY; "TRESPASSERS WILL BE PROSECUTED.")

ROAD FUND.—This was established by the Roads Act, 1920. It is made up of all licensing duties for motor vehicles levied by the County Councils, and also a proportion of the fines for motoring offences. (See HIGHWAYS.)

ROAD SERVICE LICENCE.—This is a licence required under the Road Traffic Act for public service vehicles. (See SPECIAL SUPPLEMENT "ROAD TRAFFIC.")

ROBBERY.—Strictly speaking, robbery is confined to stealing from a person with violence. It is the use of violence that distinguishes robbery from ordinary larceny. The violence may be committed immediately before or at the time of, or immediately after the stealing. It need not consist of an actual "Battery." (See BATTERY.)

Any treatment or violence or other conduct which puts the person robbed in fear is sufficient to constitute robbery.

Robbery is punishable with penal servitude for a period of not more than fourteen years, or imprisonment for not more than two years, with or without hard labour.

ROE, RICHARD.—The second of two fictional names formerly used to effect the transfer of land. (See DOE, JOHN.)

ROGUE AND VAGABOND.—Anyone found to be a rogue and vagabond may be sentenced to imprisonment for not more than three months or to pay a fine not exceeding £25.

Persons convicted of a variety of offences are deemed in law to be rogues and vagabonds and punishable as such. Examples of such offences are: betting in public places, being found in enclosed premises for an unlawful purpose and unlawful fortune telling.

ROMAN CATHOLICS.—No Roman Catholic can occupy the throne, nor can he become Lord Chancellor. Apart from this, Roman Catholics are now under no disability, save that they cannot obtain or confer preferment in the Church of England. Roman Catholic clergy may not sit in the House of Commons but may, if otherwise qualified, sit in the House of Lords. Every priest must register himself with the clerk of the peace of any district where he intends to perform ecclesiastical functions (fee, 6d.).

ROOT OF TITLE is the first document or fact and earliest in date dealt with in the Abstract of Title on a sale of land and certain interests in land. The abstract of title is an epitome of the documents and facts constituting the seller, or "Vendor's" right to the land and to sell. It is prepared by the vendor's solicitor. (See also SALE OF LAND; MORTGAGES; LANDLORD AND TENANT.)

ROULETTE.—Roulette is an unlawful game in England—unlawful, not in the sense that the mere playing of it is a punishable offence, but through the effect in law that it produces on premises in which it is played. If any building or place is kept or used for the purpose of roulette, or indeed of any other unlawful gaming, the persons conducting or responsible for the premises and their assistants may be convicted under the Gaming House Act, 1854, and fined a sum not exceeding £500. But it should be noted that an essential ingredient of this offence is the keeping of the premises for the unlawful gaming. The mere playing on an isolated occasion on private premises of an unlawful game does not constitute a "keeping" of the premises for unlawful gaming. (*See* SPECIAL SUPPLEMENT "GAMBLING.")

ROUT.—This is a disturbance of the peace by an assembly of persons who intend to do something amounting to a riot and who have started out on the way to effect their purpose but have not yet executed it. It is really an incomplete riot. (*See* RIOT.)

ROYAL ASSENT.—Before any bill passed by both Houses of Parliament can become law it must receive the Royal Assent, that is, the assent of the Crown. In practice to-day this assent is never refused. It is given either by the King in person or by commissioners appointed for that purpose.

ROYAL MARRIAGE.—Certain restrictions are imposed on the freedom of marriage of the Royal family, thus the King cannot marry a Roman Catholic on penalty of forfeiting the Crown. Again, no member of the Royal family and indeed no descendant of King George II may marry under the age of 25 or without the consent of the King, and any marriage taking place without this consent is void.

ROYAL WARRANT HOLDER.—Many tradesmen exhibit on their premises or notepaper a copy of the Royal Arms with a statement to the effect that they are "Under Royal Patronage." It is not every tradesman from whom a member of the Royal Family makes some purchase that is entitled to use the Royal Arms in this way, and it is necessary for the tradesman before using these arms to receive authority to do so. Any person who, without authority, uses the arms is liable to a fine of £50, and any person who falsely represents that goods are made by a person holding a Royal Warrant, or for the service of the King or any member of his family, or for a Government department is liable to a penalty of £20.

ROYALTIES.—Royalties are percentage or piece payments made as the consideration for the right to use some other person's property, e.g. an author of a novel usually receives 10%—25% on the published price of each volume sold. But the amount of a royalty depends in all cases, of course, upon the terms agreed between the parties (with one exception in the law of copyright, *see* COPYRIGHT).

RULE ABSOLUTE.—In proceedings in which the first step is the application for a rule nisi, the ultimate order made if the Court

Lord Russell of Killowen.

on hearing both sides decides in favour of the applicant, will be to make the order absolute. Such a rule is known as a rule absolute. (*See* RULE NISI.)

RULE NISI.—When certain remedies are required, the procedure by which they are obtained is for the person desiring them to apply to a Court—usually a Divisional Court of the King's Bench Division—asking for an order that a certain person or persons should be required to shew cause, i.e. to appear and argue before the Court, why the remedy should not be granted. The application to the Court is usually made in the first place ex parte, i.e. no notice is given to the persons against whom the order is desired of the intention to make the application. If the Court thinks, on hearing only what the applicant has to say, that there are some grounds for making the order, it will grant the rule nisi. Thereafter the case will again come up for hearing when the persons against whom the order has been made will appear and will argue that it should not be made absolute, i.e. should not be made at all. If the Court thinks that the order should be made it makes the rule absolute, that is, it orders the persons to do what the original applicant desired them. (*See* PREROGATIVE WRITS.)

RULE OF COURT.—When parties agree to submit to arbitration or to the award of an arbitrator, the submission or reward may be made a rule of Court. This takes place when the Court makes an order that the submission or award shall be conclusive.

RULES OF COURT.—It is necessary to make rules and regulations controlling the procedure of actions in the Court, and in the High Court these rules are made by a Special Rule Committee consisting of Judges, which is established under the authority of the Judicature Acts. The rules are frequently revised and are published with a very large amount of notes on cases relating to them in two annual non-official publications known popularly among Lawyers as the White Book and the Red Book respectively. Similar rules are also made for controlling procedure in the County Courts under the authority of a Committee of County Court Judges and made by the Lord Chancellor.

RUNNING DOWN CASE.—This is the name commonly applied by lawyers to actions arising out of collisions between vehicles or between a vehicle and a pedestrian. (*See* ACCIDENT; COLLISION.)

RURAL DEAN.—A rural deanery is a collection of parishes for administrative purposes within an archdeaconry. It is presided over by a rural dean. (*See* DEAN.)

RURAL DISTRICT COUNCIL.—The rural district was originally a sanitary district, but has assumed more extensive importance as a result of subsequent legislation. The district is governed by the Rural District Council, for the constitution and duties of which, *see* LOCAL GOVERNMENT.

RUSSELL, Lord, of Killowen (1832–1900).—He shone equally as an advocate and on the Bench. A tall handsome man, his cross-examination was both masterly and terrible. He represented Parnell before the Commission that considered the Pigott forgeries, defended Mrs. Maybrick, and prosecuted Adelaide Bartlett.

SACRILEGE.—This is the crime of breaking into a place of worship and committing any felony inside, or breaking out after having committed any felony inside. Any person may arrest without warrant anyone committing sacrilege. It is a felony punishable with penal servitude for life.

SALE, BILL OF.—(*See* BILL OF SALE.)

SALE OF GOODS.—One of the most common contracts entered into in every-day life is for the sale of goods and the law relating to this transaction has now been codified in the Sale of Goods Act, 1893.

What is a Sale of Goods?—A contract for the sale of goods may take either of two forms. It may be a "sale," in which case the seller at once transfers the ownership of the goods sold to the buyer, or it may be an "agreement to sell," in which case the seller undertakes to transfer the ownership of the goods to the buyer at some future time. "Goods" includes all chattels, that is, things which can be moved and can be touched—such as chairs, motorcars—except money. The goods may be in existence at the time of the contract, or they may be known as "future goods," that is, goods which the seller has to manufacture or acquire after the making of the contract. There would be a contract for the sale of future goods where a tailor agreed to make a suit for a customer.

A difficulty sometimes arises in determining whether a transaction is a sale of goods or a contract for work and materials, that is, one under which one person undertakes to carry out some work for another, using his own materials, e.g. a contract to put a new leg on to a chair with wood to be supplied by the person doing the work. This distinction is of great importance in English law and the test usually applied is that, whatever may be the value of the work or materials, the contract is regarded as a sale if the parties in entering into it contemplate that a chattel will ultimately be handed over by one to the other.

In one famous case a dentist agreed to make a set of teeth to fit the mouth of a patient and this was held to be a contract for the sale of goods and not a contract for work and materials, although the dentist had to make the teeth, because the parties intended that the dentist should deliver to the patient a chattel—that is to say, a set of teeth.

When Contract Must be in Writing.

—The importance of this distinction in English law is that where the contract is for the sale of goods over £10 in value and not for work and materials, it cannot be enforced (except in certain cases) unless there is some "evidence in writing," that is, a written document setting out its terms and signed by the party who is liable on it. Accordingly, if A agrees by word of mouth to sell B his motor-car for £100, when A brings the motor-car to B, B may refuse to take it and A cannot compel him to do so. It is important to notice, however, that this rule does not apply and the contract may be enforced if the buyer "accepts" part of the goods sold, and receives them or gives some money either in earnest or in part payment of the price.

The acceptance will be made when the buyer does anything to the goods which recognizes a pre-existing contract of sale, that is, something which he would not have done if there had not been a contract in existence. It is not necessary that he should take and keep the goods under the contract, although if he does so, there would be no difficulty in suing him for the price. If, in the case imagined above, B, when A brought the car for delivery, had looked at it and used it to go to business and had then said he would not take it—not because it was defective but merely because he had changed his mind—A would be able to sue B for the money, for B would have accepted the car. He would not have taken it and driven it away unless he had arranged to buy it.

Price Must be Money.

—Goods cannot be sold unless the person buying them has to pay money for them, and if he has not to pay money but has to give some other goods in exchange, the contract is "barter," or "exchange," and not for sale. The price may be either fixed by the contract—e.g. where a car is bought for £20—or fixed in a manner specified by the contract—as where a person buys iron at the highest market price quoted at that date—or it may be determined by the course of dealing between the parties—as where they were in the habit of selling goods to one another at cost price plus a certain percentage.

It is open to the parties in a sale to make any terms which they like, but the law lays down certain terms which are to be implied in the sale unless the parties have clearly stated that they wish these terms to be excluded from their bargain.

Conditions and Warranties.

—It is necessary here to distinguish between what the law calls a condition and a warranty. Both of these are stipulations or promises in the contract, but a condition is considered to be more essential and vital than a warranty, so that if a condition is broken by the seller, the buyer is entitled not merely to claim damages but to refuse to take the goods or to pay the price, and if he has paid it he may recover it back. A warranty, however, is a stipulation which is not considered to be so vital, and if the seller breaks such a stipulation, the buyer cannot send the goods back but must take them, and sue the seller for the damages which have been suffered through the warranty not having been kept.

It is very difficult to lay down abstract rules as to when a term is a condition and when it is a warranty. It makes no difference that the parties in the contract may have set the term out and called it a "warranty," for it may yet be so vital as to be a condition and treated as such by the Court. It is purely a question of degree. Thus if, when a car was sold, it was a term of the contract that it had new tyres and this term was broken, the law would not treat that as a condition entitling a purchaser to refuse to take the car but would compel him to take it, allowing him to claim as damages the cost of a new set of tyres from the seller. If, however, the term was that the car had six cylinders and it actually had only four, the buyer would be entitled to return the car as this would be considered so vital as to be a condition.

Can Goods be Sent Back?

—When there is a condition which has been broken the buyer is not *bound* to refuse to take the goods but may keep them and sue for damages, and this is known as treating the condition as a warranty or "waiving the condition." Moreover, where a condition has been broken the buyer must make up his mind at once whether or not he intends to keep the goods, for if he keeps them in such circumstances as to indicate that he is prepared to take them as being the goods he ordered, he will not be allowed to return them later, but will be left to sue for damages in respect of them.

Implied Terms.—There are certain conditions implied by the law in every agreement of sale even though nothing is said. It should, however, be remembered that the parties may expressly provide in their contract that these conditions shall not apply. They must, however, do this very clearly. It should be pointed out that although these implied terms are conditions and entitle the buyer to reject the goods, he is also entitled to treat the terms as warranties and claim damages instead of rejecting.

The first is that the seller has a right to sell the goods, and if afterwards it turns out that he was not entitled to do so (e.g. that they were not his property but were only on hire purchase), the buyer may repudiate the contract and claim back his money even though the seller at the time of the sale did not say in so many words: "the goods belong to me and I can sell them." It is implied. The fact that he has been using the goods for some time will not affect his right to return them, so long as he does so as soon as he finds out that the condition has been broken.

Goods Must Answer to Description. —When goods are sold by description by a seller who deals in goods of that description, there is an implied condition that they shall correspond with the description. Thus, where A buys 100 tons of Kenya coffee from B, and B delivers to him coffee which is not Kenya coffee, A can refuse to take it. It would make no difference if the coffee which is sent is better coffee, and cost more than the Kenya coffee, and that B is prepared to supply the superior coffee at the price agreed upon for the Kenya coffee. A is entitled to have the coffee named in the contract.

Sale by Sample.—Where there is a sale by sample as well as by description the goods have got to correspond with both the sample and description. Thus, in the previous sample, if a sample of Kenya coffee had been shewn, and B had sent either Kenya coffee which was not of the same quality as the sample or had sent coffee which was not Kenya coffee but was of the same quality as the sample, A could in either case refuse to take it.

Where goods are bought by description from a seller who deals in goods of that description there is a condition implied that they are of merchantable quality. Thus, if, in the case put, the coffee sent had been Kenya coffee but had been damaged by water or in some other way, A could refuse to take it on the ground that it was not of merchantable quality. Where, however, the buyer has an opportunity of examining the goods at the time of the sale to see whether or not they are of merchantable quality and does not examine them, he cannot afterwards complain. So, if A, in the case put, had seen the sack of coffee at B's warehouse and could have had it opened when he would have discovered that the coffee was defective, but did not do so because he was in a hurry, he could not afterwards complain that the coffee was bad. It should be noticed that this only applies to cases where the buyer would have found out the defect if he had looked, and if a man buys sparking plugs which have in them a flaw in the metal which could not be discovered by looking at them, he will be entitled to reject them when the flaw develops whether he has examined them at the time of sale or not.

Fitness for Particular Purpose.— When a buyer buys goods to be used for a particular purpose there will not in every case be any condition that the goods are fit for that purpose. Where, however, the purpose for which he wishes the goods is either expressly told to the seller at the time of the sale or is obvious from the nature of the goods themselves so as to shew that the buyer is relying on the seller's skill and judgment in supplying proper goods, and the goods are of a kind which the seller normally sells in his business, there is a condition implied that they are fit for the purpose.

The Picture Wire That Broke.— Thus, if a householder, who wishes to hang some pictures, goes into a shop and asks for some wire without telling the salesman that he wants to use it to hang pictures, he cannot complain if the wire does not prove to be of a sufficiently strong kind and the picture falls and is broken. (Notice that it might be an entirely different matter if the wire, instead of being of too weak a kind was the right kind of wire, but badly made, for then there would be a breach of the condition that the wire was of merchantable quality (*see above*).) If, however, the householder asks the salesman for picture wire and the salesman then sells him wire, the wire is sold for a particular purpose, and if it breaks the seller will be liable, for the buyer is relying on the judgment of the seller to give him proper wire. If this salesman had said he did not sell picture wire but that he had several kinds of wire which the buyer might think would do, and the buyer had then selected some wire himself, he would not be able to complain, for then he had not relied on the seller's skill and judgment in choosing the wire but on his own. Similarly, if he goes and asks his next door neighbour if he has any picture wire to sell and ultimately buys a length for 6d., he cannot blame his next door neighbour if the wire breaks. He cannot rely on the condition that the wire should be fit for the purpose, because it is not "in the course of the business" of the next door neighbour to sell picture wire, nor can he rely on the condition that it should be of merchantable quality because his next door neighbour does not "deal in goods of that description." (*See above*.)

No such condition applies in cases where goods are bought under their trade names. So if A buys "X's hair tonic" by that name in a chemist's shop and it causes all his hair to fall out, he cannot blame the chemist. He has got what he asked for and has relied entirely on his own skill and judgment.

When Does Buyer First Own the Goods?—The consequence of a sale—and indeed the object of it—is that some goods which have hitherto belonged to the seller should in future belong to the buyer; and in very many cases it is very important to know at what exact stage the property in the goods passes from the seller to the buyer. The property in the goods means the ownership of them, not the possession, and the buyer may have got the property in the goods while they are still on the hands of the seller and so in his possession, or the seller may retain the property in the goods although they have passed into the possession of the buyer.

It is important to know the exact moment when the property passed for two purposes:

1. If the goods are destroyed by fire or by some accident for which neither seller nor buyer is to blame, the rule is that the person

who owns the goods must bear the loss. So, if A buys a mirror from B which he sees in B's drawing room and arranges to collect the next day, and overnight the mirror falls and is broken, A must pay the price because (as will be seen below), the ownership of the mirror has passed to him.

2. If A buys a car from B and it is arranged that the property is not to pass until A has paid for the car, and A goes bankrupt before he has paid, B can claim the car back again. If, however, it was agreed that the property was to pass at once although the price was not to be paid till later, B cannot claim back the car which belongs to A's trustee in bankruptcy, but must content himself with claiming the price in A's bankruptcy, when he may receive only a few shillings in the £.

When no Provision in contract: Ascertained Goods.—Where the parties have not given any definite indication of their intention as to when the property shall pass, the law has laid down certain rules:

1. Where there is an unconditional sale of specific goods the property passes when the contract is made, and the fact that the goods have not been delivered or that payment is not yet due for them does not matter. Thus, if A goes into a shop and buys an overcoat which he says he will collect and pay for the next day, the overcoat is already his, and if anything happens to it before he gets it without the fault of the shopkeeper, e.g. if the shop is broken into during the night and the overcoat stolen, he cannot complain but must pay the price. Similarly, if the shopkeeper had to deliver the coat and it was stolen from the delivery van without any fault of the shopkeeper, or if the van was involved in a collision due to the negligence of some other driver and the coat was damaged, the purchaser would have to pay for the coat. Of course, if the loss of the coat was due to some lack of care on the part of the shopkeeper, e.g. if the delivery van was left unattended when the coat was stolen, or was involved in an accident through negligent driving, the purchaser could not be required to pay. The coat would all the same be his property but he could recover from the shopkeeper for its loss and so in effect need not pay the price.

2. Where at the time of the sale the goods are not in a deliverable state but the seller

has got to do something to them to put them in a deliverable state, the property does not pass until that thing has been done and the buyer has notice of it. Therefore, if in the previous case A had arranged with the shopkeeper to put different buttons on the coat and to let him know when it was ready, the property would not pass until the shopkeeper had told him the coat was ready.

3. Where there is a sale of specific goods in a deliverable state but the seller is bound to weigh or measure or test them in order to calculate the price, the property does not pass until that has been done and the buyer has notice of it. So if A buys all the wheat in B's warehouse—the exact amount of which is not known—at so much a ton, the property will not pass until B has had the wheat weighed, and informed A.

4. When goods are sold "on approval," or on "sale or return," the property passes to the buyer when he informs the seller that he does approve of the goods, or when he does any other act which indicates that he intends to accept them, e.g. sells them again—or if, without informing the seller that he does not intend to buy them, he retains them beyond the time fixed by the contract for their return or, if no time is fixed, beyond a reasonable time.

Unascertained Goods.—Hitherto we have been concerned only with "ascertained" goods, that is, goods which were in existence and the identity of which was known to both buyer and seller at the time of the contract. In the case of unascertained goods, that is, goods defined by description only, as a thousand tons of coal—not any particular thousand tons—or a pound of sugar—not any particular pound of sugar— or goods not yet in existence which the seller has himself to buy or manufacture, the ownership will normally pass from the seller to the buyer when the proper quantity of goods is appropriated to the contract either by the seller with the assent of the buyer, or by the buyer with the assent of the seller. The buyer's assent need not be expressly conveyed to the seller but may be implied by his conduct in not objecting. Thus, if fifteen bags of rice were bought and the seller, having no rice at the time, bought 100 bags, intending to use them to supply orders, including the order for 15 bags, no goods would be "appropriated" to the con-

tract for 15 bags by the mere delivery of the 100 bags at the seller's warehouse. No one could tell which of the 100 bags were to be used to complete the contract for 15 bags, and indeed the seller would be perfectly entitled to use none of them for that purpose but to sell them elsewhere, and to buy another 15 bags to deliver under the contract. If, however, the seller labelled 15 bags out of the 100 with the name of the buyer and informed the buyer that he had done so, these bags would be appropriated to the contract unless the buyer wrote that he objected to taking them.

When goods are to be sent by rail or by post the buyer is considered to have agreed to allow the seller to appropriate any goods he wishes by putting them in the post or delivering them to the railway company, so that they belong to the buyer after their appropriation.

How to Prevent the Property Passing.—This rule is sometimes considered undesirable by sellers as it means that the goods pass to the buyer before they have been paid for if payment is not to be made until delivery, and therefore, if the buyer should become bankrupt, his trustee could seize the goods, and the seller would have to be content to rely on his right to claim for the price in the bankruptcy. In order to avoid this the seller frequently inserts a clause in the contract to the effect that he is to retain a "right of disposal" of the goods.

This means that the goods do not belong to the buyer until he has done something, for example has paid the price, or accepted a bill of exchange for the price. If the buyer becomes bankrupt before he has done the thing required of him, the seller can claim back his goods. (*See also* LIEN; STOPPAGE IN TRANSITU.)

Sales by Persons not the Owners of the Goods.—It is a general principle of English law that a person cannot give a better title to anything than he has himself, and so, if goods do not belong to him and he wrongly and fraudulently sells them, the person who buys them from him does not get a good title, and must hand back the goods to the true owner when required to do so without any compensation. He may, of course, sue the person who sold him the goods, but in practice this right will be valueless, for that person will usually have gone bankrupt or have disappeared. Business convenience has made it necessary to introduce certain exceptions to this rule.

When the seller of goods is allowed by the buyer to remain in possession after the property in the goods has passed to the buyer, and the seller sells the goods again to someone else, that person gets a good title to them, and the buyer cannot recover them. He can, of course, sue the seller either for the return of any price paid, or for damages for not having delivered the goods sold. If A buys in a shop furniture which is to be delivered to him later, the property in the furniture will pass to him at the time of the sale; but if the shopkeeper sells the same furniture to B, who knows nothing of the sale to A, A cannot claim the furniture from B. A similar rule applies in cases where a buyer is allowed by the seller to get possession of goods which he has bought or "agreed to buy" before the property in them has passed to him; and there again if he sells them to some innocent person, that is, some person who does not know that they are not his to sell, that person gets a good title to the goods and cannot be compelled to hand them back to the original seller.

This provision is of particular importance in cases of sales on deferred payments, that is, sales on the terms that the price is to be paid by instalments, and that the property in the goods is not to pass to the buyer until he has paid the final instalment. In such cases, if the buyer sells the goods wrongly to anyone before he has paid for them, that person gets a good title. A similar provision protects purchasers from persons known as "factors." (q.v.) It should be noticed that this does not apply to what are real hire-purchase agreements, because the rule only has effect in cases where the person in possession of the goods has "bought or agreed to buy" them, and in proper hire purchase agreements the hirer does not *agree to buy* the goods but, if he pays all his instalments of hire, acquires *an option* to buy the goods by paying a final instalment, usually a nominal amount such as 5/-. He is never *bound* to buy the goods, but is merely *entitled* to do so if he wishes, so that he is never a person who has "agreed to buy." Thus, if he sells the goods to someone else before he has paid all the instalments, that

person must hand them back to the real owner.

An Old Rule.—Where goods are sold in "market overt," which includes a sale in any shop in the City of London in which goods of that class are exposed for sale, the buyer gets a good title so long as he acts in good faith even though the seller did not own the goods. (*See* MARKET OVERT.)

Must Seller Deliver or Must Buyer Collect?—The parties can make any arrangements they please as to whether the seller is to deliver the goods to the buyer or the buyer is to collect the goods from the seller. If the seller is bound to deliver, he must pay the cost; if the buyer is bound to collect, the expense is his. If they do not make any special arrangement, the general rule is that it is the buyer's duty to collect the goods from the seller's place of business, or his residence if he does not have a place of business.

The Lazy Messenger-boy.—When the seller sends goods to the buyer's house or place of business and delivers them to a person *apparently* authorized to receive them who misappropriates them, the loss does not fall on him but on the buyer. Thus, if A orders a diamond ring to be delivered at his house and the messenger-boy delivers the ring to a maid at the door, the seller cannot be held responsible if the maid steals the ring, and the buyer must still pay the price. The position would be the same if the maid was not a maid at all, but a thief who had broken into the house and disguised herself as a maid in order to get the ring. If, however, the messenger-boy, being of a lazy disposition, to save himself the trouble of walking up an avenue to the buyer's house handed the ring to a gardener who was working in the garden who promised to take it up to the house, or to a postman who was going up to deliver letters, the seller, and not the buyer would be responsible if the gardener or the postman misappropriated the ring, for neither of these persons is "a person apparently authorized" to receive the goods. Delivery must be made at the time specified in the contract or within a reasonable time if no specified time is fixed by the contract, and at a reasonable time of day. What is reasonable will depend on the circumstances—thus, in a business it would be during ordinary business hours.

What is a Good Delivery.—The seller has got to deliver to the buyer the exact amount that has been ordered and neither more nor less. Thus, if the buyer has ordered a dozen bottles of wine and the seller sends 11, the buyer is not bound to accept them and the same applies if the seller sends 13. The buyer *may*, of course, accept either the 11 or the 13, or he may accept a dozen and send back 1. The other deliveries are not made in performance of the contract but are really fresh offers made by the seller to the buyer which the buyer may accept by keeping the goods. If he does, of course, he will have to pay for them at the price per bottle fixed by the contract. A buyer cannot be compelled to accept delivery by instalments, and therefore, if the seller sends 11 bottles and says the other is coming to-morrow, the buyer may refuse to take the 11, but if the seller sent the full 12, even after the 11 have been rejected, the buyer would have to take them so long as the time for delivery under the contract has not elapsed. When goods are delivered to the buyer which he is entitled to reject either because they are not the right quantity or quality or have been delivered too late, he is not bound to send them back to the seller but must inform the seller he does not intend to keep them. It is for the seller to collect them.

What Buyer must Do if He Wishes to Reject.—When a buyer considers that he is entitled to reject goods in this way he must be careful to do nothing which might indicate that he has in fact accepted them, because if he once is held to have accepted the goods, he will be unable to return them and claim back his price however defective they may be, although he still may sue the seller for damages. The buyer will be deemed to have accepted goods in the following cases:

1. If he informs the seller that he has accepted them;

2. If he does any act to the goods which is inconsistent with the ownership of the seller. If the seller delivers furs which are in a dirty condition and which the buyer is therefore entitled to reject, the buyer will lose his right and will be held to have accepted the goods if he sends them out to have them cleaned. In many cases where the buyer is in urgent need of the goods this is the most practical course for him to take, but it should be remembered that if he does so and the cleaning turns out to be unsatisfactory, he cannot then send the goods back to the seller, although, of course, he could claim damages from him. The wisest practical course to take in such a case is for the buyer to communicate with the seller, and to say that he refuses to take the goods and to suggest to the seller that he is prepared to consider taking them if they are cleaned. If the seller consents to this course, the buyer will be entitled to reject the goods if after being cleaned they are still unsatisfactory.

3. If the buyer retains the goods for more than a reasonable time without intimating to the seller that he has rejected them so that if goods are delivered and a man allows them to lie in his warehouse without telling the seller that he does not intend to accept them, he cannot later reject them.

When goods are sent to a house or business unasked, as frequently happens in the case of fountain-pens, the householder is not required to return them to the person who has sent them or to inform him that he does not intend to take them, because this is not a delivery under a contract of sale, for there has been no agreement to buy the goods, but is merely an offer by the person sending the goods which the householder can accept or refuse as he pleases. It makes no difference if the letter accompanying the goods requests the householder to return them if he is not satisfied with them. He is not bound to do so. He may not, however, refuse to hand the goods over to anyone who calls for them, and if he uses the goods, he will be taken to have accepted the offer made by the sending of the goods and will have to pay for them.

When is Payment Due?—The general rule about payment is that the goods have got to be paid for when the buyer gets possession of them, but this, of course, may be altered by arrangement. Thus, credit may be given to the buyer or he may even be required to pay for them before they are delivered.

Rights of Seller.—The seller, if the contract is not complied with, has two classes of rights or remedies. The first class is against the buyer and the second class entitles the seller to seize the goods or sell them.

Rights Against Buyer.—With regard to the first class, the seller can sue the buyer for the price of the goods when that is due according to the contract, and this may be before the property in the goods has passed if the contract so provides. If no provision is made, the action for the price cannot be brought until the property in the goods has passed to the buyer, but notice that it is the property that is the determining factor not the passing of possession, and so a seller may sue for goods before they have been delivered.

Instead of suing for the price and requiring the buyer to take the goods, the seller, when a buyer refuses to take them and pay for them, may accept the position that the goods are not going to belong to the buyer and may sue him for damages for not having accepted them. These damages will normally be the difference between the market price of the goods at the time when the buyer should have accepted them and the contract price. Thus, if the buyer has agreed to pay £20 for some flour and the market price at the time when it should have been delivered is only £15, the damages will be £5. If it should happen that the market price is higher than the contract price, e.g. is £25, the seller will not be able to recover any damages, because in theory he could have sold the goods in the market at a higher price than he would have got from the buyer and so has suffered no loss. (*See* DAMAGES.)

Rights against Goods.—The rights which the seller has against the goods are the following:

1. A lien for the price, that is, a right to retain the goods as long as they are in his possession until the price is paid. When the goods have been sold on credit the seller cannot claim to exercise his lien until the time allowed for credit has expired unless in cases where the buyer becomes insolvent. (*See* LIEN.)

2. A right of stoppage in transitu. (*See* STOPPAGE IN TRANSITU.)

3. A right of resale. The seller can sell the goods to some third party, but he must notify the buyer that he is going to do so and give the buyer a reasonable time to pay the price even though the time fixed by the contract has elapsed except in cases where the goods are perishable, and he must therefore act at once, e.g. fruit, or where there is a term in the contract *expressly* reserving to the seller a right of resale in case the buyer fails to pay the price at the time fixed.

4. A right of withholding delivery. When property in the goods has passed to the buyer the seller must exercise his right of lien, but when property has not passed he has a right of withholding delivery which gives him the same power and arises under the same circumstances as the right of lien. (*See* STOPPAGE IN TRANSITU.)

Rights of Buyer.—The buyer has naturally no remedies against the goods, and all his rights are to sue the seller for breach of contract.

If the seller does not deliver when he should do, the buyer may do one of three things:

1. If he has paid, he can recover the price.

2. Whether or not he has paid the price he can sue the seller for damages for non-delivery which will be normally the difference between the market price of the goods and the contract price. (*See* DAMAGES.)

3. Occasionally he may be able to compel the seller to deliver the goods to him by an action for specific performance (q.v.), but this remedy will only be allowed where damages would not compensate the buyer for the seller's failure to deliver the goods, e.g. where he could not take the money paid as damages and with it buy other goods in the market and so be in the same position as if the seller had delivered the goods.

Thus, if the contract is to deliver a pound of tea or a thousand tons of coal, specific performance would not be allowed, but if the contract was for the delivery of an antique snuff box supposed to have been used by Bonnie Prince Charlie, specific performance would be allowed because no amount of damages would enable the seller to replace the article which he should have had under the contract.

Where the seller does deliver the goods but they are either not delivered in time or are not in accordance with the contract, the buyer's rights will depend upon whether the term of the contract which has been broken is a condition or merely a warranty. (*See above.*) (*See* CONDITION; CONTRACT; DAMAGES; LIEN; SPECIFIC PERFORMANCE; STOPPAGE IN TRANSITU; WARRANTY.)

SALE OF GOODS (SCOTS LAW). —The law of Scotland on this subject corresponds very closely to that of England. The distinction between the conditions and warranties is, however, not known in Scotland, and a buyer is entitled to reject the goods and treat the contract as repudiated whenever any material part of the contract is broken. A breach of warranty is deemed to be a failure to perform a material part of the contract.

SALE OF LAND.—The methods by which land is transferred by the seller, who is called the "Vendor," to the Purchaser on a sale follow fixed rules and come within the term "Conveyancing," which, however, comprises a large number of other transactions relating to property and rights in the nature of property involving the use of a document.

A sale may be brought about either by private treaty, or by auction.

In the case of a sale by private treaty, the vendor and the purchaser, or their respective representatives (usually solicitors or estate agents) agree upon a price and, as a rule, enter into a preliminary agreement which should be stated to be subject to the drawing up of a formal contract, which will contain any special terms which are to be binding on the parties in carrying through the sale. The formal contract is then prepared by the vendor's solicitor.

Auction.—In the case of a sale by auction, before the sale takes place, the vendor's solicitor must draw up Particulars and Conditions of Sale. The Particulars contain a full description of the property and should refer to any peculiarities or other matters which might be considered of importance to an intending purchaser. Any misdescription or inaccuracy might entitle the person to whom the property is sold by auction to refuse to complete the sale and repudiate his agreement to purchase; or there might arise a claim for damages against the vendor. The Conditions set out the terms to which the sale is subject.

The purchaser is generally the highest bidder, whose bid must, however, reach the reserve, or minimum price, if any, fixed by the vendor. Such reserve price is not disclosed before the sale.

Checking the Title Deeds. — The next steps vary according to whether the land is (1) Unregistered Land: or (2)

Registered Land. In respect of certain districts, official registries exist in which full particulars of land and the ownership thereof are registered. This is the case for London and Eastbourne, where registration of land is compulsory. Elsewhere it is optional.

(1) In the case of Unregistered Land, the procedure is governed by the practice which has gradually evolved by rules laid down in decided cases heard in courts, and by the terms of Acts of Parliament. The vendor's solicitor prepares the Abstract of Title, which is an epitome of the documents and facts constituting the vendor's title, i.e. it proves his claim to ownership and right to sell. If there is no agreement to the contrary, the abstract of title must cover the 30 years immediately preceding the sale. But the parties may agree on a shorter period. The earliest document is called the "Root of Title."

On receipt of the abstract of title, the purchaser's solicitor will check it by an inspection of the originals of the documents which have been epitomised, wherever they may be.

Either before or after inspecting the documents, the purchaser's solicitor will compile a list of queries which arise from his consideration of the vendor's title to the property, as disclosed by the abstract of title. These queries are termed "Requisitions on Title."

When the purchaser's solicitor is satisfied with the title, he drafts the form of document by which the land is to be transferred by the vendor to the purchaser. This document is the "Conveyance." He sends the draft to the vendor's solicitor for approval. After the wording has been agreed, the conveyance is engrossed, i.e. a fair copy is made. This is executed by the vendor. By the expression "execute the conveyance" is meant that all persons who must sign the documents because they are one of the contracting parties, must, in addition to signing, seal and deliver the document. In the old days they used actually to affix their own private seals and then hand over the document. At the present time the actual physical operations are dispensed with and the party puts the index finger of his right hand on a small circular piece of paper which has been stuck on the document opposite his signature and on the right. This represents

Lord Sankey.

the seal. He then says the words "I deliver this as my act and deed," and this completes the operation. The witness to the execution also signs the conveyance.

An appointment is made to complete the sale at the office of the vendor's solicitor, or at such other place which the vendor may nominate, or the parties agree upon. The purchaser's solicitor attends with the balance of the purchase price either in cash, or, by arrangement, in the form of a banker's draft. If there are any small outgoings, such as rates, taxes, ground rent, etc., to be adjusted, the vendor's solicitor, shortly before the day fixed for completion, sends a statement shewing the amount due to or from the vendor to the purchaser's solicitor, and on the completion the necessary adjustment is made. In return for the balance of the purchase-money, the purchaser's solicitor receives from the vendor's solicitor the conveyance and the title deeds in the vendor's possession, except that if any such deeds relate to other land belonging to the vendor which he is not selling to the purchaser, they will not be handed over. In that case the vendor gives an undertaking in the con-

veyance that he will produce them to the purchaser when required and keep them safely. This is called an undertaking for production and safe custody.

Registered Land.—(2) In the case of Registered Land, the procedure to be followed is laid down by the Land Registration Act, 1925.

SALE OR RETURN.—Goods are frequently sold on terms that if the purchaser is unable to resell them, he may return them to the person who sold them to him. (*See* SALE OF GOODS.)

SAMPLE, SALE BY.—(*See* SALE OF GOODS.)

SANITARY INSPECTOR.—A Sanitary Inspector must be appointed by every local authority to act as their investigating officer in all cases relating to the healthy conditions of dwelling-houses and other premises in their district. The sanitary inspector makes a report to the local authority and to the medical officer of health upon houses which are in an insanitary condition or which are in a condition making them dangerous to the health of the inmates. (*See* HOUSING; PUBLIC HEALTH.)

SANKEY, Lord (1866-).—A Judge in the King's Bench Division for fourteen years, he had just become a Lord Justice of Appeal when he was made Lord Chancellor in 1929. He took a leading part in the Indian Conferences of 1930 and 1931.

SCAVENGING.—The cleansing of streets and the removal of refuse is usually undertaken by the local authority of each district, as part of its duties with regard to the protection of the health of the inhabitants.

Every local authority may make bye-laws which require the occupiers of premises to keep the footways and pavements adjoining their premises clean by the removal of snow or filth.

In London every sanitary authority for the various districts must arrange for the removal of house refuse at regular periods. (*See* LOCAL GOVERNMENT; PUBLIC HEALTH.)

SCHEDULE OF DILAPIDATIONS.—Leases of land and buildings contain a number of conditions, called "Covenants," a usual one being to impose on the "Lessee," who is the person to whom the lease is granted, the obligation to keep the property in repair. Power is then usually given to the Lessor, who is the landlord, to enter, or send a representative, on the property from time to time in order to examine the condition of the same. If he finds that repairs have not been carried out, a list of the work required, namely a "Schedule of Dilapidations," is sent to the lessee, together with a notice informing him that the work must be done within two months, and, as a rule, setting out the covenant in the lease which imposes the obligation to repair on the lessee. (*See also* LANDLORD AND TENANT.)

SCHOOL.—All children between the ages of 5 and 14 (or in some districts 6 and 14) must attend a suitable school for the purpose of receiving elementary instruction in reading, writing and arithmetic. (*See* EDUCATION.)

SCHOOLMASTERS. — A schoolmaster is bound to educate his pupil, and for that purpose is given a quasi-parental authority over him, with power of reasonable punishment. (*See* EDUCATION; TEACHERS.)

SCIENTER.—This means knowledge in law. For instance, if a person is injured by the domestic animal of another he cannot recover damages for his injury from the owner unless he shews that the latter knew that the animal was of a mischievous disposition. The knowledge of the owner as to this would be described as *scienter*. (*See* ANIMAL.)

SCOTLAND YARD. — The headquarters of the Metropolitan Police are situated at New Scotland Yard at Whitehall. The Commissioner and his assistants have their offices there, together with the central administrative departments of the headquarters and the investigation departments. (*See* SPECIAL SUPPLEMENT "THE POLICE.")

SCOTS LAW.—The main features in which Scots law differs from English law are noted under their proper headings throughout this book. It is possible, however, in a very general way to state that in all matters relating to family relationship and land law the law of Scotland differs very widely from that of England, but that in the sphere of commercial law, e.g. such matters as contracts, sales of goods, bills of exchange, it is in most respects the same as English law. Even in these matters, however, it is never safe to assume that Scots law governing any point does not differ from English law.

Family and Land Law. — The marriage laws in Scotland are much freer than those in England, and many forms of marriage are recognized which would be of no effect in England. Further, the consequences of marriage so far as the property of the husband or wife is concerned also differ considerably from English law. (*See* MARRIAGE [SCOTS LAW].)

In land law the feudal system developed on different lines in Scotland from those which it followed in England. In addition, there has been in existence in Scotland for many hundreds of years a complete system requiring registration of all documents affecting land. A modified form of registration on somewhat similar lines has been introduced into England in recent years. The advantages of registration are obvious.

Scotland Yard as seen from the Thames Embankment.

Commercial Law.—The main difference in commercial law is the absence in Scots law of the doctrine of consideration so fundamental in the English conception of contract, i.e. the doctrine that a contract which is gratuitous will not be enforced unless it is entered into by a document under seal called a deed. (*See* BANKRUPTCY [SCOTS LAW]; BILL OF EXCHANGE [SCOTS LAW]; CONTRACT [SCOTS LAW]; DAMAGES [SCOTS LAW]; INTESTACY [SCOTS LAW]; MARRIAGE [SCOTS LAW].)

SEA.—No country or person owns the sea or any part of it. Nations exercise certain jurisdiction over their own territorial waters (q.v.) but do not own them. Offences committed at sea are, in general, triable according to the law of the country to which the ship on which the offence takes place belongs. Certain offences, such as piracy, are triable in the English Courts whatever may be the nationality of the pirates or of their ships.

SEASHORE. — The seashore is strictly speaking the ground between high- and low-water mark. It may be privately owned, and in many cases is, but in the absence of an owner who can trace his title to a grant, it belongs to the Crown. Ownership of the seashore, however, cannot prejudice the right of every person to sail or fish over it when covered by the sea. On the other hand, the public have no right to walk across the land from boats except to avoid the perils of the sea. While this applies to the public at large, in most places there is a legal custom permitting local fishermen lawfully to cross the seashore.

The public, however, have no right to shoot on the seashore, or to collect seaweed or other articles thereon. Sand and gravel on it are the property of the owner, while, in general, portions of wrecked vessels when washed up belong to the Crown. The public have no legal right to use the seashore for bathing if the owner objects.

SEARCH WARRANTS.—A search warrant is an authority issued by a Justice of the Peace empowering a police constable, or other person as directed, to enter upon any premises named in the warrant for the purpose of searching. The person executing the search warrant may enter the premises by means of force if he cannot gain access otherwise. He may take away any article he finds on the premises which is mentioned in the warrant, or which relates to the charge in respect of which the warrant is issued. He may also arrest any person whose name is in the warrant or in whose possession any articles named are found. It is essential that when a search is carried out under a warrant one of the officers carrying it out should have the warrant with him. If the occupier on the premises requires to hear the warrant read, the officer executing it must do so.

Although it is, in most cases, unlawful to force one's way into premises without a search warrant, nevertheless there are some offences which justify this being done. For instance, if it is reasonably suspected that a murder is being committed on private premises, any police officer or, indeed, any other person would be justified in entering upon the premises without a warrant, to prevent the commission of the crime.

SEARCHES.—The solicitor acting for the purchaser of land must satisfy himself that the seller, or "vendor's" "title" is in order, that is to say, that the land is his to sell. One part of his investigations will be to make "searches" or enquiries at a number of Official Registries in order to ascertain what information affecting the land is registered there, if any. (*See* also SALE OF LAND.)

SEASON TICKET.—Season ticket holders have the right to travel between two stations for a period of time on as many occasions as they please. Their tickets are not, however, usually valid for journeys other than that between the two stations, but in practice the companies are usually prepared to accept the tickets as valid and to charge any excess. Season ticket holders have no more right to a seat than any other travellers. (*See* RAILWAY PASSENGERS.)

SECRET COMMISSION.—The law forbids persons to make secret commissions when acting as agents. This is because an agent is supposed to use his best endeavours for his principal and to have his interest alone at heart. If any agent does receive any secret commission, his principal can recover from him the whole amount so received. Moreover, most secret commissions amount to corruption. (*See* BRIBERY.)

SECRETARY OF STATE.—There are seven Secretaries of State—for the

Home Department, for Foreign Affairs, for the Dominions and for the Colonies, for India, for War, for Air, and for Scotland.

SECURED CREDITORS.—A creditor is said to be secured when he is entitled to be paid his debt out of certain assets of the debtor—for example, where the debtor has mortgaged to him a piece of land, or has pledged with him some goods in security for the debt. (*See* BANKRUPTCY; DEBENTURE; WINDING-UP.)

SECURITY FOR COSTS. — In some cases a litigant may be required, before he is allowed to prosecute his claim, to pay into Court some money which the person whom he is suing may look to, should his defence succeed, for the purpose of paying the costs he incurs in defending the action. It would obviously be very hard to require a person who is bringing an action to provide security in all cases, for he may well have a good cause of action and yet have no ready money.

Security may be required: (1) where the plaintiff claims more than £20 in contract or more than £10 in tort and the defendant objects to trial in the County Court, and applies for a trial in the High Court, and the Judge certifies that some important question of law, or fact is likely to arise. In such a case the defendant is required to give security for the amount claimed and the cost of the trial in the High Court.

(2) A plaintiff who does not reside in England or Wales must give security.

(3) Where the defendant neither resides nor carries on business within twenty miles of the Court in which he is sued, he may make an application claiming that the plaintiff should give security for costs to which the defendant will be put.

(4) Where an action is brought in a High Court for tort (that is, damages for some wrongful act), a defendant may be able to shew, by calling evidence, that the plaintiff, should he lose the case, has no means of paying the defendant's costs, and in that event the High Court Judge may order the case to be tried in the County Court unless the plaintiff gives security for the defendant's costs.

(5) Where a limited company is plaintiff, and it can be shewn that there is reason to believe that the company has not sufficient assets to pay the defendant's costs should he succeed in his defence, security may be ordered.

(6) Where either party during the action applies for discovery by interrogatories or otherwise, i.e. requires the other side either to answer in writing certain questions on oath relating to the case before the actual hearing, or else requires him to state on oath what documents he has in his possession. The security required here is small in amount.

(7) When an appeal is brought from a County Court Judge's decision security may be required where the action was brought on behalf of an infant by a next friend—i.e. by some relation of the infant—and where the next friend is insolvent or where the appellant is a bankrupt or a married woman who has no property of her own.

(8) The mere fact that a litigant has no visible means of paying costs is not a ground for ordinary security even in the case of appeal unless the appeal be absolutely without merits.

SEDITION.—Sedition must be distinguished from High Treason (q.v.). Conduct aimed at stirring up strife and ill-feeling between the classes, or at producing civil commotions or public disorder, or at bringing the King or his government into hatred or contempt with the people is seditious and punishable as sedition. The crime may be committed by word of mouth, or by acts, or by writing.

Every subject has the right of freely and publicly discussing political matters provided he does not directly or indirectly incite others to violence or unlawfully intend to produce any of the results set out above. It is only when the proper limits of political discussion are exceeded that the crime of sedition is committed.

It is not seditious to publish in England anything directed against any foreign government. The law of sedition is designed for the protection of the public peace at home and not abroad.

SEISIN.—Seisin was the old legal word for possession, and the person in possession of property was said to be "seised" of it. In course of time it came to be distinguished from mere or bare possession, and came to mean only possession which was lawful. It is no longer used in any strict legal sense.

SELDEN, John (1584-1654).—One of the most famous of English Jurists, he was in favour of the popular party, and was several times imprisoned in the Tower of London, once for his share in the drafting of the Petition of Right. His first legal treatise was published at the age of twenty-two.

SENTENCE. — A sentence is the punishment inflicted on a person for the commission of a criminal offence.

SEPARATION AGREEMENT.— A separation agreement between a husband and wife is perfectly lawful provided an actual immediate separation is intended, or has already taken place. On the other hand, an agreement for a separation which may take place in the future is invalid, as it is regarded as being contrary to public policy. Further, if an agreement is made for the parties to separate, and they do not in fact separate, then the agreement becomes void, and cannot be relied upon subsequently in the event of a later separation. If a husband and wife decide to live separate and apart, it is advisable in the interests of both parties for an agreement to be recorded in writing and signed by them.

In the event of there being any default in payment of any periodical sums provided for by the agreement, the proper course is to sue, either in the High Court of Justice or in the County Court, according to the amount that is owing. In the event of there being a breach of the agreement in respect of molestation, the party molested may apply to the High Court of Justice for an injunction restraining the other from committing further breaches of the agreement.

The existence of a separation agreement does not bar either party subsequently commencing proceedings for divorce in the event of circumstances justifying such a course arising after the making of the agreement. (*See* SPECIAL SUPPLEMENT "DIVORCE.")

SEPARATION ORDER.—A Separation Order is part of the relief that can be obtained in the Police Court by a married woman against her husband. It is similar in its effect to a judicial separation. The latter can only be obtained in the High Court of Justice. A separation order relieves a woman of the duty of living with her husband and protects her from him should he attempt

John Selden.

to require her to do so. It places her as regards property in exactly the same position as if she were unmarried. It can, if the magistrates think fit, be accompanied by an order for the husband to make to her periodical payments for the support of her and her children. The maximum amounts that can be ordered are £2 weekly for the wife and ten shillings weekly for each child. Orders can also be made as to the custody of the children. If it is proved that the wife has committed adultery, no separation or maintenance order may be made, or if already made must be discharged. An exception, however, is made to this if the conduct of the husband has substantially led to the wife's adultery.

A separation order may be made on any of the following grounds: a conviction for aggravated assault, desertion, persistent cruelty, wilful failure to provide reasonable maintenance for the wife or infant children, and habitual drunkenness.

The procedure for obtaining a separation order is for the wife to apply at the Police Court for the district in which she resides for a summons against her husband. The summons, when granted, must set out the particular grounds upon which the wife asks for the order, e.g. desertion. A date is fixed for the hearing of the summons. The wife must then attend and give evidence upon oath of the matters of which she complains. She should, where necessary, bring witnesses to support her case. This is particularly desirable where she complains of persistent cruelty. The husband is then allowed to present his case and the bench gives its decision. In a suitable case, a woman may obtain an order for her husband to make her some interim payments pending the conclusion of the case. (*See* DESERTION; AND SPECIAL SUPPLEMENT "DIVORCE.")

SEQUESTRATION, ECCLESIASTICAL.—Sequestration is the taking of the proceeds of a Church of England benefice by an officer appointed by the bishop, while the position of the incumbent remains otherwise the same.

SEQUESTRATION (SCOTS LAW).—In Scotland a person is not made bankrupt when he is unable to pay his debts but is sequestrated. For convenience, however, the subject has been dealt with under Bankruptcy (Scots Law). (*See* BANKRUPTCY [SCOTS LAW].)

SERVANTS. — (*See* MASTER AND SERVANT.)

SERVITUDE (SCOTS LAW).—A servitude corresponds to what is called an easement in English law and is a burden on lands or houses imposed in favour of the owner of other land or houses. The property entitled to the benefit of the servitude is known as the dominant tenement, and that which is subject to the servitude as the servient tenement. Servitudes may be either positive or negative. A positive servitude entitles the owner of the dominant tenement to exercise certain active rights over the servient tenement, e.g. a right of way. A negative servitude does not entitle the owner of the dominant tenement to do any act but merely prohibits the owner of the servient tenement from doing something which he would otherwise be entitled to do. Thus, a right enjoyed by a dominant tenement to have a certain flow of light to its windows uninterrupted by the servient tenement is a negative servitude.

SET-OFF.—Where a defendant in an action in the High Court or County Court has a claim against the plaintiff for a debt or definitely ascertained sum of money, and this claim is in the nature of a contra-account against the plaintiff, it is known as a Set-Off and may be tried at the same time as the original action against the defendant, provided that notice of the set-off has been given to the plaintiff.

It differs from a Counterclaim, in that it is a real defence to the action, and if the defendant in an action succeeds in establishing a set-off as great as, or greater than the plaintiff's claim, he is entitled to all his costs. (*See* COUNTY COURT PROCEDURE; HIGH COURT PROCEDURE; PLEADINGS.)

SETTLED ACCOUNT.—When two parties have in writing balanced the accounts existing between them and accepted that balance as correct, the account is said to have been settled. The fact that an account has been settled is a good defence to an action for an account (*see* ACCOUNTS), though, if there are grave errors in the account, the items may be examined and the account corrected accordingly.

SETTLED LAND.—Settled land is land held under a settlement. A settlement is a disposition of property amongst two or more persons in such a manner that they will be entitled to the enjoyment of the property in succession to each other, but so that they will not (subject to certain exceptions) be able to deal with the property so as to affect the rights of each other. There are still a certain number of settlements of land. These are called strict settlements if their object is to keep the land in the family as far as possible and to provide for its passing as a whole from father to eldest son in the direct line. Under a strict settlement the eldest son takes practically the whole of the real property (land); younger children are given lump sum portions. (*See* SETTLEMENT.)

SETTLEMENT. — Property can be settled on a number of people so that each enjoys the income from it in succession but cannot dispose of the property itself. This is called a settlement. If an owner of property desires to settle it, he may do it by his will, or during his lifetime by deed. The method of effecting a settlement is to transfer the property to trustees upon the various trusts desired, e.g. to pay the income to A for his life, then to B, and finally to hand over the whole property to B's children. There is a limit imposed by law on the time during which property may be tied up in this way. Property can be settled for any period provided it does not exceed the lifetime of a living person and twenty-one years afterwards. (*See* TRUST.)

Another meaning of the word settlement is the compromise of an action when the parties in it have come to terms.

SETTLEMENT (MARRIAGE).—Until comparatively recent times, when a woman married, all her property belonged to her husband. Since, according to English law, a woman has no claim on the property of her husband on his death and he is free to leave her entirely destitute, there was thus a considerable risk, in cases where the wife was possessed of property before her marriage which passed to the husband on the marriage, that she might be left destitute after his death. In order to avoid this, it became the custom to enter into marriage settlements and even though such settlements are no longer so necessary, since a wife may hold property of her own, and her property does not automatically pass to her husband on marriage, it is still the practice to enter into marriage settlements.

Bankruptcy.—Considerable protection is given to settlements made before marriage and in consideration of marriage in the event of the bankruptcy of the person making the settlement. (*See* POST-NUPTIAL SETTLEMENT.)

SETTLEMENT (POOR LAW).—If a person wishes to obtain poor relief otherwise than as a casual poor person he must shew that he has a settlement in the county or county borough to whose council he has made his application.

A person is now regarded as settled in the county or county borough in which he was born until it is shewn that he has derived or acquired a settlement elsewhere, and the county or county borough in which a person is last settled is regarded as his county or county borough of settlement.

How a Settlement is Derived.—A settlement may be derived from a parent or a husband, and until a person acquires a settlement of his own or derives one from a husband, he (or she) takes and follows the settlement of his father until the age of sixteen if he is a legitimate child; if he is illegitimate he takes the settlement of his mother until the age of sixteen. At the

age of sixteen he retains his settlement thus acquired, and does not change with his parent.

How a Settlement may be Acquired.—A person may acquire a settlement in a county or county borough if:—

(a) he resides in it for three years; or

(b) if he is bound as an apprentice by a stamped deed, and resides for forty days in any county or county borough; or

(c) has an estate within the county, resides there for forty days and does not move farther than ten miles from the county; or

(d) if he rents and occupies for a whole year a tenement consisting of a separate dwelling-house at a rent of not less than £10, pays the rent himself or at least £10 thereof, is assessed to and pays the general rate in respect of that tenement for one year, and resides in the county for forty days; or

(e) if he pays the public taxes or local rates in respect of any tenement of the yearly value of £10 and resides in the county or county borough in which the tenement is situated for forty days.

(*See* ESTOPPEL; POOR LAW.)

SETTLING DAY.—When a transaction is entered into on the Stock Exchange, the parties do not usually intend that the shares shall be delivered or the money paid for them at once, but the transaction, unless anything to the contrary is stated, is arranged to be completed on the next settling day. There are usually two settling days in each month one about the middle and the other about the end. (*See* STOCK EXCHANGE.)

SEVERAL. — When a number of persons are liable under some contract or other obligation they may be liable either jointly or jointly and severally. (*See* JOINT AND SEVERAL.)

SEXTON.—The sexton is appointed by the parochial church council and the incumbent acting jointly. The sexton may be male or female. Payment is made sometimes by fees, sometimes by salary. His duties may include both the care of the graveyard, the care of the church and property therein, and the ringing of the church bells.

SHARES.—The capital of a company

usually consists of shares which entitle the holders of them to receive part of the profits when declared as dividends, and also to take their proportionate share of the property of the company when the company is wound up.

Issue for Less than Face Value.— When shares are issued by a company, as distinct from when they are sold in the market from one shareholder to another, they must not be issued at a discount, i.e. at less than their face value, and they must be issued in exchange for cash.

It is, however, possible to issue shares at a discount if the issue is authorized by a resolution of a general meeting of the company and is sanctioned by the Court.

Issue not for Cash.—It is always possible to issue shares otherwise than for cash so long as certain formalities are observed. The agreement to do so must be in writing and must be registered with the Registrar of Companies within one month of the date when it is entered into. Shares are frequently issued otherwise than for cash in cases where the company is purchasing a business, and the sellers agree to take so many shares instead of money as the purchase price.

Minimum Subscription.—(*See* MINI-MUM SUBSCRIPTION.)

Transfers.—A transfer of shares from one shareholder to another is quite a different thing from an allotment of shares when first issued by the company to a person who has applied for them. Every shareholder has a right to transfer his shares and the actual transfer will be in the form prescribed by the company's articles.

How to Sell Shares.—The transfer of shares usually takes place in three stages. First of all a contract is made for their sale. If the shares are dealt in on the Stock Exchange this will be made through a broker there. The actual transfer will be made some days later when the formal transfer document is signed by the seller and handed to the buyer together with the share certificate. The next stage is when the buyer sends the share certificate and the transfer form to the company and requests them to register him as the shareholder of these shares. The company is bound to insert his name on the register and send him another share certificate made out in his own name within two months.

Until the transfer has been registered by the company, the seller remains the shareholder in the eyes of the company.

Dividend Rights.—It may be that when the agreement is made the company has declared a dividend on the shares which has not yet been paid but will be paid in a short time. In such a case, the buyer and seller should agree at the time of the sale who is to get this dividend. In any event it will be paid in the first place by the company to the seller, as the share is still registered in his name in the books of the company. If they decide that the seller shall retain it, then the sale is said to be "ex dividend;" if the seller when he receives it from the company is to hand it over to the buyer, the transaction is "cum dividend." When no special arrangement is made, the seller is entitled to any dividend declared before the date of the agreement of sale, even though it is not payable until after the transfer, and the buyer is entitled to any dividend declared after the date of the agreement. If the dividend is declared before the transfer is registered the buyer will have to call on the seller to hand it over to him. (*See* CAPITAL; COMPANIES; DIVIDEND; MINIMUM SUBSCRIPTION; PREFERENCE QUALIFICATION SHARES; SHARES; SHARE CERTIFICATE; WINDING UP.)

SHARE CERTIFICATE. — Every member of a company has a right to a share certificate certifying that he holds so many shares in the company, and when shares are transferred the purchaser is entitled to have a new certificate sent to him by the company within 2 months of the time when he sends them his transfer. If the share certificate is lost, the company will issue a new one to the shareholder if he can prove to them satisfactorily that the certificate has been lost or destroyed. (*See* CAPITAL; SHARES; SHARE WARRANTS.)

SHARE PUSHING.—In recent years a great many investors have lost their money through buying shares which are suggested to them by unscrupulous finance houses and which are of no value whatsoever. In order to put a stop to this the law has now forbidden anyone to go round from house to house offering shares either for subscription, i.e. shares in a new company, or for sale. It is also forbidden, without going round in person, to send any written offer to sell shares to anybody unless full particulars of the shares are given, with the dividends that have been paid, the names of directors and very largely the same information as is required to be inserted in a prospectus. (*See* PROSPECTUS.)

SHARE WARRANT.—When the shares of a company are fully paid, i.e. when the full amount of the nominal value has been paid by the shareholder to the company, the company may issue share warrants instead of shares. A share warrant differs from a share in that the property in it can be handed from one person to another simply by handing over the piece of paper which is the share warrant certificate and without any registration in the company's books as is necessary in the case of shares. (*See* CAPITAL; SHARES.)

SHEEP.—Sheep are domestic animals and accordingly can be owned.

Dogs that worry sheep may be shot by the owner of the sheep if it is necessary for the protection of the sheep, and the owner of a dog that has done damage to sheep is liable for any damage it has done. (*See* ANIMAL; CATTLE; CRUELTY TO ANIMALS; DOG.)

SHERIFF.—A Sheriff is a county official. His duties are to carry out the orders of the High Court of Justice and to make arrangements for the sittings of that Court in various parts of the country. Thus, he has to supervise the execution of judgments, including the carrying out of sentences of death. He also has to arrange for the attendance of jurors at Assizes. He has certain duties to perform in connection with the attendance of Judges at assizes. He has to provide for their proper accommodation and for their transport protection whilst on circuit.

SHERIFF (SCOTS LAW).— The Sheriff (known also as the Sheriff Principal), with the assistance of the Sheriff-Substitute, carries out many of the duties which are in England performed by the English sheriff, the Recorder and the County Court Judge. At the present day his main duties are administrative, his judicial functions being performed for him by the Sheriff-Substitute. (*See* SHERIFF COURT [SCOTS LAW]; SHERIFF-SUBSTITUTE [SCOTS LAW].)

SHERIFF-COURT (SCOTS LAW). —Scotland is divided into a number of sheriffdoms each with one or more Sheriff-Courts. The official who presides as Judge in this Court is not, however, the Sheriff, who is, in most cases, an advocate in busy practice in Edinburgh, but the Sheriff-Substitute, who resides in the district of the Court and is a trained lawyer.

Whereas the English County Court has, with some exceptions, a jurisdiction limited to claims involving not more than £100, the jurisdiction of the Sheriff-Court is unlimited in matters concerning movable rights —i.e. actions relating to claims for damages either for breach of contract or for reparation, landlord and tenant, partnership, and all mercantile transactions. The Court cannot, however, try any case relating to status, and so such matters as marriage, divorce and legitimacy are outside its jurisdiction.

In matters relating to heritage (i.e. land) the Court has also unlimited jurisdiction but if the land exceeds £1,000 in value or £50 a year in annual value either party may have the case removed to the Court of Session.

SHERIFF'S COURT. — This is a Court which is held by the under-sheriff for each County and for each City which is entitled to a sheriff. The Court is known as the Sheriff's Court.

The Sheriff's Court to-day has no original jurisdiction, but it is used in two cases in assisting the processes of the High Court and County Court.

In those cases where a plaintiff asks for damages against the defendant and the defendant fails to put in an appearance or to defend the action, the Judge of the Court where the action would have been tried, sends the action to the under-sheriff, whose duty it is to call a jury, and on an appropriate day to assess the amount of damages to which the litigant is entitled.

The Sheriff's Court is also under a duty when called upon to sit in order to discover what lands within the County or district belong to a judgment debtor against whose lands a writ of execution has been issued. (*See* EXECUTION; WRIT OF ELEGIT.)

SHERIFF-SUBSTITUTE (SCOTS LAW).—The office of Sheriff-Substitute corresponds roughly to the English County Court Judge. He now performs practically all the duties which were originally carried out by the Sheriff. (*See* SHERIFF [SCOTS LAW].)

SWEARING IN THE SHERIFFS

This picture shows the quaint old ceremony of swearing in the Sheriffs before the Cursitor Baron at the Court of Exchequer at Westminster. The most interesting feature of the ceremony was that at the same time as the new Sheriffs took office, and those retiring rendered an account of their services, they also paid to the King's Remembrancer what are believed to be the two oldest quit rents in England—for the Moors in Salop, and for the Forge in London. The Senior Alderman would cut two faggots, one with a bill hook, and one with a hatchet. The actual rent of the Moors appeared to have been two knives, but these were substituted for a bill hook and a hatchet. The Alderman would then count aloud the six horseshoes and sixty-one nails which constituted the rent of the forge. This ceremony was abolished in 1859.

He is appointed for life by the Crown, on the recommendation of the Secretary of State for Scotland and the Lord Advocate, and he must be an advocate or law agent of at least five years' standing. He must reside within his sheriffdom and after his appointment cannot practice as an advocate.

The Sheriff-Substitute may perform any duty imposed on the Sheriff if delegated to him. He presides in the local Sheriff Court where he hears both civil and summary criminal cases and also in the Small Debt Court. An appeal lies from his decision, in civil cases, either to the Inner House of the Court of Session or to the Sheriff. (*See* COURT OF SESSION; SHERIFF [SCOTS LAW]; SHERIFF-COURT [SCOTS LAW]; SMALL DEBT COURT [SCOTS LAW].)

SHIPPING.—No ship can be entitled to the privileges of a British ship unless she is owned wholly by persons of the following description:

(*a*) Natural born British subjects.

(*b*) Persons naturalized as British subjects.

(*c*) Persons made denizens by letters of denization (this method of becoming a British subject is now obsolete).

(*d*) Bodies Corporate established under and subject to the laws of some part of the British Dominions and having their principal place of business in these Dominions.

Registration.—Every British ship must, unless exempted, be registered and unless so registered is not entitled to be recognized as a British ship.

Owners.—When the ship is registered it is necessary also to register certain persons as her owners. No more than sixty-four individuals are entitled to be registered at the same time as owners of any one ship, and for this purpose the ship is divided into sixty-four shares. No person can be registered as owner of less than one share or of any fractional part of a share, but any number of persons up to five may together be registered as joint owners of a ship or of any share in her. Such joint owners are considered as only one person for the purpose of calculating the sixty-four persons who may own the ship.

Transfer.—The only method in which a ship or any share in a ship can be transferred to a person qualified to own a British ship is by bill of sale. (*See* BILL OF SALE [SHIP].)

Passengers.—For the protection of passengers many regulations have been made relating to the condition of ships in which passengers may be carried. These regulations, however, will not usually be material in determining whether a passenger has any claim against the master or owner of ship in respect of anything relating to his carriage as a passenger. The important element for this is the contract which has been made between him and the shipowner, for it is this which regulates his rights. A shipowner may be a common carrier of goods —that is, he may not be entitled to refuse to carry any goods of the class he is accustomed to carry which are brought to him for carriage—but he is not a common carrier of passengers and is not obliged to carry any at all unless he wishes to do so. It may be, however, that if he does hold himself out as being willing to carry passengers he cannot refuse to carry such as offer themselves if there is room in the ship, and provided that the passenger is a fit person to be carried.

Liability.—The liability for passengers is less than for goods. The shipowner does not guarantee as an absolute liability that the passengers will be safely carried. His position is the same as that of a carrier of passengers on land, and he is bound merely to use all reasonable care in the navigation of the ship by himself and his servants. He is also required to provide a ship which is as fit and as seaworthy as proper care can make her. All of these requirements may be altered by the express terms of the contract, and a passenger will be bound by the terms of this contract even if they are contained in some printed conditions which he has not read, so long as reasonable steps are taken to bring to his notice the fact that the conditions exist.

The master has absolute control over the ship and its passengers, and he can require them to obey his orders and even to work the ship in an emergency. If they refuse, he may imprison them if there is no other method of ensuring the safety of the ship, but obviously this extreme power could only be exercised in very special circumstances.

Safety Provisions.—Numerous provisions have been made by international convention for the safety of life at sea. The majority of these apply to any passenger ship, the keel of which was laid on or after the 1st July 1931 or which was converted to passenger service on or after that date. Lifebuoys and buoyant apparatus must be provided in adequate numbers, and there must be accommodation in boats for all persons on board and in addition buoyant apparatus for 25 % of the persons on board.

Wireless Telegraphy must be provided on all passenger steamers of five thousand tons gross tonnage or upwards, and wireless telegraphy certificates and safety certificates must be obtained. The steering directions which were formerly to the effect that the order "starboard" or to the right was given when it was desired that the helm itself should be moved in that direction but that the head of the ship should be moved to "port" or to the left have been altered for the sake of international uniformity. Now it is compulsory to give an order directed to the head of the ship and not the helm. Thus, if it is desired to move the head of the ship to "starboard" the order must be "starboard," and if it is desired to move the head of the ship to "port" the order must be "port," the helm being moved oppositely in each case.

Load-Line. — Every ship must be marked with a load-line indicating the depth to which she may be submerged without danger when fully loaded. (*See* Articles [Ships]; Bill of Sale [Ships]; Carriage by Sea; Seaman.)

SHIP (SALE OF LIQUOR).—A justices' licence is not required for the sale of intoxicating liquor on board passenger vessels. A passenger vessel licence authorizes the sale of intoxicating liquor to passengers for consumption on the vessel while it is engaged in carrying passengers. While, however, a passenger ship is moored or lying at anchor within the jurisdiction of a licensing authority, it would appear that the permitted hours in force within such jurisdiction would apply to the ship. (*See* Permitted Hours and for other places where justices' licences are not required *see* Intoxicating Liquor; Canteens; Restaurants.)

SHOOTING.—The law relating to game is contained in a series of Acts of Parliament, and the definition of the term "game" differs in each. (*See* Deer; Game; Gun Licences; Rabbits; Shot-gun.)

SHOP.—The law relating to shops is concerned mainly with regulations about the hours during which a shop may remain open for the service of customers, and about the number of hours for which assistants may be employed in shops.

A shop for the purposes of the Shop Acts includes all premises where any retail business or trade is carried on. Retail trade or business includes the business of a barber or hairdresser, the sale of intoxicating liquors or refreshments, and retail sales by auction. It does not include the sale of programmes or catalogues at theatres or other places of amusement.

A Shop Assistant includes any person wholly or mainly employed in a shop in connection with the serving of customers, or the receiving of orders, or the despatch of goods.

The provisions of the Shop Acts do not apply to premises where Post Office business is carried on exclusively, nor to premises used for a trade fair or bazaar devoted to charity.

General Closing Hours.—All shops, with certain specified exceptions, must be closed for the serving of customers not later than 8 p.m. save that in one day of the week they may remain open until 9 p.m. The day upon which the closing hour is fixed at 9 p.m. is known as the "late" day. Unless the local authority fix some other day the late day is always Saturday.

Shops where the business carried on is that of confectionery, i.e. table waters, sweets, chocolates, or ice cream, may remain open until 9 p.m., or 10 p.m. on the late day.

Where the business carried on is that of retailing tobacco, cigarettes and smokers' requisites, the local authority may substitute later hours if they are satisfied that such substitution is desired by at least two-thirds of the shopkeepers concerned. The hours may be 9.30 p.m. and 10 p.m. on the late day.

In Holiday Resorts and Sea Fishing centres, the local authority may substitute later hours for a period not exceeding four months in one year to meet the pressure of seasonal business. If such later hours are permitted, then the assistants in the shop concerned must be given a fortnight's holiday on full pay. The following goods and transactions are not affected by the closing hour:

The sale after the closing hour of:—

(a) Meals or Refreshments (including table waters, sweets, chocolates, sugar confectionery, and ice cream) for consumption on the premises or, in the case of refreshments sold on railway premises, for consumption on the trains. Tobacco supplied at a meal for immediate consumption is counted as part of the meal.

(b) Newly cooked provisions and cooked or partly cooked tripe to be consumed off the premises.

(c) Intoxicating liquors consumed on or off the premises. (See LICENSING.)

(d) Tobacco, table-water or matches on licensed premises during the hours during which intoxicating liquor is permitted by law to be sold on the premises.

(e) Tobacco, matches, table waters, sweets, chocolates, or other sugar confectionery or ice cream, at any time during the performance in any theatre, cinema, music hall or other similar place of entertainment; so long as the sale is to a bona fide member of the audience, and takes place in a part of the building to which no other members of the public have access.

(f) Medicine or medical or surgical appliances so long as the shop is kept open only for such time as is necessary for serving the customers.

(g) Newspapers, periodicals, and books from the bookstalls of such terminal and main line stations as may be approved by the Secretary of State.

(h) Aircraft, motor, or cycle supplies or accessories for immediate use, so long as the shop is kept open only for so long as is sufficient for the service of the customer.

(i) Victuals, stores, or other necessaries required by any naval, military or air force authority for His Majesty's forces or required for any ship on her arrival at, or immediately before her departure from a port, so long as the shop is only kept open for the time necessary to the serving of the customer.

(j) The transaction after the closing hour of any form of post office business.

The provisions of the acts relating to the general closing hours may be suspended by the Secretary of State during the Christmas season or in connection with special occasions.

Any failure to comply with the provisions of a closing order or the breach of a condition imposed by any order made under the Shop Acts, makes the occupier liable to a fine of £5 on the first offence, and £20 for the second offence.

No offence against a closing order is committed by serving a customer after the closing hour, who was in the shop before the closing hour, or where the article supplied was required because of illness.

Half-day Closing.—All shops, with certain specified exceptions, must be closed for the serving of customers, not later than one o'clock in the afternoon on one day every week.

The local authority may fix the day on which shops are to be closed and that day may be the same for all shops, or different days for different classes of shops; the early closing day may be different for different periods of the year.

Shops where post office business is carried on in addition to any other business do not have to close on the weekly half-holiday for post office business, but the shop must, to secure this exemption, be a telegraph office.

Shops where the following trades or businesses are carried on are exempt from the necessity of having an early closing day.

The sale of:—Intoxicating liquors by retail, refreshments, motor, cycle and air-craft supplies and accessories to travellers, newspapers and periodicals, meat, fish, milk, cream, bread, confectionery, fruit, vegetables, flowers, and other articles of perishable quality, tobacco and smokers' requisites, medicines, medical appliances, surgical appliances, and business carried on at an exhibition or show if the local authority certifies that such trade is only subsidiary to the main purpose of the exhibition.

Assistants.—No young person may be employed in a shop for more than seventy-four hours including meal times, in one week. A young person must not be employed in a shop who has already been employed on the same day for the maximum number of hours permitted in a Factory or Workshop. In a shop where a young person is employed, a notice must be posted up in a conspicuous place stating the number of hours during the week in which a young person may lawfully be employed. This provision applies to whole-sale shops and warehouses where assistants are employed, just as if they were shops in accordance with the statutory definition set out above.

A young person is a person under the age of eighteen years.

A shop assistant must on at least one day in each week cease to be employed after half past one o'clock, except during the week preceding a Bank Holiday, if the shop assistant is not employed on the Bank Holiday, and is not employed beyond 1.30 p.m. on one day in the following week in addition to the Bank Holiday.

Refreshment Houses.—If the occupier of premises where refreshments are retailed, adopts the provisions of the Act of 1913, and the assistants are wholly or mainly employed in connection with the sale of intoxicating liquors or refreshments for consumption on the premises, then the assistants' hours are different.

Under the provisions of that Act, no assistant may be employed for more than sixty-five hours in one week, excluding meal times. Every assistant must be allowed (i) thirty-two whole holidays on a week day, of which two must be given in each month, and must comprise a holiday on full pay of at least six consecutive days (ii) twenty-six whole holidays on Sunday so distributed that at least one out of every three consecutive Sundays is a whole holiday.

Meal Intervals.—Where the hours of employment include the hours from 11.30 a.m. to 2.30 p.m. each assistant must be allowed an interval of three-quarters of an hour for dinner within those hours if the assistant takes the meal on the premises, or an interval of a full hour if the meal is taken elsewhere. If the assistant is employed between the hours of 4 p.m. and 7 p.m. then he or she must be allowed an interval of half an hour for tea during those hours.

The penalty for non-compliance with any of these provisions is £1 for a first offence, £5 for a second and £10 for a third offence.

An employer who employs female assist-ants in premises used in connection with a retail trade must provide behind the counter, or in some other suitable position, not less than one seat for every three female assistants. The penalty for disregarding this provision is a maximum of £3 for a first offence and not less then £1 and not more than £5 for any subsequent offence. (*See* FACTORY.)

SHOP CLUB.—A Society formed to provide benefits to persons who work in a factory, or a shop, or a warehouse. These societies are sometimes known as "Thrift Clubs." Membership is usually confined to persons actually employed in a particular factory or shop, but if the rules do not forbid it, a workman who has left the place of employment connected with his club, may, at his option, remain a member of the club, or have the amount of his share of the club funds paid over to him.

It is an offence punishable by a fine not exceeding £5 for an employer to make it a condition of employing a person that he or she must join a shop club, unless such club is registered and certified by the Registrar of Friendly Societies.

A shop club may be registered if the registrar is satisfied that it affords substantial benefits to the workmen in the form of contributions by the employer in addition to those paid by the workmen. The registrar must be satisfied that three-fourths of the workmen desire the club to be registered before he may register it. (*See* FRIENDLY SOCIETY.)

SHORT CAUSE.—A special list is kept in the King's Bench Division called the Short Cause List, and into this list are put cases which require an early trial and which are not likely to take up very much time. If the plaintiff has applied for summary judgment, i.e. has adopted the procedure under which the defendant is compelled at a very early stage to disclose that he has a good cause of defence, the master, if he decides that the defendant has shewn some grounds of defence, may send the case to the short cause list.

In the Chancery Division a case may be heard as a short cause if the Counsel in charge of the case certifies that it is proper in his opinion to be so heard.

SHOT GUN.—Any person who uses or even carries a gun outside his own house

Sir John Simon.

and garden, must possess a gun licence. A gun for this purpose includes any firearm such as an air-gun or a toy pistol.

The only persons who are exempted from holding a gun licence are: (1) holders of a game licence (q.v.) which is current; (2) persons carrying a gun for the holder of a gun licence or game licence; (3) occupiers of land using or carrying a gun on his land only for the purpose of killing vermin or scaring birds, or anyone using a gun for that purpose by the orders of the occupier, if the occupier himself holds either a gun licence or a game licence.

Gun licences are obtainable at a price of 10/- from the local police station and are current until the next 31st July when they must be renewed. Carrying or using a gun without a licence, or refusing to show a gun licence when it is demanded by a police constable, is an offence punishable with a fine not exceeding £10. Anyone found guilty of poaching (q.v.) forfeits his gun licence.

In addition to a gun licence, anyone who has a firearm on his premises must obtain a permit, which can be obtained for any good reason from the local police station; but none is needed for a smooth-bored gun. (*See* FIREARMS; GAME; GAME LICENCES.)

SICKNESS BENEFIT.—Sickness benefit is the weekly sum payable under the National Health Insurance Scheme to insured persons when they are prevented from working owing to sickness or disease. It is payable on and after the fourth day of incapacity and for a minimum period of 4 days and a maximum period of 26 weeks, including the first four days of incapacity. It is payable upon certificate from the panel doctor. (*See* NATIONAL HEALTH INSURANCE.)

SILK.—A King's Counsel is sometimes referred to as a "Silk." This is so because he wears a silk gown, while a junior barrister wears a stuff one. When a barrister becomes a King's Counsel he is said to "take silk."

SIMON, Sir John (1873-   ).—He is known to the public alike for his great political and legal career, and possesses one of the most brilliant intellects of the century. At the bar his work was mainly on the civil side, but he is noted for the magnificent speech he made in defence in the Malcolm murder trial. He led for the defence in Rex v. Lord Kylsant.

SIMONY.—Simony is the trafficking in ecclesiastical dignities or benefices for money. Any transaction attended by simony is void, and any person who, by virtue of such a transaction, has acquired any benefice, becomes prohibited by law from taking any advantage from it. All clergymen on institution to a benefice are required to make a declaration against simony; and any breach of this declaration renders the offender liable to proceedings being taken against him.

SIMPLE LARCENY.—Larceny may be either simple or compound. Simple larceny is stealing unaccompanied by aggravating circumstances. Compound larceny, on the other hand, is stealing accompanied by circumstances rendering the offence more serious: for example, where violence is used in order to effect a crime, or where things are stolen from special places—such as ships or enclosed premises—or where the thing stolen is something which the law regards as requiring special protection, such as cattle.

SINE DIE.—This is a Latin expression meaning without date fixed. When any case or other legal matter is adjourned without any date being fixed for the resumed hearing, it is said to be adjourned sine die.

SITTINGS.—Until 1873 the legal year was divided into terms, but since that time the division into sittings has been substituted. There are in each year four sittings, the Michaelmas (October 12th—temporarily October 1st—to December 21st), Hilary (January 11th to the Wednesday before Easter, Easter (from the Tuesday after Easter week until the Friday before Whit Sunday), and Trinity (from the Tuesday after Whitsun week until July 31st.) (*See* TERMS; VACATION.)

SLANDER.—A defamatory statement, that is a statement concerning some person which has a tendency to diminish the good opinion which others have of that person, and to expose him to public ridicule, hatred or contempt. A slander is a defamatory statement, made verbally, or in some other transitory form such as gestures. As a general rule, a slander is not actionable without proof of actual damage, that is to say, unless the person complaining of the slander is able to prove that he has suffered some financial loss as a result of the statement. To this rule there are four important exceptions.

(1) Where the slander is a statement charging a person with a crime which is punishable corporally, i.e. by imprisonment.

(2) Where the slander imputes unchastity or adultery to any woman;

(3) Where the slander imputes that a person is suffering from a contagious disease;

(4) Where the slander is made in relation to a person's office trade, or profession or trade. (*See* DEFAMATION.)

SLANDER (SCOTS LAW). — In Scots Law the distinction between defamatory statements which are verbal (slander), and those which are in writing (libel) is not found, and any statement which is defamatory may be the subject of an action, even though the person injured cannot prove that he has suffered actual financial loss through the statement.

SLANDER OF GOODS.—If one person falsely and maliciously depreciates the goods or merchandise of another, and causes a financial loss to that other, the remedy in law which may lie to the person wronged is known as an action for Slander of Goods.

SLANDER OF TITLE. — If one person makes a false and malicious statement concerning another person's title to goods or property, and that other person suffers a financial loss as a result of that false statement, such a statement is known in law as an Injurious Falsehood, and an action

for Slander of Goods or Slander of Title would probably lie. Thus, if B advertised a freehold house for sale, and A falsely said that the freehold of the house, which B had advertised, did not belong to B, and as a result of the statement, some person who would have bought the house did not buy it, then B would probably be entitled to bring an action for slander of title against A, and so obtain compensation in the form of damages for the wrong done to him. (*See* DEFAMATION; MALICIOUS FALSEHOOD; SLANDER OF GOODS.)

SLATE CLUB.—A slate club is a society which lives only from year to year, and at the end of each year wipes its transactions "off the slate." A small amount of the funds may be left over to the coming year, but it is not usually sufficient to be regarded as a reserve to meet any future claims.

After meeting claims for sickness and death which have arisen during the year, the remainder of the funds are divided up among the members.

A slate club is a kind of friendly society and it may be registered as such, provided there is an express provision in the rules that all claims are to be met which are outstanding before the division takes place. A slate club, even when registered, is not bound to take any steps to provide for possible future claims, outside its year of business. (*See* FRIENDLY SOCIETY.)

SLAUGHTER-HOUSE.—Any building used as a slaughter-house must be registered with the local sanitary authority, who keeps a special register for such purpose.

A licence is granted by the authority empowering premises to be used as a slaughter-house, and no premises may be used as a slaughter-house until such a licence is obtained. Anyone using premises without a licence is liable to a penalty of £5. Slaughter-houses must be inspected by an inspector of the local authority from time to time, to see that they are kept in a clean and proper state and that no cruelty in the methods of slaughtering is allowed to occur. (*See* PUBLIC HEALTH; KNACKERS.)

SLUM.—The law does not specifically recognise the word slum, but it is fully aware of the existence of housing conditions which make up what is called a slum, and a substantial portion of its provisions is taken up by attempts to solve a problem which is as much the concern of the law as the prevention of crime. (*See* HOUSING; PUBLIC HEALTH.)

SMALL DEBT COURT (SCOTS LAW).—This is a Court held by the Sheriff-Substitute for the purpose of hearing cases in which debts for amounts up to £20 are claimed.

SMUGGLING. — Smuggling is the secret importation into the country of dutiable or prohibited articles. A customs officer may search for undeclared articles any ship in any port of the United Kingdom or the Channel Islands, or any person on any such ship or who has landed from one.

If any passenger, on being asked by a customs officer whether he has any dutiable articles, does not disclose all he has in luggage or on his person, he is liable to forfeit them and also to pay £100 or treble the value of the smuggled goods. Similar penalties are applicable in any other form of fraudulent evasion of customs duties.

SODOMY.—This is a felony punishable by penal servitude for life.

SOLDIER.—A soldier of the Regular Army is subject to Military Law during the whole period of his engagement. If he deserts, he is liable to arrest by the civil police and to be handed over to the military authorities. A soldier may be arrested and tried by Court Martial within three months of his discharge for any offence committed whilst subject to military law.

Soldiers are subject to the ordinary law of the land. They may be tried in the ordinary Criminal Courts for crimes and sued in the Civil Courts in respect of debts or other matters. No soldier may, however, be compelled to appear in person or be taken away from his unit in respect of any debt under £30. Army pay cannot be stopped for civil debts.

When any maintenance or affiliation order is made against a soldier, the Army Council may direct that he shall be subjected to certain stoppages of pay to meet the amount of the order. (*See* MILITARY LAW.)

SOLICITOR.—The legal profession in England is divided into two classes, solicitors and barristers, each of which performs different functions. The distinction may be somewhat loosely stated by saying that it is the solicitor's duty to concern himsel. with matters which do not go into Court,

and to prepare cases which he instructs a barrister to present in Court, whereas it is the barrister's duty to appear in Court. A solicitor is, above all, an officer of the Court, and this imposes on him many important duties, and in particular the duty on all occasions of doing nothing which may mislead the Court.

Admission of Solicitors.—A solicitor is admitted after having served under Articles as an articled clerk and passed certain examinations held under the management of the Law Society.

Discipline.—The Master of the Rolls has appointed a committee from among the members and ex-members of the Council of the Law Society known as the Disciplinary Committee, and it is this committee which hears any allegations made against solicitors. It has power to suspend or strike off the rolls any solicitor. The cases in which a solicitor may be struck off the rolls are where he has committed any crime or has been guilty of professional misconduct. An appeal lies against any order made by the committee to the High Court, either by the solicitor himself or by the person applying to have him struck off. The Master of the Rolls has power at any time, if he thinks fit, to order the registrar to replace on the roll the name of a solicitor whose name has been struck off or removed from the roll.

Practising Certificates. — Every solicitor who desires to practise must obtain a practising certificate, and in order to do so, must apply to the registrar of the Law Society by writing, stating the name and place of his business and date of his admission, and signed by himself or his partner, or, if the place of business is more than twenty miles from London, by his London agent on his behalf, and must at the same time produce to the registrar a duly signed duplicate of the declaration.

The Law List, which is a list published by the authority of the Commissioners of Inland Revenue, is taken as evidence in any Court that the persons named therein as solicitors holding certificates were in fact solicitors and did in fact hold the certificates.

Qualifications and Privileges.—No person is entitled to act as a solicitor unless his name is on the roll and he has also in force a duly stamped practising certificate.

No unqualified person is entitled to act as a solicitor or as such to sue out any writ, or process, or commence, or carry on any litigation in the name of any other person or in his own name, and if any person does so act he is guilty of a misdemeanour and contempt of court and in addition is liable to a penalty of £50, recoverable by action.

Any person who has not in force a practising certificate who wilfully pretends to be, or takes or uses any name, title, addition or description implying that he is qualified to act as a solicitor is liable to a fine of £10. Further, any person not being a barrister or solicitor, who, for any fee or gain or reward, draws or prepares any document relating to real or personal estate or any legal proceeding is liable to a fine of £50. This provision does not apply to public officers acting in the course of their duty or to persons employed merely to engross, that is, write out any document. The expression "document" does not include a Will nor an agreement under hand only, i.e. not under seal, nor a Letter or Power of Attorney nor a transfer of stock which does not contain any trust or limitation of the stock. Unqualified persons may charge fees for drawing these documents and may, of course, draw any document so long as they do not charge fees. Unqualified persons are also guilty of offences if for any fee or gain or reward they prepare any instrument of transfer or charge for the purposes of the Land Restriction Act, or make any application or lodge any document for registration under that Act, or if they prepare any papers on which to found or oppose a grant of Probate or of Letters of Administration. Where any person acts as a solicitor when he is not qualified to do so, he is not entitled to recover any costs in respect of anything done by him.

Remuneration.—The work which a solicitor does is divided for the purpose of remuneration into contentious and non-contentious business. Contentious business includes such matters as a solicitor does in any Court, whether as a solicitor or as an advocate, and generally matters connected with litigation. Non-contentious business includes any business connected with sales, purchases, leases, mortgages, settlements and any other matters of conveyancing.

Agreements.—In either of these cases a solicitor may make an agreement with his client with regard to the remuneration which he is to receive, and may provide that the remuneration shall be a gross sum or by salary or otherwise. In the case of non-contentious business the remuneration may be by a percentage, but it is not permissible for a solicitor to agree to be remunerated by a share of any property recovered in litigation. The agreement must be in writing and signed by the client or his agent for that purpose. Where the solicitor wishes to recover in the case of work done under an agreement for non-contentious matters, he may bring an action in the ordinary way, but in the case of agreements for contentious matters he is not entitled to sue but must apply for an order of the Court directing the money to be paid. Any provision in such an agreement that the solicitor shall not be liable for negligence is void.

The Court, before enforcing the agreement, will consider whether it is fair and reasonable, and if they do not consider it such, may declare it to be void. Where the business covered by the agreement is business done in an action, the solicitor shall not be entitled to receive the amount due until the agreement has been examined and been allowed by a Taxing Officer of the Court. Where the amount agreed for under the agreement has been paid to the solicitor, the person making the payment may at any time within twelve months apply to the Court, and if he can shew that there are special circumstances requiring the agreement to be re-opened, the Court will re-open the agreement and it will then be necessary to consider whether or not it is fair and reasonable and the amounts under it properly incurred by reference to a taxation.

Any agreement by a solicitor which involves any purchase by him of any interest in any contentious matter, or any agreement by which a solicitor agrees to carry on any action for payment only in the event of success is invalid.

Where no Agreement.—Where there is no special agreement, the solicitor must deliver a detailed bill of costs. No action can be brought by a solicitor to recover any costs due to him until a month after the bill has been delivered. The bill must be signed by the solicitor or a partner and delivered to the party who is to be charged therewith either personally or by post. If the party disputes the amount of the bill, he may apply within one month to the Court to have the bill taxed, i.e. each item considered by an official called a taxing master, and for an order that no action be commenced until the taxation is complete. Even if no application is made within a month, the Court has still a discretion to order the taxation of the bill; but if application is made within the month, the order for taxation will follow automatically. If, however, twelve months have expired from the delivery of the bill or if the bill has been paid, no order for taxation will be made except in special cases, and in no event can any order be made more than twelve months after the bill has been paid.

Scales of Remuneration: Non-contentious Work — Conveyancing Matters.—The fees to which solicitors are entitled for conveyancing matters are fixed by a scale established in 1882, and altered from time to time. At the present time a solicitor is entitled to the scale charges and also to an additional 20%.

Solicitor may choose Payment by Time and Labour instead of Scale Charges.—When the business which the solicitor is conducting is one which falls within some of the definite fees included in the scale charges, calculated on the value of the property, the solicitor may, before undertaking the business, communicate with the client and elect that he shall be paid on the basis of fees calculated by time and folio. Unless, however, the solicitor gives the client this intimation he can charge only according to the fixed scales.

It should be appreciated that these amounts have now been increased by 20% in respect of all business done after November 30th, 1932. In respect of business done before that date, the rates were increased by $33\frac{1}{3}\%$.

Where a solicitor has elected to be paid by a gross sum instead of detailed charges, the client at any time within twelve months after delivery of the charges or within one month after payment, may require a detailed bill of charges.

Contentious Business.—It has been noticed above that a solicitor may make a special agreement as to contentious business, which must be in writing signed by the client, and that this agreement must be approved by a taxing officer before it can be enforced. It is very difficult, if not impossible, to determine beforehand what the costs are likely to be in any litigation.

Where no such agreement, the solicitor must present his bill calculated in accordance with a prescribed scale. A scale fee has been prescribed for almost every act which the solicitor will be called upon to do during the course of an action. All the above items are now subject to an increase of 25%.

Duty to Client.—The solicitor is bound to exercise proper care in carrying out all matters on behalf of his client, and if he fails to do so he will be liable for damages for negligence. He cannot by any agreement provide that he is not to be liable for negligence. If, however, he chooses on the client's instruction to take the advice of a barrister on a matter, he cannot be made liable for damages for acting on that advice even though it should turn out to be wrong advice. The barrister is not liable for negligence in any event.

Lien.—A solicitor is entitled to retain all papers belonging to his clients until the money due to him for costs is paid. This is known as his lien. He may also obtain a charging order from the Court, which charges any property recovered or preserved through the solicitor's instrumentality and entitles the solicitor to be paid his costs out of that property.

SOLICITOR (SCOTS LAW).—Solicitors in Scotland are controlled by a General Council which is elected by various societies of a local character carrying out the functions of solicitors throughout Scotland. Each member of the Council must be a member of the Society by whom he is elected.

SOLICITOR-GENERAL.—The Solicitor-General is one of the two law officers of the Crown. He is junior to the Attorney-General, and is subject to his direction. He is always a King's Counsel, and is usually a Member of Parliament. His duties are similar to those of the Attorney-General (q.v.).

SOLICITING.—Any common prostitute who solicits passers-by for immoral purposes may be arrested without warrant by any constable. The maximum punishment that may be inflicted is a fine of forty shillings or imprisonment for fourteen days. The offence may be committed in any place of public resort.

SOMERSET HOUSE. — This is a large building in the Strand, London, in which are many public offices—in particular the Inland Revenue Office, Probates of Wills, Companies, and the office at which are kept the registers of births, deaths and marriages.

SPECIAL CASE.—Either the prosecutor or the defendant may appeal on a point of law from a decision of a Court of Summary Jurisdiction by way of special case. The procedure is for the justices to state their findings of fact, and to ask for the decision of the High Court of Justice as to whether on those findings their decision was correct in law. The legal questions so raised are then argued before a Divisional Court of the King's Bench Division and a decision given. A similar method of appeal exists in the case of decisions of Quarter Sessions on appeals from Courts of Summary Jurisdiction.

SPECIAL CONSTABLE.—When on duty a special constable exercises powers similar to those of any other constable. Resisting a special constable renders the offender liable to a fine of £20. It is also an offence without authority to wear the dress of, or pose as a special constable. (*See* SPECIAL SUPPLEMENT "THE POLICE.")

SPECIAL DAMAGE. — Where a person is bringing an action and claiming damages, these may be either general or special. Special damages are the actual financial loss which the plaintiff has sustained by reason of the matter in respect of which he is bringing his action. He must prove each item on these damages.

General damages, on the other hand, are matters which do not amount to any definite financial loss, and therefore cannot be proved in detail, but which have to be calculated to some extent by guess work by the Court. Thus, if a person has been injured in a motor accident, his special damages will probably consist of doctor's bill and medical services during the period that he was ill, and also the oss of his wages or earnings through being incapacitated during that period. He must establish the amount of these special damages. In addition, however, he will be entitled to general damages for the pain and suffering he has sustained through the accident and also, if his injury is likely to continue for some time or to incapacitate him permanently, he will be entitled to general damages to compensate him for that incapacity. (*See* DAMAGES.)

SPECIAL DEFAULT SUMMONS. —Where a plaintiff in a County Court action has a claim against a defendant for a debt or ascertained sum of money greater than £10, he may, at the time of entering the plaint, file an affidavit setting out briefly the facts upon which he relies as constituting his claim, and issue a Special Default Summons instead of an ordinary summons.

If the defendant does not within 10 days after service of the Special Default Summons file an affidavit stating that he intends to defend the action, the plaintiff may sign judgment against him forthwith. (*See* COUNTY COURT PROCEDURE.)

SPECIAL DEFENCE.—As a general rule the defendant to an action in the County Court is not required to give to the plaintiff any notice of the facts on which he intends to rely in defence to the claim; but, where the defendant is relying on certain specified facts which are called special defences, notice must be given. (*See* COUNTY COURT PROCEDURE.)

SPECIAL EXEMPTION ORDER. —This is an order which allows the holder of an on-licence to keep his premises open after permitted hours on any special occasion or occasions. It can be obtained from a Petty Session Court, or, in the metropolis, from the Commissioner of Police. It cannot be obtained by the holder of an off-licence. As to what is a special occasion, that is a matter for the Court or Commissioner. A ball or dinner is the usual occasion, and Christmas and Christmas Eve have both been held to be special occasions, though summer time has not. (*See* GENERAL EXEMPTION ORDER; PERMITTED HOURS.)

SPECIAL JURY.—(*See* JURY.)

SPECIAL LICENCE. — The Archbishop of Canterbury has the right of granting a special licence for a marriage to take place anywhere in England and in any place. A marriage by special licence may be solemnised in any building named even though it is not a church or chapel and without the publication of banns. A special licence cannot, of course, legalize a marriage between persons who cannot lawfully marry each other.

SPECIALLY ENDORSED WRIT.

—Where the plaintiff in an action considers that there is no defence to the action, he may obtain judgment very speedily by means of what is known as a specially endorsed writ. If the defendant enters an appearance to the writ, the plaintiff may take out a summons requiring the defendant to disclose on affidavit what his defence is. The summons is then heard by a Judge called a master who, unless he is satisfied that the defendant has disclosed some defence to the action, will give judgment for the plaintiff.

The master does not try the case, but merely assumes for the purpose of the summons that the facts alleged by the defendant in his affidavit are true. If the master is of the opinion that on those facts the defendant might succeed in his defence, he will not give judgment, but will direct the case to be tried in the ordinary way.

Almost any claim may be included in a specially endorsed writ in this way except claims for libel or slander, malicious prosecution, false imprisonment, seduction, breach of promise, or actions in which the plaintiff alleges fraud. In all these cases the plaintiff cannot proceed by this speedy method, but must issue his writ with an ordinary endorsement.

SPECIALTY DEBT.

—Where a sum of money is due under a document under seal, i.e. a deed, it is called a specialty debt. It is not barred under the Statute of Limitations until twenty years have elapsed.

SPECIFIC PERFORMANCE. —

Where a party to a contract refuses to carry out his promises the party wronged may bring an action in the Court for an order for specific performance, i.e. for an order by the Court that the party in default shall carry out his promises.

In order that he may be entitled to specific performance, the party wronged must be in a position to shew that the granting of mere money damages would not be a sufficient compensation for the failure to fulfil the contract. Thus, if A agrees to sell B a ton of potatoes, and subsequently fails to deliver

them, it is quite clear that pecuniary compensation will be ample remedy for B, since he may buy his potatoes from someone else, and if he recovers the extra price that he has been obliged to pay as damages (q.v.) he is in no worse position than if A had fulfilled the contract. On the other hand, if A agrees to sell B a house at No. 26, Acacia Avenue, and then fails or refuses to do so, B cannot buy this particular house, which is the one which he wants, from anyone else. Accordingly, damages for breach of contract would not be sufficient compensation, and in a case of this nature, B would be entitled to an order for specific performance. (*See* BREACH OF CONTRACT.)

SPEAKER. —

The Speaker is the Member of Parliament who presides over debates in the House of Commons. The Speaker is elected by members of that House from among their own number. Perhaps the most important legal duty of the Speaker is that of declaring, under the provisions of the Parliament Act, what are or are not money bills.

SPIES.

—The present law governing spying in this country is contained mainly in the Official Secrets Acts of 1911 and 1920. These Acts lay down very severe penalties for any spying prejudicial to the safety or interests of the State, and grant to the police extensive powers in the detection of spies.

Certain places are, by the Acts, created prohibited places, and the mere approach to, or being in the neighbourhood of, any prohibited place for any purpose prejudicial to the safety or interests of the State is a felony, punishable with penal servitude for not more than fourteen years. Prohibited places include all arsenals, camps, dockyards, or similar establishments belonging to, or occupied by the Crown, and all places used by the Crown for the manufacture or storage of munitions of war, or of plans or similar documents relating thereto. A similar offence is committed by anyone who, for the purpose of spying, makes any sketch or note which might be directly or indirectly useful to an enemy; or who collects or communicates to any other person, by speech or writing, any secret official code word, or any model or document, or any information which might be directly or indirectly useful to an enemy.

The acts provide facilities for proving these offences. If anyone is charged with any of these offences it is not necessary for the prosecution to prove the commission of any particular act, tending to shew a purpose prejudicial to the safety and interests of the State; but if, from the circumstances of the case or the conduct of the accused, or his known character, it appears that such was his purpose, he may be convicted. Further, once it is shewn that a person has, without lawful authority, done any of the acts set out above, it is for him, and not for the prosecution, to prove the purpose for which it was done.

SPILSBURY, Sir Bernard (1878-).—There is hardly a murder trial of any consequence in which Sir Bernard fails to appear as an important witness for the Crown. As Home Office Pathologist, he was first brought to public notice by his evidence in the Crippen case in 1910, and since then has appeared in many famous trials, among them the Seddons, Smith, Bywaters, Thompson, Vacquier, Greenwood and Rouse.

SPRING GUNS.—No person is permitted, even on his own land, to set any spring gun or other trap, with the intention of injuring any person coming in contact with it. It would be no defence for a landowner who had committed this offence to plead that it could only injure trespassers, because this provision is intended primarily for the protection of trespassers. Even though a landowner does not set a gun himself, but merely permits such an article to remain set after finding it on premises which he has acquired, he commits this offence. The offence is punishable with penal servitude.

It is not, however, illegal to set traps of the kind which are used for the purpose of destroying vermin, provided the intention is merely the destruction of vermin, and not injury to human beings. Again, it is permissible to set spring guns or man-traps inside a dwelling-house provided that they are solely for the protection of the dwelling-house, and are not set during the day-time.

STAMP DUTIES. — When dealing with documents that are intended to have any legal effect, it is important to remember that the stamping of documents has been adopted as a method of obtaining revenue. Almost every type of legal document met

Sir Bernard Spilsbury.

with in everyday practice is liable to duty, and must bear an adhesive or impressed stamp to shew that the duty has been paid. A common illustration is a cheque. A cheque is a bill of exchange that is payable on demand. Such bills are made liable to duty by the Stamp Acts. A cheque therefore has a twopenny revenue stamp impressed on it.

The adhesive stamps used for postal purposes may be used for a stamp duty of an amount not exceeding two shillings and sixpence when stamping instruments of certain classes. In particular they may be used on the following:—Bills of exchange for the payment of money on demand, copies or extracts from a register, leases or agreements for a definite term not exceeding one year at a rent not exceeding £40, receipts. Where the amount of the duty is more than two shillings and sixpence, adhesive stamps issued only for revenue purposes must be used.

Penalties.—The Stamp Acts introduce three ways of compelling persons to stamp the instruments which they execute. (1) Fines are imposed on persons who execute certain instruments, when they have not been previously stamped in the proper way. (2) A money penalty much greater than the original duty must be paid if it is sought to stamp an instrument after execution. (3) An unstamped document cannot be used in evidence in any Court until the amount of the unpaid duty and the appropriate penalty have been paid (in practice an undertaking by the solicitor in the case that the amounts will be paid, is accepted). It is the duty of the Judge to take notice of the fact that a document tendered in evidence is unstamped, and it is immaterial that both parties are willing to allow it to be used. As might be expected, this provision does not apply to criminal proceedings, where unstamped documents may be used in evidence.

Exemptions.—Certain instruments are exempted from stamp duty if they fall within certain specific exemptions. Exemptions are of two important classes, general and special. Instruments covered by general exemptions are exempt from all stamp duty. A special exemption arises when a particular instrument of a class is exempted by statute from a duty that is imposed upon the class of instruments as a whole. The main general exemptions are:—transfer of shares in government stock or funds, instruments for the disposition of a ship, or share or interest in a ship, and testamentary dispositions.

Affidavits and Statutory Declarations.—These are liable to a duty of 2s. 6d. If, however, they are made for the purpose of being used in any Court or before any official of any Court they are exempt. Other exemptions are (1) When they are required by law; (2) When they accompany an application for a patent.

Agreement or Memorandum of Agreement.—These are liable to a duty of 6d. if they do not come under some other heading that renders them liable to a specific charge. A 6d. postage stamp may be used and should be cancelled by signature over it. The words "agreement or memorandum of agreement" do not cover every document that may refer to, or be evidence of a contract. A stamp is only needed when the parties to a contract draw up a document that is intended to be one containing substantially all the terms by which they are to be bound. They may have reached an agreement previously or only at the time when the document is drawn up. On the other hand, when a document is really a mere proposal made by one party to the other that may or may not be accepted, it is not covered by the above words. Once, however, there is a firm contract, any document that is drawn up and contains material terms will be chargeable. When an agreement is only reached after correspondence written by both parties, only one letter need be stamped. A receipt or acknowledgment of a debt is not liable to be stamped under this head unless it really embodies the terms of an agreement. Agreements are exempt from stamp duty in the following cases:—(1) When the value of the subject-matter is less than £5. (2) An agreement for the hire of any labourer or servant (as to the definition of servant, see MASTER AND SERVANT). (3) An agreement made for, or relating to, the sale of goods or merchandise. This exemption does not apply to agreements for work and labour (see CONTRACT), or to hire-purchase agreements.

Lease.—(1) For any definite term not exceeding a year of a dwelling-house at a rent of not more than £40 a year—1d. (2) A lease of any furnished dwelling-house or apartment for a definite term less than a year at a rent of more than £25 for the term—5s. 0d. (3) Any other type of lease where a rent is paid—if the rent does not exceed £5 p.a.—1s. 0d.

Rent exceeds £5 but not £10				2s. 0d.
,,	,, £10	,,	£15	3s. 0d.
,,	,, £15	,,	£20	4s. 0d.
,,	,, £20	,,	£25	5s. 0d.
,,	,, £25	,,	£50	10s. 0d.
,,	,, £50	,,	£75	15s. 0d.
,,	,, £75	,,	£100	£1 0s. 0d.

For every additional £50 or fractional part of £50 a further 10s. must be added.

The table given above applies when the term does not exceed 35 years, or is for an indefinite period. These figures must be multiplied by six when the term exceeds 35 but not 100 years; they must be multiplied by twelve when the term exceeds 100 years. Agreements for a lease for a term of not more than thirty-five years or any indefinite term, are charged with the same duty as an actual lease for a similar period. Then if a lease is entered into after the agreement, it is only chargeable with a duty of sixpence if the terms of the lease are the same as those of the agreement.

Letter of Allotment.—A letter of allotment of any shares of any proposed company is liable to a duty of sixpence when the nominal amount which is allotted is not less than five pounds.

Licence for Marriage.—Special licence—£5 0s. 0d.

Ordinary licence—10s. 0d.

Power of Attorney.—Where this is solely for the purpose of voting at a meeting by proxy, a duty of one penny is payable. Otherwise there is a general provision imposing a duty of ten shillings.

Receipts.—There is a duty of twopence on a receipt for amounts of £2 and upwards. The duty is payable, even though there is no formal receipt given, if some note or memorandum is handed over and is retained by the person paying the money. The stamp on the receipt should be cancelled by the person giving the receipt before he hands it over. A receipt that is given unstamped may be stamped with an impressed stamp on the following terms: (1) Within 14 days on payment of the duty and a penalty of £5; (2) Within one month on payment of the duty and a penalty of £10. A fine of £10 will be incurred by any person who—(1) Gives an unstamped receipt; (2) Refuses to give a stamped receipt; (3) Divides the amount payable, with intent to evade the duty.

STATEMENT OF AFFAIRS.—

When a debtor has filed a petition to have himself made bankrupt or when he is made bankrupt, a receiving order is made in a petition filed by a creditor; and the debtor must make out and submit in two copies to the Official Receiver a statement of affairs. This must be done within 3 days if the debtor is the petitioner, or 7 days if the petition is by a creditor, but this time may be extended by the Official Receiver. If the debtor is unable to make out his own statement of affairs, the Official Receiver will give him assistance. The statement of affairs must be in the form prescribed and the debtor must swear an affidavit that the statements in it are true. It sets out the debtor's assets, debts and liabilities, the names, residences and occupations of his creditors, what security they have, if any, and the times when the securities were given. If the debtor neglects without any reasonable excuse to file this statement of affairs, he may at once be adjudicated bankrupt. A similar statement must be prepared by the directors of a company which is being wound up. (*See* BANKRUPTCY; WINDING UP.)

STATEMENT OF CLAIM.—

Statement of Claim is a document in which the Plaintiff in an action in the High Court sets out the facts upon which he relies as constituting his claim and the relief or remedy which he asks the Court to grant him at trial. (*See* HIGH COURT PROCEDURE; PLEADINGS.)

STATUTE.—

A Statute is an Act of Parliament (q.v.). Things done by express permission of a statute are described as statutory.

STATUTORY OWNER.—

Parliament has recently provided that no matter how many persons may have interests in the same piece of land, how it may be settled, or who may be the owner of it, there must always be somebody with power to sell the legal ownership. This person is called the estate owner. He may be one of six different classes:—

An absolute legal fee simple owner;

A legal fee simple owner whose estate is encumbered with equitable interests;

A mortgagor;

A tenant for life under a settlement;

Trustees for sale;

A statutory owner.

The last named is the person who, whenever a minor under the age of twenty-one is entitled to land, becomes the owner of that land for all purposes of management and sale. He is, of course, a trustee for the minor. In the case of a sale to a minor, the vendor becomes the statutory owner; in a settlement, the trustees of the settlement; and under a will, the personal representatives of the deceased.

STAY OF EXECUTION.—

In the normal way in an action in the High Court execution may issue immediately judgment has been entered; and in the County Court after the expiry of 14 days after entry of judgment. It is open, however, to the judgment debtor to apply for a stay of execution either at the trial, after delivery of judgment, or upon application by summons at any time after the trial.

The usual grounds for applying for a stay of execution are when the judgment debtor intends to appeal, for the mere fact of giving a notice of appeal does not operate as a stay. Another ground in the County Court may be where the judgment debtor wishes to be granted a right to pay the debt by instalments.

Applications after trial for the granting of a stay of execution are made in the County Court direct to the Judge after obtaining a summons from the Registrar's Office, and in the High Court to the Court which gave the judgment. (*See* APPEAL FROM COUNTY COURT; APPEAL FROM HIGH COURT; EXECUTION.)

STEALING. (*See* LARCENY.)

STEP-CHILDREN.—A man is liable to maintain his step-children until they reach the age of sixteen or until the death of their mother, whichever is the earlier date; if the step-father dies, the mother is liable to maintain them; whether or not the father dies, the grand-parents must provide for them, if they are able and the father is unable to do so. The duties and rights of a step-father towards his step-children are practically the same as those of a father towards his children born in wedlock, e.g. he must see that they are educated, and must provide adequate food, clothing and medical aid. (*See also* FATHER; MOTHER.)

STILL-BORN INFANT.—A still-born infant is one born after the twenty-eighth week of pregnancy, and which did not shew any sign of life as part of a separate existence. A still-born infant must be registered just as any infant born alive, and must not be buried until the registrar's certificate has been given.

STIPENDIARY MAGISTRATE.—In London and certain of the big towns, most of the duties of the Justice of the Peace are performed by paid magistrates. These are whole time appointments and are held by barristers. In London such magistrates are called Metropolitan Police Magistrates. In boroughs outside London they are described as Stipendiary Magistrates. Such magistrates have all the powers exercised by ordinary unpaid magistrates in Petty Sessions.

STOCK.—When shares have been fully paid they may be converted into stock. The only advantage of stock over shares is that whereas it is only possible to deal in units of a certain number of shares (e.g. 100 or 1,000), stock may be split up into any smaller amounts desired, e.g. it is possible to buy £5 4s. 0d. worth of stock. Stock may be either registered in the books of the company (in which case it is like ordinary shares) or it may be payable to bearer, in which case it resembles share warrants. (*See* SHARES.)

STOCK EXCHANGE.—The Stock Exchange is a building in Throgmorton Street in London where the members meet for the purpose of dealing in shares. The public are not admitted. The Stock Exchange is owned by the persons who hold shares in it who must all be members. It is governed by a committee elected annually by the members. The committee has very wide powers of regulating business transactions and is responsible generally for the maintenance of good order. It has set up rules and insists that all dealings between members shall be according to these rules. It may expel or suspend any member violating the rules, or for other improper conduct. It also adjudicates between members cn disputes arising. Any member of the public may complain to the committee of the conduct of any member, and the committee may then hold a formal investigation.

The committee also publish an Official List of the price of shares made up from the bargains in the shares which have taken place, and no share can be quoted on the Stock Exchange in the Official List unless it complies with certain requirements of the committee designed to protect the public and to ensure, as far as possible, that the concern is genuine.

Members may be either brokers or jobbers. A broker acts on behalf of members of the public as their agent and receives for his trouble a commission on the amount of the transaction. The broker deals with a jobber. The jobber does not deal as an agent for anybody but on his own behalf, and usually the jobber specializes in one particular market or class of shares. Jobbers can only deal with brokers or with other jobbers in the Stock Exchange but they are, of course, entitled to make bargains with members of the public who are not members of the Stock Exchange so long as these bargains are not made in the house itself. When a jobber quotes a price of shares he usually gives two figures, a higher one at which he is prepared to sell and a lower one at which he is prepared to buy. Thus he may quote War Loan at $102\frac{1}{2}$ to $102\frac{3}{4}$. This means that he is prepared to buy at $102\frac{1}{2}$ but will only sell at $102\frac{3}{4}$. He takes his profit from ,he difference between those prices.

The Course of Business.—Although a broker is acting only as agent, he is yet considered to be liable personally so far as the Stock Exchange is concerned and, therefore, if his principal is unable to pay the broker, will himself be liable. Bargains, unless otherwise stated, are made and intended to be carried out on the settling day of the current account, and the parties must be ready to complete their bargains on that day. If the buyer or seller is unwilling to do so, he may be able to carry over or postpone the carrying out of his obligations until the next settling day by what is known as "carrying over." This is done on the first day of each settlement (known as "contango" day) and is at the making-up price, that is, at the price of the particular security arrived at according to the rules of the house at the time of the carrying over. Unless the making up price is exactly the same as the original contract price, one of the parties must pay to the other the difference between the two prices and these differences are paid on settling day.

The crowd outside the Stock Exchange during a financial crisis.

Transfer.—The transaction on the Stock Exchange is only the contract for the purchase of shares and does not affect the transfer of the property in the shares themselves. In order to do this, it is necessary for the seller to execute a transfer in favour of the buyer. (*See* SHARES.)

Default.—If the broker who has been employed by a client is unable to meet his obligations, the client's bargains are not affected and he will be able to enforce the transaction against the jobber with whom the broker has contracted on his behalf. Where a jobber defaults the client has no remedy against the broker.

Speculating.—Many persons enter into transactions on the Stock Exchange which are of a speculative nature. Thus, they may buy shares which they know quite well they will not be able to pay for in the expectation that the value of the shares will rise before the settling day, when they will be required to pay, and that they will, therefore, be able to sell the shares again at a higher price than they paid for them before the settling day arrives.

Transactions of this kind are perfectly legal and enforceable, and are distinguished from gaming and wagering contracts, which are not enforceable and are void. The distinction is that in gaming and wagering contract neither party is bound legally or enters into any binding legal obligation to take or deliver the shares. The intention of the parties does not matter, and the mere fact that one of them does not intend to fulfil his bargain, but intends to sell the shares again before settling day arrives, will not make the transaction one of gaming and wagering so long as the party is legally bound or has made a contract, the effect of which is to bind him to take up the shares and pay for them if required to do so. It is practically impossible to make a contract on the Stock Exchange which is void as being a gaming or wagering contract, for such a contract would not be made in accordance with the rules of the Stock Exchange.

Rigging the Market.—Rigging the market consists in arranging, by one method or another, for transactions and dealings to be carried out in the shares at a price which is not genuine. A very simple form of this is for a person who is interested in a company to instruct one broker to sell certain shares

Threadneedle Street—The Financial Centre of the World.

in it at a particular price and to instruct another broker to buy the same number of shares at the same price. The result will be that the first broker offers the shares in the market at that price where they are bought by jobbers who resell to the other broker, and there thus appears to be a genuine dealing in the shares which, of course, would appear on the official Stock Exchange list and might induce persons to believe that this was the true price of the shares. Where a person has been induced to buy shares by reading a false market price of this kind he may bring an action for fraud, and the person who has sold him the shares and rigged the market is guilty of obtaining money by false pretences. Where several persons are engaged in such a scheme they would all be guilty of conspiracy.

It should be noticed that there is nothing illegal in persons pooling shares and then instructing a broker to sell them at not less than a certain price and to buy all that are offered at that price. This also has the effect of artificially raising the price of a share. (*See* JOBBER; SHARES.)

STOLEN PROPERTY.—(*See* RESTITUTION OF PROPERTY.)

STONE-THROWING.—Any person who wantonly throws any stone or other missile in any street or any public place in a town may, on summary conviction, be required to pay a fine of forty shillings.

STOP ORDER.—Where money or stock has been paid into Court and is standing in the name of the Paymaster-General, any person wishing to prevent transfers of the money or stock without notice to himself may obtain a stop order.

STOPPAGE IN TRANSITU.—Where goods have been sold and where the property, i.e. ownership in them, has passed to the buyer, but where they are still in the possession of some carrier—e.g. a railway company—who is taking them from the seller to the buyer, the seller may, if the buyer becomes insolvent, stop the goods while they are in transit and take back possession of them.

It is only an *unpaid* seller who can exercise this right and a seller is not considered unpaid if he has accepted a bill of exchange which is not yet due, or if the whole of the price has been paid or tendered to him. For the purpose of stoppage in transitu the buyer is considered to be insolvent when he has either ceased to pay his debts in the ordinary course of business or cannot pay his debts as they become due. It is immaterial whether or not he has committed an act of bankruptcy or has been made a bankrupt.

Transit.—Goods are deemed to be in course of transit from the time when they are delivered to a carrier for the purpose of transmission to the buyer until the buyer takes delivery of them from the carrier. (*See* SALE OF GOODS.)

STRAY ANIMALS.—If cattle or similar animals by straying on the highway cause danger or annoyance to the users of it, anyone may take them and impound them in the local cattle pound. The owner of any such animals becomes liable to a fine not exceeding 40/-, plus the expense of feeding the animals whilst in the pound; if this is not paid within three days the impounded animals may be sold, provided notice has been given in the local newspaper of such impending sale.

STREET.—The word "street" by statute may include roads, lanes and paths which are not fronted by houses, and also roads, courts, alleys and squares which are private property and over which the public has no right or passage.

STREET BETTING.—It is illegal for persons to loiter in streets or other public places for the purpose of taking or paying bets. This applies not only to public highways, but to any public park, or any ground to which the public have a right to enter. It does not, however, apply to any racecourse on any day on which racing is taking place thereat.

Any person who is found making bets in any public place may be arrested by any police constable without warrant, and any document found in his possession relating to betting may be seized and forfeited by him. The offence is triable in a summary manner and is punishable by a fine. A third conviction for this offence may be punished by imprisonment without the option of a fine.

STREET COLLECTIONS.—Police authorities may make regulations governing street collections and "flag days" for charitable purposes. It is usual for the police to require a permit to be granted for each collection of this kind and only to grant this where the collection is not likely to cause an obstruction to the highway or footpath or any annoyance to passers-by. Regulations usually ensure also that the collection shall be carried on in a bona fide way: collecting receptacles must be used and the services of all collectors, etc., must be given gratuitously.

STREET MUSIC.—Street music produced by organ-grinders and similar persons is controlled by local bye-laws. Boroughs may prohibit the playing of music in the streets to the nuisance of residents and may render it an offence for any musician to continue playing after a resident or police constable has required him to desist. Contravention of such a bye-law may be punished by a fine of £5.

STREET TRADING.—Trading in the streets is subject to various bye-laws and, in general, street traders require a licence from the local authority. Local authorities have power to allow certain streets to be used as markets and to allot positions to traders for their stalls. Local education authorities may prescribe the conditions under which persons under sixteen years of age may trade in the streets. These conditions may include the wearing of badges and the determination of the times and places at which persons may carry on street trading.

STRIKE.—A strike is the name given to the action of workmen who agree together not to continue working for their employer and, in pursuance of that agreement, cease work simultaneously. A workman is lawfully entitled to strike at the end of the period for which he has agreed to work, and there is nothing illegal about the actions of any person who persuades men to determine their contracts of employment by giving proper notice, and to refuse to undertake a further term of employment except on certain conditions. If, however, a workman strikes or leaves his employment before the end of his contract, then he has committed a breach of contract and may be sued by his employer for damages.

There are certain provisions of the law relating to strikes which are applicable only to certain classes of workmen.

If a person employed by a local authority or company having the duty of supplying gas, water or electricity to a city, borough or place, wilfully breaks his contract of service with such local authority, knowing that the consequence of his doing so, whether alone or together with his fellow-workers, will be to deprive the inhabitants of their supply of gas or water, he commits an offence. The penalty upon conviction is a fine not exceeding £20 or prison for a maximum period of three months. Such workers are liable to the same penalty if they break their contracts knowing that their action in so doing is likely to endanger human life, or expose valuable property to the risk of damage.

Strike Rules.—A Trade Union may have amongst its rules provision for the maintenance of strikers and the funds may be applied for such a purpose provided it is a lawful strike. It is illegal and in breach of trust to apply trade union funds for the support of strikers who have ceased work in breach of their contracts, and anyone having an interest in the funds may apply to the Court for an injunction restraining the trustees from so using the funds.

A Trade Union rule which enables the committee to compel members to strike, or penalize them for not striking is an illegal rule, for it goes too far in restraint of trade by depriving a man entirely of his freedom of choice as to how he will dispose of his labour.

General Strike.—The Trade Union and Trade Disputes Act, 1927, lays it down that a strike is illegal if it has any object other than the furtherance of a trade dispute *within the trade or industry in which the strikers are engaged*, and if it is a strike designed to coerce the Government, either directly or indirectly, by inflicting hardships upon the whole community.

Non-Strikers.—A person refusing to take part in an illegal strike cannot be expelled from his trade union or made to pay any penalty, or be deprived of his right to a benefit or placed at a disadvantage as compared with his fellow-members.

The Courts are not debarred from enforcing the member's rights by reason of the fact that his rights arise under one of the agreements declared by law to be unenforceable by the Courts.

The Court may, instead of ordering an expelled member to be restored to membership, order that he be paid compensation or damages out of the trade union funds. (*See* TRADE DISPUTE; TRADE UNION.)

STRIKING OFF THE ROLL.— A solicitor is liable to be struck off the roll of solicitors either by the High Court or by the Disciplinary Committee of the Law Society if he is guilty of a criminal offence or of professional misconduct. (*See* SOLICITOR.)

STUFF GOWN.—While a King's Counsel wears a silk gown in Court, a junior counsel wears one made of stuff; hence the expression Stuff Gownsman.

SUB-LEASE.—Where a person who is himself a Lessee or tenant of land, grants to another a Lease, which must be a less interest than his own, no matter how small the difference, such interest is called a Sub- or Under-Lease. (*See also* LANDLORD AND TENANT.)

SUBORNATION.—The procuring of another to commit perjury. Any one guilty of this offence may be proceeded against and punished in the same way as the person who actually gives the perjured evidence. (*See* PERJURY.)

SUBPŒNA.—A Subpœna is an order directing the person on whom it is served to attend at a specified Court for the purpose of giving evidence or producing documents. At the time of serving a subpœna, sufficient money, called conduct money, should be handed to the witness to cover his or her expenses in reaching the Court. It is contempt of Court for a person on whom a subpœna has been properly served to fail to attend.

SUBROGATION.—Where one party has agreed to indemnify another in a certain event against loss and is called on, when the event happens, to make good the indemnity, he is entitled to all rights of action against other persons which the person indemnified may have in respect of the loss; and in order to enable him to enforce these rights of action, is entitled to be substituted for the person indemnified in respect of them. This substitution is known as subrogation.

Subrogation most usually arises in the case of insurance policies. (*See* INSURANCE.)

SUBSTITUTED SERVICE.— Where it is impracticable for a writ of summons, or any other summons, or a petition in the Probate, Admiralty and Divorce Division to be served personally upon a party in the ordinary way, application may be made to the Court for an order for substituted service. The Court must be satisfied by affidavit that an attempt has been made to serve the defendant personally and that such service has been impossible to obtain. A common way of satisfying the Court upon this point is to show that three appointments have been made with the defendant and that he has failed to keep any of them.

The usual method of substituted service ordered by the Court is the sending of the writ or summons to the defendant's usual address by registered post; but if his address is unknown, service may be made with the Court's permission by means of advertisements in the papers, etc. (*See* COUNTY COURT PROCEDURE; HIGH COURT PROCEDURE; WRIT OF SUMMONS.)

SUCCESSION.—(*See* INTESTACY.)

SUCCESSION DUTY.—All lands, whether freehold or leasehold, are liable to succession duty when they pass on death from one person to another. So also is all personalty (i.e. property other than lands), when legacy duty is not payable thereon. It does not matter that the person receiving the property (called the "successor") does not receive it immediately on the death of the person who left it to him (the "predecessor"). E.g., if money is left to a man's widow until she marries again, and then is to go to his child, the child will have to pay duty when the widow marries again, even though it be twenty years later. The duty is payable when the property passes by reason of an intestacy no less than when by a will. But the property must pass gratuitously: if Smith had agreed with Robinson that, if Robinson would give him five pounds, he (Smith) would leave him his house in his will, no duty would be payable on that house when, on Smith's death, it passes by Smith's will to Robinson.

The duty falls due as soon as the successor actually receives the property, and this, as has been mentioned above, may be years after the death of the predecessor. The successor is personally liable for the duty.

Payment of the duty is by eight half-yearly instalments, and the first payment must be made a year from the time when the successor took possession of the property. But in the case of property other than land, the whole amount must be paid on taking possession.

The percentage rate by which the amount to be paid is calculated varies according to the relationship of the successor towards the deceased. Where the successor was husband or wife, or direct descendant or ancestor of the predecessor, 1%; where the successor was brother, sister, niece or nephew of the predecessor, 5%; and in all other cases, 10%. But, except in the case

of husband or wife and in the case of leaseholds, all these duties will be raised by 1½% if no estate duty (q.v.) is paid on the estate.

There are numerous exemptions from duty. For example, where the total value of all successions on the same death does not exceed £100, or where the whole of the estate does not exceed £1,000 in value, no succession duty is payable at all. Furthermore, the 1% duty is remitted when (i) the value of the whole of the deceased's property upon which estate duty is payable does not exceed £15,000, or (ii) where the total amount of all benefits derived by the successor from the predecessor does not exceed £1,000 (or, in the case of the predecessor's widow or infant child, £2,000). (*See* ESTATE DUTY; LEGACY DUTY.)

SUFFRAGAN.—A suffragan bishop assists the diocesan bishop in his diocese. He is consecrated, but has no temporal power. He is "The Bishop" not "The Lord Bishop" of X. He has, in consequence, no right to a seat in the House of Lords. It is rare for a suffragan to be raised to the rank of diocesan.

SUI JURIS.—This is a Latin expression taken from Roman law.

In English law the expression is applied to a person who is independent of any authority limiting his legal rights. Of course, at the present time most persons of full age are "sui juris." The wife is no longer dependent upon her husband for her legal rights. Persons of unsound mind, and convicts, however, can sue only through the medium of a representative appointed to look after their interests. The same applies to all persons under the age of 21.

SUICIDE.—Self-murder. This is a felony, but for obvious reasons it is never punished, the offender being of necessity dead. An attempt to commit suicide is a misdemeanour, punishable by imprisonment. If two or more people agree to commit suicide together at the same time, and one of them for any reason survives, he may be convicted of murder. Cases of this kind are popularly described as "Suicide Pacts."

SUICIDE CLAUSE.—Policies of life insurance frequently provide that nothing shall be payable under them if the death of the person insured is caused by his own suicide. In some cases, however, it is provided that payment will be made even in the case of suicide so long as the suicide does not take place within a specified period from the commencement of the policy, e.g. a year or thirteen months. (*See* LIFE INSURANCE.)

SUMMARY DILIGENCE (SCOTS LAW).—In certain cases it is possible in Scots law to seize a debtor's property for a debt without first bringing an action in the Courts. Seizure of the property in this way is said to be summary diligence. It is available when a bill of exchange is dishonoured either by non-acceptance or non-payment.

SUMMARY JURISDICTION.—The criminal jurisdiction of England and Wales is of two kinds. There is the jurisdiction of the higher Court which tries cases of seriousness by means of juries. Cases of this kind are said to be tried on indictment. Minor offences are dealt with in what is popularly known as the Police Court. They are tried by magistrates who do not have the assistance of juries. Such Courts are correctly described as Courts of Summary Jurisdiction. There are certain offences which must be tried on indictment. Magistrates, however, have the power to try them with the consent of the accused person, if they think that such a course is proper, having regard to the nature of the charge and the antecedents of the prisoner.

SUMMARY ORDER IN LUNACY.—This is a special order which may be made for the detention of lunatics who are paupers or who are found wandering at large. (*See* DETENTION OF LUNATICS.)

SUMMER TIME.—Summer time, first introduced as a temporary measure during the war, has now a permanent place in English law. It commences at two a.m. on the Sunday after the third Saturday in April, or, if that should be Easter day, then the Sunday after the second Saturday in April. It ends at 2 a.m. on the Sunday following the first Saturday in October. Summer time is one hour in advance of Greenwich mean time.

SUMMING UP.—Whenever a case is tried by a Judge and jury, it is the duty of the Judge, at the conclusion of the evidence and after the addresses of counsel on both sides, to sum up to the jury. In his summing up, the Judge should tell the jury what

is the law applicable to the case, and what are the issues which they have to decide. He should then summarize the evidence on both sides, and the bearing of one portion of evidence on another. In summing up, a Judge is bound to be impartial, and although he may communicate to the jury his own view in regard to any particular fact, he should make it clear to them that while he has to decide questions of law, it is entirely for the jury to decide any questions of fact.

SUMMONS.—A summons is the general term applied to any document addressed by a Court to a litigant calling upon him to appear before the Court to answer a claim made against him.

The word is applied equally to a County Court Summons by which an action is started under the rules of County Court Procedure (q.v.), to the High Court Summons by means of which Interlocutory Proceedings are prosecuted under the rules of High Court Procedure (q.v.), and to a Police Court summons by which a person accused of a criminal offence may be brought before the Court. The distinction between these two types of summons should be borne in mind, and each should be carefully distinguished between the summons issued by a Petty Sessional Court by which criminal and quasi-criminal proceedings are instituted.

A High Court action is commenced by a Writ of Summons (q.v.). (*See* COUNTY COURT PROCEDURE; HIGH COURT PROCEDURE; WRIT OF SUMMONS.)

SUNDAY.—In early times the legislature attempted to enforce the use of Sunday as a day of rest. Under the Act of Uniformity, 1552, members of the Church of England are still required by law to attend divine service on Sundays and under a number of Lord's Day Observance Acts it is still illegal to work or take part in certain pastimes on Sunday.

The most important of these Acts, the Sunday Observance Act, 1677, forbids tradesmen, workmen, drovers and others from carrying on their business on Sunday under pain of a fine of 5/- or two hours in the stocks. A later Act, however, has provided that no prosecution may be brought under this Act without the consent of a police official or magistrate. Consequently, the Act is virtually dead and

Sunday trading generally is now seldom interfered with. The Act itself allows the sale of milk between certain hours and of food in inns and cookshops while other statutes allow bakers to work till 1.30 p.m.

Under the Factories and Workshops Acts it is illegal to employ women or children on Sundays except in creameries or where the workers are Jews observing a different Sabbath.

With regard to Sunday entertainment, an Act of 1780 made it illegal to use a house for public entertainment on Sunday and offenders were liable to pay up to £200 to anyone who cared to sue for it, the person suing being known as a "common informer." This Act, however, was virtually killed by another which gave the Crown power to remit any penalty imposed by it, but it still remains law, with modifications. The chief modification was made by the Sunday Entertainments Act (1932). This Act enables local councils, if their electors do not object, to license Sunday cinematograph entertainments. The Act provides that the employees must be given some other whole day's holiday in place of Sunday, while a percentage of the profits must be devoted to charity and to the Cinematograph Fund. Similar powers are given for licensing Sunday musical entertainments and the Sunday opening of museums, galleries, gardens, lectures and debates is legalized.

Under the Game Act, only rabbits may be shot on Sunday.

The hours of sale for alcohol are restricted on Sunday to five instead of the usual eight. There is no Sunday opening of public houses at all in Wales.

For all Court proceedings and for public bodies Sunday is a dies non, that is to say, a day on which no transactions may be carried out. On that day no legal process can be served nor any arrest made except in cases of treason, felony, and breach of the peace, though magistrates may, on Sunday, issue warrants for arrest or search.

Sunday is reckoned from midnight to midnight. Where the law provides for something to be done within a period of less than six days, a Sunday does not count as one of them.

SUPER TAX.—(*See* SPECIAL SUPPLEMENT "INCOME TAX.")

SUPREME COURT OF JUDICATURE.—This is the official name given to all those Courts which sit in the Royal Courts of Justice, Strand, and in the Assize Courts throughout the country, and to the final Court of Appeal in England and Scotland, the House of Lords. All actions without limit of size or nature with certain exceptions may be tried, appealed against and finally decided upon in one of the branches of the Supreme Court of Judicature. (*See* COURT OF APPEAL; COURTS; HIGH COURT OF JUSTICE; HOUSE OF LORDS.)

SURETY.—Where a person is to be released on bail (*see* BAIL), he is usually required to find one or more persons as sureties for his appearance when required. A surety is required to enter into a bond called a recognisance whereby he agrees to forfeit the amount for which he goes bail if the person for whom he pledges himself does not appear. In addition to the case of bail, sureties are required where persons are bound over to keep the peace, or to be on good behaviour, or for similar purposes.

SURRENDER.—Where a tenant wishes to escape from the obligations of a lease it is possible for him to arrange to surrender the lease to the landlord. This can only be done with the landlord's consent, for once the surrender has taken place the tenant's liability under the lease ceases. Where a tenant wishes to leave a house before the end of his lease it is a great advantage if he can induce the landlord to accept a surrender of the old lease and grant a new lease to some other person who may be found by the tenant. If the tenant merely assigns his old lease to the person who is to take his place his liability under the lease does not cease, for he may be called upon to carry out the obligations contained in the lease should the person to whom it has been transferred fail to do so.

Insurance.—In insurance the word has another meaning. Life insurance policies usually provide that the person insured may terminate his liability under the policy and also that of the insurance company by surrendering his policy for a fixed sum of money. Unless there is a provision in the policy for surrender, the insured will not be entitled to claim to surrender.

Policies usually have no surrender value until a certain number of years' premiums has been paid. The exact number differs in the case of various companies but is usually one, two, or three. The amount received on a surrender of a policy will be less than the amount of premiums paid. Some companies not only allow surrender but also include in their policies fixed sums at which they will be prepared to accept the surrender of the policies in each year. In such a case the surrender values are said to be guaranteed. (*See* LIFE INSURANCE; LANDLORD AND TENANT.)

SURROGATE.—A Surrogate is a substitute appointed by the Chancellor of a diocese to hold Consistory Courts in his absence. He must be a man of some skill in ecclesiastical law, a favourer of true religion and a man of modest and honest conversation. (*See also* CONSISTORY COURT; DIOCESE.)

SURTAX.—(*See* SPECIAL SUPPLEMENT "INCOME TAX.")

SURVIVOR.—Where several persons are killed in the same disaster there is, in the absence of evidence, no presumption that one survived the other. (*See* PRESUMPTION OF DEATH.)

SWEEPSTAKES.—There is really no distinction in principle between a sweepstake and a lottery. (*See* LOTTERY.) The Lotteries Act, 1833, provides that any person who sells tickets in any lottery not authorized by Parliament is liable to be convicted as a rogue and vagabond. A privately conducted sweepstake, as in a club, however, does not necessarily involve the sale of any tickets and somewhat different considerations apply. In general it may be said that there is a distinction to be drawn between public and private sweepstakes, and that, at any rate in practice, the latter are not made the subject of prosecutions. (*See* SPECIAL SUPPLEMENT "GAMBLING.")

SWEETS.—This is the name given to any liquor made from fruit and sugar which has undergone a process of fermentation in its manufacture.

It is most usually applied to British wines. (*See* INTOXICATING LIQUOR.)

SYNAGOGUE.—A synagogue should be certified in writing to the Registrar General, but there is no obligation so to do. Certain advantages, however, accrue from certification which make such a course advisable.

In particular, the secretary of a synagogue has statutory powers and duties as to marriage register, books, etc., if he has been confirmed in his office by a certificate from the President of the London Committee of Deputies of the British Jews.

T ABLE "A."—A model form of articles of association (q.v.)—i.e. internal regulations—which may be adopted by companies who do not wish to go to the trouble of preparing special articles of their own is prescribed by the Companies Act, and is called Table "A." This is not suitable for private companies (q.v.) because it does not contain the necessary limitation on their powers. (*See* ARTICLES OF ASSOCIATION; COMPANIES.)

TACKING.—The right to tack is a right which can be exercised in certain circumstances by a man who has lent two separate sums of money at different times on the security of mortgages of the same property. Prima facie mortgages are entitled to be paid off out of the proceeds of sale of the mortgaged property in the order in which they were created. Tacking alters this order. It is a right to treat the second advance as if it had been made at the same time as the first in order that, if the borrower should prove insolvent and the mortgaged property had to be sold, both the advances may be paid off in full before any other advance by any other person is considered. It can only apply where there have been at least three advances on the security of the same property; two of which have been made by the same person but at different dates, while the third has been made by a different person at some time in between the other advances. If A lends money on a mortgage of Blackacre to B, then C lends money on a mortgage of the same property, and lastly A lends a further sum also on a mortgage of the same property, A may be able to get both his loans paid off in full before C is entitled to be paid anything.

This right to tack can only be exercised in the following cases:

(i) If C consented at the time when A made his second loan.

(ii) If, at the time when A made his second loan, he had no knowledge that there had been any intervening mortgage to C. But if C had registered his mortgage in the Registry at Lincoln Inn Fields by that date, A cannot usually say that he had no knowledge of it. In the case of mortgages to banks, however, and other mortgages which are stated to be made for the purpose of providing security for further advances, the fact that the intervening mortgage (C's in the example) was registered before the further advance was made does not of itself prove that A had knowledge of it. In such cases it is necessary to shew that he had actual knowledge.

TAIL.—An estate tail is an estate in land which descends from father to son in the direct line, and in the event of a complete failure of issue will revert to the original owner.

Formerly nothing could be done to prevent an estate tail from passing, on the death of its owner, to his eldest son. The owner could neither dispose of it during his life nor by his will. For some time, however, it has been possible to "bar" (bring to an end) the entail, and the position now is that the owner can do so either during his life or by his will. He can, therefore, dispose of property in which he has an estate tail nearly as freely as if he were the fee simple owner. (*See* ENTAIL.)

TAVERNS.—(*See* INTOXICATING LIQUOR; PUBLIC HOUSES.)

TAXATION OF COSTS.—Where a solicitor makes a special agreement with his client as to the amount of remuneration which is to be paid to him, the agreement is valid, but the client in certain cases may apply to the Court to have the amount payable reduced. Where there is no agreement, the solicitor makes the claim for his costs by delivering a bill, and the client is then entitled to object to the items in the bill and claim to have the costs taxed. The client must make his claim within a month of the delivery of the bill, and if he claims within this period the Court will order the taxation. In the taxation the solicitor will have to justify the charges he has made, will

have to prove that they actually were incurred, and that the amounts are reasonable. The official before whom the taxing takes place, who is the registrar in the County Courts and a taxing master in the High Court, will allow or disallow each item.

If the client fails to apply for taxation within a month of delivery of the bill, an application may still be made either by the solicitor or the client, and the Court has power to order taxation. If, however, twelve months have expired from delivery of the bill, or if the bill has been paid, no order will be made on the application of the client except in special circumstances, and in no event will any order be made after the expiration of twelve months from the payment of the bill.

A client should be cautious before he applies for taxation, because unless he manages to reduce the bill by as much as one-sixth of the total amount he will have to bear the costs of the taxation, although, of course, he will not have to pay more than the reduced amount on the bill.

When the certificate of a taxing officer has been obtained, it is, unless it is set aside or altered by the Court, final as to the amount of costs due.

Principles of Taxation.—Costs may be taxed on any one of three principles. Firstly, as between party and party, secondly, as between solicitor and client, and thirdly, as indemnity costs. Taxation between party and party takes place when one party is called upon to pay the costs incurred by the other party in litigation. In a taxation of this kind the taxing master is very careful only to allow what is reasonable, and to cut down all fees and disbursements to the lowest possible amount. For example, if the victorious party has briefed a very expensive barrister to whom he has paid a hundred guineas, the taxing master will probably not allow that amount in taxation between party and party, but might reduce it, say, to thirty guineas. The result would be that the defeated party would have to pay thirty guineas of this item while the successful party would have to provide the other seventy guineas. In taxation between solicitor and client, the taxing master is less strict to disallow items on the ground that the charges are excessive, and would not, for example, in the case given above reduce the amount of the barrister's fee unless it was grossly improper. Indemnity costs include all expenses to which the client has been put by reason of litigation.

Where a litigant succeeds the usual order for the costs will be that his opponent must pay him costs taxed as between party and party. In certain cases, however, the costs which the opponent is ordered to pay may be those taxed either on a solicitor and client basis, or on an indemnity basis. An order for taxation on these scales will, however, only be made in cases where the proceedings were unwarranted, or where the unsuccessful party has been guilty of some misconduct. (*See* Costs in County Court; Costs in High Court; Solicitor.)

TAXES.—The money required for the national expenditure is obtained by taxes. Taxes may be either local or national. Local taxation consists solely of rates. National taxation takes many forms. It may be direct or indirect. Direct taxation is imposed on the person who is required to pay it; an illustration of this is income tax. Indirect taxes are imposed on some person on the expectation that he will be able to pass the burden of paying in whole or in part to some other person. Thus, the tax on tobacco is paid in the first place by the importer or manufacturer, but it is intended that he should not bear the burden of the tax himself, but should pass it on to some other person. (*See* Special Supplement "Income Tax.")

TAXI-CABS.—A taxi-cab is subject to police regulation and control. It is an offence for any driver of a taxi-cab to refuse without reasonable excuse to take a hirer to any place within the district in which he is plying for hire. If it has conveyed any persons suffering from an infectious disease, the driver or owner of the cab must at once cause it to be disinfected. A driver may refuse to carry any person suffering from such an infectious disease unless he has paid the cost of disinfection. It is a criminal offence for any person who has hired a taxi-cab to refuse to pay the authorized fare just as it is for the taxi-driver to demand more than the authorized fare. If the hirer and the driver agree that more is to be paid, this agreement is not binding, and the hirer can recover from the driver anything that he has paid him over and above what is proper.

TEACHER.—Grants are made by the Board of Education to Universities and Colleges to provide for the training of teachers. Grants are also made to intending teachers to enable them to undergo training at such institutions. The intending teacher must undertake in consideration of the grant to follow the profession of teacher for a specified period, and on failure to do so must repay the amount of the grant to the Board. The amount may be recovered through the Court as a debt due to the Crown, and the undertaking is binding on the intending teacher even though he is an infant and therefore not liable as a general rule in his contracts.

The Contract of Employment.— In general, the contract of employment between teachers and those employing them is governed by the rules applying to the relation of Master and Servant (q.v.), but there are certain exceptional rules applying to teachers.

Local education authorities have power to appoint officers, including teachers, but the contract may be put an end to by the local authority at its pleasure and without notice to the teacher. Though the contract may provide for reasonable notice of dismissal being given, nevertheless the local authority must so exercise their power that the contract must be framed so as to allow them to dismiss the teacher at their pleasure and without notice.

In non-provided elementary schools (*see* Education), the consent of the local authority is necessary to the dismissal of a teacher by the managers of the school unless the dismissal is on grounds connected with religious instruction given at the school. The giving of the consent, however, is a question concerning only the local authority and the managers, and the fact that consent has not been given will not of itself entitle the teacher dismissed to sue the managers for wrongful dismissal. Thus, unless the local authority intervenes, the managers have in practice power to appoint and dismiss teachers as they please. The contract of employment is with the managers, so that the local authority cannot be sued for arrears of salary by the teacher, even though, in fact, the salary is paid by the local authority.

No teacher at a public elementary school can be required under his contract of employment as part of his duties to supervise, or assist, or to abstain from supervising or assisting in the provision of meals for children, or the collection of the cost thereof. The local authority has power to provide conveyances for teachers, or to contribute towards travelling expenses where they consider it necessary and reasonable to do so.

In endowed schools, the contract of employment is made with the governing bodies. Subject to any special provisions in a scheme or contract of employment, a master shall not be dismissed except at the end of a school term, and except after two months' notice given by the governing body. A master may, however, be dismissed without notice for misconduct or other good or urgent cause.

Teachers and Pupils.—There is a general duty on the teacher to use care in his relations with his pupils. The relation between the teacher and his employers is that of master and servant, so that not only will the teacher be liable for negligence towards his pupils, but his employers also will be liable for the teacher's negligence if committed in the course of his employment.

Contract to Educate.—It is an implied term in every such contract that the master will educate the child, so long as the child is not guilty of conduct which would justify the master in expelling him. In expelling a child, the master must act in good faith and on reasonable grounds. Apart from questions of, e.g. wrongful imprisonment of the child, wrongful expulsion does not of itself constitute a tort—i.e. wrong—giving rise to an action for damages.

Where the contract provides for a term's notice, or payment of one term's fees before removal of a child, if no notice is given the master can sue for the fees. Further, in cases of expulsion for good cause, the schoolmaster is entitled to the whole term's fees.

Punishment.—The duty of a schoolmaster to his pupils is that of a careful father to whom the parent delegates his authority and control in so far as is necessary for the welfare of the pupil. The master may therefore inflict moderate and reasonable punishment, but if it prove excessive, the master may be liable to an action for damages and to criminal proceedings. This power of moderate and reasonable punishment may be reasonably delegated to assistant teachers, prefects and monitors. The authority to punish extends not only to offences committed by the pupil on the school premises, but also to acts done by the pupil on his way to and from school, e.g. smoking on his way to school.

Salaries and Pensions.—In 1920 a national scheme of salaries for elementary and secondary teachers was drawn up by a committee under the chairmanship of Lord Burnham, known as the Burnham Scale. In the case of pensions there is a statutory scheme now in existence under which pensions and allowances are paid to teachers in respect of the following services:

(a) Recognized Service (R. Service), i.e. service as a teacher before the Teachers Superannuation Act, 1925, as recognized by the Board of Education.

(b) Contributory Service (C. Service), i.e. service as a teacher after 1925 which the Board determines to be full time service.

The Board must grant superannuation allowances to teachers who have attained the age of 60, and have been employed for the requisite periods in R. or C. Service or who, having been employed for 10 years in R. or C. Service, have, before reaching the age of 65 years, become permanently incapable, in mind or body, of teaching. The allowances granted are as follows:

(a) An annuity for life, together with a lump sum, both based on salary and length of service.

(b) Short service gratuities in the case of a teacher who has not qualified for superannuation.

(c) Death gratuities when the teacher has served five years in R. or C. Service and has died in service.

The allowance is payable quarterly, and no allowance or gratuity can be disposed of in favour of others or taken in bankruptcy. The grant, however, may be refused or reduced if the teachers have been dismissed for misconduct.

The teacher in C. Service must pay 5% of his salary for the time being and the employer must pay the same sum. Where a teacher ceases to be employed in C. or R. Service for one year, he is entitled to be repaid the balance of his contributions. (*See* CONTRACT; EDUCATION; LOCAL GOVERNMENT; MASTER AND SERVANT; NEGLIGENCE; TRUST.)

TELEGRAPH.—For the purposes of the law a telephone is a telegraph, and the rules which apply to them are identical. The Postmaster-General has a monopoly (except as to companies existing before 1869, which, however, he can purchase under compulsory powers) of the collection, transmission and delivery of telegrams within the United Kingdom, and between it and the Channel Islands, the Isle of Man and the Irish Free State; this monopoly does not extend to foreign or Imperial telegrams outside these boundaries.

Private lines are permissible if they are used only or generally for the private or business purposes of their owner; they may be used on occasion by strangers without infringing the law, provided no charge of any sort is made, but such lines must be used for the private or business purposes of one person only. A line between doctor and chemist, ticket agency and theatre, householders, police and local authorities would infringe the monopoly, but a line between house and office, a head office and branch would not.

The Postmaster-General may also grant licences to private persons or companies to work a private telegraphic or telephonic line. Where wireless is relayed on a commercial basis (i.e. for a charge), if more than one house is supplied, or if any of the lines cross a public street the same rules apply, and it is necessary to get special permission from the Postmaster-General (in addition to the ordinary wireless licences for the set and each separate extension). But special permission is not necessary if the distribution is confined to one house or block of flats, no matter how big.

The special powers of the Postmaster-General to erect posts and wire, etc., and to enter on private land, which are discussed below, cannot be invoked by a private licensee; he must get the express consent of the owner and tenant of every property over which he desires to place a wire or erect a post or bracket, and the tenant or owner is entitled to refuse him permission to enter at all upon his land. Any tenant or owner who is threatened by such a

licensee may apply to the Chancery Division of the High Court for an injunction to restrain the latter from infringing his rights. Such an injunction cannot be obtained in the County Court unless it is ancillary to a claim for damages which does not exceed £100. If entry is made upon land or any posts, etc., are erected upon it before an injunction has been obtained, the occupier of the land has two alternative remedies: (1) He may cut down whatever has been erected, though he cannot recover the expense of doing so; (2) he may bring an action for trespass to land and/or damages for the inconvenience, etc., caused by the wires or posts, the presence of which amounts in law to a nuisance.

If the defendant does not remove the offending things after damages have once been recovered against him, another action may be brought for the continuance of the nuisance and this may be repeated indefinitely.

The Postmaster-General has special statutory powers to "place and maintain telegraphs (including telephones) and posts under, in, upon, over, along or across private land or buildings." The consent of the owner or occupier must first be obtained. If this is not given within two months, provision is made for the decision of the dispute by a special tribunal. Even where nothing is to be placed on a man's land his consent is sometimes necessary before any work may legally be done. Thus, the consent of the owner, tenant or occupier is necessary before a wire may be put less than six feet over a dwelling-house or over a drive or approach, or a post placed within ten yards of a dwelling-house, or in such a way as to obstruct the owner's means of access to his property unless it is erected in a street, and the local authority has already consented to the work being done. If, after any telegraphic apparatus has been placed on or over his land, a landowner wishes to make alterations to his property, he may apply to the Postmaster-General and require the latter to move the apparatus so far as may be necessary within fourteen days.

Offences under the Telegraph Acts.—In order to protect Post Office property a number of things have been declared offences under the Telegraph Acts. Amongst them are: causing wilful or malicious damage to telegraph posts or other apparatus (an extra heavy penalty of £20 a day is provided if this results in an interruption of telegraphic communication); obstructing Post Office officials in their work, or fixing unauthorized notices to telegraph posts, exchange, etc. The apparatus which is installed when a private telephone is fitted remains the property of the Post Office, and it is an offence wilfully or maliciously to damage it. If the damage is accidental, the subscriber is liable to pay to the Post Office the cost of putting it in order, and he is generally required to make a deposit to cover such contingencies in addition to paying a yearly rental. To take away or sell any telephone apparatus, whether fitted in a house or not, would, of course, be theft. Since such apparatus is the property of the Government it is not subject to distress, and cannot be seized by a landlord or judgment creditor.

There is another class of offences which are created to protect the interests of those who use the telegraphic or telephonic services. It is an offence for any employee of the Post Office to disclose the contents of any telegram, or wilfully or negligently to omit or delay delivery; and for any person, whether an employee or not, to forge or alter a telegram, or to deliver it with knowledge that it is forged, or indeed to deliver as a telegram any message or communication which is not, in fact, a telegram. The Post Office keep all inland telegrams for three months, but may only produce them to the sender or addressee unless served with a subpoena to produce them in Court.

The sender of a telegram may have it re-telegraphed back from the delivery office on payment of an additional fee, but he cannot get a copy of the repeated telegram; the addressee may always have a telegram repeated without charge at any time within three months of the date on which it was sent.

The Postmaster-General is not liable for any loss or damage which may be caused by the delay or non-delivery of a telegram, or for any mistakes in transmission; though the sender of a telegram might be able to recover any damage he has suffered by Petition of Right from the King. It seems likely that the individual officer of the Post Office whose carelessness caused the

loss could be sued by either the sender or the addressee. In the case of telegrams to foreign countries and cables the position is rather different, as these may pass over the lines of private companies; if this is the case, the company can be sued by both the sender and the receiver. Such companies, however, generally limit their liability to repeated telegrams and a maximum sum. Telegrams may be in any language or in code, but the Post Office will not accept indecent or obscene messages, or very offensive ones. The sender of a defamatory statement by telegraph is deemed to "publish" it to the Post Office officials; the libel being the original telegram as handed in for transmission. (*See* POST OFFICE.)

TELEPHONE.—Since the law on this subject is for the most part the same as the law about telegraphs, it is discussed under that head (q.v.), but there are one or two special rules relating to the telephone.

Subscribers who are more than two miles from an exchange may be required to contribute towards the cost of connecting them up with it, and some payment is usually required for alterations and removals. In addition to the annual rent, a subscriber is required to make a deposit of two thirds of the estimated amount of a quarter's fees and charges. No charge is made for disconnecting a subscriber temporarily, but a charge of five shillings is made if this is done because the account has not been paid. A subscriber is not legally liable to pay for more than the calls actually made from his instrument, but the Post Office have installed machines to check and count calls, and if there appears to be an inaccuracy it is seldom of much use to contest it unless it is a glaring one. All the apparatus installed remains the property of the Postmaster-General and the subscriber is bound to replace it at his own cost if it is broken or injured in any way, whether intentionally (which would be an offence), or accidentally (as by fire). No alterations or attachments to telephonic apparatus may be made without the consent of the Postmaster-General.

For particulars of the services and facilities offered, see the Post Office guide or a telephone directory. (*See* POST OFFICE; TELEGRAPH.)

TEMPORARY PATIENT. — It is now possible for a person who is suffering from some mental disease to be received into a mental institution for treatment without being certified as a lunatic. This not only prevents the stigma of "lunatic" from attaching, but also enables the patient to receive treatment at an early stage in his illness when the treatment may lead to prevention or cure. Where the patient is in sufficiently good health mentally to make up his own mind, he can decide for himself to go into the institution, and will be known as a voluntary patient (q.v.). Where, however, the patient is not in a fit state mentally to make up his mind to go into the institution of his own free will, he may be sent there for a short time without his consent, and will then be known as a temporary patient. (*See* LUNATICS; VOLUNTARY PATIENT.)

TENANT. — (*See* LANDLORD AND TENANT.)

TENANT IN COMMON.—Tenants in common are persons who own the same land at the same time. They are deemed in law each to be the owner of an as yet undivided share of the land; until division they are all entitled to use the whole of the land. A tenant in common may deal with his share by sale or mortgage, and may dispose of it in his will. (*See* JOINT TENANTS.)

TENANT RIGHTS.—A great deal was done in 1927 to remedy the harshness of English law bearing on the tenant of business premises, and in the case of agricultural buildings similar provisions are contained in the Agricultural Holdings Acts.

In business premises which are not agricultural, the tenant is now entitled to compensation when he leaves the tenancy in respect of any improvements made by him or his predecessors in title, which he is not entitled to remove as fixtures, but which add to the letting value of the holding. (*See* IMPROVEMENTS.)

Compensation for Goodwill.—Where a tenant has been carrying on a business for not less than five years, and where by reason of his having so carried on the business goodwill has become attached to the premises so that they could be let at a higher rent than they would have realized otherwise, the tenant at the end of his tenancy may claim compensation for this goodwill (q.v.).

New Lease.—Where a tenant who is entitled to compensation for goodwill as above, alleges that the amount of compensation would not compensate him for the loss he may, in certain cases, demand from the landlord a new lease of the premises instead of compensation. (*See* FIXTURES; GOODWILL; IMPROVEMENTS; LANDLORD AND TENANT.)

TENANTABLE REPAIR.—A tenant under a lease often agrees to keep the premises in "tenantable" repair or "good tenantable" repair. The exact extent of this obligation is that he must keep the premises in such repair as, having regard to the age, character, and locality of the house, will make them reasonably fit for the occupation of a reasonable tenant of the class who would be likely to take them. (*See* LANDLORD AND TENANT.)

TENDER.—Where a person who has undertaken to carry out some obligation or pay money under a contract offers to do so, but where the other party refuses to accept the performance of the contract tendered, the party tendering, if he is later sued for not having carried out his obligations, may successfully defend the proceedings by proving that he offered to do so. This defence is known as tender, and special notice must be given of it when it is raised in the County Court. (*See* SPECIAL DEFENCE.)

Tender of Money. — Where the obligation is one to pay money, the full amount due must be produced and offered unconditionally, unless the person to whom the money is due dispenses with the production of it—e.g. by saying he will not accept it if it were offered. The money due must be tendered with legal tender, i.e. gold up to any amount, silver up to forty shillings, copper up to a shilling and Bank of England notes up to any amount. The amount tendered must be the exact amount due—i.e. no change must be necessary or demanded. Tender by cheque is good in most cases if the only objection made by the creditor is that the amount is insufficient.

Where a debtor has tendered money which has been refused and is afterwards sued, he should pay the money into court and plead tender. The creditor will thereafter obtain the money in the action but will have to pay the costs. The following is an example of tender: A does work for B, and claims that B owes him £50 in respect of the work. B says that the proper charge is £30 and tenders that to A. A refuses the amount, saying it is insufficient, and sues B for £50. B should plead tender and pay £30 into court. If A succeeds in recovering more than £30, he will get judgment against B, but if he recovers only £30, he will receive that money out of court and will have to pay the costs incurred by B.

Tender in other Cases.—Where the obligation is not to pay money but to do some act, and the person liable to do the act—e.g. to deliver goods—takes the goods for delivery to the purchaser, who refuses to accept them, saying they are not in accordance with the contract, the seller, if he is later sued for failure to deliver the goods, may plead that he tendered them and offered to deliver them, and that will be a defence to the action if it be proved that the goods were in accordance with the contract and should have been accepted. In addition, the seller may sue the purchaser for any loss he has suffered through the failure to accept the goods.

Tender of Amends.—Where a public authority is sued for damages for any act done in pursuance or intended execution of any public duty, or for any neglect in the execution of such duty, the authority may tender amends—i.e. reasonable compensation—before the commencement of the action. If this compensation is refused, and the action is then brought and the plaintiff does not recover more than the sum tendered, he is deprived of costs; and the defendant is entitled to the costs to be taxed as between solicitor and client, i.e. on a scale very much in favour of the defendant. Even if no amends have been tendered, the Court may award costs to the defendant solicitor and client, if it is of the opinion that the plaintiff did not give the defendant a sufficient opportunity of tendering amends before commencing the action. (*See* LEGAL TENDER.)

TENEMENT.—The word tenement means any property held by a tenant in land whether dwellings or vacant land.

TENURE.—As a result of the influence of the Feudal system upon the English land law, it has always been firmly established that every owner of land holds it by some form of tenure from the King. In practical life this tenure is of no importance whatsoever.

In feudal times there were many different kinds of tenure; but only ones which survived for long were copyhold and socage tenure.

Copyhold tenure was abolished in 1925, and the only one which now remains is socage tenure. (*See* COPYHOLD.)

TERCE (SCOTS LAW).—This is the right which a married woman has in the heritable property, i.e. land of her deceased husband. She is entitled to enjoy for her life the interest or income from one third of the land which he owned at the time of his death. (*See* MARRIED WOMAN [SCOTS LAW].)

TERM (LAW).—There are four law terms in England. These are Hilary, Easter, Trinity, and Michaelmas. During these periods the High Court of Justice sits for the trial of actions and the disposal of other legal business. (*See* SITTINGS.)

TERM (SCOTS LAW).—The period at which rent or other periodical payments are due in Scotland are called the term days and correspond to the English Quarter Days. The term days are Whit Sunday, May 15th, and Martinmas, November 11th.

TERM OF YEARS.—In the law of real property this means an estate or interest in land to be enjoyed for a fixed period. Thus a lease for a period of time is a term of years. A term of years is one of the two estates in land which are now capable of existing as legal estates, and not merely as equitable interests. The other estate in land is an estate in fee simple. (*See* LANDLORD AND TENANT.)

TERRITORIAL ARMY.—The Territorial Force was created in 1907, its name being changed to the Territorial Army in 1921. Establishment and organization are in the hands of the County Associations, but training and command are the province of the military authorities.

A recruit joins the Territorial Army for four years. He serves in the County unit he selects on enlistment. The County Associations may permit re-engagement up to a further four years. Soldiers of the Territorial Army are required to attend a prescribed number of drills, and undergo a minimum period of training annually, unless exempted by superior authority. Failure to comply with these requirements in the absence of reasonable excuse, such as sickness, renders an offender liable to a fine not exceeding £5. When at drills, or in training, soldiers of the Territorial Army are subject to Military Law (q.v.), and may be tried by Court Martial for offences committed whilst so subject.

In time of war or other national emergency the Crown may cause the Territorial Army to be embodied, and all members are then required to join and serve with their units. When so embodied, the legal position of the Territorial Army is similar in most respects to that of the Regular Army.

TERRITORIAL WATERS. — The sea is not part of any state, but in international law the right of states to control the sea within three miles of their coasts is recognized. These portions of the sea so controlled are known as territorial waters.

TESTAMENTARY GUARDIAN. —A testamentary guardian is a guardian appointed by a parent for his children by his will. The guardian may refuse to accept the office, but having accepted it must continue with it. A testamentary guardian may be removed by the Court at any time.

TESTAMENTARY WRITING.— This has the same meaning as a will. It should be noted, however, that any testamentary writing must be executed with the same formalities as a will if it is to be valid. Formerly the word testament was used to indicate a disposition of personal property by will, and the word will was used in the case of real property. To-day, however, the word will is used in both cases. (*See* WILL.)

THEATRES.—All places, except booths or portable theatres, kept for the public performance of stage plays require a licence, or authority by "letters patent," and anyone keeping such a place without a licence— there are very few patent theatres—commits an offence, and renders himself liable to a fine of £20 for every day upon which it was kept open without authority. One performance is sufficient to make a person liable. Also any person who for hire shall allow, or present, or take part in a play (and where any money or reward is taken for admission any actor therein shall be deemed to be acting for hire) in an unlicensed place, shall be liable to be convicted and fined £10 for every day upon which he offends.

A theatre licence is granted in London, Windsor and Brighton by the Lord Chamberlain, and also in such places as the King occasionally resides, but in the last case only while he is in residence, the ordinary licence then being suspended. In places outside these areas the licensing authority is the county or borough council who, however, may delegate their authority to the local justices. In the case of a theatre duly licensed, a justices' licence is not necessary for the sale by retail of intoxicating liquor. But, of course, theatre licences are sometimes refused unless an undertaking is given not to retail intoxicants. Where there is not such an undertaking, intoxicating liquor must not be sold except while the theatre is open and being used as a place of entertainment. Even while being so used intoxicating liquor can only be sold to bona fide users, and then only during the permitted hours.

The manager of a theatre may refuse to sell a ticket for any performance to any individual. The purchaser of a ticket is entitled to room in the portion of the theatre for which he has paid; if there is no such room his money must be refunded. The holder of a ticket may be removed if he behaves improperly. Spontaneous expressions of approval or disapproval of the performance do not constitute improper conduct, provided they do not interfere with the enjoyment of the performance by other members of the audience. (*See* THEATRICAL EMPLOYERS.)

THEATRICAL EMPLOYERS.— Every theatrical employer must register with the local authority and provide certain prescribed particulars. Before registering, the employer must insert in two different issues of a London newspaper devoted to the Stage a notice of his intention to register. On registration the employer receives a certificate of registration.

Any theatrical employer commits an offence who, during the course of an engagement, abandons his performers, or who carries on his business without registration, or who supplies incorrect particulars on applying for registration. These offences may be punished by imprisonment for a period not exceeding three months and also by a fine of not more than £50. In addition, the Court may order that any registration certificate he may possess shall be revoked.

These provisions do not apply to persons who do not employ more than two performers at a time.

THEFT.—This is a popular expression used to cover all forms of larceny. (*See* LARCENY.)

THIRD PARTY INSURANCE (Bankruptcy and Winding-Up).—By a very wise rule of the law it is now provided that where a person is injured, and in consequence has a claim against an individual debtor or a limited company, in respect of which the debtor or company has taken out a policy of insurance, the injured person, if the debtor becomes bankrupt or the company is wound up, is not required to claim against the insolvent estate of the debtor or company, but can claim the money due direct from the insurance company. Before this change in the law was made in 1930, the insurance company, who were bound only to indemnify the person they had insured (that is, the bankrupt or company, not the injured person), would pay the money to the trustee in bankruptcy or liquidator, who would not pay it out to the injured person, but would use it as the ordinary assets of the estate for the benefit of all the creditors. Thus, the injured person when claiming for the amount to which he was entitled might receive only a few shillings in the pound.

This will readily be seen by taking a concrete example. Suppose a man has been knocked down by a motor-car and injured. He claims damages against the owner of the car and recovers a judgment for £5,000 against the person injuring him. That person is insured, and the insurance company are prepared to pay him £5,000 so that he may hand it over to the person he has injured. Assume, however, that the person causing the injury becomes bankrupt, and that his total assets are £10,000 plus the money due by the insurance company, namely, £5,000, and that his creditors are claiming for £20,000 apart from the claim by the injured person. Under the old law the creditors, including the injured person, with total claims for £25,000 would all share in the £15,000 of assets, so that the injured person would receive only twelve shillings in the £. To-day, however, the injured person receives his £5,000 direct from the insurance company, and the other

creditors have to be content with the other assets of the debtor, receiving, in the case imagined, 10/- in the £. (*See* TRUSTEE IN BANKRUPTCY; WINDING-UP.)

THIRD PARTY PROCEDURE.—Where a defendant in an action in the High Court or in the County Court claims that he is entitled to a contribution or an indemnity from a third person not already a party to the action, in respect of the claim made against him, or where in the High Court, but not in the County Court, he claims that the subject matter in dispute is substantially the same as a dispute which has arisen between him and a third person, he is entitled to make the third person a party to the action, and to have the question of the contribution or indemnity, etc., decided at the same time as the action by the plaintiff against him.

This process is known as Third Party Procedure. The defendant, upon application to a Master in the High Court, or upon notice to the Registrar in the County Court, is entitled to serve upon the third person a Third Party Notice setting out the nature of the defendant's claim against the third party. If the third party wishes to dispute the defendant's claim against him, he must take steps similar to those which he would have taken if the third party notice were a writ of summons or County Court summons, and at the trial of the action the issues between the defendant and the third party will be tried and judgment given in much the same way as if it were an ordinary separate action. (*See* COUNTY COURT PROCEDURE; HIGH COURT PROCEDURE.)

THREATS.—A threat, if unlawful, may render the person who makes it subject to criminal proceedings. The most serious form of threat is one used in an endeavour to extort money. This is, of course, blackmail (q.v.), which in certain forms may be punished by penal servitude for life. Other serious forms of threats are sending letters threatening to murder or to burn houses. Offences of this kind are felonies punishable by penal servitude for ten years.

Threats falling short of these grave crimes may be made the subject of complaint in a Police Court and a summary remedy obtained. Anyone who on reasonable grounds is in bodily fear from threats that he or his family will be physically ill-treated may complain to justices. On being satisfied that the fear is real and well grounded, the justices must require the person guilty of the threats to enter into a recognizance (q.v.) to keep the peace and behave properly towards the complainant.

In addition to constituting a crime, unlawful threats may render any contract entered into under the effect of them unenforceable in law. Threats of physical injury or false imprisonment would certainly have this effect and be held as constituting duress.

On the other hand, it must be remembered that many threats are perfectly lawful, being merely the exercise of a legal right, e.g. the foreclosure of a mortgage or the termination of a tenancy.

TICHBORNE CLAIMANT. The Claimant.

In April, 1854, Roger Tichborne, a member of one of the oldest Roman Catholic families in England, heir to the Tichborne baronetcy and considerable estates, sailed from Rio in South America bound for Jamaica on board the "Bella." The ship was wrecked and nothing was heard of him for eleven years. To everyone but his poor, imaginative mother it was clear that he was lost, but she advertised continually in newspapers all over the world, offering a reward for any person who could give information of her son, and in 1865 a man came forward from Australia claiming to be Roger Tichborne, and started legal proceedings in Chancery to dispossess his relations and obtain his estates. He found many supporters of his claim, among them "Old Bogle," a negro who had been servant to the Tichborne family, and was able to give him valuable information about family affairs.

The Civil Action.—The action of ejectment was tried before Chief Justice Bovil at the Common Pleas, Sergeant Ballantine and Hardinge Giffard, K.C. (later Lord Halsbury), led for the Claimant, and the newly appointed Attorney-General, Sir John Coleridge, with the famous cross-examiner, Mr. Henry Hawkins, Q.C. (later Lord Brampton), for the trustees of the estate, the defendants. The trial of the action lasted over a hundred days, and over a hundred witnesses swore that the claimant was Roger Tichborne. Public opinion was greatly in his favour, the one fact that Lady

Tichborne, "his mother," had recognized him, carrying more weight than the overwhelming testimony brought forward by the defence which shewed clearly that the claimant was an impostor, a man named Arthur Orton, the son of a Wapping butcher.

Identity.—The real Roger Tichborne was born in Paris, his mother being half French, and spoke that language perfectly; he had been to a public school, and served later in the Fifth Dragoon Guards. He was a slim English gentleman who spoke with rather a foreign accent, but who wrote cultured and frequent letters to his relations and friends, and who, before leaving for America, had declared his honourable love to his cousin Kate.

The claimant was a coarse, illiterate man weighing nearly twenty stone. His spelling and writing were totally different from Roger's; he was not recognized by any members of his family, nor did he recognize them. He could not speak a word of French. On landing in England he had disguised himself and set off to trace the Orton family down in Wapping. He was married to a servant girl who could neither read nor write, and the ceremony had been performed in a Protestant church. He declared that his cousin Kate, now a married woman, had been enceinte by him.

Perjury.—The jury rejected his claim and Orton was immediately arrested on charges of perjury and forgery. The indictment charged him with falsely swearing that he was Roger Tichborne, that he had seduced his cousin Kate, and that he was not Arthur Orton. The trial was presided over by Chief Justice Cockburn, and lasted for 188 days. Henry Hawkins, Q.C., led for the prosecution, and Orton was defended by Dr. Kenealy. Found guilty, he was sentenced to fourteen years' penal servitude. And in 1898, Orton died, a worthless adventurer who had divided the whole nation into two camps and been the cause of the most protracted and expensive litigation of modern times. His finances, which, besides the money he obtained from "his mother," who died during the course of the case, depended mainly on the charity and goodwill of his supporters, were helped by the issuing of the famous Tichborne Bonds, which needless to say, did not prove a very satisfactory investment for those who took them up!

TICKET.—Tickets are frequently issued for travel, cloak rooms or garages subject to special conditions which are not always printed on the ticket itself, but to which reference is made on the ticket by some statement such as "issued subject to conditions" in time tables, etc. The person taking the ticket is usually bound by these conditions and that is so even if he has not read them. (*See* CLOAK ROOM; RAILWAY PASSENGERS.)

TICKET OF LEAVE. — This, a popular expression, used in connection with the release on licence of convicts of good behaviour before the expiration of their sentences. A man who has served three-fourths of a sentence of penal servitude may, if his conduct warrants it, be released on licence. This licence contains conditions as to his behaviour and may be revoked or forfeited on breach of those conditions. (*See* PENAL SERVITUDE.)

TIME.—When a fixed time in days is allowed for anything to be done, the day from which the period starts is not generally counted, though the last day is. In the absence of any special provision governing the particular rule or contract, Sundays and holidays count as other days. Fractions of days are ignored in the computation of time for most legal purposes.

TIME IMMEMORIAL.—In the 12th and 13th centuries it was the practice of Parliament to enact at more or less regular intervals that no action should be brought about facts which were of more than a certain age. Instead of doing what is now the practice under the Statutes of Limitation, and providing that after a definite number of years a right of action was to be lost, a date, such as the accession or death of a king, was fixed upon, and it was provided that no action might be brought for anything which happened before this date.

These Acts of Parliament were said to fix the date of legal memory; because the act directed the Judges not to remember anything which had happened before the date named in them. The last one to be passed fixed 1189, the date of the accession of Richard II. It was later repealed and a new act passed, but by then the limits of legal memory had become fixed at 1189.

Any right which can be shewn to have been exercised from before this date is said to have been exercised from time immemorial, and proof that it has been so exercised conclusively establishes that it is lawful.

This curious rule is still of importance whenever attempts are made to prove that a custom exists in any particular locality varying the general law of the land. The success of the attempt to establish that the custom is lawful will depend on whether it can be traced back to time immemorial.

It is also important in the law of prescription.

TIME TABLE.—Railway companies and other carriers of passengers publish time tables which indicate the time at which trains, or other vehicles, are expected to arrive or depart. It is always stated, however, in the time table that the company do not guarantee the arrival or departure of the trains at the time indicated, and where there is such a provision a passenger who suffers loss through being delayed in his journey by a train being late cannot recover damages.

TIPSTAFF.—This is the name applied to an officer of the Court whose duty it is to take into custody any persons committed by the Court for contempt.

TITHE.—Tithes gain their origin from the idea that one-tenth of the fruits of the earth should be paid to the ministers of the Church for their support. In the course of centuries many land holdings became freed from the burden of yielding tithes, and many tithes passed into the hands of persons in no way connected with the Church's ministrations. At the present time where tithes are payable at all, they take the form of a tithe rent charge. This is a fixed annual sum payable in most cases to Queen Anne's Bounty. This annual sum now includes a small amount payable to a sinking fund in redemption of the rent charge. While this latter is a compulsory payment, the rent charge can be voluntarily redeemed by a lump sum payment the amount of which can be fixed by agreement.

Tithe rent charge is payable by the owner of lands, and not by the occupier. It is recoverable only through the County Court. The County Court bailiff may levy distress under an order of the Court on lands occupied by the owner of the land in respect of which the rent charge is payable, or collect the rent payable for the land in question.

TITLE DEEDS.—The title deeds of a property are the deeds by means of which it has been transferred or otherwise dealt with in the past. The deeds are treated almost as part of the property, and they pass along with it to any person to whom it is sold, given or left.

So much are they part of the property that at one time it was impossible to steal them, for one could not, in law, steal real property. It is now a crime to take title deeds unlawfully.

A very common way of making mortgages in order to borrow money is to deposit the title deeds of a property with the lender. This constitutes an equitable mortgage. A mere deposit of the deeds, however, without any intention of creating a mortgage—as for instance a deposit in the strong room of a bank or a solicitor—will not affect the property.

TOBACCO.—Tobacco is, on importation into the United Kingdom, subject to customs duties at rates varying according to the form in which it is imported. On re-export, the duty on manufactured tobacco may be claimed back; this is known as "drawback."

Growers and curers of tobacco in the United Kingdom must obtain an annual licence (five shillings), and excise duties are payable on tobacco so grown.

Manufacturers of tobacco must take out a licence, the fee for which depends upon the amount of tobacco received by the applicant for manufacture in the previous year. No manufacturer may have on his premises any earths, leaves, wood or other substitutes for tobacco, nor any tobacco containing more than 32% moisture.

Sellers of tobacco must, under penalty of £50, take out licences (which expire on 5th July in each year), in respect of their premises (fee: 5/3). Tobacco must not be hawked.

Sellers of tobacco must, under penalty of £20, place signboards not more than three feet above the principal entrance to their premises, on which, in letters publicly visible and at least one inch long, the full name of the seller, and a statement that he is licensed to sell tobacco, must be painted.

TOLLS.—The charges made by dock and canal companies for traffic conveyed by them are called tolls. The word was originally applied to the money which had to be paid by persons using turnpike roads, and this money was paid at toll bars. The word is also used to indicate the money which may be paid to the owner of a market by persons using the market.

TORT.—This is a legal expression covering all classes of wrongs to individuals other than those arising out of personal relationship or a contract.

Breach of contract is not a tort, nor is any wrong arising out of the relationship of husband and wife a tort. Any other infringements of individuals' rights by another, is a tort. For instance, libel, assault, trespass, nuisance, are all torts.

A person who commits a tort is described as a "Tortfeasor." Any act constituting a tort is described as a "Tortious act."

TOWN CLERK.—Each borough has an official called a Town Clerk as its chief officer. He carries into effect the decisions of the Borough Council and acts as its representative. The appointment is a whole-time one. The practice is to appoint solicitors, as Town Clerks have much legal business to transact, and also act as legal advisers to the governing body of the borough. (*See* LOCAL GOVERNMENT.)

TOWN COUNCIL.—The term Town Council is applied to Urban District Councils and to Borough Councils. (*See* BOROUGH COUNCIL; LOCAL GOVERNMENT; URBAN DISTRICT COUNCIL.)

TOWN PLANNING.—The importance of planning out a town and not letting it grow up in a haphazard fashion was first recognized by Parliament in the Housing and Town Planning Act, 1909. Since that Act there have been a number of Acts passed which have dealt further with the problem, and at the present day the law upon the subject is contained in the Town and Country Planning Act, 1932.

Under that Act schemes may be made by a local authority with respect to any land, whether there are buildings on it or not, with the general object of controlling the development of the land comprised in the area to which the scheme is to apply. The considerations which are to influence the local authority in preparing a scheme, are the preservation of objects of historical, architectural or artistic interest, the securing of proper sanitary conditions, and the improving of the amenities of the district.

A local authority may either by a resolution prepare a scheme, or else they may adopt with or without modification a scheme prepared by all or any of the owners of any land within their district.

The resolution incorporating the scheme must be submitted to the Minister of Health for his approval, and if it is approved by him, then it must be laid before both Houses of Parliament. The scheme comes into force within twenty-one days after it has been laid before Parliament, unless either House resolves that it ought not to be passed. When the scheme has been approved by the Minister, the local authority must put a notice in a local newspaper, naming a place where a copy of the scheme and a map of the area may be seen.

If complaint is made by a person aggrieved by the scheme, then the Minister of Health directs one of his inspectors to hold a local enquiry and hear evidence upon the subject. If no complaint is made, the Minister may confirm the scheme or make such modifications in it as he sees fit. He must not, however, substantially increase the expense of the scheme by his modifications.

A Town Planning Scheme may provide for a large number of matters, such as the laying out of streets, the building of new houses, or the alteration of existing ones, the control of advertisement hoardings, petrol stations, and any objects of a like nature which, unless regulated, would tend to destroy or impair the amenities of the district comprised in the scheme.

In order to ensure the satisfactory working of schemes, the local authorities have been given power to purchase compulsorily land comprised in the area to which the scheme applies if such land is required for securing a satisfactory frontage along an existing or projected highway, or for securing the satisfactory development of any land included in the scheme.

Persons whose property is injuriously affected, or whose trade or business is disturbed, may claim compensation within the time laid down in the scheme. The claim is made by serving upon the local authority from whom the amount is to be claimed, a notice in writing stating the grounds of the claim and the amount thereof. Conversely, a local authority who have carried out the provisions of a scheme and thereby greatly improved or increased the value of some property comprised in the area, may claim compensation for betterment from the owner of the property. (*See* BUILDING SCHEME; HOUSING; LOCAL GOVERNMENT.)

TRADE DISPUTE.—A Trade Dispute is any dispute between employers and workmen, or between workmen and workmen about:—

(1) The employment or non-employment,
(2) the terms of the employment,
(3) the conditions of labour of any person.

A dispute between employers and employers is not a trade dispute.

A dispute between union and non-union workmen is a trade dispute, and so is a dispute between two unions as to the employment by an employer of a person not in one of the unions.

The dispute must be about something fairly definite, and not a mere personal quarrel, or grumbling or agitation. It is always a question of fact which must be decided by the jury whether there was a trade dispute in existence or imminent at the time of the doing of an act about which an action may be brought.

When there is a Trade Dispute.— If a person does an act which causes damage to another, or induces another to do an act which causes damage to a third person, in the ordinary way he is liable to pay damages to the person injured. (*See* TORT.) If, however, the act was done in furtherance or contemplation of a trade dispute, then it is not actionable, and the person doing it may escape liability for the harmful consequences of his act.

The same immunity is extended to a combination of persons agreeing together to do some act which causes harm to a person, provided that the act was done in contemplation or furtherance of a trade dispute, and even if the motive for doing the act was the malicious one of ruining the person acted against rather than the furthering or protection of their own interests. This immunity was conferred by the Trade Disputes Act, 1906. If, however, the doing of the act by either an individual or a combination is accompanied by threats or violence, then the protection given by the Act is withdrawn, and an action will be maintainable since an injury has been done over and above the kind of injury which is protected by the Act.

An example.—(1) A induces B, C, D, and E to cease working for X because X is employing V, a non-union workman. This is in furtherance of a trade dispute. No action can be brought against A.

(2) A, B, C and D, combine together and threaten X that if he does not dismiss V from his employment they will beat him. They do, in fact, beat him. This is an Act in furtherance of a trade dispute, but accompanied by threats and violence. No protection against action for assault is afforded by Trade Disputes Act.

When there is no Trade Dispute.— An individual is liable for the consequences of his tortious acts unless he is a member or an official of a trade union, and the act was committed on behalf of a trade union. (*See* TRADE UNION.)

An act which would be actionable at law if committed by an individual is naturally actionable if done by a number of persons combining together.

If a number of persons combine to do an act which would be perfectly lawful if done by an individual, such act of the combination may nevertheless be actionable at the instance of a person damaged by it. The reason for this is that the greater extent of the injury which may be done to a person by the combination of a number of persons of itself gives him a right of action.

An example.—(1) A, a wholesale distributor of newspapers cuts off supplies from B, a retailer. Not actionable.

(2) A, B, C and D combine together and each cut off supplies from X because they are jealous of his success. Actionable.

The law regards an interference with a man in his trade as prima facie actionable, and requires that persons combining to do so should justify their action. This they may do by shewing that their action was taken to protect their own trade interests and not to injure the person who has in fact been

damaged. If the injured person can prove that the action of the combination was simply for the malicious purpose of ruining him, and not for the furtherance of any trade object, then he is entitled to succeed in an action for damages against the combination.

The Act of 1927.—It is important to observe that a trade dispute as defined by this act is confined to narrower limits than those laid down by the Act of 1906. In this act, a trade dispute is one confined to the industry in which strikers are engaged. That is to say, if persons strike in furtherance of a trade dispute in an industry other than their own, their action is illegal and they are not protected from liability for the consequences of any acts they may commit while so striking, by the provisions of the Act of 1906. If they assist strikers in some other industry by actions other than a strike, then it seems they are still protected. (*See* BLACK LIST; CONSPIRACY; STRIKE; TRADE DISPUTE; TORT.)

TRADE FIXTURES.—The ordinary rule of law as regards fixtures, i.e. chattels or goods affixed to premises, is that they belong to the landlord and cannot be removed by the tenant at the end of his tenancy. To this rule there are many exceptions, one of which is that where the fixture has been brought on to the premises by the tenant for the purposes of some trade carried on by him there, the fixtures may be removed if the removal will not injure the premises. Where fixtures cannot be removed in this way, the tenant may now claim compensation for them as improvements. (*See* FIXTURES; IMPROVEMENTS.)

TRADE MARKS.—The Trade Marks Act defines a trade mark as "a device, brand, heading, label, ticket, name, signature, word, letter, numeral or any combination thereof used in connection with goods of the proprietor of the trade mark by virtue of manufacture, selection, certification, dealing with or offering for sale." As appears from this definition, trade marks are not confined to indicating the origin or the manufacture of goods. They are used by importers, wholesalers and others on whose judgment in buying their customers rely, and they may be used to shew simply that the goods were sold by a particular trader or store.

How Acquired.—Trade marks are

acquired either by use or by registration as a trade mark in the Registry kept by the Trade Mark Registrar in the Patent Office at 25, Southampton Buildings, London. There are special registers for marks used in the cutlery and cotton trades at Sheffield and Manchester, respectively.

Trade marks which have been acquired by use alone, and have not been registered, can be protected by means of the common law action of passing off. This may be brought against anyone who attempts to pass off his goods as the goods of the person who brings the action. No man is entitled to steal another's trade by deceiving customers into believing that they are buying the latter's goods. It is immaterial whether he achieves the deception by copying trade marks, by getting up his goods in a particular way or by trading under a deceptive name; there have even been a few cases in which a man who traded under his own name has been held guilty of passing off, but in all of them it was clearly shewn that he intended to deceive the public. In order to succeed in an action for passing off it is necessary to prove that the public were in fact deceived.

Where the trade mark has been registered the rights of the proprietor are much wider; it is therefore necessary to know what may be registered.

Registers.—There are two registers of trade marks in the Patent Office, the A register and the B register. In order to be capable of registration in the A register a mark must consist of one of the following things:—

(i) The name of a real person or firm, treated in some special manner. The name alone in ordinary letters would not be sufficient. The reason for this is the hardship that registration of a name might cause to other persons of the same name.

(ii) A signature.

(iii) An invented word. Words which are descriptive of the goods in connection with which the mark is to be used, such as "perfection," "quick-firing," "the best," can never be registered because it would not be fair to give to one trader a monopoly of them. If, however, he invents a word to describe his goods there can be no objection to this provided that

the word is a genuine invention and is not just a combination of two or more words or a phonetic spelling of an ordinary word. Names which have been coined by the inventor of a patented article to describe it cannot be registered, and will become public property when the patent expires.

Registration of foreign words is not permitted if in their natural meaning they are descriptive of the goods.

(iv) A word which has no direct reference to the goods.

No objection can be raised to the registration of words which are not in any sense descriptive because it could not affect the rights of any other trader. For instance, the word "sailing" would probably be accepted for registration in connection with matches, but perhaps not for bicycles, and certainly not for model yachts.

Geographical names and surnames cannot be registered under this head though they are sometimes admissible under one of the others.

(v) Any other distinctive mark, including a geographical name. Under this head fall the numerous pictorial marks which are now so common. Almost any device, drawing or reproduction is registerable, but if it is a drawing of the articles in connection with which the mark is to be used, there must be some distinctive feature about it either in the arrangement of the articles or in the other parts of the picture.

(vi) Any word or mark which was in use before 1875 and has been continuously applied up to the date of the application for registration.

The Registrar has a discretion whether or not to allow any particular application for registration, but in exercising it he must keep within certain definite bounds. The grounds for refusing to permit registration are three:—

(a) That the application is scandalous; that is, objectionable or ridiculous.

(b) That it is contrary to morality or law.

(c) That it resembles another mark which

is already registered for the same class of goods.

There are fifty different classes of goods in the Trade Mark Register amongst which are distributed every possible kind of article. When applying for registration, the applicant states which articles he intends to use the mark on, and when it is registered he will only be protected as to goods of that sort. The fact that a mark has been registered for goods in one of the fifty classes does not mean that protection will be gained for its use on all other articles in the same class. This is important, because it follows that an application by a different person to register a similar mark for different goods in the same class will not necessarily fail.

In determining whether a mark proposed for registration resembles one which is already registered, the Registrar will look at the general idea of the mark. He will not examine the two marks for minute differences, but will take into consideration the general effect of each. He will consider the circumstances in which the marks will be used in actual trading and the types of customers who are accustomed to buy the goods in question. Trade customers and those in expensive trades are usually credited with greater intelligence, and it is assumed that slight similarities between two marks will not deceive them. But illiterate, native or very poor customers are easily misled, and the Registrar will be quick to refuse a mark which might confuse them if it is to be used on goods which they buy. Regard is paid not only to the appearance of the mark in draft and in actual use, but also to its effect upon the ear.

It is possible to register a mark in colour, but the rule is that the mark must be of such a nature that it would be distinctive even though it was colourless. In determining whether one coloured mark too closely resembles another, little attention is therefore paid to the actual colours.

Before refusing to register a mark, the Registrar must give the applicant an opportunity of being heard in support of his application.

An appeal lies from any decision of the Registrar either to the Board of Trade or to the Court. The applicant may elect which of these he will appeal to; both of them have

power, in appropriate cases, to cancel a registration.

The fact that any particular mark is not capable of registration, or is refused by the Registrar does not necessarily affect the right to bring an action for passing off.

How to Apply. — Applications for registration should be made to the Registrar, stating the goods in connection with which the mark is to be used. He will institute an official search to make sure that the mark does not resemble any other registered for the same or similar goods. There is no guarantee that this search is accurate.

The proprietor of a registered mark may apply for the separate registration of individual parts of it, or of other marks which resemble it. These will be registered as associated marks, but they can only be owned together with the principal mark. Where part of a mark is not registrable, the Registrar may require the applicant as a condition of registration to disclaim that part. In order to register "motorine" or "absorbine" applicants have been forced to disclaim the exclusive right to the use of the words "motor" and "absorb." The same principles would apply where part of a new mark resembles a mark already registered. Disclaimer of that part would be required. In certain circumstances, as, for instance, where marks have been used only in particular districts, the Registrar may require a disclaimer of any intention to use the marks in other districts. A disclaimer is entered on the register and prevents any action being brought for the infringement of the mark in respect of the use or imitation of the disclaimed part or its use in a disclaimed district. It does not, however, affect any right the proprietor may have to bring an action for passing off.

The only persons who may apply for registration are those who used the mark in the past to distinguish their goods or have invented a new mark which they intend to use after registration. They may apply through agents.

Where two or more persons apply for the same mark for the same goods, the Registrar may refer the whole matter to the Court; but if he is satisfied that there has been bona fide user of the mark by both or all of them, he may register them as concurrent proprietors. If they desire to use the mark on different kinds of goods no difficulty will arise.

Objections.—On receipt of the application for registration, the Registrar causes it to be advertised in the *Trade Marks and Patents Gazette.* Any person who desires to object may do so by giving notice to the Registrar setting out his reasons. The grounds of objection are:—

(i) That the mark ought not to be registered for one of the reasons set out above.

(ii) That the mark is an infringement of some right of the objector.

Objections will be allowed from any person who shews that he is the proprietor of a similar mark which is registered for similar goods, or that he uses a similar mark but has not registered it and that the new mark will cause confusion.

An application may also be made at any time by any person interested to remove a mark from the register on the ground that the proprietor had no intention of using it when he registered it, or that he has not made a bona fide use of it since then.

Registration in Part B is procured in the same way, and the same rules of procedure apply as for Part A; but the class of marks which can be registered is much wider. It is not necessary, in order to register in Part B, to shew that the mark comes within one of the six classes set out above. On the other hand, it is necessary to shew that the mark has actually been used for two years. Provided user for this period can be shewn, any mark may be registered in Part B (in addition, if desired, to registration in Part A), provided only that it is not confusing or deceptive, and does not too closely resemble a mark registered for the same kind of goods.

Effect of Registration.—The effect of registration varies slightly according as to whether it is in Part A or B. If it is in Part A, then, subject only to the fact that the registration itself may be attacked on the ground that the mark was never suitable, proof of registration alone establishes the exclusive right to the use of the mark on the goods in question. Whereas, if it is Part B, registration only affords prima facie proof that the person registered is entitled to the exclusive use of the mark, and it will still be open to an opponent to prove in any way

he can (and not merely by shewing that the mark was not suitable for registration), that the registered owner is not in fact so entitled.

Any one registration lasts for fourteen years from the date of the application and may be renewed indefinitely for further periods of fourteen years on payment of small renewal fees.

If the proprietor dies or his title devolves on another, notice should be given to the Registrar who will make the requisite alterations.

Trade marks can be assigned or sold even though the mark consists of the original owner's signature or name; but they can only be dealt in as ancillary to the goodwill of the business. They can never be assigned alone.

The registered proprietor of a trade mark is entitled to the exclusive use of the mark in connection with the goods for which it was registered. If a competitor uses the same or a similar mark the proprietor has the following remedies:

He may apply to the Court for an injunction to restrain the infringer from using the mark in the future; it is not necessary to shew that the defendant knew he was infringing the plaintiff's mark, but the Court will only grant an injunction if it considers that further infringements are possible. The Court will also order that all infringing marks be destroyed and that the infringer shall hand over to the proprietor all stamps, dies, etc., employed to make them.

If the proprietor can shew that the infringer knew he was infringing a registered mark, he will be entitled to plain damages. These will be estimated, at his election, either by determining the amount of the damage which he has himself suffered through loss of trade, etc., or by investigating the profits which the defendant made out of his use of the mark and ordering him to account for them to the proprietor.

In addition to the possible grounds of defence already referred to, a defendant can always establish a good defence and set up his right to the use of the mark if he can shew that he was using it himself before the proprietor's mark was registered and has continued to use it ever since.

TRADE UNION. What is a Trade Union ?—The words "Trade Union" signify to the majority of people an organization representative of the workers in a particular branch of industry—e.g. the National Union of Railwaymen—and many people think of a trade union as a body of persons mainly concerned with political activities.

Legal meaning.—In law the term "Trade Union" means any combination of persons, whether temporary or permanent, which has for its principal objects the following activities:—

(a) The regulation of the relations between workmen and employers, between workmen and workmen, and between employers and employers.

(b) The fixing of conditions for, and the imposition of restrictions upon, the method of conducting any trade or business.

(c) The provision of benefits to members.

Statutory Objects.—These three main activities are called the Statutory Objects, because they are laid down in the Trade Union Act Amendment Act, 1876, as being lawful objects for the furtherance of which a combination of persons may be formed.

Trade Unions before the year 1871. —Before the passing of the Trade Union Act, 1871, a combination of persons for the purpose of imposing restrictive conditions upon the conduct of a trade or business or of interfering in the relations between workmen and master was an unlawful combination, since its activities were held to be in restraint of trade. Trade unions existed, but they were mainly concerned with the provision of benefits to members, and the payment of strike pay, such objects not being regarded as being in restraint of trade.

The difference made by the passing of the Trade Union Acts, 1871 and 1876.—Trade unions formed for the purpose of furthering any of the three main objects set out above acquired a recognized status in the eyes of the law, provided they conformed to certain statutory requirements (*see below*), and, in consequence, they were freed from many of the disabilities under which they had previously worked. Registered trade unions can now own property, prosecute servants for embezzling funds and enforce most contracts made with them.

Contracts and Agreements which a Trade Union cannot enforce in a Law Court.—The following agreements

can lawfully be made by trade unions, but the Courts of law will not interfere in any action which may be brought to enforce the agreements or obtain damages for the breach of them.

(1) Any agreement between members of a union concerning the conditions on which any members for the time being shall or shall not sell their goods, transact business, employ or be employed.

(2) Any agreement for the payment by any person of any subscription or penalty to a union.

(3) Any agreement for the applying of the funds of a union to provide benefits to members, that is to say, sick, accident, or strike pay.

Note.—This means that a member cannot sue a trade union for any benefit which is due to him. He can, however, get the Court to declare that by the rules of the union he is entitled to a benefit. (On forfeiture of benefits through disobedience to instructions to strike, *see* TRADE DISPUTES.)

(4) Any agreement for the use of the funds of the union to provide contributions to any employer or workman not a member of the union in return for his undertaking to obey the rules and resolutions of the union.

(5) Any agreement for the application of the funds of a union to pay a fine imposed upon anyone by a Court of law.

(6) Any agreement made between one union and another.

(7) Any bond to secure the performance of any of these agreements which are so declared to be unenforceable.

Important.—These agreements are unenforceable by either side, i.e. the party other than the trade union is debarred from enforcing them in a law Court, just in the same way as a trade union is debarred.

How is a Trade Union formed?— Seven or more members of an organization who subscribe their names to its rules may register the union.

What is the effect of Registration.— Registration is not compulsory in order to form a lawful trade union, but a registered trade union acquires privileges which are not open to unregistered trade unions.

An Important Case.—The Taff Vale case decided that a registered trade union, being an entity recognized by law, has the right to the exclusive use of its registered name and can sue and be sued in that name.

How and Where to Register.—An application to register a trade union must be sent, together with a printed copy of the rules and a list of the titles and names of the officers, to the Chief Registrar of Friendly Societies, whose office is at 17, North Audley Street, London, W.1.

The Registrar, upon being satisfied that the union has complied with the regulations relating to registration, must register the union and the rules. The Registrar may not register a trade union unless in his opinion the principal objects of the union are "Statutory Objects."

Certificate of Registration.—When the Registrar registers a trade union he issues a Certificate, which is conclusive evidence that the regulations regarding registry have been complied with. A trade union which does not desire to be registered may apply to the Registrar for a certificate declaring that it is, by reason of its rules and objects, a trade union within the meaning of the Trade Union Act, 1913. If the Registrar refuses to grant a certificate to an unregistered trade union applying for the same, or refuses to register a trade union, then an appeal may be made to the High Court against his decision.

A certificate may be withdrawn or cancelled by the Registrar either at the request of the trade union itself, or if he is satisfied that it was obtained by fraud, or if in his opinion the rules and constitution of the union have been so altered that the principal objects of the union are no longer "Statutory Objects."

Requirements of the Law: What must the Rules contain?—The rules of every registered trade union must contain the following:—

(1) NAME.—The name of the union and its place of meeting for business.

(2) OBJECTS.—The whole of the objects for which the union is to be formed, the purposes for which its funds are to be used, the conditions which entitle a member to receive benefits, and the fines and forfeitures to be imposed on any one of its members.

(3) RULES.—The manner of making, altering, amending or deleting the rules themselves.

(4) COMMITTEE AND TRUSTEES.—Provision for the appointment and removal of a general committee of management, of a trustee or trustees, of a treasurer and other officers.

(5) THE FUNDS.—Provision for the investment of the funds of the union and for an annual audit of the accounts.

(6) THE BOOKS.—Provision for the inspection of the books and list of members of the union by every person having an interest in the funds.

(7) DISSOLVING THE UNION.—Provision for the way in which the union is to be dissolved.

Important.—A copy of the rules *must* be delivered to any person requesting it on payment of a maximum sum of one shilling. It is an offence to give to any member or intending member of a registered trade union a copy of the rules other than those in existence for the time being, pretending that these are the existing rules or that there are no other rules.

Membership of a Trade Union: How to become a member.—A person becomes a member of a trade union when his entrance fee and subscription are accepted by the union and when he receives a card of membership.

Who may not become Members.—An infant under the age of sixteen years may not be a member of a trade union.

A member of a Police Force may not become a member of a trade union, but if he was a member before he joined the Force he may, with the consent of a Chief Officer of Police, continue to be a member of his union.

Civil Servants are, by the Trade Disputes Act, 1927, forbidden to become members of any organization of which the principal object is the influencing of the pay or conditions of service of the members, unless such organization confines its membership to persons employed by the Crown.

A Civil Servant who was a member of a trade union six months or more before the coming into effect of the Trade Disputes Act may remain a member, if any benefit was due to him under the rules of the union.

Expulsion from Membership.—A member cannot be expelled from membership unless the rules so provide, and if there is a power of expulsion contained in the rules, then he must be given a hearing before expulsion. '(*See also* TRADE DISPUTE.)

Trade Union Property.—A registered trade union may hold an unlimited amount of personal property, e.g. money, stocks and shares, but it may only purchase or lease land to a maximum extent of one acre, and such property must be for purposes connected with the administration of the business of the union, e.g. for an office or headquarters.

Who holds Trade Union Property? —All the real and personal estate of a registered trade union is vested in the trustees of the union, and they hold it on behalf of, and for the benefit of, the union and its members.

A trustee is only liable to account for money actually received by him on behalf of the union, and is not liable for any deficiency which may arise in the general funds of the union.

The Main Objects of a Trade Union.—A trade union usually has two main spheres of activity (a) Political, (b) Non-Political.

A. Political Objects.—Political objects were not included in the original Trade Union Acts of 1871 and 1876, which defined the Statutory Objects of trade unions; but, by the Trade Union Act, 1913, the funds of a trade union were permitted to be used for certain political objects subject to some specified safeguards.

Objects Permitted by the Act of 1913.—Money belonging to the union may be expended upon:—

(1) Payment of expenses incurred directly or indirectly by a candidate or prospective candidate for election to Parliament or to any public office, before, during, or after the election in connection with his candidature or election.

(2) The holding of any meeting or the distribution of any literature in support of any such candidate or prospective candidate.

(3) The maintenance of any person who is a member of Parliament or of any person who holds public office.

(4) Registration of electors or the selection of a candidate for Parliament or any public office.

(5) Holding of political meetings or on the distribution of political literature or political documents of any kind.

Ballot.—A trade union may not apply its funds in the furtherance of any of these political objects, unless such furtherance has been approved as an object of the union by a resolution passed on a ballot of members.

Political Fund.—The rules of a trade union which desires to apply its funds towards the furtherance of any of the political objects enumerated above, must provide for the creation of a separate political fund.

It must be a rule of a trade union that any member shall be exempt from contributions to its political fund unless he delivers written notice of his willingness to contribute.

An Important Case.—The Osborne Case decided that it was not within the powers of a trade union to levy a compulsory contribution from its members for the purpose of supporting representatives in Parliament.

A member must not be excluded from any benefits, nor subjected directly or indirectly to any disadvantage as compared with the other members of the union, by reason of his unwillingness to contribute to the political fund.

B. Non-Political Objects.—The non-political activities are mainly covered by the "Statutory Objects," that is to say, they include such subjects as the protection of the interests of members in questions relating to wages, conditions of working, payment of sick and accident benefit, and maintenance during strikes. (*See* FRIENDLY SOCIETY; STRIKES; TRADE DISPUTE.)

Such activities of trade unions are not allowed to be unrestricted by the law, and, in the event of the actions of members of a union being held to have been done in pursuance of a conspiracy maliciously to ruin a person in his trade rather than in pursuance of a legitimate trade object, then the members committing the acts are not freed from liability, because they are members of a union and did the acts on its behalf or for its benefit. (*See also* CONSPIRACY; STRIKES; TRADE DISPUTE.)

An Important Case.—L was a butcher and M was one of his best customers. Q intimidated M into ceasing to deal with L because L employed non-union labour. It was decided that the words "trade dispute between employer and workmen" in Section 3 of the Trade Disputes Act, 1906, do not include a dispute between members of a trade union and an employer of non-union workmen; and that the action of Q was not done in furtherance of a trade dispute, but was part of a conspiracy to ruin L.

Law Suits by or against Trade Unions.—A registered trade union may, except in one case (*see below*), sue or be sued in its registered name, and a trade union whether it is registered or unregistered, may sue or be sued in a representative action, if the parties are fairly representative of the union. (*See* PARTIES.)

Who Sues for a Trade Union.—The trustees of a registered trade union may bring or defend any action concerning the property of the union, but they must sue and be sued in their own names, adding thereunto the title of their office, e.g. "A. B. Jones, trustee of the Amalgamated Society of...................."

Important.—In a claim for damages against a trade union the trustees should be sued; they are entitled to be repaid out of the funds of the union.

A Trade Union cannot be Sued for a Tort.—This is the exception referred to above.

No action may be brought against a trade union in its registered name in respect of a tort alleged to have been committed by or on behalf of the union or one of its branches. (*See* "TORT" for fuller explanation of the term.)

This complete immunity from actions in tort was conferred upon trade unions by the Trade Disputes Act, 1906, but it makes no difference to the immunity that the act was done when there was no trade dispute either in existence or in contemplation.

The meaning of this freedom of a trade union is that a trade union cannot be sued for damages for, e.g. a trespass or a libel in its registered name. The trustees may be sued for damages, provided the tort was not committed by a person on behalf of the union in contemplation, or in furtherance of a trade dispute. (*See* TRADE DISPUTE.)

What is the liability of a Trade Union for the acts of its Officials?—The officials of a trade union can only make the union liable for the consequences of their acts if they had authority to do the particular act or acts. It follows that an official has no authority to do something which his union may not lawfully do.

An Important Case.—Brown was the district delegate of a union. It was held that he was not the agent of the union to make it liable for his acts in the absence of evidence that direct authority had expressly been given to him. (*See* BLACK-LIST; CONSPIRACY; FRIENDLY SOCIETY; STRIKES; TRADE DISPUTE; TORT.)

TRANSCRIPT. — When a shorthand note is taken of the proceedings of a trial, the document containing the typewritten record is called the transcript. In criminal cases tried at assizes or quarter sessions a transcript of the evidence and summing up can be obtained on payment. In civil actions a shorthand note is not usually taken, but the parties can arrange amongst themselves for one to be taken, and in such circumstances they can obtain the transcript from the firm of shorthand writers engaged.

TRANSFER OF JUSTICES' LICENCES.—In certain specified events it is permissible to transfer a justices' licence from one person to another. This is done at the Transfer Sessions which are held once a year. The permission of the justices must be obtained to transfer a justices' licence. (*See* INTOXICATING LIQUOR; and PROTECTION ORDER.)

TREASON.—The only kind of Treason now properly so called is High Treason. (*See* HIGH TREASON.)

TREASON FELONY.—This is an offence similar to High Treason, though not so serious in its character or punishment. Any person who plans or incites others to depose the King, or to levy war against him, or to intimidate Parliament can be convicted of treason-felony and be sentenced to penal servitude for life. (*See* HIGH TREASON.)

TREASURE TROVE. — When precious metals in bullion or other form are found hidden anywhere they are called treasure trove. If the owner cannot be found, treasure trove becomes the property of the Crown. It should be noted that treasure trove is confined to articles that have been hidden by some person and not articles that have been merely mislaid or lost. If they have been actually hidden, then they are treasure trove even though they are in a private house or on other private property. It is an offence for any person who finds treasure trove to fail to report what he has found to the coroner of the district in which he found it. It is the duty of the coroner, if there is any doubt as to whether the articles found are treasure trove or not, to hold an inquest on the point.

TREASURY SOLICITOR.—A permanent public official whose duties include acting as solicitor to various Government departments and providing legal representation to protect the interests of the public in certain cases. The person holding the office of Treasury Solicitor also holds that of King's Proctor.

TREES, OVERHANGING.—A person who allows a tree from his garden to overhang that of his neighbour is technically guilty of a nuisance, but no action can be brought unless the neighbour can shew some actual financial loss caused by the overhanging tree, which is unlikely. The neighbour, however, is entitled to cut away the branches that overhang, although it is probably not advisable for him to do so without first requesting the occupier of the land to cut the branches himself. If trees which overhang property collapse and do damage, the occupier of the land will only be liable if he has in some way been negligent, e.g. if he ought to have known that the trees were insecure and had done nothing to prevent them falling. Where dangerous trees, such as yew trees, project into the property of another, and cattle eat the leaves and die, the person occupying the land on which the trees are may be liable to pay damages.

TRESPASS.—In English law trespass has a much wider meaning than in ordinary speech, for it includes not only trespass to land but also trespass to chattels or goods, and trespass to the person. Thus, an assault is, technically, trespass to the person. In the case of land, any person trespasses who goes on the land occupied by some other person or remains upon the land or places any material object on it without justification. Trespass is an offence against posses-sion, and it is immaterial who is the owner of the land on which the trespass takes place. Thus, a landlord may be guilty of trespassing on the property which he has let to his tenant while the tenant is lawfully in possession.

It is not necessary that actual damage should have been suffered before an action for trespass can be brought. Thus, if A walks across B's land even though he keeps to a path, B is entitled to bring an action against A claiming damages. The damages which would be given in such a case would be very small, but the trespasser might be required to pay the costs of the action.

Trespass to Goods. — Trespass to goods consists of committing without lawful justification any act of direct physical interference with a chattel in the possession of another person. The act need not cause damage to the chattel, for it is trespass to remove a chattel even though damage is not done. Trespass to goods, like trespass to land, is an offence against possession and not against ownership and therefore a person who has possession of goods, even though he is not the owner, may sue for trespass to them. Thus, if A hires a car which B takes away without A's authority A may sue for trespass. This is the case even though B is the owner of the car.

"TRESPASSERS WILL BE PRO-SECUTED."—This notice, which is so frequently seen on boards in woods and private land has been called by a Judge a "wooden lie," for no prosecution (which is a criminal proceeding), can in general be brought against a trespasser. The position is different when the person trespassing does so in pursuit of game, or when in his trespass he does damage to the land, e.g. walks through a standing crop of corn—or where the land is of some special kind, e.g. in the occupation of a railway company.

The only remedy for trespass is to bring an action claiming damages in a Civil Court (not a prosecution), against the trespasser, but in an ordinary case the damages recovered would be nominal, e.g. a farthing. The usual object of these notices threatening a prosecution for trespass is not to prevent persons from coming on the land, but to prevent them from establishing a *right* to come on the land by creating a right of way. No right of way can be claimed unless the owner of the land acquiesces in the use of his land; and if persons were in the habit of using the path on the land to the knowledge of the owner, it might be inferred that the owner acquiesced in the use if he did nothing to prevent it. The erection of notices threatening a prosecution makes it quite clear that the use is against the will of the owner, and, in consequence, it is not unusual for owners not to interfere with persons using paths in an orderly way so long as the presence of these notices makes it clear that they are not doing so by permission of the owner.

A recent act (The Right of Way Act, 1932) now enables owners of land to make it clear that they are not granting new rights of way to the public, by filing declarations to this effect at stated intervals. This act came into force on January 1st, 1934, and it seems likely that landowners will be more willing to allow to the public access to their lands since they can prevent any *right* to use the land being created by means of the declaration. (*See* HIGHWAYS; RIGHT OF WAY.)

TRINITY MASTERS.—The Trinity Masters constitute Trinity House and are a company of Masters of ships on whom are imposed many duties relating to the sea. Trinity House was originally incorporated in the reign of Henry VIII.

Trinity House exercises control over lighthouses and over pilots. Where there is no local piloting authority the pilots are appointed by Trinity House.

TROVER.—The action of trover lies for wrongs done to personal chattels. Conversion consists in an act of wilful interference with the chattel without lawful justification whereby any person entitled to the chattel is deprived of it. Conversion may take place either by the wrongful taking of a chattel or by detaining it wrongfully or by disposing of it wrongfully. It is not necessary that the person converting should know that he is acting wrongly by so doing. Thus, if the hire purchaser of a motor car sells the car when he is not entitled to do so to X, who takes it in all innocence and pays for it and later sells the car to Y, X (and also Y) is guilty of conversion in selling the car, and may be called upon to pay damages to the person to whom the car belongs, namely, the other party to the hire purchase agreement.

TRUCK.—The name given to the system of paying wages for service by goods rather than by cash. As a system it had been in operation for many centuries, and the evils of its operation as regards the workman had been observed as far back as the fifteenth century in a statute of 1464. The legal position is now governed by the Truck Acts of 1831, 1887, and 1896 which impose restrictions upon the methods in which wages may be paid. These statutes prohibit the payment of wages to certain defined workmen in any form other than cash, which must be current coin of the realm. Bank notes or cheques drawn upon a bank within fifteen miles of the place of payment satisfy the requirements and are regarded as current coin.

The Truck Acts apply to any workman who comes under the following heads: A labourer, servant in husbandry, journeyman, artificer, handicraftsman, miner, or a person otherwise engaged in manual labour. The definition does not include a domestic or menial servant, and the provisions of the Acts do not therefore apply to them.

If an employer makes a payment to a workman in respect of wages earned by the workman, by the delivery of goods, it is illegal and does not constitute a payment of wages, even though the workman has chosen to take goods instead of cash.

Any contract to employ a workman which provides that the whole or any part of the wages are to be payable in goods is an illegal contract and has no effect in law. If, in pursuance of such an illegal contract, or even without an express contract, the workman receives goods as part of his wages, he is still entitled to recover from his employer the portion of his wages not paid in cash, and he cannot be sued by his employer for the price of the goods thus delivered to him. No contract may be made between an employer and a workman which provides that wages shall be laid out or expended in a particular way.

The acts provide that the whole of the wages earned by a workman are to be paid over to him in cash, but this provision does not prevent certain deductions being made which are permitted by statute. Thus, deductions may be made in respect of fuel, medicine, medical attendance, and also for the payment of the education fees of the workman's child. (*See also* FACTORY.)

The penalty for a contravention of the provisions of the Truck Act is a fine not exceeding £10 for the first offence, and not less than £10 and not exceeding £20 for a second offence.

If an offence is committed without the knowledge of an employer, he may be exempted from penalty upon the conviction of the actual offender. (*See* FACTORY.)

TRUE BILL.—It was the practice for a grand jury, whenever they presented a case for trial, to return what was described as a "True Bill." Grand juries, however, have now been abolished.

TRUST.—This is the legal term given to the holding of property by one person for the benefit of another. The person so holding property is called a trustee and the person for whose benefit the property is held is called a beneficiary or cestui que trust.

Trusts are of two kinds, Express and Implied. An express trust arises upon an express declaration of trust by the owner of any property, as where A declares himself a trustee of some property for B, or transfers the property to C with a direction that C shall hold it upon trust for B. An implied trust arises when a person acquires or holds property in such circumstances that the law requires him to hold it in trust for some other person, as where the objects for which a trust was created fail, for example, by the death of all the beneficiaries without issue (in which case the law requires the trustee to hold the property in trust for the person who originally created the trust), or where a trustee obtains a renewal in his own name of a lease held by him as a trustee and the law requires him to hold the new lease in trust for the beneficiaries of the old lease.

Creation of an Express Trust.— In order to create a valid express trust six conditions must be fulfilled:—

(i) The person creating the trust must be capable in law of alienating (i.e. parting with and transferring) the property, the subject of the proposed trust, to the extent necessary to fulfil the expressed object of the trust.

(ii) The beneficiary or cestui que trust must be capable in law of holding the property to the extent to which it is being held in trust for him.

(iii) A declaration of trust which sufficiently indicates the creator's intention.

(iv) A declaration which sufficiently defines the subject matter of the trust.

(v) A declaration which sufficiently defines the object or the person or persons to be benefited by the trust.

(vi) In the case of land or of any interest therein, the Law of Property Act, 1925, provides "a declaration of trust respecting any land or any interest therein must be manifested and proved by some writing signed by some person who is able to declare such trust or by his will." The statute lays down a rule of evidence, and it is not necessary that the trust should be declared in writing in the first instance; it is sufficient if there be some writing signed by the proper party in existence at the date when an action is brought to enforce the trust.

Limitation of Trusts.—Private ownership of property necessarily carries with it the right of the owner to dispose of the whole interest in his property either inter vivos (i.e. during his lifetime) or on death. Public policy, however, requires that this power of disposition should not be abused and from early times the law has discouraged dispositions of property which unreasonably fetter the future devolution or enjoyment of that property.

The most important limitation of the right to dispose freely of property by the creation of a trust is the so-called Rule against Perpetuities. Under this rule every future estate or interest in any kind of property must vest in the beneficiary or beneficiaries during the life of a person, or the survivor of any number of persons in being named in the trust instrument, and twenty-one years from the termination of such life; if no such person is named in the trust instrument, the estate or interest must vest within twenty-one years of the time of its creation. For the purposes of this rule, a child *en ventre de sa mère* at the time of the creation of an estate or interest is deemed to be a person in being. The time of creation of an estate or interest is the time of execution of the instrument creating the estate or interest, except in the case of the creation of an estate or interest by will, when the time of the death of the testator is deemed to be the time of creation.

Any estate or interest which at the time of its creation does not necessarily satisfy and continue to satisfy the above rule is void from its creation.

The Rule against Perpetuities applies to all private property, the right of ownership of which is governed by English law with the following exceptions:—

(i) Certain perpetual interests created in praesenti (i.e. to take effect immediately) such as easements and profits à prendre (q.v.) rent charges; covenants and conditions binding land; customary rights; charities; and interests held by corporations.

(ii) Vested interests, including those which come into possession in futuro, i.e. at a future date.

(iii) Certain estates or interests otherwise too remote, a right of destruction of which is given to the owner of another estate by operation of law; for example, a remainder after an estate tail.

(iv) Certain Charitable Gifts arising in futuro; for example, a gift over —otherwise too remote—from one charity to another. But other future gifts to charities and gifts over to persons after gifts to charities are subject to the rule.

(v) Personal contracts.

(vi) Interests given by operation of law; for example, rights of escheat.

(vii) Certain Rights of Entry and of Re-entry in leases which are necessarily co-extensive with legal estates and interests not themselves subject to the operation of the rule.

(viii) Interests which, though in expression too remote, must in fact vest within the perpetuity period.

The general effect of a void limitation is that the instrument takes effect as if the void limitation had been omitted altogether, and every limitation that is dependent upon the void limitation is itself void.

Enforcement of Trusts.—A trust is completely constituted when the trust property has been vested in trustees for the benefit of the beneficiaries; until this has been done the trust is incompletely constituted. This distinction is important from the point of view of the enforcement of trusts, since a completely constituted trust is enforced whether any valuable consideration has been given for its creation or not; whereas an incompletely constituted trust will only be enforced if value has been given.

Revocation of Trusts.—Unless a power of revocation is inserted in the trust instrument, a completely constituted trust can only be revoked if it was obtained by fraud or undue influence, or if it was executed under a fundamental mistake or misapprehension as to its effect. To the above rule, however, there is an exception in the case of a conveyance by a debtor to a trustee upon trust for his creditors. Such a conveyance is sometimes treated as an arrangement made by the debtor for his own personal convenience and accommodation—for the payment of his own debts in an order prescribed by himself, over which he retains power and control. Such a trust is sometimes spoken of as "illusory." There are, however, four cases in which such a conveyance does create an enforceable trust in favour of the creditors or some of them:—

(i) Where any creditor is a party to the deed of conveyance and executes it, the deed will be irrevocable as to that creditor, and enforceable by him.

(ii) If the trust is communicated to the creditors or any of them and they assent thereto and either act thereon or are thereby induced to forbear to enforce their ordinary remedies, the deed is irrevocable as to, and enforceable by them.

(iii) If it appears from the trust instrument that the intention of the debtor is to create a trust and not merely a convenient method of paying his debts, the trust will be enforceable by the creditors.

(iv) If the trust is created for the payment of the debts after the death of the debtor, and the debtor dies without revoking the trust, it will be enforceable by the creditors.

Rectification of Trusts.—If, by mistake, the trust instrument does not express the intention of the creator, the Court according to the circumstances will rectify or cancel the trust.

Termination of Trust.—A trust ceases when the trustee no longer holds any property for the benefit of another and his duties and liabilities in his capacity as trustee have also ceased. A trustee's duties and liabilities do not necessarily cease because he no longer holds property for the benefit of another, because he may have disposed of property wrongfully, in which case he remains liable to the beneficiaries for his breach of trust, and so as it is possible to identify or follow the proceeds of the wrongful disposition the beneficiaries are entitled thereto. The conditions under which a person ceases to be a trustee are dealt with under the heading TRUSTEE.

TRUSTEE.—A person who holds property for the benefit of another is said to be the trustee of that property for the other. The capacity of a person to be a trustee is co-extensive with the capacity to hold property. A person may be one of the trustees and one of the beneficiaries of the same property, but he cannot be both the sole trustee and the sole beneficiary.

Appointment of Trustees.—Trustees may be appointed:—

(i) By being named in the trust instrument.

(ii) By some person who has a power to appoint new trustees, either under the trust instrument or under the Trustee Act, 1925. Under this act, the person or persons nominated for the purpose of appointing new trustees by the trust instrument, or, if there is no such person, or no such person able and willing to act, then the survivor or continuing trustees or trustee for the time being, or the personal representatives of the last surviving or continuing trustee, may by writing during his lifetime appoint any person or persons, including himself in the last mentioned case, to be a trustee or trustees in the place of any trustee who is dead, or remains out of the United Kingdom for more than twelve months, or desires to be discharged, or refuses, or is unfit, to act, or is incapable of acting, or is an infant.

(iii) By the beneficiaries if they are all of age and between them entitled to the whole beneficial interest.

(iv) By the Court. The High Court has extensive powers of appointing a new trustee or new trustees either in substitution for, or in addition to any existing trustee or trustees, or although there is no existing trustee. The appointment can be made whenever it is found inexpedient, difficult, or impracticable to appoint a new trustee without the help of the Court; as where a trustee is convicted of felony, or is a lunatic or defective, or is bankrupt, or is a corporation which is in liquidation or has been dissolved.

The number of trustees of a settlement of land or of a trust for sale of land is limited. If on 1st January, 1926, there were more than four trustees, no new trustees can be appointed until the number is reduced to less than four. If the settlement or trust is made after that date, the number must not, in any case, exceed four, and if more than four are appointed, the first four named who are able and willing to act will alone be the trustees.

A person is legally constituted a trustee who (1) has been duly appointed by one or other of the above modes, and (2) has accepted the trust either expressly or by acting in the execution of it. A person who has not been legally constituted a trustee, nevertheless becomes what is called a constructive trustee in the following cases:—

(i) Where, for want of a legally constituted trustee, trust property becomes in law vested in him.

(ii) Where he holds or acquires property in such circumstances that the law requires him to hold it in trust for some other person.

(iii) Where he intermeddles with and acts as a trustee of trust property, in which case he is also called a trustee de son tort.

Custodian Trustee. — A custodian trustee is a trustee to whom the trust property is transferred as if he were sole trustee, whilst the management of the trust property and the exercise of all powers and discretions under the trust remain vested in the other trustees as managing trustees. He has the custody of all the trust securities and documents of title, but the managing trustees have free access thereto and are entitled to take copies and extracts. The custodian trusteeship may be determined by an order of the Court upon the application of the custodian trustee or any managing trustee or beneficiary, upon proof that such determination is generally desired by the beneficiaries or is otherwise expedient. The Public Trustee, if he consents to act as such, and is duly appointed under the provisions of the Public Trustee Act, 1906 (*see* PUBLIC TRUSTEE), may act as custodian trustee, and any incorporated banking or guarantee or trust company, or other body corporate which is for the time being empowered to undertake trusts, may also act as custodian trustee in like manner as the Public Trustee, provided that it does not state or hold out that any liability in respect of any act or omission on its part, when so acting, will attach either to the Public Trustee or the Consolidated Fund of the United Kingdom.

Judicial Trustee. — The Court has power on the application of the creator or a trustee or a beneficiary, to appoint any fit and proper person nominated in the application, or an official of the Court (usually the Official Solicitor), to be a judicial trustee to act alone or jointly with any other person, and, for sufficient cause, in place of all or any existing trustees. A judicial trustee must, as soon as practicable after his appointment, furnish the Court with a complete statement of the trust property, and must from time to time give to the Court all information necessary for keeping the statement correct. Where a judicial trustee is so appointed, special provisions apply to the keeping of the trust accounts and bank accounts and the deposit and custody of all trust documents of title. The Court may at any time, either with or without any request of the judicial trustee, give directions as to the trust or its administration, or order an inquiry into the administration or any dealing or transaction of a judicial trustee. A judicial trustee receives such remuneration as is fixed by the Court.

Public Trustee. — (*See* PUBLIC TRUSTEE.)

Disclaimer by Trustee. — A person appointed a trustee is not bound to accept his appointment, but may disclaim the trust at any time before he has done anything shewing his intention to accept it. No formal act or instrument is necessary to effect the disclaimer. It may be by word of mouth or inferred from conduct, or from the fact that a long time has elapsed since the appointment and the trustee has done nothing, but it is usual and convenient to disclaim by deed, and in the case of a married woman a deed is necessary to enable her to disclaim an estate or interest in land. The disclaimer must be of the whole of the trust, a disclaimer of part is ineffectual. Once the trust is accepted, either expressly or impliedly, disclaimer is impossible. A person impliedly accepts his appointment as trustee if he interferes with the trust property, or otherwise acts in the trust, or allows proceedings in reference to the trust property to be carried on in his name.

Retirement of Trustees. — A trustee who has accepted the trust cannot disclaim, but he may obtain a release from his trusteeship in the followings ways:—

(i) Unless negatived by the trust instrument (if any), a trustee may retire by deed from the trust, provided that after his discharge there will be either a Trust Corporation or at least two individuals (not counting a custodian trustee) to act as trustees to perform the trust, and provided that his co-trustees and the person (if any), empowered to appoint new trustees consent by deed to his retirement. In such a case everything necessary to vest the trust property in the continuing trustees must be done. Such vesting is effected by an order of the Court as regards certain interests in land and property which is only transferable in books kept by a company or other body, or in other manner directed by, or under an Act of Parliament, and is effected as regards all other property by a vesting declaration made by the retiring and continuing trustees.

(ii) A trustee may retire upon the appointment of the Public Trustee as an ordinary trustee. (*See* PUBLIC TRUSTEE.)

(iii) In certain cases, for example, where a trustee has served for a long time and is of advanced age and in failing health, or if much litigation has taken place, or other difficult circumstances have arisen in connection with the trust and were not contemplated and did not exist at the time when he accepted the trust, a trustee, if he cannot otherwise obtain his discharge, may apply for it to the Court of Chancery in an action to administer the trust.

The retirement of a trustee does not terminate his liability as such to third parties unless he has taken the necessary steps (e.g. in the case of shares, of having them transferred out of his own name), to get rid of those liabilities.

A trustee must not retire if he knows that some breach of trust is contemplated by the continuing trustees. If he does so, he may be held liable for the consequences of the breach of trust in spite of his retirement.

Duties of Trustees.—It is a trustee's duty to conduct the business of the trust in such a way as an ordinary prudent man would conduct his own. In addition, he must conform to any directions given to him in the trust instrument and to the rules of law and equity governing the management and disposition of trust property. If all the beneficiaries are of age and between them entitled to the whole beneficial interest, a trustee must comply with any direction given by them in which they all concur.

Trustees cannot shift their duties on to others, but they may employ and pay an agent to perform duties in connection with the administration of the trust whenever, as prudent men of business, they would do so on their own behalf; and they may, unless forbidden by the trust instrument, employ and pay an agent, whether a solicitor, banker, stockbroker or other person, to transact any business or to do any act required to be transacted or done in the execution of the trust or the administration of the testator's or intestate's estate, including the receipt and payment of money, and will be entitled to be allowed and paid all charges and expenses so incurred. They will not be responsible for the default of any such agent if he was employed in good faith. Further, a trustee who intends to remain out of the United Kingdom for a period exceeding one month, may, by power of attorney, delegate to any person the execution or exercise during his absence of all or any trusts, powers or discretions vested in him as such trustee, either alone or jointly with any other person or persons; but he

cannot appoint his sole co-trustee unless the co-trustee is a trust corporation. The trustee remains liable for the acts and defaults of his attorney. The power of attorney only comes into operation if and when the trustee actually leaves the United Kingdom, and it is automatically revoked by his return. The power of attorney must be attested by at least one witness, and must be filed at the Central Office within ten days after its execution, together with a statutory declaration that the trustee intends to remain out of the United Kingdom for more than a month.

In order to escape liability for any loss consequent upon the employment of an agent in connection with the business of a trust, trustees must have exercised ordinary prudence in their selection of such agent and in their subsequent supervision of the performance of his duties, and must not employ him in matters not connected with his usual business.

The primary duty of a trustee is to acquaint himself with, and get possession of the trust property and to place it in a state of security.

Where there are two or more trustees, the trust property should be placed under the joint control of all of them. It is a breach of trust for trustees to leave one of their number in sole control of the trust property. Thus securities payable to bearer should be deposited in a bank in the joint names of the trustees, though one trustee may safely be left in possession of non-negotiable securities and title-deeds.

A trustee must be faithful to the trust and must not undertake a duty or put himself in a position which is inconsistent with his duty as a trustee, or act in a manner inconsistent with that duty. Thus, he must not use his position for his personal advantage, and must not enter into transactions in which he has, or may have, an interest which conflicts with the interests of the beneficiaries. This rule applies to all persons who stand in a position of trust or, as it is sometimes called, a fiduciary position; and all such persons whether agents, solicitors, guardians, partners, directors of companies, managing owners of ships, etc., must refund with interest all profits made by them by means of their fiduciary position, unless the profit is made with the full knowledge and approval of the persons to whom they owe a duty or stand in a position of trust.

Another duty of a trustee is to keep accurate accounts of the trust property and to produce them to the beneficiaries when required together with all necessary information affecting the trust property.

Trustees may cause the accounts to be examined or audited by an independent accountant, but such an audit should not be taken more often than once in every three years unless special circumstances require a more frequent audit.

Any trustee or beneficiary may apply once in any one year to the Public Trustee for an investigation and audit of the trust accounts.

A further duty of a trustee is promptly to invest all capital trust money coming into his hands, unless the trust instrument otherwise directs. He is liable for any loss occurring as a consequence of his investing such moneys improperly or of his delaying the investment for an unreasonable length of time.

The nature of the property in which a trustee may invest trust funds is governed by the trust instrument and by the Trustee Act, 1925. A trustee may invest in any property which the trust instrument expressly authorizes, provided the trustee bona fide exercises his discretion for the benefit of the trust. Apart from investments authorized by the trust instrument, a trustee is in general limited to so-called gilt-edged securities, that is to say:—Parliamentary stocks or public funds or Government securities of the United Kingdom; real securities of the United Kingdom (including first mortgages on freehold land but not second mortgages nor land itself); stock of the Bank of England or the Bank of Ireland; India Seven, Five and a half, Four and a half, Three and a half, Three, and Two and a half per cent. stock, or any future issues of such stock; securities the interest of which is guaranteed by Parliament; London County Council stock or Metropolitan Water stock; debenture, or rent-charge, or guaranteed or preference stock of any railway in the United Kingdom incorporated by special Act of Parliament, and having during each of the ten years last before the date of investment paid a dividend at the rate of not less than three per centum on its ordinary stock;

debenture stock of any railway company in India owning or operating a railway in that country, the interest in sterling on which is paid or guaranteed by the Secretary of State in Council of India; certain Indian Railway annuities; debenture or guaranteed or preference stock of any company in the United Kingdom, established for the supply of water for profit, and incorporated by special Act of Parliament or by Royal Charter, and having during each of the ten years last past before the date of investment paid a dividend of not less than five per centum on its ordinary stock; nominal or inscribed stock of any municipal borough, having, according to the returns of the last census prior to the date of investment, a population exceeding fifty thousand; or by any County Council, or by any Commissioners incorporated by Act of Parliament for the purpose of supplying water, and having a compulsory power of levying rates over an area having, according to the returns of the last census prior to the date of investment, a population exceeding fifty thousand; stocks, funds or securities authorized under the Colonial Stock Act, 1900; local housing bonds; stocks or securities issued in respect of any loan raised by the Government of Northern Ireland; and any of the securities authorized for the investment of cash under the control of the Court.

Trustees may vary any investments for other like investments, and also, may continue any authorized investment, notwithstanding that, since the investment of the trust funds therein, they may have ceased to be authorized investments.

Maintenance of Infants.—The Court has power to allow maintenance to an infant out of property in which he has an interest, and in special circumstances will do so even though the trust instrument contains a direction to accumulate the income for a period allowed by law. But the Court will not usually make an allowance to the father for this purpose, since a father is bound in law to support his children. If, however, the father is not able to give the child an upbringing suitable to the child's expectant fortune, he may be granted an allowance. A mother is not under a similar obligation, and will usually be granted an allowance. Trustees have wide powers of using income for a child's maintenance, education and benefit, without any application to the Court.

Powers of Trustees.—A trustee must exercise all such lawful powers as are given him by the trust instrument in good faith and for the purposes for which they were given. Similarly, where the trust instrument gives him a discretion he must exercise it in accordance with any directions contained therein. But, subject to any express directions in the trust instrument, a trustee may do all acts which are reasonable and proper for the realization and protection of the trust property.

Subject always to any express provision in the trust instrument, the trustee or trustees for the time being of any trust may, if he or they think fit, accept any composition or any security, real or personal, for any property, real or personal, which he or they have claimed, and may allow any time for payment of any debt, and may compromise, compound, abandon, submit to arbitration, or otherwise settle any debt, account, claim or thing whatever relating to the trust.

The power of a trustee to repair and improve the trust property, and the question whether he is entitled to do so out of capital or income, depend on the terms of the trust instrument. Generally speaking, leasehold property should be kept in repair out of income.

In the absence of any direction or power in the trust instrument a trustee should apply to the Court, which will direct the execution of necessary or proper repairs or improvements, and also direct whether the cost is to be paid out of or apportioned between capital and income.

Subject to any direction in the trust instrument, a trustee of leaseholds which by covenant or contract, or by custom or usual practice, are renewable from time to time, may, if he think fit, and must, if required so to do by any beneficiary, use his best endeavours from time to time to obtain a renewed lease on the accustomed and reasonable terms, and may do all proper and requisite acts for that purpose.

Except in the case of property of which he is the legal owner and which he is expressly authorized to repair or repair out of income of capital, and except where he is authorized by the trust instrument to apply capital money for any purpose or in any manner, a trustee can only mortgage the trust property to the extent authorized by the trust instrument.

Where a trustee holds property on trust for sale, or exercises a power of sale contained in the trust instrument, he must endeavour to sell the property to the best advantage and must not offer it for sale in a manner that may lessen its value or prejudice the sale. He ought to ascertain its estimated value, and unless the trust instrument directs him to sell in any event, he ought not to sell at an undervalue.

A trustee having a power of sale cannot give a third person an option to buy at a fixed figure at a future date, because, if the property increases in value in the meantime, the trust estate will lose the increment, whereas if it deteriorates the option will not be exercised.

A power of sale includes a power of postponing the sale unless a contrary intention appears from the trust instrument, and also a power to sell separately any part of the property.

Unless forbidden so to do by the trust instrument, a trustee may insure in his discretion any building or other insurable property against loss or damage by fire. Moneys recovered under such a policy are treated as being held upon the same trusts and for the same purposes as the property insured.

Rights of Trustees.—Apart from any express provision in the trust instrument, a trustee is only entitled to remuneration for his work in the following cases:—(1) by agreement with the beneficiaries, provided they are all of age; but the Court looks with suspicion upon any such agreement. (2) If the trust is more than ordinarily burdensome, the Court may sanction a commission being paid or allowed. (3) A judicial trustee may be paid such remuneration as the Court may assign him. (4) The Public Trustee is allowed to charge such fees as are fixed by the Treasury. (5) A corporation appointed by the Court may charge such remuneration as the Court authorizes. (6) A solicitor-trustee is entitled to his profit costs when he acts as solicitor in an action or other legal proceeding on behalf of himself and his co-trustee, except so far as the costs have been increased by his being one of the parties. Although not entitled to remuneration, a trustee may reimburse himself, or pay, or discharge out of the trust property all expenses, costs or liabilities incurred in, or about, the execution of the trusts or powers contained in the trust instrument.

When it is difficult for trustees to obtain a discharge, they or the majority of them may pay into Court any money or securities, and the receipt of the proper officer of the Court is a sufficient discharge for such money or securities.

Breaches of Trust.—Any act in contravention, excess, neglect or default of the duties imposed on a trustee by the trust instrument, or his acquiescence in a similar act by one of his co-trustees, constitutes a breach of trust. As a general rule a trustee is liable in respect of any loss occurring as a consequence of any breach of trust brought about by his own wilful default, that is to say, if he knew and intended to commit or acquiesce in a breach of his duty or was recklessly careless in not caring whether his or his co-trustee's actions constituted a breach of duty or not. An innocent trustee is not responsible for a breach of trust by his co-trustee. As between themselves the loss is borne by all the trustees equally, so that if one trustee pays more than his share, he can, except where all have been guilty of fraud, obtain repayment from the others. In three cases, however a trustee must indemnify his co-trustees:—

(1) Where he alone has received trust money and misappropriated it. (2) Where he is a solicitor-trustee, and the breach of trust was committed on his advice. (3) Where he is also a beneficiary, the loss will be made good so far as possible out of his beneficial interest.

The Court may relieve a trustee from personal liability in respect of a breach of trust if he acted honestly and reasonably, and ought fairly to be excused for the breach of trust and for omitting to obtain the directions of the Court in the matter in which he committed such breach.

A trustee may plead the Statute of Limitations in an action brought against him for breach of trust, and time begins to run from the date when the breach was committed except where the beneficiary is under a disability—e.g. is under 21 years of age, in which case time runs from the cessation of the disability, or where the beneficiary's interest is reversionary, in which case time only begins to run when his interest falls into possession.

A trustee will also be freed from liability for a breach of trust (1) by his subsequent bankruptcy and discharge; (2) by the beneficiary's confirmation, acquiescence or concurrence in the breach, or by his subsequent release of the trustee.

TRUSTEE IN BANKRUPTCY.— When an adjudication order (q.v.) is made against a debtor "adjudging" him bankrupt, all his property is taken from him and handed over to a trustee who sells it and distributes it for the benefit of the creditors.

The trustee is appointed by the creditors usually at the first meeting of creditors when they have resolved that the debtor is to be adjudicated bankrupt. If the creditors do not appoint a trustee the appointment may be made by the Board of Trade. The Official Receiver acts as trustee until the trustee is appointed. Objection may be taken to the appointment of a trustee on the ground that he is not fit to act, as where he has previously been removed from the office of trustee for neglecting his duty, or on the ground that he is so closely connected with, or related to the bankrupt or a creditor that it will be difficult for him to deal fairly and impartially with the interest of the creditors as a whole.

A trustee may be removed by the creditors if they pass an ordinary resolution, i.e. by a bare majority of their number calculated according to value—i.e. not by the number of creditors but by the value of the debts for which each has proved in the bankruptcy, or by the Board of Trade where he is acting improperly. The trustee acts generally under the direction of a committee of inspection of the creditors.

Powers.—The trustee has power to do most acts which arise in the bankruptcy without obtaining the permission of any person and at his own discretion, but for certain purposes he must get the permission of the committee of inspection or of the Board of Trade if no committee has been appointed. The most important of these are the following:—

1. To carry on the bankrupt's business, but permission can only be given for the purpose of having the business wound up

and sold. It cannot be carried on indefinitely for the benefit of the creditors.

2. To bring or defend any legal proceedings relating to the bankrupt's property.

3. To raise any money by giving to the lender a security over the bankrupt's property.

4. To compromise any debts due by the bankrupt or to him, i.e. to accept 15/- in the £ from a debtor of the bankrupt if it does not appear that any more can be obtained, or to agree to pay one of the creditors of the bankrupt a lump sum of money in settlement of his debt instead of the dividend which would be paid to him out of the estate.

5. To appoint the bankrupt to carry on his business for the benefit of the creditors.

6. To make to the bankrupt a cash allowance out of the proceeds of his property or business to support himself and his family.

Banking.—Very strict rules have been made controlling the dealings of a trustee with money he has obtained. The trustee must pay all money into an account called the Bankrupt Estate Account at the Bank of England unless special permission has been given by the Board of Trade to pay money into a bank in the district where the debtor has lived or has carried on his business. He must not keep more than £50 in his possession for more than 10 days without paying it into the bank unless he gets special permission from the Board of Trade, and if he does so without permission he may lose his remuneration or be removed from his office and will be liable to pay interest at 20% per annum on the amount over £50.

Remuneration.—The trustee is entitled to remuneration for his work, and this is fixed either by the creditors or by the committee of inspection. It is usually a commission or percentage calculated in part on the total value of the property collected by the trustee, and in part on the amount which he distributes as dividends to the creditors.

Books.—The trustee must keep proper books which are subject to strict audits by the committee of inspection every month, and by the Board of Trade at the end of 6 months from the date of the receiving order and every 6 months thereafter. The trustee must also send to the Board of Trade at least once a year a report as to the progress he is making in the distribution of the estate.

Release.—The trustee will be entitled to be released from his office when he has realized all the property that he thinks is capable of realization and has distributed a final dividend. He will also be entitled to be released if a composition has been accepted by the creditors (in which case he will not have been required to collect and distribute the debtor's property) or if he has resigned or been removed from office. The release is made by order of the Board of Trade and will not become effective until the trustee has handed over to the Official Receiver all the documents which have come into his possession relating to the estate of the bankrupt.

Property passing to Trustee.—The property which passes to the trustee is, in general, all property which belonged to the bankrupt at the commencement of the bankruptcy or which he acquired before he is discharged, and all property within the "possession, order, or disposition" of the bankrupt. The date from which the property passes, under the doctrine known as "relation back," is not the date of the adjudication order, but the date of the earliest act of bankruptcy (q.v.), within 3 months before the presentation of the petition. Thus, if a petition were presented on 1st July on a bankruptcy notice served in June and, during the investigation of the bankrupt's affairs, it was discovered that he had committed an act of bankruptcy in April by making a fraudulent conveyance (q.v.) of his property, the trustees would be entitled to the property which the debtor had in April, for that is the date which is reckoned to be the commencement of the bankruptcy. If this rule were carried out without any qualifications, it would lead to great hardship, for where someone had bought goods from the debtor in April and had paid for them, he would be compelled to hand the goods back to the trustee, and although he would be entitled to claim for the price he had paid, his claim would probably not be of much value to him and he would receive only a few shillings in the £.

It has therefore been provided that where payments are made by the debtor to one of his creditors, or where goods are delivered to the debtor or by him to any person for value (that is, not as a gift), or where he has made any contract, the transaction will not be interfered with by the trustee so long as it took place before the date of the receiving order, and so long as the person claiming the property did not know at the time that the debtor had committed the act of bankruptcy. In the case of payments of money or delivery of goods *to* the debtor, the transaction is given a still wider protection, for so long as these are carried on in the ordinary course of business and are made before any receiving order has been made, or before the person paying the money or sending the goods to the debtor has notice that a bankruptcy petition has been presented, the payment or delivery of goods is considered to be a good fulfilment of any obligation that that person was under towards the debtor, and he cannot be compelled to pay again even though he may have known that an act of bankruptcy had been committed.

Property Trustee may Claim.— There is certain property of the debtor which, although it does not pass to the trustee in the first place, may yet be claimed by him from the persons to whom it has been given. Thus, where property has been transferred by the debtor to any person otherwise than in good faith or otherwise than for good or valuable consideration, the trustee may have the transaction made void and claim the property back as fraudulent conveyance or voluntary settlement. Again, where a creditor has been fraudulently preferred to the other creditors—i.e. paid before them—with the deliberate object of putting him in a better position than they are, the money paid to him may also be claimed by the trustee.

Execution.—When a creditor has issued execution against any property of a debtor (that is, has taken the appropriate legal procedure with a view to having the property sold and the proceeds paid to him in satisfaction of his debt), he will not be able to retain the money which he has got in this way unless the execution was completed before the date of the receiving order and before notice of any act of bankruptcy on which a petition could have been presented or of the presentation of the petition itself.

Where a Sheriff is engaged on behalf of a judgment creditor in seizing the goods of a debtor in execution he must hand over the goods to the trustee if he is notified that a receiving order has been made. Moreover, where the judgment on which the Sheriff is acting is for more than £20, and the Sheriff sells goods in payment of it, or if money is paid to him to avoid the goods being sold, he must keep the money for 14 days, and if within that time he is notified that a petition has been presented and a receiving order is made, he must hand over the money to the trustee.

Settlements.—The trustee is also entitled in certain cases to set aside settlements made by the bankrupt on his property before he became bankrupt. A settlement takes place when property is transferred with the object of it being preserved or retained, e.g. where money is handed over for the purpose of being spent, this is not a settlement, but where jewels or shares are given, the transaction is a settlement.

When the settlement is a gift, that is to say, where the debtor receives nothing in exchange for it and there is no consideration, it is void in all cases if made within 2 years before the bankruptcy; and where it is made more than 2 years but within 10 years before the bankruptcy, it will be void unless it can be proved that the debtor was solvent when he made it, i.e. could have paid all his debts at that time without the aid of the property he gave away, and that the whole interest of the debtor in the property is transferred by the gift.

Where the settlement is made before, and in contemplation, and in consideration of marriage, e.g. where a father settles property on his son who is about to be married, or where a man settles property in trustees for his wife, the transaction will be good whatever may have been the intention of the person conveying the property so long as the person receiving it did not know that it was intended to be in fraud of creditors. In the same way a settlement made in favour of a purchaser in good faith and for valuable consideration is also protected. (*See* VOLUNTARY SETTLEMENT.)

Assignment of Book Debts.—If a debtor transfers to some other person the debts which are owed to him in his business —called an assignment of book debts—the transaction will be void so far as concerns any debt not paid to the person in whose favour the transfer was made at the commencement of the bankruptcy unless the transaction is registered as a bill of sale. This does not apply to assignment of book debts from specified creditors nor does it apply to debts which are included when a business is sold.

Apparent Possession.—It is possible for the trustee to obtain and use for the benefit of the creditors property which has not belonged to the bankrupt at all under what is known as the Doctrine of Apparent Possession. This applies when a person whether engaged in trade or not has in his possession goods which belong to someone else and are held by him in virtue of a bill of sale which has not been registered.

Reputed Ownership.—A somewhat similar provision applies in the case of persons who are carrying on some trade, and is known as the Reputed Ownership Clause. Under this, all goods which at the beginning of the bankruptcy were in the possession of the bankrupt, or under his control with the consent of the true owner and used by the bankrupt in his business in such a way that he is the reputed owner of them, may be taken by the trustee and used to pay the bankrupt's debts. The basis on which this rule is founded is that where a man is seen to be using goods in his business persons dealing with him are likely to assume that they belong to him, and therefore to give him credit which they would not otherwise have given.

Accordingly, the person to whom the goods belong is considered to be assisting the bankrupt in obtaining this credit and cannot complain if the goods are taken from him. He will, of course, be entitled to claim as a creditor against the bankrupt's estate for the value of the goods. The principle also applies to book debts which are due or are becoming due in the future to the bankrupt in his business. In many cases where property is claimed under this clause the true owner succeeds in keeping it from the trustee by shewing that there was a well-known custom that persons in the position of the debtor should have in their possession goods not belonging to them, and that therefore the creditors who have dealt with the debtor would not be misled into thinking that the goods were his property because they would know of the custom. Thus the presumption would not arise in

the case of warehousemen who must naturally have on their premises goods belonging to others, and it is also recognized that hotel keepers frequently hire the furniture in their hotels.

Property not Passing to Trustee. Trust Property.—Certain property which has belonged to the bankrupt does not pass to the trustee. Thus, property which the bankrupt has held on trust for some other person is not regarded as being his. It is difficult in some cases to tell whether property which the bankrupt has is trust property or not. Where, for example, he has paid trust money into his own bank account the rule is that so long as there is in the account any money at all it is regarded as belonging to the trust and not to the bankrupt.

Tools of Trade.—The tools of trade of a workman and the necessary wearing apparel and bedding of the debtor and his family to the value of £20 do not pass to the trustee, nor does property which the bankrupt obtained by mistake or fraud. Such property may be claimed back by the person who was mistaken or defrauded.

It is possible that money or other property may be left to a person on the terms that he is to enjoy the use of it only until he becomes bankrupt. This must be done, however, in such a way as not only to provide that the bankrupt's interest in the property will cease on his bankruptcy, but the document giving the property must also state that when the debtor does become bankrupt some other person is to get an interest in the property. It is not possible to settle money on oneself in such a way that it goes over to some other person when bankruptcy happens, but something very near to this can be done by directing property to be paid to a trustee and instructing the trustee to pay the income to *one or more* certain specified persons at his discretion, one of them being the person giving the property.

Earnings during Bankruptcy.—The personal earnings of a bankrupt during his bankruptcy, so far as they are required reasonably for his own support and that of his family, do not pass to the trustee; but where the bankrupt carries on a business as distinct from earning money by his own labour his profits will pass. Further the trustee may in any case apply to the Court for an order that the bankrupt should be required to pay over his income or part of it to the trustee, and an officer of the army or navy, or civil servant may also be required to hand over any half pay or pension, or a part of it, if the chief officer of the government department concerned gives his consent.

Personal Rights of Action.—Where rights of action are purely personal to the bankrupt and do not affect his property, that is, for example, where he has been libelled or slandered or where he has been injured in a street accident, the right of action does not pass to the trustee, but the bankrupt may sue and recover damages for himself.

Creditors and Dividends.—In the administration of the estate the trustee will require proofs from the creditors as to their debts, and will satisfy himself that the debts are really due. When he has collected the money available from the estate or some part of it, he will proceed to divide it among the creditors by declaring a dividend. Frequently there will be more than one dividend, and the first dividend must be declared in four months after the conclusion of the first meeting of creditors, and subsequent dividends at intervals of not more than 6 months thereafter. When a trustee has got any dividend in his possession which has not been claimed by a creditor he must pay it into the Bankruptcy Estates Account at the Bank of England.

Interest.—In considering claims made by creditors the bankrupt will frequently find that interest is claimed on a debt. Under the ordinary law and apart from bankruptcy, interest is not payable on any debt unless there is an agreement in that particular case to pay interest, or where mercantile custom allows it—for example where it is due on a bill of exchange. Where the interest rate agreed upon is over 5 % per annum a creditor, unless he is a money lender, can reckon his debt at the full amount due for all purposes of voting at meetings, but when he wishes to claim to share in dividends the interest is cut down to 5 %. In the case of money lenders the interest is never calculated at more than 5 % either for voting or for dividend. In all cases, however, where there is some money left over after all the creditors have been paid on this basis, the creditor for interest,

whether he is a money lender or not, will be entitled to be paid as a deferred creditor. There are many restrictions in addition on the amount which may be claimed in respect of interest by a money lender, and a trustee in bankruptcy has got power to apply to the Court to have reopened transactions between the money lender and the debtor with a view to shewing that the rate of interest which the money lender has charged is excessive. For the purpose of determining this, and for the purpose of claiming in the bankruptcy the money lender is, when dealing with sums that have been repaid by the debtor, not entitled to claim that any part of a sum which is partly interest and partly repayment of capital is to be reckoned as interest beyond what would be due as interest on the amount of capital repaid. Thus, if a debtor who had borrowed money, £1,000 at 50 % per annum, after a year had repaid £100, the money lender would naturally wish to divide that into £50 interest due and £50 of repaid capital. He would not, however, be able to do this but would have to take £66 13s. 4d., as return of capital and the remaining £33 6s. 8d. as the interest due.

Deferred Debts.—The debts which are entitled to be paid in preference to others are the same as the preferred debts in the case of the winding up of a company. (*See* PREFERRED CREDITORS.) There are, however, certain debts which are not to be repaid until after all the others, i.e. deferred debts. These are:—

1. A loan the rate of interest of which varies with the profits of the business carried on by the debtor.

2. Any money due in respect of the sale of the goodwill of a business, the amount payable pending on the profits.

3. A loan by a husband to a wife or by a wife to a husband for the purposes of any trade or business carried on by her or him, as the case may be.

Provable Debts.—As a general rule, all debts which persons may have against the debtor may be proved for in his bankruptcy —i.e. the creditor may claim the amount of money due and receive his proper share of whatever money is available to pay creditors. Thus, all debts incurred before the receiving order, whether payable before it or not, may be proved whether they are present or future, (i.e. whether they are due now or in a year's time) certain or contingent. A contingent debt is one which may or may not become due. For example, if an annuity has been granted payable on the 1st of December in each year, the annuitant (that is, the person entitled to the money) will not be able to claim any money in respect of any year unless he lives until the 1st of December in that year. It is difficult to estimate the value of these debts in many cases, but as the object of the bankruptcy acts is to free a debtor from all possible liabilities, the trustee must endeavour to put some value on the debt and the creditor will be entitled to receive a dividend on that amount. If the value of a contingent debt cannot be estimated, the Court will make an order to that effect and the creditor will not be able to prove in the bankruptcy, nor will the debtor be freed from the debt, but such a situation rarely arises, and the Court has even estimated an annuity which was to cease to be payable on the remarriage of the person entitled to it.

By a rule which does not appear to be very logical damages which are unliquidated and are in respect of a tort, i.e. a wrong, cannot be proved in the bankruptcy unless the creditor has obtained judgment in the Court and in that way make his damages liquidated before the receiving order. This rule most usually applies to cases where injuries have been done to third persons by negligence, and so far as injuries arising from motor cars are concerned, the rule to-day has little practicable effect because the liability of the bankrupt is now transferred to any insurance company who may have insured the bankrupt against such liabilities. (See THIRD PARTY INSURANCE.) This rule has undoubtedly removed a great hardship. Prior to 1930 if a person were injured by a bankrupt and recovered damages for, e.g.

£5,000 against him he would not receive that money even though the bankrupt was insured against the liability. The insurance company would pay the money to the bankrupt's trustee, who would use it not to pay the injured person in particular but for the benefit of all the creditors, of whom, of course, the injured person would be one. If, therefore, the assets of the bankrupt apart from this policy were £1,000 and the total debts apart from that of the injured person were £4,000, all the creditors, including the injured person, would have received 13/4 in the £ on their debts. Since the change in law, however, the ordinary creditors would have to be content with receiving 5/– in the £, being what would come to them from the £1,000 of assets, and the injured person claims against the insurance company direct.

Other debts which are not provable in bankruptcy are:

1. Debts contracted by the debtor with a creditor who knew that the debtor had committed an act of bankruptcy within 3 months before the petition was presented.

2. Alimony awarded to a wife.

3. Illegal debts, e.g. bets and debts barred by the Statute of Limitations, i.e. by the lapse of time. (See ACT OF BANKRUPTCY; BANKRUPTCY.)

TUBERCULOSIS.—Power exists for the compulsory transfer to hospital of persons suffering from tuberculosis. The procedure to be followed is for the local authority to apply to a court of summary jurisdiction for an order directing the removal to hospital of the sufferer. The Court may, however, only make such an order when it is satisfied that the condition and circumstances of the patient are such that a real danger of infection of other persons exists. Any person who disobeys or who obstructs the execution of an order is liable to be punished by a fine.

UBERRIMAE FIDEI.—This is a Latin expression meaning, "Of the utmost confidence." It is used in connection with contracts requiring full disclosure by one or both of the parties of every fact relevant to the making of the contract. Such contracts are said to be "Uberrimae Fidei."

Contracts of insurance are so described because it is the duty of the insured to disclose to the insurer every fact which might influence the latter in making a contract of insurance, or in fixing the premium.

ULTRA VIRES.—This is a Latin

expression meaning, "Beyond the lawful power." The expression is frequently used when considering regulations made by local authorities. For instance, various local authorities and public utility companies have power to make bye-laws. A railway company may make bye-laws governing the conduct of persons using the railway. A bye-law may not go beyond the power given to the authority that makes it, and if it does, the Courts can declare it "Ultra Vires."

The expression is also used in connection with companies. (*See* COMPANIES.)

ULTRA VIRES (COMPANIES).—

Any act of a company is said to be ultra vires when it is "beyond the powers" of the person who has done it. The word is used in two senses in law. Firstly, an act may be "ultra vires the company," in the sense that the company has not got power to do the act under its Memorandum of Association (q.v.) or, secondly, it may be "ultra vires the directors" in the sense that, although the company has got power to do the act, yet it has not authorized the directors to do the act on its behalf as its agents, but has required that the act when done should be carried out in some more formal way, e.g. by a resolution of the company itself.

Ultra Vires the Company.— An instance of an act which is ultra vires the company would be provided where a company had power under its memorandum to build railway engines but had no power to manufacture motor-cars. If such a company bought materials for the purpose of manufacturing motor-cars, the act would be ultra vires and void. It would have no effect whatsoever on the legal position of the company. Thus, the company would not be liable on the contracts which had been entered into to buy the material, and if its directors had paid out money to any persons for material, the effect would be not that the company had paid it out, but that the directors had taken the company's money and used it for purposes not those of the company, with the result that they would have to replace the money themselves. When an act is ultra vires in this sense, it is not possible for the company to adopt it, even if all the shareholders meet and agree to do so, and the only way in which the

company can get power to do acts which are not in its memorandum is by altering its memorandum and having the alteration confirmed by the Court. (*See* MEMORANDUM OF ASSOCIATION.)

Ultra Vires the Directors.—When the word ultra vires is used in the second sense, that is, as being "beyond the powers" of the directors, the effect is somewhat different. The position is the same as when any agent, such as is a director, acts in a way which is not authorized by his principal, i.e. the company, and the director is liable for damages to the person with whom he has entered into the contract because he has, by entering into the contract, guaranteed that he has the company's authority to do so. The company, on the other hand, is not liable on the contract but it may become so if it ratifies the contract, that is to say, if, after it has full knowledge of what the director has done, it approves it at a meeting of shareholders and agrees to be bound by his acts. The powers of the directors are set out in the Articles of Association (q.v.), and if a director acts in a way which is not authorized by the articles he will be acting ultra vires. It may be, however, that even in such a case the company will be bound, for if the director occupies a position, e.g. as managing director —from which it would naturally be assumed that he had authority to enter into ordinary contracts on behalf of the company, and if the person who is contracting with him does not know of the clause in the articles of association limiting his authority to make contracts, the company will be bound on the basis that it has "held the director out" as having authority, i.e. has allowed him to occupy a position which is usually only filled by persons who have authority to do such acts. (*See* COMPANIES; DIRECTOR.)

UMPIRE.—Under the Unemployment Insurance Scheme, provision is made for the determination of claims to benefit by insured contributors.

The local Insurance Officer makes the first decision and there is an appeal from his decision to a Court of Referees. A further appeal may be made to the umpire who is appointed by the Crown.

An appeal to an umpire may only be brought by an insurance officer, an association of employees of which the claimant is a member, or by the claimant himself. A claimant can only bring an appeal himself, if he is given leave to do so by the chairman of the Court of Referees, or if the decision of that Court is not unanimous. An appeal must be made to the umpire within six months of the decision of the Court of Referees and the decision of the umpire is final. (*See* REFEREES; AND SPECIAL SUPPLEMENT "UNEMPLOYMENT INSURANCE.")

UNBORN INFANT. — For certain legal purposes a baby is regarded as being in existence before it is born. Once a child is conceived, it is capable of inheritance, and its interests may, where necessary, be protected by the appointment of a guardian.

UNBURIED ANIMALS. — No person may allow the carcass of any horse, sheep or swine to remain unburied in any place to which dogs can gain access.

UNDER-LEASE. — When a person who is himself a lessee of land grants a lease to some other person, that lease is called a sub-lease or under-lease. (*See* LANDLORD AND TENANT.)

UNDER-SHERIFF. — To assist him in the performance of his duties a Sheriff (q.v.) may have an Under-Sheriff. He is usually a solicitor, and he is responsible for the enforcement of judgments of the Civil Courts.

UNDERTAKING. — An undertaking is a promise given in Court by a party to an action to do or refrain from doing something. Undertakings are usually given to avoid the necessity of drawing up formal orders by the Court. If the party giving it is represented by counsel, the undertaking is given by counsel on behalf of his client. If an undertaking is broken the offender may be dealt with for contempt of Court.

UNDERWRITER. — An underwriter in Marine Insurance is the person who subscribes his name to the policy and agrees to bear part of the loss. In Company Law an underwriter is the person who agrees to take up a certain number of shares which are being issued in the event of the public not taking them up, but he will not be required to take any shares otherwise. The remuneration of an underwriter is by a commission on the amount of shares which he agrees to underwrite. (*See* UNDERWRITING COMMISSION.)

UNDERWRITING COMMISSION. — When a company is inviting members of the public to take shares from it (usually when it is first formed), it is very important to the company that a sufficient number of persons should apply for shares to enable all the shares available to be allotted, for if this does not happen the issue will fail, and the great deal of money which has been spent on it will be wasted. As an insurance against this those engaged in the promotion of the company usually underwrite a certain number of shares, that is, they enter into agreements with persons called underwriters who agree for a certain sum of money paid to them, called a commission, to take up and apply for a certain number of shares should members of the public not do so. If the issue is a success and all the shares are applied for by members of the public, the underwriters will not be called upon to do anything, but will retain their commission. If the issue is not a success, they will have to take up and pay for the number of shares which they have agreed to underwrite.

To some extent underwriting represents the issue of shares at a discount, for an underwriter who has agreed to underwrite shares for 5% commission and is required to take them up will, in fact, only pay 95% of the nominal value for them. Further, the rate at which underwriters are prepared to underwrite an issue is a very good indication of what the business world considers the prospects of the company are, and for that reason underwriting commission is required to be disclosed in the prospectus (q.v.). The law also limits the rate of commission which may be paid. This must not be more than 10% but if a lower figure is fixed by the Articles of Association of the company, then the rate of commission is limited to that lower figure. Frequently underwriters enter into sub-underwriting contracts with other persons who agree to take so many shares from the underwriters if they are called upon to fulfil their agreement. (*See* CAPITAL; COMPANIES; SHARES.)

UNDISCHARGED BANKRUPT. — From the time when a person is first adjudicated bankrupt until the Court makes an order discharging him he is an undischarged bankrupt.

He is subject to some disabilities; where he either alone or jointly with some other person obtains credit to the extent of £10 or upwards without informing the person from whom he obtains the credit that he is an undischarged bankrupt, or where he engages in any trade or business other than that in which he was adjudicated bankrupt, and fails to disclose to all persons with whom he enters into business transactions the name under which he was adjudicated—he is guilty of a criminal offence and liable to twelve months imprisonment. A person who is an undischarged bankrupt cannot act as director of a company without the leave of the Court. Undischarged bankrupts cannot sit in Parliament, nor can they hold any office such as Mayor, Alderman or Councillor. (*See* BANKRUPTCY.)

UNDUE INFLUENCE.—In many cases where the inducement to enter into a contract does not amount to duress (q.v.) it may amount to undue influence. In cases where a child enters into a contract with his parent or guardian, or a person enters into a contract with his solicitor, his doctor or his trustee, the contract is voidable (*See* VOID AND VOIDABLE), i.e. cannot be enforced unless the parent or guardian, solicitor, doctor, or trustee can shew that he has not taken advantage of his position to obtain a benefit which he would not otherwise have had.

This does not mean that perfectly valid contracts cannot be entered into between these parties, but it does mean that the Court will look very carefully at such contracts before it allows of their being enforced, and in the particular case of the solicitor, the client may refuse to be bound by the contract unless the solicitor can shew not only that the contract was a perfectly fair one, but also that the client had competent outside advice.

Although in these cases the Court makes the party who is in a position to influence the other party prove that the contract was fair, it is not necessary that the parties should be in these particular relationships in order for a contract to be set aside for undue influence. Wherever it can be shewn that one of the parties to a contract has obtained a complete influence over the will of another, as a nurse or housekeeper may obtain an influence over an old man, or as an older friend may obtain an influence over a young man, it is open to the person influenced to avoid the contract if the contract is clearly

unfair to the weaker party. (*See* CONTRACT; DURESS; FRAUD.)

UNEMPLOYMENT INSURANCE. —(*See* SPECIAL SUPPLEMENT "UNEMPLOYMENT INSURANCE.")

UNIFORMS.—No person not serving in the armed forces of the Crown may wear any uniform of those forces or any dress having the appearance of any such uniform. Similarly, it is an offence for any unauthorized person to wear any dress resembling any uniform of the armed forces in such a manner and in such circumstances as would be liable to bring contempt upon it. It is to be noted that it is lawful for naval, military or air-force uniforms to be worn by persons taking part in plays or similar performances. The prohibition against wearing unauthorized uniforms is not confined to those of the armed forces. Similar rules govern the wearing of police uniforms or other dress having the appearance of police uniform.

UNITED KINGDOM.—Since the creation of the Irish Free State, the United Kingdom now consists of Great Britain and Northern Ireland. There is, of course, a separate Parliament for Northern Ireland, but its powers are limited and certain subjects of wide application are reserved for the Parliament at Westminster.

UNIVERSITY COURTS. — The Courts of the Chancellors of the Universities of Oxford and Cambridge have jurisdiction to try misdemeanours committed by resident members of the University and their servants. Where a prosecution is commenced in the ordinary course the Chancellor may have it removed to his own Courts. In Cambridge the jurisdiction of the Court only exists where all parties are members of the University, and the Court has fallen into disuse.

UNLAWFUL ASSEMBLY.—An assembly of three or more persons who are gathered together either to commit some unlawful act, or else to do some lawful act in a manner which is likely to cause persons of normal courage and firmness to apprehend a breach of the peace. An unlawful assembly may be dispersed by forcible means, though the force used must not be of a kind likely to cause death or serious injury.

An unlawful assembly must be distinguished from a riot (q.v.), to disperse which greater force may lawfully be used

UNSOUND MIND.—A person is said to be of unsound mind when he is either a lunatic or an idiot. A person may either be of unsound mind not so found by inquisition or a person of unsound mind so found. Persons of the latter class have been subjected to a formal inquiry as to their sanity. A person may be a lunatic although he is not of unsound mind so found by inquisition. (*See* LUNATICS.)

UPSET PRICE.—Upset price is the lowest fixed price at which in auction sales the seller is willing that the bidding should be started and sold if no higher bids can be obtained. It differs from a reserve price in that it is disclosed before the auction, so that the bidders know that it is no use bidding unless they are prepared to offer at least the upset price.

URBAN DISTRICT COUNCIL.—An urban district was originally an area administered by a sanitary authority, but the importance of such districts has now been greatly extended. Each district is governed by the urban district council, for the constitution, duties and powers of which, *see* LOCAL GOVERNMENT.

URGENCY ORDER.—When it is not desirable to take the usual steps to secure the detention of a lunatic by means of a reception order, and where some more speedy method is necessary, an urgency order may be obtained. This is of a temporary character and only available where the person to be detained is dangerous to himself or to others. It remains in force for only seven days, or, if an application has been made for a reception order, until that application has been heard. (*See* DETENTION OF LUNATICS.)

USE AND OCCUPATION.—Where a tenant continues to occupy land after his tenancy has come to an end he is liable to an action by his landlord of use and occupation. Under this action what the landlord will recover will be in effect the rent. (*See* LANDLORD AND TENANT.)

USER.—The person having the enjoyment of any property is said to have the user of it.

USURY.—There were formerly certain Acts of Parliament called "The Usury Laws" which prohibited the charging of interest at a higher rate than 5%. These statutes were all repealed in 1854, and there is now no absolute limit to the amount of interest that may be charged. Relief may, however, be given to the borrower where the rate of interest is excessive, and, in the case of licensed money-lenders, a rate of over 48% is presumed to be excessive unless the money-lender can shew exceptional circumstances to justify the high rate. (*See* MONEY-LENDERS; MONEY-LENDING.)

UTTER BARRISTER.—Barristers are divided into two classes—King's Counsel and Junior Barristers. King's Counsel are allowed in Court to sit within the bar, that is to say, in the first row reserved for counsel, junior barristers having to appear behind the bar, and for this reason are called Outer or Utter Barristers.

UTTERING.—This expression is used to cover the issue by a person of some article in circumstances which he knows to be criminal. Thus, if a person presents for payment a forged cheque, the act of presenting it constitutes uttering. So also when counterfeit coin is handed for exchange or in payment it is uttered. Again, a person who sends a threatening letter is said to utter it. Uttering with guilty knowledge is, in general, punishable in the same way as the unlawful making of the article itself. Thus a person may be liable to a serious penalty for uttering a forged cheque, just as the forger himself may be.

VACATION.—The periods during which the Law Courts in London are closed are called vacations. The vacations are four in number, the Long Vacation, the Christmas Vacation, the Easter Vacation, and the Whitsun Vacation. The long vacation begins on the 1st August and ends on the 11th October. In order to increase the speed of legal business the long vacation was made to end on the 1st October in 1933. The Christmas vacation lasts from the 24th December to the 6th January, the Easter vacation from Good Friday to Easter Tuesday, and the Whitsun vacation from the Saturday before Whitsunday to the Tuesday after Whitsunday.

VACATION JUDGE.—When the Courts are not sitting for any considerable period, it is customary for one of the Judges of the High Court of Justice to remain in London to deal with matters of an urgent nature. Such a Judge is called a Vacation Judge. He sits in Court from time to time to deal with urgent business that must be disposed of. Matters of extreme urgency may be placed before the vacation Judge out of Court, and indeed, if necessary, at his own home.

VACCINATIONS.—The parent of every child born in England must, within six months of the birth of the child, have it vaccinated by a medical practitioner and if such vaccination is unsuccessful, or does "not take" then the child must be again vaccinated. If a child is three times unsuccessfully vaccinated, then the medical practitioner must give the parent a certificate of unsusceptibility, and the parent is then no longer required to have the child vaccinated. If the parent of the child is dead, or ill, or absent abroad then the person having the custody of the child must see that it is vaccinated.

Any parent or person having the custody of a child may, within four months of the birth of the child, make a declaration that he conscientiously believes that vaccination would be bad for the health of the child, and send such declaration to the vaccination officer of the district. He is then exempt from the obligation of having the child vaccinated.

The statutory declaration should be as follows:—

"I . . . . . . of . . . . . . in the
"Parish of . . . . . . County of . . . . . .
"being the parent of a child named
". . . . . who was born on the . . . day
"of . . . . . . do hereby solemnly and
"sincerely declare that I conscientiously
"believe that vaccination would be pre-
"judicial to the health of the child and
"I make this solemn declaration con-
"scientiously believing the same to be
"true and by virtue of the provisions of
"the Statutory Declaration Act, 1835.
"Dated this 14th day of December, 1933.
      "Signed . . . . .
"Declared before me at . . . . . . on the
"14th day of December, 1933.
     "A Commissioner for Oaths."

A child may be vaccinated by any registered medical practitioner or without any charge by the public vaccinator. The public vaccinator is a doctor with whom the local authority have made a contract for his services as vaccinator for the district.

The public vaccinator of the district must, if the parent of a child requires it, visit the home of the child for the purpose of vaccinating it, but the vaccination may be carried out at the surgery of the public vaccinator if the person concerned desires. If the public vaccinator thinks that a child vaccinated by him requires medical treatment in consequence of the vaccination, he must, if the person having the custody of the child consents, attend the child and prescribe any required treatment.

If the vaccination is performed by a doctor who is not the public vaccinator then the doctor, after ascertaining that the operation has been successful, must deliver to the parent a certificate of successful vaccination signed by him, and the parent must then send on the certificate within a week to the vaccination officer of the district. If the vaccination is performed by the public vaccinator, then he must send a certificate of successful vaccination to the vaccination officer.

If the public vaccinator or any other qualified doctor is of opinion that a child is not in a fit or proper state to be successfully vaccinated, he must give a certificate which is called a certificate of postponement of vaccination.

The certificate lasts for two months and may be renewed for further periods until the public vaccinator or other doctor considers that the child is fit to be vaccinated.

The public vaccinator is not allowed to charge a parent any fee for the vaccination of a child where such vaccination was done within the district for which he has been appointed by the local authority.

Re-vaccination is not compulsory, but any person desiring to be vaccinated may apply to the public vaccinator for such vaccination, and is entitled to have it done without charge. If, however, any person neglects to return for an inspection to ascertain whether the operation has been successful, when requested to do so by the public vaccinator, then he may charge a fee of 2/6. (*See* INFECTIOUS DISEASE; PUBLIC HEALTH.)

VALUABLE CONSIDERATION.—

The law requires that there should be for every contract or obligation which is to be enforced some valuable consideration unless the contract is made under seal, i.e. by a deed. A valuable consideration consists of money or money's worth. A promise of marriage is valuable consideration, and so a marriage settlement which is made in contemplation of marriage is made for valuable consideration. Valuable consideration is distinguished from good consideration, which is in reality no consideration at all. Good consideration is founded on relationship or natural love and affection. (*See* CONSIDERATION.)

VALUER.—(*See* APPRAISER.)

VENDOR is the seller of property, the person buying being called the "Purchaser." The seller of a lease, however, is called the "Assignor" and the buyer the "Assignee." The person creating a lease is the "Lessor" and the person to whom it is granted the "Lessee." (*See also* LANDLORD AND TENANT; SALE OF GOODS; SALE OF LAND.)

VENEREAL DISEASE.—It is defamatory to say of a person that he or she is suffering from venereal disease. If anyone is falsely defamed in this way, damages can be recovered for libel (q.v.), or slander (q.v.), as the case may be. Such a statement is one of the exceptions to the rule that in slander a plaintiff must prove actual damage.

It is a punishable offence for anyone other than a qualified medical practitioner to give treatment or advice for venereal disease for reward direct or indirect. Nor may any advertisement for treatment for such disease be exhibited except those sanctioned by local authorities.

The contraction by a husband or wife of venereal disease after marriage, is, on proof by the other spouse of freedom therefrom, evidence of adultery sufficient in most cases to justify a divorce. (*See* SPECIAL SUPPLEMENT "DIVORCE.")

VENUE. — Special rules govern the places at which cases can be tried. The place of trial is called the venue. Venue used to be of great importance, as criminal cases could then only be tried in the county in which the offence was committed. Recent legislation, however, has rendered venue of much less importance to-day, and a person may now be tried at the most convenient place.

VERDICT.—When a jury in any civil or criminal case return an answer as to any question of fact, they are said to give a verdict.

In criminal cases juries are only allowed to return verdicts of "Guilty" or "Not Guilty." The Scottish verdict of "Not Proven" is unknown in English law.

In civil cases it is frequently the practice for juries to answer a series of questions put to them by the Judge. Upon the answers to these questions the Judge can then give judgment as a question of law.

Juries must always be unanimous in their verdict, although in civil actions there is power by agreement between the parties to the action to accept the verdict of a majority of the jury.

VERGER.—A verger is strictly the official who carries a "verge" or mace before a bishop. Commonly he is the person who takes care of the interior of the fabric of the church. He is the servant of the parochial church council who should guard against their liabilities under the Workmen's Compensation Act by insurance.

VESTING DEED.—Under the provisions of the Settled Land Act and the Law of Property Act of 1925, it is provided that whenever land is either settled or held upon trust for sale, the documents relating to the settlement or trust shall be divided into two classes. On the one hand there is the document that sets out the terms of the trust or settlement, and on the other there is the vesting deed. The latter is a bare declaration that the property in question is vested in X or Y as tenant for life under the settlement or as trustee for sale. It contains no mention of the terms of the trust and is kept as simple and short as possible. If the property is sold, the vesting deed is the only one which is shewn to the purchaser; the trust instrument is never produced or handed over to him.

VESTING ORDER.—A vesting order is an order of the Court that certain property shall be transferred to a particular person. It operates as an immediate transfer.

VESTRY.—Any person whose name appears in the rate-book of a parish or who occupies land so rated is automatically a member of the parish Vestry. A company so rated may appoint a representative to vote in vestry. The incumbent is also a member, and he or the churchwardens summon vestry meetings by affixing a notice in the church porch. The incumbent is chairman of the meeting. Voting is usually conducted by a show of hands, but if a poll is demanded it must be held, each member then having a right to one vote unless the amount he is rated at exceeds £50, when he has one vote for every complete £25, but never more than six votes.

The majority of the powers formerly possessed by the vestry were transferred in 1921 to the Parochial Church Council (see PARISH, ECCLESIASTICAL); but certain functions are still retained by the vestry in respect of the election of churchwardens and under the Burial Acts. The vestry clerk is the secretary to the vestry.

VETERINARY SURGEON. — No person is entitled to practise as a veterinary surgeon, or to treat animals for injuries or diseases, unless he is registered upon the Register of Veterinary Surgeons kept by the Royal College of Veterinary Surgeons. In order to qualify for registration the candidate must pass the examinations held by the college.

Although no one may practise as a veterinary surgeon without being registered, there is nothing to prevent unqualified persons from undertaking to cure the diseases of animals, but such persons are not entitled to sue for their fees in a Court of Law, and if any unqualified person describes himself as a Veterinary Surgeon, or in any other words which might induce the public to believe that he is properly qualified and registered, he is liable to a penalty not exceeding £20.

It is not necessary to be a registered veterinary surgeon in order to keep a boarding home for animals, and unregistered persons can recover their charges for board though not for any veterinary treatment given to animals while at the home.

The profession of veterinary surgeon is governed by the Royal College of Veterinary Surgeons in the same manner as the profession of medicine is governed by the General Medical Council, and the College has the power of removing or restoring the names of veterinary surgeons to the register as a punishment for professional misconduct. (See REGISTERED MEDICAL PRACTITIONER.)

VEXATIOUS LITIGATION.— There is power to restrain those peculiar people whose love of going to law is so great that they become habitual litigants. The method is for the Attorney-General to make application in the High Court of Justice for an order that the person complained of shall not start any proceedings in any Civil Court without the leave of a Judge. Such an order will only be made when the Court is satisfied that the person complained of has continually started proceedings of a vexatious character and without reasonable grounds. The person complained of can be heard in his or her defence and, if without means, may be assigned counsel.

In Criminal Cases.—The above provisions do not apply to criminal proceedings. These, however, are covered by the Vexatious Indictments Act, 1859. This act forbids anyone to present a bill of indictment alleging any of the crimes enumerated in the act, unless the magistrates have committed the accused person for trial, or the Attorney-General has sanctioned the proceedings. In some cases the authority of the Director of Public Prosecutions is necessary. The offences covered by the act include:—obtaining goods or money by false pretences, perjury, corruption, conspiracy, criminal libel, keeping a disorderly house, and any kind of indecent assault.

VILLAGE.—A village is not, like a borough, a separate legal entity for the purposes of administration, but forms part of the parish in which it is situated. For certain purposes, however, a village may have a separate existence, e.g. it is possible for a gift to be made for the benefit of the inhabitants of a village, as, for example, when money is given for the building and maintenance of a village hall. Such a gift is deemed to be made for a charitable purpose, and thereby certain advantages accrue, e.g. the income of investments made for such a purpose is not subject to income tax.

Village Greens.—Village greens in rural parishes are owned by the Parish Council, or, if there is no Parish Council, by the Parish Meeting; in urban parishes, they are owned by the Urban District Council or the County Borough Council. A green may be the subject of a "scheme" under the Commons Act, 1899, which means that the Urban or Rural District Council may make bye-laws and regulations for the prevention of nuisances and the preservation of order on the green, and may expend money on the drainage, levelling, and improvement of the green. At least three months' notice of the intended scheme must be given by the insertion of two advertisements within one week in a local newspaper, and the posting of notices in two or more places on the green, etc. Printed copies of the scheme must be obtainable at the Council's office at the cost of not more than sixpence. Objections or suggestions as to the scheme must be sent to the Board of Agriculture, and, at the expiration of the three months, the Board will consider the objections or hold an enquiry before approving of the scheme. The scheme may be vetoed by the person or persons entitled to the soil of the green as Lord of the Manor or otherwise, or by persons representing at least one third in value of such interests in the green as are affected.

When once the scheme has been made, the District Council that made it may transfer all its powers of management to the Parish Council.

VIVA VOCE.—"By word of mouth." Evidence may be given either by affidavit or viva voce. In most trials in the Courts the right to give evidence by affidavit is limited and is subject to special rules.

VIVISECTION.—Vivisection, which means the performance of an experiment which is calculated to give pain upon a living vertebrate animal, may only be performed by persons who are licensed to do so.

An applicant for a licence must forward an application form, signed by the presdient of one of the learned medical societies, to the Home Secretary, and must state the nature of the experiments for which the licence is required. The Home Secretary may attach conditions to the grant of the licence, and may require (and generally does require) that the place where the experiments are to be made shall be registered. No experiments may be performed except for the purpose of scientific discovery, with the object of preventing suffering or prolonging life, and no experiment upon living animals may be made for practice in surgery, or for illustrating lectures, unless it has been shewn upon the certificate of application that such experiments are absolutely necessary for the advancement of medical knowledge.

Experiments performed under licence are subject to very strict conditions. In the ordinary way no experiment may be performed unless the animal is under an anæsthetic sufficient to prevent it feeling pain, and it must be killed immediately after the experiment if there is any likelihood of it suffering pain after it has come out of the anæsthetic.

Horses, asses, mules, cats and dogs may not be the subject of experiments, unless a further certificate is given that the experiment will be of value only if it is performed upon these animals, while experiments without anæsthetics and experiments in which the animal is permitted to live after the experiment even though suffering pain, must not be performed unless a certificate has been given that it is absolutely necessary for the purpose of the research.

No stray dog may be used for vivisection. (*See* Cruelty to Animals.)

VOID AND VOIDABLE.—A void contract is one which is destitute of any legal effect. It cannot be enforced and no person can take any rights under it. A voidable contract is one which one of the parties may make void or put an end to at his option. Until he makes it void the contract is good and binding. Examples of a void contract are contracts by an infant to buy goods which are not necessaries, and gambling contracts, also contracts entered into under some fundamental mistake by the parties.

It is sometimes very important to know whether a contract is void or merely voidable; for a person who has rights under a voidable contract may transfer them to another at any time before the contract is made void, and that other will acquire a good title if he does not know of the defect which makes the contract voidable. Thus, if A induces B to sell him goods by some fraud the contract is voidable and B may make it void by claiming back the goods from A. If, however, before this has happened, A has resold the goods to X, B cannot claim back the goods from X, and if A has not paid him the price will have to stand the loss. At the time when X took the goods A had a title to them though it was a voidable title and therefore X acquired a good title. If, on the other hand, the contract had been void, e.g. had been entered into under some fundamental mistake, A never had any title

[729]

to the goods which he could transfer to X, and B could claim back the goods from X or from anyone who has them.

Contracts may also be void because of some illegality. A contract may be illegal either:—

(a) Because of something relating to its formation, e.g. when a loan is made by an unregistered money-lender; or

(b) because it is a contract to do an illegal act, e.g. to commit a burglary; or

(c) because the act to be done under the contract, although not illegal, is against public policy.

When a contract is illegal the law declares it to be void, and will give no effect to it whatsoever. Thus, if one of the parties had paid some money or done some act under the contract, he cannot enforce it against the other party or recover his money. So if A promises B £5 to commit a burglary and pays B the money, he cannot recover the £5 if B does not do what he has promised. In one well-known case the secretary of a Charitable Institution promised a wealthy man that if he gave a large sum of money to the charity he would receive a knighthood. The money was given but the person giving the money received no knighthood, and he claimed to have the money repaid to him. It was held that he was not entitled to recover anything.

Any contract to impede the proper administration of justice is illegal, and thus a contract by which a thief agreed to return stolen property, provided that he was not prosecuted, could not be enforced. Contracts which involve trading with the enemy, that is, with a person living in enemy territory during a time of war are also illegal, as are contracts in restraint of trade (q.v.), and gaining contracts.

A contract affecting the freedom of marriage will be regarded as illegal and also what is known as a marriage brocage contract, that is, a contract to introduce a man and woman to each other with a view to their subsequent marriage. In marriage brocage contracts an exception is made to the general rule that money paid under an illegal contract cannot be recovered, and it has been held that, even if part of the purpose of the contract has been carried out by the introduction being effected, the money paid may be recovered. (See CONTRACT; RESTRAINT OF TRADE.)

VOLENTI NON FIT INJURIA.— This is a Latin expression meaning that there can be no injury where there has been consent.

Persons may agree to enter upon premises that they know to be dangerous, or they may take part in some game or competition or display of a patently dangerous character. In such cases, if it is shewn that they knowingly and voluntarily exposed themselves to risk, they cannot afterwards complain and recover damages if that risk materialises.

For instance, if a person engages in a boxing match and suffers injury, he cannot sue his opponent for the injury sustained, because by engaging in that match he agreed to take the risk of suffering that injury. Of course, it would be otherwise if his opponent had been guilty of any unfair conduct, as in such a case for obvious reasons the maxim would not apply.

VOLUNTARY CONVEYANCE.— Any transfer of property for which no valuable consideration is given is a voluntary conveyance. Thus a gift is a voluntary conveyance. Any creditor of a person who has made the conveyance may have the conveyance set aside if he can shew that it was not made in good faith or was made with the intention of depriving creditors of the goods conveyed. It will then be a fraudulent conveyance in the eyes of the law. (See BANKRUPTCY.)

VOLUNTARY MENTAL PATIENTS.—Until 1930 it was almost impossible for anybody to receive treatment in a mental hospital or similar institution for diseases of the mind without first incurring the stigma of certification as a person of unsound mind. A person had to wait until he was definitely mad before treatment could be given. In 1930 the Mental Treatment Act went some way towards minimising this stigma by providing a new terminology (lunatics should now be called "persons of unsound mind," paupers, "rate-aided persons," and asylums "mental hospitals"), but it also provided for the treatment of mental disease in certain cases in the early stages without any certification as a voluntary or temporary patient.

Voluntary Patient.—Where the person

who suffers from such a disease yet remains capable of making up his own mind and of understanding what he is doing, he may, of his own initiative, apply to be received into a house licensed under the Lunacy Acts, or into a mental hospital or institution, or, if the Lunacy Board of Control have given their approval and consent to its being used for this purpose, into a nursing home or other house or place. Alternatively, such a person may place himself as a single patient in the care of a person who has previously been approved by the Board of Control. He is called a voluntary patient. (*See* ASYLUMS; and BOARD OF CONTROL IN LUNACY).

If the patient is over sixteen years of age he must make an application in writing to the institution or person under whose care he wishes to be; such an application need not be accompanied by a medical certificate. If he is under sixteen years of age his parent or guardian must apply, but their application must be accompanied by a medical certificate given not more than fourteen days before the application by the patient's usual doctor. This does *not* certify the patient as insane. If this is impracticable a certificate must be obtained from a doctor previously approved by the Board of Control.

A voluntary patient may lawfully be detained against his will once he has entered a mental hospital or home, but he is entitled to give notice in writing of his desire to leave and must then be allowed to do so within 72 hours. In the case of a person under sixteen, this notice must be given by the parent or guardian of the patient. If the patient's illness becomes worse and he becomes incapable of expressing his willingness to remain, or of giving the requisite notice in writing of his intention to leave, he must not be detained (unless a proper reception order is made against him) for more than 28 days. If, however, he recovers sufficiently within that time to be once more capable of expressing his willingness to remain, this rule will cease to apply. This test—that of capability of expression—apparently applies to persons under sixteen so that if they became worse they could not be detained beyond 28 days even though it is not their willingness that is material but that of their parent or

guardian. It is specially provided that relatives or friends of a voluntary patient who wish to be near the patient may be boarded in the same institution. The Commissioners in Lunacy (Board of Control) may visit any place in which a voluntary patient is detained and have power to order his release or the institution of proceedings to have him certified as of unsound mind.

Temporary Patients. — Where the disease has progressed so far that the patient is incapable of making the decision himself of going into a home for treatment and becoming a voluntary patient, but it is believed that proper treatment would effect a cure or at any rate bring about a substantial improvement *within six months,* he may be sent without his consent and without any reception order and detained in any mental hospital or approved home. He is called a temporary patient. Alternatively he may be placed in the care of an approved guardian as a single patient, though in such a case the approval of the Lunacy Board is necessary, not only as to the guardian himself, but also as to his taking charge of this particular patient. Application in writing must be made to the hospital or home concerned. Wherever possible it should be made by the husband or wife or near relative of the patient, but it can be made by a friend or even by a Local Authority. Two medical certificates are necessary. The doctors, one of whom must be a doctor approved by the Board of Control, must have visited the patient not more than 14 days before his reception into the mental hospital or home, and their visits must have been within five days of each other (they need not, therefore, both have been present at the same time). Each certificate must state that the doctor giving it believes that the patient is likely to benefit from a course of temporary treatment. The patient is not certified insane.

If the patient, while so detained without his consent, recovers sufficiently to become capable of making up his own mind and expressing himself, he must not be detained for more than 28 days unless he has a relapse within that time. In no case may a temporary patient be detained for more than twelve months. In the first place eight months detention only is allowed, but if at the end of that time the Board of Control believe that a continuation of the treatment would probably result in early recovery they may authorize further detention and treatment for an additional period not exceeding six months.

Temporary patients may be visited at any time by the Commissioners of the Board of Control; they *must* also be visited within two months of their reception into the mental hospital by two members of the local visiting Committee (a committee appointed by Local Authorities to visit and control mental hospitals and institutions) or by two visitors (Inspectors) from the Board of Control. The visitors, after seeing the patient, must either give a written statement to the manager of the hospital etc., that they consider the patient in question a proper case for temporary treatment or must immediately report their disapproval to the Board of Control.

A commissioner of the Board of Control or any three "visitors" may at any time order the discharge of a temporary patient, and the Board may also order proceedings to be taken for his certification. A patient's discharge may also be obtained by an application by the person who originally applied for his reception: such an application can only be refused if the medical officer certifies that the patient is "dangerous and not fit to be at large." This certificate may be overridden by the Board of Control.

On recovery of the patient notice must be sent to the person who procured his reception. (*See* CERTIFICATION OF LUNATICS; DETENTION OF LUNATICS; LUNATICS.)

VOLUNTARY SETTLEMENT.— Gifts of property which are made by a man who is in financial difficulties may be set aside as voluntary settlements. The distinction between a conveyance and a settlement is that in a settlement the property given is intended to be kept in the form in which it is given and not to be used. Thus a gift of money would normally not be a settlement, but a gift of shares or jewellery would be a settlement. Settlements may be attacked either under the common law or under the bankruptcy laws.

Common Law.—Any settlement made by a man in order to delay, hinder, or defraud his creditors is void against the creditors. Assignments for value are clearly not included because the man's estate cannot

be said to suffer if, for example, he has obtained money in exchange for the goods he has settled. The assignment of the whole of the man's property for the benefit of one creditor or several creditors to the exclusion of others is clearly fraudulent because it is bound to prejudice the other excluded creditors.

Bankruptcy Law.—Any settlement (not being a settlement made in favour of a purchaser or incumbrancer in good faith and for valuable consideration, or a settlement made before and in consideration of marriage, or a settlement made on, or for the wife or children of the settlor, of property which had accrued to the settlor after marriage, in right of his wife), shall, if the settlor becomes bankrupt within two years after the date of the settlement, be void against his trustee in bankruptcy; and if he becomes bankrupt at any time within ten years after the date of the settlement shall be void against the trustee in bankruptcy unless the parties claiming under the settlement can prove (1) that the person making the settlement had enough property to pay all his debts at the time when he made the settlement without the aid of the property comprised in the settlement and further (2) that the person making the settlement retained no interest in the property after the settlement. There are certain other exceptions to this applicable in the case of marriage settlements. (*See* MARRIAGE SETTLEMENT.)

The effect of a settlement being made void in this way is that the persons who are entitled to the property under the settlement must give it up to the trustee. They may, however, claim as creditors of the bankrupt in respect of the money which they have given up, but their claims are preferred to those of all other creditors for valuable consideration.

VOLUNTEER.—A person who takes property under a voluntary conveyance is called a volunteer.

VOTING. Parliamentary Elections: History.—The qualifications for voting, which had remained unaltered for 400 years, have been so completely changed during the last 100 years that, before coming to the position to-day, a brief consideration of reforms during that period is required. Not only were qualifications for electors entirely altered, but the constituencies were re-arranged and stringent laws made to control the conduct of elections so as to prevent bribery, corruption and excessive expenditure—the most important reform in this connection being the introduction of the secret ballot in 1872. Prior to this date constituencies were so arranged that many had less than 100 electors and some were entirely controlled by one big land-owner, e.g. Old Sarum, which consisted merely of ploughed field. The re-distribution of seats in 1832, 1867, 1884 and finally in 1918 gave more seats to the towns with increasing populations, and constituencies were eventually arranged so that now each member represents an equal number of electors.

From 1430 to 1832 the right to vote was confined in county constituencies to a very limited number of property owners, and in borough constituencies the qualifications were both limited and chaotic, with the result that in 1832 there were only half a million electors compared to the almost universal suffrage of to-day. In 1832 the ownership qualification in county constituencies was extended to cover all types of ownership provided the property was over a certain value, and occupiers were given the right to vote if they paid £50 p.a. rent, while in borough constituencies occupation of property of sufficient value was made the sole qualification. In 1867 the ownership and occupational qualifications in county constituencies were extended, while in borough constituencies all rate-paying house-holders were given the vote, in addition to occupiers of lodgings of sufficient value. In 1884 the position was much simplified by the qualifications in county and borough constituencies being assimilated, and persons who resided in houses by virtue of their employment were given the right to vote provided their employer did not live there also. Finally in 1918 practically universal male suffrage was established.

Women's Right to Vote.—Meanwhile during this period women had been demanding the vote. Bills for this purpose were introduced in 1867 and 1884, the latter only being defeated through Gladstone's influence, and in 1887 women were allowed to vote at County Council elections. In 1906 the militant suffragette movement began and

this, by lawful and unlawful means, kept its cause continually before the public. Eventually in 1918 women were given a limited right to vote. This right was confined to women over 30 who were either the wives of electors or were themselves the occupiers of a house of any value or of other property of the annual value of £5. Finally in 1928 women were given equal rights with men.

Present Position: The Right to Vote.—Since 1928 any person of either sex over the age of 21, who is not subject to any legal incapacity, is entitled to vote in the constituency in which he or she is on the register of voters. Nobody is entitled to vote whose name is not on the annual register in force at the date of the election. There is a separate register for each constituency and a new register comes into force on October 15th of each year.

The following persons are under a legal incapacity to vote:—

(i) Minors.

(ii) Peers.

(iii) Unnaturalized aliens.

(iv) Lunatics.

(v) Persons convicted of treason or any felony for which they were sentenced to penal servitude or sent to prison for any period with hard labour, or for more than 12 months without, until they have served their sentence or been pardoned. Persons convicted of a misdemeanour may vote, but the fact that they are in prison may prevent them from doing so.

(vi) Persons convicted of a corrupt or illegal practice at an election within the previous seven or five years respectively. (*See* ELECTION AGENT.)

(vii) Persons twice convicted of bribery, or receiving bribes, as a public official.

Subject to these legal incapacities, any person is entitled to have his or her name on the register if either;

(i) he or she is, on June 1st, resident in the constituency and has during the preceding 3 months been resident in or near the constituency; or if

(ii) he or she occupies on June 1st business premises, of the annual value of at least £10, for the purpose of his or her business profession or trade and has, during the preceding 3 months, done so in or near the constituency; or if

(iii) he or she is the husband or wife of a person entitled to vote as the occupier of business premises.

The register is compiled by means of a house to house enquiry: If any qualified person is omitted from the register he should apply before August 7th to the local registration officer, who will on request supply an official form of application which must be used. The registration officer is the town clerk of the borough or the clerk of the county council. Once a person is on the register he is entitled to vote until a new register is published even if he no longer possesses a residential or business qualification.

The Method of Voting.—At a General Election polling in all constituencies takes place on the same day, i.e. the ninth day after nomination day. Every constituency is divided into polling districts and each polling district has a number of polling stations.

Every person wishing to vote must attend at the polling station to which he has been allotted during the hours of the poll. The poll is open from 8 a.m. to 8 p.m., unless it is extended by one hour at either or both ends at the request of one of the candidates.

If, by reason of his occupation or because he is in the Army, Navy or Air Force, any elector may be prevented from voting, he can, if he has had his name put on the absent list, vote by post or proxy. (*See* PROXY.)

On arrival at the polling station a voter will be given a ballot paper containing the names of the candidates and a private compartment will be provided so that he can vote in secret. Nobody except the voter is admitted to the compartment, with the exception of blind persons who are entitled to take a companion in to vote for them. (*See* BLINDNESS.)

The voter should make no mark on the ballot paper other than a cross against the name of the candidate (or in a constituency returning two members, the candidates) for whom he wishes to vote.

A ballot paper is invalid if—

(i) it is not stamped with the official stamp;

(ii) the voter has voted for more candidates than he is entitled to;

(iii) it contains no vote;

(iv) it is uncertain for which candidate the vote is intended;

(v) it bears any mark by which the voter can be identified.

If a voter inadvertently spoils his ballot paper he can obtain another from the presiding officer at the polling station on delivering up the spoilt paper.

When the voter has recorded his cross he must fold up the ballot paper and place it in the ballot box. The ballot is thus absolutely secret and it is impossible for anyone to discover how a person has voted.

It is a corrupt practice for a voter to apply for a ballot paper in any name but his own, or in his own name when he has already voted. Anyone so doing, or any person persuading him to do so, is liable to a term of two years' hard labour as well as the other consequences of being guilty of a corrupt practice. (*See* ELECTION AGENT.)

If any person has the right to vote in respect of one or more qualifications, e.g. business and University, as well as a residential qualification, he can vote twice, and twice only, and one vote must be in respect of the residential qualification. It is an illegal practice for anyone to vote or attempt to vote in more constituencies than he is entitled, or at all if he knows he is disqualified from voting. The penalty is a fine up to a maximum of £100 together with the other penalties of illegal practices. (*See* ELECTION AGENT.)

University Elections.—Every person of either sex who is of full age and not subject to any of the afore-mentioned legal incapacities who has received a degree (other than an honorary degree) at a University, is entitled to vote at the election of the Parliamentary representatives of that University.

Polling at a University election is conducted quite differently from ordinary elections.

Those entitled to vote can do so in person, by post or by proxy (*see* PROXY). The poll must be open for five days and for at least four hours a day between 8 a.m. and 8 p.m. Anyone not voting in person must comply with all the requirements set out in the voting paper, and his signature must be witnessed.

All the University constituencies in England return more than one member, and they are elected by a complicated system of proportional representation. A voter must, therefore, place a "1" instead of a cross against the candidate whom he wishes elected, and can express his alternative preferences by placing numbers against the other candidates.

Local Government Elections.—A local government election is an election for any county council, municipal or metropolitan borough council, district or parish council.

Every person over the age of 21 who is on the register of local government electors is entitled to vote if he or she is not under any legal incapacity. The legal incapacities are the same as in Parliamentary elections except that peers can vote. Any person with the requisite residential qualifications is, if not under a legal incapacity, entitled to be placed on the register of local government electors which is compiled at the same time and in the same way as the Parliamentary register.

The qualification is occupational. Any person is so qualified who on June 1st occupied, as owner or tenant, any land or premises in the local government area or has occupied land or premises in that area during the preceding 3 months; or who is the wife or husband of anyone so qualified, provided they both live on the premises.

A lodger is, for this purpose, deemed to be a tenant if the room or rooms occupied were let unfurnished, but not if they were let furnished.

A person who by virtue of his employment inhabits any dwelling-house where his employer does not live is counted as a tenant.

A person cannot vote twice in an area although he may be registered in more than one division or ward in that area.

The procedure and law in regard to voting in local government elections is exactly the same as that in Parliamentary elections except that polling hours are always between 8 a.m. and 8 p.m., and there is no voting by post or proxy. (*See* ELECTIONS; ELECTION AGENT; PROXY.)

VULGAR ABUSE. — Words which would otherwise be regarded as defamatory will not be so considered if they are merely in the nature of vulgar abuse, and would not be taken by any person hearing them to bear the meaning which they might otherwise have. (*See* DEFAMATION; SLANDER.)

WAGER.—A wager is really a bet, which is the hazarding of a sum of money or some article to abide the result of some uncertain event. Money or things won by wagers are not recoverable in law. (*See* SPECIAL SUPPLEMENT "GAMBLING.")

WAGES.—A servant is not entitled to be paid for his work unless there is an express or implied agreement by the master to pay wages. Generally such an agreement can be implied from the circumstances wherever there is an express or implied request by the master to perform work, even though no sum is fixed. In such cases the servant is entitled to recover a reasonable reward for his services. If the services are said to have been given free, it is for the master to prove it.

Additional Wages.—When a servant is engaged to do certain work at a fixed wage, any promise to pay additional wages is usually void for want of consideration.

Further, a servant cannot claim additional wages merely because he has performed additional services of the same kind as he was already bound to perform.

When Wages can be Claimed.—If the servant has, by his contract, to do a definite piece of work or complete a fixed period of time he must do so before any wages are recoverable, unless by custom or agreement he is entitled to wages before completion, or from time to time. Where a master breaks a contract, the servant is certainly entitled to wages up to the date of dismissal (*see* WRONGFUL DISMISSAL), and, subject to the rule that a person bringing an action must minimise his damage as far as possible, probably up to the end of the term of service agreed in the contract. (*See* MASTER AND SERVANT.)

Where a servant breaks the contract, he is not entitled to any wages other than those which have actually accrued due, i.e. he is paid up to his last pay day, but no more.

Where wages are paid in proportion to the work done, the master usually, but not necessarily, has to provide work. There is a presumption that when a servant has left for a considerable time and nothing has been heard of him, all wages have been duly paid.

The Action for Wages.—This should be brought against the master, or his executor or administrator. Being an action for a specific sum, as distinct from an action for damages, it should be brought in the County Court unless for over £100. Where the amount is less than £10, the action may, by the Employers and Workmen Act, 1875, be brought in a Police or Magistrate's Court.

Deduction from, and Payment of Wages.—In certain trades, wages must be paid in money, and the master cannot deduct any sum due to him. In other trades wages do not have to be paid in money. They cannot be paid in, or in the garden of any public house, beer house or such place. The penalty is a fine.

Minimum Wage.—The trades of sugar confectionery, food-preserving, shirtmaking, embroidery of linen or cotton, machine ironing in laundries, hollow ware-making, tailoring, cardboard box-making, machine lace-making and chair-making, have a minimum wage fixed under a trade board. A joint district board fixes a miner's minimum wage, and a committee of the county settles that payable to agricultural workers.

Illness and Holidays. — Wages, it is often said, must be paid during temporary illness. This however, is true only in "very peculiar" cases; for when the performance of work is the consideration for the wages, then a failure to perform (though being through illness there is no breach of contract), disentitles the servant to wages. This is the general rule at the present day, and further, by the rules of most friendly societies, sick pay is given in place of wages, and the servant is not entitled to both.

Illness may be such as to justify dismissal. Holidays with or without wages are a matter for arrangement between the master and servant in every case.

Tips.— In many trades these are looked upon as part, or even as the whole of the wages, and where this is so, a claim may be made for their loss in an action for wrongful dismissal.

In trades where the noxious custom does not exist, the giving of a tip is dangerous, as it may be construed as the crime of corrupting or endeavouring to corrupt or bribe the servant.

WAGES (BANKRUPTCY AND WINDING UP).—When wages are due to a workman or servant by an employer who has gone bankrupt, or by a company which is being wound up, a certain proportion of them will be paid as preferred debts, i.e. before any other debts. A clerk or servant will be entitled to be preferred in this way for a maximum of £50 if that is due for the period within 4 months before the receiving order or winding up order, and a workman or labourer is entitled to the same preference for an amount not exceeding £25 and for two months before the same dates. (*See* BANKRUPTCY; PREFERRED DEBTS; WINDING UP.)

WALL. — Although the owner of land is not permitted to set traps for trespassers upon it, he is entitled to erect walls or fences upon it to keep them off, and he may place spikes, broken glass, etc. upon these walls to make them more efficacious.

If the wall adjoins a highway and is permitted to fall into disrepair it may become a public nuisance, and its proprietor will then be liable for any damage it causes, particularly to children who may be tempted to play upon it.

Where a wall is common to two buildings, it is called a party wall. (*See* ADJOINING OWNERS; FENCE; PARTY-WALL.)

WAR CHARITIES.—No person may make any public appeal for any war charity, or raise money by means of any entertainment for it, unless the responsible authority of the charity has authorized it. Further, all war charities for which money is raised by such means must be registered with the local authority. If any war charity is not properly carried on, there is power for the Charity Commissioners to take control of it. (*See* CHARITY COMMISSIONERS.)

A war charity is any fund or institution having among its objects any charitable purpose connected with the Great War.

WARD.—A minor, i.e. person under twenty-one, who is under the protection of a guardian is said to be the ward of that guardian. A minor under the protection of the Court is called a Ward in Chancery, or a Ward of Court. A person becomes a Ward of Court if there is any property belonging to him under the protection of the Court, or if any application has been made to the Court on his behalf.

WARRANT.—A warrant is a document issued by some authority authorizing some person to do something by virtue of it. The most familiar example is that of a warrant of arrest, which is a document issued by a Justice of the Peace authorizing a constable to arrest a person on a charge.

WARRANTY.—A warranty is a promise made in a contract. It is distinguished from a condition. A condition is a promise made in the contract going to the root of the contract, i.e. as to some matter so vital that, if the condition be not fulfilled, the other party to the contract is entitled to refuse to be bound by it. Where a warranty is broken, the other party to the contract is not entitled to refuse to be bound but is only entitled to claim damages.

Many warranties are implied in the sale of goods, e.g. that the thing sold is fit to use, and is the property of the vendor and that he has a right to sell it. Where a condition is broken, the person who is entitled to refuse to be bound by the contract may choose, if he pleases, to continue with the contract but to sue for the damages he has suffered. If he does this he is said to treat the condition as a warranty. (*See* CONTRACT; SALE OF GOODS.)

WARRANTY OF AUTHORITY.—Any person who makes a contract as agent for another is said to warrant—i.e. promise that he has in fact authority from that other to enter into the contract. If he has not in fact authority he may be sued by the person with whom he has contracted for damages for breach of warranty of authority. The amount of damages recovered will be the loss sustained by the other party through not being able to enforce the contract against the person whose agent the other contracting party held himself out to be. Directors who enter into contracts on behalf of a company, when they are not authorized to do so by the Articles of the company, may be sued for damages for a breach of this warranty. (*See* PRINCIPAL AND AGENT.)

WASTE.—In the old days before covenants by a tenant to repair became usual, the law developed a rule that any occupier of land who was not the absolute owner of it but had only a limited interest,

e.g. a life interest, must not permit it to fall into decay or alter its character in any material way. Such a failure to repair or alteration is called waste. A tenant under a lease, or a tenant for life under a settlement was subject to this rule.

The old rules with regard to waste still exist, but in practice they are unimportant, as the position between landlord and tenant is always governed by express agreement, and every settlement provides that the tenant for life shall be unimpeachable for waste; that is, shall not be bound by this rule, except as to actions which are obviously and clearly harmful to the property. Permissive waste is letting the property fall into disrepair. Voluntary waste is changing the nature of the property; if the result is to improve it, it is called "ameliorative" waste, and no complaint can be made in respect of it.

WATCH COMMITTEE.—Borough police forces are controlled by a board called the Watch Committee. (*See* SPECIAL SUPPLEMENT "THE POLICE.")

WATER.—The supply of water to any particular district is usually provided by an undertaking body, and such body may be either the local authority, e.g. the borough council, or a company empowered by Parliament to supply water. The duty of ensuring that there is an adequate supply of wholesome water for domestic use in each district rests upon the local authority for the district. If the local authority fails to carry out this duty, then the Minister of Health may appoint some person to do it. If there is no water supply company willing to supply the district, then the local authority may construct their own waterworks or hire one from some company.

If there is a company empowered by Act of Parliament to supply water operating in the district, and that company is willing to give the necessary supply, then the local authority must not build a waterworks to compete with them. In pursuance of its duty a local authority may require the owner of a house within its district to obtain a proper water supply for such house, and to do all the work necessary to ensure such supply. They must serve a notice upon the owner containing the requirements, but they can only serve such a notice if their surveyor reports that the house is without a proper supply and that water can be supplied to the house at a cost not exceeding the water rate for the district. Where an owner receives a notice from the district council stating that there is not an available supply of wholesome water within a reasonable distance from his house and requiring him to provide one, he may raise any of the following objections:—

(1) That there is already a sufficient water supply.
(2) That it is impossible to provide the supply at a reasonable cost.
(3) That the authority ought itself to provide a supply of water for the area in which his house is situated.

If he raises either of the first two objections, then the matter is decided by the local justices, but if he raises the last of these objections, then the matter must be referred to the Minister of Health who may either cancel the requirements of the notice or confirm them by an order. In London an occupied dwelling-house without a proper and sufficient supply of water is deemed to be unfit for human habitation.

Every owner, or occupier of a dwelling-house within the area of supply who has laid the necessary communication pipes and paid the water rate payable is entitled to receive from the water undertakers a sufficient supply of water for domestic purposes. Domestic purposes includes all the ordinary uses to which water is put, e.g. for baths or lavatories, and in country districts it usually includes the use of water for the washing of a carriage or motor car kept for private purposes, and the watering of a garden. In London where the water is supplied by the Metropolitan Water Board, the term domestic purposes does not include the washing of carriages nor the watering of gardens by a hose.

Failure to supply water to an owner or occupier of a house who is entitled to receive it having paid, or offered to pay his water rate, unless such failure is occasioned by frost, or unusual drought or other unavoidable cause makes the water undertakers liable to a penalty of £10.

What are Water Rates?—The charge for water supplied for domestic purposes usually takes the form of a rate based upon the value of the premises to which the supply is given. Water rates can be re-

covered by the water suppliers in a court of summary jurisdiction, that is before the magistrates, from the person who receives or uses the supply of water. If the rates are not paid, then the suppliers have power to cut off the water supply from the house except in the case where the owner, and not the occupier of the house is liable to pay the water rate.

The occupier can be proceeded against to recover the water rate, but he must first be given notice to pay the rate out of any rent due from him to the owner. If he fails to pay, then it may be recovered from him in the Court, and he can then deduct the amount he has had to pay from any rent that may be due from him to the owner.

Wastage and Pollution of Water Supply.—It is an offence to waste water supplied by an undertaking body either by allowing any of the pipes or cisterns to be out of repair, or by using the pipes or closets in such a way as will contaminate the supply by foul air. The penalty for the offence is £5, and it is payable to the undertaking body. Every local sanitary authority is responsible for making bye-laws to secure the cleanliness and freedom from pollution of tanks and cisterns used for storing water for domestic purposes, and these bye-laws usually provide that drains and sewers shall be constructed in such a way as not to contaminate or pollute the water supply.

An offence is committed by any person who bathes in any stream, reservoir, aqueduct, or watercourse belonging to a water company or local authority. Similarly it is an offence to wash a dog in any such stream, or to throw any rubbish or filth into it, or to wash any cloth, leather, skin, or other clothes in such water. Water from a sink, sewer, drain, steam engine or boiler must not be allowed to flow into any stream which is used by a water supply body. The penalty for each of these offences is a sum of £5 which is forfeited to the water supplying undertakers. (*See* LOCAL GOVERNMENT; PUBLIC HEALTH.)

WEAR AND TEAR.—Where a person acquires a right to use property of another either under a lease of land or on the hire of a chattel, it is frequently stated that he will maintain the article or land in good repair "reasonable use, wear and tear excepted." In such cases the expression means that the tenant or hirer is not liable for any damage or waste to the thing hired caused by ordinary reasonable use. Thus, in a house the fact that wall-paper becomes scratched or faded would be reasonable wear and tear, but if the wall-paper were cut with a knife by the mischievous son of the tenant, such damage would not be "reasonable wear and tear."

WEDDING PRESENTS.—It is curious that there is no clear decision in English Law as to the ownership, (as between husband and wife), of wedding presents. The correct view probably is that presents given by the friends of the husband become his property, those given by the friends of the wife become hers, and those given by mutual friends become the joint property of husband and wife.

WELSHING.—The Welsher is a not uncommon form of undesirable met upon racecourses. Welshing is really a criminal offence, being a form of larceny by a trick. (*See* LARCENY.)

If a man accepts bets, never intending to pay anything in any event, he can be convicted of larceny by a trick. It should be noticed that this does not in any way mean that the law assists persons to recover money won at betting. Winners from a bookmaker have no legal right to enforce payment, but, nevertheless, if a bookmaker extracts money from the public by means of the trick of pretending that he is running a bookmaker's business, yet never intending to pay at all, the criminal (as distinct from the civil) law comes into motion with the result indicated above.

WEIGHTS AND MEASURES.— It is not lawful to use any measure for the sale of goods, except the Imperial Weights and Measures. Anything sold by weight must be sold by Avoirdupois weight, except gold and silver, platinum, diamonds or precious stones, or articles made of these substances, which may be sold by Troy weight. Apothecaries' Weight may be used in the sale of drugs.

It is an offence for any person to use, or have in his possession for using, in trade, any weight or measure which is not a correct one. Fraudulent use of any weight or measure renders the offender liable to a fine of £5, or, on a second conviction, to one of £20. Every weight or measure used in trade must

be stamped by an inspector of weights and measures, to shew that it is a correct one; and it is an offence for any person to use for this purpose any weight or measure which is not so stamped. Facilities must be given at all reasonable times to allow inspectors of weights and measures to examine any weights or measures which are used for the purpose of trade. Any obstruction of an inspector renders the offender liable to a fine of £5, or, a second offence, £10. (*See* FALSE WEIGHTS.)

WHIPPING.—Whipping at one time could be inflicted on any person convicted of misdemeanour. Since 1820 the whipping of females has been prohibited. The whipping of males is now only permitted in the case of certain specified offences. These include various crimes of violence such as robbery, and certain offences connected with what is popularly termed the White Slave Traffic.

WHITE SLAVE TRAFFIC.— This is a popular term applied to the procuration of women for immoral purposes. It is applied particularly to the practice of enticing women to leave the country so that they may commence a career of prostitution abroad. Concerted international efforts have been made to suppress this traffic, and there is in force an International Agreement to this end. It is a serious criminal offence for any person to procure or attempt to procure any women for such purposes. (*See* PROCURATION.)

WHITSUNDAY.—This is one of the two Term Days in Scotland. It falls on the 15th May for the purpose of payment of rent, but for the purpose of entering into the premises let, or leaving them at the end of the tenancy, Whitsunday is the 28th May and is known as the removal term. Whitsunday, it will be observed, is not necessarily a Sunday and is entirely distinct from the English Whit Sunday, being one word and not two.

WHOLE BLOOD.—Persons may be related either in the whole blood or in the half blood. Persons are related in the whole blood who have the same mother and father, and in the half blood where they have only one parent in common, i.e. are stepbrothers or sisters.

WIDOWS' PENSION.—The widow of a man who died after the 4th day of

January 1926 and was insured under the National Health Insurance Scheme, is entitled to a pension of ten shillings per week, subject to the fulfilment of certain conditions which are:—

(a) One hundred and four weeks must have elapsed, and one hundred and four contributions must have been paid by the husband or on his behalf since the time when he first became insured.

(b) Where two hundred and eight weeks or more have elapsed since the date of his entry into insurance, that the number of contributions paid during the three contribution years before his death represent an average of at least twenty-six contributions per year.

(c) The husband must have been resident in Great Britain for a period of two years immediately prior to the date of his death, and his last employment must have been in Great Britain.

This pension is payable until the widow remarries or attains the age of seventy. If a children's allowance is being paid with the pension it is not affected by re-marriage. When the widow becomes seventy she then receives an Old Age Pension.

Some hard cases arose out of the operation of these conditions, and special provision has had to be made in later Acts of Parliament to meet these cases.

Thus, a woman whose husband died before 4th January, 1926, receives a pension as if her husband had died immediately after that date and been under seventy at the time, provided that she has not married again before the 4th January, 1926, and that there was at that date one child under the age of fourteen living, either of the marriage, or of any former marriage of either parent.

Similarly, if the husband dies after the 4th January, 1926, but was seventy years of age before that date, and would have been entitled to an Old Age Pension, then the widow receives a pension. There must, however, be at least one child of the marriage living, under the age of fourteen, and the deceased husband's occupation must have been such that he would have been regarded as insured under the act of 1925 if it had then been in force. This pension and that granted under the conditions just set out ceases to be payable when the youngest or only child attains the age of sixteen, or upon the 31st of July following the child's sixteenth birthday if it is still at school. Further, a woman whose husband died before the 4th January, 1926, receives a pension at the age of fifty-five provided that her husband:—

(a) Was within the three years before his death registered as a member of an approved society or was a deposit contributor; or

(b) her husband's normal occupation at some time within the three years before his death was an employment in respect of which contributions would have been payable if the 1925 Act had then been in force.

Disqualification from receiving a Pension.—A widow cannot receive a pension if and for so long as she and another person are living together as man and wife; or if she is in prison under the order of any Court of law; or if she is an inmate of a workhouse or a lunatic asylum.

Pension money is not payable to any person while that person is absent from Great Britain, nor is it payable if it is not claimed within three months after the date when it is due to be paid.

How to Claim a Pension.—In order to obtain a Widow's Pension it is necessary to fill up a form which can be obtained at any Post Office. When the form is filled up it must be delivered to the Postmaster at the Post Office at which the claimant wishes the pension to be paid. If any difficulty is experienced in filling up the form, or in deciding whether a claim can be made, ask the Postmaster in a Post Office. It is an offence to make any false statement or representation to obtain a pension for oneself or anyone else, and the offender is liable to six months' imprisonment with hard labour. Pensions are paid weekly on each Tuesday at a Post Office and are paid by means of a Pension Order.

Service Widows' Pension.—Pensions are paid to widows of officers and men who served in the Great War, and were either killed on active service or died of wounds within seven years after receiving the wounds, or died of a disease contracted during the War or aggravated by War service. The pension varies according to the rank of the dead husband, and also

Sir Ernest Wild.

according to whether the widow is over or under forty years of age, or has children who qualify for an allowance. The officers' widows' pension varies from £800 per annum for the widow of a Field-Marshal to £120 per annum for the widow of a Second-Lieutenant. A children's allowance of £30 per annum is payable in respect of each child until it reaches the age of sixteen.

The widow of a Warrant Officer, Class I, receives a pension of forty shillings per week if she is over forty years of age, or has children available for a children's allowance, but if she is under forty and has no children then the pension is thirty shillings.

The amount of pension decreases according to the rank of the husband, and the lowest pension is twenty-six shillings and eightpence per week which is paid to the widow of a private soldier, a naval rating below a Second Class Petty-Officer and a Class F Airman. This pension is decreased to twenty shillings per week if the widow is under forty and has no children available for a children's allowance. The children's allowance for widows other than officers' widows is ten shillings per week for the eldest child, seven and sixpence per week for the second child, and six shillings per week for any other child, and is payable until the children reach sixteen years of age.

Service widows pensions are not claimable as of right, but are given as a reward for the services of the deceased husband. Once they are awarded, however, the widow has a legal right to be paid. These pensions, and the disablement pensions paid to ex-servicemen are administered by the Ministry of Pensions. (*See* NATIONAL HEALTH INSURANCE; PENSION; OLD AGE PENSION.)

WILD, Sir Ernest (1869-   ).—Has been the Recorder of London since 1922. He sits at the Old Bailey and has become noted for his efforts to suppress crimes of violence in this country. Before reaching the Bench he was a distinguished advocate and appeared in many notable trials.

WILD BIRDS.—Every wild bird in England and Wales which does not come into the category of game (q.v.) is protected from being killed or taken between the dates March 1st and August 1st in each year. The penalty for breaking these regulations depends upon the rarity of the bird, and for the rarer birds, including all forms of wild duck, widgeon, owls, gulls, cuckoos, woodpeckers etc., the maximum penalty is £1, for other birds such as sparrows, thrushes, blackbirds etc., there is a reprimand or maximum penalty of 5/-. The exception to this rule is that a landowner or any person authorized by him may kill wild birds which do not belong to the rarer class, and hence it is not illegal for a gamekeeper to kill such birds as hawks, crows, blackbacked gulls, jays, etc., during the close season.

It is a further offence to have in one's possession after the 15th March of each year a wild bird that has been recently killed or taken, while to sell or to have in one's possession plover's eggs between the 1st March and the 1st August of any year is an offence punishable with a fine not exceeding £5.

In many counties there are further regulations preventing the killing of certain wild birds at all, or altering the close seasons for different birds in the county. Other local regulations may prohibit the taking of the eggs of certain birds, or may abolish the close season for any species of bird. These regulations are generally published on the notice boards of the local police station or County Offices, and since they vary for each county, persons wishing to catch wild birds or to go birds nesting should satisfy themselves that no regulation applies to the birds or their eggs in the area in which the person dwells. The penalty for breaches of these regulations is a maximum fine of £1.

In addition to these prohibitions various methods of capturing birds at any time are illegal on the grounds of cruelty. (*See* CRUELTY TO ANIMALS.)

Apart from these special provisions designed for the protection of wild birds, the general law relating to them is the same as that applying to any other wild animals (*See* ANIMAL; CRUELTY TO ANIMALS; GAME.)

WILLS.—The principle by which a person may give binding directions for the disposal of his property after death is of very great antiquity, and although under the feudal system land was not generally capable of being dealt with by means of a will, this restriction gradually vanished, and to-day there is no property either real or personal in which a person has more than a life's interest which he cannot bequeath to anyone he wishes. The exceptions to this, of course, are annuities and all other interests which end at the death of the owner of them, a nomination to benefit due under the rules of a Friendly Society or under National Health Insurance.

Any adult, male or female, who is over twenty-one and is not insane may make a will under the laws of England, but a person who dies domiciled abroad is dependent upon the law of the country where he is domiciled for the validity of his will. No person who is under twenty-one years of age can make a will except a soldier or member of the Air Force while he is actually on active service, or a seaman or member of the merchant marine while he is actually at sea. No person may make a valid will while he is insane, but if, having been insane he makes a will during a lucid interval, the will will be valid.

Form of a Will.—Every will must be in writing. It may be written in ink or pencil, typewritten or printed and it may be made partly on a specially printed form with the blanks filled up in hand-writing.

The person making a will must sign it in the presence of two witnesses. Normally he will sign his full signature, but if he is unable to write, he may make a mark, or some other person may guide his hand in making his signature or mark, or may even make the mark or signature himself provided that the person whose will it is, acknowledges that it is his signature in the presence of the witnesses. This should only be done if the testator is too weak to sign himself.

The witnesses must be present at the time that the signature is made, and must see it being made, though it is sufficient if after the signature has been made in their absence, the testator acknowledges that it is his signature in their presence. It is vital that the witnesses should be present at the same time. The signature of the testator must appear at the foot of the will, and anything that is written below his signature will not count as part of the will and will be invalid.

Any person can be a witness of a will, but it is most important to remember that a witness cannot take any benefit under a will, and if anyone who has been left a gift or legacy under the will signs his name to it as a witness, he will be unable to take the legacy. The same applies to husbands and wives of witnesses, who also are not entitled to take any benefit under a will. Both witnesses must be present at the same time and should sign their names as witnesses in the presence of the testator. They, too, may make a mark if unable to sign their names.

It is usual to place against the signature of the witnesses, a clause known as an "attestation clause" shewing that these rules have been carried out strictly, and if this is done, the executor as explained below can get probate of the will more easily. A convenient form of attestation clause to which the witnesses can put their signatures runs as follows:

"Signed by the above-named A.B. as his last will in the presence of us, the undersigned, both being present at the same time, who, at his request and in his presence and in the presence of each other have hereunto subscribed our names as witnesses."

A will should never contain alterations or interlineations, for unless these are signed

I, JOHN GRAY of 999 Crayford Road Ealing hereby revoke all former Wills and Codicils and DECLARE this to be my last Will —————————————————————————————————

1. I APPOINT JANE GRAY my wife and her brother JOHN BROWN of 999 Blackford Road Ealing in the County of Middlesex to be the EXECUTORS AND TRUSTEES of this my Will and GUARDIANS of my infant children —————————————————————

2. I BEQUEATH Fifty pounds to my sister Esther Gray and my gold cuff links with the white stone to my friend Joseph White of Greylands Hampstead in both cases free of duty ————

3. I DEVISE AND BEQUEATH all the residue of my property to my Trustees on trust to sell call in and convert the same into money (with power in their discretion to postpone such calling in and conversion) and to invest the same in their names in any of the investments authorised by law and to stand possessed of such investments and of all parts of my estate for the time being unsold (hereinafter called my residuary estate) ————

(a) Upon trust to pay the income thereof to my wife for her life and after her death ——————————————————————

(b) Upon trust to pay and divide the capital and income of my residuary estate among my children in such shares as my said wife shall by deed or will or codicil appoint and subject to any such appointment upon trust to pay and divide the same among all my children living at my death in equal shares

IN WITNESS whereof I have hereunto set my hand this day of   One thousand nine hundred and thirty

SIGNED by the above named JOHN GRAY)
as his last Will in the presence of)
us present at the same time who in)   *John Gray.*
his presence and in the presence of)
each other have hereunto subscribed)
our names as witnesses

Frank H. Connett. 500 Horton Avenue Redford
Builder.
Roger Westby, 776 Upper Dorman Lane, Matley
Clerk.

Form of Will leaving property to wife for life, and on her death to children.

or initialled by the testator and both witnesses they are presumed to have been made after the will was signed and are of no effect. If any alterations are to be made they should be signed and witnessed in exactly the same manner as if the will itself were being made.

Codicils. — After making a will, a testator very often wishes to alter some details in it with changing circumstances. Any alteration however small will be invalid unless it is made with the same ceremony as to signature and witnesses as the will itself. This is generally done in a codicil, which is any document duly signed by the testator in the presence of two witnesses who themselves sign it, and intended to be read with a will. It should generally be attached to the will itself, but this is not strictly necessary and a second will, if it does not expressly revoke a previous will and is not wholly inconsistent with it, will be treated as a codicil.

When the provisions in the codicil contradict the provisions of the previous will they are taken as cancelling it as far as the inconsistent clauses are concerned, and any further codicils bearing a later date inconsistent with the will or earlier codicils have the same effect.

Any number of codicils may be made to a will, but if they change the terms of the original will to any great extent, it is wiser to make a fresh will and to revoke the old one.

Alterations of Wills.—No will is binding upon a testator until his death, and no promise that he makes not to change it can bind him except in certain cases where he enters into a definite contract for good consideration not to do so. Accordingly he can at any time, up to the very moment of his death alter it in detail, provided he complies with the necessary forms, or revoke it entirely in one of the manners set out below.

A will may be altered by the testator completely obliterating any part of it, but it must be so thoroughly obliterated that it is impossible to see what were the words which are removed. A better way, however, is to make alterations and interlineations in the will, and these must be signed or initialled and witnessed by two witnesses who must also append their signatures or initials.

Most alterations however are made by codicils which, as explained above, have the effect of nullifying any previous will or codicil to the extent that the provisions of the new codicil are inconsistent with the provisions of the old document.

Revocation and Cancellation of Wills.—It is most important to realize that every will is revoked by a subsequent marriage, even if it is expressly made in contemplation of a proposed marriage. Therefore any person upon marriage should make a new will altogether, though it is possible, if it is not desired to change the provisions of the old will to execute a codicil signed and witnessed in the ordinary way after marriage, stating that the provisions of the old will are intended still to apply.

Wills may also be cancelled by destruction. In such a case they should be wholly destroyed and thrown away, for the mere passing of a pen or pencil through the whole will and writing "cancelled" across it, does not serve to revoke a will. Accidental destruction will not revoke a will, unless it was done with intent to cancel.

Finally, wills may be revoked by saying so in writing, signed and witnessed with the same formalities as the will itself. Whenever a testator wishes to make a wholly new will instead of altering an old one by means of a codicil, he should expressly state at the beginning of the new will that he revokes all previous wills, codicils and other testamentary instruments heretofore made by him.

Soldiers' and Sailors' Wills.—The only persons in this country who are entitled to forego the formalities of signature and witnessing of a will are soldiers and members of the Air Force while they are *actually* on active service, and sailors and members of the merchant marine while *actually* at sea. Although it will save a vast amount of trouble if their wills are in writing and signed and witnessed, they are perfectly good wills even if not signed and witnessed at all, or even if made by word of mouth to another person.

Terms used in Wills.—Wills are legal documents, and accordingly the words that are used in wills and in any discussion of wills are technical terms which have a precise meaning. The property of the testator is often called his estate, and that portion of his property or estate which

This is the last Will and Testament

——————————— of me ———————————

JOHN BROWN of 1000 Redford Road Warminster I HEREBY REVOKE all
former wills and testamentary disposition made by me and by
this last Will GIVE DEVISE AND BEQUEATH all my real and
personal estate whatsoever and wheresoever to my wife [or "to
my son "John" or "to my sister Jane" as the case may be]
absolutely and appoint her [or him] sole executrix of this my
Will —————————————————————————————————————

    IN WITNESS whereof I have hereunto set my hand this
day of   One thousand nine hundred and thirty———

SIGNED by the above named JOHN
BROWN as his last Will in the
presence of us present at the
same time who in his presence
and in the presence of each
other have hereunto subscribed
our names as witnesses

John Brown

Charles John Hornsby. 10 Smoulie Avenue. Woolwich
Schoolmaster

Winifred Green   355 Turnpike Lane. Northampton.
Nurse.

Short Form of Will leaving all property to one person.

consists of interests in freehold land is called real estate, the rest of his property of all kinds, including leaseholds and interests in leasehold land is called his personal estate or personal property, while leaseholds and interests in leaseholds are sometimes called chattels real, to distinguish them from other forms of personal property.

The persons who receive property under a will are called beneficiaries or legatees, and the property which they receive is called a gift or legacy. Sometimes the word legacy is used in a restricted sense meaning a gift by will of a specific sum of money or a specific article, but this use is incorrect, and a legacy is any gift or any share of property left by a will.

A legacy may be specific, when it is of a definite thing whether it be a definite chattel, piece of land, block of shares, leasehold property or anything else that is definite, or it may be general where it is a specified sum of money, sometimes called a pecuniary legacy or anything of a particular kind provided that the actual thing is not identified.

It may on the other hand be a share of whatever is left over when the specific and general legacies have been paid. In such a case it is generally called a residuary gift, while the person who receives it is called a residuary legatee, and the portion of the estate out of which it is paid, i.e. all the remainder of the testator's property after the legacies have been paid is called the residue of the estate. (*See* LEGACIES.)

Contents of a Will.—Owing to the complicated legal decisions governing wills it is most unwise for the layman to attempt to make one himself, but if the will is very simple, and amounts only to the giving of a few bequests or legacies and the leaving of the rest of the property to one or more persons, the will may be made upon one of the printed forms that can be bought at most stationers, and its contents should be arranged in the following order.

1. Express revocation of all previous wills, e.g. "I, X Y of Z, hereby revoke all other wills, codicils and testamentary documents heretofore made by me and declare this to be my last will and testament."

2. Appointment of executors, e.g. "I appoint A B of C and E F of G to be the executors and trustees of this my will."

3. Gifts of specific things, e.g. "I give and bequeath my gold watch to my eldest son W Y and I give and bequeath my signet ring to my daughter V Y."

4. Gifts of sums of money, e.g. "I give and bequeath the sum of £100 free of all duties to my servant Q R."

5. Gift of the residue of the property, e.g. "I give and bequeath all the residue of my property real and personal to my dear wife U Y absolutely."

6. Signature.

7. Attestation and witnesses' signature.

Naturally the greatest care should be taken to identify exactly the property to be bequeathed and the persons to whom it is intended that the property should pass. Vague words such as "money" should not be used, and if the testator possesses leaseholds and freeholds in land, he should remember that leaseholds are personal property, whereas freeholds are real property. Accordingly, if he wants some beneficiary to take all his interests in land, he must state in his will that he is bequeathing "leasehold property, and real property," for if he refers to the latter alone, only the freehold interests will pass. If the testator wishes to bequeath everything that he possesses, he should for choice use the words "all my property real and personal whatsoever."

Stating Property in Proportion.— Another point to be borne in mind is that the will does not come into operation until after the testator's death, though it may be made very many years before his death. Accordingly in making his will he should endeavour to provide for the property that he will possess at his death, and not merely for what he possesses at the time at which he makes the will. If he has ceased to own property which he bequeaths specifically to some person by his will, the gift will lapse and the beneficiary will receive nothing at all. For this reason, wherever possible a testator should not bequeath either specific property or specific sums of money, but should give definite proportions of his total property, since these will all increase or diminish in the same ratio, whereas if he gives a legacy of £100 to some person, under the impression that it amounts only to a small portion of his estate, he may find that at the time of his death the £100 legacy exhausts nearly the whole of his estate, and that the person to whom he thought he was giving a substantial sum as a share of the residue will get practically nothing.

The person to whom the gift is made should be identified always by name and wherever possible by his address as well. For if a legacy is left in such terms that it might be payable to two different persons, as for example where a testator leaves a legacy to "my nephew George" where he has two nephews called George, and there is no way of telling which of his nephews he intended, the gift is void for uncertainty, and neither of the nephews called George will get anything at all.

This sort of thing frequently happens when there is what is called a "class gift," i.e. where the testator leaves a portion of his estate or a certain sum of money to a definite class of persons. Prima facie this sort of gift vests in the beneficiaries at the death of the testator, and so if a testator leaves a legacy to "My grandchildren in equal shares" only those grandchildren who have been born at the date of his death will receive a share, though the testator may have intended that all his children's children should receive shares.

This rule as to the identification of beneficiaries is relaxed only in the case of charities. If the Court is convinced that the testator's intention was to leave money to a charity, even though the will describes the charity by the wrong name, it will be entitled to receive the legacy, and even if there is no charity in existence of that name or description, the charity most similar in nature to that intended will benefit instead.

In connection with the identity of the beneficiaries under a will, the testator should also bear in mind that the will will come into operation at his death, and not before then. Accordingly if he leaves money to a person who dies before him, the gift will lapse, whereas the testator may have wished the children of the beneficiary to take the gift in such circumstances. Accordingly, wherever a testator wishes to arrange that the children of a beneficiary should receive his share if the beneficiary should happen to die before the testator, he should remember to state so specifically in his will.

One of the most important things to be dealt with in a will is the appointment of executors, since the object of a will is to enable a living person to give directions as to the way his property shall be dealt with after his death, and the persons who will have the duty of dealing with it will be his executors, or if he fails to appoint any, his administrators. Accordingly he should take great care that they are appointed by the will, and this is the first clause, after the revoking of any previous wills, that should appear in the document.

Not more than four or, if any of the beneficiaries is an infant or any beneficiary is given a life interest in any property, less than two executors should be appointed; but if the testator's property is being left outright without any questions of infancy or trusts arising, one person *may* act as sole executor, though it is always wiser to have two. The consent of executors should be asked before naming them in the will, as this may save expense and difficulty after the death of the testator.

Testators often wish to retain control of their property after their death, but there are limits which the law imposes upon this and which must be strictly observed or there will be a danger of the whole gift failing.

Although it is perfectly proper and usual to leave property to one person for life to enjoy the *income* from the property alone during his or her life, and to pass the property to another person after the death of the owner of the life interest (this being very desirable where the testator leaves a spouse as well as children), yet the law does not permit property to be tied up in this way for a period longer than 21 years after the death of a person who is alive at the date of the death of the testator. An example of the working of this may make it clear: A testator dies leaving a married son. He wishes to leave the property to his son for life, and after the son's death to the son's children but so that they will not obtain control of their money until they are old enough to be responsible. In such a case he may leave it tied up in the control of trustees for the children until they reach the age of twenty-one, but if, like many people, he thinks that young persons should not have control of large sums of money until they are 25, he cannot leave the property in the hands of trustees until each child reaches the age of 25 because that might happen more than 21 years after the death of the son, and would so offend against the rule. For the son might die when one of the children was less than 4 years old, and the provision is void wherever there is even a possibility of the rule being broken.

Another rule of a similar nature is designed to prevent the accumulation of interest upon property, and accordingly it is not generally permissible to leave property to trustees with a direction that they are to add the income to the capital and so let the sum accumulate for a period greater than 21 years.

Again, if a testator wishes to make sure that a legacy shall be used in a particular manner, he should state quite definitely in his will that he is leaving it on trust for that particular purpose, for as a general rule the expression of a hope that the money should be used in a particular way will not ensure that it is so used. Thus, if he wants to make sure that his wife for instance, shall hand on his property to his children after his death, he should give her a life interest only, and should not rely on such words as "I desire that" or "I am confident that she will leave my property to my children after her death, or that she will deal fairly by my children." There is no more fruitful source of litigation than such a direction contained in a will, and a testator who wishes his directions to be observed should make sure that they will be either by leaving money to trustees to carry out his wishes, or by making the gift conditional upon his wishes being carried out.

But there are certain conditions that he cannot impose. All conditions that are immoral or contrary to public policy are void, and among these is a condition that a person shall not marry at all, though it is possible to give a woman an interest in property until her marriage; and it is not unlawful to make a condition against a widow marrying again, or against a woman marrying one particular person or a member of one particular class of persons such as a sailor, or a Roman Catholic.

Likewise a condition giving a legacy to any person on condition that he or she shall take no steps to upset the will is always void, unless some provision is made for the legacy to go to someone else if the condition

is not complied with; and even if this is done, such a condition will not in general prevent the beneficiary taking steps to dispute the will if the Court thinks that it is reasonable that he or she should do so.

Further, as well as giving legacies, a testator should make provision for the rest of his estate after the legacies have been granted: in other words he should make a residuary legatee to whom the rest of his estate which is not exhausted in legacies will be granted. If he does not do so, considerable expense will be involved, as he will be treated, so far as the residuary estate is concerned, as if he had not made a will at all.

Important Points to Remember.— Even when the testator employs a solicitor who will see that his will does not offend against the various rules of law just mentioned and other less commonly infringed rules, there are various important points that he should bear in mind, and of which he should inform the solicitor. If he is drawing up his own will with the assistance of one of the will forms obtainable at many stationers he should pay even greater attention to these, and if in doubt should make the simplest will possible. The points are probably best dealt with in the following order.

1. If any previous wills have been made, they should be revoked in the clearest possible language.

2. If the testator wants to leave any directions as to the way in which he wishes to be buried, whether he wishes for an elaborate funeral and the like, he should state this in his will. It is not actually binding on his executors, but they will generally follow out his wishes.

3. If the testator is married he should consider whether there is any doubt as to the legality of his marriage, and if he has children whether there is any question as to their legitimacy. If they are illegitimate, and he wishes them to receive a legacy under his will he must mention them by name and not by describing them as his "children." Also, if there is any likelihood of the birth of other children, he should make provision for them as well.

4. He should then run over in his mind the property which he possesses and decide whether there is one particular portion

which he wishes to be used for the payment of his debts, death duties, etc. If he makes no special fund for these payments they will be paid out of his residuary estate. If he has property in land he should remember that unless he says something in the will to the contrary, the persons to whom he bequeaths the land will have to pay the succession duty payable on it, and as they may not be able to do this without selling some of the land, he should provide a fund from which the succession duty is to be paid if he wishes them to have the whole value of the land. Again, if some of his land is mortgaged he must decide whether he wishes the mortgage to be paid off out of the rest of his estate, or whether he wishes the beneficiary taking the land to take it subject to the mortgage, in which case he need make no special provision, for this is what happens unless he uses words to the contrary in his will. When reckoning up his property he should always make allowances for debts, testamentary expenses and death duties.

5. Turning then to the question of his widow he should bear in mind that it may be some little time before a life income is available for her, and it may be convenient for him to leave a small legacy payable immediately to tide her over the first few weeks after his death. That provided for, he must decide whether he wishes to give her a sum of money or a portion of land outright, or whether he wishes her to have the benefit of the income only of all or part of his property during her life. If he is going to do this he should also decide whether he wishes her to have the same amount if she should marry again. He may wish either to reduce the amount payable to her, or to stop it entirely. This he can only do by appointing trustees, and leaving his estate on trust to pay the income to his widow; but if he wishes to avoid having his money tied up in a trust, he can solve the problem of providing for his widow during her lifetime by leaving a sum of money to be expended upon purchasing an annuity for her of a fixed amount and leaving the rest of his estate free from trusts.

6. If the testator has children, he must decide upon the share in the property which he wishes to give to each of them. He may wish them to take their shares immediately upon his death, in which case he need not leave the property on trust, but if he wishes them not to take any share until they are 21 he should leave the money upon trust as he must do in any case if he is arranging that his widow should have the income of some of the property for life instead of buying her an annuity. Where the children are not to be entitled to their shares until they are 21 he should make some provision for their education before that date, either by making the widow responsible for maintaining them, or by giving the trustees a right to advance the money to the children as they require it for their advancement or education. This he may do quite briefly by bequeathing their shares to the executors as trustees to divide among the children "upon the statutory trusts." He should also bear in mind the rule mentioned above about advancement, and if he has already advanced money to some of the children he should make it clear whether he wishes the amount which has already been advanced to them to be deducted from their shares or not.

7. A testator may also wish to make provision for his grandchildren in which case he will be bound to create a trust unless the grandchildren are already living. He should, in any case, decide whether he wishes the share of any child who predeceases him to go to that child's children or not.

8. If he intends to leave a legacy to one of his debtors or creditors he should bear in mind the rules as to debts and legacies, and if he wishes the legacy to be independent of any debts or credits he should state so in the will.

9. Having settled the general principles of the manner in which he wishes his property to be divided among his family, he should decide whether he wishes to leave any legacies of specific things. Often there is a family heirloom or memento he wishes one particular member of the family to have. These he should leave as specific legacies (q.v.).

10. To friends and servants or to charities he may wish to make gifts of money, and if he is doing so he should decide whether he wishes them to receive the legacies free of legacy duty or not. If he says nothing in his will about this, the legatees will be obliged to pay the duty themselves. Accordingly, if he wishes his friend X to receive a gift of £100 net, he should remember that he must leave him the legacy "free of all duties."

11. If he is intending to leave an annuity to his widow or to some other person, he should decide how the annuity is to be raised, whether it is to be raised from his general estate, from his landed property or from the proceeds of some particular investment. If he is intending to leave the residue of his property either directly to one person, or in shares between several persons, or subject to life interests and the like, he should decide whether he wishes the property to be retained by his executors and trustees in its present state, or whether he wishes property such as leaseholds, or freeholds, stocks and shares and the like to be turned into money and invested in safe trustee stocks. Unless he particularly mentions that it should be retained as it is, it will be the duty of the executors to realize the property and re-invest it in safe securities.

13. If the testator leaves a business, he should decide whether he wishes his wife or children or his executors to carry it on, and if he gives them power to carry it on he should take care to leave ample funds for them to use in it, otherwise their powers to carry it on will be thwarted.

14. Finally he should decide what powers to give to his executors and trustees. If one of them is a solicitor it should be remembered that he cannot charge for his services unless he is specially empowered to do so, and accordingly provision should be made for this. Provision should also be made for trustees, assuming that he has left some of his property on trust, to have discretion as to the investments that they make, unless the testator wishes the proceeds of his property to be invested only in gilt-edged stock. It is also most important and will save a great deal of expense in the long run if he makes provision for the appointment of new trustees to take the place of any who die or who refuse to act.

Effect of a Will.—A will has no effect whatever until the testator has died. Before that time he can revoke it, destroy it, alter it as he wishes, but upon the moment of his death it comes into operation, and when probate has been obtained it has the effect of vesting all the estate and interest of the deceased in the executors for the purpose of carrying out the provisions of the will. On this subject *see* EXECUTORS AND ADMINI-STRATORS. (*See also* CODICIL; LEGACIES; PROBATE OF WILLS; TRUSTS; TRUSTEE.)

WINDING-UP.—A Company is an artificial legal person which the law allows to be brought into existence on certain documents being registered with the Registrar of Companies, and it is therefore necessary for the law to provide also for some method by which the existence of this artificial legal person can be brought to an end, for a company, unlike an ordinary human being, cannot die a natural death. The method by which the law has allowed a company to cease to exist is by its dissolution, but before the dissolution can take place it is necessary for all the money belonging to a company to be collected and to be paid to the persons who are entitled to it, whether they are creditors or shareholders. This preliminary process is known as the winding-up of the company.

It by no means follows that when a company is wound up it is insolvent, i.e. cannot pay its debts, although very often in practice this is the reason why a company is wound up, for the law will not allow a company to go on trading and defrauding its creditors when it has no money to pay their debts any more than it will allow an individual who is insolvent to do so. The company in such a case may be wound up and the individual may be made bankrupt.

A company may be wound up in one of three ways:—

1. By an order made by the Court. This is called a compulsory winding-up.

2. Voluntarily. This is by the shareholders or the creditors without the assistance of the Court.

3. Under the supervision of the Court. This method is to some extent a combination of the other two and is not often met with in practice.

By the Court.—A company may be wound up by the Court in cases where it is unable to pay its debts, or where the number of the shareholders falls below 7 in the case of a public company or 2 in the case of a private company. If anyone wishes to wind up a company on the ground that it cannot pay its debts, he usually proves either that he is a creditor to whom the company owes £50 or more, and that he has sent to the company a demand for payment which has not been complied with within 3 weeks, or that he has brought an action against the company and has obtained a judgment on that action which has not been paid. A creditor is the person who will usually present a petition on these grounds, but it is possible for a shareholder also to ask for a company to be wound up although he cannot do so in all cases unless he has held his shares for 6 out of the last 18 months.

The more usual method in cases where a shareholder wishes to have the company wound up is for the company to be wound up voluntarily. A petition is frequently presented to wind up a company where the creditor does not really want the company wound up at all, but hopes that by presenting a petition, and threatening to wind it up, he may induce the directors to pay to him the amount of his debt out of their own pockets.

Voluntary.—A voluntary winding-up is usually brought about when a company passes a special resolution to the effect that it is to be wound up. But it may be wound up by an ordinary resolution if the company has been formed for some particular purpose, e.g. the production of a play, and that purpose has come to an end, or by an extraordinary resolution when the grounds of the winding-up are that the company is unable to pay its debts. There are now two kinds of voluntary winding-up:—

1. A members' voluntary winding-up.
2. A creditors' voluntary winding-up.

The first of these takes place when the directors of a company make a statutory declaration—i.e. a solemn statement—that in their opinion the company will be able to pay its debts in full within 1 year and send this to the Registrar of companies. The advantages of a members' voluntary winding-up are that the proceedings are controlled entirely by the shareholders themselves, and not by the creditors, who are not considered to be interested since their debts will be paid in full in any event.

A creditors' voluntary winding-up takes place in every case where the declaration of solvency by the directors has not been made, and in it it is the creditors rather than the members who exercise a control over the proceedings.

The effect of any winding-up is to put an end to the carrying on of the business of the company except for the purpose of having it sold as a going concern, for if the company stopped carrying on its business it would lose its customers and its goodwill which is a great part of the value of any business, and it is therefore allowed to carry on its business until someone comes forward to buy it. No shares can be transferred from one shareholder to another after a winding-up has commenced without consent of the liquidator, and accordingly members who are liable on calls on their shares cannot escape their liability by transferring their shares to other persons.

One of the first things which has to be done in the winding-up is to appoint some person to act as liquidator of the company. It is his duty to collect all the company's property and to sell it and to divide up the money received among the creditors and shareholders. (*See* COMPANIES.)

WINDOW-CLEANING.—In any town or urban district it is an offence for any householder to order, or permit any servant to stand on a window-sill for the purpose of doing anything to the outside of the window. This does not, however, apply to windows in basements.

WITHOUT PREJUDICE.—(*See* PREJUDICE, WITHOUT.)

WITHOUT RECOURSE. — The drawer or endorser of a Bill of Exchange may add these words to his signature, and if he does so he excludes himself from any personal liability on the bill. Thus, if an endorser uses these words and the bill is not paid by the acceptor when presented for payment, the endorser is not liable.

WITHOUT RESERVE.—When property is sold by auction without reserve this means that neither the vendor nor any person on his behalf will bid at the auction, and that the property will be sold to the highest bidder.

WITNESS.—Any person who is required to testify before any Court or similar tribunal is called a witness. A witness can be required to attend before a Court if he is served with a subpœna (q.v.), and sufficient conduct money to take him to the Court. The witness is required to remain available at the Court until he gives his evidence, and indeed until the conclusion of the case unless the tribunal gives him permission to leave.

A witness is required to take such form of oath as is binding upon his conscience, and it is his duty to indicate this form before he is sworn. A witness who refuses to answer questions properly put to him may be dealt with for Contempt of Court. A witness may decline to answer any questions which shew that he could be convicted of some criminal offence.

WOOLSACK.—The seat in the House of Lords on which the Lord Chancellor sits is known as the Woolsack. The word is also applied to the office of Lord Chancellor.

WORKING MEN'S CLUB.—A society formed by workmen for the purpose of social intercourse, mutual assistance and recreation. It is usually somewhat more of a club than a friendly society, but if the rules provide for the payment of benefits to members, it may be registered with the Chief Registrar of Friendly Societies.

If intoxicating liquor is supplied to members of the club, then the club must be registered under the Licensing Acts. (*See* FRIENDLY SOCIETY; LICENSING.)

WORKMEN'S COMPENSATION. —If a workman sustains personal injury by reason of an accident which occurs when he is engaged in his employment then his employer is liable to pay him compensation. But no compensation is payable:—

(1) If the injury does not disable the workman for three days at least from earning full wages.

(2) If the accident causing the injury occurred because of the serious and wilful misconduct of the injured workman; but if the workman dies, or is permanently disabled by the accident, then his claim is not barred under this exception.

A claim for compensation is not the only remedy available to a workman, for in two cases he can, if he chooses, proceed by way of an ordinary civil action; if he is injured by the personal negligence or wilful act of his employer or of some person for whose act or default the employer is liable, then he may either claim compensation or sue the employer for damages. The workman must make his choice for he cannot do both. If, however, he brings a civil action against his employer and fails in the action he may request the Court to assess the compensation which would have been payable to him under the Workmen's Compensation Act, and he may then claim compensation from his employer. Compensation can, however, only be assessed in this way by the Court if the injury which the workman sustained, and in respect of which he sued the employer, was one for which the employer would have been liable to pay him compensation.

The Court may, in its discretion, deduct all or part of the costs incurred by the workman's bringing the action from the amount of compensation which it awards.

Similarly, if the workman sustained injury in circumstances which create a legal liability to pay damages in some person other than his employer, then he may take action against that person to recover damages and against his employer to recover compensation, but he cannot recover both damages and compensation. When a workman is employed by a contractor who is engaged to do work undertaken by another person, usually called the principal, then in the event of injury the workman may claim compensation from the principal, who is for the purposes of compensation regarded as his employer. He may also claim compensation from the contractor by whom he was directly employed, the object of this double remedy being to ensure that the workman shall receive his compensation, and not be deprived of it by reason of the inability of the contractor to pay it. If the principal is thus rendered liable to pay compensation to a workman employed by a contractor, he is entitled to be repaid by the contractor any sums he may have to pay, because, but for this special provision, the contractor would have been solely liable.

The one exception is where the contractor contracts to thresh, plough, or do other agricultural labour, and he provides and uses his own mechanically-driven machinery, then he alone is liable to pay compensation to a workman injured.

What must the Workman Prove?— In order to entitle a workman to make a claim for compensation he must have sustained the injury in an accident "arising out of, and in the course of his employment." It is necessary for the person claiming compensation to prove that the accident arose out of, or occurred in, the course of the workman's employment.

It is usually necessary to decide whether the workman was actually engaged in his employment at the time when the accident occurred, and sometimes it has to be decided whether the workman had commenced the work for which he was employed, or had ceased work. Some examples from decided cases will make this clearer:—

(a) An engineer had to go aboard a ship at night to attend to the boilers, and in the darkness he fell overboard, and was drowned. This was held to be an accident in the course of his employment.

(b) A workman is injured in a street accident before he reaches his place of employment, such an accident occurred outside the course of his employment. The position would be different if the workman was injured in an accident while travelling in a train or omnibus specially provided by his employers to bring him to, or take him away from, his place of employment.

Each case must be decided upon the particular facts, and it is impossible to lay down any rules upon the subject. One general test can be applied to assist in deciding the question: "Was it part of the injured person's employment to risk, or to do that act which caused his injury?" If the answer is "Yes," then the accident arose out of his employment.

When the workman has established that the accident arose out of, or in the course of, his employment, then it is for the employer to prove that the accident occurred by reason of the injured workman's serious and wilful misconduct if he relies upon that ground as a defence to the claim.

What is Serious and Wilful Misconduct.—Whether the workman's conduct amounted to serious and wilful misconduct is again a question of fact which must be decided in each particular case. Two contrasting examples may help to indicate what amounts to serious and wilful misconduct and what does not:—

(1) A workman used a lift without a load when there was a notice posted up forbidding workmen to use the lift unless they were in charge of a load. He was injured, and it was held that the mere breach of the rule did not constitute serious and wilful misconduct, since the danger to him was not increased by his disregard of the rule.

(2) An engine driver left the footplate of his engine while it was moving, thereby disobeying an express rule of his employers. He was injured, and this was held to be serious and wilful misconduct because he had greatly increased the danger of his employment by his action.

If the accident which caused the injury to the workman would have occurred, quite apart from the action of the workman, then the fact that there was misconduct upon the part of the workman does not affect his claim to compensation.

Serious and wilful misconduct cannot be used as a defence by an employer to a claim by the dependants of a workman who has died as the result of the accident, nor to a claim by a workman for compensation when he has been permanently disabled by the accident.

Who is an Employer ?—For the purposes of the Workmen's Compensation Act, 1925, which contains the law upon this subject, an employer is any person who has the right to the services of another by reason of a contract, and the expression employer includes any body of persons or a corporation, and where the workman is employed by a club and engaged or paid through the club, the manager or members of the managing committee. (*See* MASTER AND SERVANT.)

If a person is engaged in a vehicle or vessel plying for hire, the use of which is obtained from the owner by a contract of bailment, for example, a taxi-cab, then his employer is the owner of the vehicle or vessel.

Who is a Workman ?—A workman is any person who has entered into a contract of service or apprenticeship with an employer, either to do manual labour or clerical work; the contract may be an express one or implied, and it may be oral or in writing. The following persons are, however, outside the scope of the Compensation Act:—

(a) A person not employed for manual labour who is paid more than £350 per annum.

(b) A person whose employment is casual, and is not employed for purposes connected with the employer's trade or business. This exception does not include persons who are employed for the purposes of a game or for recreation and are engaged or paid through a club, e.g. caddies at a golf club.

(c) A member of a police force.

(d) An outworker: that is, a person to whom articles or materials are given out to be made up, cleaned, altered, or repaired in his own home, or in premises not under the control or management of the person who gives out the material or articles.

(e) A member of the employer's own family living in his house.

How to Make a Claim.—If an injury is caused to a workman by an accident during his employment then *notice* of the accident must be given to his employer as soon as possible after the accident. The notice may be either a verbal one or a written one, and may be given to the employer or to any foreman or official under whose supervision the workman worked, or to a person whom the employer appoints for the purpose. The notice must give the name and address of the person injured, the cause of the injury and the date on which the accident happened, e.g.:—

To the A Colliery Company (Employer) 70, Smith Street, —town.

Please take notice that on the 20th day of October, 193–, John Jones, of 104, Blank Road, Blank town, who was a workman in your employment, was personally injured by a fall of coal.

Yours truly,
MARTHA JONES (Signature).

21st day of October, 193–.

The fact that notice was not given, or that the notice given was inaccurate, will not be a bar to the workman's right to claim compensation if it is proved that the employer knew of the accident from some other source, or had either himself, or by some person on his behalf, reported the accident to an Inspector of Factories, or if the accident had been entered in a register kept at a mine, quarry, factory or workshop. Even if the employer was unaware of the accident from any of these sources, the fact that no notice has been given will not affect the workman's rights unless the employer can shew that he has been prejudiced in defending the claim by reason of the lack of notice.

When notice has been given, the employer

will usually, in a clear case where he does not dispute his liability, commence the payment of compensation, either upon a scale agreed between himself and the injured workman or, in default of an agreement, in accordance with the award of an arbitrator appointed for the purpose of deciding the question.

If, however, the workman receives no compensation, then he must make his claim within six months from the date of the accident or, if death results, then his dependents must claim within six months from the date of his death. If, however, the failure to make a claim within the time was due to a mistake or other reasonable cause, the rights of the workman, or his dependants, will not be barred. As a general rule, the employer and the workman can agree between themselves as to the amount that should be payable, but if they are unable to come to an agreement, the Act provides legal machinery for the settlement of their dispute. The method provided is that of arbitration by:—

(1) A representative committee of the employers and workmen which in some cases is appointed as a standing committee for such work; or

(2) A single arbitrator to be agreed upon between the parties; or

(3) The County Court Judge or an arbitrator appointed by him. Where a question has been decided by an arbitrator in accordance with the provisions of the act, a memorandum of his decision must be sent to the registrar of the County Court. The registrar then records it in a special register, and the memorandum then becomes enforceable as a County Court judgment.

To Whom is the Compensation Payable?—Compensation is payable to the injured workman himself when the injury incapacitates him. If he is killed, or dies as the result of the accident, then the compensation is payable to his dependants. The dependants who are entitled to claim compensation are such of the members of the workman's family who were altogether or partially dependent upon his earnings at the time of his death. The members of the family include the father, mother, grandfather, grandmother, step-father, step-mother, son, daughter, step-son, step-daughter, grandson, grand-daughter, brother, half-brother, sister, and half-sister. An illegitimate child is included among the dependants, and the parent or grandparent of an illegitimate child may be dependent upon him.

An applicant for compensation in respect of the death of a workman, because of his partial dependency upon the earnings of the deceased, must shew that he was dependent for the ordinary necessaries of life, and not only that he has lost some pecuniary benefit.

Amount of Compensation. — The amounts which are payable by way of compensation for an injury to a workman are calculated in accordance with the rules which are laid down in the Compensation Act of 1925. The method of calculation and the amount payable vary according to whether the workman died, or was totally or partially disabled by the accident.

Death.—When death results from the injury the compensation is paid to the dependants in a lump sum which is calculated in accordance with the following rules:—

(1) If there are dependants who were wholly dependent upon the earnings of the dead workman, then the lump sum is to be an amount equal to the total earnings of the workman in his particular employment during the three years immediately preceding the injury, or the sum of £200 if that is a larger sum. The total amount payable must not, however, exceed £300.

(2) If the workman has been employed for less than three years by the same employer, then the sum is to be arrived at by multiplying his average weekly earnings during the period of his actual employment by a hundred and fifty-six.

(3) If any weekly payments were made to the workman before his death, then the amount of such payments must be deducted, but not to the extent of making the lump sum less than £200.

(4) If the workman leaves no dependants wholly dependent upon his earnings, but leaves some partly dependent upon him, then the lump sum payable is to be agreed between the employer and the dependants. The

sum thus agreed must not be larger than the amount which would have been payable if there had been dependants wholly dependent upon the workman. If the parties cannot agree upon the amount, then it is to be settled by arbitration (*see above*).

(5) If the workman leaves no dependants of any kind, then the lump sum is to be an amount equal to the expenses of the medical attendance and burial, but not exceeding £15.

The Children's Allowance.—If a workman leaves a widow or another member of his family over fifteen years of age, wholly or partially dependent upon his earnings, and in addition leaves one or more children under the age of fifteen so dependent, then an extra sum is payable which is called the children's allowance. This allowance is calculated as follows:—

(1) If the widow or other member of the family, and the child or children were wholly dependent upon the workman's earnings, then the children's allowance shall be in respect of each child under fifteen years, fifteen per cent. of the workman's average weekly earnings multiplied by the number of weeks which will elapse from the day of his death until each child reaches its fifteenth birthday. If the average earnings were less than one pound or more than two pounds per week, then the wages are taken to be one pound and two pounds respectively. The children's allowance and the lump sum must not exceed six hundred pounds when added together.

(2) If the widow or other member of the family, and the child or children were partially dependent upon the workman's earnings then the allowance is to be an agreed proportion of the sum payable under the foregoing rule. If the sum cannot be agreed, then it must be determined by arbitration.

(3) No deduction is to be made from the children's allowance in respect of weekly payments made before the workman's death unless those payments have been redeemed by payment of a lump sum.

The dependants claiming compensation

must prove that the workman died from injuries received in the accident, but it is not necessary that it should be proved that the death was the natural consequence of the injury. For example, a man died under an anæsthetic which was administered to perform an operation necessitated by his injury. Death was held to have resulted from the injuries received in the accident.

Compensation for Disablement.— Compensation for total or partial disablement resulting from an accident is payable weekly during the incapacity and is calculated as follows:—

Total Incapacity.—The weekly payment shall be a sum not exceeding fifty per cent. of the workman's average weekly earnings during the twelve months previous to the accident, or if he has not been so long employed by the same employer, then the average for the period during which he has been in that employment. If the maximum amount payable under the above method of calculation is less than twenty-five shillings, then the workman is entitled to an addition which shall be one-half of the difference between the maximum sum thus payable and twenty-five shillings, or his average weekly earnings, whichever is the less. An example will make this clear: Suppose the workman earned on an average thirty-eight shillings per week, then he would be entitled to nineteen shillings, the maximum under the fifty per cent. basis, plus one half of six shillings, i.e. three shillings, making a total of twenty-two shillings altogether. Suppose his earnings were twenty-two shillings per week, then he would receive eleven shillings plus half of eleven shillings, i.e. five shillings and sixpence, making a total of sixteen shillings and sixpence. The five shillings and sixpence in this instance is half the difference between the maximum payable under the fifty per cent. basis, i.e. eleven shillings, and his average weekly earnings, twenty-two shillings.

Partial Incapacity.—This calculation is at first sight very complicated, but it can be made clearer by examples. The payment for partial incapacity is calculated by reference to the amount that would have been payable if the capacity had been complete, and the amount which the workman is still able to earn despite his injuries. The payment is made in this way:—

(a) If the maximum sum payable would have been twenty-five shillings or over in the case of total incapacity, then for partial incapacity the amount payable is half the difference between the average weekly earnings before the accident, and the average weekly amount which the workman is earning or is able to earn in some suitable employment after the accident. Example:—

	£	s.	d.
Average weekly earnings before accident	3	0	0
Average weekly earnings since accident	1	10	0
Compensation payable.		15	0

(b) If the maximum sum payable for total incapacity would have been less than twenty-five shillings, then the weekly payment is to be a sum bearing the same proportion to the difference between his present earnings and his earnings before the accident, as the maximum sum payable upon total incapacity bears to his average weekly earnings before the accident. Example:—

Average pre-accident weekly earnings....	46/-
Average present weekly earnings	26/-
Difference between these payments.....	20/-
Maximum weekly payment in event of total incapacity..........	24/-

The Compensation C
is, C : 20 :: 24 : 46,
i.e. 46C— 480/-
C— 10/5.2

In no case may the weekly payment exceed thirty shillings.

It is important to note that, where a workman has recovered sufficiently from an injury as to be fit for employment of a certain kind, or has taken all reasonable steps to obtain and has failed to obtain such work, then if he proves to the satisfaction of the County Court Judge that he cannot obtain such work because of his injury and has made every effort to obtain it, the County Court Judge shall order that in such a case his incapacity shall be regarded as total.

What are Average Weekly Earnings.—Where the injured workman has been working for some time under the same employer and in the same grade of employment, then there is little difficulty in computing what his average weekly earnings were. Complications arise when the workman has only been employed with the particular employer for a very short time, and when this is the case, his average weekly earnings are regarded as being the same as another workman in the same grade and in the same employment, who has been in that employment sufficiently long to enable an average to be calculated. If there is no workman in the same employment with whose earnings a comparison can be made, then the arbitrator deciding the question may refer to the earnings of workmen employed in the same type of employment in the district.

If a workman is employed and receives wages from two different employers under separate contracts with them, the earnings from both sources must be included when a calculation is made of his average weekly earnings. There must be a contract of service with each employer, and any earnings of the workman coming from casual employment during his spare time are not to be included for the purposes of calculation. When compensation is fixed upon the basis of a workman's average weekly earnings, he is entitled to request his employer to give him a list of the payments which have been included when the calculation was made.

There are several points which are of importance when considering whether a workman is still entitled to compensation which was being paid to him. Thus a workman whose continued incapacity was due to his neglect to comply with certain medical directions which were given him was deprived of compensation.

Similarly, a workman who refused an offer by his employer of suitable light work had his compensation reduced to the amount he would have received if he had accepted the light work and the earnings attached to it. A workman is justified in refusing an offer of light work if he honestly believes that it will not be suitable in view of his state of health, and if he is supported in his belief by his own medical practitioner. Suitability of employment for an injured or partially incapacitated workman is always a question of fact which has to be decided by the arbitrator in case of a dispute.

A Declaration of Liability.—This is a very useful safeguard for the future to a workman who has received an injury during his employment, but has either suffered no pecuniary loss at the time because his employer is still paying him full wages, or the injury has not at present incapacitated him. The principle of granting a declaration is that the workman may have received an injury of such a nature that it may develop in the future and lessen his earning capacity. The workman may apply for the declaration himself by asking his employers to submit to a declaration of liability, or the declaration may be awarded when he claims compensation, or when an application is made to review the weekly payments which were being made to him. The declaration sets out that the workman has received an injury in an accident arising out of, and in the course of his employment, that there is no present incapacity or loss of earnings, but that there is a reasonable probability that incapacity lessening his powers of earning will develop in the future. When the declaration is signed by the employer it should be filed in the local County Court for future reference.

Redemption of Weekly Payments by a Lump Sum.—If an employer has been making weekly payments to an injured workman for not less than six months he may apply to redeem the liability to make such payments by the payment to the workman of a lump sum.

If the incapacity of the workman is permanent then the lump sum must be such an amount as would, if invested in the purchase of an annuity from the National Debt Commissioners, bring in an annual amount to the workman equal to seventy-five per cent. of the amount he would receive in a year from weekly payments. Incapacity is considered to be permanent if it is reasonably probable that the amount of the weekly payments will never vary. This provision with regard to the amount of the lump sum does not apply when the injured workman is under twenty-one at the time of the application for redemption. In the case of non-permanent incapacity, the lump sum may be any amount which is settled by arbitration. Where a lump sum is paid to redeem payments payable to an infant, it must be paid into Court, but the workman upon attaining twenty-one years of age has an absolute right to have it paid out to him. When the arbitrator is deciding what amount should be paid to an infant to redeem weekly payments, he must take into account the special right that an infant has of demanding a review of the weekly payments on the basis of his probable earnings when he attains twenty-one. This is more fully explained below.

If the redemption of weekly payments is effected by an agreement between the workman and the employer, then such agreement must be registered at the County Court, otherwise the employer does not escape his liability to make weekly payments. If the redemption is effected by the award of an arbitrator, then such award is recorded at the County Court. The agreement and award are recorded on special forms which may be obtained at the office in any County Court.

Review of Weekly Payments.— Weekly payments may be reviewed at the request of either the employer or the workman, and may on such review, be stopped, lessened or increased. The review may be made by agreement between the parties concerned, or if they cannot agree, then it is done by an arbitrator.

If the injured workman was under the age of twenty-one when the accident happened, and a review is made more than six months after the accident, then if application to review is made before or within six months after the workman's twenty-first birthday, the weekly payment may be increased to the amount which would have been payable had the workman been earning the wages which he would, in all probability, have been earning but for his injury.

If a review takes place more than six months after the accident, or it is proved that the average earnings of the workman, had he remained in his employment, would have been greater or less by twenty per cent. than his actual pre-accident earnings, then the weekly payment may be varied in accordance with such increase or decrease.

Before any application for a review can be heard, there must have been a change in the circumstances of the case since the payments were awarded or agreed upon.

Stoppage of Payments.— An employer may, however, stop or lessen the weekly payments without any agreement or finding by an arbitrator in the following cases:—

(1) Where a workman who has been receiving a weekly payment in respect of total incapacity has actually returned to work.

(2) Where the weekly earnings of a partially incapacitated workman who has been receiving compensation have actually increased.

(3) Where the employer has sent to the workman a copy of the certificate of the medical practitioner who has examined him and certified him to have wholly or partly recovered, together with a notice of the employer's intention at the end of ten days from the sending of the notice to end or diminish the weekly payment by an amount stated. If the workman makes no objection to the notice, or if he does not send to the employer a medical certificate stating the contrary view, then the payment may be ended or diminished at the end of the ten days period. If, however, the workman before the end of the ten days sends the employer a report of a medical practitioner disagreeing with the opinion expressed in the employer's certificate, then the weekly payment must not be diminished except in so far as such diminishing would be in accordance with the report of the workman's doctor, or with the report of the medical referee who decides the dispute. The employer may, after making the application for a settlement of the dispute by a medical referee, pay into Court the amount of each weekly payment if his application is to have the weekly payment stopped; or where his application is to have the weekly payment decreased, he may pay into Court so much of the money as is in dispute. The sums thus paid into Court are paid over to the employer or the workman in accordance with the finding of the medical referee.

The Medical Examination.— Where a workman has given notice of an accident to his employer, and his employer requires him to submit to a medical examination by a qualified doctor provided and paid for by the employer, the workman must submit himself, and if he refuses to do so, then his right to compensation is suspended until such examination has taken place. Similarly a workman who is receiving weekly payments may be required by his employer periodically to submit to a medical examination, and if he refuses to do so his right to such weekly payment is suspended until he complies. If a workman has been examined by a medical practitioner on behalf of the employer and by his own medical man, and the parties cannot come to an agreement as to the condition of the workman, then the registrar of the County Court may, on the application of both parties, refer the matter to a medical referee.

Bankruptcy of Employer.—If an employer is insured in respect of any liability he may incur to pay compensation to his workmen, and he becomes bankrupt or makes a composition with his creditors, then an injured workman steps into the shoes of his employer, and he has all the rights of his employer against the insurers.

The insurers thereupon have all the rights of; and are subject to the same liabilities as the employer, save that they are not liable to the workman to any greater extent than the employer would have been.

If the amount which the insurers are liable to pay is less than the amount which the workman could claim from his employer, then the workman can prove in the bankruptcy of the employer as an ordinary creditor for the balance. The position is the same if the employer is a company and is wound up or has a receiver appointed; the workman can recover any balance not covered by the insurance from the liquidator or the receiver.

Repayment of Poor Relief.—If a local authority has granted out-door relief to a workman while he is waiting for a settlement of his claim to compensation, and if such relief would not have been granted supposing compensation had been paid, or if more relief has been given than would have been granted had compensation been paid, then the local authority may give notice of such relief payments to the person liable to pay compensation. When the person liable to pay compensation receives

such a notice, he must repay to the local authority the amount expended in relief, but not in excess of the amount he would have had to pay as compensation to the workman.

Contracting-Out of the Workmen's Compensation Act, 1925, is not permitted except by way of a Certified Scheme. (*See* CERTIFIED SCHEME; INDUSTRIAL DISEASE; INSURANCE; NEGLIGENCE.)

WORKMEN'S COMPENSATION (BANKRUPTCY AND WINDING-UP).

—Persons to whom payments are due for injuries received during their work under the Workmen's Compensation Act are entitled to be treated as preferred creditors, i.e. to be paid before the other creditors—when the employer from whom the money is due becomes bankrupt or, if the employer is a limited company, is wound up. The preference extends to all amounts which are due to the workmen as compensation.

When the employer has not carried the risk of these injuries himself, but has taken out an insurance policy covering them with some insurance company, the workman's position is different. He is not entitled to claim at all against the employer, but must claim directly against the insurance company for the amount due to him.

Where the amount which is due is payable in weekly payments, the total amount payable in bankruptcy or in the winding-up will be calculated according to the rules for redemption of these weekly payments under the Workmen's Compensation Acts. (*See* BANKRUPTCY; PREFERRED CREDITORS; THIRD PARTY INSURANCE; WINDING-UP; WORKMEN'S COMPENSATION.)

WORKHOUSE.—Every county and county borough council is under a duty to provide an institution for the reception of poor persons who are not granted out-door relief, but are adjudged to be entitled to poor relief. These institutions have received the name of workhouses probably because an inmate, whose state of health permits him to do so, is required to perform some task in return for his food and lodging.

Each council appoints a person as master of the workhouse, and he has servants and other officers under his control. Every institution is governed by a management committee and that committee has control over the master and other officers. Each council also appoints a visiting, or house committee which has to undertake the visitation and inspection of the institution. Two or more members of the house committee must inspect the institution and its stores at least once a fortnight, and some of their visits during the year must be surprise ones. During their visit the members of the committee are required to hear any complaints of the inmates and to interview any inmates who have been admitted since their last visit.

The house committee reports to the management committee the results of each inspection, and every half year they must present to the management committee a full report concerning the management of the institution, the state of the buildings and the conduct of the officers with any recommendations which they see fit to make.

Admission to a Workhouse. — A person can only be admitted to a workhouse in one of the following ways:—

(a) By an order of the council signed by the clerk and dated at least six days before the day of admission.

(b) By an order signed by the relieving officer and dated at least six days before the day of admission.

(c) By the master of the workhouse:

　(i) Without an order in case of urgent necessity;

　(ii) when he is duly transferred from another establishment;

　(iii) when he is brought to the workhouse under an order of removal from another county.

If the master refuses to admit any person to the workhouse he must send a written report containing his reasons to the house committee which they must consider at their next meeting.

The Minister of Health makes a code of regulations with regard to workhouses covering the conduct of inmates, the diet to be administered, the tasks to be performed and the punishments for offences against the rules. A county council may prescribe the tasks to be performed by the inmates within the limits of the rules laid down by the Minister.

When a person is admitted to a workhouse he must be bathed, cleansed and suitably clothed either in his own, or fresh clothes. As soon as possible after his admission he must be medically examined and a report written by the medical officer. Every person admitted is given a task to be performed in accordance with his capacity, but he must not be given a task to do which in the opinion of the medical officer is dangerous to his health.

Discharge from the Workhouse. — An inmate of a workhouse may discharge himself from it at any time provided he gives reasonable notice to the master of his intention to do so, and that the medical officer does not object on the grounds of the inmate's health. If the head of a family all of whom are inmates of a workhouse discharges himself, then all the members of the family are automatically discharged, unless one of them is sick and is detained by the advice of the medical officer. Temporary leave of absence may be allowed to an inmate by the master.

A child, other than infant, must not be detained longer than six weeks in an institution unless he is in a sick ward, or unless the medical officer has certified that it would be for the good of his health that he should be retained. When a child is discharged from a workhouse he is usually boarded out by the council, or if he is of sufficient age he may be apprenticed to a trade.

A workhouse is divided up into classes in accordance with the age and sex of the inmates, and no one is allowed to go into any quarter other than his own without permission. If, however, a husband and wife are admitted to a workhouse and both are over the age of sixty, they are allowed to live together. Similarly, if a husband and wife are admitted and one of them is infirm or sick or over sixty years, the council may permit them to live together.

Offences and Punishments. — An inmate of a workhouse commits an offence if he:—

(a) Makes any noise when silence is ordered to be kept;

(b) uses any obscene or profane language;

(c) insults any person by words or action;

(d) threatens to assault any one;

(e) fails to cleanse himself;

(f) refuses, or neglects to perform the task which he has been required to do;

(g) pretends to be ill;

(h) misbehaves when on his way to or from a place of public worship outside the workhouse;

(i) returns after the appointed time when he has been granted temporary leave of absence;

(j) wilfully disobeys any order.

If he commits any of these offences he is regarded as disorderly. If he is regarded as a disorderly person the master may withdraw any privileges to which he was entitled, and may also put him on a ration of bread for a maximum period of forty-eight hours instead of his dinner. If he commits any of these offences twice within a week or does something more serious like insulting a member of the visiting committee, damaging tools or materials, or getting drunk, he is to be regarded as refractory. The management committee may then order that he is to be put in solitary confinement with or without deprivation of his dinner, for a period not exceeding twenty-four hours. In addition to these punishments he may be taken before a justice of the peace and charged with drunkenness or misbehaviour, and if convicted may be sent to prison for a maximum period of fourteen days. If he is convicted of an assault upon a poor law officer while that officer was doing his duty, he may be sent to prison for a maximum period of two years.

A child may be placed in solitary confinement, but not during the hours of darkness, and he may also receive corporal punishment, if not an infant, but under the age of fourteen. The punishment must be inflicted by the master himself or by someone specially appointed by him, and there must be at least two officers present including the master. Corporal punishment must not be inflicted until two hours have elapsed since the commission of the offence. No adult person may be subjected to corporal punishment, and if the master orders or himself administers such punishment to an adult, he is liable upon conviction to a fine of £20. (*See* CASUAL WARD; LOCAL GOVERNMENT; POOR LAW.)

WORKSHOP means any of the following premises or places, namely:—hat works, rope works, bakehouses, lace warehouses, shipbuilding yards, quarries, pit banks, dry cleaning works, carpet beating works, bottle washing works and laundries, where no mechanical power is used to assist the process of manufacture. The essence of a workshop as compared with a factory is the absence of mechanical power, but this is not a hard and fast distinction since there are certain premises which are classed as non-texile factories even if they have no mechanical power to assist in the process of manufacture. These premises are print works, bleaching and dyeing works, earthenware works, lucifer match works, percussion-cap works, cartridge works, paper-staining works, fustian-cutting works, blast furnaces, copper mills, iron mills, foundries, metal and india-rubber works, paper mills, glass works, tobacco factories, letterpress printing works, book-binding works, flax scutch mills and electrical stations.

Any premises in which manual labour is exercised in the way of making, altering, repairing, ornamenting, finishing or adapting for sale any article, are workshops.

The legal provisions relating to workshops are all contained in the Factory and Workshops Act, 1901, and the succeeding acts which have added to the provisions of that act. (*See* FACTORY.)

WOUNDING.—There are various kinds of wounding constituting criminal offences. The most serious of these is wounding with intent to murder. This is a felony punishable with penal servitude for life. A slightly less serious offence is wounding with intent to maim, disfigure or disable, or with intent to resist lawful apprehension. This, also, is punishable with penal servitude for life. Another wounding offence is described as unlawful wounding.

In order to convict a person for any wounding offence it must be shewn that he actually, by means of stabbing or cutting, caused an incised wound, as distinct from a mere bruise or laceration. The skin must be actually broken. It is, however, sufficient if the internal skin is cut; for instance, a blow with the fist causing the teeth to cut the inside of the cheek or lip would constitute a wounding in law.

WRIT OF SUMMONS.—A writ of summons is the method by which nearly every action in the High Court of Justice is commenced. An intending plaintiff may obtain such a writ by applying at the Central

Office at the Royal Courts of Justice, Strand, London, or at a District Registry. It is addressed upon the face of it to the defendant, and calls upon him to enter an appearance at the Court in order to give his reasons why the plaintiff should not obtain the relief demanded. Upon the back of a writ, in the case of an ordinary writ, is a statement of the nature of the remedy which the plaintiff is seeking from the defendant, e.g. "The plaintiff's claim is for damages for breach of contract."

The writ must be served upon the defendant personally, which is done by handing it to the defendant, or if the defendant is a company, by leaving it at the registered office, though in most cases the defendant's solicitor agrees to accept service of the writ by post on his behalf. If personal service or service through a solicitor is not practicable, substituted service may be granted by permission of the Court. (*See* SUBSTITUTED SERVICE.)

If the defendant does not within ten days of the service of the writ enter an appearance by filing an appearance at the central office or District Registry, the plaintiff is entitled to sign judgment against the defendant by default, in which case, if the claim is for a definite ascertained sum of money, he may proceed to enforce his judgment immediately, or if the claim is for general damages or for a sum of money not yet ascertained, the plaintiff obtains an Interlocutory Judgment, and the case then goes to a Sheriff's Court (q.v.) for the amount of the damages to be ascertained. In such a case the defendant is permitted to be heard at the Sheriff's Court, and to argue as to the amount of the damages, though he is not allowed to deny the fact of his liability to pay some damages.

If the defendant enters an appearance to the Writ of Summons, it is the duty of the plaintiff to take out a summons for directions, and the action proceeds through its ordinary stages to trial and judgment.

Specially Endorsed Writs. —Wherever the plaintiff's claim is of a simple nature and does not involve an allegation of fraud, or libel or slander, seduction, etc., the plaintiff is entitled to issue a specially endorsed writ. In such a case, the Statement of Claim is endorsed upon the back of the writ in exactly the same manner as if it were a Statement of Claim delivered in an ordinary action. Such a writ is served in the same manner as an ordinary writ, and the defendant must enter an appearance in the ordinary manner, or judgment will be given against him in default.

When the defendant has appeared, however, it is open to the plaintiff to take out a summons for judgment, for which purpose he must make an affidavit verifying his cause of action, and stating that he believes that there is no true defence to the action. If he does this, the defendant at the hearing of the summons or before, must make and file an affidavit in which he sets out on oath the grounds for his defence and asks for leave to defend the action.

The summons is heard before a Master, and if the Master comes to the conclusion that there is not in fact any real defence to the action he may give the plaintiff leave to sign the judgment forthwith. If, on the other hand, he comes to the conclusion that there is some ground upon which the action might be defended, then, although he may not think that the defendant's prospects of success are high, he will give leave to defend and will make such orders as to pleadings and other interlocutory matters as he might have made upon a summons for directions (q.v.).

The advantage of specially endorsing a writ, is that it enables a plaintiff to prevent delay in recovering his rights where the defendant has no real defence. Therefore, if the plaintiff in fact knows that the defendant has a good ground of defence, and that there is a real dispute between the parties, he gains no benefit by taking out a summons of the nature referred to above, but may proceed in the ordinary way to take out a summons for directions as if the writ has been endorsed in the ordinary way. (*See* HIGH COURT PROCEDURE; SUBSTITUTED SERVICE.)

WRIT OR OATH (SCOTS LAW). —In certain cases, facts in Scots law can only be proved by writ or oath, and not by the verbal evidence of witnesses. Proof by writ or oath requires that the person bringing the action should either produce some document in which the person he is suing admits the claim, either expressly or by inference, or admits the fact desired to be proved, or by referring to the oath of the person he is suing. That person is compelled to answer on oath all questions he may be asked which are directed to establish the truth of the fact desired to be proved. (*See* CONTRACT [SCOTS LAW]; WRITTEN CONTRACTS [SCOTS LAW].)

WRITER TO THE SIGNET (SCOTS LAW).—In Scotland there is a society known as the Society of Writers to the Signet. Together with numerous other societies they carry out the duties of solicitors in Scotland. All members of the society are "law agents" and as such are now also solicitors. A person does not need to be a Writer to the Signet in order to be a solicitor or law agent.

WRITTEN CONTRACTS.— There are a large number of contracts which are not enforceable in English law unless they are made in writing and signed by the person whom it is wished to render liable upon the contract.

The chief of these are:—
(1) Bills of Exchange (q.v.).
(2) Assignment of Shares. (*See* SHARES.)
(3) Marine Insurance Contracts. (*See* MARINE INSURANCE.)
(4) Promises by executors to pay damages out of their own pockets. (*See* EXECUTORS.)
(5) Contracts of Guarantee. (*See* GUARANTEE.)
(6) Agreements made in consideration of marriage. (*See* HUSBAND AND WIFE.)
(7) Contracts for the sale of land or interests in land. (*See* LAND.)
(8) Contracts for the sale of goods of a value greater than £10, except in certain circumstances. (*See* SALE OF GOODS.)
(9) Contracts not to be performed within a year. This class does not include contracts which may possibly be completely performed by both parties within a year, even though it is unlikely that they will be performed in that time. Thus a contract by A to pay B £100 a year during his lifetime does not come within this category, since B may die before the year is finished, and accordingly the contract may be performed within a year. It does include, however, a contract by A to employ B for one year, starting from the day after the contract is made, since that contract cannot be

fully performed until one year and one day after the contract has been made. Persons entering into yearly employment starting at any time after the contract of employment is made, should therefore be careful to see that the contract is made in writing. (*See* PERIOD CONTRACTS.)

The rules which deal with numbers (4) to (8) of these contracts do not require that the actual contract should have been made in writing. It is merely a rule which demands that before an attempt is made by one of the parties to the contract to enforce it against the other in a Court of Law, he shall be in a position to produce a written document signed by the other party or someone authorized by the other party which contains all the terms of the agreement.

Thus there may be a perfectly valid agreement between the two parties which is not in writing, but because one of the parties has not signed some document in which the terms of the contract are contained, the other party cannot enforce the obligations created by it in a Court of Law.

The requirement of a written document does not mean that there must be something in the nature of a formal agreement. The agreement may have been made in a number of letters passing between the parties, and in such a case if the letters clearly refer to each other, the contract is contained in all of them, and all of the letters together constitute the written record of the contract that is required.

Again, the written record of the terms of the contract need not be made at the time of the agreement at all. It is sufficient that a written record has been made at some time before the date on which one of the parties wishes to enforce the contract in a Court. Thus A and B may come to a verbal agreement that A shall guarantee C's debt to B, and some months afterwards A may sign a letter in which he sets out the terms of the agreement. That letter will be a sufficient written record of the agreement for the purposes of permitting B to sue upon the contract in Court.

A further example will show the limits to which this rule applies. A enters into a verbal agreement with B to guarantee C's debt to B. Nothing is placed in writing at the time and some months afterwards A wishes to release himself from his obligation and writes to B a letter in which he says, "You may remember that some time ago I promised to guarantee C's debt to you up to £100, if you refrained from suing him. I have now decided that I can no longer undertake this, and I hereby give you notice that I consider my obligation at an end." This letter, if signed by A, is sufficient written record of the contract to enable B to sue on the contract, even though the terms are contained in a letter in which A is repudiating liability under the contract.

But the written document to be used for this purpose must fulfil certain conditions. In the first place it must be signed by the person whom it is sought to make liable, or by someone authorized by him to enter into the contract. Thus, if A and B enter into a verbal agreement which comes within this rule, and B, either at the time or later, writes down the terms of the contract and signs it himself while A does not sign it, A can enforce the contract against B, but B cannot enforce it against A.

Again, the document must contain all the terms of the contract, that is to say, the parties to the contract must be named, the subject matter of the contract must be identified, and the consideration stated. Where the contract, as is so often the case, is contained in a number of letters, where one letter refers to another, then that other letter may also be considered as part of the written document, and it oftens happens that where a letter containing the contract is addressed merely to "Dear Sir," then the envelope in which the letter was contained is part of the written record of the contract for the purpose of identifying the party to whom it was addressed, and thus fulfilling the condition that the names of both parties to the contract must appear in the written record before one of the parties may enforce it in a court of law.

Part Performance.—The operation of the rule that requires written records of certain contracts in order to make them enforceable, would often cause great injustice if it were not for a legal doctrine known as the doctrine of part performance. In certain cases where one of the parties to a verbal contract which ought to be recorded in writing has done certain things in pursuance of the contract, and has been permitted to do so by the other party, relying upon the contract being valid, the Court will enforce it despite the fact that there does not exist a record in writing of the transaction.

Before the Court will do this, however, there are certain conditions which must be fulfilled. In the first place the things done must have been quite clearly done in reliance on the contract; in the second place they must be things of such a kind as to render it highly unjust that the other party should be able to escape his liability because of the absence of writing; and in the third place they must be acts done in pursuance of a contract the Court could have enforced.

All these contracts are dealt with in detail under their respective headings. *See* BILL OF EXCHANGE; CONTRACT; EXECUTORS; GUARANTEE; HUSBAND AND WIFE; LAND; MARINE INSURANCE; PERIOD CONTRACTS; SALE OF GOODS.)

WRITTEN CONTRACTS (SCOTS LAW).—In Scots law certain contracts must be entered into in writing and certain other contracts, although they do not require to be entered into in writing, can only be enforced if the person seeking to enforce them can produce some written document in which the person he is suing admits the obligation, or if he induces that person to admit the obligation on oath.

Contracts made in Writing.—Where contracts are required to be made in writing, the writing must be either probative or holograph. A probative writing is one executed with certain formalities signed on each page by the person granting it and witnessed by two witnesses. A holograph contract is one written entirely in the hand of the person who is being sued. Contracts which must be constituted in writing in this way are all contracts relating to land with the exception of leases for not more than a year, contracts which the parties have agreed to put in writing, contracts of service for more than a year and guarantees.

Contracts requiring Written Proof.—Contracts which, although they need not be entered into in writing must yet be proved by some written document which may have been drawn up after the time of the contract or by the oath of the person sued, are loans over £8 6s. 8d., and all gratuitous promises. (*See* CONTRACT [SCOTS LAW]; WRIT OR OATH [SCOTS LAW].)

WRONGFUL DISMISSAL.

WRONGFUL DISMISSAL.—When a servant has been engaged for a definite length of time and there is no provision or custom enabling the agreement to be ended by notice, the servant cannot be dismissed before the end of the period. When, on the other hand, there is such a provision or custom about notice, it must be observed. In all other cases reasonable notice must be given to a servant. If a master discharges a servant summarily without observing whichever of these three rules applies to the particular contract of employment, he commits a breach of that contract, for which he can be sued by his servant, provided, of course, that instant dismissal is not justified by the servant's misconduct, wilful disobedience, incompetence, or permanent disability, or by some other good and legal reason.

Remedies.—When a servant is thus wrongfully dismissed he has alternative courses open to him: He may either sue the master for breach of contract in an action for wrongful dismissal, or he may sue to recover the wages for the period during which he has served right up to the day of dismissal. In the latter action the amount which is sued for can be easily ascertained by a simple piece of arithmetic, but no more than the sum so arrived at can be recovered, whereas in an action for wrongful dismissal other damage to the servant can be taken into account when assessing the sum which he shall be paid. The servant must choose one remedy or the other, he cannot have both.

There are also those cases in which wages can, by agreement, be given to the servant in lieu of notice. Here, instant dismissal is not wrongful, and consequently the servant's remedy is to sue for the wages which should have been given in lieu of notice. Such wages are a debt due from the master from the time of dismissal.

Although in many cases an order called an injunction can be obtained from the Court to prevent a breach of contract, such an order will never be given to prevent a wrongful dismissal.

Damages Recoverable.—In an action for wrongful dismissal, not only wages up to the time of discharge can be recovered if they are unpaid, but also a further sum to indemnify the servant for any loss he suffers by reason of his master's breach of contract. The question to be decided is, "What damage has the servant suffered?" Occasionally there is no damage, for example, where the servant at once secures equally good or even better employment elsewhere; and it is the duty of the servant upon dismissal, as in every other kind of breach of contract, to minimise the damage, that is, to endeavour to the best of his ability to secure employment. He need not, however, accept employment of a different kind, or in a lower position than that which he has lost, and it should be noted that the amount of his wages is immaterial in deciding whether employment is, or is not, similar.

Where no new employment could reasonably have been obtained, the damages for a wrongful dismissal are assessed by considering the chances of finding another situation, and thus calculating the time which will probably elapse before the servant is earning wages once again. In addition, any other benefits to which the servant would be entitled in his old employment, such as tips are taken into account together with the amount of his fare home; but no compensation is ever recoverable for injured feelings or for supposed damage to reputation caused by the dismissal. (*See* MASTER AND SERVANT; WRITTEN CONTRACTS.)

YEAR AND A DAY.

YEAR AND A DAY.—For many purposes in old legal rules, acts are required to take place within "a year and a day" of certain other acts. The exact reason for this is somewhat obscure, but it is probably due to the desire that there should be no doubt that a full year had elapsed. The period is still of importance in some cases as for example in the rule that before any person can be charged with murder the person he is accused of killing must have died within a year and a day of the time when the blow was inflicted. Thus, if A assaulted B with a knife on the 1st June in one year and B did not die at once, but died at some time after the 2nd June in the next year, A could not be charged with having caused his death even though responsible.

THE POLICE

by

MAJ.-GEN. SIR WYNDHAM CHILDS, K.C.M.G., K.B.E.

MANY people regard the law as an oppression and an irritation, and to many, indeed, it is because inevitably our laws are the result of conflicting opinion. For example, some people think that teetotalism should be enforced by law. America thought so and eventually realized she had made a mistake. Some people wish to restrict our moral life on puritanical lines and others do not.

Be that as it may, and good or bad as our laws may be, they are the result of the expression of the will of the majority, and if the minority rebel against those laws, the intervention of the police becomes inevitable.

Our police are in fact public servants, charged with the duty of maintaining for the public, liberty, protection and the enforcement of that social code which is commonly called the "law."

It is not possible to present an adequate survey of the Police without first tracing the history which has led up to the establishment of the police forces of this country.

History.—As long ago as the reign of Edward I, attempts were made to introduce an organization to deal with crime and to protect the subject. Two hundred years later the City and Borough of Westminster attempted an improvement, but about the year 1800 the condition of London and, indeed, the whole of England was such that highway robbery, murder, burglary and every kind of violent crime made it vital for the individual citizen to protect himself and his belongings.

The preservation of peace then rested upon local endeavour. Parishes, townships, etc. were responsible for electing every year a "constable" (he had other titles such as "tithingman," "borsholder," etc.). The office was not a paid one and could not be avoided and in the event of the failure of a parish to provide a constable, Justices of the Peace could do so themselves.

It is here convenient to refer to the ancient office of "High Sheriff" which is still maintained to this day. The office is one of very great antiquity and it is interesting to recall that in the year 1170 there was an "inquest of Sheriffs" to inquire into the activities of certain sheriffs who had abused their powers.

He was, in fact, the King's Deputy, charged with the duty of executing the King's writs and armed with the power of calling out the Posse Comitatus—a body of armed citizens. Originally the appointment would appear to have been by popular election, but nowadays his election is governed by an ancient ceremony known as the "Pricking of the Sheriffs." This takes place annually on the "Morrow of St. Martin" (12th November). Three names are submitted to His Majesty by the Chancellor of the Exchequer and the Judges of the King's Bench Division, and from those three names the King makes his selection by pricking a hole with a bodkin opposite the name on the parchment sheet which he has selected.

The qualifications for the office are the possession of a "sufficiency of land," and the office is obligatory and practically cannot be avoided. In the old days a sheriff was an official armed with the most extensive powers and charged with the most important duties, but to-day those powers and duties have been somewhat reduced. He still remains responsible for the execution of writs, for the carrying out of executions and for the attendance on the Judges at Assizes; and in this connection it is amusing to mention that he is required to provide the Judge with a "certain amount of stately ceremony," and can be fined either by that Judge or by the High Court if he has failed in that regard! It is usual for a sheriff to entertain, during the Assizes, the Grand Jury (now defunct), members of the

Sir Robert Peel, Founder of the modern Police Force.

Bar, etc., and the officials of the Court. The office is an annual one, but under certain conditions a sheriff may be required to continue a second year of office.

The Bow Street Runners.—No serious attempts were made to create any police force until about 1828 when the condition of London and the country as a whole had become impossible. The parish constables were impotent and, in London the so-called "Bow Street Runners" were the only people charged with the reponsibility of the arrest of criminals. Known in those days as "Robin Red Breasts" because of the scarlet waistcoats which they wore, they were the servants of the magistrates and, in fact, the ancestors of the present Criminal Investigation Department. It was computed at that time that out of every twenty-two persons in the United Kingdom one was a criminal. In 1829, however, the Metropolitan Police Force was formed by Sir Robert Peel, and in 1835 provincial

forces were established on similar lines.

When it was proposed to introduce this system there was great popular opposition, as the view then largely held was that this was merely a scheme to enslave the people. The Act went through, however, and the Metropolitan Police Force was born.

The Present Organization.—The present organization of our police forces is as follows:—

The Metropolitan Police are administered by the Home Secretary. The Commissioner and the Assistant Commissioners, however, hold office directly under the Crown. Subordinate officers derive their authority from the Commissioner, but it is usual for the Home Secretary to sanction or approve the appointments of Deputy Assistant Commissioners and Chief Constables. The City Police is, however, a separate force and is responsible for an area of about one square mile of the County of London. It is administered by the Lord Mayor, and numbers about 1,100 in strength as opposed to the Metropolitan Police Force which numbers about 20,000 officers and men. In the Provinces the police forces consist of County Police, City Police and Borough Police, administered by Chief Constables who serve in the Counties under the standing joint committees and in the Cities and Boroughs under the Watch committees.

The standing joint committees of the Counties are composed half of representatives of the County Council and half of Justices of the Peace. The Watch committees, on the other hand, are committees of the Town Council elected annually. Nowadays there are sixty County Police forces and 121 separate City and Borough forces.

Finance.—The cost of the maintenance of our police forces is (with the exception of the Metropolitan Police) borne entirely by the ratepayer with the proviso, however, that if a force after inspection by one of H.M. Inspectors of Constabulary is found to be efficient, the State makes a grant of 50% of the cost of maintenance, and it is interesting to recall that on occasions that grant has been withheld.

In so far as the Metropolitan Police is concerned, however, the expenses are met by a rate levied by the Commissioner and by contributions from the Exchequer.

The finances of the Force are administered by an official named the Receiver, who is the treasurer of the Metropolitan Police Fund. All police property of every description is vested in the Receiver who also pays the salaries and wages of the members of the Metropolitan Police Force and the civil staff of New Scotland Yard. The Receiver, with the approval of the Secretary of State, can sell, let or mortgage any property vested in him. The Commissioner, on the other hand, merely administers the bodies of the officers and constables under his control and does not even possess the chair in which he sits, as that belongs to the Receiver! Why the office of Receiver was originally created under the Act of 1829 is not quite clear, but it is interesting to note that at that time he had to give a bond with two securities to His Majesty for the "faithful performance of his duty, and for the due application of all moneys paid to him"—in other words, he had to enter into a sort of Fidelity Bond. Originally (in 1829) there was no Commissioner, but there were two Justices of the Peace who administered the Metropolitan Police Force. It may be shrewdly suspected that in those days the authorities were a little suspicious and set up a system under which the "Justices" did not have the opportunity of handling any money!

It is interesting to recite some of the preamble to the act of 1829 as it shows the condition of London in those days. It ran as follows:—"Whereas offences against property have of late increased . . . and the local establishment of nightly watch and nightly police have been found inadequate to the prevention and detection of crime by reason of the frequent unfitness of the individuals employed, the insufficiency of their number, the limited sphere of their authority and their want of connection and co-operation with each other, and whereas it is expedient to substitute a new and more efficient system . . . and to constitute an office of police which, acting under the immediate authority of one of His Majesty's principal Secretaries of State, shall direct and control the whole of such new system of police . . . be it therefore enacted," etc.

The Metropolitan Police Force remains

A photograph of one of the original "Peelers" enforcing a punishment now out of date—imprisonment in the Stocks.

to-day under the immediate authority of the Home Secretary. With the exception of the office of receiver, provincial police forces are organized on similar lines to those which obtain in the Metropolitan Police, but there is a tendency towards amalgamation of the smaller Borough police forces with the neighbouring more powerful City or County organizations.

I do not think that we shall ever see in this country a national police force such as the French gendarmerie, but I certainly consider it highly probable that there will, in the near future, be very great amalgamations and that Borough and small County police forces will entirely disappear.

The Criminal Investigation Department.—The Metropolitan Police Force organization broadly consists of the Uniform Branch, who perform the duties familiar to the man in the street and are the preventers of crime, as opposed to the Criminal Investigation Department who do not wear uniform and who detect crime. The rest of New Scotland Yard consists of administrative departments such as the Carriage Department which deals inter alia with the licensing of taxi drivers and their cabs, the Lost Property Office, etc.

It is interesting to recall that when the Metropolitan Police Force was first formed there was no Criminal Investigation Department. The "Robin Red Breasts," to whom reference has been made above, disappeared when the police force was formed and it was not until fifteen years after the Act that the then Home Secretary set up the first elements of the present famous Criminal Investigation Department. The department at its birth consisted of three inspectors and nine sergeants. To-day it consists of close on 1,000 officers.

Finger-print Identification.—

One of the milestones in the history of the Criminal Investigation Department was the

Sir Edward Henry who instituted the finger-print identification system.

setting up of the finger-print identification system by the late Sir Edward Henry the then Commissioner of Police. The use of finger-prints as a means of identification has been common for centuries and even to-day natives in some countries give a receipt for their pay by leaving an impression of their thumb on the pay sheet; but Sir Edward Henry introduced a system of classification which enabled rapid identification possible. It is not possible in this short work minutely to explain the method of classification, but it is sufficient to say that finger prints naturally

fall into certain groups or types, and although the collection at New Scotland Yard numbers something over 500,000 prints, identification is a matter of minutes—indeed, so expert are some of the officers that they are able to memorise certain finger prints. It must be remembered, however, that unless the finger prints of an individual have previously been secured and classified, the discovery of prints at (e.g.) the scene of a burglary carry the police no further in their investigations.

In addition the Criminal Record Office at New Scotland Yard contains the dossier of all convicted criminals, and its services are required in producing photographs for primary identification. The Photographic Department of the Criminal Investigation Department also plays a most important part in the detection of crime, as it is usual in all important cases, such as murders, for the most complete set of photographs to be taken before the body is finally disturbed when removed.

The method of the selection of recruits to the Criminal Investigation Department still remains somewhat primitive. There is no direct enlistment but the officers are selected from the uniform branch and undergo a probationary attachment, but have to have served for a certain period in the uniform branch and have been employed in plain clothes (e.g. on winter patrols) before selection. The system is perfectly sound in many ways but, unfortunately, produces a more or less "stock-size" detective owing to the physical standard which is imposed upon all officers of the Metropolitan Police.

The use of women police in the Criminal Investigation Department has never been

Examining finger-prints through a microscope in Scotland Yard.

extensive and needs only passing reference.

The Mounted Police.—There is another department at New Scotland Yard which is well known to the public, and that is the Mounted Police. Many attempts have been made to do away with it, fortunately without success, as they are of the very greatest value in dealing with disorder and also with vast crowds of law-abiding citizens, and it will be remembered by many that one Mounted Police officer was able, at a cup-tie final at Wembley, to prevent disaster when the crowd got out of hand.

In so far as the internal economy of the Metropolitan Police is concerned, unmarried police officers live in section houses (a form of barracks), and married officers live in their own private residences, but they receive an allowance towards the payment of their rent, which is known colloquially as rent aid.

All police officers in the United Kingdom serve under a disciplinary code governed by regulations made by the Home Secretary under his statutory powers. The service is pensionable and the rates of pension depend broadly on the period of service and the rank held at the time of retirement. Every

police officer from the Commissioner downwards contributes a percentage of his salary towards his own pension, and the deduction made from his pay on that account is known as the "rateable deduction."

The Police Federation.—It will not be out of place here to refer to the history which led up to the establishment of the Police Federation.

In 1916 there was manifest growing unrest not only in the Metropolitan Police Force but in some of the great provincial cities. The grievances under which the police suffered, largely of a financial nature, were evident, as the rates of pay at that time in operation were not sufficient to maintain a police officer in a state of respectability commensurate with his position.

An organization known as the National Union of Police and Prison Officials was set up in order to support and represent the officers' grievances. Nothing was done to relieve them, however, and as a result there was a strike. As a consequence of that strike the Police Act of 1919 was passed which prohibited any police officer belonging to any union and at the same time set up the Police Federation. The object of the Act was to enable members of the police forces in England and Wales to consider and bring

A Section of the Finger-print Library at Scotland Yard.

The famous siege of Sidney Street in 1910, when the military were called out to aid
the police in dislodging a desperate gang of criminals.

to the notice of the police authorities and the Secretaries of State all matters affecting their welfare and efficiency, other than questions of discipline and promotion affecting individuals. The Federation consists of all members of the police forces below the rank of lieutenant, and there are three Branch Boards, one for constables, one for sergeants, and one for inspectors. The members of these boards are elected by secret ballot annually. The Act of 1919 prohibited any police officer from being a member of any trade union, and the Police Federation was set up in order to enable all police officers to possess a statutory method of ventilating their grievances.

The Special Constabulary.—A passing word as to the genesis of the force known as the Special Constabulary will, I think, be of interest.

Special constables were recognized by statute as long ago as the reign of Charles II, and Justices of the Peace were entitled to appoint such constables if there was reasonable cause to suppose that there was likely to be such disturbances of the peace as to warrant that action. This principle, was extended under the Special Constables Act of 1831, which culminated in the Act of 1914, which allowed the appointment of special constables during the War, although there was no apprehension of riot or disturbance.

To-day the Special Constabulary remain a permanent auxiliary to the regular police force of the country. In addition to this auxiliary force, police forces are entitled to lend, in an emergency, officers to other police forces, a provision of the law which is much used when strikes or riots are prevalent. The officers lent have the same authority as constables when serving with another police force as they have when serving with their own.

Maintenance of Order.—I will now pass to some of the most important duties which fall to the police forces to perform. The maintenance of law and order during civil disturbances, strikes, riots, etc., is primarily the duty of the police, but if it is considered that the situation has got out of hand and beyond the power of the police to cope with, the services of the military may be requisitioned. There are certain formalities in this connection which are too technical to mention, but, broadly speaking, except in a sudden emergency, an officer is prohibited from ordering out troops in assistance of the civil power without a requisition in writing or by telegram from the civil authority. In the Metropolitan Police district that authority is the Commissioner or an Assistant Commissioner of Police; in English counties the senior magistrate or, in an emergency, any magistrate; in English cities and boroughs the mayor or, in case of an emergency, any magistrate having jurisdiction in the city or borough.

On the arrival of the troops at the place mentioned in the requisition, the officer commanding the troops exercises his discretion as to the necessity for intervention. The magistrate is required to meet the troops on arrival in order that, if the disturbance amounts to a riot and the officer in command decides to intervene, the magistrate may read the proclamation under the Riot Act. The reading of the riot proclamation has a two-fold purpose—firstly, it conveys a warning and, secondly, it involves the legal consequence that those who do not disperse within one hour are guilty of felony. There is no obligation, however, on the officer in command of the troops, if the situation is serious, either to read the proclamation or to wait until the hour has expired. It rests with the magistrate, however, to decide that the police are unable to cope with the riot and to request the commander of the troops to take action. The responsibility then entirely falls upon the military officer in command and it is interesting to quote the King's Regulations on the subject. "If an officer thinks it unnecessary to take immediate action, it is not obligatory upon him to do so, nor will he continue any action longer than he thinks absolutely necessary. All commands to the troops will be given by the officer. The troops will not on any account fire except by word

of command of their officer who, if it becomes necessary to order the troops to fire, will exercise a humane discretion in deciding both the number of rounds and object to be aimed at." Happily in this country, although we have passed through vast upheavals, it has seldom been necessary for the military to "take action."

A Constable's Duties.—It is not, I think, realized that a constable derives his authority from the law and the law alone, and no superior authority can extend or restrict his powers. He is responsible to the law for all his acts or for any misuse of his authority, and he cannot shelter behind the suggestion that he is obeying orders. He serves, of course, under a severe disciplinary code which permits of his dismissal (inter alia) for disobedience of orders, but those orders can only relate to administrative matters in connection with the organization of his force and cannot, under any circumstances, refer to the duties imposed upon a constable by the law.

It is a popular misconception that a policeman is only entitled to arrest a person because he is a policeman. That is far from being the case. Any civilian is entitled to

Inside Bow Street Police Station a century ago.

arrest, and indeed it is his duty to arrest, any person who is committing or who has committed a treason or a felony. The same applies in order to prevent a breach of the peace which is taking place or is about to take place. Again, if there is what is known in old phraseology as a "hue and cry" (which is in fact the immediate pursuit of a felon), a similar right and duty falls upon the civilian. On the other hand, a constable's powers of arrest are three-fold. First, the power above mentioned which vests in him as a civilian, with the addition that under Common Law a constable has the right of arresting on reasonable suspicion that a treason or a felony has been committed; second, the power to arrest under statutes which specially provide for that circumstance; and, third, to arrest under the warrant of a magistrate. In this latter case the constable is bound to execute the arrest and has no discretion. There are various local, one might almost say parochial, statutes in various cities and boroughs where a special power of arrest is conveyed under the Town Police Clauses Acts and, in London, under the Metropolitan Police Act of 1829. In such cases a constable can arrest for various and minor offences committed "within his view."

The natural sequence of an arrest is obviously search, and it is an interesting fact that there is no statutory power to search an arrested person nor the dwelling of an arrested person. From time immemorial, however, the police have made a practice of doing so and there is a consensus of opinion that it has obtained for so long as to have become part of the Common Law.

There are many duties which fall to the police of a domestic nature, such as the regulation of traffic, the enforcement of administrative orders connected, e.g. with foot and mouth disease, leaving the carcasses of animals unburied, dealing with offences under the Road Transport Act, trundling barrows or hoops along pavements, leaving coal holes open, shaking mats after 8 o'clock in the morning, etc., etc., which unfortunately absorb too much of a police officer's time. Many of these duties have to be neglected for the simple reason that Parliament is continually passing new legislation which requires the police to enforce it without granting an increase of establishment to the police forces concerned.

Statements to the Police.—I will now turn to a matter connected with the duties of the police which formed the subject of grave controversy for some years and has, as a matter of fact, been dealt with as recently as 1929 by a Royal Commission, and that is the methods under which the police secure the information which subsequently becomes the evidence upon which a prosecution is based. It is chiefly when the police are called upon to interrogate a suspected person, or to take a statement from a suspected person or a person who has in fact been arrested and charged with an offence, that trouble may possibly arise. It is a fundamental principle of our laws that no one should be compelled to incriminate himself and a confession is held to be an "*admission, made at any time by a person charged with a crime, stating or suggesting the inference that he committed that crime,*" and no confession is deemed to be voluntary if it appears to have been caused by an inducement, threat or promise proceeding from a person in authority.

Such was the uncertainty of the law and so conflicting were the rulings of different Courts in regard to the admissibility of confessions that in 1912 the Judges of the King's Bench Division, at the request of the then Home Secretary, drew up rules for the guidance of police officers. It was made clear at the time that the rules had not the force of law and were merely advisory. It was pointed out, however, that statements obtained contrary to the spirit of those rules might be rejected as evidence by the presiding Judge. The rules were circulated by the Home Office to all police authorities stating that they had been approved by His Majesty's Judges in regard to "statements by persons suspected of crime or by prisoners in police custody." These rules have never been authoritatively questioned and remain to-day as a guide to the police. They are as follows:—

1. When a police officer is endeavouring to discover the author of a crime there is no objection to his putting questions in respect thereof to any person or persons, whether suspected or not, from whom he thinks that useful information might be obtained.

2. Whenever a police officer has made up his mind to charge a person with a crime, he should first caution such person before asking any questions or further questions as the case may be.

3. Persons in custody should not be questioned without the usual caution being first administered.

The manifest difficulty of a police officer, of course, is to satisfy a Judge as to the precise moment when he (the police officer) "made up his mind to charge." Be that as it may, the advice—and, I may say, invaluable advice—contained in those rules is followed to-day and there is no reason to think that there will ever be any change in practice.

Probably the most difficult task that falls to the lot of a police officer is the taking of a statement from a suspected or an arrested person. On occasions an equal difficulty is experienced in taking a statement from a witness for the prosecution whose personal character is involved. By this I do not mean a person who has been directly or indirectly involved in a crime and who has, in colloquial words, "turned King's evidence," but a person who, under cross-examination, might have to admit that he or she is a disreputable character.

I have come to the conclusion after some years' experience, that no innocent person is endangered if he speaks the truth, but unfortunately some people accused of an offence are apt to attempt to improve the truth and thereby to incur grave suspicion and to imperil themselves. It is my experience that many criminals, if not most, after arrest and a period of cogitation in the cell express a desire to "make a statement." That statement is the result of a carefully thought out excuse, but frequently it has proved their undoing. It takes a brilliant brain to be a consistent and successful liar. When Browne and Kennedy were arrested and charged with the murder of P.C. Gutteridge, they both desired to make statements, and did so. Each tried to incriminate the other and both were hanged. I have known of other cases where a perfectly innocent person has made a lying statement to account for his movements, which only involved him in further suspicion and the police in further inquiry, merely because for domestic reasons he did not desire his wife to be aware of how he actually had occupied his time. It is the practice of the police in taking statements from suspected or arrested persons, and indeed from any person whatever, laboriously to record in longhand all that that person may say. But inevitably the officer taking the statement is bound to put questions in order to elucidate matters, and therein lies the danger as, when the statement is put in as evidence, it may be suggested by a defending counsel that those questions were put for the purpose of causing the person concerned to incriminate himself. For some reason which I have never yet been able to fathom, criminals under suspicion or arrest seldom seem to desire to write out a statement themselves and to hand it to the police officer. It is customary for the police to require the person concerned to initial every sheet, and at the end of the statement to sign a declaration that it has been read over to them and is correct.

There is a difference, and a very material difference, between a statement made by an accused or suspected person and that made by a potential witness, as in the latter case the statement is really only a "proof of evidence" which will eventually be submitted to the prosecuting authority and may or may not be used. It is interesting to recall that arising out of a statement taken from a potential witness for the prosecution, an upheaval occurred in the House of Commons which resulted in a special Commission of Inquiry and eventually The Royal Commission on Police Powers and Procedure which rendered their report in March, 1929. The circumstances were simple. A man had been arrested and charged with an offence. He was brought before a magistrate and gave evidence. During the tendering of that evidence the magistrate stopped the case, dismissed the charges against him and the lady who was concerned, and awarded costs against the police. Subsequently the then Home Secretary under pressure in the House of Commons, sent the papers to the Director of Public Prosecutions for his consideration as to whether the police officers concerned had committed perjury. The gentleman concerned absolutely refused to give any statement whatever to the police and he, of course, was a most material witness in the event of proceedings for perjury against the police officers. The lady, however, gave a statement and suggestions were made that her statement had been obtained in such a way and under such circumstances that it could not be deemed to be voluntary and that the statement in itself involved her own personal character and reputation. No proceedings for perjury, however, ensued, but as a result, the Royal Commission, which I have mentioned above, were charged with the duty of inquiring into the practice followed in interrogating or taking statements from persons interviewed in the course of the investigation of crime, and to report whether, in their opinion, such powers and duties were properly exercised and discharged with due regard to the rights and liberties of the subject, the interests of justice and the observance of the Judge's rules both in the letter and the spirit. The Royal Commission rendered their report in due course and made certain recommendations but no action has ever been taken on the reports and the situation remains in statu quo.

The Character of Prisoners.— The protection which is given by our laws to an accused person in regard to safeguarding him against incriminating himself is, of course, extended when he takes his trial. A man may have thirty or forty convictions recorded against him and yet neither the magistrate at the preliminary hearing nor the jury at the subsequent trial, if it occurs, are aware of that fact until after the verdict. A criminal's character apart from his convictions cannot be referred to unless he himself has, in fact, "put his character into issue"—that is to say, suggested in the witness box that he is a man of good character, when counsel in cross-examination is entitled to put questions to him suggesting that he is not. An interesting example of where, in my judgment, the law failed, was the Rouse case. Rouse, it will be remembered, was charged with murder arising out of the discovery of the charred body of a man, or what remained of a man, in a burnt out motorcar. It was necessary to suggest a motive for the crime and when Rouse appeared before the magistrate at the preliminary hearing, evidence was given as to his immoral life to prove that he

had every motive for "disappearance" (the burnt body being intended to be taken for his own). The result was that although, of course, this evidence was never led when he ultimately took his trial at the Old Bailey, yet, as it had been fully reported in the Press at the time of the magisterial inquiry, every member of the jury must have known of Rouse's character, not only before he was convicted, but also before he actually appeared in the dock.

Prior to the passing of the Criminal Evidence Act, 1898, no doubt following the principle that no accused man should be required to incriminate himself, a person accused (e.g. of murder), could not give evidence himself in his own defence. He could make a statement from the dock but that statement was not on oath and was not, therefore, liable to cross-examination by prosecuting counsel, nor could he be led by his own counsel when making it. When the law was changed, however, the accused person was entitled, if he chose, to give evidence on his own behalf and the mere procedure under which that evidence is given is an example of the meticulous fairness of our Courts. The evidence is not given from the dock; the accused person leaves the dock and enters the same witness box as that which is occupied by the witnesses of the prosecution. He is designedly removed from the atmosphere of arrest and restraint; no police officer stands by his side in the witness box. He takes the oath and is examined by his own counsel and gives his story of the episode. On the other hand, he is liable to be subjected to cross-examination, and it is the opinion of many eminent criminal lawyers that many a criminal would have gone scot free if he had not availed himself of the privilege of giving evidence himself! The point, of course, is that if he *does not* give evidence it is competent for the prosecuting counsel to comment upon that fact and this must inevitably convey an inference to the jury and influence them in their verdict. In the old days the statement from the dock was privileged and protected. Be that as it may, the passing of the Criminal Evidence Act was only another example of English Justice. Contrast the position of an accused murderer giving evidence in the witness box with that of the wretched Van der Lubbe who

Keeping order on London's great waterway. River police patrolling the Thames.

spent practically the whole of his time awaiting trial, and indeed during his trial, chained like a wild animal, shouted down and intimidated by the Judge.

Charging Prisoners.—I have indicated previously the powers of arrest which are inherent in the constable by common law, by statute and by warrant. I will now deal with the events which follow arrest— that is, the "charging of the prisoner" —or the refusal of the charge. A discretion, of which he cannot divest himself and which he must exercise, is given to every station officer to accept or refuse a charge. Delay may arise before the station officer is able to obtain sufficient corroboration to warrant him in accepting the charge. In other words, in certain cases there manifestly must be delay before the station officer can make up his mind in what direction his discretion should be exercised. If there is going to be any appreciable delay, the law provides a remedy, as, under the Criminal Justice Act of 1925, a station officer can admit a prisoner to bail before charging, under obligation to return to that or any other Police Station at some time

which is specified, in order that the investigation of the charge may be further pursued.

When the station officer has decided to accept a charge the prisoner is either confined in the cells to appear at the Court next morning, or the station officer may exercise his discretion in granting bail for the prisoner's appearance before a magistrate the following morning. The law requires the prisoner's appearance the following morning and no station officer can extend the period. If the station officer refuses to accept the charge, the prisoner is immediately released and a record is made of the case in the "Refused Charge Book." In all such cases, of course, it is open to the person concerned to bring an action for wrongful arrest and false imprisonment against the police officer who arrested him— a remedy which has seldom been utilised.

Identification Parades.—Closely allied to the principles which are observed in the taking of statements is the method under which identification parades are conducted. It is often vital for the successful prosecution of the charge, that an accused or suspected person should be identified by the complainant or by witnesses. Frequently, as mentioned before, photographs produced by the Criminal Record Office are of great value. It is not the practice of the police, however, to produce a particular photograph and say "Is that the man?" On the other hand, a number of photographs of different persons are produced, and the witness is asked to select the photograph of the person whom he considers to be the person concerned in the crime. In regard to personal identification, the practice is to endeavour to secure a number of persons of similar build and physique and to require the suspected person to stand in a line with those other persons. The complainant or witness is then required to pick out the suspect. The detective officer in charge of the case is never allowed to conduct the parade and the most scrupulous care is observed to prevent any form of prompting. It is, of course, a well-known fact that many experienced criminals are able to so distort their features and thus escape identification.

The Director of Public Prosecutions.—The Department of the Director of Public Prosecutions was set up in 1879 and the Director carries out his statutory duties under the superintendence of the Attorney-General. Broadly speaking, the director is required to take up all cases and to prosecute where the offence is punishable with death, as also all cases in which he may be so directed by a Secretary of State or the Attorney-General. He also takes up cases where in his opinion a prosecution is required in the public interest, as also cases which appear to be of importance or difficulty, and cases where there has been a refusal or failure of a person to proceed with a prosecution. He gives advice and assistance to officers of the police, clerks to Justices and other persons concerned in criminal proceedings.

The office of the director is situated in London, but country cases are frequently dealt with by the director's agents, who are usually local solicitors. The department is in no way a "detective organization" as it has no machinery for making inquiries itself and that rests with the police force concerned.

During the course of the investigation of the case the director naturally issues such instructions as he may deem desirable as to the nature of the inquiries to be carried out, and it is the practice of the police forces to lend to the director detective officers who are at his absolute disposal for that purpose.

At the time of the Royal Commission on Police Powers and Procedure there was a popular feeling that the director's department should be an investigating department as well as a prosecuting one, but no change has ever been made and I think rightly so. The director's duty is to present the cases at Court, see that the necessary technical evidence is available and that counsel are properly instructed at the trial. As matters stand at present it is a great safeguard to the interests of justice that the statements obtained by the police are minutely scrutinised in the director's department and it may be taken for granted that if it appeared that any statements were improperly or indiscreetly obtained, they would be immediately rejected.

There is another objection, rather of a financial nature, to the director's department being an investigating one, as that would of necessity make it imperative to retain a large staff of detective officers ready to proceed at one moment, e.g. to Penzance and at another, e.g. to Newcastle-on-Tyne to go into a question of potential murder. The police machinery for assisting the Director is, in my judgment, adequate, and there seems no likelihood of the present system being altered in the direction of extending the activities of the Director of Public Prosecutions to investigation as well as to prosecution. Where the Director does not intervene, police prosecutions are carried out in important cases by solicitors and in minor cases by superintendent, or even by the constable who laid the information. Great objections are often raised, however, to police officers themselves conducting cases. I think that this practice is objectionable and I know that my view is very largely shared by the legal profession. It is much better that the constable who laid the information should give his evidence, and the Clerk to the Magistrate should see that the necessary witnesses are called and examined (under his advice if necessary) by the magistrates hearing the case. I myself have actually heard a superintendent of police presuming to "sum up for the Prosecution" and address the Bench.

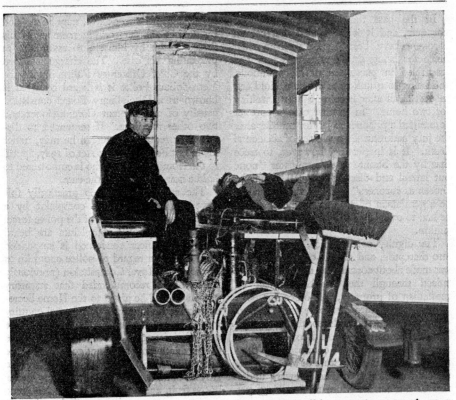

The interior of a Flying Squad van, where every possible emergency such as a break-down, an accident, etc., is prepared against.

Coroners' Inquests.—Another preliminary to a prosecution by the police is in certain cases the coroner's inquest, and many chief officers of police would, I think, welcome the abolition of that process of law, or at any rate a curtailment of its activities to the extent of finding that a person's death was not a natural one, and recording no observations as to the circumstances under which the death occurred.

It is a fact that a coroner can by putting a series of indiscreet and leading questions based largely on the information he has previously received from the police, give a suspected person who appears before him as a witness a pretty good idea of the evidence which the police have accumulated, and thereby place him on his guard. Coroners nowadays, however, under recent legislation have power to adjourn sine die in cases where the police are conducting an enquiry. In ancient times, however, when police forces were non-existent or practically so, it was frequently convenient and in the interests of Justice that a suspected person should be arrested on a coroner's warrant after the verdict of the jury that murder had been committed either by some person or persons unknown, or by the suspect.

It may be of interest to recall the genesis of the system of coroners' inquests. In ancient times when everybody looked after himself and carried lethal weapons, it was not at all unusual to find persons lying dead in the King's highway or elsewhere, and it obviously fell to somebody's lot to identify the body if possible, and to make some enquiry as to the cause of death. It may not be known that certain high officials are, by virtue of their office, "coroners," notably the Lord Chief Justice of England and the Judges of the High Court. The earliest statutory reference to coroners occurs in the reign of Edward I, and it is interesting to note that even to-day a coroner when he is engaged in the discharge of his official duties is privileged from arrest.

In the past there were coroners and coroners, and it is on record that certain coroners have been removed from their office for being drunk when the jury had assembled in pursuance of his summons, and being so drunk as to refuse to hold any inquest at all after keeping the jury waiting for two hours. In another case, a coroner committed a prisoner to jail for murder after the jury had returned a verdict of accidental death. It is interesting, however, to trace that by the Statute of Westminster "none but lawful and discreet knights should be chosen as coroners" and the coroner had to be a gentleman of property—that is to say he had to own lands to the value of £20 per annum.

The dignity of the office, however, fell into disrepute, and the following comment was made about coroners at the time: "now indeed through the culpable neglect of gentlemen of property, this office has been suffered to fall into disrepute and get into low and indigent hands so that although formerly no coroners would condescend to be paid for serving their countries and they were by the aforesaid Statute of Westminster expressly forbidden to take a reward under pain of a great forfeiture to the King, yet for many years past they have only desired to be chosen for their perquisites."

The Police and the Public.—
It is appropriate to close this article with a reference to the relations which exist between the public and the police—how to help them in the execution of their duties and how, if necessary, to complain of their conduct. As I briefly mentioned before, every police officer serves under a disciplinary code and can be punished for offences against that code.

He may be dismissed, required to resign, reduced in rank, reduced in rate of pay, subjected to forfeiture of merit or good-conduct badges (except such as have been granted for an act of courage or bravery), fined, reprimanded or cautioned. If a complaint is made against a police officer he is entitled to a full enquiry. The charge against him must be in writing and he may call any witnesses he may desire on his own

behalf and, if he so desires, may be assisted by having another serving member of his force, chosen by himself, to assist him in presenting his case. The charge is heard by the Chief Officer of Police but in the Metropolitan Police it is heard by what is known as a Disciplinary Board consisting usually of an Assistant Commissioner and two other members. If sentenced to dismissal or required to resign he may, under the recent Police Appeals Act of 1927, appeal to the Home Secretary who is empowered to hold a new inquiry into the case.

The same procedure is practically followed in the case of a complaint by a civilian against a member of the police force, although frequently complaints are heard before the officer concerned is suspended from duty. In regard to police enquiries as a whole, the Royal Commission (previously referred to), recommended that statutory powers should be given to the Home Secretary to set up at any time a formal enquiry into matters concerning police discipline and administration with power to require the production of papers and to take evidence on oath. The recommendations of the Royal Commission, however, have never borne fruit, and it is to be hoped that some day this recommendation will be adopted. In the Army a Military Court of Inquiry can be set up at any time to enquire into any matter, and under certain conditions civilians may be summoned to appear under subpœna, and similar machinery should exist in the police forces of this country.

An aspect of civilized life which requires more than passing reference is the liability of any law-abiding citizen to be involved in a charge, for example, through mistaken identity. In every police station there will be found a notice in big print on the wall telling an accused person his rights; the right to communicate with his friends and relatives or solicitor, with his own doctor, etc., etc. Indeed it is a happy reflection to be able to conclude this article with the suggestion and submission that English law and police procedure are unique among the nations of the world in securing to the citizen liberty, peace and justice.

ROAD TRAFFIC*

By

The Rt. Hon. HERBERT MORRISON, j.p., l.c.c.

TYPES OF MOTOR VEHICLES.
—Motor vehicles are divided into heavy and light locomotives, motor-tractors, heavy motor-cars, motor-cars, motor-cycles and invalid carriages.

"Heavy motor-cars" are vehicles with a weight unladen over 2½ tons, which are constructed to carry a load or passengers and are not classed as "motor-cars." "Motor-cars" are vehicles whose unladen weight does not exceed 3 tons (if constructed solely for the carriage of passengers and their effects and adapted to carry not more than 7 passengers and a driver, and fitted with the prescribed tyres) and 2½ tons in every other case. "Motor-cycles" are vehicles not over 8 cwt. in weight when unladen which have less than four wheels and are not classed as invalid carriages. It follows, therefore, that a tricar may be a motor-cycle. "Invalid carriages" are vehicles of unladen weight not over 5 cwt. specially made for use by persons suffering from some physical disability, e.g. the loss of a limb.

There is an enormous mass of law dealing with motor-vehicles upon the public highway. The most important provisions relate to the various licences which are required, and to the insurance policy to be taken out against certain accidents. Certain licences are required for all vehicles, irrespective of the purpose for which they are being used, while other licences are required in addition for certain vehicles used for certain purposes, e.g. Public Service vehicles. Further, not only the vehicles must be licensed but the drivers also. Here again there is one licence which all drivers require, and in addition certain special licences which may be required by drivers of certain vehicles.

Registration and Licensing.—The first duties of the owner of a motor-vehicle are to have it registered and to obtain the proper excise licence for it. Where he is buying a new car he must apply for registration to the County Council of the district in which he proposes to keep the vehicle, or to the Council in whose area the car is at the time.

As a result of this application he will receive a registration book. This sets out in considerable detail a description of the car, and if at any later time the vehicle is altered in such a way as to render inaccurate the entries on the licence, or to require a higher rate of duty, information must be sent to the Council. The book must at any time be produced for inspection to a Police Officer or Local Taxation Officer.

Change of Ownership, etc.—When a vehicle is sold, or the ownership is changed in some way, the seller must hand the Registration Book to the purchaser and must also notify the change of ownership to the council by whom the vehicle was last registered. The purchaser must insert in the book his name and address and send the registration book to the council. It will be returned to him in due course.

Where the owner of a vehicle changes his address he must put his new address in the book and send it to the council and if the vehicle is broken up, destroyed, or sent permanently out of Great Britain, the council must be notified and the book sent to them.

Loss of Book.—When a book is lost, destroyed, defaced or becomes illegible a new one must be obtained from the council, and if the old book is found after it has been lost and replaced, the owner must do all he can to get possession of it, if it is not in his possession, and return it to the council. It is a serious offence to supply false information in applying for a licence, or in notifying the council as to any change in registration, or fraudulently to alter or use, or fraudulently

* Note.—The various sections of the law as stated in this supplement include the provisions of the Road Traffic Act, 1934. Different sections of this Act come into force on different dates fixed by the Minister of Transport.

lend or allow to be used by any other person any registration book, licence, or identification mark.

Who May Examine Register.—Any person who wishes to obtain the registered particulars of a vehicle may do so on applying to the council and shewing some reasonable cause, e.g. that he wishes to find out the owner of a particular car whose number he has taken and against whom he wishes to bring proceedings. The fee is a shilling. The police may examine the register without fee. Where emergency medical treatment has been given by a doctor or hospital to any person injured on the road, the police will supply the doctor or hospital with the number, and name and address of the owner of any motor vehicle concerned in the injury, so that a claim for payment for the emergency treatment may be made (*see below*).

Warning—It is quite wrong to assume that because a certain person is registered as the owner of a vehicle he is entitled to sell it. In particular, when a vehicle is taken on hire purchase, it is always registered in the name of the hirer. Until he has paid all his instalments he has, however, no right to sell it. Prospective purchasers of second-hand cars should, therefore, never rely on the registration book as proof of ownership of the car, for if they buy the car and it turns out later that the person from whom they bought it had no right to sell it, e.g. because he merely had it on hire purchase, they will be compelled to hand back the car, or the value of it, to the hire-purchase company without any compensation. They will, of course, have rights against the person who sold them the car, but these will be of little value to them in practice, since he will probably have disappeared or be without any money.

Identification Marks.—Each vehicle is given an Identification Mark for its number plates by the council when it is registered and this must be fixed to it in letters and figures of a certain size. The mark must be kept clear, but a driver who is charged with failing to keep it clear will not be convicted if he proves that he has taken all reasonable steps to prevent it from being obscured. Drivers of vehicles should remember that the mark must be visible at all times and should be careful

when they are carrying luggage on a carrier behind that it is placed in such a position that their rear number plates are not obscured. Drivers sometimes chalk their number on the luggage on the carrier when the proper plate is obscured by the carrier, but technically they are not entitled to do so for their identification marks should be shewn either on a flat plate or on some flat unbroken rectangular surface *forming part of the vehicle itself.* Probably, however, no objection would be taken so long as the chalk marks were clear.

Road Fund Licences.—Licences must be taken for every motor vehicle as evidence that the proper amount of excise duty has been paid. These licences differ entirely from the licences required when vehicles are being used for special purposes—e.g. public service vehicles. The ordinary licences are of three kinds—the usual Road Fund licence, General Trade licence, and Limited Trade licence. At the time of the taking out of the licence the driver must produce his insurance certificate to shew that an insurance policy against certain risks has been taken out with some Insurance Company. (*See below*, INSURANCE.)

Licences may be taken out either for the whole or remainder of a year from January 1st to December 31st, or for one or more of the quarterly periods. The year is divided for licensing purposes into quarters ending March 24, June 30, September 30, and December 31. The first quarter is made to end on March 24, so that the second quarter may always include the Easter holidays. Licences may be surrendered and a refund claimed.

Licences may be renewed at the offices of the appropriate County or County Borough Council and at certain post offices.

MOTOR-CARS AND HEAVY MOTOR-CARS

Petrol-driven goods vehicles	If fitted entirely with pneumatic tyres			If fitted with solid tyres		
	£	s.	d.	£	s.	d.
Unladen weight not over 12 cwt	10	0	0	10	0	0
12 cwt to 1 ton	15	0	0	15	0	0
1 to 1½ tons	20	0	0	20	0	0
1½ to 2 tons	25	0	0	25	0	0
2 to 2½ tons	30	0	0	40	0	0
2½ to 3 tons	35	0	0	46	13	4
3 to 4 tons	50	0	0	66	13	4
Over 4 tons—For first 4 tons	50	0	0	66	13	4

Petrol-driven goods vehicles	If fitted entirely with pneumatic tyres £ s. d.	If fitted with solid tyres £ s. d.
For each additional ton or part of a ton in excess of 4 tons . .	20 0 0	26 13 4

Goods vehicles used solely for certain special purposes and those driven by other means than petrol engines are charged with duty at different rates.

Private motor-cars.

Not exceeding 6 horse-power or electrically propelled . . £6

Exceeding 6 horse-power . . £1 for each unit or part of a unit of horse-power.

On and after January 1st, 1935, only three-quarters of the above amount is payable in the case of private cars.

Motor-Cycles, etc.—Motor-cycles (including motor-scooters and cycles with an attachment for propelling the same by mechanical power) not exceeding 8 cwt. in weight unladen.

	Before Jan. 1st, 1935 £ s. d.	On or after Jan. 1st, 1935 £ s. d.
Where the cylinder capacity of the engine:		
(a) does not exceed 150 c.c. .	15 0	12 0
(b) exceeds 150 c.c. but under 250 c.c.	1 10 0	1 2 6
(c) exceeds 250 c.c. .	3 0 0	2 5 0

Where a bicycle over 250 c.c. was licensed before January 1, 1933, and does not exceed 224 lbs in weight unladen, the duty before January 1st, 1935, was £1 10s. 0d. and on or after that date is £1 2s. 6d.

Trailers or side-cars:		
additional duty .	1 0 0	15 0
Tricycles . .	4 0 0	4 0 0
Invalid Carriages .	5 0	5 0
Motor Mowing Machines . .	5 0	5 0

Certain vehicles do not require a licence. These are vehicles belonging to the Crown, motor ambulances, fire engines, etc., and vehicles used for the carrying of voters free of charge to and from the polls at Parliamentary and Local Government elections. These last must, however, be insured.

Trade Licences.—Manufacturers, repairers or dealers in motor vehicles obtain licences of a special kind known as trade licences. No vehicle with a trade licence must be used by anybody except the person to whom it is issued, or some servant of his, or a prospective purchaser of the vehicle, or unless the licensee or some person in his employment is present and in charge of the vehicle. Where a vehicle has accommodation for only one person, e.g. a motor-cycle, a prospective purchaser may use it for testing or trial. A trade licence may be taken out either in respect of all vehicles used by the licensee or in respect of all vehicles used by him of the cycle, tricycle or invalid carriage type.

Trade licences are of two kinds:

(1) General Trade Licence. This must not be used for carrying passengers for profit or reward. A general trade licence for all vehicles costs £25 and for all cycles, tricycles and invalid carriages £5.

(2) Limited Trade Licence. This can only be used for certain purposes:

(1) test or trial during or after construction or repair or by a prospective customer;

(2) proceeding to and from a public weighbridge or any place for registration or inspection;

(3) delivery to a purchaser or to another maker, dealer or repairer;

(4) proceeding to or from a workshop;

(5) towing a vehicle which has broken down on a road;

(6) proceeding to or from a railway station or a wharf for the purposes of transport, or to or from a storage place or sale-room.

Even during these journeys certain regulations apply. A book must be kept in which particulars of the purposes for which the vehicle is to be used must be entered in duplicate on each occasion before it is used, and a copy of the entry must be carried on the vehicle and produced if required. No passengers for profit or reward can be carried and not more than two persons in addition to the driver must be carried and each of those must be either an employee or a prospective purchaser. On Sundays, Bank Holidays, and Public Holidays, no passenger may be carried at all. No goods can be carried in the course of trade or for delivery or removal, but a load of ballast may be carried to test the vehicle.

Limited trade licences for all vehicles cost £5 and for cycles—including tricycles weighing not more than 8 cwt. and invalids' carriages—the cost is £1. It will be appreciated that these trade licences, unlike the ordinary licences, are not confined to one vehicle but may be removed from one vehicle to another as required by the licensee.

Driving Licences.—It is an offence for any person to drive a motor vehicle on the road unless he holds a driving licence or to employ any driver who is not licensed. The maximum penalty is a fine of £20 for a first offence, and a fine of £50 or three months' imprisonment for subsequent offences.

The licence is obtained from the Council of the County or County Borough in which the driver lives. Unlike the excise licence, it does not expire at the end of the calendar year but remains in force until 12 months from the date when it is first issued.

All persons who apply for a licence must make a declaration as to their physical fitness. Persons who are physically fit and who held a licence for some time before April 1, 1934, may obtain a licence without any driving test, but all other persons— i.e. those who held licences before April 1, 1934, if they are not physically fit, and all persons who did not hold a licence before that date, whether they are physically fit or not—must pass a test.

To enable an applicant who has to undergo a test to acquire proficiency he is entitled to a provisional licence which costs 5/-. This is valid for 3 months, but it can only be used when the person to whom it is issued is driving under the supervision of a competent instructor, and this instructor must also, except in the case of a motor-cycle or invalid carriage, be present in the vehicle with the driver.

Age Limits.—No person under 16 may drive any motor vehicle; persons between 16 and 17 may drive motor-cycles and invalid carriages; any person over 17 can drive an ordinary motor-car, but no person under 21 can drive a heavy motor vehicle.

Production of Licences.—Every person driving a motor vehicle on the road must produce his licence for examination to any police constable so as to enable the constable to ascertain the name and address of the holder, the date of issue and the Council by whom it was issued, under a penalty of a fine not exceeding £5. A driver who has not got his licence in his possession may escape from any liability to fine by producing the licence within five days in person at some police station named by him at the time he was asked to produce the licence. Drivers should remember this provision where they have been unable to produce their licence when travelling away from home, and should select a police station at some place where they are likely to be within the five days and which will give them time to have their licence sent to them. The licence must be produced in person and it is not enough to send it by post.

Endorsement.—A person who is convicted of certain motoring offences may have the fact of the conviction endorsed on the driving licence. For certain offences the licence must be endorsed—e.g. dangerous or careless driving, or exceeding speed limit.

A person whose licence has been endorsed may obtain a clean licence, i.e. a licence free from endorsement, after a certain period of time. The period will vary with the nature of the conviction for which the licence was endorsed. Where the endorsement is in consequence of a conviction for exceeding the speed limit a clean licence may be obtained at any time after one year from the date of the endorsement, if at the time of the endorsement the driver had a clean licence or a licence only endorsed for speed limit offences, and if, during the year since the endorsement, no further endorsement has been made. Where the endorsement was imposed not in respect of an offence against the speed limit but for some other offence, the application for a clean licence cannot be made until three years after the endorsement, and only then if, during those three years, no other endorsement has been made. For this purpose speed limit endorsements are not counted if they are more than one year before the date of application. Where a person has been disqualified from driving he cannot count the period of his disqualification in the three years or one year period as the case may be.

Disqualification.—A person may be disqualified from driving for any offence under the Road Traffic Act, 1930, but not for a breach of regulations made under Powers given in that Act. With certain exceptions (*see below*) the disqualification may be for any period up to the life of the driver. Where a person is convicted of promoting or taking part in racing or speed trials on the road, being incapable of proper control of the vehicle through drink or drugs, or of using a vehicle when it is not properly insured, he *must* be disqualified from driving for at least 12 months unless the Court for special reasons remits the disqualification. Some disqualification on a second conviction for dangerous driving must also be imposed unless there are special circumstances. On a first conviction for careless driving the disqualification cannot be for more than one month, and on a second conviction three months. When the driver has, within the three years before his conviction for careless driving, been convicted of reckless or dangerous driving, he is for this purpose treated as if that previous conviction had been for careless driving. No disqualification can be imposed for first or second offences against the speed limit.

When the disqualification is imposed the licence must be handed to the Court and will be forwarded to the Council which issued it and who retain it until the disqualification ceases. It is a serious offence to drive a motor vehicle when disqualified and the maximum penalty is a £50 fine or six months' imprisonment, or both.

When a driver has been disqualified he may apply to the Court at any time after six months of the disqualification has elapsed and ask that his licence may be restored to him, and if his application is refused, he may apply again after another three months. If no application of this kind is granted at this time the disqualification will expire automatically at the end of the time for which it was imposed.

A person who is convicted of reckless, dangerous or careless driving may be disqualified from holding a licence until he passes the driving test. A disqualification of this nature may be imposed even though the person has already passed the test—e.g. when he obtains his licence. A person disqualified in this manner may obtain a provisional licence (*see above*).

Insurance.—It has now been made compulsory for every person who uses, or allows any other person to use a motor vehicle on the road to have in force a policy of insurance in respect of certain third-party risks. Failure to have a vehicle properly insured is regarded as a very serious offence and is punished by a fine not exceeding £50 or imprisonment for not more than three months, or both fine and imprisonment. The convicted person must also be disqualified for 12 months except in special cases.

It should be noticed that the motorist is not required to insure against all third-party risks but only against any liability which he may incur in respect of the death or bodily injury of certain persons. This includes liability to pay fees for emergency medical treatment to these persons (*see below*). The policy need not cover liability to persons who are being carried as passengers, except where they are being carried for hire or reward or under a contract of employment. A man is thus not required to insure against any injury to himself, nor to his chauffeur while driving the car nor to passengers who are being carried without payment. Insurance is not required against damage to vehicles or other property. It should perhaps be pointed out that the provisions as to insurance do not affect the ordinary rules of liability of the motorist or of his insurance company. He is still only liable when he has caused damage through negligence in his driving.

Liability of Insurance Companies. —When compulsory insurance was introduced in 1930 the object of the legislature was to protect persons who were injured by the negligent driving of another from being unable to recover any damages because the person responsible had no money. It was thought that they would be able to claim against the insurance company. This object has frequently been defeated by the insurance company inserting in the policy provisions entitling them to repudiate liability on very trifling grounds. Thus, the insurance company might rely on a clause in the policy under which the insured person warranted the truth of certain statements in his proposal form, and if any of these statements turned out to be untrue— e.g. if he had stated his age wrongly—the insurance company might technically be able to repudiate.

This right of the insurance company to repudiate liability has been limited in several ways so far as any third person injured is concerned. It should be clearly understood, however, that the right to repudiate is in no way affected so far as the insured is concerned. The insurance company may have to pay damages to an injured third person even in cases where they are entitled to repudiate, but in such cases they are damages they have paid from the insured person. If he has no money, then the right to recover is valueless, but it is the insurance company and not the injured person who suffers.

The restrictions in the right to repudiate are of three kinds. Firstly, there are certain grounds upon which the insurance company can never rely; secondly, there are grounds upon which they may be prevented from relying if the injured person takes certain steps; and thirdly, there are grounds upon which they can rely if they themselves take proper proceedings in Court.

Grounds upon which Company cannot rely.—The insurance company can never escape liability to the injured person by alleging that the insured person has failed to do or has done something *after* the accident which, according to the terms of the policy, releases them from liability. Thus it is frequently provided that the insured must give notice of the accident within a certain time. His failure to do this cannot now prevent any injured person from recovering from the insurance company, although the insurance company may be able to recover the money paid from their insured. Again, any terms of a policy which restrict the insurance of the person insured by reference to any of the following matters are of no effect so far as the liability of the insurance company to the injured person is concerned:—

(a) Age, physical or mental condition of the persons driving the vehicle; or

(b) the condition of the vehicle; or

(c) the number of persons carried in the vehicle; or

(d) the weight or physical characteristics of the goods carried in the vehicle; or

(e) the time at which or the areas within which the vehicle is used; or

(f) the horse-power or value of the vehicle; or

(g) the carrying on the vehicle of any particular apparatus; or

(h) the carrying on the vehicle of any particular means of identification other than any means of identification required to be carried by or under the Roads Act, 1920.

Grounds which may be relied on unless injured person takes certain steps.—Provided that the injured person takes certain steps (*see below*) the insurance company cannot repudiate liability after the accident on any grounds except that the policy was obtained by non-disclosure of a material fact—i.e. by the failure of the insured person to tell the insurance company something which he ought to have told them, e.g. that he had had many accidents— or by a representation of fact which was false in some material particular. A material fact is one which is of such a nature as to influence the judgment of a prudent insurance company in determining whether or not it will take the risk, and if so, at what premium and on what conditions. The effect of this is, roughly, that the insurance company cannot repudiate liability to the injured person for trifling mis-statements.

An injured person who is bringing an action in respect of his injuries, and who wishes to prevent the insurance company from repudiating liability on immaterial and trifling grounds, must give notice to the company either before he commences proceedings or within 7 days afterwards.

Grounds upon which Company may rely.—The insurance company may still, even against an injured person, repudiate liability on the ground that the policy was obtained by non-disclosure of a material fact or by a representation of fact which was false in some material particular. The company must, however, bring an action asserting the right to repudiate either before the injured person commences his action for damages or within three months after that time. The insurance company must also, in cases where the injured person's action for damages is commenced before their action to repudiate, give notice to the injured person within 7 days after the commencement of the insurance company's action, specifying the non-disclosure or false representation on which the company intends to rely.

In order to enable injured persons to find out the insurance company of the person against whom they wish to bring action, all persons against whom claims are made in respect of which they are bound to insure must, on demand, state whether or not they were insured and give particulars of the policy.

The liability of the insurance company under the above provisions arises only when the insured person has a certificate of insurance in force at the time of the accident. The provision will therefore not apply if *before* the accident out of which the claim arises the policy was cancelled by mutual consent or by virtue of any provision in it, and either the certificate was handed back to the insurance company before the accident or within 14 days afterwards, or within 14 days the insurance company began proceedings against the insured person to compel him to surrender the certificate.

Insurance Certificate.—The driver of every vehicle must have with him his insurance certificate and must produce it to a police officer. The maximum penalty is a fine of £20 for a first offence and £50 or three months' imprisonment for later offences. He may, however, escape from a conviction in cases where he is unable to produce it when asked, if he produces it to a police station within five days, and the rules applicable to the production of driving licences as set out above also apply here. When an insurance policy is cancelled the motorist must give back his certificate to the insurance company within seven days. A policy of insurance is of no effect until a certificate of insurance is issued.

Offences.—The offences connected with the driving of motor vehicles are innumerable. The most important are dangerous driving, careless driving, and driving while under the influence of drink or drugs. The penalties given below for various offences are the maximum penalties which can be imposed, and in most cases a penalty much smaller than the maximum will in fact be imposed.

Dangerous Driving.—Any person who drives a vehicle on the road recklessly or at a speed or in a manner which is dangerous to the public, is guilty of dangerous driving. On summary convictions—i.e. in a Police Court—the maximum penalty is a fine of £50 or four months' imprisonment for a first offence and for a second or subsequent offence the fine may be increased to £100, and both fine and imprisonment may be imposed. If the offence is tried on indictment—i.e. before a jury, the maximum sentence is two years' imprisonment or a fine, or both imprisonment and fine. All the circumstances of the case must be taken into account in determining whether the driving is dangerous or not, and in particular the nature, condition and use of the road and the amount of traffic which is actually, or might reasonably be expected to be on the road at the time.

It is by no means necessary that any damage should have been caused before a prosecution can be brought, and, indeed, a man may be prosecuted for dangerous driving although there is no other traffic on the road at the time. The driver may be disqualified for a first conviction, and on a second or subsequent conviction he must be disqualified unless the Court considers that there are special circumstances in the case. The licence must in any event be endorsed even on a first conviction. It is an offence to incite any other person to drive dangerously, and so a man who urges a taxi-driver to drive at a very fast speed in order to keep an appointment may himself be liable to a fine. A person who incites another to drive dangerously is liable to disqualification and to have his licence endorsed.

Careless Driving.—It is an offence to drive without due care and attention or without reasonable consideration for other persons using the road. The punishment is a fine not exceeding £20 for a first offence, and for subsequent offences a fine not exceeding £50 or three months' imprisonment. Disqualification may be imposed for any offence, but for a first offence the maximum period is one month and for a second offence three months.

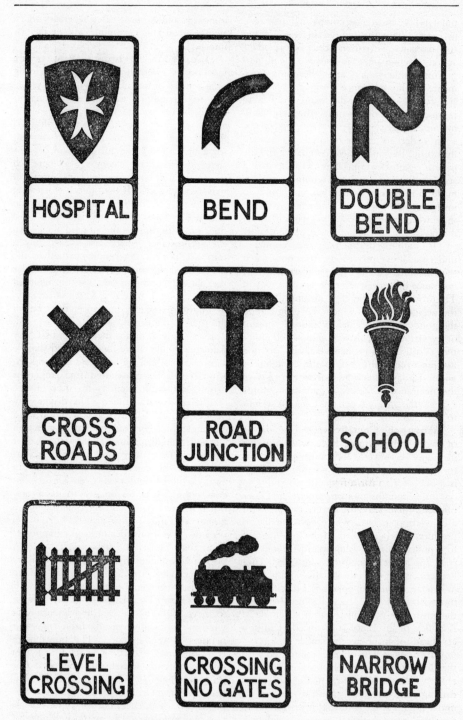

A Selection of the most recent Road Signs approved by the Ministry of Transport.

These are a selection from the most recent set of traffic signs approved and authorized by the Ministry of Transport. Instructions for their correct installation and use are issued to every County Council, County Borough Council, the Common Council of the City of London, Metropolitan Borough Councils, Town Councils and Urban District Councils.

Though at the time these were issued in December, 1933, local authorities were not required to remove existing traffic signs except those which actually conflicted with the new regulations, they were asked to augment and replace them as soon as possible.

The Ministry of Transport aims at making the roads as safe as possible for both pedestrians and motorists by issuing clear directions to motorists who may be uncertain of their route, the type of road they are on, or are about to join, and also to warn them of obstructions, dangers, etc., ahead.

It is urged that signs should not be used unnecessarily, and that those approved by the Ministry should not be augmented by other warnings, as these only tend to puzzle both pedestrians and motorists, and often cause them to ignore such notices altogether.

The signs shown on these pages explain themselves. The majority are warnings to motorists informing them what is ahead. One that is new in form and now very frequently seen is the "Major Road Ahead." Collisions often occurred where a motorist emerged unexpectedly from a comparatively quiet road into a busy stream of swift-moving traffic.

Where a person is prosecuted for either of the above offences, or for exceeding the speed limit, he will not be convicted unless he was either warned at the time of the offence that he might be prosecuted, or he received a summons within 14 days of the offence, or within that period of 14 days a notice of the intended prosecution was served on or sent by registered post to him or to the registered owner. Where, however, the Court is satisfied that the police could not reasonably have discovered the name and address of the accused or of the registered owner within the time, or that the accused has by his own conduct contributed to the failure to give him the proper notification, this defence will not be available. Further, in all cases it is for the accused to prove that no notice was given within the proper time.

A person who is alleged to have been driving dangerously or carelessly must give his name and address to any person who has reasonable grounds for asking him—e.g. another motorist who has suffered damage or a risk of damage through the dangerous or careless driving. It is an offence to refuse to give the name and address or to give a false name and address. A police officer may arrest without a warrant any person whom he sees driving dangerously or carelessly, unless that person gives his name and address or produces his licence for examination.

Speed Limits.—The maximum speed at which a vehicle may be driven will depend on the class of vehicle and whether it is used for passengers or goods. There is, however, one general speed limit applying to all motor vehicles. No motor vehicle must be driven on a road in what is known as a "built-up area" at a speed exceeding 30 miles an hour. A road is considered to be in a "built-up area" if it has on it a system of street lighting with lamps not more than 200 yards apart, but roads answering this description may be excluded from the speed limit restrictions, and, on the other hand, the speed limit may be applied to a road which does not answer the above description if the proper authority makes an order to that effect. The maximum penalty for an offence against this speed limit is a fine of £20 for a first offence and £50 for later offences. Local authorities

must put up traffic signs to indicate to motorists when they are entering and leaving a road to which the speed limit applies.

While all vehicles are subject to the above speed limit when in "built-up areas," many vehicles—practically all vehicles except private motor-cars and cycles—must comply with a speed limit whether or not they are in a "built-up area" and irrespective of the time of the day at which they are being driven.

The speed limits applicable are:—

Class of Vehicle.	Maximum Speed. Miles per Hour

1. Passenger vehicles, i.e., vehicles constructed solely for the carriage of passengers and their effects:—

(1) If the vehicle is a heavy motor-car or is adapted to carry more than seven passengers, exclusive of the driver, and all the wheels are fitted with pneumatic tyres and the vehicle is not drawing a trailer . . 30

(2) If the vehicle is adapted to carry not more than seven passengers, exclusive of the driver, and is not a heavy motor-car and is drawing a two-wheeled trailer, and all the wheels of the vehicle and trailer are fitted with pneumatic tyres . . 30

(3) Invalid carriages . . . 20

(4) In any other case (except a vehicle all the wheels of which are fitted with pneumatic tyres and which is adapted to carry not more than seven passengers exclusive of the driver and which is not drawing a trailer) . 20

2. Goods vehicles, that is to say, vehicles constructed or adapted for use for the conveyance of goods or burden of any description:—

(1) When not drawing a trailer—

(a) Motor-cars and motor-cycles if all wheels fitted with pneumatic tyres; and

(b) Heavy motor-cars, constructed or adapted for the conveyance of horses and their attendants and used solely for that purpose, if all the wheels are fitted with pneumatic tyres 30

Class of Vehicle.	Maximum Speed. Miles per Hour.

(c) Heavy motor-cars not having a body fitted thereon, not carrying any load other than that required for the purposes of testing and not exceeding 5 tons in weight unladen, if all the wheels are fitted with pneumatic tyres . . 30

(d) (i) Motor-cars, if all the wheels are not fitted with pneumatic tyres but are fitted with soft or elastic tyres; and . . .

(ii) Heavy motor-cars, if all the wheels are fitted with pneumatic or soft or elastic tyres . . . 20

(iii) Motor-cars not exceeding in weight one ton unladen, if all the wheels are fitted with pneumatic or soft or elastic tyres . 30

(2) When drawing a trailer—

(a) if all the wheels both of the drawing vehicle and of the trailer are fitted with pneumatic tyres, or if the trailer is attached to the drawing vehicle by partial superimposition in such manner as to cause a substantial part of the weight to be borne by the vehicle, and all the wheels both of the drawing vehicle and of the trailer are fitted with soft or elastic tyres . . 20

(b) if all the wheels both of the drawing vehicle and of the trailer are not fitted with pneumatic tyres but are fitted with soft or elastic tyres 12

(3) In any other case . . . 5

3. Locomotives and motor tractors—

(1) Heavy locomotives . . 5

(2) Light locomotives—

(a) When not drawing a trailer or not drawing more than two trailers, if all the wheels both of the locomotive and of any trailer drawn by it

Class of Vehicle.	Maximum Speed. Miles per Hour.

have soft or elastic tyres 12

(b) In any other case . . 5

(3) Motor tractors—

(a) When not drawing a trailer, if all the wheels of the tractor are fitted with pneumatic or soft or elastic tyres . 20

(b) When drawing a trailer—

(i) if all the wheels both of the tractor and of the trailer drawn by it are fitted with pneumatic tyres . . 20

(ii) if all the wheels both of the tractor and of the trailer drawn by it are fitted with soft or elastic tyres . . 12

(c) In any other case . . 5

A conviction for exceeding the speed limit must be endorsed on the driving licence of the offender. The motorist cannot be disqualified from driving on a first or second conviction for exceeding the speed limit.

Fire Engines, etc. — Fire engines, ambulances and police cars are exempted from the speed limit in all cases where the observance of the limit would be likely to hinder the use of the vehicle for the purpose for which it was being used.

Drunkenness.—To drive or attempt to drive or be in charge of a motor vehicle on a road or other public place while under the influence of drink or drugs to such an extent as to be incapable of having proper control of the vehicle is a very serious offence. The punishment, if the case is tried in the Police Court, is a fine of £50 or four months' imprisonment for a first conviction; and on a later conviction the fine may be increased to £100. When the offence is tried on indictment—i.e. before a jury—the maximum penalty is imprisonment for six months, or a fine, or both imprisonment and fine. A person convicted must further be disqualified from holding a driving licence for at least 12 months unless some special circumstances are present. The licence must be endorsed. Any person committing this offence may be arrested without a warrant. It should be remembered that a person is considered in charge of a motor vehicle even though he is not actually driving or even trying to do so. Thus a person who, being conscious that he was not in a fit state to drive, stopped the car at the side of the road and went to sleep until he recovered, would be guilty of an offence. It seems probable that he would not be guilty of that offence in such a case if he drove his car into a field instead of leaving it on the road.

Road Racing.—Any person promoting or taking part in a race or trial of speed between motor vehicles on a public highway is liable to a maximum penalty of three months' imprisonment or £50 fine, or both, and will be disqualified for at least 12 months except in special cases.

Pillion Riding.—A pillion passenger may be carried on a motor-cycle; but where the motor-cycle has no side-car, not more than one person must be carried on the pillion and that person must sit astride on a proper seat securely fixed on the cycle behind the driver's seat. The penalty for this offence is a fine not exceeding £5 on the first conviction and £10 for later convictions.

Construction of Motor Vehicles.— Detailed regulations have been brought into force prescribing such matters as maximum dimensions and weights of the various types of motor vehicles and other matters relating to their construction. Such matters do not frequently concern the private driver as he is naturally in the hands of the manufacturers, but it should be remembered that if a vehicle in fact infringes some regulation, e.g. by not having an efficient silencer, the driver may be prosecuted, and it is no defence for him to prove that the vehicle is as supplied to him by the manufacturers.

Brakes.—Every motor vehicle except motor-cycles with or without side-cars and invalid carriages, must have an efficient system of brakes which operate to prevent two at least of the wheels from revolving when the vehicle is not being driven—e.g. is parked. In the case of vehicles with only three wheels, one at least must be prevented from revolving when the vehicle is not being driven. A motor-car must have two entirely independent and efficient braking systems in good working order, or one efficient braking system having two independent means of operation. The brakes must be kept in good and efficient

order and properly adjusted. When the vehicle is left standing one of the brakes must be left on. Motor-cycles must have two braking systems or one system with two independent means of operation so constructed that failure of any single part will not prevent the brakes on one wheel from stopping the motor-cycle within a reasonable distance.

Driving Mirrors.— Every vehicle except a motor cycle, must have a reflecting mirror. The mirror may be either in the centre of the vehicle or at the side, but where it is in the centre it should be remembered that as the only means of vision is through the window at the back the vision will be obscured when the car is being driven with that window covered—e.g. when the blind is pulled down in night driving. It is not usual, however, for the police to prosecute in such cases.

Windscreen.—All glass fitted to the windscreen or outside windows facing to the front of a motor vehicle, except glass on the upper deck of a double-deck vehicle, must be safety glass. This does not apply until January 1, 1937, to vehicles registered on or before January 1, 1932.

Tyres.—All motor-cars whose unladen weight exceeds 1 ton must have pneumatic tyres, but this does not apply until after January 1, 1940, to motor-cars registered on or before January 2, 1933, if they have soft or elastic tyres. Motor-cycles must have pneumatic tyres.

Horn.—Every motor vehicle must carry an instrument capable of giving audible and sufficient warning of its approach and position. The driver must use this horn when necessary. It is, however, an offence to sound a horn when the vehicle is stationary unless this is necessary on the grounds of safety. Persons in vehicles outside a house who sound a horn in order to attract the attention of persons inside the house are therefore guilty of an offence.

Lighting.—During the hours of darkness every vehicle must have two white front lamps and one red rear lamp which are visible from a reasonable distance. The hours of darkness are, during summer-time, the time between one hour after sunset and one hour before sunrise, and, during the rest of the year, the time between half an hour after sunset and half an hour before

Road safety for pedestrians. (Top) "School" warning sign adapted to ensure safe street crossings for children. (Bottom) "Safety Lanes" in a busy London street.

sunrise. No light carried by a vehicle other than a dipping headlight must be moved by swivelling, deflecting or otherwise whilst the vehicle is in motion. Headlamps may, however, be fitted which turn with the steering wheel. The identification mark on the rear of the car must be kept illuminated after dark.

Motor-cycles must have two white lights in front if they have a side-car attached, and one white light when they are solo. A rear light is necessary in every case.

Automatic Lights and Police Signals.—It is an offence for any person not to obey signals given by a police officer or an automatic light signal. The penalty is a fine not exceeding £20 for a first offence or £50 or three months' imprisonment for later offences. Every motorist must stop when requested to do so by a constable in uniform.

Parking.—Local authorities have made bye-laws regulating the places where vehicles may be parked and the length of time they may be left in those places. These bye-laws are enforced by fines. In addition, any person leaving a vehicle elsewhere than at a recognized parking place may be guilty of obstructing the road. *The maximum penalty is a fine of £20.* Obstruction may take place although there is some person left in the vehicle in charge of it. It is also an offence to stop a vehicle in a position in which it is dangerous to others.

No person may drive a vehicle on to any common land, moor land or other land not being part of a road except for the purpose of saving life, extinguishing fire or other like emergency or for the purpose of parking the vehicle—when it may be driven on to land within 15 yards of a road. Although leaving a vehicle within 15 yards of the road is not an offence, yet it may constitute a trespass for which an action might be brought and the driver of the car must move the vehicle if requested to do so.

Control.—No person must drive a vehicle in a position from which he has not full control of it. Thus it might be an offence for three persons to sit in front of a car if the driver were in any way interfered with. The driver must also be in such a position that he has a full view of the road and traffic ahead.

Noise.—No vehicle must be used in such a way as to cause excessive noise which could have been avoided by reasonable care. In particular an efficient silencer must be fitted. Any person who uses or allows to be used a vehicle which is excessively noisy, either because it is badly made or in bad repair or because it has a load which is badly packed, e.g. milk cans not properly secured—is guilty of an offence. The horn must not be sounded when the vehicle is stationary and the engine must be stopped, if necessary, for the prevention of noise except when held up in the traffic.

Reversing.—In Oxford Street, London, reversing is forbidden altogether, and generally it is an offence to reverse a vehicle more than is necessary.

Towing.—When one vehicle is towing another the distance between them must not exceed 15 feet and the tow ropes must be made easily distinguishable. When a vehicle is being towed it must bear upon it the identification mark of the towing vehicle in place of its own marks.

Accidents.—When an accident takes place which causes damage or injury to any person, vehicle, or animal (which includes horse, cattle, ass, mule, sheep, pig, goat, or dog, but not a cat), owing to the presence of a motor vehicle on the road, the driver of the vehicle must stop. He must also give his name and address, the name and address of the owner of the car and the identification marks of the car to any person who asks him with reasonable grounds for doing so—e.g. someone who has been injured. If he does not give his name and address to some such person, he must report the accident at a police station or to a police constable as soon as he reasonably can, and in any case within 24 hours. If he does not do so he is guilty of an offence and liable to a fine of not more than £20 for a first offence and £50 or three months' imprisonment for later offences. If the accident has caused personal injury to any other person the driver must not only give his name and address and the particulars mentioned above, but must produce his insurance certificate within 24 hours. If he cannot do this, he may escape liability by producing the certificate within 5 days at some police station selected by himself, but otherwise he will be liable to the same punishment as is mentioned above. It should be noticed that where the accident does not cause damage to any person, vehicle, or animal, but only to property such as a fence or gate, the accident need not be reported. Where an accident takes place which causes damage only to the vehicle of the person driving, it should in strict law be reported, but in practice this is not usually done. Further, there is no need to report the accident to the police or to produce the insurance certificate to the police if the name and address is given and the insurance certificate produced to some person who asks for the information at the time of the accident.

Claims.—When a claim is made against any person in respect of any liability against which he is compelled to insure, he must, if he is asked, state whether or not he was insured or would have been insured against that liability but for his policy being repudiated, and give particulars relating to the policy as stated in his certificate of insurance. This is to enable the injured person to intimate his claim direct to the insurance company (*see above*).

Medical Treatment.—Great hardship has been caused to doctors and to hospitals who are called on to render assistance to persons who are injured as a result of motor accidents in that very frequently the injured persons have no money to pay for the treatment. Until recently there was, as a rule, no method by which the doctor or hospital could recover the money from the person in charge of any motor vehicle which caused the accident. It is now, however, possible for the doctor to recover the fee of 12/6 from the person driving the vehicle at the time in respect of each person to whom he gives emergency treatment, and in addition 6d. for every mile or part of a mile over two miles which he has to come in order to give the treatment. When the treatment is given in a hospital, the hospital are in the same way entitled to claim a fee.

A claim for this fee either by a doctor or by a hospital may be made at the time when the treatment is given, and, if not made at that time, must be made in writing within seven days by registered post or by delivery. The police are bound to give the doctor or the hospital every assistance to enable them to discover the name of the registered owner of the vehicle.

Where an accident occurs which is not the fault of the person against whom a claim for a fee is made, he is nevertheless bound to pay it in the first place, but he may recover it from the person responsible for the accident. The insurance policy required for the vehicle must cover the liability to make payments of this kind, and also the payment of a sum not exceeding £25 to any hospital in which any person injured or killed on a road has received treatment to the knowledge of the insurance company. It should be noticed that the driver is not liable to make this latter payment but only his insurance company.

Bicycles.—The regulations relating to motor vehicles do not apply to bicycles. A bicycle must not, however, be ridden on the footway, penalty 40/-. Not more than one person may be carried on a bicycle unless it is constructed or adapted for carrying more than one person, e.g. a tandem, on penalty of a fine of £5 for a first offence and £10 for later offences. Bicycles must carry a white front lamp but do not need to carry a red rear lamp if an unobscured and efficient red reflector is carried instead. Persons who sell reflectors which do not comply with the regulations are liable to a fine of £5 for a first offence and £10 for later offences. The Minister of Transport may make regulations compelling bicycles either to have a large white surface on the rear mudguard as well as a reflector or to carry a red rear lamp, and he may also regulate the brakes of bicycles.

Public Service Vehicles. — Motor vehicles, such as omnibuses and charabancs, used for carrying paying passengers, are known as public service vehicles. These require special licences and their drivers and conductors must also have special licences in addition, in the case of the driver, to the ordinary driving licence.

Public service vehicles may be either stage carriages, express carriages, or contract carriages. Stage carriages are vehicles, such as omnibuses, which carry passengers at separate fares, some of which are less than one shilling. Express carriages are charabancs carrying passengers at separate fares, no fare for ordinary passengers being less than one shilling. Vehicles may still be express carriages although special fares of less than one shilling are charged in the case of children, workmen or students. A motor vehicle adapted to carry less than 8 passengers is not a stage or express carriage merely because it carries passengers at separate fares on occasions of race meetings, public gatherings, and other like special occasions. Contract carriages are vehicles hired as a whole, e.g. a charabanc engaged for a party of people.

Passengers are considered to be carried at separate fares, and therefore the vehicles in which they are carried are considered to be stage carriages or express carriages, even though the fares are paid not to the owner of the vehicle but to some other person, and even though the fares include payment in respect of something in addition to the journey.

Difficulties arise when a party is formed to go on a certain motor trip, the members of the party each paying a sum of money to the person who is getting up the trip and he making the arrangements with the owner of the vehicle for the hire of the vehicle as a whole. Is the vehicle a stage or express carriage, or is it a contract carriage? As a rule the vehicle is a stage or express carriage, but special provisions have been made to meet the needs of purely private parties. When the vehicle is being used for carrying a private party on a special occasion the mere fact that the members of the party have made separate payments does not make the vehicle a stage carriage or express carriage. A vehicle is only considered as being used for carrying a private party on a special occasion when:—

(a) the person making the arrangements for bringing the party together is not the holder of a public service vehicle licence for the vehicle, or an agent of

his and acts without any remuneration;

(b) the journey is not advertised to the public;

(c) all the passengers, in the case of a journey to a particular destination, must be carried to or near to that destination, or, in the case of a tour, for the greater part of the journey;

(d) the fares for the journey must not differ on the basis of distance or time;

(e) in the case of a journey to a particular destination no person must be carried who frequently, or as a matter of routine, travels to that destination at or about the time of day at which the journey is made.

Public Service Vehicle Licences.— Each of these vehicles requires a public service vehicle licence, which will only be granted if the vehicle is maintained in a proper condition and passes the inspection of an examiner.

Road Service Licences.—This does not relate to the vehicle but to the route on which it is to operate. No person may run a public service vehicle on any route unless he has a road service licence in respect of that route.

Drivers' and Conductors' Licences. —Special licences are required for drivers and conductors of public service vehicles and for drivers of heavy goods vehicles. No person can obtain a driver's licence until he is 21 nor a conductor's licence until he is 18.

Applications.—Applications for all of these licences must be made to the traffic commissioners of the district. As to special licences for goods and other vehicles, *see* CARRIERS' LICENCES; HACKNEY CARRIAGE.

DIVORCE

UNTIL 1857 the only method of obtaining a divorce permitting re-marriage was by a private Act of Parliament. The cost of such a proceeding was enormous and was a luxury reserved for the very rich. It is of interest to note that between the years 1715 and 1852 the total number of marriages dissolved in this country was less than two hundred. By the Matrimonial Causes Act, 1857, however, the High Court of Justice was granted the power of granting decrees of divorce en-titling the parties to remarry.

At the present time, the matrimonial jurisdiction of the High Court of Justice is exercised mainly by the Probate Divorce and Admiralty Division. This Division deals with the validity of marriages, and the grant of relief on account of matrimonial offences. Suits of the first class are those for jactitation, (which literally means "boast-ing,") and nullity of marriage. The second class are for divorce, restitution of conjugal rights, and judicial separation. It will be convenient to consider all these under their separate heads:—

1. **Jactitation of Marriage.**—Suits in respect of jactitation are very uncommon nowadays. If a person persistently main-tains that he or she has been married to another, the person of whom it is said can ask the Court to command the other to cease making the allegation.

2. **Nullity of Marriage.**—A decree of nullity of marriage must be distinguished from one of divorce. In the first case the Court holds that there never was in fact a complete and valid marriage, in the second it dissolves an existing marriage. Marriages may be incomplete and invalid on several grounds. In some cases they are void from the beginning, in others they can be rendered void on the application of one of the parties. The latter class are described as voidable.

Marriages are void if there was absence of consent on the part of one or both of the parties. Thus, if a person is married when in such a state of intoxication as to be unable to give any real consent, the ceremony is void. It is equally so if his consent is obtained by threats of violence, or fraud as to the nature of the ceremony. On the other hand misrepresentation on other matters has no legal effect. Marriages are void also if performed contrary to the law governing their celebration, or if between persons within the prohibited degrees, or (if after the 10th Mary, 1929), with a person under sixteen years of age, or a person so mentally deficient as to be unable lawfully to marry, or one already married.

A marriage is voidable if, when the ceremony is performed, one of the parties is physically unable to consummate it, and such inability is incurable. In such cases, however, only the other party may ask for the decree of nullity. It should be noted that mere sterility does not constitute grounds for a decree.

3. **Divorce.**—At the present time a divorce may be granted on the ground of adultery by the husband or wife. Desertion, or cruelty, or other matrimonial offences are not in themselves sufficient to allow the Court to dissolve a marriage, though they may entitle a petitioner to a judicial separa-tion. In addition to adultery, certain un-natural offences constitute grounds for divorce.

A person cannot, of course, ask for a divorce on the ground of his or her own adultery. The right is that of the innocent party. But if a petitioner who proves adultery by the other spouse, has himself committed adultery, he is not necessarily prevented from obtaining a divorce. In such a case, however, it is essential that at the time of presenting the petition, he makes a full disclosure in writing to the Court of all adultery committed by himself, and the circumstances leading to it. If this be done the Judge has a discretion which he may exercise in the petitioner's favour to grant him a decree, notwithstanding his own adultery. When both parties are petitioning for divorce on the ground of the other's adultery, and each admits adultery and asks for the discretion of the Court to be exercised in his or her favour, the Court has the task of deciding which should be granted the decree.

The effect of a divorce is that both parties may marry again. This, however, cannot be done immediately after the hearing. At the hearing a decree nisi of dissolution is pronounced, and this is provisional only. At the expiration of six months application may be made to make the decree absolute, and if this be granted, the divorce becomes effective. In special circumstances, the Court will allow the six months' period to be reduced. If the petitioner commits adultery before the decree has been made absolute, the decree nisi may be revoked.

There are several bars to a petition for divorce. The adultery may, of course, be denied, and in this connection it may be noted that the petitioner has not merely to allege, but to prove the adultery. If it be shewn that the petitioner connived at the adultery, the petition must be dismissed. Connivance consists of assistance or conduct intentionally directed to procure the adultery of the other spouse. Again, if the parties are in collusion to deceive the Court or effect some agreement by which the case is not defended, the Court has no option but to dismiss the petition. A similar result is produced when the adultery complained of has been condoned. Condonation takes place when the innocent spouse with full knowledge of the other's matrimonial offences forgives them and returns to conjugal cohabitation. Mere verbal forgiveness does not in itself constitute condonation, but resumption of marital relations, even without expressions of forgiveness, is conclusive evidence of condonation.

In certain cases even though adultery be proved, the Court has a discretion as to whether to grant a divorce or not. This is so where the conduct of the petitioner has conduced to the adultery complained of. Neglect or cruelty may have this effect, but it must be remembered that each case has to be considered on its own facts. Another ground on which a decree may be refused is undue delay in bringing the divorce proceedings. Where there has been long delay after the petitioner has learnt of the adultery the Court must consider the motives behind the delay. If the reason is shewn to be lack of funds, the Court will regard it with sympathy, but nowadays the work of the Poor Persons' Committee is reducing the cases in which such a plea can validly be advanced. A further discretionary bar is the petitioner's own adultery, which has already been dealt with above.

In divorce proceedings, the husband and wife are the principal parties, being called the petitioner and the respondent as the case may be. Where the wife is the petitioner, the woman with whom she alleges the adultery was committed is called "the woman named." She can, if she wishes, intervene in the proceedings to deny the allegations made against her. Where the husband is the petitioner, the other man is called "the co-respondent." As such, he is always a party to the suit. In addition to obtaining a divorce from his wife, a husband may recover damages from a co-respondent who, knowing her to be a married woman, has seduced her. A co-respondent may in such circumstances be directed to pay the costs of the proceedings.

4. **Judicial Separation.**—A decree of judicial separation may be granted on the grounds of adultery, cruelty, or desertion. Such a decree does not dissolve the marriage, and the parties are not rendered free to marry again. It does, however, provide that they need not cohabit, and usually carries with it orders relating to maintenance of the wife and custody of the children. The rules governing the absolute and discretionary bars applicable to divorce proceedings in general apply also to proceedings for judicial separation.

5. **Restitution of Conjugal Rights.**—If a husband or wife refuses to live with the other in spite of genuine requests to do so, the party deserted may obtain a decree for the restitution of conjugal rights. Refusal to comply with this decree constitutes desertion.

Matrimonial Offences.—The chief matrimonial offences are adultery, cruelty, and desertion. These must each be separately considered.

1. **Adultery.**—A single act of adultery is sufficient to constitute this matrimonial offence. Of necessity such conduct can seldom be directly proved. A confession by the guilty spouse is always strong evidence, but in general some evidence in addition is required. In most cases adultery is regarded as established if association of an intimate character is proved, coupled with opportunity to commit adultery. Did the

An Agreement made the twenty second
day of July One
thousand nine hundred
and thirty ——
BETWEEN GEORGE
HUNTER of 2276
Randolph Crescent Bremcaster (hereinafter called the husband) of the
one part and ELIZABETH MARGARET HUNTER his wife (hereinafter called
the Wife) of the other part WHEREBY IT IS AGREED as follows :-

1.   THE husband and wife shall for the future live apart from each
other and the wife shall be freed from the control of the husband
The wife shall have the custody of the three children of the marriage

2.   NEITHER the husband nor the Wife shall molest or annoy or
interfere with the other or endeavour to compel the other to cohabit
or live with him or her by any proceedings or in any manner
whatsoever

3.   THE husband will pay to the wife for the support and maintenance
of herself (so long as she shall lead a chaste life) the weekly sum
of ONE POUND and for the support and maintenance of each of the said
children while under the age of sixteen a further weekly sum of
SEVEN SHILLINGS AND SIXPENCE

4.   THE wife shall out of the said allowance or otherwise support
herself and the said children and in case the husband shall at any
time or times hereafter be called upon to pay and shall pay any debt
which the wife shall have incurred then the husband may deduct the
amount of such payment from any sums thereafter payable to the wife
hereunder whether in respect of herself or in respect of the said
children

5.   IN case the husband and wife shall at any time hereafter come
together and cohabit or if their marriage shall be dissolved this
agreement shall thenceforth determine

        I N   W I T N E S S   whereof the parties hereto have hereunto
set their hands the day and year first before written

S I G N E D by the above named   }
GEORGE HUNTER in the presence of :)   *George Hunter.*

    Ralph Gray,
        962, Randolph Crescent, Bremcaster.
                        Bank Clerk.

S I G N E D by the above named   )
ELIZABETH MARGARET HUNTER in the   )   *Elizabeth Hunter.*
presence of :-   )

    T Stewart Scown
        17ᴬ Ibslon Park Place
                Lanchester
                    Barristers Clerk

A Specimen Separation Agreement.

parties by their behaviour indicate a relationship in which illicit intercourse was likely, and did they seek and find an occasion from their behaviour on which such intercourse may reasonably be inferred?

Sometimes a husband seeks to establish adultery on the part of his wife by proving that she gave birth to a child of which he could not possibly be the father. In the famous case of Russell *v* Russell, the House of Lords laid down the rule that no husband can himself give evidence to shew that he has not had during the marriage marital relations with his wife, if the effect of such evidence would be to shew her offspring to be illegitimate. Evidence having this result can be given by other witnesses. Thus a husband can call persons to say that at the time material to the paternity of the child, while his wife was in England, he was abroad.

Where a husband and wife have been judicially separated, there is no longer any presumption that a child born to the wife is the child of the husband, and adultery may be inferred from such an event. A similar rule applies where the parties are living separately in accordance with the provisions of a separation deed.

The law forbids forcing a husband or wife to admit adultery. No questions may be put in cross-examination to a respondent tending to prove adultery until he or she has already denied committing it.

2. Cruelty.—To constitute cruelty in law there must be conduct which has either affected the health of the other party, or is reasonably likely to have that effect. In some cases a single act may be sufficient if it causes serious bodily injury. Most cases of cruelty, however, arise from a course of conduct having a cumulative effect. There need not necessarily be any actual physical violence at all. Threats of violence if sufficiently repeated may be sufficient, and in some cases persistent threats of false accusations. Mere neglect or preference for other persons cannot constitute cruelty. In itself drunkenness is not cruelty, but, of course, violent behaviour when in a drunken condition may well amount to it.

A wife as well as a husband may be guilty of cruelty. It is the practice of the Courts to require some corroboration of a petitioner's allegations of cruelty. This can be afforded by a doctor who attended the petitioner, or

by persons to whom the petitioner has complained at the time of the alleged cruelty, or of course by actual eye-witnesses.

3. Desertion.—A spouse deserts the other when he or she ceases to live with the other contrary to the wishes of the other and without just cause. If they separate by mutual consent, one spouse cannot afterwards complain that by refusing to return to cohabitation, the other is guilty of desertion. But for a separation to have this effect, it must be intended to be a permanent ending of conjugal relationship. If on account of business or duty the parties have to live separately for a time, such absence does not constitute separation by mutual consent. When circumstances render resumption of cohabitation possible, refusal by one to return to it may be desertion.

There is no desertion unless the deserting party actually leaves the other. If they continue living in the same house though marital intercourse is refused, there is no desertion. There may, however, be special circumstances amounting virtually to living in separate houses. Thus where a husband refused to have anything to do with his wife, and required her to live in a self-contained part of his house having a separate entrance, his conduct was held to constitute desertion.

The party who actually departs from the other is not necessarily the one guilty of desertion. If one party pursues a course of conduct with the intention of causing the other to depart, he is the deserting party and not the other.

Questions of great difficulty frequently arise where one party having deserted the other repents of it, and asks the other to resume cohabitation. If this request is refused, the Court may have to decide whether the refusal was justified. This will depend on the conduct of the parties before the desertion commenced. If there is a genuine regret for past misbehaviour, and a real desire to start afresh, a spouse who refuses to receive back the deserting party cannot afterwards complain of desertion.

To obtain a decree of judicial separation in the High Court of Justice on the ground of desertion, the desertion must have lasted for two years. If, however, proceedings are brought in the Police Court for a separation order, such an order may be made though the desertion has lasted a shorter period.

The Procedure of the Divorce Court.—Proceedings in the Divorce Court are commenced by a petition setting out in proper form the particulars of the marriage, the matrimonial offences complained of, and the relief asked for. The respondent then files an answer stating his or her defence, if any, to the allegations. The respondent may, in the answer, set up cross charges, and on them ask for a divorce or judicial separation against the petitioner. If this is done, the petitioner files a reply containing the defence to the cross charges. When these pleadings are complete the case may be set down for trial. At the trial the judge may make a decree or dismiss the petition, and may make such order as to the costs of the proceedings as may be necessary.

The King's Proctor.—The King's Proctor is an official whose duties include the scrutiny of divorce proceedings with a view to bringing to the notice of the Court, any collusion or other matters of which it should be aware. The reason for the existence of such an office is that divorce is a matter of interest to the community as well as the parties. In ordinary actions the parties can be left to fight out, or compromise their disputes as they wish, but in matrimonial disputes it is thought that the actual parties, not being the only people affected, should not be left without some supervision aimed at preventing abuse of the facilities offered by the Courts. If the King's Proctor becomes aware of any material fact not known to the Court when it pronounced a decree nisi, it is his duty to intervene and bring it to the notice of the Court.

Costs in the Divorce Court.— The costs of a suit, of course, vary enormously according to its nature, the number of witnesses, whether it is defended or not, etc. A wife who is a petitioner or respondent and who has not sufficient property of her own, can frequently obtain an order at any early stage that her husband give security for a considerable part of her costs. If she succeeds, the Judge usually orders the husband to pay her costs. Even if she fails, her solicitor is nevertheless usually allowed the costs up to the amount of the security ordered by the Judge.

If a wife fails, and has enough property of her own, the husband can sometimes obtain an order for her to pay his costs. A co-respondent who is found guilty of adultery, and who knew that the respondent was a married woman can be ordered to pay the whole costs of the proceedings.

Money Payments to Wives.—A husband is bound to support his wife even though she has divorced him. If a husband divorces his wife, she has no further claim on him, though sometimes the Court will only grant a husband a decree if he, to save the wife from starvation, makes her some small compassionate allowance.

The duty of supporting the wife, however, is qualified by possession by her of means of her own, or ability to earn a living. The method by which maintenance figures are arrived at is to add together the husband's and the wife's incomes, including in the wife's her ability to earn. (Here it should be noted that a wife burdened by young children or who is elderly, has little or no earning capacity.) A proportion of the total joint incomes is then fixed as the amount proper for the support of the wife. If her own income is below that proportion, the husband is ordered to pay sufficient to bring it up to that proportion.

Allowances are of two kinds: Pending suit, and permanent. The first is, as the name implies, pending the trial of the case. It is properly called *alimony pendente lite.* The proportion usually thought proper for the support of the wife is about one fifth of the joint incomes. After a divorce or a judicial separation, permanent orders are made, their correct names being maintenance and permanent alimony respectively. The amounts are larger than for alimony pendente lite, the usual proportion being about one-third of the joint incomes.

Applications for alimony or maintenance are made by means of petitions. The means of the parties are then enquired into by one of the Registrars of the Divorce Division who fixes the proper figure after, where necessary, hearing evidence. Orders for payment can be enforced in much the same way as High Court judgments.

Children.—When parties who have children under sixteen years of age are divorced or judicially separated, the Court decides on their custody. In determining this question, the Judge has to consider primarily the welfare and interests of the children. Usually custody is granted to the innocent party, it being considered that he or she can provide the environment best suited for the bringing up of children. But where a child is very young, the claims of the mother often override the consideration of her guilt.

A guilty parent, however, is seldom completely barred from seeing his or her children. Though custody be granted to one parent, the other may be allowed access to the children for limited and stated periods. This access may be for short visits to the child's home only, or may in some cases extend to receiving the child for long holiday periods.

In deciding questions of custody and access, a Judge may conduct an enquiry in his private room. He may examine the claims of persons other than the parents, and may interview the child in the absence of its parents in order to ascertain its own views.

A husband is always required to provide suitable maintenance for his children. When the wife is granted custody, it is usual to make him pay to her such periodical sum as is decided to be proper for this purpose.

The Matrimonial Jurisdiction of the Police Courts.—A quick and cheap method by which wives can obtain relief in respect of matrimonial wrongs is in the Police Court. But it must be noted that the Police Court has no power to try divorce cases, or to dissolve marriages. Moreover, the Police Court can entertain only applications by wives, and not by husbands.

Any married woman can obtain an order against her husband if he has been convicted of a serious assault upon her, if he has deserted her, if he has been guilty of persistent cruelty to her, if he has wilfully neglected to provide reasonable maintenance for her or her infant children, or if he has been found to be in law an habitual drunkard.

The Court may make a separation order having the effect of a judicial separation, and may order the husband to pay to her a sum not exceeding £2 weekly for her maintenance. The Court may also grant her the custody of the children of the marriage, and direct the husband to pay her a sum of not more than ten shillings a week for the support of each child. If disobeyed, these orders for payment can be enforced by imprisonment.

It will be observed that the matrimonial offences here set out differ somewhat from those that can be made the subject of complaint in the High Court of Justice. Adultery on the part of the husband is not a ground in itself for granting the wife any order in the Police Court. Desertion is common to both jurisdictions, and the principles governing it the same. So far as cruelty is concerned, the Police Court can entertain complaints based upon it if it is persistent or consists of an aggravated assault.

A special word is necessary as to the offence of wilful failure to maintain, which is not in itself a ground for a decree in the High Court. It must be noted that the failure must be *wilful*, that is to say, the husband must be shewn to have the means to maintain, or at any rate the possibility of earning sufficient means. It must also be remembered that it is for the husband to decide the scale of living he wishes himself and his family to adopt; the question therefore is not what maintenance is usual to a person of his means, but whether he has failed to provide any reasonable maintenance.

There is an important provision that no order can be made if the wife has committed adultery, or, if made, it is to be revoked if adultery be proved. If, however, the adultery has been condoned or connived at by the husband, or if by his wilful neglect or misconduct he has conduced to it, this provision is not enforceable. When adultery in this connection is in question, the principles which govern proof of it in the High Court apply in the same way in the Police Court.

RENT RESTRICTIONS

OWING to the shortage of houses during and after the War, it was necessary to pass legislation preventing landlords from turning out of their premises tenants of houses of low value, and also limiting the landlords' right to raise the rents of these premises. The effect of the Acts in force until 1933 was that, generally speaking, all houses were given the above protection if the standard rent (which was usually the rent on the 3rd August, 1914, *see below*) or the rateable value was not greater than £105 in London, £78 in other places in England, and £90 in Scotland.

From 1923 until 1933, there was in force a process of gradual decontrol, that is, it was possible for individual houses to cease to be controlled, i.e. governed by the Acts, in certain cases, the most important of which was where the tenant left and the landlord recovered possession.

In this way, by 1933, a very large number of houses had ceased to be governed by the Acts. It was found, however, that by that year, although the supply of the larger houses within the Acts was then sufficient to meet the demand, and that it was therefore no longer necessary to protect the tenants or control the rent of these houses, yet in the case of the very smallest houses there was still a great shortage, and therefore that it was undesirable to continue this process of decontrol by individual houses in the case of these very small houses. Accordingly, in 1933, an Act was passed, which did two things. Firstly, it removed, as from 29th September, 1933 (Scotland 28th November, 1933), all protection from the larger type of house, i.e. houses whose recoverable rent (*see below*), and rateable value *both* exceeded £45 a year in London or Scotland, or £35 a year elsewhere on the "appointed day." (The appointed day is the 6th April, 1931, in the County of London, 1st April, 1931, throughout the rest of England, and 16th May, 1931, in Scotland.) The recoverable rent means the amount to which the landlord was entitled to raise the rent under the provisions of the earlier Rent Acts (*see below*).) Houses of this type are now known as Class A houses.

Secondly, the Act of 1933 prevented any more of the smallest houses from being deprived of the protection of the Acts piecemeal by the operation of the decontrol of individual houses. After 18th July, 1933, no decontrol is possible of houses whose rateable value did not exceed £20 in London, £13 in the rest of England and £26 5s. in Scotland, on the appointed day. (*See above.*)

Houses of this class which had been already decontrolled before 18th July, 1933, were not brought back within the control again, but no decontrol of houses still within the Acts on that date was possible. Houses of this class are known as Class C houses.

There is still left the class of houses between Class A and Class C, namely those the rateable value of which on the appointed day exceeded £20 in London, £13 in the rest of England, and £26 5s. in Scotland, but which do not fall within Class A, i.e. which do not have a recoverable rent or rateable value over £45 in London, etc., as set out above. These houses in Class B remain unaffected by the 1933 Act. They may still be decontrolled, but until they are decontrolled they are protected.

It is thus necessary to consider not only the 1933 Act, but also the provisions of the earlier Rent Acts.

Dwelling Houses within the Acts. —Before 1933, the houses within the Acts were all those where either the "standard" rent or the rateable value on a certain date did not exceed £105 in London, £90 in Scotland, and £78 elsewhere. The standard rent is the rent at which the house was let on the 3rd August, 1914, or, where the house was not let on that date, the rent at which it was last let before that date. Where the house was first let after that date, then the standard rent is the rent at the time of first letting. (*See below.*) The date at which the rateable value of any house within the Act is taken is also the 3rd August, 1914.

Since the 1933 Act has deprived the larger houses of protection, it follows that to-day, no house will be within the Acts if its recoverable rent (which differs from the standard rent, *see above*), *and* its rateable value (on the appointed day, *see above*, not on 3rd August, 1914), are over £45 a year in London or Scotland, and £35 elsewhere.

Note firstly, that both the recoverable rent and rateable value must be above the amount; if either is below, the house may still be protected; and secondly, that it does not follow necessarily that a house is protected because its recoverable rent or rateable value are below these amounts. In any case it may have lost its protection by what is known as decontrol before 29th September, 1933, or, if it is a Class B house, by decontrol before or after that date.

Dwelling-house.—A dwelling-house does not mean only self-contained buildings. A single room or a flat will be a dwelling-house if it is let as a dwelling. The Acts do not apply, however, to premises used solely for business purposes, but they apply to premises of which part only is used for business, e.g. to a shop with a house over. Nor do the Acts apply in any of the following cases:—

1. Houses where land is included in the letting, if the rateable value (in 1914, as above), of the land is one quarter or more of the rateable value of the house or premises.

2. Where the rent is less than two-thirds of the rateable value (in 1914, as above). This excludes from the operation of the Acts all houses let on long leases at a ground rent.

3. Where the letting includes payments in respect of board, attendance, or use of furniture, so long as the amount payable for the attendance or the furniture forms a substantial portion of the whole rent paid. Thus, a house will not lose protection merely because a tenant has in it some linoleum belonging to the landlord, or is entitled to some small services, such as the bringing up of coal.

4. Where the house is one which was erected after the 2nd April, 1919, or was in the course of erection at that date, or was then being or has since that date been reconstructed by being converted into two or more separate and self-contained flats.

5. Since the 29th September, 1933, the Acts do not apply to any on-licensed premises.

To all houses not within these provisions the Acts originally applied, but from 1923 to 18th July, 1933, it was possible for any house within the Acts to be removed from them by what has been called "decontrol"; since 1933, it is still possible for Class B houses (*see above*) to be decontrolled; but this is not now possible in the case of Class C houses. It is therefore necessary to consider decontrol.

Decontrol.—Any house might be decontrolled between 1923 and 18th July, 1933, and a Class B may still be decontrolled in any of the following ways:—

1. Where the landlord on the 31st of July, 1923, was in possession of the house, or came into possession of it at any time after that date. Possession for this purpose means actual possession, and a mere change of tenancy on one tenant going out and another coming in without any interval between will not amount to possession by the landlord for purposes of decontrol.

On the other hand it is probably not necessary for the landlord or his agent actually to enter on the premises, so long as there is a gap between one tenant going out and another coming in.

But it is certainly wise for a landlord who wishes to decontrol premises to enter either by himself or by some agent, such as a caretaker or a decorator. Even if this is not done, however, it may be enough if the landlord has received the key from the tenant and if there is some gap before the new tenant goes in.

Who is a Landlord?—Difficult points arise in determining who is a landlord for these purposes. Where A lets a house of six rooms to B, and B sub-lets three of the rooms to C, and three to D, there is no doubt that in ordinary speech C and D will refer to B as their landlord, and B will refer to A as his landlord. Suppose, therefore, that C gives up his three rooms so that B is in possession of them and may let them again—are the three rooms which form a dwelling-house taken out of the Act, i.e. decontrolled—because landlord B is in possession? It is expressly provided that in this case the three rooms are not decontrolled by reason of B being in possession of them.

Suppose, again, that B, instead of letting all the rooms in the house, has only let three to C and has lived in the remaining three himself. If C leaves, and B enters into possession, the effect will be the same as in the case already considered, and C's rooms will not be decontrolled.

Suppose, again, that it is B who gives up the house, leaving C in occupation of the three rooms sublet to him, B's three rooms will then be in the possession of landlord A, and are decontrolled; but C's three rooms are not decontrolled. There are really three dwelling-houses in existence: firstly, the whole house let by A to B, secondly, C's three rooms, and thirdly B's three rooms. The result of B leaving will be that his three rooms will become decontrolled, but not the three rooms occupied by C. If B sublets the whole house to C, and C leaves, it is probable but not certain that the house will be decontrolled.

It should be noticed in this connection that it is still possible for a Class C house to be decontrolled by the landlord having possession in one case. Where A lets a dwelling-house which is not of Class C to B, and B divides it and sublets it in smaller dwelling-houses which come within Class C, the smaller dwelling-houses may still be decontrolled by the landlord coming into possession of them. Where, however, the sub-dividing into smaller houses is done, not by a tenant but by the landlord himself, the ordinary rules apply. The houses, being Class C, are not now liable to decontrol.

Suppose that the person who is letting the house has not let it before 1923, but has been in possession of it as occupier since that time, is he a landlord in possession, although at the time when he was in possession, he had never had any tenant? It has been held that the fact that the premises have not been previously let at the time when the "landlord" has possession will not prevent them being decontrolled. In the same way, if, instead of letting the whole house, the owner lets part only of it which he has never previously let before, but has occupied himself, that part is decontrolled. In all the above examples, the result would be the same if the landlord himself held under a lease instead of as a freeholder, so long as he was paying a rent which was less than two-thirds of the rateable value—e.g. a ground rent.

Decontrol by a New Lease.—Where the landlord, after 31st July, 1923, grants to the tenant a lease of the house for not less than two years, or enters into an agreement for such a lease, the lease being one which is not due to expire before one year after the date fixed at the time when the lease is granted for expiration of the Acts, the house is decontrolled. At the present time the Acts are due to expire on the 24th June, 1938, in England, and 28th May, 1938, in Scotland, so that the lease, in order to decontrol the house, must expire before the 24th June, 1939, in England, or 28th May, 1939, in Scotland.

The theory of decontrol in this way is that a tenant who obtains a definite tenure on a fixed rent for a lengthy period, does not require the protection of the Acts. In this case also protection is given to sub-tenants, and if A lets a dwelling-house to B who sublets parts of it to C and occupies part himself, a lease granted by A to B will not decontrol the house occupied by C, but only the part occupied by B.

Protection of the Acts.—Tenants of the houses which are within the Acts are afforded protection in two respects. Firstly, they cannot be put out of possession except in certain circumstances, and secondly, the landlord is only entitled to increase the rent up to a certain amount and in a certain manner.

Right to Retain Possession.—No tenant whose house is protected by the Act can be put out of possession except by an order of the Court. The Court will only make an order in cases where it considers it reasonable to do so, and either (a) it has been satisfied that there is suitable alternative accommodation available for the tenant, or (b) it has been proved that one or other of the following events has taken place:—

1. The tenant has failed to pay rent, or has broken some other obligation of his tenancy. In this case the Court does not usually make an order that the tenant should give up the possession of the premises at once, but makes an order which is suspended from having any operation so long as the tenant pays the current rent and some proportion of the arrears of rent, or remedies the other breach of the terms of his tenancy.

If the tenant keeps up the payments under this order he will not in fact be deprived of his house. Where he fails to keep the payment up, another application should be made to the Court for possession. Even on the hearing of this application the Court will frequently give the tenant further time to pay the arrears.

2. Where the tenant, or some person residing with him, has been guilty of conduct which is a nuisance or annoyance to adjoining occupiers, or has been convicted of using the premises, or allowing them to be used, for an immoral or illegal purpose, or where through the conduct or neglect of the tenant or such other person, the condition of the dwelling-house has deteriorated. Where the acts complained of have been done not by the tenant, but by some lodger or sub-tenant of his, the Court will not make any order for possession unless it is satisfied that the tenant has not done all he might have done to have the lodger or sub-tenant removed from the premises. The general effect of this is that a tenant may lose the possession of the premises if he, or any person for whom he is in any way responsible, uses them improperly or damages them.

3. Where the tenant has given notice to quit, and in consequence the landlord has arranged to sell or let the house, or has taken any other steps as a result of which he would in the opinion of the Court be seriously prejudiced if he could not obtain possession. Thus, if a tenant informs his landlord that he intends to leave, and later changes his mind, the landlord can only recover possession, if in the meantime he has undertaken some liabilities—e.g. by selling the premises with vacant possession —which he would not be able to carry out owing to the tenant's refusal to leave.

4. Where the tenant *without the consent of the landlord* has at any time after the 31st of July, 1923, assigned or sublet the whole of the dwelling-house, or has sublet part of it when the remainder is already sublet. Even if there is no express provision against assigning or sub-letting in the tenancy agreement, this provision will apply. If there is a provision in the terms of the letting preventing the tenant from sub-letting or assigning, his conduct in doing so will be a breach of the obligations of his

tenancy and will also fall under heading 1, above.

5. Where the dwelling-house includes premises with an off-licence, and the tenant has committed an offence as holder of the licence, or has not conducted the business to the satisfaction of the licensing justices or the police authority, or has carried it on in a manner detrimental to the public interest, or where the renewal of the licence has been refused.

It should be remembered that premises with an on-licence are now outside the Acts altogether. (*See above.*)

6. Where the dwelling-house is so overcrowded as to be dangerous or injurious to the health of the persons living in it, and the Court is satisfied that the tenant could have prevented this over-crowding and has not done so.

7. (*a*) Where the dwelling-house is reasonably required by the landlord as a residence for some person employed whole time, either by the landlord or by some tenant of the landlord; and (*b*) where *either* the tenant, whom it is desired to remove from the premises, was himself employed by the landlord or a former landlord, and where the house was let to him in consequence of that employment which has ceased; *or* where the Court is satisfied that the person for whom the house is required is to be employed by the landlord on an agricultural holding, or in repairs, or building works on an agricultural holding.

8. Where the landlord has become landlord in some way otherwise than by purchasing the house at a date after the 11th July, 1931, he may obtain possession in certain cases where he wishes to use it as a residence for himself, or any son, or daughter of his over 18, or his father or mother. The Court, however, will not make an order on this ground if, in view of the positions of landlord and tenant, greater hardship would be caused to the tenant by granting the order and turning him out than would be caused to the landlord by refusing it. It should be noticed that no landlord who has purchased the premises since the date mentioned can rely on this provision, but a landlord who has acquired the premises otherwise than by purchasing them—e.g. by succeeding to them under a will or on intestacy, even after that date—may rely on that provision.

9. Where the tenant has sublet part of his premises, and is charging an amount in excess of the recoverable rent, i.e. the rent permitted under the Act. (*See below.*) The object of this is to prevent tenants from profiteering by paying a small rent themselves and sub-letting a part at a large profit. It should be noticed that under heading 4 above, the tenant may be put out of possession where he has sublet the whole house without the landlord's consent whether or not the rent charge is excessive.

It should always be remembered that even if the landlord succeeds in proving one or other of the above sets of facts, the Court is not bound to make an order unless it considers it reasonable to do so. In practice, this gives to the Court a very wide discretion which is exercised in some districts in favour of the landlord, and in others in favour of the tenant.

Alternative Accommodation.—

Even though the landlord cannot prove any of the above facts, he may still obtain possession from his tenant if he proves to the Court that there is suitable alternative accommodation available for the tenant. Even here, however, the Court will not make an order unless it thinks it is reasonable to do so.

The landlord may prove to the Court that there is suitable alternative accommodation in either of two ways. The simplest and most conclusive method is for him to obtain a certificate from the housing authority of the area stating that the authority will provide suitable accommodation for the tenant. Where the landlord has not obtained a certificate to this effect, he must call evidence to satisfy the Court that there is available for the tenant either another house controlled by the Acts or, if it is not within the Acts, e.g. has been decontrolled, that it gives the tenant a similar degree of security of tenure as would a house within the Act. To satisfy this last provision it would probably be necessary that the tenant should get a lease of a suitable house for a period not expiring before the date fixed for the expiry of the protection of the Acts. At present this is 24th June, 1938 in England, and 28th May, 1938, in Scotland.

In any case, the Court must be satisfied that the alternative accommodation offered is suitable to the needs of the tenant and his family in that it is near the place where they work, and that it is either similar as regards rental and extent to any dwelling-houses provided in the neighbourhood by any housing authority for persons whose requirements are similar to those of the tenant in question, or that it is otherwise reasonably suitable to the means and the needs of the tenant. A certificate may be obtained from the housing authority on this matter also.

Statutory Tenancy Notices.—It
should be remembered that so long as a tenant is holding under a contract with the landlord, this contractual tenancy must be brought to an end by a notice to quit before the landlord takes proceedings to recover possession under one of the above provisions. Where, however, some act has taken place, putting an end to the contractual tenancy—e.g. the service by the landlord of a notice increasing the rent of the tenant—it is not strictly necessary to serve the tenant with a notice to quit, for the tenant has ceased to hold under his contract with the landlord, and now holds by virtue of the Acts (statutes), and is known as a statutory tenant. It is always wise, however, for the landlord to serve a notice to quit before taking proceedings even in these cases.

After this notice has been served, the landlord is not prejudiced or prevented from recovering possession merely because he accepts rent for the period after the date of the expiry of the notice, as he would be in the case of an ordinary tenancy not governed by the Rent Acts. (*See* LANDLORD AND TENANT.)

Where a tenant has been a statutory tenant of a house of class A—i.e. a house to which the Acts cease to apply on the 29th September, 1933—a special notice must be served on him by the landlord if he wishes to recover possession. This notice must be in writing, and must inform the tenant either that he must give up possession of the house on the date mentioned in the notice, or that he will be required to give up possession unless before that time he comes to an agreement with the landlord for a new tenancy.

The notice must expire not earlier than one month after the date it is given. Where the tenant wishes to give up possession, he must give notice in accordance with the requirements of his original contract of tenancy, if any notice was mentioned in that; or if no notice was mentioned there, as is probably the case, he must give three months' notice.

Increases of Rent.—The protection against increase of rent above a certain amount is the other great benefit given by the Acts to the tenant. Any landlord who wishes to increase the rent of his tenant must be careful to see not only that the amount of the increase is authorised, but that the proper notices relating to increases are given.

Amount of Increases.—The rent on which all increases are calculated is the standard rent, which is the rent at which the premises were let on the 3rd August, 1914, if they were let at that time. If they were not let at that time, the standard rent will be the rent at which they were let before that date. If they were never let till after that date, the standard rent is the rent at which they were first let. It will frequently happen that a house, which was let as a whole at the time when the standard rent should be calculated, is now split up into several smaller dwelling-houses, and it is necessary to determine the standard rent of these smaller dwelling-houses. This will be done by apportioning the rent of the whole house among the smaller houses into which it is now divided. Since it is now many years since the 3rd August, 1914, it will often be very difficult indeed to find out what the rent of the house was on that date, and in these cases the Court will fix the rent with reference to the rent of other similar houses in the neighbourhood. Where it is necessary to apportion the rent of one large house among several smaller houses, an application for the apportionment should be made to the Court if the rent cannot be agreed.

The following are the grounds upon which the rent may be increased:—

Expenditure on Improvements.— Where the landlord has since the 4th August, 1914, spent money in improving, or in carrying out, structural alterations to the house, he may increase the rent up to 6 per cent. of the standard rent, if the expenditure was before the 2nd of July, 1920, and 8 per cent. if the expenditure was after that date.

This does not include expenditure on decorations or repairs, but it does include expenditure on additional, or improved fixtures or fittings, if these were carried out after the 18th July, 1933.

The tenant is always entitled to apply to the Court against the increase if he can shew that the expenditure was unnecessary, and that he has not given his consent in writing to it, where he was the tenant at the time when the expenditure was incurred. Where there was no tenant at the time of the expenditure, e.g. because the landlord was in possession, or the premises were empty, the first tenant after that time may also apply if he became a tenant without notice of the nature and extent of the alterations, the amount of the expenditure, and of the increase in rent resulting.

Increase for Rates.—Where the landlord pays the rates, he may increase the rent by the amount which the rates have increased since the 3rd August, 1914, or the first period when rates were paid thereafter.

General Increase.—A general increase in addition to these amounts is allowed which must not exceed 15 per cent. This percentage, however, is not calculated in all cases on the standard rent, but on what is called the net rent. This simply means the standard rent less the proportion of it which the landlord has got to pay away in rates. If the landlord does not pay the rates but the tenant does so, the standard rent will be the same as the net rent.

In addition to the above general increase, the landlord may increase the rent by an amount not exceeding 5 per cent. of the net rent where he is liable for repairs. This, of course, is intended to compensate the landlord for the increased cost of repairs since 1914.

The combined effect of these last two provisions is that where the landlord does the repairs, as is usually the case, he may add to the rent 40 per cent. of the net rent. In cases where premises are sublet, the tenant who has sublet is entitled to charge his subtenant an amount not exceeding 10 per cent., and the landlord can claim from his tenant of the whole house an additional 5 per cent. of the net rent.

Method of Increase.—The first thing the landlord who wishes to increase a tenant's rent has to consider is whether the

Rent and Mortgage Interest Restrictions Acts, 1920 to 1933.

R.R. No. 1.

Notice of Increase
of Rent.

The Solicitors'
Law Stationery Society,
Limited,
22 Chancery Lane, W.C.2,
27 & 28 Walbrook, E.C.4,
49 Bedford Row, W.C.1,
6 Victoria Street, S.W.1,
15 Hanover Street, W.1,
19 & 21 North John St.,
Liverpool, 2.

29925.27-3-34

Date *July 28* 193—

To *William Smith*, tenant of *

999, Blake Street, London

TAKE NOTICE that the rent of the above premises will as from

August 6, 193— be (¹) *8/—* per *week* [and as

from *August 27th* be *10/—* per *week*].

Details showing how this rent is made up are given below.

(Signed) *Alfred Nelson*
(Landlord or Agent for Landlord.)

(Address) *697 Rodeney Street*
Chatham

* Insert full address.

		£	s.	d.	
(a) Standard Rent of the premises ..		7	6		per *week*
(b) 40 (²) per cent. of £ —: 5s. — d. (the net rent of the premises) ..		2	—		" "
(c) (³) per cent. of £ — s. d. spent on improvements not including decorations and repairs to the premises					" "
(d) (⁴) Increase of rates payable by the landlord in respect of the premises from £ 5 : 4 s. — d. in 19/4 to £ 6 : 10 s. — d. for the current rating period		6	"	"	
(e) (⁵) per cent. of £ — : s. d. being the net rent of the sub-tenancies (if any) in the house			"	"	
Total rent		—	10	—	—

Note (1).—Any increase of rent over the standard rent under heads (b), (c) and (d) can only be charged after notice has been given by the landlord in the statutory form of notice or a form substantially to the same effect. At least four weeks' notice must be given in the case of an increase under heads (b) and (c), but only one week's notice is necessary in the case of an increase under head (d). Where a valid notice of increase has been served on any tenant (whether in the form prescribed by the Act of 1920 or, in future, in this form), the increase may be continued without further notice to any subsequent tenant.

Note (2).—The maximum permitted increase under head (b) is 40 per cent. of the net rent. If the tenant considers that the premises are not in a reasonable state of repair he can apply to the sanitary authority for a certificate to that effect. (A fee of one shilling is chargeable on an application for a certificate, but if the certificate is granted the shilling can be deducted from the rent.) Where a certificate is granted, and the tenant serves a copy of it on the landlord, the tenant may withhold that part of the increase in the rent set out under (b) above until the landlord has executed the necessary repairs to the satisfaction of the sanitary authority.

If, however, the landlord can prove to the County Court that the condition of the house is due to the tenant's neglect or default or breach of agreement, he may be able to recover all or part of the money withheld.

Instead of withholding the amount under (b) the tenant may apply direct to the County Court for an Order suspending this amount. In that case, he must satisfy the Court, by producing a certificate from the sanitary authority, or in some other manner, that the house is not in a reasonable state of repair.

The address of the sanitary authority is *Town Hall Chelsea*

Note (3).—The maximum permitted increase under head (c) is 6 per cent. of the cost if the work was done before 2nd July, 1920, and 8 per cent. if done after that date. If the tenant claims that the work was unnecessary or the cost excessive, he can apply to the County Court for an Order reducing the part of the increase in rent set out under (c), but an order can only be made if he was the tenant when the work was done and had not consented to it in writing, or was the first tenant after the work was done, and was not informed of the nature and cost of the improvements and the increased rent chargeable before taking the house.

Note (4).—The maximum permitted increase under head (d) is the increase in the current rates payable by the landlord over the corresponding amount paid in the rating period which included the 3rd August, 1914, or, if for some reason no rates were payable for that rating period, the period when rates first became payable thereafter.

Note (5).—Where part of a house is lawfully sub-let, the maximum permitted increase chargeable by the landlord of the whole house under head (e) is 5 per cent. of the net rent of the part sub-let; the maximum permitted increase chargeable by the tenant who has sub-let the part is 10 per cent. of the net rent of the part sub-let.

This form may be purchased from the Solicitors' Law Stationery Society, Limited, 22 Chancery Lane, W.C.2.

Notice of Increase of Rent for house controlled by the Rent Acts.

tenant is still holding under some contract with him. If so, this contract must come to an end before the rent can be increased. Thus, if a tenant has a lease, his rent cannot be increased until the lease comes to an end. In the case of a weekly tenant, a notice of increase of rent is in itself sufficient, and it is unnecessary to terminate the tenancy beforehand by serving an ordinary notice to quit.

The Notice. — The landlord must serve on the tenant a notice in the form set out in the Acts, of his intention to increase the rent. This notice cannot become effective for four weeks after it has been given, except in cases where the increase is made on the ground of the increase of the rates, where only one week's notice is required. Where the notice is wrong in form, the Court may remedy it and in most cases probably will.

Recovery of Rent.—Where the landlord charges the tenant too much rent, or has not given a proper notice of increase, he cannot recover the extra rent from his tenant, and the tenant is entitled to claim back from the landlord any over-payment of rent, but in no case for more than six months.

Registration of Houses.—In the case of houses in Class C, i.e. those which cannot now be decontrolled if they were not decontrolled before the 18th July, 1933, a register is kept in which the landlord of every house of that class decontrolled on that date may be registered. The effect of this registration should be carefully noticed. It must have taken place before 18th October, 1933, except in cases where the landlord obtains a certificate from a County Court permitting him to register later on proving that he has some reasonable excuse for his delay in registering. Even when a house is registered, it does not by any means follow that it is decontrolled; and if the landlord should desire to establish this he must prove it by evidence in the ordinary way as set out above. The only advantage of registration is that if a tenant desires to take a house he may be quite satisfied that it is still controlled if he does *not* find it in the register.

Rent Books.—Every rent book relating to a house within the Acts must have in it a notice containing certain information. The most important of this is the address of the premises, the name and address of the landlord and any agent, the amount of the standard rent, the amount by which the current rent has been increased over the net rent in respect of the general increases and repairs increases, a statement that the tenant or landlord or sub-tenant can apply to the Court if there is disagreement as to the rent, the address of the local sanitary authority, and a statement that the tenant may apply to the sanitary authority (if the premises are not in a reasonable state of repair), for a certificate to that effect. The tenant must also, if he sublets any part of the premises unfurnished, give the landlord particulars of the sub-letting, including the rent, within 14 days. The tenant must also be informed that if he overcharges his sub-tenant, he may lose possession of the premises.

If the rent book does not contain the above requirements the landlord may be fined £10.

When the tenant obtains a certificate from the sanitary authority to the effect that the premises are not in a reasonable state of repair, he is entitled to serve a copy of it on the landlord, and may then deduct from his rent the amount which is stated in the notice in his rent book as being paid in respect of the increases permitted by the Acts.

Distress.—Not only is a landlord prevented from increasing the amount of the tenant's rent except by notice and in the proper amounts, but he is also prevented from levying distress without the consent of the Court. (*See* DISTRESS.)

Court.—Whatever may be the amount of the claim, all proceedings relating to premises covered by the Rent Act may be brought in the County Court, and a person who brings such proceedings in the High Court will not be able to recover any costs.

GAMBLING

GAMBLING in all its various forms is a subject that rouses strong and bitterly opposed feelings. On the one hand many people regard it as one of the most serious social evils of the day. They point to the dreadful tragedies that may follow in its wake, to its peculiarly infectious nature, and to its weakening effect upon the national character. On the other hand great numbers of people resent interference through the power of the law in their private affairs. They deny the moral right of the State to deprive the steady majority of their innocent pleasures merely to protect the weak-willed few from their own follies. They point also to the disastrous effect the imposition of penalties in respect of acts in which vast portions of the population see no moral wrong may have upon popular respect for the law and the police.

These conflicting views are impossible to reconcile. On one part of the question, however, most people agree. That is the part which the Civil Courts should be allowed to play in the settlement of disputes over gambling transactions. It is generally conceded nowadays that, whether or not the criminal law should be used to suppress various forms of gambling, winners of bets should not be permitted to invoke the aid of the law to force losers to pay. At any rate the loser claims the protection of the law. In other words there is at the present time little or no public demand for the "debt of honour" to be made legally enforceable.

So far as the use of the criminal law to reduce the evils of gambling is concerned there is a middle view that has recently gained many responsible adherents. Supporters of this view concede the general right of the individual to select his own moral code, but they hold that at the same time persons should be discouraged from exploiting the gambling instincts of their fellows for their own personal profit. By this course, they argue, the liberty of the individual will be preserved, while the spread of gambling to dangerous dimensions will be avoided.

It will be convenient to consider the present law governing gambling under two main heads: first, the rights of individuals in respect of bets won and lost; and secondly, the extent to which the criminal law controls gambling in its various forms.

The Recovery of Bets in the Law Courts.—Up to the first half of the nineteenth century many bets or wagers were regarded very much like any other contracts. But in 1845 the Gaming Act of that year laid down that all contracts by way of gaming and wagering should be void. Probably the best definition of such contracts was supplied by the famous Mr. Justice Hawkins in a case tried in 1892. In that case he said: "It is not easy to define with precision what amounts to a wagering contract, nor the narrow line of demarcation which separates a wagering from an ordinary contract; but according to my view, a wagering contract is one by which two persons, professing to hold opposite views touching the issue of a future uncertain event, mutually agree that, dependent upon the determination of that event, one shall win from the other, and that other shall pay or hand over to him, a sum of money or other stake; neither of the contracting parties having any other interest in that contract other than the sum or stake he will so win or lose, there being no real consideration for the making of such contract by either of the parties. It is essential to a wagering contract that each party may under it either win or lose, whether he will win or lose being dependent on the issue of the event, and therefore remaining uncertain until that issue is known. If either of the parties may win but cannot lose, or may lose but cannot win, it is not a wagering contract."

Whilst no action can be brought to enforce any wagering contract, nevertheless once a bet or other wager has been paid it cannot be recovered back. This, however, is subject to a qualification in the case of money paid as deposits on bets for certain sporting events if paid at premises used for the purpose of betting with persons resorting thereto. This qualification is provided by the Betting Act 1853, section 5 of which enacts "Any money or valuable thing received . . . as a deposit on any bet, or as, or for the consideration for any such assurance, undertaking, promise, or agreement . . . shall be deemed to have been received to, or for the use of the person from whom the same was received, and such money or valuable thing, or the value thereof, may be recovered accordingly, with full costs of suit, in any Court of competent jurisdiction.".

Where the parties to a wager hand their bets to a stakeholder to abide the result of the event the winner cannot sue the stakeholder for anything more than his own stake. Either party may recover his own stake by action even after the event, e.g. the race, has taken place. On the other hand, if the stakeholder in fact hands over to the winner the loser's stake, the latter has no redress unless he revoked the stakeholder's authority before the money was paid over. Should the stakeholder be himself a party to the wager the person depositing the stake with him can in law revoke his authority at any time up to the moment when the stakeholder, if the winner, appropriates it to himself. Usually this moment not unnaturally turns out to be that of the notification of the result of the race, or other event in question. In such a case, however, the right to appropriate covers only money lodged and not anything given by way of security only.

The law declines to assist not merely the winners of bets but also those who lend money for betting. No one who lends money knowing that it is to be used for betting can recover even the principal back by action. This rule is strictly applied, so that where counters are borrowed for betting the redemption of them for cash cannot afterwards be enforced. It is interesting to note that an action can be maintained in the English Courts for the return of money lent in France for the purpose of betting. The reason for this, at first sight anomalous distinction, is that the Statutes directed against card playing in England do not apply to France.

While money lent for betting cannot be recovered no such rule applies to money lent to pay betting liabilities already incurred. The distinction is sometimes a fine one, but if the money is lent for gaming

at the time and at the place at which the play is in progress, it cannot in any circumstances be recovered.

The law does not assume, in the absence of evidence, that all loans to persons engaged in betting are for the purpose of betting. Thus money lent to a bookmaker can be recovered unless there is evidence that it must have been lent for betting. This is so because a bookmaker, of necessity, may require money for purposes other than betting.

Cheques.—The law governing cheques and securities given in respect of betting transactions is very complicated. In general it may be said that no security given upon any wager or bet is enforceable between the actual parties to the wager or bet. But in certain circumstances a third party who has purchased a cheque given in respect of a wager can enforce payment of it against the person who issued it. Whether or not this can be done depends on the nature of the wager for which it was originally given. If it was given in payment of losses incurred in the playing of any of the games or pastimes enumerated in a Statute passed in the reign of Queen Anne, even a person who in complete ignorance of its origin has purchased it cannot sue upon it. It is otherwise if it was given for other forms of wagering. It is of interest to note that the modern sport of Greyhound Racing is covered by the Statute of Anne.

Promises Based on Fresh Consideration.—Although betting winnings as such cannot be recovered in a Court of Law, promises to pay losses can sometimes be enforced. Refusal to pay a debt of honour is a matter many people try to avoid at all costs. Any publicity given to such a refusal may in some cases lead to social or professional ruin. Frequently, therefore, persons who owe gambling debts bargain with their creditors in order to get time to pay. The new agreements so arrived at are sometimes enforceable. The rule has thus been laid down by a famous Judge: "While the plaintiff cannot sue for the recovery of money won by him by betting, nor on a bond, bill, note or cheque given to pay the money lost, he can sue upon a new contract, not tainted with illegality and made for good consideration, if he can prove such a contract."

If, therefore, there is a new contract whereby the creditor agrees in consideration of a promise to pay the whole, or part of the gambling debt, to forbear to do something he has a legal right to do, the new contract can be enforced. But the forbearance must be refraining from doing something effective. Mere forbearance to sue on an unenforceable act does not constitute fresh consideration sufficient to make enforceable any contract based upon it alone. But if the creditor agrees to forego or postpone any right he has of declaring the debtor a defaulter, or of reporting the facts to somebody exercising powers which the debtor does not wish to be directed against him, there may well be sufficient new consideration. As another Judge famous for his learning said: "Any lawful act done or forborne by the plaintiff at his request and for the benefit of the defendant is a sufficient consideration to support a promise to pay by the defendant.

"All betting is not illegal because in certain places and under certain conditions it is made an offence by Act of Parliament, nor because bets which were enforceable as contracts at common law have been made by statute unenforceable as void or on an illegal consideration. There is certainly nothing illegal in paying or receiving payment of a lost bet; it is one thing for the law to refuse to assist either party in their folly, if they will bet, it is quite another thing to forbid the loser to keep his word.

"Lost bets are still regarded as debts of honour; in other words, all honourable men regard the payment of money lost on a bet as a duty of imperfect obligation, and the payment of bets is indirectly enforced by the social stigma attached to a defaulter, and also by certain disqualifications consequent on posting. There is nothing illegal in an unpaid winner calling to his aid those resources, and, if so, there is nothing illegal in his agreement not to do so in consideration of the payment of the amount lost. Although the law will not enforce payment of a bet, it will not restrain the winner from putting in force, such extra-legal remedies as he may have by posting the defaulter or otherwise."

Betting Commissions.—Just as wagering agreements are not enforceable between the parties that make them, so also agents cannot recover in Courts of Law anything in the nature of a commission for services in connection with any such agreements. The same applies where an agent pays, or promises to pay bets incurred by him on behalf of a principal. Even though he has paid a third party his winnings on a bet made on behalf of his principal, he cannot recover the amount from his principal, but, if the latter declines to pay, he must bear the loss himself. On the other hand, if the principal wins a bet, the agent must pay over to him any money he receives from a third party in respect of it. This is so because the agent receives the money as agent for his principal and as such must account to him for anything he receives on his behalf.

Betting Partnerships.—There remains to consider the question of partnerships formed for the purpose of carrying on betting businesses. Betting not being in itself a forbidden activity, it follows that partnerships for such purposes are not illegal. But difficulty may arise in enforcing the rights of one partner against the other. For instance, if one partner pays betting losses from money supplied by himself he cannot, for the reasons set out above, recover at law any contribution from the other partner.

Gambling and Criminal Law.—This part of the subject can conveniently be considered under three heads: Lotteries, Gaming, and Betting.

Lotteries.—A lottery may take many forms. It may be a huge national sweepstake financed by contributions amounting to hundreds of thousands of pounds and collected from all portions of the globe; or it may be a simple raffle held at a parochial sale of work involving subscriptions amounting to but a few shillings. Whatever the form may be, if one characteristic is present it is a lottery. That characteristic is the distribution in consideration of a contribution of a prize or prizes by chance. Public Lotteries in this country are at present illegal. It is a punishable offence to organise a public lottery, or to advertise a scheme for one, or to sell tickets or chances for one. Further, search warrants may be issued authorising the police to search any premises where it is reasonably suspected that a lottery is being conducted. It is to be noted that the prohibition governing advertising lotteries or selling tickets for them is not confined to lotteries organized in Great Britain. Lotteries organized in foreign countries or in other parts of the British Empire, even though lawful in the places where they are organized, are equally affected by the prohibition.

The object of the organizers does not affect the illegal nature of lotteries. Though they may not be run for private profit, and though a large share of the contributions are devoted to charitable purposes, they nevertheless remain illegal with all the consequences set out above.

For any scheme to be a lottery there must, of course, be contributions from the persons taking part. A mere distribution entirely gratis of prizes by some charitable person does not constitute a lottery, even though he arrives at the identity of the prize winners by lot or chance. But the mere fact that some only of those taking part receive free tickets or make no contribution does not render a scheme not a lottery provided contributions are received from others.

Contributions need not take the form of direct payments for tickets. If tickets or chances are given as part of an inducement to people to make other and lawful purchases, the scheme remains capable of being a lottery. Thus, the distribution by lot of cash or other prizes amongst purchasers of some article as part of a scheme to advertise it may well constitute a lottery.

In order to decide in each particular case whether a scheme is lawful or not it is necessary to examine it as a whole. Once it is clear that persons may be actuated, even in part, to purchase the article by the hope of gaining thereby a chance of winning a prize, the scheme takes on the nature of a lottery.

A word is necessary as to the question of distribution by chance—an essential ingredient of a lottery, it will be remembered. If distribution is based upon skill, as in the case of newspaper and other competitions, whereby competitors submit solutions involving the exercise of skill or judgment, there is no lottery. This is so even though there is a considerable element of luck involved in addition to the skill. In general it may be said that wherever there is any substantial element of skill required, a scheme becomes not a lottery but a lawful competition.

Gaming.—It is, with few exceptions, not generally unlawful to play games in this country even for stakes. The criminal law governing gaming is directed mainly against gambling in public places or in gaming houses. A gaming-house is by Act of Parliament declared to be any house, office, room or place which is opened, used or kept for the purpose of unlawful gaming. "Unlawful gaming" in this connection means gaming for stakes upon games of pure chance. Where there is an element of skill the gaming, with certain exceptions specified by Statute, is not unlawful.

The Gaming Houses Act of 1854 enacts that the owner, or occupier, or person having the use of a gaming-house, who uses it for unlawful gaming may, on summary conviction be sentenced to pay a fine not exceeding £500, or to be imprisoned with or without hard labour for twelve months. Similar penalties may be inflicted on such persons who, though not themselves taking any part in the management, knowingly permit the premises to be used for unlawful gaming. Also, anyone who in any manner assists in the conduct of the premises for such a purpose may be punished in the same way.

It is to be noted that for the offence to be committed the premises must be habitually used for unlawful gaming. The use of a private house on a single occasion, of course, does not amount to habitual use. On the other hand, premises may be a gaming house even though they are not exclusively or even mainly used for gaming. The use on any premises of an automatic machine from which on payment prizes may be obtained by pure chance, as distinct from skill, would render the premises a gaming-house. Again, the fact that the persons using the premises are members of a club does not prevent that club from becoming a gaming house if the other considerations are present.

It remains to note that special provisions in addition to the foregoing apply to premises licensed for alcoholic refreshment. It is an offence for any licensed publican to permit any gaming to take place on licensed premises. It will be observed that in the case of licensed premises it is not necessary that there shall be habitual use. The offence may be committed on a single isolated occasion.

Gaming in public places is also forbidden. In this connection, public places include all highways and open spaces which the public may enter. The essential part of this offence is the use of money or any instrument of gaming in the course of playing any game of chance. The offence is committed though the play takes place in a vehicle, including probably a private motor-car. Railway carriages are public places for this purpose.

Betting.—The racing of horses and greyhounds is a lawful pastime. Betting upon such and other events is, however, subject to considerable restrictions.

It is an offence for anyone to frequent any street or other public place for the purpose of paying or receiving bets, whether on behalf of himself or of some other person. In this connection a public place has a wide meaning and includes all ground to which the public have access.

So far as other premises are concerned, the law is in a curious state. There is a great distinction drawn between betting at a race-course and betting elsewhere. As regards betting away from the course, it is lawful only if it is carried on by letter, telegram, or telephone. This result is produced by the Betting Act of 1853, which enacts that no house, office or other place may be used for the purpose of the owner, occupier or anyone using it, conducting thereat the business of betting with persons resorting thereto. If any place is kept for this purpose it may be treated as a common gaming-house, and the penalties for such be inflicted. It will be observed that the business must be that of betting with persons who actually resort thereto, and this means actual physically attending as distinct from mere correspondence.

The Betting Act of 1853 goes on to prohibit the keeping of any place for the purpose of any money being received on account of a bet on any race, fight, game, sport or exercise, in other words, ready money as distinct from credit betting. On the other hand a place may lawfully be used for the purpose of paying bets made in a lawful manner.

Race-Course Betting.—Betting at race-courses is controlled by the Race-course Betting Act, 1928. This Act set up a Race-course Betting Control Board with extensive powers of control. The Board consists of a chairman appointed by the Home Secretary, and members selected by various government offices, the National Hunt Committee, the Race-course Association, Ltd., the Jockey Club, and the Committee of Tattersalls. The powers and duties of the Board include the approval and grant of certificates in respect of race-courses. The Board may, as a condition of the grant of a certificate, require the management of a course to provide a place where bookmakers may carry on their business and to which the public may resort for the purpose of betting. The Act provides that the Betting Act, 1853 (which it will be remembered forbids ready-money betting to be carried on in any "place") shall not apply to any race-course approved by the Board on days on which horse-races take place.

The Act also recognizes and legalizes the totalisator under certain conditions. "Notwithstanding any rule of law or enactment to the contrary, it shall be lawful on any approved race-course, and whether in a building or not;

(a) For the Race-course Betting Control Board and any person authorized by them to set up and keep a totalisator;

(b) for the Board and any person authorized by them to operate, in accordance with the provisions of this Act, and for the purpose of effecting betting transactions on horse-races only, a totalisator on days when horse-races, but no other races, take place on the race-course;

(c) for any person to effect betting transactions by means of a totalisator lawfully operated."

The Act confers on the Board power to establish a totalisator fund into which must be paid such a percentage of the receipts as the Board may determine. The fund is to be used in accordance with a scheme prepared by the Board and approved by the Home Secretary for purposes conducive to the improvement of needs of horses or the sport of horse-racing.

The Act makes special provision for the prevention of betting at approved race-courses by persons under the age of seventeen. It is made an offence punishable by a fine not exceeding £5 to bet with anyone under that age by means of a totalisator or otherwise.

It is an offence to send any advertisement relating to betting to any person under twenty-one years of age. Where the letter is addressed to any place of education, the sender is, in the absence of an explanation by him, presumed to know that the addressee is under age.

A word is necessary as to the position of that unpopular person the "welsher." Although no one can be forced by law to pay a bet he has lost, yet the conduct of a defaulting bookmaker may be such that it amounts to a crime. If a person holds himself out as willing to take bets and never intends to pay even the deposits if he loses, his acceptance of the bets amounts to stealing the money he receives and he may be convicted of larceny by a trick. (*See* LARCENY BY TRICK *under* LARCENY.) Of course, for a conviction to be obtained, the evidence of fraudulent intention must be clear. Mere failure to pay his losses is not enough, proof must be given that at the time of receiving the money he intended in any event to decamp. Disappearance before the result of the race is known is, of course, very strong evidence of this. It may be added that even a welsher may not be assaulted by his victims, though if he has committed the felony of larceny he may be arrested.

Ready Money Football Betting.— It is an offence for anyone to write, print, publish or knowingly circulate any advertisement or coupon relating to ready money football betting. It should be noted that this offence may be committed anywhere in the United Kingdom, not being confined to public places, streets, or betting premises. The punishment is a fine not exceeding £25 for the first offence, or £100 for subsequent offences.

Gambling on the Stock Exchange.— —A Stock Exchange transaction may constitute gaming in law, just as much as a game of poker. When it does, the same legal principles apply, namely, that the winner cannot in a Court of Law recover his winnings from the loser, or sue him upon any security he has received from him. In practice, of course, it is extremely difficult to shew that a Stock Exchange transaction is a gaming one. A purchaser of shares may, in fact, never intend to take them up, but merely to sell them before he is required to produce the cash, yet it is usually impossible to establish his intention as a matter of fact. This is much easier to effect where the agreement is merely one to pay "differences," that is to say, to settle for the difference between the price on one day and that on another. But even then the transaction has to be examined to find out whether it was one of gaming or not.

UNEMPLOYMENT INSURANCE

PROVISION by the law for the insurance against periods of unemployment on the part of workpeople was first made in the year 1911. Since that year the problem of providing a satisfactory scheme has constantly exercised the ingenuity and patience of Parliament, and has naturally necessitated a great deal of legislation.

In 1920 a serious effort was made to solve the problem by the passing of the Unemployment Insurance Act, 1920, and, although that act has required amendment every year since its passing, yet it constitutes the foundation of the scheme, and is still referred to as the principal act of the Unemployment Insurance Scheme.

The problem of providing for the maintenance of the unemployed became really acute following the trade depression which commenced in 1929, and this year Parliament has made one more effort to put the scheme in order and to provide something approaching a final solution of the problem. The present act recognizes that the problem is a twofold one, namely, the provision of a self-supporting Insurance Scheme, and the provision of a method for assisting and rehabilitating persons who have been without employment for long periods.

The law is now divided into two categories, that which deals with insurance, and that which deals with assistance, and it can be most conveniently explained under these two main headings.

Who are included in the Insurance Scheme.—Every person, with the exception of those detailed later, between the school leaving age and the age of sixty-five who is employed under a contract of service in Great Britain must be insured against periods of unemployment; this provision includes any apprentice who receives payment for his services, and also the master and members of the crew of any ship registered in Great Britain.

Every person who is employed under these conditions is regarded as being in an insurable occupation, but a person who is employed in any of the following ways is regarded as being in an uninsurable occupation, and does not require to be insured:—

(a) Persons employed in agriculture, horticulture and forestry.

(b) Persons employed in domestic service unless they are employed at a place such as an hotel, which is carried on for the purposes of gain.

(c) Civil servants.

(d) Persons who are not manual workers and who are receiving a salary of more than two-hundred-and-fifty pounds per annum.

(e) Female nurses and probationers.

(f) Regular sailors, soldiers and airmen of His Majesty's Forces.

(g) Members of a Police Force, except the short-service members of the Metropolitan Police Force.

(h) Teachers in recognized or contributory service.

(i) Persons employed as commission agents, provided that they are mainly dependent for their living upon some other occupation.

(j) Persons employed casually for private purposes.

(k) Persons employed by their parents and receiving no wages.

(l) Persons maintained by the employer, and not receiving wages.

(m) Persons employed by a Local Authority under an arrangement made between the Authority and a Poor Law Authority.

(n) Share fishermen wholly remunerated by share.

(o) Persons exempted from insurance under a Certificate of Exemption granted by the Minister of Labour. Certificates can only be granted to Government Departments, Public and Local Authorities, Railway Companies and Public Utility Companies such as Gas and Water Companies, and can be granted only in respect of the permanent employees of such companies who have pension rights secured to them by Act of Parliament.

The Minister of Labour may, if he is satisfied that two types of employment, one of which is insurable and the other uninsurable, are similar from the point of view of the terms and conditions of the service, make regulations including the uninsurable occupation among the insurable occupations, or taking the insurable occupation out of the scope of the Acts.

This power is given to the minister to prevent anomalies and hardships arising as a consequence of the operation of the Insurance Scheme.

Who Makes Contributions. — Unemployment Insurance Benefits are paid out

present weekly rates of contribution made to the Unemployment Fund by each of the three contributors.

How Contributions are Made.— The employer of a person who is in an insurable occupation is responsible for paying the joint contribution of himself and the employee. Failure to do so entails a serious penalty.

The method of payment is by fixing unemployment insurance stamps to an unemployment book issued in the name of the employee.

The employer may deduct the employee's contribution from his wages each week, but he must make the deduction only from the wages paid for the period to which

Class of Employed Persons.	Employee's Contribution.	Employer's Contribution.	Exchequer Contribution.	Total.
Men aged 21 and under 65 . .	1od.	1od.	1od.	2/6
Young Men aged 18 and under 21.	9d.	9d.	9d.	2/3
Women aged 21 and under 65 .	9d.	9d.	9d.	2/3
Young Women aged 18 and under 21	8d.	8d.	8d.	2/0
Boys between 16 and 18 years .	5d.	5d.	5d.	1/3
Girls between 16 and 18 years .	4½d.	4½d.	4½d.	1/1½
Boys and Girls under 16 years .	2d.	2d.	2d.	6d.

of a fund called the Unemployment Fund, which is placed under the control and management of the Minister of Labour; the minister, however, is to be advised and assisted by a special permanent body called the Unemployment Insurance Statutory Committee, whose duty it is to make reports and recommendations to the Minister of Labour upon the financial condition of the fund.

The fund itself is made up of contributions from the employees, employers, and the Exchequer.

The table on this page indicates the

the contributions apply. In the majority of cases this is one week.

A weekly contribution must be paid for each week, during any part of which a person is employed, but if the employee is employed in two insurable occupations in one week, only one contribution is required and must be paid by the employer who first employs him.

Every person who enters an insurable occupation must obtain an unemployment book if he does not already possess one, and must hand it to his employer when he starts work with him. When the employment terminates, the employer must hand back the book to the employee stamped up to date.

When an employed person attains the age of sixty-five he is no longer required to make any contribution to the fund, but if he remains in employment, his employer must still pay the employer's contribution to the fund.

The Unemployment Insurance Statutory Committee may, when they consider the fund to be solvent, and when the debt of the fund is paid off, recommend to the Minister of Labour that the rates of contribution from employer and employee should be lowered.

The Right to Benefit.—An insured person who is between the ages of sixteen and sixty-five and is unemployed is entitled to receive benefit provided he fulfils the necessary statutory conditions and is not disqualified under the Insurance Acts from receiving it.

The statutory conditions which an applicant must fulfil are:—

1. That not less than thirty contributions have been paid in respect of the two years immediately preceding the date when he makes application for benefit from the fund.

   If he has been receiving a disability pension for a disability sustained during the Great War during the relevant two years, and by reason of the disability fails to satisfy this condition, he need only prove the payment of ten contributions instead of thirty.

2. That he applies for benefit in the prescribed manner and proves that since the date of the application he has been continuously unemployed. This means that he must make a claim at an Employment Exchange, sign the necessary documents and deposit his unemployment book with the officials at the Exchange.

   A man may still be regarded as unemployed although he is engaged in some occupation which he normally followed outside his ordinary working hours provided he does not earn by this other occupation more than three shillings and fourpence a day.

3. That he is capable of work and available for work. If, however, he is attending an authorized course, or a course of instruction approved by the Minister of Labour, he is not to be regarded as unavailable for work but may take a job.

4. That if the Minister of Labour has, for the purpose of giving him an opportunity of becoming or keeping fit for entry into, or return to, regular employment, required him to attend an authorized course, he proves that he duly attended, or that he had good cause for not attending, e.g. that he was ill.

An insured contributor who satisfies these conditions is not immediately entitled to benefit, for he has to go through a waiting period of six days during which no money is payable. Once a claimant has completed a waiting period he does not have to go through it again provided his unemployment is "continuous." Continuous, for the purpose of the Insurance Acts, means any three days of unemployment within six consecutive days, or any two periods of three continuous days if those periods are not separated from each other by more than ten weeks.

An insured contributor who fulfils all these conditions becomes entitled to receive in a benefit year, benefit for periods which total in all one hundred and fifty-six days, that is to say, he can be unemployed for one hundred and fifty-six days in one year and receive benefit in respect of all those days. He may also receive additional benefit in one benefit year if he has been in insurable occupation for five years previous to his claim. For every five contributions paid in respect of him during the preceding five years he receives three days' additional benefit; but if he has been in receipt of benefit during any one of those five years, then he loses one day's additional benefit for every five days that he received it previously.

The effect of this provision is that people with good contribution records receive additional benefit after they have exhausted their one hundred and fifty-six days, and if a man has made no claim for benefit throughout the preceding five years, then he will be entitled in that case to a second period of one hundred and fifty-six days' benefit in one year.

How one may be Disqualified for Benefit.—An applicant may be disqualified from receiving benefit if:—

(*a*) It is proved by an officer of the Ministry of Labour that he has, without good cause, failed to apply for, or refused to accept, a suitable situation notified to him by an Employment Exchange, or other recognized agency, as vacant or about to become vacant, or that he has neglected to avail himself of a reasonable opportunity of suitable employment, or that he has without good cause failed to carry out any written directions given to him by an officer of an Employment Exchange with a view to assisting him to find suitable employment.

The maximum period of disqualification under this provision is six weeks, and the claimant must be disqualified from obtaining benefit by the decision of a Court of Referees or the Umpire.

(*b*) He has lost employment by reason of a stoppage of work which was due to a trade dispute at the premises at which he was employed. This disqualification does not apply if the insured contributor can prove to the authorities to whom he applies:—

(i) That he is not himself participating in, or financing the trade dispute which has caused the stoppage and;

(ii) that the persons who are participating in the dispute do not include members of his own grade or class who were employed before the stoppage at the premises where the stoppage is taking place.

(*c*) He loses his employment through his own misconduct, or if he voluntarily leaves the employment without good cause. The longest period of disqualification in a case such as this is six weeks.

(*d*) He is an inmate of any prison, or workhouse, or other institution supported out of public funds.

(*e*) He is resident temporarily or permanently outside the United Kingdom.

(*f*) He is receiving sickness or disablement benefit under the National Health Insurance Scheme, or a pension under the Blind Persons Act, 1920.

What is the Amount of Benefit.— If an insured contributor successfully proves that he fulfils all the conditions, and is not disqualified by any of the provisions which are stated above, then he receives benefit in accordance with the following scale:—

Class of Insured Person.	Rate of Benefit per week.	
Persons of 21 years and upwards and young men and women receiving additional dependants' benefit:—	*s.*	*d.*
Men	17	0
Women	15	0
Persons between 18 and 21 years not in receipt of additional dependants' allowance:—		
Young Men	14	0
Young Women	12	0
Persons between 17 and 18 years of age:—		
Boys	9	0
Girls	7	6

Class of Insured Person.	Rate of Benefit per week.
	s. d.
Persons under the age of 17 years:—	
Boys	6 0
Girls	5 0
Dependants' Benefit:—	
For an adult dependant	8 0
For a child dependant	2 0

Dependants' benefit is payable to a claimant in respect of his wife if living with him, and wholly or mainly maintained by him, or in respect of a female person residing with him if she has the care of his children. It is also payable in certain circumstances in respect of the parents of a claimant if they were wholly or mainly maintained by him. A dependent child for whom extra benefit may be claimed is defined by the Unemployment Insurance Acts, as:—

The child, younger brother, or younger sister of a claimant who is:—

(a) Under the age of fourteen and is maintained wholly or mainly by him, or

(b) is between the ages of fourteen and sixteen and is maintained wholly or mainly by him, and is either (i) under full-time instruction at a day school or (ii) is unable to receive such instruction by reason of physical or mental infirmity, or

(c) is between fourteen and sixteen years of age, and when unemployed is maintained by the claimant. This dependant must, however, be himself entitled to benefit under the Insurance Scheme in order that dependants' benefit shall become payable in respect of him.

How Claims are Decided.—All claims for benefit by an insured contributor are referred in the first place to an insurance officer, who may on his own authority allow any claim for benefit. If the insurance officer is not satisfied that such a claim for benefit should be allowed, he must refer it, if possible, within fourteen days to a Court of Referees.

The insurance officer may disallow a claim if he is of opinion that the claimant is disqualified by reason of a trade dispute, but if he does so, the claimant has a right to appeal to a Court of Referees within twenty-one days.

A claimant for benefit whose claim has been disallowed by the Court of Referees may appeal to the Umpire, who is an officer appointed by the Crown, without leave if the decision of the referees was not unanimous, and otherwise he may appeal only with leave of the chairman of the Court of Referees.

Training and Instruction.—Local authorities are now required to submit to the Minister of Labour proposals for the provision of courses of instruction and training for persons between the school-leaving age and the age of eighteen, who are capable of work and have no work or only intermittent employment. If the Minister approves of the proposals, then the local authorities may proceed with the provision of courses.

The Minister may also provide such courses of instruction for persons who are over eighteen years of age, and may pay the persons attending them. The expenses of these courses may be partly defrayed out of the Unemployment Fund. The various local authorities bear the remainder of the costs.

Unemployment Assistance.—A new method has been evolved for dealing with the problem of the able-bodied unemployed who have exhausted their benefit rights under the insurance scheme, and who, up to the time of the passing of the Unemployment Insurance Act, 1934, were receiving transitional payments through the Public Assistance Committees.

An Unemployment Assistance Board has been constituted by the Act of 1934, and its main duties consist of making provision for the re-entry into insurable occupation of persons who have been for a long period without employment, and for the paying to such persons of allowances until such time as they secure employment once more.

The Board is to be assisted in the performance of its duties with knowledge of local conditions of labour and industry.

The persons who come within the scope of the Board's activities are those between the ages of sixteen and sixty-five who are either normally occupied in an employment in respect of which contributions are payable under the Widows', Orphans', and Old Age Contributory Pensions Scheme, or who, not having been engaged in any occupation since the age of sixteen, might reasonably have expected to be employed in an insurable occupation, but for the industrial circumstances of the district in which they happen to reside.

Any question whether a person is, or is not a person coming within the sphere of the Board's activities is decided by the officers of the Board.

How to Get an Allowance.—If a person proves that:—

(i) He is registered for employment in the prescribed manner and has made proper application for an allowance;

(ii) that he has no work or only such work as is insufficient to enable him to earn his living and support himself with the necessities of life;

(iii) that he is in need of an allowance; then an allowance may be granted to him. It will not be granted to

him if he is disqualified from receiving unemployment benefit by reason of misconduct, or refusal to carry out reasonable directions given to him for the purpose of finding himself permanent work.

It will be noted that the Means Test is applied to the case of every applicant for an allowance, and certain rules are laid down by the Act of 1934 for the assessment of an applicant's needs.

An applicant may be granted an allowance while he is attending a course of training, and payments may be made to members of his family while he is resident at a training centre. The allowance may be paid, subject to the conditions that the applicant attends a training course provided by the local authority for the district in which he resides.

The allowances are to be paid out of an Unemployment Assistance Fund which is to be maintained by contributions from the Exchequer and from the local authorities of each district in proportion to the calls which they make upon it.

It is an offence to make any false statement or representation with a view to obtaining either unemployment benefit, or an unemployment allowance, and any offender upon conviction may be sentenced to prison for a maximum period of three months. (*See also* OLD AGE PENSION; OUT-DOOR RELIEF; POOR LAW; REFEREES; UMPIRE.)

INCOME TAX

THE method by which by far the greater part of the revenue acquired by the Government of the country is obtained is by a tax on the income of all persons in the country. The tax is calculated in two ways, firstly as income tax proper at a standard rate in the pound and, secondly, by an additional income tax known as surtax calculated on all income over £2,000 a year at a rate varying with the amount of the income. These two taxes are not mutually exclusive, and a person whose income is liable to surtax will have in addition to pay the ordinary income tax.

What is Income?—The Courts have stated very frequently that income tax is a tax upon income. This may appear to be obvious, but it is by no means easy in all cases to determine whether a sum of money which has been received is income or capital. It is not all money which a person may receive that is income for the purposes of income tax.

1. **Voluntary Gifts.**—As a general rule a gift is not liable to income tax. Thus, if a parent makes a present of money to his child, no tax is payable by the child. The parent, of course, will not be entitled to deduct the payment from his own income for the purpose of calculating his income tax, and so will in effect pay tax himself on the amount of the gift. Where, however, the voluntary payment or gift is made by an employer to an employee in some trade or business it may well be that the employee will have to include the gift in his return for income tax, and in that case the employer will, of course, be entitled to charge up the amount of the gift as an expense of his business.

Gifts to employees will in all cases be regarded as income if they are paid because the person receiving the money is an employee. Thus Christmas boxes distributed to a staff are part of the income of the staff, and are assessable as income. It should be noticed that it is immaterial whether the person receiving the money has any right to it or not. Wherever the real ground of making the gift is some service rendered by the person to whom it is given, the gift will be taxable. Thus tips are liable to taxation. A gift to an employee is much less likely to be taxable if it is given on his retirement, even though it is given not merely on one occasion, but annually after he has retired as a voluntary pension.

It has been held that a benefit granted to a professional cricketer by his cricket club was not taxable, but where a professional footballer received a proportion of the transfer fee for his transfer from one club to another (to which he was entitled by the rules of the Football Association), the amount paid was held to be liable to taxation.

2. **Lump Sum Payments.**—Where these are made by way of compensation for injury received by the person to whom they are paid, they are not assessable unless they are paid in the form of an annuity. The person who pays them, however, may be entitled to deduct them from his profits as a business expense in cases where the person to whom they are paid is his employee, and also in other cases where the payment of such sums may be said to be part of the ordinary business expenses of the employer, e.g. when he is engaged in carrying out a passenger 'bus or railway service. To-day, however, this is of less importance, as in such cases the risks will invariably be carried by an insurance company.

Where under an accident policy payments are received by an injured person in respect of his injury periodically for some time, the person receiving them may be required to pay tax. Where compensation or damages are payable to a servant as salary or wages in lieu of notice, the servant will usually have to include this in his income tax return, except in cases where the payment is in respect of the time after the employment had ceased.

3. **Payments under Insurance Policies.**—Amounts received under a life policy are not taxable. In the case of Fire and Burglary Policies the amounts received must be included if the policy is taken out in connection with some business, but not if it is merely in respect of the private

premises or belongings of the insured person. Where the amounts received are taxable in this way, the amount of the premiums will be allowed as a deduction in calculating the taxable profits of the business.

4. Casual Profits.—Profits out of transactions which form no part of the business of the person entering into them, but are merely isolated and not likely to recur, at any rate frequently, are not taxable. Thus transactions on the Stock Exchange in the buying and selling of shares, or the purchase of any property and re-sale at a profit, are not liable to taxation. If, however, the transaction is not an isolated one but takes place frequently so that it becomes part of the business of the person carrying it out, he will be required to pay tax on his profits. He will have the corresponding benefit that he will be entitled to charge any losses, and to deduct them from any profits he may make in any other business he is carrying out. Thus, betting gains or an amount won in a sweepstake would not normally be taxable, nor would prizes won in newspaper competitions, although, if the entering for such competitions became so frequent as to be regarded as part of the business of the person receiving the prizes, it might be liable to taxation.

5. Receipts which cannot be converted into Money.—A person may be employed on the terms that he receives in addition to his wages in cash, either the free use of a house, or board and lodging. The question may arise whether the value of the house or the board and lodging is to be taken into account. This will depend on whether the additional benefit can be turned into cash by the person receiving it. Thus, if a man is employed on the terms that he receives £500 a year and a free house, the value of the house would have to be included if he was not compelled to live elsewhere. But the value of the house would not be included where he had no alternative but to live in the house. Where the wages are divided so that one part is wages proper and the other part is to be considered as payment out of which the servant may maintain himself, tax must be paid on the full amount.

6. Letting Unfurnished Rooms.—A person who lets unfurnished rooms is not required to return the amounts received as part of his income. He will already be paying tax on the house of which the rooms form part under Schedule A. The position is different if the rooms are let furnished, or if any service is given in addition to the unfurnished rooms.

7. Legacies.—No tax is payable on legacies unless they take the form of an annuity. If the money received by legacy is invested and bears interest, income tax will be payable on that.

8. Scholarships.—Income received on scholarships is not liable to taxation.

9. Pensions.—As a general rule pensions which are paid in respect of past services are assessable. Old Age Pensions are also assessable. For the purpose of determining whether or not a pension is taxable, it is immaterial that it is paid out of a Superannuation Fund. War pensions, in so far as they are given for wounds or disabilities, are exempt from tax; but pensions paid to widows or to mothers whose husbands or children were killed are liable to taxation.

Who Pays Income Tax? — All persons who reside in the United Kingdom, that is, Great Britain and Northern Ireland, will be liable to income tax on all income they receive, whether it arises from some source within the United Kingdom or not. Further, persons who do not reside in the United Kingdom will be liable to tax in respect of any money received by them from any property in the United Kingdom or any profits earned by them in the United Kingdom. It will be seen from this that persons cannot escape from income tax by living outside the United Kingdom, e.g. in Jersey, if their income arises from some source inside the United Kingdom.

How Income Tax is Levied.—The responsibility of a levy and collection of income tax is in the hands of the Inland Revenue Department whose headquarters is at Somerset House. Locally, income tax is under the control of Inspectors of Taxes, and it is in their office that the work of assessing the various incomes of the residents in the district and obtaining from them proper returns is carried out. The actual collection of the tax is in the hands of another officer known as the Collector of Taxes.

Income Tax Return.—Every person whose income is such as to make him liable to income tax is required to make a return. He is not excused merely because no demand is sent to him, for notices requiring returns are exhibited in churches, and this is a sufficient demand. The return made is for the income tax year, which is from April 6th in one year to April 5th in the next. For the purposes of making a return the sources of income are divided into five Schedules called respectively A, B, C, D, and E.

Schedule A.—This tax is known as Property Tax and is levied on all rent or other income arising from the ownership of land. It is calculated not on the actual amount of rent received in every case, but on what is known as the "annual value," which is the amount which the property would bring in, if it were let on the terms that the landlord should pay all repairs and the tenant should pay all the rates. This annual value is fixed every five years. Even if the property is not let at all but is occupied by its owner, he will have to pay Schedule A income tax on its annual value. This tax is payable on the 1st January in each year.

Certain deductions are allowed from the annual value before the tax is calculated. By far the most important of these is the repairs allowance. In the case of land this is a deduction of one-eighth of the annual value, but in the case of houses and buildings the calculation of the necessary deduction is more complicated.

	ALLOWANCE.
Gross assessment not over £40 . . .	One-fourth.
Gross assessment over £40 but not over £50 .	£10.
Gross assessment over £50 but not over £100 .	One-fifth.
Gross assessment over £100	£20 plus one-sixth of the excess over £100.

Where the actual amount spent on repairs is greater than that allowed, the taxpayer may in certain cases claim relief. He must, however, prove that his average expenditure on repairs and maintenance for a period of five years exceeded the allowance as above calculated. Other deductions have also to be made in respect of land tax, tithes, and rates for drainage, fencing or embanking. The repairs allowance is intended to include not only the actual cost of repairs but also of the maintenance of the property generally, e.g. the expenses of collecting the rent.

Where the tenant has undertaken to pay the cost of repairs and where, therefore, the rent actually received is lower than the gross assessment, the landlord will not be entitled to claim in respect of a repairs allowance any sum greater than the amount by which the assessment exceeds the actual rent. On the other hand, where the owner pays out of the rent which he receives any rates, taxes, etc., the amount of these must be deducted before the annual value is calculated.

Who pays Schedule A?—The person on whom the assessment in respect of Schedule A is made is not the owner but the occupier. The occupier, if he is a tenant, must pay the tax in the first place, but is entitled to deduct it from his next payment of rent, so it is the landlord who bears the burden of it in the end. This does not apply to dwelling-houses in the occupation of tenants of which the annual value is less than £10, nor to land let for a period less than a year, nor to houses and buildings let in separate apartments and occupied by two or more persons separately, e.g. flats. In such cases the landlord pays the Schedule A tax direct, and the tenant pays the full amount of his rent without any deduction. In addition, the landlord may always apply to the clerk to the General Commissioners before July 31st in any year, requiring that he should be assessed as the occupier of the premises, and in this case also he will be entitled to his rent in full. Where the occupier is also the owner he pays the tax in the ordinary way, and as there is no rent from which he can deduct it, he bears the burden himself.

The tenant will normally receive the demand for Schedule A tax in January and, after he has paid it, is entitled to deduct the amount he has paid from the next instalment of his rent. It should be noticed that the deduction must be made from the next instalment, and not from later instalments, and that it cannot be made until the tenant has himself paid the tax.

Where the assessment is greater than the rent, the tax can only be deducted on an amount equal to the rent. Thus, where a person occupies premises at a less rent than the annual value (i.e. presumably the proper rent), he is required to pay part of the Schedule A assessment himself without being able to recover it. The deduction is not limited to the amount of tax on any one instalment of rent, and if the instalment of rent next due after the payment of Schedule A is for any reason not sufficiently large to enable all the tax to be deducted from it, a deduction of the balance may be made from later instalments.

Schedule B.—This is known as the farmer's tax. It applies to all land including farmhouses and buildings which are used for the purpose of husbandry. The tax is calculated on the annual value arrived at for the purposes of Schedule A without any deductions on account of maintenance allowances, etc.—i.e. the gross annual value. Where, however, the land is not used for the purposes of husbandry, the assessment will be one-third of the gross annual value.

Where a farmer is taxed on this basis, and he proves that his actual profits for the year are less than the assessable value as calculated for the purposes of Schedule B, he may have the tax reduced to the amount which would be due if he had been taxed on his actual profits for the year; and if he has in fact paid more, he may recover the difference. In addition to this, any farmer, by giving notice in writing to the Inspector of Taxes not later than the 5th June in any year, may claim to be assessed under Schedule D, i.e. on his actual profits, instead of under Schedule B. If he does this he will calculate his profits in the same way as any person carrying on any other business. (*See below.*)

Schedule C.—Schedule C is not of great practical importance to the average taxpayer. There is included in it all income arising from the public revenue of the United Kingdom or of any foreign State, Dominion or Colony. Income from all these sources is taxed at the source (*see below*), that is, the person paying the income deducts from it the amount of tax due at the standard rate before making payment. This does not apply to War Loan. The interest due on War Loan is paid in full and must be returned under Schedule D.

Schedule D.—Schedule D includes all profits made from the carrying on of a business or received from certain miscellaneous sources, and this schedule and Schedule E are by far the most important schedules to the average income taxpayer.

Schedule D has six cases applicable to different types of income.

Case I.—Into this case fall all profits arising from trades carried on in the United Kingdom by any person, and trades carried on outside the United Kingdom by persons who reside in the United Kingdom. Normally the basis of assessment is not the profits of the year in which the tax is paid, but the profits of the previous year from April 6th to April 5th, inclusive.

Case II.—Case II covers the profits of professions and vocations and is assessed on the profits of the previous year in the same way as Case I.

Calculation of Profits.— When a business man calculates his profits for any year, the figure at which he arrives will not necessarily be the profits for income tax purposes. Many items which a prudent business man will incur and deduct as expenses from his gross profits for the purpose of calculating his net profits will not be allowed as deductions for the purposes of income tax, and will have to be what is called "added back," that is, added on again to the profits as arrived at by him. This, of course, is exactly the same as if they had never been deducted at all. The only expenses which he is entitled to deduct are those which have been wholly and necessarily incurred for the purposes of the trade, business or profession.

What May Be Deducted. — Any expenditure which involves the investment of more capital as distinguished from revenue expenses, cannot be deducted. Thus, the money spent in alterations to the premises or extensions is not an expense for income tax.

Personal Expenditure.—The personal living expenses of the proprietor of the business cannot be deducted, nor are any drawings by him in the nature of wages or otherwise, nor his life insurance premiums (*See below.*)

Income Tax.— The amount paid in the year of assessment for income tax cannot be deducted, as this is regarded as part of the personal expenses of the proprietor.

Expenses of Removing Business.— These may be allowed in cases where the removal is compulsory, i.e. due to expiry of lease.

Subscriptions.—These may be de-

Somerset House. The Headquarters of the
Board of Inland Revenue.

ducted only in cases where they were incurred for the carrying on of the business. Thus, subscriptions to trade associations are usually allowed, but not subscriptions which are made merely in the hope of obtaining further business, e.g. subscriptions to clubs —nor charitable subscriptions unless they are paid to secure benefits for employees, e.g. to a local hospital to obtain certain treatment for employees.

Reserves and Legal Expenses.—No reserves can be deducted even though they may be proper items placed to reserve in the accounts, except when they are intended to meet expenses already incurred—e.g. rent not yet due—or for specified bad debts (*see below*). Nor may legal expenses incurred otherwise than in the ordinary course of trading be deducted. Thus, the expenses of collecting debts or defending actions will be allowed, but not the expenses of leases.

Current Expenses.—Current expenses such as the salaries and wages, commission, stationery, etc., may be deducted, but not any salary or wages drawn by the proprietor of the business.

Bad and Doubtful Debts.—Where a debt is written off as bad, the amount of it may be deducted. Where the practice of the business is merely to set up a *general* reserve for doubtful debts, the deduction of this reserve will not be allowed. Where an allowance is desired, the *specific* debt considered doubtful must be indicated, and a reasonable reserve against *that debt* will be allowed. Where a bad or doubtful debt is paid in a later year, the amount of it must be added to the profits of that year.

Insurance Premiums.—The amount of fire and burglary insurance premiums may be deducted if they relate to the business premises or stock. Premiums paid in respect of insurance against liability under the Workmen's Compensation Act may be deducted, but no deduction can be made for premiums in respect of life or personal accident insurance. A special allowance is, however, given in respect of life insurance. (*See below.*) When a loss occurs which is covered by insurance—e.g. fire—the amount of the loss may be deducted from the profits, but any amount received from the insurance company must be included in the profits. Where part of the loss is not covered by insurance, a deduction may be made in respect of this loss.

Rent or Annual Value.—Where the person carrying on the business is assessed under Schedule A (*see above*), in respect of the premises where the business is carried on, he is entitled to deduct the amount of the net annual value from his profits. Where he not only carries on business on the premises, but also lives there himself, he will not be entitled to deduct the full amount of the Schedule A assessment, but only a proportion of it. The exact proportion which will be attributed to the part occupied by himself will depend on the facts of each case; but in practice it is usual to allow two-thirds of the net annual value as a business expense. Where the person carrying on the business pays rent and is not assessable under Schedule A, the amount of the rent will be deducted (or a proportion on the same principles as above, where the premises are also used for other than business purposes).

Travelling Expenses. — These may be deducted where they are incurred wholly, necessarily and exclusively in carrying on the business. Nothing can be deducted in respect of travelling expenses between the residence of the taxpayer and his place of business, but expenses will be allowed which have been incurred in visiting customers, or in going from a warehouse to a factory. Where the travelling involves hotel expenses, these will usually be allowed, but in some cases a proportion of them will be disallowed on the ground that the tax-payer, by living at the hotel has been saved a certain amount of expense which he would otherwise have had to incur in living at his home.

Entertainment Expenses.—These are not allowed to be deducted.

Wear and Tear.—No sums written off for depreciation of plant or machinery may be claimed, but in place thereof a wear and tear allowance is available, calculated at a percentage on the cost varying with the nature of the goods whose depreciation is under consideration.

Special rates of depreciation have been fixed by the Inland Revenue authorities for different trades. In the case of fixtures and fittings it is usual for the tax-payer to charge the actual cost of repair and renewal instead of a percentage allowance, and this also applies to trade implements, such as barrows or scaffolding, and other utensils used in the business. The wear and tear allowance is confined, therefore, to plant and machinery.

When plant or machinery requires to be replaced, an allowance may be claimed for obsolescence in cases where the plant or machinery has either been scrapped or sold, and has been replaced. The amount allowed will be the value of the machinery as written down by the various annual deductions in respect of depreciation.

Schedule D, Cases 3, 4, 5 and 6. —Case 3 includes profits of an uncertain value, the most important of which are bank interest, and the interest received on securities of the British Government which are not assessed under Schedule C, and in particular, War Loan. Cases 4 and 5 deal with income arising outside the United Kingdom, while Case 6 is a sweeping case including all profits or gains not coming within any other case or schedule but which are nevertheless income for the purposes of income tax. The most important of these is the profit derived from letting furnished rooms.

Schedule E.—Within this Schedule falls all income earned in employment, and this is known as the "salaries tax." It includes not only salaries, but all wages, fees, perquisites, commission, bonuses and remuneration generally. This is also calculated not on the remuneration of the current year, but on that of the preceding year, so that a person whose salary has been increased in any year will in that year pay only the tax on the smaller income formerly enjoyed unless the increase in salary is due to a change in employment. (*See below.*) In the same way if the income is reduced, the tax payable is on the larger income of the previous year. Returns are made in this case not only by the persons employed, but also by the employers.

Weekly Wage Earners.—There are certain exceptions to this method of assessment. Weekly wage earners employed by way of manual labour are assessed half yearly, the two halves of the year ending on the 5th October and 5th April, respectively. Persons coming within this exception are manual labourers whose remuneration is calculated by reference to the hour, day,

week, or any period less than a month, or whose wages, however calculated, are paid daily or weekly or at any interval less than a month. Clerks, typists and shop assistants and persons engaged in similar employment are not within the exception, for they are not considered to be engaged in manual labour. Persons within this exception are assessed on the actual earnings of the half year. They are entitled to one-half of the appropriate allowances. (*See below.*)

The weekly wage earner is required to pay his tax on the 1st January and the 1st July respectively. If he wishes, he may do so by income tax stamps, and should apply to the Collector of Taxes. The payment in this case will be spread over thirteen weeks. In the event of a person paying tax in respect of the first half-year, but through unemployment not being liable to tax for the year as a whole, repayment should be claimed.

What Expenses May Be Deducted. —The principles of deduction here are the same as those already considered in the case of a business. Where an expense is necessarily incurred in the earning of the wage and is borne by the wage earner, it may be deducted. Thus a commercial traveller can claim his travelling expenses, taxicabs, fares, etc. Entertainment expenses cannot be allowed. A manual worker may deduct the sums required for his tools, or special clothes required for his work. The amounts allowed as deductions in respect of these items have been agreed between the trade unions and the income tax authorities, and any weekly wage earner who wishes to check the amount deducted should apply to his trade union for information on the subject.

New Businesses and Employments: Losses.—Where a person is starting a business he obviously cannot be taxed on the ordinary principles during the first year, as he has not any profits of the previous year on which the tax may be calculated. In such a case during the first year the assessment will be calculated on the profits he has actually made from the date when he began his business until April 5th following; in the second year he will be taxed again on the profits of the first year (as being the "previous year"); in the third and subsequent years he will be taxed on the profits of the previous year in the ordinary way.

He may, however, apply in writing to the Inspector at any time within two years of the second year of assessment for the purpose of having the assessment for the second year calculated on the actual profits of that year instead of on the profits of the first year. When he does this, the assessment of the third year will also be taxed on the actual profits of that year, instead of on the profits of the second year.

Thus, the effect is that if a man makes the necessary application, he may in the first three years of his business be taxed on the actual profits of the years instead of on the profits of the previous year. Where application has been made in this way it may be revoked at any time within twelve months of the end of the third year of assessment.

Giving up a Business.—Similar problems arise when a tax-payer gives up a business which he has been carrying on. Then the tax of the year in which the business ceased will be calculated on the actual profits from the 6th April to the date when the business ceased, instead of on the profits of the previous year. The Inland Revenue have, however, a right in cases where the profits of the previous year exceed those of the year in which the business ceased, to make an additional assessment on the amount of the excess. This has the effect of making the tax-payer pay on the profits of the previous year, and the whole effect is that in practice he will pay tax either on the profits of the year in which the business ceased, or on the profits of the previous year, whichever are the greater.

Commencement of Employment. —When a tax-payer is first employed he will pay tax in that year on his actual income during the year, that is, from the date of commencement to 5th April following. In the second year he again pays on the actual income, except in cases where the employment began on 6th April. In such cases tax is calculated on the income of the previous year. In the third year he will again pay on the actual earnings if he makes a claim to that effect within twelve months of the end of the year; but if no claim is made he will pay on the earnings of the second year. Thereafter he will be assessed on the earnings of the preceding year in the ordinary way.

Change of Employment.—When the employment is changed, and the tax-payer goes to work for a new employer, he is considered as entering into a new employment and the above rules will apply. When the change in the employment is merely promotion under the same employers, it is not regarded as new employment unless it involves a distinct change of duties.

Losses.—Where a loss is incurred in a business the tax-payer may set off the loss against any other income—e.g. from investments—which he may receive during the year. If he has no other income, he may carry forward the loss and set it off against any profits which he may make for the next six years.

Calculation of Tax: Charges and Allowances. — Charges. — When the profits or salary have been ascertained, and all proper deductions made in accordance with the above provisions, the tax-payer does not require to pay tax on the full amount of the remaining figure but is entitled to certain allowances. All the various sources of income which the tax-payer has will be collected together and embodied by him in his return, and the resultant figure, less what are known as annual charges, is called the statutory income.

These charges are not matters which the tax-payer would have been entitled to deduct as part of the expenses of his business, but they are payments reducing the amount of income actually retained by him. The best known of these is interest paid to a Building Society. Thus suppose a tax-payer carries on a business, his gross profits are £500 but against that he is entitled to deduct £300 in respect of allowable expenses on the principles set out above. His profits for income tax purposes will therefore be £200; suppose, however, that he owns a house of the annual value, after the deduction of the repairs and other allowances, of £40, his total income will therefore be £240. If he pays £20 a year to a Building Society or to a mortgagee this sum will be deducted as a charge on his income. Thus his position for income tax purposes will be:

Profits of business . . .	£200
Annual value of house . .	40
	£240
Less Building Society interest	20
Statutory Income . . .	£220

Where the payment to the building society is partly in respect of interest and partly in respect of repayment of capital, only the amount due in respect of interest may be deducted.

Allowances.—The tax-payer is still not required to pay tax on the full amount of this statutory income, for he is entitled to deduct from it certain sums called allowances intended to make the tax bear some relation to the burdens which there are upon his income. The allowances in question are earned income allowance, personal allowance, child allowance, dependent relative allowance, and allowances in respect of insurance premiums on life policies, and age allowance.

Earned Income Allowance.—Where any part of the income of a tax-payer is earned by him as distinct from being derived from investments, he is entitled to an allowance which at the present time is one-fifth of the net amount of the earned income after the deduction of all expenses. The maximum allowance is £300, so that no additional income allowance can be claimed where the earned income is over £1,500. The applications of these principles to the illustration above would be as follows:—

Statutory Income . . . £220
Earned Income Allowance
 (being one-fifth of £200) . £40

Personal Allowance. — Every tax-payer is entitled to deduct a personal allowance. In the case of the single man the amount is £100 and in the case of a married man £150. In addition, a married man where his income includes any *earned* income of his wife (*see* HUSBAND AND WIFE, below), is entitled to deduct four-fifths of the wife's earned income up to a maximum of £45. As one-fifth of the wife's earned income will already have been deducted in the earned income allowance, the result is that the total earned income of the wife is deducted up to a maximum of £45.

Child Allowance.— A tax-payer who has a child or stepchild under 16 years of age, or if over 16 receiving full-time instruction at a university, college, school or other educational establishment, is entitled to an allowance of £50 for the first child, and £40 each for any others. The allowance cannot be claimed in the case of a child which has income of its own exceeding £50 a year, but any income of the child which is derived from scholarships is not included for the purpose of calculating the £50.

Housekeeper Allowance.—An individual is not entitled to any allowance merely because he requires to employ a housekeeper to look after his household, but where the tax-payer is a widower or widow *and* has living with him (or her), some female relative of his own, or of his deceased wife (or husband) to look after some child, or (in the case of a widower), to act as house-keeper, he is entitled to deduct £50 from his income as housekeeper's allowance. Where no female relative is available, and another person is employed as housekeeper, the allowance may be claimed. It cannot however, be claimed on the above grounds by an unmarried person. An unmarried person may claim a like deduction of £50 where he has in his charge some young brothers or sisters, and where he has living with him—for the purpose of looking after these children—either his widowed mother, or some other female relative whom he maintains at his own expense.

Dependent Relative Allowance.— Where the tax-payer maintains at his own expense any relative of his or of his wife whose total income is not greater than £50 a year, and who is either incapacitated by old age or infirmity, or is his widowed mother, or his wife's mother, whether incapacitated or not, he is entitled to a further allowance of £25 a year. If the taxpayer himself is also incapacitated by old age or infirmity and has his daughter living with him to look after him, he may likewise claim the allowance of £25.

Age Allowance.—Where a tax-payer, whose income is not over £500 a year, is himself over 65 years of age at the commencement of the year in which the assessment is made (or where his wife lives with him and is over that age), he is entitled to an allowance of one-fifth on his income just as if it were earned income. If the income is in fact earned, and the tax-payer therefore already entitled to deduct one-fifth as earned income allowance, he cannot claim the benefit of this age allowance which therefore only applies to cases where the tax-payer is in receipt of unearned, i.e. investment income. The limitation of this right to persons whose income is not over £500 might work hardship in the case of persons whose income is just over that amount, and accordingly it is provided that any tax-payer whose income is over £500, but who would otherwise be entitled to the age allowance, may claim to have his income tax reduced to the amount which would have been payable had his income been exactly £500, plus half the amount by which the total income exceeds £500. It will be noticed that what has to be added is not the tax on half that excess, but half of the actual excess itself.

Taxable Income.—When all allowances have been deducted on the above lines, the amount which remains is known as the taxable income of the tax-payer, and it is on this that he is required to pay tax. The rate at which tax is payable is called the standard rate of income tax and is fixed by the Finance Act of each year.

The rate fixed for the year 1934–5 is 4/6 in the £1. The tax-payer is not, however, required to pay at this standard rate on the full amount of his taxable income. He is entitled to pay at a reduced rate on the first £175 of his taxable income, and at the standard rate only on the balance. The reduced rate is 2s. 3d. in the £ on the first £175 of taxable income.

Insurance Policies.—A tax-payer who has insured his own life, or that of his wife, is entitled to deduct from the amount of tax otherwise payable by him a sum calculated at the appropriate rate on the amount of the premiums of the year. The rate will depend upon the date when the insurance policy was taken out. If the policy was taken out before the 22nd June, 1916, the amount to be deducted will be half of the standard rate (*see above*) on the amount of the premiums. Where the policy was taken out on or after that date, the amount to be deducted will be dependent on the total income of the tax-payer. If the total income does not exceed £1,000, a deduction will be made at half the standard rate; if the income is between £1,000 and £2,000, three-fourths of the standard rate, and where the income exceeds £2,000, the deduction is at the full standard rate.

Where the policy does not secure the payment of a capital sum at death, whether in addition to any other benefit or not, no claim can be made in the case of policies taken out after 22nd June, 1916, and even

in the case of policies before that date, the allowance is limited to premiums not over £100. The amount of the premiums claimed must not exceed 7 per cent. in the total amount insured, and also must not exceed one sixth of the taxpayer's total income.

In cases where the income is a small amount above one of the limits fixing the rate of the tax—i.e. £1,000 or £2,000—relief, called Marginal Relief, is allowed to the tax-payer on the same principle as in the case of age allowance where his income is slightly over £500. (*See above.*)

Trade Union and Pension Contributions.—A deduction of the proportion of trade union contributions which is paid in respect of life insurance is allowed, and also a lump sum deduction in respect of contributions under the Widows', Orphans', and Old Age Pensions Act to the extent of £1 for a man and 10/– for a woman.

Income Taxed by Deduction: Repayment Claims.—One of the most convenient methods of collecting income tax is to require that where one person is bound to pay to another a sum of money, he shall not pay the full sum that is owing, but shall first deduct the amount of income tax at the standard rate and pay only the balance to the person to whom he owes the money. The income tax deducted he will be required to pay to the Revenue Authorities. This does not apply to payment of debts due for trading, but it applies to almost all classes of unearned income such as dividends from shares or other securities, to rent or ground rent, to annuities and payments out of settled funds and to certain salaries, the most important of which are those payable to railway employees and to public officials. The provision as to salaries does not, however, apply to employees of railway companies who are engaged in manual labour.

When tax is deducted in this way it is always deducted at the full standard rate irrespective of the income of the person to whom the money is paid. If he is not liable to pay any income tax it will be necessary for him to claim back from the state the tax which has been deducted from him. Even if his income is liable to some tax he may not be liable to tax at the full standard rate and in this case also a repayment claim will have to be made. To meet the convenience of persons who would be seriously inconvenienced if they were deprived of their tax until the end of the income tax year, claims for repayment may be made by instalments during the course of the year and a final claim immediately after 5th April. The appropriate form, which will vary according to the total income of the claimant and as to whether or not he has made a return of his income, should be obtained from the inspector of taxes of the district. With the claim, the certificates vouching for the fact that income tax has been deducted should be sent. Where these certificates have been lost, duplicates may be obtained if application is made to the inspector of taxes.

Husband and Wife.—For all purposes of income tax and surtax, a husband and wife are assessed together, or, in other words, the husband must include all income received by his wife during the year in his own returns, and is liable to pay tax on that. He is, of course, entitled to a personal allowance of £150 instead of £100.

Year of Marriage.—The wife makes a separate return as to her income from the 6th of April up to the date of marriage, and is entitled to any allowances available. Her husband is not concerned with the income of this period. The husband, when he makes his return for the year, will include all his own income for the whole year, and also his wife's from date of marriage up to the next 5th April. The husband will be entitled against this to a full personal allowance of £150 as a married man, but there will not be any personal allowance, of course, in respect of his wife. It should be noticed that so long as the marriage takes place within the year of assessment, even if so late as 4th April, the husband is entitled to his full allowance as a married man for the year.

Separate Assessment.—A husband and wife may wish to be separately assessed. This will not make any difference to the total tax liability, but the wife will be able to claim personally the benefit of a proper proportion of the various allowances. Where the wife has a private unearned income from which tax is deducted at the source, this method may be of benefit to her if any repayment is due in respect of the tax so deducted, for instead of the amount due to her being used to reduce the husband's tax liability, he will have to discharge his liability in full, and the wife will receive her repayment in full. The final position of the family is the same as if there had been no separate assessment, but some part of the tax which the husband pays is received back by the wife instead of being deducted from the husband's liability in the first place.

If husband and wife wish to be separately assessed in this way, either should apply in writing to the local inspector of taxes at any time within six months before the 6th of July in the year of assessment. Once notice has been given in this way it will remain good until revoked.

Separated and Divorced Persons.—When a husband and wife have been divorced, or are living apart under a deed of separation, or by agreement, they are regarded as single persons for tax purposes, and each of them is therefore entitled to a full personal allowance of £100. If the husband pays the wife any alimony, the normal rule is that, except where the payment is being made under an order of the Court or a legal deed of separation, the husband must pay the amount named in full without deduction; but he is treated as if he had deducted the amount of tax due and is liable for that to the authorities, the payment being regarded as a nett amount. This does not apply to amounts paid otherwise than under order of the Court of a legal deed of separation. The husband may deduct from his total income any sum paid in respect of alimony or maintenance.

Wife's Earnings.—The husband, in the first place, must return any earnings of his wife as part of his income, but he is entitled to relief which will, in effect, prevent him from being liable in cases where the wife's income is small. A husband is entitled to earned income relief on the whole income, his own and his wife's which is earned to the extent of one-fifth (*see above*). In addition, he is entitled to deduct four-fifths of the wife's earned income up to a maximum of £45.

Appeals.—When the tax-payer considers that his assessment is higher than it should be—e.g. that certain items of expenditure which he has included as part of his business expenses have not been allowed—his wisest course is to communicate either personally or by letter with the Inspector of Taxes in his district, and endeavour to induce the Inspector to allow the items. This should be done without delay, i.e. within two or three days of the receipt of the assessment. If the inspector will not make the allowances, the tax-payer has a right of appeal. He must give notice of his intention to appeal to the Inspector of Taxes in writing within twenty-one days from the date appearing on the notice of assessment, but there is power to extend this time where it can be shewn that the omission to give notice in time was the result of sickness, absence or other reasonable cause.

Appeal lies normally to the General Commissioners but appeals may be made to the Special Commissioners instead of the General Commissioners under Schedules D or E. The General Commissioners are local persons who give their services without payment. The Special Commissioners are trained experts who are centred in London but who visit different districts to hear appeals. When the notice of appeal is given, reasons should be stated in it. Where the appeal involves any investigation of the books of the tax payer, he will be well advised to go to an accountant and obtain from him a proper statement of his accounts as shewn by the books. If no books have been kept, an accountant may still be able to draw up accounts from pass books, invoices and paying-in slips, and these documents should certainly be shewn to the Inspector.

In very many cases the result will be that an arrangement will be come to with the inspector which will render further prosecution of the appeal unnecessary. If the appeal continues, the appellant will receive a notice notifying him of the time and place of the meeting of the Commissioners, and he should attend there. He may be represented either by a barrister, solicitor or an accountant, or if he pleases may appear in person, but in any case should have with him all papers and documents necessary to establish his claim.

Collection and Payment.—Tax is payable in two equal instalments on January 1st and July 1st, respectively, except in the case of Schedule A, which is payable in full on January 1st, and in the case of weekly wage earners, when it may be paid by instalments by means of income tax stamps. (*See above.*) In respect of Schedule D tax, discount is allowed on any sum prepaid at the rate of $2\frac{1}{2}$ per cent. per annum. Money orders may be obtained free of charge at any post office in those cases where the amount due does not exceed £40.

Proceedings.—After thirty-eight days from the time when the tax becomes due, proceedings may be taken to recover it, either by distress, or in a Police Court. The proceedings in the Police Court must be taken within six months of the time when the tax became due, and are not available if the amount of tax is over £50. When Police Court proceedings are taken, the taxpayer is usually ordered to pay by instalments, and on default may be sent to prison. Proceedings may also be taken in the High Court.

Surtax.—Surtax is an additional income tax on all incomes over £2,000. The rate at which this tax is payable varies, being 1/– in the £ on the first £500 over £2,000, and gradually increasing until it reaches 7/6 in the £ on any part of the income over £52,000, plus, in all cases, 10 per cent. on the duty payable as calculated above. No allowances in addition to those made for income tax are made from the income before calculation of surtax. A surtax payer has also to pay tax calculated at the ordinary rates upon his income.